LOUISIANA

A Guide to the State

LOUISIANA

A Guide to the State

NEW REVISED EDITION
HARRY HANSEN, *Editor*

Originally Compiled by the Federal Writers' Program
of the Work Projects Administration
of the State of Louisiana

AMERICAN GUIDE SERIES

ILLUSTRATED

HASTINGS HOUSE • *Publishers* • *New York*

FIRST PUBLISHED IN 1941

ISBN: 8038-4272-4
Library of Congress Catalogue Card Number: 75-158007
Copyright © 1971 by Hastings House, Publishers, Inc.
Copyright © 1941 by the Louisiana Library Commission at Baton Rouge
Printed in the United States of America

A Note About the New Edition

When the Federal Writers' Program was formed by the Work Projects Administration in the days of economic distress to "give employment to professionally trained writers, journalists, and research workers," no one could foretell what admirable results would be disclosed when *Louisiana, A Guide to the State,* was first published. Not only did the book provide a unified survey of a land lavishly endowed by nature, but it presented a wealth of picturesque detail about people and places, legends and folklore, aspirations and results. The public immediately acclaimed it, and it has been in demand ever since.

Sponsors of the project were the Louisiana Library Commission—now the Louisiana State Library—in the person of its Executive Secretary, Miss Essae Martha Culver, and the Louisiana State University, represented by its Acting President, Paul M. Hebert. The general plan of the American Guide Series was devised by Henry G. Alsberg. Lyle Saxon was State Supervisor, Edward Dreyer Assistant State Supervisor and Darvey W. Wixon Unit Supervisor. Those who contributed to the work or evalued its contents, were authors, editors, educators, librarians, and artists, of top rank in the State.

The compilers of this edition recognize the unique character of the opening essays in this *Guide,* and have left them intact except for a few timely emendations. In updating the Cities and Towns, and the Tours, they have tried to record the tremendous changes that have taken place in education, industry, general culture, and social readjustment, in a land still full of promise after more than 300 years of exploration and settlement.

Contents

Part I. Louisiana: Past and Present

Part II. Cities and Towns

Part III. Tours

Page

Part IV. Appendices

Maps

Illustrations

General Information

Boundaries: Louisiana is bounded on the north by the state of Arkansas, on the east by Mississippi, on the west by Texas, and on the south by the Gulf of Mexico. It has an area of 48,523 square miles, and ranks 31st in area in the United States. There are 3,417 square miles of water surface in the State, and the length of the coast and the mainland and islands is approximately 1,700 miles. The State is divided into two parts, with the city of Alexandria as the geographic center. To the south are bayous and marshes bordering on the Gulf, and a predominantly Catholic and French population. To the north the State is Anglo-Saxon and Protestant, with gentle rolling hills, forests, and wide delta lands. The influence of both French and Spanish cultures is found in south Louisiana; the Creoles, descendants of early French and Spanish settlers, and the Acadians, descended from French exiles from Nova Scotia, who came to Louisiana in the 1750's and 60's. The population of the northern part of the State is mainly descended from pioneers from neighboring states. The total population of Louisiana in 1970 was 3,643,180, an increase of 386,158, or 11.9 percent, from the 3,257,022 total of 1960. Louisiana was classified as an urban state for the first time as a result of the 1950 census when the percentage of city inhabitants was 54.8; in 1960 this increased to 63.3 percent.

Louisiana has a network of approximately 4,260 miles of primary roads designated on the map with the suffix US. These constitute 27 percent of the 16,000 miles of State-maintained highways. About 10 percent of these highways was four-lane in 1970; new lanes were continually being added.

Driving Regulations: Tourists visiting Louisiana and possessing valid driving licenses issued by their home states or counties may drive in Louisiana for a period of 90 days. They must carry their licenses.

Residents of Louisiana must be at least 15 years of age, give proof of date of birth, and pass an examination. A chauffeur's license is needed by anyone driving a vehicle weighing more than 3,500 lbs. or driving for other owners or for hire, and the holder must be 18 years old and pass an examination.

Any member of the U. S. Armed Forces stationed outside of Louisiana is not required to renew a license during the period of service and 60 days thereafter. He must carry his license and evidence that he is a member of the Armed Forces.

The law requires any person who drives or rides upon a motorcycle to wear a helmet of an approved design. Both driver and passenger must have the chin strap of the helmet properly fastened and there must be foot rests for the passenger.

The rules of the road are explicit but based on common sense and fairly uniform with those of other states. Automobiles and buses may drive up to 60 *m.* per hr. in rural areas and 70 *m.* on multilane highways. Trucks must observe a limit of 50 *m.* and a vehicle pulling a house trailer is limited to 45. A driver may not pass a school bus when it is servicing passengers. Drivers are warned not to drive while under the influence of intoxicants or narcotics. Accidents involving personal injury or property damage of $100 must be reported to police in a city or to State police.

The *Drivers Guide* is issued by the Drivers' License Division of the Department of Public Safety, Baton Rouge, La. It has most specific directions for safe driving and the driver's responsibilities.

HUNTING

For all forms of hunting and fishing that take place within the boundaries of Louisiana the State has enacted a thick compendium of regulations that are administered by the Louisiana Wild Life & Fisheries Commission. Wildlife is a boon to the State in various ways, not the least of which is the income derived from the sale of licenses and the expenditures of sportsmen. The object of regulation is conservation—the proper management of fur, game, and fish to assure trapper, hunter, and fisherman a sufficient supply without exhausting the species. The State can prescribe during what weeks deer can be taken with bow and arrow, and how long a catfish must be in order to grace a meal, but when it faces the prime ambition of hardy sportsmen, landing the big game fish of the Gulf of Mexico, it regulates not size but weight, equipment of motor boats and gear. The phrase *paradise for fishermen* is often applied to Louisiana, and it has as much right to it as the other states that line the Gulf, but even more so when considering the immense resources of the fresh-water bayous and swamps.

Deer hunting is subject to regulations that cover every aspect of the sport. The bag permitted is one legal deer per day, five per season. A legal buck is defined as a deer with antlers not less than 3 inches long. A doe may not be killed unless the prohibition is lifted for special reasons. Spotted fawns are protected. Still hunting prohibits the use of dogs in areas so designated, including wildlife management or refuge areas; in all other areas dogs may be used. It is stated that "the use of organized drivers and standers, in which drivers make noises by shouting, whistling, discharging firecrackers, striking objects together, using horns or other noisemakers, or the use of vehicles and horses in attempting to take deer on any wildlife management area, is prohibited."

Archery season is usually from October to the first week in January. Deer of either sex may be killed by bow and arrow in the area designated, and guns may not be carried at that time.

Daily permits are required in many places and may be obtained from stations on or near the wildlife management areas. Deer killed where daily permits are necessary must be checked at a weighing station.

The black bear, once prolific in Louisiana, has been disappearing because his woods are being cut down. In 1964 the Louisiana Wild Life & Fisheries Commission closed the hunting season on bear in order to restock such woods as were left. The state of Minnesota offered bears if the Louisiana men would trap them. The Louisiana Commission introduced 156 animals from 1964 to 1967 in Madison, Tensas, and Pointe Coupee Parishes. Of this number 35 have been killed, some by motor cars and some by bullets, not by licensed hunters.

Rabbits are fair game for five months, from October 1 to February 28. The daily bag limit is 8, total catch 16. A still hunt is prescribed, but use may be made of beagles. Squirrels are hunted from early October to January; the daily limit is 8, total 16. Raccoon may be hunted only for a week in September and a week in January at Russell Sage, and special permits must be obtained from District 11 office in Monroe.

General Provisions for Hunting Game Birds: Bait and live decoys may not be used. Hunters of ducks and geese who are 16 and over must obtain a Federal waterfowl stamp at a Post Office. Use of shotguns larger than 10 gauge or holding more than 3 shells is prohibited. A hunter must retrieve every bird he shoots. There is a permanent closed season on swan, whooping, and sandhill cranes; kildeer, prairie chicken, upland plover or papabotte, black bellied and golden plover, and any shore birds except woodcock and Wilson's or jacksnipe. It is unlawful to kill any grosbec or other herons, egrets and cranes. However, certain destructive birds are classified as outlaws: cormorants, vultures (buzzards), crows, redwing black birds, sparrows, starlings; also grackles and bobolinks that damage crops.

The turkey season runs from late March to middle of April and is subject to detailed geographical restrictions in northern and eastern parishes of the State, schedule available from the Louisiana Wild Life & Fisheries Commission. Gobblers only may be hunted; the daily limit is one gobbler, season limit, two gobblers; still hunting only. Use of dogs, baiting or rifles and shooting of birds from moving or stationary vehicles are illegal.

The quail season runs from late November to late February. Only recognizable breeds of bird dogs and retrievers are permitted in quail and migratory bird hunting. Hunting from duck blinds and tree stands and the use of spurs for tree climbing are prohibited.

Seasons and bag limits for migratory birds are carefully specified by the Commission, which will provide details for doves, teal, ducks, coots, geese, rails and other species.

Licenses: All basic hunting licenses exclude big game, deer, and turkey hunting. Season resident license, $2, non-resident, $25; non-resident license for 5 consecutive days, $5. Big game, resident and non-resident, additional, $2. Hunting club, $5; commercial hunting preserve, pen-raised birds only, $200; game breeder, $10. Exceptions: A non-resident from a state that has a reciprocal hunting agreement may hunt after he gets his reciprocal hunting license in Louisiana. Members of the U. S. Armed Forces on military duty are treated as residents. Any person 60 years old or older who has lived in the State 2 years min. may get a license free. Persons under 16, resident or non-resident, do not need a license or have to pay fees to fish or hunt and will be issued a permit and tags to hunt deer or turkey on request.

Hunting Statistics: In a typical year, 1968–69, 442,863 hunting licenses were issued in Louisiana. Resident season licenses numbered 315,467, an increase of 3,983 over the previous year; big game licenses numbered 120,725, an increase of 1,106. The largest number of $2 licenses 20,523, was issued in East Baton Rouge Parish, where 6,982 were for big game also at $2. In Ouachita Parish 9,030 licenses out of 15,200 were for big game; in Caddo Parish 7,957 out of 17,830 were for big game. Calcasie issued 17,277; Orleans 15,267.

Motor boat certificates issued for the same period were 17,072 for outboard motors and 1,727 for inboard. Withdrawn were 1,436 inboard and 9,360 outboard permits.

Address the Louisiana Wild Life & Fisheries Commission, 400 Royal St., New Orleans, La., 70130. Additional information on wildlife management areas, including maps, may be obtained by writing any District Office of the Commission at the following places: P. O. Box 915, Minden, 71035; P. O. Box 4004, Ouachita Station, Monroe, 71201; P. O. Box 278, Tioga, 71477; P. O. Box 426, Ferriday, 71334; 1213 North Lakeshore Drive, Lake Charles, 70601; P. O. Box 593, Opelousas, 70570; P. O. Box 14526, Southeast Station, Baton Rouge, 70804.

FISHING

Fresh Water Game Fish: There is no closed season for fresh water game fish in Louisiana. The daily creel limits are: Black bass, 15; striped bass, 2; walleye, 2; white bass (bar fish), 25; yellow bass and crappie (white perch, speckled perch, sac-a-lait) combined, 50; sunfish (perch, bream, goggle-eye, bluegill) 100. No more than 2 days' creel limit may be possessed except where permitted by arrangement with bordering states. No fresh water game fish may be sold within the State of Louisiana. Bait seines, 30 ft. or less; dip nets, and minnow traps for taking minnows and shrimp are permitted.

Fresh Water Commercial Fish: Size limits: Buffalofish, 16 in. min.; gaspergou, 12 in. min.; paddlefish, 15 lbs.; catfish, blue, yellow or goujon, 14 in. min.; catfish, channel, eel, or willow, 13 in. min.

April and May are closed season for bullfrogs and lagoon frogs. Frogs may be taken by aid of jack light and devices that do not puncture the skin, but use of spears is prohibited and hunters may not carry firearms during night hunting.

There are prohibitions against taking fish by means of spears, poisons, explosives, guns, bows and arrows, and traps, but garfish may be taken by all these devices except explosives. A barbless spear may be used for taking flounder. No one may use wood baskets or slatt traps, and no fyke nets, wings or leaders, seines, gill nets, or trammel nets may be set within 500 ft. of the mouth of any inlet or pass. Wings and leaders are permitted on hoop nets in overflowed areas beyond the actual bed of stream or lake.

No pollution of water by industrial or other wastes is permitted when they kill fish or their food or are otherwise detrimental to the interest of the State.

Salt Water Fish: Size limits: Speckled sea trout, 10 in. min.; redfish, 16 in. min.; sheepshead, 10 in. min.; hardshell crabs, 5 in. wide; softshell crabs, 4½ in. wide; diamond-back terrapin, 6 in. long. No limitations on other species. These limits do not apply to persons fishing solely for home consumption, not for sale. Traps for terrapin are prohibited and there may be no shipping between April 15 and June 15. No turtle eggs except those of the mobilian turtle may be taken.

Fees and Licenses: Typical fees, expiring June 30, 1971: Resident, $2; non-resident, $6; non-resident 7 consecutive days, $3. A non-resident from a state that has reciprocal agreements with Louisiana may fish in Louisiana after he gets his reciprocal fishing license. Members of the U. S. Armed Forces on military duty are treated as residents. Any person 60 years old or older who has lived in the State 2 years min. may get a license free. A non-resident who owns property on a lake and spends 30 days min. on it may obtain a resident license.

The amateur is lucky. The lone resident who uses a rod for a fishing pole or a hook and line without a reel or artificial bait needs no license. And the householder fishing solely to provide his dinner may take in one day 25 buffalofish and catfish in the aggregate.

TRAPPING

First of all for the trapper to remember—no alligators. Trapping alligator is out for the present. Anyone coming to Louisiana to stalk the alligator for his valuable hide had best return home. And poaching is dangerous and unlawful.

The trapping season for fur is usually from December 1 to February 28. The basic tax is $2; the resident fur buyer pays $25; the non-resident fur buyer pays $100; the resident fur dealer must deposit $500 and pays $150; the non-resident fur dealer must deposit $1,000 and pay $300.

There is a State severance tax on all skins and hides, which must be paid by the dealer or the trapper shipping his own catch out of the State. The tax is 1¢ on skin of bob cat, coyote, ring-tailed cat, muskrat, opossum, raccoon, skunk and spotted skunk; 2¢ on nutria or coypu; 10¢ on mink; 25¢ on otter.

There are restrictions on areas, which may be obtained from the Wild Life Commission.

Motor Boat Registration: All motor boats with engines of more than 10 hp must be registered. No vessel may be operated without required safety equipment and life-saving devices for every person on board. All accidents of more than $100 damage must be reported. Certificates with numbers for the initial three-year period are: Dealer, $25; rental, first three, each $5, additional, each $3; individual and commercial, each $5.

RECREATION

Louisiana has but one National Park, the Chalmette National Historical Park on the site of the Battle of New Orleans. But it has eight State parks, eight historical monuments, and two waysides, all with facilities for recreation, such as camping, fishing, picnics, following trails, etc. There are many parish and municipal parks, and scores of localities that have special accommodations for fishing and outings.

The following State installations, listed by the Chamber of Commerce of the New Orleans Area, are followed by initials that designate their facilities: C—cabins; CA—camping area; BH—beach; BT—boating; F—fishing; PT—pits and tables; PL—pool; RR—restrooms; S—shelters.

STATE PARKS

Chemin-A-Haut. La 139, 10 m. north of Bastrop, near the Arkansas border (C, CA, BH, BT, F, PL, PT, RR, S).

Chicot. 8 m. north of Ville Platte off US 167; 6,000 acres, including a beautiful lake (C, CA, BT, F, PT, RR, S).

Fairview-Riverside. 2½ m. south of Madisonville (S, PT, BT, F, RR, CA).

Fontainebleau. US 190, 3 m. east of Mandeville. Camping and picnic areas, nature trails and a beach on Lake Pontchartrain.

Lake Bistineau. La 163, 20 m. southwest of Minden and US 80 (C, CA, BT, F, PT, RR, S).

Lake Bruin. 4 m. north of St. Joseph off US 604 (CA, BT, F, PT, RR, S).

Sam Houston. Off US 171 north of Lake Charles on La 378 (CA, C, BT, F, PT, RR, S).

Longfellow-Evangeline. St. Martinville, on La 31, 7 m. east of US 90. Located in the heart of Louisiana's Cajun Country, this park is the locale of the poem, "Evangeline" (CA, PL, PT, RR, S).

HISTORIC MONUMENTS

Audubon Memorial. 30 m. north of Baton Rouge, off US 61, 3 m. south of St. Francisville on La 965. In this area John James Audubon completed many of his *Birds of America* series (PT, RR, S).

Earl Kempt Long. Winnfield, 3 blocks off US 167.

Edward Douglass White. La 1, 4 m. north of Thibodaux (PT, RR).

Fort Jackson. National Historical Monument. Just off La No. 25, 5 m. below Buras. Approximately two hours' drive from New Orleans. Scene of major engagement between Confederate land batteries and a Union fleet (BT, PT, F, RR).

Fort Pike. US 90, 30 m. east of New Orleans. Built between 1819 and 1828 (BT, F, PT, RR).

Fort Jesup. 6 m. east of Many off La 6 (PT, RR, S).

Mansfield. La 175, 4 m. south of Mansfield and US 84 (PT, RR).

Marskville. On La 1, 30 m. southwest of Alexandria. Site of prehistoric Indian mounds (PT, RR, S).

WAYSIDES

Bogue Falaya. Covington, on US 190, on Bogue Falaya River (BH, F, PT, RR, S).

Abita Springs. On La 59, across Lake Pontchartrain from New Orleans. Famous mineral spring (PT, RR, S).

Many parish, municipal and area groups provide publicly-operated camping facilities. Included are: Cotile Reservoir, approximately 21 miles west of Alexandria on La. Hwy. 1200; Oil City Park on Caddo Lake, Hwy. 1; Belmont Camp Ground, near New Iberia; Cheniere Lake Park, 5 miles west of Monroe, off Hwy. 80; North Beach, 34 miles south of Lake Charles; Catahoula Parish Veterans Memorial Park, on La. 124 near Harrisonburg; Lake D'Arbonne, 5 miles east of Farmerville off Hwy. 2; Rutherford Beach, south on Hwy. 27 from Creole; Holly Beach, near Cameron; Bayou Bodcau Reservoir, 8 miles north on La. 157 near Bellevue.

TAXES

State Income Tax: The tax rate on individuals is 2% on the first $10,000 of net income; 4% on the next $40,000 of net income; 6% on all net income above $50,000—all on net after exemptions. Nonresidents pay only on income derived from Louisiana sources. Exemptions are $2,500 for a single person, $5,000 for a married person or head of family; $4,000 for each dependent. The State grants practically the same deductions as provided for in the Federal Income Tax Law. Federal income tax payments or net income taxes paid to other states are deductible.

The State Sales and Use Tax is 2% with numerous exemptions benefiting major industries or products, such as shipbuilding and repairing, servicing of vessels engaged in interstate commerce, gasoline, natural gas, electric power, water, steam, and merchandise bought for resale. 2% of the tax collected may be retained as compensation for collecting and remitting. Most cities have a sales tax of 2%, as in New Orleans, and a school tax usually of 1%, with the vendor's compensation of 1% for the collecting.

STATE SYMBOLS

The Great Seal: The Great Seal of Louisiana was adopted in 1902. It has a pelican with its head turned to the left, feeding three young in its nest. Over the head of the pelican are Union, Justice; below the nest is Confidence. Around the border of the Seal are the words State of Louisiana.

The State Flag. The State Flag was adopted in 1912 and consists of a field of solid blue on which is superimposed the pelican and its young in white and gold from the State Seal. Below the pelican a white ribbon bears the State Motto: Union, Justice, Confidence.

The State Flower. This is the magnolia—*magnolia grandiflora*—adopted in 1900. An effort in the Legislature to make the native Louisiana iris the official flower was defeated in 1950.

The State Song. A new official State song was adopted by the Legislature in 1970: "Give Me Louisiana," by Miss Doralice Fontane of Baton Rouge.

The State Bird. The pelican is considered the State bird by virtue of its position on the Great Seal and the Flag. Louisiana is often referred to as the Pelican State.

The gradual disappearance of the brown pelican, the official State bird, from the coasts of Louisiana, prompted an investigation in 1968 at Rockefeller Wildlife Refuge to determine the cause. The study was initiated by the Louisiana Wild Life & Fisheries Commission, the State Bureau of Sports Fisheries & Wildlife, the Audubon Society, and a number of other protective organizations. Fifty fledgling pelicans were obtained from Cocoa, Florida, and released in covered flying pens at Rockefeller Refuge and the Marine Laboratory at Grand Terre Island. The birds did well at Grand Terre but some became ill and died at Rockefeller, where concentrations of chlorinated hydrocarbons were found in the brain and liver. However, all causes of the migration of the State bird have not yet been determined.

WAR STATISTICS

Louisiana casualties in World War II are reported officially as follows: ARMY: Killed in action, 1,999; died of wounds, 349; died of injuries, 19; died non battle, 1,324; finding of death, 259. Missing, 19. NAVY: Died in combat, 1,019; died in prison camp, 18; missing, 14; wounded, 1,351. Total dead and missing, Army and Navy, 5,015.

Louisiana casualties in the Korean War: Killed in action, 596. Wounded, but not mortally, 1,760.

Louisiana casualties in the Vietnam War: In 1961–1967, inclusive, the Army lost 136 from hostile action and 27 from other causes; Navy, 7, and 7; Marine Corps, 90 and 16; Air Force 5 and 5. Totals, 238 and 55, or 293.

In 1968 Army lost 133 from hostile action, 22 from other causes; Navy, 8 and 2; Marine Corps, 69 and 2; Air Force, 3 and 2. Totals, 213 and 28, or 241.

In 1969 Army lost 101 from hostile action, 23 from other causes; Navy, 5 and 3; Marine Corps, 29 and 6; Air Force, 3; Coast Guard 1. Totals 139 and 32, or 171.

In 1970, January Through September: Army 51 from hostile actions, 22 from other causes; Navy, 1 and 1; Marine Corps, 6 and 4; Air Force, 2 and 1; Totals, 62 and 28, or 90. Total losses, 1961 through Sept., 1970, 795. Data courtesy Office of the Adjutant General, Military Dept., State of Louisiana, New Orleans.

Calendar of Annual Events

Festivals dominate the off-duty activities of Louisianians. Just as rodeos stir the blood of spectators in Texas and Colorado, so pageants and pageantry annually arouse the enthusiasm of hundreds of thousands in the State and in the South. In all the revelry associated with Mardi Gras New Orleans stands preeminent, but dozens of other cities and towns greet the season with some sort of exercises. Visitors will discover that Louisiana has rodeos too, but except for a few horse shows these are fishing rodeos, and just what part the fish play in them the visitor must find out for himself.

The list that follows is a selection from the *State Calendar of Events* published by the Louisiana Tourist Development Commission, Baton Rouge, 70804. It deals chiefly with outdoor events, and does not include plays, concerts, exhibits in museums and college athletic activities, which are found in the complete list.

JANUARY

First Week—The Mardi Gras Carnival Season begins traditionally on Twelfth Night (January 6) and accelerates during the month until it reaches full steam in February. The Louisiana Tourist Commission says: "Carnival in New Orleans is a special stew which starts simmering late in December, works up to a slow boil in January and early February, and really heats up in the week or so preceding Shrove Tuesday." January 1 is also a big day for New Orleans on account of the Sugar Bowl football classic.

Second Week—Louisiana Fur & Wildlife Festival, Cameron; Louisiana Square Dance Festival, North Iberia; Battle of New Orleans reenactment, Jan. 11, Chalmette National Park.

Third Week—Louisiana Polled Hereford Show, Alexandria; State Junior Miss Pageant finals, Houma; Southwest Louisiana Camellia Show, Lafayette; Ruston Men's Camellia Show, Ruston; Carnival Parade, Slidell.

Fourth Week—Mardi Gras Street Parades begin in New Orleans and suburbs, including Choctaw River Parade and Choctaw Street Parade, Algiers; Men's Camellia Club Show, Shreveport; Ozone Camellia Show, Slidell.

FEBRUARY

First Week until Lent, usually 10 days: (1) Carnival Parades in New Orleans. Krewe of Carrollton, Krewe of Okeanos, Krewe of Alla (Gretna, Algiers), Krewe of Juno, (Arabi, Chalmette). (2) Krewe of Freret, Krewe of Hercules (Gentilly). (3) Krewe of Pegasus. (4) Krewe of Babylon. (5) Krewe of Momus, Krewe of Jupiter (Chalmette, Arabi). (6) Krewe of Diana (Metarie), Krewe of Hermes. (7) Krewe of Iris, Krewe of Greta (Gretna) Krewe of Endymion. Krewe of Jason (Harahan). (8) Krewe of Thoth, Krewe of Venus, Krewe of

Mid-city, Krewe of Poseidon (Harvey, Marrero, Westwego), Bacchas, Zeus (Metarie). (9) Krewe of Proteus. (10) Krewe of Zulu, Krewe of Arabi, Krewe of Rex, Krewe of Orleanians, Crescent City, Krewe of Cronus (Algiers) Krewe of Comus.

Other Carnival Parades: Krewe of Olympia and Lions Club Mardi Gras Parade, Covington. Krewe of Hyacinths, Houma. Carnival Parade, Montegut. Ozone Camellia Show, Slidell; Beauty Pageant, Hammond: Men's Camellia Club spring show, Shreveport.

Second Week—Parish and District Livestock Show, Alexandria. Courrir du Mardi Gras, Church Point; same at Eunice, Ville Platte and Mamou. St. Mary's Parish Junior Fair and Livestock Show, Franklin. Mardi Gras celebration, Lafayette. Frontier Days, Logansport. Fashion Festival, St. Mary's Dominican College, New Orleans.

Third Week—Louisiana Rodeo Assn. Rodeo, Alexandria. New Orleans District Livestock Show, Arabi; Southwest District Fat Stock Show and Rodeo, Lake Charles; Louisiana Federated Music Club Festival, Pineville. State Band Festival, Ruston. Bird Art, Louisiana State Exhibit Museum, Shreveport.

Fourth Week—Louisiana State University Livestock Show and Rodeo, Baton Rouge; Northeast Louisiana Livestock Show, Delphi. Parish Spring Livestock Show, Natchitoches. All District Band Festival, Ruston. Southwest Louisiana District Fat Stock Show and Rodeo, Lake Charles.

MARCH

First Week—Caddo Parish Science Fair, Shreveport; Ballet Festival, Lafayette: Fort Polk Graduation Parade, Leesville; Redbud Festival, Vivian, including golf, bowling and bridge tournaments, flower shows, parades and a fishing derby.

Second Week—Livestock Show & Rodeo, Louisiana State University, Baton Rouge. Roundup Parade, Baton Rouge. Spring Pilgrimage historical tour, Baton Rouge; Miss Minden Pageant, Minden.

Third Week—Regional Social Science Fair, Louisiana State University, Alexandria; North Louisiana Broiler & Swine Show, Grambling.

Fourth Week— Southeastern Indian Festival, Baton Rouge. Miss Houma and Teen Miss Houma Pageants, Houma. Dogwood Festival, Tour of Homes, Bogalusa. Easter Sunrise Choral Pageant, Many, Easter Morning.

APRIL

First Week—Paint Horse Club Show, Alexandria: Miss Baton Rouge Pageant. Dogwood Festival, Bogalusa. Spring Garden Tour, Covington. Evangeline Downs Race Season opens, runs through July, Lafayette. Spring Fiesta, 15 days, in New Orleans, with tours of Vieux Carre, Garden District, patios by candlelight, Fiesta Queen coronation in Jackson Square, Bayou Teche tour. Dogwood Drive, Plain Dealing, Fresh & Saltwater Rodeo, Houma. Miss Lafayette Pageant, Lafayette. Louisiana State Science Fair, Baton Rouge. Spring Garden Tours, Shreveport.

Second Week—Miss Bossier Pageant, Bossier City. Fishing Rodeo, Colfax. Jaycee Air Show, Houma Air Base. Fair Assn. Rodeo, Lafayette. Arabian Horse Show, Lafayette. Cochon de Lair Festival, Mansura. Crosstrailers Square Dances, Monroe. Dixieland Gem & Mineral Show, New Orleans. Bayou Lafourche Tour, New Orleans. Chandeleur Ho Fishing Rodeo, Breton Island.

Third Week—DeSota Parish Tour of Homes, Mansfield. Easter Egg Knocking Festival, Marksville. Square Dance Festival, Baton Rouge. East Ascension Strawberry Festival, Gonzales. Jazz & Heritage Festival, New Orleans. Miss Thibodaux Beauty Pageant. Firemen's Fair, Thibodaux. Miss Northeast Pageant, Monroe. Holiday in Dixie, Shreveport. Greater New Orleans Open Golf Tourney. Southeast Louisiana Cyridustrial Futurame, Hammond.

Fourth Week—All Arabian Horse Show, University Coliseum, Baton Rouge.

AUGUST

First Week—National Appaloosa Horse Show, LSU, Baton Rouge. Fishing Contest, Campti. Hilltop Motorcyle Racing, La 80, Shreveport, continues weekends.
Second Week—Horse Show, Saddle & Bridle Horsemen's Club, Greensburg. Sailboat Races, Mandeville. State Fair Pitch Softball Tourney, Monroe. Square Dance Festival, New Iberia. Rodeo Cowboys Assn. Rodeo, Springhill.
Third Week—Home and Garden Week, LSU, Baton Rouge. Delcambre Shrimp Festival. Empire-Southwest Pass Tarpon Rodeo, Empire. President's Cup Golf Tourney, Lake Charles. South Lafource Oyster Festival, Larose. Deep South Rodeo, Winnsboro. Shreveport Drag Races, La 171. Southern Yacht Club Regatta, New Orleans.

SEPTEMBER

First Week—Fishing Rodeo, Abbeville. North Louisiana Cotton Festival & Fair, Bastrop. Fishing Contest, Campti. Invitational Regatta, Mandeville. Louisiana Shrimp & Petroleum Festival, Morgan City. Fishing Rodeo, Slidell.
Second Week—Women's Invitational Golf, Lake Charles. Men's Golf Club Championship Tourney, Lake Charles. Shrine Circus, Shreveport.
Third Week—Red River Parish Fair, Coushatta. Beauregard Parish Fair, De Ridder. Northwest Louisiana Dairy Festival & Claiborne Parish Fair, Haynesville. LaSalle Parish Fair, Jena. Championship Rodeo, Monroe. Toledo Fall Festival, Many. Cotton Festival, Bastrop. Lafourche Parish Agricultural & Livestock Show, Raceland.
Fourth Week—Tangipahoa Parish Fair, Amite, into October. Jaycee Fair & Forest Festival, Minden, into October. West Louisiana Forestry Festival, Leesville, into October. Winn Parish Fair, Winnsboro, into October. Catahoula Parish Fair, Jonesville. Sugar Cane Fair & Festival, New Iberia.

OCTOBER

First Week—Terrebone Parish Fair & Rodeo, Houma. Lake Charles Yacht Club fall series begins. West Louisiana Forestry Festival, Leesville, from September. Toledo Fall Festival, Many. Louisiana Livestock & Pasture Festival, Marksville. Fair and Forest Festival, Minden. Ouachita Valley Quarter Horse Show, Monroe. Natchitoches Parish Fair & Rodeo, Natchitoches. Winn Parish Fair, Winnfield. Calcasieu-Cameron Bi-parish Free Fair, Sulphur. Hilltop Bowl summer stock races, Shreveport. Young Men's Business Club Air Show, Lake Charles. West Baton Rouge Parish Fair, Port Allen. Festival of Beauties, Youngsville.
Second Week—International Rice Festival, with Frog Derby, Crowley. Rapides Parish Fair, Alexandria. Outboard Racing Championships, Alexandria. Louisiana Appaloosa Point Show, Alexandria. Tangipahoa Parish Fair, Amite. Washington Parish Free Fair, Franklinton. LaSalle Parish Fair, Jena. Vermilion Parish Fair & Festival, Kaplan. Tourist Appreciation Day, Natchitoches. Ladies State Amateur Golf Tournament, Lake Charles. Grand National Bass Tourney, Toledo Lake, Logansport. Jackson Point Junior Livestock Show, Jonesboro. Livingston Parish Fair, Livingston. Allen Parish Fair, Oberlin. North Louisiana State Fair, Ruston. Shreveport Rose Society, Shreveport. Sports Car Rally, Slidell. North Central District Fair, Olla.
Third Week—St. Tammany Parish Fair, Covington. Louisiana State Bowling Jamboree, Monroe. Yambilee Festival, Opelousas. Caddo Parish Fair & Junior Livestock Show, Shreveport. Louisiana State Fair, 2 weeks, Shreveport. Dairy Festival & Fair, Abbeville. Louisiana Cotton Festival, Ville Platte.
Fourth Week—Louisiana Rodeo Assn. Alexandria. Louisiana Swine Festival, Basile, into November. Greater Baton Rouge State Fair & Trade Show, Baton Rouge. Hungarian Folk Festival, Albany.

Art Associates Annual House Tour, Lake Charles. Stockmen's Show, Lafaye
Spring Water Show, Natchitoches. International Auto Show, Rivergate, N
Orleans. Crawfish Jubilee, Pierre Park. Open Skeet Shoot, South Louisiana G
Club, Bridge City.

MAY

"The rustle of crawfish and song of birds permeate the land. Now
the azalea, first flowery commitment of spring, has made its presence
known. This season the State earns its sobriquet of Sportsman's Paradise
as anglers haunt Louisiana's bays, lakes, rivers, and Gulf Coast for pis-
catorial excitement, including the simple but unique sport of crawfishing."

First Week—Elks Club Bayou Boat Cruise, Slidell. Louisiana Crawfish Festi-
val, Breaux Bridge. Spring Festival, Gueydon. Claiborne Parish Jubilee, Homer.
Paint Stock Horse Assn., Lafayette. Kiwanis Ladies Pro Golf Tourney, Shreve-
port.
Second Week—Appaloosa Horse Show, Alexandria. Louisiana Guernsey
Cattle Show, Alexandria. Intercollegiate Invitation Golf Tourney, Baton Rouge.
Championship Piroque Races, Lafitte.
Third Week—American Kennel Club Dog Show, Louisiana State University,
Baton Rouge. Pine Tree Festival, Walker.
Fourth Week—Contraband Days Celebration, Lake Charles; continues into
June. Shreveport Power Squadron, Evangeline Bayou Country Cruise joined
with Louisiana and Texas squadrons from Lake Charles via Calcasieu River
and Intracoastal Waterways to New Orleans.

JUNE

First Week—Amicus Club Rodeo, Alexandria. Shreveport Power Squadron
Cruise, stops at Houma, Intercoastal City; continues to New Orleans.
Second Week—Food Festival, New Orleans. Nicholls Golf Classic, Thibodaux.
Jambalaya Festival, Gonzales.
Third Week—Gulf Coast Oil Golf Tourney, Lafayette. Monroe Air Show,
Selman Field, Monroe.
Fourth Week—Miss Louisiana Pageant, Monroe. Peach Festival, Ruston.

JULY

First Week—Louisiana Junior Championship Golf, Alexandria. Kraft Golf
Tourney, Bastrop. American Youth Festival, Baton Rouge. Golden Meadow
Tarpon Rodeo, Golden Meadow. Southwest Louisiana Deep Sea & Inland Fish-
ing Rodeo, Cameron. Fishing Contest, Campti, all month. Cattlemen's Rodeo,
Church Point. International Regatta, Mandeville. Fishing Rodeo, Cypremont
Point Beach Landing, New Iberia. Hilltop Motorcycle Racing, La. 80. Sailboat
Racing, Cross Lake, Shreveport.
Second Week—Soybean Festival, Jonesville. Bastille Day celebration, Kaplan.
Gospel Singing Jubilee, Monroe. Louisiana Skeet Championships, Shreveport.
Third Week—Sailboat Race Lake Pontchartrain, Mandeville. Square Dance
Festival, Rivergate, New Orleans. Royal Lipizaner Horse Show, New Orleans.
Fourth Week—Bayou Blue-Coteau Fair, Houma. Louisiana Golf Club matches,
Lafayette. Watermelon Festival, Farmerville. National Inboard Boat Races,
Morgan City.

NOVEMBER

First Week—Livestock Show & Dixie Horse Show Jubilee, Louisiana State Univ., Baton Rouge; Louisiana Pecan Festival, Colfax; Lake Charles Yacht Club fall series, Lake Charles; International Acadian Festival, Plaquemine; Louisiana State Fair, Shreveport (from October); Louisiana Swine Festival, Basile.

Third Week—National Quarter Horse Show, All Student Rodeo, Baton Rouge; Shrine Circus, New Orleans; Sailboat Racing, Shreveport.

Fourth Week—Racing Season opens, Thanksgiving Day through March, Fair Grounds, New Orleans; Sailboat Races, Cross Lake, Shreveport, continuing weekends.

DECEMBER

First Week—Christmas Festival opens; river show, Natchitoches; Christmas month, Tallulah.

Second Week—Christmas Parade, Lafayette; Festival of Lights, Hodges Gardens; Christmas Tour of Homes, Bogalusa.

Third Week—Midwinter Sports Carnival, New Orleans, continues into January.

Fourth Week—Sugar Bowl Parade, New Orleans.

PART I

Louisiana: Past and Present

The Many Sides of Louisiana

IF you will look at a map you will see that Louisiana resembles a boot with its frayed toe dipping into the Gulf of Mexico. The State is bounded on the east by Mississippi, on the north by Arkansas, and on the west by Texas. The Mississippi River flows between Mississippi and Louisiana for half the length of the State and then passes entirely into Louisiana. The vast delta and the spreading mouth of the great stream lie wholly within the State. Somewhat larger than New York State, Louisiana has an area of 50,820 square miles, of which 7,409 are water. Large areas are actually below sea level, and for great stretches, channelled by levees, the Mississippi is higher than the surrounding land.

North and South Louisiana are entirely unlike. Shreveport, the second largest city resembles Dallas, Texas more than it does New Orleans; and the countryside with its rolling hills and pine and hardwood forests resembles Arkansas. The eastern portion of north Louisiana takes on the color of the Mississippi River and the traveler finds cotton plantations and stately houses standing in groves of trees. Monroe is the largest city of this section.

Alexandria, a thriving town in the center of the State, is distinctly American; yet only seventy miles west is Natchitoches, the oldest town in the State. Natchitoches, founded in 1714, four full years before New Orleans, has a flavor undeniably French. It was first a fort on the road which led from Mexico to the Mississippi. One of the antique iron crosses in the cemetery tells of an unknown Spanish lady who died on that road at the beginning of the eighteenth century. This is a rich cotton-growing country and there are many plantations along Red River and Cane River.

In Louisiana the traveler must remember that old towns and old houses will always be found near a river, or bayou, as water was the chief means of transportation in the early days. Modern highways make traveling easier, but those who wish to visit older places must take the less frequented roads.

Southern Louisiana takes its character from the French-speaking people who settled the vast, wet terrain, and who in the eighteenth century penetrated its rivers and bayous to make homes in the jungle-like forests. This part of the State is a lush land of great fecundity.

New Orleans was a French and Spanish city a century old before it became part of the United States. It stood on a peninsula bounded by the Mississippi River, Lake Pontchartrain and the reedy marshland that stretched south to the Gulf of Mexico. Founded by the French in 1718, it remained a possession of France until 1769, when it was taken under Spanish rule. In 1803 it became a part of the United States by right of the Louisiana Purchase. Even today French culture and French customs persist, though the city has spread out far beyond the boundaries of the Vieux Carré, the old town of iron lace, balconies, and courtyards. And the Creoles, proud white descendants of the original French and Spanish settlers, have given New Orleans a world-wide reputation for good food and drink, and good living.

It is significant that the most colorful celebration is Mardi Gras. At Carnival time the city enters a season of gaiety with nightly balls and other festivities from Twelfth Night through Shrove Tuesday, a season which culminates with a week of street pageantry, and with general masking in the streets on Mardi Gras itself. Another colorful ceremony is that of the decoration of the graves on All Saints' Day, when all of the cemeteries are filled with flowers and are crowded with people from early morning until nightfall.

Mardi Gras and All Saints' Day are observed throughout south and southwest Louisiana. In the Acadian country west of New Orleans, maskers ride about on horses on Shrove Tuesday and there are numerous dances and balls; and on All Saints' Day even the humblest country cemetery is decorated with wreaths and bouquets.

West of New Orleans, in the parishes which fringe the Gulf, one finds the Acadians, descendants of families that were driven from Nova Scotia in 1755. They were country-bred people, and it is natural that they should have settled in that fertile land along Bayou Teche. The Cajuns, as they are nicknamed, are, like the land, prolific. They remain to a large extent an agricultural people, and they still speak French. There are Negroes in the Teche country who can speak no English, having been born and brought up among the French-speaking Acadians.

The Teche country is as beautiful as any in the State. Winding roads follow winding bayous, and old white columned plantation houses, many restored for their tourist interest, stand at the ends of avenues of trees. The rich black earth is renewed to fertility each year by the thousands of Negro laborers who work in the sugar cane fields. As one rides along the roads one can see large sugar mills standing like islands in a sea of waving green cane.

In this peaceful country, huge live oak trees are draped with Spanish moss, and the bayous are covered with purple water hyacinths that in some areas impede navigation. Magnolia trees flaunt their large white flowers, and the cypress grows in water, surrounded by its upturned roots, or "knees." There are birds and bees in every thicket, and the streams are full of crawfish. Turtles sun themselves on logs. In the swamps the bull frogs bellow all night, and the trilling of the tree frogs sounds like thousands of tiny shrill bells all ringing together.

The people are friendly and pleasant. Families are large and the aunts, uncles, and cousins are legion. Names are musical, and nicknames are frequently quaint and amusing. Life passes placidly and people still retain their old customs and the old civilities.

Lafayette is the largest town in the Acadian country. Every Cajun knows the folk song *Allons à Lafayette.* Dancing is the most popular pastime. Country dances are called *Fais-dodo* literally "go to sleep"—or an all night party.

New Iberia is another pleasant Louisiana town, where there are numerous fine old houses, and there life seems easy and good. Near New Iberia is Avery Island, a wonderful bird sanctuary, where the herons flourish unharmed and the tourist may see a great colony of egrets. Farther south on islands in the Gulf and westward along the coast are many refuges for wildlife, including the vast Rockefeller Refuge in Vermilion and Cameron Parishes.

But the placid life of rural Louisiana is being crowded back by the feverish activity of modern industry, most of it based on petroleum, natural gas, and sulphur. Thousands of oil wells are producing, the most spectacular being the offshore platforms in the Gulf. A huge petrochemical industry around Lake Charles and extending from Baton Rouge to New Orleans is bringing immense wealth to the State.

North of New Orleans, across Lake Pontchartrain, is a great pine forest, with white sandy-bottomed rivers and many health-giving springs. St. Tammany Parish is noted for its Ozone Belt of health resorts, where many New Orleanians have country homes. Here one finds white people predominating—unlike the cane and cotton land along the Mississippi— and truck farms replace plantations. Strawberries are a large crop and there are groves of tung-oil trees. Going farther to the north and west, the traveler finds Baton Rouge, the State capital, a modern city deriving its prosperity from the oil refineries near by. Here is Louisiana State University. Baton Rouge was much in the nation's headlines during the lifetime of Huey P. Long, that fiery and picturesque figure who dominated Louisiana for the five years before his death in 1935. The visitor is usually interested in the towering Capitol that he built, and in his grave and monument on the grounds.

North of Baton Rouge are two of the State's most beautiful parishes: East and West Feliciana. These are "English-speaking" parishes in that they were settled by English families at the time of the American Revolution; families who came here while this land was still Spanish territory. A parish is synomonous with a county elsewhere.

The last section of Louisiana is that strange land of marsh and islands which lies south of New Orleans. Within a few miles of the city the traveler enters a primitive country of shrimpers and fishermen, who live as simply as their grandfathers did. Here are communities of men and women who have among them descendants of Lafitte's smugglers and pirates. The salt marshes conceal the houses of hundreds of muskrat trappers, for Louisiana is one of the richest fur-bearing States in the union. Here, too, live the fishermen whose haul of fish, shrimp, crabs, and oysters supply the city of New Orleans and many other parts of the United States.

This is known as the Barataria section, and is a sea marsh stretching some sixty miles southward to the Gulf. And beyond lies a bright archipelago of tropical islands, where few men live and where both sea and sky are filled with seagulls, terns, and other waterfowl.

To thousands of visitors New Orleans is the city of miracles. Here is historic evidence of the most romantic sort, as well as the peak of modernity. The food it serves, the entertainment it offers; finally the energies bound up with its shipping, which make it the second largest port on the continent, are not duplicated in the American scene.

Natural Setting

LOUISIANA lies wholly within the Gulf Coastal Plain and is the only State that extends in part over three major sections of that physiographic province: the East Gulf Coastal Plain, the Mississippi Alluvial Plain, and the West Gulf Coastal Plain. The more elevated areas east and west of the Alluvial Plain are known as the Upland Districts and consist of three main divisions: the Uplands of the Florida Parishes, north of Lake Pontchartrain and east of the Mississippi; the West Louisiana Uplands, west of the Red and Calcasieu Rivers; and the North Louisiana Uplands, a wedge-shaped area lying roughly between the Red and Ouachita Rivers. Near the coast, the delta formations of the Alluvial Plain lying east of Vermilion Bay and the low formations of the West Gulf Coastal Plain (Cameron-Vermilion Marshes or Wet Prairies) make up the Coastal-Delta Section. The higher arable portions of the Mississippi Alluvial Plain and the valleys of the Red and Ouachita Rivers are known as the Valley Lands.

The physiographic features of the State consist of pine hills, bluffs, prairies, coastal marshes, and alluvial plains. Rolling hill country, studded with longleaf and shortleaf pine, is found in each of the upland regions. Ranging in elevation from 100 to 300 feet in the southernmost uplands, the hills rise to a maximum of a little more than 400 feet near the Arkansas boundary. Except for conspicuous differences of elevation at successive terraces, or where the hills border valleys, the uplands slope gently toward the coast, the average incline being about two feet to the mile. Two high points west of the Mississippi rise above 400 feet: the Kisatchie Hills on the Natchitoches-Vernon Parish line and an area in the southern part of Claiborne Parish. Picturesque hills, bluffs, and ravines occur along the streams and valleys, the most notable being Grand Écore Bluff in Natchitoches Parish, the Tunica Hills in West Feliciana Parish, and the gorges known as Fluker's Cave and Fricke's Cave in St. Helena and Washington Parishes.

Bluffs border the Mississippi Alluvial Plain to the east and west of the river. On the east side the bluffs rise to an elevation of over 300 feet in the Tunica Hills east of Angola and end somewhat south of Baton Rouge at an elevation only slightly above the valley floor. West of the Alluvial Plain a lower chain of bluffs extends in a broken line from Oak Grove to Lafayette. The bluff lands slope away from the Mississippi Valley on each side, their drainage being away from the river.

The prairie lands in southwest Louisiana make up a flat sloping plain declining in elevation from 60 feet near Mamou to sea level at White Lake, the descent averaging a foot to the mile. There are no pronounced relief features.

A wide fringe of coastal marshes extends along the 1,500-mile coast line of Louisiana. Close growths of sedge, grass, and rushes make up a flat treeless plain dotted with thousands of shallow salt water lakes and lagoons. Except where the delta is encroaching on the sea, the marshes are bordered on the seaward side by barrier beaches, composed mainly of fine sand, which rise to a crest and support groves of live oak on their inner slopes. Sand and shell ridges, sometimes rising several feet above the general level, are to be found throughout the marshes. Called *chênières* because of the oak groves usually found growing on them, they represent former barrier beaches. Good examples are Grand Chênière and Pecan Island in southwest Louisiana. Drainage of the marsh areas is effected by sloughs and drainage bayous. In the coastal region proper the marshes are generally salt or brackish, the transition from fresh water being very gradual.

In addition to the *chênières,* the "land islands" of Louisiana are positive topographic features of great importance both to topographers and geologists because they represent the surface expression of underlying salt masses. These "land islands" are usually a mile or more in diameter and rise to a maximum height of 196 feet (Avery Island) above the general level of the surrounding marshes.

In southwestern Louisiana, extending along a line bearing S. 49° E. from a place ten miles west of New Iberia to the mouth of Atchafalaya River, are five distinct surface mounds known as the "Five Islands" of

Louisiana: Jefferson Island, Avery Island, Weeks Island, Côte Blanche, and Belle Isle.

The Mississippi Alluvial Plain extends southward along the river in a broad belt with an average width of about 50 miles. Narrow in the north, it widens considerably below Baton Rouge, where it swings south-eastward to form the delta. From the Arkansas Line, where the elevation is 115 feet, the flood plain slopes gradually to sea level at the Gulf of Mexico, the drop in the river over its 569-mile course through the State being about 2½ inches to the mile. The variations in the topography of the Alluvial Plain consist mainly of a series of ridges and basins. Along the main river and its distributaries, or natural outlets, the ridges are termed "natural levees." The arable lands of the high elevation sloping away from the river compose the "frontlands," the relief of which is altered in many places by meanders, cutoffs, and oxbow lakes. The intervening area between the frontlands and the bordering swamps is known as the "backlands," a region of fine silt and clay. When the level of the backlands dips below the mean water table, swamps are found. They vary from shallow swamps, characterized by a variety of hardwoods, to deeper, more permanent, cypress-tupelo swamps. Since the drainage in the Alluvial Plain is away from the master streams, the swamps, as a rule, do not drain into the Mississippi River, but serve merely as catch-basins for overflow waters and rainfall. In the delta proper, there are, in addition to the swamps, wide expanses of treeless water areas—marshes, lagoons, and lakes.

The most important rivers in the State are the Mississippi, Red, Ouachita, Sabine, and Pearl. A peculiar feature of many streams is the fact that they run upon a higher elevation than their flood plains. This is especially true of the Mississippi, which meanders through Louisiana between ridges built up by successive depositions of silt. The river is of little value, therefore, as a drainage channel for the State, its only tributary on the west being Red River, and on the east, Bayou Sara and Thompson's Creek. Were it not for a continuous line of levees, one-third of the total area of the State would be flooded by the Mississippi whenever bankfull stage was exceeded.

Numerous bayous—flood distributaries and drainage streams for swamps—make up a drainage network for the State. Of these, Teche, Macon, Lafourche, and Bœuf are the largest. The bayous, in most instances, are distributaries rather than tributaries of streams, and as such act as auxiliary outlets. Those found in the catch-basin swamps along the Mississippi and in the Tensas River and Lake des Allemands areas serve as drainage outlets for overflow waters.

Three classes of lakes occur. Coastal lagoons, existing as arms of the sea isolated behind barrier beaches or surrounded by deltaic ridges, are found in the delta. Lying at sea level, they have a slight tidal action, although storms and varying winds cause greater rises and falls than the regular tides. Barataria Bay and Lakes Pontchartrain, Maurepas, and Salvador are typical of such lagoons. Oxbow lakes, resulting from cutoff meanders of the Mississippi River, are found throughout the Alluvial Plain. Their characteristic shape is that of a crescent, and their width that of the river from which they were cut off. The lakes found in the Red River Valley, of which Caddo, Bistineau, and Black are typical, were formed as a result of the damming of Red River by the Great Raft. Their level is dependent now upon that of Red River, high water resulting in a flooding of the lakes by backwater.

CLIMATE

Louisiana has a semitropical climate that is remarkably equable over large areas. Variations in daily temperature are determined by soil differences, distance from the Gulf of Mexico, and, to a slight degree, by differences in elevation.

The mean temperature for the State as a whole is 67.4°; for northern Louisiana, 65.2°; and for southern Louisiana, where prevailing southerly winds and a network of bays, bayous, and lakes are moderating influences, 68.2°. January is the coldest month, with an average of 53.2° in the southern section and 48.3° in the northern section, while July and August are the warmest, with temperatures averaging approximately 82° in both northern and southern sections. There is, however, a greater daily fluctuation in the northern section in summer, the days being hotter and the nights cooler. At Shreveport a maximum of 100°, or higher, has been recorded frequently; in New Orleans, 100°, or higher, has been recorded rarely. The highest temperature recorded was at Plain Dealing in August, 1936: 114°. The lowest was at Minden, Feb. 13, 1899: −16°.

High winds, preceding areas of high barometric pressure, are experienced every winter. These high pressure areas, which move into Louisiana from the northwest, rotate in a clockwise direction, and, as the centers usually pass to the northward of most points in Louisiana, the wind generally shifts from the south by way of west to the north. As the fall in temperature is most noticeable when the wind shifts to the northwest, the storms are commonly called "northwesters."

Snow is rare in southern Louisiana, especially near the coast, but occasional falls are recorded in the northern part of the State. Whenever snow falls in the southern section it usually amounts to little more than a few flurries with the flakes melting as they touch the ground. In the northern section snow falls on an average of about once a year, the annual unmelted fall ranging from about 1 inch in central Louisiana to 3.3 near the northern border.

The average rainfall for the State over a 48-year period is 55.45 inches. The mean precipitation at New Orleans is 59.3 inches a year; at Shreveport, 43.37 inches. The most serious long-period drought, mainly affecting north Louisiana, extended from June to November 1924, with 5.69 inches or only about one-fourth the normal for the period, being recorded. Droughts rarely occur in southern Louisiana. Most of the heavy rainfalls occur during the warm season as the result of thunderstorms and tropical cyclones.

At long intervals strong cyclonic winds, accompanied by high tides and torrential rains, occur in connection with the tropical storms that visit the Gulf Coast from July through September or early October. These storms, which generally approach from the southwest, usually strike some part of the Louisiana coast every 4 or 5 years; and dangerous storms, with winds reaching velocities of 100 miles an hour, have been frequent in recent years.

In the 1960–1970 decade Louisiana suffered heavy losses from four major hurricanes, which destroyed habitations, wrecked offshore oil drilling equipment, damaged thousands of small fishing craft, and hurt oyster beds so severely that production was badly curtailed. The storms were hurricanes Ethel, Sept. 15, 1960, which hit the mouth of the Mississippi River and Plaquemines Parish; Hilda, especially severe in St. Mary Parish and Vermilion Bay, killing 18 and injuring 115 at Larose in Lafourche Parish; Betsy, Sept. 9, 1965, at Grand Isle and Jefferson Parish, which destroyed Grand Pass Camp of the Louisiana Wild Life & Fisheries Commission and other laboratory installations and killed 61 persons; and Camille, Aug. 17–18, in Plaquemines and St. Bernard Parishes, with total devastation from Buras to Venice, and heavy damage to commercial fisheries along the Rigolets and Lake Pontchartrain.

Covering an area 200 to 300 miles in diameter, the storms rotate in a counter-clockwise direction. The wind to the right of the storm center moves in the same general direction as the storm center itself, and as the forward speed of the storm as a whole is about 12 to 15 miles an hour, it may blow some 25 to 30 miles an hour stronger on the right side of the storm than on the left. As these high winds move over the Gulf they develop swells of great size and length. The largest waves, ranging from 20 to 50 feet in height, depending upon the velocity of the wind, form to the right of the storm center. They travel at a speed of more than 40 miles an hour, about three times the speed of the storm center, and approach the coast as great swells far in advance of the storm and even against adverse winds. The storm centers tend to pass to the east of the mouth of the Mississippi River, and New Orleans and the Louisiana coast are thus more frequently within the less violent left-hand half of tropical storms.

A characteristic of hurricane winds is their irregular, gusty nature. An observer on the right hand front of the storm center notes that the wind shifts from a northerly to a southerly direction by way of east; on the left side the shift is by way of west. Easterly winds of great velocity, accompanied by heavy rains, immediately precede the most dangerous period of the storm.

GEOLOGY AND PALEONTOLOGY

Geologically considered, Louisiana as it appears today is a young area. Much of it consists of marine and alluvial sediments deposited after the principal structural features of surrounding regions had assumed their final form. Subsidence of the original structures was so great that few if any of the basic formations are visible. Most of such rocks as appear on the surface, as well as the cores brought up in the drilling of oil wells, show that the structures, even at great depths, are comparatively recent ones. Most observable evidence belongs to the latter part of the Mesozoic era and to the Cenozoic era, the final and shortest major unit in geologic time.

Because the younger rocks conceal the older record, the history in the earlier eras of what is now Louisiana can be known only by inference from the evidence of adjacent States. It is certain, however, that this area had a long and varied history preceding the more recent era.

A long interval elapsed between the closing of the Mesozoic era and the accumulation of the earliest Tertiary deposits of Cenozoic age in Louisiana. Where wells have been drilled, it has been shown that the basal Tertiary lies on an eroded surface where strata ranging in age from late upper Cretaceous to early Comanchean of the lower Cretaceous have been truncated, or cut across, to form the floor on which deposits of later age were built up.

The dawn of Tertiary times in Louisiana showed this region occupying part of a large trough flooded by water and known as the Mississippi Embayment. Sedimentation and uplift contracted and ultimately obliterated the depressed area and resulted in continued and widespread advances and retreats of the invading Gulf waters.

The existing faults, folds, and salt domes were formed immediately following the completion of Miocene deposits of the Tertiary beds. The Gulf then receded far beyond the present shore line, erosion intensified, and the Quaternary period began with the entire region covered with a mantle of Pleistocene sands and gravel. The succeeding Recent period has been occupied largely with the removal of this debris.

The rocks exposed at the surface in Louisiana consist almost entirely of clay, sand, and marl beds. These materials, except for the flood-plain deposits along present-day streams, were laid down in the Gulf of Mexico or near gulf level, when that body of water was much larger than it is now and covered broad portions of the Gulf coastal States. Some of the beds represent ancient deltas of the Mississippi River and of other large streams of the region; others represent deposits in marine water "offshore" from the ancient deltas.

The relationship and distribution of the beds indicate a progressive but gradual retreat of the Gulf and an accompanying rise of the northern part of the State. As the beds became dry land and rose higher and higher, stream erosion produced the hill lands. Due to these changes the oldest beds are found in the northern part of the State, with overlying and progressively younger beds southward. The youngest deposits are found along the coast and in the alluvial valleys of the present streams.

The table on the following page gives a generalized section of the beds, or formations, at the surface in Louisiana and southern Arkansas. The columns at the left show the intervals of geologic time during which the beds formed; the right-hand column gives the geological names of the rock units. These units range in thickness from twenty or thirty feet to several thousand feet.

The chief structural features of the Louisiana geologic formations are the Sabine uplift, a prominent and broad uplift centering in northwestern Louisiana; the Monroe uplift, a similar structure in northeastern Louisiana; the Angelina-Caldwell flexure, a fold, or line of weakness dating from Tertiary times, extending from Sabine Parish across north-central Louisiana to Caldwell Parish; the Mobile-Tunica flexure, a fold of rather recent formation, extending from near Mobile Bay, Alabama, eastward to the Tunica Hills of the northern Feliciana Parishes of Louisiana; 11 interior salt domes in north Louisiana; and not less than 100 salt domes in the coastal area.

During the Cretaceous period near the close of the Mesozoic era, strata consisting of hard crystalline limestone, gypsum, salt, sulphur, and marls were deposited at the bottom of the inland sea in an area comprising a large part of Louisiana. These strata were nearly always accompanied by salt beds, which, when exposed by erosion, were bare of vegetation. The old salt works of Webster, Bienville, and Winn Parishes are proof of this; and enormous deposits of nearly pure salt were discovered in the 11 salt domes of that section.

The great pressure of the thick Tertiary and Quaternary deposits subsequently laid down along the coast is believed to have been a factor in driving upward the great columns of rock salt which form the numerous salt domes of the Louisiana coastal area. The most widely accepted theory is that a prehistoric salt bed, similar to that of the Great Salt Lake in Utah, has been depressed and buried under the enormous ac-

OBSERVABLE SURFACE FORMATIONS IN LOUISIANA

ERA		PERIOD (*Descending Time*)	FORMATION (*Rock Units*)
Cenozoic	Quaternary	Recent	Alluvium
		Pleistocene	Terraces along streams Port Hudson—Beaumont Clays Citronelle Gravels
	Tertiary	Pliocene	Undivided
		Miocene	Fleming Clays and Sands Catahoula Discorbis zone* Heterostegina zone* Marginulina zone*
		Oligocene	Vicksburg
		Eocene	Jackson Claiborne Sabine Midway
Mesozoic		Upper Cretaceous	Arkadelphia Clay Nacatoch Sand Saratoga Chalk Marlbrook Marl Anona Chalk Ozan Brownstown Marl Tokio (Woodbine) Eagleford
		Lower Cretaceous (Comanchean)	Washita Fredericksburg Upper Glen Rose Trinity Anhydrite Zone Lower Glen Rose Travis Peak
Paleozoic			None

* Sub-surface equivalents of Catahoula

cumulation, during millions of years, of the alluvial deposits of the Mississippi River. The great pressure of this deposit, which is estimated to be from 5 to 6 miles in depth, has caused the salt to become plastic and to seek relief by flowing upward through the surrounding rocks. In a few cases, the rising salt columns have perforated the entire 25,000 or more feet of superimposed strata; these outcrops, each usually with an overlying crust, are known as the "Five Islands," the salt mines of which produce most of Louisiana's rock salt.

Salt domes, or plugs, are an important element in the origin of the south Louisiana oil fields. The oil was formed in the bedded rocks as they were deposited, and finally accumulated in the porous and permeable sand layers. As a salt plug moved upward through the bedded rocks, it arched the beds above into dome-shaped structures, and where it cut through these beds they remained up-arched against the flank of the salt. If the domed beds or the beds abutting against the salt were oil-bearing sands, the oil would migrate up the slope of the beds and accumulate in the highest part of the dome above the salt, or in the upper end of the bed, against the side of the salt. In these places it would remain trapped until tapped by wells.

The salt core is sometimes topped with a cap, from a few feet to several hundred feet in thickness, consisting of various minerals, or combinations of minerals, such as limestone, gypsum, anhydrite, sulphur, galena, sphalerite, pyrite, and petroleum. Besides petroleum, the accompanying sandy strata contain vast quantities of natural gas.

The majority of the intruded salt masses have no surface expression, but a few have superficially manifested themselves by sunken areas. The absence of a surface expression has been the motivating reason for the rapid development and application of a new science, geophysical prospecting, which not only detects but measures and determines the shape, size, and location of these masses even when buried under thousands of feet of sediment and water.

On the flanks of the Sabine uplift, in northern Louisiana, are some oil pools localized chiefly by anticlinal structure, including high spots on the uplift and independent domes and anticlines grouped around it. Areal limitations of sand bodies and variation in permeability of reservoir rock, however, have been factors in determining the positions and extent of most of the pools of this district.

The powerful forces which produced the Sabine uplift caused many fractures and folds and gave north Louisiana the basis for its future drainage system. Similar forces produced the Monroe uplift in the northeastern part of the State, the two areas being separated by the immense Ouachita-Mississippi Basin. Extensive shallow swamps and coastal marshes in this basin furnished ideal conditions for preserving forest remains and other vegetable debris, which are represented today by the lignite deposits of north Louisiana.

Northwestern Louisiana slowly emerged, and rivers and creeks began sculpturing a topography similar to that of the present day. But again the scene changed, and another submergence took place. Muddy, shallow seas prevailed, and a heavy deposit of gray clays was placed over the former dry land. These clays rest upon the deeply eroded surfaces of the Wilcox, Claiborne, and Cockfield formations. They are of great economic importance, being the water-carrying beds for the springs and wells of north Louisiana. They enter into the composition of the soils of the creek bottoms, and the water coming from them is remarkably pure.

Deposits known as the Jackson formation rest upon the Cockfield formation. Unlike the deposits mentioned above, which have a dip conforming to the Sabine uplift, the Jackson strata have a general southward dip conforming to the Angelina-Caldwell flexure. They run in a band about 30 miles wide across the southern portion of the hills of north Louisiana and outcrop in many places, frequently protruding like islands, especially along their northern boundary, through a thick cover of red, sandy clay formed later. The Jackson strata make up calcareous soils, which consist for the most part of tough, yellow, fossil-bearing marls grading into gray clays. Frequently, white and yellow limestone boulders are scattered over the outcrops; more rarely, limestone ledges a few feet in thickness cap the hills. Fossil bones of the Zeuglodon, a whalelike mammal, have been found, and the formation is considered one of the best for the collection of upper Eocene fossils. Fossil Foraminifera are numerous both in kind and number.

The Vicksburg Oligocene deposits overlie the Jackson, but there is no difference in the topography of the territory they occupy, nor in their vegetation. They consist of yellow fossil-bearing marls and exhibit the same black prairies, but their fossils show them to belong to a later geological horizon.

South of the Vicksburg deposits are outcrops of the Catahoula formation, which form a prominent hilly belt across the State in the parishes of Vernon, Sabine, Natchitoches, Grant, La Salle, and Catahoula, terminating at Sicily Island. The belt is made up of sandstones, clay stones, and massive clays, which overtop the southern border of the Vicksburg marls. The area consists of steep hills and bluffs which frequently rise more than 150 feet above the surrounding country. The former plain structure has been preserved, however, as a plateau, in which the rivers have cut wide valleys with steep walls, and the tributaries, deep ravines.

Above the Catahoula formation, and completing the Miocene deposits, lie the Fleming clays and sands. The term Fleming at one time was used to refer to the 5,000 to 8,000 feet of sediments lying between the Citronelle gravels of the Pleistocene and the Discorbis zone of the Miocene. Lately Fleming is being used to name the clays and sands between the Discorbis zone and the Pliocene. As the study of microfauna and microfossils has progressed, tentative zones have been set up within the Fleming, such as the *Potamides matsoni* and *Rangia johnsoni* zones. The Fleming covers southern Louisiana; its northern boundary being a curve extending through northern Calcasieu, southern Beauregard, central Allen and Evangeline, southern St. Landry, central Pointe Coupée, northern Livingston, and southern Tangipahoa and St. Tammany Parishes.

Little is known about the Pliocene, which lies between the Fleming and the Pleistocene. Interpretation is rendered difficult because the only described Pliocene microfauna available for correlation is a small one from the comparatively thin Caloosahatchee marl of southern Florida. Besides this, most of the knowledge of the Pliocene sediments of Louisiana comes from wells drilled on the piercement type domes, where the section is only partially represented. The horizon of the Pliocene covers southern Louisiana, and extends northward to end in a slanting line which cuts across southern Beauregard, Allen and Evangeline, central St. Landry and Pointe Coupée, southern West and East Feliciana, central St. Helena, northern Tangipahoa, and central Washington Parishes.

Pleistocene sands and gravels, known as the Drift, cover a vast surface area of the State. Strata are found at Avery Island overlying the salt beds and underlying the Bluff strata. Excavations have revealed fossilized bones and some nearly complete skeletons of species of mastodon, elephant, horse, and species of mylodon and megalonyx (giant sloths). Rising northward, the Drift becomes more or less abundant through the uplands of the State. It spreads a thin sheet over extreme north Louisiana, forms immense deposits centrally, and thins out again over the Catahoula deposits. Silicified corals, Favosites, and Cyathophyllum have been found among these gravels north of Alexandria.

Plant fossils are abundant in several of the Louisiana formations; the identifications include various extinct species of ferns, grasses, sedges, walnuts, oaks, elms, mulberries, figs, magnolias, laurels, hollies, heaths, dogwoods, and olives.

Blue clay, calcareous silts, and brown loams, deposited in or bordering the large bottoms during the Recent period by streams which immediately antedate those of the present time, may be classified together as the Port Hudson-Beaumont formations. Strictly speaking, they are not all alluvial. The clays were deposited as thick strata in sluggish, shallow estuaries running well up to Cairo, Illinois, along the Mississippi and up to Shreveport along Red River Valley. The width of the ancient Mississippi flood plain extended almost to Monroe on the west and to

Vicksburg on the east. At the present day, in spite of the fact that the rivers have been depositing their alluvium on top of the blue clay, large areas are still uncovered. When cultivated, these clays give rise to the famous "buckshot" soils.

The formation of Louisiana's bluffs accounts for the high uplands, 10 to 15 miles in width, which wall the Mississippi River. During the Pleistocene there were four epochs of alluviation, separated by distinct erosional intervals occurring in the Deltaic plain region of Louisiana. The deposits of this period have been correlated with interglacial stages, while the erosional intervals coincide with glacial advances. These four alluvial surfaces, called "Terrace," are named Prairie, Montgomery, Bently, and Williana.

Each terrace starts as a thin layer of silt deposited along the banks in the back reaches of streams, but as the streams advance toward the coast the deposit becomes thicker and broader until it is a wide seaward-sloping surface, which forms a distinctive topographic belt more or less paralleling the alignment of the present coastal marshes. The older surfaces, such as the Bently and Williana, are more steeply inclined than the younger surfaces, which indicates continual regional tilting. This is partially due to the localized uplift along the Mobile-Tunica flexure.

A detailed study of the lower terraces has yet to be undertaken, and just how rich they may be in fossils is not known. The Prairie, or youngest terrace, however, is represented by buckshot clay, a dark colored, gummy soil containing calcareous and ferruginous concretions, fossil woods of oak, bamboo, hard pine, mulberry, hickory, cypress, persimmon, tulip, poplar, elm, and such northern species as white spruce, larch, and white cedar; fossil fruits and seeds of the buttercup, rose, grape, carrot, honeysuckle, and plantain; and fossilized bones of the tapir, elephant, and peccary.

The limits of the Deltaic plain are very irregular, and it is practically impossible to give definite boundaries. This is partly due to the fact that bounding distributaries were inconsistent in position and subject to abandonment, bifurcation, and sudden relegation to an interior position. Roughly, the delta spread between the Pearl and Sabine Rivers. Its northern boundary started in northern Calcasieu Parish; swept sharply north into southern Vernon and Rapides and Central Avoyelles Parishes; then dropped again to enter central Pointe Coupée, East and West Feliciana and St. Helena Parishes; and finally dropped still farther south to cross central Tangipahoa and St. Tammany Parishes.

In the marshes of the southern part of the State, the floods and tides of the Recent period have deposited mud, clay, and sand, with fossil shells similar to those of living species, on top of the blue clay of the Beaumont formation. These marshes are still in the process of formation and are overflowed daily by the tides. Near the rivers and along the banks of bayous that represent former river beds, the alluvium brought down by the floods has been piled upon this clay as deltaic fingers, elevating the adjacent surfaces above the level of the marshes and making arable land. In addition, wave-built barrier beaches are forming along the coast. Sand dunes rise along the crests of these beaches wherever they are exposed to the prevailing winds.

In Louisiana, except for the alluvial deposits at the mouth of the Mississippi, the shore line is receding at a rate of from 6 to 125 feet a year, irrespective of hurricanes, which can cause a retreat of several hundred feet in a few hours. Two factors cause this recession: (1) the regional tilting brought on by the weight of the growing Mississippi delta, which causes the lands about it to dip more sharply and become submerged; (2) the ease with which the low-lying shore is eroded, as is shown by the greater depth of the recession on those portions of the shore line which are more exposed to the prevailing winds and waves. Indeed, so noticeable and rapid has been the subsidence of the mainland, that many of the old plantations have become a region fit only for trapping, hunting and fishing.

Except in the delta, the shore line of southern Louisiana is generally sandy; there are numerous sand and shell ridges extending for miles parallel to the shore either in close proximity to the Gulf or some distance inland. Because of the recession of the coast line, similar ridges are now developing along the Gulf border, just above and below mean tide. Some distance out in the Gulf the same force is at work making the Sabine Shoals. Isle Dernière and Timbalier, Ship, Cat, and Chandeleur Islands will eventually become island ridges like Pecan Island and Grand Chênière in southwest Louisiana or like the less elevated and less conspicuous sand and shell ridges that traverse Orleans Parish near the south shore of Lake Pontchartrain.

Equally interesting in this portion of the State are the numerous shallow lakes and bays. A complete series of beds showing a transition from purely salt to brackish, or even fresh-water, characterizes the submerged areas. The strictly marine Fulgur, Natica, and Arca shells give place successively to brackish water oysters and Mactra, Rangia, and fresh-water Unio, indicating that the land area of this part of Louisiana, during recent geological periods, has passed through a succession of stages similar to that in existence today. A number of extensive swamp areas have the appearance of being old lake beds from which the waters are nearly drained off. The water and oil wells of the region seldom fail to reveal masses of Rangia shells at some depth.

In some places there has been a continual loading and consequent depression of the Gulf's border, giving rise to uplifts in adjacent regions. The shifting of the mouth of the river and the resulting change of loading point has brought about a shifting of regions of depression and upheaval. If the region of uplift is some distance from the coast, the uplifting produces shallow sounds, bays, or lakes, according to its extent. These, when finally filled with clays derived from the sediments of inflowing rivers, pass from the sea-marsh stage into prairies.

NATURAL RESOURCES AND CONSERVATION

An unusual combination of diversified natural resources occurs in Louisiana. Rich alluvial soils and a favorable climate produce a great variety of agricultural products and valuable forests; salt, sulphur, oil, and natural gas are found in widespread areas; lakes, rivers, and the Gulf provide fresh-water fish and sea food, as well as sand, gravel, and shells; game and fur-bearing animals abound.

Extremely fertile soils are the State's basic resource. In addition to their abundance of plant food, most Louisiana soils are warm and porous. As crop and timber lands, the heavy deposits of silt in the alluvial basins along the Mississippi River and other streams are among the best in the world. Next in soil value are the sands and sandy loams of the uplands. They produce a large part of the staple crops of the State. In all, approximately one-seventh of the land area—5,000,000 acres—is under cultivation.

Louisiana's land conservation program is concerned with protection against overflow of land in constant use. Comprehensive waterway control plans now in process of completion will assure this. Flood control acts passed by Congress in 1928 and 1936 provide for protection for the greater part of the eastern half of the State from maximum flood levels in the Mississippi. Floodways providing for the diversion of high water whenever the levee system is threatened have been constructed in the Tensas basin in northeastern Louisiana and in the Atchafalaya basin in south-central Louisiana; the Bonnet Carré Spillway just above New Orleans makes possible the diversion of water from the Mississippi to the Gulf by way of Lake Pontchartrain.

The principal mineral resources are salt, sulphur, petroleum, and natural gas. Of the approximately 100 salt dome formations so far discovered, most are located in the southern part of the State. The largest deposits are under the "Five Islands," which are actually hills, in St. Mary, Iberia, and Vermilion Parishes. Oil in commercial quantities has come from nearly half of them. The largest sulphur deposits are at Grande Écaille, 45 miles south of New Orleans, and at Jefferson Island. Sulphur is also found in salt domes in Iberia, Assumption, Cameron, Iberville, Lafourche, St. Mary, Terrebonne, and Plaquemines Parishes. In Winn and Evangeline Parishes the cap rock of the salt domes is more than 90 per cent limestone. In 1937 the two open-pit quarries produced 408,433 tons of lime rock.

The oil supplies lie chiefly in the northwestern part of the State, where they are found in extensive fields, and in the Gulf Coast region, where they occur principally in connection with salt domes. Among the past and present oil fields in North Louisiana are Rodessa, Cotton Valley, Caddo-Pine Island, Shreveport, Lisbon, Haynesville, Homer, Urania, and Zwolle. The principal south Louisiana oil fields are Jennings, Lafitte, Iowa, Iberia, White Castle, Caillou Island, Ville Platte, Charenton, East Hackberry, Tepetate, Jeanerette, and Bosco. Offshore more than 4,600 oil and gas wells are producing.

The greatest natural gas field is in the northeastern section, including the parishes of Ouachita, Union, Morehouse, Richland, and East and West Carroll. The proven areas are chiefly in three distinct districts: the largest north of Monroe, the others in Richland Parish and along the East and West Carroll Parish line.

Louisiana's scenic beauty lies chiefly in its vegetation and its bodies of water. Most of the State would lack picturesqueness without the conspicuous massing and intermingling of pine, cypress, magnolia, and live oak. Forests and plant areas achieve striking contrasts. This arises from the fact that in Louisiana a difference of a few feet in elevation often makes a great difference in the nature of the soil and its degree of moisture.

There are about 150 species of trees in the State, including 15 species of oak, five of hickory, five of pine, several species of magnolia, ash, maple, elm, and willow, and one each of beech, yellow poplar, sycamore, cottonwood, sweet gum, hackberry, tupelo, upland black gum, and swamp black gum.

The cypress which grows most abundantly in swamps, achieves its most vivid effect on the borders of some of the lakes, especially near the coast. It flanks the shores in a continuous panel of deep green, shot with the gray of Spanish moss. Occasional "ghost" forests of towering cypresses, killed by the inroads of salt water, give a haunting touch to the mute wilderness. The cypress is readily distinguished by its feathery green foliage and out-flaring base. The roots push themselves above the water for air and are called "knees." Tupelo gum, when the trees are bare, is often mistaken for cypress because it, too, grows abundantly in swamps and has an enlarged trunk. Its foliage, however, is entirely different.

The live oak is indigenous to the coastal strip of Louisiana, occurring naturally as far north as the mouth of Red River. Transplanted trees thrive fairly well north of this, though never attaining as great a size as in southern Louisiana; here the live oak, hung with Spanish moss, is planted in avenues and groves on most plantations and grows wild in fringes along the low ridges, the higher banks of lakes and bayous, and some of the shell beaches of the coast. Natural groves on the higher alluvial deposits have a spectacular beauty marked by the pattern of light and shadows on the ground beneath the trees and among the trunks, branches, and crowns. The largest trees, some of which have diameters of more than six feet at the base and a spread of more than 200 feet, grow on open land.

Several oaks in Louisiana rival the live oak in size and beauty. Although none has as great a spread, the height of most of them averages much more than that of the live oak. The most widely distributed of these is the water oak (*Quercus nigra*), which grows in any rich soil and is especially notable as a shade tree on lawns and streets. Its bark is smoother than that of the live oak, and the leaves less leathery but larger and often lobed at the apex, especially in new growth.

The large-flowered magnolia, a native forest tree growing principally in the southern half of Louisiana, is transplanted in all parts of the State. Its natural situation is on rich, well-drained ridges in the lower districts and along the banks of streams in pine uplands, where it mingles with oak and hickory.

Shade and ornamental trees, some European, some tropical, are most conspicuous in New Orleans and some other cities of the State. Camphor trees (*Cinnamomum camphorum*) are widely used as shade trees along the sidewalks of New Orleans; old, well-established trees can resist temperatures as low as 15° Fahrenheit, though the leaves freeze with that degree of cold. The tallowtree is a peculiar exotic growing in New Orleans. Varnish tree, or Firmania, is present in New Orleans as well as in Shreveport and other upland towns and cities. Ailanthus grows well in Shreveport and other places. The China tree is found throughout the State. Bananas grow very well at the Gulf Coast, but the leaves die with a killing frost. A native-grown stock of oranges has become hardy in extreme southern Louisiana and produces a commercially important crop. The bitter orange grows as an ornamental plant in many gardens. Oleanders and crape myrtles are widely grown, especially in the southern half of the State. Palms from many parts of the world have been planted successfully in New Orleans.

More than half of the area of Louisiana is at present forest land. There are some virgin or nearly virgin stands, but most of the timber areas have been cut over and are in various stages of re-growth.

The forests fall roughly into four major types: (1) shortleaf pine uplands; (2) slash and longleaf pine flats and hills; (3) hardwood forests in alluvial basins; (4) cypress and tupelo swamps.

In the parishes of northwest Louisiana grow some of the finest stands of loblolly and shortleaf pine timber in the Nation; much of it is used in construction throughout the South. These species are also much used in pulpwood manufacture, and the center of Louisiana's pulp and kraft paper industry is situated in this region.

Hardwood is found principally in Red River Valley, in a broad belt along the Mississippi River almost to the Gulf, and in the adjoining basins of other streams. The more northern hardwood tracts are probably as rich in timber as the upland pine districts. Here, many million feet of hardwood, including oak, red gum, ash, and elm, are logged annually and shipped to the North and East for manufacture into furniture, interior trim, and various other items.

Towards the south this hardwood belt gives way partly to extensive cypress swamps. Much of the timber in this area has been cut, and a great deal of the second growth is tupelo and other water-loving hardwoods.

In the southern half of the State, on each side of the hardwood belt, are the longleaf and slash pine forests. Most of the virgin longleaf pine has been cut, but some reforestation is in progress.

Forest conservation has made notable progress in Louisiana. The Department of Conservation maintains a successful forest fire patrol system in the pine regions, where fire is a constant menace. The Kisatchie National Forest, in four divisions in central Louisiana, embraces 900,000 acres. The State and several of the larger lumber companies have extensive reforestation areas in the pine districts. The Southern Forest Survey of the U. S. Forest Service has its headquarters in New Orleans, where are also located the offices of the largest of the Nation's nine forest experiment stations. They carry on their work in co-operation with one another, with the State division of forestry, and with lumber companies.

PLANT LIFE

The most varied wild-flower display appears during the warmer months in the pine woods, where the ground is bright with deergrass, ground orchids, phlox, mints, asters, St. Johnswort, false foxgloves, wild peas, and stargrass. In spring, on the slopes and bottoms of the upland sections is an abundance of yellow jasmine, wild azalea, silverbell, dogwood, and redbud. The flowers of the crossvine and trumpetvine are the most conspicuous blooms in the wooded lowland districts.

The fresh-water marshes sometimes have more flowers than the pinewoods, but their variety is not as great. Flowers of the wild mallow, or hibiscus, in white, and changing shades of rose and carmine, cover wide stretches. Blue pickerelweed, white arrowhead, irises, scattered spider lilies, masses of lavender water hyacinth, and occasional rafts of yellow pond lilies, and white water lilies intensify the color and luxuriance of the marshes. Here, in quiet shallow lakes, there are frequently rich growths of the native lotus, or water chinquapin, known in Louisiana as *graines-a-volée*.

Although the introduced water hyacinth (*Piaropus crassipes*) produces a remarkable spectacle with its acres of lavender blossoms, it is often a serious impediment to navigation. Its floating leaves cover the shallow lakes and slow-flowing bayous with almost impenetrable masses, sometimes thick enough to bear a man of average weight. The water hyacinth cannot live in brackish water, and continued high tides cause sufficient salinity to kill it in some streams. Other waterways are cleared by means of dredges or by spraying with a mixture of oil and soda.

Irises in great abundance and variety of color grow in freshwater marshes and swampy areas; most abundant are the giant blue and the copper-colored. Many plants believed to be hybrids have flowers in different shades of wine purple; and there are also variations, including yellow sports, which cover a great range of colors.

Spanish moss, or "long moss" (*Tillandsia usneoides*), grows profusely in southern Louisiana and more rarely in the northernmost part of the State. Common along water courses, it drapes the Gulf Coast cypresses and live oaks, and, less freely, pecans, elms, water oaks, and other trees. Spanish moss is not, botanically speaking, a moss, but a seed-producing plant of the pineapple family. It has minute, lily-like, straw-colored flowers, with correspondingly small oval pods. It also reproduces by division: as the parent plant swings to and fro strands break off, find new resting places, and continue their life cycle. Contrary to general opinion Spanish moss is not a parasite; as an epiphyte, or air-feeding plant, it merely uses trees as an anchor.

Wild cane is characteristic of the low ridge lands that traverse the swamps. Its growth is very dense, and individual plants sometimes reach a height of ten feet or more. Palmettoes grow most abundantly in flat, moist hardwood districts and in the level pinewoods nearest the coast.

ANIMAL LIFE

A richly varied animal life finds attractive habitats in Louisiana: tidal marshes, dry prairies, tupelo-cypress swamps near the coast, large tracts of backwater woodlands in the interior, and pine-forested flats and hills. The coastal and river basin districts are notable for their wild life. Recognition of threats to the continued safety of numerous species has caused the State to provide supervision and protection through the Louisiana Wild Life & Fisheries Commission, while Federal agencies and foundations support extensive refuge areas.

Muskrats are abundant in the Louisiana marshes; they are the chief source of supply for the extensive Louisiana fur industry. The number reaching the American fur market from Louisiana every year is about three times that coming from the rest of the United States and Canada. The Louisiana muskrat is a distinct species, *Fiber rivalicius.* It is a compactly built little animal, with an average body length of twelve inches and a ten-inch tail. The head is relatively wide, with round ears that project above the fur; the eyes are small, bright, and beady. The body is covered with a soft underfur interspersed with long, stiff, glistening guard hairs, which overlie and practically conceal the fur on the upper surface and sides of the body. The color is a dark brownish black, with reddish or golden tints on the sides, and a white or silver belly. The animal is a prolific breeder, producing from three to five litters a year, with an average of about four "kits" to a litter.

The alligator is most typical of the coastal bayous and lagoons, but it also frequents all lowland streams and other inland waters. It seldom, if ever, ventures into salt water. Its numbers have been greatly reduced by the demands of the leather novelty trade, to such an extent that hunting alligators is presently outlawed and habitats are guarded against poaching.

Most of the deer of Louisiana are found in the wooded swamps. The principal districts are along Atchafalaya River, in the wooded localities near the Mississippi in Southeastern Louisiana, and in the Tensas Basin swamps. Black bear, have become rare and cannot be hunted. Bear from Minnesota have been introduced to restock the species. The cougar, or "panther," inhabits only the northeastern part of the State. The wild cat, raccoon, and mink, though rather general, are most common in the lowland wooded districts, where the skunk and the opossum are also to be found.

Abundant in the wet lands, open or wooded, is the water hare, or swamp rabbit, and the gray squirrel; if the timber is tall and dense and includes oak and hickory, the fox squirrel is also present. In the Tensas Basin there is a very dark type of timber wolf; but wolves, though appearing in various parts of Louisiana, are among its rarer animals. The gray fox is more plentiful but inhabits only the upland localities. Beavers have a few small colonies on some of the swifter creeks of the State. The otter is more common and frequents lowland streams. Wild hogs are hunted in the vicinity of Lake Maurepas. Thousands of wild horses are to be found in the remote sections of southwestern Louisiana.

The Louisiana coastal region is the greatest winter resort in North America for wild ducks and geese. Mallard, pintail, teal, gadwall, scaup, and shoveller are especially plentiful, and scatter by thousands over the great marsh areas. Most of the blue geese in North America are believed to winter on the Louisiana coast, finding a congenial environment about the mouths of the Mississippi River and on the low shell banks of the flats of the western coast.

As a measure of national conservation, several large preserves have been established in Louisiana for the great number of wild fowl visiting the State. They include the Delta Migratory Waterfowl Refuge near the mouth of the Mississippi; Marsh Island, off Vermilion Bay with the Russell Sage Refuge; the Rockefeller Wild Life Refuge, west of Vermilion Bay; and the Sabine Wildlife and the Lacassine Federal Refuge in Cameron Parish; the Paul J. Ramey Refuge in Vermilion Parish.

Sea birds congregate in great numbers about low beaches and shell islands near the coast. The most familiar are the brown pelican, laughing gull, royal tern, and black skimmer. Many species of sandpipers, plovers, and other shore birds frequent these localities. The fate of the brown pelican, the State bird, has caused much concern. Formerly it nested on mud lumps at the mouth of the Mississippi. The last nesting was observed in 1961 on North Island of the Chandeleur chain. In 1968 wildlife protective agencies united to bring pelicans back to Louisiana. Pelicans obtained from Cocoa, Florida, were established at Rockefeller Refuge and the Marine Laboratory on Grand Terre Island, and the program is continuing.

The Louisiana heron is a characteristic species in the immediate vicinity of the coast. The Wilson snipe is unusually plentiful in many Louisiana marshes and wet meadowlands during the winter months. The woodcock finds fewer feeding grounds in the marsh than in the low, boggy woods back from the coast. Marsh wrens, seaside sparrows, red-winged blackbirds, and boat-tailed grackles are practically the only representatives of the passerine, or perching, type of bird-life found regularly in the marsh section.

In submerged cypress brakes and similar places, herons and related birds gather in nesting colonies, often of great extent. The little blue heron, American egret, and yellow-crowned night heron are the more familiar species. The snowy egret has found a refuge on Avery Island, where it is protected, and has become a major tourist attraction. The wood duck abounds in the dense growths of cypress, tupelo, and other swamp trees near the larger lowland lakes and streams. The so-called upland plover, known in Louisiana as a "papabotte," prefers prairies and lowland pastures, and was formerly a plentiful and much-prized game bird. The tree swallow is also abundant in the lowlands.

The bald eagle is as rare in Louisiana as elsewhere, its habitat being the coastal cypress swamps, where there are sites for its nests and an abundance of the fish on which it feeds. While both the turkey vulture and black vulture are present throughout Louisiana, the black vulture is more abundant in the lower part of the State, especially near the coast.

Capital and Environs

LOUISIANA STATE CAPITOL, BATON ROUGE. SEEN FROM THE STATUE OF HUEY P. LONG (BRONZE ON MARBLE) AT HIS GRAVE IN CAPITOL PARK

HISTORIC PENTAGON BARRACKS, WITH ONE UNIT MISSING, BATON ROUGE

ONE UNIT OF PENTAGON BARRACKS, BATON ROUGE

THE PATRIOT, STATUARY AT STATE CAPITOL DEPICTS SOLDIER
KEEPING WATCH WHILE PEOPLE MOURN THE HEROIC DEAD

Louisiana Tourist Development Commission

NEW MISSISSIPPI RIVER BRIDGE AT BATON ROUGE,
ROUTE OF INTERSTATE 10

DOWNTOWN BATON ROUGE, FROM THE CAPITOL. THE TALL
BUILDINGS ARE THE STATE EDUCATION BLDG. AND THE
STATE BANK OF LOUISIANA

Louisiana Tourist Development Commission

VICTORIAN GOTHIC LANDMARK: OLD STATE CAPITOL, BATON ROUGE

STAINED GLASS DOME OVER STAIRCASE, OLD STATE CAPITOL

TOMB OF EMMELINE LABICH, "EVANGELINE," ST. MARTINVILLE

TIGER STADIUM, LSU, MEN'S DORMITORY INSIDE, BATON ROUGE

MEMORIAL TOWER, LOUISIANA STATE UNIVERSITY, BATON ROUGE

The dense, moist forests of the Tensas Basin are probably the only regions of Louisiana where the rare ivory-billed woodpecker survives. The pileated woodpecker is a common inhabitant of the swamps. The same woods teem in summer with the yellow-billed cuckoo, and a number of smaller birds, among them the Acadian flycatcher, white-eyed vireo, and hooded and prothonotary warblers. The cardinal, while prevalent throughout Louisiana, is most abundant in low wooded districts.

At one time Louisiana had more than 1,000,000 wild turkeys ranging over river bottoms near pine woods and swamps, but by the 1940's they were down to about 1,500. A restocking program with wild trapped birds has been progressing since 1963. Southern whippoorwill (chuckwill's-widow), flicker, thrasher, catbird, wood thrush, Baltimore oriole, tanagers, and buntings are common in the bluff lands. The red-cockaded woodpecker, Bachman sparrow, chipping sparrow, bluebird, pine warbler, and brown-headed nuthatch are typical of the pinelands.

Fish and other aquatic life range from the porpoises and dolphins of the Gulf to the small game fish of upland streams. Giant rays, sharks, jewfish, tarpon, jackfish, and king mackerel abound in the deep waters off the coast. In the shallower bays and offshore waters are redfish, pompaño, speckled sea trout, flounder, croaker, sheepshead, and Spanish mackerel.

Shrimp proliferate in the estuarine waters of Louisiana to such an extent that commercial shrimp production is between 60,000,000 and 80,000,000 pounds annually. The white shrimp, *penaeus setiferus,* is the most valuable, but the brown shrimp, *penaeus aztecus,* is also cultivated. At one time shrimp developed east of the Mississippi River, but the supply there has diminished greatly. Extensive protective measures have been instituted to keep shrimp beds clear of pollution by pesticide residue and oil waste. Louisiana oysters come from protected bayous, coves, and small bays along the coast, where the waters have the proper degrees of salinity. A great number of blue crabs (*Callinectes sapidus*) and crawfish are found in southern sections of the State. Bullfrogs attain a size and degree of abundance that make Louisiana the foremost frog-catching State.

In the deeper streams are large catfish, especially the blue, or Mississippi catfish, and the yellow catfish. Paddlefish, or "spoon-billed cat," a relative of the sturgeon, are plentiful in some of the shallower lakes, and are valued principally for their roe, from which a form of caviar is made.

The choupique (*Amia calva*), also called the bowfin and grindle, is found in sluggish streams and ponds in the marshy regions of Louisiana. The single living member of an entire order of fishes, the choupique's family history dates back to the age of the Dinosaur. The fish is remarkably tough and because of the peculiar construction of its swim bladder is able to breathe air and live in mud. Some have been ploughed up alive in fields weeks after floodwaters have receded.

The principle fresh-water game fish of Louisiana are the large-mouthed black bass, or "green trout," white crappie ("white perch"), black crappie or calico bass, barfish, yellow bass (sometimes mistaken for the striped bass), and the warmouth and other small bass, or sunfish, known locally as "perch." Near the coast, except for large-mouthed black bass and sunfish, there are few fresh-water game fish.

Turtles, snakes, and other reptiles are plentiful and mostly harmless; the water moccasin is the only common poisonous snake. The most dangerous is the rare cane rattler, a southern variety of the timber rattlesnake. The loggerhead snapping turtle, the largest fresh-water species in Louisiana, attains a weight of 50 pounds or more. Green and other sea turtles are fairly common along the beaches of the coastal islands.

First Americans

ARCHEOLOGICAL evidence unearthed at mortuary and domiciliary mounds near Marksville by the U. S. National Museum in 1933 indicates that a prehistoric race, culturally superior to the Indians found by the earliest European explorers, inhabited Louisiana in the distant past. These Marksville People, whom archeologists sometimes associate with the Hopewell People of the Ohio Valley, were slender and small of stature. They were agriculturists and lived in semi-subterranean houses in villages frequently enclosed by earth embankments and usually built on bluffs bordering streams. Their ceremonial buildings were apparently erected on rectangular earthworks, similar in shape to the stone pyramids of Central America. The artifacts found at several village sites in Louisiana show that these primitive Americans made use of copper, probably transported from the Great Lakes region, galena from the Ozark Mountains, and shells from the Gulf of Mexico. Their pottery was artistically decorated with birds and geometric figures.

Material from a recently excavated Indian mound in La Salle Parish, near Archie, dates from the early Marksville period. Many skeletons and fragments of pottery were found, but only one vessel was intact. Archeologists have been able to determine the period to which they belong by the designs on the pottery.

Recent evidence of another prehistoric Indian culture, discovered by WPA archeologists near Lake Catherine, seems to antedate the Marksville period. This find, which has been named the Tchefuncte because of a similar find near Lake Pontchartrain in the Tchefuncte State Park, includes bits of pottery, arrowheads, and a few human bones. Of especial interest is the fact that the people of the Tchefuncte period were a long-headed race who did not practice the custom of head flattening characteristic of the Marksville period. Their pottery, too, is thicker and cruder than that of the later group.

Succeeding the Marksville People in the prehistoric period were the Deasonville and Coles Creek primitives, remains of whose culture have been found in various places in eastern Louisiana. These groups were contemporaries, and, as far as archeologists can determine, were the ancestors of the Indians met by the European explorers.

Accounts of the Indians left by the early Spanish and French explorers and missionaries form the basis of our knowledge of the historic period. Interesting and valuable as these accounts are, however, they contain many gaps, are seldom accurate, and often reflect the character and background of the narrator. Some approached the Indian from the viewpoint of civilization and found him a brutal savage; others tended to idealize the simple native as man in his natural and finest state. The missionaries seldom agreed with the soldiers, nor the soldiers with the traders, when it came to describing the Indian.

The Indian himself, possessing no form of writing, naturally had no clear record of his history. In common with all primitive people, the tribal memory was preserved in oral form, as tradition; and facts tended to become confused with legend.

The Indians of Louisiana were a semi-sedentary people and were related culturally to the tribes of the Eastern Maize Area. They lived in relatively permanent villages on the banks of rivers and bayous and raised crops in extensive fields. Maize, or Indian corn, of which several kinds seem to have been cultivated, was the most important crop. Pumpkins, melons, and beans were also domesticated. The Indian supplemented his diet with the grain of cane and millet, the seeds of the palmetto and the pond lily, and with chestnuts, black walnuts, persimmons, wild beans, and fungi. Tobacco was an important crop and was carefully planted and tended, being used in Indian rituals and ceremonies as well as for ordinary smoking.

In some places it was easy to clear the land by burning the cane, but on wooded ground it was more difficult; here, the underbrush was removed by pulling and hacking, the bark from the larger trees was stripped off about two feet from the ground, and when it was sufficiently dry, the whole area was burned over. Cultivation was done with a long stick, curved at one end and flattened, not unlike the modern hockey stick. With this tool the Indian could dig or hoe to some extent. The shoulder blades of buffalo were sometimes used for this purpose. In planting seeds the Indians either jabbed a hole in the ground with a sharp pointed stick or scooped out the earth with their hands. Most of the cultivation seems to have been done by the women, though there were certain crops, such as tobacco for ritualistic purposes, which were considered appropriate for masculine labor. Work in the fields tended to be communal, and elaborate ceremonials and rituals attended planting and harvesting.

Among the animals hunted for food, bear and deer were favorites. In the northern part of the State buffaloes were hunted, and in the southwest, alligators. Rabbits and squirrels were often killed with the blowgun, an extremely accurate weapon at short range. Turkeys were treed with the aid of dogs and then shot down; hitting a bird on the wing was apparently beyond the skill of the average bowman.

Fresh- and salt-water creatures were important to the Indian, particularly in the southern part of the State, where they must have replaced land animals as a chief food. Great piles of clam shells have been found in every village site throughout the coastal regions. Fishing, however, was practiced throughout the entire State. Large fish, such as the catfish, were speared, shot, or caught with lines. In shooting fish, arrows were attached to a wooden float and retrieved. Nets were looped of cedar bast, the strong tough under-fiber serving admirably for that purpose. Fish traps with a funnel-shaped entrance were also used.

The only boat used by the Louisiana Indians, so far as it is known, was the dugout canoe, or pirogue, crudely fashioned with fire and primitive tools from cypress logs and bearing little resemblance to the light, slim pirogue used along the bayous by trappers and fishermen.

Instead of the familiar cone-shaped tepee, uncommon in Louisiana, there were several varieties of semi-permanent houses. The simplest were constructed of poles thatched with palmetto leaves. More pretentious dwellings had mud-plastered walls with dome roofs covered with palmetto leaves or grass. A common feature of Indian dwellings was the granary, usually built like a dovecote on poles 15 or 16 feet high, and well polished to prevent mice from climbing them.

Pots, bowls, and dishes were made of clay. The potter's wheel was unknown and all pottery was hand-worked. All shapes and sizes were made: pots, bowls, jugs, storage vessels, plates and dishes, and great containers holding "forty pints" for keeping bear oil. Mantles were woven from bark or nettles; beautiful patterns were developed, and feather work for ceremonial robes and articles was very elaborate. Indian women could spin a little, and used buffalo wool. The dressing of skins was an important work and a variety of colorful effects was achieved in red, yellow, green, and blue paints. Deerskin was used principally for articles of clothing, varying from a breechcloth to a cape for men, and from short petticoats, worn alone, to ample overgarments for women; young girls wore a breechcloth resembling a very small apron. Foot covering was not ordinarily considered necessary, though a kind of deerskin moccasin was employed in traveling.

Children's heads were flattened by strapping them to a board and pulling bands tightly across the skulls. This practice was by no means common in Louisiana. Babies were generally secured to a board, on which they could be conveniently rocked, carried, fed, or placed in an upright position. From youth, the Indians carefully plucked all the hair from their bodies. Tattooing was almost universally practiced by both sexes. The designs were symbolic, and to the initiate the pattern on a warrior's body was an index to his life and achievements. Indian men wore their hair according to the fashion of their tribe—sometimes shaved on the right, sometimes on the left, and at other times entirely shaved except for a tuft at the top, which was worn in a long lock down the back. The women, whose hair was very black, generally wore it long and thick. Body ornaments—necklaces, bracelets, anklets, earrings, and even nose pieces—were affected by both sexes. Men painted their bodies in a manner provided by their various rituals, but the women seem to have indulged in the custom from the mere love of ornament.

The Indian could count to 10 but not beyond, except by indicating two 10's, three 10's, and so on. Ten 10's, or 100, seems to have been his limit, though it is possible that by using sticks he could indicate higher figures. Appointments were kept by means of sticks: each party to a meeting would be given a bundle of twigs that had been counted out beforehand; one would be removed each night until but one remained, showing that the appointed day had been reached. Calendar time was calculated by the moon.

A number of games were played, some of the tribes possessing community athletic fields or a kind of "village green." The chunkey game, general in America, was common throughout Louisiana. It was played with a small, flat disk and a long stick crooked at one end. The object of the game was to throw the disk and the stick in such a way that when they came to rest the disk was inside the curved portion of the stick. The Indian appears to have been an inveterate gambler. An exciting contest would be enlivened by the shouts and cries of players and spectators, and it might end, on occasion, with the loser staking his wife on a last desperate gamble to repair his fortune. The women also had their games, one of which was played with bits of corn. In contrast to the men's they were notable for their quietness and the absence of gambling.

On a linguistic basis ethnologists have grouped Louisiana Indians in three families: The Tunican in the coastal region and in the northeast, the Muskhogean in the east-central and southeast, and the Caddoan in the northwest corner of the State.

The Chitimacha, Attakapa, Opelousa, Koroa, Chawasha, and Washa tribes made up the Tunican family. Except for the Koroa, who lived in northeast Louisiana, the Tunican tribes inhabited the coastal regions.

The Chitimacha were a relatively large tribe, occupying as many as 15 or more known village sites. Their name may have been derived from *Teu'ti'ima'ca* (those having cooking vessels), or from their name for Grand River, *Ce'ti*. The Chitimacha have a long history of association and conflict with the French, and more is known of their language and customs than of most Louisiana tribes. Culturally, they followed the general pattern of the lower Mississippi Valley Indians, save for their greater dependence on food taken from the water.

A system of nobility prevailed in the tribe, with the chiefs and their descendants constituting the aristocracy; a requirement that nobles marry only within their class undoubtedly hastened the depletion of the race. *Thoume Kene* (Great Spirit) ruled over the Chitimacha universe, unseen and impersonal. In addition, each Indian had a personal guardian, or "totem," embodied in some animal who became his helper. No Indian ever killed the animal that was his totem, since he considered that animal sacred.

Typical names among the tribesmen were White Flower, Shout-at-Night, Bluebird, Catfish Mouth, and Three-Legged. An early chief, called by the French *Soulier Rouge* (red shoe), known for his noble character, was the hero of a Louisiana novel in French, *Soulier Rouge,* which appeared in a magazine called *La Violette* in 1849–50.

The Chitimacha excelled as craftsmen, making handsome bracelets, shoulder and breast pieces from copper, and nose ornaments from gold and silver; their basketry, which they still make, was perhaps the finest of all the lower Mississippi Indians. They were also proficient in weaving, pottery-making, and woodworking.

The Attakapa, whose name is derived from a Choctaw word meaning "man-eater," were regarded as cannibals by early historians. Such a reputation was largely undeserved, though the Attakapa were probably inferior in most respects to their neighbors and apparently did indulge in some ritualistic form of cannibalism. They were, as a matter of fact, a settled, agricultural people inhabiting one general region. The settlements of the Attakapa were not intruded upon by the main body of white settlers until the end of the eighteenth century. They were then discovered in three main divisions: on Vermilion River and Bay, on the Mermentau River and its branches, and on Calcasieu River and Lake. The name of the tribe came to have a loose geographical meaning, referring to south-central and southwestern Louisiana, and in time it represented the political division comprising the parishes of St. Mary, St. Martin, Iberia, Lafayette, and Vermilion. Only six of the once great Attakapa tribe remain, all in Calcasieu Parish.

Little is known of the Opelousa, Washa, Chawasha, and Koroa Indians. They were small tribes and offered little opposition to white encroachment. Through frequent migration and amalgamation with other tribes they eventually lost their identity.

Of the Muskhogean tribes living in Louisiana there were the Houma,

Choctaw, Acolapissa, Taënsa, Avoyel, Tangipahoa, Okelousa, Bayogoula, and Quinipissa. All lived in the east-central part of the State on
or near the Mississippi.

Tonti speaks of the Houma Indians, who used the red crayfish as
their war emblem, as "the bravest savages on the river." It was at
one of their villages that Iberville ended his exploratory journey up the
Mississippi in 1699. In 1706 a Tunican tribe settled among the Houma
and immediately carried out a massacre of their hosts, forcing the
survivors to seek new homes. They lived for a while on Bayou St. John,
near what later became New Orleans, before moving into the southern
part of Ascension Parish, where they occupied the Little and Great
Houma villages, the former on the Mississippi a few miles below the
head of Bayou Lafourche, the latter about a mile and a half inland.
During this period the Houma absorbed the remnants of the Bayogoula
and Acolapissa tribes, and at some later time moved into Terrebonne
Parish. Here they occupied six settlements, supplementing hunting and
fishing with work on the plantations during the sugar season. They
mingled extensively with other Indians and today offer a remarkable
example of a growing Indian tribe—125 in 1910; 639 in 1920; 936
in 1930.

The Choctaw, one of the first tribes with whom the French made
an alliance, occupied a small area in Louisiana north of Lake Pontchartrain between the Pearl and Tangipahoa Rivers. Having little liking for warfare, the Choctaw lived as peacefully as the times permitted
with their white and Indian neighbors. They traded freely at the French
Market in New Orleans, selling cane baskets, hides, blowguns, trinkets,
and gumbo filé, a seasoning made of powdered sassafras leaves which has
become closely associated with Creole cuisine. Through Père Adrien
Rouquette, a poet and Roman Catholic priest who lived among them
at intervals from 1845 to 1887 and who built several chapels in their
territory, the Choctaws were instructed in Catholicism and encouraged
in their good neighborliness. Many of Father Rouquette's romantic
poems deal with Choctaw life. About 100 Choctaw, of various degrees
of racial purity, now reside in Louisiana. They live in two small groups
in St. Tammany and La Salle Parishes.

The Acolapissa (those who listen and see or those who look out
for people) originally lived on Pearl River, 10 or 12 miles from its
mouth. In 1702 or 1705 they moved to the north shore of Lake
Pontchartrain in company with the Natchitoche from the west, whose
crops had been ruined and who, upon applying to St. Denis for aid,
were assigned to that locality. For some obscure reason the Acolapissa
massacred many of the Natchitoche while the latter were preparing to
accompany St. Denis to their old lands. Apparently no action was taken

against the tribe, which in 1718 joined other tribes in a settlement on the Mississippi about 13 leagues above New Orleans.

The Taënsa were first discovered by the French living on the shore of Lake Joseph about "three leagues from the eastern end." In 1706 they were forced to move south, probably near Edgard or Manchac. Before 1744, however, they had moved across to the Tensas River, to which they gave their name. After several other migrations and a last stand on Bayou Bœuf, they either died out, intermingled with other tribes, or left the State.

The remainder of the Muskhogean family in Louisiana—the Avoyel, Tangipahoa, Okelousa, Bayogoula, and Quinipissa—were all small tribes that either died out or were absorbed by other tribes in the early nineteenth century.

The Caddoan confederacy of tribes, represented in Louisiana by the Kadohadacho, Natchitoche, Yatasi, Adai, Doustioni, and Washita, resided in the northwest section of the State. They were among the first Indians encountered by the white men within the United States, being visited by De Soto in 1541. Situated as they were, between the French and Spanish colonies, they were subjected to the worst influences of both. For years the Caddoan territory was the disputed "no man's land" between the colonial empires. The several tribes seem to have favored the French, with whom they carried on an extensive trade in merchandise stolen from the Spaniards of the Southwest. In 1835 the Caddo signed a treaty with the United States, relinquishing their lands in northwest Louisiana for $80,000. Many of them migrated to Texas; but in 1838 Texas pioneers invaded Caddo Parish in a campaign against the Indians. A new treaty was signed at Shreveport that year, in which the Caddo surrendered their guns to the Texans and agreed to remain in Louisiana, at the expense of Texas, until Indian troubles on the northern boundary were settled. In 1859 they narrowly escaped a general massacre projected by the whites. After a forced march of 15 days they reached safety on the Wichita River in the Oklahoma Territory. There the boundaries of their new homelands were fixed in 1872.

There were about 1,500 persons in the State classified as Indians in the census report of 1930. This indicates about a 100 percent increase since 1900, when it was feared that the race was on the verge of complete extinction. It is doubtful, however, whether many of this number were of pure blood. Louisiana has but one government reservation and, consequently, such groups as survive tend to mingle with and adapt their lives to the white man. The 130 Koasati (Coushatta) Indians living in Allen Parish are not native to the State, their ancestors having migrated here from Alabama in 1799.

The Indian has made many contributions to the State. Numerous bayous, rivers, and towns have been given names taken from his language. The early settlers benefited greatly by agricultural methods taught them by the Indian; some of our most popular food is of the same origin. The large number of mounds scattered over Louisiana still command great interest. Many have been investigated, but Louisiana continues to present a large field for archeological research.

History

ACCORDING to several fantastic and geographically obscure accounts, the mouth of the Mississippi and littoral Louisiana were discovered by Spanish adventurers not long after Columbus found the way to the New World. In the spirit of the times, when the discovery of anything less than El Dorado or the Fountain of Youth embarrassed Spanish explorers, Alvarez de Pineda, in 1519, reported that he had come across a great river (presumably the Mississippi) laden with gold and bordered by numerous villages inhabited by pigmies and giants wearing golden ornaments. The "Rio del Espiritu Santo," as Pineda called the river, and by which name the Mississippi was known to Spaniards in the early sixteenth century, may also have been visited by Cabeza de Vaca and the survivors of the Narvaez expedition in 1528.

Hernando de Soto, acknowledged discoverer of the Mississippi, is credited with being the first European to have entered what is now the State of Louisiana. During the winter of 1541–42 his expedition traveled through Arkansas and northern Louisiana in the Ouachita and Red River country over a route that has never been exactly determined. After De Soto's death, his successor, Luis de Moscoso, set out with what few men remained of the expedition on an overland journey across Louisiana to Mexico. They finally abandoned the attempt and returned to the Mississippi, where they built boats and descended to the Gulf.

Father Dávilla y Padilla, author of a history of the Province of Santiago published in Madrid in 1596, tells of a Dominican lay-brother, Marcos de Mena, who was shipwrecked in 1553 with 300 others off the Gulf Coast. The survivors were attacked by Indians, and de Mena was wounded by seven arrows. Although he was not quite dead, his companions buried him in a shallow grave on the beach and left an opening through which he might breathe until he died. But de Mena regained his strength and left his premature entombment, only to find that his companions had been slain by the Indians. He finally reached Mexico after a perilous journey across Louisiana and Texas.

For more than a century, while Spanish *conquistadores* searched the Southwest for the riches of Cibola and French missionaries explored the upper valley, lower Louisiana lay neglected. France at last claimed the territory in 1682, when La Salle and a band of 50 men descended to the mouth of the Mississippi. On April 9 of that year, on the bank of the river three leagues from the Gulf, the expedition erected a cross, and a column bearing the arms of France with an inscription claiming the territory in the name of Louis XIV, in whose honor the entire tributary system of the Mississippi was named "Louisiana."

Two years after the acquisition of this vast territory France took steps toward securing the mouth of the river against Spain and England. For that purpose La Salle was sent out with a colonizing expedition in 1684. Sailing too far westward, he landed at Matagorda Bay, Texas, in the belief that it was the western channel of the Mississippi. After a fruitless search for the river, La Salle abandoned the project and set out on an overland journey to Canada, during which he was treacherously killed by his own men.

A second expedition left France in 1698 under Pierre Le Moyne, Sieur d'Iberville. Arriving at Mobile Bay in February 1699, the French learned from the Indians that the Mississippi was a short distance to the west. Anchoring the fleet off Ship Island, Iberville and a small party set out in boats for the mouth of the river, which they entered on March 2, 1699. The next day, Shrove Tuesday, the party started upstream, the appropriate name of Mardi Gras being given to a bayou 12 miles up the river. The following Friday they arrived at the present site of New Orleans, where a buffalo was killed, a cross erected, and trees were marked. Above Istrouma (Baton Rouge), a place named for the tall, red pole that marked the boundary of the Houma and Bayogoula hunting grounds, the expedition effected a short cut, christened Pointe Coupée, across the neck of a great bend of the Mississippi. Near the mouth of Red River the party turned back, Iberville returning by way of Bayou Manchac through Lakes Maurepas and Pontchartrain. His brother, Sieur de Bienville, continued down the Mississippi to obtain a letter left with a Mongoulacha chief in 1685 by Tonti, who had come from Canada to join La Salle's colony.

Even as Iberville sailed, two English ships were on the way to explore the mouth of the Mississippi. In a great turn of the river just below the site of New Orleans, Bienville, returning in September 1699 from an exploratory trip, encountered one of them at anchor. In a parley with the English captain, Bienville dissuaded him from proceeding up the river by stating that his was but a small detachment of a large French force stationed upstream. The English weighed anchor and turned about. The bend in the river has since been known as English Turn.

Further exploratory work in Louisiana was carried on by Catholic missionaries, *voyageurs* from the upper valley, and *coureurs de bois*, who traded with the Indians and supplied the small settlement at Biloxi with fur pelts, without which the colony would have languished, since its early settlers were men whose chief interests lay not in agriculture and colonization but in acquiring wealth. From time to time small parties were sent out to establish amicable relations with the neighboring Indians and to forward the fur trade. Perhaps the most important man engaged in this work was Juchereau de St. Denis, who traveled extensively in western Louisiana and Mexico in an effort to develop trade with the Spaniards of the Southwest. To protect French territory in the Red River country against Spanish encroachment he established Fort St. Jean Baptiste (Natchitoches) about 1714, at the termination of the Great Raft, the huge log jam that blocked navigation from that point north on Red River. At Los Adais, about 14 miles southwest of Natchitoches, Spain established a mission in 1717 and a fort in 1721. Up to the transfer of Louisiana to Spain in 1763, France controlled the major portion of what is now the State of Louisiana, while Spain governed a narrow strip paralleling Sabine River. Until 1773, Los Adais, a Louisiana settlement, served as the capital of the Spanish province of Texas.

Little attempt was made under Louis XIV to colonize the province, the expectation being that the region, like Spanish Central-American possessions, would yield large revenues in the form of gold and silver. Disillusioned in that respect, and finding the maintenance of the colony too expensive, the French Government in 1712 consigned trading rights in Louisiana to Antoine Crozat, a wealthy French merchant. A charter was granted, the government reorganized, a certain number of settlers imported each year, and efforts were made to establish profitable trade.

Crozat's venture was far from a financial success. He relinquished his concession in 1717 to the Company of the West, a trading company controlled by John Law, whose financial schemes were then in great favor in France. Reorganized in 1719 as the Company of the Indies, Law's colonial enterprise did much toward colonizing Louisiana. Glowing accounts, picturing Louisiana as a veritable paradise, were circulated in Europe, and thousands of gullible settlers were lured to the colony. Disappointed though they were at finding nothing but a wilderness, many of these colonists remained to till the fertile land and make their fortunes.

The original intention of founding a city near the mouth of the Mississippi to secure the river and Louisiana against covetous Spain and England was finally carried out, about 1718, with the establishment of New Orleans 30 leagues (about 100 miles) from the Gulf, at a point where the proximity of Bayou St. John afforded a convenient portage to Lake Pontchartrain. Named in honor of the Regent of France, Philippe, Duc d'Orléans, the town became the capital of Louisiana in 1723.

To minimize the danger arising from the presence of large numbers of Negro slaves, Governor Bienville, in 1724, promulgated the *Code Noir,* a set of laws drawn up for regulation of Negroes on the island of Santo Domingo. Its provisions were not, on the whole, severe, the most stringent penalties being imposed for offenses imperiling the safety of whites; otherwise, slaves were protected from the possible cruelty and injustice of their masters. Additional provisions provided for the expulsion of Jews from the colony under penalty of imprisonment and confiscation of property, and the establishment of the Catholic religion as the State faith.

The peace of the colony was suddenly disturbed in December 1729 when a half-famished refugee electrified New Orleans with the news of a massacre of the whites by the Natchez Indians at Fort Rosalie (Natchez). Hasty preparations were made for the defense of New Orleans, and couriers raced into the outlying country to warn the settlers. Governor Périer secured assistance from the Choctaw, who, swooping down on the Natchez while they were still celebrating their victory, killed 60 warriors and rescued many prisoners.

The Indian problem was but one of many that embarrassed French administration in Louisiana. Revenue from commerce was so meager that the mother country constantly had to subsidize the colony. Comparatively few settlers migrated to the territory; by mid-century, except for plantations along the river and small settlements clustered about military posts scattered through the vast Mississippi Valley, Louisiana still remained an uninhabited wilderness. With the loss of Canada to England in the Seven Years' War (1756–63), France readily disposed of the unprofitable colony, untenably isolated by British and Spanish holdings in North America.

The transfer of Louisiana to Spain, officially confirmed by the Treaty of Paris (1763), was actually consummated in 1762, when Louis XV, in order to prevent the territory from falling into the hands of the English, made a gift of the "Island of New Orleans" and all Louisiana lying west of the Mississippi to his cousin, Charles III of Spain. To England were ceded the French settlements east of the river, except the "Island," and all of Spanish Florida and West Florida.

Spain rather reluctantly accepted Louisiana. The transfer was kept secret for a time, and it was not until 1764 that French officials in Louisiana were informed of the transaction. The transfer was, naturally, unpopular with the French colonists. A petition was sent to France requesting that the king rescind the cession; although sponsored by the aged Bienville, this movement came to naught. Antonio de Ulloa, the Spanish commissioner sent to take over the colony, arrived at New Orleans in March 1766. His entry on a stormy day with only 90 soldiers was not impressive. Smouldering contempt for Spanish authority and indignation against commercial restrictions finally broke out in revolt.

In the 10-month period that Louisiana, the first colony in America to revolt against a European power, enjoyed freedom from foreign rule, no essential steps were taken to preserve the independence won in the bloodless rebellion. There were some among the rebels who proposed to found a republic under a "Protector," but more cautious Louisianians, fearing foreign intervention, especially on the part of Great Britain, spoke against the scheme. Whatever notions of severance from Spain the colonists entertained were dispelled by the arrival in August 1769 of 24 men-of-war and more than 2,000 soldiers, under the command of Count Alexander O'Reilly. One of his first acts—intended to instill respect for Spain—was the execution of six of the leaders of the October rebellion.

After his power had been established, O'Reilly instituted changes in government, abolishing the Superior Council and substituting the *Cabildo* (*see Government*), in its stead. Less imperious than the soubriquet "Bloody" accorded him by Louisianians would indicate, O'Reilly, in laying the foundation of Spanish administration in Louisiana, left the colony essentially as it was before the cession to Spain. Except for the substitution of the Spanish language as the official tongue, the adoption of Spanish law, and a few minor changes, the government resembled that under the French regime. As under France, the mercantilist theory was adhered to in the regulation of commerce, Spain being substituted as the sole country—the Spanish colony of Cuba excepted—with which Louisiana could trade.

In the 30-year period following 1760 about 4,000 Acadians, who had been expelled from their settlement in Nova Scotia by the British in 1755, came to Louisiana. Of French descent, they were readily welcomed by the Creoles, whose sympathy following their own transfer to Spain naturally went out to victims of colonial disruption. Successive groups of Acadians settled in southern Louisiana, particularly in the Attakapas District. Their descendants, known today as "Cajuns," form a large part of Louisiana's French stock.

At the outbreak of the American Revolution, Spain, ever eager to humble England, permitted Spanish officials in Louisiana to aid the rebellious American colonists. Munitions and supplies were sent to the Atlantic colonies from New Orleans, where agents of the Continental Congress were allowed to establish bases. One of these, Oliver Pollock, by forwarding credit and directing the shipment of supplies, made it possible for George Rogers Clark and other American patriots to wrest the western country from the British. Bernardo de Galvez, acting governor of Louisiana at the time, further aided the Revolution by permitting James Willing to use New Orleans as a base in pillaging and terrorizing the Loyalists in West Florida. Upon the declaration of war between Spain and England in 1779, Galvez, with a small body of recruits, captured Manchac, Baton Rouge, and Natchez in little more than a month. By May 10, 1781, Mobile and Pensacola had been taken and both Floridas were added to Spanish Louisiana. For the first time in its history the area now comprising the State came under one flag. The northern boundary of West Florida, set at 31° by the treaty of Madrid in 1795, ultimately became the State Line east of the Mississippi.

During the Spanish regime Louisiana depended increasingly for the bulk of its commerce upon the settlers in the Ohio Valley. The trade had always been held illegal, but enough smuggling was carried on, with the connivance of Spanish officials, to satisfy both the merchants at New Orleans and the traders of the upper valley. The merchandise not permitted to be sent directly to New Orleans was sold in British territory at Manchac. After Spain acquired the Floridas and had little reason to fear British encroachment, its friendliness toward the new American republic languished. Though the treaty drawn up between Great Britain and the United States gave each country free navigation of the Mississippi, Spain, claiming it had not been a party to the agreement, denied the right and refused to open the Mississippi to either country.

A large increase in the population of the Ohio country following the Revolution intensified the Mississippi question. A greater number of flatboatmen each year clamored for unrestricted commerce at New Orleans, and though some were able to win trading rights through collusion in Spanish intrigues, many were denied passage through Spanish territory. Seizure and confiscation of numerous cargoes irritated the Kentuckians and Tennesseans, who proposed either to take New Orleans by force or secede from the Union and join Spain.

The problem was settled, for the time being, by the treaty of 1795, which allowed American traders free navigation of the Mississippi from its source to its mouth and a "right to deposit" (permission to store and reship) goods in New Orleans, for three years; at the expiration of the period these privileges were continued. In less than five years the number of ships and river boats arriving at New Orleans more than doubled. Sudden revocation of trading rights by the Spanish intendant, Don Juan Ventura Morales, in 1802, produced such agitation among the Americans, who appeared on the verge of invading Louisiana, that Governor Salcedo restored freedom of navigation. The United States, aware at last of the full import of the Mississippi question, began negotiations for the purchase of the Floridas and the Island of New Orleans from France, which by the Treaty of San Ildefonso (1801) had regained Louisiana.

At the close of the eighteenth century, except for New Orleans, Natchitoches, Baton Rouge, Opelousas, St. Martinville, Lafayette, New Iberia, Monroe, Alexandria, and a few isolated trading posts, the area now comprising the State of Louisiana was still relatively undeveloped. Population centered along the Mississippi and Red Rivers and the bayous of the southern section. Only hunters and trappers had penetrated into the wilderness of northwest Louisiana. What the territory lacked in numbers, however, it made up for in diversity of inhabitants. Isleños, brought over from the Canary Islands during Galvez's administration, lived as trappers and fishermen at Terre aux Bœuf below New Orleans and in the Teche country. Descendants of the German settlers who had been sent to Louisiana by John Law tilled their farms on the German Coast, a 40-mile strip of territory on the Mississippi 20 miles above New Orleans. Along Bayous Teche, Vermilion, and Lafourche and scattered throughout southern Louisiana lived the Acadians. American settlers, who had migrated to the region while it belonged to Great Britain (1763–79), inhabited West Florida on the east bank of the Mississippi, north of New Orleans. After the French Revolution numerous Royalists fled to Louisiana, where they were given generous grants of land along the Mississippi in the northern part of the State. New Orleans, the largest city in Louisiana and the most important in the entire Valley, had a population of less than 10,000.

Spanish officials in Louisiana were not formally notified of the transfer of the province to France until the arrival in March 1803 of Pierre Clement de Laussat, the prefect sent by Napoleon to take over the colony. Although Louisiana was predominantly French, there was little enthusiasm over the reclamation of the province by the mother country. Spanish silver seemed much more stable than fluctuating French assignats; merchants of New Orleans, dissatisfied as they were with the reactionary Spanish commercial policy, feared the possibility of new regulations; citizens accustomed to an orderly Spanish regime viewed with alarm a change in government that would bring them under the control of *revolutionnaires* led by Napoleon. As the agent of an anti-Catholic government, Laussat was considered so dangerous that many of the Ursuline nuns fled to Havana.

Meanwhile, unknown to Louisianians, negotiations for the purchase of Louisiana were under way between Napoleon and the United States.

The sale was completed on April 30, 1803. For 80,000,000 francs, roughly $15,000,000, the United States acquired more than 1,000,000 square miles of territory and 90,000 inhabitants.

Within 20 days (November 30–December 20, 1803) Louisiana changed hands twice. On November 30, amid much ceremony at the Place d'Armes, Laussat formally assumed control in the name of the French Republic. Twenty days later William C. C. Claiborne and General James Wilkinson, agents of the United States, took over Louisiana from Laussat at the Cabildo.

The transfer of the colony to the United States was as unsatisfactory to Louisianians as the prospect of French rule had been. Claiborne, who surrounded himself with American officials, was disliked as governor because of his unfamiliarity with the customs and language of the people. Once again the introduction of a new language and strange customs affronted the Creoles, whose acquaintance with rowdy American rivermen led them to look askance at immigrants from the States.

A division of the purchased territory was made by Congress in 1804. The part lying north of 33°, the present northern boundary of the State, became the District of Louisiana, and the portion lying south was called the Territory of Orleans. Both the eastern and western boundaries of the Territory of Orleans, the nucleus of the State of Louisiana, were in dispute. In acquiring Louisiana from France the United States contended that it had purchased the entire area formerly comprising French Louisiana. Spain contested the claims to West Florida and the Sabine River area. While negotiations were under way Spain held the Florida Parishes, the territory east of the Mississippi and north of Lakes Maurepas and Pontchartrain. On the west, the United States set Sabine River as the boundary of the Territory of Orleans, while Spain claimed a line farther east along the Arroyo Hondo, a creek halfway between Natchitoches and Los Adais. After the Louisiana Purchase both Spain and the United States sought to strengthen their claims by military occupation. A truce was effected in 1806, whereby the corridor between the disputed boundaries was regarded as a neutral strip pending solution of the controversy.

Louisiana was disturbed in the winter of 1806 by a number of wild rumors concerning a filibustering expedition headed by Aaron Burr. It was reported that he and a formidable body of recruits intended either to separate the western country from the United States or Mexico from Spain. New Orleans was to be used as a base, the banks there plundered, and Louisiana revolutionized. New Orleans was fortified under the supervision of General James Wilkinson, who exposed Burr, his erstwhile friend and confidant. Actually, Burr had only 60 to 80 men under his command. He succeeded in getting his flotilla of flatboats as far as

Bayou Pierre, a short distance above Natchez, where he was arrested and his band dispersed. Concern over possible insurrection and war with Spain quickly subsided.

The danger of war again arose in 1810 when the American settlers of the Florida Parishes rebelled against Spain. Baton Rouge, the seat of government, was taken by the insurrectionists in September. The Spanish authorities retired to Pensacola, and the revolutionists, meeting in convention, proclaimed West Florida "a free and independent State." A republic was set up, a constitution adopted, and application made for admission to the United States. Taking advantage of the revolt to settle the boundary dispute, President Madison in October proclaimed West Florida part of the United States and ordered Claiborne to take possession.

The census of 1810 revealed that the Territory of Orleans, with a population of 76,556, was eligible for admission to the Union as a State. After prolonged debate, in which it was brought out by eastern antagonists that the admission of a State in which the inhabitants were foreigners of doubtful allegiance, was a violation of the constitution and a menace to the Union, Congress finally authorized the general assembly of the Territory of Orleans to call a special election of representatives for the purpose of formulating a constitution. A convention of 45 delegates representing 19 parishes met at New Orleans in 1811 and drew up a constitution modeled after that of Kentucky. On April 30, 1812, Louisiana was granted statehood. West Florida, with Pearl River as the eastern boundary, was incorporated in the State. The present boundaries were established in 1819 when Spain finally relinquished its claim to the territory east of Sabine River.

In the winter of 1814, at the end of the War of 1812, while packets sped across the Atlantic bearing news of the signing of peace at Ghent in December, Louisianians, under the command of General Andrew Jackson, and with the assistance of volunteers from Kentucky, Tennessee, and Mississippi, defended New Orleans against a British force of Wellington's veterans commanded by General Sir Edward Pakenham. An ineffectual campaign against Jackson had been waged from the British base at Pensacola during the summer of 1814, but no move had been made toward New Orleans. An unsuccessful attempt was made by the British to enlist the aid of the Baratarian pirates, who had scoffed at American efforts to suppress their buccaneering operations along the Louisiana coast. Arriving off Chandeleur Island on December 10, the British defeated five American gunboats detailed in Lake Borgne for scouting purposes and succeeded on December 23 in advancing unseen up Bayou Bienvenue to within seven miles of New Orleans. Jackson lost no time in checking the enemy's advance. Every available detachment in town, including Choctaw Indians, Baratarians, and free Negroes, swung down the levee to meet the invaders. After preliminary skirmishes the British were completely routed in the Battle of New Orleans, January 8, 1815 (see Tour 8).

American enterprise soon became apparent in the progress made by the State after the War of 1812. Traders from the upper valley, taking advantage of steam propulsion (the first steamboat to navigate the Mississippi arrived at New Orleans in 1812), increased their tonnage, and New Orleans began to boom as a port. Steamboat arrivals at the city increased in number from 21 in 1814 to 1,573 in 1840, and tonnage, exclusive of unrecorded freight rafted down the river, jumped from 67,560 tons in 1814 to 537,400 tons in 1840. By that time New Orleans had become the fourth city in the nation and stood second only to New York as a port. Towns sprang up in the outlying parishes and numerous planters from neighboring Southern States migrated to Louisiana with their slaves to take advantage of the fertile land. Cotton and sugar enriched many plantation owners.

Meanwhile, in the early nineteenth century, Captain Henry Shreve's work in clearing Red River of the immense raft of driftwood that had obstructed it for centuries opened that river to navigation and encouraged settlement in the hitherto unpopulated northwestern part of the State. The evacuation of the district by the Caddo Indians, who in 1835 sold their lands to the United States for $80,000, resulted in the rapid settlement of the territory. Shreveport, founded in 1837 by Captain Shreve and seven associates, soon became an important trading center. With Natchitoches and Alexandria as other thriving commercial centers, Red River rapidly developed as the second most important artery.

A more democratic constitution was adopted by the State in 1845. Under it the electoral franchise was broadened through the elimination of property qualifications, and provision was made for the election of the governor by direct popular vote. Except for the constitution of 1868, the seven other constitutions that Louisiana has adopted since 1845 (see Government) have been based upon the document of that year.

As the gateway to the Southwest, Louisiana played a prominent part in the expansionist movement that brought on the Mexican War. Many of its citizens joined the American wagon trains that rumbled across the State over the San Antonio Trace into Texas. To protect the frontier, Cantonment Jesup was established west of Natchitoches in 1822 and Cantonment Atkinson at Lake Charles in 1830. When Texas voted for annexation in 1845 General Zachary Taylor, then in command at Fort Jesup, moved into Texas. At this critical juncture John Slidell of Louisiana was sent as minister to Mexico to adjust the boundary dispute. Mexico refused to receive him and war started soon afterward.

After the war New Orleans became a base for filibusters operating against Cuba and other Latin-American countries. In 1850 and 1851 Narciso Lopez organized two expeditions in the city to wrest Cuba from Spain. Both expeditions reached Cuba but met with little success. News of the execution of Lopez and many of his followers incited riots in New Orleans, in which Spanish cigar stores and the consulate were mobbed. William Walker, who tyrannized over Nicaragua in 1855–56, was tried and acquitted for his filibustering in New Orleans in 1857. For years thereafter Louisiana harbored jingoes clamoring for intervention in Central American politics.

Following the lead of South Carolina and other Southern states, Louisiana seceded from the Union on January 26, 1861. For six weeks, before it joined the Confederacy, the State existed as an independent republic under its own flag. Immediate steps toward mobilization were taken. The militia was called out, the U. S. Mint and Customhouse were seized in New Orleans, and the military posts of the State were taken over. Thousands of native sons under such able leaders as Beauregard, Bragg, Polk, and Taylor hurried to the Virginia battlefields.

For a year after the outbreak of the war Louisiana remained undisturbed by warfare within its borders. In April 1862, however, David G. Farragut, a former resident of Louisiana, led an expedition of 44 ships up the Mississippi with the intention of taking New Orleans, closing the Confederacy's main source of supplies, and severing the South. After a five-day bombardment of Forts Jackson and St. Philip near the mouth of the river, Farragut successfully took 17 ships past the forts on the night of April 24 and two days later occupied New Orleans without opposition. On May 1, General Benjamin F. Butler brought up 15,000 Federal troops and began his dictatorial and highly unpopular military rule of the city.

Farragut continued up the Mississippi, taking Baton Rouge and Bayou Sara. A desperate effort to recover Baton Rouge for use as a base for supplies sent from the Red River Valley was made by a Confederate force of 3,000 men under General John C. Breckinridge. It failed because of the breakdown, five miles above town, of the *Arkansas,* an iron-clad ram with which the Confederates hoped to drive off the Federal gunboats supporting the Baton Rouge garrison.

Up to the early part of 1863 practically all of Louisiana west of the Mississippi was still under Confederate control. Opelousas was then the capital of what remained of Louisiana. Under General Dick Taylor, son of Zachary Taylor, the Confederates had kept Butler bottled in New Orleans and the surrounding parishes east of the river, but were unable to prevent his successor, General Nathaniel P. Banks, from taking possession of southern Louisiana as far west as Berwick Bay. As the Federals neared Opelousas the capital was removed to Shreveport.

In 1864 Taylor and his small army were successful in frustrating a Federal attempt to take Shreveport and conquer the Red River territory. Two Union forces, one sent up Red River and another up Bayou Teche, succeeded under Banks in penetrating as far as Mansfield, where they were defeated in a bloody engagement and driven back to Alexandria in disorderly retreat. After that there was little fighting in Louisiana.

During the war the State had two governments. The portion of western Louisiana still under Confederate control was governed first from Opelousas and later from Shreveport under the administrations of Thomas O. Moore and Henry W. Allen. Federal-controlled Louisiana, with the capital at New Orleans, was administered by Military Governor General George Shepley and later by Michael Hahn. Although the Emancipation Proclamation of January 1, 1863, granted freedom to slaves in the territory held by the Confederates, slavery was preserved in the 13 parishes occupied by the Federal troops. Slavery was abolished formally by the constitutional convention in 1864. The constitution drawn up by this Republican body was proclaimed a model for "rebel" States, but nevertheless failed to gain Congressional approval. It continued in use, however, as a basis of government until a "reconstruction" constitution was adopted in 1868.

After the war, and with the complete surrender of Louisiana, the State was once more united under one government administered by a succession of military governors. Conforming to the Reconstruction Acts of March 21 and 23, 1867, a constitution in keeping with the Thirteenth, Fourteenth, and Fifteenth Amendments was drawn up for the State. Negroes were granted equality and full social and civil rights. Retributive action in withholding the franchise was taken against persons too active in sponsoring the Confederate cause. Louisiana was thereafter readmitted to the Union.

With the inauguration in 1868 of Governor H. C. Warmoth and Lieutenant Governor Oscar Dunn, a Negro, there began a period of racial strife, official plundering, crushing taxation, scandalous bribery, and official disregard for the rights of whites. The State bonded debt increased from $10,000,000 to $50,000,000 within eight years, taxes rose 450 percent, a single session of the legislature cost $900,000, and the proceeds of a public school fund were divided among embezzlers. Public affairs were controlled by "carpetbaggers," Northern fortune hunters who flocked into the South during Reconstruction to take advantage of the confusion, and Negroes organized in Union Leagues directed by whites. Few native white Louisianians had any voice in governmental affairs.

To curb the Negroes and their white instigators, an organization known as the Knights of the White Camellia was formed at Franklin in 1867. It and the Ku Klux Klan sought by intimidation, and often by violence, to keep Negroes out of office. Later, a more powerful organization, the White League, was instrumental in overthrowing carpetbag rule.

The despoilers of the State began to quarrel among themselves, and in 1872 split into two factions. In the gubernatorial election of that year Warmoth and his followers, calling themselves Liberal Republicans, united with the Democrats to support their candidate, John McEnery, against the Radical standard bearer, W. P. Kellogg. McEnery received a majority of the votes, but the Radicals, supported by President Grant, placed Kellogg in office with the aid of Federal troops. The Democrats and their Republican allies were not entirely shut out, however, since they set up their government at the City Hall in New Orleans, a city then serving as a two-fold capital.

Opposition to carpetbag tyranny now began to be expressed in violence. At Colfax, Grant Parish, a bloody riot occurred in April 1873 when a band of white men from Grant and the neighboring parishes sought to regain the courthouse and offices taken from them during a Negro uprising. Three whites and about 120 Negroes were killed before the Negroes were finally ejected. At New Orleans on September 14, 1874, the White League, which had pledged itself to restore self-government to Louisiana, met and defeated Kellogg's Metropolitan Police. Although the Democrats were in complete control of the city and had installed themselves in the State House, victory was short-lived. The Radicals, aided once more by Grant, resumed control.

In 1877, after the inauguration of President Hayes, carpetbag rule was lifted. Federal troops were withdrawn and home rule was restored under Governor Francis T. Nicholls. In reconstructing itself the State adopted a new constitution (1879) in which the threat of a large Negro vote was minimized by restricting the powers of the legislature and increasing the appointive power of the governor. Baton Rouge again became the capital of Louisiana in 1882.

Louisiana slowly recovered from the economic chaos that prostrated the State during the Civil War and Reconstruction periods. An important factor in this recovery was the work done by Captain James B. Eads in deepening the channel at the mouth of the Mississippi (*see Tour 1A*). Railroad expansion soon followed the increased facilities of the port. By 1880 five trunk lines served New Orleans; three years later, with the completion of a line linking New Orleans with California, the city had rail service with the East, North, and West. Steamboat traffic fell off steadily in the face of railroad competition, railroad tonnage increasing from 937,634 tons in 1880 to 5,500,000 tons in 1899, but both helped New Orleans to regain most of its former commercial importance.

No less important in the development of the State was the work carried on after 1870 in rebuilding and improving the levees along the Mississippi. Much levee construction had been accomplished by 1882, but the great flood of that year, sweeping through 284 crevasses and washing away 56 miles of levee, proved flood control work done up to then lamentably inadequate. To provide for more efficient control, a convention, attended by representatives of all States interested in the work, met at Baton Rouge the following year. The Federal Government and the States concerned pooled their efforts and resources and embarked upon a concerted and aggressive campaign to control the river.

A serious drawback to the progress of Louisiana—one as destructive as the recurrent floods that have ravaged the lower Mississippi Valley— was the frequency of yellow fever epidemics in the larger cities and towns. Almost yearly, from early summer to late fall, a small percentage of the population died of the disease; and at intervals epidemics of devastating proportions swept from town to town claiming large numbers of Louisianians. In 1853, during the worst plague in the history of the State, 11,000 persons were said to have perished in New Orleans alone. On August 22 there was an average of one death every five minutes. Small towns were almost wiped out, and farming and commerce were neglected until late fall. Despite efforts to control the spread of yellow fever through quarantine methods and sanitation, epidemics continued to harass the State up to 1905. During the epidemic of that year a screening ordinance, sponsored by Dr. Quitman Kohnke, was passed in New Orleans, in recognition of the discovery by Dr. Carlos Finlay that the fever germ was carried by mosquitoes. The ordinance provided for the screening of cisterns in order to prevent mosquito breeding. The Finlay theory, advanced in 1881, was validated in Cuba in 1900. Since its application in Louisiana the State has been free of yellow fever.

After 1900 Louisiana entered upon an era of commercial and industrial expansion. Abundant natural resources, including oil, sulphur, salt and natural gas, were discovered throughout the State. Towns sprang up almost overnight as industries boomed. Refineries, carbonblack factories, and chemical plants, were set up near the major gas and oil fields. To the ever-broadening industrial scene new industries, lured to the State by low-priced fuel and cheap labor, were added. Transportation facilities kept pace with industrial development; railroad trunk lines were constructed to every section of the State, roads improved, and canals dug to form a network of waterways. The increased commercial activity of Louisiana's three deep-water ports—New Orleans, Baton Rouge and Lake Charles—revealed the growing prosperity of the State.

During the World War Louisiana responded as patriotically as her sister States. Several important military camps were established in the State, thousands of men entered service, and various civic organizations led the citizenry in a full-hearted response to the Government's appeal for money and war supplies. More than $200,000,000 was subscribed during the various Liberty Loan drives of 1917 and 1918. Worthy of especial mention are the Jennings Cavalry, which served as the Headquarters Troop of the 42nd Rainbow Division, the Tulane Medical Unit (Base Hospital No. 24), staffed by 150 Louisiana nurses, and the Loyola Medical Unit (Base Hospital No. 102), which served on the Italian front.

The levee system, though greatly improved after 1883, again proved inadequate in 1927. In the great flood of that year hundreds of square miles of land were inundated, principally in northern and south-central Louisiana. To save New Orleans the levee at Caernarvon below the city was dynamited. With the aid of huge Federal appropriations, the State has completed flood control projects ensuring protection against flood stages higher than that of 1927.

From 1928 to 1935 Louisiana's history was influenced largely by Huey P. Long, the State's most energetic political figure. Soon after his inauguration as governor in 1928 he built up a powerful political machine and became the virtual dictator of the State—the popular idol of his followers and the bitter enemy of his political opponents. In the Senate (1930-35) he attained nation-wide attention. As the champion of the Share the Wealth program, through which he proposed to redistribute the nation's wealth, Long succeeded in amassing a large following. Until his career was cut short through assassination in Baton Rouge in 1935, Long ruled the State with an absolutism rarely seen in American politics. Louisiana is indebted to his regime for many public improvements: the highways were modernized, the State University and hospitals greatly enlarged, a sea wall, airport, bridge, and spillway built at New Orleans, and free textbooks distributed to school children. He also built the great new Capitol in Baton Rouge.

Shortly after Long's death his political machine began to crumble. Governor O. K. Allen, who had entered office when Long went to the Senate, died, and James A. Noe, Lieutenant Governor, served the remainder of the term. Richard W. Leche was elected to succeed him in May, 1936. In 1939 Leche resigned, and Earl Long, Lieutenant Governor and brother of Huey, came into power to complete the term. During this year, after a series of spectacular Federal indictments of many leading political figures, the Long machine was disrupted, and in 1940 a reform party elected Sam Jones Governor.

With the co-operation of Federal agencies the State weathered the great depression. New industries have come to the State as a result of publicized industrial advantages, and these, together with the large appropriations allotted by the Federal Government for public works and the stimulation of employment, have kept Louisiana prospering. The opening of offshore oil wells and the easy access to supplies of fresh water made Louisiana the center of a huge petrochemical industry that brought billions of dollars into the State.

Government

THE inhabitants of Louisiana, during more than two centuries of political development, have experienced divers forms of government under the rule of France, Spain, Great Britain, and the United States. In addition to an abortive revolt against Spanish authority, in 1768, six orderly changes were made during the colonial period: Louis XIV to Antoine Crozat in 1712; Crozat to the Company of the West in 1717; the Company of the West (known as the Company of the Indies after 1719) to Louis XV in 1731; France to Spain in 1763; Spain to France and France to the United States in 1803. After nine years of territorial government, Louisiana entered the Union (1812), only to secede in 1861, to join the Confederate States of America (1861–65). A transitional period of provisional government during the War between the States and under the Reconstruction Acts of March 21 and 23, 1867, preceded readmission to the Union. That portion of Louisiana lying east of the Mississippi and north of Lake Pontchartrain, referred to as the Florida Parishes, has been under Great Britain and Spain, and for two and one-half months in 1810, following a revolt against Spain, enjoyed autonomy as the Republic of West Florida.

Upon its establishment in 1699 as one of the crown colonies of New France, Louisiana was given a government similar to that of all the French possessions in the New World. A governor, appointed by the king as his representative, regulated the affairs of the colony and exercised military and administrative authority, enforced by the soldiery of which he was the head. His dictatorial authority also embraced judicial and legislative powers, limited to a great extent, however, by the fact that all ordinances and royal edicts emanated from France. A codification of ancient French law, the *Custom of Paris,* was adopted.

In 1712 Antoine Crozat, a French merchant, was granted exclusive trading rights in the colony, and Louisiana was given a charter and its first constitution. A Superior Council of five members was formed to act in an administrative capacity. Successive revisions under the Company of the West (successor to Crozat) and the Company of the Indies increased the power and functions of the council, which was composed, at that time, of the directors of the trading companies. Lower courts were established for the administration of justice, and a right of appeal to the Superior Council was granted. In 1724 the *Code Noir,* a compilation drawn up for the regulation of Negroes on the island of Santo Domingo, was promulgated in Louisiana.

In 1731 the Company of the Indies relinquished its charter and Louisiana once more became a crown colony. The Superior Council was reorganized to consist of an intendant, *procureur-général* (King's Attorney), registrar of the province, and six prominent citizens. In conjunction with the governor and *ordonnateur,* whose duties were concerned with commerce, the supervision of royal property, and the management of the stroehouse, the council discharged the executive, legislative, and judicial affairs of the colony. The outlying districts were governed by commandants appointed by the governor.

Under Spanish rule centralization of power in the hands of a few officials, lack of a legislative body, and bureaucracy continued to characterize the government. French law was abolished and supplanted by the law in force in other Spanish colonies. The executive department consisted of the governor, assisted by an intendant, auditor of war, auditor of the intendancy, comptroller, and various minor officials. Both civil and military powers were vested in the governor, who appointed commandants in the same capacity for each parish or district. The Superior Council of the French regime was replaced by a legislative and quasi-administrative council called the *Cabildo,* which was composed of six *regidores perpetuales,* two *alcaldes,* an attorney-general *syndic,* and a clerk. Its judicial function was limited to the jurisdiction of appeals from the *alcaldes* courts set up in New Orleans and the chief towns of the province. Laws came either directly from Spain, the Captain General of Cuba, the *Audencia de Habana* (Cuban administrative council), or from the governor himself, who at the outset of his term promulgated a list of laws in an inaugural address.

On March 26, 1806, the Territory of Orleans was set up by the United States as a governmental unit in the administration of the region acquired by the Louisiana Purchase. William C. C. Claiborne was appointed governor and given dictatorial powers, taking over all the civil, military, and judicial functions of the short-lived (November 30–December 20, 1803) French government established by Laussat. On March 2, 1805, a government similar to that of the Mississippi Territory was given to the Territory of Orleans; legislative powers were vested in a house of representatives and a legislative council; a superior court, several inferior courts, and justices of the peace administered justice. The governor's secretary and judges of the superior court were appointed by the President of the United States, who also appointed the members of the legislative council for five-year terms from a list of ten candidates submitted by the U. S. House of Representatives.

In gaining admission to the Union, Louisiana on January 22, 1812, drafted a constitution in keeping with the organic law established by other states. Modeled after that of Kentucky, the document provided for clearly defined executive, legislative, and judicial departments. A formal bill of rights was lacking, the assumption being that the attainment of American citizenship entailed all the rights and privileges enjoyed under the Constitution of the United States; a recapitulation was made, however, of the rights of *habeas corpus,* jury trial, and bail in all but capital cases. A bicameral legislature, called the General Assembly of the State of Louisiana, consisting of a senate and a house of representatives, was established. The governor was elected by the general assembly from the two candidates receiving the largest popular vote. The judiciary consisted of a supreme court and a number of inferior courts set up by the legislature. Two distinct features set off Louisiana from the rest of the Union: (1) the retention of the *Code Napoléon* in contradistinction to the English common law adopted throughout the United States; (2) the use of parish as the term for governmental units called counties elsewhere.

During the 30 years following admission to the Union, Louisiana outgrew the organic law set up in 1812. In response to popular sentiment favoring a more democratic constitution, a convention was convened in 1845 for the purpose of revising the outmoded document. Radical changes were made; the electoral franchise was broadened through the elimination of property qualifications; the governor was elected by direct popular vote, and succession provided for by the creation of the office of lieutenant governor. The most noteworthy achievements of the convention were the creation of the office of State Superintendent of Public Education and the establishment of a free public school system.

A further democratization was effected in 1852, whereby the appointive power of the governor was greatly restricted by the election by popular vote of a number of officials. Public welfare was enhanced by provisions for the safekeeping of educational funds, State aid for public improvements, the creation of a board of public works, fixing of a State debt limit of $8,000,000, and a further liberalization of the electoral franchise.

In 1861, after Louisiana had seceded from the Union, a single change —the substitution of the words Confederate States for United States— was made in the constitution of 1852.

During the last years of the War between the States two governments held sway in the State. Governor Hahn, the Federal incumbent, called a convention in 1864 composed entirely of Republicans for the formulation of a constitution, the chief provision of which was the abolition of slavery, but which also made extensive amendments to the constitution of 1852. Although the North proclaimed the document a model for Southern States, Congress failed to approve it, and it continued in use merely as the basis of a provisional government.

Under the Reconstruction Acts of March 21 and March 23, 1867, action was taken toward the composition of an organic law in keeping with the constitutional provisions set up by the Federal Government in the Thirteenth, Fourteenth, and Fifteenth Amendments. In 1868 a convention of 98 delegates, equally divided between Negroes and whites, drew up a constitution with a bill of rights granting the Negro equality and full social and civil rights. All male adult citizens of the United States were granted the right to vote, except: (a) persons convicted of crime or under interdict; (b) holders for 1 year of a Confederate office; (c) registered enemies of the United States; (d) publishers of treasonable newspaper articles or preachers of subversive sermons; (e) those who voted for or signed the ordinance of secession of any state. In addition, voters were required to show a certificate stating that they considered the rebellion morally and politically wrong. All State officials were obliged to take an oath guaranteeing the civil and political equality of all men, regardless of race, color, or previous condition of servitude.

The end of carpetbag rule in Louisiana brought about a new constitution drawn up in 1879, in which the possible effects of a large Negro vote were minimized by restrictions placed upon the legislature, and by an increase in the appointive power of the governor, who was able, thereby, to control parish government.

As the result of an exceedingly high Negro vote in the election of 1896, a convention was called in 1898 for the express purpose of disfranchising as many Negroes as possible without violating the Fifteenth Amendment. For that purpose, educational and property qualifications for voters were imposed. Only those able to read and write, to reckon time and to remember dates and places, or owners of property of $300 value were permitted to vote. An "understanding clause," requiring a knowledge of essential facts, was appended. In order to safeguard the illiterate and impoverished white vote, a "grandfather clause" was added, providing that no man who had voted on or before January 1, 1867, his son or grandson, nor any foreigner, resident of the State for five years and naturalized before January 1, 1898, could be deprived of the franchise because of his failure to pass the educational and property qualifications.

A need was felt in 1913 for a constitution in which the legislature should have a freer rein. The convention convened for that purpose overstepped its authority and revised the entire constitution. It was tacitly understood, however, that the revision was of a provisional nature and that a new constitution was to be drafted in the near future. The convention of 1921, therefore, assumed extensive powers in rewriting the organic law, but did not make any radical changes in the former document. Provisions for education, the creation of a better road system, changes in suffrage, and the reorganization of the judicial department were the chief features of the new constitution.

The government of Louisiana, both State and local, does not differ, functionally, to any great extent, from that existing in the other states in the Union. The outstanding difference is that found in the judicial system. The State has retained the laws of France and Spain, expressed in its civil law, in preference to the English common law. The Civil Code, as drawn up in 1808 in answer to a popular demand for the retention of the written Continental law, is a codification of French and Spanish modifications of ancient Roman law as developed in Louisiana under the influence of the *Custom of Paris,* the edicts of the French kings, the Royal Schedules of Spain, and the *Siete Partidas*. A project of the *Code Napoléon* was used in the redaction of the civil law. Louisiana has, therefore, a written law of great antiquity. Its constitutions have zealously safeguarded, since statehood, the basic law evolved during the century of French and Spanish domination, although modifications showing the influence of English common law have been made.

As a result of the singular evolution of its jurisprudence, Louisiana's judicial system differs from that of other States, although the tendency has been, in constitutional revision, to effect a greater similarity to the judicial machinery in operation elsewhere. To that end, criminal procedure and rules of evidence have been adopted, for the most part, from English common law, and the court system has been patterned after that of the nation as a whole.

The present system, as established by the constitution of 1921, reposes the judicial power in a supreme court, courts of appeal, district courts, and other lesser tribunals as provided for by legislation. The supreme court is composed of a chief justice and six associate justices, representing a like number of supreme court districts. Provision is made for the court to sit in divisions of three, and while in *en banc* (quorum present) session to call upon judges of the courts of appeal or district courts to sit in any case. It has both original and appellate jurisdiction. The courts of appeal, consisting of three judges each, have appellate jurisdiction over three divisions of the State. Courts of an intermediate grade are the district courts for the parishes, having original jurisdiction in civil and criminal cases and appellate jurisdiction over appeals from justices of the peace; the civil and criminal district courts of Orleans Parish; and parish juvenile courts. Among the petty tribunals are the justices of the peace, police magistrates, mayors' courts, and the municipal courts. In addition, there is a certain amount of quasi-judicial procedure delegated to such agencies as the public service commission and the tax commission.

The executive power is vested in a governor, lieutenant governor, auditor, treasurer, secretary of state, registrar of the land office, commissioner of agriculture and immigration, and commissioner of conservation. The governor is elected for a four-year term; his succession in office is provided for by the consecutive advancement of the lieutenant governor, the president *pro tempore* of the senate, and the secretary of state, the governor is paid $20,000 a year; the lieutenant governor $16,500; the secretary of state $18,700. Of the more than 80 State boards and commissions, only two are elective, one in part. The Reorganization Act of 1940 consolidated them under 20 departments.

Louisiana's legislature consists of a senate of 39 members and a house of representatives of 105 members. Members of both houses are elected for four-year terms. The legislature meets for 60 calendar days in even years, and 30 calendar days in odd years, in May at Baton Rouge. Members receive $50 per day and mileage during the 60-day session of 10¢ a mile for 8 round trips. When the legislature is not in session members receive $250 a month as expense allowance. Special sessions may be convoked by the governor on extraordinary occasions or by petition of two-thirds of the members of both houses. Both in its structure and the restrictions placed upon it by the constitution, the legislature of Louisiana is similar to that operating in other States.

In Louisiana local governmental units, known elsewhere as counties, are called parishes. Originally they were ecclesiastical units set up by O'Reilly, Spanish provisional governor of Louisiana (1669–70), in conjunction with 11 administrative districts. As Louisiana developed, it was found that the districts were too large and that the smaller religious divisions were more suitable. As a consequence, when Louisiana became a State, the term parish was taken over with the name of the region to which it had applied under the Church.

The governing body in the parish is the police jury, composed of from 5 to 16 members elected for four-year terms. It acts in a legislative, administrative, and quasi-judicial capacity in much the same manner as do county boards of supervisors or commissioners elsewhere.

In municipal government the cities of Louisiana follow the pattern of mayor and aldermen prescribed in 1896. All cities except New Orleans are divided into four wards, having a total of not more than nine and not less than five aldermen. Commission-manager governments are permitted but have not been tried in the large cities. With the multiplication of boards and commissions the executive power has been extended, but appropriations from revenue need the approval of the city council. The sales tax has been applied generally and bond issues are voted for special purposes within legal limits. In the 1950–1970 period Louisiana cities experienced much municipal construction, larger revenue, and a gradual increase in taxes.

New Orleans had a commission form of government from 1912 to 1950, consisting of five men elected by popular vote. In November, 1952, the voters ratified the Home Rule Charter, which provides for a Mayor, an Administrative Officer with executive powers but appointed by the Mayor, and a Council of seven members, five elected from municipal districts and two from the city at large. Terms for Mayor and Councilmen are four years and the Mayor may not serve more than two terms. The Mayor's salary is $20,000 a year and he has a contingent fund for expenses, and the Chief Administrative Officer earns $17,500. Councilmen earn $7,500 and may not hold any other office. The Council levies all taxes.

Until 1970 a voter in Louisiana had to be 21 years old, but new legislation by Congress made the age 18 for national elections. A voter must be a citizen, not a convict. The Voting Rights Act of 1965 suspended literacy tests and other devices to determine qualification of voters in any state or county that had them in force on Nov. 1, 1964, and where less than 50 percent of the voting-age population was registered or voted in the Presidential election. Louisiana demanded residence of one year in the State, 6 months in the parish, 3 months in the precinct. For municipal elections 4 months residence in the precinct was prescribed.

LOUISIANA ELECTIONS SINCE 1940

1940: Roosevelt, D., 319,751; Willkie, R., 52,446. 1944: Roosevelt, D., 281,664; Dewey, R., 67,750. 1948: Thurmond, States Rights, 204,290; Truman, D., 136,344; Dewey, R., 72,657; Wallace, Prog., 3,035. 1952: Eisenhower, R., 306,925; Stevenson, D., 345,027. 1956: Eisenhower, R., 320,047; Stevenson, D., 345,027. Andrews, States Rights, 44,520. 1960: Kennedy, D., 407,339; Nixon, R., 230,380; States Rights (unpledged) 169,572. 1964: Johnson, D., 387,068; Goldwater, R., 509,225. 1968: Nixon, R., 259,668; Humphrey, D., 317,814; Wallace, 536,779.

The four largest parishes voted as follows in 1968 national election: Orleans: Humphrey, 72,663; Nixon, 48,225; Wallace, 58,884.
East Baton Rouge: Humphrey, 21,772; Nixon, 21,770; Wallace, 35,951.
Calcasieu: Humphrey, 14,751; Nixon, 9,590; Wallace, 20, 274.
Caddo: Humphrey, 17,811; Nixon, 21,242; Wallace, 28,439.

Agriculture

AGRICULTURE remains an important income-producing part of the Louisiana economy, despite the wealth gained from oil. In 1964 the U. S. Dept. of Commerce listed 10,411,045 acres devoted to agriculture in Louisiana, and in 1969 reported total cash receipts from marketing as $934,467,000, of which $317,837,000 came from crops, $274,374,000 from livestock, and $52,266,000 from Government subsidies. Sugar cane, rice, cotton, and corn are most important crops. The favorable climate and fertile alluvial soil make it possible to raise almost every crop indigenous to the Western Hemisphere. The State ranks first in the nation in the production of sugar cane, rice, strawberries, shallots, perique tobacco, and white clover; fourth in sweet potatoes; fifth in oranges and pecans; and seventh in cotton.

The early French colonists, given generous tracts of land along the Mississippi and the larger bayous, imported slaves and bond servants to work their large holdings. Emulating their English neighbors on the southern Atlantic seaboard, they adopted the plantation system. Under this system, with individual landholders employing hundreds of slaves, crops were cultivated on a large scale. Each plantation was a self-sufficient agricultural unit.

Indigo was at first the most important export crop. A wild species was found by the French in the high, wooded sections of interior Louisiana. The qualities of this plant as a dye product had been known to western Europe for a century or more and a large market in France was open to Louisiana planters. A few of the more farsighted planted some of the wild seeds on their land and were successful in cultivating it. In 1722 a ship was dispatched to Cape Français with a cargo of plants to be exchanged for seed for general planting.

The commercial manufacture of the dye was begun by Father Nicholas de Beaubois, a Jesuit priest, who developed on the Jesuit plantation a process similar to that in use today. In the wake of Father de Beaubois' success the industry was firmly established, and indigo became one of the Colony's important crops. By 1754, forty-seven planters were producing about 82,000 pounds annually. A caterpillar plague destroyed the crop in 1793 and the cultivation of indigo was set back.

The invention of the cotton gin in 1792 and the discovery of a method of refining sugar on a commercial scale in 1795 turned the attention of indigo growers to sugar cane and cotton, hardier and more profitable crops. Napoleon, seeking to restore agricultural prosperity after the return of the Colony to France, urged the revival of indigo cultivation and recommended crop rotation as a means of preserving soil fertility, but indigo never regained its former importance. It is no longer grown commercially, and that which grows wild in some sections of southern Louisiana is the bane of the rice farmer.

Bienville, in one of his first reports to Paris in 1700, mentioned the planting of a few stalks of sugar cane on the site of what was later to be New Orleans. In 1742 the Jesuits imported from Santo Domingo to their plantation adjacent to New Orleans a quantity of sugar cane and a number of skilled Negroes. Various unsuccessful attempts were made to granulate marketable sugar, but it was not until 1795 that Étienne de Boré on his plantation above New Orleans perfected a method of refining sugar on a commercial scale.

Sugar cane cultivation on a large scale is successful only upon the alluvial soils in the south-central region, a portion of the State known as the Sugar Bowl. Louisiana produce 88 percent of all sugar cane raised in the United States. In 1966 it produced more than 7,800,000 net tons, a yield of approx. 25 tons per acre.

Cotton was first planted in Louisiana in 1718 by Emanuel Prudhomme on his plantation near Natchitoches. It was not grown to any extent, however, until the invention of the cotton gin (1792) made production profitable. By 1809 it was the principal crop of the Red River Valley and the Opelousas District. While it remains a staple crop it has decreased in production in recent years. In 1966 it produced 450,000 bales.

The Louisiana planter was favored by the proximity of New Orleans, one of the world's largest cotton markets, to which he could ship his cotton by cheap steamboat transportation on the network of waterways leading to the city. As the price of cotton mounted, more and more land was devoted to its cultivation, and though the War between the States seriously disrupted planting for a time, cotton growing was resumed on an ever-increasing scale.

The fertile soil and mild climate of Louisiana are particularly adapted to the growth of cotton. The rich, loamy alluvial soils in central and northern Louisiana, especially along the Mississippi and in the valleys of the Red, Ouachita, and Tensas Rivers, are the most suitable. Crops grow successfully, however, in thinner, as well as stiffer, soils, with the aid of special cultivation and fertilization. Short-staple upland cotton is grown almost exclusively. It is hardier in growth and the fiber less subject to deterioration than in the case of the long-staple, or sea-island, type. There are a few localities near the coast where the latter variety has been produced, but the amount is negligible.

Practically all of the State's irrigated land is devoted to the production of rice. Climate is hardly a factor in the rice crop, but the need for irrigation has limited the rice area to districts in which there is a convenient water supply as well as fertility of soil. The prairie section of southwestern Louisiana offers favorable soil conditions, and while lacking large streams, permits of comparatively cheap irrigation by means of canals, many of which traverse this region.

Rice was introduced in Louisiana about the beginning of the eighteenth century, and by 1726 was commercially important enough to be exported to Europe. By 1866 the State was producing 50,000 barrels a year. Irrigation projects begun in 1880 so stimulated production that by 1914 the State was producing 4,000,000 barrels a year. In 1887 Dr. Seaman A. Knapp joined J. B. Watkins in promoting an extensive colonization project in southwestern Louisiana, bringing several hundred Midwestern farmers of German, Swedish, and Danish descent to settle a million and a half acres in the Louisiana Rice Belt. In 1898 the U. S. Government sent Dr. Knapp to Japan to study rice culture, and as a result Japanese rice replaced the Honduran rice formerly planted in the State. In 1966 the Louisiana crop was more than 21,000,000 cwt.

Corn, best adapted to alluvial lands, is the fourth most important crop in Louisiana, Although corn is planted in the rotation system on some sugar plantations, there is probably less corn acreage in southern than in northern Louisiana.

Besides cotton, the more northerly parishes of Louisiana produce the greater part of the oats, alfalfa, Irish potatoes, and peaches grown in the State. The southern districts raise not only all the rice and practically all the sugar cane but a greater proportion of the sweet potatoes, most of the truck, all the oranges, and practically all the strawberries.

There are numerous truck-growing areas in the State. Cabbage, cauliflower, kale, broccoli, mustard, turnips, Spanish and Bermuda onions, garlic, bell and hot peppers, tomatoes, eggplants, burr artichokes, radishes, lettuce, spinach, cucumbers, peas, beans, and okra are some of the vegetables that come from Louisiana fields. The area immediately surrounding New Orleans is the great truck district.

Strawberries, considering the shortness of the season, are relatively more valuable than truck. The berries from Tangipahoa and neighboring parishes are firm, large, and fine-flavored, and make up a very large part of the Louisiana crop. The Louisiana berry is ready for market at a favorable time, just after the Florida crop is exhausted and before crops in other States have reached maturity.

The culture of strawberries in the Florida Parishes was introduced by the Illinois Central Railroad, which sent agricultural experts to determine the most favorable crop for this section. After years of experimentation, it was found that the soil and climate were suited to the cultivation of strawberries. In 1866 plants were furnished to several farmers for test purposes. Within a few years production had increased to such an extent that the railroad introduced express service to Northern markets, and by 1900 trainloads of berries were being shipped daily during the season.

The pecan is the principal orchard tree of the State. Although widely cultivated, the nut is still found growing wild in bottomlands, and more of these reach the market than the cultivated variety.

It is said that the first instance of scientific pecan cultivation in Louisiana, and probably in the world, was the trunk grafting of 16 trees of a variety later named the Centennial by Antoine, a slave gardener on Telesphore J. Roman's Oak Alley Plantation in St. James Parish in 1846. Several other gardeners copied his methods. In 1878, in Madison Parish, Sam Jones became the butt of jokes because he planted "50 acres of good cotton land" in pecans. However, this orchard, the oldest planted, is still bearing today, having many times proved the foresight of its originator. Various growers have named individual varieties, among those originated in Louisiana being: the Money Maker, Frotscher, Van Deman, Carman, James, Centennial, Caspiana, Claremont, Steckler, and Teche.

While pecans are highly profitable, the growers are faced with problems of insect pests and bacterial and fungus diseases. The Federal Government has taken cognizance of these hazards and has established stations for research in soil chemistry, entomology and bacteriology at Shreveport and other points. In spite of the problems involved in producing the nut, pecans offer attractive returns for growers. The necessary passage of several years between planting and profitable yield is probably the chief factor limiting the number of persons undertaking their cultivation.

The largest orange district is the Plaquemines Parish "frontlands," especially those on the western side of the Mississippi River. Early in the history of this section, probably about 1750, orange growing was introduced. Only recently, however, have large-scale operations been undertaken. The growth and development of the citrus industry in this region has been remarkable. The Louisiana sweet orange is the principal variety grown in the State. Mandarins, tangerines, kumkuats, Satsumas, and grapefruit are also grown.

A 1,000-acre area near Lutcher is said to be the only locality in the world in which perique tobacco is grown. The tobacco is black and strong and is used principally for blending and mixing with milder varieties. It was first grown by the Indians, and after 1776 was cultivated by the Acadian settlers of St. James Parish, one of whom, Pierre Chenet, or "Perique" as he was nicknamed, introduced it commercially. The major portion of the annual crop is shipped to England, Canada, and Norway.

Other Louisiana agricultural specialties are shallots, vetivert, and Creole Easter lily bulbs. About 98 percent of all commercial shipments of shallots in the United States comes from a district within a 100-mile radius of New Orleans. Shallots, usually called "green onions," sell from November to April in all of the leading markets of the United States and Canada. Vetivert, an ornamental East Indian grass, the roots of which give off a pleasant aroma and yield an oil used in the manufacture of perfume, is grown in commercial quantities in Tangipahoa Parish. More than 1,000,000 Creole Easter lily bulbs are grown annually in the orange belt of Plaquemines Parish, where they are prepared for sale throughout the Nation. Although American experimentation with this bulb has been in progress for more than 20 years, it was not until 1923 that domestic production on a large scale was begun. In former years florists imported the bulbs chiefly from Japan, but they were frequently diseased upon arrival. The U. S. Department of Agriculture made an effort to find an area in the United States where the bulbs could be grown, and after several years the climatic conditions and the salt and sulphur content of the soil of southern Louisiana were found satisfactory.

The cut-over pinelands, river bottoms, and coastal marshes of the State offer fine range conditions for the raising of livestock. It is said that cattle raising in southwestern Louisiana began before it did in Texas, and that the stock of the early Texas herds came from this section. Tradition even asserts that the longhorn originated in Louisiana instead of Texas.

Most of the State's beef cattle graze on open ranges in the southwestern section and along the Red and Ouachita Rivers. The mild winter makes winter housing unnecessary, and in localities where flies and mosquitoes are a menace cross-breeding with Brahma stock has produced a strain more or less immune to insects. The introduction of Hereford and Aberdeen-Angus breeds has also improved the native stock. Dairy cows, of which there are 245,000 (1965), are confined to small farm herds.

During the nineteenth century heavier breeds of horses were brought to Louisiana from Mississippi, Kentucky, and the older States and bred with the wild horses (locally called Creole ponies) of southwest Louisiana and the Texas mustangs. Percherons and Shetlands—the largest and smallest of horses—were bred with wild mares and the mares set free to rejoin the herds. The herds of wild horses were a source of much annoyance when the tick eradication program was begun in Louisiana. Catching and dipping them was difficult and uncertain, and finally many were shot.

Louisiana's 171,000 hogs are raised on farms throughout the State, the greatest concentration being in the Delta and the Rice Belt. The favorite breeds are the Poland China, Hampshire, and Duroc-Jersey. Free-ranging, or wood hogs, which forage unattended in the river bottoms of the Black and Tensas, are rounded up once a year.

Much of the cut-over pineland of the State is devoted to the raising of sheep. A number of breeds have been introduced, but the most satisfactory have been the Rambouillet and Corriedale. Louisiana's sheep have decreased in recent years, the 102,000 of 1961 having shrunk to 67,000 in 1965.

Since its inception in 1914, agricultural extension work has made notable strides in Louisiana. The improvements in agriculture made in the last quarter century reflect the work of State and Federal agencies in teaching scientific farming. The soil-depleting, economically unsound "one-crop system" has given way to crop rotation and diversified farming; soil conservation practices have been adopted, many farms having engaged in contour cultivation, terracing, and drainage control; production has been increased through a more efficient use of land; the introduction of purebred sires has improved livestock; rural electrification, and instruction in home economics have improved rural living conditions.

State and Federal crop experiment stations, distributed throughout the State, conduct research in cotton, sugar cane, and rice, as well as in specialty crops and livestock. County and home demonstration agents work in every parish. 4-H Clubs compete in achievement contests, exhibit at fairs, and attend short courses at Louisiana State University.

Commerce, Industry, and Labor

COMMERCE had a slow start at the opening of the eighteenth century, because the colony that Iberville established at Biloxi in 1699 was unable to provide for itself. When this enterprise proved too expensive to the Crown, trading rights in the colony were consigned in 1712 to a French merchant, Antoine Crozat, with the stipulation that a specified number of settlers and food for their maintenance were to be sent to Louisiana yearly. Under Crozat's management, a profitable trade was carried on with the Indians; pelts, procured from them in exchange for guns, knives, and brandy, were shipped to France at a substantial profit. Lumber and tobacco were added to the exports, and an effort was made to render the colony self-supporting through improved agriculture.

Commerce, despite restrictions of trade with foreign countries, increased steadily, trade relations, both legal and illegal, being maintained with France, England, Spain, Mexico, Florida, and the West Indies. Barques and brigantines, one of which was built in the colony in 1704, were plying the Mississippi as early as 1713. Trade with the Ohio country brought increasing amounts of merchandise to New Orleans for transshipment to France. As settlers crossed the Allegheny Mountains and developed the Middle West, New Orleans began to grow rapidly as the commercial port of the Mississippi. The bulk of cargoes shipped in exchange for slaves and European merchandise consisted of lumber, pitch, tar, brick, rice, indigo, sugar cane, cotton, sassafras, and fur pelts.

With the lifting of trade restrictions on Mississippi commerce following the Louisiana Purchase, and the appearance of the steamboat (1812), New Orleans forged ahead commercially. Cotton, grain, sugar, and slaves formed the bulk of trade. Today ships from every seaport in the world enter the State's three deep-water ports—New Orleans, Baton Rouge, and Lake Charles. Barge service on the Mississippi connects the State with ports on the Great Lakes. A 280-mile intracoastal waterway provides communication with numerous inland shipping points on Louisiana's 4,794 miles of navigable waterways. Fourteen major interstate railroads, numerous bus and motor freight lines, and 18 air transport lines complete the commercial facilities. In 1968 the Port of New Orleans alone handled 113,511,052 short tons of foreign, coastwise, and internal shipping. Leading exports are petroleum products, iron, steel, corn, and cotton; leading imports, sugar, bananas, coffee, and bauxite. Foreign and coastwise traffic handled at Baton Rouge, which in 1968 amounted to 37,872,394 short tons, consists almost entirely of crude oil, petroleum products, and chemicals. Foreign and coastwise traffic at Lake Charles totaled 15,451,523 short tons for the same year, with crude oil, rice, lumber, and chemicals the leading items.

For two centuries before the discovery of oil, Louisiana's industries were devoted almost exclusively to the processing of agricultural products. Before Eli Whitney's cotton gin (1792) and Étienne de Boré's successful granulation of sugar (1795), the only industry of importance was the manufacture of dye from indigo. This had involved many difficulties, and planters turned eagerly to the more profitable sugar cane and cotton.

Early planters were unsuccessful in refining the juice of sugar cane, their product turning into muscovado, a milk sugar resembling marmalade. When Étienne de Boré succeeded in refining cane on a large scale the sugar industry began. Discovering the method of boiling cane juice to the concentration point at which it granulates, de Boré converted his crop into a $12,000 profit, a success that stimulated quantity production among other planters.

In 1802 New Orleans had only one sugar refinery, "where brown sugar was transformed into white sugar of fine appearance," yet by 1830, one-half to two-thirds of United States sugar was supplied by Louisiana. No large refineries were built, however, until after the War between the States. During the 1880's the famous Louisiana House was built on the river front at New Orleans; this refinery had a capacity of 6,000 barrels daily and employed about 800 men. Today, its successor, the American Sugar Refinery at Chalmette, is said to be the largest in the world.

Louisiana has always led the nation in the production of cane sugar. In 1966 sugar cane for sugar and seed amounted to 7,875,000 net tons.

Total crop value, including seed and sirup, was $66,000,000. Sirup production was 1,500,000 gallons. In 1969 the United States produced 22,592,000 tons of sugar and seed from cane.

At first cottonseed was discarded as worthless, but after 1835 the chartering of the Louisiana Cottonseed Oil Factory began the important industry of oil and seed cake manufacture. Before the 1860's this industry did not expand, but from 1865 to 1885 it became one of the most important in the State.

Efforts to make New Orleans a great cotton cloth manufacturing center have been made since the 1860's. In 1869 the lessees of the State Penitentiary installed looms; in 1870 two mills were built in New Orleans, and by 1894 four cotton mills were doing a business of $1,500,000 a year. But cotton milling has never become important in Louisiana.

The cleaning and polishing of rice developed as an industry after 1869. In 1870 there were seven steam mills in the rice country and two in New Orleans. By 1880 the number of mills in the city had increased to six, and in 1900 the industry was worth $5,000,000 a year. There has been great expansion since. Today, the State's rice mills, located near the source of supply in southwestern Louisiana, handle the crop that in 1966 reached a record of 21,100,000 cwt., a yield per acre of 3,750 lbs. (23.1 bbl.) the crop was valued at $102,000,000.

After the war many small manufacturing establishments came into being as the State entered a period of industrial growth. This period saw the establishment of lumber mills, steam bakeries, candy factories, boot and shoe factories, brick factories, flour and corn meal mills, carriage and wagon factories, and many others.

Commercial mining of sulphur began in 1905 at Sulphur in Calcasieu Parish. The Frasch system was first employed at this field, which, until production began in Texas in 1914, supplied 75 percent of the nation's sulphur. The product obtained was 99 percent pure and was put on the market unrefined. In 1924, after 9,500,000 tons had been mined, the field was exhausted. Production began at Jefferson Island in 1932 and at Grand Écaille in 1933; two other mines are at Garden Island Bay on the lower Mississippi and at Lake Pelto. Use of sulphur has been increasing for making fertilizer. Sulphur is converted into sulphuric acid for processing local phosphate rock into fertilizer in Florida. A sulphur research laboratory is located in Belle Chasse.

Salt deposits, worked by the Indians long before De Soto discovered Louisiana, are being mined extensively. Salt is being used increasingly by the chemical industry. In 1965 Louisiana produced 256,000 short tons of evaporated salt worth $6,293,000; 3,016,000 short tons of rock salt worth $17,828,000, and 4,854,000 short tons of brine worth $17,691,000.

Louisiana's papermaking industry, confined to the manufacture of "kraft," or wrapping paper, is based on its large supply of loblolly and shortleaf pine. A large part of the forest resources supports the naval stores industry, which for many years has been centered in the South, where abundant stands of yellow pine contribute to the manufacture of soap, paint, varnish, turpentine, resin, printer's ink, oil, grease, wax, linoleum, and drugs. Important to this industry, too, is the manufacture of tung oil, for the production of which large tracts of cutover land are being reforested with tung trees.

The gathering, curing, and ginning of Spanish moss provides employment for many Louisianians. Spanish moss is used in mattresses and in upholstering furniture and automobiles.

Fur production is a highly profitable industry and has been growing with the increased demand for unusual, plucked, and sports furs. The Louisiana Wild Life & Fisheries Commission reported that in the 1968–69 season 3,419,040 pelts brought $6,063,514, and 11,660,000 lbs. of meat brought $1,100,000, a total of $7,163,514. In the 1967–68 season the revenue was $3,712,324. There is a premium on muskrat, for casual and sports wear; nutria, raccoon, and opossum. In 1968–69, 1,556,754 muskrat skins earned $1,500,000, a 67% increase; 1,754,028 nutria skins earned $3,762,084, a 57% increase.

Production of oysters and shrimp is a big part of commercial fisheries. The industry is subject to damage from storms and water pollution, and is carefully supervised by the Louisiana Wild Life & Fisheries Commission, which had a big task in restoring oyster seed beds ruined by Hurricane Camille. In 1968 freshwater fisheries yielded 13,274,164 lbs., worth $2,619,572 to fishermen, and saltwater fisheries yielded 713,714,824 lbs., worth $37,540,191 to fishermen. The largest quantities were of buffalo fish, catfish and bullheads, and crawfish; also menhadden, crabs, shrimp, and oysters. St. Bernard Parish led in the barrels of oysters produced; other producing parishes were Terrebonne, LaFourche, Plaquemines, and Jefferson.

OIL, GAS AND PETROCHEMICALS

Louisiana ranks second among the states as a producer of oil and natural gas, being surpassed only by Texas. It supplies approx. 28 percent of all natural gas marketed and ranks second as producer of natural gas liquids. The value of its mineral output has surpassed $3 billion for a number of years.

As early as 1812 seepage of oil and gas had been observed. In 1839 the *American Journal of Science* had referred to springs of petroleum along the Calcasieu River. On Oct. 5, 1865, J. W. Mallet paid $20,000 for the first oil and gas lease on Louisiana land, which he transferred to the Louisiana Petroleum & Coal Co. on June 1, 1866. That concern drilled to a depth of 1,230 ft. and found traces of oil and sulphur. It ran out of funds in June, 1869. Other attempts were fruitless.

In 1899 Captain Anthony F. Lucas drilled for oil in the Anse le Butte area near Breaux Bridge, then moved to Texas to test a field south of Beaumont. On Jan. 10,1901, his well exploded with a most spectacular gusher, the famous Spindletop. It created an immense sensation, and as a great crowd of prospectors, land speculators, and gamblers converged on the Texas field more cautious operators hurried to secure rights to the areas in Louisiana where oil seepage had been found. So great was the fever that by the end of 1901 76 companies with capital of $44,063,000 had been formed in Louisiana to drill for oil. The Heywood brothers struck oil at 1,800 ft. 6 miles north of Jennings, but the well sanded up. Next year they found a producing well at Anse le Butte, as did the Moresi brothers of Jennerette. In 1902 five wells produced 548,617 bbl. of oil valued at $188,985, less than 35¢ per bbl.

On March 28, 1906, first commercial production was established in Caddo Parish. Total production that year was over 9 million bbl. Most of this was moved by railway, but such handling was costly and local refineries became a necessity. The first was built east of Jennings. In 1909 Standard Oil Co. of New Jersey built a refinery at Baton Rouge and brought oil from Oklahoma by pipeline. This became the nucleus of the present plant of Humble Oil & Refining Co., largest in the country.

The discovery and utilization of natural gas in Louisiana was similar to that of oil. Gas seepage had been noted in 1812, when a geologist reported an "island" on fire for at least three months. An ice plant operator in Shreveport dug a well for water but found it too salty; later he saw a "wind" issuing from the well and lighted it. He had the gas piped to his plant and used for illumination. In May, 1908, gas from the Caddo field was piped to Shreveport and sold at 35¢ per 1,000 cubic ft. for domestic use, and 17.5¢ for industrial purposes.

The oil and gas industry became a major resource of the U. S. Army and the Navy during World War II. At that time it ranked fifth in production in the country, producing 93.6 million bbl. of oil. It operated 5,101 wells and accounted for 25 percent of the State's income. But this was only a fraction of the expansion to come. Not only was Louisiana floating on a sea of oil but there was evidence that the mineral extended far out under the Gulf of Mexico.

Drilling in the water had been tried offshore at Creole in 1938, but it was not until Nov. 14, 1947, that a 900-bbl. well was brought in 12 miles off the coast by Ship Shoal Block 32. Underwater operations called for much more complicated methods than those used on land, but the industry mastered its problems and production of oil and gas soared. On Jan. 1, 1968, Louisiana had 30,670 oil and 9,036 gas wells; of these

4,771 oil and 945 gas wells were offshore. In the preceding year they had produced 673,956,273 bbl. of crude oil, of which 262,534,935 bbl. came from offshore.

Louisiana ranks third among the states in refining and processing minerals. In September, 1968, it processed more than 1,200,000 bbl. of crude per day. Oil and gas were produced in 58 of the State's 64 parishes. Gas processing was being done in 126 plants with a capacity one-fourth of the national total. Natural gas is the primary fuel for industry, which uses 90 percent of the State supply annually.

During the 1960 decade Louisiana averaged 48,000 employed in petroleum and natural gas products, 23,600 in the chemical industry, and 10,600 in petroleum refining.

The U. S. Dept. of the Interior Bureau of Mines reported that in 1968 Louisiana's employment in petroleum production, refining and related industries averaged 102,300 persons, an increase of 1,950. Oil and gas operations provided 92.3 percent of employment and 92.8 percent of wages derived from the mineral industry.

During the 1960–1970 decade national corporations invested heavily in the lower Mississippi River areas. In the environs of New Orleans new construction averaged approx. $500,000,000 a year. The most important development, which drew attention to the facilities of east Orleans Parish, was the huge Michoud operation of the National Aeronautics & Space Administration (NASA), established in 1961 and employing 10,000 to 12,000. (*See New Orleans*).

An important factor was completion of the Mississippi River-Gulf Outlet, which supplemented the Intracoastal Waterway. The building of the Michoud plant brought other industries to the area. The Louisiana Cement Co., a division of the Oklahoma Cement Co. of Tulsa, built on Michoud Slip opposite the NASA. Air Products & Chemicals, Inc., adjacent to the Michoud site built a plant to supply liquid oxygen to the NASA Mississippi Test Facility, and also to manufacture liquid hydrogen, nitrogen and argon. Air Reduction Sales Co. moved into the same area to produce industrial gases.

The Kaiser Aluminum & Chemical Co. was responsible for large investments in Louisiana. Expansion of its facilities took place at the Chalmette plant in St. Bernard Parish. At Norco Kaiser built a plant to process petroleum coke. At Gramercy it completed a new alumina plant and another to make isocyanates.

One of the largest chemical fertilizer plants ever built was completed by the National Phosphate Corp., a subsidiary of Hooker Chemical Corp. near Hahnville. It included a chlorine-caustic soda operation and a chlorinated solvents plant. The investment was placed at $35,000,000. Other huge outlays were made by Gulf Oil Co. for a processing complex near Venice, where Humble Oil & Refining built its Delta Gas plant for processing natural gas. Dow Chemical Co., Louisiana Division, located at Plaquemine, where it makes ethylene, propylene, polyolefin, chlorine, and caustic. Geismar is the site of large plants of Socony Mobil Oil Co., Union Oil Co., Monochem, Inc., and the Borden Chemical Co.; it also has plants of the Wyandotte Chemical Corp. and the U. S. Rubber Co.-Naugatuck Chemical Co. The Monsanto Corp. is making diammonium phosphate fertilizer and nitrates at Luling.

The Shell Oil Co. has its principal refinery at Norco and with Shell Chemical Co. makes ethylene, ethylene oxide and derivatives. Texaco has built a new refinery north of the Sunshine Bridge on the east bank and Skelly Oil Co. has a site some distance below the Bridge. The American Cyanide Co. is located at Fortier. One of the largest chemical operations is the Pontchartrain plant of E. I. du Pont de Nemours on the east bank near Laplace, where it makes adiponitrile, used in producing nylon. The plant cost $24,000,000. These industries of recent construction add to the huge concentration of chemical installations upriver toward Baton Rouge; other large refineries are located near the city of Lake Charles and in Caddo Parish.

SHIPBUILDING

As a maritime State Louisiana has a large investment in shipbuilding and in manufacturing equipment for ships and providing repairs and replacement. During recent years more than 10,000 have been employed in the primary occupations, with many other thousands in auxiliary work. Avondale Shipyards, Inc., builds vessels for the U. S. Navy and cargo ships and employs approx. 5,000, with a payroll as high as $35,000,-000 annually. In the mid-1960's it had a contract for 21 ocean-going freighters for Lykes Bros. Steamship Co. and its affiliate, Gulf & South American Steamship Co., costing $197,000,000. Avondale has five divisions: Its shipbuilding yards; a service foundry; the Harvey Repair Yard, which makes and repairs propellers; Avoncraft, which makes porcelain steel products, and the Bayou Black division at Morgan City, which builds barges and equipment for offshore oil production. Todd Shipyards has its principal establishment on the Mississippi below New Orleans. Equitable Equipment Company builds barges, tugs, diving equipment, and pleasure cruisers. It delivers tugs as far away as Nigeria.

EMPLOYMENT

Louisiana had 3,643,180 people on April 1, 1970, according to the Decennial Census. Its work force averaged 1,316,830 in 1969 and its unemployed 69,400, making the total employed 1,295,800. The unemployed averaged 5.1 percent. These figures reflected only slightly the drop in employment noted in national statistics. Five years before, the number employed had increased 43 percent over 1964 and the unemployed, 62,000, totaled 5 percent.

The number of Louisianians who drew pay from government sources in 1965 was 171,700, up 8.3 percent over 1964. Of this total the Federal Government employed 27,900, and State and local services employed 143,800, up 7.8 percent over 1964. In the subsequent years the totals grew larger; in 1969 governments employed 207,400; of this number the Federals had 30,900, and State and local services 176,500, 3.2 percent over 1968.

Contract construction was busy in the 1960 decade. In 1965, 76,850 were employed. By 1968 there was an average of 89,300 employed in construction, but 1969 showed a drop of 7.1 percent, to 83,000.

Louisiana has a Workmen's Compensation Law that covers employees in factories, mills, building construction and other hazardous occupations. For a major disability 65 percent of wages will be paid for not longer than 300 weeks. If the disability is permanent this will be paid for 400 weeks. If a fatality results death benefits are paid to survivors for 400 weeks. Minimum weekly disability payments are $10; maximum, $35. The employer furnishes hospital and medical services not to exceed $2,500 in value. In the event of the death of an employee the employer pays burial expenses not to exceed $600.

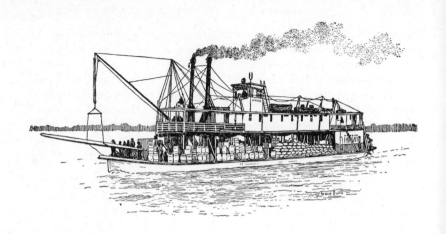

Transportation

LOUISIANA has experienced every form of transportation known to man. The character of the land dictated the need of devices to cross waterways. Its inhabitants have used the hollowed-out tree trunk, the canoe and the pirogue; the raft, rowboat, barge, sailboat, scow, side-wheel and stern-wheel steamboat. They have used the flatboat, canalboat, shrimpers' tug, wooden and steel-bottomed freight and passenger steamship and motor vessel. The newest in this category is a tender especially adapted to serve offshore oil stations. The State has known the horse and donkey as carriers, the Indian's drag, the cart, wagon, automobile, motorcycle, motor truck, railroad car and airplane.

Transportation did not present so grave a problem to the early settlers of Louisiana as it did to those of other frontier areas of America. Navigable streams ran to every section of the State, and the French and Spanish, following the example of the Indians, used this network of waterways as their principal means of communication. Their only effort at road building was the construction of levees, the tops of which were used as roadways.

For travel on land the pioneers made use of well-marked routes: migratory paths of buffalo herds and Indian trails. The buffalo paths ran in astonishingly straight lines, were often worn five or six feet deep, and were wide enough for two wagons to travel abreast. Indian trails, though much less well defined, were far more numerous. They led from one Indian settlement to another, and were soon used by the settlers.

During the nineteenth century, with the influx of Anglo-Saxon immigrants from other sections of the United States, great wagons, carrying pioneers and their families, began rumbling over this network of Indian trails, buffalo paths, and levees.

The natural formation of the Gulf Coast provided few adequate landing places for even small sailing vessels. Even in fair weather a ship might be stranded on sand bars at the mouth of the Mississippi. Then, after getting safely through the passes, it needed 20 to 70 days to travel a hundred-odd tortuous miles upstream against the current before Nouvelle Orléans was reached—and this after 80 to 100 days had been spent in traversing the Atlantic and the Gulf of Mexico.

From the Indians the French settlers borrowed the idea of the dugout, or *pirogue,* building it on a larger scale. Huge cottonwood and cypress trees were felled and the great logs hollowed out by fire. Although surprisingly large *pirogues* were built—the largest were said to have had a displacement of 50 tons—their limited capacity gave rise to a demand for other types of boats. The keelboat came into use about 1742. It was from 60 to 70 ft. long, had a beam of 15 to 18 ft., and drew only 20 to 30 inches of water. Toward the end of the French domination the *radeau,* a boat resembling the flatboat, began to be used on the Mississippi and its tributaries. Both the keelboat and the *radeau* were usually poled or rowed up and down stream. Sails were used whenever possible, but were hardly dependable on a river voyage.

Until superseded by the steamboat, these craft served the settlers of the upper valley as the principal means of getting hides, corn, wheat, livestock, lumber, and whisky to market. The levees at New Orleans were lined with the picturesque boats, whose standard signal, indicating that the proprietor was ready to do business, was a bottle of whisky strung up on a pole. Brokers would then make bids for the entire outfit, including the flatboat, which was dismantled for its lumber.

A large proportion of north, central, and east Louisiana was settled by pioneers from other sections of the United States who had migrated by water. First a large flatboat was built from timbers hewn from the virgin forests. Then families, with livestock, produce, and household belongings, floated on the current in search of new locations. Such voyages were for many years fraught with danger; Indians and pirates lurked around every bend, while the river town swarmed with swindlers and gamblers.

As commerce continued to grow, the problem of upstream navigation became more and more acute. The difficulties encountered in coaxing a clumsy craft up a winding river, against both wind and current, can be imagined. The time required for a trip from New Orleans to the Illinois country varied from three to four months, but the return trip could be made downstream in 12 to 15 days. One attempt was made to propel a boat upstream by means of horses walking a treadmill, but between New Orleans and Natchez several horses were completely broken down, and the idea was discarded.

STEAMBOATS

In January 1812, the first steamboat to be seen on the Mississippi arrived in New Orleans amid great excitement. Built in Pittsburgh by Nicholas J. Roosevelt, agent of Livingston and Fulton, the *New Orleans,* as the boat was called, was 20 ft. wide, 116 ft. long, and weighed 400 tons. Surviving the terrors of the New Madrid earthquake, the *New Orleans* gained for its owners the sole right of building and navigating steamboats on the Mississippi, a monopoly offered by the Territory of Orleans in 1811 to whoever should be successful in propelling a boat of 70 tons or more, four miles an hour in still water. The boat was put into service on a run between New Orleans and Natchez. In a short time steamboats supplanted other river craft.

An outstanding personality in steamboating was Captain Henry Shreve, for whom Shreveport was named. He was responsible for opening the Red and Sabine Rivers to navigation by removing sunken trees. Shreve developed the first successful "snagboat." He was also a pioneer builder of large river craft; his custom of naming the passengers' rooms after states of the Union is said to have been the origin of the term "stateroom."

Improvements and refinements in river boats came with time, including the introduction of the gangway in place of a few loose boards laid between deck and wharf, of the whistle, of steam at the capstan instead of manpower, of coal, of multiple engines, and, finally, of electricity. The period from 1830 to 1860 was the golden age of the steamboat. Vessels of 1,500 tons were not uncommon. Copious food and fine orchestras were featured on the floating palaces, whose passengers came from all walks of life—planters, pioneers, businessmen and their wives, as well as prostitutes and professional gamblers.

One by one the packet steamers disappeared. In their wake came towboats moving an acre or so of barges with a tonnage equivalent to several hundred carloads of freight. Completion of the final links in the Lakes-to-the-Gulf inland waterway system has greatly stimulated barge traffic in recent years; it is now possible for a tow of barges to go from New Orleans up the Mississippi to any point on the Great Lakes and beyond.

THE RAILROAD ERA

On January 20, 1830, the Pontchartrain Railroad Company was authorized by the State legislature to build a road from New Orleans to the lake. Construction started March 10, 1830. A roadway 150 ft. wide was built in a straight line from the river to a point on the lake, where a wharf was erected. Horses were used for motive power, and the first run was made on April 23, 1831. Thereafter the train made its daily 4½-mile trip on a 1½-hour schedule. On Sundays it ran all day to accommodate crowds of excursionists.

In 1832 the company imported a "steam car" from England. It hauled 12 coaches with accommodations for more than 300 persons. In 1880 the road was absorbed by the Louisville & Nashville Railroad, under whose control it ran until 1932.

The New Orleans & Carrollton Railroad, a trolley system, began its service in 1835. It ran from Baronne and Canal Streets in New Orleans to the village of Carrollton. Steam dummies were used after 1845 to haul the train from Carrollton to Tivoli Circle (Lee Circle), from which point horses completed the run to Canal Street. In 1894, after the line had been taken over by the public utilities interests of New Orleans, electricity was applied.

Although planters, who had always experienced great difficulty in transporting their cotton over the almost impassable roads of the back country, clamored for railroads, construction in Louisiana lagged during the period preceding 1850. In that year only five roads, with a total mileage of 79.5 miles, were in operation. The alarming reduction in river traffic and volume of foreign trade at New Orleans, caused by the diversion of freight in the upper Mississippi Valley to the East via railroads and the Erie Canal, and the omission of the city from plans being projected for a railroad to run north from Mobile to connect with the Illinois Central at Cairo, finally aroused public interest in railroad construction on a large scale. At the Southwestern Railroad Convention, February 1852, plans were drawn up for a road to run from New Orleans to Nashville, via Jackson, Mississippi. The legislatures of Louisiana and Mississippi granted charters for construction of the Jackson & Great Northern. In 1858 a grand-opening run was made to Canton, north of Jackson.

Construction ceased in 1861, and it was not until 1873, after consolidation with the Mississippi Central, that the first through train ran from New Orleans to Chicago. Reorganized in 1875 as the Chicago, St. Louis & New Orleans Railroad, it was taken over two years later by the Illinois Central.

Construction of a road to the West, to link New Orleans and California, began with the organization of the New Orleans, Opelousas, &

Great Western Railroad in 1853. A company known as the Southern Pacific, a forerunner of the present organization, was chartered in 1855, with the stipulation that track was to be laid to El Paso, Texas, within 10 years and to the Pacific within 15 years. By 1854 the railroad extended from Algiers 52 miles west to Lafourche Crossing, and three years later it ran to Morgan City, from which point freight was transported to Texas by boat. The company was taken over by Charles Morgan, steamship magnate, in 1869. The first through service between New Orleans and California began in 1883. The Southern Pacific System acquired possession of the route in 1885.

A large part of the effectiveness of the Port of New Orleans has been due to the long haul facilities of its eight trunkline railroads. They are the Gulf, Mobile & Ohio, the Illinois Central, the Kansas City Southern Lines, the Louisville & Nashville, the Missouri Pacific, the Southern Pacific, the Southern Railway System, and the Texas & Pacific. These roads move freight to and from the wharves via the New Orleans Public Belt Railroad, which carries freight cars between a central yard and dockside or industrial terminals. The railroads are still able to prove their usefulness despite the intense competition from trucks. Their passenger business has been greatly curtailed. The Union Passenger Terminal in New Orleans, opened in 1954 at a cost of $16,000,000, now shares its railroad offices with those of Greyhound bus lines. In 1940 the railroads had more than 5,000 miles of track in Louisiana; in 1970 Class I roads had less than 3,500. In 1964 employment on interstate lines averaged 9,500; in 1968 the figure was 8,400, and in 1969 8,100. In the meantime employment in other means of transportation, including aviation, went from 49,800 in 1965 to 56,300 in 1969.

HIGHWAYS AND AIRPLANES

The State first undertook the construction of highways in 1911; from 1911 to 1922 activities were devoted primarily to improvements of the principal highways radiating from the larger municipalities. Most of the roads built were gravel-surfaced. Between 1922 and 1928 the State Highway Commission had completed 51 miles of various types of pavement.

In 1928 Governor Huey P. Long launched the most comprehensive paving program ever undertaken in the Deep South. Between 1929 and 1936, under the Long-Allen Administration, 9,800 miles of paved and graveled roads were built, involving an expenditure of approximately $140,000,000. Today, more than 400 toll-free bridges cross the State's waterways. One is the Huey P. Long Bridge across the Mississippi River, on the outskirts of New Orleans. A similar structure crossing the river at Baton Rouge was completed in August, 1940, and a second bridge, carrying Interstate 10, in 1969. In 1938 the State purchased the Watson-Williams Bridge, across Lake Pontchartrain, renamed it the Robert S. Maestri Bridge, and made it toll free. The Greater New Orleans Bridge was opened in 1945.

Airplanes were first seen in New Orleans in the spring of 1910, when Louis Taulhan made an exhibition flight at City Park Race Track. An international aviation tournament was held at the Park Dec. 24, 1910, to Jan. 2, 1911, during which two aviators were killed in crashes. A mile was made in 57 seconds and a height of 7,125 ft. was attained. The second official air mail trip in the United States was made by George Mestach between New Orleans and Baton Rouge on April 10, 1912, in one hour and 32 seconds.

In the period since World War II airplanes have become the principal media for passenger services. More than 200 major and minor airports are available and more than one-half of the planes in use are single-engine executive craft that have been found most helpful by industries and off-shore oil platforms. The New Orleans International Airport at Moisant Field is the busiest terminal in the State, with well over 200 arrivals and departures daily, and up to 2,000,000 passengers using it annually. Besides having direct lines to Europe it is a principal station for Central and South American lines. There is continuous construction of new facilities, extensions to the main terminal building, enlargement of runways, and provision for cargo. The New Orleans Lakefront Airport, formerly Shusan, has been enlarged by reclaiming land from Lake Pontchartrain. Alvin Callender Field in New Orleans is the U. S. Naval Air Station. The largest runways for military planes are at Barksdale Air Force Base at Bossier City. The principal aircraft activity outside of New Orleans is at Shreveport, Lake Charles, Baton Rouge, Lafayette, Alexandria, Winnsboro, and New Iberia.

Racial Elements

THE Louisiana Creole is a descendant of the French or Spanish settlers of the State. The oldest and proudest families today trace their ancestry to those French or Spanish Colonials. Although Creole, in a restricted sense, is applicable only to persons of French or Spanish descent, the term, in the course of time, has come to be used in speaking of various Creole possessions and products, for example: Creole pralines, Creole lettuce, Creole horses. When applied as an adjective to food, such as *shrimps Creole,* it has an unmistakable Spanish flavor.

The Creoles are chiefly of French descent; Spain sent comparatively few colonists to Louisiana. Most of the French settlers came directly from France, although a great many migrated to Louisiana from various French possessions in America, especially from Nova Scotia and Santo Domingo.

Of the Colonial French, the Acadians form the most homogeneous group. Approximately 4,000 settled in Louisiana after the English dispersion of the Nova Scotia settlement in 1755. Coming in small groups over a 30-year period (1760–90), the Acadians settled in the Attakapas country of southwestern Louisiana, along Bayous Teche, Lafourche, and Vermilion, and below New Orleans, in Plaquemines Parish. Along with other French stock, their descendants now live in south-central and southeastern Louisiana and are popularly known as Cajuns (a corruption of Acadian). Today, the terms Creole and Cajun are used-colloquially as synonyms for French-speaking city people and French-speaking country people.

Two centuries of linguistic intercourse have molded the dialects of the French settlers of Louisiana into two rather distinct types: that spoken by the cultured Creoles, an approximation of pure French, and the patois spoken by the Acadian descendants. In the latter dialect, archaic French forms have been retained, and to these have been added words and inflections, borrowed from English, Spanish, German, Negro, and Indian neighbors. No absolutely definite line can be drawn between the two dialects, however, since both have augmented their native language from the same foreign sources.

In many places in southern Louisiana, French is more often heard than English, and French is the household language of families who have been in Louisiana for generations. Many Negroes speak French or at least a French patois, known as Gombo, and it is not unusual in such towns as Lafayette and St. Martinville to find Negroes who cannot speak English.

In St. Bernard Parish are to be found the Isleños, Canary Islanders brought to Louisiana by Governor Galvez in the 1770's. In spite of intermixture with other nationalities, principally the French, they have retained the Spanish language and many of their native customs. Trappers and fishermen for the most part, they live along the bayous and swamps on the fringe of the delta.

Negroes inhabit almost every portion of Louisiana and are in the majority in eight parishes and practically half the population in five others (*Louisiana Almanac, 1969*). The nonwhites have a majority in East Carroll, De Soto, Medina, Pointe Coupée, St. Helena, St. John the Baptist, Tensas, and West Feliciana; the races are about even in Claiborne, East Feliciana, Iberville, St. James, and West Baton Rouge Parishes.

Because of the constant interbreeding of the various Negro racial strains imported as slaves during the Colonial period, it is quite impossible today to determine the African origins of the Louisiana Negro. It is apparent only that most of them are descendants of West African tribes. Mixture with both Europeans and Indians has further modified Negro stock. In southern Louisiana, more so than elsewhere in the South, intermixture of Negroes and whites was not taboo.

Between 1719 and 1722 many German colonists were sent to Louisiana by John Law. They settled along a 40-mile stretch of the Mississippi about 30 miles above New Orleans, on what subsequently became known as the German Coast. As time passed these early Germans were almost completely absorbed by their Latin neighbors, who even transformed the German family names by pronouncing them in French and Spanish.

The central and northern sections of the State are inhabited largely by persons of English, Scottish, and Irish descent whose ancestors came to Louisiana during the westward movement of the latter half of the eighteenth and the first half of the nineteenth centuries. Typical American pioneers, these immigrants came chiefly from near-by Southern States. In East and West Feliciana Parishes, in the vicinity of St. Francisville, there are many descendants of English Royalists who moved into the section, then under Spanish rule, during the American Revolution.

Under the Black Code, Jews were excluded from Louisiana, and although a few merchants were permitted to carry on business in New Orleans during the Spanish regime, it was not until after the barrier against them was raised following the Louisiana Purchase that Jews began to settle in Louisiana. By 1905 there were about 12,000 in the State. Since then the Jewish population has increased steadily.

The foreign-born whites were 30,557, in 1960, of whom Italians, 5,470, were the largest number. They have settled principally in New Orleans, Baton Rouge, and Shreveport. Other groups include 3,091 Germans, 1,357 French, 2,622 English, 760 Russians, and some Central and South Americans. Most of these have settled in the larger towns of the State. A few hundred Dalmatians and Slavonians live along the Mississippi in the vicinity of Buras. Small colonies of Czechs have settled at Kolin and Libuse, near Alexandria, and a group of Hungarians live at Arpadon, near Hammond. Of the few Chinese and Filipinos living in the State a number have formed colonies in the Barataria Bay area. Manila Village, Leon Rojas, and Bayou Cholas, all populated by Filipinos, and the Chinese settlement of Bayou Defon are small communities of shrimp fishermen.

At Grand Isle and in the surrounding country descendants of Lafitte's corsairs speak a French-Spanish patois, and represent a mixture of French, Portuguese, Spanish, and Filipino.

Of the 3,587 Indians (1960 census) living in the State, the largest groups are the Houma, living in Terrebonne Parish; Coushatta, Allen Parish; Choctaw, St. Tammany and La Salle Parishes, and Chitimacha, St. Mary Parish.

Folkways

OLD villagers will tell you that when a Louisianian dies and goes to Heaven and finds there is no gumbo, he comes right back. Anyway, in the full of the moon at Kenilworth Plantation, a couple stroll up and down the stairs, restless, perhaps because they have no heads. At Ingleside chains bang and clang all night, field bells toll, and an elderly ghost known as Uncle Naplander Richardson plays old-fashioned tunes on the piano. At Myrtle an inquisitive old lady, wearing a bright green bonnet, wanders from room to room, raising the mosquito *baire* and peering into the faces of sleepers. On the wide porch of Conrad Plantation ghosts play music and sing spirituals at twilight. A plantation without a ghost would be worse off than a plantation without a rosewood piano that had been used as a horse trough by the Federals, or one that boasted no carved mahogany staircase marked by hoof prints when those "damn Yankees" rode up to the second floor. Every house in New Orleans' French Quarter has its ghosts; the most widely known are the tortured slaves who wail and groan and rattle the chains that bind them to the walls in the Haunted House of Madame LaLaurie. From Pearl River music emanates each spring. An orchestra was drowned there. On Raccourci cutoff, a nineteen-mile short cut in the Mississippi, there is even the ghost of a steamboat. Trapped in the cutoff the night the river changed its course, the old paddle-wheeler can be heard on foggy nights, its signal bell jangling and the pilot cursing his luck.

If you are troubled with ghosts, hang a horseshoe on your front or back door, burn sawdust and sprinkle the ashes in the corners of the house, burn two white candles on the floor in front of your fireplace, turn your pockets inside out, and never pass a cemetery unless you are holding a little child by the hand. If you are still bothered, confront the ghosts and tell them you are angry and perhaps they will go away. Otherwise turn around three times and spit on them. If you are afraid of a dead person, pin two new straight pins in the form of a cross on the corpse or place a bottle of white chicken feathers on the grave, and, unless his *gris gris* is stronger than yours, he won't haunt you.

Among the more irritating ghosts are those who guard buried treasure. Every bayou, every tiny island, every swamp in the State undoubtedly conceals pirate treasure; every Indian mound is filled with precious loot; every plantation garden hides valuables buried by faithful retainers at the first cry of "Yankees is coming." But the pirates killed and buried a minor member of their crew along with their gold; the Indians, an enemy brave; and the shade of a faithful retainer walks in the garden, jealous of his knowledge.

They all add to the problem. And the job of controlling spirits is complicated, requiring, among other things, a thorough command of the *Book of Moses, 'Tit Albert,* and *The Little Lost Friend,* and an adequate supply of *Special Delivery Oil.* Without a ghost, treasure hunting is difficult enough. "You can't talk or even sweat too much when you dig. You can't take no tobacco or whisky. You can't have no stained hands. You can't have nothing to do with no women for four days. You gotta go with an open mind. You gotta be clean in heart and spirit."

Treasures have been found in many places: German coins at Bayou Chicot near Opelousas, English silver at Ruston, Spanish doubloons at Baton Rouge and New Orleans. And the quest is of perennial interest. A treasure hunt at Pecan Island reached such enthusiastic proportions that giant oak trees were uprooted and pits left which are still visible today. A plantation house on the river road near St. Rose has been totally razed by treasure hunters, its ground floor torn up tile by tile.

Many of the legends concerning treasure are connected with the pirate, Jean Lafitte. On stormy nights Lafitte still sometimes appears at Destréhan Plantation, cryptically points a bony finger at the hearth and then vanishes. Most of the time, however, he is content to lie in his grave at the cemetery where the Bayou of the Geese meets Bayou Barataria, side by side with Napoleon and John Paul Jones. There are persons who will vouch for all three.

This bayou country is the heart of the territory settled by the sturdy Bretons after their exile from Nova Scotia. The Acadians, called Cajuns now by everyone in the State including themselves, are a thrifty, hardy, fun-loving, but devoutly religious folk, who work, play, and make love with equal enthusiasm, marry young, and cheerfully demonstrate extreme fecundity. One aged lady in a Cajun parish counted eight hundred lineal descendants, blood relatives all. Twenty-five children from a single pair of parents is not unusual.

And these offspring are often named with complete abandon. Pseudo-Grecian appellations are popular; literally hundreds of Achilles, Ulysses, Télémaques, and Télesphores live along the bayous. One proud parent named a son Déus, a daughter, Déussa. Other families achieve a novel effect by dubbing the youngsters with names starting with an identical letter. To Miss Perpetuée Mayard, who married Lastie Broussard, an Abbeville attorney, were born sixteen children named Odile, Odelia, Odalia, Olive, Oliver, Olivia, Ophelia, Odelin, Octave, Octavia, Ovide, Onesia, Olita, Otta, Omea and finally—and perhaps in desperation—Opta. Besides this there is a tremendous passion for nicknames and few children are ever called by anything else; every Cajun family boasts members known as Titi, Mannie, Lala, Noonoon, Tootsie, Bootsie, Bos or Coon.

Love of race and family is deeply rooted in the Cajun heart. No other people can so accurately relate just who is their *cousine*—perhaps because practically everyone is. *Tantes* (aunts), *nainaines* (godmothers), and *parrains* (godfathers), are treated with great respect. When a death occurs within the family, mourning is strict and conspicuous, no matter how distant the relationship. Black-bordered announcements of the death are tacked on trees and posts along the highways and black is worn for every cousin, aunt, uncle or godparent. Widows must wear trailing veils for at least a year and black for three years. Some women are never out of mourning.

Until the first World War most Cajun families displayed little interest in English. Today, their use of that language is amusing and picturesque, to say the least. Sometimes it is intentionally exaggerated, as in the timeworn but often used request: "You see ma cow down by de bayou you push heem home, yes. He been gone tree day now—yesterday, today, and tomorrow!" But just the other night at *Sweet Poulou's,* a café near Laplace, a lady was heard to lament, "It ain't much fun being married twice as old as yourself to a man, no." And there is the little boy who, returning from confession and rubbing his knees after more Our Fathers and Hail Marys than he had expected, exclaimed, "That Father Étienne! He is a hard man, yes. He ain't no softshell crab!"

The Cajuns' pleasure-loving nature is manifested in the community gatherings, dances, and peculiar sports that are integral parts of bayou life. Of these, the annual pirogue race at Bayou Barataria is the most widely known. On this occasion trappers and fishermen from all over the southern part of the State meet to show their skill in handling those frail boats, hollowed out of single logs, in which they travel with amazing speed.

Particularly popular are *fais-dodos,* big Saturday night dances. A traveller in the 1870's thus describes such a dance:

> The neighborhood ball is orderly and well conducted, with whole families attending. A section known as the *parc aux petits* is provided for the babies so that mothers can keep a careful watch on their older daughters, while the fathers enjoy a quiet game of cards in an adjoining room. The old women also come to play cards, each carrying with her a bag of coins. Some of the mothers are quite young to be relegated to places against the walls; and, as they follow the dance with sparkling eyes, . . .
> During the evening a supper of chicken gumbo with rice and hot black coffee is served. When the musicians at length grow weary, they go outside and, firing pistol shots into the air, cry, 'Le bal est fini!' Otherwise, the dance-loving Acadians would never go home.

A country dance is generally known today among the Cajuns as a *fais-dodo* (literally, go to sleep); possibly because the dancers stay up all night and sometimes fall asleep while still dancing; possibly because the mothers sing *fais-dodos* (lullabies) to put the younger children to sleep so that they themselves can leave the *parc aux petits* for the dance floor.

Fais dodo, Minette,	Go to sleep, Kitten,
Trois piti coohon dulaite;	Three little suckling-pigs;
Fais dodo, mon piti babe,	Go to sleep, my little baby,
Jiska l'âge de quinze ans.	Until the age of fifteen years.
Quan quinze ans aura passe;	When fifteen years have passed;
Minette va so marier.	Kitten will marry.

Swing bands, radios, and record players have penetrated the Cajun country, but at the genuine *fais-dodo* the music of the fiddle, the accordion, and the triangle (sometimes called the "ting-a-ling") is always featured; for the Acadian retains his love for these instruments and often possesses rare skill in playing them. A full orchestra includes also the guitar and harmonica.

So popular is dancing that even the *Loup-garous* of the State hold a ball. Annually at Bayou Goula, they meet and indulge in no end of weird carryings-on. Half human, half wolf, the *Loup-garou* is the first cousin of the werewolf of Central Europe and his habits are just as curious and fiendish. Some *Loup-garous* are souls under a curse, others, self-imposed vampires. The most efficient one recorded is a gentleman who turned himself into a mule and ploughed his own farm. If a *Loup-garou* drinks your blood you will become one of his kind. The best protection is salt which, when thrown upon these loathsome creatures, reduces them to ashes.

Among the other monsters who frequent southern Louisiana is the

Létiche of Terrebonne Parish, the soul of an unbaptized infant who swims the bayous, upsetting pirogues whenever possible. Mermaids also swim up the bayous from the coast, and Cajun children have grown quite used to them.

The Creoles form another large French-speaking group of Louisianians. They are city folk in contrast with the Cajuns, who are country folk. White descendants of the Colonial French and Spanish settlers, the Creoles include many of the oldest families of the State and remain a proud and clannish group. It is still possible in New Orleans to find old ladies who will shrug their shoulders over some debutante of the season and explain that she is acceptable, perhaps, to the "Americans" but hardly to "downtown society." A young person being introduced to an elderly Creole is almost always asked: "And what was your mother's name before her marriage?" And the possessor of an uncomprisingly non-Creole name will find his reception much warmer if he can produce a mother who was a De la Something.

Creoles have a humor all their own. For example they say that every Creole considers himself *sorti de la cuisse de Jupiter*—born from the thigh of Jupiter; his family invariably one of *les bonnes familles*. Yet the Creole invented at least seven terms to describe degrees of dowdiness among his cousins and acquaintances of which *chacalata* (one who stubbornly refused to accept new ideas or customs) is the best known.

Among themselves, Creoles are warm, affectionate, extremely loyal. *La famille* is the very core of their life, and like the humbler Cajuns, this extends to the utmost limits of relationships. The Creole is skilled in the fine art of having a good time within the family circle. A Creole lady may not always have had the advantages of an elaborate education but she can always "entertain a parlour."

Although much of their charm lies in the manner of their telling, Creole stories are endlessly amusing. There is this story of an old lady discussing an approaching marriage:

"Azalée—she is not as young as she used to be. One might have thought by now she would have thrown her corset on top the *armoire* (i.e., given up the struggle of keeping herself attractive to men). But she is a lady. She is related to people who are related to me. In fact, my chère, she is almost related to me. She is a *real* lady!"

Holidays are celebrated with gusto by Creoles. Christmas was formerly celebrated strictly as a religious festival, the gift giving taking place on New Year's. On the morning of this day, before receiving his presents, each child presented his parents with a carefully prepared *compliment de jour de l'an*—a sheet of pink paper adorned with tinsel and fat cherubs on which was written in a childish hand in French a verse like the following:

My dear Papa, my dear Mama,
I wish you a Happy and Prosperous New Year.
I will be a good little boy.
I will not tease my little sister any more.
I love you with all my heart.

Creoles, with few exceptions, are Roman Catholic. Name days, the feast days of the saints for whom they are named, are always celebrated. The most important feast day is that of Marie, for most families possess at least one daughter with Marie in her name, and innumerable *Tante* and *Cousine* Maries.

The Cajuns are also predominantly Catholic as are the large groups of Italians who have come to the State in the last fifty years. And the Catholic Church with its ceremonies and pageants adds interest to the lives of even non-Catholics.

The blessing of the sugar cane crop and of the shrimp fleet are always noteworthy. The first takes place at harvest time, which is also the time of replanting; the second, just before the fleet sails out into the Gulf for the catch. Hundreds of small boats gayly decorated with flags tie up at one of several bayou villages. The elaborately designed vestments of the priests, the gleaming crozier, the fluttering flags, and the green water hyacinths floating idly by, all add color to the scene as the Bishop waves his aspergillum in the direction of boats named variously the *St. Ann,* the *Three Brothers,* and even the *Mae West.*

The bayou banks are crowded with visitors, the boats with proud fishermen and their families. Everybody is dressed up. Here and there a Cajun woman has struggled into her corset (perhaps for the first time in a year) to proudly exhibit a new pink dress, but has found shoes too much of an effort. She is only momentarily embarrassed when from a neighboring boat her little niece screams, "Regardez Tante Naomi with her bare feets!" After the ceremony everyone feasts on boiled shrimp.

On All Saints' Day, November first, cemeteries throughout the State are turned into flower gardens as tombs and graves are bedecked with bouquets and wreaths. The chrysanthemum is the favorite flower. In the Cajun parishes the evening assumes an eerie aspect as hundreds of candles are lighted in the graveyards. In New Orleans the downtown cemeteries are particularly festive. Women weep and gossip, men discuss local politics, children run in and out the crisscross aisles; venders on the *banquette* hawk gumbo, snowballs, pralines, peanuts, taffy candy, hot dogs, apples on a stick, balloons, mechanical birds, and toy skeletons.

In September the Italians of Kenner and Harvey honor St. Rosalie in a procession in which barefoot men and women march, carrying a life-sized statue of the saint. On the nineteenth of March Italians in New Orleans and elsewhere erect elaborate altars in honor of St. Joseph. The altars are composed of tier upon tier of specially prepared delicacies.

Louisiana Houses

Louisiana Tourist Development Commission, Baton Rouge
GOVERNOR'S MANSION, BATON ROUGE, SOUTH FACADE

GOVERNOR'S MANSION, BATON ROUGE, SOUTHWEST VIEW
Louisiana Tourist Development Commission, Baton Rouge

Louisiana Tourist Development Commission, Baton Rouge

PARLOR, GOVERNOR'S MANSION, BATON ROUGE

STAIRCASE IN FOYER, GOVERNOR'S MANSION, BATON ROUGE

SAN FRANCISCO PLANTATION HOUSE (1850) AN EXAMPLE
OF STEAMBOAT GOTHIC

HOUMAS HOUSE, ASCENSION PARISH, 1840

MADEWOOD PLANTATION HOUSE ON BAYOU LAFOURCHE,
NAPOLEONVILLE

THE MYRTLES, NEAR ST. FRANCISVILLE, AMID SPANISH MOSS

Tourist Guide of Opelousas

MAGNOLIA RIDGE, BUILT BY CAPT. LEWIS D. PRESCOTT, C. S. A.

OAK ALLEY, NEAR VACHERIE, ST. JAMES PARISH

Richard Koch Photo

GARDEN OF SACRED HEART ACADEMY, GRAND COTEAU

ROQUE HOUSE (18TH CENT.). NOW A MUSEUM, NATCHITOCHES

They are announced in the classified ads of the local newspapers, and thousands of people come to view them every year and to take away blessed bread and lucky beans. Afterwards most of the food is distributed among the poor. In all of the Catholic communities other saints' days are celebrated. Throughout the State there are many shrines; St. Roch's and Our Lady of Prompt Succor in New Orleans, St. John Berchmans at Grand Coteau, and St. Amico's in Donaldsonville are among the better known.

In the central and northern part of the State most of the natives are of Anglo-Saxon descent and Protestants. Folkways approach more generally those of the neighboring states. Logrollings, corn huskings, and quilting bees are popular. The hog butchering season is an occasion for celebrations. Many families raise hogs, chiefly for home consumption. On butchering days the family giving the party invites several friends and their children. Each adult guest is adept at one of the processes of preparing the pig—making sausage, rendering lard, baking hams, etc. The festivity begins at dawn, and by noon large quantities of pork dishes are ready to be served, eaten, and washed down by quarts of homemade wine. Beef clubs, active from May to October, operate in much the same manner. In the vicinity of Dry Prong singing conventions and revivals are held in brushwood arbors during the "lay-by" season of July and August.

Another old custom popular during the Christmas season is that of shooting the *papagai*. The *papagai* is a target cut out in the shape of a cow. Marksmen try their skill by shooting at that particular cut that they desire. Wooden chickens, turkeys, or ducks are sometimes substituted.

Crop signs, weather signs, folk remedies and the like play their part in the daily life of Louisiana: "When there is a large cotton crop, there is a small pecan crop. Plenty of thunder makes more sugar in the cane. When 'dirt daubers' build low down, a drought is to come. The roaring of an alligator is a sure sign of rain. A pepper bush in the yard brings good luck. It is bad luck to have Spanish daggers growing near the house. If a woman has a lot of girl-children, she will have a boy-child if she moves her bed into another corner. Bathe children in orange-flower tea for 'nerves.' A tea made by boiling roots of the Blue Flag (wild iris) is good for pneumonia. Garlic in a bag around the neck will cure colic. You will have bad luck if you keep funeral notices. Kill a lizard on a grave, ain't no charm your life can save."

Ever a source of myth and legend, the Mississippi has contributed much to the folklore of Louisiana. The remarkable prowess of John Henry is too well known to be repeated here, but that of his spiritual sister, Annie Christmas, is less familiar.

Annie was a black gal who stood six feet eight inches without shoes, weighed over two hundred pounds and wore a neat mustache. She could carry a barrel of flour under each arm and another balanced on her head. Once she towed a keelboat from New Orleans to Natchez on a dead run. She wore a necklace of every ear, nose and eye she had gouged off of men in fights. Usually she dressed and worked as a man, but sometimes she primped up, shaved her mustache, filled her barge with fancy women from New Orleans and operated a floating brothel up and down the Mississippi. When she died her body was placed on a barge by her twelve coal black sons and all of them floated down the river and out to the sea, never to be seen again.

In many parts of Louisiana the Negro is as different from his brethren in other states as is the Cajun from the Ozark hillbilly or the New England farmer. Latin influence and Catholicism have permeated deeply. French Negro is a common term. In many sections Negroes speak a corrupted French known as Gombo. Among them lore and legend assume a Gallic flavor and *Brer Rabbit* becomes *Compère Lapin.*

From Africa the slaves brought primitive music and dances and these, in various modifications, continued to play an important part in their life in the New World. On many of the plantations slaves were allowed to give "balls" on holidays and in New Orleans Congo Square was set aside for their use.

Alcée Fortier has described a New Year's celebration on a plantation:

The musical instruments were, first, a barrel with one end covered with an ox-hide,—this was the drum; then two sticks and the jawbone of a mule, with the teeth still on it,—this was the violin. The principal musician bestrode the barrel and began to beat on the hide, singing as loud as he could. He beat with his hands, with his feet, and sometimes, when quite carried away by his enthusiasm, with his head also. The second musician took the sticks and beat on the wood of the barrel, while the third made a dreadful music by rattling the teeth of the jawbone with a stick. Five or six men stood around the musicians and sang without stopping. . . . These dancing-songs generally consisted of one phrase, repeated for hours on the same air.

In the dance called *carabiné*, which was quite graceful, the man took his *danseuse* by the hand, and made her turn around very rapidly for more than an hour, the woman waving a red handkerchief over her head, and every one singing,—

Madame Gobar, en sortant di bal,
Madame Gobar, tiyon li tombé.

Madame Gobar, coming out of the ball,
Madame Gobar, her head-handkerchief fell.

The other dance, called *pilé Chactas,* was not as graceful as the *carabiné,* but was more strange. The woman had to dance almost without moving her feet. It was the man who did all the work; turning around her, kneeling down, making the most grotesque and extraordinary faces, writhing like a serpent, while the woman was almost immovable. After a little while, however, she began to get excited, and untying her neckerchief, she waved it around gracefully, and finally ended by wiping off the perspiration from the face of her *danseur,* and also from the faces of the musicians. . . .

On Sundays the slaves of New Orleans gathered in Congo Square for similar entertainments. The music of the *bamboula* (a drum made of a goat skin stretched across a hollow log) and the *banza* (a crude bass fiddle) was helped out by clapping hands and stamping feet. Men and women danced until exhausted. A favorite dance was the *Calinda,* to which the singers improvised words ending in the refrain:

> Dansé Calinda, boudoum, boudoum!
> Dansé Calinda, boudoum, boudoum!

Dancing was supposed to cease at dusk but often continued later. At nine o'clock a cannon in the center of the Square was fired, and any Negro found on the streets after that hour without his master or a permit was thrown into prison. Eventually the sensual nature of the Dance Congo caused its prohibition.

Congo Square early became associated with the practice of Voodooism, perhaps the most interesting of all phases of Louisiana folklore. Originally an African cult in which the powers of evil were worshipped in the form of a large snake, Voodooism sprang up wherever African slaves were imported and conditions were favorable. For almost two centuries in Louisiana the lives of most Negroes and many whites were influenced by the activities of the Voodoos.

Of the series of Kings and Queens who ruled the Voodoos of New Orleans in the nineteenth century, none is better known than Marie Laveau, who flourished just before and for some time after the War between the States. On St. John's Eve, June 23rd, the occasion of the most spectacular of the Voodoo saturnalias, Marie reigned in some hidden place near the entrance of Bayou St. John into Lake Pontchartrain. Here she sat, a handsome mulatress holding the serpent in its box before an altar. While a cauldron seethed with witches' brew she would chant:

> L'Appé vinie, li Grand Zombi
> L'Appé vinie, pou' fe' gris-gris!
>
> He is coming the Great Zombi
> He is coming to make gris-gris.

Then into the clearing would leap a Negro carrying a small black coffin. And at sight of him the celebrants would bound into the air screaming, "Li Grand Zombi! Li Grand Zombi!" The evil contents of the cauldron were distributed, live pigeons and chickens torn limb from limb, until faces and teeth and hands and bodies were smeared with blood. Then the Voodooists would dance and whirl and scream until many of them fell to the ground unconscious.

Eventually public sentiment drove Voodoo into its present secret existence. Today it is hard to witness a Voodoo ceremony; but it is not impossible. Voodoo charms and *gris-gris* are still bought. If you know where to go, there are drug stores in many of the larger towns where you can buy Love Powders, Get-Together Drops, Boss-Fix Powder, Easy Life Powder, Come To Me Powder, Devil Oil, Controlling Oil, and Dice Special. If you are white and prosperous, your cook may have better luck in obtaining the charm you desire.

Today Voodoo practices are frequently blended with rituals borrowed from established Christian denominations in the cults that spring up wherever there is a large Negro population. Of these cults the "spiritualists" are the most numerous. Practically all of the "Temples" organized by some self-appointed "Mother" or "Father" use the statues, candles, and incense of the Roman Catholic ritual. The congregations sing Protestant hymns accompanied by the clapping of hands and the stamping of feet. Members "fall out" and "talk in the unknown tongue" while the leaders summon the ghosts of departed relatives and heal ailments. On the side there is frequently a brisk business in *gris-gris*.

Negro superstitions are numerous throughout the State:

To keep a man at home: Write his name on paper, put it in a cocoanut shell and roll the shell.

To make a love powder, catch live humming birds, gut them without first killing them, dry the heart and powder it. Then sprinkle the powder on a person and he can't help loving you after that. Another way—a bit simpler—is to pin a lock of his hair to an unseen part of your clothing.

To make a person move: Take a dead black cat, remove its hair, wrap it in silver paper, stuff its mouth with lemons that have been painted with melted red wax and crayon, perform incantations over it and then put it under the person's house. "With that cat under his house he'll move right out."

To drive a person crazy: Take nine dusts, including goofer (dust from a grave), dead cow, cat, rabbit, chinaball leaves and others, mix with red ash and call the devil into the middle of it at midnight. The devil stands in the middle and guides his evil work himself. "He can make you leave yo' insides right on yo' front step."

Not all Louisiana Negroes "get religion" of the Voodoo variety; many prefer the good old-fashioned revival style, especially along the outer edges of the State, where the Negro more closely resembles those in Mississippi and Arkansas. Among them there is much testifying, singing, and shouting during services. The good sisters dance about, shake their skirts and cry, "Preach it! Lay it on me!" Often healing is part of the ceremonies. Music is likely to embrace a full orchestra and choir, who swing the old hymns while the congregation trucks and shuffles and gets "hot."

And it is wonderful. Religion is a living, breathing thing to these people, and God is a close friend, to be often addressed in the easy, familiar fashion of the *marchande* who, crossing the ferry at West-wego with a basket of blackberries on her head, expressed appreciation for blessings received with, "I thanks you, my Lawd, I thanks you my rockin' chair, I thanks you my leanin' post, I thanks you my hot loaf of bread."

Social Life and Social Welfare

THE first social events in Louisiana were the entertainments and feasts given to the French by the Indians. In 1699 Iberville, exploring the Mississippi northward, came upon the village of the Houma in the Tunica hills in what is now West Feliciana Parish. Iberville's report gives the following account of the entertainment provided: "At 4 o'clock in the evening they gave a formal ball for us in the middle of the square, where the entire village was assembled. They brought into the midst of the assembly drums (and) chychycouchy, which are gourds, in which are dry seeds, and with sticks for holding them; they make a little noise and serve to mark the time . . . A short time afterward there came 20 young people of from 20 to 30 years old, and 15 of the prettiest young girls magnificently adorned after their manner, entirely naked, having only their breechcloths on, which they wore above a kind of belt . . . The young men were naked, having only a belt like the girls, which concealed them in part, they being well daubed with paint and their hair well provided with bunches of feathers. Many had pieces of copper in the form of flattened plates, two and three together fastened to their belts, and hanging as far down as the knee, which made a noise and assisted in marking the time. They danced like that for three hours in a very active and sprightly manner."

With the settlement of New Orleans almost 20 years later and the acquisition of the colony by Antoine Crozat, Negro slaves were introduced into Louisiana to work the plantations that every year became more numerous. New Orleans was at this time little more than a fortified garrison, and white women were scarce. Some of the soldiers married Indian women, but this did not prove a popular expedient. Others associated with Negresses, and their half-white progeny, who were generally free, gave rise to a new class—the free people of color. In many instances the strain became whiter through the generations, the mulatto women proving more desirable than the pure Negro.

The French Government recognized the colony's need and sent over women gathered from the prisons of Paris. Many of these died in transit or succumbed to the rigour of the life in the New World. In addition, a few unfortunate aristocrats came to Louisiana under *lettres de cachet* and spent the remainder of their days in exile from France.

The first group of the *filles à la cassette* (Fr. casket girls), girls of better antecedents, who came willingly to Louisiana, arrived in 1728. These were peasant girls of honest parentage, or orphans from the asylums of Paris. They were so called because of the small chests of clothes and linens allotted to them by the French Government. The Ursuline nuns, who had arrived the previous year, cared for them until they were married. To help matters along, soldiers who married were given their discharge, a plot of land, a cow, provisions, and a rifle. Sister Hachard of the Ursulines wrote in 1728 that "the women, while ignorant about things concerning their salvation, are not so about vanity. . . . The generality . . . are dressed in stuffs of damask full of ribbons, notwithstanding the dearness, for these stuffs usually cost in this country three times more than in France. Women here, as elsewhere, paint white and red, to hide the wrinkles of their faces, on which they also wear beauty spots. The demon possesses here a great empire."

In 1743 Bienville resigned as governor and was succeeded by the Marquis de Vaudreuil, who changed the social life of New Orleans from that of a drab military outpost to a gay and brilliant society. The Grand Marquis ruled from 1743 to 1752, and the legends of the gaieties that characterized his reign persist today. He seems to have begun the tradition that was later to become so much a part of the city—a tradition of pleasure. Charles Gayarré in his *History of Louisiana* describes the times: "His administration, if small things may be compared with great ones, was for Louisiana, with regard to splendour, luxury, military display, and expenses of every kind, what the reign of Louis XIV had been for France. He was a man of patrician birth and high breeding, who liked to live in a manner worthy of his rank. Remarkable for his personal graces and comeliness, for the dignity of his bearing and the fascination of his address, he was fond of pomp, show and pleasure; surrounded by a host of brilliant officers, of whom he was the idol, he loved to keep up a miniature court, a distant imitation of that of Versailles; and long after he had departed, old people were fond of talking of the exquisitely refined manners, the magnificent balls, the splendidly uniformed troops, the high-born young officers, and many other unparalleled things they had seen in the days of the *Great Marquis.*"

The 30 years from 1760 to 1790 saw the gradual infiltration of the outcast Acadians from northern Canada. They settled in southwestern Louisiana near Opelousas and along Bayou Teche in the ancient country of the Attakapa. There they established customs and ways of living peculiar to themselves, and their descendants today form a picturesque unit in the racial composition of the State. During the French Revolution a number of refugees settled in this part of Louisiana; and the number of barons, marquises, counts, and countesses in St. Martinville earned for it the title of Le Petit Paris.

During the Spanish domination in the last quarter of the eighteenth century an effort was made to inject Spanish culture into the Colony, but the predominantly French population refused to conform, and in time even absorbed through marriage some of the high government officials. There is, however, in New Orleans a Spanish air about much of the architecture. A great deal of the present Vieux Carré was rebuilt after the fire of 1788, and the Spanish influence is especially to be noticed in the Cabildo, Presbytère, and Cathedral, all of which date from the last years of Spanish rule (*see Architecture*). The Spanish influence is also to be noted in Natchitoches.

The journal of the Baron de Pontalba gives a picture of the social life in New Orleans during the governorship of the Baron de Carondelet. There seems to have been a continuous round of bathing and fishing parties, subscription balls, and card parties, at which ladies were "seriously offended" at those who did not allow them to win at "Bourre" or "Coq."

"May 18, 1795—Another boisterous party at Gentilly. Tremoulet took charge of getting it up. A list was passed around in the circle of Madame la Baronne (de Carondelet). . . .

"Ask my little Tintin if he has forgotten our little crayfish parties: tell him I saw one this morning that interested me far more than the party at Gentilly. His little cousins d'Aunoy with Céleste la Jonchere were fishing for them, catching five or six on their line at one time.

"May 24, 1795—. . . I went this evening to the card party (at Madame Carondelet's); Madame Landry, Madame Gauthier, Madame Macarty and others were there. The ladies are now reconciled to *Madame la Baronne,* whom they find very tactful. In fact you cannot find ladies more amiable in society, more friendly, more simple, more affable, than these who now frequent her parties and who are attached to her.

"June 18, 1795—I was invited to another bathing party today at Madame Macarty's. . . . The ladies go at eleven in the morning and pass two hours in the water, going under head and all."

By October, Madame Macarty had a full house of overnight guests, including the governor, Baron de Carondelet. At night the ladies played pranks on the men, going to the latter's rooms and making a great racket at their doors. "This afternoon," continues the Baron, "they all went on horseback to the Laporte Crevasse with all their young men; they ran races and committed all sorts of extravagances."

When the Mississippi River was thrown open to inland traffic during the Spanish regime many Kentuckians and Americans from other States came down the river in their flatboats to trade at New Orleans. These crude "Kaintucks" presented a violent contrast to the emerging Creole society with its polished manners and European background. They found diversion in gambling houses, and were as much antagonized by the elegance of the Creoles as the Creoles were offended by their dress and rough habits.

The growing class of *gens de couleur* began to provide the Colony with a problem. So great became the beauty and the luxury of women of color, that in 1788 Governor Miro passed an ordinance which is one of the most extraordinary documents on file in Louisiana. The directory of that year shows 1,500 "unmarried women of color, all free, living in little houses near the ramparts," and Governor Miro's ordinance made it "an evidence of misconduct" if one of these women walked abroad in silk, jewels, or "plumes"; by so doing the woman was "liable for punishment." The only head covering which the ordinance allowed them was the madras handkerchief or *tignon*. Many of these women were quadroons or even lighter in color; from all reports they were very beautiful, and lived as mistresses with white men. The children of such unions were, of course, free, and many were educated in Paris. Toward the middle of the nineteenth century these educated free men of color wrote plays and poetry, were musicians of note, and participated in a culture that was far above that of the Negroes. The free people of color themselves frequently owned slaves.

The institution which continued and regulated the "code" by which mistresses were acquired was the "Quadroon Ball," to which mothers brought their daughters for inspection by the rich planters of the colony. After dancing and preliminary conversations, the suitor would approach the mother and make all arrangements. These *femmes de couleur* were reared in the strictest morality—they were in no sense prostitutes. There was always a legacy or cash settlement in case the young man should marry or die. In many cases the relationship was kept up after marriage, bringing about untold jealousy and hatred between the women of both social strata. The quadroon balls were, however, much gayer than the more formal entertainments of "society."

Almost without exception the travellers who visited New Orleans during the period condemn this popular institution with much moral indignation; but in defense of the Creoles it may be said that such convenient relationships were often an outlet from *mariages de convenance* and were conducted with a *savoir faire* that did justice to the breeding of all parties concerned.

From the very beginning travellers were impressed by the cosmopolitan atmosphere of the city, whose inhabitants they described as a gay mixture of Creoles, French, English, Spanish, Germans, and Italians, who liked to dance, drink, and gamble. Berquin Duvallon in his *Vue* of 1802 says that the mania for dancing kept a public ball going twice a week during the winter, at which dancing lasted from seven until "cock crowing the next morning."

"This hall is about 80 feet long by 30 feet wide; on both sides of that narrow tube are built graded seats or sorts of loges where the mothers and the young girls who are not dancing are seated. These girls decorate the wall, as it is expressed here, and are called 'bredouilles' [wallflowers]. Finally called down to participate in the dance, they immediately change their manners and expressions; seated on those benches they look miserable, they have long faces, sad expressions, the eyes showing sadness and deception. The closer they get to the dance floor, the happier they look. As they get down from seat to seat they become animated and gay, their eyes show happiness and their entire behavior is that of mirth and joy. Finally when they reach the floor they are completely 'débredouillées' [set free]."

A manuscript memoir by Thomas C. Nicholls, then 17 years old, of New Orleans in 1805 describes an amusing custom: "During our sojourn in the city we attended one of the grand balls. This afforded us an opportunity of seeing the fashion and beauty of the country. The day was rainy and disagreeable, and the ballroom was situated at the farther extremity of the city. How the ladies were to reach the ballroom we could not divine, as hacks and public vehicles were then unknown. But the means proved more simple and easy than we, in our ignorance, could have conceived them to be. . . .

"Everything prepared, the order was given to march; when, to my horror and amazement, the young ladies doffed their shoes and stockings, which were carefully tied up in silk handkerchiefs, and took up the line of march, barefooted, for the ballroom. After paddling through mud and mire, lighted by lanterns carried by the negro slaves, we reached the scene of action without accident. The young ladies halted before the door and shook one foot after another in a pool of water close by. After repeating this process some half a dozen times, the feet were freed of the accumulated mud and were in a proper state to be wiped dry by the slaves who had carried towels for the purpose. Then silk stockings and satin slippers were put on again, cloaks were thrown aside, tucked-up trains were let down, and the ladies entered the ballroom, dry-shod and lovely in the candlelight."

When sated with dancing the general public found entertainment at the numerous French theaters, and later at the English theaters and at the French Opera.

Of all the celebrations however, those of the Carnival season, which date back to the beginning of the Colony, were gayest. Street parades began in New Orleans in 1838 and continue to this day.

The Carnival season remains one of the most elaborate and formal social seasons in existence any place in America. Twelfth Night is the official beginning of Carnival, but balls have become so numerous that in short seasons they sometimes start before Christmas. Almost every night of the season there is a ball somewhere, with king and queen and court, and everyone is interested in seeing which débutantes are honored.

The first street parade takes place on the Wednesday before Mardi Gras. There are other parades on Thursday, Friday, Saturday, and Monday, all followed by balls. On Mardi Gras (Shrove or Fat Tuesday) there are many parades and general street masking. The next day is Ash Wednesday, the first of the forty days of Lent.

The celebration of Mardi Gras is not confined to New Orleans. Wherever the French influence has been felt there are masquerades of some kind. Lafayette has its own street parades. In the country district around Natchitoches elderly men and women attend private masked balls; and on Fat Tuesday in such outlying districts as Golden Meadow, many a Cajun trapper dons his wife's bonnet and a pair of rabbit-skin gloves in preparation for a spree.

Outside of the towns and cities social life centered about the great plantations. All along the rivers and bayous were estates ranging from 500 to 10,000 acres, their magnificent mansions testifying to the wealth of their owners. Large-scale farming was highly profitable, and before the close of the eighteenth century, Louisiana's aristocratic landowners had achieved a social organization rivaled only in feudal times. Three classes composed each plantation unit: the planter and his family, the household servants, and the field hands. Slaves were housed in the Negro quarter, usually two rows of one- or two-room white-washed cabins arranged along a street some distance from the "big house." A bell called the slaves to work and to special assemblies. Every large plantation had an overseer's house, store, and smokehouses, a jail, hospital, chapel, and burial ground. The "big house," about which the life of the plantation centered, ranged from a simple raised Creole cottage to a colonnaded mansion (*see Architecture*) with separate kitchens.

The master, with an overseer who managed the slaves, ruled the plantation very much like a feudal lord. The raising of cotton, sugar cane, or rice, maintenance of a racing stable, fox and deer hunting, politics, and transacting sales with his New Orleans factor, kept the plantation owner, who was affectionately known to his slaves as "maître," or "massa," well occupied. *Madame la maîtresse,* or "old missy" as she was invariably called, played an important role in the plantation's management. With often as many as 200 slaves under her supervision, the planter's wife gave them clothing, necessary comforts for their cabins, and attention and advice in illness and trouble.

On the great plantations life was also very gay at times. The arrival of a steamboat or the coming of distinguished visitors was a time for general rejoicing, and the slaves who were attached to the "big house" seemed to enjoy the time of excitement as much as the owner and his family. Great distances separated the plantations and visits often extended over weeks. Sometimes whole families would swoop down, filling the spare rooms and making the mansion ring with lively chatter and laughter. Parties and "frolicks" were given, and often there were barbecues or a dance. Formal balls were always great affairs; musicians were brought from New Orleans or some near-by town, and the guests flocked in from neighboring plantations. A week or so prior to a social function, a slave set forth with a basket of delicately penned invitations. Invited ladies had the privilege of going through the lot to see who the other guests would be—a nice morsel of gossip for the day.

Louise Butler in the *Louisiana Historical Quarterly* has described such a fête: "But it was at the planter's own receptions, called balls or parties, that he most shone. Beautiful women, gorgeous costumes in real lace, real silk or hand-embroidered lavishness, jewels, plumes, made the scene, according to an eye witness who attended such a function in the extreme youth of the 19th century, splendid beyond imagination. Then delightsome music filled the air. Then the staircase was garlanded in roses all the way up its three-stories extent, vases on mantels and brackets filled with flowers not fresher nor fairer than the young faces flocking from the distant rooms to cluster in the ballroom. The gentlemen, ornamental, but not quite so ornamental, before descending from their dressing room, had sampled old bottles of Scotch or Irish, so quite a number were mellow, not to say slightly over-ripe when they did appear. About midnight supper was announced and the hostess led the way to the dining room. Of the menu, the cold meats, salads, salmis, galantines quaking in jellied seclusion, an infinite variety of *à las,* were served from side tables leaving the huge expanse of carved oak, besilvered, be-linened and be-laced, for flowers trailing from the tall silver *épergne* in the center to the corsage bouquet at each plate; fruits, cakes in pyramids or layers or only solid deliciousness, iced and ornamented; custards, pies, jellies, creams, Charlotte Russes encircling a veritable Mont Blanc of whipped cream dotted with red cherry stars; towers of nougat or carmel, sorbets and ice cream served in little baskets woven of candied orange peel and topped with sugared rose leaves or violets.

"Various wines in cut glass decanters, each with its name carved in the silver grapeleaf suspended from its neck, champagne frappéed, were deftly poured by the waiters into goldtraced or Bohemian glasses.

"Illuminating the whole were wax candles in crystal or bronze chandeliers, and, on the table, in silver or delicate Dresden candelabra.

"More dancing followed supper and just at dawn when the guests were leaving after this

> Night of wit and wine, of laughter and guitars
> Was emptied of its music,

a plate of hot gumbo, a cup of black coffee and enchanting memories sustained them on the long drive to their abodes."

Funerals were also attended by invitation only. These were delivered to friends and close associates by a horseman. A funeral invitation of 1859, still extant, is lithographed on the pale blue folded note paper of that period, old-fashioned wedding size, with black bars joined by delicate long corner ornamentations and a small scene, including the setting sun, a leaning tombstone, and weeping willows, above the French wording.

Christmas was eagerly looked forward to, especially by the slaves. On this morning, the cry of "Chrismus gifth'" resounded through the "big house." New Year's calls were religiously made by the gentlemen, who, dressed in their best, began a round of brief visits at eleven o'clock in the morning. Eggnog and cake were served in the parlor and brandy and whisky in the dining room.

Many of the plantation owners had town houses or made frequent visits to New Orleans for "the season." In the summer their city cousins visited the plantations or perhaps together they spent some time at one of the resorts on the Gulf. One of the most popular of these in the fifties was Last Island. Its tragic destruction in the storm of 1856 is described by Lafcadio Hearn in *Chita*.

The Negro slaves—the economic basis for the plantation system—were allowed to have balls or dances of their own, and in general were well treated. It was to the economic advantage of the planter to keep his workers in good condition.

An overseer with a whip watched over the Negroes in the field and the whipping post was the usual mode of punishment. Usually, there was a specific number of lashes for a given offense, such as running away. Bennett H. Barrow, a successful planter of West Feliciana Parish, gives in his diary an account of everyday life on the plantation. Barrow seems to have had the care of his slaves at heart, but was often severe in his punishment. He kept blooded dogs for hunting, and raced his thorough-bred horses at all the tracks from St. Francisville to New Orleans. He won many races with his "Josh Bell" at the old Metairie track. The English-speaking planters, like Barrow, hunted the fox, deer, and bear in the forests surrounding the plantations. Father south, alligator hunting was popular, but often the hunting parties found rare sport in rounding up escaped slaves who had remained in the vicinity to be near their women and food. Sometimes a camp, with many comforts fetched from the quarters, would be located in the swamps. The runaway was generally treed by the dogs; but the planters seldom shot to kill as the slave was too valuable as property.

Harriet Martineau, who visited New Orleans for a short time in 1835, gives her impressions in *Retrospect of Western Travel:* "I could never get out of the way of the horrors of slavery in this region. Under one form or another, they met me in every house, in every street,—everywhere but in the intelligence pages of the newspapers, where I might read on in perfect security of exemption from the subject. In the advertising columns, there were offers of rewards for runaways, restored dead or alive; and notices of the capture of a fugitive with so many bands on his limbs and shoulders, and so many scars on his back."

Before the war, Negro meant slave—after, "those whose complexions were noticeably dark." Even the Negroes themselves made post-bellum distinctions. They were either "free men of color" or "freedmen of color" —persons who had always been free or recently emancipated slaves. People of mixed blood struggled to retain their position of social superiority over the blacks, but finding this impossible, except for a few groups, the old order of the *gens de couleur* was submerged beneath a vast element designated as colored people. A few mixed-blood communities, whose residents make it a point of honor not to fraternize with Negroes, are found today in various parts of the State (*see Racial Elements*).

The plantation system disintegrated after the abolition of slavery, and the large holdings were gradually broken up into tenant farms or were operated by absentee owners through the sharecropper system. Many old families held on for a number of years, but today most of the great plantation houses are deserted, or occupied by sharecroppers. The share-cropper pays with one half of his crop for the use of the land. The land-lord owns the implements and livestock, extends the tenant credit for food and fuel at the plantation store, but the latter must supply his own seed and fertilizer. The tenant farmer is a little more independent—

he pays rent in cash and owns his own equipment, but often he suffers the same lack of living comforts and endures the same meager, unbalanced diet. Both dread age and infirmity that eventually deprives them of the land.

The whipping post and those necessaries of the torture chamber—wheel, rack, and branding irons—were all part of the legal machinery of justice during the eighteenth century. In 1724 the Black Code (in force until the War between the States) provided for cutting off ears, hamstringing, and branding of runaway slaves. A third offense carried the death penalty. Even suicides were "indicted, tried, convicted and sentenced to be deprived of Christian burial and to lie rotting and blackening on the face of the earth." A Natchitoches murderer was sentenced to be broken on the wheel and then hanged. Just before execution the judges modified the sentence, allowing the culprit to be hanged first and broken on the wheel afterwards.

An investigation in 1818 of the old Spanish Calabozo in New Orleans found the convicts "not provided for as humanity would dictate since many were destitute of clothing and others were almost destroyed by vermin." Debtors were confined with the blackest criminals. Entrance and exit fees as well as board and lodging payments were required of the prisoners. In 1861 a debtor was free after 90 days imprisonment, provided his keep for the interim had been paid.

The vicious practice of leasing and sub-leasing the convicts to private contractors was begun in 1844. Under this system, conditions in the various camps were frightful—a ten-year penalty was considered a life sentence, and in many instances the only escape was death. The mortality rate in 1881 was 14 percent; and when the State abolished leasing and took over the camps in 1901 all of the prisoners in one camp were found dying of smallpox. Since that time there has been a steady improvement in prison conditions. Today the State Penitentiary at Angola is entirely self-supporting. The men work on a great cotton and sugar plantation, which for the last five years has been operated at a profit. There are no cell blocks, except for incorrigibles, the convicts sleeping in large dormitories.

SOCIAL WELFARE

Social welfare in Louisiana, lacking the English poor-law background of the Atlantic colonies, devolved almost entirely upon religious organizations and social-minded philanthropists until local and State responsibility was assumed in the late nineteenth century. The Ursuline nuns, who arrived in New Orleans in 1727, pioneered in social work. They were specifically charged in France with caring for the sick and sheltering dependent young girls. Under their supervision the first orphanage in the Colony was founded after the Natchez Massacre (1729). Jean Louis, a retired sailor, supplied funds in 1735 for the establishment in New Orleans of a hospital for the poor. Forerunner of Charity Hospital, this institution was financed entirely by private funds until taken over by the State in 1814. The *Loge de Charité,* an early poorhouse, was in existence prior to the Spanish Acquisition, and Governor Miro (1785–91) established a lepers' hospital on Bayou St. John. Charity Hospital served as a refuge for dependent children and the homeless poor as well as for the sick, its population reflecting not only the health of the community but the social and economic conditions of the city and State as well.

Aside from the Ursulines, the earliest official reference to the care of the poor and sick is found in the New Orleans city charter of 1812, whereby police officers were instructed to visit inns, taverns, vessels, and other places, and to search out sick and poor persons in order to furnish them treatment and relief at Charity Hospital. Although an act introduced in the legislature in 1817, to "Provide Support for the Relief of the Poor," was not passed, some measure of public assistance existed, chiefly in the form of subsidies granted to private institutions. Dependent children seem to have benefited most. In 1824, in transferring 24 orphans from the Ursuline Convent to the Poydras Female Asylum, founded by Julien Poydras in 1817, the Mayor of New Orleans contracted to pay the asylum $1,600 annually for the education, clothing, board, and lodging of the orphans. A share of the proceeds derived from the State tax on gambling was allotted to the Society for the Relief of Destitute Boys, incorporated in 1825.

An asylum for indigent colored children was established in 1838 through the generosity of Madame Bernard Couvent, free woman of color; this asylum and a home for women were taken over by the Sisters of the Holy Family (colored), whose work was greatly aided by the beneficence of Thomy Lafon, Negro philanthropist. The Marianites of the Holy Cross arrived in Louisiana in 1848 to assume charge of St. Mary's Asylum. In 1851 they established Our Lady of the Holy Cross Industrial School and Model Farm for Girls. During this period the Good Shepherd nuns came to New Orleans and were assigned to an institution for the care and correction of delinquent girls.

The Apprenticeship Act of 1865 provided that sheriffs, justices of the peace, and other civil officers of the State were to report to the district courts the names of all males under 21 years and females under 18 years who were orphans or whose parents or tutors were without means to support them, so that they could be apprenticed. By 1870 State appropriations to private institutions amounted to $98,250, distributed among 44 organizations representing all sectarian groups. More than half of these institutions cared for orphans; many of the others took the form of mutual benefit organizations, which provided burial funds and cared for and assisted sick and dependent members.

In 1870 a bill for the relief of the poor was rejected by the legislature as "calculated to encourage laziness, and make the State of Louisiana a receptacle for the poor of other States." The danger was overlooked by the Parish of Natchitoches, which in 1874 provided for the establishment of a poorhouse—action that anticipated the first State-wide poor law, passed in 1880 in compliance with the provision of the Constitution of 1879 making it obligatory for each parish to support its own poor and infirm. The act of 1880 provided that the police juries ascertain the names, situation, and condition, and provide for the entire support of those utterly destitute and helpless and the partial support or assistance of others, with the qualification "that police juries and parish officers shall not at public expense, support or aid any persons as paupers except such as are infirm, sick or disabled." Poor farms were to be leased or bought, with the provision that they were to be wholly or in part self-sustaining. Local taxation provided the funds.

The Poor Law of 1880 was supplemented in 1916 by an act directing that in parishes having cities between 25,000 and 100,000 population there be set aside by the police jury 10 percent of all fines and forfeiture of bonds collected by the District Court for violations of State laws, and likewise by the city council, together to constitute an alms fund for the care of the indigent in those parishes and cities.

From time to time, after the turn of the century, laws such as the Mothers' Pension, Workers' Compensation, and various child welfare statutes were adopted. Community Chests, organized during the post-World-War development of that movement, function in the larger cities of the State with the approval of all religions. Social service in Louisiana has been improved by the influence of the Tulane University School of Social Work, founded in 1921 and financially assisted in 1927 to graduate proportions by the Rockefeller Foundation. A Graduate School of Public Welfare Administration was established at Louisiana State University in 1937.

The first State-wide system of relief was established as a result of the nation-wide depression in 1932 when an Unemployment Relief Committee was organized to supervise relief from funds received from the Federal Reconstruction Finance Corporation. By 1935, under pressure from the Federal Emergency Relief Administration, local parish welfare agencies had been set up in every parish. These were later absorbed into the Department of Public Welfare.

The Welfare Organization Act, approved June 26, 1936, created a State Department of Public Welfare to "administer or supervise all forms of public assistance including general home relief, outdoor and indoor care for persons in need, old age assistance, aid to dependent children, aid to the blind, and to the crippled and otherwise handicapped—and such other welfare activities or services as may be vested in it." The department acts as an agent for the Federal Government in welfare activities in the State and in the administration of funds granted for social assistance. Parish departments administer to local needs, taking applications and making assignments as aid is required. The Board of Public Welfare has as members representatives of the eight Congressional districts.

An important activity of the State Commissioner of Labor, aided by a Board of Review consisting of three members appointed by the Governor, is the administration of unemployment compensation. Contributions from employers and employees are deposited in an Unemployment Compensation Fund, credited in favor of the State by the Secretary of the Treasury of the United States, in accordance with the provisions of the Social Security Act.

Other social legislation approved during the 1936 session provides for retirement and pension funds for State Police and for superannuated and incapacitated school teachers. Supplementing the governmental agencies are numerous religious and non-sectarian agencies and institutions.

Since government agencies assumed the bulk of the relief load, private agencies, in line with the general trend, turned their attention to constructive and educational work aimed at the prevention of social breakdown. Louisiana has State societies for educational work for the handicapped, and for the prevention of tuberculosis, blindness, and the social diseases. Child and family welfare agencies, neighborhood settlements, and young people's associations have concerned themselves with work to keep people out of trouble or prevent them from getting into it again. The Louisiana State Conference of Social Welfare, established in 1916, functions as a discussion group for sponsors and workers in public and private social agencies.

Education

IN 1725, only seven years after the founding of New Orleans, the
Capuchin superior, Father Raphael, wrote to France for official
approval of "un petit collège" which he had established for the infant
colony. Father Raphael hoped the Company of the Indies would sanction
his purchase of a school building for 3,000 livres, and explained his ambitious design: "The house that has been bought is too small for the plan
that I have of forming a little seminary of 12 or 15 pupils who are now
in the Colony of age and in a position to be admitted to it. I am yet assured of only seven but I do not doubt that the others who are at distant
posts will soon present themselves." This school, located on St. Ann
Street between Royal and Chartres, was the first in the Colony. A year
later, matters had not progressed as they should, and Father Raphael
complained that "the majority of the inhabitants who are in a position
to send their children to school seem satisfied to have them taught to read
and write and regard all the rest as useless. However, there are 5 or 6
of them pursuing other subjects and succeeding wonderfully in them."
By 1731 Father Raphael was being sued for the third time for non-
payment of the 3,000 livres. The Company of the Indies finally "liqui-
dated the obligation."

Education for girls began in 1727 when Father Beaubois, the superior of the Jesuits in Louisiana, persuaded the Ursuline nuns to open
a convent in New Orleans. Nine professed nuns, a novice, and two

postulants arrived. The nuns began their school immediately. The first contingent of 30 *filles à la cassette* (Fr., casket girls), who arrived the following year, were placed in their charge, and boarded until their marriage. In 1734 when the Ursulines moved to their beautiful convent on Chartres Street, there were "20 boarders, 3 parlor boarders, 3 orphans, 7 slave boarders to be instructed for baptism and first communion and many black and Indian women who attended every day for two hours." At first the curriculum included reading, writing, catechism, and needlework, but later was extended to include French, English, geography, arithmetic, history, and housework.

In 1730 the Ursulines were host to the unfortunate refugees from the massacre at Fort Rosalie, and later they befriended many of the Acadians expelled from Canada. The Ursuline convent, which is still standing on Chartres Street, was vacated in 1824 for a larger school farther down the river, and in 1912 the nuns moved to State St.

When Bienville was about to leave the Colony for the last time in 1742 he petitioned the Crown for a college to be run by the Jesuits, and pointed out how "seriously expensive it is for those who send their children to France to be educated," and that moreover "it is even to be feared from this circumstance that the Creoles thus educated abroad will imbibe a dislike for their native country, and will come back to it only to receive and convert into cash what property may be left to them by their parents." There were, at this time in Louisiana only some 3,500 persons, scattered over a large territory, and the petition was refused.

After Bienville's departure and before the coming of the Spaniards in 1766, private schools for boys were operated in all parts of the city and Colony. Often the master was an itinerant school teacher who found board and lodging in the house of his pupils' parents. The Spaniards made some attempt to establish schools in their new territory, but the response of the French population (although some 50 percent of the adults could neither read nor write) was not encouraging. Governor Miro, reporting on the state of the schools in 1788, writes that in 1772 there had come from Spain four teachers to establish a school in New Orleans. There was a "Professor of the rudiments of the Latin language," a teacher of grammar, and a teacher of reading and writing. After discussing the difficulties of getting the colonists to send their children to the school, Miro concludes: ". . . no pupil ever presented himself for the Latin class. A few came to be taught reading and writing only. These never exceeded 30, and frequently dwindled down to six." At this time, however, there were eight private schools in the city, frequented by 400 children of both sexes.

Three years later the Santo Domingan revolt was to send many pupils and teachers to Louisiana. These refugees of 1791 are an important element in the early cultural history of the State. They gave

New Orleans its first professional theater, its first newspaper, and many teachers of the more elegant accomplishments: fencing, dancing, and music. The Spanish Ursulines who came over to join their French sisters were forced to "content themselves with the feeble achievement of extorting Spanish catechism from girls who recited with tears because they were compelled to use Spanish.

After the acquisition of Louisiana by the United States, one public school was established in the city in 1804; it served 50 children from poor families, instructing them in French, Spanish, reading, writing and ciphering. But the public schools were doomed to failure because of the stigma of poverty attached to those who attended them; even the very poor often kept their children at home rather than advertise publicly their circumstances. The sons of the rich planters were still educated abroad, and the daughters were sent to the Ursulines.

By 1805 there was a plan to establish a College of Orleans in the city to give instruction in Latin, Greek, English, French, and Spanish, as well as in the sciences, philosophy, and literature. This ambitious project was to be financed by two public lotteries, and was to include preparatory academies and public libraries in the different parishes. There was also a system of help for the indigent and a plan for girls' schools. The whole project fell through when the lotteries failed, but it was revived in 1811 and the College of Orleans became a reality. The State legislature appropriated $39,000 and licensed gambling houses to provide additional funds. Two thousand dollars were appropriated for a school or academy in each parish, and in 1813 the lottery was again authorized to support the project. The College of Orleans was located where St. Augustine's Church now stands (St. Claude and Governor Nicholls Streets). By 1823, when a committee examined the students of the College of Orleans, there were 44 boarding and 35 day pupils. The examinations were in English, French, Greek, Latin, geography, arithmetic, elements of geometry, and algebra. One of the later directors was Lakanal, a member of the council that voted to execute Louis XVI, and there were other refugees who gave a revolutionary tone to the faculty. Because of this many of the Creole families withdrew their boys from the college.

Under the legislative act of 1808 Pointe Coupée was the only parish to establish public schools. Public funds allotted for education were then assigned to provide for indigent children in private institutions, as this was regarded as the simplest, cheapest method of reaching the children who needed and would accept free instruction. This subsidized system prevailed for nearly a century. Private tutoring and plantation schools were still popular among the wealthy Creoles and the American settlers. Itinerant teachers of dancing, music, and art continued to make their rounds through the parishes, and private schools flourished in the prosperous sections. A school of this type was conducted by John James Audubon and his wife in West Feliciana Parish. In fact Audubon's success as a dancing teacher helped him to finance the publication of his great ornithological work, *The Birds of America*.

The Academy of Natchitoches and the College of Rapides were established in 1819, and in 1820 the College of Baton Rouge was founded. At Grand Coteau, St. Landry Parish, the Sisters of the Sacred Heart established in 1821 the Sacred Heart Academy for girls. A general school act of the same year provided free textbooks and tuition to eight indigent children of each school district, but this provision only served to increase the unpleasant feeling that persisted regarding free instruction. In 1824 a movement was begun to reorganize the State school system. The new note of non-sectarianism was sounded by the Academy of Ouachita, which catered to "all shades of religious belief."

Even more indicative of the gradual transfer of power to the American elements in Louisiana was the founding in 1825 of the College of Louisiana with funds diverted from the allotment of the College of Orleans and an additional amount appropriated by East and West Feliciana Parishes. The location was at Jackson, in the Felicianas, and among a predominantly English-speaking group. The attendance soon averaged 85 to 100 boys, and included among its students the future president of the Confederate States, Jefferson Davis.

The balance of the original appropriation for the College of Orleans was used in 1826 to create two elementary schools and a central high school in New Orleans. After 1827 a lottery was authorized to raise $40,000 for educational purposes in the State, and this remained the mode of financing for some time. Many private and religious schools were founded in this period: St. Michael's, founded by the Sacred Heart nuns at Convent (1825); the Academy of Covington (1828); Clinton Female Academy (1830); and the College of Franklin at Opelousas (1831). In New Orleans many small schools were operating.

The College of Jefferson, (*see Tour 10B*), a compromise between the College of Orleans and the College of Louisiana, was founded at Convent in 1831. It was free from religious bias and seemed to realize Bienville's dream for a great university. There were 7,000 volumes in the library, and by 1842 the attendance averaged 170 students. The buildings were severely damaged by fire March 6, 1842. The college functioned until 1927 when it became a religious retreat.

A general school act in 1833 established a State library and required the Secretary of State to furnish free textbooks to the needy. The Medical College of New Orleans, later Tulane University, opened in 1835; a deaf and dumb institute at Baton Rouge and St. Charles College (Jesuit) at Grand Coteau were founded in 1838. Despite these new opportunities many plantation schools still thrived, and wealthy Louisianians continued to send their children to institutions of Virginia, Maryland, Pennsylvania, Kentucky, and even Ireland and France. Even free Negroes when their wealth permitted, educated their sons abroad; some of these young men were brilliant students at the Imperial Conservatory and L'École Polytechnique in Paris. During this period the Sisters of the Holy Family, a colored Catholic order of nuns founded in 1842, organized classes for the instruction of their race.

Public instruction began in 1841 when city and State joined forces to provide funds for free New Orleans schools. A State superintendent of education was appointed in 1845. Country schools were supervised by parish superintendents, and parishes, divided into school districts of 40 pupils each, received financial aid for their schools from poll-tax receipts.

In 1845 the College of Louisiana at Jackson merged with Mississippi College and became the present Centenary of Shreveport. In 1847 the Medical College at New Orleans added academic and scientific courses to its curriculum and was taken over by the State as the University of Louisiana. A large State seminary was planned near Alexandria in 1847, but it did not materialize until some years later. After an absence of more than 80 years, the Jesuits returned to New Orleans, and in 1849 established the College of the Immaculate Conception for young men; this grew to be one of the most important colleges in the State, numbering among its students such men as Chief Justice Edward Douglas White and Judge Pierre Crabites of the Louisiana State University faculty. The Marianites of the Holy Cross established an industrial school for indigent girls in 1851, and in the early 1850's founded what became the Academy of the Holy Angels. The Holy Cross nuns established St. Basil's Academy at Plaquemine (1856), and Immaculate Conception, Opelousas (1858). In New Orleans the Sisters of Charity founded in 1860 St. Simeon's Select School for young ladies in what was then the Saulet Plantation House, now Mercy Hospital.

John McDonogh's contribution in 1850 to public education by which New Orleans received $750,000, enabled that city to erect 36 school buildings. The Christian Brothers established St. Mary's College in New Orleans in 1855 and in 1856 Colonel George Soulé opened his commercial college, which also offered academic courses. The first normal school in New Orleans began in the Girls' High School in 1858. Offering courses in medicine, law and sciences, the State Seminary of Learning was established in 1860 near Alexandria with Colonel William Tecumseh Sherman at its head. The seminary was transferred in 1869 to Baton Rouge and renamed Louisiana State University. A Federal land grant, voted in 1862 by Congress for each State, was accepted in 1866 by the carpetbag legislature to be used for the establishment of an agricultural and mechanical college. This became a reality in 1874 and is now part of Louisiana State University.

The Confederate legislature of 1862 appropriated $485,000 for free schools; later, on an order of the governor, because textbooks were contraband, pamphlets were issued.

St. Mary's Dominican, the first Catholic women's college in Louisiana, was founded in 1865 by the Sisters of St. Dominic, in Greenville, Jefferson Parish, now uptown New Orleans. Jared Y. Sanders authorized the normal department of this college in 1910.

Reconstruction policies provided joint schools for white and Negro children and white parents withdrew their offspring from the schools. A girls' high school for both races, established during Reconstruction in the Haunted House at 1140 Royal Street, came to an end in the 1870's, when members of the White League invaded the building and removed all girls of mixed blood.

Negro education advanced under the carpetbaggers. In New Orleans, in the 1870's, Flint Medical College (later Flint-Goodridge Hospital) and three universities—Leland (Baptist); Straight (Congregationalist); New Orleans University (Methodist), which advertised for students of all creeds and races, were organized. Southern University, a State organization, was established in New Orleans in 1880 and moved to Scotlandville near Baton Rouge in 1914. It now has branches in New Orleans and Shreveport. Xavier university was founded for Negro education by Roman Catholic women in 1925. Straight and the New Orleans University combined in 1929 to form Dillard University, opened in 1935.

In 1870, Houma College, established in 1861 under Protestant supervision, lost favor and the Holy Cross nuns were called in to found the St. Francis de Sales Academy. A similar incident occurred in Franklin in 1871, when the same sisters were placed in a former Methodist institution, later St. John's Academy. The Marianites of the Holy Cross also established St. Charles Academy at Lake Charles in 1882, a school for Negroes at Plaquemine in 1882, and the Sacred Heart Academy at Morgan City in 1893.

Northwestern State College, founded at Natchitoches in 1884 as a normal school, became a university in 1970.

In 1884, from funds donated by Paul Tulane, Louisiana University at New Orleans was expanded under the name of Tulane University. The H. Sophie Newcomb College for girls, founded in 1886 by Mrs. Josephine Louise Newcomb, became a part of Tulane University at its founder's request. Louisiana State Normal School was established in 1884 at Natchitoches. In New Orleans, Sophie B. Wright began her free night school, and five years later, in 1889, opened the Home Institute on Camp Street, a private school for young girls of the wealthier families. In its advertisements, Carnatz Institute, a similar school of the Garden District, offered modern comforts of plumbing along with professors of science and logic, while the Holy Cross Academy of the Holy Angels in downtown New Orleans provided "baths during summer for $2."

Outside New Orleans, several institutions of higher learning developed around the turn of the century. Louisiana Polytechnic Institute at Ruston (1894); Southwestern Louisiana Institute, now University of Southwestern Louisiana, at Lafayette (1901); and Louisiana College at Pineville in 1906.

Loyola of the South (Jesuit) was established at New Orleans in 1904 and consolidated with the College of the Immaculate Conception in 1911. It became a university in 1912. It is coeducational and enrolls more than 4,000. Southeastern Louisiana College, founded 1925 at Hammond, became a university in 1970.

EDUCATION SINCE WORLD WAR II

In the decades following World War II public education in Louisiana experienced an expansion similar to that in other states. In the 1960–70 decade attendance in white and Negro schools nearly doubled, and only the nonpublic schools showed a decrease. In 1968–69 registration, which is slightly larger than average, attendance reached a total of 890,311 pupils; of this number 545,329 were white and 344,482 Negro; nonpublic schools reported registration of 138,542, of whom 118,276 were white and 20,266 Negro. Thus more than 1,000,000 pupils attended grades from kindergarten to 12; 50,611 were graduated from public and nonpublic high schools, of whom 35,159 were white and 15,452 Negro, all categories showing increases.

Free textbooks are advantages given Louisiana children. The increase in the distribution of textbooks may be seen by comparing the figures for 1958, when they cost the State Department of Education $2,334,075, with those for 1968–69, when they cost $5,329,498, or $5.18 per pupil.

School lunches are another helpful contribution to public education in Louisiana. In the 1968–69 period the public schools served 107,-589,283 lunches and the nonpublic schools served 13,678,238, a total of 121,267,521. It cost the State $10,861,247, denominational and private school children being included, and the Federal Government contributed $6,955,676. The National School Milk Program cost $622,654. In past years the Federal contribution in general has been 10 to 15 percent of the totals.

The State gives strong support to trade and vocational-technical schools and to institutions for the handicapped. The State Dept. of

Education supervises 34 such schools. In 1969 it cost $6,853,804 to finance the operations, of which the Federal Government supplied $1,792,955. There are two State schools for the blind and the deaf in Baton Rouge, and two at Southern University. The State school for Spastic Children is at Alexandria. The Northeast Cerebral Palsy school is at Monroe. In many cases vocational-technical courses are arranged to suit the hours of adults with daytime occupations. Of 36,870 enrolled, 23,866 attended evening extension classes. In 1969 the Federal Government contributed $5,503,489 to the total expenditures of $16,138,199.

In the field of higher education Louisiana administrators have risen fully to their opportunities. With the help of Federal funds new buildings have been erected all over the State, most of them with large areas of fenestration, flourescent lighting and air conditioning. Requests for community colleges have been increasing, and the Louisiana State University has started two-year branches at Alexandria, Eunice and Shreveport, with the object of expanding to four years; this occurred at Lake Charles, where McNeese was a branch of LSU until taken over by the State Board of Education as a four-year college in 1950.

An important contribution to public education was the establishment of Louisiana State University in New Orleans in 1956. Located on 178 acres bordering Lake Pontchartrain, early plans envisioned a completely functioning university of 10,000 students; by spring, 1970, 9,156 were enrolled. The first senior class from a four-year course was graduated in 1962. LSU had organized its Medical Center in New Orleans with the School of Medicine in 1931 and added the School of Dentistry in 1968. It organized a School of Medicine at Shreveport in 1969, and had a School of Veterinary Medicine ready by 1970.

An opportunity to enroll more Negroes for higher education came when Southern University, a State institution at Scotlandville, East Baton Rouge Parish, opened a new branch in New Orleans, not far from LSU, and another in Shreveport. Southern had been founded in New Orleans, then removed to Baton Rouge, where it enrolls up to 7,000 annually. New buildings are being financed by State and Federal funds.

The high prestige of research study, and the opportunities opened by grants and endowments, have drawn many scholars from the classroom and thus reduced the number dedicated to the teaching of youth. Some colleges have voted incentives to develop teaching. There also have been efforts to recruit undergraduates who appear promising for careers in teaching in the liberal arts and sciences. The Graduate School has assumed greater importance and efforts have been made to raise the quality of work needed for higher degrees. The recognition that living cost often inhibits a scholarly career has led to easier admissions for gifted students.

Another development is the movement to admit citizens past college age to courses in continuing education, thus enlarging the capacities of those who never had a chance to improve their capabilities.

When the United States Supreme Court ruled in May, 1954 and May, 1955, that public schools must not discriminate between races, it made State and local authorities responsible for desegregation. The decisions brought about many difficult readjustments in Louisiana. Here segregation of the races in the public schools was based on long practice and worked with little friction. The State always had provided well for its Negro population, which in some parishes equalled or exceeded the white. The decisions of the Supreme Court met with some opposition, but the State Legislature and the Federal district courts upheld desegregation. In 1960 the State Legislature passed 28 bills dealing with desegregation. That year New Orleans schools were integrated. In 1962 Archbishop Rummel of New Orleans ordered desegregation of all Roman Catholic schools in his jurisdiction. There were demonstrations of protest against desegregation of public schools, and in one clash advocates and opponents picketed the Capitol.

As elsewhere, the people of Louisiana resented forced hauling of pupils to distant places to achieve what was called racial balance. The neighborhood school had been considered the logical place for a child ever since schools were founded. Busing proved the principal obstacle to integration. Some parents withheld their children from school and opened classes in vacant stores and houses. Others kept children out of school for a few weeks, then reluctantly sent them back. New private academies sprang up, but they charged tuition fees and did not receive State or Federal support. There was an effort to build new denominational schools and enlarge others, from kindergarten up, but the churches did not oppose desegregation. It was estimated by schoolmen in 1970 that less than one in seven children attended private or church-affiliated elementary and secondary schools.

SPREAD OF THE LIBRARIES

A powerful agency for spreading the use and love of books to every part of Louisiana is the LOUISIANA STATE LIBRARY, which in 1969 saw the culmination of its efforts to place a library system in every parish in the State. Since 1925 the State Library—called the Louisiana Library Commission until 1946—had sent books, equipment, and trained personnel to parish seats to demonstrate the operation of a library and encourage local leaders to place it on a permanent basis. Jefferson Davis, Assumption, and West Carroll were the last of the 64 parishes to vote taxes to support libraries. The action of Jefferson Davis, in voting a tax of 2.5 mils, was typical of the action taken by most parishes. Only one parish, St. Landry, rejected support for a library by a narrow margin, whereupon the cities of Opelousas and Eunice cooperated to form a system, appropriating part of their sales tax for this purpose.

The activities of the State library have been augmented by Federal funds, the latest of which enabled it to extend library service to State institutions such as the Louisiana State Penitentiary at Angola, and to the physically handicapped, including the blind. The State Library is one of 46 regional center libraries that cooperate with the Library of Congress in promoting service to the blind and handicapped. Federal funds matched with local funds made possible the erection of new public library buildings and additions. The State Library retains close ties with all libraries, giving supervisory service and advice on request, establishing a processing center to serve the parishes, supplying reading lists, explanatory pamphlets, slides and color films, and information to news media, including television. It has provided inter-library loans and increased its information and reference facilities to benefit industries and local governments.

Extending a regional library system in the State was the next step in making books more accessible. In July, 1970, the State Library started the Trail Blazer Library System of Northeast Louisiana, on an experimental basis, bringing into it three academic and 13 public libraries in 13 parishes. Center of the system is Ouachita Parish Public Library at Monroe.

Libraries in the public schools also have been enlarging their collections. Orleans Parish has the largest number, 135, with nearly 1,000,000 books. No other parish comes close to the 100 mark. Total volumes in 1969 were 8,176,604, compared with 7,548,976 the year before.

There is an increased annual expenditure for school libraries in the parishes. In 1969 there were 967 libraries and 534 fulltime librarians in predominantly white schools and 302 libraries and 350 fulltime librarians in Negro schools. The white schools had 5,978,067 books net (after removal of worn copies); the Negro schools had 2,197,031 books net. Expenditures for all school libraries reached $11,266,314, compared with $10,433,467 the year before.

Religion

THE earliest missionaries to the Floridas, the Gulf Coast, and the territory now called Louisiana and Texas were Spanish priests who accompanied explorers of the early sixteenth century. Some of the early expeditions never reached the coast of Louisiana, and those that did often met shipwreck or disaster at the hands of hostile Indians. The expedition of De Narvaez (1528) was chronicled by Cabeza de Vaca, who reports the presence of several secular priests and five Franciscans. Among the Franciscans was Father Juan Suarez, Bishop-designate of Florida and first resident bishop in the territory that became the United States, whose spiritual jurisdiction included Louisiana. In attempting to reach Mexico with de Vaca and the survivors of the expedition, he either drowned at the mouth of the Mississippi or, as some historians assert, died of starvation and exposure at Matagorda Bay, Texas. Many representatives of religious orders accompanied De Soto on his tragic expedition of 1539. A few Indians were converted by these priests, but none of the missionaries lived to reach Mexico.

For 120 years after De Soto, no further colonization efforts were made, but in 1673 the French Jesuit Father Marquette, accompanied by Joliet, explored the Mississippi southward as far as the Arkansas River. This tentative effort was followed in 1682 by the expedition of Robert Cavelier, Sieur de La Salle, who explored the Mississippi to its mouth. Father Zenobius Membre, a Franciscan Recollect, accom-

panied La Salle and preached to the Indians. He was present when
La Salle took possession of Louisiana in the name of the French King
and the Christian Church. La Salle was murdered by his own men
on the second expedition, and Father Zenobius was subsequently killed
by the Indians.

After La Salle's discovery, missionary work was planned by the
Franciscan Recollects, who worked under the authority of the Bishop of
Quebec. Little was accomplished, however, until secular priests from
the Seminary of Quebec were assigned to Louisiana. The first mission
was among the Tensa Indians at what is now Newellton, Louisiana.
Father Davion, the best known of these, was Vicar-General of the lower
Mississippi Valley, and both he and Father St. Cosme were well known
to the Indians before Iberville's arrival. St. Cosme was later murdered
by the Indians, but Father Davion continued his work until 1722.

In 1699 Sieur d'Iberville established the first permanent colony of
Frenchmen in the lower valley, and from this post near Biloxi he
explored the Mississippi River, accompanied by Father Anastase Douay,
a Recollect. Father Du Ru, a Jesuit missionary, was with Iberville
on his second voyage and fulfilled the latter's wish made on an earlier
voyage: "I regret not having a Jesuit missionary who would know the
savage language in a very short time." In 1700 Father Du Ru built
at the village of the Houma, near what is now Angola (*see Tour 10A*),
the first Catholic chapel in the lower Mississippi Valley and named it
in honor of St. Francis Xavier. During these first years missionaries
from many orders accomplished heroic work among the Indians. They
suffered constant physical hardship and lived in imminent danger of
martyrdom. By 1717 the Spanish missionaries, moving eastward from
Mexico, had established the Los Adayes Mission on the Red River, 21
miles from Natchitoches. Father Antonio Margil, the founder, had
established missions throughout northern Mexico and Texas. The
French, however, were jealous of Spanish encroachment and sacked
the mission in 1719, although the good fathers had ministered to the
French post at Natchitoches in the absence of missionaries.

The Black Code, formulated by Bienville in 1724, prohibited the
practice of any religion but the Catholic, and in 1727 the Ursuline
nuns arrived in New Orleans to establish a convent and school for the
women of the Colony. Under the Company of the Indies the territory
was divided in 1722 among the three religious orders concerned. The
territory south of the Ohio and east of the Mississippi was given to
the Carmelites, that north of the Ohio to the Jesuits, and that west
of the Mississippi to the Capuchins. The Carmelite territory was shortly
afterwards given to the Capuchins, who then exercised authority over
the whole valley south of the Ohio. The Jesuits had been so successful,
however, in their work among the Indians that the Company of the

Indies invited them to take charge of all Indians in the Colony and permitted them to come to New Orleans to establish a house. This resulted in charges of infringement on the jurisdiction of the Capuchins, but a compromise was effected that left the Jesuits free to carry on missionary work without interfering with the authority of the Capuchins at New Orleans. Thirty-seven years later, in 1763, the Jesuits were expelled from Louisiana because of political difficulties in France. Their successful plantation, which extended south of what is now Common Street in New Orleans, and which had supported much of their work among the Indians, was confiscated. The Jesuits did not return to Louisiana until 1837, but their subsequent endeavors have been highly successful.

In 1763 Louisiana passed into the hands of the Spanish, but it was not until 1772 that a group of Spanish Capuchins arrived from Cuba to take over the religious control from their French colleagues. The austere and haughty Spaniards were disliked by the French population. After considerable friction and an attempted ouster of Father Dagobert, the French pastor, the Spaniards resigned themselves to his authority until his death in 1776. Among the second group of Spanish Capuchins, who arrived in 1781, was a monk, Antonio de Sedella, the famed Père Antoine, who for almost half a century was the storm center of ecclesiastical difficulties in New Orleans. He was made pastor of the Church of St. Louis in 1785, and in 1787 received his appointment as Commissary of the Inquisition for Louisiana. Père Antoine soon got into conflict with Governor Miro and his own superior, Auxiliary Bishop Cirillo of the Diocese of Havana, Louisiana, and the Floridas. The Inquisition was feared and disliked by the Colonial authorities because its reputation discouraged American settlers. Miro was anxious to get rid of Père Antoine and at length ordered him to leave the Colony. Père Antoine responded by invoking his own authority as Commissary of the Inquisition; the controversy was only resolved when the troops ordered to enforce the Inquisition, conducted the surprised friar to a boat bound for Cadiz. Two years later Miro was replaced as governor, and Père Antoine in 1795 returned to the Colony, where, until his death in 1829, he remained as the highly popular pastor of the St. Louis Cathedral, despite the attempt of American church authorities to remove him.

An episcopal diocess, embracing the immense area from the Gulf to Canada and from the Texas province to the Mississippi, was formed in 1793 with the seat at New Orleans. Don Almonester y Roxas donated funds for the rebuilding of the parish Church of St. Louis, which had been destroyed by fire in 1788; this more substantial and enlarged edifice became the St. Louis Cathedral. After 1803, when the United States bought Louisiana from Napoleon, the diocese passed under the temporary jurisdiction of Bishop Carroll of Baltimore. Many years of ecclesiastical confusion followed, during which Père Antoine had himself elected pastor at a mass meeting in the Cathedral. Finally Bishop Carroll delegated Father William Louis Dubourg, a Frenchman born in Santo Domingo and a refugee to Spain from the Reign of Terror in Paris, as administrator in Louisiana. In 1815, Dubourg helped Jackson marshal forces for the Battle of New Orleans and greeted the general on his return from the field with a service of thanksgiving in the Cathedral. That same year Dubourg was appointed Bishop of New Orleans.

Louisiana became an archdiocese in 1850 with New Orleans as the seat; today the State contains three ecclesiastical districts: the Archdiocese of New Orleans, lying between the Pearl and Atchafalaya Rivers, and from the Gulf to the northern boundary of Pointe Coupée Parish; the Diocese of Lafayette, the section between the Atchafalaya and the Sabine, from the Gulf to the northern boundaries of Beauregard, Allen, Evangeline, and St. Landry Parishes; and the Diocese of Alexandria, which includes all of north Louisiana.

Today only about half of the people of Louisiana are Catholics, but the early prevalence of Catholicism has left many of its customs among the people of other denominations. In the southern part of the State and especially in New Orleans, which is predominantly Catholic, place and street names, colorful celebrations like the Mardi Gras, All Saints' Day, and other holidays, and even the menus of restaurants and non-Catholic homes, show the influence of the rules and rituals of this religion. Another interesting carry-over of Catholicism is the fact that the civil subdivisions of the State are called parishes instead of counties.

After the sale of Louisiana to the United States, freedom of worship supplanted the single authority of the Catholic Church. Even before this, however, Protestantism had made tentative efforts to establish itself in the Colony. In 1799 Bailey E. Chaney, a Baptist minister, was arrested by the Spanish officials for conducting services at an Anglo-Saxon settlement near Baton Rouge. Protestants were permitted to live in Louisiana but were prohibited from practicing their religion in public assemblies. Ministers from several denominations came after 1803 to work among the Indians and the Negroes. Joseph Willis, a mulatto Baptist preacher, conducted meetings in 1804 at Vermilion (now Lafayette), but was forced to leave because of his race. In 1812 Willis returned to Bayou Chicot (*see Tour 15b*) and organized the first Baptist church west of the Mississippi. A month earlier, his colleagues in the Florida Parishes had organized the Half Moon Bluff Church, the first Baptist church in the State, near the Bogue Chitto River in Washington Parish. During this same year Cornelius Paulding, a Baptist layman, came to New Orleans to engage in business. He donated space in one of his buildings for Baptist meetings and arranged for traveling ministers to hold services. In 1834 the First Baptist Church was established in New Orleans, and in 1854, with funds provided by Paulding's will, the Coliseum Place Baptist Congregation was founded.

In New Orleans during the early years of the nineteenth century Protestants were scarce, but in 1805 a group of them assembled in Francisques' ballroom and formed the first Protestant congregation in New Orleans. Forty-five Episcopalians, seven Presbyterians, and one Methodist voted to affiliate with the Episcopal Church. Their first minister was the Reverend Philander Chase of New York. The church was known as Christ Church and was the first incorporated Episcopal church in the Mississippi Valley. The present Christ Church Cathedral is its successor.

Elisha Bowman, a Methodist missionary, arrived soon after, but he was unsuccessful in his efforts to establish a church, largely because of the hostility of the Episcopalians, and he left the "ungodly city of New Orleans," where he heard people on the streets "pouring out heavy curses on the Methodists," to try "the watery waste and the pathless desert." William Winans, another Methodist, came in 1814 and was sufficiently successful as teacher and preacher to be invited by the Episcopalians to preach to them. Winans did so, but was soon supplanted by James Hull, an Irishman, who, it seems, was fitted to be either lawyer or clergyman, depending on the occasion. Winans described him as "a boon companion at wine, and an adroit whist player." Unfortunately for Winans, "the fashionable and gay" elements of the congregation were charmed with Hull, and they invited him to take over the pulpit. The severer members offered a position to Winans, but because of the rules of the Methodists he was unable to accept it. A small church was built in 1830, but by 1836 there were only 50 white Methodists in the city. In the next decade Methodism grew rapidly and by 1850 there were 13 small congregations, including a Beer Garden Chappel on Enghien Street (now Almonaster Avenue).

Many self-styled preachers who came down the Mississippi by barge and keelboat were medicine men like Lorenzo Dow. These itinerant enthusiasts gathered crowds by religious exhortations in order to sell their wares. Dow, a Methodist evangelist, preached in the Attakapa country as early as 1803, and after meetings sold a concoction called Lorenzo Dow's Family Medicine. A. P. Hudson, in his *Humour of the Old Deep South,* has recorded a typical sermon, "The Harp of a Thousand Strings," which is attributed to a flatboat merchant who docked his craft at Water Proof, Louisiana, during the twenties or thirties.

But the most colorful phase of early Protestantism in Louisiana concerns the Presbyterians and the Reverend Theodore Clapp. In 1820 the Presbyterians organized a church with the Reverend Sylvester Larned as pastor. Larned had entertained the Catholic clergy in a body on one occasion, and Clapp, who succeeded him, so far fell beneath the spell of Catholicism as to declare that were it not for his ideas on the Trinity he would not hesitate to enter the Catholic Church. In 1829 Clapp was dismissed by his congregation, and in 1831 he was officially deposed. Clapp's Unitarian doctrines were pleasing to some of his old congregation and they followed him; but it was necessary for Judah Touro, the noted Jewish philanthropist, to maintain his church and salary for a number of years. In time, Parson Clapp's Church ranked with the St. Charles Theater and the French Opera as a show-place in New Orleans. Clapp's church was chartered in 1853 as the First Congregational Unitarian Church and later was called the Church of the Messiah. The present Unitarian Church in New Orleans is descended from this congregation. Clapp's *Autobiographical Sketches* (1857) is an extremely vivid account of the New Orleans of his day.

The Presbyterians were not disorganized, however, and during the forties and the fifties some six churches were founded. Dr. Benjamin M. Palmer, a prominent leader of this church, was active in spreading Confederate sentiment among the American population in Louisiana.

There probably were Lutherans among the early German colonists, but congregations of this denomination were not assembled until after immigration increased in 1830. German settlers remained chiefly in New Orleans, making the city the center of Lutheran activities. Christ Chapel, established in 1830, and three other Lutheran churches flourished in the city before 1860.

In the prosperous years of the nineteenth century Protestantism expanded throughout Louisiana. Some of the leading churches of the present day were erected at this time. In New Orleans the Episcopalians organized St. Paul's (1838), Annunciation (1844), and Trinity (1848). From the pastors of Trinity Church, built in 1855, some of the Episcopal bishops of other States have been supplied. The Reverend Leonidas Polk, first Bishop of Louisiana, was rector of the church from 1855 to 1861. Polk had been appointed a missionary bishop of the Southwest when the diocese was organized in 1838, and under him the Episcopal church in Louisiana became a vital religious force. He established churches at Shreveport, along the Red River, along Bayous Teche and Lafourche, at Plaquemine, Opelousas, Thibodaux, Napoleonville, and Donaldsonville. After his consecration as Bishop of Louisiana in 1841 many new Episcopal districts in New Orleans were organized, and with Bishop Elliott he began the movement to establish the University of the South at Sewanee, Tennessee. Polk became a lieutenant general in the Confederate Army and was known as the "fighting bishop." He was killed in action at Pine Mountain, Marietta, Georgia.

A few Jews were in Colonial Louisiana, despite the Black Code's ruling against them. By 1803 a considerable increase was shown, but the early rabbis generally had to support themselves by additional work.

Dr. I. Roley Marks, one of the first rabbis, was also captain of a fire engine and an actor in a theater. There is also a story that Dr. Marks' predecessor, unable to find a Jewish maiden to his fancy, married a Catholic woman. Upon the rabbi's death, a good deal of persuasion was needed to prevent the weeping widow from placing a crucifix in the coffin with her husband. In 1828 a group organized the Shaaray Chesed (Gates of Mercy) congregation, which tradition claims was established by Jacob da Silva Solis, a trader who was unable to find any *matzoth* (unleavened bread) in New Orleans at Passover. In the old city of Lafayette (upper New Orleans), Shaaray Tefilah (Gates of Prayer) was organized about 1845 by Abraham de Joung, a Portuguese Jew; the Dispersed of Judah (now Touro Synagogue) was founded in 1847. A reform movement, proposing secession from the orthodox faith, began in 1864 among the New Orleans Jews. This materialized in 1871 with the establishment of Temple Sinai. Today, Jewish congregations are found only in the larger communities.

During the Colonial period Negroes were reared in the Catholic faith, and rear pews in most of the churches were set aside for them. Some of the early Protestant congregations emulated this custom, but soon gave it up. Occasionally, a branch church was maintained for the Negroes. In early New Orleans the Methodists made great progress among the Negroes, and in 1830 the Wesley Church, which is still functioning, was founded. Prior to the War between the States there were three other African Methodist churches and one Episcopal church for colored Protestants in the city. The Catholic Church has since established separate Negro churches, and in many instances these are presided over by Negro Catholic priests.

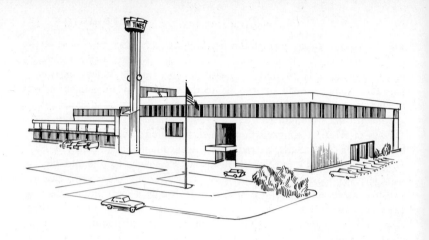

Communications Services

PRINTING came to Louisiana in 1764 when Denis Braud, a New Orleans merchant, was granted an exclusive privilege by the Superior Council. There are records of twenty impressions made by him between 1764 and 1770; among them is the *Mémoire* of the citizens of Louisiana protesting to Louis XV the transfer of their province to Spain. After 1770 there is no trace of Braud's press, and it is not until 1777 that we find the signature of Antoine Boudousquie, *Imprimeur du Roi et du Cabildo,* and printer of the famous *Code Noir.* Ten publications can be traced to Boudousquie between 1777 and 1782, but no records of printing in the intervening years before 1794 are extant.

In 1794 Louis Duclot, a refugee printer from Santo Domingo, gave Louisiana its first newspaper, *Le Moniteur de la Louisiane.* Its motto was *"Bombolio, Clangor, Stridor, Tarantara, Murmur,"* and it was published irregularly as a weekly, semi-weekly, and tri-weekly for a little more than two decades. Until 1803 *Le Moniteur* was the only journal, but in seven years following eight others appeared in New Orleans. Hardiest was *L'Ami des lois et journal du soir,* which, established in 1809, survived through various managements and names until 1834, when it was merged with *L'Abeille de la Nouvelle Orléans.* *L'Abeille* was founded in 1827 by François Delaup, and continued publication until 1923 (*see Literature*).

The *Union or New Orleans Advertiser and Price Current* was

established by James Lyon & Co., on December 13, 1803. The paper and printer's shop were bought by James M. Bradford, son of David Bradford, pioneer printer of Kentucky, who, on December 20, 1804, brought out the *Orleans Gazette.* John Mowry had established the *Louisiana Gazette* on July 27, 1804, to which a French section was added in 1817. Bradford became territorial printer, a post which he lost in 1809 because of political differences with Governor Claiborne. Soon afterwards he went to St. Francisville, where he established the *Time Piece* (1811), the first newspaper to be published in the Florida Parishes. The early papers paid little attention to local happenings because these were usually known to the public long before the sheet was lifted from its handpress; their editors used the shears more often than the pen, and much of their material consisted of items clipped from other publications, both foreign and domestic. But in 1835 the *True American,* which closely followed politics and news, revolutionized the journalistic profession in Louisiana.

In the rural parishes the earliest newspapers arrived less than two decades behind those of New Orleans. The first to appear were the *Louisiana Planter* (1810), the *Red River Planter* (1813) in Alexandria, and the *Time Piece* (1811) already mentioned. *La Gazette de Baton Rouge* published its first issue in 1819, and 5 years later *Le Courrier de Natchitoches* and the *Gazette des Attakapas* (St. Martinville) appeared. The first newspaper in Monroe was the *Louisianian,* founded in 1822. The pioneer of Caddo Parish was the *Red River Patriot and Shreveport Literary Register,* first published in 1839. Established in 1842, the Baton Rouge *Advocate* still appears as the *Morning Advocate.* The *Sugar Planter,* founded in 1856, was the first farm or trade journal in the State. The Abbeville *Meridional* was founded in the same year.

Most of these rural journals were printed on a fairly good grade of paper, using the six-column form. There was a rather well-developed system of classified advertising in which the "cards" of professional men were published. These, as well as the mercantile advertisements, were only a column wide, the larger spaces of one-third and one-half page width being taken by visiting attractions such as circuses and menageries. Under the cut of a figure of a running Negro, who evidently had all his worldly goods in a bundle slung at the end of a stick, appeared the notices of runaway slaves. Besides a detailed description, such advertisements often explained the type of work in which the slave specialized, and even his gait when walking.

As early as 1836 a Louisiana newspaper "scooped" the world when the *Red River Herald* printed the first account of the fall of the Alamo; but the more usual fare consisted of controversies waged in print over political and personal questions. These differences were often settled by duels. War halted political bickering, however, and welded the press into a driving force for the defense of the Confederate cause. Yet continuous publication was endangered as materials were exhausted and the finances of the patrons suffered with the fortunes of war. The Opelousas *Courier,* rather than discontinue publication, limited subscriptions to persons living in the parish. A small number were printed on wrapping paper, and the February 1864 issues were printed on the back of gaily-patterned wallpaper. The War between the States practically ended the flourishing period of the journals printed in French.

In metropolitan New Orleans, where journalism attained its greatest development in the State, the *Times-Picayune,* which in 1937 celebrated its centennial, is typical of the succession of mergers undergone by the local papers. Established as the *Picayune* after the pattern of the "penny press" of the North, it sold for a picayune, a small coin worth about 6¼¢. During the Mexican War the *Picayune* repeatedly "scooped" the world, printing the news, brought by pony express, before the official dispatches reached Washington. When the *Crescent* (1848) was suppressed in 1863 by Federal military authorities, the New Orleans *Times* was established in the old plant and soon became known as one of the most brilliantly edited American newspapers. In 1881 it was combined with the more prosperous *Democrat* (1875) to become the *Times-Democrat.* The combined publication was merged with the *Picayune* in 1914 and became the present *Times-Picayune.*

The New Orleans *States,* founded January 3, 1880, by Major Henry J. Hearsey and known as the *Daily States,* was purchased by the Times-Picayune Publishing Co. in 1933 and continued as an afternoon newspaper. Its Sunday issue was combined with the Sunday edition of the *Times-Picayune.*

One of the most colorful chapters in Southern newspaper history is that of the New Orleans *Item,* founded in 1877 by twelve journeymen printers who banded together to create their own publication. A year later Lafcadio Hearn changed the *Daily City Item* from a dry, colorless sheet to a sparkling mirror of local and national events, literary criticism, dramatic reviews, poems, and cartoons. In 1894 Dominic O'Malley became master of the paper's policy, and scathing editorials denouncing political scandals followed. Fist fights, cane lashings, and threats made at gun point were frequent occurrences.

In 1958 the Times-Picayune Co. bought the New Orleans *Item* and merged it with the *States* to form the New Orleans *States-Item.* In June, 1962, Samuel I. Newhouse, publisher of 17 successful newspapers, acquired most of the company's outstanding shares of stock for $41,100,000 in what *Editor & Publisher* termed the biggest cash deal in a newspaper property. Newhouse, with headquarters in New York

City, followed his practice of letting local management determine the policies of his newspapers.

In January, 1968, the company moved into a new plant at 3800 Howard Avenue that represents the peak of functional planning. The editorial departments of the two newspapers operate independently. The mechanical departments employ devices that have simplified processes, such as high-speed automatic machines that set market quotations from tape and teletype machines that cast 12 lines per minute from tape. Display advertising is processed by the complex Photon machine, directed by an operator at a console that resembles "a gigantic automatic mind." The pressroom has three Hoe Colormatic presses, each of nine units, double-decked and in one section triple-decked, 45 ft. tall and nearly one block long, each unit capable of printing 70,000 papers per hour, or 210,000 in all.

Supplementing the news services is the library, a depository of information that can be produced at a moment's notice. Not only are millions of clippings available, but the files of the newspapers from 1837 are reproduced on microfilm, and there are thousands of photographs.

The New Orleans headquarters of the Associated Press occupies a section of the building with batteries of teletype machines and perforators handing approx. 500,000 words daily from near and far places.

A number of Louisiana newspapers have merged in recent years, but others have been established and the number remains between 20 and 22 dailies. The number of weeklies is much larger; they served the needs of many small communities and also deal with professional and business interests, such as labor, trade, shipping, oil and gas, education, libraries, religious and cultural themes.

The principal daily newspapers of the State are the Alexandria *Town Talk*, Bastrop *Enterprise*, Baton Rouge *Morning Advocate* and *State-Times*, Bogaluse *Daily News*, Crowley *Daily Signal*, Franklin *Banner Tribune*, Hammond *Daily Star*, Jennings *Daily News*, Lafayette *Daily Advertising*, Lake Charles *American Press*, Monroe *News Star-World*, Morgan City *Daily Review*, New Iberia *Daily Iberian*, Opelousas *Daily World*, Ruston *Daily Leader*, and Shreveport *Times-Journal*. The *Daily Journal of Commerce* is an important New Orleans publication.

The *Louisiana Weekly*, published in New Orleans, is the best-known Negro organ in the State. Others are the Alexandria *News-Leader*, the Baton Rouge *News-Leader*, the Bossier City *Hurricane*, the Monroe *News-Leader*, and the Shreveport *Sun*.

Many outstanding journalistic and literary figures have been associated with New Orleans newspapers and magazines. The list includes James L. Freaner, Walt Whitman, Mark Twain, Lafcadio Hearn,

George W. Cable, Henry Castellanos, Mollie E. M. Davis, G. W. Kendall, Mark Bigney, Pearl Rivers (Mrs. E. J. Holbrook), Julia Wetheril (Mrs. Marion Baker), Mrs. Elizabeth Lyle Saxon, Elizabeth Bisland Wetmore, Catherine Cole (Mrs. Martha R. Field), Don Jose Quintero, Henry Guy Carleton, and Henry Rightor. More recent writers have been Dorothy Dix (Mrs. Elizabeth M. Gilmer), whose column of advice to the lovelorn appeared in the *Picayune* for over 40 years, Helen Pitkin Schertz, Flo Field, Lyle Saxon, Roark Bradford, John McClure, Hermann B. Deutsch, Meigs Frost, K. T. Knoblock, Bruce Manning, Gwen Bristow (Mrs. Manning), William Faulkner, Hamilton Basso, Carl Carmer and many others.

American Progress, founded by Huey P. Long in 1933, was succeeded as the voice of the State administration by *Progress,* which suspended publication in February, 1940. In the same month the Opelousas *Daily World* received national notice as the only "offset" daily in the United States. The *Federationist* was the official organ of the Louisiana Federation of Labor, and the *Catholic Action of the South* the leading diocesan organ.

Dramatic and musical reviews have been popular. Pioneers included *L'Entr'Acte, Le Coup d'œil, La Loge d'opéra,* all of course in French, as were their most important successors, such as *La Violette, Les Véillées louisianaises,* and *La Revue louisianaise.* The most solid and representative magazine of the time was *De Bow's Review,* which enjoyed a long life (1846–80); it stood for the industrialization of the South while emphasizing its commercial, agricultural, manufacturing, natural, and literary resources. *Le Journal de la Société médicale de la Nouvelle Orléans* (1839–40) was the first medical journal published in New Orleans. In 1844 Doctors Erasmus D. Fenner and A. Hester began the *New Orleans Medical and Surgical Journal.* The *Louisiana Journal of Education* appeared in 1879, and the *American Clubman* was published in 1897.

Toward the end of the century Regina Morphy, niece of the famous chess champion, was active in the publication of a women's magazine. Later, the *New Citizen* (1911–14) and the *Woman's Era* (1910–11) were both characteristic of the movement for woman suffrage.

RADIO AND TELEVISION

In 1922, shortly after the successful inauguration of commercial broadcasting by station KDKA of Pittsburgh, WAAB, of the Coliseum Place Baptist Church, and WWL, of Loyola University, began operations in New Orleans. WAAB became WJBO in 1927, and in 1934 moved to Baton Rouge.

During the twenties, KWKH became one of the most popular stations in southwestern United States, not only because of its early use of high power but also because of the extremely energetic personality of its first owner, W. K. Henderson, a retired ironmonger, who nightly regaled listeners with a coffee-selling plan which was part of his personal fight against the spread of chain stores throughout the State.

Joseph Uhalt opened a five watt station, WCBE, at New Orleans, in July 1923. In 1928 this station became WDSU. WDSU was the first station in Louisiana to broadcast from an airplane and from a ship at sea. It also was the first to broadcast a Southern League baseball game. It became an important link in the intrastate hook-up known as the Louisiana Network, which was used for matters of special local interest such as L. S. U. football games and political campaigning. In the summer of 1934, through station WDSU, Huey P. Long conducted his historic "investigation" of New Orleans.

Chain broadcasting began in the State in 1926 when Joseph Uhalt carried the National Broadcasting Company's programs for a period of 90 days; but regular service did not go into effect until the autumn of 1927, on WSMB.

In 1969–70 there were 80 radio stations and 17 television stations in Louisiana. The largest number was in New Orleans, which had 15 radio and 5 television stations. Of radio stations, Baton Rouge and Shreveport had 9 each; Monroe had 6, Lake Charles and Lafayette 5 each, and Alexandria had 4. In New Orleans the principal television channels were WDSU and WWL. Other cities with more than one television station were Baton Rouge, Lafayette, Lake Charles, and Shreveport, each 2.

Sports and Recreation

ONE of Louisiana's greatest assets is its variety of recreational facilities. Hunting and fishing are exceptionally good; golf courses, tennis courts, and bathing beaches or pools are available in or near all the larger cities; recreation areas with facilities for picnicking, camping, hiking, swimming, boating, and fishing have been provided for the public in Kisatchie National Forest, State Forest, and in several State parks. Unusual sports are pirogue racing, tarpon rodeos, and wolf hunting, while bloodier fare is provided by cock fights. During the Mid-Winter Sports Carnival, at year-end in New Orleans, tennis and golf tournaments, boxing, track, basketball, and yacht racing are topped off with the Sugar Bowl Game, a football classic, between the leading team of the South and of some other section of the country. Horse racing draws crowds to the Fair Grounds track in New Orleans and Evangeline Downs in Lafayette. In March many of the country's best amateur and professional golfers participate in the annual New Orleans Open Golf Tournament.

Hunting and fishing are the greatest attractions to the thousands of winter vacationists. Three types of hunting grounds are available: coastal marshes for ducks, geese, snipe, and rabbits; interior wooded swamps and ridgelands for bear, deer, squirrel, and woodcock; and upland areas for rabbits, squirrels, quail, and doves. There are also three types of fishing: Gulf of Mexico for deep-sea species, such as tarpon, king mackerel, jewfish, and sharks; coastal lagoon for redfish, sea trout, and sheepshead; and fresh-water bayous and upland streams for black bass, crappie, yellow bass, barfish, warmouth bass, and sunfish (perch).

The temperament of early Louisianians is perhaps best reflected in their sports. Public entertainment of the early nineteenth century, when American frontiersmen were flocking to the new territory, was of an exciting and brutal nature. Love of combat, whetted by frequent recourse to sword or pistol, whenever honor was impugned, was vicariously enjoyed by pitting animals against each other. Bulls, bears, dogs, cocks, and alligators were baited for the amusement of rawboned flatboatmen and Creole dandies, who demanded plenty of action. The cruelty of exposing a bear, a bull or a jackass to attacks of bulldogs gradually converted legislators to their prohibition.

Horse racing early became a major sport. Few planters were without a stable of thoroughbreds and many had their own courses, on which match races for huge stakes were run between the horses of rival planters. New Orleans, with five tracks in operation during the winter season, was the racing capital of the Nation in the 1850's. Every winter, turf enthusiasts of Kentucky and Tennessee came to the State to race their horses against Louisiana favorites.

Women as well as men were great riders and lovers of horses. One of them, in advance of her times, was arrested in 1850 for "riding on horseback, on the levee, straddling the horse, and causing a great scandal" among the large crowds she attracted.

A companion sport of racing, one in which fine horses were displayed to best advantage, was the "ring tournament" of the latter part of the nineteenth century. At these tourneys, which were attended by a great deal of pageantry imitative of the age of chivalry, "knights" in colorful costumes, mounted on caparisoned steeds, tilted at rings suspended at intervals along a straightaway. The honor of presiding at the ball that usually followed the tourney and of crowning the tournament queen went to the horseman collecting the most rings. The "peasantry," in their turn, engaged in "gander-pulling": riders, galloping by a goose suspended by its feet, endeavored to seize the bird's neck and yank off its head. As often as not, stout-necked geese ignominiously unseated the assailants.

Dueling, while not a sport, was treated so in some instances. There is the case of a duel on horseback, which was fought in the year 1836, and later described in the *New Orleans Times* of June 20, 1869. Both principals in the combat were Creoles, but one—a Lieutenant Shamburg —was a soldier whose superior had forbidden fighting on the "field of honor." Accordingly, when Adolph Cuvillier challenged him, he chose horses and lances for the combat, which was held on the Carrollton Race Course.

Duels were also fought with the bowie-knife, a weapon with a nine-inch blade and guarded handle said to have been designed by Resin Bowie, brother of Colonel James Bowie of Rapides Parish. Colonel Jim took a fancy to the knife and made it famous by dexterously cutting down Major Norris Wright in the celebrated duel at Vidalia in 1827. It was a particularly murderous weapon when used by duelists slashing at each other across a handkerchief held at the corners.

During the steamboat era competition among rival steamboat lines gave rise to a form of racing and betting that occasioned international interest. The usual time of departure from New Orleans was 5 o'clock in the afternoon, and since the first boats to arrive at any landing were most apt to get the bulk of the freight, races usually resulted. Most of these contests were spontaneous, but often the more famous steamers engaged in prearranged races on which great sums of money were wagered. Such was that between the *Robert E. Lee* and the *Natchez.* Starting from New Orleans on June 30, 1870, the two steamed nip and tuck to St. Louis, the *Lee* winning by 3 hours and 44 minutes, in 3 days 18 hours and 14 minutes. During the frenzied excitement of this race, signal guns were fired by the contestants as they passed towns and their positions were relayed to an anxious world by telegraph operators; bonfires on shore signaled the progress by night, and by day watchers on plantation house belvederes strained to see the columns of black smoke before the steamers came in view "round the bend."

Tall tales are told of gambling, back in the steamboat days. But gambling has always been popular throughout the State. Claude Robin, a visitor to Louisiana in 1802, wrote:

> Gambling is the principal source of amusement for the men, and there are many gambling houses in New Orleans, fortunes are lost overnight, rich men play for high stakes, and lose freely. The captain of a vessel loses more than he has made on his entire voyage, and often bets the ship's money. The planter who has come to sell his crop, on which he expects to buy supplies for his family for the year, and clothes for his slaves, is forced to return without provisions, unless he borrows money at a ruinous rate of interest, but gamble they must.

The oldest men's club in New Orleans, the exclusive Boston Club, was organized in the early American days for the card game Boston, said to have been invented by French army officers in Massachusetts during the American Revolution. Herbert Asbury in *Sucker's Progress* reports that New Orleans was the first port of poker in the United States—the name being a derivative of the French *Poque* (a similar game) and some of its original rules coming from as far away as Persia.

Despite Government efforts to subdue it, the gaming fever ran high following the United States' purchase of the territory, and the continued popularity of the "palaces of chance," eventually led to the State-authorized Louisiana lottery, instituted in 1868 to replenish finances dissipated by the War between the States. From small beginnings, the lottery grew to a capital grand prize of $600,000, which could be awarded twice a year, on a $40-ticket, and to monthly and semi-monthly schemes which totaled $28,000,000. The lottery was outlawed in 1895.

It is said that Louisiana first introduced the game of craps to the nation. Edward Larocque Tinker wrote that Bernard Xavier Philippe de Marigny de Mandeville (1785–1868), the son of a wealthy Louisiana-Creole planter, learned Hazard in London and introduced it on his return; the game was then Americanized into craps by the rivermen from the term "Johnny Crapeau" used for the French. Asbury, however, declares that the same dice game was known as crabs, krabs, craps, or kreps, both in England and on the European continent at that time. At any rate, Baron de Marigny did subdivide his plantation, probably, as Tinker says, because of gaming losses and, in naming the streets, designated part of the present Burgundy Street of New Orleans as Craps Street.

Lotto, also called Keno remains a popular form of gambling throughout southern Louisiana and Bingo is played for fun and for raising funds.

Paul Morphy, one of the greatest chess players of all time, was born in New Orleans and spent most of his life there. Competing at the American Chess Congress in 1857 he became recognized as the foremost American player. During 1858 and 1859 he toured Europe, vanquishing all comers, and establishing himself as world champion. In 1872 he published *Games of Chess*.

A sport popular among the Creoles of the nineteenth century was raquette, a game adopted from the Indians. An exceedingly rough-and-tumble game, it was played on a large field between teams composed of from 5 to 100 members. A ball about the size of a golf ball, made of India rubber or of rags covered with buckskin, was tossed up at the "bomboula," a pole erected in the center of the playing field, to start the game. Each player had two rackets—a short one for scooping the ball from the ground and a longer one for throwing it. A point, or "pelotte," was scored whenever a team succeeded in driving the ball against the goal, a high, narrow sheet of tin that resounded sharply when struck. At the end of the game the victorious team carried its captain around the field, singing a victory song in Creole patois, each verse being accompanied by the club cry, a forerunner of the college yell of today.

During the 1890's and from 1910 to 1915 New Orleans was the boxing center of America. In those two periods world's championship bouts in every division were fought in the city. The State was one of the first to legalize prize fighting (1890), and it was in Crowley's

Lane, in St. Bernard Parish, that Louis Nuckols and Charles Carroll engaged in the first contest in America in which gloves were worn. The longest bout in the history of prize fighting was that staged in New Orleans on April 6, 1893, between Andy Bowen and Jack Burke, who battled 7 hours and 19 minutes to a 110-round draw. Wearily the reporter for the *Daily Picayune* wrote: "At 3 o'clock the men were still fighting. The eighty-ninth round had been reached, Bowen was said to have a broken wrist, and some of the spectators bethought themselves of breakfast. Owing to the length of the contest and the lateness of the hour, it is not advisable to describe the fight further, or to wait for the result."

The 145-round fight between Harry Bell of Liverpool and Steve O'Donnell of New Orleans, held under the oaks in City Park in 1860, was longer in terms of rounds, but lasted only 2 hours and 10 minutes, since a round in those bare-knuckle days terminated with a knock-down and frequently was very short. On three successive nights in September 1892 three world's championship fights were held at the Olympic Club in New Orleans. The highlight of the carnival was the memorable fight between James J. Corbett and John L. Sullivan, the former winning by a knockout in 21 rounds. Wrestling is a minor entertainment and there are regular matches in the Civic Center in Monroe.

Inauguration of the rain check in baseball, as well as of Ladies Day, is credited to Abner Powell, manager of the first New Orleans Southern League baseball team in 1887. A world's automobile speed record was established by Ralph DePalma in New Orleans in 1909, when he drove 50 miles around the mile dirt track at the rate of 60 miles an hour. Jimmy Wedell of New Orleans, at the time of his death, 1934, held the world speed record for land planes.

Two of the most popular race tracks in the South are those of the Louisiana Jockey Club at the Fair Grounds in New Orleans and the Evangeline Downs in Lafayette. The long New Orleans season opens on Thanksgiving Day and lasts until April. Its handicaps are the Thanksgiving, Crescent City, Tenacious, Pont Alba, Sugar Bowl, and Louisiana Futurity. In 1972 it observed its centennial. The Evangeline Downs track opens in April and has had its season extended into September. Its big race, the Evangeline Quarter Horse Futurity, is run at 2 p.m. on Independence Day for a purse of $150,000. On its last day the Louisiana Futurity is run for $60,000. In 1969 betting at its mutuel windows averaged $241,000 a day. The track runs only three afternoon cards, all others start at 7:30 P.M.

Yachting is a regular summer sport on Lake Pontchartrain and Lake Charles, and there are cruises and races on the Mississippi River and on some of the bayous. The Southern Yacht Club and the City Yacht Club of New Orleans sponsor weekend races on Lake Pontchartrain. Mandeville on the opposite shore has races and a regatta in July, August, and September. The Shreveport Yacht Club has International Sailboat Races on Cross Lake July 4. Lake Charles Yacht Club has a fall series of races in October-November. Novel contests are the World Championship Pirogue Races off Lafitte in May.

There are many fine golf courses, public and private, in Louisiana. The Greater New Orleans Open Golf Tourney takes place in April at Lakewood with champion golfers competing for $125,000 in prize money. There are numerous other tourneys in New Orleans. The Gulf Coast Oil Golf Tourney takes place at Lafayette in June. The Nicholls Golf Club Classic is played at the Bayou Country Club at Thibodaux in June. Summer events include the Louisiana Junior Championship at the Alexandria Country Club; the Kraft Golf Tourney at Morehouse Country Club in Bastrop; the Lafayette Golf Cup matches at Acadian Hills Club in Lafayette; the International Golf Meet of the Palmetto Club in Shreveport; the President's Golf Tourney of the Lake Charles Country Club; the Invitational Tourney for Women and the Men's Championship Contest, both at the Lake Charles Country Club; the Kiwanis Ladies Pro Golf Tourney at Huntington Park Club in Shreveport, and many others.

Spectator sports, athletic contests, and competitive racing on land and water have become important activities in the lives of Louisianians. The biggest draws are football games, college and professional, which jam the stadia. The major localities are the Sugar Bowl Stadium at Tulane University in New Orleans where the Sugar Bowl Classic takes place on January 1, and the Tiger Stadium in Baton Rouge, home base of the LSU teams. These will be surpassed in size by the Domed Stadium, or New Orleans Superdrome, on which work was begun in July, 1970. It will seat 80,000 and will be the home base of the Saints of the National Football League. Most of the big stadia are associated with colleges and are used also for track events and festivals. Among them are Rapides Coliseum at Alexandria, Southern Stadium, Memorial Stadium, and LSU Coliseum at Baton Rouge; Cowboy Stadium at Lake Charles, Brown Stadium at Ruston, and Fair Grounds Stadium at Shreveport. The Grantland Rice Bowl postseason game sponsored by the National Collegiate Athletic Assn. is held annually at Memorial Stadium and draws a crowd of 20,000.

Basketball has become the most popular year-around college sport and calls for smaller arenas than football. Teams come from the South and places as far away as Pittsburgh, Providence, R.I., Milwaukee, and Hawaii. Professional baseball is played regularly in New Orleans, Baton Rouge and other large cities.

Architecture

THE early building in Louisiana evolved out of the materials on hand, the exigencies of the climate, and the needs of the colonists. The actual methods of building were the heritage of Europe, and, later, of the West Indies, but the forms that developed remain today as proof of an original growth.

New Orleans and Natchitoches, the first white settlements in Louisiana, were both founded in the first quarter of the eighteenth century; but little of the building before 1794 is still standing, as New Orleans was visited by disastrous fires in 1788 and 1794, and Natchitoches by one in 1823. Yet examples of the different types remain to record the stages of development.

The Indians plastered their huts with clay kneaded with "Spanish beard" (Spanish moss), and covered them with the bark of the cypress or with palmetto. And the earliest buildings constructed by the white settlers were rude cabins of split cypress boards, with a filler of clay and moss. Hardly an example of this *bousillage* type of construction remains in New Orleans, but on the river road between New Orleans and Baton Rouge, and along Cane River, in the vicinity of Natchitoches, a number of buildings which date from the eighteenth century reveal clay and moss walls within a frame of cypress posts. No covering was used and the structural frame is visible in the completed wall. One of the oldest houses in Natchitoches has clay walls utilizing deer hair instead of moss as a binder.

Because of the abundance of good clay on the shores of Lake Pontchartrain, brick kilns were soon constructed to supply New Orleans and its vicinity. These first bricks, while far superior to the former construction in wood and clay, were soft and porous, which, in the wet semitropical climate of the lower delta, rendered them unfit for permanent building. In addition, the first mortar, compounded from clamshell lime, disintegrated when wet. To overcome these disadvantages the *briqueté entre poteaux* (bricks between posts) structure became popular. In this type of house the wall space between the framework of heavy cypress posts and diagonal struts was filled with bricks and mortar, and the whole covered with a smooth plaster to prevent the absorption and infiltration of moisture. A typical example of this construction, dating from the last half of the eighteenth century, may be seen in the Lafitte Blacksmith Shop at Bourbon and St. Philip Streets, New Orleans. This building is especially interesting as the plaster has fallen away in spots to reveal the structural detail, and the roof is cut by dormers showing early utilization of the attic space. It is a square single-story building, which, at the time of its construction, was divided into four rooms of equal size, two of which were used as a shop.

Split cypress shingles or a thatch of palmetto leaves covered the earliest houses; but after the second fire in 1794 the governor, Baron de Carondelet, offered a premium to builders for the use of tile to lessen the fire hazard. First in use were the tapered half-cylinders of Spanish tile which were cradled on beveled rafters and made tight by flashing and chinking with mortar. The French pan tiles were also used extensively and may still be seen on the old building at the corner of Bourbon and Pauger Streets.

The larger houses of this early period, such as Madame John's Legacy, 632 Dumaine Street, New Orleans, reveal another striking characteristic of Louisiana architecture which had its inception in necessity. This house (1728?) and other plantation houses in the bottomlands of Louisiana were raised above the ground some six to eight feet on brick piers—a precaution against the periodic flooding. Other characteristics of the Louisiana-type house were a wide gallery, generally supported on brick piers with slender cypress colonnettes extending from the gallery to the eaves of the hipped roof; a stair within the confines of the gallery; the absence of a hallway; and a floor plan that made use of both stair and gallery as the means of communication for the rooms. There are few examples of such houses more than two stories and a half, *i.e.,* a basement, a main floor, and an attic. Later, when necessity for building in fear of flooding had passed, the "raised cottage" style, as it came to be known, persisted as a popular mode of construction. The main floor was raised higher and the basement converted into a dining-room and an office. Columns and colonnettes began to vary. Bermuda, near Natchitoches, is one of the few remaining examples of the open lower-floor type. Examples of the enclosed lower floor are numerous: Parlange near New Roads, the Parker House and the Schertz House on Bayou St. John, New Orleans, and Melrose near Natchitoches. The Westfeldt House, 2340 Prytania Street, New Orleans, built in the early 1820's as a plantation house, reveals the transition of the style with the use of Greek Revival detail to embellish the façade. The colonnettes have given way to square columns with a formal entablature.

After 1830 Louisiana entered on the great boom period of river commerce and agricultural prosperity, and the plantation houses of this later era differ widely from their earlier prototypes. The Greek Revival had made its way south; and it is an interesting architectural fact that whereas this style is today sometimes bemoaned as a "paper" architecture that created Greek temples of dubious merit as buildings, it found a true functional expression in the plantation houses of the deep South. The façade of a Greek temple plastered on buildings of all descriptions often reveals only pretentiousness and bad taste, but the adaptation of this style to Louisiana was at once happy and charming. The "colossal order," or two-story column from the ground to the roof, now became the rule in place of the more horizontal façade described above. Isolated as the building was and surrounded by great oak and pecan trees, the large column found a proper setting, and became the most recognizable characteristic of the plantation house. Galleries now surrounded the house on all sides, protecting the walls and windows from extremes of heat and from rain.

Kitchens, offices, and other quarters were contained in numerous outbuildings which were located a short distance from the main house. In addition, there were often twin *garçonnières* or *pigeonniers* to balance the plan. The *garçonnières* housed the young bachelors of the family and male guests; the *pigeonniers* were dovecotes. Still farther back from the "big house" were the slave quarters—a long row or double row of frame or brick cabins still in many cases used by field hands who are descendants of the original slaves. Most of the brick quarters have disappeared, but examples may yet be seen at Magnolia near Natchitoches, and Woodland near West Pointe à la Hache.

Floor plans of these later houses reveal a significant change: a wide central hall bisects the house from front to back with high-ceilinged rooms opening on to it from each side; and very often the stair becomes an integral part of the house as it ascends gracefully from the central hall in a manner reminiscent of the same feature in the Colonial houses of Virginia and the Carolinas. Dormers are more widely used. Notable examples are Belle Chasse and Three Oaks near New Orleans, Belle Hélène near Geismar, and the Hermitage near Darrow. There is often a crowning belvedere, or widow's walk, from which the inhabitants could watch the coming and going of steamboats. This is illustrated by Burnside Plantation near Burnside, and Seven Oaks near New Orleans.

In the Feliciana Parishes, which were largely settled by Scotch-English pioneers from Virginia and the Carolinas, the architecture reflects the Georgian heritage; many of its features are borrowed from the Colonial architecture of the Atlantic seaboard. Gable roofs are frequent and many houses are close parallels to contemporary Virginia houses with gable roofs and outside chimneys. Often the house is raised a few feet off the ground on stout brick piers and the steeply pitched roof shows the characteristic eaves extension which forms a gallery and adds a Louisiana touch. Typical houses are Wakefield in West Feliciana and Asphodel in East Feliciana. A larger type is Waverly, also in West Feliciana. This house is a two-story frame structure with a gabled roof, flanking outside chimneys, and galleries on both floors across the front. The more pretentious design, such as the Chase House in Clinton, reveals a two-story façade with a front-facing gable supported by columns that extend both stories with a fine doorway of Greek detail surmounted by a graceful fanlight. Identical wings, one story in height and duplicating the design of the main house, flank it on each side. Many of these houses have in addition the central hall characteristic of the Atlantic seaboard, which later became a prominent feature of the building in all sections of the State. Many are clapboarded frame with shingled roofs and wooden columns but the larger houses are often of brick. Other such houses may be found in the Teche country. The Hebrard House at Opelousas is noteworthy, but the best known is the Shadows on the Teche at New Iberia, which, however, duplicates the floor plan of the indigenous raised cottage.

In the last period of Louisiana plantation building, before the War between the States had wiped out the great wealth which made such mansions possible, the Greek Revival had completely conquered the taste of Louisianians. Belle Grove near White Castle was a striking example of the final exuberance of this style. This building was designed by the famous Louisiana architect, James Gallier, Jr., and built in 1857. It was a raised two-story mansion designed on a grandiose scale with a gabled portico supported by full-length Corinthian columns on the front and one side. There was a central hall and a great stair with 70 rooms finished with very fine plaster detail. Not classic in design, but expressive of the prosperity of the period, is Afton Villa in West Feliciana Parish, a highly ornate Victorian-Gothic mansion, set in terraced gardens.

For distinctive urban dwellings two sections of New Orleans are of architectural importance: the Vieux Carré, or French Quarter, where Spanish and French influences combined to form a unique Creole style, and the Garden District, which reveals the influence of the Greek Revival upon the large town houses built by the Americans in that section of the city settled by them after 1820. A third section of the city, the Bayou St. John neighborhood, is interesting because of the number of plantation houses that survive.

Adrien de Pauger, assistant of Bienville's engineer, Le Blond de la Tour, laid out Nouvelle Orléans as a rectangle lying along the river-bank, and surrounded by a rampart with forts at the strategic corners. The result of this enclosure, necessary for protection, was to crowd the growing city into a given space. Thus Madame John's Legacy, mentioned above, is essentially a plantation house in the midst of the city. The later building, which grew up around the turn of the eighteenth century, much of which is still standing in the French Quarter, makes use of the party wall or continuous building. For this reason most of the roofs in the old city slope to the street and to the court, not on all sides as the Lafitte shop and Madame John's. This crowding of the buildings into a given area gave rise to the most distinctive of all the Louisiana forms—the courtyard house. Brick was the universal medium of construction, often with a covering of smooth cement, which, in the beginning a necessity, later became the style; when not cemented the brick facing was painted.

At first the small single-story building was built on the ground, and the full width of the lot opened onto a rear court. Generally a two-story outbuilding faced it across this court, the upper story being used for slave quarters, the lower for a kitchen. Frequently the gabled roof of the main building was heightened and broken by dormers in order to make additional living quarters. This constituted the typical Creole cottage. Later the larger houses utilized an L-plan formed by the addition of a wing running down one side of the court and sometimes across the rear. From the street the *porte-cochère* gave access through an arched and flagstoned drive to the court. Stairs at one side of this drive and just off the court ascended to the living quarters above. The rest of the building on the ground floor was given over to a shop or used as dining rooms. Kitchen and slave quarters were on the ground floor of the wing. The stair hall on each floor was lighted by a large casement window, half of which was utilized as a door onto the gallery of the wing, and the whole surmounted by a large fanlight which admitted light into the interior rooms of the house. The successive levels of the wing were lower than those of the main house and necessitated a step-down from each floor to the gallery.

French windows opened from the main rooms onto balconies which ran across the face of the building, and which were either supported by wrought-iron brackets or slim iron columns extending to the street. The result in either case was to shade the *banquette* (sidewalk) from both sun and rain as well as supply a safe vantage point for the occupants of the house. Doors were often of solid cypress and the

French windows were protected by blinds which successfully excluded the hot sun and rain without cutting off the circulation of air. Heavy brick walls made these houses cool; high ceilings added to the effect of spaciousness and kept the rooms comfortable during the long summer months. Detail work in plaster and wood was universally fine in the better houses where the interiors reveal a restraint reminiscent of the Adam brothers. Many of the earlier houses have beautifully proportioned wooden mantels. Expensive marble mantels of classic design were later features.

The French Quarter houses offered adequate protection to the enclosed court in the rear where a high standard of living might be carried on in true privacy. Balconies, which were the most distinctive single feature about the house, added the only decoration to an otherwise severe façade. Wrought-iron railings and decorative panels were used in the first years of the nineteenth century, but later the cast-iron "lace" became almost universal. These balconies give to a street in the Vieux Carré a distinctive atmosphere. Bow and arrows, trailing roses, grape vines, and the popular acorn motif are only a few of the many designs to be seen today.

The advent of the Greek Revival in New Orleans left its mark upon some of the houses of the French Quarter without changing in any way their essential individuality. Doorways were flanked by columns and the decorative detail of cornices and window pediments reveal the classic motifs in all their variety. Le Petit Salon on St. Peter Street is a fine example of the adaptiveness of the style on a house that is essentially the same as its neighbors. The classic example is, of course, the two Pontalba Buildings designed by James Gallier, Sr., and built in 1849. These buildings were conceived as units and as such lent themselves readily to the order and symmetry which is essential to the feeling for classic design. Yet the design does not resemble the more lavish representations of much of the earlier building of the Greek Revival in the United States. The feeling of the buildings is essentially French, and the restraint of classic ornament individualizes the façades rather than reproduces detail from the temples of Greece. The delicate iron pilasters of the lower floors and the graceful cast iron of the balconies relieve an otherwise severe expanse of red brick and pedimented windows.

In the Garden District of New Orleans the Greek Revival found its fullest expression. Here the larger building sites allowed the house to be surrounded by a garden, and the presence of large oaks and magnolias provided an ideal setting for the large conception that is generally coincident with this style. Much of the building in the Garden District is of wood, but many of the larger houses are brick with decorative detail and the columns of wood; in many cases stucco covers the brick. Ironwork is used here more sparingly but achieves in many instances an aesthetic quality of rare charm. Some façades exhibit the delicate cast-iron columns and iron railings found in the French Quarter. Often a frame house will use the iron gallery between wooden columns, or a larger house with two-story columns in wood will utilize ironwork for the side gallery to achieve pleasant results. The L-plan town house with double parlors, side hall, and separate carriage house and servants' quarters was most popular. And it is noteworthy that the spaciousness of the outbuildings makes them today suitable for renovation as modern apartments. Fences were popular and usually of cast iron, sometimes set in a foundation of brick and stucco. There are a few houses in this section in the style of the French Renaissance; noteworthy is the old Newcomb College on Washington Avenue, formerly a private residence and later the Baptist Bible Institute. This house was surrounded with a formal garden embellished by statuary of nymphs, gods, and goddesses.

After the War between the States and the subsequent slow recovery of building, many of the traditional methods and styles gave way before the bad taste of the late nineteenth century. The steamboat with its reputation for gaudy luxury had left its mark. Retired captains built homes in conscious imitation of the boats they loved. An example may be seen gaily facing the Mississippi at 400 Egania Street, New Orleans. Houses whose builders had no such formal intention grew to look like steamboats "coming round the bend." The gingerbread embellishment made possible by the band saw was attached to every surface; couple this to the sudden desire for romantic effects as achieved by fake forms, add turrets, gables, bay windows, and colored glass and the result is "steamboat Gothic," that unfortunate "style" the remnants of whose popularity still remain in many cities of the State. New Orleans in particular has an unusual display of grotesque late nineteenth-century architecture. San Francisco Plantation in St. John the Baptist Parish is an example of "steamboat Gothic" applied to a traditional plantation building.

The most noteworthy of the early public buildings are also to be found in New Orleans. The old Ursuline Convent, later known as the Archbishopric, 1114 Chartres Street, is an excellently preserved example of the original French construction. A simple French Renaissance building, it was completed in 1734 and for a long time was said to be the oldest building in the Mississippi Valley, a claim now disputed by Madam John's Legacy.

Dating from the Spanish period are the Cabildo, the St. Louis Cathedral, and the Presbytère, all facing Jackson Square. The Cabildo, erected in 1795, and its counterpart, the Presbytère, completed some years later, were originally designed in the Spanish style as flat-roofed buildings with arched colonnades. The Spanish effect was marred, however, by the addition in 1847 of incongruous French mansard roofs. The Cathedral, originally a Spanish provincial church in brick and stucco with hexagonal flanking towers, has undergone many changes in façade since its completion in 1794. In 1820 Benjamin H. Latrobe added a central belfry. Jacques N. B. de Pouilly enlarged the church in 1850. The present façade, with some later modifications, dates from that time.

Benjamin H. Latrobe, the father of the Greek Revival in America, who came to New Orleans in 1819 to finish a waterworks started by his son, is represented in the city by the Louisiana State Bank, 401 Royal Street, constructed from a design submitted by him a short time before he died of yellow fever in 1820. De Pouilly's best work in New Orleans was the St. Louis Hotel, remarkable for its great dome constructed of earthenware pots whose axes were laid along the radial axes of the dome and were held in place by a light frame of wrought iron and the key action of their position. The one known remaining structure of De Poilly's is St. Augustine's Church at St. Claude Avenue and Bayou Road. This has been renovated and altered to some extent.

The Galliers, father and son, the most famous of the New Orleans architects of the last century, were the chief exponents of the classic style. Gallier, Sr., designer of the Pontalba Buildings, the original St. Charles Hotel, and many residences and public buildings, is best remembered for Gallier Hall, the former City Hall. The younger Gallier, while in partnership with his father, conformed to the Greek Revival style, but after he took over the business in 1851 his work exhibited an individual note. His best work was the French Opera House, erected in 1859 and destroyed by fire in 1919.

With the exception of these buildings and a few fine Greek Revival designs, such as the Clinton Courthouse and the Courthouse at Homer, public buildings in Louisiana are monotonous in the sameness of their design. The most popular type is a combination of the Greek and Roman styles. The plan is generally a Greek cross with columned porticoes on the four sides and the center of the building crowned with a dome—the whole vaguely reminiscent of the Pantheon. Then there is the simple Greek temple, with variants utilizing only a colonnaded portico on the most important front. The Old State Capitol at Baton Rouge, however, Gothic Revival in style, was designed by James Harrison Dakin as a medieval castle with towers and machicolations that commanded the Mississippi in both directions.

Other nineteenth-century architects who worked in Louisiana include Charles B. Dakin, brother of James; Isadore de Pouilly, brother of Jacques; Henry Howard, who built Madewood on Bayou Lafourche; William Strickland, who designed the old Mint in New Orleans; James and William Freret; and Lewis Reynolds. Triscini and Soldini, Swiss-Italians who came to Natchitoches in the 1830's, had considerable influence on the architecture of that city.

The middle of the nineteenth century produced many fine brick churches in Louisiana. They are notable for the general excellence of design and the unusual craftsmanship displayed in their construction. Christ Church (Episcopal), Napoleonville, was built in 1853 and is a Gothic building of red brick surmounted by a small steeple. The walls are buttressed and the windows are stained glass. St. John's Episcopal Church (1844) at Thibodaux is a small brick church with a hipped slate roof surmounted by a wooden tower reminiscent of the designs so familiar in New England. St Mary's Episcopal Church (1857) in West Feliciana Parish and St. Stephen's (1859) in Pointe Coupée Parish are both small brick churches of a modified Gothic design with a front bell tower. Noteworthy is the small frame Church of the Nativity (1859) at Rosedale. It has no tower but the window and door arches are Gothic and the steeply pitched roof creates an excellent effect. Trinity Church (1857) at Natchitoches is a small but beautifully designed building in a modified Romanesque with a flanking square tower. Grace Church (1858) in St. Francisville is a brick building in modified Gothic with a bell tower flanking the rear. The Church of the Immaculate Conception (1838), Natchitoches, is a Spanish building with twin towers topped by domes and a larger dome covering the altar apse.

According to N. C. Curtis, (*New Orleans, Its Houses, Shops and Public Buildings,* 1933), the Redemptorist churches in New Orleans built in the 1850's are as fine in their use of brick as the fifteenth-century churches of Rome. St. Mary's is in the baroque style and the most imposing structure, but the twin towers of St. Alphonsus are architecturally finer. St. Patrick's (1833) on Camp Street is said to be modeled after York Minster in England. It is a large brick building covered with rough stucco and is embellished by murals on the interior. Another interesting building is the Jesuit Church on Baronne Street. It was built in 1857 and rebuilt (Wogan and Bernard, Architects) on practically the same lines in 1927. The building is essentially a Spanish church in the traditional design with flanking towers and a domed apse, but the decorative motifs are Moorish. The columns and altar are Eastern and the towers are capped with onion domes characteristic of the Levant.

The floor plans of most of the larger churches are basilican. Vaulting, except in rare instances, is accomplished by means of the pitched roof of heavy timbers covered with slate. Excellent vaulting in brick may be observed at any of the numerous brick forts in Louisiana. Groin-vault chambers are reached through barrel-vault corridors and the general excellence of the craftsmanship is in evidence. Fort Pike at the Rigolets may easily be studied, as it has been cleared of underbrush and is open as a State park.

The Negro churches of Louisiana, which may be seen in all sections of the State, are generally rectangular frame buildings with gable roofs surmounted by a tower of some description. The church may be small and in such a sad state of repair that the whole is leaning at a crazy angle, yet there is always a tower in evidence. Often it is a front tower rising from the ground, but a more inexpensive tower supported on brackets near the peak of the gable and extending a respectable distance above it is a common substitute. No two towers are exactly alike.

Another interesting phase of Louisiana building is seen in the cemeteries of the State. Due to the condition of the soil, the dead in the lower Mississippi Valley are buried above ground in buildings employing in miniature the methods of everyday construction. Here in the cemeteries may be found simple dwellings of brick covered with stucco, surmounted by gabled roofs and surrounded by wrought-iron fences. A modification of this "house" type of tomb is the shelter of latticework topped by a gable roof that is occasionally built over graves in country cemeteries. All types of tombs, from the simple horizontal slab to the elaborate mausoleum, can be seen in family cemeteries on old plantations. A simple form of interment in crowded city cemeteries consists of rows of "ovens," each nicely vaulted and employing the party wall that is so characteristic of the French Quarter of New Orleans. Sometimes by way of embellishment there is a wrought-iron cross or a stone cherub. In the latter part of the nineteenth century grandiose mausoleums became the style. Greek temples in granite and marble now face Egyptian palaces and sandstone monuments across the tree-lined avenues of the cemeteries.

Public buildings of the first part of the twentieth century were generally in the Neo-Classic style, but here and there may be seen a bad copy of Richardsonian Romanesque which borrowed the more obvious faults without understanding the essential fineness of Richardson's contribution to American architecture. It is interesting to note that although Henry Hobson Richardson was born just above New Orleans in St. James Parish, the only design of his in the South is the Howard Library, New Orleans, a fine building of brown sandstone completed three years after his death (1886) from a design found among his papers. The building is aesthetically gratifying and illustrates the fine feeling for material which Richardson possessed. After the bad eclecticism of the nineteenth century it was necessary to learn the art of true building all over again. Richardson showed the way by adapting materials to the forms.

Architects who were not native, but examples of whose work reached New Orleans, include James Gamble Rogers, Daniel H. Burnham,

Louis Sullivan, and Albert Kahn. Local architects included Albert Toledano, Samuel Stanhope Labouisse, Francis J. MacDonnell, and Frank Churchill.

The small house in Louisiana is a single-story frame building whose chief characteristic is the built-in front porch. The roof, forming a common cover for both house and porch, is gabled, with the chimney either at the side or in the center of the building. These simple forms of building are still found in the city, where the house seems merely to have been turned on its end to fit the narrow building lot. The "shotgun" house, in which the rooms are one behind the other and the doors separating each are in line, so that a shot fired in the front entrance would go out the rear, and the "camelback" house, one-story in front and two stories in the rear, are also found in New Orleans.

Another interesting form, characteristic of the low marshy sections of the State, is the oysterman's hut, which is built over the water on pilings and reached along a precarious elevated plank-walk. In Barataria Bay entire hamlets inhabited by fishermen engaged in the shrimp industry are elevated on platforms on low-lying, marshy islands. The same principle is used in constructing bathing pavilions which fringe the lakefront near New Orleans. These houses (many of them are dwellings) are built over the water on pilings and usually include a wide gallery that surrounds the entire building. A railed walk also on pilings leads out from the shore to the house. The trapper's house, found on the edge of the coastal marshes, is often only a frame thatched with palmetto leaves, roofed with tarpaper, and flanked by a chimney of mud and sticks.

Better houses in the cities represent a variety of types. Sometimes public taste runs to New England farmhouses, which may be seen side by side with English, Georgian, and Spanish villas. These styles are, of course, excellent in themselves, but their presence in Louisiana, where it is essential to build for the peculiarities of the climate, seems out of place. There are some strictly modern buildings carrying out Le Corbusier's axiom that a house is a machine to live in.

Among noteworthy modern public buildings are those of Louisiana State University in Baton Rouge, which are a modified Italian Romanesque complete with campanile. The effect is of a miniature city. The earlier buildings were by Theodore F. Link; most of the later buildings are the work of Weiss, Dreyfous, and Seiferth. The Agricultural Center and several minor structures are by Edward F. Neild, who is also the designer of the Caddo Parish Courthouse at Shreveport. After World War II, however, the University departed from the uniform style.

Interesting restorations of plantation houses (Oak Alley in St. James Parish and the Hurst House in New Orleans) are the work of Armstrong and Koch. The same firm built Le Petit Théâtre du Vieux Carré, a modern building which fits so well into the general pattern of the French Quarter that is frequently mistaken for an old one.

Skyscraper building in New Orleans is famous among architects and engineers for the peculiarity of the foundations. Because of the nature of the soil, it is necessary to rest these large buildings on pilings driven far below the surface. Pioneers in this field include Thomas Sully (the Hennen Building and the third St. Charles Hotel) and the Stone brothers (the Maison Blanche Building). Like most American cities, the first skyscrapers of New Orleans disclosed the architect's reluctance to depart from traditional forms.

The foregoing survey of architecture was prepared for the original edition of this *Guide* in 1940. It reflects most admirably the changing practices of the 19th century and later, when tradition was still followed, and gives only one small hint of the coming break with eclecticism. In its last paragraph it mentions only two examples of "the new international style," the Municipal Incinerator in Shreveport and the grain elevators in New Orleans.

Since that time architects have adopted the radical use of steel and glass exploited by Gropius, Le Corbusier, Mies van der Rohe and their followers in high-rise office and apartment buildings. New technology and materials, prefabrication, automatic services, daylight lighting, and self-contained atmosphere, plus easy money from banks, foundations and the United States Government, made the revolution possible.

The classical City Hall of Gallier represented the majesty of the law, but the oblong banks of glass of New Orleans' new City Hall more truly suggest the vast amount of routine work in municipal administration. Huge rectangles such as the International Trade Mart, the Shell office building, and the Louisiana State Bank in Baton Rouge, rise skyward free of their neighbors, the cathedrals of commercial enterprise. The State of Louisiana was in step with the future when it erected its Capitol in 1932. Its office buildings are quadrilaterals or oblongs, such as the State Board of Education Bldg., the State Department of Highways Bldg., and the State Land and Natural Resources Bldg. in Baton Rouge. Colleges have deserted classicism and Mediterranean gables for unadorned structures that disclose their use through their windows. Railroad stations, once monumental, have flattened out, but attempts to transfer their authoritative character to airports have been baffled by the problems of detached depots and endless corridors to runways.

Another adaptation of modern technology is to the sports arena and convention hall. The basic object of the Greek and Roman amphitheater remains—to make the central action visible to great numbers of spectators; the innovation lies in increasing that visibility, intensifying sound and light, and providing shelter under one roof without structural interference. Easy access, regulated temperature, movable banks of seats, space for parking cars are advantages, while the façades reflect the freedom of design available to architects.

The tools that make possible the new office buildings apply also to high-rise apartments, which are devices to overcome the high cost of land. Quadrilateral towers make possible individual porches on each side. Sometimes the tower becomes circular, as in the Fountain of Shreveport, where apartments are sliced like pie. Rows of apartment buildings have plain façades, as in the Fischer Buildings of New Orleans; economies are made by the uniform installation of complete service units. Detached dwellings show little variation from conformity; usually they are 1 or 1½ stories, low ceilinged with garage integrated or attached.

The sprawling plantation houses, with their columnar porches, have become museum pieces. With the rise of tourism their importance as examples of a more opulent period has increased. Today they are restored and treasured. Their best examplar stands on grounds of the State Capitol in Baton Rouge—the Governor's Mansion, opened in 1968, a white house with tall white columns rising to the roof. It is a remainder of an unhurried past, when acquisitiveness was tempered by gracious living.

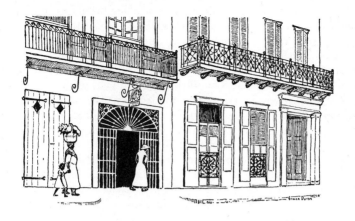

Art

DRAFTSMEN and map makers accompanied all of the early explorers, and an artist named Miguel Garcia is credited with having come to the Colony with Bienville; but the first person known actually to have sketched in Louisiana was A. de Batz, who made crude drawings of Indians as early as 1732. Unsigned illustrations in the chronicle of Le Page du Pratz, who lived at Fort de la Boulaye and later on Bayou St. John and among the Natchez, appear to be in De Batz' style or the work of an equally untrained person; these drawings were published in 1759. Dumont de Montigny, who was in Louisiana between 1719 and 1737, also made crude sketches for his verse history.

During Governor Kerlerec's regime (1753–63), an unknown artist made a crayon portrait of the governor. A contemporary painter portrayed Don Luis de Unzaga, Spain's ruler of the Colony from 1770 to 1777. For more than 20 years, F. Godefroid, whose son was also an artist, painted in New Orleans. His portrait of Don Pedro Rousseau, captain of the brig *Galveztown* of the Spanish Navy, completed in 1780, and that of Michel Fortin, a Master Mason, completed in 1800, hang in the Cabildo. Ferdinand Latizar, reputed to have been a Mexican, is said to have lived in Louisiana between 1790 and 1830. Many of his family portraits still survive. In 1796 Francisco Salazar made a full-length, signed study, now in the St. Louis Cathedral collection, of Don Almonester y Roxas. Two pictures hanging in the Cabildo and credited to a "contemporary French artist," represent Antoine Philippe de

Marigny de Mandeville, *décédé* 1779, and his brother, Pierre, richest man in the Colony, who died in 1800. Louis Godefroy (1810) is said to have painted the portraits, now in the Louisiana State Museum, of Lieutenant Michel Dragon and his daughter, Marianne.

With the American acquisition considerable impetus was given to art. Painters flocked to New Orleans, the center of Creole culture. John Wesley Jarvis (1780–1835), the reckless, roistering, liquor-loving nephew of the founder of Methodism, came from England and in 1816 arrived in New Orleans with Henry Inman as an apprentice. Before reaching the city, Jarvis had established a reputation, having painted John Randolph of Roanoke, Governor De Witt Clinton, and Commodores Perry and McDonough. In his dirty Rue Conti studio, Jarvis, who charged $100 for a head and $150 for a head and hands, turned out six portraits a week by painting the subject and turning the canvas over to Inman, who filled in the background. Jarvis was on friendly terms with the Lafittes, and a painting on wood, said to depict these brothers and attributed to Jarvis, may be seen in the Cabildo. Here also are portraits attributed to him of Mayor Roffignac and Governor Armand Beauvais.

When Old Hickory defeated the British at Chalmette in 1815, Jean François Vallée, a French artist, made a miniature of the general that Andrew Jackson said was his best likeness. A sketch of Jackson, drawn by Thomas Sully "immediately after the battle," would seem to prove that the artist visited New Orleans, a point long disputed.

Ambrose Duval, who portrayed Governor Claiborne, was in New Orleans prior to the 1820's. About this time, Joseph H. Bush, a pupil of Sully, spent his winters painting portraits in New Orleans and Natchez. William West visited New Orleans previous to his trip to England, where he studied under Benjamin West. Twenty years later 40,000 people paid admission to see the latter's *Christ Healing the Sick,* then on exhibition at the St. Louis Cathedral. This picture was also exhibited in Franklin and New Iberia.

Between 1820 and 1830, John Vanderlyn resided in the Creole City. Louis Antoine Collas worked here for a decade, painting many portraits and miniatures. Chester Harding, a self-taught painter from Massachusetts, visited Louisiana about 1820. In 1841 he maintained a studio at Canal and Camp Streets, New Orleans. He was acknowledged as among the leading portrait painters of his time. Alexander Wilson was in Louisiana during this period; and, on January 6, 1821, Jean Jacques Audubon, the great naturalist, accompanied by the artist, Joseph Mason, arrived in New Orleans and established a studio on Ursuline near Chartres, to which he soon attracted a few pupils. In this city, Audubon met an Italian artist who introduced him to a theater manager, a half-crazed painter of birds, and Vanderlyn, Wilson, Inman and Jarvis.

Education

LIBRARY, LOUISIANA STATE UNIVERSITY, BATON ROUGE

INTERIOR NEW LAW LIBRARY, LOUISIANA STATE UNIVERSITY

Information Services, LSU

CLASSICAL FACADE, LAW BUILDING, LOUISIANA STATE UNIVERSITY

EAST ENTRANCE, LAW CENTER, LOUISIANA STATE UNIVERSITY

Information Services, LSU

Information Services, LSU

LIFE SCIENCES BUILDING, LOUISIANA STATE UNIVERSITY

SAMUEL H. LOCKETT HALL, LOUISIANA STATE UNIVERSITY

Information Services, LSU

TULANE CAMPUS AND RICHARDSON MEMORIAL BUILDING

University Relations, Tulane

BUTLER HOUSE,
MODERN DORMITORY
FOR WOMEN, TULANE

A CORNER OF THE
NEW HOWARD-TILTON
LIBRARY AT TULANE

University Relations, Tulane

Centenary College, Shreveport

GEODESIC DOME FOR PHYSICAL EDUCATION CENTER,
CENTENARY COLLEGE

STUDENT LOUNGE, NICHOLLS STATE COLLEGE, THIBODAUX

Nicholls State Information Office

Northwestern State University

LARGEST CLASSROOM BUILDING IN STATE, NORTHWESTERN
STATE UNIVERSITY, NATCHITOCHES

NORTHEAST LOUISIANA UNIVERSITY AT MONROE
Roger Kelley Photo, Monroe Chamber of Commerce

Architect's Model, Northwestern State University
TEACHER EDUCATION CENTER, NORTHWESTERN STATE UNIVERSITY, NATCHITOCHES

HISTORIC ACADEMY OF THE SACRED HEART, GRAND COTEAU
Louisiana Tourist Development Commission

Jarvis, seeing in Audubon a possible rival, promised to give him some background work, a promise he later overlooked.

Audubon remained in New Orleans until June. He then went to St. Francisville, but returned in October and rented a house on Dauphine Street, where he brought his family in December 1821. Audubon retained the friendship of Inman, Wilson, and Vanderlyn. While in New York, in 1823, Audubon posed for the body of Vanderlyn's painting of General Jackson. In his journal Audubon wrote: "Prince Canino (Charles Lucien Bonaparte) engaged me to superintend his drawings intended for publication (for *American Ornithology*), but my terms being much dearer than Alexander Wilson asked, I was asked to discontinue the work."

It is probable that the Italian whom Audubon met in New Orleans was Signor Fogliardi, scenic designer of the St. Philip Theater. This artist opened the first art academy in New Orleans, with good results according to the standards of the classical school. Beltrami, a visitor to the city in 1822, described Fogliardi's own decorations as "superb." As early as 1830, Antonio Mondelli, a pupil of Perego of Milan, was designing scenes for Caldwell's American Theater.

A portrait painter named Elijah Metcalf, represented in the Cabildo, lived on Magazine Street just above Common in 1822; and in the latter 1820's Matthew Harris Jouett, a pupil of Gilbert Stuart, painted in New Orleans and visited Natchez and other towns along the river. He made a portrait of Lafayette on his visit to Louisiana (1824–25). Jean Joseph Vaudechamps, who painted General Plauché as early as 1820, remained in New Orleans long enough to transfer to canvas the likenesses of several of the Marignys, Forstalls, De Lesseps, and other Orleanians. Jules Lion painted and made lithographs between 1830 and 1845. His engravings of early prominent citizens have historical value. An unusually interesting pastel by Lion is a portrait of a white gentleman clasping hands with what is obviously his mulatto son.

George Catlin, the great portrayer of Indians, had a studio at 78 Chartres Street in 1835. A painting, signed by Catlin and said to be of Marie Laveau, the voodoo queen, is extant. Both the signature and the identity of the sitter, however, have been questioned. In this connection it is amusing to note that at least four different portraits, which do not in the least resemble each other, have been claimed as likenesses of Marie; and it has become something of a joke in New Orleans that the owner of any unidentified portrait of a woman of color with her head wrapped in a tignon will almost invariably put forth a similar claim.

Dominique Canova came to paint murals in the old St. Louis Hotel. He taught in the city between 1838 and 1869 and decorated the church of the bishopric and the walls of the Washington Avenue home of James Robb, later the Baptist Bible Institute.

James H. Beard painted portraits here in the late thirties. His

Master Bain, which depicts a scion of the Bain family (from which the West Feliciana town of Bains gets its name) wearing a torn straw hat, was probably inspired by Sully's famous *Boy With a Torn Straw Hat.*

George Cook founded the first art society in New Orleans in 1840. Thomas Trevor Fowler worked in New Orleans in 1840–42. He painted the portraits of President Harrison and Henry Clay which now hang in the City Hall. In 1843 Theodore Sidney Moise painted at Customhouse and Royal Streets. In 1844, together with Jacques Amans, he won a $1,000 prize awarded by the Municipal Government for the best equestrian painting of Andrew Jackson. Amans also did a portrait of the philanthropist, *Margaret* (*see New Orleans*). A. D. Rinck had a studio in the Upper Pontalba Building, and Garbeille, a sculptor and caricaturist, made statues for the Cathedral and a series of caricatures of local personages for *La Revue louisianaise.* In 1845 G. D. Coulon, painter of portraits and Negro studies, was already well known.

Art collecting began in New Orleans in 1844 when the National Art Gallery of Paintings, which existed until the War between the States, was organized. In 1847 the Duke of Tuscany's collection of old masters—Rubens, Raphaël, Van Dyck, and others—was shipped to New Orleans from Italy with the intention of founding a permanent art gallery. The venture was unsuccessful, but all of the pictures were sold to wealthy Louisianians. Years later, in 1892, the Creole Art Gallery offered a religious painting which it claimed was a part of this 1847 exhibition. A catalogue description reads: "This painting has had a romantic career; Ougarratti and Cagnolatti stole it from Don Carlos J. Masoni, Consul of Tuscany; the thieves were prosecuted and died in our city jail. The Pirate Lafitte and his lieutenant, Juan Barrillas, sold it to a Spanish Jew by the name of Pablo Francisco Fernendez, and it was at last found in the hands of Cagnolatti's mistress, Celeste, a quadroon." This picture, with its remarkably checkered career, was listed as *"The Ascension of Angels Visit Mary,* by A. Carracci."

In the late forties Alfred Boisseau of Paris was in Louisiana. Among his many paintings are *The Creole, The Negro Barber,* and the *March of the Indians in Louisiana.*

According to the *Crescent,* March 14, 1849, Hiram Powers' *Slave* was then being displayed at the State House, while adjoining the hall where it was shown, Mr. Kellogg, who was engaged in painting *The Greek Girl,* had an exhibition of his pictures. *The Circassian,* an engraving by Calamatta of Paris, was also on exhibit. Upon the first occupation of Baton Rouge during the War between the States, Powers' statue of Washington was taken by General Butler from the old Capitol and removed to Washington.

A. G. Powers (1851) made a full-length study of General Zachary Taylor, and portraits of Judah P. Benjamin and of Placide Canonge, director of the French Opera. George P. A. Healy (1813–94) worked at 127 Canal Street in 1852 and painted the Cabildo picture of Major General Thomas. Healy was a portrait painter of international repute; his subjects included Webster, Lincoln, Grant, and Louis Philippe. In 1860 he was assisted by his brother Thomas, who also painted in Natchez. John Wood Dodge was in the city at this time, and gave an exhibition of miniatures and portraits; also here was Gaston de Pontalba, the Baroness' son, a painter, draftsman, carver, and musician. William H. Baker lived at 123 Canal Street in 1855, and during this same year, F. Haug, said to have been "an artist of merit," designed very rich "different" murals for the New Orleans Savings Institute, at Canal and Baronne Streets. Medallions of famous persons, including Washington, De Soto, Morse, Bismarck, Napoleon, Newton, Edmund Burke, and others, formed the frieze, and genre subjects adorned the ceiling. Randolph Lux also did miniatures on porcelain in the 1860's; all that remains of his work in New Orleans are a few portraits delicately painted on tall coffee cups. Edward Arnold painted portraits and boat studies. Ernest Ciceri, designer of the French Opera murals in 1859, taught classes in the city. Francisco Bernard came to the city at the invitation of a group of planters and remained to paint many portraits, still lifes, and landscapes. The sale of the James Robb Collection in 1859 brought about a more widespread distribution of art works throughout the State. The collection included items once in the possession of Joseph Bonaparte.

The war-ravaged sixties and the destructive policies of the carpetbag regime were discouraging to all professions; yet even thus handicapped, painters continued to work in New Orleans. Enoch Wood Perry (1831–1915) executed portraits of John Slidell and President Jefferson Davis. George William Sullivan, a native of Ireland, painted portraits and studies of market types in the manner of Murillo. E. D. B. Fabrino Julio studied under Bonnat in France and worked in New Orleans during these turbulent days; in 1871 he completed in St. Louis his canvas depicting the *Last Meeting of Lee and Jackson,* which Mark Twain mentions having seen on one of his down-river trips. It is now in the Louisiana State Museum. Richard Clague, born in New Orleans in 1821, produced Louisiana landscapes that have become well-known. Samuel Walker, many of whose small representations of Negro types and portraits are found throughout Louisiana, sold his work for trifling sums. Benjamin Franklin Reinhardt painted here throughout the sixties and was elected to the National Academy of Design in 1871.

Erasme Humbrecht came to New Orleans in 1872 to work on murals in the St. Louis Cathedral, and he also decorated the walls of the St. Peter and Paul Church. Victor Pierson, painter of hunting and other outdoor scenes, and Paul Poincy, a native Orleanian, collaborated in 1872 in painting a huge oil canvas of the *Volunteer Firemen's Parade.* Organization members paid to have their likenesses inserted in this "mug-book." Leon Pomerade made the reproductions of old masterpieces on the walls of St. Patrick's Church; and in 1876 Leon Fremaux published a book entitled *New Orleans Characters.* Alexander Alaux (b. 1851 France) came to Louisiana at the age of six. He studied under Ciceri and Bernard, and painted uninterruptedly until his death in 1932. A large panorama of *De Soto's Discovery of the Mississippi,* designed for the Mississippi State Capitol, was completed with the assistance of his daughters, Marie and Louise.

In 1873 Degas, the great French impressionist, visited his uncle and two younger brothers, all of whom worked at the Cotton Exchange in New Orleans. Degas painted his relatives during office hours, and the picture, *Le Bureau de Coton a Nouvelle Orléans,* is now in the museum at Pau. *The Woman With the Chinese Vase* is also said to have been painted while Degas was in New Orleans.

The second art association in New Orleans was the Art Union founded in 1880 by Charles Wellington Boyle, later curator of the Delgado Museum. During this period Andres Molinary was holding well-attended classes at his Carondelet Street studio. His wife, Marie Seebold Molinary, was also an artist. William H. Buck was a popular painter during the latter nineteenth century. August Norieri, a painter of marine subjects, depicted the steamboats *Robert E. Lee* and *Natchez,* and left paintings of Camp Street and the Old Spanish Fort Hotel. Lafcadio Hearn did wood-block caricatures for the *Item* in 1881.

The Southern Art Union dissolved in 1883, possibly because some of the ladies wanted to inject "art embroidery" into its exhibitions. The Southern Artists' League, founded in 1885, was reorganized a few weeks later under the name of The Artists' Association and brought down interesting shows from the North. One of the most ardent workers in a campaign to consolidate the city's art groups was Bror Anders Wikstrom, a Scandinavian, who designed carnival parades and produced both land and seascapes in and around New Orleans. Edward Livingston and Marshall J. Smith were also active in promoting organized art. Achille Peretti worked on portraits and bird studies and designed the murals after Raphaël in the St. John the Baptist Church. J. L. Viavant depicted the flight of ducks over the marshes and other wildlife subjects. A. G. Heaton made a portrait of Winnie Davis, the daughter of Jefferson Davis. George Inness and William Keith were both in New Orleans in the eighties. In 1882 Joseph Pennell came to illustrate some of Cable's stories, and, in 1886, William Hamilton Gibson made drawings for Charles Dudley Warner's magazine articles on New Orleans and the

Cotton Exposition. Another illustrator, Harry Fenn, came to illustrate in color Maurice Thompson's *My Winter Garden*.

In 1883 William Woodward came to teach art at Tulane University; his brother Ellsworth followed. Together they founded the School of Art at Newcomb College, and strongly influenced art in Louisiana and the South. A volume of *French Quarter Etchings* by William Woodward, based on his color studies of 40 years earlier was published in 1938. Ellsworth Woodward was president of the Art Association of New Orleans, the Isaac Delgado Museum of Art, and the Southern States Art League.

At the turn of the century, Alexander J. Drysdale, son of a Christ Church rector, had a studio in the Board of Trade Building. He operated a veritable one-man factory that turned out innumerable copies of his sketches of Louisiana lowlands—misty blue and green landscapes seemingly seen through soft rainfall. It is said that Drysdale lined up his boards, canvases or paper, and painted in series of skies, then in like manner filled in the greens and other colors.

John Pemberton, a native of New Orleans, designed the figures over the door of the Louisiana Building on Gravier Street in New Orleans, and made the sketches of Negroes now in the Round Table Club. Patrick M. Westfeldt was an excellent amateur water colorist.

Catherine A. Carl, who did most of her painting abroad, was a native of New Orleans. She spent many years in the Orient and painted a number of portraits of the Empress Dowager Tse Hsi of China. Percival Leonard Rosseau, born in Pointe Coupée Parish, won prizes at the Paris Salon in the early 1900's.

In 1905 the Artists' Association and the Arts and Exhibition Club, founded by the Woodward brothers in the late nineteenth century, merged into the Art Association of New Orleans. Funds were donated to the city by Isaac Delgado, a sugar broker, for the erection of an art museum. It was completed in 1911 and placed under the supervision of the Art Association. The Delgado today houses loan and gift collections as well as contemporary exhibitions.

The demolition of the old St. Louis Hotel was indirectly instrumental in bringing a revival of art interest to New Orleans. Protests against the destruction of the hotel started a movement to preserve the French Quarter and to make it an art center. Among the organizations that grew out of this movement were Le Petit Théâtre du Vieux Carré, Le Petit Salon, and the Arts and Crafts Club.

Alberta Kinsey, who came from Fizzleville, Ohio, and several other artists, including Brice Sewell and Belle Lawrason, wanted to study life drawing; accordingly, a group was organized with Harry Nolan as instructor. From this the art colony expanded and went rapidly ahead.

In 1921 a group of artists led by Gertrude Roberts Smith of Newcomb College, Lydia Brown, a portrait painter, Nina Harper, painter of the Vieux Carré, and others, formed the Artists' Guild to hold exhibitions and sales for three months in the old Mortgage Office building, Royal and Conti Streets. Here, Clarence Millet of Hahnville, St. Charles Parish, held his first one-man show, and sold enough pictures to go north and study. The Guild disbanded to allow the Arts and Crafts Club to be formed in May, 1921. Several art partons, including Sarah E. Henderson, Mrs. Martha Gasquet Westfeldt, and Mrs. William Mason Smith, lent their aid to the art movement. The club developed in 1926 into the New Orleans Art School.

Among the artists who have visited or lived and worked in Louisiana in the present century, many distinguished names are found. Between 1914 and 1922, Luis Graner painted Louisiana scenes. Robert W. Grafton and L. O. Griffith painted a series of New Orleans studies, now to be seen at the St. Charles Hotel. Globe-trotting George O. "Pop" Hart came annually to Louisiana, where he produced some of his most interesting paintings and caricatures.

Elizabeth Telling, pencil-portrait artist, exhibited in the Arts and Crafts Gallery. Several water colors of Vieux Carré subjects give evidence of the sojourns of Anne Goththwaite in New Orleans. Helen M. Turner of the National Academy of Design painted the Little Theater's portrait of Mrs. Oscar Nixon. Wayman Adams, nationally known portrait painter, made the study of Grace King now at the Delgado, and painted Mayor Martin Behrman for the City Hall in 1926. Ronald Hargrave produced many fine colored etchings while in New Orleans. Gerry Peirce was once an instructor in the New Orleans Art School. Will Stevens has been connected with Newcomb College. Knute Heldner, painter and woodcarver, lived for some time in New Orleans.

William P. Spratling formerly taught in Tulane University and the Arts and Crafts classes. A book of his caricatures of local celebrities (*Sherwood Anderson and Other Famous Creoles*, New Orleans, 1926), drawn at a time when the French Quarter was a second Greenwich Village, was arranged by William Faulkner. Spratling did the illustrations for *Old Plantation Houses in Louisiana* (1926), the text of which was written by Natalie Scott. Leslie Powell taught water color at Tulane and the New Orleans Art School and executed panels for the S. J. Peters High School. Baroness Lucienne de St. Mart, miniature painter, had a studio for several years in the lower Pontalba Building, where she was constantly being pestered by tourists and house hunters who thought she was the Baroness de Pontalba who erected the apartments in 1848. Harry Nolan founded the New Orleans Art League with Gideon T. Stanton, former State Director of the Federal Art Project.

Charles W. Bein, an outstanding water-colorist, was for some time director of the New Orleans Art School. Daniel W. Whitney, former portrait and life teacher of the New Orleans Art School, conducted classes for the WPA. Charles Reinike was associated with an Academy of Art at 630 Toulouse Street.

Charles Woodward Hutson, writer, teacher, and Confederate veteran, began painting at an advanced age. At 85, he was awarded the Benjamin Prize for his *Banks of the Boguefalaya,* and he continued to paint until a short time before his death in 1936. His daughter, Ethel Hutson, also an artist, became connected with the Delgado Museum and the Southern States Art League. Frank Schneider made many copies and restorations for the Cabildo. Nell Pomeroy O'Brien, a student of William Woodward and Wayman Adams, is represented in the Civil Courts' gallery of Louisiana justices.

Xavier Gonzales was designer of the *Story of Aviation,* murals at the New Orleans Airport. Ella Wood did the murals at the Army Supply Base and in the Louisiana State Museum. Boyd Cruise and Josephine Crawford have exhibited in local galleries and elsewhere. Olive Leonhardt, satirist, published a book of drawings, *New Orleans, Drawn and Quartered* in 1938. E. H. Suydam sketched throughout the State and his illustrations for Lyle Saxon's books are well known. Among the many others who have worked in New Orleans are Douglas Brown, E. B. Baker, Alberta Collier, Leonard Flettrich, Edward Schoenberger, Rita Hovey-King, Myron Lechay, Jeannette Le Bœuf, Clayre Barr, Julius Woeltz, Dr. Marion Souchon, Morris Henry Hobbs, and Robert Mayfield.

New Orleans has long been a favorite subject for photographers. Arnold Genthe's picture book, *Impressions of Old New Orleans* (1926), and the photographs of Eugene Delcroix, John N. Teunisson, Wood Whitesell, Clarence Laughlin, and Rudolph Hertzberg are particularly noteworthy.

Important early monuments were designed and executed outside of New Orleans. Adolphe Bouchard worked at 97 Rampart Street in the fifties. Achille Perelli made bust studies, including one of himself which is now in the Cabildo. For the Cotton Exposition (1884) a firm of New Orleans stonecutters carved a representation of Lot's wife out of a ten-foot block of salt from the mines at Petit Anse (Avery Island). In 1889 a Parisian sculptor, Joseph Domenget, had a studio at 146 Chartres Street and Romeo Celli, an Italian sculptor, lived for many years in the French Quarter. Albert Rieker designed the heads of Beauregard, Claiborne, La Salle, Livingston, and Zachary Taylor for the State Capitol's base window pediments. Angela Gregory designed decorative figures for the New Orleans Criminal Courts Building and the State Capitol's window heads of Benjamin, Gayarré, Gottschalk, Jefferson, Touro, and White. Juanita Gonzales designed the heads of

Governor Nicholls and General Dick Taylor for the same building. Enrique Alferez, a Mexican, executed designs for the Charity Hospital Medical Center and the State Capitol. He also completed a fountain at the New Orleans Airport.

The Delgado Museum at City Park and the Louisiana State Museum in the Cabildo and Presbytère have the largest public exhibits. Annually, in conjunction with the Spring Fiesta, an open-air artists' bazaar is held in the alleys surrounding the Cathedral, and the Louisiana artists are well represented in traveling shows and exhibitions in the North and East.

From New Orleans as a center the early painters made trips up and down the river, enjoying the hospitality of the great plantations, and painting family portraits. Audubon was associated with the Louisiana countryside. In the manor houses of the Felicianas, where in the 1820's both he and his wife taught school, he completed many of the drawings for his *Birds of America*. In 1823 Audubon, his son Victor, and the Pennsylvania artist, John Steen, made a portrait-painting tour in Louisiana and Mississippi. Portraits in oil were $50, miniatures $30.

As late as the sixties, the traveling artist was a familiar figure. The following notice, which appeared in the *Tri-Weekly Advocate* of Baton Rouge in 1867, is typical: "Attention is called to the card of J. W. Petty. Most perfect and life-like pictures are produced by this gentleman and as his stay in this city is limited, all those who are desirous of getting their handsome countenances counterfeited to the life, had best not let the grass grow under their feet."

Many of the family portraits to be seen in the old plantation houses were painted outside of the State. Most of the Sully portraits were executed in Philadelphia. Not a few portraits were painted abroad, especially in Paris, where many of the Creoles were educated. In this group a particularly interesting one is that of Emmanuel Prudhomme at Bermuda Plantation, in which the subject, having been the first man in this section to raise cotton on a large scale, is depicted proudly holding a cotton boll.

More than one rich planter had a private museum. An amusing story is told of Nicholas Noel Destréhan, who lived in great luxury on his estate at Harvey, Louisiana. Regularly on Sunday afternoons he took his three little daughters to his private gallery to instruct them in the beauties of sculpture; but always they were preceded by a slave who carefully draped each figure in a mother-hubbard so that only head, hands, and feet were visible. Such instances of extraordinary modesty persist. It is related that a citizen of Shreveport, newly rich on oil, brought back from Europe nude statues for his lawn. Presently they were up for the whole town to see, but dressed in breechcloths made by his wife.

In recent years the large towns have been developing their own art colonies; and the development of regionalism in Louisiana art today accounts for the new attitude being shown by the State officials toward commissioning local artists for important work in the State. In 1932, when the new Louisiana State Capitol was constructed during the governorship of Huey P. Long, the execution of the important architectural decorations of the building was assigned to such sculptors as Lee Lawrie, Weinman, Ellerhusen, and Lorado Taft, and the painters Jules Guerin and Louis J. Borgo—men who had never lived in the State. This led to criticism by native artists.

Since then most of the important new buildings of the State have been decorated by Louisiana artists. Conrad Albrizio executed murals for the State Office Building in Baton Rouge, the State Exhibits Building in Shreveport, and the De Ridder Post Office. Duncan Ferguson was employed on the State Office Building, the Agriculture Center of Louisiana State University, the post office building at Leesville, the Charity Hospital at Pineville, and the Louisiana Polytechnic Institute at Ruston.

The Teche country holds an enviable place in Louisiana art. It is a lure to many far and wide. Joseph Jefferson, famous Rip Van Winkle of yesteryear, painted at his Jefferson Island home, and declared he would rather paint than act. Weeks Hall of The Shadows at New Iberia, became an artist of distinction. James Gebert, Ines De Blanc, and Jack Kahn were also New Iberians. Paul Froelich of Philadelphia, winner of the 1924 Benjamin Prize, worked there.

George Isvolsky spent much time painting on Grand Isle. At Lafayette, Emily Huger and Harriet Joor taught art in the Southwestern Institute. The illustrator George B. Petty, was born in Abbeville. A. J. Angman, a Swedish artist, who formerly painted in New Orleans, later moved his studio to Lake Charles.

There were artists in the Cane River Country as early at the eighteenth century. In 1760 Michel Dégoût, a "Master sculptor of Paris," who resided at Natchitoches, murdered M'sieu' Crête with a sculptor's chisel. Perhaps the first sculptor in Louisiana, Dégoût was executed in the Place d'Armes, New Orleans, February 1, 1766. In 1921 the Natchitoches Art Colony was established by Gladys Breazeale and Irma Sompayrac. It functioned as a summer school and vacation resort for artists until 1937.

Pottery is perhaps the oldest craft in Louisiana. Evidences of the ceramic art of prehistoric Indian tribes have been unearthed from time to time in various parts of the State. Present-day Indians, however, are proficient in basketry rather than pottery, using reeds, cane, strips of native wood, pine straw, and *latanier* (palmetto). The Koasati of Allen Parish and the Chitimacha, near Charenton, are skilled in basketry. The palmetto is used by natives all over the State in making hats, baskets, and fans. Corn shucks are frequently woven into rugs and chair seats.

Fine embroideries and lace-making were brought over by the Ursulines in 1727, and have been continued by other religious orders as well. In the nineteenth century Attakapa cottonade was a popular cotton cloth of indigo interwoven with white. In the Teche country "Cajun homespun" is still made on hand looms used by eighteenth-century weavers.

Lucien Marçon made wax figures at St. Ann Street between Bourbon and Royal in 1858. In the last half of the nineteenth century, convents and private schools offered courses in "wax work." Francisco Vargas of New Orleans won first prize for his modeling in wax at the New Orleans Cotton Centennial in 1884, and at the Louisiana Exposition in St. Louis in 1904. His daughter, Mrs. Maria Maftio, specialized in figurines of New Orleans street characters.

In the late eighties china was manufactured in New Orleans by the Hernandez brothers, who came from Sèvres. In 1887 the ceramic department of Newcomb College was founded. Especially noteworthy was the work of Joseph Meyer. Among those who worked in the Newcomb Pottery were Paul E. Cox, Kenneth Smith, Henrietta Bailey, Sadie Irvine, and Anna Frances Simpson. Other potters of distinction included Mrs. Bentley Nicholson, Majorie Callender, Martha Gasquet Westfeldt of New Orleans, and John and Lois Mahier, who formed the Forest Studios in Baton Rouge.

Excellent work has been accomplished by the Newcomb metalcraft students trained by Mary Butler. Louise Jordan Hemenway of Alexandria, Rosalie Roos Wiener (formerly of Opelousas), Juanita Mauras, Miriam Levy, and Lawrence Schernecker, all of New Orleans, made jewelry and metal objects. Elizabeth Black Carmer (Mrs. Carl) formerly taught metalcraft at the New Orleans Art School. Among those who have worked in leather are Lota L. Troy, Eunice Baccich, and Sally Holt.

Wood craftsmanship has come down from the dugouts of the Indians and the pirogues of the earlier settlers—hand-hewn from solid tree trunks. At a later date many of the slaves became skilled craftsmen, as the woodwork of old plantation houses erected by slave labor indicate. Two carved chickens which have been entered in the Index of American Design are said to have been the work of a slave of the pirate Jean Lafitte. In the first half of the nineteenth century Pierre Joseph Landry of Iberville Parish made wood carvings of allegorical figures. His *Cycle of Life* and a head of himself, as well as several other pieces, are in the Cabildo. Also there is a large wooden figure of a Negro slave pounding simples in a drug mortar. One of the most interesting exhibits, however, is the 9½-foot clock designed by Valsin B. Marmillion of St. James Parish and built by slave labor in 1833. A figure of a Negro boy with a hammer, made of lead and weighing 80 pounds, strikes the bell at intervals of an hour.

Seignouret, Mallard, and Siebrecht were famous furniture designers and cabinet makers in New Orleans. Seignouret chairs, similar to the fiddleback, are very rare today. Mallard's bedroom suites, ornate center and *duchesse* dressing tables are still popular. Napoleon III parlor sets by Siebrecht are neat and graceful.

Throughout the State many fine wood carvers work in conjunction with cabinet makers. The reproductions of antiques made in New Orleans are famous. In Kolin, a little town near Alexandria, the late Matt Vlasek, a Bohemian, executed designs for church carvings, and made excellent life-size models of birds and animals. At Libuse, nearby, William Pospisil, another Bohemian, conducted his trade; some of his work may be seen in St. James Episcopal Church at Alexandria.

The Cabildo has an interesting pair of wooden angels, which formerly hung from the ceiling of the Catholic church in Opelousas, and a carved cypress Madonna and child made in 1872. The churches throughout the State have always furnished an outlet for the decorative instincts of both professional and amateur; particularly worthy of note is an altar made of *bagasse* and shells in the Church of St. Michael at Convent.

Cast and wrought ironwork in Louisiana forms one of the most popular means of ornamentation. Many of the balconies in the French Quarter of New Orleans date from the late eighteenth and early nineteenth centuries (*see Architecture*). In general, the wrought iron can be distinguished by its simpler design; the more ornate oak and grapevine motifs are cast iron. Many of the door knockers and foot scrapers are wrought iron, and in the courtyards and cemeteries there are numerous pieces of cast-iron furniture. There is even an iron tomb in one of the New Orleans cemeteries. In many sections there can still be seen hitching posts of cast iron, either a horse's head or a more elaborate figure of a Negro jockey. In the Cabildo is a pine knot flare holder of wrought iron. This device was used on the levees to signal steamboats and as a means of lighting during the loading or unloading of cargo at night. Here also is a wrought-iron collar with three bells attached, used to subdue an unruly or runaway slave.

Every plantation boasted a large cast-iron bell to call the Negroes in from the field and to announce unusual events. It was the custom to cast silver dollars in the molten iron so that the finished product might have a more pleasing ring. At the Cabildo is the bell from Bernard de Marigny's Fontainebleau Plantation, cast in 1825. The Cabildo is also the custodian of a perique tobacco cutter of about 1850, a remarkable specimen of plantation craftsmanship. The blade is steel; the handle is bone inlaid with brass and elaborately picked out with French fired-enamel beads, which were part of the hereditary collections of such beads common in Louisiana. Drawings of this, as well as of many other examples of Louisiana crafts, were made by the Art Project of the WPA for inclusion in the Index of American Design.

In the pine-covered sections of the Florida Parishes, particularly in St. Tammany, the natives make ornaments by dipping flowers, fruits, vegetables, pine cones, and other articles in molten rosin at the turpentine stills. Objects thus dipped take on a glossy texture and are preserved indefinitely. In the swamp sections cypress knees are sawed off the trees, hollowed, and made into hanging flower pots by boring holes in them. Knees, with a few more holes, when mounted on base boards, serve as bird houses.

Jay Remy Broussard has been director of the State of Louisiana Art Commission since 1947. His headquarters are in the Old Capitol, Baton Rouge, where art exhibits are also held. He has been associated with the New Orleans Art Association and the Fine Arts faculty of Louisiana State University and has been a juror of selection and award for many of the major regional and national art exhibitions, including the Lowe Gallery awards.

Tom Cavanagh has been associate professor of fine arts at Louisiana State University since 1957. His paintings are in the collections at Isaac Delgado Museum of Art, the Nelson Gallery in Kansas City, the Kansas State College of Manhattan, the Joslyn Gallery, and elsewhere.

Arthur C. Morgan, sculptor of Shreveport, created the bronze figure of Edward D. White, Chief Justice of the United States, for the U. S. Capitol in Washington, the Earl K. Long monument in Winnfield, and the Henry Miller Shreve monument on the River Parkway in Shreveport. He was born on Riverton Plantation in Ascension Parish, was director of the Art Department at Centenary College 1928–33, and director of the Southwestern Institute of Art since 1933. Morgan's work is also to be seen at the U. S. Postoffice and Court House at Alexandria, the Terrebonne Parish Courthouse in Houma, the Civic Theater in Shreveport and the First Federal Savings & Loan Assn. building in Shreveport.

Gladys B. Morgan (Mrs. Arthur C.) did a notable series of water colors for Louisiana Magazine in 1961. She organized the Art Colony of New Iberia in June, 1964. Also active in Shreveport is Joseph Travis Stevens, illuminator and engrosser.

Miss Lyn Emery of New Orleans has won distinction as a sculptor of liturgical themes. Her work includes the following examples in New Orleans: statues, fonts and stations of the Cross, in St. James Major Church, the Church of St. Catherine of Siena, Grace Episcopal Church, Holy Cross High School, and the Mossy Home. She has contributed a sculptured fountain and monument to the Civic Center.

Ida Kohlmeyer (Mrs. Hugh), a native of New Orleans, who has been instructor of drawing and painting at Newcomb College, has been represented in many galleries and exhibits.

Mrs. Caroline Durieux, painter and lithographer, born in New Orleans, has had her work included in the Fifty Prints of the Year and Fifty Books of the Year, and is represented in painting collections of the New York Public Library and the Bibliotheque Nationale of Paris. She was at one time State Director of the Louisiana Art Project and illustrated the *New Orleans City Guide* produced by the Federal Writers Project in 1937. According to *Who's Who in Art* Mrs. Durieux developed "electron printing" from radioactive drawing in collaboration with Dr. Harry Wheeler, and developed the Clichés-Verre Techniques in collaboration with Dr. Christman, emeritus professor of Fine Arts at Louisiana State University.

Janice R. Sachse, who was born in New Orleans and lives in Baton Rouge, has been the recipient of a number of awards that included purchase of her paintings. She has exhibited frequently in New Orleans and Baton Rouge, at the Louisiana Art Commission, the Isaac Delgado Museum of Art, and galleries in St. Louis, Memphis, Monroe.

Paul Arthur Dufour, member of the art faculty of Louisiana State University in Baton Rouge, has won distinction for his accomplishments in liturgical art. His stained glass may be viewed at the Capital Bank & Trust Co. in Baton Rouge, and at the Caldwell Bank & Trust Co. in Columbia, La. He has won recognition from the Louisiana State University Council on Research, the Louisiana Art Commission, the Currier Gallery and Yale University.

Among artists living in New Orleans are Jacques van Aalten, a painter who was born in Belgium; J. L. Steg, professor of art at Tulane University; Pat Tringio, painter and head of the Painting and Drawing Division at Tulane; and W. Joseph Fulton, museum director, who is represented in collections at Isaac Delgado Museum of Art and Louisiana State Museum. James Rogers Lamantia, a collector and architect who lives in New Orleans, was a winner of the Prix de Rome. James Bernard Byrnes is director of the Delgado Museum.

Jean Seidenberg, who has been active as sculptor, designer, painter, and photographer, lives in New Orleans. Her mosaic mural is in the Motel de Ville, and sculpture is in the Simon-Diaz Clinic, the James Derham Junior High School, the Oil & Gas Bldg., and International House, all in New Orleans; also at Philips Area Junior High School, Union Bethel Church and the Lakewood Country Club, Algiers.

Literature

THE chronicles of the Spanish *conquistadores* in the first half of the 16th century and the accounts of the French colonization under La Salle a century later comprise the earliest literature concerned with Louisiana. After the founding of New Orleans in 1718 an indigenous literature began to grow, but it was not until the establishment of a printing press in the Colony in 1764 that local original writings began to appear. These first efforts disclosed that Louisiana's culture, like that of most colonial states, was an imposed European culture. Most of the Colonists had been born in Europe, and their children were sent there to be educated. Thus the culture of Louisiana bore the imprint of France and Spain; and during the late 18th and early 19th centuries its literature either followed the neo-classic ideal, or viewed the Indians in the forest through the highly colored glass of French romanticism.

As late as 1850 most of the literature of the State was written in French, though English had made great progress since the Louisiana Purchase in 1803. The Civil War was to witness the crystallization of the Creole tradition and the succession of English as the literary language. After the war the English-speaking peoples, under the leadership of George W. Cable and Grace King, discovered Creole local color, and from that time on the Creoles have been fighting a losing battle to preserve French as a literary medium. Outside of these traditions were the writers from other sections of the United States who visited Louisiana during the last half of the century. These men were influenced by the State and have contributed to its literature; perhaps the most important was Lefcadio Hearn, whose Mediterranean blood gave him an affinity with Louisiana's Latin culture.

In 1542 Alvar Nuñez Cabeza de Vaca published in Spain his account of the ill-fated Narvaez expedition of 1528, and in 1557 a Portuguese Gentleman of Elvas published his *True Relation,* an account of De Soto's discovery of the Mississipppi. These were followed by *La Florida del Ynca* (1605), a narrative of great charm by a Peruvian, Garcilaso de la Vega, who combined fact and chivalric romance to color the account given him by one of De Soto's men. Grace King's *De Soto and His Men in the Land of Florida* (1898) is based on Garcilaso's romantic tale. Chief among the French chroniclers were Father Hennepin, Henri Joutel, and Henri Tonti, at different times connected with La Salle's expeditions. André Pénicaut, who came to Iberville in 1699 and remained until 1722, wrote *Annals of Louisiana,* and Father Paul Du Ru, who arrived at the same time, kept a day by day account in his *Journal.* Father Charlevoix, a Jesuit priest, describes a journey made to Louisiana shortly after 1720, and Bénard de La Harpe tells of explorations through the Red River country and Texas from 1718 to 1723. Diron D'Artaguette's *Journal* (1722–23) is well known. Le Page du Pratz, Captain Jean Bossu, and Dumont de Montigny, in works published in the mid-eighteenth century, give valuable information about the customs of the Indians and the natural history of Louisiana. Madeleine Hachard, one of the Ursuline nuns who came to New Orleans in 1727, wrote letters to her father in Rouen about her work in the city. The letters of Marie Tranchepain, the Mother Superior of the convent, have been preserved.

Bienville's letters are noteworthy, as are the accounts sent to him by his lieutenants, D'Artaguette and Maurepas. Dumont de Montigny, who came to Louisiana in 1719, wrote a prose *Mémoire* and a history in verse. The latter, which remained in manuscript until 1931, consists of four lays, and treats with considerable humor and satire "everything that happened in Louisiana from 1716 to 1741." A general history of Louisiana was written by Guy Soniat du Fossat, a Frenchman who came to New Orleans in 1751. His history, not published until 1903, covers the period from the foundation of the Colony to the year 1791. There was no other history written until 1827 when François-Xavier Martin's *History of Louisiana from the Earliest Period* was published in New Orleans. Although written in English, this two-volume work based on the early documents of the explorers served as the model for the later histories written in French. Charles Gayarré, in 1830, published his *Essai historique sur la Louisiane,* and 30 years later followed it with a two-volume history, *Histoire de la Louisiane,* in which most of the material was drawn from contemporary documents. Alexandre Barde's *Histoire des comités de vigilance aux Attakapas* (1861) is a well-written account of the activities of the vigilantes in the region about St. Martinville. It is rich in legends and traditions of the Attakapas country and its inhabitants, the Acadians.

Besides these formal historical works much of the drama of early Louisiana history is found in its poetry, plays, and historical novels. In 1777 Boudousquie printed in pamphlet form Julien Poydras' *Epitre à Don Bernard de Galvez* and *Le Dieu et les nayades du Fleuve St. Louis*. In 1779 appeared Poydras' *La Prise du morne du Baton Rouge*. This is a strictly neo-classic poem, with a river god and naiads celebrating Galvez' taking of the English fort at Baton Rouge. Berquin Duvallon, a refugee from Santo Domingo, published several poems between 1802 and 1806. In 1814 Paul Le Blanc de Villeneufve published a drama in Alexandrine verse called *La Fête du Petit-Blé, ou l'héroisme de Poucha-Houmma*, which treats of strange customs among the Indians.

The period of Louisiana history that has always attracted much notice and aroused the patriotism of its people was the conspiracy of a group of French citizens to overthrow Spanish authority in 1768 and the subsequent execution of six leaders of the group. In 1839 Auguste Lussan published *Les Martyrs de la Louisiane,* a tragedy in verse on the subject; and in 1849 Armand Garreau's novel, *Louisiana,* also an account of the tragedy, appeared in Charles Testut's *Veillées louisianaises*. In 1845 appeared Urbain David's epic poem, *Les Anglais à la Louisiane en 1814 et 1815*. In 1849 Testut published serially *St. Denis,* a novel dealing with the Chevalier St. Denis, who in 1714 led an expedition into Mexico. Testut is also the author of *Calisto,* many of the scenes of which are laid in Carrollton. The Choctaw and Chickasaw wars between 1734 and 1738 have been treated imaginatively in a novel, *Soulier Rouge* (the name of a Choctaw chief), which appeared serially in *La Violette* during 1849. In 1850 L. Placide Canonge published the play, *France et Espagne,* which seems to be a dramatization of Garreau's *Louisiana*. Canonge also wrote librettos for several successful operas. In 1852 Charles O. Dugué published a drama, *Mila, ou la mort de la Salle*.

The romanticism which had swept over France and England in the early days of the 19th century soon reached Louisiana. Chateaubriand's novels, *Atala* (1801) and *René* (1803), laid in Louisiana, captured the imagination of the colonists and colored much of the literature that followed. Where Poydras had domiciled a river god and his naiads in the Mississippi, the new writers copied the lush, exotic descriptions of the romantics. The Indian became the noble red man, the living symbol of the natural man, and his life in the forest seemed the approach to the good life. Of this romanticism of Chateaubriand, the Rouquette brothers, Dominique and Adrien, were ardent enthusiasts. Dominique, born at Bayou Lacombe in 1810, expressed his passionate love of Louisiana landscapes in novels and poems. While in Paris in 1839 he published *Meschacébéennes (Mississippians)*, a book of poems dealing with the State. He returned to Louisiana the same year, and in 1856 published another volume of poetry, *Fleurs d'Amérique*. Dominique loved the Choctaw and whenever he speaks of their customs or their bravery he sees them as men in an unspoiled state of nature, surrounded by great pine forests and the waters of his beloved Louisiana lakes. Adrien Rouquette, his brother, born in New Orleans in 1813, published his first book of poems, *Les Savanes, poésies américaines,* in Paris in 1840. He was also a lover of nature, and in middle age, after he had become a missionary to the Choctaw Indians, Adrien published *La Nouvelle Atala,* the story of a young girl who gave herself up to the Spirit of Nature and went to seek peace and happiness among the Indians.

Dr. Alfred Mercier's *Erato,* a book of poetry, appeared in 1840. Tullius St. Ceran was another popular writer of this period. He published *Rien-ou-Moi* in 1837, and in 1840, *Les Louisianaises.* Many of his poems appeared in *L'Abeille* between 1831 and 1836. The versatile Dr. Mercier, who continued to write in French long after English had become the accepted literary medium, presents in *L'Habitation Saint-Ybars* (1881) an impartial picture of the conditions on Louisiana plantations during ante-bellum boom times. Madame Sidonie de la Houssaye, one of the most prolific of the French writers of the post-war period, wrote short stories and novels, using the Acadians as subjects. The best known of her works is *Pouponne et Balthazar* (1888).

The most important among the French newspapers in which literary material was published were *Le Courrier de la Louisiane* and *L'Abeille de la Nouvelle Orléans. Le Courrier,* which ran, except for short periods, from 1807 to 1860, published the work of such men as Alexandre Barde, Adolphe Calonge, and Charles Bléton. *L'Abeille,* the most famous of the French reviews, ran continuously from 1827 to 1923, and published not only much poetry but many local and European novels. Of the later period of French culture, the outstanding publication is *Les Comptes rendus de l'Athénée louisianais,* the official journal of the *Athénée Louisianais,* a literary group founded by Dr. Mercier and devoted to the preservation of the French language in Louisiana. Alcée Fortier (1856–1914) made contributions to the literature of the State in both French and English. His works include *Sept grands auteurs du dix-neuvième siècle* (1890), *Histoire de la littérature française* (1893), *Louisiana Studies* (1894), *Contes louisianais en patois créole* (1900), and a *History of Louisiana* (1904). A contemporary, the foreign-born German scholar, John Hanno Deiler, wrote much on the Germans in Louisiana.

During the first half of the 19th century Louisiana received visits from many distinguished writers from the northern and eastern States. Among these were John James Audubon and Vincent Nolte, a European banker and speculator in cotton, whose journal of his stay in New Orleans was used by Hervey Allen as the source for parts of *Anthony Adverse*. Walt Whitman's short visit to Louisiana in the spring of 1848 is considered by his biographers as an important period of his life. While here he worked for the New Orleans *Crescent* and published in its pages the series of articles on his trip down the Ohio and Mississippi Rivers known as "Excerpts from a Traveller's Notebook." John Erskine has written a romance on Whitman's stay in Louisiana: *The Start of the Road* (1938). Samuel L. Clemens traveled the Mississippi from 1857 to 1861 as a river pilot and spent much time in New Orleans at the end of each trip. His letters reveal his love of the city, and one of his contributions to the New Orleans *Crescent* resulted in his subsequent use of Mark Twain as a pen name. His *Life on the Mississippi* was written after a visit 21 years later.

After the Civil War, George W. Cable, born in New Orleans of New England parents, exploited local color, then fashionable in American fiction. Cable chose Creoles of Louisiana as characters for his novels and short stories. For his pains he incurred the enmity of the people he had thought to honor, discovering that Creoles "never forgave a public mention." His best known works are his collection of short stories, *Old Creole Days* (1879), and the novel, *The Grandissimes* (1879).

Because she disagreed with Cable's interpretation of the Creoles, Grace King began writing on similar themes. Though Anglo-Saxon by birth, she was Creole in sympathy, and her stories contained in *Monsieur Motte* (1888), *Tales of a Time and Place* (1892), and *Balcony Stories* (1892), give a more flattering picture of Creole life.

One of Grace King's best known works was *New Orleans; the Place and the People* (1907). Interesting memoirs of New Orleans include *New Orleans As It Was* (1896) by Henry C. Castellanos and Eliza Ripley's *Social Life in Old New Orleans* (1912).

Women have been unusually active in literary production in the State, and several wrote paper-back novels on a large scale. The most prolific was Eliza Ann Dupuy, who began in the 1850's and produced 38 novels in quick succession (such as *All For Love; or, The Outlaw's Bride* and *The Cancelled Will—Why Did He Marry Her?*); Mrs. Mary Edwards Bryan, who flourished in the 80's, wrote 20 (*The Bayou Bride* and *Three Girls*); and, on a somewhat higher literary level, Jeannette Ritchie Walworth produced 30 (*Forgiven At Last* and *Dead Men's Shoes*). Although residents of Louisiana for a large part of their lives, none of the three was a native of the State.

Later women writers whose work possessed genuine literary merit include Mollie E. Moore Davis (*The Little Chevalier* and *The Queen's*

Garden), Ruth McEnery Stuart (*Solomon Crow's Christmas Pockets and Other Tales* and *The Story of Babette*), and Cecelia Viets Jamison (*Lady Jane* and *Toinette's Philip*), whose children's stories are eagerly read to this day.

Adah Isaacs Menken, who was born near New Orleans was the author of a volume of posthumously published poems: *Infelicia*. Other women poets included Mary Ashley Townsend (Xariffa) and Mrs. Elizabeth Poitevant Nicholson (Pearl Rivers). Elizabeth Bisland Wetmore wrote both poetry and prose. Martha R. Field (Catherine Cole) was a well-known journalist. Her daughter, Flo Field, is the author of the play *A La Creole*. Dorothy Dix lived in New Orleans many years. Helen Pitkin Schertz wrote *An Angel by Brevet,* a novel of voodoo in New Orleans.

Visiting writers to Louisiana have usually made New Orleans their headquarters. Lafcadio Hearn, having steeped himself in the French writers of the later romantic period, was thoroughly Galic in style as well as sympathy. Alone he forms a link between the old and the new cultures in Louisiana. His *Chita* (1889), a fantasy of the destruction of Last Island, a fashionable resort on the Gulf of Mexico, is among his best work done here. In addition, he published *Gombo Zhèbes* (1885), a collection of Creole proverbs. Some of his best translations were done during his stay in New Orleans, notably that of Theophile Gautier's collection of short stories, *One of Cleopatra's Nights* (1882). He later lived in Japan. Leona Queyrouse Barel wrote *The Idyll, My Personal Reminiscences of Lafcadio Hearn* in 1933.

Other visitors included O. Henry, Eugene Field, Joaquin Miller, Frank Stockton, and Winston Churchill of *The Crisis,* all of whom have presented New Orleans and Louisiana to their readers. Thomas Bailey Aldrich reversed the process and went North to write later of boyhood memories of New Orleans in *Story of A Bad Boy*. Brander Matthews, born in New Orleans, became a New York critic.

Among recent and contemporary writers who have touched the State and left their imprint, however brief, in essay and story collections are: John Galsworthy, "The Old Time Place" in *The Inn of Tranquility;* Sherwood Anderson, "A Meeting South" in *Sherwood Anderson's Notebook;* and Joseph Hergesheimer in *Quiet Cities*. Hergesheimer's *Swords and Roses* is also partly of Louisiana origin. Herbert Asbury wrote *The French Quarter*. E. Merton Coulter edited *The Other Half of New Orleans* (1939). Rex Beach and Harris Dickson have used the New Orleans locale in fiction, one concerned with Mardi Gras and the Mafia, the other with early legends and the Battle of New Orleans.

In 1921 the *Double Dealer,* published in New Orleans, struck a new and forceful note. Among its contributors were Sherwood Anderson,

William Faulkner, Ernest Hemingway, Jean Toomer, and Thornton Wilder. Among the New Orleanians associated with the magazine were Julius Friend, Basil Thompson, John McClure, Albert Goldstein, and Lillian Marcus.

The Teche and its inhabitants have been immortalized by Longfellow's *Evangeline.* Cable's *Bonaventure* deals with this section, as does Kate Chopin's *Bayou Folk,* S. A. E. Dorsey's *Panola,* and Robert Olivier's *Pierre of the Teche.* The names Teche and Attakapas are applied to the section of southwest Louisiana settled by the Acadians. Walter Coquille is known for his Bayou Pom Pom stories in Cajun dialect. An earlier writer, James J. McLoughlin, wrote newspaper letters in the patois under the name of Jack Lafaience. *Madame Toussaint's Wedding Day* by Thad St. Martin of Houma, is a story of the Cajun fishermen and trappers along the Louisiana coast.

Scholarly works dealing with French speech in Louisiana include Jay K. Ditchy's *Les Acadiens louisianais et leur parler* and William A. Read's *Louisiana French.* Dudley Le Blanc is the author of *The True Story of the Acadians.*

The Lafitte Country and the Barataria Country are interchangeable terms for the section of the State lying south of New Orleans, where the pirates had their headquarters in the first decades of the nineteenth century. Not less than 20 writers, some native Louisianians, have written novels laid in this section. Among them are Robert W. Chambers' *The Rake and the Hussy,* J. Frank Dobie's *Coronado's Children,* Charles Tenney Jackson's *Captain Sazarac,* and Marie Devereaux's *Lafitte of Louisiana.* Lyle Saxon's *Lafitte the Pirate* is a biographical study.

A plantation in the Natchitoches region was the scene of Harriet Beecher Stowe's *Uncle Tom's Cabin.* It is a disputed point whether or not Mrs. Stowe ever visited this part of the State, but a spot at Chopin is pointed out as the actual site of the cabin. Kate Chopin, short story writer, lived for a time at Cloutierville. She is the author of *Bayou Folk.* Ada Jack Carver wrote stories concerning the Redbones of the region. Lyle Saxon's *Children of Strangers* is a novel dealing with Cane River mulattoes.

E. P. O'Donnell's *Green Margins* portrays the fisherfolk and orange growers of the region below New Orleans. Clara Bush's *The Grinding,* Elma Godchaux's *Stubborn Roots,* and Clelie Huggins' *Point Noir* are all concerned with sugar cane plantations. Stella Perry's *Come Home* is a romance of the Louisiana rice lands. Charles Martin's *Unequal to Song* is a novel of southwest Louisiana. Evans Wall wrote novels with Louisiana settings including *The No-Nation Girl* and *River God.* Dr. Hewitt Leonard Ballowe wrote short stories about the Buras region. E. A. McIlhenny wrote nature studies of Avery Island including *Bird City* and *The Autobiography of an Egret.*

Roark Bradford, Louisianian by residence, who died in 1948, was one of the best interpreters of the plantation Negro. Among his books with a Louisiana setting are *This Side of Jordan, John Henry, Kingdom Coming,* and *Ol' Man Adam an' His Chillun,* which served as the basis for Marc Connelly's play, *The Green Pastures.*

Lyle Saxon also wrote *Father Mississippi, Fabulous New Orleans,* and *Old Louisiana,* and his later books included *Gumbo Ya Ya,* and *The Friends of Joe Gilmore.* He was State Supervisor of the Federal Writers Project. His death in 1946, at 55, was widely mourned.

Robert Emmet Kennedy has written humorous stories of Negro life in East Green, a Negro settlement supposedly located in Gretna. His short stories, *Black Cameos* and his novel, *Red Bean Row* use Negro dialect.

Edward Larocque Tinker of New York contributed generously to Louisiana's literature. His *Lafcadio Hearn's American Days, Les Ecrits de la langue française en Louisiane,* and his tetralogy of New Orleans novels are examples of his versatility.

Hamilton Basso wrote novels dealing with Louisiana: *Relics and Angels, Cinnamon Seed* and *Days Before Lent.* He also wrote *Beauregard, the Great Creole.* Other biographical works by Louisiana writers include Pierce Butler's *Judah P. Benjamin;* Meigs Frosts's *A Marine Tells It to You;* Hermann B. Deutsch's *The Incredible Yanqui,* a biography of Lee Christmas; James Wilkinson's *Wilkinson, Soldier and Pioneer,* and James E. Edmonds' *Fighting Fools.* Deutsch also wrote *The Wedge,* a novel laid in Mexico.

Stanley Clisby Arthur has written *Old New Orleans,* an account of the French quarter, and *Audubon, an Intimate Life of the American Woodsman.* John Smith Kendall is the author of *A History of New Orleans.* Many authors use similar titles. Oliver Evans' *New Orleans* is a book of essays with pictures, and Stuart M. Lynn's *New Orleans* is pictures with explanatory text.

Frans Blom is author of *The Conquest of the Yucatan* and collaborator with Oliver La Farge, who began his successful career in New Orleans, in *Tribes and Temples.* Judge Pierre Crabites has written many volumes on political subjects including *Beneš, Statesman of Central Europe,* and *Unhappy Spain.*

Poets include John McClure, who is also a critic, the epigrammatist Richard Kirk (*A Tallow Dip, Penny Wise*), and John Fineran (*Minority Opinion*). While in New Orleans Carl Carmer wrote *French Town* (1928).

Fannie Heaslip Lea was born in New Orleans and books with local settings are *Jaconetta Stories* (1912) and *Chloe Malone* (1916). Louise Hubert Guyol has written much about New Orleans, especially for children. Beth Brown (Mrs. John Barry) is the author of *For Men*

Only, a story of the restricted district of New Orleans. Willson Whitman wrote *Contradance,* a novel based on the life of John McDonogh.

Gwen Bristow's Plantation Trilogy—*Deep Summer, The Handsome Road* and *This Side of Glory*—deals with the evolution of two plantation families. Mary Barrow Linfield has written *Japonica Grove* and *Day of Victory.* Julia Truett Yenni is the author of *Never Say Goodbye* and *This is Me, Kathie.* Mystery stories by Gwen Bristow and her husband, Bruce Manning, and others by Kenneth T. Knoblock, author also of *A Winter in Mallorca,* have Louisiana settings. Innis Patterson is the author of two detective novels.

Lillian Hellman, playwright, whose *The Children's Hour* and *The Little Foxes* have had wide acclaim, is a native of New Orleans. More recently she wrote *Toys in the Attic.*

Non-fiction includes Mary Mims' *The Awakening Community,* written in collaboration with Georgia Moritz, and *France d'Amérique* by Simone Delery and Gladys Anne Renshaw.

Among other publications by Louisiana authors are: *Chien Nègre* by Nemours Henry Nunez; *One was Valiant* by Doris Kent LeBlanc; *Between the Devil* by Murrel Edmunds, and *Why Babies?* by Rachel V. Campbell.

In 1931 John E. Uhler created a local sensation with his novel *Cane Juice,* which concerned student life in the Louisiana State University. Huey P. Long's *Every Man a King* (1933) and *My First Days in the White House* (1935) started many controversies. Hilda Phelps Hammond wrote *Let Freedom Ring* (1936), an attack on Long. Both novelists and biographers have found Long a subject for analysis and tragedy.

In 1939 two books that received wide critical acclaim came out of Baton Rouge: *Night Rider* by Robert Penn Warren and *Pale Horse, Pale Rider* by Katherine Anne Porter.

Negro literature prior to the 1860's was confined to educated freedmen. The slaves told animal stories and sang patois songs, much of which became a part of the written literature of Louisiana through the efforts of such white writers as Alfred Mercier, Alcée Fortier, Charles Testut, George W. Cable, Lafcadio Hearn, Mrs. Emilie Lejeune, and others.

The writings of Free Negroes, which began to be published with the founding of *L'Album littéraire, Journal des jeunes gens* (1843), the first review by Negroes in the State, was not the voice of a downtrodden group striving for freedom, but rather that of a cultured society concerned with the personal verities of life. *Les Cenelles,* a collection of love songs, was the first anthology of Negro verse in America. It appeared in 1845 and was dedicated *Au beau sexe louisianais.* Seventeen poets contributed, including Armand Lanusse, Joanni Questy, Camille Thierry, Pierre Dalcour, and Victor Séjour. Dalcour, Thierry, and Séjour later went to France where they achieved literary distinction. Twenty-one of Séjour's plays were presented in Paris.

The second phase of Negro literature in Louisiana opens with the founding in 1862 in New Orleans of *L'Union*, a newspaper of the free colored group. By this date a marked change in social status had taken place, and the pages of *L'Union*, later the *Tribune de la Nouvelle Orléans*, carried the voice of the socially awakened Negro. Paul Trévigne served as editor on both papers; Adolph Duhart was a leading contributor to the *Tribune*. With the failure of the *Tribune* a few years later, able Negro writers took up the defense of their race in the columns of P. B. S. Pinchbeck's newspaper, the New Orleans *Louisianian* (1870–81) and its successor, the New Orleans *Crusader* (1890–97).

Madame Louisa R. Lamotte was born in New Orleans but spent her youth in France. She became directress of the *Collège de jeunes filles d'Abbeville*, [France], which position she held for 40 years. She was the author of *Recueil de questions orates posées au examens du brevet de capacité pendant les années 1897 et 1880*.

The late Alice Ruth Moore, born in New Orleans, was among the first Louisiana Negro writers of the modern literary period. She married Paul Laurence Dunbar, the Negro poet, and her first volume was *The Goodness of St. Rocque, and Other Stories*.

Rodolphe L. Desdunes published in 1911 *Nos hommes et notre histoire*, a short history of the free people of color of Louisiana and their descendants. Charles Barthelemy Rousseve is the author of *The Negro in Louisiana* (1937).

Louisiana and New Orleans continued to be favorite topics of the State's authors after World War II, both in fiction and descriptive writings. The Louisiana State University Press continued to give a hearing to scholarly studies of political and economic conditions in the South and to cast new light on personalities and issues of the Confederate period.

The *Southern Review* has filled an important place in presenting original work and literary criticism. Its first issue, in July, 1935, contained contributions by Aldous Huxley, Ford Madox Ford, Richard Aldington, John Gould Fletcher, Herbert Agar, Jesse Stuart, and John Peale Bishop. Robert Penn Warren, one of its founders, former member of LSU faculty, has continued to augment his remarkable output of poetry, fiction, literary and social criticism, and in 1970 added the National Award for Literature to his string of 13 awards since 1936, including Pulitzer prizes for both poetry and fiction. His books *All the King's Men, Segregation, The Inner Conflict in the South*, and *Who Speaks for the Negro?* were closely related to events. His newest work is *Audubon, A Vision*.

T. Harry Williams has built a solid career as a historian and biographer of Civil War and later American times since he joined Louisiana State University in 1941. From *Lincoln and the Radicals* he progressed to *Lincoln and His Generals;* 20 years later he wrote *McClellan, Sherman and Grant.* He has written *P. T. G. Beauregard, Napoleon in Gray; Romance and Realism in Southern Politics; America at War, Every Man a King.* He edited Lincoln's speeches, the *Military Memoirs of a Confederate, E. P. Alexander;* the *Diary of President Hayes,* and wrote *Hayes of the 23rd.* He was director of the Civil War Centennial Assn.

In 1969 he published *Huey Long, A Biography,* which won the unusual distinction of getting both the Pulitzer Prize and the National Book Award.

Tennessee Williams is not a Louisianian but once lived in New Orleans and gave so much publicity to it in *A Street Car Named Desire* that a car of that line is now in a New Orleans museum. He is Mississippi-born and has the South in his mouth, as was demonstrated in *27 Wagonsfull of Cotton.*

Hamilton Basso added to his creative work with *The Light Infantry Ball, Sun in Capricorn,* and *The View from Pompey's Head* before his death. Roark Bradford's *The Green Roller* was published in 1949, after his death.

In fiction Truman Capote, who was born in New Orleans, has become known for virtuosity and style. His *The Glass Harp* became a play; he wrote *Breakfast at Tiffany's, Other Voices Other Rooms,* and published collections of short stories. In 1966 he produced a journalistic tour de force, *Cold Blood,* a meticulous report of the behavior of two murderers who made him their confidante before going to execution. It became a sensational best-seller and provided Capote with means to become a New York host on a large scale.

Frances Parkinson Keyes, who lived in Beauregard's house in the Vieux Carré, often employed Louisiana settings for her novels. These included *Crescent Carnival, Dinner at Antoine's, Steamboat Gothic,* based on the house San Francisco at Garyville, and *The River Road.* She wrote the text for *All This is Louisiana,* photos by Elenore Morgen. When she died she left funds to care for the Beauregard House.

James Kern Feibleman, a native of New Orleans, is a scholar with experience in business and broadcasting, who has been chairman of the Department of Philosophy at Tulane University and author of many books of philosophy and social import, including recently *The Foundations of Empiricism,* and *Mankind Behaving; Human Needs and Material Culture.* He is the husband of Shirley Ann Grau and the father of Peter S. Feibleman, both novelists.

Shirley Ann Grau won the Pulitzer Prize for fiction in 1965 for

The Keepers of the House. She began publishing in 1955 with *The Black Prince and Other Stories,* followed by *The Hard Blue Sky* and *The House in Coliseum Street.* Her story "Hunter's Home" appeared in *The Best Short Stories of 1958.*

Peter S. Feibleman has written *The Daughters of Necessity* and *Strangers and Graves, Four Short Novels,* and a play, *Tiger, Tiger, Burning Bright,* which was produced on Broadway.

Arna Bontemps, born in Alexandria, writes prose and poetry and has made the Negro his special study. Since publishing his first book, *Black Thunder,* in 1936, he has been a prolific writer, issuing among others a biography, *Frederick Douglass; The Story of the Negro, Famous Negro Athletes, A Book of Negro Folklore, 100 Years of Negro Freedom, American Negro Poetry,* and recently *Anyplace But Here.*

Ernest Gaines, born in Louisiana and now living in San Francisco is the author of *Bloodline* (short stories); *Of Love and Dust* and *Catherine Carmier.* In 1958 he won the Wallace Stegner Creative Writing Fellowship at Stanford.

A prolific writer on southern themes is Harnett Kane, who was born in New Orleans. He has written novels and historical and descriptive books. Among the latter are *The Bayous of Louisiana, Deep Delta Country, Natchez on the Mississippi, The Ursulines, Nuns of Adventure,* and *Place du Tivoli, a History of Lee Circle.* In 1966 he published *Young Mark Twain and the Mississippi.*

Hodding Carter, who has won the Pulitzer Prize for editorial writing, and is editor of the *Louisiana Almanac,* also writes about Southern and Louisiana subjects, as in *Gold Coast Country, Lower Mississippi, Robert E. Lee and the Road of Honor, The South Strikes Back, Southern Legacy,* and *John Law Wasn't So Wrong.* New Orleans and Louisiana are favorite topics of John Churchill Chase, who writes with a touch of humor in *Frenchmen, Desire, Good Children, and Other Streets of New Orleans,* and has written *Louisiana Purchase, America's Best Buy, The New Orleans Story,* and *Musee Conti, New Orleans' Historic Wax Museum.*

Charles L. Bufour, whose *The Night the War Was Lost* appeared in 1960, has also written about New Orleans; his other books include *Highlights of a Century of Service on Southern Waters, The Mexican War,* and *Gentle Tiger; the Life of Roberdeau Wheat.*

A New Orleans novelist with a score of novels to her credit is Sallie Lee Bell, who wrote many of her stories in the 1950's and more recently has published *The Hidden Treasure, The Shattered Wall,* and *Love That Lingers.* Arthemise Goertz is the author of *Give Us Our Dreams, A Dream of Fuji,* and a number of other novels.

Charles East won the Henry H. Bellaman award for a book of short stories, *Where the Music Was,* in 1965. He is a native of Mississippi and now editor of the Louisiana State University Press. His stories have been published in *Mademoiselle, Yale Review, Virginia Quarterly Review,* and *Antioch Review.*

John William Corrington was born in Tennessee and grew up in Louisiana. He is professor of Literature at Loyola University in New Orleans and author of *The Upper Hand, And Wait for the Night,* and *The Lonesome Traveler and Other Stories.* In 1961 he won the Charioteer Poetry Award for a book of poems, *Where We Are.*

Percy Walker, who has lived in Louisiana for more than 20 years, won the 1962 National Book Award for fiction with *The Moviegoer.* Alexander Federoff, a native of Louisiana, lives in California and writes novels, plays and movie scripts, including *This Side of the Angels* and *Falling Through the Night.*

Robert Tallant (1909–1957), wrote frequently on New Orleans themes. His fifteen books included *Mardi Gras, Lafitte and the Battle of New Orleans, Voodoo in New Orleans, Evangeline and the Acadians,* and three novels about Mrs. Candy, beginning with *Mrs. Candy and Saturday Night.*

William Jay Smith, poet, who wrote *Typewriter Town* in 1960, is consultant in American letters to the Library of Congress.

A great deal of original writing and commentary on historical, literary, and political subjects and current affairs, is being provided by a group of scholarly magazines, most of them published quarterly. They include *Southern Review,* published at the University in Baton Rouge; *Louisiana History,* organ of the Louisiana Historical Assn. of Baton Rouge; *Acadiana Profile,* a bi-monthly magazine for bi-lingual Louisiana, published in Lafayette; *Louisiana Heritage,* of Alexandria; *Louisiana Studies* of Louisiana Studies Institute of Northwestern State University, Natchitoches; the *LSU Journal of Sociology,* of the Dept. of Rural Sociology, Louisiana State University, Baton Rouge; *New Orleans Review* of Loyola University, a quarterly, and *New Orleans Magazine,* a monthly.

Music and the Origins of Jazz

SOMETIMES it goes on all day. The song may change, but the rhythm, which is an integral part of any sustained activity on the part of the Negro, is always present. Throughout the State, in the cities as well as in the rural districts, the system is the same. The pace is set by a leader, and the actual work punctuates the replies of the workers:

Git it a-goin', Emma T.

It is the voice of the "top hand" among the field crew, chopping cotton on a Louisiana plantation. There is a moment's quiet, then a throaty contralto begins in a plaintively minor key:

Po' lil' Jesus.

Then all the hands join in harmony, the hoes falling rhythmically at the end of the line:

Hail Lawd!

a pause, and the voice of the leader again:

They bound him with a haltuh.

Hoes poised, the field crew answer:

Hail Lawd!

Why do they sing like that?

It rest 'um, suh. It rest 'um, and it undo knots in the muscle.

Work songs, however, comprise only a relatively small portion of Negro folk music. There are, in addition, the so-called "sinful songs" and, of course, the spirituals. Each type has its genesis in the need of a special activity or occasion, and there is a close intrinsic and musical relationship between each genre.

The spiritual is perhaps the most characteristic, and is present wherever there are Negroes—in the "sanctified" church, at home, at work, and even during the few hours before bedtime that the tired worker spends "settin' on the gal'ry." The spiritual is characterized by its syncopated phrasing, its minor key, its relatively close intervals, and, above all, its repetition of both music and words.

It is the rhythmic repetition of word and sound that gives the spiritual its hypnotic effect. In times of high religious fervor, the singer frequently reaches a state near auto-hypnosis, the refrain producing an effect somewhat like that of the African witch doctor's incantation. A good example is the "shout" spiritual *If I Had My Way I'd Tear the Buildin' Down*:

> If I had my way oh Lawdy, Lawdy,
> If I had my way oh Lawdy, Lawdy,
> If I had my way oh Lawdy, Lawdy,
> I'd tear the buildin' down.

Some of the best known spirituals among Louisiana Negroes are: *There's a Man Goin' Round Takin' Names, He Never Said a Mumblin' Word, Jesus Goin' to Make Up My Dyin' Bed, Gospel Train, Whilst the Blood Runnin' Warm in Your Veins,* and *I Got Religion and I Can't Sit Down.* Published collections of Louisiana spirituals include R. Emmet Kennedy's *Mellows* and *More Mellows,* and E. A. McIlhenny's *Befo' de War Spirituals.*

A highly religious Negro limits his music to work songs and spirituals; other music is called "sinful" or "worldly" music. To this large class belong the "blues," the "honky-tonk tunes," the reels, the "hollers," and the ballads that the Negro has adapted for his own use. Here is a good example of a blues:

> Say you know you didn't want me
> The day you lay across ma bed
>
> You was drinkin' bad liquor
> An' talkin' out of your head
>
> But I rather see a coffin comin' to ma back do',
> Than to heah you sayin' you don't want me no mo'.

Spiritual or blues, reel or work song, there is an unmistakable sameness about the Negro folk song. The idiom rarely changes, though the tempo, of course, may vary greatly; and the performer feels at liberty to *ad lib* words, music, and phrasing.

Occasionally one encounters a real Negro minstrel—one whose only apparent livelihood is the money given him on the street by those who stop to listen. These singers frequently make up their own songs, though the bulk of their material is usually inherited from other sources. Such a one is Huddie Ledbetter, born in Mooringsport, Louisiana, in 1885, who had a book devoted to him by John and Alan Lomax, called *Negro Folks Songs as Sung by Lead Belly* (1936).

There are three folk traditions in Louisiana which, linguistically and culturally, are derived from the French—the Creole, the Acadian (Cajun), and the Gumbo—and each group has developed its own music.

The Negro slaves of the Creoles had their difficulties with French, much as they did with English, and the dialect their misunderstanding ears made of French is called "Gumbo." Of course, these Negroes sang; in the kitchen, in the nursery, in the stable, song went with them. And it was natural that the white owners should, on occasion, speak as their slaves did. Such talk was amusing, and often more pointed than their own formal French; it was also necessary to make the slaves understand orders. Thrown into close contact, it is not surprising that the Creole found much to delight him in the little songs his slaves invented.

In contrast to other Negro folk music, the Gumbo songs show a noticeable lack of religious themes, preferring instead such wordly and sophisticated topics as the amorous adventures of well-known local characters, satirical sketches of familiar personages, or pure love lyrics, usually of a plaintive nature.

"Dansé, Calinda, din, sin, boum, BOUM!" was a popular refrain for Gumbo songs and used with many different verses.

Today among the Creoles and the descendants of their slaves, Gumbo songs are still to be heard. Among the best known are *Po' Piti Mamzel Zizi,* a love song of heartbreak and tenderness, and the taunt song, *Toucoutou.* The latter was composed by Joseph Beaumont, a free man of color, and based on an actual court case in New Orleans just before the War between the States.

A number of such songs are to be found in *Bayou Ballads,* arranged by Mina Monroe and Kurt Schindler (Shirmer, New York, 1921), and in *Creole Songs from New Orleans,* arranged by Clara G. Peterson (Grunewald, New Orleans, 1902).

The Cajun, with his accordion, is still a pleasant figure in the folk music of the south-central part of the State, especially in the vicinity of Lafayette and St. Martinville. Fiddle, guitar, and *les fers* (steel triangles) usually complete the simple orchestra for the *fais-dodos,* or public dances. *Fais-dodo* is the French equivalent for the English "go to sleep" and is a common enough refrain in lullabies both in France and Canada. Its added meaning, that of a dance, is a French colloquialism among the Acadians. The musicians are themselves referred to as *fais-dodos* and live a life comparable to that of medieval troubadours, traveling about the Cajun settlements, living on the bounty of those who enjoy their music. Usually there are two or three, seldom more than four players in a company.

Not all of the music is dance music. There are "les chansons de guerre," "d'amour," "de mariage," "de joie," and "les chansons rondes," the last named being songs sung for the games which are substituted for dancing during the Lenten season. Musically, the songs are very simple, consisting of 16 measures repeated over and over; frequently they are obviously derivative in nature. In World War I Louisiana Cajun soldiers astonished the peasants of Normandy by breaking into "native" airs on the march. The words, however, are often original with the *fais-dodos*. When they are hungry, they sing of food; when they are in love, they sing of their sweethearts. The words "come with the music."

Allons à Lafayette is a good example of such improvising:

Allons à Lafayette	Let's go to Lafayette
J'ai pou' changer ton nom	I must change your name
On va t'app'ler Madame,	You will be called Madame,
Madame Canaille Comeaux.	Madame Canaille Comeaux.

Another amusing song concerns the particularly vicious mosquitoes of the bayou country, called *maringouins* by the Cajuns:

Les maringouins a tout mangé ma belle,
Et y ont laissé juste les deux gros orteils;
Y les ont pris pou' faire des bouchone d'bouteilles.

Ton papa 'semb'é ein éléphant,
Et ta maman 'semb'é ein automobile,
Ton 'ti fràre 'semb'é ein bullfrog.

The maringouins have eaten up my sweetheart,
They have only left the two big toes;
They took them to make corks for bottles.

You papa looks like an elephant,
And your mama like an automobile,
Your little brother looks like a bullfrog.

Louisiana French Folk Songs by Irène Thérèse Whitfield (Louisiana State University Press, 1939) is the most comprehensive collection of such songs. It also lists phonograph recordings and songs collected by other writers.

One of the most popular forms of musical entertainment in northern Louisiana is community singing. An old custom of the Anglo-Saxons of the uplands, singing conventions have spread to many sections of the State. Usually one of the Evangelical churches, particularly the Baptist, has a hand in organizing these get-togethers, although secular as well as religious songs are sung by the groups. In Vernon, La Salle, Ouachita, Tensas, and Sabine Parishes singing conventions sometimes last for several days and are accompanied by picnics, barbecues, and similar pleasures. Probably the largest of these musical gatherings is the annual convention sponsored by the Shreveport Chamber of Commerce, held on the fourth Saturday and Sunday of each April and attended by as many as 10,000 persons. Loud speakers broadcast special numbers to the audience, and visual music slides are used to enable singers to follow the song leader. Outstanding musicians, trios, and vocal soloists appear at the conventions, and concerts by college bands are frequently given.

The innate musical aptitude of Louisianians is shown by the facility with which songs of purely topical appeal are produced. Many songs, published by the Werlein, Grunewald, and A. E. Blackmar Companies of New Orleans, were written during the War between the States; a few of the titles are J. E. Gleffer's *Grand March of the Southern Confederacy*, H. MacCarthy's *Bonny Blue Flag*, Blackmar's *A Southern Marseillaise*, H. Walther's *Our Country's Call*, and James Pierpont's *We Conquer or Die*. *I Wish I was in Dixie*, adopted as the battle song of the Confederacy, was first published by Werlein after the song had been sung in New Orleans in the fall of 1860. The published version differed somewhat from the original, which is generally conceded to have been a "walk around" song composed by Dan Emmet in 1859 for Bryant's Minstrels. The words of *Maryland, My Maryland* were composed by James Ryder Randall, of Baltimore, on April 26, 1861, at Poydras College, Pointe Coupée Parish.

Other compositions inspired by topical events of various periods were Auguste Davis' *People's Rights Quick Step*, E. A. Langbecker's *Gold Standard March*, Senna Duty Furloa's *16 to 1 March*, and *The Car Driver's Union March Victory*, as played by Professor Frank Fabregas' Great Louisiana Field Artillery Brass and Reed Band. Not in the same category, but none the less interesting, are Louis Blake's *Dr. Tichenor's Antiseptic March* and Regina Morphy Votier's *Louisiana Oyster Commission Waltz*.

Aside from these formal compositions, there are various songs of the ballad type which have their inspiration in events of the day. One striking example is a song made up during the famous Lebœuf murder trial at Franklin in St. Mary Parish—*Sweet Piroguin' Mama, Don't You Angle-Iron Me*—the title of which suggests the manner in which the murder of Mr. Lebœuf was accomplished.

Formal music has a rich tradition in Louisiana. After the coming of the first theatrical troop to the State in 1791, operatic arias and musical programs, romantic or comic, multiplied as theater after theater rose in New Orleans. At almost every performance given in the early French theaters, a short opera was presented along with the dramatic fare; sometimes the program consisted of a one-act comedy followed by a three-act opera. The enthusiastic reception accorded musicians and singers soon attracted the world's best artists. Mlle. Julie Calvé appeared at the Orléans Theater in 1837. Ole Bull and the Frenchman,

Vieuxtemps, noted violinists of the day, competed before partisan American and Creole audiences in the 1840's. Jenny Lind, under the management of P. T. Barnum, sang before overflow crowds during an extended engagement in 1851. Seats for her first concert were sold at auction, the first going to a Canal Street hatter for $240. Public adoration was such that an enterprising merchant sold Jenny Lind Shirts and Jenny Lind Cravats.

Although New Orleans was the musical center of the State, interest was not lacking in the parishes. The Countess Von Leon, for instance, a German aristocrat who settled in the little town of Minden in the thirties, taught all the children to play the piano. Before the first instrument arrived in town the music-loving lady had lost no time, and childish fingers were already practicing scales and melodies on a keyboard painted on a plank.

In the middle of the nineteenth century, New Orleans, already recognized as a leading musical center of the country, augmented its musical prestige with the establishment of the French Opera Company, one of the South's greatest contributions to music. The French Opera House, an imposing structure of Italian architecture designed by Gallier, Jr., was erected in 1859 and opened in December of that year with *Guillaume Tell*. Under the direction of Charles Boudousquie, husband of Julie Calvé, opera had a glittering beginning.

During the summer many of the artists vacationed at St. Martinville where they presented operas for the entertainment of the citizens of the "little Paris of America."

Opera, as popular as the drama of that day, differed from it in that more solid works were in demand; the majority of operas presented were the accepted classics of Europe. For many years opera remained almost wholly French in atmosphere and selection; a few German and Italian operas, however, diversified the list. More than a dozen operas had their first American presentation in New Orleans. They included: Meyerbeer's *Les Huguenots,* Gounod's *La Reine de Saba* and *La Tribut de Zamora*, Massenet's *Hérodiade, Werther,* and *Don Quichotte,* Saint-Saën's *Samson and Delilah,* and Lalo's *Le Roi d'Ys.* American debuts of great singers also took place in the city. Adelina Patti, after an apprenticeship tour of the West Indies under the aegis of Louis Moreau Gottschalk, Louisiana's first great musician, made her operatic debut in 1860 at the French Opera. Caterina Marco, born in New Orleans in 1853, made her American debut in New York in 1872 and three years later shared honors with Patti in Moscow. While singing in a concert in New York in 1927, she was acclaimed America's oldest prima donna.

Only the War between the States could curtail to any extent the complete success of opera among music-loving Orleanians and their visitors; and even the black days of Reconstruction did not entirely discourage production, which lasted, though with a somewhat dwindling sparkle, until the destruction of the opera house by fire in 1919.

With the wealth of folk music at their disposal and with a strong European tradition firmly established, Louisiana composers quickly developed a distinctive idiom. Among the early composers, Louis Moreau Gottschalk and Ernest Guiraud, both born in New Orleans, are particularly noteworthy. Of the two, Gottschalk (1829–69) is the best known, not only because of his extensive European and American reputation as a pianist and conductor, but more so because he composed voluminously, employing an idiom adapted from the Negro and Creole music heard in New Orleans when he was a boy. At eight years of age he gave a benefit concert in the city; five years later he went to Paris, where he entered the Conservatory. By the time he was 15 he had already written two of his best known compositions—*Bananier* and *Bamboula*, both descriptive of New Orleans sights and sounds. Considered by many as the greatest concert pianist of his day, he traveled three continents, giving thousands of concerts, many of them before royalty. Gottschalk composed one symphony, one cantata, and two operas which were never performed, but he preferred and built his reputation on his short piano compositions which contained Louisiana themes. His *La Morte, Trémole Étude, Tarantella, Le Banjo, Pasquinade, Radreuse,* and *The Last Hope,* are well known.

Ernest Guiraud (1837–92), who spent his boyhood and early manhood in New Orleans, where he composed his first opera, *Le Roi David,* at the age of 15, gained his reputation in Paris. He won the Prix de Rome, as his father had before him, taught at the Paris Conservatory, and was eventually made a member of the French Academy. He is best known for *Sylvia,* the *Kobold, Carnaval,* and *Piccolino.*

Other early composers who were important in the development of Louisiana music were: Emile Johns, who lived in New Orleans in the 1820's, and won recognition through his *Album louisianais,* a collection of original pieces and the first known volume of Louisiana music; Gregorio Curto, one of the first European musicians to migrate to New Orleans (1830), and a successful teacher of voice and composer of liturgical music; and Theodore von La Hache, organist at various New Orleans churches and composer of many ballads and marches.

During the middle of the nineteenth century New Orleans also produced a number of free Negroes who were accomplished musicians. Several of them were educated in France, to which they eventually returned. Lucien Lambert, pianist and composer, left New Orleans for France and later for Brazil. His brother, Sidney Lambert, also a pianist, was decorated by the King of Portugal. Edmond Dédé, violinist, born in New Orleans, became the director of an orchestra in

Bordeaux. Other Negro musicians included Basile Bares, Samuel Snaer, E. V. McCarthy, and Dennis Auguste. Before the War between the States the Philharmonic Society, an association of free colored people, boasted more than 100 members who were skilled amateur musicians.

After the war music groups and societies disbanded, theaters closed, and even the French Opera Company gave but periodic performances.

In the eighties German singing clubs were very active. In 1888 the United Singers of New Orleans participated with marked success in the twenty-fifth National Saengerfest of the North American Saengerbund at St. Louis. In 1890 the twenty-sixth National Saengerfest was held in New Orleans.

The revival of interest in music at the turn of the century may be attributed to able instructors, some of them born in Louisiana, others from Europe. They included Dr. Giuseppe Ferrata, for many years connected with Newcomb College; Otto Weber, Mark Kaiser, Erneste Gargano, Mme. James Feodor, Florian Schaffter, and Mme. Eugenie Wehrmann-Schaffner.

Lena Little, Sam Franko, and Nathan Franko, all natives of New Orleans, achieved international reputation, the first as a singer, the other two as violinists and conductors. Henry Albert Lang, pianist and composer, was also born in New Orleans.

Since 1900, new vitality and new motifs have been noticeable in the work of Louisiana composers, the result of a direction given music by the adaptation of the folk idiom to more sophisticated expression. Notable among these compositions are *Street Cries* and a composition for organ called *Bayou Song,* by Ferdinand Dunkley; *Danse louisianaise,* by Christian Jordan; *Orchestral Variations on a Louisiana Folk Theme,* by Helen Gunderson; *Songs from Creole Land,* by Henri Wehrmann; and the operetta, *Louisiana,* by Ruth Carlton and Edith McLennan. In addition to these are the works of Dana Suesse of Shreveport, Robert MacGimsey of Alexandria, Katherine Blair of Lake Charles, and Owen Reed of the Louisiana State University School of Music. Ferde Grofe, though not a native, portrayed something of the feeling and beauty of New Orleans in the Mardi Gras section of his *Mississippi Suite,* as did John Beach in a pantomime ballet of the same name, and Charles Cadman in his *Dark Dancers of the Mardi Gras.* Beach's *Orleans Alley* is well known. Houry Gilbert's ballet *Place Congo* was given at the Metropolitan in 1918. Jacques Wolfe composed *Swamp River Suite* and the musical score for Roark Bradford's *John Henry.* Other noteable musicians have been Harry Burk, accordion; Elizabeth Garrett, the blind musician whose anthem, *O Fair New Mexico,* became the official song of that State; James G. Heller, born in New Orleans, composer and critic in Cincinnati; Rose Hicks, of Minden; Claire Coci and Edward Larmann, organists; Adrian Freiche, Albert Kirst, and M. Lubowski, violinists; Genevive Pitot, pianist; Elizabetta M. S. de Pate, first woman symphony conductor in South America, and W. B. Clarke, who for 45 years directed the music department of the Louisiana State School for the Blind.

Other Louisiana singers of note are Edna Thomas, mezzo-soprano, who gained a reputation both in America and Europe for her Negro spirituals, folk songs, and New Orleans street cries; Sidney Raynor, Kitty Carlisle, Rose Dirmann, Marguerite Castellanos Taggart, Bernadine Wolf, and Julian Lafaye, who acted in Hollywood as John Carroll.

JAZZ is generally said to have had its origin in New Orleans around 1900, although the term first gained currency in Chicago. Various elements of Louisiana's musical background went into its composition. The Negro contributed blues—a folk music that found expression in early jazz in such pieces as *Livery Stable Blues, Basin Street Blues,* and *Careless Love.* Strange as it may seem, Negro funerals afforded a favorite occasion for the playing of both blues and "hot" music. On the way to the burial a slow blues, or lament, would be played, while on the return march the band, which usually included such indispensable jazz instruments as the trombone, cornet, clarinet, and drums, would strike up some lively tune of the "hot" variety. From brass band music, especially that played by Carnival bands, came the four-beat time that also influenced jazz. Thus the clarinet chorus of *High Society Blues,* a favorite among swing fans, has its derivation, supposedly, in a piccolo passage of a Sousa march.

It was ragtime, however, that served as the medium for jazz; for it was in improvising this popular music, lending rhythmic emphasis and variety, that "hot" music of the distinctive New Orleans style was born. Its original exponents were the ragtime bands that played at Milneburg, at the races, at house parties, and in wagons on the streets. Among the first of these bands were Jack "Papa" Laine's, Buddy Bolden's, and John Robichaux's—orchestras which included musicians who read as well as improvised music and were capable enough to double in military and brass bands and at formal balls. But jazz was also turned out by "spasm" bands composed of improvising "ear" men. These nondescript bands played in honky-tonks in the red light district, in front of theaters, and on the streets, ballyhooing prize fights and commercial products. One of the earliest was that headed by Emile "Stale Bread" Lacoume, an Exchange Alley newsboy. "Stale Bread," with six or seven other boys bearing such colorful nicknames as "Warm Gravy," "Family Haircut," "Whiskey," and "Seven Colors," beat out rhythm on home-made instruments—a bass fiddle constructed of half a barrel, a soap-box guitar, a cheese-box banjo, and a serving-tray mandolin, to which were added a zither, harmonicas, and an assortment of bells and whistles.

Of humble origin, jazz kept to the environment of its birth and only emerged to a higher plane when Northern talent scouts in 1914 saw commercial possibilities in it. Which of the bands was the first to introduce jazz to Chicago is open to debate. The Original Creole Band, organized by Bill Johnson, started on a series of vaudeville tours as early as 1911. By 1917 at least five—Tom Brown's, George Schilling's, Freddy Keppard's, Manuel Perez's, and the Dixieland Band —had played in Chicago cafes. Of these the Dixieland Band, a 5-piece unit led by Dominick LaRocca (trumpet) and composed of Larry Shields (clarinet), Edwin B. Edwards (trombone), Henry Ragas (piano), and Tony Sbarbaro (drums), was the first to attain prominence. None of the Dixieland musicians could read or write a note of music, but the tantalizing manner in which they improvised *Tiger Rag, Milneburg Joys, Clarinet Marmalade, Sensation Rag,* and other New Orleans classics soon had Chicago dancing to a livelier tempo. In 1916 they went to New York, opening at Reisenweber's, where they attained the popularity that carried them to Europe.

It was in Chicago in 1915 that the word "jazz" (originally spelt "Jass") was first applied to the New Orleans style of music. To encourage the orchestra to play livelier, dancers would exhort the musicians to "jass it up," and in a short time the term was extended to the type of music called for. The word is of uncertain origin. Many improbable explanations have been offered such as: standard French, *jaser* (to gossip); *Jasper* (the name of a dancing slave on a plantation near New Orleans); *Chaz* (Charles) Washington (a Vicksburg drummer). Whatever its origin it had for years been used in the sense of "to enliven," "to get hot." It also had a sexual meaning. In the early nineteen hundreds it was a word that could not be used in the presence of a lady. Several of the New Orleans bands playing in Chicago added it to their names, and it was as the Original Dixieland Jazz Band that LaRocca and his boys scored a hit in New York. As early as 1917 music publishers in New Orleans were calling the new music "jazz"; in that year Williams & Piron designated as such *Brown Skin Who You For?, Mama's Baby Boy, Long, Long Time Before You See My Face Again, Call Me Shine,* and others. At the same time the Original Dixieland Jazz Band was making recordings of *Livery Stable Blues* and other "jazz" pieces.

From Chicago and New York "hot" music spread through the Nation, constantly vitalized by a host of New Orleans jazz artists. Its popularity as a new music craze and the imputation that New Orleans was its birthplace aroused the indignation of certain Orleanians. A *Times-Picayune* editorial of June 20, 1918, "Jass and Jassism," condemned "this particular form of musical vice" and urged that the city "be last to accept the atrocity in polite society, and where it has crept in . . . make it a point of civic honor to suppress it." But though it was disavowed in the city of its birth, "hot" jazz in the best New Orleans tradition continued to pour out of the city, conveyed by such popular bands as the New Orleans Rhythm Kings, King Oliver's (Creole) Jazz Band, the Crescent City Jazzers, and the Creole Jazz Band.

A great number of jazz artists have come from Louisiana. Perhaps the best known is Louis Armstrong, whose trumpet technique and "scat" style of singing have had great influence upon the development of "hot" style. Among the other "hot" men from the State were Henry Allen, Jr., Ray Bauduc, Sidney Bechet, Abbie Brunies, George Brunies, Johnny Dodds, Irving Fazola, George (Pops) Foster, Tommy Ladnier, Nappy Lamare, Wingy Mannone, Paul Mares, Eddie Miller, Jelly Roll Morton, King Olivier, Edward (Kid) Ory, Roy Palmer, Louis Prima, Leon Rappolo, Zutty Singleton, Emil Stein, and Clarence Williams. Singers include Gene Austin, the Boswell Sisters, Jerry Cooper, Dorothy Lamour, and Loretta Lee. Of the 26 musicians chosen by Paul Whiteman for his All-American Swing Band in 1938, three were Louisianians—Armstrong (trumpet), Bauduc (drums), and Miller (tenor saxophone). An album called "New Orleans Memories" was recorded by Jelly Roll Morton.

Today jazz is regarded in New Orleans as the true forerunner of popular musical expression. The improvisors long since have traveled the erratic road to rock and roll and hard rock, and have elaborated the sounds that brought more millions to the Liverpool Beatles than were acquired by men who struck oil. All kinds of pop music may be heard in Bourbon Street (*see Vieux Carré under* NEW ORLEANS) but the true doctrine is enshrined in the Jazz Museum of the New Orleans Jazz Club at the Royal Sonesta Hotel, where fans may hear recordings by the leading musicians and bands of the 20th century.

The Theater

THE first professional theatrical performances in Louisiana were given by a troupe of Santo Domingan refugees in New Orleans in 1791.

Amateur productions, however, date from 1753. In that year, Le-Blanc Villeneufve, an ex-officer in the French army who was employed by his government in work among the Choctaw Indians, heard the story of a tribal father's sacrifice for his son. Villeneufve was so impressed by the dramatic quality of the tale that he cast it into a play, *Le Père indian,* which was presented in the governor's mansion.

The professionals from Santo Domingo were singing actors, menbers of a homeless troupe headed by Louis Tabary. Their earliest performances were held in improvised tents, private homes, rented halls and warehouses; but they soon converted a room on the second floor of a St. Peter Street house into a permanent theater. It was called variously El Coliseo, La Salle de Comédie (1793), and Le Spectacle (1806), and was popularly known as the St. Pierre. Although Louisiana was a Spanish colony at that time, performances were given in French. The actors, most of whom were republicans, frequently insulted the royalist playgoers by singing the *Carmagnole* and *Ça-Ira,* rousing songs of the French Revolution. Disturbances between the players and the audience often occurred, and the playhouse was closed temporarily either for that reason or because the actors were bold enough to compare Governor Carondelet to a suckling pig.

Reopened, the theaters employed amateurs to take the place of certain of the professionals who had moved on. A writer of the time refers to the actors in *The Death of Caesar* as having "repeatedly stabbed the enemy of Roman freedom in the person of an old colonist— an ex-army man resident in this country for fifty years."

Trouble with the authorities continued, and in 1806 censorship was established by an ordinance which required the mayor or a representative to attend all performances.

Two other French playhouses operated in early nineteenth-century New Orleans—the St. Philip (1808) and the Orleans (1813). Performances at these houses usually began about 6:30 in the evening and lasted until midnight. Troupes were small and there was much doubling. In the comedy *We Do What We Can and Not What We Want,* one of the St. Pierre actors, St. Martin, played eight different parts. An evening's program often included an opera, a serious drama, and a comedy, with song and skit specialties sandwiched between the longer numbers. The theaters were open several nights each week, but Sunday's bill seems to have been the best.

The earliest notice of English drama occurs in the newspaper accounts of 1806. In that year a Mr. Rannie gave performances of *The Doctor's Courtship, A New Way to Pay Old Debts,* and *The Unfortunate Gentleman, or The Ghost's Return.* During 1807 and 1808, the French Players treated the English-speaking populace to patriotic tableaux and pantomime, *The Portrait of Washington* and *American Independence, Homage to the Memory of Washington.* But not until 1811 and the arrival of William Duff and his "American Company" did the local English-speaking peoples again hear their native tongue in the theater. Duff arranged with the French players to give two performances a week at the St. Philip Street Theater. Later, Duff moved to the Condé Ballroom and here performed that long-time favorite of the theatergoers of the Atlantic seaboard, *The Two Hunters and the Dairy Maid.* In 1817 an American company under a Mr. Cargill presented "Shakespeare's very justly celebrated, and much admired tragedy of Othello The Moor of Venice."

Two rather unusual events occurred in 1816. A Mr. Turpin opened public baths, including a tank for a water show "planned by Leriche, ex-architect to the king of Westphalia and civil engineer of his theaters." On January 15 of that year, a concert re-enactment of the Battle of New Orleans of the previous January was produced in the Condé Ballroom.

In the fall of 1818 the Orleans Theater, which had burned in 1816, reopened, and French performances were resumed with no English competitors. The second Orleans, which like other early theaters took its name from the street on which it stood, was far superior to any which had preceded it and was one of the first homes of grand opera in America. Above an elevated and commodious parquet, which was almost encircled by *Loges grillés,* rose two tiers of boxes and a gallery. Supper rooms and ballrooms, which formed a part of the same building, connected with the theater proper, and the parquet was often floored over and used for additional dancing space. The Orleans, which existed until 1866, was devoted primarily to opera, companies for which were recruited from Paris. Two grand and two comic operas were presented each week. The other evenings were given over to dramatic performances, usually vaudeville or musical *comedietas.*

A notable event at the Orleans was the performance given in Lafayette's honor in April 1825. Casimir de Lavigne's five-act comedy, *L'École des vieillards,* was presented, Lafayette arriving for the last two acts. After the play, the entire cast sang a song composed for the occasion.

On January 13, 1818, Noah M. Ludlow and his American Theatrical Commonwealth Company, having come to the city by keelboat from Nashville, opened at the St. Philip Street Theater with Tobin's *The Honeymoon* and the farce, *The Hotel, or A Servant with Two Masters.* Circumstances favored their success, for the Orleans had not yet been rebuilt, and they were able to alternate with the French company at the St. Philip, playing Monday, Wednesday, Friday, and Saturday evenings. At the end of the season, the company divided a profit of $3,000 and was praised in the *Louisiana Gazette* (April 25, 1818):

> It is with regret every friend to New Orleans will hear of the departure on next Thursday, of the American players. Their private deportment, while among us, has been so universally correct, that not even the tongue of slander has dared to assail it. Their merit too, as performers, though criticized rather severely by the fastidious few, has always been respectable, and indeed much greater than the support given could reasonably have looked for. The propriety of encouraging a national theatre in this city, is believed to be incontrovertible. The strangers who annually repair hither in such numbers, are often at a loss how to spend an evening rationally. A well conducted stage is always productive of good effects on the manners of a people.

In 1819 Aaron Phillips brought a makeshift company he had organized in New York and engaged the Orleans for its off nights. He was playing with little success when a second English-speaking company arrived in 1820, under the leadership of James H. Caldwell. This company, recruited in England and the East, was superior to Phillips', and it was not long before Caldwell took over Phillips and most of his players and assumed the contract for the Orleans. The most celebrated members of Caldwell's company were Thomas A. Cooper, the foremost American actor of the time, Junius Brutus Booth, who first played his famous Brutus in New Orleans, and who won the admiration of the French population by his interpretation of Racine's *Andromache* and Mrs. Cornelia Burke, Joe Jefferson's mother. In 1821 Mrs. Burke played Blanche of Devon in *The Lady of the Lake,* a melodrama adapted from Scott's poem. Dramatizations of Scott's works were frequently presented by Caldwell, additional evidence of a popularity which Mark Twain was later to call the "Sir Walter disease."

Caldwell settled in New Orleans, and from there dominated the theatrical life of the Mississippi Valley as well as of the city. In 1823 he built the first American playhouse in New Orleans. It was in such a remote part of the city—Camp Street between Gravier and Poydras—that he had to lay sidewalks for his patrons—gunwales of ships, about 2½ feet wide. When the American Theater opened in January 1824, it was lighted with gas, the first building in New Orleans to be so illuminated. For 16 years the best actors in America appeared there as stars, supported by a splendid stock company. Edwin Forrest, then 18, became a member of the company soon after the opening of the theater, Joe Cowell, star of Europe and New York, George Holland, James E. Murdock, Charlotte Cushman, Lola Montez, and many others who achieved national fame were members of Caldwell's stock companies through the years.

The decade between 1830 and 1840 was a flourishing period for the theater in New Orleans. American plays became increasingly popular and the French theaters were still well attended. The following item from the *Daily Picayune,* May 22, 1838, headed "Down-Town Theatres" describes the latter:

There are no less than three French Theatres at present in successful operation below Saint Louis street—the Théâtre d'Orléans, Théâtre Marigny, and Théâtre d'Élèves. We "dropped in" at the latter establishment on Sunday evening, and were much pleased with the manner in which some of the lighter French vaudevilles are brought out. The theatre is at the corner of Champs Élysées and Rue des Grands Hommes, and boasts the attractions of one or two very pretty women and good actresses, besides Mons. Victorin, the best eccentric commedian who has ever appeared upon the boards of a French theatre in this city.

The Théâtre Marigny is also on Champs Élysées, two squares further back, and is intended for the amusement of the colored population, who flock there nightly in great numbers. Many white people also attend this establishment, the best order being observed, and the performances giving general satisfaction. We remained but a few moments in this theatre—another time we shall see and say more.

Davis' Théâtre d'Orléans is too well known to need any notice as to location or the character of the performances.

In 1835 Caldwell built the St. Charles Theater, "the most beautiful theater in America." It had 4,000 seats, 47 boxes, and a mammoth chandelier weighing 4,200 pounds, made up of 250 gas lights and 23,300 cut-glass drops. The greatest stars of the time appeared there; but its glory was short-lived, for in 1842 it was destroyed by fire. Its rival, the New American, built in 1840 on Poydras Street by Noah Ludlow and Sol Smith, bitter competitors of Caldwell, also burned shortly afterwards. On the site of Caldwell's St. Charles Theater, Ludlow and Smith immediately built a second "St. Charles." More famous actors appeared on its stage than on any other in the South: Junius Brutus Booth, his son, Edwin Booth, Joe Jefferson, J. H. McVicker, Charles Keane and his wife, Ellen Tree, Jenny Lind, Charles Macready, Charlotte Cushman, Lotta Crabtree, Fanny Ellsler, the Kembles, Mary Anderson, and many others. Adelina Patti sang there during the Cotton Centennial Exposition in 1885. The second St. Charles was familiarly called Old Drury. When the building burned in 1899, Dr. George K. Pratt, the owner, rebuilt a replica of the old edifice to house the productions of the Orpheum Circuit. When the Orpheum was erected, the Pratt theater was renamed the St. Charles, and housed stock companies, road shows, and motion pictures.

Caldwell took over the rebuilt New American in 1842, and later had a hand in the erection of the Varieties, which opened in 1849 under the management of Tom Placide, the actor. Five years later it, too, burned, and was reopened as the Gaiety, under the management of Dion Boucicault. When it was completely destroyed in 1870, its owners built the Grand Opera House on Canal Street. Lawrence Barrett was for many years its manager, and played there for the first time the classical repertoire which later gained him lasting fame.

In the meantime, in 1859, the French Opera House had been erected in the old quarter of the city. It was a magnificent structure, built for social as well as cultural purposes and, unlike the Canal Street theater, which was devoted to drama, was intended and used almost entirely for operatic presentations.

There were many less important theaters in New Orleans during the latter half of the nineteenth century. The Academy of Music, next door to the St. Charles, opened in 1853 as an amphitheater under the management of Dan Rice, the circus king. In 1842 a German troupe arrived in New Orleans and for a number of months produced farces and one-act numbers in Fulda's Restaurant. Calling their company the German National Theater, in 1843 this group transferred activities to Otto's Restaurant, where they gave more involved German productions directed by Louise Thielemann. But in a brief space of time the company went on the rocks; and the German element lacked a theater until, in 1849, a theatrical company organized in the old City of Lafayette, and Mrs. Thielemann returned to present German dramas, musical comedies, and farces. Another German troupe of the middle fifties, according to press items, "attacked" Schiller and Goethe. During the sixties, the German theaters were doing their best business. An

Italian theater, two small French theaters, and a theater for Negroes also found sufficient popularity to exist and prosper.

Le Théâtre Français opened in 1844 with a drama titled *Diegarias*. Irish farces and other comedies were given in 1865 at the Pelican Theater, of which W. E. Anderton was manager.

From time to time in the old theaters, benefit performances were given for certain actors. The following from the *Daily Picayune,* August 23, 1861, is an advance notice of one of these shows:

The Zouaves at the Old Orleans Theatre:—The artist Zouaves will give a performance on Sunday evening next at the Old Orleans Theatre, for the benefit of Leon, the youngest member of the company, whose personifications of Parisian grisettes are so much admired. For this occasion the prices of admission are reduced, though the bill is attractive enough to render this measure unnecessary. The performance will commence with the vaudeville of "No smoke without a fire," in which Leon will play the part of Suzanna. Then Mr. Gautier will sing the parody of Lucia of Lammermoor; Mr. Frederick will sing the patriotic war cry "Manassas, Louisianians, forward!" Then will come the burlesque, "The fury of love," and the duo, "The companions in arms." The whole will conclude with exercises of bayonet fencing and other portions of the Zouave drill, the vaudeville of "The night bell," and the popular rondeau of the Zouzous. Persons who will not like this bill are certainly hard to please.

In 1899 the Tulane Theater took its place among the city's best; Julia Marlowe, George Arliss, Richard Mansfield, Anna Held, Maude Adams, Sarah Bernhardt, De Wolf Hopper, Minnie Maddern Fiske, Clay Clement, Robert Mantell, Otis Skinner, Guy Bates-Post, Chauncey Olcott, Olga Nethersole, Henrietta Crossman, Mrs. Leslie Carter, Charlotte Walker, Sir Johnston Forbes-Robertson, Louis Mann, Walter Hampden, Fritz Lieber, Margaret Anglin, the Barrymores, and Katharine Cornell appeared there. The Tulane was demolished in February 1937. The Crescent, a sister theater, next to the Tulane, torn down at the same time, presented lesser shows and rounded out its existence with vaudeville bills, motion pictures, and girl shows.

At the beginning of this century, Walter Baldwin, a pioneer in popular-priced stock, introduced it in New Orleans with his Baldwin-Melville Stock Company (the Melville of the firm, his wife, was a sister of Rose Melville, the famous Sis Hopkins). Later the Baldwin Theater (the Dauphine) was erected for the company. At the Grand Opera House, William Farnum and Lester Lonergan were Baldwin's most popular matinee idols. At the Baldwin, Bert Lytell played leads. William Farnum also acted at the Lyric, originally Wenger's Music Hall, a German beer-serving place of amusement. The Lyric ended its days as a Negro road-show theater. The Elysium, built for Lester Lonergan was another popular playhouse. The Baldwin Theater was known as the Bunting, when Emma Bunting's company occupied it just before the first World War. Later, as a burlesque house it was called the Dauphine.

The early stock companies of the Grand Opera, Baldwin, Lyric, and Elysium presented only plays by the best playwrights and dramatizations of leading authors' works. Burlesque shows—Wheel Road Show presentations—were offered at the Greenwald, another early twentieth-century theater. This house was later used by miscellaneous troupes, including the Bunting Company; just prior to World War I, it became a unit of a vaudeville circuit under its later name, the Palace. After a siege of semi-darkness, broken by occasional road and circuit stock companies, the Palace was re-opened in 1936 as a Negro motion-picture house.

During the heyday of the theater in early twentieth-century New Orleans, two other playhouses functioned. Welch's Hippodrome, on the river side of Baronne near Lafayette, was taken over by Lew Rose, who operated it under the name of the Winter Garden as an inexpensive family amusement place. Musical comedies, dramas, and vaudeville were presented. The admission price was 10 cents "all over the house." Rose sometimes gave 10 acts on an evening's bill and boasted to players who registered complaints that their numbers were worth only a penny apiece to him. Amateur night began in New Orleans at the Winter Garden, where the cry of "Get the hook!" reverberated for the first time in the city.

The Schubert, later the Lafayette, built just after the turn of the century, offered the best New York road shows. Early New Orleans suburban picture shows, with stage facilities, booked stock companies that played one-night stands in and out of the city.

Early Louisiana theaters made provisions for colored patrons and had special prices for slaves and servants accompanying their owners. White persons of the wealthier class had their way lighted by slave torch and lantern bearers, and it was often necessary for Negro attendants to carry the ladies' shoes. The bad condition of the streets made barefoot walking more practical. Slaves occupied the upper gallery, or cheapest section, later erroneously known as "the pit." The free people of color had a whole tier, usually the second, allotted to them. In the 1830's, as indicated in the item from the *Picayune* quoted above, a playhouse operated especially for the colored population, but white patrons were also admitted. Around this same time, there was a much discussed and disputed Negro actress appearing in New Orleans, who is variously reputed to have toured the United States before leaving for Paris and whose existence has been vehemently denied. According to Desdunes, who says her name was Virginia Girodeau, she played tragic roles at the Theater of the Renaissance in New Orleans and was a contemporary of Armand Lanusse and Edmund Orso (1830–60). In 1856 an "amazing African giant," a "breath-taking specimen of humanity," 16 feet high, was presented at Campbell's Theater, and "Blind Tom" (Thomas Green Tethune), a grotesque 10-year-old Negro prodigy who had displayed musical talent at the age of two, was exhibited in 1860 at Spalding and Roger's Museum and Amphitheater.

Just after the War between the States, Negro actors and musicians performed at the Orleans Theater in plays and musical programs by Creole Negro composers; these programs included the works of Victor Séjour, Adolphe Duhart, Edmond Dédé, Samuel Snaër, Basile Barès, Florian Hewlett, Eugene Victor Macarty, and Charles Véque. The latter was also a comedian. Such performances were lengthy affairs, usually staged for benefits. In the early twentieth century, a Negro theatrical troupe presented Shakespearean drama in the Negro Pythian Hall. When the Lyric was given over to the Negro population, Negro actors from the North performed here.

New Orleans was the birthplace of several noted theatrical figures. Mark Smith, born here in 1829 while his father, Sol Smith, acted at Caldwell's American, achieved fame as a light comedian in the East and in England. Lucille and Helen Western were both natives of the city. Cora Urquhart Potter and Edward H. Sothern were born here in 1859. The latter, born while his parents were on tour in the city, was educated in England and did not return to New Orleans until he was 19, when he played an important role in a local theater. Sothern appeared in many of his own plays and became recognized as America's leading Shakespearean actor. Mrs. Potter, usually playing in comedies, toured the United States, India, Australia, South America, and England. Minnie Maddern Fiske, celebrated exponent of Ibsen and noted also for other roles such as Tess of the D'Ubervilles and Becky Sharp, was born in New Orleans in 1865. In 1868 Robert Edeson was born in New Orleans while his father was playing a season in stock. Sydney Shields, for many years Walker Whiteside's leading lady, was born in New Orleans in 1888.

Though less brilliant, there was theatrical activity in the State outside New Orleans even in early days. Probably the earliest was at St. Martinville. In the 1790's an influx of aristocratic French *émigrés* made the little bayou town a center of wealth and culture. Cable quotes a contemporary diary which mentions an early performance of the *Barber of Seville*. Later, during the summer months, vacationing opera singers and actors from New Orleans presented opera and drama in a small theater. The New Orleans *Bee* for August 1850 reports on the success "brilliant and way beyond all hope conceived" of a group of artists from the Orleans Theater who, "seeking to benefit during the slack season, formed a society and went bag and baggage to St. Martinville to run the music hall of the locality." Among the noted actors who maintained homes and vacationed in the region was Joseph Jefferson, famed as the world's greatest Rip Van Winkle. On Jefferson Island, named in his honor, he built a home which still stands and which he called Bob Acres after his part in Sheridan's *The Rivals*.

Towns and villages lying along the rivers and bayous were particularly favored by theatrical companies, for after the Ludlow company's successful river trip to New Orleans, others adopted that mode of travel. In 1830, Sol Smith's brother, Lemuel, toured the towns near New Orleans during the summer months with a company which played the following season under Caldwell's management in New Orleans. In many places they performed in empty sheds and warehouses, though by the thirties there were regular playhouses in some of the towns. In 1837 John S. Potter, actor-manager, built a theater in Natchitoches. Potter was the father of the playhouse in the South, building theaters all over Tennessee, Mississippi, and Louisiana. The diary of William S. Tourney throws a bit of light on the theater in Natchitoches 100 years ago: "April 13, 1839. Went to the theatre in Trudeaux Street . . . play, 'Warlock of the Elms,' horribly mutilated; miserable performers." Tourney was probably a more severe critic than the majority of the audience that night, for he made frequent trips to New Orleans, where he saw superior performances.

Shreveport witnessed the first dramatic appearance of Adah Isaacs Menken, born in Milneburg, a suburb of New Orleans, about 1835. In March 1857 she made her debut at J. S. Charles' theater as Pauline in *The Lady of Lyons*. Success followed success as she rapidly won acclaim in both America and Europe. Her sensational private life kept her continually before the public—an austere Victorian world that looked askance at her four or more marriages, her alliances with John Heenan, popular prize fighter of the day, her arrest as a Secessionist, and her scandalizing performance as a scantily clad "Mazeppa," the first woman to attempt the role and the first performer to ride a horse in the scene in which a dummy had always been used.

In 1860 George F. Pike, a prominent citizen of Baton Rouge, was planning to erect a mansion, but when the war intervened, he ran up a large, barn-like structure instead. This served as a hospital during hostilities, and later the upper floor was used as an auditorium for social affairs, political meetings, and theatrical perfomances. In 1899 the material from this building was used in the Elks' Theater. Well-known popular plays were presented there until it burned.

In 1888 Dr. Frank Wallace, with a company of three comedians and banjoists, arrived in Baton Rouge to conduct vaudeville and free tooth extraction tournaments to lure purchasers for his Wild West Bitters. Wallace ran into difficulties with the local dentists but he pacified them with the consoling idea that they would be able to replace the teeth he pulled.

Circuses and other spectacular exhibits were always popular. About one of the earliest of these, which performed in Congo Square in New Orleans, the French-speaking Negroes made up a patois song:

C'est Michié Cayétane
Qui sorti la Havane
Avec so chouals et so macacs!
Li gagnin ein homme qui dancé dans sac;
Li gagnin qui dansé si yé la main;
Li gagnin zaut' à choual qui boi' di vin:
Li gagnin oussi ein zeine zolie mamzelle
Qui monté choual sans bride et sans selle;—
Pou di tou' ça mo pas capabe,—
Mais mo souvien ein qui valé sab'.
Yé n'en oussi tout sort bétail:
Yé pas montré pou' la négrail
Qui ya pou' dochans—dos-brulés
Qui fé tapaze—et pou' birlé
Ces gros mesdames et gros michiés
Qui ménein là tous p'tis yé
    'Oir Michié Cayétane
    Qui vivé la Havane
    Avec so chouals et so macacs.

It is Monsieur Gaëtano
Who comes out from Havana
With his horses and his monkeys!
He has a man who dances in a sack;
He has one who dances on his hands;
He has another who drinks wine on horseback:
He also has a pretty young lady
Who rides a horse without bridle or saddle:
To tell you all about it, I'm not able,—
But I remember one who swallowed a sword.
There are all sorts of animals, too:—
They did not show to nigger-folk
What they showed to the trash—the burnt-backs (poor whites)
Who make so much noise—nor what they had to amuse
All those fine ladies and gentlemen
Who take all their little children along with them
    To see Monsieur Gaëtano
    Who lives in Havana
    With his horses and monkeys.

Barnum writes in his *Recollections:* "The New Orleans papers of March 19, 1838, announced the arrival of the 'Steamer Ceres, Captain Barnum, with a theatrical company.' After a week's performances, we started for the Attakapas country. At Opelousas we exchanged the steamer for sugar and molasses; our company was disbanded, and I started for home." Barnum was not very popular among the parish folk, who much preferred Dan Rice's company or Colonel Ames' New

Orleans Menagerie and Circus, which included such attractions as "Signorita Ella Eugenia, the Fairy Lion Queen."

The period also brought "Grand Balloon Ascensions." The *Creole* of October 14, 1848, printed the following advertisement:

> Miss Emma V....... The Celebrated Aeronaut From Bordeaux.
> Informs the inhabitants of St. Martinsville and the vicinity that she will exhibit one ascension, in a superb Balloon, one hundred feet in length, and three hundred feet in circumference; the balloon is imported from France. She will make her ascension on Thursday next, 19th. October, 1848, at 4 o'clock P.M. from the residence of M. Diogene Bossier.
> Price of admission, 75 cents. Children and servants, 40 cents. Seats prepared for the ladies.

The minstrel show was popular in Louisiana as early as the 1820's and, though classified for some time among extra-theatrical activities, it was soon introduced as a balance to many heavy dramatic bills. Early mention is made of minstrel shows even in the northern part of the State. Performances in Shreveport were especially frequent at Brewer's Hall, Crisp's Gaity, and at the Grand Opera House. New Orleans was the mecca for many troupes and the home of a large number of famous burnt-cork artists. Debuts in the city led to eastern circuit contracts. Performances closing long and honorable careers took place also in Louisiana, where celebrities came to perform as a climax to their fame.

It was in New Orleans in 1849 that John Washington Smith, one of the earliest and best of the black faces, wrote *Old Bob Ridley,* a song added permanently to many minstrel show repertoires. In 1852 Charles H. Duprez, one of the greatest of the early managers, made his debut with Carle, Duprez, and Green's Minstrels. George Washington Dixon, among the first and best known of the impersonators, closed his career, begun in 1827, when he died in New Orleans in 1861. It was Dixon who claimed to be the author of the "Zip Coon" song, a popular bit of traditional minstrelsy based on "Old Corn Meal," a Louisiana Negro whose prototype was introduced into the minstrel show on the New Orleans stage. Jim Johnson (Gallegher), old-time minstrel banjoist, and Ben Cotton, one of minstrelsy's immortals, traveled the Mississippi for years on the showboat *Banjo.* Montgomery and Stone's first appearance was in New Orleans in 1895. Billy Carter, the banjoist, was born in St. Bernard Parish and made his debut in New Orleans. Warren Richards (Richard A. Warren), the tenor with Duprez and Benedict's Minstrels, was born in New Orleans, as were Luke Schoolcraft and John Queen (McQueen), whose coon ditties (*Get Your Habits On, All Alone,* etc.) were very popular in their time. McIntyre and Heath's Minstrels, recruited from various parts of Louisiana, were among the "local boys who made good."

Showboats carrying dramatic, minstrel, and circus companies visited plantations in the interior. Dan Rice made annual trips along the Mississippi and adjacent waterways with his circus, usually playing the river towns. In 1842, on his first trip, he contracted yellow fever and was treated by a physician at Bayou Sara while his troupe performed without him. In 1852 Rice's circus performed only at the plantations along the way, giving afternoon performances daily, as the planters would not permit their slaves to be out at night. Planters often allowed their entire menage to attend the performances; one paid 201 admissions, for himself and his slaves.

In February 1861, the month following Louisiana's secession from the Union, the Baton Rouge *Weekly Gazette and Comet* announced the arrival of " 'the most novel, unique and extraordinary exhibition upon earth,' over which Dan Rice, Esq., presides with his ancient grace, ease and elegance." The account went on to state that "everybody wants to see the performing Rhinoceros, who during his visit to the Crescent City, has been trained to dance the 'secession polka.' Mr. Rice is an enterprising young man. He will stop at Bruley Landing, to bring along with him the people of that vicinity to the Show." Rice was a Union sympathizer during the War between the States, a fact his Southern friends found hard to forget. When he attempted to perform at Shreveport in 1868, public disfavor was so great that his entire company, the band and canvasmen included, refused to work.

The showboat era reached its height between 1870 and 1890. Beginning as little more than flatboats with rude houses, ridge roofs, and a staff floating a flag marked "Theater" as their only proof of identity, the showboats grew in time into "floating palaces." Many of the later boats had names such as the *Cotton Blossom,* the *Daisy Bell,* the *River Maid,* and the *Water Queen. French's Sensation,* which claimed "the only woman pilot" on the Mississippi, in the person of the wife of the captain, created a final spectacular performance in 1900 when it went up in flames at Elmwood Plantation on Red River. The *Golden Rod* was typical in construction. The stage was 40 by 24 feet, the auditorium 40 by 162 feet. At the opposite end from the stage the box office and lobby opened onto a short deck from which the gangplank ran ashore. There were staterooms for women and married couples, back stage or built over the roof; bachelors lived in a towboat which attended the theater craft. The regular tour was to tow up the Mississippi to Hastings, Minnesota, and then to run down the whole length of the river, finishing the season in the bayous and canals of Louisiana. At first, admissions were negligible, and boats would cruise leisurely along the river until a sufficient audience gathered on the bank to warrant their pulling up to shore for a performance. Arrangements grew steadily more formal. The coming of the showboat was announced by messenger many hours ahead. The music of the calliopes heralded the boat's appearance. With bands crashing a march and multicolored flags, the boat pulled up to a landing. Then fields, sugar houses, and kitchens would be deserted as everyone poured out to see the spectacle.

The chief drama on the bill of fare was likely to be *Lena Rivers, East Lynne, St. Elmo,* or *Tempest and Sunshine;* melodrama on the showboats was as popular as on the stage. Musical entertainments were more numerous, but in general the same taste, if a less critical one, was served. Performances were lengthy. Almost everybody but the engineer and pilot took part in the show. Those who did not act served as stage hands and ushers or sold peanuts and candy during the single performance given before the showboat moved on early the next morning. Showboat performances were given on the river at New Orleans as late as 1931, and on the New Basin Canal in 1940.

New Orleans had one of the earliest Little Theaters in the country. In 1891 Madame Rosa Salomon da Ponte, a noted beauty, built and equipped a miniature theater on the spacious grounds of Roselawn, her St. Charles Avenue mansion. She engaged a director and presented plays —usually melodramas—for several years.

Founded in 1916 as the Drawing Room Players, Le Petit Théâtre du Vieux Carré of New Orleans started with one-act performances in private homes and rented halls. In 1930, as part of a concerted movement among French-speaking residents to maintain French culture in New Orleans, Le Petit Théâtre du Reveil Français was established after Le Petit Théâtre du Vieux Carré discontinued producing French plays. The Group Theater, organized in 1934, suspended operation in 1938. It was reorganized in December 1939 under the name of the New Group Theater. The Civic Theater, the Theater Guild, the Algiers Little Theater, the local branch of the National Catholic Theater Conference, and many school and college dramatic clubs became increasingly active.

The Federal Theater, a WPA project, begun in New Orleans in 1936, presented professional performances at the St. Charles Theater until the abolition of the project. The WPA Recreation Center, a separate project, continued to present outdoor pageants, specialty numbers, and one-act marionette shows.

In the decades following 1940, when the foregoing historical sketch was first published, the theater in Louisiana gained a number of advantages. Cities and towns with colleges were assured of seeing experimental and traditional plays, and the larger cities had more frequent opportunities to attend performances by national touring companies of Broadway musical and dramatic hits. The latter were helped by the building of civic centers, which usually provided halls for the performing arts capable of being adapted to large and medium-sized audiences.

In New Orleans big musicals are booked in the Municipal Auditorium, which has been modernized as part of the new Cultural Center. Among the productions that have appeared there are *Show Boat, Cabaret, I Do, I Do, On a Clear Day You Can See Forever,* and *Holiday on Ice.* Here, too, are staged the performances of grand opera. New Orleans has maintained its annual season of opera through several decades, usually offering works from the classical repertory with choruses trained locally and leading roles taken by artists from the Metropolitan and New York Civic and other organizations. Recent bills have included *Faust, Madame Butterfly, Don Pasquale, Tosca, Arabella,* and Verdi's *Atilla.* Similarly the Shreveport Symphony Society usually produces three bills of opera annually, performing *La Traviata,* the *Barber of Seville, Lucia di Lammermoor,* and *La Voix Humaine* of Poulenc in recent seasons. The Opera Guild of Lafayette has sung *Susannah,* among others. Opera workshops flourish at colleges in New Orleans, Baton Rouge, and Monroe, and programs of operatic arias are given frequently in college and civic auditoriums.

At Le Petit Theatre in New Orleans there is a variety of plays. The Gallery Circle Theater offers in "high camp" such thrillers as *Dracula* and *Little Murders;* Loyola has an active Opera Workshop and has staged *Volpone,* among others; Xavier has put on *Harvey* and *Silvain;* Louisiana State University has a diversity of dramatic fare at its Lakefront, Union, Cabaret, and Repertory Theaters; there are plays at St. Mary's Dominican, Tulane and Southern.

Shreveport has the Port Players, Little Theatre, Marjorie Lyons Playhouse of Centenary College and summer melodrama of the Gaslight Players. Baton Rouge profits by the numerous dramatic bills of Louisiana State University, just as Lake Charles does by McNeese and Ruston by the Teche Theatre Players. There are regular bills at the Civic Center in Monroe, the Barn in Covington, the Town and Gown Players at Hammond; others at Slidell, Grambling, Lafayette, and Morgan City.

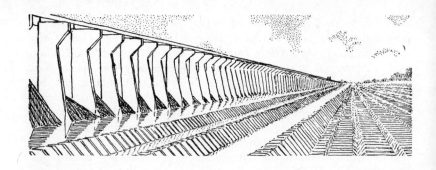

Science

THE State of Louisiana is so richly endowed in natural resources that for several centuries their users considered them inexhaustible. But the rapid pace of industry, augmented by the discovery of vast quantities of oil and natural gas, has alerted authorities to the need for guarding a misuse of the common treasure. Controls have been tightened ever since municipalities became aware that their drinking water and food supplies were being endangered by the reckless disposal of industrial wastes.

Before this became evident the greatest danger was from floods. When the winter snows in the North began melting in the spring the waters of a whole mid-continent descended on Louisiana. The Mississippi River has been known to overflow its banks ever since 1543, when De La Vega, the historian of Hernando de Soto's expedition, described a big one. Ever since the river has been challenging men along its banks to contain it. Research has proved that it has moved its delta numerous times, destroying old channels and carving new ones.

Attempts to control the river began on a large scale with Federal help in 1879, when the U. S. Army Corps of Engineers was given the task of constructing and maintaining the levee system. Levees were standardized and undermining was prevented by sinking willow mats along the banks. But the inadequacies were exposed when the great flood of 1927 swept through the State and New Orleans was saved only after the levee had been dynamited at Caernarvon below the city. Cutoffs straightened the river and provided a more rapid run-off of high water, an outlet channel for Mississippi and Red River flood waters was built in the Atchafalaya Basin, and New Orleans was protected by the construction a short distance above the city of the Bonnet Carré Spillway, a floodway used during threatening flood stages to divert a maximum of 250,000 cubic feet of water a second from the Mississippi to Lake Pontchartrain. An additional precautionary measure is the Morganza Floodway, which connects with the Atchafalaya Floodway. The Bonnet Carré Spillway was used most successfully during the big flood of 1937, and again in 1945 and 1950, when the waters were less dangerous.

Engineers of the Mississippi River Commission determined in 1950 that there was imminent danger of the Mississippi breaking through its controls at Old River, 80 miles above Baton Rouge, and flowing through the Atchafalaya River. This would be a catastrophe of major proportions, destroying the petrochemical industry along its banks, wiping out towns and making a new delta out of an area filled with tremendous natural and biological resources. The Old River was a seven-mile link between the Mississippi and the Red and Atchafalaya Rivers, created by Captain Henry Shreve when he cut off a loop of the Mississippi in 1831.

In September, 1954, Congress authorized building of new controls that would regulate the flow of flood waters into the Atchafalaya Basin and eliminate the danger from Old River. In 1963 the engineers closed Old River by building a dam with a base 1,500 ft. wide rising 100 feet above the bed of the river. A navigation lock was constructed south of the junction of the Old River and the Mississippi to serve an inland waterway.

The maintenance of a channel at the mouth of the Mississippi deep enough to permit the entrance of large ships has been another difficult task. Prior to the construction of jetties, several unsuccessful attempts were made to increase the depth of the passes by dredging with buckets, dragging with harrows, and blasting. As early as 1721 Adrien de Pauger, Colonial engineer, suggested that a system of jetties be constructed to narrow and deepen the entrance; but it was not until a century and a half later that the proposal was put into effect by James B. Eads, whose "no cure, no pay" jetty system (*see Tour 1A*) provided a permanently deep channel. A wall of willow mattresses, stone, and debris was erected on each side of the proposed channel. Controlling the current, the jetties forced the river to cut and maintain its own channel. By 1880 a depth of 32 feet was reached. Today, the river is 4,100 ft. wide at Pilottown, with a depth of 39 to 42 ft. At New Orleans Ferry the river is 1,700 ft. wide and 87 to 165 ft. deep.

Louisiana has pioneered in organizing research in geology and geography of river flood plains, deltas and coastal plains. Studies that contributed to the expansion of petroleum production were carried on at Louisiana State University in the 1920's. In 1931 the Louisiana Geological Survey was organized in the School of Geology. A decade later the School was the center for geological research for the Mississippi

River Commission. In 1953 the LSU Coastal Studies Institute was formed and specialists were enabled by grants from the Office of Naval Research and foundations to extend their studies beyond the marshes and deltas of Louisiana to far places. Louisiana's seafood industry has benefited directly from its studies. A major contribution to the coastal studies was made in 1968 by a Sea Grant from the National Science Foundation. The Sea Grant program is intended to improve sea products, increase consumption, and study the possibilities of the marine environment.

In the decades following World War II the State of Louisiana became sharply aware of industrial practices that endangered one of its most important resources, the fresh water supply by which men live and industries function. The billions of gallons of water that daily flowed through its rivers nurtured human beings, fisheries and wildlife, but they also served the needs of the petrochemical plants, sugar mills, and pulp and paper producers. In the 1950 and 1960 decades millions of dollars were invested in new industries that found unlimited access to water one of the major reasons for locating in Louisiana.

For many years industries had dumped their waste products into the rivers, and as long as the rivers were able to absorb them there was little damage to the environment. But industries grew so rapidly and so large that the balance was changed and the water supply became endangered. About 70 percent of industrial discharges went into the Mississippi River, 20 percent into the waters around Lake Charles, and 10 percent into the Red, Atchafalaya, Vermilion, and Ouachita Rivers and their tributaries. The ravages of pollution became evident.

The State concentrated the energies of a group of agencies on the major problem, under the supervision of the Stream Control Commission, an ex-officio body composed of the Commissioner of Wildlife & Fisheries, the President of the State Board of Health, the Commissioner of Agriculture, the Executive Director of the Dept. of Commerce & Industry, the Attorney General, the Commissioner of Conservation, and the Director of the Dept. of Public Works. The Water Pollution Control Division of the Louisiana Wildlife & Fisheries Commission became the principal agency for testing water for its potable qualities, making chemical and biological surveys of rivers, carrying on surveillance of oil pollution in the coastal areas, and cooperating with industries to eliminate contamination by treating waste before it reached the rivers.

The Water Pollution Control Division developed cooperation with industrial and municipal leaders to aid waste abatement. Attempts to remove harmful elements from large bodies of contaminated water proved incredibly difficult; the effective method obviously was to control pollution at its source. Major industries agreed and began treatment of wastes in their own plants. In some instances where industries ignored the laws legal proceedings were instituted to gain compliance.

The Water Pollution Control Division bases its effectiveness on two well-equipped biological and chemical laboratories at Louisiana State University, Baton Rouge. Their principal function is to make chemical and biological analyses of waste materials submitted by the investigators. These include oil and pesticide residues, gravel pit washings, process and wash water from sugar mills, pulp and paper mills, and food processing plants; oil drilling mud and salt water brine from petroleum production fields; sewerage, septic tank and slaughterhouse effuents. The principal analysis determines the amount of oxygen required by microorganisms (bacteria) to decompose a given amount of waste. Inorganic wastes need stronger treatment, usually physical or chemical separation. Modern instrumentation has provided means for detecting concentrations of materials never before thought possible. Substances once thought free of contamination are proved to contain harmful materials.

Modern technology provides new methods for analyzing examples difficult to handle. They include the gas chromatography, the infrared spectrophotometer for identifying oil residues; the bioassay method of testing the tolerance of fish to certain toxicity, and the atomic absorption spectrophotometer, for determining the concentration of metallic and semi-metallic elements in solution or in very fine suspension.

Those cities in Louisiana which are dependent upon the Mississippi for drinking water have overcome great difficulties. Wells, cisterns, and crude waterworks were used at first but failed to satisfy the needs of growing cities. Cisterns for rain water were in use in New Orleans as late as 1916, but advances toward a purer and more reliable supply were made much earlier. Between 1892 and 1900 much valuable information concerning methods of purification was gathered by George G. Earl of the New Orleans Sewerage and Water Board, and an experimental purification plant was established at Audubon Park. The modern and highly efficient system in use today in New Orleans is the result of these long years of experimentation. Water is pumped from the river into open reservoirs, where it is permitted to settle before passing through a battery of filters to be purified with a chlorine treatment.

Along with these advances, which brought adequate drainage, sewage systems, and water supplies to the low-lying cities of the State, came the final phase in the control of such dread diseases as yellow fever, once chronically epidemic in the lower Mississippi Valley.

The *Louisiana Spectator* for August 20, 1853, thus reported an ineffectual attempt at a "scientific" cure for the fevers then raging: "The authorities of our city ordered, on Thursday, the firing of cannon and burning of tar in each district with the view of purifying the atmosphere. For a few hours the booming of cannon echoing from all parts of New Orleans, broke painfully upon the ear, giving us the impression that we occupied a beleaguered town." Such desperate remedies were not, however, without some efficacy. Malaria and yellow fever were linked even then to the oppressive tropical atmosphere, and exploding cannon, burning tar, or a garland of garlic around the neck were all sufficiently odoriferous to discourage the tiger-striped *aedes aegypti* and *anopheles* mosquitoes, which a later day was to reveal as carriers of the fever parasites. As early as 1727 Father Du Poisson, a Jesuit missionary, had voiced a complaint against these pests that is still valid. "The plague of Egypt," he said, "was not more cruel. . . . This little insect has caused more swearing since the French have been in Mississippi than had previously taken place in all the rest of the world."

Swearing endures but science has conquered yellow fever. Although the discovery of the yellow fever carrier was made in Havana, many of the problems of practical control in large cities were solved in New Orleans. Quarantine and disinfecting methods instrumental in checking the fearful toll of yellow fever epidemics were introduced by Samuel Chopin, C. B. White, A. W. Perry, and others. Dr. Charles Faget contributed an indispensable diagnostic sign of yellow fever—fall of the pulse rate during the first days of the disease. The last epidemic in Louisiana occurred in 1905. Although means of transmittal and prevention were then known, the general public was still unacquainted with them, and an educational program was undertaken to bring about control of the disease. The Tulane School of Tropical Medicine, organized at Tulane University by Dr. Creighton Wellman in 1912, carried on the fight against tropical diseases.

In other fields of medicine Louisiana physicians and surgeons have made many notable contributions: C. C. Bass and F. M. Johns developed the cultivation of the plasmodium of malarial fever; A. W. de Roaldes established the first eye, ear, nose, and throat hospital in the South; C. A. Luzenburg removed a gangrenous bowel in hernia; François Prevost performed one of the first Caesarian sections in America; A. W. Smyth ligated the innominate artery; J. L. Riddell invented the binocular microscope; Edmund Souchon developed two methods of retaining the color of muscles and organs in the preservation of anatomic dissections, founded the Souchon Museum of Anatomy at Tulane, and did much original work on aneurysm of the sub-clavian artery and aorta; Warren Stone did work on aneurysm and rib resection to secure permanent drainage in empyema.

Standford E. Chaille was for many years dean of the Tulane Medical School. Ernest S. Lewis, Confederate officer, was a pioneer in gynecology. C. Jeff Miller, Professor of Gynecology at Tulane for many years, was president of the American College of Surgeons. Among the many others who made noteworthy contributions in the field of medicine are C. F. Dubourg, Tobias Gibson Richardson, H. C. Schmidt, Compton, Albert Baldwin Miles, Joseph Jones, F. W. Parham, E. D. Martin, Marion Sims Souchon, Robert Clyde Lynch, Carroll Woolsey Allen, Henry Dickson Bruns, and Oscar Dowling.

Rudolph Matas, a world-famous surgeon, particularly in the field of blood-vessel surgery, has made many contributions to medical science —a method of reducing and securing fixation of zygomatic fractures, an original method of blocking nerves in regional anaesthesia, the application of spinal subarachnoid anaesthesia for surgical purposes, and others.

The fight against leprosy in the United States has been centered in the U. S. Leprosarium at Carville, Louisiana. This hospital or colony was established in 1894 by the State of Louisiana and put in charge of the Sisters of Charity. In 1921 it was taken over by the Federal Government (*see Tour 10B*).

Since the visit of William Bartram, whose descriptions of Louisiana plant life appeared in his *Travels* (1791), Louisiana has attracted many botanists. Among them were Thomas Drummond and Emmanuel Hartmann, who collected specimens here in the early part of the nineteenth century and have left their names to some of our wild flowers. The Reverend A. B. Langlois of Pointe à la Hache won considerable renown in the study of rare plants and new species peculiar to the Mississippi Delta. He left a herbarium of more than 5,000 species, and in 1892 published a catalog of 1,200 varieties of fungi which he had found in the State. John James Audubon was in Louisiana for an extended period, and it was here that he did much of his ornithological work. The late Professor Reginald Cocks of Tulane was a well-known botanist. Caroline Dormon is the author and illustrator of *Wild Flowers of Louisiana* (1934). Percy Viosca, Jr., has published widely on the habits of reptiles, amphibians, and fishes.

Plant culture has been concentrated in the improvement of agricultural products. In early times the colonists of Louisiana used sugar cane chiefly for the production of tafia, a kind of rum. Dubreuil, de Mazan, Destréhan, Mendez, and Solis, among others, experimented in converting cane juice into sugar, achieving a "marmalade," a brownish milk sugar of poor quality; but it was not until Étienne de Boré successfully granulated cane on a commercial basis in 1795 that the sugar industry became important. Improvements in refining soon followed. John J. Coiron introduced steam power in 1822, and in the 1830's the vacuum pan and condensing column, along with the "multiple effect" process invented by Norbert Rillieux of New Orleans, revolutionized the industry. The use of bisulphate of lime for bleaching was introduced in

1840, and in 1844 the centrifugal machine for separating molasses from sugar replaced the old cone drip method, accomplishing in minutes what previously required days. Hand in hand with improvements in refining went experimentation in the cultivation of cane varieties and the development of superior types of cane. The Malabar was discarded in the 1820's for the purple and striped canes, which, to some extent, were superseded in 1872 by White Java. Dr. W. C. Stubbs, of the Sugar Experiment Station of New Orleans, in 1886 produced the D74 and D95 varieties, and in following years introduced other cane types of increased sucrose content and tonnage yield. Between 1912 and 1926 the mosaic disease, which affects the chlorophyll in the cane, causing starvation of the stalk, attacked all varieties and almost completely disrupted growing. P.O.J. (Proefstation Oost Java) canes, which were resistant to this particular disease, were then introduced. Intensive experimentation by Federal and State agricultural specialists has improved upon this Javanese import and developed new strains suitable to all localities. Methods of controlling and exterminating the cane borer and the cane beetle are constantly being studied. Other important results of scientific research in the sugar industry are the utilization of bagasse, the waste product of cane, in manufacturing celotex, a building material, and the manufacture of industrial alcohol from molasses.

Improvement in rice and cotton cultivation has been equally dependent upon science. Systematic study of varieties, the elimination of diseases, the control of the boll weevil, and the introduction of improved methods of cultivation have steadily increased production and quality. In rice cultivation, Sol L. Wright of Crowley has made noteworthy contributions in selection study. Most varieties grown in the United States at the present time were developed by him. Development of cotton strains has been a slow process. Colonel F. Robiew and G. W. Brannon originated special strains, but it was not until 1926 that Harry Bates Brown, professor of cotton breeding at the Louisiana State University, began a series of tests which gave Southern planters types of cotton specially suited to soil, insect, and climatic conditions. Brown is the author of *Cotton,* an authoritative book on this staple. As in the sugar industry, much of the profit from cotton and rice is now derived from byproducts; research by industrial establishments in conjunction with the Louisiana Farm Chemurgic Council each year adds to the utilization of Louisiana's three major crops. Interesting experimentation is also conducted in the control of diseases of the pecan tree.

The Southern Forest Experiment Station, in conjunction with the State Conservation Department and various other organizations, carries on botanical research and reforestation. The Federal Government built the Southern Regional Laboratory of Research in New Orleans which will establish chemical, physical and biological bases for the search and preliminary manufacture of non-edible products from Southern surplus crops. Cotton, sweet potatoes, and peanuts will be the first three tested in the South.

Louisiana has opened a fertile field for scientific research in the commercial extraction of oil, gas, sulphur, and salt. An important method that changed an industry is the Frasch process of sulphur extraction, which was devised by Herman Frasch in the 1890's to extract sulphur from deposits lying too deep for ordinary mining. Heated water is injected through pipes into the low-lying beds, and the molten sulphur is brought to the surface by the use of compressed air.

At the Delgado Trades School in 1936 students under the direction of Byron Armstrong built the Delgado Maid, a speed plane that attained, unofficially, 420 miles per hour before crashing. A second plane, the Delgado Flash, a smaller ship, broke the world's record for planes of its class. A model of the Delgado Flash is displayed at the Smithsonian Institution.

Numbers of native sons have sought scientific opportunities outside of the State. Among them is R. J. Thompson, research engineer and inventor of the Acorn tube, a midget radio mechanism which won him the Morris Liebman Memorial Prize in 1936. He was born in Roanoke, Louisiana.

Much important meteorological data has been compiled and published in Louisiana. The work of Dr. Isaac M. Cline, district forecaster and director of the Louisiana section of the U. S. Weather Bureau from 1900 to 1935, is particularly noteworthy. His treatise, *Tropical Cyclones,* is esteemed as an outstanding contribution to the science. Seismological data is recorded at the Nicholas D. Burke Seismological Observatory of Loyola University, New Orleans, where vertical and horizontal instruments of the Weichert astatic type are under observation.

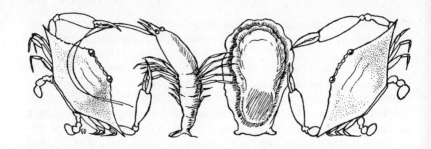

Cuisine

WILLIAM MAKEPEACE THACKERAY found New Orleans "the city of the world where you can eat and drink the most and suffer the least." But although Louisiana's reputation for fine food is in part based on the excellent fare served in the internationally famed restaurants of New Orleans, it is in reality founded upon the culinary art of the Creoles.

From the very beginning the people of Louisiana would tolerate no nonsense about food. This is amusingly illustrated in what has become known as the "petticoat insurrection." In 1706 Bienville appealed to the Bishop of Quebec for girls to be sent to Louisiana to become wives of the settlers. His request was granted; but soon Bienville was writing in his dispatches:

> The males in the colony begin, through habit, to be reconciled to corn, as an article of nourishment, but the females, who are mostly Parisians, have for this kind of food a dogged aversion, which has not yet been subdued. Hence, they inveigh bitterly against the Bishop of Quebec, who they say enticed them away from home, under the pretext of sending them to enjoy the milk and honey of the land of promise.

These "females" swore to leave the Colony at the first opportunity if the food did not improve. Today, their descendants set luscious tables with Creole dishes that have evolved over a period of more than two centuries and represent a triumphant synthesis of the French love for delicacies and the Spanish taste for pungent seasoning. To the French and Spanish influences must be added the culinary skill of the Negro. Important also have been the roots and herbs contributed by the Indians, particularly the Choctaw, whose powder prepared from sassafras leaves—called *filé* by the Creoles—is an ingredient of gumbo.

Creole cooking today is found at its best in the vicinity of New Orleans and in the Teche country; but its excellencies may be enjoyed throughout southern Louisiana and in all other parts of the State where the French influence has penetrated.

Nature has been exceptionally kind to the Louisiana cook. Vegetables in great variety are available throughout the year. Among those usually unfamiliar to visitors are: the *mirliton* (vegetable pear), which is prepared in the same way as squash or egg plant, and frequently stuffed with crabmeat or shrimp; okra, used as an alternative for *filé* in gumbo; and cushaw (neck pumpkin), usually cut in squares and baked in the skin, or mashed and baked in a casserole. Fresh- and salt-water fish, shrimp, oysters, crabs, crayfish, turtles, and frogs are plentiful and cheap. Formerly, when game was sold at markets, snipe, quail, grouse, wild turkey, deer, raccoon, opossum, and a wide variety of wild-fowl were important items in the Creole menu. Now, only rabbits, raccoon, and opossum may be sold, and the housewife's supply of game depends upon her husband's hunting.

Well stocked as the larder may be, it is the seasoning that makes Creole food distinctive. Onions, garlic, bay leaf, celery, red, green, black and cayenne pepper, parsley, thyme, shallots, basil, cloves, nutmeg, and allspice are used in different combinations. Several of the most important of these items are often bundled in a "seasoning bunch" and sold at vegetable markets for five or ten cents. The various seasonings are mixed in a *roux,* the basis of many Creole dishes, which is made by the careful browning of flour in melted butter or lard. With patient simmering, the ingredients blend in a composite seasoning. A condiment much in use, and one contributed by the "German Creoles," is Creole mustard, a preparation made locally of distilled vinegar, salt, and mustard seed imported from Austria and Holland. It has a distinct horse-radish flavor.

Gravies and sauces abound. Besides the bottled preparations, the manufacture of which is an important Louisiana industry, there are tomato, wine, tartar, barbecue, cocktail, and numerous other piquant mixtures. The tendency is towards hot condiments, and the visitor early learns to respect what in local restaurant parlance is termed "hot stuff," a pepper sauce manufactured in Louisiana from cayenne or tabasco pepper. The peppers are grown principally in the parishes of St. Martin, Iberia, and Lafayette. One of the earliest of the hot sauces was named after Maunsel White, a planter who was very fond of the raw oysters served at the old Gem Restaurant in New Orleans and who carried with him a small bottle of sauce made by his slaves.

In the preparation of sea food Creole cuisine is at its best. Mark Twain spoke of the pompano cooked in Louisiana as being "delicious as the less criminal forms of sin," and Thackeray and Irvin S. Cobb found New Orleans *bouillabaisse* unexcelled. The latter is a fish chowder made of two kinds of fish, usually redfish and red snapper, cooked with crabs, crayfish, shrimp, wine, and appropriate seasoning. Redfish prepared as a *courtbouillon* is a similar but simpler dish. Crayfish bisque is a soup full of crayfish heads stuffed with the meat of the tails. Boiled crayfish are also popular. In season, Negroes line the highways to sell their catch to passing motorists. Oysters are eaten on the half shell, in cocktails, fried, baked, stewed, stuffed, in soup, in dressings, and à la Rockefeller. With crabs and shrimp, they are cooked in gumbo, the most distinctive Creole dish. Chicken, veal, or ham are often substituted for shellfish in gumbo, but the basic recipe remains the same, a thick soup prepared with okra or *filé*. The Creole, it has been said, puts everything into gumbo except the Creole. Gombo Zhèbes, a herb gumbo made with seven greens and salt meat or ham, is considered a lucky dish to eat on Holy Thursday. Shrimp (river and lake) and crabs are served in many ways. The latter are considered more of a delicacy in the soft-shell state. "Soft-shells" and "busters" (shedding crabs from which the old shell is pried off) are coated with cracker meal and fried in deep fat. They are then devoured, shell and all. Soft-shell turtle is another delicacy. Frog legs are fried a golden brown and served on crisp lettuce with tartar sauce and lemon.

In addition to sea food, game, and domestic fowl, there are a variety of roasts, and such elaborate dishes as *daube glacée,* jellied veal made with pig's and calf's feet. The French trait of economy is often called upon to balance an over-drawn budget, in which case *soup-en-famille* is cooked. This is a vegetable soup cooked with *bouilli,* a beef brisket, which is served hot or cold, garnished with the vegetables of the soup.

Rice is used by Louisianians as Irish potatoes are used elsewhere. Every Creole dinner includes rice, whether it be served with red beans (a good-luck dish on Monday) or gumbo, as *riz au lait* (a dessert made of rice boiled in milk), in *jambalaya* (rice cooked with ham, sausage, shrimp, or oysters), or simply with gravy. A degree of skill is required to bring out the full tastiness of rice. The best results are obtained by boiling it rapidly without stirring in salted water until tender, rinsing with cold water, and steaming in a colander over boiling water until the grains stand apart. *Calas tout chaud,* an old favorite, are hot rice cakes fried in deep fat and sprinkled with powdered sugar. They were once sold by Negro street hawkers along with *batons amandes* (almond sticks), and *estomacs mulâtres* (mulatto stomachs), a kind of gingerbread made with flour and cane syrup. *Pain-patate,* a kind of cake made of sweet potatoes, was also sold on the streets. Today a popular dish in New Orleans restaurants is *pommes soufflées,* puffed Irish potatoes.

Grits (hominy) is to breakfast what rice is to dinner. There are two varieties—yellow and white—and two grades—coarse and fine. Coarse white grits is considered best, but whatever kind is used, it is boiled as a mush and served with eggs, bacon, sausage, liver, or *grillades* (cooked veal squares). Leftover grits is sliced and fried. Stale bread is made into *pain perdu* (lost bread). A favorite breakfast dish of the Acadians is *coush-coush caillé* (cornbread and clabber). Another popular dairy product is cream cheese, made of clabber drained in perforated molds.

The perfect complement to a Creole meal is Creole dripped coffee. It is brewed to perfection in New Orleans; but though good coffee can be had in most homes in Louisiana, it is not always at its best in restaurants and cafes, connoisseurs being able to reckon their distance from New Orleans by the quality of the coffee they drink in the hinterland. Many natives will not travel without a supply of coffee and their own coffee pot. There is an old Creole saying that "good coffee and the Protestant religion can seldom if ever be found together." Creole coffee differs from "Northern" coffee in that it is a darker roast, is ground finer for dripping, and contains 10 to 20 percent chicory, from which it derives body. It is best described by an old adage:

Noir comme le Diable,	Black as the devil,
Fort comme la mort,	Strong as death,
Doux comme l'amour,	Sweet as love,
Chaud comme l'enfer!	Hot as Hell!

A taste for it has to be acquired, as does the art of making it. For each cup of coffee a tablespoon of coffee is placed in the strainer of a drip pot. A spoonful of boiling water at a time is slowly, very slowly, dripped through the grounds. Once dripped, the coffee must never be allowed to boil. To be good, the *café noir* thus made should be strong enough to stain a cup. *Café au lait* (coffee with milk) is coffee to which hot milk, not cream, is added, the proportion being about half and half. *Brioche,* a local coffee cake, is an excellent accompaniment. At formal dinners, and during the holiday season, *café brûlot* is served, a mixture of coffee, spices, citrus peel, and burning brandy; it creates an effective scene when the lights are turned out and the shadows play on the faces of the guests.

Numerous fruits are grown in Louisiana. One of the favorites is the tree-ripened Celeste fig, which unfortunately does not stand shipping and has to be marketed as a preserve. The *mespilus* (Japanese plum or loquat) requires very little care and is a favorite local fruit. A preserve is made from the Japanese plum, but it is more flavorsome eaten raw. From the jujube, a species of guava, preserves and paste are made. An excellent marmalade is made from kumquats. Louisiana oranges, especially the Louisiana Sweet, are justly celebrated. Sour oranges are preserved. A syrup made from the orange flower is used as a sedative for colds, as a flavoring, and as a drink. An unusual candy is prepared by separating orange flowers, dropping them into simple syrup, and placing spoonfuls on squares of waxed paper to harden. Violets are also candied. Strawberries are raised for national consumption in Tangipahoa and neighboring parishes. Strawberry preserves, strawberry wine, and strawberry syrup are popular. Bananas and plantains are imported from Central America; the latter are fried and used as a side dish.

The pomegranate is grown both as a fruit tree and as a flowering shrub; grenadine is made from the fruit. A purple syrup served with crushed ice as a cooling drink, or in sherbets and cocktails, is made from the maypop, or passion flower. Preserves are prepared from blackberries, dewberries, mayhaws, muscadines, and scuppernongs. Blackberries cooked in pastry turnovers are known as "niggers in a blanket." The pecan, the most savory and nutritious of Louisiana nuts, is used in stuffing for fowl and in salads, desserts, and candies. It is the main ingredient of the famous pecan praline, a waferlike candy made of sugar, molasses, cream, butter, and nuts.

Molasses, the cooked syrup of the sugar cane, is used in cakes and candies and in a variety of other ways. *La cuite* is the thick syrup just before it turns to sugar; mixed with halves of pecans, it is an old favorite. The open-kettle method of refining sugar is necessary for the making of *la cuite* and *sirop de batterie,* the purest and finest of cane syrups. *Vin de canne* is an alcoholic beverage made from fermenting cane juice.

The Louisianian makes wines and liqueurs from almost anything from which he can extract juice. Most of the fruits already mentioned, as well as watermelons, pecans, rose geraniums, and many strange things are used for this purpose. The orange wine manufactured in the vicinity of Buras is particularly good. Creole beer, or *bière douce* (sweet beer), is made from the skin of the pineapple, with sugar, rice, and water added. Negroes once sold it at stands in Congo Square in New Orleans, where on hot summer evenings ladies and gentlemen would stop to enjoy a glass of this cooling beverage. Today, in hot weather children enjoy "snowballs," a confection made of crushed ice and brightly colored syrups.

A traveler in Louisiana in the days before the War between the States tells of a visit to Burnside Plantation where he was awakened in the morning by a slave with a mint julep. Presently the slave disappeared and returned with a second julep, explaining that the dew was heavy that morning and the drink was good for warding off fever. When the third julep arrived the guest was told that he had better take it because it was "the last drink that will be served before break-fast."

The thirst for things cooling and alcoholic has been responsible for the invention of several famous drinks. The cocktail is said to have been invented by Antoine Peychaud, a New Orleans apothecary, in the early nineteenth century. The name supposedly derives from the *coquetier* (egg cup) in which he served his cognac and bitters. The most celebrated of New Orleans cocktails—the Sazerac—is a mixture of whisky, bitters and sugar, served in a glass rinsed with absinthe. Here is a dialogue which appeared in the newspapers in the eighties:

> When you get to New Orleans, my Son, drink a Sazerac cocktail for me and one for yourself.
> And a third one?
> For the devil, my Son, for no living mortal can accomplish that.

Excellent, too, are the Ramos Gin Fizz (gin, egg white, powdered sugar, lemon and lime juice, orange flower water, sweet cream, and soda water) and the Roffignac (whisky, Hembarig, grenadine, or raspberry syrup, and seltzer or soda water), named in honor of Louis Philippe Joseph de Roffignac, an early mayor of New Orleans. Wine, or baba cake, a porous cake dipped in claret or rum, is a typical Louisiana confection.

As one goes farther north in Louisiana the cooking more and more resembles that of the South in general. But there are few places where Creole methods have not had some influence. In the vicinity of Natchitoches, the Spanish influence is particularly noticeable. Some of the dishes recall the old days when ex-slaves sold tamales along with coffee in the stalls of the public market. Incidentally, it is interesting to note that truffles can be found on the old Cane River Lake bank after a spring shower.

The Monroe area is famous for its barbecues. The meat is broiled slowly over hickory or other hardwood embers and owes its distinctive flavor to the sauce with which it is basted. Usually fifteen or more ingredients are used in preparing these sauces. A popular "country dish" of this section of the State is pot liquor and corn pone, loudly acclaimed by the late Senator Huey P. Long. Pot liquor is the water in which greens, such as cabbage, turnip tops, collards, and beet tops, and a piece of salt meat, pickled pork, or ham have been boiled. Corn pone, plain corn bread baked in a long pan, is covered with the pot liquor and eaten with a spoon, as a soup, the meat and greens serving as a side dish.

Although Negroes contribute much to the excellency of Louisiana food, acting as cooks in many restaurants and in private families, they have their own preferences when they cook for themselves. Their principal foods are sweet potatoes, fried, boiled, or baked; chitterlings, boiled, stewed, or in salads; cabbage, collards, mustard greens, and turnip greens smothered in lard with salt meat or pig tails, and eaten with corn meal dumplings (meal, water, and salt) cooked in the greens; pork in all forms, the year round; 'possum baked with sweet potatoes; fish; and corn bread and sweet bread (a large flat biscuit with sugar added). Though they often can afford better food, some Negroes never lose their love for this simple fare.

Among themselves, Negroes frequently have amusing names for dishes. A "coal yard" is a cup of black coffee. "Red and white" is red beans and rice. Pork chops are known as "flat cars." A "drunk coon" is a baked coon sprinkled with gin and served in a dish with sweet potatoes. A "Sunday breakdown" is fried chicken and grits.

PART II

Cities and Towns

Abbeville

Air Services: Abbeville Municipal Airport, north of La 141, east of Veazey Rd. Facilities include helicopter ports in Kaplan and Intercoastal City.

Highways: US 167 connects with US 90 and Interstate 10 at Lafayette (21 *m*) and has jct. with La 14 at Abbeville. La 14 connects with US 90 at New Iberia (32 *m.*). The Hug-the-Coast route, Brownsville, Texas, to New Orleans, to be segment of US 11. New Orleans is 157 *m.* east, Lake Charles 74 *m.* west.

Railroad: Southern Pacific Ry., Railroad Ave. & S. Main St.

Waterways: Vermilion River, Gulf Intracoastal Waterway, Fresh Water Bayou Channel.

Information: Abbeville Meridional, weekly; Abbeville Chamber of Commerce, 111 N. Jefferson; Abbeville Harbor & Terminal District, P. O. Box 5 Abbeville; Vermilion Parish Library.

Recreation: 2 swimming pools, 2 recreation centers, 2 parks. Boating, hunting. Fresh-water fishing, and salt-water fishing in Gulf of Mexico. Abbeville Country Club, west of limits on La 14.

Events: Spring Flower Show; Dairy Festival and Fair; Abbeville Fishing Rodeo.

ABBEVILLE (20 alt., 10,996 pop. 1970; 10,414, 1960, increase 5.8%) seat of Vermilion Parish, is an example of a quiet rural center, undisturbed among its massive live oaks, transformed into a bustling, energetic community by the exploitation of oil and natural gas in its parish and offshore drilling. When the first edition of this *Guide* appeared it described Abbeville as "the quiet center of a fertile rice-growing area." It still relies on rice for much of its income, but its quiet has given way to the rumble of trucks and airplanes, the handling of freight on its waterways, and the steady movement of labor to new sites of employment.

Abbeville was founded because Pere Antoine Desire Megret, pastor of a church in Vermilionville, now Lafayette, was at odds with the board of his church. For years he had traveled by pirogue and by horseback over the region. Finally he decided to build a church at the village of Pont-Perry (Perry's Bridge) on Vermilion River. But obstacles arose that caused the priest to determine to found a new settlement for his church. For $900 he obtained a plot of land between Pont-Perry and Vermilion and on a bluff overlooking the river built St. Marie Madeleine's Chapel in 1845. He laid out streets and small farm plots, which were sold with the provision that buyers pay an annual "interest" to the little church. The village plan was patterned after the old towns of

Provence, with narrow, winding streets and a central square. Soon there was a thriving village, composed largely of descendants of the Acadians who had come to Louisiana from Nova Scotia between 1766 and 1775. Besides the settlers of French extraction there were a few Spanish. For a time the settlement was called La Chapelle, but the name was changed after a few years to Abbeville. Meanwhile Pont-Perry faded into insignificance.

In 1852 Megret installed his assistant and protégé, Valcort Veazey, in Abbeville as publisher of *The Independent,* the first newspaper of Vermilion Parish. The following year Megret was forced to return to Vermilionville because a serious epidemic of yellow fever had stricken his former parishioners. He himself succumbed to the fever, the last victim of that particular epidemic. A few months later Veazey gave up the idea of becoming a priest and married a wealthy widow; he afterward said, "It was just as noble to save the property of a woman so charming as it was to save souls."

The sustaining industry of the region in those days was cattle raising. Shortly after the incorporation of Abbeville in 1850, bands of marauding cattle thieves threatened to break the long undisturbed peace of the country and bring on a form of civil war (*see Lafayette*). An ordinance was passed requiring anyone bringing beef to market in Abbeville also to bring the hides, with brands, to show that the meat was not from stolen cattle. In Abbeville, as in other southwestern Louisiana towns, *comités de vigilance* (vigilance committees) were organized, and finally stamped out the cattle thieves.

In the last quarter of the nineteenth century the surrounding country turned from cattle raising to rice culture, and there was an influx of Anglo-Saxon mid-westerners, who adapted themselves readily to the customs and traditions of the Latin community. Intermarriage has brought about an almost complete fusion between the two racial strains.

Abbeville and its vicinity were portrayed in Stella Perry's *Come Home* (1923), a romance of the rice fields.

The oil and natural gas industry is steadily expanding in Vermilion Parish. It usually ranks third in the State in value of natural gas and second in value of natural gas liquids produced. Drilling of wells continues, on the land and offshore. Vermilion Parish also leads the State in the production of rice, which accounts for 75% of its agricultural income. Abbeville has rice mills, dryers and storage warehouses, and large-size packaging operations. A large kettle syrup mill in Abbeville sends cane syrup to all parts of the country. The city is also the seat of the Vermilion Dairymen's Cooperative Creamery and stages an annual Dairy Festival. Beef cattle and cotton, corn, potatoes, and fruits are also substantial products of the parish and contribute to Abbeville's employment and banking strength.

One of the largest rice mills in the United States is operated by Riviana Foods, Inc., in S. Washington St. This organization also has the only solvent extraction rice milling process.

Another industry of special interest is the C. S. Steen Syrup Mill,

121 N. Main St., one of the few large remaining syrup mills. This firm also operates the first cane cleaning plant built.

The Vermilion River flows through Abbeville and the Freshwater Bayou Deepwater Channel, being built by the Corps of Engineers U. S. A. will serve a port facility to be constructed in the Abbeville area. Besides serving the oil and gas industries it will give sports fishermen direct access to the Gulf, where tarpon and marlin are found in abundance. The east-west Gulf Intracoastal Waterway connects with the Vermilion River and carries millions of tons of freight between the Sabine and the Mississippi Rivers.

In recent years the community has made provision for considerable expansion of the health facilities of Abbeville. The principal addition has been the ABBEVILLE GENERAL HOSPITAL, with an initial cost of $1,800,-000. It is a three-story, 75-bed institution, built with four equidistant wings so as to reach a maximum of light and air, and be capable of supporting additional floors. The Vermilion Parish Health Unit has its headquarters in Abbeville.

A bond issue of $1,250,000 was used recently for the development of the educational plant, which includes two high schools and four elementary schools. A parochial school system is maintained by the Roman Catholic Church. The GULF AREA VOCATIONAL-TECHNICAL SCHOOL, established by the State Dept. of Education in 1952, trains students in skills often needed in local industry.

POINTS OF INTEREST

MADELEINE SQUARE, in the center of town, is a well-landscaped, tree-shaded public square.

ST. MARIE MADELEINE'S CHURCH (Roman Catholic), across from Madeleine Square, facing Port St., occupies the site of Abbe Megret's chapel which was destroyed by fire in 1854. The present church, designed by a Canadian and dedicated in 1910, replaces the second church to burn on the site. The brick structure has a deep red color, the same red that Acadians are fond of for their roofs. The steeple, with heavy iron cross, is so tall that some consider it a dangerous hazard; its chimes toll the hours, the mellow and silvery notes mingling with the subdued hum of the business section, only a block away.

McPHERSON GROUNDS, 419 Fairview Ave., left of the Bamboo Grove, is a garden in which there are many azaleas, camellias, wistarias, and other flowers. Valcourt Coulée (named for Valcourt Veazey), winding through the garden, is lined with fern and iris. Another fine iris garden is that of W. B. MACMILLAN, 211 N. Washington St.

The EDWARDS HOUSE, 337 N. State St., is the birthplace of the illustrator George B. Petty. The house is a yellow frame structure, the oldest part of which was built in the eighties. On this site, under the moss-laden oaks, duels were fought in the old days, and it was here that Megret held open-air mass before his chapel was built. The cleats nailed to an old oak (R) supported a sort of platform upon which the missionary priest stood when saying mass.

The LOUSIANA STATE RICE MILL (*visitors admitted*), Railroad Ave., between S. Jefferson and S. Washington Sts., is one of the largest in the State.

VERMILION PARISH LIBRARY, organized 1941, occupies a two-story headquarters building of cream-colored brick in contemporary design erected in 1951. Its activities extend to branch libraries in Delcambre, Erath, Gueydan, Kaplan, Maurice and Pecan Island; other communities are reached by bookmobile, which serves public and parochial elementary schools and some high schools. In 1969 the library had 55,563 volumes, a genealogical collection, recordings, periodicals and the beginning of an art collection. It is supported by a tax of 3 mills on the total parish assessment, which, after stated deductions, gives the library about $124,236 annually for operation. The library has reciprocal arrangements with the South Central Region of Libraries and can draw on the facilities of the Louisiana State Library.

The branch libraries in Kaplan and Gueydan were built by the municipalities. Delcambre is located in both Iberia and Vermilion Parishes and the branch there gets financial support from both. The Pecan Island branch is located on a ridge in the Gulf Coast marches and two intracoastal canals separate it from the mainland.

Alexandria-Pineville

Air Services: Delta Air Lines, 6 flights daily; Trans-Texas Airways, 4 flights daily; Air East Airlines, 5 flights daily, New Orleans round trip; Esler Field, 10 *m.* east; Buhlow Lake Airport, 2 *m.* north of Pineville, light planes.

Highways: La 1, US 71, to Shreveport, 135 *m.;* to Baton Rouge, 107 *m.* Also US 165, 167; La 28.

Bus Lines: Continental Trailways, 6th & Jackson, Alexandria; Salter Bus Line. Alexandria Municipal Bus Lines. Independent lines to Pineville, Tioga, Smithville, Wardville, and England AFB.

Railroads: Missouri Pacific, and Texas & Pacific, daily passenger services, joint terminal, 10th & Jackson Sts. Kansas City Southern and Louisiana & Arkansas, daily passenger services, 2nd & Casson Sts.; Rock Island and Southern Pacific, freight.

Information: Alexandria-Pineville Chamber of Commerce, Jackson St. Alexandria *Daily Town Talk* (afternoon except Sunday); The *Pineville News* (weekly); *Alexandria New-Leader* (weekly); 4 radio stations, 5 television channels.

Churches: 87, representing 17 denominations.

Climate: Mean average temperature 67.8°; average monthly high, July, 83.1°; average monthly low, January, 51.9°.

Recreation: City Park, Alexandria, 100 acres, is fully equipped with facilities for swimming, games, golf, baseball and other outdoor activities; the same is true of City Park, Pineville, Buhlow Lake, north of Pineville and across the Red River from Alexandria, has 265 acres and a depth of 8 ft. for water sports. Golf also at Alexandria Golf & Country Club and Rapides Golf & Country Club. A large Federal game reserve is located north of Alexandria. About 20 *m.* west is Cotile Reservoir and Recreation Area, with 100 picnic sites, boat dock and launching ramp, pavilions and supplies. West of Alexandria 14 *m.* is the Hot Wells Spa, operated by the State.

Annual Events: See newspapers for specific dates. Northwest Symphony Orchestra concerts; Basketball, Louisiana College; Social Science Fair, LSU, Mar.; Paint Horse Club Show, Apr.; Central Louisiana Garden Forum, spring; Polled Hereford Show, fall; Louisiana Guernsey Show, fall; Camp Beauregard encampment, July–Aug.; Appaloosa Horse Show, fall; Rapides Parish & District Livestock Show, Oct. Athletic contests at LSU and Louisiana College.

ALEXANDRIA (79 alt., 41,557 pop. 1970) seat of Rapides Parish, is located on the north bank of the Red River, 135 *m.* below Shreveport, opposite the city of PINEVILLE (95 alt., 8,951 pop. 1970), on the south bank. The two communities are practically at the geographical center of Louisiana and developed from the earliest trade routes. Alexandria had 40,270 people in 1960, and its gain in a decade was 2.7 percent; contiguous with it is Southwest Alexandria, 3,151 pop., unincorporated. Pineville in 1960 had 8,636; its 1970 gain was 3.6 percent.

The parish takes its name from Les Rapides, the French designation for the limestone rapids that once created a portage in the Red River. The 1970 census gave Rapides Parish 118,078, up 6 percent over 111,-351, the 1960 figure. The parish is about equally divided between urban and rural population, and the number of nonwhites is more than one-third. Four other places have slightly more than 4,000 people each: Spring Hill, 4,671; Buckeye, 4,437; Samtown (unincorporated) 4,210, and Cotile, 4,111.

Alexandria and Pineville cooperate in many of their business and cultural activities, but have separate municipal governments: Alexandria has a mayor and commissioners, Pineville a mayor and aldermen. Industries include mills that make specialized wood products such as skis, and plants that process fresh-water fish. The area has good freshwater fishing and Beechwood Fish Hatchery at Forest Hill regularly stocks lakes and streams. Timber is not as profitable as formerly because much of the forest has been cut, but reforestation is being pursued and a State Forest is 10 *m.* south on US 165. Alexandria has a branch of Louisiana State University, a State-supported Trade School, and the Louisiana State School for Spastic Children. Pineville has Louisiana College, a Baptist institution, and a Veterans Administration Hospital. Camp Beauregard, a 9,000-acre military reservation, is located in Rapides Parish.

The two cities are known for their attractive residential sections and for the luxuriant displays of flowers in season, especially camellia, azalea, jasmine, magnolia and wistaria. They have more than the usual number of garden clubs, which are responsible for annual exhibits and awards.

Louis Juchereau de St. Denis, Canadian-born explorer, who was sent to the Red River area by Governor Cadillac in 1713 to arrange trade relations with the Spaniards, is believed to have started trading at Pineville. He founded Fort St. Jean Baptiste at the later Natchitoches, which was then on the Red River. A small French group of soldiers was placed at the rapids about 1723.

In the 1760's a group of Appalache Indians, unwilling to live under the British, to whom their land near Mobile was ceded in 1763, moved to Les Rapides, where a chapel, known as St. Louis des Appalages, was established for them by the Capuchins. By this time, various racial strains were already represented at the settlement. French soldiers, from Canada, had taken up land grants and become small-scale planters and traders, and the first Acadian exiles had arrived. Spanish officials and traders established themselves at the post after the transfer of Louisiana from France to Spain. After the Louisiana Purchase transferred the territory to the United States settlers from the east coast began to move in.

Around the year 1800 two men from Pennsylvania established the trading firm of Miller & Fulton. In 1805 Alexander Fulton surveyed and plotted a town and named it Alexandria after his daughter. In 1807 Rapides Parish was established and Alexandria was made the seat of government. The town was incorporated in 1819 and received a charter from the legislature in 1832. It grew as a trading center. Adjacent forests were cut down to provide lumber for fast-growing New Orleans, and vast acreages were planted in cotton, sugar cane, and other crops. Pineville, though it was the site of the original settlement, grew much slower than Alexandria and was not incorporated until 1878.

Under French and Spanish rule all religious exercises except the Roman Catholic had been banned. The first Protestant minister to preach in Alexandria was a former blacksmith, John Shrock, who nearly precipitated a riot when he held a service at the courthouse in 1814. By the middle of the nineteenth century several Protestant denominations had built churches in the town. Only the Catholic church was left standing at the close of the War between the States, and that remained because of the defiant opposition of Father J. G. Bellier, an ex-cavalryman and accomplished fencer.

In 1819 a school with the ambitious name, College of Rapides, was established on land donated by John Casson. With the opening of a bank in 1824, Alexandria began to take on the air of a metropolis for central Louisiana.

In the same year the Reverend Timothy Flint arrived from Massachusetts and made the following announcement:

The subscribers take leave respectfully to inform the public that they are jointly employed by the Trustees of the College of Rapides, as Instructors of that institution. They teach all the elementary branches together with Latin, Greek and French languages, with the use of Globes, History and Elocution. The writing department is superintended by Mr. Gunning and that of Languages by Mr. Flint, who will shortly be fitted to receive a number of pupils as boarders, who can, if desired, retire with him in the pinewoods. The misses will be under the care of Mrs. Flint, who will teach plain and ornamental needle work. Music and painting will be taught if sufficient encouragement be given. They pledge themselves to watch with unremitting diligence over the comfort, health and improvement of their pupils.

Among Flint's numerous writings is a novel called *Francis Berrian, or A Young Mexican Patriot,* which was based on the Mexican experiences of Judge Henry Adams Bullard of Alexandria.

What is said to have been the first railroad west of the Mississippi River was begun in 1837 by a planter, Ralph Smith-Smith. Approximately 40 miles long, the line ran from Alexandria southward to Bayou Hauffpauer, near Cheneyville, and brought cotton and sugar cane from the plantations of lower Rapides Parish to steamboats on Red River. In 1849 a steam ferry between Pineville and Alexandria replaced a ferry powered by blind horses that plodded around a circular treadmill.

Through the years an extensive and lucrative business developed in transporting steamboat cargoes around the rapids. Loaded vessels of average size could negotiate the shoals, especially during periods of low water, only by lightening their draft. In the early 1850's Herbert Flint constructed a tramway around the rapids, only to be all but ruined when Congress appropriated funds for deepening the channel in 1854.

The outbreak of the War between the States found Alexandria and Pineville at the height of their ante-bellum prosperity. The Louisiana Seminary of Learning, forerunner of the Louisiana State University, had been established on the outskirts of Pineville in 1860. William Tecumseh Sherman, its first superintendent, in applying for the position, gave as references Colonel Braxton Bragg, Major P. G. T. Beauregard, and Richard Taylor, son of President Zachary Taylor—all Louisiana residents who became generals in the War between the States. Sherman resigned when Louisiana seceded from the Union in 1861, returning north to become a general in the Federal Army.

During General Banks' first invasion of Red River Valley, in the spring and summer of 1864, Alexandria and Pineville were occupied by Federal soldiers, almost without bloodshed. In the absence of a force strong enough to challenge the Federals, the towns submitted quietly.

But the rapids presented a serious obstacle to continuance of the Federal invasion. Finally the idea of damming Red River was conceived. Cotton gins, sugar houses, and other structures were demolished to provide materials; and rails, cross ties, bridge timbers, and rolling stock of the Red River Railroad were dismantled and dumped into the river. After a few weeks, the Federal gunboats and troops pressed onward to Natchitoches and Mansfield, only to suffer defeat at the Battle of Mansfield (*see Tour 19b*). Retreating, the Federals fired Alexandria, May 13, 1864, destroying nearly all of the town.

At one time during the campaign the Federals took, among others, two fine horses, Edmund Burke and Childe Harrold, belonging to Major Seip of Oak Isle Plantation, on Big Bayou. James T. Flint, grandson of Timothy, went out to Big Bayou to see Generals Banks and Smith and, on the strength of the fact that both generals and Timothy Flint had come from Massachusetts, the horses were returned. They were taken to Mexico City for safety and became the favorite mounts of the ill-fated Maximilian and Carlotta. In 1867 when Flint told his Negro body servant, Aleck, that Maximilian was to be shot, the latter said, "Marse Jimmie, I can put him (Maximilian) on Edmund Burke and I will ride Childe Harrold and before sunrise in the morning I can get him across the Rio Grande and Eagle Pass on Texas soil." Maximilian, it is said, was informed of the plan but declined to desert his comrades.

POINTS OF INTEREST IN ALEXANDRIA AND PINEVILLE

The CITY HALL of Alexandria, 915 Main St., includes in its attractive modern structure the new CONVENTION HALL, containing 11,200 sq. ft. of open floor space and managed by the Alexandria-Rapides Conventions Commission. There is nothing in the present building reminiscent of the four-sided City Hall with Corinthian columns and red tile dome that stood here from 1909 on. The Convention Hall can seat 1,300 in the auditorium with stage, and 1,600 with stage removed, has space for five bays and 37 exhibit booths, and can seat 1,000 at a banquet.

The RAPIDES PARISH COURTHOUSE, Second St., between Washington and Lee Sts., is a buff brick structure with a portico that has archways beneath and Corinthian columns above. From the upper-floor windows one can obtain an excellent view of Red River and the new levee system.

The FEDERAL COURTHOUSE AND POST OFFICE BUILDING, Fifth St., between Washington and Murray Sts., is a modern reinforced steel and concrete structure, built in 1933. Bronze grillwork over the entrance depicts the evolution of mail transportation.

Alexandria has added numerous motels and motor hotels in the last 20 years. Most of these are easy of access on MacArthur Drive 2 to 5 miles from mid-town. Included are Congress Inn, Holiday Inn, Howard Johnson's Motor Lodge, Fleur de Lis, Ramada Inn, Travelodge. Hotel Bentley, in DeSoto St., 300 rooms, is said to have been erected by Joe Bentley, a wealthy lumberman, because he was not allowed to keep his dog in a hotel.

ESLER FIELD, Alexandria's airport, has opened a new Terminal Bldg., 2 stories of glass and steel, built at a cost of $565,800. The airport serves 10,000 passengers a month. The Field originated in 1930 as a base of the National Guard for Central Louisiana and was used during World War II by the USAF for training.

The RAPIDES PARISH LIBRARY, Washington St. at Fourth, opened its new Main Library building June 30, 1965. This fine structure of precast concrete with exposed quartz aggregate and glass, is also the administrative hq for the Parish Library System. The building cost $333,000 out of $600,000 for the total project, has 20,000 sq. ft. and a capacity of 100,000 vols. The system has four branches inside the Alexandria-Pineville city limits—the Main Library, Thornton, Community Center, and Pineville. Four other branches are located in Boyce, Tioga, Glenmora, and LeCompte. Two bookmobiles serve outlying areas. The system has an income of $375,000 annually from the property tax, and book circulation for a typical year, 1969, reached 364,000 books, with 2,888 on interlibrary loan; there were 25,500 calls on the reference and reading aid service. With the addition of its records, art prints, newspaper microfilms, and periodicals the Library provides a reference center for the entire parish. The Alexandria Public Library, which was built in 1907 from donations by S. S. Bryan and the Carnegie Foundation, became a part of the Parish system in May, 1956.

The CITY ZOO, off Masonic Drive in Bringhurst Park, Alexandria, is a fully stocked municipal undertaking, largest in State next to New Orleans. The park also contains an amusement area, nine-hole golf course, tennis courts, baseball diamonds, model-airplane field, picnic and playgrounds.

The MEDICAL FACILITIES of Alexandria-Pineville constitute

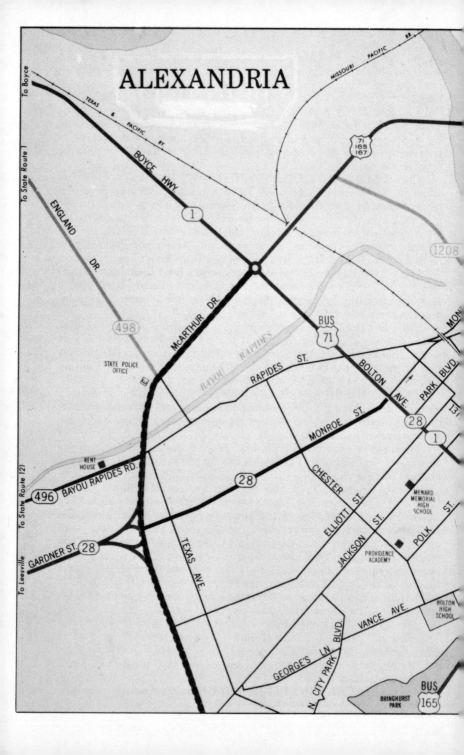

ALEXANDRIA

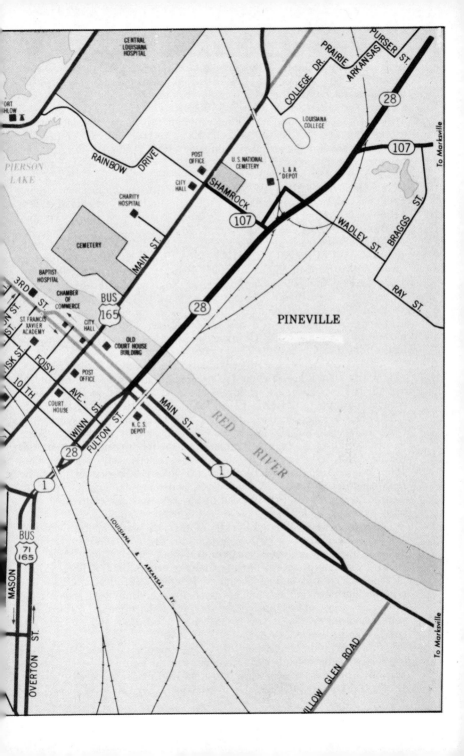

an important asset for the wellbeing of Central Louisiana. Easily accessible are seven hospitals, six major specialized institutions, 14 clinics, and 11 nursing homes. BAPTIST HOSPITAL, Alexandria, is operated by the Louisiana Baptist State Convention, has 221 beds, and serves 10,000 patients annually. ST. FRANCIS CABRINI HOSPITAL, Alexandria, has 126 beds, and a training program for X-ray and laboratory technicians. HUEY P. LONG CHARITY HOSPITAL, Pineville, 288 beds, cares for the acutely ill indigent within a nine-parish area, and has out-patient clinics in numerous ailments, including alcoholism. It treats 9,000 in-patients and 87,000 out-patients annually. CENTRAL LOUISIANA STATE HOSPITAL, Pineville, maintains more than 3,000 beds and an average daily census of mentally ill patients of 2,685 (1966). Its out-patient psychiatric clinic, the Forest Glen Mental Health Treatment Center, has a state-wide reputation.

Within easy reach of both cities on combined highways US 71 and 167 is the VETERANS ADMINISTRATION HOSPITAL for the care and treatment of eligible veterans. It has 498 beds and serves about 3,500 patients annually. The hospital at England Air Force Base has 50 beds, and the Murrell Clinic & Hospital, a private undertaking, has 38 beds. The 11 nursing homes of both cities provide more than 600 beds for permanent residents and convalescents. More than 4,000 employees of these medical facilities earn $13,000,000 a year, while the institutions spend an average of $17,000,000 annually.

The ALEXANDRIA-PINEVILLE GUIDANCE CENTER is a community mental health clinic for emotionally disturbed children up to age 18. It treats about 500 children a year. It is located in the building occupied by the REHABILITATION CENTER OF RAPIDES PARISH, on Leesville Highway, La 28. The latter is a community clinic for speech and physical therapy, giving priority to children. Also within easy distance are the Louisiana School for Spastic Children and the Pinecrest State School for the mentally defective and epileptic. The John Eskew Training School is devoted to rehabilitation of mentally retarded children on a day school basis, and the John Eskew Training Center takes the mentally retarded of 16 years and older for evaluation with a view of employment.

The ALEXANDRIA TRADE SCHOOL was established by the Louisiana Legislature in 1938 to help youths and adults acquire training enabling them to get employment in appliance repair, automobole mechanics, drafting, practical nursing, radio-television, and welding. Most of the instruction is individual and students may enroll at any time except for business training and practical nursing. Employed people may attend part-time classes during the day or in the evening. As this is a state school instruction is free to residents. More than 500 students are enrolled annually.

The State Industrial School for Girls is located at Pineville.

A new center of higher education for central Louisiana became available in September, 1960, when the first students enrolled in the new two-year commuter college, LOUISIANA STATE UNIVERSITY

AT ALEXANDRIA. At that time 327 students registered for a fresh-man program that included 36 courses of study in 16 fields. The college was authorized in 1959 by the Louisiana Legislature, which appropriated $650,000 for a start. The campus is in the Red River Valley, five miles south of Alexandria on US 71, a beautiful tract of 3,114 acres originally known as Oakland Plantation, which had been deeded to the University in 1945 by the Federal Government for use as a school of vocational agriculture. That school, the Dean Lee Agricultural Center, had been operated under the direction of Dr. C. L. Mondart until it was discontinued in 1959. Its main brick building was converted into classrooms and a bookstore; a dormitory was turned into administrative offices, and two frame buildings were erected to house laboratories and the library. In 1963 452 were enrolled; by 1970 the number was reaching for the 1,000 mark.

With the support of the Legislature and enthusiastic sponsorship by Alexandria citizens, LSUA has been developing complete college facili-ties. A master plan was commissioned of architects Garron, Heinberg, and Brocato & Glanker & Broadwell. The first new building was Oak-land Hall, followed by a science building with 45,000 sq. ft. of space, and the Library, which quickly acquired 25,000 vols. and has room for 150,000.

Dean Martin D. Woodin of LSUA pointed out that the opening of the college meant the return of higher education to Central Louisiana after 91 years. The Louisiana State Seminary of Learning & Military Academy was located on the site of the present Veterans Hospital in Pineville 1860–1869. When the main building was destroyed by fire the seminary was removed to Baton Rouge.

LOUISIANA COLLEGE, a private, coeducational college of the liberal arts and sciences, occupies a wooded campus of 81 acres on the north side of the Red River in Pineville. It is owned by the Louisiana Baptist Convention and has among its alumni many Baptist ministers of Louisiana. It welcomes students of all faiths but chapel attendance is compulsory and every student must attend Sunday services at the church of his choice. Enrollment exceeds 1,100 and there are more than 60 mem-bers of the faculty.

The college was opened in 1906 as the successor of two earlier Bap-tist institutions going back to 1852 and 1857. It has an endowment of $2,800,000. Alexandria Hall, its administrative center, is a three-story building with a portico of Corinthian columns, erected in 1918. In re-cent decades new structures and rebuilding of old ones have greatly expanded the facilities. Cottingham Hall, women's dormitory, received new additions in 1964. Tudor Hall for men was opened in 1958 and received a new wing in 1964. The Morgan W. Walker Student Center and the Richard W. Norton Memorial Library are important to campus life. The Weathersby Fine Arts Building, for the arts, music and speech, was opened in 1961 and considered exceptionally beautiful and func-tional. The H. O. West Physical Education Building, completed in 1965, has a basketball gymnasium that seats 4,800. Other new buildings are the Maintenance Building, 1966, and the Science-Mathematics Building, 1967. The college also completed the Married Students Apartments in 1967.

Louisiana College has two semesters a year and a summer session. The approximate cost per semester is $600 for a student residing in a dormitory, and $350 for a day student (1970).

ST. FRANCIS XAVIER CATHEDRAL (Roman Catholic), Fourth St., between Beauregard and Fisk Sts., is a red brick building with a tall bell tower flanked by two small gables surmounted by crosses. The building was erected in 1898. The grounds were part of the Flint-Thomas plantation and the site of a home that in 1866 served as the headquarters of General George A. Custer, at that time stationed in Alexandria. ST. FRANCIS XAVIER ACADEMY, Fourth and Fisk Sts., was founded in 1858, closed during the War and reopened in 1872.

ST. JAMES EPISCOPAL CHURCH, Bolton Ave., between Albert and Murray Sts., erected in 1926, is a red brick building with a square bell tower on the left. The stained-glass windows portray consecutively the life of Christ and the Church. The reredos is of native walnut. During the War between the States when the first church, which stood about a mile away, was burned by the Federals, the silver Eucharistic service, presented by the ladies of the congregation in 1847 and still in use, was saved by being hidden in a cistern. On another occasion it was secured against Federal marauders by being entrusted to a Catholic priest, who hid it in his garden.

MOUNT OLIVET CHAPEL (Episcopal), Main St., between Hardtner and Ball Sts., Pineville is a small white frame building with a portico supported by two angled wooden columns. It was erected in 1857 and at one time served as barracks for the Federals. On the sides and at the rear of the chapel is the cemetery.

A TRAVELERS' CHAPEL in the form of a four-sided cone has been placed on MacArthur Drive (US 71, 165,167) by the Alexandria Rotary Club for the use of wayfarers. It is nondenominational and provides a list of church services.

The PINEVILLE NATIONAL CEMETERY, bounded by Shamrock Ave., Sanders, Reagan, and Main Sts., is one of four national cemeteries in Louisiana and was established in 1867. The list of wars and battles, a part of whose dead are buried here, reads like a cross section of American history. Included are the Indian, Mexican, Civil, Spanish-American, and World Wars. A gray granite monument marks a trench containing the remains of 1,537 unknown Federal soldiers removed from Brownsville, Texas, in 1911. On Memorial Day impressive joint services are held here by various military organizations.

In the front left hand side of the RAPIDES CEMETERY in Pineville, is the grave of Enemund Meullion (1737–1820) commander of the Fort of Rapides under the Spanish regime.

ENGLAND AIR FORCE BASE, hq of the First Air Commando Wing, on England Dr. northwest of Alexandria, occupies the site of the Alexandria Municipal Airport, which was leased in 1939 by the USAF to become an emergency auxiliary for the Pollock Army Air Base. During World War II it was expanded as a training field for B-17 and B-29 Bomber Groups. During the Korean hostilities it was under the Tactical Air Command and then grew from a Wing hq to Divisional status in 1964. For a time it had two tactical fighter wings of the 834th Air Division, the 401st, which was sent to Spain, and the 3rd, which went to Vietnam. The 3rd Tactical Fighter Wing of the Division took command of the base Aug. 1, 1966. The military strength at that time was 5,476, and the military payroll $11,800,000 a year; the civilian employees, 498, received $2,667,185. The Alexandria-Pineville community profited also by Base expenditures, which run to more than $6,500,000, and by construction, which averaged $500,000 a year 1863 to 1968. The Base has a 55-bed hospital, a 517-seat theater, a library with 14,000 books, a golf course, and a chapel for Catholic-Protestant-Jewish services.

The BOYCE HOME, 105 Main St., Pineville, served during the War between the States as headquarters for Confederate troops. It was fired on by Federal gunboats and one shell exploded in the dining-room. Evidence of the shelling has been erased in various remodelings. Courts-martial were held here, and those condemned to death were shot on the sand bars above the bridge. The house is now a white, one-and-one-half-story frame cottage with a steep gabled roof and four square columns on the gallery Several of the foundation pillars are of homemade brick held together by mortar in which deer hair is the retaining element. On the front elevation is some finely-turned paneling.

HOT WELLS SPA, a curative mineral resort operated by the State Dept. of Hospitals is located near Hot Wells, 14 *m.* west of Alexandria in the Kisatchie National Forest. It is reached via La 496 from Alexandria. Hot water at 116° was accidentally discovered in 1913 by an employee of an oil-drilling crew, whose rash disappeared when he washed his hands in the water. An analysis disclosed 21 minerals in the water. The Spa has dressing room with individual electric heat boxes, massage rooms and cooling rooms, swimming pool and picnic areas.

COTILE RESERVOIR & RECREATIONAL AREA, about 20 *m.* west of Alexandria on La 46 and La 1200, adjoins the Hot Wells Spa. The reservoir has a surface area of 1,775 acres and a maximum depth of 25 ft.; 400 acres are cleared for sailing, boating, and water skiing, while 4 75-ft. boat lanes provide access to 1,375 wooded areas suitable for hunting and fishing. The recreational area has 55 spaces for camping and 100 picnic sites. There are 2 pavilions, a boat dock and launching ramp.

FORT BUHLOW, on the Pineville side of Red River near the O. K. Allen Bridge, was built during the Civil War to repel an expected third invasion by Union troops, but was never used. It has become a favorite picnic area. Adjacent LAKE BUHLOW, established in recent years by an earthen dam on Rocky Bayou, is a popular spot for boating, swimming, water skiing and fishing.

Baton Rouge

Airlines: Delta Airlines, Southern Airways, Texas International, at Ryan Airport, north on US 61 and US 67 to Harding Blvd, then to Ryan access road. Downtown Airport for private planes, east on Florida Blvd to Lobdell Ave.

Bus Lines: Continental Trailways, 222 North Blvd.; Greyhound Bus Lines, 220 St. Philip.

Highways: Int. 10 crosses New Bridge, west to Port Allen and La 1; US 61 (Airline Highway) to New Orleans, 80 *m.* south, St. Francisville north. US 190 to jct. with US 90 at Mississippi border, west to Opelousas, Beaumont, Texas. La 1 south along west bank of River and Bayou Laforche to Grand Isle; northwest to Alexandria, Natchitoches, Shreveport, 237 *m.* La 73, Jefferson Highway; La 30, La 42, La 67, La 37.

Railroads: Illinois Central, Kansas City Southern, Missouri Pacific; west of River, Texas & Pacific. Freight service handles 300,000 tons monthly.

Waterways: The North Bridge is head of navigation on the Mississippi River, which provides a 40-ft. channel to the Gulf of Mexico and more than supplies needs of industry and municipality. Port of Greater Baton Rouge includes Port Allen on west bank; latter has terminal locks of the Baton Rouge Barge Canal; Port Allen-Morgan City Cutoff Canal links up with Gulf Intracoastal Waterway.

Information: Morning Advocate and *State Times* (evening), Capital City Press, 525 Lafayette St. Baton Rouge Chamber of Commerce, 564 Laurel St. Louisiana Tourist Development Commission, The Pentagon. Louisiana State Library, East Baton Rouge Parish Library. All major radio networks, 2 television channels.

Accommodations: 3 hotels close to Capitol and business district; 11 inns and motor lodges, including national chains, on Airline Highway. Four hospitals with 1,204 beds.

Recreation: There are 7 recreation centers; 28 large and small parks led by City Park, Dalrymple Dr.; 5 public swimming pools, 5 golf courses, 24 tennis installations. Private swimming pools and golf courses are located at Sherwood Forest Country Club, Baton Rouge Country Club, Piedmont Club, Louisiana State University. Most of the larger motor inns have swimming pools.

Special Events: Consult calendar of Louisiana State University for football, basketball, track and other sport schedules; also for livestock exhibitions and rodeos; also for cultural events such as lectures, plays, concerts and conferences. Watch newspapers for important legislative meetings at Capitol. LSU Roundup Parade, Mar.; Spring Historical Tour, Mar.; Indian Festival, Mar.; Miss Baton Rouge Pageant, April; Louisiana State Fair, April; Square Dance Groups, April; All Arabian Horse Show, Coliseum, LSU, April; American Kennel Club Show, May; Appaloose Horse Show, LSU, Aug.; Homes & Gardens Week, Aug.; Greater Baton Rouge State Fair, Oct.; Dixie Horse Show, LSU, Nov.; All Student Rodeo, Nov. The Baton Rouge Little Theater produces five plays each season.

BATON ROUGE (51 alt., 165,963 pop. 1970), capital of Louisiana and seat of East Baton Rouge Parish, is the second largest city in the State, the farthest inland port of the Gulf of Mexico and head of deep-water navigation on the Mississippi River, and the apex of the huge petrochemical industry that extends for nearly 100 miles along the river to New Orleans. Its Port handles the second largest tonnage in the State and the seventh largest in the United States, and ranks second nationally in grain shipments. It is the center for a huge pipeline system, intake and outgo, and has the State's peak effort in higher education in Louisiana State University, and the supervision of public libraries in the Louisiana State Library.

Before Baton Rouge began to expand the Humble Oil Company unit of Standard Oil Company was the only major refinery in its environs. In 1950 it had 125,629 pop. By 1960, when industry was multiplying, the city had 152,419. During the decade of 1960–1970 the petrochemical industry invested approx. $1 billion in plants down river; it accounted for 10 percent of the work force of Baton Rouge. State employment reached 18 percent; city retail sales had doubled and bank resources has risen 181 percent.

All public institutions of learning, including primary and secondary schools, added to their physical plants and church schools kept pace. The 19,000 pupils who had marched to school in East Baton Rouge Parish (county) in 1948 had increased to 69,347, and the teaching staff had expanded from 600 to 2,959. By 1970 Louisiana State University enrolled more than 15,000 students in Baton Rouge alone, and Southern University in the suburb of Scotlandville, predominantly Negro, enrolled 7,600. Two vocational schools operated daytime and evening classes training workers for advancement in industry .

HISTORY

Baton Rouge has lived under seven different governments: French, English, Spanish, West Floridian, Louisiana, Confederate, and American.

In the year 1722, Paul Penicaut, a ship's carpenter, returned from Louisiana to Paris, and published his *Relation,* which includes an account of his voyage of exploration under the leadership of Pierre Le Moyne d'Iberville (1699–1700). Five leagues above "le Manchac," he writes, "we found very high banks, which are called Bluffs in that country, and in the savage tongue 'Istrouma' which signifies *Baton Rouge* (Red Stick), because there is in this place a reddened post, which the savages have placed, to mark the division of the lands of two nations, namely: that of the Bayogoulas from which we came, and the other about 30 leagues higher than Baton Rouge, called the Oumas." In such fashion did Baton Rouge receive its name; and in name only is existed until about 1719, when the French built a fort and established a military post to subdue the Indian tribes. At that time Louisiana was in the hands of the Company of the Indies, and Baton Rouge was included in a grant to Diron d'Artaguette, who made an unsuccessful attempt to change its name to Dironbourg. When, in 1763, the Treaty of Paris ended the Seven Years War, Baton Rouge was included in the territory ceded to Great Britain and became a part of West Florida, one of the "four distinct and separate governments" proclaimed by King George III on October 7, 1763, in his newly obtained "extensive and valuable acquisitions in America."

During England's domination Baton Rouge was renamed New Richmond; but the majority of the inhabitants in the district remained French. England made the port a point of origin for contraband commerce with Spanish Louisiana.

The crosses of St. George and St. Andrew floated over the town until the Revolutionary War, when Don Bernardo de Galvez, Spanish Governor of Louisiana, captured Fort Bute on Bayou Manchac and advanced to overpower the British garrison and seize their hurriedly constructed redoubt in the First Battle of Baton Rouge, September 21, 1779. Galvez forced the evacuation of other forts in the district and by the spring of 1781 the whole of West Florida was ruled by Spain. Nineteen years later Spain, by a secret treaty, retroceded Louisiana to France; but when Napoleon, in 1803, sold Louisiana to the United States, Spain retained West Florida, claiming that this was an independent territory and not a part of Louisiana.

The population was still only a few hundred in 1810, when the American-born citizens of the surrounding parishes captured the somewhat dilapidated Spanish fort and the town, and raised the flag of the West Florida Republic. Thus took place the Second Battle of Baton Rouge on September 23, 1810. Three months later Governor Claiborne annexed the new republic proclaiming "that so much of the territory of Orleans as lies south of the Mississippi Territory and east of the River Mississippi, and extending to the River Perdido, should constitute one county to be known and called by the name of Feliciana." In April 1811, the County of Feliciana was divided into six parishes, East Baton Rouge being the second named; and and by an Act of Congress, approved April 8, 1812, Louisiana was admitted into the Union. In 1817 the town of Baton Rouge was incorporated, and in 1849 it became the capital of the State.

At the outbreak of the War between the States, the citizens of Baton Rouge numbered about 5,500, the population having doubled since 1820. Joseph H. Ingraham, a traveler of that period, called the town the "rural and Franco-American Capital of Louisiana." "The place is small," he stated, "but flanked by the United States Barracks on one side and by the Capitol on the other." In between was a miscellaneous cluster of unpainted buildings, a few handsome dwellings, the penitentiary, and three churches. South of the capitol stood the newly erected School for the Deaf. The coming of steamboats helped interstate transportation, and a vast trade with the upper Mississippi and Missouri Valleys was opened to the lower river ports.

But war cut short the brief quarter-century of progress and Baton Rouge reverted to the role of a strategic point. On January 26, 1861, the United States Barracks were peacefully surrendered and Louisiana entered the Confederacy. For more than a year Baton Rouge was touched by rumors of war only; but the fall of New Orleans on May 1, 1862, opened the Mississippi to the Federal forces as far as Vicksburg. Union gunboats steamed up the river, passing on their way flatboats of flaming cotton—saturated with whisky to make them burn more surely. The Union troops stopped only long enough to raise the United States flag over the barracks and went on to Vicksburg. They returned two weeks later and occupied the town.

While the war lasted Baton Rouge was almost continually held by Union forces without opposition or even serious menace—except for the grave and bloody Confederate attack in the Third Battle of Baton Rouge, August 5, 1862. By this assault the Confederates hoped to regain control of the Mississippi River from Baton Rouge to Vicksburg and pave the way for the recapture of New Orleans.

The battle was short but sharp, and the losses were heavy on both sides. The Confederates, under Major General Breckinridge, approached through the thick woods surrounding the city over the Greenwell Springs Road and in a dense fog advanced so close to the Union camp that they could hear a field band playing the grand march from *Norma*. Brigadier General Williams, Union commander, had been expecting the attack, but the fog covered the movements of the troops. The Confederates opened the engagement, and for four hours the battle raged back and forth, a fierce hand-to-hand struggle—its center, the cemetery in the grove of magnolias. General Williams was killed, and among the Confederate losses was Lieutenant Alexander H. Todd, half-brother of Mrs. Lincoln and the youngest of three Todd brothers who died in the Confederate ranks. The Union gunboats on the river—their fire directed by a signaler in the capitol tower—raked the Confederate lines; and as the day wore on, General Breckinridge listened anxiously for the guns of the ram *Arkansas,* finally withdrawing his men to Ward's Creek, on the outskirts of the town, to await her arrival. Late in the afternoon word reached him that the *Arkansas* had disabled her engine and was lying helpless in a bend of the river, about five miles above Baton Rouge. He ordered his command to retire to Comite River—and the battle was over. Next morning the Union gunboat *Essex* set out to engage the *Arkansas* and found her a mere wreck, still burning, having been fired by her crew to prevent capture.

Owing to war conditions the seat of government in Louisiana had been moved first to Opelousas, then to Alexandria, and finally in 1862 to Shreveport. During the winter following the battle, the capitol was used as quarters by Union troops. In December the building was gutted by fire. It was not rebuilt until 1880–82, when the seat of government was returned to Baton Rouge.

Baton Rouge is at the northern end of what business agencies call the Petrochemical Gold Coast, more than 100 miles of huge industrial plants on both sides of the Mississippi River down to New Orleans. North of Baton Rouge on US 61, which US 190 joins as far as the northern bridge, the landscape once devoted to cotton and sugar cane is filled with refinery installations, and what seems an endless farm of oil storage tanks. They bear names of national repute: Humble Oil & Refining Co., Ethyl Corp., Allied Chemical Corp., Uniroyal, Inc., Enjay, Stauffer Chemical Co., Cook Chemical Co., Copolymer Rubber & Chemical Co., Foster Grant Co., Schuylkill Products Co., Reynolds Metal Co. A number of these corporations have built additional plants farther south. This concentration of industry is based on the Louisiana production of petroleum, natural gas, and salt, the copious supply of water for processing, and the advantages of water transportation. Inland waterways carry barge traffic many hundreds of miles; deep-water transport is made possible by the 40-ft.-deep river channel to the Gulf of Mexico.

The Esso plant of Humble Oil & Refining Co. opened at Baton Rouge in 1909 and was the first to locate there. It chose high ground to avoid floods, a danger since thwarted elsewhere by levees and spillways. It had no neighbors until 1935. The Copolymer Rubber & Chemical Corp. was the first Government-built rubber plant to be operated during World War II. It opened in March, 1943, and was owned by seven medium-sized rubber manufacturing companies. After the war it produced "cold rubber," a product of butadiene and styrene. The plant became a private corporation in 1955.

The real growth of manufacturers came with the development of petrochemicals after World War II, and the years 1956–58 and 1964–1970 were boom years. In some instances products such as ethylene, propylene, acetylene, chlorine, ammonia, and benzene, needed by neighboring plants are supplied through pipelines connecting them.

The concentration of plants brings with it acute problems of air and water pollution, which both industry and the State Legislature have made subjects of special study.

To obtain skilled workers for employment in the industries of the area the State through its Department of Education provides vocational-technical training. The Baton Rouge Vocational-Technical School and the Capital Area Vocational School are in the city; others are located in Greensburg, New Roads, and Plaquemine. The Baton Rouge school enrolls more than 400 men and women in day training and 1,200 employed workers in night classes. Classes are also conducted in the plants. The schools began with training for war work in 1942. No tuition or free are charged Louisiana residents; outsiders pay $50 a month for day training.

Education under sectarian auspices is provided by five church organizations several of which have built new high schools. The Roman Catholic Diocese of Baton Rouge provides elementary and secondary education in 8 parishes (counties). In East Baton Rouge Parish it has 4 high schools, 1 junior high school, and 14 elementary schools. Attendance in the 1969–70 year was 8,257 students, with a faculty of 383. There is a special facility for exceptional children. The Episcopal High School built a new plant costing $1,300,000 and enrolled 366 for 1969–

70. It has a college preparatory program for grades 5 to 12. The St. James Episcopal Day School had an enrollment of 312. Trinity Baptist School enrolled 150 through sixth grade. First Lutheran School had 70 pupils for grades 1–6 and Trinity Lutheran Church operated a kindergarten. Baton Rouge Junior Academy of the Seventh Day Adventist Church enrolled 138 in grades 1–10. Several other private schools were available. Harwicke-MacMasters School enrolled 398 in course from kindergarten through high school. Central Private School, elementary, had 73 students. About 30 other kindergartens and day schools are in operation.

A new bridge across the Mississippi River to carry highway Interstate 10 from Baton Rouge to Port Allen was completed in March, 1968, at a cost of $46,000,000. It has the third largest cantilever span in the country, 1,235 ft., surpassed only by the Greater New Orleans Bridge and the San Francisco-Oakland Bay Bridge. Caissons for four piers were sunk 140 ft. below the surface of the river. The bridge is located south of downtown Baton Rouge. It carries six lanes of traffic to a large cloverleaf junction in Port Allen, where one of the routes is the important northwest-south highway La 1, which crosses the State from Shreveport to Grand Isle. The bridge was financed by the State Department of Highways and the Federal Bureau of Public Roads and has been called the most expensive piece of highway construction ever built in Louisiana.

The North Baton Rouge Bridge, in the heart of the industrial district, is at the head of deepwater navigation. It was opened in 1940, is 12,211 ft. long and carries four lanes of US 190 and the tracks of the Texas & Pacific Ry. It cost $10,000,000. A river light one and one-tenth miles above the bridge has been named for an author, Ben Lucien Burman, author of Steamboat Round the Bend and other books about river life, including the popular Catfish Bend series.

POINTS OF INTEREST

The LOUISIANA STATE CAPITOL (*open daily, 7–7; tower, 10–5*), situated on the edge of University Lake, at the north end of Third St., is surrounded by a landscaped 50-acre park. The main elevation faces south toward the city of Baton Rouge, with a long vista of colorful gardens enclosed in an avenue of *Magnolia grandiflora,* Louisiana's State flower. The miles of walks and drives within the grounds are bordered with a great variety of trees and shrubs, and the extensive lawn areas are outlined with beds of flowers and flowering bulbs, so planted that, whatever the season, there is always color.

This, the most famous of modern buildings in Louisiana, combines a great monument with the functions of an office structure. It rises 34 stories and 450 feet and at the top flies the flag of the United States. Criticized for its cost in 1932, it is commended today because "only $5,000,000" was expended for what would demand many millions more now.

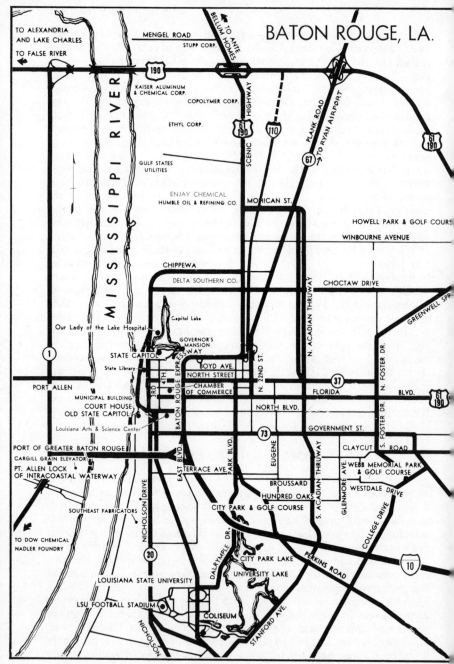

BATON ROUGE, LA.

TO ALEXANDRIA
AND LAKE CHARLES

TO FALSE RIVER

MENGEL ROAD

STUPP CORP.

TO ANTE BELLUM HOMES

190

KAISER ALUMINUM
& CHEMICAL CORP.

COPOLYMER CORP.

ETHYL CORP.

SCENIC HIGHWAY

61
190

110

PLANK ROAD

TO RYAN AIRPORT

67

61
190

GULF STATES
UTILITIES

ENJAY CHEMICAL
HUMBLE OIL & REFINING CO.

MOHICAN ST.

HOWELL PARK & GOLF COURSE

WINBOURNE AVENUE

M I S S I S S I P P I   R I V E R

CHIPPEWA

DELTA SOUTHERN CO.

CHOCTAW DRIVE

GREENWELL SPR.

Capitol Lake

Our Lady of the Lake Hospital

GOVERNOR'S
MANSION
WAY

1

STATE CAPITOL

State Library

BOYD AVE.

NORTH STREET

N. 22ND ST.

N. ACADIAN THRUWAY

N. FOSTER DR.

PORT ALLEN

MUNICIPAL BUILDING
COURT HOUSE,
OLD STATE CAPITOL

Louisiana Arts & Science Center

4TH

3RD

BATON ROUGE EXPRESSWAY

CHAMBER
OF COMMERCE

NORTH BLVD.

37

FLORIDA

BLVD.

61
190

GOVERNMENT ST.

PORT OF GREATER BATON ROUGE

CARGILL GRAIN ELEVATOR

PT. ALLEN LOCK
OF INTRACOASTAL WATERWAY

EAST BLVD.

PARK BLVD.

73

EUGENE

S. ACADIAN THRUWAY

GLENMORE AVE.

S. FOSTER DR.

CLAYCUT

ROAD

WEBB MEMORIAL PARK
& GOLF COURSE

WESTDALE DRIVE

SOUTHEAST FABRICATORS

TERRACE AVE.

BROUSSARD

HUNDRED OAKS

CITY PARK & GOLF COURSE

COLLEGE DRIVE

TO DOW CHEMICAL
NADLER FOUNDRY

NICHOLSON DRIVE

30

DALRYMPLE DR.

CITY PARK LAKE

UNIVERSITY LAKE

PERKINS ROAD

10

LOUISIANA STATE UNIVERSITY

LSU FOOTBALL STADIUM

COLISEUM

NICHOLSON

STANFORD AVE.

Baton Rouge Chamber of Commerce

Constructed of Alabama limestone, the Capitol is a modern adaptation of classical motifs. More than 30 varieties of marble and stone are used in the interior, some having been imported from Italy, France, Greece, Spain, and Belgium. The building also contains the work of many sculptors and painters, among whom are Ulric H. Ellerhusen, Adolph A. Weinman, Lewis Borgo, Andrew Mackey, Jules Guerin, Angela Gregory, Juanita Gonzales, Conrad Albrizio, Albert Rieker, and the Piccirilli brothers.

A broad flight of 48 granite steps—each inscribed with the name of state and date of admission to the Union—leads up to the main entrance. The steps are flanked by monumental sculptures designed by Lorado Taft: *The Patriots* and *The Pioneers*. When completed the first 13 steps bore the names of the 13 original states of the Union, and the rest had the names and dates of admission of all up to 48 states. On the top step is the motto *E Pluribus Unum*. When Alaska and Hawaii became states their names were inscribed on the same level as the motto.

The massive bronze entrance doors, nearly 50 feet in height, are ornamented with bas-reliefs by Lee Lawrie and surmounted by the seal of Louisiana. Through these doors one enters MEMORIAL HALL, which contains in sculpture and color a symbolic and historic record of Louisiana. An interesting feature is the circular bronze plaque in the center of the floor on which is outlined a product map of the State. The main portals to the west wing, housing the Senate, and to the east wing, housing the House of Representatives, are framed by murals symbolizing the abundance of the earth, and the four sets of bronze doors are divided into 48 panels, each panel depicting a scene from Louisiana's history. The interiors of the legislative chambers and of all other important rooms are treated with dignity; and, although each has its own individual mark, all are in harmony with the design as a whole. Three rooms of particular interest are the State Supreme Court, the Circuit Court of Appeals, and the Law Library—all on the fourth floor—which are characterized by an exquisite simplicity of design and ornamentation and a rich use of color.

The site of the building included sections of the abandoned American cemetery, in which, by means of ground radio, metal caskets were located and removed. The detector also revealed the resting place of a copper chest filled with coins; among them was one of the four silver half dollars minted at the New Orleans Mint by the Confederate States of America.

Directly in the center of the sunken garden, which the Capitol faces, is the GRAVE OF HUEY P. LONG, surmounted by a 12-foot bronze statue executed by Charles Keck of New York and erected in 1940 with a $50,000 appropriation made by the Legislature in 1938. Portrayed in bas-relief on the marble base are scenes from the political life of the Senator and former Governor, who stands above, beside miniatures of the State Capitol and the Mississippi River bridge named for him at New Orleans. Russell Long, his son, posed for the statue.

On the Capitol grounds is a marker commemorating the SITE OF

THE HOME OF ZACHARY TAYLOR (727 Lafayette St. is the actual site), commandant of the barracks at the time of his election in 1848 to the Presidency of the United States. Taylor (1784–1850) had long been a Louisiana citizen when he left his plantation for the White House. He came to New Orleans in 1808, at the age of 24, as first lieutenant in the 7th Infantry, under General James Wilkinson. He served in the War of 1812, the Black Hawk War, and the Seminole War. Between 1808 and 1822 he established Forts Selden and Jesup, and purchased a cotton plantation near Bayou Sara. He returned to the service for the Mexican War and became a major general. On his Baton Rouge plantation he received news of his nomination and election to the Presidency in 1848. He died two years later of typhus.

Facing Capitol Park on North St. are several white-painted brick buildings once part of the 51 occupied by Louisiana State University. They were used by the Louisiana Highway Commission until it moved to its new building east of Capitol Lake. Today they shelter the State Mineral Board and other official agencies. South of them the State has erected two tall office structures, the 14-story DEPARTMENT OF EDUCATION and the 16-story LAND AND NATURAL RESOURCES BLDG. West of Capitol Park stand the Capitol Annex, a utilitarian building; the completely restored Pentagon group, and the Department of Welfare Bldg.

The PENTAGON, west of the Capitol on Third St., is a group of four two-story buildings arranged as a pentagon with the fifth side open toward the river. They were built in 1819–29 as barracks for the U. S. Army. The identical buildings are of brick, painted pink, with white Doric columns supporting galleries on both sides.

A fort was built near this spot in 1719 by the French. In 1799 the British threw up a redoubt at the approach of the Spaniards under Galvez. The Spaniards constructed Fort San Carlos, a group of wooden buildings inside a stockade. A marble slab at the end of Building D says this fort was captured Sept. 23, 1810, by forces of the Republic of West Florida. In 1825 General Lafayette visited the Pentagon. During its use as barracks many famous soldiers were quartered here, including Robert E. Lee, Thomas Jackson, Braxton Bragg, Wade Hampton, Jefferson Davis, Philip Sheridan, and John A. LeJeune. When Louisiana seceded from the Union the barracks were occupied by Confederate troops, who gave them up when the Federals came in 1862.

In 1886 the Pentagon was lent to the State for use of the University. In 1906 it was conveyed to the University by the U. S. Congress and made into dormitories for women. It is still owned by the University and contains apartments and offices, including those of the Louisiana Tourist Development Commission.

The LOUISIANA STATE LIBRARY, 760 North Third St. in the Capitol Complex is a five-story structure of modern functional design opened in 1958. It has an auditorium, meeting rooms, and space for 350,000 volumes. Included in its collection are thousands of talking books, recordings, and films.

The Louisiana Library Commission was established by the State Legislature in 1920. Its name was changed to the Louisiana State Library in 1946. The latter title had been used by the Supreme Court Library at New Orleans, which then became the Law Library of Louisiana.

The Louisiana State Library has been the principal agent in establishing parish library systems in each of the 64 parishes of Louisiana. The method pursued was to place a demonstration collection of books in an interested parish, supply trained personnel, and enlist intelligent local support, so that citizens might observe the usefulness of the library before asking the voters to approve a small tax to maintain it. There were only five inadequate libraries in Louisiana communities when Miss Essae Martha Culver became State Librarian in 1925. She applied the demonstration plan for thirty-seven years and Miss Sallie Farrell, her successor, carried it forward to completion. The plan comprises a central library in the parish seat, which is administrative head and supply center; a number of branch libraries in promising locations, and bookmobile service. The State Library has many other functions, such as enlarging the use of books, maintaining a legislative reference service, cooperating with the Library of Congress in service to the blind and handicapped, placing libraries in institutions, and establishing new outlets.

One of the agencies that cooperated with the State Library Commission in extending services was the Library Service Project of the Work Projects Administration, 1939–42. WPA funds paid librarians who supervised thousands of workers, mostly clerical, who needed work; the funds also helped increase book collections. One valuable offshoot was the Federal Writers Project, which prepared the *Louisiana State Guide* under the sponsorship of the State Library Commission and the Louisiana State University; the *New Orleans City Guide,* and a book on Louisiana folklore, *Gumbo Ya-Ya.*

EAST BATON ROUGE PARISH LIBRARY has its Main Branch and Parish Library headquarters at 700 Laurel St. It was established in 1939 with 3,500 volumes, and its building was erected in the same year. At the beginning of 1970 it had 237,837 catalogued books, 672 microfilmed periodicals, 11 newspapers and 326 magazines, and a circulation of 855,072 books. Besides its Main Branch it has seven others and extensive bookmobile services, all on a budget of $525,127.

Five citizens and the Mayor-President of the City-Parish make up the Board of Control. Support comes from an annual appropriation from the General Expenditure Fund for the City-Parish. The Parish Library works energetically to present the advantages of the system to the citizens and has had a substantial annual increase in circulation. An instance of its usefulness is the demand made on its reference service, which answered 87,714 questions for school business and general purposes in 1969. Among them were inquiries about nuclear power, building bird houses and a smoke house, civil service, breeding rabbits, goats, and cattle, mental retardation, and how to make a speech.

The Mid-City Branch, 7711 Goodwood Blvd., has the newest of the buildings and the Main Branch plans to be placed there. The Parish

Library is also planning a south branch. In pointing out its usefulness the Library reported that it cost the citizens of Baton Rouge only $2.28 per capita in 1969, which might buy one book or one magazine, but actually made each person a part-owner in eight libraries and two bookmobiles.

The HUEY P. LONG MEMORIAL LIBRARY is located in the Capitol and is under the supervision of the Attorney General. The public has access to the collection. Also in Baton Rouge is the LAW LI-BRARY OF LOUISIANA STATE UNIVERSITY, which is designated by statute as a depository of records and briefs of the Louisiana Courts of Appeal.

The OLD ARSENAL MUSEUM is the designation since 1962 of the Arsenal that dates back to 1835, when it was the third powder magazine in the military area. It is a low building surrounded by a 10-ft. brick wall and stands near an Indian mound and Capitol Lake. The lake was called Bayou Grosse once and University Lake later, and is believed to have been the "small river which resembled a lake" where Iberville and Bienville landed on March 17, 1690, and saw the "red stick," that separated the hunting grounds of the Houma and the Bayou Goula Indians. The building has walls 54 inches thick and the roof is 4 ft. thick. The exhibits include firearms, household utensils, quilts, letters and papers, with memorabilia of Robert E. Lee, Jefferson Davis, and Confederate times. Mannequins illustrate period costumes of Louisiana's past. *Open daily except Mondays, free.*

Between the Museum and the Lake is a mound, possibly of Indian origin, where military officers and their families were buried at one time. A popular legend tells of a duel between two officers who fought to the death and were buried in the mound, with their bloodstained swords at their sides.

Beyond the eastern end of Capitol Lake on Baton Rouge Expressway are the Governor's Mansion and the big office building of recent date of the Louisiana Department of Highways. Farther on is MEMORIAL STADIUM. There is a junction with US 61 and US 190, which are joined until US 190 turns west. US 61 proceeds north to a junction with Harding Blvd., which runs east to RYAN AIRPORT, the principal airport for commercial lines.

The GOVERNOR'S MANSION, located east of Capitol Lake, was completed in 1962 and first occupied by Governor and Mrs. John J. McKeithen. It is a perfected example of the columnar style developed in the big plantation houses. Eighteen tall white doric columns rise two stories to the low gambrel roof, eight of them gracing the front facade. Dormers protrude from the roof. The entrance door has a fanlight and there are four French windows opening on the porch, with full-length green shutters, and five windows on the second-floor front with shutters and ironwork. The interior expresses the restrained elegance of the period. The Great Seal of the State is visible in the marble floor of the entrance hall. The State Drawing Room has copies of 18th-century Sheraton furniture and a 5-ft. 30-branch chandelier of 1830 restrung with old French handcut crystals. The State Dining Room has a 21-ft. table and normally seats 24 guests, but can accommodate 48. Mrs. McKeithen, in a brochure describing the Mansion wrote: "We selected a plain old English pattern of silver and had the State Seal etched in each handle. The informal family dining area is off the sitting room. The family living room is separated from the State rooms by a foyer. It, too carries on the Louisiana traditions, being paneled in famous tidewater cypress. The mantle was inspired by an old one from an antebellum plantation home." The grounds have a large garden with a succession of blooms. The Mansion is used for receptions and conferences and is open to visitors when not needed for official occasions.

The OLD STATE CAPITOL, North Blvd. and St. Philip St., is a castellated Gothic structure standing on a terraced bluff overlooking the Mississippi River. It was rebuilt in 1882 after the plans of the original building, which was built in 1847–50 and destroyed by fire in 1862. The old State House contained a notable collection of books, paintings, and statuary. Many of these went up in flames; the rest had been removed prior to the fire by order of General Benjamin F. Butler. Among the latter were the more valuable books of the State Library and the statue of George Washington, executed by Hiram Powers for the State in 1852.

When James H. Dakin designed the first capitol he avoided the prevailing Graeco-Roman design and adapted a Tudor Gothic plan. The building is four stories high and has four low battlemented towers. At one time these were topped by elaborate cast-iron turrets. The chief building material is cement-covered brick, but granite and other stone are used in the steps and elsewhere. Foliated traceries adorn the doors and windows and are repeated in the design of the cast-iron fence that encloses the grounds. The exterior walls are painted gray with aluminum and black ornamentation. From the central hall, which is flagged in black and white marble, an iron stairway winds to the second floor, which is roofed by a dome of colored glass supported by a single iron column. Colored glass and other baroque ornamentation are also used in the old Senate and House of Representatives chambers. The executive chambers were once equipped with furnishings that had been shipped from Europe to the Emperor Maximilian of Mexico, some of which may be seen at the Cabildo in New Orleans.

Mark Twain reached Baton Rouge in the 1880's, when the Capitol, a "sham castle," was being restored; he considered it pathetic that "this architectural falsehood" should be "undergoing restoration and perpetuation in our day, when it would have been so easy to let dynamite finish what a charitable fire began," and he damned it as a "sustainer of maudlin Middle-Age romanticism." He praised the magnolia trees on the grounds but thought their sweet scent overpowering.

Inscriptions on the entrance walls rehearse the diverse fortunes of the building. They relate that it was *burned* December 28, 1862, and stood, a hollow shell until 1882, when it became the seat of the State government and was so used until 1932. In the late 1930's it was hq of the Work Projects Administration. In 1936 it was *restored* by Governor

Richard W. Leche; in 1946–47 it was *rehabilitated,* and on November 11, 1947, Governor Jimmie H. Davis *dedicated* it to the soldiers of World War II. In 1956 it was *remodeled* by Governor Earl H. Long. In 1969 it was *rededicated* "to all veterans who died in our nation's wars" by Governor John J. McKeithen. In 1970 the Louisiana Art Commission had its offices there and art exhibitions were given in the Senate Chamber.

On the grounds a circular structure shelters a French railroad freight car of the famous "40 & 8" variety—forty men and eight horses capacity —used by the AEF in World War I. It was presented by France February 22, 1947, and accepted by the Old State Capitol Memorial Commission at exercises on January 12, 1949, at which Drew Pearson spoke.

West of the entrance gate is the grave of BRIG. GENERAL HENRY WATKINS ALLEN, Confederate Governor of Louisiana (1864–65) who died in Mexico City in 1866 and was buried in his Confederate uniform.

The ARTS AND SCIENCE CENTER on North Blvd. between Royal and St. Charles Sts. occupies the former Governor's Mansion built in 1930 by Governor Huey P. Long. It is a Georgian besign in brick and stucco and has a portico with four white Corinthian columns. It has exhibitions of paintings, a museum, a concert hall, and a large PLANETARIUM with lectures. Among the exhibits are a miniature furniture collection, dioramas of Baton Rouge, and replicas of early dwellings and a country store. The Center has increased its facilities by opening RIVERSIDE CENTER in the former Illinois Central Ry. station on Front St. Exhibits include an aerospace display by NASA, and paintings by Noel Rockmore.

The LOUISIANA STATE BANK occupies a new 24-story building that has some novel architectural features. Designed by Curtis & Davis of New Orleans, it is a 21-story tower on a 3-story base, built of reinforced concrete. Eight exterior columns, two to a side, give support to the walls and eliminate as many as 20 interior columns, thus providing greater floor space. The visitor approaching it may wonder at the utility of two one-story rectangular brick structures with convex bases, that stand at two sides of the building. They contain skylights that illuminate the banking floor below ground level. The building, completed in 1968, cost approximately $10,000,000. This is typical of the new tall buildings that are towering like lighthouses over two-story stores and parking lots. Among others are the Republic Tower, the Blue Cross Bldg., and the All-American Assurance Co.

CITY PARK, north of City Park Lake, and through which wind Dalrymple Drive and Park Boulevard, is a landscaped area containing a golf course, tennis courts, and a swimming pool, which in winter is used as a skating rink. At the northern entrance to the park is a Spanish-American War Memorial, a concrete representation of a ship's prow, in which is imbedded the figurehead of the U.S.S. *Louisiana.* The brass medallion, emblazoned with the seal of the United States, was presented to the State in 1910.

On the grounds of the Dufrocq School, Dufrocq and Spain Sts., is a marble tablet saying Governor Henry Watkins Allen, Acting Color Bearer for 9th La. Battalion, was wounded near this spot during the Battle of Baton Rouge. August 5th, 1862.

The NATIONAL CEMETERY, N. Dufrocq, between Convention and Florida Sts., contains the graves of nearly 2,000 United States soldiers.

MAGNOLIA CEMETERY, N. Dufrocq, between Florida and Main Sts., was the scene of the fiercest fighting in the Battle of Baton Rouge. The Confederates, hidden behind tombs and trees, launched the attack against the Union forces. After the battle, "behind a beautiful tomb, with effigies of infant children kneeling, twelve dead rebels were ound in one heap." The tomb, in the front part of the cemetery to the left, is topped by portrait statues of three children of William H. and Mary E. Crenshaw.

The BATON ROUGE ZOO, opened in March, 1970, is operated by the Recreation & Parks Commission on Thomas Road near La 19. It has 140 animals in proper settings, including an elephant compound, and an island for the monkey exhibit.

The LAURENS COLE ARBORETUM, opened in May, 1970, is a legacy to the city by Cole and comprises his house and 16 acres of trees and shrubs native to Louisiana. It is sponsored by the Civic Beautification Council of Garden Clubs.

ST. JOSEPH'S CHURCH (Roman Catholic), corner Church and Main Sts., is a gray cement-covered brick structure in the Gothic tradition.

On the feast of St. Sylvester, December 31, 1721, the Jesuit Father, François Xavier de Charlevoix, on his way from Quebec to New Orleans, landed at Diron d'Artaguette's plantation and, on an improvished altar, celebrated Mass on New Year's Day, 1722. This was the first celebration of Mass in Baton Rouge. Prior to 1792, however, when Father Carlos Burke arrived, Roman Catholics in Baton Rouge had no resident pastor or organized congregation, but were visited at intervals by missionary priests, or by clergymen from the Church of St. Francis in Pointe Coupée, founded in the early 18th century. Near Baton Rouge, too, were the parochial churches of St. Gabriel near Manchac and St. Bernard at Galveztown.

The land on which the present church stands was donated by Don Antonio Gras, a Spanish settler, who subdivided the surrounding property. The first church was a small frame building that was replaced in the 1830's by a more elaborate structure with a tall steeple and town clock; but even this did not long accommodate the growing congregation, and in 1853 the cornerstone was laid for a third church. In 1924 this was completely remodeled and enlarged into the present building.

ST. JAMES EPISCOPAL CHURCH, corner Church and Convention Sts., is a red brick Gothic structure almost completely covered by ivy. The intricate panels behind the altar were carved by Dr. J. S. Tucker, rector from 1899 to 1906.

The DOUGHERTY-PRESCOTT HOUSE, 741 North St.,

was the home of Colonel Arthur Taylor Prescott and dates from about 1840. The house is of red brick with massive square plastered-brick columns, supporting a hipped roof on all four sides. The front gallery on the second floor has a handsome cast-iron railing. During the War between the States, Union cavalry rode their horses up the front steps into the house, and the hoof prints are still embedded in the floors. The troops determined to burn the house and piled firewood under the stairway; but they desisted when it was pointed out that the place would make an excellent hospital.

Another place, the S. G. LAYCOCK HOUSE, on Goodwood Ave. near the Downtown Airport, a white cement-covered brick, dates from 1856. The land is supposed to have been given to Thomas Hutchings by George III in the 1770's.

LOUISIANA STATE UNIVERSITY

The most popular objective of visitors to the main campus of the LOUISIANA STATE UNIVERSITY and Agricultural & Mechanical College in South Baton Rouge is that STADIUM where the Tigers win their football victories and where, on occasion, Dr. Billy Graham exhorts the crowds. But the visitor with a scholastic bent is more likely to aim for the MEMORIAL TOWER, which contains both a clock and an information office. At the approach stands the marble foundation stone of the University's predecessor, the Louisiana State Seminary of Learning & Military Academy, which opened in Pineville on January 2, 1860, with William T. Sherman as its first superintendent. Despite the strong feelings the South has had against Sherman, the University remembers that eventually he presented it with two cannon that had fired on Fort Sumter when carrying out the orders of Louisiana's Napoleon in gray, General P. T. G. Beauregard. They stand today in front of the Military & Air Science Bldg.

The first seminary burned down in 1869, and the school moved to Baton Rouge. In 1870 it became the State University; in 1877 it added the Agricultural & Mechanical College of New Orleans. It moved into the Pentagon Barracks and occupied 51 buildings in what is now Capitol Park. By 1925 LSU turned to its present location, concentrating on a 300-acre tract one-half mile east of the Mississippi River out of 1,944 acres mostly part of the Magnolia Mound Plantation of Armand Duplantier, with adjoining property increasing the University's holdings to 2,800 acres. Here it erected buildings in a style adapted from the domestic architecture of northern Italy, with tan stucco walls and red-tiled roofs, over which rises a 175-ft. campanile, built in 1923 as a memorial to the veterans of World War I, with American Legion support.

Here is the core of a system of higher education that reaches across the State. In 1969 it enrolled 28,363 students and had a faculty of 3,128, of whom 15,873 students and 1,451 faculty members were located at Baton Rouge. Its second largest unit was LSU at New Orleans, begun 1958 on the shores of Lake Pontchartrain and already enrolling 9,156 students. It operated a Medical Center in New Orleans, with the School of Medicine since 1931, to which was added the School of Dentistry in 1968, and jurisdiction over the School of Medicine in Shreveport since 1969. It had established a group of two-year colleges, LSU at Alexandria in 1960, LSU at Eunice in 1967, and LSU in Shreveport in 1967. It has legislative authorization for two additional two-year colleges, one east central and one in St. Tammany Parish. It conducts 14 agricultural experiment stations and has a Cooperative Extension Service in each of the 64 parishes. President of the University is John A. Hunter, appointed 1962.

As a land grant college LSU recognizes a responsibility to the people off campus. Of the three functions, to teach, to carry on research, and to serve the public interest, the last has led the university into many fields of activity. Among them is aerospace engineering, begun in 1968; farm equipment management, closely related to agribusiness; chemical engineering, which may deal with the health of sugar cane; nuclear energy technology, computer technology, and environmental science, which deals with problems of air and water pollution and their effect on the human organism. The University cooperates with other institutions in tropical studies and conducts research on diseases in its Dept. of Tropical Medicine. To train students for international commitments the University conducts the Area Studies Programs.

The 100th anniversary of the organization as Louisiana State University was observed on March 16, 1970, when the administration could point to three major academic buildings to add to the campus: SAMUEL L. LOCKETT HALL, the LIFE SCIENCES BLDG., and the LAW CENTER. The ASSEMBLY CENTER, was being built near the Tiger Stadium.

The College of Business Administration doubled its enrollment in five years during the 1960 decade. The scattered facilities of this college and the inadequate housing of the College of Engineering have led the University authorities to plan a Center for Engineering and Business Administration, to occupy a 12-acre tract on the southwest edge of the campus. The LSU Foundation began a drive to raise $4,000,000 toward a possible cost of $14,700,000 for the whole project.

To meet its new needs the administration departed from the domestic Italian design of its original campus and boldly adopted the modern construction that uses large areas of concrete and glass. In the 1960–70 decade the Board of Supervisors supported the educators in asking the Legislature for millions for expansion of the LSU System, looking to the State for 80 percent of its income.

The LSU UNION, one of the largest buildings on the campus, was opened in January, 1964. It quickly became popular as the center for student services, informal meetings and relaxation. In the Browsing Room students may read books, newspapers, and magazines daily from 10 a.m. to 11 p.m.; in the Music Listening Room they may choose the recordings; in the TV Lounge they may look at films. The Union contains the Union Theater, Art Gallery, Arts and Crafts Shop, the Plantation Room for table service, Tiger Lair for snacks, Cafeteria for quick service. The Union meets all the general needs of students and is open to visitors as well.

The LIFE SCIENCES BLDG., in use by January, 1970, is another new structure with no resemblance to other new ones except in its feeling of solidity and strength. A 6-story mass of pre-cast concrete panels, it houses laboratories and classrooms of the departments of Zoology & Physiology, Botany & Plant Pathology, Entomology, Microbiology, and Experimental Psychology. The University calls it "the largest, most complex academic structure ever built on the Baton Rouge campus." August Perez & Associates of New Orleans were the architects, and it cost $7,302,973, of which $319,510 was for movable equipment.

SAMUEL L. LOCKETT HALL is a huge quadrilateral that brings a new look to its location, between Journalism Bldg. and Prescott Hall. It is four stories tall and houses 31 classrooms and 125 faculty offices. There are seven large lecture rooms in the basement, which is made of reinforced concrete. The superstructure is of steel with brick facing. The top floor houses the Mathematics Department.

The LAW CENTER, a massive rectangular building of concrete, steel and glass, fronts on the Law Circle off East Campus Drive. Opened in 1970, it became the dominant functional unit of a complex comprising also the formal, pillared Law School of 1930, with which it is connected, and the planned Law Residence Hall, a dormitory for law students. The Center has four levels and 133.795 sq. ft. and cost $4,300,-000. The right half of the ground floor has the Library, with its main reading room and a circular staircase; the library continues on the three floors above it. On the third floor a ramp leads to the redesigned older Law Bldg. and the Civil Law collection donated by Col. John H. Tucker, Jr., of Shreveport.

The LIBRARY of the University occupies a building of modern design erected in 1958 at a cost of $3,500,000. It stands opposite the Memorial Tower and has a floor area of 324 ft. by 192 ft. It houses approximately 1,000,000 volumes and regularly receives more than 13,000 periodicals, magazines and serial titles. It devotes half a floor of space to each collection of the humanities, social sciences, and science, and places the main collection on open shelves. It can accommodate 2,000 readers and has separate facilities for private study.

Special collections include the LOUISIANA ROOM, which contains material dealing with State interests, including the writings of its authors, and other items related to the Lower Mississippi Valley. Another is the DEPT. OF ARCHIVES & MANUSCRIPTS, nearly 3,000,000 items of primary source material on all phases of human activity, among them professional and business records, account books, and records of State and parish governmental units. The David S. Blondheim collection has about 4,000 items on the dialects of France. The Richard T. Ely collection of economic items has 7,500 volumes and 10,000 pamphlets. The Jules M. Burguieres collection deals with sugar. The Warren L. Jones collection has more than 3,200 items on Abraham Lincoln and his times.

The Library School Library is located in the Library. There are microfilms, newspaper files, and listening rooms for the use of recordings.

One of the valuable publishing outlets is the LOUISIANA STATE UNIVERSITY PRESS, established in August, 1935, which publishes numerous books of scholarly and general interest dealing with the culture and history of the South. Among its regular publications are the *Southern Biography Series, Southern Literary Studies,* the *Library of Southern Civilization,* and *A History of the South.* It issues between 40 and 50 titles annually.

The University welcomes visitors and suggests they will find objects of interest in the Museum of Natural Science, the Geology & Anthropology Museum, the Library, the Greek Theater, the Planetarium and the Union. They may dine at Union, Hatcher Hall, Laville Dining Hall, and North Highland Cafeteria.

The MUSEUM OF NATURAL SCIENCE, in the west wing of Foster Hall, provides a vast amount of information about wildlife in its habitat groups, identification panels, three-dimensional biologic exhibits, and research collections. The realistic presentation of waterfowl in a Louisiana marsh in the spring is amplified by the sounds emanating from geese and other animals, and by explanatory panels. The Gallery of Louisiana Birds contains examples of practically everyone of the 403 species. Nearly 100,000 mammals, birds, reptiles, amphibians, and fishes are included in the research collection. The Museum is open weekdays 8–5 except Saturdays 8 to noon; Sundays, 2–5. In the summer it is closed on Saturday.

The TIGER STADIUM, a great arena for spectator sports, has seats for more than 67,000 fans at football games, and serves another useful purpose the year around, for below its concrete stands are dormitories for nearly 1,500 men.

Fees for students on all campuses were increased effective the second semester of the 1968–69 sessions. There are two semesters a year and a summer program. Louisiana residents pay $160 per semester at Baton Rouge except that Law School fees are $225. At New Orleans students pay $130; at Alexandria, Eunice and Shreveport they pay $90. Nonresident undergraduates pay $410 per semester; law students $530; social welfare students, $510; Graduate school students, $260. At Alexandria, Eunice and Shreveport they pay $340. At the Medical Center Louisiana residents pay $800 a year, which is also the fee for dentistry; nursing costs $370. Nonresidents pay $2,000 a year for medicine and dentistry; nursing, $870 a year. There are smaller fees for part-time registration. University fees for the summer term are $95. There are fees for field courses in forestry, geology, and zoology. An average student living in the Baton Rouge area spends about $580 above fees, room and board per school year. An out-of-town student spends about $1,500 a year extra. Married students spend about $2,500.

SOUTHERN UNIVERSITY and Agricultural & Mechanical College is located at Scotlandville, 5.5 *m.* north of the Baton Rouge line on US 61. *See pages 508–509.*

Bossier City

Air Services: Braniff International, Delta Air Lines, Trans-Texas Airways, Royale Airlines, at Greater Shreveport Municipal Airport.

Bus Line: Continental Trailways.

Highways: I-20 principal east-west route; La 3, north; US 71, south; US 79 and 80. I-22 bypass under construction.

Railroads: Illinois Central, Cotton Belt, Texas & Pacific, Kansas City Southern, Southern Pacific.

Information and Accommodations: Bossier *Tribune* and Bossier *Press* (weekly). Bossier Chamber of Commerce, 710 Benton Road, phone (318) 746-0252. General Hospital; 38 churches, 13 denominations.

Parks and Recreation: Fort Smith Park, Bearcat Drive, and Walbrook Park, Alameda Drive, with swimming pools, baseball diamonds, football fields, tennis. A Starfish F 94 jet airplane, donated to the City by Barksdale Air Force Base, on permanent exhibition.

BOSSIER CITY, 70.9 *m.* (180 alt., 41,595 pop. 1970; 32,776, 1960, inc. 26.9%) is located on the east bank of the Red River, opposite the city of Shreveport, with which it is connected by bridges and maintains close industrial and business relations. For many years while Shreveport was expanding into the metropolis of Northwestern Louisiana, Bossier City remained a small settlement. In 1940, when Shreveport was close to 100,000 population, Bossier City had only 5,786; but in subsequent years it attracted industries; in 1950 it had 15,470 people and changed from a town to a city. By 1960 it had 32,776.

Bossier City developed a group of public-spirited citizens who bought 22,000 acres of land that had been farmed to cotton and invited the United States Government to establish a reservation for the Air Force. The development of BARKSDALE AIR FORCE BASE just beyond the city line has helped materially to build its economic welfare.

Bossier Parish was formed in 1843 from the Natchitoches District and named for General Pierre Evariste Jean Baptiste Bossier. At the time Bossier City was little more than Cane's Landing, with settlers strung out on the hills of Caddo Parish and the site of Shreveport across the river. The county seat went to Benton, a town with a few hundred people, whose only competitor was Bellevue. Bossier Parish became a profitable place for growing cotton; some 720,000 acres were planted to cotton, much of it in river bottoms, returning an annual income as high as $12,000,000 in recent years.

After World II ended the opportunity came for Bossier City to grow. It now has the Bossier Industrial Foundation to help get industries for the city. It has become the center for night-life for the adjacent parishes. In the evenings, from the Red River Bridge and east along US 80 for 2½ miles, a blaze of neon lights indicates the way to the restaurants and entertainment. This is as much an outlet for Shreveport as for Bossier City. In the booster literature that is characteristic of cities that solicit conventions to come their way, the mayors of both cities join in recommending their advantages. The convention facilities of Shreveport (*see article*) are supplemented by cocktail lounges and dining places in Bossier City.

Recent public construction has included the General Hospital, the Bossier Parish Library, and the Airline High School, the latter costing $2,250,000. Since 1957 the city's water has come via a filtering plant and storage in a 117-acre reservoir that holds 700,000,000 gallons of Red River water.

A new CITY HALL is being financed in Bossier City as part of a $10,820,000 capital improvement bond issue approved by the voters. The city will apply a tax of 7 mills for 25 years and $3,300,000 from Federal funds. The old Courthouse of Bossier Parish in Benton also is being replaced with a new five-story building on a 15-acre tract.

Bossier City has its own well-equipped Library, which is part of the BOSSIER PARISH LIBRARY, organized in 1940. This also has libraries in Benton, Plain Dealing, and Haughton. Buildings were constructed in 1959. The Parish has upwards of 35,000 volumes and subscribes to 112 periodicals, and had a circulation of 102,131 in 1969. The Bossier City Library is open Monday through Thursday, 9–8, Friday, 9–6, and Saturday, 9–5.

The BOSSIER CITY GENERAL HOSPITAL, Airline Drive and Shed Road, was built at a cost of more than $2,000,000 raised by one-half of a 1-cent sales tax, effective Jan. 1, 1964. The other half of the tax was used for improved fire and police protection. Thomas R. Meredith, architect of the hospital, applied the design of "in the round," by means of which ten rooms are placed in a circle with the nurse's station at the hub.

In 1970 Bossier City obtained a Federal grant of $800,000 to begin construction of the NORTHWEST LOUISIANA SCHOOL FOR THE MENTALLY RETARDED. Its location is a 90-acre site two miles off Shed Road donated by the John D. Caruthers family. It will serve about 750 children from the northwestern parishes and comprise a complex of buildings costing $7,500,000. Included in the first group will be a 108-bed unit for non-abulatory patients. The Bossier Parish

School Board built its Mental Retardation Laboratory and Child Study Center on Viking Drive in 1970. Thomas Meredith was the architect.

One of the newly built churches in Bossier City is ST. JUDE'S ROMAN CATHOLIC CHURCH on Viking Drive east of Airline High School. Wiener, Morgan & O'Neal were the architects and cost was $370,000. TRINITY LUTHERAN CHURCH was erected at Van Deeman St. and Curtis Loop.

Among new industries in Bossier City is a pilot plant of the California firm of Levi Strauss & Co., on Douglas Drive, producing exclusively "Levis for gals," which started its machines with an order for 8,000 pairs of pants.

BARKSDALE AIR FORCE BASE, named for Eugene Barksdale of Mississippi, flyer in World War I, adjoins Bossier City for 9½ miles. It is hq. for the Second Air Force Base of the Strategic Air Command. The Second Bomb Wing has direct control of the tactical units and is supported by the Second Combat Support Group. In April, 1970, the U. S. Government closed Westover Air Force Base of the 8th Air Force in Massachusetts and about 350 of its personnel was transferred to Barksdale. Also the Second AFB took command of 15 additional units located throughout the country and having about 35,000 personnel. The change was expected to save $15,300,000 a year.

Bossier Base, an installation since 1953, of the Defense Atomic Support Agency (DASA) was transferred to the Headquarters Command and called Barksdale East. The transfer meant that it would keep only the number of nuclear bombs needed for Barksdale, with the excess removed to other bases. This was expected to save more than $2,000,000 annually for the U. S. Government.

Barksdale AFB was located here after public-spirited citizens bought 22,000 acres of cotton land and gave it to the Federal Government for a military reservation. It became known as Barksdale Field and the first units to use it was the 20th Pursuit Group, operating single-engine P-12 interceptors. Prior to Pearl Harbor the base was a flying school for the Army Air Corps. In 1961 it received the first GAM-77 Hound Dog missiles, with which B-52 bombers were equipped.

During the summer of 1970 the Second Air Force cooperated in a summer camp program for 200 teen-age boys from low-income areas, providing dormitories at Barksdale East. Expenses were paid by local businessmen. The Base Command also started construction of a new child care center.

Barksdale AFB strongly influences the wellbeing of the city. When the military personnel at a given time was 6,736, the dependents numbered 15,000; 768 civilians were employed and paid $4,100,000 a year; the military pay was $38,600 a year. It was estimated the Base added $42,000,000 a year to the economy.

As is the case in other cities, Bossier City people are moving into new residential developments along the highways. Tall Timbers, on US 80 East, covers 100 acres with more than 200 dwellings, some on a small lake.

A bridge across the Red River carries the Broadmoor-Barksdale Highway from Shreveport directly to a junction with US 71 and to Barksdale AFB. In 1970 the authorities gave a contract for the building of a new two-lane bridge span south of the former bridge to the T. L. James Construction Co. of Ruston, for $4,047,800. The bridge was planned to be completed in 1972 and to carry 17,500 vehicles a day between Shreveport and Bossier City.

Houma

Highways and Waterways: US 90, 57 *m.* to New Orleans; La 24 to Thibadoux and thence La 1 to Baton Rouge, 83 *m.* La 56 and La 57 to Lake Boudreaux and Terrebonne Bay. Gulf Intracoastal Waterway, connecting with Gulf via Houma Navigation Canal.

Motor Bus and Truck Services: Teche Greyhound Bus Lines, 14 buses daily; 4 interurban lines for rural areas; 15 truck lines.

Churches and Hospitals: 16 Protestant and 15 Catholic churches: 8 Catholic chapels in Terrebonne Parish. Terrebonne General Hospital, 200 beds; Terrebonne Mental Health Center, succeeded Guidance Center, Jan. 1, 1968.

Information: Terrebonne Press, issued Tuesdays; *Houma Courier,* issued Fridays. Houma-Terrebonne Chamber of Commerce, 603 Belanger St.

Recreation Facilities: 12 parks, most of them with tables, barbecue pits and playgrounds; 2 municipal swimming pools; youth center; 12 lighted fields for baseball, softball, football, for 66 teams, all ages. Basketball, National Guard Armory; bowling, softball. Deep-sea fishing via chartered and rented boats.

Events: Louisiana Junior Miss Pageant, January. Fishing Rodeo, June. Shrimp Fete, July. Tarpon Rodeo, July. Redfish Rodeo, October. Annual Fair and Western Rodeo, October. Municipal Christmas party for school children, December. Concerts by New Orleans Philharmonic-Symphony Orchestra, winter.

HOUMA (12 alt., 30,912 pop. 1970; 22,561, 1960, inc. 37.1%) is the seat of Terrebonne Parish and named from the Houmas (*red*) Indians, who settled here in the early 18th century. It is the principal distributing point for huge petroleum and gas products and a processing center for sea food, especially shrimp.

Houma profits by its location on the Gulf Intracoastal Canal and gets direct connection with the Gulf of Mexico by the Houma Navigation Canal, a 36-mile channel with a depth of 16 ft. and surface width of 300 ft. This gives access to the great oil fields to the south. In 1965 Terrebonne Parish produced 63,788,857 bbl. of crude oil and 12,242,698 bbl. of condensate, as well as 484,802,876 cu. ft. of natural gas. Depths range from shallow wells of 2,000 to 4,000 ft. to those of 10,000 to 12,000 ft. In 1965–66 fiscal year Terrebonne Parish collected more than $29,000,000 in severance taxes, second in the State.

Caillou Island Field, discovered 1930, is the largest producer. Tidewater Oil Co. has a plant in Houma for removing butane and propane. Freeport Sulphur Co. operates a sulphur mining plant on a man-made island in Lake Pelto, using natural gas. Houma owns three gas-producing wells, which supply the municipality.

The shrimp fleet, which supplies Houma's canneries, starts out each season by invoking the blessing of the fleet, a rite carried here from Brittany 150 years ago. The prosperity of the industry is based on two agencies: the application in the 1980's of a shrimp drying process by Lee Yim, a Cantonese immigrant, which enabled shipment without spoilage, and the trawl, introduced in 1917, which multiplied the catch. In July, 1967, the American Shrimp Canners Assn. observed the 100th anniversary of successful canning of shrimp at Grand Terre. During spring, 1967, the harvest of brown shrimp was 12,699,551 lbs., worth $1,814,220 to the fishermen.

Terrebonne Parish is located on the Gulf of Mexico and has an area of 1,336 sq. m. of land and 557 sq. m. of water. It is the third largest parish in Louisiana and has a variety of terrain, with prairie and woods in the north and bayous and salt marshes in the south, but its altitude is only 12 ft. above sea level. The Houmas tribe arrived here some time in the 18th century. In 1765, 250 exiled Acadians came via Santo Domingo and were settled in the area by Captain Deutrine. The Parish was created in 1822. Prominent among the early families were the names of Thibodaux, Barras, Sheivin, Duplantis and Prevost. Houma was incorporated March 16, 1843. In 1858 the town officials were authorized to impose a tax not exceeding $500.

The forerunners of the present highway system were the cordelle roads, making use of old tow paths. When there was not enough wind to take the sail-powered barges upstream, horses on the tow paths pulled them. Prior to 1854 steamboats plied on the Bayou Lafourche from Houma to Donaldsonville on the Mississippi. Stage lines ran to Thibodaux and made connections with New Orleans.

Etienne de Boré perfected a process for granulating sugar in 1794, and refining of sugar and molasses became an important local industry.

The Lirette Oil Field, originally known as the Old Houma Gas Field, is located about 18 miles southeast of Houma and is the oldest producing field in the parish. It was discovered by surface indications and gas seepage, and until 1927 was the source of supply for the Southern Gas Company of Houma. Then the gas was exhausted, but other fields provided a new supply.

Houma was occupied by both Confederate and Union troops during 1861–65. A number of ante-bellum houses exist in Terrebonne Parish.

Two large halls were completed in 1957. The MUNICIPAL AUDITORIUM, suitable for conventions, seats 2,000. The DUMAS AUDITORIUM seats 800 and has a stage and a library. LE PETIT THEATRE DE TERREBONNE, a non-professional group with more than 800 members, produces five plays a year in the Old City Hall on East Main St. A new Regional Mental Health Center has been built in Houma.

Noteworthy is the attention given the welfare of children in city and parish. The SOUTH LOUISIANA TRADE SCHOOL offers vocational courses. The City Athletic Program provides baseball contests for youngsters 8 to 12, and 13 to 15. Bantam football for boys and Bantam basketball for girls brings out 24 teams. Bowling instructions are given up to

300 children during 10-week periods. The city sponsors an arts-and-crafts course during the summer and a soft ball league for girls. This is supplemented by the recreation program of Terrebonne Parish, which directs seasonal parties for all ages. The Louisiana Junior Miss Pageant, held every January in Houma, appeals directly to teen-agers.

The Roman Catholic parish of St. Francis de Sales was organized in 1847. The present edifice at the foot of Church St. is of recent construction. Planters formed the first Protestant Episcopal Church in 1855 and held services in the old Courthouse. The Presbyterian Church dates from 1848, the Methodist from 1850, the Baptist from 1870. Most of the people of Houma are Catholics, and the church maintains schools, with an attendance in Terrebonne Parish of around 3,000 against 18,000 in the public schools. The South Terrebonne High School, opened September, 1961, cost $1,896,590 and has a 50-acre campus.

TERREBONNE PARISH LIBRARY has its Main Library at 424 Roussell St., corner of Verret, in Houma, and branches at East Houma (1311 Grand Caillou Hwy.), Carver (Dumas Memorial Center), Bourg, Montegut, Point au Chene, and Chauvin. It operates two bookmobiles out of the East Houma library. New functional buildings were completed at East Houma and Chauvin in 1969, when 329,-285 books were circulated. The total number of volumes in the Parish system was 86,299. The East Houma Branch has the largest building in the system, erected at a cost of $325,000.

The activities of the Parish library include successful reading programs for children, story hours, exhibits by the Terrebonne Fine Art Guild, and additions to films, which have more than 12,000 viewers annually; microfilms, of which there are now more than 331, records and art prints.

The POINTE-AU-CHIEN WILDLIFE MANAGEMENT AREA is located 15 miles southeast of Houma in Terrebonne and Lafourche Parishes. It has 27,504 acres and was opened in October, 1968, by the Louisiana Wild Life & Fisheries Commission. Access to the area can be obtained by driving to Pointe-au-Chien from Houma on La 55 and La 665. A boat launching ramp is provided at the end of the road at Pointe-au-Chien and this provides marine access into the area through Grand Bayou and St. Jean Charles Canal.

Lafayette

Air Services: Lafayette Airport, John Glenn Drive. Trans-Texas Airways, 10 flights daily; Longhorn Airlines, 4 flights daily; Air East Airlines, 5 flights daily. Texas International offers daily jet service to Dallas–Fort Worth. Petroleum Helicopters, Inc., serves the oil industry. There are two private air services.

Buses: Teche Greyhound Line, City Transit System, 5 interstate truck lines.

Highways: US 90, south and west; US 167 connects with US 190 at Opelousas for Baton Rouge, 87 *m.;* I-10 under construction from Orange, Texas to Baton Rouge via Lafayette; La routes 89, 94, 182.

Railroad: Southern Pacific, W. Grant St. near Jefferson.

Waterway: Vermilion River, connection with Intracoastal Waterway, and Gulf.

Information: Greater Lafayette Chamber of Commerce; Industrial Foundation of Lafayette; *The Daily Advertiser; Southwest Register* (weekly); 6 radio stations, 2 television stations, with principal national networks.

Accommodations: 1 hotel, Evangeline, 302 Jefferson; 10 motels; 5 hospitals of 858-bed capacity.

Churches and Halls: 48 churches, 17 denominations. Blackham Coliseum, (U. of SW Louisiana) seats 6,500; Municipal Auditorium, seats 2,332.

Amusements and Recreation: 4 movie houses, 1 drive-in theater, 3 18-hole golf courses, 2 driving ranges, 12 public tennis courts, 19 recreation areas, 3 public swimming pools, 1 bowling alley, little theater, community concert association.

Annual Events: Mardi Gras, South La. Midwinter Fair, Iris Show, La. Gulf Coast Oil Exposition (odd years), Gulf Coast Oil Center Golf Tourney, Azalea Trail, Christmas Parade, Tourist Appreciation Day, Chamber of Commerce Golf Tournament, Cajun Classic-PGA, Southwestern Relays, Greater Lafayette Tennis Tournament, Lafayette-Oil City Relays (high school state-wide invitational); Gulf Coast Petroleum League Bowling Tournament, Jaycee Junior Golf Tournament, Southwest Louisiana Bridge Tournament, Southwest Open Chess Tournament, Evangeline Downs Race Meet, April-September.

LAFAYETTE (25–40 alt., 68,908 pop. 1970; 40,400, 1960, inc. 70.8%), seat of Lafayette Parish, is one of the fastest growing commercial centers in Louisiana. To 33,541 people in 1950 it added 35,367 in 20 years of growth and annexation. The principal forces for expansion came from the prospering oil and natural gas areas offshore from Iberia and Vermilion parishes, and the concentration of offices of these industries, representing 700 companies and employing about 5,000 white-collar workers. Considerable growth also was marked in the processing of food, cotton, sugar and molasses, and the rich crops of sugar cane, rice and yams, cattle and dairying in adjoining parishes, and packing of fresh and saltwater fish, such as shrimp, crab, oysters and crayfish.

Lafayette calls itself the Capital of Acadiana, for this area became the homeland for the majority of the French refugees from Acadia, and the Cajun spirit and goodwill is carefully cherished by their descendants and successors. The local Cajun dialect has never died out in the six parishes, Vermilion, Iberia, St. Martin, St. Landry, Acadia, and Lafayette.

The first families to clear the present town site are believed to have been those of Andrew Martin and Jean and Marin Mouton, who arrived during the 1770's. Salvator and Anne (Bastoroche) Mouton came from Halifax, Nova Scotia, with the young Jean. Marin was born in Louisiana. According to George W. Cable's version, Anne, fleeing the English persecution in Nova Scotia with her children, took refuge in a forest and subsisted for 10 days on roots and berries before making her escape.

Like the Moutons, other early colonists were almost exclusively French, many of them the sons and daughters of exiled Acadians. They first named the village Vermilionville, after near-by Bayou Vermilion (Fr., cinnamon-red).

The first written word of the settlement is found in the report of the missionary, Père Michael Bernard Barrière, who wrote in 1804 that he often stopped at "the large plantation of Jean Mouton," whom he further identified as "l'oncle dit chapeau" (the uncle known by his hat). Two branches of the Mouton family have long been differentiated as the "Chapeau (hat) Moutons," the descendents of Jean, and "Capuchon (colloq. Fr., cap) Moutons," the descendents of Marin— a result of one brother's habit of wearing a hat, the other a homespun cap. The Mouton family has produced many men prominent in Louisiana history. Alexandre, Jean's son, was a U. S. Senator, the first Democratic governor of Louisiana, and the presiding officer of the Secession convention.

Vermilionville was laid out as the seat of Lafayette Parish in 1824 by Jean Mouton, who donated land for the courthouse and the Catholic church. It was incorporated in 1836 and about 1840 acquired a branch of the Union Bank of Louisiana. In 1842 Vermilionville Academy was established, to continue until 1872, when it was sold and the proceeds were used for free public schools. By 1846, a weekly newspaper, L'Impartial, was being published in both French and English.

Early activity in this section centered around cattle raising, jeopardized just before the War between the States by a highly organized band of cattle thieves. Ruin threatened the Acadian ranchers when the rustlers grew so bold they began to corral entire herds in daylight. The bandits were largely "foreigners." Numbered among them were wild young sons of Acadian families, attracted by easy money and adventure.

Obtaining little satisfaction from law enforcement agencies, the cattle raisers finally organized a force of 4,000 vigilantes under Major Orilian St. Julien and Alfred Mouton, a West Point graduate. The rustlers formed an organization of "anti-vigilantes." In September, 1859, after several minor skirmishes, they took refuge at an ammunition cache on a farm on Bayou Queue de Tortue. The vigilantes dragged up a formidable-looking cannon, in the face of which the bandits took flight. Some 200 of them were captured, the leaders hanged, and the others flogged until they agreed to leave the State. The local youths were let off with lashing and promises to reform. Barde's *Histoire des Comités de Vigilance aux Attakapas* offers an interesting account of the incident.

Retarded by two yellow fever epidemics and Civil War engagements, Vermilionville remained little more than a village, until the construction of the New Orleans, Opelousas & Great Western Railway in 1878, and its extension to Houston, Texas, in 1881. In 1884 the name was changed to Lafayette.

In spring and early summer a wealth of flowers—azaleas, roses, wistaria, crape myrtle, camellias, and purple magnolias—bloom in the gardens of nearly every home in Lafayette. Plain but substantial buildings are typical of the town's Acadian traditions. Modern brick buildings house business establishments, but there is no superfluous ornamentation about them.

Old customs remain. Afternoon coffee, served with ceremony about 3 o'clock, is still called a *collation*. In former days, delicious homemade *sirops,* or heavy wines, and pastry triumphs such as the *oreille de cochon* (pig's ear) and *beignes* (glorified doughnuts, or fritters) appeared with the coffee. Today the *collation* usually consists of freshly dripped black coffee, often sweetened in the pot, and served alone or with a simple pastry.

French is still the language of Lafayette. Both a patois and the correct language are heard, even among Negroes, some of whom do not speak English. During World War I, men from this and other south Louisiana towns served as interpreters and billeting officers for the American Expeditionary Forces in France.

To keep alive Acadian traditions and to establish relations with their far-flung countrymen, the Association of Louisiana Acadians, under the leadership of Dudley J. LeBlanc of Lafayette, was organized about 1930. Pilgrimages to Grande Prè, Nova Scotia, were made and in return Nova Scotia Acadians have come to Louisiana.

Lafayette is the home of the Live Oak Society, an organization of more than 50 huge trees in Louisiana, Mississippi, and Texas, believed to be at least a century old. The society, which has a junior branch of slightly younger trees, was founded by the late Edwin L. Stevens, president of Southwestern Louisiana Institute. Tree specialists declare a live oak measuring 17 feet in girth 4 feet from the roots is 100 years old. This estimation where documentary proof is unavailable, determines the membership of the oak. Each member of the Live Oak Society has an "attorney" or sponsor, who secures its history and guarantees its preservation. The "president" of the organization is the Locke Breaux Oak at Hahnville (*see Tour 11a*).

The constitution of the society provides for annual dues of 25 acorns from each tree, to be planted in a live oak nursery. Another provision declares "Members shall not be whitewashed. Violations of this law shall be punished by expulsion—and the attorneys for such members shall be disbarred from practice."

POINTS OF INTEREST

The UNIVERSITY OF SOUTHWESTERN LOUISIANA is located on a 735-acre campus, the main part of which is bounded by University Ave., Johnston, St. Mary and McKinley Sts. It was established in 1898 and is the largest of the State institutions of higher learning under the Louisiana State Board of Education. The campus is known for its fine plantings of azaleas, camellias, moss-draped oaks and native cypress. Here are the 20th Century Oaks, planted by the University's first president on the first day of this century. On part of the main campus is Cypress Lake, a natural swamp area, where every kind of Louisiana swamp growth has been cultivated.

There are six undergraduate colleges, a Graduate School and a University College for night and special classes. Beyond the master's degree is a Specialist in Education degree. The Ph.D. is offered in English, history, biology, microbiology, and mathematics, with options in statistics and computer science. In the spring, 1970, the University had an enrollment of 9,159, and a faculty of 511.

Nearly 80 buildings, many of recent construction, serve the needs of the University. Across St. Mary's Blvd. is the main DUPRE LIBRARY, which recently has been enlarged. There are more than 250,000 volumes in the library system, which includes the Stephens Library for undergraduates, the Engineering Library in Madison Hall, and the Horticulture Library in the Ira S. Nelson Horticulture Center. The Southwestern Archives in Dupre Library have the Louisiana Colonial Records and other historical materials. The French heritage is carefully preserved and La Maison Acadienne Francaise is a center for cultural studies.

The COMPUTING CENTER has teaching and research for its primary functions. Major sports activities take place in McNASPY STADIUM. There are a College of Nursing and a College of Commerce, and the School of Home Economics prepares students for gainful employment.

The physical plant has been expanded in keeping with the increase in enrollment and programs of study. Of recent construction are Angelle Hall for music; Maxim Doucet Hall, for mathematics and education; the modern Dupre Library building; Martin Hall, administration building, computer science and audio-visual center; E. A. Martin Dining Hall; F. G. Mouton Hall for the College of Commerce; and the V. L. Wharton Medical Sciences Building.

New dormitories for men and women have been built and apartments have been provided for married students. BLACKHAM COLISEUM has gained new seating areas. At a cost of $9,000,000 the athletic complex has been relocated and a new student and athletic building provided.

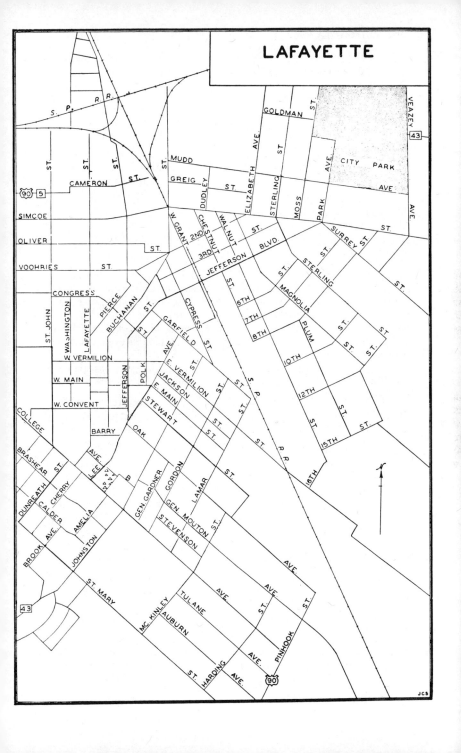

LAFAYETTE

The new Student Union has been erected near Cypress Lake. Half a dozen other structures, including the Humanities Bldg. and the Art and Architecture Bldg. are in the offing.

The horticulture and vegetable farms serve as test gardens for annuals, vegetables, and the All American Rose, Inc. The greenhouses, which have an unusual collection of orchids, have tropical plants brought from jungles of Central and South America and acclimatized for propagation and sale by nurserymen. The University has its own vegetable, dairy, poultry and animal husbandry farms and a modern creamery, which supply the two dining halls on the campus.

HEYMANN OIL CENTER in the heart of Lafayette provides physical evidence of the great concentration of oil interests in Vermilion Parish. Here between Coolidge St. and Heymann Blvd. are located the offices of the numerous producers, distributors and agencies of the South Louisiana oil and gas industries. The Center was opened in 1952.

The MUNICIPAL AUDITORIUM, 1300 S. College Road, is a center for conventions and mass activities, including operas, plays, concerts, and musicals. It can seat 2,332. It is located on Girard Park Drive adjacent to the Lafayette General Hospital. The Drive leads to McNaspby Football Field, and on St. Mary Blvd. East to Our Lady of Wisdom Chapel and the campus of the University of Southwestern Louisiana. BLACKHAM COLISEUM of the University, 2200 Johnston St., is used for some non-campus activities such as the biennial Lagcoe Show and Gulf Coast Oil Exposition.

The WAR MEMORIAL BUILDING, 2100 Jefferson St., commemorates the military sacrifice of Lafayette servicemen in World Wars I and II. It has offices of the parish, youth and community organizations, and the Lafayette Chamber of Commerce.

The MOUTON STATUE, at Lee and Jefferson Aves. In the business district, honors Brig. General Jean Jacques Alfred Mouton (1829–64) who became captain of the Acadian Guards, the first company organized in 1861, was wounded at Shiloh and died in the battle of Mansfield in 1864. The monument was erected by the United Daughters of the Confederacy in 1922.

ST. JOHN'S ROMAN CATHOLIC CATHEDRAL, 914 St. John St., was completed in 1918. It occupies the site of the first church in the parish. The building is of brick, painted red, with a white stone trim. The central tower is topped by a dome and flanked by two lesser towers, attached to the central tower and also domed. The sanctuary contains panels ornamented with life-sized paintings of St. Augustine, St. Jerome, St. Ambrose, and St. Gregory.

The CATHEDRAL OAK is a great tree that stands beside the walk that leads from the Cathedral to the old cemetery. It is 90 ft. tall, 24½ ft. round at the base, has a 160-ft. spread, and is believed to be 300 years old. In the cemetery are tombs of Jean Mouton, who died in 1834 at the age of 80, and his family.

The FIRST PRESBYTERIAN CHURCH, 323 S. Buchanan St. was built in 1878 on a lot donated by Dr. F. S. Mudd. Members of the congregation hauled the building materials from New Iberia and took part in erecting the church.

The LAFAYETTE PARISH PUBLIC LIBRARY had more than 100,000 books available in 1969 and circulated 380,152. It was serving its constituency from the Main Library in Lafayette and branches in Broussard, Scott, Cavencro, Duson—which took over the old town hall—Youngsville, and the unincorporated town of Milton. A small branch is located on the northwest side of Lafayette. The library also operates a bookmobile. A bond issue approved by the voters has made available $2,000,000 for a new five-story main building, planned by the David L. Perkins architectural firm. The site chosen is the triangle bounded by W. Congress, Pierce, and Lafayette Sts., hitherto occupied by a municipal department, which in turn moves to the evacuated library building.

LAFAYETTE GENERAL HOSPITAL is the largest and newest of the city's medical facilities. Erected in 1965, it has 200 beds; in 1967 a 10-bed intensive-care unit was added. OUR LADY OF LOURDES HOSPITAL, on St. Landry St., has 160 beds and a complete psychiatric unit. On its grounds toward Julien St. is the LAFAYETTE TUBERCULAR HOSPITAL; this and the LAFAYETTE CHARITY HOSPITAL nearby, both operated by the Louisiana State Dept. of Hospitals, provide 400 beds. Also functioning are the REHABILITATION CENTER and the LAFAYETTE MENTAL HEALTH TREATMENT CENTER.

A typical ACADIAN HOUSE, 702 W. University Ave., follows the lines of houses established after 1750. It is built of cypress and insulated with moss and mud. It was used as a school for the children of Jean Mouton, founder of the town.

EARLY ACADIAN INN, 1300 Pinhook Road (*private*), was one of the first inns in Vermilionville. It is constructed of cypress and has a fireplace of handmade brick.

LAFAYETTE MUSEUM, 1122 Lafayette St., occupies the former home of Alexandre Mouton, first Democratic governor of Louisiana. It contains notable antiques. With an Acadian cottage adjacent it is the Lafayette Tourist Center (*10–12, 3–5, closed Monday and Sunday morning; free*).

CHARLES MOUTON HOUSE, 338 N. Sterling Ave. (*private*) was built in 1848 by Charles Homére Mouton, jurist and lieutenant governor. This was once the center of a large plantation, since built up. The lower part of the house is of brick, painted white, the upper of cypress; six square plaster-covered brick pillars support the gallery and smaller square wooden pillars support the gabled roof. The oak trees along Sterling Ave. once were part of a grove in front of the house, where the field hands held a jamboree on Saturday nights, at which a Negro named Bazile became widely known for drumming a primitive African chant called *Bamboula*.

CITY PARK, 1,000 Mudd Ave., has long been a favorite recreation ground, with swimming pool, 18-hole golf course and community center. GIRARD PARK, 400 Girard Park Dr., is also a recreation center and site of the PLANETARIUM and YOUTH MUSEUM. The ground is historic because here the Confederates clashed with the army of General Nathaniel Banks when he marched through Vermilionville. Men from this area were members of the 1st company, 18th Louisiana Regt. BEAVER PARK and the LAFAYETTE PARK PLAYGROUND are located on Surrey St. just south of the Vermilion River, in an area that also contains the LOUISIANA NATIONAL GUARD ARMORY, the U. S. ARMY RESERVE and the U. S. NAVY RESERVE headquarters, and the PARISH SCHOOL ADMINISTRATION center. North of the river is the AMERICAN LEGION HOME.

The famous AZALEA TRAIL has one of its anchors in Lafayette. The visitor can walk and drive over 30 miles bordered by the rich colors of this opulently flowering shrub. Blooming starts in late February, continues into March. Camellias and iris are also on display in the spring.

OAKBOURNE COUNTRY CLUB, Nickerson Parkway and the Vermilion River, has been the home since 1958 of the Cajun Classic, the golf tournament that annually winds up the winter tour of the PGA. The annual Gulf Coast Oil Tournament is also held here. Northeast of the city, on N. Pierce St. and also reached by US 167 is the ACADIAN HILLS GOLF AND SWIMMING CLUB, with a 18-hole course.

On Breaux Bridge Highway (La 94) a number of religious institutions are situated. One is the CARMELITE MONASTERY, established here in 1936 by the cloistered Carmelites from New Orleans, who built this house in 1956. Another is the HOLY ROSARY INSTITUTE, a boarding and day school operated at 921 Breaux Bridge Hwy. by nuns of the Order of the Holy Family. Here also is IMMACULATA SEMINARY, established in 1947 to train young men for the priesthood. Another is the house of the DE LA SALLE CHRISTIAN BROTHERS, founded in 1923 and containing the juniorate, senior novitiate, and retirement home. The RECLUSE MONASTERY of the Missionary Recluses of Jesus and Mary, a French Canadian order, is located on US 167 S. (*Chapel open 6 a.m.–6 p.m.*)

EVANGELINE DOWNS is a major race track, usually open from April to August, but more recently extended into September. Its big features are the Southwest Louisiana Derby, the Southwest Louisiana

Futurity, and the $60,000 Lafayette Futurity on its final meeting. Post time is 7:30 p.m., but on Independence Day racing starts at 2 p.m., when the Evangeline Quarter Horse Futurity, a $150,000 purse, is run. The track is generally prosperous; in 1969 betting through mutuel windows averaged $241,000 a day. The clubhouse is glass-enclosed and grandstand and box seats accommodate 8,000. The track is reached on US 167 north.

POINTS OF INTEREST IN ENVIRONS

Myrtle Plantation House, 1 *m.;* Le Jardin de Mouton, 1.4 *m.;* Henri Bendel Estate, 2.2 *m.;* Pin Hook Bridge, 2.3 *m.;* Dan Debaillon Place, 3.9 *m.* (*see Tour 1c*). Carencro, 7.6 *m.* (*see Tour 15B*).

Lake Charles

Air Services: Texas International Airlines, up to 40 daily flights. Connections with all major lines. Total passengers boarded, 1969, 39,665. Lake Charles municipal Airport.

Bus Lines: Greyhound Lines, Continental Trailways.

Highways: Int. 10 (east-west); Int. 210 (bypass); US 90 (east-west); US 171 north to Shreveport; US 171 and La 378 to Sam Houston State Park; La 27 (west route) to Holly Beach and Gulf; La 27 (east route) to Cameron Parish hunting-fishing areas and jct. with La 82. La 384 to Cameron Parish east; US 165 northeast to Arkansas via Alexandria and Monroe, jct. with Int. 10 and US 90 about 14 *m.* east of Lake Charles. Mileage to Shreveport, 181; to Monroe 188; to Baton Rouge, 137; to New Orleans, 225.

Railroads: Kansas City Southern, Missouri Pacific, Southern Pacific for freight only passenger service to New Orleans and West Coast on Southern Pacific.

Information and Accommodations: American Press, evening and Sunday; Tourist Information Bureau, North Shore Beach; Greater Lake Charles Chamber of Commerce, 900 N. Lakeshore Dr. City has new motels, members of national chains; 98 churches and more than 24 denominations; 3 major hospitals —St. Patrick's, 241 beds; Lake Charles Memorial, 211 beds, Charity Hospital, 166 beds, 5 nursing homes, 333 beds.

Recreation and Tourist Attractions: The city has 20 parks and 1¼ *m.* of sandy beach on Lake Charles and supports all forms of acquatic sports. Sam Houston State Park, a 7-mile drive to the West Fork of the Calcasieu River and the Houston River, has 1,047 acres for camping and outdoor sports. Available are three golf courses, Lake Charles Golf & Country, Kayouche Coulee, and Frash Park Golf Club at Sulphur. Fishing is considered best in State; fresh-water fishing is available in Lake Charles, along the Channel, Prien Lake, Calcasieu Lake, and bayous; especially recommended are Federally managed Lacassine Refuge and Sabine Refuge, both in Cameron Parish, (La 27), free. Boats can be hired at Lake Charles and Cameron (town) for deepsea fishing. Ducks and other wildfowl can be hunted throughout the marshlands.

Special Events: Contraband Days, 8 days on Lake front late May, early June; Sailboat races, Lake Charles Yacht Club, usually Sundays in summer; Golf tournaments, Lake Charles Golf & Country Club, in June and August; Southwest Louisiana Deep Sea Fishing Rodeo, around July 4; Stock car races every Friday eve at Lake Charles Speedway; Motorcycle races on specific dates in summer, at Speedway; football and basketball competition at McNeese State College in season, band concerts on the land in June and July. Programs in fall and winter by Lake Charles Little Theater, Artists Civic Theater Studio Bayou Players, Civic Symphone Orchestra, Community Concert Assn., Civic Ballet and Lake Charles Ballet Society. Consult Tourist Information Bureau Lake Charles or Louisiana Tourist Commission, P. O. Box 44291, Baton Rouge.

LAKE CHARLES (13 alt., 77,998 pop. 1970; 63,392, 1960, inc. 23%), seat of Calcasieu Parish, is the industrial and recreation capital of Southwestern Louisiana. It is located on a broad sweep of the Calcasieu River and connected with the Gulf of Mexico by a 32-mile channel for deep-sea commerce. The Port of Lake Charles is the third largest port in the State, after New Orleans and Baton Rouge, and the 19th in the United States, an outlet for oil operations and the center of a petrochemical industry second only to that of the lower Mississippi River. Lake Charles, along which the city is built, is 2 m. wide, 3 m. long. Much of the economic wellbeing of the city has come from the plants along the Channel, with their huge outlays for construction and wages. Also a substantial growth continues in the tourist trade, which favors fresh-water fishing in the bayous and lakes and deep-sea fishing in the Gulf, and with wildfowl hunting in the marshes of Calcasieu and Cameron Parishes. The expansion of hotel accommodations, including the recent Holiday Inn, Downtowner Motor Inn, and Sheraton Chateau Charles Motor Inn, has helped the City.

Chennault Air Force Base is located on the eastern limits of Lake Charles. It was named for General Claire Chennault, a native of Louisiana. It has been recently deactivated.

The first settlers of Lake Charles are said to have been Martin Camersac LeBleu, a Bordeaux Frenchmen who arrived from Virginia about 1780, and Carlos Salia, a New Orleans Spaniard, who came a year or two later. Salia later changed his name to Charles Sallier, and as Charles or Charlie he gave his name to the lake and settlement. In 1803, Sallier married Catherine, daughter of Bartholomew LeBleu, and they are credited with building the first dwelling.

By the early part of the 19th century, the first stopping place east of Orange (then Green's Bluff), Texas, was Charlie's Lake. Consequently many a traveler stopped here. Many of those coming before 1842 took up Arroyo Hondo claims between the Calcasieu and Sabine Rivers. This part of the Louisiana Purchase was in dispute, first between Spain and the United States and, after the Mexican Revolution in 1821, between Mexico and the United States. While there was no open conflict, there was threat of trouble, and in 1830 the United States established Cantonment Atkinson in the northwest part of Lake Charles. It was named for General Henry Atkinson, the first adjutant general of the U. S. Army, appointed by President Monroe in 1822.

The settlements along and near Calcasieu River at this period were in St. Landry Parish in 1840. Calcasieu Parish was created from a portion of St. Landry in 1840. In 1852, Charlestown (an early name for Lake Charles) became the seat of Calcasieu Parish. A small wooden building, housing the government records and business, was placed on wheels at Marion, six miles up the Calcasieu River, driven by ox team to the river, transferred to a raft and floated to the desired location. The sheriff of the parish, Jacob Ryan, who, with Samuel Kirby and other settlers, effected the removal, has been called the Father of Lake Charles, and the principal street bears his name.

The town was incorporated in 1867, with a population of about 400. By 1890, following completion of the final link of the Southern Pacific Railway between New Orleans and Houston, the population had jumped to 3,200. Sawmills had been built and rice culture extended and improved.

One of the principal factors in developing the section was large-scale advertising. In 1887 Captain J. B. Watkins of New York moved his newspaper, the *American Press,* to Lake Charles and began an extensive publicity campaign for the growing city. A large portion of the paper's 10,000 circulation was mailed to Midwest farmers, and tons of pamphlets, circulars, and other printed matter were distributed. It is said that at one time Captain Watkins bought $1,000 worth of 1¢ stamps for this purpose.

Discovery of oil in the region early in the present century and the development of the Frasch method for mining sulphur displaced the lumber industry and were important factors in the industrial growth of Lake Charles. A great sulphur dome was found in 1905 at SULPHUR 8 *m.* west on US 90. Sulphur mining was extensive until 1924, when the diminished supply of the mineral made it unprofitable.

The chemical industry started at Lake Charles when the Olin Mathieson Alkali plant located there in 1933. By 1945 Cities Service Co. had built a high octane refinery, Firestone a latex plant, and the Defense Plant Corporation, with cooperation of Reconstruction Finance Corp. had facilities for producing butadiene, ammonia, and magnesium, and an oxidization unit. When the deep water channel was effective plants estimated to be worth $1 billion moved into the area. The corporations represented included Lone Star Cement, Pittsburgh Plate Glass, Hercules, Continental Oil, Continental Carbon, Davison Chemical division of W. R. Grace, Lockheed, Ancon, National Distillers & Chemical and others of like stature.

The need to expand facilities and provide new areas for the location of industry led to a bond issue for $13,000,000. This helped build the Industrial Canal, at the junction of the Ship Channel and the Intracoastal Waterway, 12 *m.* south of the city. The Canal has been dredged and provides 6,800 ft. on each bank for new plants, an area of 825 acres 10 to 12 ft. above mean low Gulf. A railspur to connect with the major lines at the Port was built with the help of the United States Government. The first industry to begin construction there was the Gulf Coast Aluminum Co., with an investment of $63,000,000.

PORT OF LAKE CHARLES

The LAKE CHARLES HARBOR AND TERMINAL DISTRICT, which controls 203 sq. m. including the cities of Lake Charles and Westlake, was created by the State Legislature in 1924. It is administered by a Board of Commissioners of five appointed by the Governor on recommendations of a nominating council of representatives of business, shipping, rice growing, Trades & Labor Council of AFL–CIO and members of the Legislature from Calcasieu Parish. The District comprises the waterfront on both sides of the Calcasieu River to the public wharves, 15 *m.*, and above the wharves, 11.5 *m.* There are 48 *m.* of frontage on deep water and 18 *m.* on shallow water. The Ship Channel meets the Intracoastal Waterway at the Industrial Canal 12 *m.* below Lake Charles. The District owns 1,292 acres, rail tracks, and Port facilities; 1 railroad, 7 truck lines and 9 barge lines handle the Port.

About 100 years ago the principal shipment from Lake Charles was lumber. Timber was felled in the pine forests farther north and tossed into the Calcasieu River, whence it gave work to 21 sawmills. Lumber was cut to fit the holds and decks of shallow-draft schooners. In 1880 the Morgan, Louisiana & Texas Railroad, in 1887 the Watkins Line (later part of Missouri Pacific), and in 1896 the Kansas City Southern, facilitated the shipment of lumber by land. As timber ran out rice became the principal commodity for shipping, and then came oil.

Unable to ship by water because of the obstructed channel to the Gulf Lakes Charles shippers had to pay the higher costs of rail transportation to reach such outlets as Galveston. In 1918 they began a campaign to get the Federal Government to deepen the channel, but the authorities decided the amount of tonnage handled did not justify the work. When the State Legislature in 1921 authorized the parishes to issue bonds for improving river channels or canals, Calcasieu Parish voted $2,750,000 to deepen the channel from Lake Charles to the Intracoastral Waterway, whence shipments could take the Waterway 22.5 *m.* west to the Sabine River and through Sabine Pass to the Gulf. This was completed in 1926. By 1928 the Federal Government took over maintenance of the channel.

Convinced that the Port had a great future the people of Lake Charles repeatedly voted bond issues for new facilities. The three railroads were invited to run a rail line to the wharves; when they refused the Port built its own 5 *m.* of main line trackage, plus yard connections. In 1931 the Port added a third wharf, 1,600 ft. long, costing $700,000.

From 1928 to 1933 the Port of Lake Charles tried vainly to get the Government to refund the construction costs of the channel. In 1934 the Port began agitation for a direct channel to the Gulf through Calcasieu Pass; this was finally accomplished by 1941. From 1956 to 1960 the Port worked to get the Government to deepen the channel. In 1960 the Corps of Engineers, USA, approved a depth of 40 ft. and a width of 400 ft., and Congress made available $17,000,000.

The type of wharf construction built here is similar to that of New Orleans. Wharves are parallel to the river bank and there is a 32-ft. apron on which two tracks make possible direct loading from car to ship. The Port can berth ten vessels and two barges at one time. Its piers and transit sheds are supported by 14 storage warehouses back of the waterfront, accessible to raidroad cars and trucks. Industries own dock facilities as a private right and no public authority is exercised over their terminals. This has proved an incentive to manufacturers to locate in the District.

The Port continues the installation of modern facilities to keep up with expansion. In 1970 it applied part of a $9,000,000 appropriation to a new handling and loading system for bulk cargoes, such as petroleum, coke, wood chips and coal. Ships can be loaded at a rate of 1,250 short tons per hour. A 1,000,000 gallon storage tank with shipside pipelines was built to hold creosote that comes by barge from Pittsburgh and other steel centers and is used to preserve wood. Other containers hold coconut oil from the Philippine Islands, to be used in soap, margerine, and food products. An unusual facility is the grinding plant for phosphate rock or bone phosphate of lime, conveyed here from Florida and used as a fertilizer ingredient; it also grinds barite ore for use as oil-drilling mud. Raw and calcined coke, an oil refinery product, is conveyed from storage to ship by belt conveyor at a rate of 450 tons per hour.

This is the major exporting port for bagged rice. The Parish of Calcasieu leads in the production of rice and Lake Charles has milled rice for many years. In 1968 the Port moved 633,232 tons. In 1969 two bulk rice storage tanks were completed.

POINTS OF INTEREST

Municipal and parish headquarters are located in the CITY HALL and the COURTHOUSE of Calcasieu Parish, that stand opposite each other on Ryan St. The City Hall, at the corner of Kirby, is a decorative red brick building with cream-colored quoins, 2 stories tall with a square clock tower that rises above the main entrance. The Courthouse occupies a landscaped area between N. Court and Gill Sts., and is a formal 2-story building of tan brick and marble trim with wide stone steps approaching a Greek porch, where four fluted Doric columns hold up the pediment, and a low dome covers the central axis. On the grounds stands a tall Ionic column of marble surmounted by the statue of a Confederate soldier. Plans include a new Police Administration Bldg. with the City Court and Jail.

A new CIVIC CENTER, comprising a coliseum seating 7,000, a theater seating 2,000, and ample exhibition space, was begun on the Lake Front in the fall of 1969 for completion January 1, 1972. The enterprise started in 1965, when a bond issue for $5,000,000 was voted for preliminary work on site and plans. An urban renewal grant of $1,400,-000 was obtained from the Dept. of Housing & Urban Development for seawall, filling and preparation of parking area, total 60 acres. In 1969 another bond issue of $10,000,000 was authorized. The south 20 acres will be landscaped; the seawall will have a seating section for viewing aquatic sports, and the parking space will accommodate 2,200 cars. All is within walking distance of hotels and shops.

At the same time the Downtown Merchants, with the help of the Office of City Planning, created the RYAN MALL, a four-block area restricted to pedestrians and provided with five multi-level pavilions for sales and exhibits. The Mall extends between Kirby St. and Mill St. and is part of Operation Heartbeat, which gave a new appearance to a hitherto congested business area. Included in the creation is an inner

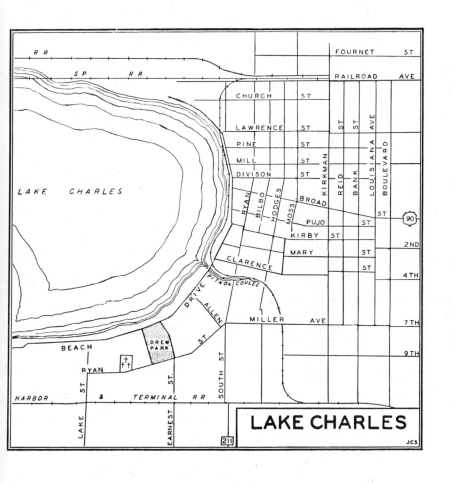

traffic loop, four lanes wide for two-way traffic, covering eight square blocks, in which vacant lots have been hard-surfaced for parking cars.

The LAKE CHARLES PUBLIC LIBRARY, 411 Pujo St., was founded in 1904 and primarily serves the city. It is one of four municipal libraries in the State. In 1969 it had 60,393 books, of which 48,334 or 80% were adult books. In that year the library circulated 117,833 books, 90,177 of which were adult and 27,656 juvenile, and nearly half of the adults called for nonfiction. As another service the library circulated 8,555 records. Cost of operation was $102,491, and $26,657, or 26%, was spent for books. The library is supported by a tax of 1½ mills.

The CALCASIEU PARISH PUBLIC LIBRARY, opened in 1944, directs its activities from 700 East Prien Road, a metal building erected in 1965, of which it is said that it lacks architectural distinction but has a high functional capacity. The Parish system has 12 branches, located in Lake Charles, Bell City, Carver, De Quincy, Hayes, Iowa, Maplewood, Moss Bluff, Starks, Sulphur, Vinton, and Westlake. The system is supported by a tax of 1½ mills.

In 1969 the Parish had 98,201 books, 58% of them adult, and circulated 459,177, of which 248,017 were adult and 211,160 juvenile. Adult fiction was 25% of the circulation. It also circulated 6,117 records, and the reference desks answered 31,865 inquiries. The summer reading club enrolls more than 3,000 children. Cost of operation was $170,946, of which $26,312 was paid for books. To get tax support the system had the able assistance of the Business & Professional Women's Club of Lake Charles.

McNEESE STATE COLLEGE, the chief collegiate institution in Southwestern Louisiana, is a four-year coeducational school with a wide range of studies in Education, Business, Humanities, Agriculture, Engineering, the Biological and Physical Sciences leading to baccalaureate degrees, and in the Division of Graduate Studies to degrees of master of arts and doctor of philosophy. A School of Continuing Education was opened in the fall of 1970, when a School of Engineering was emerging from the planning stage. The campus comprises about 700 acres and the SPECIAL EDUCATION CENTER, with buildings for administration, physical science and teacher education, occupies part of the former Chennault Air Force Base.

A two-year junior college was established in 1939 as a division of Louisiana State University. In 1940 it was taken over by the Board of Supervisors and named McNeese, commemorating John McNeese, who became the first superintendent of schools in 1888. In 1950 McNeese became a State college under the State Board of Education with a 4-year curriculum. It quickly proved its usefulness to the area. In 1963 it enrolled 2,802 students; in 1969–70 it had 4,533 and a faculty of 224.

McNeese gives strong support to the training of teachers, who will function on all levels in Louisiana. The School of Education grants degrees in the field of early childhood education, from kindergarten through third grade; its Department of Health & Physical Education trains coaches as well as teachers and includes courses for drivers. The Department of Speech offers majors in radio broadcasting and telecasting. English, French and Spanish are four-year courses. Forestry includes study in camp at DeQuincy. There are pre-dental, pre-medical, pre-pharmacy, and pre-optometry courses; also in wildlife management, home economics and nursing. The Engineering and Technological Dept. has a computing center; chemical engineering offers studies in pulp and paper making, of special local interest, and there is even a two-year course in mortuary science, to provide proficiency in funeral service, leading to the degree of associate.

Among recent additions to the physical plant is the HOLBROOK RANCH STUDENT CENTER, known as The Ranch. A 3-story AGRICULTURE BLDG. has just been completed. Two new 5-story dormitories, KING HALL for men and BURTON HALL for women, opened in the fall, 1970, are considered innovations in this style of housing; each contains 72 eight-student suites, and each suite has a living room, a study room, a double bath and four bedrooms.

The LESTER E. FRAZAR MEMORIAL LIBRARY, named after the first president of the college, is located on Contraband Bayou and is soon to receive a 4-story addition. It has been building a substantial collection of books and materials and has, among other services, the Regional Film Library, which provides films without charge to the schools of Louisiana. The *Contraband* is the student newspaper; *Arena* is a literary magazine edited by students, and *The Log* is the college annual. The student body is organized for self-government on the model of the United States.

McNeese has won a leading place in the cultural life of Lake Charles by frequent musical programs and exhibits in its Auditorium and Squires Hall. The Civil Symphony Orchestra and the Dallas Symphony Orchestra perform there; *The Messiah* is sung in December by a chorus of 240 voices; the Bayou Players produce plays and other organizations give band and operatic programs. The Fine Arts Gallery and the Auditorium Gallery have exhibits of painting and jewelry. The college also supports competitive collegiate sports and is a member of the Gulf States Conference. Its football team competes in the Cowboy Stadium. The Cowboy Marching Band is a special student feature.

SOWELA TECHNICAL INSTITUTE, the first technical institution supported by the State of Louisiana, offers students a wide variety of courses in business and industry. It teaches such subjects as aerodynamics, drafting, electronics, machine trades, data processing, nursing, with clinical experience, and numerous other bases for sound technical knowledge. It enrolls around 1,000.

The CALCASIEU PARISH SCHOOL SYSTEM represents a consolidation, since 1967, of the public schools of Lake Charles and the outlying parish. Their history is unique. In 1907 the schools of Lake Charles became independent of the parish and the two system developed side by side. A professional study of their workings a few years ago led to the recommendation that they be reunited, and this was done in July, 1967. The present system is the fifth largest in Louisiana, with 73 schools, more than 1,600 teachers, and more than 38,000 pupils. LaGrange Senior High School enrolls 1,800. The services include classes for the blind, and for those with speech and hearing difficulties, the orthopedically handicapped, the homebound, and those with learning disabilities. There are adult education for out-of-school youth, guidance counselors and vocational training. There are 10 schools in the ROMAN CATHOLIC PAROCHIAL SYSTEM, which has just voted the consolidation of its two high schools in a coeducational institution called St. Louis High School, with an enrollment of around 6,000.

Of the 98 churches in the city, the CHURCH OF THE IMMAC-ULATE CONCEPTION, the FIRST BAPTIST CHURCH, and the FIRST METHODIST CHURCH, are the bestknown houses of worship. The Church of the Immaculate Conception occupies landscaped grounds on Kirby St. and is the principal edifice for Roman Catholics, numerically the largest group in the city. The Baptist organizations have the largest number of churches. There are 25 different faiths in Lake Charles.

City Scenes

Chamber of Commerce of the New Orleans Area

CHANGING SKYLINE OF NEW ORLEANS. SHELL BLDG., 52 STORIES

AERIAL VIEW OF DOWNTOWN NEW ORLEANS, WITH ARABI
BEYOND RIVER

Louisiana Stadium & Exposition District

STADIUM SKETCHED ON PROPOSED SITE, MIDTOWN NEW ORLEANS

AERIAL VIEW OF NEW ORLEANS TRADE MART AND RIVERGATE:
CUSTOM HOUSE AT RIGHT

Chamber of Commerce of the New Orleans Area

CHARITY HOSPITAL COMPLEX, NEW ORLEANS, WITH VETERANS
ADMINISTRATION HOSPITAL, MEDICAL SCHOOLS OF TULANE UNIV.
AND LOUISIANA STATE UNIV. TOP RIGHT: CIVIC CENTER, WITH
CITY HALL AND STATE OFFICE BUILDING

From New Orleans World Trade Center, *publication of International House*
Photographs by Charles F. Weber and Samuel R. Sutton

ENTRANCE, NEW CONVENTION HALL, SHREVEPORT

NEW CONVENTION HALL AND CIVIC THEATER, SHREVEPORT

BARNWELL GARDEN AND ART CENTER ON RED RIVER PARKWAY

OUACHITA RIVER BETWEEN MONROE AND WEST MONROE

Roger Kelley Photo. Monroe Chamber of Commerce
MONROE CIVIC CENTER AND SYMPHONIC WATERFALL

Minden

Highways: US 80 and I-20 are the principal east-west routes US 79 comes from the northeast and joins US 80 to Shreveport. Others direct or close by are La 7, 159, 164, and 518.

Railroads: Illinois Central, Kansas City Southern.

Bus Line: Continental Trailways.

Airport: Municipal, with 4,000-ft. runway.

Information: Press-Herald, daily since 1966; Minden Chamber of Commerce.

Accommodations: Three modern motels on main highways. Thirty churches. Two theaters.

Recreation: The Pinehill County Club has a 9-hole golf course. The city has 4 parks, 4 swimming pools, a lighted ball park. Lake Bistineau and the Caney Lakes are within easy driving range. Facilities for bowling, tennis, fishing, camping, and water sports.

Annual Events: Flower Show, April; Bossier-Webster Fair & Forest Festival, October.

MINDEN (181 alt., 13,996 pop. 1970; 12,788, 1960, inc. 9.5%) is the trading and shipping center of a productive cotton-growing and farming district in the northwestern part of the State. It is the seat of Webster Parish, which produces around $30,000,000 worth of minerals annually, these being, in order of value, natural gas, petroleum, natural gas liquids, sand and gravel. Minden makes presses for cotton gins.

Minden was founded in 1836 as a real estate promotion by a German-American named Charles Hance Veeder, who named it after a town on the Weser River in Germany, the birthplace of Veeder's parents. Veeder left Minden to take part in the California gold rush.

Minden has a wide main street, tree-shaded residential sections, parks planted with shrubs and flowers, and a general air of comfort and well-being. Saturday in Minden finds the streets, stores, and theaters crowded with farmers and their families in town for their weekly shopping and recreation. In the vicinity are numerous small lakes and streams affording excellent fishing, boating, and picnicking sites.

Minden is about 28 *m.* east of the Shreveport-Bossier industrial area, with which it is in direct connection over US 79 and 80, and the new Interstate 20, which crosses the northern part of Louisiana to Vicksburg. Hence it profits by plants along these routes, the largest of which, the Louisiana Army Ammunition Plant, usually referred to as LAAP, is only 7 *m.* west of Minden. This is owned by the U. S. Government and operated by the Remington Office Equipment Division of Sperry Rand Corporation. It produces ammunition for the U. S. Army, Navy, and Air Force, and is the largest manufacturing employer in Northwest Louisiana. In the 12 months ended February 29, 1967, the plant had orders worth more than $54,000,000, and the payroll for February amounted to $2,700,000. The impact on the welfare of the area was marked because many of the employees live in Minden.

POINTS OF INTEREST

The new CIVIC AUDITORIUM, part of the Minden Civic Center complex, was dedicated during 9 days of varied programs beginning April 3, 1971. There were addresses, one by Mayor Moon Landrieu of New Orleans; musical and dramatic shows, a Grambling College jazz concert; a Northwest Louisiana Amateur Boxing Tournament, plays by Centenary Players, and other public entertainment. The Auditorium seats 1,300, has removable seats for spectacles, and can dine 900.

WEBSTER PARISH COURTHOUSE, Pearl and S. Broadway Sts., is a two-story stone and buff-colored brick structure with an octagonal white dome. Each side has a portico with four ionic columns.

The WEBSTER PARISH LIBRARY, 521 East & West St., is a parish-wide, locally supported public library, which profits by a close relationship with the Louisiana State Library for the use of the latter's collections. There are three branches in Minden and single ones in Cotton Valley, Dayline, Dubberly, Heflin, Sarepta, Shongaloo, Sibley, and Springhill. One bookmobile is in operation. The Headquarters Office is located in a residential area in a Spanish type stucco house, the gift of the late Mr. and Mrs. Edmund L. Steward and Miss Dell Brown. The library has been in operation since September, 1929, and is now supported by a property tax of 3 mills.

The library had a collection of 68,685 books in June, 1970, and an average annual circulation of more than 225,000. It stocks 61 magazine titles in multiple copies, 749 individual recording titles, and 40 framed pictures. A number of film projectors, tape recorders and record players may be borrowed by adults.

MINDEN SANITARIUM, Monroe and Cedar Sts., was established in 1926 as a semi-public institution. There are also four major clinics in Minden, served by ten physicians and six dentists.

GERMANTOWN COLONY site. A marker cites that 7 miles northeast on Rt. 186 are the remains of a colony founded 1835 by followers of Count Leon, who came from Germany on account of their religious beliefs and operated a communal village until 1871.

The NORTHWEST LOUISIANA VOCATIONAL SCHOOL is a training school for mechanical and allied skills benefiting those who seek employment in the area.

Caney Lakes Recreation Area, Kisatchie National Forest, 5 *m.* north on La. 159, then 2 *m.* west. Space for 29 tents, 5 trailers. Electricity, fireplaces, showers. Pets allowed. Fee.

Monroe

Air Services: Delta Airlines, 2 daily flights east to Atlanta and 2 daily flights west to Dallas. Texas International Airlines, 2 daily flights to Houston and 2 flights daily to Little Rock. Southern Airways, 3 flights daily to Memphis and 3 daily to New Orleans. Monroe Municipal Airport, 5 *m.* east of Downtown, has 6,100 ft. jet runway.

Bus Lines: Southern Continental Bus Lines, 22 daily arrivals and departures. One intercity system operating 6 a.m. to 10:20 p.m.

Railroads: Missouri Pacific Railroad; Illinois Central Railroad; Arkansas-Louisiana-Missouri Railroad.

Highways: Int. 20 and US 80 east-west; US 165 north-south; US 34, La 15, La 139, La 143.

Information: Monroe Chamber of Commerce, 102 S. Grand St. *World,* morning and Sunday; *News-Star,* evening, 411 N. 4th St. Two tv, 4 radio stations.

Organizations and Accommodations: 2 major hotels, 12 major motels, Monroe; 4 major motels West Monroe; St. Francis and 2 other hospitals; 143 churches, all denominations; 3 school systems, City, Parish and Parochial.

Recreation: Municipal golf, 2 9-hole courses; Bayou DeSiard Country Club, 18-hole course; Highland Park Country Club, West Monroe, 9 holes. Bernstein Park and Zoo; Forsythe Park, tennis and swimming; Ouachita River and bayous, swimming and fishing. Four indoor recreational centers. Frequent excursions on the *Twin Cities Queen.*

Spectator Sports: Northeast State basketball, Civic Arena, winter. Championship wrestling, Civic Center Arena, Jan., Feb., Mar. Air Show, Salmon Field, June.

Annual Events: Mardi Gras, on Shrove Tuesday; Citywide religious Sings, by Negro choirs on Good Friday; Easter Egg Hunt at Forsythe Park or Bernstein Park on Easter Sunday; Labor Day Barbecue at Bernstein Park for organized labor; Gospel singing, Civic Center. Broadway Theater Series, Civic Center Theater. Northeast Concert series with symphony orchestras. Art Shows, Masur Museum. Championship Rodeo, Civic Center; Children's Theater Festival, Northeast Louisiana State College, Miss Louisiana Pageant. Festival of Music, Civic Center Arena. Square Dance Festival.

MONROE (77 alt., 56,374 pop. 1970; 52,219, 1960, increase of 8%), fourth largest city in Louisiana, is the seat of Ouachita ("Wash-i-taw") Parish, the metropolis of northeastern Louisiana and an industrial center. It has an area of 33 sq. m. fronting 9.2 *m.* on the Ouachita River, and its neighbor, West Monroe (14,868 pop. 1870) has an area of 5.7 sq. m.

Monroe is on the big Interstate 20 highway, on a line with Shreveport. It has a mayor and commission form of government, whereas West Monroe has a mayor and aldermen.

Ouachita Parish produces petroleum, natural gas, and natural gas liquids. In 1968 the value of its mineral production was $24,791,000, a big increase over 1967, when it was $11,360,000.

The business and cultural interests of Monroe have expanded greatly since World War II and the city makes a lively bid for conventions, has considerable space available for outdoor activities, and provides programs of operatic and symphonic music. Its industrial facilities include 770 acres at Selma Field, 250 acres administered by Southwest Industrial Park, Inc., and other acreage in the Bayou DeSiard Industrial Park outside the city. Its cultural units include Masur Museum of the Arts, Ouachita Valley Museum, Strauss Playhouse, Northeast State Concerts Assn., and activities of Northeast Louisiana State College.

The MONROE CIVIC CENTER was dedicated in September, 1967, and gave the city the means of providing superior accommodations for state and national organizations. It occupies 31 acres and has three spacious buildings, the THEATRE, the ARENA, and the CONVENTION HALL. At the approach to the Center is the Anna Gray Noe Mall, and the NOE SYMPHONIC COLORFALL, a fountain costing $100,000, donated by Mr. and Mrs. James A. Noe, on which colors play to the accompaniment of melodies. At the left of the group as one enters stands the Theatre, which has seats for 2,245. In the middle is the huge Arena, its roof 70 ft. above the mall, its seating capacity 7,900, with 4,212 permanent seats. At the right is the Convention Hall, adaptable to exhibits, meetings, separate conferences and banquets. By means of moving walls the large hall can be converted into four independent rooms. The Civic Center was designed by Johns & Neel and built by Jesse F. Heard & Sons.

MONROE GOVERNMENT CENTER, built in 1966, covers four city blocks and consists of three buildings, the CITY HALL, the POLICE DEPARTMENT HEADQUARTERS and JAIL, and the CITY COURT. The City Hall is the major building, contains 29,304 sq. ft. on two levels, and cost $3,000,000. The exterior of the Hall is black granite and ornamental precast concrete with inset windows. The foyer is of Botticino marble with a terrazzo floor. The Mayor's conference room and the Council Chamber, seating 100, are panelled in walnut.

The Police Department Headquarters has 12,500 sq. ft. of office space and room in the Jail for 138 prisoners. The City Court occupies a compact one-story courtroom and office building. Beside the flagpoles in front of City Hall is a reflecting basin. Paved pedestrian malls link the buildings, and there are five major parking areas. The buildings of the Center were designed by L. Milton King and William King Stubbs of Monroe and constructed by Jesse F. Heard & Sons of West Monroe. The Center was built with part of the proceeds of a bond issue for $11,250,000, and was dedicated in October, 1966.

HISTORY

Hernando De Soto himself may have been the first white man to explore the Monroe region; he is believed to have descended the Ouachita to its junction with the Tensas, in 1542. It is also likely that Tonti, in his efforts to join La Salle in 1689, passed through the section. In 1700, more than a century and a half after De Soto's reputed visit, Bienville and St. Denis, accompanied by Canadians and Indians, doubtless visited the Monroe area, while engaged in exploring the country west of the Mississippi. Bienville's account mentions the Ouachita Indians, one of the tribes for whom the area was a popular hunting ground.

There were white settlers on Ouachita River during the first half of the eighteenth century and a few tiny settlements promoted by private colonization ventures. Although approved by the French Colonial government, these settlements received no official recognition, nor were they classed as posts of authority. On an old map supposed to show French and Spanish possessions prior to 1765 "Poste des Washitas" is written across the Ouachita Valley, but no definite spot is shown.

In February, 1783, Jean Baptiste Filhiol, or Don Juan Bautista Filhiol (1740–1821), as he was known to the Spanish, was appointed commandant of the Poste des Washitas. Although a Frenchman, Filhiol had served under Spanish Don Bernardo de Galvez against the English in Florida. Setting out from New Orleans in keelboats, Filhiol and his party of settlers and soldiers made their way up the Mississippi, Red and Black Rivers to the Ouachita country. May found them as far up the Ouachita River as Écore-à-Fabry, now Camden, Arkansas. Not finding that location satisfactory, the party returned down-stream and settled on the present site of Monroe in the year 1785.

Fearful of Indian attacks upon the few settlers he had managed to gather about him at the post, Filhiol erected a fort for their protection in 1790, which he called Fuerte (Sp. fort) Miro, in honor of the Spanish governor, Don Estevan Miro. In 1795 and 1796 two large land grants were made to the Marquis de Maison Rouge and to the Baron de Bastrop, a Hollander ennobled by Fredrick the Great. The latter grant was later to associate the names Aaron Burr, Edward Livingston, and Stephen Girard with the region. Other early settlers were the Bréards, the Chevalier D'Anemours, and Abraham Morehouse.

The little settlement of Fort Miro grew slowly, the cultivation of large crops of cotton being curtailed at first because of the difficulties and dangers of transportation. In the year 1819, however, when the steamboat *James Monroe* chugged up the Ouachita, the first steamboat ever to ascend the stream, a new and prosperous era was launched. A convivial delegation of residents headed by Judge Henry Bry visited the boat and after partaking of the hospitality of its captain, unanimously decided to change the name of Fort Miro to Monroe. Many steamboats followed the *James Monroe;* and cotton, the principal crop, became highly profitable.

It was not until 1860 that the first trains of the Vicksburg, Shreveport & Pacific ran between Vicksburg and Monroe. This line became a part of the Illinois Central System.

During the War between the States many skirmishes were fought in the neighborhood, including two in the town itself on August 2 and September 3, 1863. During the siege of Vicksburg Federal gunboats commanded by Admiral Porter steamed up the Ouachita and destroyed the courthouse and other public buildings.

Following the Reconstruction period Monroe began to enjoy a steady growth. Its industrial era did not begin, however, until after the discovery of the gas field in 1916.

POINTS OF INTEREST

NORTHEAST LOUISIANA STATE COLLEGE is located in the eastern part of Monroe on a tree-shaded campus of 150 acres through which flows the Bayou DeSiard. It has developed to a four-year coeducational institution since 1931, when it began as a junior college of the Ouachita Parish school system. After affiliation for some years with the Louisiana State University it was transferred in 1950 to the State Board of Education and called by its present name. In addition to courses in liberal arts, science, education, business administration, pharmacy, and pre-professional studies, the college in 1961 established a graduate school and in 1968 was authorized to give the degrees of doctor of philosophy and doctor of education.

In the 1960–70 decade the college pursued an extensive building program, which greatly increased its classroom and dormitory facilities. Among new academic buildings were Administration, Sandel Library, Garrett Hall, a coliseum for the Dept. of Health and Physical Education, and the School of Pharmacy. The College Union received an addition in 1962; two dining halls and a cafeteria were added, and the Brown Stadium was built in 1967. Ten new domitories have been erected since 1961.

SANDEL LIBRARY occupies a two-story structure of contemporary design on Hippolite St. It has more than 120,000 volumes, 1,730 periodicals, and 8,703 volumes on microfilm. A film library is maintained for the use of schools. The SPECIAL EDUCATION CENTER extends its services to participating parishes, giving attention to the needs of exceptional and handicapped children and their teachers. During the 1969–70 school year the college enrolled 6,845 students and had a faculty of 898.

OUACHITA PARISH PUBLIC LIBRARY, founded 1916, has its headquarters at 1800 Stubbs Ave. It operates three branch libraries and two bookmobiles. In 1969 it reported 135,312 volumes available and a circulation of 469,126, of which 74,494 were distributed by bookmobile and 205,920 were children's books.

OUACHITA PARISH COURTHOUSE, 301 S. Grand St., is a gray and white stone building with two wings and an inset colonnade of fluted Ionic columns across the second and third stories of the façade. The building was completely renovated and the two wings were added in 1968. The square was donated to Monroe by its founder, Don Juan Filhiol. In a glass case above the judge's bench in the courtroom, is the sword of Don Juan Filhiol, first commandant of the Post of Ouachita, which was presented to him by Don Estevan Miro, Governor General of the Province of Louisiana.

On the site of OLD FORT MIRO, 424 S. Grand St., stood a wooden stockade built in 1790 as a protection against unfriendly Indians.

The COOLEY HOUSE (*private*), 1011 S. Grand St., is a two-story cement-covered brick house with a brown wood trim. It was built in 1926 from a design by Walter Burley Griffin, the Chicago architect who planned Canberra, the capitol of Australia. Mr. Cooley's brother was a well-known steamboat captain on the Mississippi and Ouachita Rivers, and often brought passengers to the house as guests.

LAYTON CASTLE, in the 1300 block of S. Grand St., has within its walls part of the old Bry (pronounced Bre) House, built about 1810 by Judge Henry Bry, who came to Fort Miro in 1803. Bry was an intimate friend of Don Juan Filhiol and Baron de Bastrop, and upon occasion entertained John James Audubon. Some of the rarest specimens of camellia have grown to enormous size here.

Layton Castle was built by the widow of Robert Layton II, grandson of Henry Bry, in 1910. Its bricks are a dull pink in color, almost the same shade and texture as those of the silkworm house, built a century earlier. The principal architectural feature is a tower. Within Layton Castle are treasured lithographs and chromolithographs of pictures painted by Audubon, a small folio of Audubon's works, and other interesting volumes and documents.

The J. R. WOOTEN HOUSE (*garden open*), 2111 S. Grand St., was once the overseer's home for the Lower Pargoud Plantation. The house is one story in height with six square wooden columns across the long front gallery. Screwed into the paneled gallery ceiling are immense hand-made iron hooks from which large earthenware jugs filled with

KEY TO MONROE MAP

1. Ouachita Parish Courthouse
2. Site of Old Fort Miro
3. Cooley House
4. Layton Castle
5. J. R. Wooten House
6. U.S. Locks and Dam
7. St. Francis Sanitarium
8. Federal Building
9. Sycamore Hall
10. Stubbs House
11. Victor C. Barringer House
12. American Legion Home
13. Forsyth Park
14. Lakeside Golf and Country Club
15. Upper Pargoud Plantation House
16. Pargoud Indian Mound
17. O'Kelly House
18. Saunders Monument
19. Bernstein Park

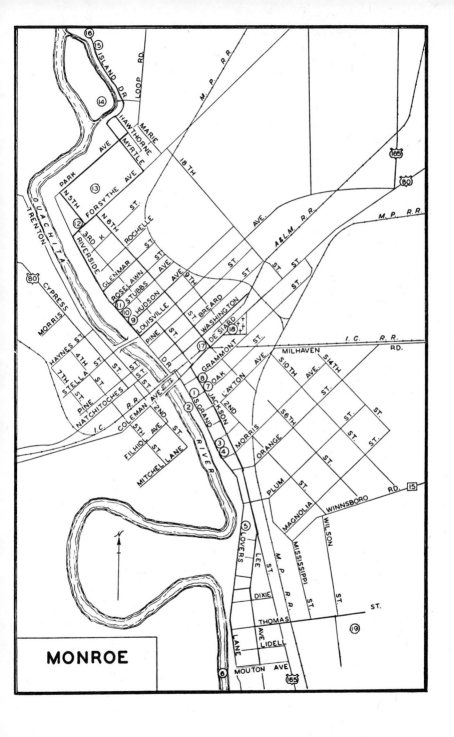

MONROE

water were suspended by iron chains and swung back and forth by boy slaves for the purpose of cooling drinking water.

The U. S. LOCKS AND DAM (*not visible at high-water stage*), S. Grand and Mouton Sts., were constructed to keep Ouachita River navigable the year round. There is fine fishing for white bass from the dam when the water is low.

The ST. FRANCIS SANITARIUM (*visiting hours 10–11 a.m., 2–4 and 7–9 p.m.*), 309 Jackson St., conducted by the Franciscan Sisters, was a gift of Father Enaut, for 51 years a resident of the community. The original four-story red brick building was begun in 1912.

The FEDERAL BUILDING, corner Jackson and Grammont Sts., a three-story modern concrete structure, houses the post office, Federal district court, and other government offices.

SYCAMORE HALL (*private*), 906 Riverside Dr., so named because of an immense sycamore tree in the front garden, was formerly owned by John Ludeling, Chief Justice of the State Supreme Court and prominent Radical politician of Reconstruction days. The original home, destroyed by fire in 1930, was said to have been haunted after the murder of Ludeling's son, a crime which attracted nationwide attention. The present house is a modern white frame structure. The gardens are among the most beautiful in Monroe.

The STUBBS HOUSE (*private*), 916 Riverside Dr., was built by Frank P. Stubbs in 1853, and is one of the oldest homes in Monroe. It is a one-story frame structure with a carriage porch. Square columns support the hipped and dormered roof. In the early spring immense wisteria vines climbing to a great height into the trees at the rear present beautiful spectacle. A patch of bamboo is unusual this far north.

The VICTOR C. BARRINGER HOUSE, 1004 Riverside Dr., houses a fine collection of Indian relics, pottery, cooking vessels, implements of war, and arrowheads.

The AMERICAN LEGION HOME, corner Forsythe Ave. and N. Fourth St., was built as a memorial to veterans of World War I. It is a red brick building with white exterior woodwork.

FORSYTHE PARK has free tennis courts, a municipal golf course, a clubhouse, bathhouses, and a swimming pool.

The LAKESIDE GOLF AND COUNTRY CLUB [*18 holes*], is situated on an island formed by Ouachita River and Lake Phillips.

The UPPER PARGOUD PLANTATION HOUSE (*open*), end of Island Dr., facing Ouachita River, is considered one of the oldest in the parish. It was built in the early nineteenth century as an overseer's home, by Hypolite Pargoud, one of Monroe's first wealthy planters and merchants. A frame structure, two stories in height, it has a gabled roof broken by wide three-windowed dormers and supported by wooden columns of the Doric order.

The PARGOUD INDIAN MOUND, 400 yards north of the Upper Pargoud Plantation House, between the levee and Ouachita River, is a relic of an Indian tribe that once made the Ouachita Valley its home. According to tradition the mound was built as a burial place for Wichita, beautiful daughter of the Indian chief, Ucita, who died after she had been deserted by Juan Ortego, a member of de Narvaez's expedition, whose life she had saved, and who married her.

The O'KELLY HOUSE (*private*), 123 N. Sixth St., occupies a portion of the De la Baume grant, acquired by the Chevalier D'Anemours in the early 1790's, and bought in 1869 or 1870 by Colonel Henry O'Kelly, who added the front part of the house about 1880. The house is surrounded by fine old trees, among which is one of the largest specimens of holly in the section. The building is a one-and-one-half-story frame structure with a wide gallery and square columns across the front, massive cypress doors, and green-shuttered windows.

SAUNDERS MONUMENT, near the entrance to the Old City Cemetery, 900 DeSiard St., was erected in memory of Sidney Saunders (1845–89) by his wife, Ann Livingston, as a rebuke to gossip concerning the marital status of the pair. The granite tomb is topped by a life-size statue of Saunders holding in his hand a scroll purporting to be his marriage license. It is inscribed,

This is to certify that Sidney W. Saunders & Ann Livingstone of Monroe in the State of La., were by me joined together in holy matrimony, March 25, 1875. 'John M. Young, justice of the peace, City of St. Louis.' Witnesses: John W. Rice, Frank Gregory.

Inscribed on the pedestal is the following:

Is it in heaven a crime to love too well? To bear too tender or too firm a heart? Sidney: I could have well forgiven that last seeming cruel act of thine (for you wanted me with you in heaven), had you with your life taken mine. Trembling and alone I tread life's dreary strand beset by envy, strife and jealousy; but mid it all, God and love of thee has staid my hand to raise that marble to thy memory. My husband: may God in mercy pardon me if, when here I come to weep and pray, all my soul and thought shall be of thee, and rapt in thee my idol from the Maker stray. Farewell: this monument is now my last adieu till we meet no more to separate. I say in heaven: for whereth you are, our boy and you, there is my heaven: for that alone your faithful, loving wife prays, watches and waits.

BERNSTEIN PARK, east end of Thomas St. on the southeastern edge of the city, is the site of the new LOUISIANA PURCHASE GARDENS AND ZOO, opened April 10, 1971, to commemorate the Louisiana Purchase. The 13 states of the Purchase are represented by characteristic flora. There are rides on a stagecoach, a train with coal-burning locomotive, and boats.

The BIBLE RESEARCH CENTER, 2004 Riverside Drive, opened in the fall, 1970, is a nonsectarian, nondenominational foundation whose object is "to allow all to discover enlightened understanding through research into the little known facts of the Bible." It provides lectures and commentaries about the Bible, has a research library, exhibition hall, reading solarium, and microfilm room. The Rare Book Room houses the Marian-Gordon-Fraser collection of rare Bibles; as well as prints; the Mapparium has ancient and rare biblical maps. There is a copy of the 1848 edition of the first translation in English of the New Testament by John Wycliffe in 1386. There are also examples of illuminated manuscripts on vellum.

MASUR MUSEUM, S. Grand St., has regular exhibits of the fine arts and subjects of cultural interest, including history and archaeology. Exhibits are changed every month from September through June. The museum is housed in a former residence built in 1929.

Natchitoches

Airport: Municipal Airport, Airport Road.

Bus Lines: Continental Trailways, 729 Third St.

Highways: La 1, north-south; US 84 to Natchez, Miss. via Winnfield; La 6 junction with US 71 at Clarence, also west to Texas.

Railroads: Texas & Pacific R.R., connection with Kansas City Southern.

Information: The *Natchitoches Times:* Natchitoches Parish Chamber of Commerce, 781 Front St.; television & radio stations.

Organizations and Accommodations: Natchitoches Parish Hospital, 501 Keyser Ave.; Geriatrics Hospital. 30 Churches orthodox and evangelical; Parish Library, 431 Jefferson St.

Recreation and Sports: Fishing in Cane River Lake, Black Lake, Clear Lake, Saline Lake. Hunting for deer, duck, quail, fox, squirrel in season. City Park and East Fifth St. Park, camping, swimming, water skiing, outdoor sports. Competitive sports at Prather Coliseum, Northwestern State University.

Special Events: Cultural programs at University during school year. Rodeo in Prather Coliseum. Garden Club spring tour, usually May. Conducted tours to historic houses and places by Assn. of Natchitoches Women for the Preservation of Historic Natchitoches; Annual Tour, second week in October; special tours by arrangement with Assn., Box 2105, Natchitoches, La., 71457. Tourist Appreciation Day, second October weekend. Christmas Festival starts first Saturday in December with parade and river show.

NATCHITOCHES (pronounced Nak'-a-tosh, 120 alt., 15,974 pop. 1970; 13,924, 1960), is the seat of Natchitoches Parish and the oldest town in Louisiana. It is located on the west bank of Cane River Lake, which was part of the main channel of the Red River until the river changed its course in 1832. Today the lake is an attractive recreation area, especially for fishing, and is regularly stocked by the Beechwood Fish Hatchery. The town is an outlet for the timber and agricultural products of Natchitoches Parish, which was formed in 1807 as one of the 12 original counties of the State. The town is especially attractive to tourists and lovers of history because of its many old houses, some decorated with ironwork and well-preserved. The parish, which has large areas of pine and hardwood, also produces much cotton.

The Natchitoches region was first explored by LaSalle, in 1687, and was settled, according to tradition, by Canary Islanders, who came by way of Mexico in 1691. Bienville and St. Denis made the first extensive exploration of the region in 1700. With the latter the early history of Natchitoches is romantically associated. Born in Canada about the same time as Bienville, Louis Juchereau de St. Denis (1676–1744) became a dominant leader. The Natchitoches were a tribe of Caddo Indians; the name means chestnut or pawpaw eaters.

In 1713 he was sent by Governor Cadillac to establish a post on Red River, with the dual purpose of bringing about amicable trade relations with the Spaniards of Texas and Mexico and of checking their territorial aspirations east of Sabine River. At an Indian village occupying the present site of Natchitoches, he left 10 picked men and a quantity of merchandise and sat out for Mexico City. Following an old buffalo trail formed by the annual migrations of the herds from the plains of Texas to the Mississippi River and its tributary bottomlands, St. Denis made rough maps as he went, blazing the trail which later became widely used as El Camino Real (*see Tour 17A*).

In 1715 a detachment of soldiers was sent to Natchitoches and a modest fort was built either late that year or early in 1716 on a low sandy ridge near the Indian village. The site chosen was the head of navigation on Red River, at the southern end of the Great Raft, a tremendous log jam which blocked navigation to the north. This was the Fort of St. Jean Baptiste.

In his efforts to establish trade relations with the Spaniards of Mexico St. Denis encountered many difficulties. On his first visit he allayed Spanish suspicion by marrying the granddaughter of Commandant Diego de Sanchez Ramon. Leaving his bride in Texas, he returned to Louisiana for merchandise for the Spanish trade. Less successful on his second visit, he was imprisoned for two months. Making his escape on a horse seized from a Spaniard, he returned to Natchitoches, and took command of the outpost.

About two years after the erection of the fort at Natchitoches, the Spanish established a military post and mission at Los Adais (*see Tour 17A*), about 14 miles to the southwest. For the two decades following 1721 the little French settlement experienced strained relations with both the Spaniards and the Natchez, the latter attacking the village on several occasions. In 1732 the Indians laid siege for 22 days. Exasperated at the stubborn resistance of St. Denis and his small garrison, they are said to have produced a captive Frenchwoman and burned her alive within sight of the fort. This act so incensed St. Denis that he sallied forth with 40 white soldiers and 100 friendly Indians. They fought furiously and defeated the besieging Natchez, killing 92 warriors. The others fled to the shores of a lake, now dry, at the foot of Sang Pour Sang Hill (*see Tour 17b*), and were completely annihilated.

The convergence of important water and land trade routes, Natchitoches early assumed commercial as well as military importance. Pack trains brought hides, dried buffalo tongue, and bars of silver from the mines of Mexico; other trails extended eastward to Natchez and southward to Opelousas. Clumsy river craft, rowed, or "cordelled" (pulled by rope), northward against the current of Red River, brought tobacco, medicine, spirits, firearms, and other products of civilization for exchange with friendly Indians. Salt produced by Indians and later by white men on Bayou Saline, about 20 miles to the northeast, was an important item of early commerce.

Trade continued to flourish under Spanish rule (1763–1803), mainly because Colonial officials wisely retained Athanase de Mézierés, French commandant of Natchitoches, under whose regime the settlement had prospered. An accomplished diplomat in Spanish and Indian relations, he cushioned the shock of transfer, otherwise unwelcome to the French settlers. So promising was the commercial outlook of Natchitoches during the last half of the eighteenth century that many predicted it would became the second largest city in Louisiana. But in 1832 Red River changed its course, leaving Natchitoches on the banks of a quiet little river, or lake, bereft of its shipping advantages, and dependent for existence solely on farm products.

Meanwhile the government of Louisiana passed back to French control, in November, 1803, and a few weeks later to the United States. When American officials came upon the scene in 1804 they found a quaint little French-Spanish town, only slightly concerned with outside affairs. There followed an influx of American settlers from New England, Kentucky, Tennessee, and North and South Carolina.

During the early period of French domination the western boundary of Louisiana had been in continual dispute with Spain, and when the United States acquired the territory it inherited the old frontier problem as well. In 1819 a treaty was negotiated fixing Sabine River as the boundary, but as an additional safeguard several American military posts were established along the frontier. Camp Salubrity (*see Tour 17b*), and Fort Seldon (*see Tour 5b*), respectively three and six miles distant, were the nearest to Natchitoches; U. S. Grant was stationed at Salubrity in 1844, when he was a second lieutenant just out of West Point.

During the War between the States Natchitoches suffered greatly, though it was spared actual combat. Curtailment of markets for cotton, virtually paralyzed the economic life of the community. Twelve companies of volunteers were mobilized in Natchitoches; of one company composed of 101 men and boys, only 17 were mustered out at the end of the war.

On their retreat from Mansfield and Pleasant Hill (*see Tour 19b*), General Banks' Federals marched through the most productive district in the Natchitoches area, that lying along the Cane River, to the southeast. The retreating Federals sacked and burned as they went, leaving scarcely a cabin in their wake.

The industrial life of Natchitoches today is based upon the production, processing, and transportation of cotton and its by-products, supplemented by the various utilities, merchandising establishments, and service facilities common to a town of its size.

POINTS OF INTEREST

The GRAVE OF ST. DENIS, founder of Natchitoches, lies beneath McClung's Drug Store, corner Front and Church Sts. The Daughters of the American Revolution have marked the store with a plaque. This section of town was built over the cemetery that extended back of the old Catholic church. The latter was a small log structure, erected soon after the founding of the town and destroyed a century later (1823) by a fire that consumed many blocks.

The site of the INN is now occupied by a business building, 104 Front St. The first building had its origin about 1759, when Jean Baptiste Prudhomme built a one-story brick residence with a long ell to the rear housing kitchen and servants' quarters. Prudhomme arrived with the French army of occupation as Docteur du Roi, and received a land grant along the banks of Red River from Louis XV. It was on this grant that the doctor's sons began the growing of cotton on a large scale, the first experiment of its kind in Louisiana. The house, which was surrounded by a high brick wall topped with jagged broken bottles and other pieces of glass, was once used as an army hospital. Frame second and attic stories were added in the early nineteenth century by a wealthy grandson, Narcisse Prudhomme, who entertained lavishly; U. S. Grant was one of his guests at the time of the Mexican War. During Reconstruction the building served as headquarters for carpetbaggers. Later

---

HISTORIC HOUSES AND SITES

1. St. Denis marker
2. Prudhomme house site
3. Prudhomme-Roquier house
4. Parish Public Library
5. DeBlieux-Prudhomme house
6. Chambord House
7. Levy-Tauzin house
8. Bayou Amulet
9. Taylor Dupleix house
10. Lemée house-Historical Assn.
11. Soldini House
12. Dranguet house
13. Northwestern Louisiana State University
14. Fort St. Jean Baptiste site & American Cemetery
15. Laureate house
16. Sullivan house
17. First Methodist Church
18. First Baptist Church
19. Pioneer fortification site
20. Trinity Episcopal Church
21. Old Market site
22. Parish Courthouse
23. Church of the Immaculate Conception
24. Catholic Cemetery
25. Masonic Lodge
26. Dr. John Sibley site
27. Bride's Cottage site
28. Old Steamboat Landing
29. Tauzin-Campbell house
30. The Magnolias
31. Rocque House Museum
32. Good Darkey statue
33, 34, 35. Old Iron Lace buildings. Behind 35, Hughes-Prudhomme bldg., Iron Spiral Stairs
36. Front Street chairs
37. Wells house

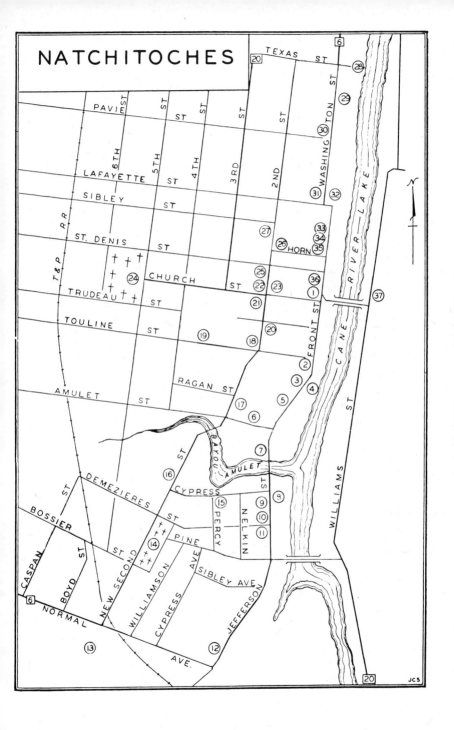

it was made an inn and continued as such until it was torn down in 1937.

The JEAN BAPTISTE PRUDHOMME HOUSE in Jefferson St., is a white frame house with six square plastered brick columns on the lower gallery and six smaller wooden columns of the same type above. The gabled roof has three dormers. The house was built by a grandson and namesake of the first Natchitoches Prudhomme.

The ST. AMANT HOUSE in Jefferson St., is a one-story brick structure built in the 1830's by Triscini and Soldini and since considerably remodeled. Triscini, a Swiss-Italian architect, came to Natchitoches from Italy and brought with him his foreman, Soldini, and 11 builders. Their influence on the architecture of Natchitoches was considerable. The house was occupied by the St. Amants, one of the wealthiest Louisiana families of the period. Miss Nezilda St. Amant was among *Les Belles de la Rivière Rouge* to whom J. Grimmer dedicated his "Grand Valse de la Société Philarmonique des Opelousas." Lieutenant U. S. Grant, who was stationed near by at Camp Salubrity in 1844, was a frequent visitor here.

The DEBLIEUX PRUDHOMME HOUSE (*private*), 424 Jefferson St., was built about 1850 for Tante Huppe, who was mentioned in the diary of Lestan Prudhomme (part of which is printed in Lyle Saxon's *Old Louisiana*), as a gift from her brother after the death of her third husband. Later it was used as a town house by various members of the family. For this reason separate outside entrances are still to be seen at each of the rooms. It is a one-and-one-half-story brick house with square wooden columns supporting a gabled and dormered roof. An interesting wooden stairway winds to the old second-story slave quarters at the left of the wing at the rear.

The CHAMARD HOUSE in Amulet St. has been remodeled many times, and has within its walls the old adobe ones which enclosed the home of André Chamard, a descendant of the royal Bourbons, who had been knighted by Louis XVI. Chamard came to Natchitoches by way of Nova Scotia sometime before 1735. One of the rooms was fitted up as a chapel, and there the priest from the mission at Los Adais, the Spanish military post a few miles to the southwest, blessed marriages contracted before the civil authorities in the settlement's earliest days. A daughter of the Chamard family, Marie, received a proposal from Joseph Tauzin in a poem of 17 verses; the marriage took place in 1792 and the poem, written in French, is still in the possession of the Chamard family.

The LÉOPOLD LEVY or TAUZIN HOUSE (*private*), 358 Jefferson St., is a two-story house, the lower floor of brick, the upper of wood. It was originally a one-story office building erected by Triscini and Soldini; the upper story was added just before the Civil War. Iron columns support the second-floor gallery which has an ornate cast-iron railing. In the gardens are rose vines, mimosas, crape myrtles, ferns, magnolias, cypresses, and many other trees and plants.

BAYOU AMULET, crossed at its confluence with Old Red River

by Jefferson St., is one of many bayous formed by the Great Raft in the early days of Natchitoches. Now crowded with vegetation, Bayou Amulet was, at one time, the head of navigation, and as such the scene of much activity. Caravans of mules and horses loaded with Mexican silver, hides, and dried buffalo tongue from the West were unloaded here and reloaded with whisky, cotton goods, and other products brought up the Red and Mississippi Rivers from New Orleans.

The TAYLOR-DE BLIEUX HOUSE, 320 Jefferson St., is a modern residence which retains the round brick columns and the fan doorway of the old De Blieux house which formerly stood on the site. Louis de Blieux advertised in the Natchitoches *Chronicle* in 1851 as follows: "For sale on arrival of ship La Jenny from Bordeaux, 40 casks of good claret wine, 100 boxes of red and white wine all subject to drawback in the stores of the Custom House in New Orleans."

The LEMÉE HOUSE, 310 Jefferson St., also built by Triscini and Soldini, was erected about 1830 for the third Natchitoches generation of the Lemée family, the first representative of which came to Natchitoches in 1769 and became a son-in-law of Louis Juchereau de St. Denis. It is a one-and-one-half-story brick structure, plastered on the front and built flush with the sidewalk. It has a cradled roof morticed together with wooden pegs in handhewn cypress logs. It has a cellar, a rarity in old Louisiana. The patio with a covered cistern is an authentic restoration. The house was bought by the City in 1943 and restored by members of the Association of Natchitoches Women for the Preservation of Historic Natchitoches, who make it their headquarters. *Open Tuesday through Saturday 10 to noon, Sunday 2–4, closed Monday.* The members, known as Ladies in Calico, not only keep records and do research, but they conduct tours to historical places. The Annual Historic Tour takes place the second weekend in October and comprises trips to the Cane River area, starting on La 494. Old Natchitoches did not have houses with tall white pillars reaching to the roof; rather it had cottages of French colonial design with hip roofs and small windows. The plantation houses often had galleries raised a low story from the ground level to get away from dampness. The more formal houses were built chiefly after 1830. The conducted tours visit such houses and localities as Starlight, Beau Fort, Oakland, Melrose, Isle Brevelle, Lakeview, and the Bayou Folk Museum.

The ROCQUE HOUSE MUSEUM, filled with historical relics and antiques, is located on the Cane River near the foot of Lafayette St. The house itself is of more than ordinary interest; it is built of cypress beams with mud and moss filling (bousillage) and was moved to this site from Isle Brevelle.

The DRANGUET HOUSE in Jefferson St., a one and one-half story brick house with round wooden columns on the gallery, said to be the first brick building in Natchitoches, was built for the Benjamin Dranguet family about 1823 and used as an apothecary by Dr. A. P. Breda.

The site of the original FORT ST. JEAN BAPTISTE is on

Jefferson St. and the Cane River bank, and is partially covered by the AMERICAN CEMETERY. A voluntary corporation called Restoration of Colonial Natchitoches, Inc., chartered 1957, has made the rebuilding of the Fort its prime objective. A museum is also projected, the whole to cost $300,000.

Earthworks may still be seen in the southern half of the American cemetery. In the early days both soldier and civilian dead were buried within the stockade, to protect the bodies from Indians. The graves were arranged in family groups and marked by iron crosses or oval stone slabs. The oldest grave bearing an inscription is said to be that of a woman of noble birth. The inscription reads:

> Ici repose Le Corps d'honorable
> Dame Marie Anne D'Artigaux
> Épouse de M. Pierre Joseph Maës
> Decedée de 26 février
> de l'année 1793 agée de 34 ans.

The LAUREATE HOUSE on Poete St., formerly called the Chaplin House, is a one-and-one-half-story white brick building with six square wooden columns covered with ivy. The fan door is similar to other Triscini and Soldini houses. During the Civil War the cellar was used to hide chickens from troops foraging in quest of food.

The SULLIVAN HOUSE, 402 New Second St., was the home of Miss Mary Campbell, who is said to have rejected U. S. Grant's suit when he was stationed at Camp Salubrity. It is a one-story frame house with a shingled gable roof supported by slender wooden posts.

The FIRST METHODIST CHURCH, southeast corner Second and Ragan Sts., is a buff stucco building erected in 1912.

The FIRST BAPTIST CHURCH, northwest corner Second and Touline Sts., is a large modern red brick structure with a red tile roof.

TRINITY EPISCOPAL CHURCH, southeast Second and Trudeau Sts., was erected with funds donated by General Watt de Peyster, of New York, and is said to be the oldest Protestant church building in north Louisiana. The corner-stone was laid in 1857 by Bishop Leonidas Polk and the first services were held the following year. It is a cream-colored brick structure with a bell tower to the left and a large medallion window.

The NATCHITOCHES PARISH COURTHOUSE at 200 Church St. is a monumental building of recent erection with offices on four levels. It contains many old records, some of which date from the time of St. Denis.

The CHURCH OF THE IMMACULATE CONCEPTION (Roman Catholic) at the northeast corner of Church and Second Sts. was built in 1856 and survived a disastrous fire that wiped out many old houses. It was called the Cathedral of St. Francis of Assisi until the Bishop of Natchitoches moved to Alexandria. It is of gray brick with twin towers topped by octagonal domes. A lower dome is surmounted by a statue of the Virgin.

The CATHOLIC CEMETERY, bounded by Fifth, Trudeau, Sixth, and St. Denis Sts., is only a little over 100 years old but contains bodies transferred from the first cemetery. Many of the tombs are raised box-like structures with horizontal slabs.

The site of DR. JOHN SIBLEY'S HOUSE, 701 Second St., is now occupied by the Commercial Hotel. The hotel includes part of the remodeled home of Dr. Sibley, a native of Boston, who was one of the influential men in the frontier days of Natchitoches, serving as both surgeon and Indian agent. He was author of *Historical Sketches of Several Indian Tribes in Louisiana,* a series of articles which gives an excellent account of Indian life. Dr. Sibley died in 1837.

The OLD STEAMBOAT LANDING, on the shore of Cane River Lake opposite Texas St., was known as the Upper Landing. It was a busy spot when Natchitoches was the head of navigation on Red River.

The JOSEPH TAUZIN or CAMPBELL HOUSE in Washington St., is the second home of Joseph Tauzin to be built on this site. The first, built for his bride, Marie Chamard, was erected in 1792, and their 10 children were born there. The house was destroyed by fire in 1840, and Tauzin immediately built a duplicate. It is a one-and-one-half-story frame cottage with Doric columns supporting a gabled roof broken by three dormers.

The LAUVE HOUSE, 902 Washington St., known as The Magnolias, was built in 1806 by Nicholas Lauve. It is a raised plantation cottage with plaster-covered brick basement supporting the frame upper story. Tall French windows open on a wide gallery and wooden columns support a gabled roof broken by two dormers. The magnolias in front of the house are said to have been planted 100 years ago by Theopile Tauzin, Sr., who bought the house in 1836 from C. Pavie. On one side of the house there are espaliers of fig trees. The original iron fence has been removed from the front of the house and placed in the attic. The furnishings include interesting heirlooms.

The BALCONY BUILDING (*open*), 120 Washington St., is a two-story gray brick building with an unsupported balcony of lace-like ironwork across the front. The windows and doors of the façade are fanlighted. The house was constructed in the 1830's by Triscini and Soldini for Alexandre Louis de Blieux, whose father, in 1804, opposed the coronation of Napoleon and fled with his sons to Louisiana. Alexandre de Blieux conducted a banking and trading establishment on the lower floor.

The GOOD DARKEY STATUE, Washington and Lafayette Sts., is a bronze figure of an old Negro—hat in hand, smiling, with shoulders bent. The sculptor was Hans Schuler of Baltimore. The inscription reads: "Erected by the City of Natchitoches in Grateful Recognition of the Arduous and Faithful Service of the Good Darkies

of Louisiana. Donor, J. L. Bryan, 1927." There is a legend that plantation Negroes late at night would ask the statue to tell them the way
home—and it did.

The DUCOURNEAU BUILDING, 612–614 Front (continua-
tion of Washington) St., is a two-story tan brick building with a gabled
and dormered roof. The ironwork on the second gallery is noteworthy.
The iron doorstep bears the date 1839 and came originally from a building which stood on the site of St. Denis' grave, and which was destroyed
by fire in 1882.

The ELKS CLUB or LACOSTE BUILDING, 736 Front St.,
once housed the Comus Club, which had its origin in 1892. The building was erected in 1852 by T. Lacoste and is said to have duplicated
a house he saw on a visit to Canada. The elaborate cast-iron grillwork
was imported from France. The house was used for balls and other
social functions.

The HUGHES or PRUDHOMME BUILDING, corner Front
and Horn Sts., is a two-story stuccoed brick building decorated with
cast-iron grillwork. It is one of three buildings so decorated with Old
Iron Lace. It was erected in 1853 by Gabriel Prudhomme. To the rear
is a second-floor gallery with rail, supports, and roof edge of wrought
iron. Ironwork stairways lead from the ground to the gallery, one a
straight flight, the other the famous SPIRAL STAIRCASE, a much
admired subject for artists and photographers.

The WELLS HOUSE, 607 Williams Ave., formerly known as the
Williams or Tauzin House, at the east end of the bridge, was erected
in 1776 on the site of the first Indian trading post. The house, which
has been remodeled, is now a white one-and-one-half-story frame building with eight columns supporting a gabled roof. At the time this house
was built the census of Natchitoches was as follows: 113 homes, 105
heads of families; 86 women; 106 infants and children; 77 youths; 84
bachelors; 100 young girls; 34 unmarried women. The walls are of
adobe mixed with deer hair; the sills and rafters of cypress are held
together by wooden pins. The windows are set with iron bars for protection against the Indians. Seven years were required for construction
of the house which originally had only two rooms with a gallery running around them. Here Sunday night dances were held, several of
which were attended by U. S. Grant.

WROUGHT IRON CHAIRS along Front St. are embossed with
fleur de lis and date 1714, year of settlement. Family names in iron
designate donors. The chairs were designed by Mrs. Olive Long Cooper
and placed on the waterfront by the Art League Beautification Foundation.

NORTHWESTERN STATE UNIVERSITY OF LOUISI-
ANA is located on a pine-clad campus of 916 acres west of College

Avenue. It was founded in 1884 as the State Normal School, and was known as Northwestern State College until June, 1970, when the State Legislature authorized the change of name to Northwestern State University. It enrolls upwards of 6,500 students annually, has a faculty of 300, and offers courses in five undergraduate schools—Business, Education, Liberal Arts, Nursing, and Science and Technology, and a Graduate School. It has a branch in Shreveport closely associated with the hospitals there, and maintains classes also in Alexandria, England Air Force Base, and Fort Polk.

Part of Northwestern's land was originally the 18th-century plantation of St. Denis. In 1832 Judge Henry Adams Bullard built a mansion that was used later by the Sacred Heart Convent. Around this site stand the 60 buildings of the campus, which has acquired a modern look because numerous new buildings have been erected as part of an $8,000,000 program. One of the most impressive is the ARTS & SCIENCE BLDG., a structure of 220 rooms, housing also the GEORGE WILLIAMSON MUSEUM of biological and geographical objects, the GAUSS ARCHIVES, and a closed circuit television system.

In 1970 the college completed its new BIOLOGICAL SCIENCES BLDG., a three-story structure west of Williamson Hall on Sibley Drive, which has 27 laboratories for research and cost $1,700,000. Other recent additions include the TEACHER-EDUCATION CENTER, actually four round buildings under one roof, including an experimental school; the PHYSICAL EDUCATION BLDG., the STUDENT UNION, and the dormitory-dining complex, which houses 1,500 and provides dining facilities for 4,000.

The administrative offices are in ROY HALL, opened 1964. They were formerly in Caldwell Hall, the oldest building on the campus, built 1906, completely rehabilitated in 1969. A new PRESIDENT'S HOUSE was completed in 1969. Plans have been approved for a new Library, to cost $3,000,000. RUSSELL LIBRARY has a collection of 170,000 books and subscribes to 1800 periodicals. It has a large collection of U. S. documents, a file on Education, more than 10,000 reels of microfilm, and 8,000 pieces of other microforms. There is a section devoted to Louisiana archives and other materials in the Louisiana Room. A branch library is maintained at the School of Nursing of the College in Shreveport.

The FINE ARTS BLDG., erected in 1939, is a center for a wide range of activities, including music, drama, and art. There are two stages, large auditoriums, band rehearsal areas, and studios.

The facilities for athletics and other outdoor activities are impressive. PRATHER COLISEUM, a gigantic, air-conditioned arena, was added in 1964. The capacity of DEMON STADIUM, built in 1939, has been increased from 7,500 to 10,500. NESOM NATATORIUM is an indoor swimming pool. Seven acres along Sibley Lake were acquired for a marina for purposes of instruction and recreation.

Northwestern still has an extensive agricultural program, with a dairy, grazing land for cattle, and cultivated field crops. A new agricultural accessory building was opened in 1970. There is a center on campus for processing dairy products, and the agricultural department provides milk, butter, ice cream, and vegetables to dining halls.

The college retains the loyal interest of many alumni, of whom 14,000 are members of the Alumni Association. More than 60,000 persons have attended the college through the years, and all 64 parishes of Louisiana are regularly represented.

Northwestern is unique in that, on the campus, there are a high school, junior high school, elementary school, kindergarten and nursery school. The elementary and kindergarten classes are operated as laboratory schools by the college. A person may begin school on the Northwestern campus at the age of 4 and continue to a doctor's degree without ever attending school off the campus.

New Iberia

Air Services: Royal Airlines to New Orleans, Baton Rouge, Shreveport and other Louisiana connections.

Highways: US 90, north-south, reaches New Orleans via Morgan City and Houma. Lafayette is 20 *m.* north. La 14, connects with Gulf Coast. Abbeville is 19 *m.* west. La 31 runs north & east.

Waterways: The city of New Iberia is 2 *m.* north of the Port of New Iberia. The Commercial Canal, 6 *m.* long connects with Intracoastal Waterway. A channel connects the Port with the Gulf of Mexico.

Railroads: Southern Pacific R. R., Railroad Ave. & Washington St.; Missouri Pacific R. R. Fulton St. and Bayou. The Southern Pacific serves the Port.

Bus Lines: Teche Greyhound, 220 W. Main St. LaPorte Bus, 929 Center St.

Information: Iberian & Jeanerette Enterprise, eve. & weekend, 926 E. Main St. New Iberia Chamber of Commerce, 127 W. Main St.

Schools and Churches: 14, public and parochial in city, 33 in parish, also Parish Trade School. 14 churches, 3 Catholic, 3 Baptist.

Parks and Recreation: City Park, 46 acres, swimming, tennis, boating, and many other facilities; West End Park, same. Community Centers in both parks. Acadian Park for Little League baseball. Fresh and salt water fishing, Spanish Lake, Lake Deuterive, Lake Fausse Point, Vermilion Bay, Gulf. Boating, hunting.

Special Events: Square Dance Festival, City Park, Aug. Sugar Cane Festival & Fair; blessing of crops, livestock and horse shows, coronation of queen, last week in September.

NEW IBERIA (19 alt., 30,147 pop. 1970; 29,062, 1960), seat of Iberia Parish, lies on the banks of the Bayou Teche, 20 miles south of Lafayette and 2 miles north of the Port of New Iberia, which has access to the Intracoastal Waterway and the Gulf of Mexico. Although a city of white-pillared houses and oaks draped with Spanish moss, suggesting leisurely living, New Iberia has shown much commercial growth in recent decades, its population increasing from 16,467 in 1950 to 29,062 in 1960, and an estimated 35,000 in 1969. Its port expedites shipments of sugar, salt, and petroleum, three principal products of Iberia Parish, which in 1964 produced more than 80,000 tons of sugar, 2,000,000 tons of salt, and 11,500,000 bbl. of oil. There are 3 mines of rock salt producing 99% pure sodium chloride; 8 oil and gas fields; a "virtually inexhaustible" deposit of clay for brick and tile, and a huge deposit of peat at Spanish Lake, with air-dried peat running to 600 tons per acre.

Numerous concerns supplying the oil industry are located in New Iberia. The city's plants include sea food canneries, makers to tabasco, pepper and spice; sugar, molasses and syrup producers, mattress makers, and foundries.

The origin of the settlement is usually ascribed to Canary Islanders who came to raise flax and hemp in their colony of Iberia, and then turned to cattle. In 1788 a census listed 190. The town, first called Iberia, was laid out by Henri Frederic Duperier, a sugar planter, and incorporated in 1839. During a yellow fever epidemic that year a Negro slave named Félicité won immortal fame for her ministrations. During the Civil War the Bayou Teche area was occupied by Major General Nathaniel P. Banks. In 1868 the Parish of Iberia was formed and New Iberia became its seat. Its position as a shipping point brought it prosperity and the title, Queen City of the Teche.

POINTS OF INTEREST

The new CIVIC CENTER is located between Main St. and the Bayou Teche, as far west as The Shadows. It brings together three public buildings designed uniformly after the colonial plantation style, the CITY HALL, the U. S. POST OFFICE, and the main building of the IBERIA PARISH LIBRARY.

The City Hall, a two-story structure, has a porch that extends the length and height of the house, with ten white pillars across the facade. There are fountains and a pool.

The Iberia Parish Library, founded 1947, entered its new building in 1966. This has both the headquarters and the New Iberia Branch. The parish system has developed in less than 20 years. The Jeanerette Branch was completed in 1952. The Loreauville Branch was completed in November, 1961; it has precast concrete panels in a modern style. The Booker T. Washington Branch is a colonial style building erected in 1955. The Delcambre Branch Library, opened in 1964, follows a traditional style. The Morton Branch Library entered a new building in 1970. The City Park Library has been housed in the Community Center, City Park, since 1959. Two bookmobiles serve the parish. In 1970 the Iberia Parish Library had 76,828 vols. available and circulated 306,238.

On the north bank of the Bayou is CITY PARK, with a large Community Building, swimming pool, children's train, tennis courts, and other facilities for leisure use. At the northeast corner of City Park on Parkview Dr. is the SUGAR CANE FESTIVAL Bldg. The opportunities for landscaping along the Bayou have been made use of also by the Iberia Golf & Country Club, which occupies a large section of land inside the curve of the Bayou.

Widely known as a fine example of Louisiana plantation house style is SHADOWS-ON-THE-TECHE, the restored town house and gardens of the Weeks plantation family, standing at Main St. and Bayou Teche. This is one of the most photographed of Louisiana houses. It was built 1831–34 by David Weeks, whose father had received a grant of thousands of acres from Carondelet in 1792. The house was occupied by the Union General Nathaniel Banks at one time during the Civil War, when the widow of the builder died there. The founder's great-grandson, Weeks Hall, bequeathed it with its antique treasures in 1958 to the National Trust for Historic Preservation. *Open daily, 9–4:30; adults $1, servicemen and children, 50¢.*

The oblong house, of a rich pinkish brick, with eight masonry columns of the Doric order on the south front, and three attic dormer windows, is of a style unusual in traditional Louisiana architecture. It is extraordinary in southern Louisiana in that it has a paved cellar. This is possible as the ground-line of the house is 20 feet above Bayou Teche at this point. The first floor is level with the ground. The brickwork is unusually fine and the bond used on the south front of the house is different from that on the other sides. The bricks were fired by slave labor. Almost all the Louisiana cypress woodwork is intact and the blinds are the original ones, unchanged after a century and more in use.

The outside staircase on the west end of the house leads from the first floor gallery to the second. This is the most typical Louisiana architectural feature of the exterior. A secondary stairway is inside. A row of three identical double wooden doors occurs in the center of the severely beautiful façade of the north, or bayou, front of the ground floor. These give access to a loggia paved in squares of marble. The house contains no central hall and the identical plans of the first and second floors consist of three rooms across and two rooms deep. The interior woodwork and plaster detail is the original.

The entrance to the grounds of almost three acres is directly from Main Street, but the entire property is hidden by a tall end dense hedge of bamboo. A rectangular formal garden to the east of the house is enclosed by clipped bamboo hedges and bordered with walks of handshaped brick. At the four corners of the garden are marble statues of the four seasons which were once in the gardens of the old Hester plantation. In the center of the grass rectangle is a clump of old camellia trees planted when the house was built. The signed marble sundial, dated 1827, is inscribed in French with the old adage, "Abundance is the daughter of economy and work."

The CHURCH OF THE EPIPHANY (Episcopal) 303 West Main St., is the oldest church still in use. It was consecrated May 6, 1858, by Bishop Leonidas Polk who was killed during the Civil War while serving as a lieutenant general in the Confederate Army. It was used as a hospital during that war. A huge fig vine that covered the facade when the church was used as a background for D. W. Griffith's film, *The White Rose,* has been removed since.

ST. PETER'S ROMAN CATHOLIC CHURCH occupies the

newest church structure. It was erected in the late 1950's on the site of the former Gothic-style structure that had served the congregation for 80 years.

The NEW IBERIA CATHOLIC HIGH SCHOOL, at Admiral Doyle Drive and De La Salle Drive, is the successor to the former St. Peter's College, which located where the Civic Center now stands.

MOUNT CARVEL CONVENT, Front St. & Duperier Ave., on the banks of the Teche, has been operated as a girls' school by the Sisters of Mount Carmel since 1872. It was built as a dwelling by Henri Frederic Duperier in 1830.

Sculpture from ancient Rome has found a home in New Iberia. Facing 119 Weeks St. stands a marble statue of the EMPEROR HADRIAN, completed about 130 A.D.

On La 86, 2 *m.* east of New Iberia, is Justine's Bottle Museum, in an old store building on the Bayou Teche. Mrs. Aleen L. Yeutter, owner, moved the store 50 *m.* downstream on two barges.

New Orleans

Areas: New Orleans covers 363.5 sq. m. of which 199.4 are land. The metropolitan area covers 2,677.5 sq. m. New Orleans is coextensive with Orleans Parish; other parishes are Jefferson, St. Bernard and St. Tammany.

Port of New Orleans: Administered by a Board of Commissioners of five appointed by the State to 6-year terms without pay (2 Canal St.). Activities at the docks are exceedingly complex and visitors are asked to keep out, for their own safety.

Air Services: New Orleans is served by 18 airlines with more than 250 daily airplane arrivals and departures at New Orleans International Airport, Moisant Field (Kenner) west on Airline Highway, US 61; also reached by Jefferson Highway, La 48, and I-10 via Williams Blvd. cloverleaf and Public Service Bus 1. The airlines are Air France, Airlift International, Alitalia, Aviateca, Braniff International, Continental, Delta, Eastern, Lufthansa, National, Pan American World, SAHSA Honduras, Southern, Taca International, Texas International, Trans World, United, and Viasa, Venezuelan International.
    The field has a 9,275-ft. runway and a modern Terminal Bldg. (1959). Corporate and private planes use New Orleans Lakefront Airport. Military needs are met at Alvin Callender Naval Air Station, used also as training field for units of Navy, Air Force, Marines, Coast Guard and National Guard.

Bus Lines: Two passenger bus lines connect with all U.S. routes. Greyhound Terminal, 1710 Tulane Ave.; Trailways Terminal, 3800 Tulane Ave. New Orleans Public Service lines in city *Consult Transit Guide & Street Map.*

Railroads: Eight trunkline railroads carry a heavy tonnage of freight, but passenger schedules have been shortened. Passengers leave from Union Passenger Terminal, Loyola Ave. facing Howard Ave. Railroads are Gulf, Mobile & Ohio, Illinois Central, Kansas City Southern, Louisville & Nashville, Missouri Pacific-Texas & Pacific, Southern Pacific, Southern Ry. Public Belt Railroad, 163 *m.* serves the Port.

Ferries: Canal St. to Algiers. Jackson Ave. to Gretna.

Cruises on River Steamers: Str. *President,* daily 2:30 to 5 p.m. M. V. *Mark Twain,* past Chalmette Battlefield and into Lafitte country, daily 11 a.m. to 4 p.m.; M. V. *Voyageur,* harbor cruises daily. All leave from Canal St. Docks.

Recreation: New Orleans Recreation Dept. (NORD) supervises scores of contests and programs in the numerous parks and playgrounds. CITY PARK, 1,500 acres, Esplanade Ave. and City Park Ave. is largest with complete facilities. Three 18-hole golf courses; tennis courts, some lighted; outdoor dance floor at Peristyle; Storyland for children with fairy tale characters and taped lectures; famous floral clock; baseball, swimming, picnic areas. AUDUBON PARK, 247 acres, has scenic riverside drive, shelters, games, unusual Zoo with 2 giraffes, 2 hippos, tigers, sloth bears, pygmy goats. Also John P. Bechtel Memorial Park for golf, and Joe W. Brown Memorial Park. In addition to outdoor activities NORD provides numerous indoor programs, including plays and square dancing.

Performing Arts: New Orleans Opera Co., 8 performances during 4 winter-spring months; Touring ballets; National touring companies, musicals and plays, Oct.–Mar.; New Orleans Philharmonic-Symphony concerts, all at Municipal Auditorium. Opera Workshop, Marquette Auditorium, Loyola Univ.; Friends of Music concerts, Tulane Univ.; Opera Ballet, May; See newspapers also for engagements at Repertory Theater, Gallery Circle Theater, Le Petit Theatre du Vieux Carré, Lakefront Theater, LSU.

Annual Events: Sugar Bowl Football Classic, January 1; Twelfth Night (King's Day and the official beginning of Carnival), January 6; Jackson Day (Battle of New Orleans) ceremonies, January 8; Mardi Gras, Shrove Tuesday, the 41st day, Sundays excluded, before Easter; parades start on preceding Wednesday with night parade of Babylon, followed by Momus on Thursday night, Hermes on Friday night, Nor (children's parade) on Saturday, Proteus on Monday night and Rex and Comus on Mardi Gras; Zulu King (Negro) and neighborhood organizations parade in various parts of the city on Mardi Gras; St. Joseph's Day (*micarême*), March 19; Spring Fiesta, and Jazz-Heritage Festival, April; Garden District Homes Tour, Old Southern Homes Tour, Spring; Sunrise Services in Tulane Stadium, Easter; New Orleans Open Golf Tournament, March or April; Lower Mississippi Valley Music Festival, Dillard University, April; Horse Show, April; Louisiana Livestock Show, April; McDonogh Day, 1st Friday in May; Confederate Memorial Day (Jefferson Davis' birthday), June 3; Southern Yacht Club Regatta, August; All Saints' Day, November 1; beginning of horse racing season, Thanksgiving; Automobile Show, December; Doll and Toy Fund Christmas Tree for poor children; Mid-Winter Sports Carnival, last week in December through first week in January.

NEW ORLEANS (4 alt., 593,471 pop. 1970, in the central city, and 452,338 in its metropolitan area of the parishes of Jefferson, St. Bernard, and St. Tammany) is the largest city in the South and the second-largest port of the nation in tonnage and value. It is the seat of Orleans Parish, with which it is coterminous. It is located on a crescent-shaped bulge of land approx. 110 *m.* up from the Gulf of Mexico on the Mississippi River, and thus is the gateway to the mid-continent. It is the principal American port trading with Latin America. Its international airport is used by 18 airlines and annually serves nearly 2,000,000 passengers. It is the business headquarters for the great oil and gas industry of Louisiana and of the petrochemical industry that stretches along the banks of the River for 100 miles to Baton Rouge, and it markets the huge crops of the fisheries.

Population Statistics. The population of New Orleans as of April 1, 1970, was 593,471, subject to minor adjustments. This was far from the actual population, but the boundaries of the central city are restricted to Orleans Parish, whereas New Orleans actually flows over the immediate parishes of Jefferson and St. Bernard, and to a slight extent over that of St. Tammany. Metarie, for example, is indistinguishable from New Orleans, of which it is a part, but its people pay their taxes at the parish seat in Gretna, which is an incorporated city of 24,875 population across the Mississippi, cut out of New Orleans like a slice out of a big pie. Kenner, next door to Metarie, where the New Orleans International

Airport is located, is an incorporated city of 29,858, up from 17,037 in 1960, some of this gain indicating what has become of the 141,133 pop. that the central city lost in 10 years.

Jefferson Parish, established Feb. 11, 1825, has an extraordinary terrain; its authority runs all the way from the crowded suburbs on the east bank by way of the strange conglomeration of cities and fishing villages of the Barataria swamps, and illogically takes in the town of Grand Isle (2,236 pop.), which geographically belongs in Lafourche Parish. This is where New Orleans gets its diamond back terrapin and its delta shrimp. Other places in Jefferson Parish that are actually tributary to New Orleans are Westwego, a city (11,402 pop.); Harahan, a city (13,037), and these unincorporated suburbs: Terry (13,832), Marrero (29,015), Jefferson Heights (16,489), Little Farms (15,713).

St. Bernard Parish is another political division that slices population from the central city. Arabi, across the River, where many New Orleans workers have their homes, and East New Orleans, are arbitrarily in St. Bernard Parish, which had 51,185 on April 1, 1970, a 59 percent increase over 32,186 of 1960. When New Orleans was already a civilized town wild oxen were roaming over St. Bernard, which was known as the Terre aux Boeufs. From 1720 on Canary Islanders settled here, worked plantations and produced the first indigo and sugar cane. New Orleans merchants developed plantation homes here. When St. Bernard Parish was formed March 31, 1807, Chalmette became the parish seat, and in time, a famous battlefield.

More than any other American city New Orleans enjoys a reputation for sustained festivity, good living, and a superior cuisine, which, augmented by major sports and a mild winter climate accounts for a large income from tourism. Foremost are the events associated with Mardi Gras Carnival, which runs from Twelfth Night to the beginning of Lent. *See Social Life and Social Welfare.* In addition to modern accommodations New Orleans offers visitors the archaeological interest of the Vieux Carré, the oldest part of the city, noted for its French domestic architecture, shops of antiques and perpetuation of the jazz tradition. The Quarter, carefully preserved and yet fully adapted to modern living, provides a pilgrimage into history. Galleries adorned with beautiful wrought-iron and cast-iron railings project over the sidewalks. Seen through hallways are decorative patios, courtyard gardens verdant with oleanders, wistaria, camellias, bananas and yucca. In the heart of the Quarter are the St. Louis Cathedral and Jackson Square, where General Andrew Jackson balances precariously on his pranching horse.

HISTORY

New Orleans was founded about 1718 by Jean Baptiste Le Moyne, Sieur de Bienville, who, with engineers Le Blond de la Tour and Adrien de Pauger, cleared the land and plotted the city along a curve of the Mississippi at a point where the river swung nearest Bayou St. John and Lake Pontchartrain.

The new settlement, named in honor of the Duc d'Orléans, Regent of France, superseded Biloxi in 1723 as the capital of the vast Colonial empire of Louisiana. At that early date it was a mere outpost housing officials, soldiers, merchants, slaves, and rivermen. To provide wives for the settlers, young women, known as *filles à la cassette* because of the small chests of clothes and linens allotted to them by the French Government, were sent to the Colony in 1728. While they were being courted, the prospective brides were under the chaperonage of six Ursuline nuns, who had come to New Orleans the year before to set up a school and to care for the sick.

During the administration of the Marquis de Vaudreuil (1743–53), New Orleans became a gay social center. The citizens copied his elegant manners and lavish entertaining, insofar as their means permitted. From that time on New Orleans became noted both for its bawdiness as a river town and for its gaiety as a cultural center dominated by a socially exclusive Creole set.

Following the partition of Louisiana between Spain and England in 1763, New Orleans became the capital of Spanish Louisiana. The citizens, angered by the transfer, coolly received Antonio de Ulloa, the Spanish commissioner sent in 1766 to establish Spanish authority. Revolt brewed for two years. In October, 1768, a petition was circulated demanding Ulloa's expulsion. The guns at the city gate were spiked on the night of the 27th and the next day a mob of 400 Acadians, German Coast settlers, and other insurgents took over the city. Expelled by the Superior Council, Ulloa sailed for Cuba, New Orleans becoming the first Colonial capital to revolt against European rule.

Independence was short-lived. On August 17, 1769, Count Alexander O'Reilly, with 24 ships and more than 2,000 men, arrived at New Orleans. In the face of so formidable a force no opposition was made, and next day, to the shouts of "Viva el Réy" the flag of Spain was raised in the Plaza de Armas.

New Orleans was almost completely destroyed by the Great Fire of 1788, which started when a taper lighted in observance of Good Friday ignited the curtain of a Chartres Street house. More than 800 houses were razed. Hardly had the city been rebuilt when a second conflagration leveled 212 buildings in 1794.

In the space of 20 days (November 30–December 20) in 1803, New Orleans witnessed the transfer of Louisiana to two nations. On the day of the formal transfer from Spain to France, November 30, 1803, the populace, which had gathered at the Place d'Armes for the flag-raising ceremony, was astonished at the announcement that the Colony had been sold to the United States. The inhabitants were antagonistic to American rule and responded with little enthusiasm when the American flag was raised 20 days later.

American enterprise aided the rapid development of New Orleans. At the time of annexation the city had a population of approximately 10,000; by 1810 it had increased to 24,552. Though the arrival of a large number of refugees from Santo Domingo was largely responsible for the increase, a great many Americans, interested in the commercial possibilities of the growing port, were annually settling in New Orleans. They lived outside the city in the Faubourg Ste. Marie, the present business section, where they developed a suburb quite different from the old French town.

The city was incorporated on February 17, 1805, and for the first time since its founding Orleanians could choose their officials. In the same year the New Orleans Library Society was formed, and the Protestants of the city, choosing an Episcopal clergyman, established Christ Church. The College of Orleans, the first institution of higher learning in Louisiana, provided for by legislative act in 1805, opened in 1811. The following year the *New Orleans* (or *Orléans*), the first steamboat to descend the Mississippi, was put into service between New Orleans and Natchez. When the State was admitted to the Union, April 30, 1812, New Orleans became the capital of Louisiana.

At the close of the War of 1812 New Orleans was belatedly attacked by a British force led by General Sir Edward Pakenham. After checking the British advance in several preliminary engagements below the city, General Andrew Jackson and his hastily organized army decisively defeated the invaders January 8, 1815, in the Battle of New Orleans (*see History and Tour 8*).

Trade on the Mississippi increased tremendously with the advent of the steamboat, and the city boomed as a cotton and slave market. By 1840 New Orleans ranked fourth in population (102,192), had the first railroad west of the Alleghenies, and was contesting with New York for first place among American ports. Streets were paved, drainage was improved, gas introduced, a steam waterworks erected. A new public school system was established in 1847, and in the same year the University of Louisiana (Tulane), established a few years earlier by the State, absorbed the Medical College of Louisiana, founded in 1835 by a group of local physicians. With the continuance of prosperity New Orleans became the cultural center of the South. Operatic and dramatic performances multiplied; many European and American artists set up studios; society reveled at magnificent balls and receptions, while the populace abandoned itself to the gaiety of Mardi Gras. There were horse and steamboat racing, cock and dog fighting, dueling, and gambling. Only recurrent yellow fever epidemics and the constant fear of floods darkened the scene.

New Orleans was intensely partisan in the War between the States, because more than any other city in the South it depended upon slavery and cotton for prosperity. As the chief port of the Confederacy, the city became an early objective of the Federals. Admiral David G. Farragut, with 25 wooden ships and 19 mortar schooners, passed through the mouth of the river in April, 1862, and crippled Forts Jackson and St. Philip below the city in a 5-day bombardment (*see Tour 11b*). Poorly defended, New Orleans was forced to surrender. In May, General Benjamin F. Butler began a dictatorial rule that lasted for the duration of the war.

From 1865 to 1877 the history of the city was characterized by racial and political strife. Carpetbaggers and scalawags, using the Negro as an instrument, fomented trouble between all classes. Riots between Negroes and whites broke out frequently as each sought to control the city government. Elections resembled military campaigns in which the Democrats, Republicans, and Radicals sought to attain office by force. For the defense of their rights white citizens formed the Crescent White League, which, after defeating the Metropolitan Police in a street battle, September 14, 1874, set up its own government. Military law was quickly established by the Federal Government, which reinstated the Reconstruction regime of Governor Kellogg. Northern sympathy was aroused, however, and in 1877, after President Hayes' election, home rule was restored to New Orleans.

In the years following Reconstruction, New Orleans slowly rebuilt. Most important to a commercial renaissance was the deepening of the channel at the mouth of the river, accomplished in the 1870's by Captain James B. Eads (*see Tour 1A*). By 1883 the city was linked by railroads with the West and North and formed the hub of a State network. Canal Street was illuminated by electric lights in 1882 and shortly after electricity came into general use. Horse cars were supplanted by trolley cars in 1892, and a purification and pumping plant completed in 1907 gave the city an ample supply of pure water. In the 20th century New Orleans developed into the great industrial and shipping capital of the South.

PORT OF NEW ORLEANS

This is the nation's second largest port and the chief port serving the Southern Hemisphere. It has more than 25 *m.* of public and private docks and facilities extending along the east bank of the Mississippi River, which is 2,000 ft. wide and 30 to 200 ft. deep. At the start of the 1970 decade the Port had approx. 48,086 linear ft. of wharf frontage and could provide 135 berths, of which 92 were operated by the Board of Commissioners of the Port, a State agency; 9 belonged to the United States Government, and 34 were privately owned.

The Port can handle 85 ships at one time. In 1968 it handled 113,-511,052 tons (2,000 lbs.), second only to the New York-New Jersey port. In a typical year 4,800 ships from 47 nations entered the Port and grain was the largest comodity exported, nearly 500,000,000 bu. being moved. Its public grain elevator has a capacity of 1,000,000 bu. a day. The Port is served by 100 steamship lines, 150 barge lines, 8 trunkline railroads with connecting Belt Line, and more than 50 truck organizations. Principal exports are petroleum products, grain, cotton, and chemicals. Principal imports are coffee, sugar, iron and steel products, bananas, and rubber.

The Henry Clay-Nashville Ave. wharf complex is 3,500 ft. long and the Port's largest facility for handling containers, breakbulk and steel cargoes. It has berth space for seven ocean-going vessels and its shed can hold 80,000 tons of cargo. The Napoleon Ave. wharf has the widest apron

—108 ft. at one berth, and crane-rail foundations. The Port has barge-mounted cranes capable of lifting up to 600 tons.

The Public Bulk Terminal, located on the Mississippi River-Gulf Outlet, which is used for transfer of cargo to and from barges and to storage, handles more than 1,000,000 tons of ores, sugar, and other dry bulk.

In 1958–63 the Board of Commissioners of the Port realized an objective of many years by completing the MISSISSIPPI RIVER-GULF OUTLET, a 76-mile channel that enables ocean-going vessels to cut 40 miles off the customary water route to New Orleans. On July 25, 1963 the *Del Sud* of the Delta Line was the first vessel through the channel. Built by the Corps of Engineers, USA, the Outlet cost $95,000,-000. The channel is 500 ft. wide and 36 ft. deep, and is protected at Breton Sound by stone dikes 3 miles long. It is crossed in eastern New Orleans by the PARIS ROAD BRIDGE, a 4-lane structure that carries La 47, which extends from Chalmette to Lake Pontchartrain. Near the New Orleans Terminal at the Industrial Canal it has a turning basin 1,000 ft. wide and 2,000 ft. long.

Here the Port authorities have begun the FRANCE ROAD TERMINAL, a complex of modern loading, unloading and storing facilities, with special provision for bulk container cargo. The first section consists of a one-berth, 830-ft. long facility, which, with cranes and container-handling devices, may cost $15,000,000. Plans call for the construction of nine ship berths, a cargo marshalling area, and consolidation sheds, on 280 acres, at an estimated total cost of $64,000,000. Eventually this is to be part of a massive program of reconstruction to build Centroport, USA, a terminal doubling the present capacity of the Port.

The Port has a full complement of traveling loaders and unloaders, conveyors, silos and warehouses. Shipments can be transferred mechanically from vessel to barge, rail car, truck, plant or warehouse. A 10,000-ton ship can be unloaded in 24 working hours, and a 1,000-ton barge in three hours. Some of the barge-mounted cranes can lift up to 600 lbs. of cargo. The extensive use of containers by shipping lines led the Port to expand wharfage and machinery to accommodate them. The Farrell Lines carry 232 containers per ship to Australia. Hapag-Lloyd, Lykes Bros., and the Holland America Line also use the wharf for container transport.

The HUEY P. LONG BRIDGE, toll free, carries US 90 across the Mississippi at Jefferson Heights. It was erected in 1935, is 4.4 miles long, has a central pier 409 ft. from foundation to peak, and cost $13,000,000.

The GREATER NEW ORLEANS BRIDGE, toll free, crosses the River from Downtown to the West Bank. It was opened in 1948 and cost $65,000,000. It is 2.12 miles long with approaches and has a cantilever span of 1,575 ft., longest in the country. It is crossed by US Branch Route 90, which becomes the West Bank Expressway and eventually joins US 90.

The construction of Interstate 10 in New Orleans called for numerous bridges, elevated roads, and cloverleaf connections. A new bridge carrying it over the Inner Harbor Navigation Canal is of cantilever truss construction with tied arch suspended span. At the point where the Canal enters Lake Pontchartrain it is spanned by the new SEABROOK BRIDGE, used by Hayne Blvd.

The GULF INTERCOASTAL WATERWAY, a barge transportation system that extends from Brownsville, Texas, to Carrabelle, Florida—and eventually will go to the Atlantic Ocean—enters the Mississippi River through several channels at New Orleans, of which the Harvey Canal on the West Bank transports many tons of oil field and shipbuilding equipment. Over 70 barge lines make use of the Intercoastal Waterway.

DOWNTOWN NEW ORLEANS

The skyline of New Orleans changed dramatically in the 1960–70 decade as one lofty office building after another rose downtown. On the waterfront between Poydras and Common Sts. came the INTERNATIONAL TRADE MART, designed by Edward Durrell Stone and intended for headquarters of foreign and domestic trade representatives that use the Port. Although its 33 stories are not the tallest in the city, its isolation on International Plaza overlooking the River gives it great distinction. The observation deck is open to visitors at 50¢ per person. The restaurant called The Top of the Mart is an objective of visitors to the metropolis. There is also a cafeteria.

In its shadow stands THE RIVERGATE, an immense exhibition facility covering six square blocks, but which, because of the elliptical character of its facade, appears much less capacious than it really is. It has four levels, two underground for 800 motor cars. Its main hall, 630 by 237 ft., has 132,500 sq. ft. of exhibition space without columns, and can seat 17,666. In its first year, 1969–70, more than 600,000 persons passed its doors. Adjacent to the Plaza is the ITM Garage, a structure of 8 levels holding 1,100 motor cars.

Foreign nations have contributed to the embellishment of International Plaza. For the Place de France, General de Gaulle, as President, and four cities—Paris, Orleans, Rheims, and Rouen, presented a gilded bronze equestrian statue of Joan of Arc, 13 ft. tall.

In 1970–71 Shell Oil Co. built the tallest office building downtown, rising 50 stories at Poydras, Carondelet and Perdido Sts., at what is called Shell Plaza. The building, which resembles One Shell Plaza of Houston, Texas, is a towering structure of steel and glass, completely changing the character of the neighborhood.

While the International Trade Mart rises over the waterfront, a much taller office building, the PLAZA TOWER, opened in 1966, dominates another area at Howard Ave. and S. Rampart St. with 45 stories. The locality had not been considered especially suited to a 510 ft. giant, which had difficulty getting occupied. Across from it on Loyola is the UNION PASSENGER TERMINAL, completed in 1954 at a cost of $16,000,000. It brought into one station the business of six railroads that had been widely separated, and eliminated nearly 100 grade crossings that had impeded traffic. Unfortunately it came at a time when passenger business was diminishing. In October, 1969, Greyhound Bus Lines took over a large share of the station, using 16 loading berths. This was the first railroad terminal in the country to be occupied by a bus line. The railroads primarily move heavy freight.

Across Julia St. and facing Loyola is the N. O. POSTOFFICE and FEDERAL OFFICE BLDG. complex, erected in 1961 at a cost of $15,000,000, and consisting of a two-story Postoffice and a 14-story office building that shelters most of the Government agencies in New Orleans. This group is within three blocks of the Civic Center.

To gain better access to International Plaza, and also to provide a better highway to connect with the new extension westward of Interstate 10, the city widened Poydras St., so that it is now 134 ft. wide, with six lanes separated by a neutral ground 22 ft. wide.

At Loyola Ave. Poydras reaches the modern, efficient-looking concentration of office buildings of the CIVIC CENTER. This is an 11-acre dominated by the 11-story CITY HALL, which has 431,-278 sq. ft. of floor space and cost $8,000,000. Adjacent is the CIVIL COURTS BLDG., a $2,500,000 construction. Another side of the Center has the STATE OFFICE BLDG. of 8 stories which cost $4,-000,000, and the STATE SUPREME COURT BLDG. Farther along on Loyola near Tulane Ave. is the Main Building of the New Orleans Public Library.

The great CHARITY HOSPITAL in Tulane Avenue at N. Claiborne Ave. dominates a complex of medical buildings near the Civic Center. The hospital traces its origin to 1736 when Jean Louis, a sailor, left a legacy for a hospital for the indigent. It passed through various vicissitudes and changes of name, was burned down and rebuilt, and eventually became one of the general hospitals supported by the State. Its core covers three city blocks and it has nearly 3,000 beds. Closely associated are the School of Medicine of Louisiana State University and the School of Medicine of Tulane University. Many of the hospitals of New Orleans have increased their services within recent years by building additions and adding departments. The newest is the Methodist Hospital, on Interstate 10 east of Downman Road, where the first unit comprised 150 beds and a total of 450 beds is in the plans.

The NEW ORLEANS PUBLIC LIBRARY moved from Lee Circle to its new modern headquarters in the Civic Center in 1958. The building cost $2,500,000. On January 1, 1969, it had a stock of 630,873 books and a circulation of 1,320,420, and was operating on a budget exceeding $1,100,000 a year. The Library is continually expanding its usefulness to every part of New Orleans through two regional branch libraries, eight neighborhood branches, and two bookmobiles. In 1969 it had budgeted expenditures of $1,198,803, of which salaries and wages accounted for the major slice of $869,921. Federal funds amounted to

$45,000. On October 23, 1968, it opened the East New Orleans Regional Branch Library in the East Gentilly district, a structure embodying the most recent planning in architecture and services, which will become the center for a regional network of libraries. The Library carries on extensive programs to concentrate public attention to the usefulness and importance of books, publishing pamphlets on current issues, supporting lectures and book luncheons, interesting children by means of puppet shows and story hours. To serve multilingual citizens the Library is building up its foreign language collections.

On neutral ground near the intersection of Loyola and Tulane Aves. lies a floral clock, 20 ft. in diameter, presented to the city by its retail jewellers and the watchmakers of Switzerland.

The urge to construct new buildings for official business also gave the New Orleans Department of Police new headquarters. In an area bounded by S, Broad, Perdido, S. White and Gravier Sts. the City completed the new POLICE ADMINISTRATION BLDG., the HOUSE OF DETENTION, the CENTRAL LOCKUP, the MUNICIPAL & TRAFFIC COURTS BLDG., and a PARKING AND MAINTENANCE GARAGE, at a cost of $9,000,000. To intensify the fight on crime the City Council authorized a "stop and frisk" ordinance, and promised anonymity to all citizens who offered information about crimes. Metal signs warning motorists to lock their cars were placed even in the Vieux Carré. The first four-year cadet class with a degree in criminology was graduated from Loyola University in 1968 and provided recruits for the police force.

After the Civic Center was completed and the Internationl Trade Mart in operation, the City began work on a CULTURE CENTER. Basic in the plan was the MUNICIPAL AUDITORIUM, erected 1930 at St. Claude and St. Ann Sts., facing Beauregard Square. On April 18, 1967, the voters approved a bond issue to enable the City to purchase land in the Auditorium area. As an initial operation the Auditorium was altered to conform with the new design. Its main area can seat 9,100 and can be divided into two halls. The main floor has 32,250 sq ft. of exhibit space and there are two other halls for exhibitions. The Auditorium was erected in 1930 to honor the soldiers of World War I. The Culture Center is to comprise new buildings and facilities for opera, symphonic concerts, and theatrical performances, lecture halls and an art gallery.

BEAUREGARD SQUARE, on N. Rampart St., between St. Peter and St. Ann Sts., was named for General P. G. T. Beauregard. The Square is the original Place Congo, where informal gatherings of Negroes more than a century ago celebrated with primitive dances believed to have had some of the later characteristics of jazz.

The new City Hall has proved so useful for transacting the city's business that no one regrets the removal of the administrative offices from the monumental Hall that served as the city's capital for 115 years. Fortunately the original building continues its usefulness as GALLIER HALL, named in honor of its architect, James Gallier, Sr., exponent of

Greek Revival architecture in the 19th century. An imposing pile of marble and granite, it faces Lafayette Square on Charles Ave., with its granite steps rising between six two-story ionic columns of white marble and four columns behind them. Its place in history is secure; Presidents, Governors, and many other famous men have been received here, and the great parades of Mardi Gras and other festivals have halted here to salute the city's executive.

Adjacent to Gallier Hall is the New Orleans Branch of the FEDERAL RESERVE BANK of Atlanta, built in 1965 at a cost of $4,000,000. It fronts on Charles Ave. and Carondelet St. Adjoining it is an extensive planting of azaleas.

INTERNATIONAL HOUSE, occupying a 10-story building at Gravier and Camp Sts., "dedicated to world peace, trade and understanding," performs an important function in furthering the trade relations of New Orleans with foreign countries. It starts off trade missions, welcomes foreign diplomats and professional delegations, helps import-export relations, and furnishes information in a number of languages. It has 2,800 members, most of them interested in foreign trade. Its language courses enroll up to 900 students studying languages of their principal customers, including Japanese.

The LOUISIANA SUPERDOME, a domed stadium planned to exceed any spectator facility ever built, began to take form in 1966 when Governor John J. McKeithan called for it and New Orleans acquired a National Football League franchise. On November 8, 1966, the State's voters endorsed a constitutional amendment creating the Louisiana Stadium & Exposition District, with authority to build a multi-purpose domed stadium in Orleans or Jefferson Parishes. In the ensuing years to 1970 the Commission, with David Dixon executive director, approved choice of a 55-acre site bounded by Poydras, S. Claiborne, Howard and S. Liberty Sts., at the intersection of Interstate 10 and Pontchartrain Expressway, and appointed Curtis & Davis, architects of New Orleans and New York; Sverdrup & Parcel, engineers of St. Louis, and Nolan, Norman & Nolan, and Edward B. Silvertein & Associates of New Orleans. Nathaniel C. Curtis, Jr., was made project director.

By 1970 the Commission had marketed $16,600,000 in bonds to cover acquisition of land and preliminary construction. The Louisiana Commission proposed to exceed the Astrodome in Houston, Texas, in attendance and revenue. Instead of 50,000 seats it would have 80,000. It would have six to eight closed-circuit television screens in full color and use movable grandstands to bring spectators closer to basketball, ice shows and entertainment.

But the cost would be huge—an estimated total bond issue of $93,-500,000, calling for payment of $6,500,000 to $7,500,000 a year. Yet the annual revenue was expected to be $15,000,000, and this did not count the calculated benefit from tourist dollars filtering into the municipal economy. Houston figured that 2,000,000 annual out-of-town visitors to the Astrodome spent an average of $40 each. The Louisiana Commission declared "a sales tax on hotel and motel rooms in Orleans and Jefferson Parishes is the backbone of Superdome financing." It called for the completion of 10,000 new hotel units.

The historic U. S. CUSTOM HOUSE is a four-story granite building at 423 Canal St. and occupies a block bounded by Canal, Decatur, Oberville and North Peter's Sts. It was erected in 1849 on a site once occupied by Fort St. Louis, which stood on the bank of the river. Its cornerstone was laid in the presence of Henry Clay. Its principal attraction is the Marble Hall on the second floor, 128 by 84 ft. and 58 ft. hall. The ceiling is constructed of ground glass plates in a white and gold iron frame supported by 14 columns of white marble. Its floor, of white and black marble, has ground glass plates inset, an early effort to carry daylight to the floor below. Part of the building was used as an office by Major Gen. Benjamin F. Butler during the Union Army occupation of New Orleans. The U. S. Passport Office is in Room 228.

The new MARRIOTT HOTEL and office building completely changes the aspect of a part of lower Canal St. above the Custom House. It is 36 stories tall, has 800 rooms and cost approx. $30,000,000.

The CHAMBER OF COMMERCE OF THE NEW ORLEANS AREA dedicated its new building at Camp and Gravier Sts. on October 6, 1969. It is a 5-story reinforced concrete structure with module interior bays, separated from contiguous buildings. Construction alone cost $1,231,192. This, the largest Chamber of Commerce in the South, serves every business and industrial interest of the five geographical areas and in addition, through well-organized committees, watches over urban affairs, legislation, foreign trade, petroleum, waterways, marketing and numerous other vital activities. Its Agricultural Department annually plans the Southeastern District Junior Livestock Show, June Dairy Month, Louisiana Beef Week, 4-H Good Provider Contest, State tours for 4-H Club winners, and puts a number of helpful programs on television and radio. The Sales-Marketing Executives, in addition to regular functions, look after youth education and co-sponsor the Junior Achievement Trade Fair. In the field of national policy the Chamber has the Americanism Committee, whose goal is "a hard-hitting, aggressive program to alert Americans to the doctrines, morals, methods, and objectives of Communism, and to educate, particularly high school and college students, in our American heritage of freedom, patriotism and the free enterprise system."

The HIBERNIA TOWER of the Hibernia Bank Bldg., 812 Gravier St., 23 floors, 355 ft. high, was the tallest building for 40 years, 1912 to 1962, when the 255 Brown Bldg., later the Five Flags, was opened.

Monuments of famous men are scattered about New Orleans and several have changed locations. The 16½ ft. bronze figure of GENERAL ROBERT E. LEE stands on top of a 60-ft. fluted marble column on a mound at Lee Circle, St. Charles St. and Howard Ave. The memorial was planned in 1870, when Lee died, but not unveiled until February 22, 1884, in the presence of Jefferson Davis and other veterans. Its shaft and base were completely rebuilt in 1954. Facing one section of Lee

Circle is the HOWARD MEMORIAL LIBRARY, 601 Howard Ave., and at 929 Camp St. is the CONFEDERATE MEMORIAL HALL, a museum (*Tues. thru Sat. 10–4, 50¢*).

The HENRY CLAY MONUMENT is a life-size bronze statue of Clay, standing with outstretched hand on a granite pedestal in the center of Lafayette Sq. It was began in 1856, four years after his death, and mounted in 1860 at a corner of Canal and Royal Sts. In 1901 it was taken to Lafayette Sq. to occupy the place of a statue of Benjamin Franklin by Hiram Powers, the marble of which had been eroding, and which was removed to the New Orleans Library, then at Lee Circle. In 1926 a citizen of Chicago, Henry Wadsworth Gustine, donated a new statue of Franklin to the Square.

Also in Lafayette Square is the city's tribute to JOHN Mc-DONOGH, a public benefactor of ante bellum days. Two children, a boy and a girl, are depicted offering flowers to the bronze figure of Mc-Donogh. He came from Baltimore when 22 years old and made his fortune in New Orleans. At his death in 1850 he divided his wealth equally between New Orleans and Baltimore, stipulating that it be used to build free schools. Each city received about $750,000, and New Orleans built 36 schools. The monument was unveiled December 29, 1898. Mc-Donogh was originally buried in the Negro section of a cemetery he had established (*see Gretna*). Later his body was removed to Baltimore. Children annually place flowers on his monument the first Friday in May.

GENERAL P. G. T. BEAUREGARD, like General Jackson, is commemorated by an equestrain monument, which stands at the entrance to City Park at Esplanade Ave. He died in 1893 and his statue was unveiled in 1915.

THE FRENCH QUARTER—VIEUX CARRÉ

The FRENCH QUARTER, or Vieux Carré (Old Square), is not only an architectural showpiece but despite its 250 years the liveliest spot in Town. Into this compact area bounded by Canal St., N. Rampart St., Esplanade Ave. and the River, thousands of visitors come daily to admire the decorative ironwork on the houses, comb the little shops for jewels and antiques, sample the Creole cuisine, and follow the beat of jazz and rock into the bars and nightclubs of Bourbon St. A walk by daylight discloses unexpected vistas: Vine-clad passages between houses; fountains playing in patios; run-down houses, and houses smelling of fresh paint. And throngs of people, from camera-laden tourists, unkempt artists, guitar-twanging bohemians, to smartly dressed patrons of specialty shops.

The French Quarter is the prime place in the United States to view the historic application of ironwork to houses. The early 19th century grills and railings are of wrought iron, some imported from France and Spain; the later ones are of cast-iron.

The importance of maintaining the traditions of the French Quarter led the City of New Orleans to name the Vieux Carré Commission to supervise new construction and restoration. Seven other organizations watch over and exploit the Vieux Carré. The Mayor's Report called the Quarter "the center of our tourist industry and sacred citadel of both our rich heritage and revered past." Awards are made for exceptional restorations. One problem faced by architects was to adapt the traditional styles to new construction of greater heights. Considered successful are the Downtowner Motor Inn at Bourdon and Toulouse Sts., and the Chateaux LeMoyne, in Dauphine and Bienville Sts. The latter has five new sections above three floors of older buildings. Similarly the Vieux Carré Hotel, on the block bounded by Bourdon, Conti, Bienville, and Royal Sts., arranged to keep the historic look with gable roofs and dormers and alternating facades. However, the Monteleone Hotel did not conform when it added six stories and a sky terrace, and the French Quarter Holiday Inn, sixth in its chain in the New Orleans area, towers 18 stories at 124 Royal St.

While many tourists visit the French Quarter for its architecture, others seek it out as the fount of jazz music, although the music heard today in Bourdon St. has changed in many ways from the simple improvisations that came out of Basin St. fifty years ago. Besides sampling the sounds that pour nightly out of the bars and clubs the visitor may hear recordings by bands past and present at the JAZZ MUSEUM of the New Orleans Jazz Club in the Royal Sonesta Hotel in Bourdon St. Its archives are still preserved at 1017 Dumaine St. *Museum hours 10–5 Monday through Saturday, and 2 p.m. Sunday.* Bands play nightly in Preservation Hall, 726 St. Peter St. Jamborees are heard every Sunday

---

KEY TO FRENCH QUARTER MAP

1. U. S. Custom House
2. Absinthe House
3. Mortgage Office
4. Old Bank of Louisiana
5. Patio Royal (Brennen's)
6. Louisiana Wild Life & Fisheries Bldg.
7. New Orleans Hotel
8. Grima House
9. Brulatour Residence
10. Court of the Two Lions
11. Antoine's
12. Court of the Two Sisters
13. Patti's Court
14. Sieur George's Hotel
15. Labranche House
16. Arts and Crafts Club

17. Ballroom, Bourbon Orleans Ramada Hotel
18. Madame John's Legacy
19. Lafitte's Blacksmith Shop
20. Haunted House
21. Old U. S. Mint
22. French Market weekend every
23. Ursuline Convent
24. Beauregard House
25. Jackson Square
26. Pontalba Buildings
27. Presbytère
28. St. Louis Cathedral Pirates Artists
29. Cabildo   Alleys
30. Little Theatre
31. Napoleon House
32. Maspero's Exchange

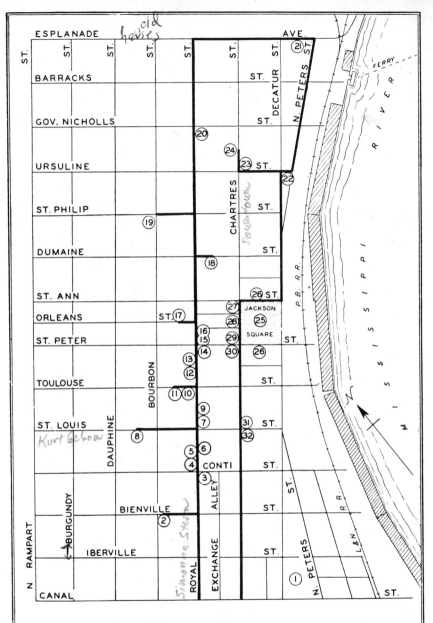

ESPLANADE old houses AVE.

BARRACKS ST.

GOV. NICHOLLS

URSULINE

ST. PHILIP

DUMAINE

ST. ANN

ORLEANS

ST. PETER

TOULOUSE

ST. LOUIS Kurt Schow

BIENVILLE

IBERVILLE

CANAL

DECATUR ST.

N. PETERS ST.

CHARTRES

Soggytown

P. B. R. R.

JACKSON SQUARE

BOURBON

DAUPHINE

BURGUNDY

N RAMPART

Simonne Skow ROYAL

ALLEY EXCHANGE

ST. PETERS ST.

L & N R R

FERRY

RIVER

MISSISSIPPI

N

FRENCH QUARTER

night in Economy Hall in the Royal Sonesta. There is jazz—and its successors—at Pete Fountain's Inn, Steve Valenti's Paddock Lounge, Al Hirt's Club, Court Tavern, Dixieland Hall, Ronnie Cole's, Famous Door, Your Father's Mustache. Some of it spills over into the Royal Orleans at Royal and St. Louis, the Blue Room of the Roosevelt, and other downtown hotels. In late spring many famous bands and musicians arrive for the International Jazz and Heritage Festival.

The LOUISIANA WILD LIFE & FISHERIES COMMIS-SION, 400 Royal St., occupies the former Civil Courts Bldg., which it purchased from the city Aug. 6, 1957. The Commission occupies the main floor for its administrative offices and the LOUISIANA WILD-LIFE MUSEUM. The building is 4 stories tall faced with marble and terra cotta. The main room of the Museum has examples of most of the 387 species of birds observed in the State. It exhibits a pair of the extinct passenger pigeon; the ivory-billed woodpecker; 25 species of ducks and geese in flight, and the extinct prairie chicken. There are mammals, fish, turtles and snakes. Of the 120,000 annual visitors many are school children. *Open free Monday through Friday, 8:30 to 5, closed on holidays.* The building also houses U. S. District Courts, the U. S. 5th District Court of Appeals, the Greater New Orleans Tourist Commission, the Gulf States Marine Fisheries Commission, the New Orleans Levee Board and the Alcoholic Beverage Control Board.

OLD SAZARAC COFFEE HOUSE, 116 Royal St., rear, was opened 1859 by John B. Schiller, who is said to have concocted the Sazarac cocktail.

MERCHANTS' EXCHANGE, 126 Royal St., built by Dakin and Gallier, is a marble-faced building once used by traders. The exchange room on the second floor became the seat of the U. S. District Court, before which William Walker was tried and acquitted in 1859 for filibustering against Nicaragua. He was shot in Honduras in 1860. Later the building was occupied by a gambling casino.

SLIDELL HOUSE, 312 Royal St., was built by the Earl of Balcanes after 1828. It was owned in 1839 by John Slidell, Louisiana politician, who became an international issue when he was removed by the U. S. Navy from a British steamship, *Trent,* while going abroad for the Confederacy. After the war he remained in France in the service of Napoleon III.

The MORTGAGE OFFICE, 334 Royal St., was built in 1826 and was the second Bank of Louisiana. It is now the home of the American Legion.

The GAZ BANK, 339 Royal St., was built in 1800 and occupied later by the Planters' Bank, and a branch of the United States Bank. In 1836 the New Orleans Gas, Light & Banking Co. acquired it. The wrought-iron balcony railings are especially fine.

The OLD BANK OF LOUISIANA, 403 Royal St., was built in 1821 from a design by Benjamin H. B. Latrobe, who had helped design a wing of the National Capital in Washington. The bank building was referred to as the Antique Dome, because of a dome of brick, covered by cement. The balcony railing has the monogram LSB.

The ROUQUETTE HOUSE, 413 Royal St., was the birthplace and home of Adrian Rouquette (1813–1877), the parish priest who as Chata-Ima served as a missionary to the Choctaw Indians. The monogram DR, for Dominique Rouquette, is worked into the railing.

The PATIO ROYAL, 417 Royal St., is believed to have been built in 1801 by Don Jose Faurie, who sold it four years later to the president of the Bank of Louisiana. In 1828 Andrew Jackson was a guest here of Martin Gordon, the owner, and next year Jackson made Gordon collector of the port of New Orleans. Later it was the boyhood home of Paul Morphy, chess expert. In 1920 it went to Tulane University and is now occupied by Brennan's French restaurant.

PEYCHAUD'S APOTHECARY, 437 Royal St., now an antique shop, was founded by a refugee from St. Dominique who made Peychaud's Bitters for use in cocktails. A local legend credits him with inventing the designation cocktail after *coquetier,* the egg-cup in which he served it.

At 520 Royal, corner of Toulouse, is the BRULATOR HOUSE, with interesting ironwork. It was built in 1816 by Francois Seignouret, a wine merchant who also designed fine furniture. In 1870 the house was leased by another wine importer, Pierre Brulator, whose name continues to be applied to the house. Its patio is open. It is now occupied by the WDSU Radio and Television Stations. Adjoining it on Toulouse is the JUDAH TOURO HOUSE.

The CASA MERIEULT, 529 Royal St., was built in 1792 by Jean Francois Merieult and is given over to shops. A patio connects with 718 Toulouse St.

The COURT OF THE TWO SISTERS, 613 Royal St., built in 1832, occupies the site of a French colonial governor's house. Two sisters conducted a store here until 1896. It is now occupied by Joseph Fein, caterer. The court connects with the patio of the Hotel Maison de Ville, 727 Toulouse.

Although the ST. LOUIS HOTEL disappeared from the corner of Royal and St. Louis Sts. 50 years ago, its site is still pointed out although now occupied by a modern hotel. The original house, which had a copper-plated dome, was erected in 1835 by the De Pouilly brothers. It burned in 1841 and was reconstructed. From 1874 to 1882 the State Legislature used it; then it became the Hotel Royal. A hurricane damaged it in 1915 and it was torn down. John Galsworthy made the old hotel the site for one of his stories. The present ROYAL ORLEANS HOTEL has 350 units and is luxuriously appointed.

The LE MONNIER HOUSE, 640 Royal St., is known also as Sieur George's House after a story placed here by George W. Cable, a favorite storyteller at the turn of the century. When its three stories were raised to four in 1876, the natives called it "the first skyscraper." It has wrought-iron balcony railings that carry the monogram YLM for Dr. Yves Le Monnier. At one time William Faulkner, the novelist, lived in a second-floor apartment.

The LABRANCHE HOUSE, 700 Royal St., was erected in 1835 by Jean Baptiste Labranche, a planter. It is notable for the oakleaf and acorn design in the railings on the two balconies.

The PIERRE THOMAS HOUSE, 712 Royal St., built in 1823, became the home of the New Orleans Arts and Crafts Club in 1932. It has a vista of the Garden of St. Anthony at the rear of the Cathedral.

The MILTENBERGER HOUSE, 910 Royal St., at Dumaine, is one of three erected by the widow of Dr. Christian Miltenberger, who acted as surgeon at the Battle of New Orleans. The iron railings have an oakleaf and acorn design. It is of interest as the birthplace of Alice Heine, granddaughter of Alphonse Miltenberger, who married Prince Louis of Monaco and thus became the first American-born princess to preside there. A divorce in 1902 ended the marriage.

The CORNSTALK GATE and barrier in front of 915 Royal St. has acquired distinction because of the elaborate design of cornstalks, morning glory blossoms, vines and pumpkins in cast iron.

The ABSINTHE HOUSE, 238 Bourdon St., corner of Bienville, built after 1806, was a tavern where patrons could sip absinthe, a distillation of wormwood oil and anise, later prohibited as damaging to the nervous system. Cayetano Ferrer is credited with having originated absinthe frappe. One of the numerous Andrew Jackson legends is associated with an upstairs room, where Jackson is said to have met the pirate Lafitte and persuaded him to help defend New Orleans in 1815.

JUDAH BENJAMIN HOUSE, 327 Bourbon St., was built in 1835 by Auguste St. Martin, father of the wife of Judah P. Benjamin, who attained eminence in law and as U. S. Senator from Louisiana, and Secretary of State of the Confederate States. After the war he established himself as a lawyer in England.

LAFCADIO HEARN is associated with the house at 516 Bourdon St., where he had rooms while employed on a local newspaper. The house has iron railings on two balconies.

JEAN LAFITTE'S BLACKSMITH SHOP, 911 Bourbon St., is said to date from 1772 and to have been used by the Lafitte brothers, smugglers, but recent research has cast doubt on this.

The LEPRETE MANSION, 716 Dauphine St., at Orleans, is an object of much tourist interest because of the lavish use of iron on the two upper balconies. It was built in 1835 by Dr. Joseph Coulon Gardette and sold four years later to Jean Bapiste LePrete, whose family lived here for forty years, after which it was occupied by a bank and the New Orleans Academy of Art.

The MUSEE CONTI, 917 Conti St., is a wax museum containing effigies of historical figures and other memorials.

North of Royal at 713 St. Louis St. is ANTOINE'S, a nationally-known restaurant, built in 1840 and bought by Antoine Alciatore in 1868. It originated oysters Rockefeller and pompano en papillote.

MADAME JOHN'S LEGACY, 628 Dumaine St., is owned by

the Louisiana State Museum. It is built like a raised cottage with a hip roof with dormers. It has been traced back to Jean Pascal, a French sea captain, who built it in 1728 and was killed by Natchez Indians in 1729.

North on Toulouse and across Bourdon St. is the recently built motor inn, LE DOWNTOWNER DU VIEUX CARRÉ, with a facade one block long. This stands on the site of the FRENCH OPERA HOUSE, designed by James Gallier, Sr., and famous for its acoustics. It seated 1,800 and was opened in 1859 with *Guillaume Tell*. Dear to the Orleanians is the story of how Adelina Patti made a brilliant debut as Lucia on December 10, 1860. She was living at the time at 631 Royal St., a house known today as PATTI'S COURT, after the fine patio in the rear. The Opera House burned down in 1919.

The COURT OF THE TWO LIONS, 708 Toulouse St., corner of Royal, gets its name from two crouching lions atop gate posts of the courtyard. The house was built in 1798 by Don Juan Francisco Merieult, and sold twenty years later to Vincent Nolte, whose adventures, related in *Fifty Years in Both Hemispheres*, became a source for Hervey Allen's novel, *Anthony Adverse*. Robert Edeson, the actor, was born here, and Winston Churchill, the American author, used the house as a setting in *The Crossing*.

The GRIMA HOUSE, 818 St. Louis St., dates from the 1820's and has a fine patio, garden and stable. It is the home of the Christian Women's Exchange. Continuing across Dauphine St. to the corner of St. Louis St., here is the AUDUBON COTTAGES, where John James Audubon worked on some of the plates for his *Birds of America* in 1821–22. He also rented a room briefly at 822 Barracks St.

MASPERO'S EXCHANGE, 440 Chartres St., was the old Exchange Coffee House, where males of all professions met in the early 19th century to gossip and refresh themselves. It was built in 1788 and is said to have been a rendezvous of the Lafitte brothers. When General Jackson was fined $1,000 for contempt of court for failing to end an emergency he here thanked his followers and refused to accept their tender of the fine.

The NAPOLEON HOUSE, 500 Chartres St., and another house at 514 Chartres, are the subjects of legends associated with Napoleon Bonapart. The first is a spacious 3-story house with a cupola, and an oft-repeated tale says it was prepared to shelter Napoleon if his escape from St. Helena could be managed. The *New Orleans City Guide* of the American Guide Series quotes an authority who believes the legend rests on the enthusiasm that greeted the news that Napoleon had escaped from Elba. The report reached Mayor Nicholas Girod during a performance at a theater, where he made a speech welcoming Napoleon and offered to place his house at the Emperor's disposal. Dr. Francois Antommarchi, Napoleon's physician at St. Helena, lived in this house in 1834 and administered to the needs of the poor without charge. The second house at 514 Chartres is sometimes said to have been built for Napoleon, but the aforesaid *Guide* says it was built a year after Napoleon's death.

The PHARMACEUTICAL MUSEUM, 514 Chartres St., has exhibits related to the history of medicine in New Orleans.

The BEAUREGARD HOUSE, 1113 Chartres St., is widely known as the one-time home of General P. G. T. Beauregard (1818–1893). It has one story above a raised basement and two flanking staircases of stone protected by wrought-iron railings. It was built in 1827 by Joseph Le Carpentier, and in 1837 became the birthplace of Paul Morphy, famous chess champion. In recent years it has had the care of the late New Orleans writer, Francis Parkinson Keyes, and the Beauregard Foundation. General Beauregard also lived, 1867–1875, in a two-story house at 934 Royal St.

The URSULINE CONVENT, 1114 Chartres St., opposite the Beauregard House, was opened in 1734 and occupied by the Ursuline nuns until 1824. Thereafter the building became a school for boys, a temporary home for the State Legislature, the Archbishop's Palace, and a presbytery of St. Mary's Italian Church, built in 1846. A parochial school is located in the rear of the courtyard.

The BOURBON ORLEANS RAMADA, a recently completed building between Orleans and St. Ann Sts., has a famous address, 717 Orleans St. Here stood a house that has been identified as the site of the Quadroon Balls of ante-bellum days, at which young men-about-town danced with—and fought over—lovely women of mixed races. The State occupied the house briefly in 1828 and in 1881 the property was bought for Negro nuns. The new hotel, an example of adaptation of French Quarter architecture, has incorporated the Quadroon Ballroom, which is used for weddings and social gatherings. Most of the original decorations have been retained, including the double stairway leading from the lobby to the ballroom, which is believed to be 150 years old.

The HAUNTED HOUSE, 1140 Royal St., was built by Dr. Louis LaLaurie in 1832. He was the third husband of Delphine Macarty, a woman known for her extreme cruelty to slaves. She grew up in Chalmette, where her father, the Chevalier de Macarty, was known as a cruel slavemaster. Her mother was murdered by slaves. When a fire occurred in the McLaurie house seven slaves in miserable condition were uncovered, and Delphine and her husband were compelled to leave town because of adverse public feeling. This provided the basis for stories of strange noises and wailing. The three-story, French empire-style house later served as headquarters for the Union Army, a gambling casino, and the first unit of a welfare movement founded by William J. Warrington.

Every visitor interested in Old New Orleans arrives eventually at JACKSON SQUARE, the landscaped oasis bounded by Chartres, St. Peter, St. Ann, and Decatur Sts. This was the Plaza de Armas of the Spanish administration, and the Place d'Armes of the French. Facing the Square on Chartres is the CATHEDRAL OF ST. LOUIS, so designated in 1793 and more recently named a basilica. A parish church on this site was destroyed by a hurricane in 1723; a second church burned down in 1788. Don Andreas Almonester y Roxas, a Spanish nobleman, offered to build a new church if a mass were said for the repose of his soul every Sunday; his offer was accepted and his remains now rest under the altar of the Sacred Heart. The edifice had two lateral towers when De Pouilly enlarged it in 1851 and added steeples and a portico.

On its St. Peter flank stands the CABILDO, headquarters of the Spanish administration, which lost two buildings by fire before the present one was erected in 1795. In a large room on the second floor the formal transfer of the Louisiana Territory from France to the United States took place in 1803, soon after the French had taken over from the Spaniards. The Spanish royal arms in the pediment was replaced by the American eagle. It houses historical and art collections of the LOUISIANA STATE MUSEUM. Among its many historical objects is the death mask of Napoleon Bonaparte, presented to the City in 1834 by Dr. Francois Antommarchi, who made the original plaster cast at Napoleon's bier on May 5, 1821.

At the St. Ann side of the Cathedral stands the PRESBYTÈRE, a building that in its Spanish-Moorish design resembles the Cabildo. It contains natural science collections of the LOUISIANA STATE MUSEUM. Don Almonester had begun building this house and had erected one story in 1794 when fire destroyed the Cabildo. This delayed construction generally, and in the interim Don Almonester died. The second floor was completed by the Federal Government in 1813. Mansard roofs were placed on both the Cabildo and the Presbytère in 1847, and the Cabildo received a cupola. In 1963 the State spent $700,000 for restoration, and the rejuvenated Presbytère was rededicated by Governor Jimmie H. Davis and Mayor Victor H. Shiro of New Orleans on December 5, 1963.

The Baroness de Pontalba, daughter of Don Almonester, brought about the conversion of the Place d'Armes into the present Square after 1849. That year she built the two PONTALBA BUILDINGS along two sides of the Square at right angles to Chartres St. These impressive brick buildings, three stories and an attic in height and decorated with iron railings from France, were designed by James Gallier, Sr., and carry the monogran AP for Almonester and Pontalba. One is owned by the City of New Orleans and one by the State. The lower Pontalba building has the Louisiana State Museum and a library containing historical material, open for reference purposes Tuesday to Saturday, 9–4.

The Baroness promoted the landscaping of the Square and in 1856 helped finance the bronze equestrian statue of General Andrew Jackson, made by Clark Mills. It faces the Upper Pontalba building and is noteworthy in sculpture because the 10-ton horse and rider are supported solely on the horse's hind legs. Jackson laid the cornerstone for the pedestal in 1840 but did not live to see the completed statue. The pedestal bears the legend: *The Union Must and Shall Be Preserved,* placed there by Major General Benjamin F. Butler, Union commander in New Orleans, and is a free rendering of Jackson's famous toast: *Our Federal Union: It Must Be Preserved.*

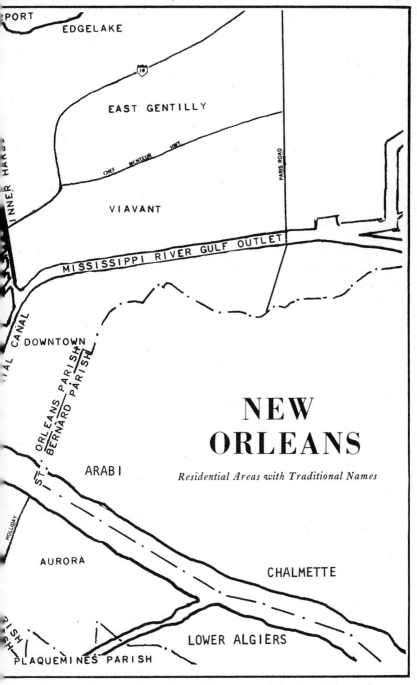

NEW ORLEANS

Residential Areas with Traditional Names

Research & Statistics Dept., Chamber of Commerce of the New Orleans Area

The LITTLE THEATRE, 616 St. Peter St., is a comparatively recent building in the French Quarter style. It seats 500 and is known for its picturesque patio.

At 632 St. Peter St. Tennessee Williams, the dramatist, occupied an apartment. His play, *A Streetcar Named Desire,* gets its title from the former Desire line, which ran past the cemetery to the Elysian Fields, and is now Bus No. 10 of the New Orleans Public Service, Inc.

The OLD SPANISH STABLES at 716 Governor Nicholls St., are not Spanish in origin but stables built by Judge Gallien Preval in 1934. Sherwood Anderson in the 1920's lived at 715 Gov. Nicholls St.

Of the two alleys beside the Cathedral, Orleans Alley and St. Anthony's Alley, the former within recent years has been called PIRATE'S ALLEY for no good reason. It is, however, the exhibit and market place of artists, who display their paintings on fences and walls. A special effort on behalf of Louisiana artists is made during the Spring Fiesta.

The FRENCH MARKET begins at St. Ann St. on Decatur St. along the River and extends on North Peter St. to Barracks St., a collection of five buildings containing stalls filled with farm produce and coffee stands. Fresh fruits and vegetables are trucked in daily from the alluvial farms, and fresh fish and meats are available. The Market, located here since Spanish times, is filled with spectacular activity, especially on weekend evenings, and is greatly favored by tourists.

The OLD UNITED STATES MINT, Esplanade Ave. and Decatur St., was built in 1836 at a cost of $182,000. It is three stories tall, classical revival in design, built of stuccoed brick trimmed with granite, and has an ionic portico. Here, beginning in 1837, the United States Government minted coins without charge from gold and silver brought by individual owners. The Mint was operated from 1838 to 1860 and from 1878 to 1910. After various uses it became a Federal prison in 1931.

The Mint has a special place in Civil War history because it was here that William Mumford and others tore down the United States flag after Admiral David G. Farragut, USN, had occupied New Orleans on April 25, 1862. Major General Benjamin F. Butler, commander of the Federal troops, had Mumford arrested, tried by court martial, and hanged just below the flag staff.

New Orleans has not been celebrated as a city of churches, but it is a place where all demoninations have flourished. Jesuit missionaries arrived with Iberville and Bienville and one of the first huts was a house of worship. In 1724 Bienville made Catholicism the state religion, and with the energetic work of a number of religious orders this became the dominant faith. Today it is represented by many large and small houses of worship. Notable among them is the Church of the Immaculate Conception, 132 Baronne St., founded in 1857 and said to be the first church so designated. Two churches, St. Alphonsus, 2030 Constance St., and St. Mary's Assumption, Josephine St. near Constance, with associated schools are administered by the Redemptorist Fathers, who established the original St. Mary's in 1844 in a German community. The churches are admirable examples of baroque brick architecture. St. Patrick's Church, 712 Camp St., is said to have been modeled after the York Minster in England.

Christ Church Cathedral, 2919 St. Charles Ave., has a congregation that dates back to 1805, when the Protestants of New Orleans organized. The denominations voted to unite in a common church and the Episcopalians being the more numerous, a clergyman of their group was chosen minister. The St. Charles Ave. Presbyterian Church, corner of State St., French Gothic in design, was erected in 1930. The Rayne Memorial Methodist Episcopal Church, 3900 St. Charles Ave., at General Taylor St., is a brick building in the Gothic perpendicular style. Felicity United Methodist Church, 1818 Chestnut St. is the present name of the former Felicity Street Methodist congregation.

St. Paul's Evangelical Lutheran Church, Port and Burgundy Sts. dates its origin back to 1843 and originally had services in German. Temple Sinai, 6221 St. Charles Ave., is an adaptation of Byzantine architecture with a domed roof over an auditorium that seats 1,000. It was the first Reform congregation when organized in 1872.

GARDEN DISTRICT AND BEYOND

The GARDEN DISTRICT is a residential area of New Orleans generally designated as extending from Jackson Ave. to Louisiana Ave. and St. Charles Ave. to Magazine St. It retains many fine old houses remarkable for their size and upkeep, standing amid decorative tropical vegetation. This was known in ante bellum days as the American colony, as distinct from the Creole aristocracy of the Vieux Carre. There are houses of Greek Revival and Georgian design, and houses with two-story pillars and porches of gleaming white paint—an occupant of one of these showplaces confided recently that it has cost her $9,000 to have the house repainted. Among houses of historic interest is the Forsyth at 1134 First St., where Jefferson Davis died in 1889. At that time it was occupied by Judge Charles Emerson Fenner. It was built in the 1850's by the judge's father-in-law, J. H. Payne.

CYPRESS GROVE and GREENWOOD CEMETERIES, at the intersection of Canal and City Park Ave., and METAIRIE CEMETERY, Metairie Rd. (continuation of City Park Ave.) and Pontchartrain Blvd., are among the most beautiful burial grounds in the city. The dissimilarity to the typical American cemetery is explained by the fact that the sogginess of the land underlying the city in former times made burial beneath the surface difficult. Tomb burial was therefore resorted to, each family using the same tomb for generations through the simple expedient of burning the coffins after a suitable expiration of time and despositing the bones in a crypt. Modern drainage makes interment within the ground possible, but long-established custom prevails.

AUDUBON PARK, named for John James Audubon, is located on 247 acres between St. Charles St. and the River, opposite the campus of Tulane University. It occupies part of the DeBore plantation, on which sugar was first granulated in 1794. The Audubon Sugar School was begun here in 1891 and transferred to Louisiana State University in 1899, and is today active on the Baton Rouge campus. Audubon Park has numerous facilities for recreation and outdoor fun; its ZOO has not only a pair of giraffes but a pair of hippos.

LAKE PONTCHARTRAIN, named by Iberville for the French Minister of Marine, is an important element in the recreation program of New Orleans. On its shores are drives, parks, beaches, an airport, an amusement park, a college, a yacht harbor, and residential sections. It would be a freshwater lake were it not for the tides from the Gulf that enter from Lake Borgne through Chef Menteur Pass and the Rigolets (*Rigolees*). The lake is fed by bayous and covers 630 sq. mi., about half the size of Rhode Island. It has a maximum depth of 15 ft. It is connected with the Mississippi by the Inner Harbor Navigation Canal (Industrial Canal), opened in 1923.

Hayne Blvd. runs along the base of the lake and carries Transit Line 17, crossing the canal over the new Seabrook bridge. Just before the bridge the NEW ORLEANS AIRPORT (Shushan Airport) extends into the lake on a big triangle of filled-in land, built in 1935 and extended whenever runways are to be lengthened. Entrance is at Downman Road, which joins Chef Menteur Highway and Interstate 10. The airport is used by the U. S. Army and the U. S. Navy, by executive planes and some commercial ones. Among facilities a well-appointed Administration Bldg., which contains murals by Xavier Gonzales depicting New Orleans history. On the west side of the Airport is the Civil Air Patrol.

After Seabrook Bridge the Lake Shore Drive follows the curve of the Lake, passing the U. S. Naval Reserve Training Station, the Gulf South Research Institute, the Pontchartrain Beach, and the Pontchartrain Amusement Park. A stepped concrete seawall extends for about six miles along the lake. Then come the new buildings of the LOUISIANA STATE UNIVERSITY IN NEW ORLEANS, on a campus that borders the landscaped London Canal on the west. Lake Shore Drive continues on BAYOU ST. JOHN, on the west bank of which are the U. S. Coast Guard and Captain of the Port.

Bayou St. John is a historic waterway. Here the Spanish government built an outpost of brick that still was able to shelter a garrison when the British invaded in 1814. In later years it fell into ruin, but the area continued to be called Spanish Fort. East of the Bayou Alexander Milne developed his town of Milneburg, now largely covered by Gentilly; the Milne Municipal Boys' Home, 5420 Franklin Ave., was named in his honor. In 1831 the Pontchartrain Railroad was built to the mouth of the Bayou, which became the port of steamers that crossed the lake. A tavern located there sheltered some notable guests who entered New Orleans by the back door, among them the novelist Thackeray, who testified that he consumed a bouillabaisse "than which a better was never eaten at Marseilles." For years a resort flourished here, with a theater and a casino; it has since disappeared.

The Bayou St. John marks the east boundary of CITY PARK, which extends west to Orleans Blvd. and south from Robert E. Lee Blvd. to City Park Ave. Near the Park entrance at Beauregard Circle is the equestrian monument of General P. G. T. Beauregard, by sculptor Alexander Doyle, erected in 1915. The effective landscaping is largely the work of nature, which has preserved groves of venerable oaks hung with Spanish moss. The Dueling Oaks, near which duels were fought a century ago, and the Suicide Oak, where disconsolate men ended their lives, stand near the ISAAC DELGADO MUSEUM OF ART. The Park contains a Stadium, a Riding Academy, two 18-hole golf courses, and lagoons. The DELGADO TRADE & TECHNICAL INSTI-TUTE adjoins the Park on the west and the SOUTHERN RE-GIONAL RESEARCH LABORATORY of the U. S. Dept. of Agri-culture is located in the northeast corner.

The ISAAC DELGADO MUSEUM OF ART stands on Lelong Ave. in City Park, a fine example of adaptation of the classic Greek to a design by Samuel A. Marx, Chicago architect. The Museum was opened in 1912, a legacy of a Jamaica-born sugar planter, who was interested in founding a trade school for boys, now the Technical In-stitute, and in building a wing at Charity Hospital. The Museum build-ing cost $150,000. It is maintained by the City of New Orleans, dona-tions from individuals and art associations, and dues from 1,000 members. Its combined income in 1969 was $325,256. The annual number of visi-tors exceeds 70,000.

Since the first donation of French salon and Barbizon paintings and sculpture the Museum has acquired examples of art of many schools. It has a special concentration of pre-Columbian masterpieces from Mex-ico, Central and South America, and collections of Spanish colonial work, contemporary American and Latin American painting and sculpture, and Louisiana and Colonial American painting. There is a Samuel H. Kress collection of Italian Renaissance and Baroque art. The Woodward sketches of the Vieux Carré, 1885, are preserved. As the value of the Museum increased the municipality authorized a full-time professional staff with a curator of education, allocated $135,000 for renovation and supported a bond issue to pay for a new wing to cost $1,400,000. It also earmarked $15,000 a year for purchases to complete permanent collec-tions. In 1965 the Museum acquired Edgar Degas' *Portrait of Estelle* by public subscription and staged a Degas exhibition. Degas had painted this in New Orleans in 1872. The activities of the Museum include tours for high school and adult groups, programs for grammar schools, film showings, seminars, and publication of catalogues.

Near City Park are the FAIR GROUNDS, where Louisiana Jockey Club holds horse races on weekends beginning on Thanksgiving Day and extending into March, and sometimes later. The popularity of this track is shown by its large attendance and big betting. In a typical year more than 600,000 attend the season and betting takes in $35,000,000 to $40,000,000. The tax revenue, as high as $2,500,000, is divided between the City, the State, Louisiana State University, Delgado Trades Institute, and other agencies. This is the home of the $50,000 New Orleans Handicap and the $40,000 Louisiana Derby.

From Bayou St. John the Lake Shore Drive continues west through residential areas to WEST END PARK and the CITY YACHT HARBOR, where the City Yacht Club and the Southern Yacht Club are located. Here also Pontchartrain Blvd. reaches the lake. This is a popular area for watching the week-end boat races, the Southern Club's spring regatta and the fall races of the Gulf Yacht Assn. This northwest corner of Orleans Parish inspired the subdividers to name the streets, Amethyst, Topaz, Crystal, Beryl, Turquoise, Emerald, and other gems. At the end of West End Park is the boundary between Orleans and Jefferson Parishes. Across the Metairie Canal in Jefferson is a night spot known as Bucktown, made up of bars, snack stands, and restaurants, and where at least one establishment, the My-O-My, offers shockers for the curious.

From this point westward the land is protected by levees. By turning left from Lake Shore Dr. the motorist can reach Veterans Memorial Highway or Interstate 10, which join the Greater New Orleans Expressway to the LAKE PONTCHARTRAIN CAUSEWAY, the most spectacular highway in the South. This crosses more than 23 miles of water to St. Tammany Parish on the north shore, near the towns of Mandeville, Covington and Madisonville and junction with US 190 and La 22. The Causeway has two bascule spans and three elevations for boats, and a motorist out of sight of land has the sensation of being at sea. Before the Causeway was opened on August 30, 1956, traffic had to follow the shores of the lake. On June 16, 1964, six persons died when a bus fell into the lake after two barges had collided and damaged the Causeway. The Causeway cost $51,000,000 and proved so profitable that a parallel road was built and opened in April, 1969.

COLLEGES AND UNIVERSITIES

DILLARD UNIVERSITY, 2300 Gentilly Boulevard, began its existence under this name on a new 63-acre campus in 1935, and a fine group of administrative and classroom buildings has been erected since. It was formed by the merger of New Orleans University, founded 1869 by the Freedmen's Bureau for the higher education of Negroes, and Straight University, founded by the American Missionary Society of New York. Dillard is coeducational and supported by the Congregational and Methodist Churches and private endowments, and gives baccalaureate degrees in Education, the Humanities, the Natural Sciences, the Social Sciences, and in nursing and the allied arts. In recent years it erected the Stern Science Hall at a cost of more than $600,000, and the Lawless Memorial Chapel at a cost of $525,000. A typical enrollment was 920, with a faculty of 68. Flint-Goodrich Hospital is a unit of the university.

LOUISIANA STATE UNIVERSITY IN NEW ORLEANS. In 1956 the State Legislature voted to extend the extraordinary educational facilities of Louisiana State University to New Orleans. Land for the campus was acquired facing Lake Pontchartrain west of New Orleans Airport and in five years more than 3,000 students were enrolled. By 1970 9,156 were receiving instruction there and in the School of Medicine. The New Orleans campus has six academic units: the Junior Division, the Colleges of Liberal Arts, Business Administration, Science, and Education, and the Graduate Division. Regular credit courses are given in the Evening Division for those who cannot attend in daytime.

The addition of new departments and courses goes on uninterruptedly as LSU-NO opens new opportunities for scholarly training, research and service to the community. In its report for the Biennium 1966–68 the Board of Supervisors cited the creation of a Department of Secretarial Science, and another of Engineering Science; the extension of the Ph.D. degree to chemistry and of master to theater and dramatic literature, government, economics, applied physics, biological science, and mathematics; the starting of an Audio-Visual Center to make films and slides available to instructors. The Special Education Center was active in promoting educational opportunities for exceptional children. A computer research center was established. New buildings continue to rise as the appropriations became available—the Administrative Bldg., the Student Center, the Library, and the Health, Physical, & Recreation Education Bldg., and the General Purpose Classroom Bldg. The two-story Library, which cost $2,500,000, can hold about 470,000 volumes and at present is half full. A city of learning has grown up beside a residential district and the noisier Pontchartrain Amusement Park and Bathing Beach.

The SCHOOL OF MEDICINE of LOUISIANA STATE UNIVERSITY has its headquarters in an 8-story building at 1542 Tulane Ave., adjacent to the Charity Hospital. It also has a 10-story residential center for single and married students three blocks away, which can accommodate 140 single men, 64 single women, and 133 married students. The School was opened in 1932 and offers a four-year program, after pre-medical work, leading to the degrees of doctor of medicine, master of science, doctor of philosophy, and bachelor of science in nursing. For physicians who wish to abreast advance in their profession it has refresher and evening courses.

The School conducts laboratory and clinical research in a large number of health subjects. Its preoccupation with tropical medicine made it the base laboratory of the International Center for Research and Training in San Jose, Costa Rica, where LSU helped develop a medical school.

The MEDICAL CENTER of the University in New Orleans is located in about 30 buildings, old and new, on Florida Ave. The Main Bldg. has been enlarged and new structures to accommodate laboratories and classrooms have been added from year to year. In 1964 the Center acquired a 22-acre tract from the Federal Government, valued at $2,-000,000. It had several frame buildings of the former Bienville Homes. In 1969 the University began erection of the SCHOOL OF DENTISTRY, authorized more than a decade before. August Perez & Associates of New Orleans were the architects and Gervais F. Favrot & Co. obtained the building contract for $11,119,000. The main nine-story structure contains the basic sciences and clinical division, and a lower wing has administrative offices. The total cost was estimated at $12,-700,000. Dr. William H. Stewart, Surgeon General of the United States Public Health Service, an alumnus of LSU, has been named Chancellor of the Medical Center succeeding Dr. William W. Frye, who retired after 20 years as head.

The LOUISE S. McGEHEE SCHOOL FOR GIRLS, 2343 Prytania St., (private) occupies a house built for Bradish Johnston in 1870 by James Freret. The building is a fine example of free Renaissance design. Its Arts and Science Bldg., recently erected, contains chemistry and physics laboratories.

LOYOLA UNIVERSITY IN NEW ORLEANS, 6863 St. Charles Ave. is a privately supported coeducational institution conducted by the Jesuit order. It is the largest Catholic university in the South and open to students of all faiths. It developed from a number of college organizations going back to 1849 and became Loyola University in 1911. The College of Arts and Sciences is the central unit, with a wide selection of courses from chemistry to journalism, political science, speech and television, with a graduate division in biological sciences and education. The College of Business Administration gives baccalaureate and master degrees, and the School of Law gives the degree of bachelor of laws. The School of Dentistry treats 60,000 patients annually and conducts clinics at the Charity Hospital. A two-year certificate course in dental hygiene is open only to women. There is a College of Music, an Evening Division leading to degrees, and an Institute of Industrial Relations. Its Main Library was completed in 1950 at a cost of about $900,-000, and Loyola Field House, where the Sugar Bowl basketball tournaments are held, was erected in 1954 at a cost of $600,000. In a recent typical year Loyola enrolled 4,736 and had a faculty of 275.

NEW ORLEANS BAPTIST THEOLOGICAL SEMINARY, 3939 Chef Menteur Highway, began in 1917 as the Baptist Bible Institute and received its present title from the Southern Baptist Convention in 1946. The Seminary has three schools: the School of Theology, which trains ministers, missionaries, and teachers; the school of Religious Education, which prepares teachers and administrators in the religious field, and the School of Church Music. It has a campus of 75 acres.

NOTRE DAME SEMINARY, 2091 South Carrollton Ave., is a diocesan institution for the instruction of students for the priesthood, conducted by the Fathers of the Society of Mary. It awards the degrees of bachelor of arts and master of arts. An applicant must have completed two years of classical studies in college and be sponsored by a bishop. Residence halls are located on the campus, which embraces ten city squares.

ST. MARY'S DOMINICAN COLLEGE, 7214 St. Charles Ave., is a Catholic liberal arts college for women conducted by the Sisters of St. Dominic. Dominican Sisters from Ireland began teaching in New Orleans in 1860; a later Dominican Academy granted teachers' certificates, and in 1910 the College was authorized to grant degrees after four-years of instruction. Ten new buildings are to be erected on its campus by 1980. It enrolls about 550 and accommodates 180 in residence halls.

SOUTHERN UNIVERSITY IN NEW ORLEANS, 6400 Press Drive, is a branch of Southern University and A. & M. College in Baton Rouge (Scotlandville), and was created by the State Legislature in 1956. It is a coeducational commuter college for Negroes, located at Pontchartrain Park. It gives baccalaureate degrees in the Divisions of Commerce, Humanities, Science, and the Social Sciences. In 1964 Southern opened its new library, a two-story structure costing $700,000 and capable of holding 600 readers and 100,000 volumes.

TULANE UNIVERSITY, a major university devoting special attention to Latin American studies in education and medicine, has its main campus on St. Charles Ave., where also is located Newcomb College, its fine arts college for women. Tulane was founded in 1834 by a group of physicians as a medical college to combat tropical diseases. It was endowed by Paul Tulane in 1882 and the State assumed control in 1884. Its off-campus interests are the Tulane School of Medicine in Tulane Ave., the Tulane Delta Regional Primate Research Center, 35 miles north of New Orleans, and the Riverside Research Laboratories for advanced training in space and computer sciences and environmental engineering. In 1970–71 it enrolled 7,115 in regular courses and 1,161 in Newcomb College.

Tulane has strongly supported its Graduate School, which offers 31 programs of study leading to the doctorate. It has introduced innovations in teaching, so that "science must be taught as a dynamic entity," unifying botany and biology for example, speeding up progress toward graduate degrees, and emphasizing training of college teachers. It is closely associated with Latin American needs—its Division of Hygiene—Tropical Medicine has wide effectiveness, and since 1961 it has conducted a center for medical research and training in coopertaion with the Republic of Colombia. It developed the Modern Language Laboratory for teaching language, and its University School and other seminars offers adult education—even teaching the "new math" to parents. It supports the Junior Year Abroad programs.

The Riverside Laboratories are located in the F. Edward Herbert Center of 364 acres at Belle Chasse, south of New Orleans on La 23 and are for advance training in space and the computer sciences and environmental engineering. The Center was named for the Representative from the First Congressional District who obtained the land from the Federal Government.

In recent decades Tulane has constructed about 30 new buildings or additions to existing buildings and completely rehabilitated its physical plant. In the late 1960's it organized its Forward Fund and set a goal of $24,400,000, which it reached. This included a $6,000,000 grant from the Ford Foundation contingent on this being matched, two for one, in cash over a three-year period, which was done. The University allocated

$12,770,000 of the Forward Fund to new construction, $8,400,000 to academic needs and special equipment, and $3,300,000 to endowment. The first building constructed under this plan was the new Howard-Tilton Memorial Library, at a corner of Freret St. and Newcomb Place in 1968. The library has room for 1,200,000 volumes and seats for 1,385 users. It now houses 700,000 bound volumes, and more than 750,000 auxiliary items, such as letters, documents, recordings and microfilm. It receives 5,200 periodicals. Tulane, Loyola, and LSU cooperate in the purchase and use of microfilm materials. The new library cost $6,200,-000, and Federal grants were $1,734,500. The former library became the Joseph Merrick Jones Library and serves the Tulane School of Law.

The Latin American Library is located on the fourth floor of the Howard-Tilton Library. Here also are the manuscripts, rare books, the Louisiana collection and the Archive of New Orleans Jazz.

Other recent structures of great usefulness are the University Chapel, the Theatre & Speech Bldg., two Medical School Bldgs., a Field House, the Richardson Dining Hall, the 12-story J. Blanc Monroe Hall for men, costing nearly $2,000,000, and the Pierce Butler Hall for Newcomb women.

At the Tulane Stadium the Green Wave football games are played and the annual Sugar Bowl Classic takes place. It is bound by Willow and Calhoun Sts., Audubon Blvd., and South Clairborne Ave. It was begun in 1926 with 35,000 seats, was given a second deck in 1939 and expanded to 80,985 seats in 1947. It is floodlighted for night games.

The TULANE SCHOOL OF MEDICINE occupies a city block on Tulane Ave., next to Charity Hospital. It has three units: Hutchinson Memorial Bldg., Libby Memorial Bldg., and Burthe-Cottam Memorial Bldg. A seven-story garage accommodating 500 cars, is attached to the Libby Bldg. The School of Medicine has a Division of Medical Computing Sciences, an office of Biochemical Communications, the Graphic Arts Laboratories established as a memorial for Leon M. Wolf; the Souchon Museum of Anatomy, and a television broadcasting station that sends programs of instruction. The Rudolph Matas Medical Library in the Hutchinson Bldg. has more than 110,000 volumes and receives 1,650 medical and scientific journals annually.

The Orleans Parish Medical Society has its offices in the Hutchinson Bldg. The Dept. of the Army, USA, maintains an editorial office for the history of the Medical Dept. of the Army in World War II, of which 16 volumes have been prepared at Tulane.

In 1969 the TULANE MEDICAL CENTER was established to guide the expansion of the school. The School of Public Health and Tropical Medicine was added.

XAVIER UNIVERSITY OF LOUISIANA, 7325 Palmetto St., is a coeducational institution for Negroes operated by the Sisters of the Blessed Sacrament. In 1954 it extended admission to persons irrespective of race. It has a College of Arts and Sciences, a College of Pharmacy, and a Graduate School. The Department of Music conducts a conservatory program for intensive musical study. Students in engineering may prepare for three years in the liberal arts courses and then transfer to an engineering college for two years of work toward an engineering degree. In the spring, 1969, Xavier enrolled 1,320 students and had a faculty of 131.

ON THE WEST BANK

New Orleans is called the Crescent City because its older sections are located inside a crescent formed by the Mississippi River and called the East Bank, although on the map it appears to be north. On the West Bank are residential and industrial areas, of which ALGIERS is directly opposite Downtown and the Vieux Carré. It is reached by the Greater New Orleans Bridge and a Canal St. ferry. It starts at the boundary of Jefferson Parish and Gretna and extends 12 miles down river, opposite Chalmette.

Algiers was Crown property in 1717 and developed as plantation land under various proprietors. The dry dock industry started here in 1837 and the U. S. Naval Station was opened in 1849. The Shell Marine Dock is located near the point where the river turns. Some distance farther on are the Todd Shipyards. The dry docks extend down to the Quarantine Anchorage and the U. S. Quarantine Station. Opposite the Naval Station on General Meyer Ave. is the Touro-Shakespeare Memorial Home for the aged donated by Judah Touro and Jos. Shakespeare. Algiers has both a MacArthur Blvd. and a General De Gaulle Drive, the latter connecting with West Bank Expressway (BR 90 and Int. 10).

The Algiers Regional Branch Public Library, opened in 1968, on Holiday Drive was the first of the series of regional libraries planned for New Orleans. It cost $482,000 to build and stock and was partly financed by Federal funds.

Adjoining Algiers on the southwest is Jefferson Parish and the incorporated city of GRETNA (24,875 pop. 1970). This was originally a village of German immigrants called Mechanicsham, owned by Nicholas Drestrehan. It has a Memorial Arch opposite the Courthouse, Huey P. Long Blvd., dedicated to the Jefferson Parish war dead. It became a parish seat in 1884 and was often called the Free State of Jefferson because unrestricted gambling went on there. It began to be called Gretna, after Gretna Green in Scotland, where runaway couples found quick marriages easy. Mechanicsham and the adjoining village of McDonoghville were incorporated in 1913 as Gretna. Jefferson Parish has built new additions to the Courthouse.

McDonoghville had been laid out by John McDonogh, the benefactor of New Orleans schools, whose monument stands in Lafayette Square. At the age of 22 McDonogh came to New Orleans from Baltimore and quickly made a fortune. After an unfortunate love affair he retired to McDonoghville and reputedly became a bitter miser. At his death in 1850 he divided his wealth between New Orleans and Baltimore for the building of free public schools. New Orleans built 36 out of a legacy of about $750,000.

The McDonogh Cemetery, on the parish line, was begun by Mc-Donogh for his slaves. He was the first white person buried there, but in 1860 his body was removed to Baltimore. Whites and blacks rested side by side until 1891 when Mayor Joseph Shakespeare of New Orleans, a commissioner of the estate, ordered segregation. The McDonogh Cenotaph is a marble vault with McDonogh's rules for guidance in his life inscribed on one side. The last lines read: "The conclusion at which I have arrived is that without temperance there is no health, without virtue no order, without religion no happiness, and that the sum of our being is to live wisely, soberly, and righteously." Here, as in New Orleans, school children place flowers on the first Friday in May, which is called Founders Day.

Next to Gretna upriver is unincorporated HARVEY, (6,347 pop. 1970) which has several canals used for industrial purposes and the main HARVEY CANAL, which provides the connection of the Intracoastal Waterway with the Mississippi River by means of locks at its mouth. Its connections with the Barataria area of oil fields and fishing villages is described in Tour 11D. The Barataria Blvd. is the dividing line between Harvey and MARRERO, (21,095 pop. 1970, unincorporated) and also divides the grounds of the Hope Haven Institute, with this institution in Marrero and the General Hospital in Harvey. Adjoining Marrero upstream is WESTWEGO, (11,402 pop. 1970), which lies opposite the Audubon Park and University area of New Orleans.

NASA AT MICHOUD

The industrial capacity of New Orleans received a tremendous boost in 1961 when the National Aeronautics & Space Administration established the MICHOUD ASSEMBLY FACILITY, a segment of the George C. Marshall Space Flight Center, on 900 acres 15 miles east of Downtown. This production site for the Saturn rocket boosters for space exploration became in a few years the largest single industrial operation in Louisiana. The physical plant expanded to huge proportions; there rose a MANUFACTURING BLDG., covering 43 acres, a 21-story VERTICAL ASSEMBLY BLDG. a four position S-IC Final Stage Test Facility, an ENGINEERING AND OFFICE BLDG. housing 4,000 contracting personnel; a HAZARDOUS MATERIAL STORAGE BLDG., a VERTICAL COMPONENT SUPPLY BLDG., a 1,200 seat cafeteria, and supplementary structures.

Prime contracts at Michoud passed the first billion dollar mark in the first four years of operation. They were carried out by four major contractors: Chrysler Space Division, Boeing Launch Systems Branch, Mason-Rust, and Telecomputing Services, Inc., of Ling-Temco-Vought.

Before a booster is ready for delivery it is taken to the Marshall Space Flight Center at Huntsville, Ala., on the NASA barge *Promise* for static firing tests, then returned to Michoud. The first completed Saturn rocket booster was shipped to Cape Kennedy Feb. 22, 1965. The influence of Michoud on the economy of New Orleans is illustrated in

━━

Le Vieux Carré – The Old Quarter

━━

Chamber of Commerce of the New Orleans Area

ST. PETER ST., VIEUX CARRE, FROM PONTALBA BALCONY.
CABILDO AT RIGHT

ST. LOUIS CATHEDRAL, JACKSON SQUARE. GENERAL ANDREW
JACKSON STATUE, JACKSON SQUARE

Chamber of Commerce of the New Orleans Area

MILTENBERGER MANSION, VIEUX CARRE, FAMOUS FOR IRONWORK

FRENCH STYLE LAMP POST,
IRONWORK, AND FLOURISHING
BANANA, VIEUX CARRE

Chamber of Commerce of the New Orleans Area

SPACIOUS FOUNTAIN PATIO, VIEUX CARRE

SHADED PATIO IN THE VIEUX CARRE

Chamber of Commerce of the New Orleans Area

NATIONAL BANK OF COMMERCE BRANCH, ROYAL AND
BIENVILLE STS.

OLD FRENCH MARKET WITH COFFEE STAND, VIEUX CARRE

Louisiana Tourist Development Commission

JAZZ MUSICIANS ON BOURBON STREET

DIXIELAND JAZZ AT PRESERVATION HALL

Louisiana Tourist Development Commission

Louisiana Tourist Development Commission

LEADER OF
MARCHING JAZZ
BAND AT FUNERAL,
NEW ORLEANS

GRAND MARSHAL
AT FUNERAL OF
JAZZ MUSICIAN

this official summary: In 1966 23,000 jobs in the plants, construction industries and services received $155,000,000 in salaries and wages; consumer spending was estimated at $103,000,000. More than 35,000 visitors tour Michoud annually.

At the Michoud Steam Electric Generating Station the New Orleans Public Service installed the largest electric generating unit in the South. It can produce 560,000 kilowatts and cost $40,000,000.

The NASA Michoud complex has spurred the exploitation of a large area in Eastern New Orleans, where thousands of houses have been erected. One development, New Orleans East, comprises 32,000 acres and will serve both industrial and residential needs. Another, Lake Forest, 5,000 acres, is located along Int. 10 between Paris Road and Downman Road.

Opelousas

Highways: Opelousas is at the intersection of two major highways, US 190, which crosses the state east-west, from Covington to Beaumont, Texas, and US 167, which come from Ruston and Alexandria in the north and proceeds to Lafayette, continuing south as US 90. Contributing State highways are La 31, 104, 357, 742, and 749.

Bus Lines: Teche Greyhound and Continental Trailways. There are seven motor freight lines.

Railroads: Missouri Pacific, passenger and freight; Southern Pacific and Texas & Pacific, freight.

Airport: A Class IV private and instruction field with runways of 4,000 to 4,500 ft. equipped for night use.

Waterway: Port facilities at Krotz Springs on the Atchafalaya River, with barge channel connecting with Intercoastal Waterway and Mississippi River.

Information and Accommodations: World, evenings and Sunday except Saturday and Monday, 127 N. Market St. Opelousas Assn. of Commerce, P.O. Box 109. Two hospitals & Cerebral Palsy Clinic. Churches, 25, representing 13 denominations. Two hotels, 7 motels. Opelousas Tourist Center & Museum, 163 West Landry St.

Recreation: South City Park and North City Park have all the necessary facilities for swimming, wading, tennis, games. Indian Hills Country Club, golf. Yambilee Bowl, 16-lane bowling. Chicot State Park, 25 *m.* north, all park facilities plus overnight lodging. Fishing, boating, squirrel and duck hunting, with or without guides, consult Opelousas Tourist Center.

Special Events: Mardi Gras, Shrove Tuesday, Louisiana Yambilee, October.

OPELOUSAS (71 alt., 20,121 pop. 1970; 17,417, 1960) seat of St. Landry Parish, is a prospering industrial and distribution center in Acadian Louisiana. It profits from the cotton, beef, sweet potatoes, rice, corn, swine and dairy products raised in the Parish and has oil and gas refineries, food packing, cotton seed processing, fertilizer and drug manufacturing. Three railroads, two of them carrying passengers as well as freight, serve the city, and agricultural tonnage can be placed on barges at Krotz Springs, 19 *m.* east, on the Atchafalaya River. Though Opelousas has attracted peoples of many foreign countries it had a basic Acadian strain and retains strong French elements in its culture and speech. Its big harvest festival in October, the Louisiana Yambilee, celebrates yams, or sweet potatoes, the second largest farm earner in the Parish.

St. Landry Parish is the center of crawfish farming. In this part of Louisiana the crawfish (never pronounced crayfish by the natives) is cultivated for commercial profit. It is often rotated with rice in the same fields.

An Indian trading post is said to have been established in the Opelousas wilderness in 1720. This historic fact enabled the city to celebrate its 250th anniversary in June, 1970. In the vicinity were several villages of Opelousa Indians, a branch of the reputedly cannibalistic Attakapa family. The traders exchanged whisky, guns, and other products of civilization for hides and furs, and built up a lucrative business. Before long other French settlers were drawn to the fertile surrounding lands.

Shortly after the Spanish assumed control of Louisiana in 1769, the settlement was made the governing center of the District of Opelousas, which comprised the whole of southwestern Louisiana. A company of soldiers was stationed here and the village officially became El Poste de Opelousas. But except for the Spanish soldiers who settled in the neighborhood after their military terms expired, there were few Spanish immigrants, and the town and country remained essentially French.

With increasing settlement of the Opelousas country stock raising became the major activity. At first cattle and hides were transported to the New Orleans market by a long water route, by way of Bayou Courtableau, Bayou Teche, Atchafalaya River, the open Gulf, and up the Mississippi River; but during the latter quarter of the eighteenth-century the Spanish connected their far-flung New World possessions with a system of trails. What has become known as the Old Spanish Trail crossed southwestern Louisiana about 20 miles to the south; Opelousas was connected with it by branches extending southward and westward. By the end of the century great herds of cattle moved from Opelousas to New Orleans for transshipment abroad. In the fall of 1803, when the United States came into possession of Louisiana, Opelousas was made the seat of the County of Opelousas, one of the 12 divisions of the Territory of Orleans; in 1807 the counties were renamed parishes, and the County of Opelousas became St. Landry Parish. In 1821 the town of Opelousas was incorporated.

Elisha Bowman, a Methodist minister who was unable to find a place to preach in New Orleans, left that "ungodly city" and traveled to the Opelousas country in 1806. A letter written in January of that year gives the following account of the district:

> I find the people very much dissatisfied with the American Government, and we have a constant talk of war. The Spaniards are fortifying themselves all round the coast; and three-fourths of the people hope they will get this country again. This I hope will never be the case.
> Three-fourths of the inhabitants of this country, I suppose, are French. And as to the country, it is entirely level, and, I suppose, three-fourths prairie. The people are rich in cattle. They have from one or two or three thousand head of cattle to a farmer; and notwithstanding their large stocks, you might with ease carry on your back all that you could find in many of their houses.
> About eighty miles from here, I am informed, there is a considerable settlement of American people; but I cannot get to them at this time, as the swamps

are swimming for miles; but as soon as the waters fall, I intend to visit them. I have great difficulties in this country, as there are no laws to suppress vice of any kind; so that the Sabbath is spent in frolicking and gambling.

Sometime later cotton growing began to supplant stock raising as the most important industry. The prairies were gradually fenced off and made into modest cotton farms, in contrast with the great plantations closer to the Mississippi River.

Opelousas shared in the quarter-century of prosperity that preceded the Civil War. But with the capture of New Orleans and Federal occupation of the Teche country to the south early in the war, there was great difficulty in shipping its products where they were most needed by the Confederates. After the occupation of Baton Rouge by the Federals in 1863, Opelousas became for a time the capital of the State. One legislative session was held here in the old Lecompte Hotel, which stood near the present site of the post office. A short time later the capital was moved to Shreveport, to be safe from the advancing Federals.

Reconstruction was a period of much turbulence in Opelousas—social, economic, and political. Racial conflict became most acute in 1868, with the outbreak of rioting between native whites and Negroes aided by carpetbaggers. The climax was precipitated by publication of attacks against prominent Southerners by Emerson Bentley, editor of the Opelousas *Progress*. He charged that the Democrats were attempting to wean the Negroes from the Republican party and were organizing them under their own leadership. A group of citizens called upon the editor, and, receiving no promise of retraction, took him out and flogged him. As erroneous reports spread that Bentley had been killed, Negroes and other sympathizers armed and demonstrated in the streets. Several days passed before order was restored by the white authorities.

The first railroad to Opelousas was built in 1882, when Morgan's Louisiana and Texas Railroad, now part of the Southern Pacific System, was completed between Opelousas and Lafayette.

Opelousas reflects the stable prosperity of a rich surrounding farm country in which the raising of cotton, rice, sugar cane, sweet potatoes, pecans, forage, and livestock occupies most of the inhabitants. Business in Opelousas itself centers around the merchandizing and shipping of these products as well as in the provisioning of the producers. A minor but active industry is the gathering and processing of Spanish moss, which is used as an upholstering material. There are several ginneries Opelousas for the decortication of the moss fibers.

As the seat of Colonial, country, and parish governments, Opelousas has been the scene of many celebrated court battles, and the practice of law has long been considered the leading profession. The State Supreme Court convened in Opelousas until 1898, and for more than a century the town has been one of the seats of the Federal court for the western district of Louisiana. Procedure in the lower courts reflects the mixed racial outlook of the inhabitants, and court formality has many times been disrupted with displays of volatile Latin tempers.

POINTS OF INTEREST

ST. LANDRY PARISH COURTHOUSE, Court St., between Landry and Bellevue Sts., was erected in 1940 on the site of an earlier courthouse built in 1886. Opposite the courthouse on Court St. is the site of the Lecompte Hotel, which became the seat of State government for several months in 1862–63 when official records were moved from Baton Rouge to Opelousas during the Civil War.

ST. LANDRY ROMAN CATHOLIC CHURCH at Main and Church Sts., is a Gothic structure of red brick built in 1909, replacing a church built in 1828. The first church in the Opelousas area was moved from Bayou Courtableau to this site in 1769, the year Spanish rule began, and early documents in the church archives are written in a fine Spanish script. The French came back a year before the Louisiana Purchase was enacted in 1803; in 1805 Opelousas territory was named St. Landry Parish, after the patron saint.

The JIM BOWIE HOUSE, 163 West Landry St., is a Museum and Tourist Guide Center opened in July, 1958, by the City and the Kiwanis Club. It is a two-room office built in 1850 by Homere Mouton, Lt. Governor 1858–60, and was used by Governor Thomas O. Moore, 1862–1863, when Opelousas was temporarily the capital of Louisiana. It stands on land once owned by Rezin Bowie, father of Jim. The Jim Bowie Oak, 16 ft. in circumference, is believed to be 300 years old. Jim Bowie, born in Tennessee, was 8 years old when his family came to a plantation at Bayou Boeuf. Bowie left when about 19 and died in defense of the Alamo, Mar. 6, 1836.

The Museum has on display artifacts that testify to the long stay of the Indian tribes in this area, and objects associated with the years of settlement and growth, from the time when the Acadians came here from Canada to that of Huey Long.

The GOVERNOR'S MANSION is the name often applied to a fine example of Greek Revival architecture at Grolee and Liberty Sts., which was the residence of Lt. Governor Mouton when Opelousas was the capital. Another stately mansion in the Greek Revival mode is the DIETLEIN HOUSE, at Main and Landry Sts., which has four fluted Doric columns two stories tall. A variant of the style is the ESTORGE HOUSE, Market & Block Sts., built by Pierre Labyche in the 1830s. It is notable for its *trompe d'oeil* ceilings. The HEBRARD HOUSE, 304 Bellevue St., said to be the oldest residence in Opelousas, has been converted to offices. Almost as venerable is a two-story brick building on Bellevue St. at Courthouse Square that was built for office purposes. The COMEAU HOUSE on West Bellevue St. was erected by Dr. James Ray in 1853.

An admirable example of a formal Greek Revival house is the DU-BUISSON HOUSE at Court and Block Sts., built on the site of an earlier mansion. Numerous other residences have survived the vicissitudes of the years and are carefully maintained. Some perpetuate French

Colonial style, notably the house on the RINGROSE PLANTATION, on Prudhomme Lane, built by Michel Prudhomme in 1770, where an antique dovecote, or *pigeoniere,* is still in use. Another house was built by Andre Prudhomme in the early 1800's for his bride, Virginie Gabriel, and their initials are perpetuated on the marbled plaster walls of the parlor. It is occupied by Mrs. Guy Jackson.

The OPELOUSAS-EUNICE PUBLIC LIBRARY is a unique example of cooperation between city libraries 20 miles apart. The only twin-city library in Louisiana operates from part of a sales tax voted in each city. On April 11, 1967, both councils adopted identical resolutions agreeing to maintain and operate the bi-city library. On August 25, 1969 the Opelousas Public Library entered its new building at the corners of Main, Grolee and Union Sts. The Eunice Public Library is located at 216 South Second St. in Eunice. The two libraries are staffed by nine people, and the library system is governed by a board of commissioners appointed by the city councils of Opelousas and Eunice, 3 from Opelousas and 2 from Eunice, with the mayor of each town a member ex officio.

Opelousas in 1970 had 21,425 volumes and a circulation of 68,589, and had available films, recordings, pamphlets, periodicals and other materials for study, information or entertainment. The system has access to the resources of the Louisiana State Library, which issues a State library reading certificate to the individual who reads 12 books on different subjects chosen from a reading list prepared by the State Library.

The Opelousas building houses both the Opelousas branch and headquarters for the bi-city system. It was designed by Hamilton, Meyer & Associates, Opelousas architects. Its style blends with Acadian-type homes and buildings traditional in this part of the South. It was designed to use an ancient method of construction to create the heavy massive feeling of masonry and yet achieve openings that allow natural light to penetrate interior spaces. A combination of three slate colors on the roof and its naturally inherent weight quality gives the entire second floor a visual feeling of one roof. The grays, black and reddish browns on the exterior are sharply separated from the dark browns and shades of green of the landscaping by placing the building upon a white concrete pedestal.

The Eunice Public Library is housed in a building furnished by the city. It had a circulation of 52,043 in 1969.

The FORT HAMILTON OAK, a venerable tree 24 ft. in diameter and possibly 300 years old, stands at the junction of US 190 and US 167, about a quarter of a mile from the eastern limits of Opelousas. Its name commemorates a fort that stood about one mile north of the tree. The fort was built by the Spaniards to protect Opelousas from the Indians. It was called Fort Hamilton after the American settlers arrived. Part of it was the home of Judge Seth Lewis, first district judge in Louisiana, who was appointed in 1813 and served 27 years. Confederate troops were trained here when the Civil War began and later Union troops were stationed here.

The site of the COLLEGE OF FRANKLIN, named for Benjamin Franklin and opened in 1836, is opposite the present City Electric Light & Water plant. It was begun as a school for the children of English-speaking planters. In 1845 it became a school for the Opelousas Indians, and after the latter moved away it was discontinued.

The MARY JANE, a steam locomotive with a record of fifty years of usefulness, today has a plot on Court House Square as a relic of superceded transportation. Built in 1904 by the Davenport, Ia., Iron Works, it was a woodburner and its best speed was 25 miles an hour. In 1959 civic organizations in Opelousas bought it and prolonged its career as an industrial monument.

Ruston

Highways: I-20 and US 80 are the leading east-west highways; US 167 runs north-south, connecting with La 2, and La 33 runs northeast from Ruston. The city is 70 *m.* east of Shreveport, 31 *m.* west of Monroe, 204 *m.* north of Baton Rouge.

Railroads: Illinois Central and Rock Island.

Bus Line: Continental Trailways.

Airport: Area air services and 4,000 ft. runway.

Information and Accommodations: Ruston Leader, evening daily; Ruston Chamber of Commerce. Motels on highways.

Recreation: Ruston has 83 acres devoted to parks. City Park, downtown, has a Greek theater with 200 seats. There is a Municipal swimming pool. Woodland Park has boating, fishing, and picnic areas. There are facilities for baseball, tennis, football, basketball, archery, and bowling. The Ruston Country Club has a 9-hole golf course and a swimming pool. There is wild game hunting in season. The Ruston Park & Recreation Board oversees recreation.

Special Events: Peach Festival, June; Lincoln Parish Fair, October. Garden pilgrimage, April. Lecture-concert series by the Louisiana Tech Concert Assn.

RUSTON (311 alt., 17,365 pop. 1970; 13,991, 1960; inc. 24%) is the seat of Lincoln Parish. A center for dairy, farm products, and lumbering, in recent years it has added three distillate plants, the Diamond Industries, with an annual output of 15,000,000 broom and mop handles; the Dowell division of Dow Chemical Co., a maker of glass containers and a producer of metal chairs and picnic equipment. With the expansion of peach orchards in five northern parishes Ruston in 1950 became the site of the annual Louisiana Peach Festival, held late in June, with naming of a queen and princess, and parades. With the discovery of oil and gas in the parish drill rigs have been appearing on farmland. The parish nets about $26,000,000 to $30,000,000 in mineral values annually and drilling is increasing.

The PEACH FESTIVAL, held annually the last week in June, highlights the successful growing of peaches in Lincoln and adjoining parishes. Of 23 varieties harvested in about 1,000 acres the Dixie Gem is one-fourth of the crop. It ripens usually for 15 days beginning June 8. Peaches are harvested several days before they are soft ripe. They gain much of their size if there is moisture during the final days; when this does not come naturally it is provided by irrigation. No. 1 grade peach is 2 in. or more in diameter. To keep up this quality growers thin the crop in the spring by eliminating thousands of bushels of small fruit. It costs a grower about $400 an acre to prune, thin, fight disease, harvest, buy containers, and pack the crop, which then goes to Louisiana markets and wholesalers by truck. At the Festival visitors are told that "the tree-ripened fruit is different—ripened by the sun, full of sugar, defuzzed, ready to eat."

During the early French regime the Ruston area was inhabited by Ouachita and Caddo Indians, visited by occasional *coureurs de bois* (Fr., forest runners), as white hunters and trappers of the period were called. Even under the Spanish Domination few ventured so far into the wilderness, away from streams providing navigation facilities.

Following the Louisiana Purchase a few settlers entered the district, coming westward from Georgia, South Carolina, and Alabama. There was no longer the threat of hostile Indians; and the pine hills teemed with game, though the soil was less fertile than along Ouachita River to the east or Red River to the south and west. About 1825 a stage line, ran about five miles north of the present site of Ruston, connecting Monroe with El Paso, Texas.

The War between the States found the Ruston area sparsely settled with modest farms; the only town or village of any consequence in the vicinity was Vienna, five miles to the north on the stage line. No actual fighting occurred in the neighborhood.

In 1873 a carpetbag-controlled Republican State legislature created a new parish from portions of Jackson, Union, Claiborne, Bienville, and Ouachita, naming it in honor of President Lincoln, whose name was anathema among the native whites.

The year 1884 saw the birth of the town of Ruston as a way-station and townsite subdivision of 80 acres belonging to a large landowner named Robert E. Russ, on the main line of the Shreveport, Vicksburg & Pacific Railroad, now the Illinois Central. In exchange for its right-of-way through Russ' property, the railroad had its engineers survey and plot the town site. Space for schools, courthouse, and cemetery was set aside, and Russ began selling building lots to prospective residents.

POINTS OF INTEREST

LOUISIANA POLYTECHNIC INSTITUTE occupies a main campus of 213 acres out of 891 ½ acres in the western part of Ruston, and has a physical plant that includes many new buildings erected in the late 1960s from a fund of $14,000,000. Of this amount $2,000,000 was allotted to a new athletic complex, comprising a stadium seating 23,318, a field house, two practice fields, and ten lighted tennis courts. Founded in 1894 Louisiana Tech now has a faculty of 367 and an enrollment of 6,500 to 7,000 students annually. Its component parts are the schools of Agriculture & Forestry, Arts and Sciences, Business Administration, Education, and Engineering. Its graduate program has been expanding since 1958 and in 1968 it was authorized to develop a program leading to the degree of Ph.D.

Representative of the practical uses to which a modern building is put is the George T. Madison Hall of the School of Arts & Sciences, erected 1967. A three-story brick building, it holds 45 classrooms, 100 faculty offices, a television studio, and an auditorium. It is built around a courtyard that has palm trees and fountains. Four other buildings serve the Arts & Sciences.

The School of Agriculture & Forestry has at its disposal not only the facilities of the main campus for instruction in the basic sciences but the agriculture & forestry campus for practical studies in agronomy, horticulture and forestry, where are located a sawmill, a dry kiln, a woodworking shop, a dairy processing plant, a fire tower, a weather station, farm machinery, orchards and nurseries, as well as meat animals. Here are Reese Hall, which has, among other facilities, a forestry library of more than 3,000 books and 15,000 publications.

The School of Engineering has many appliances used in studies in chemical, electrical, industrial, mechanical and petroleum engineering. Louisiana Tech has been active in the field of computers for many years. The School of Business Administration captures the interest of about 1,500 students annually. Of the students in the School of Education about 50 percent train for elementary teaching. Home Economics is attractive to many students and covers a wide range of studies, such as child development, fashion merchandising, institution management, and the responsibilities of family life.

GRAMBLING COLLEGE, on US 80 5 miles west of Ruston, was founded in 1901 as a college of higher education for Negroes and is supported by the State. It has three major divisions: Applied Sciences and Technology, with courses in Agriculture, Business, Home Economics, and Industrial Arts; Education, with courses in Elementary Education, Health, Physical Education and Recreation, and Liberal Arts, with courses in Music, Science and Mathematics, Social Science, Speech and Drama. There about 250 in the faculty and enrollment is around 3,500.

LINCOLN PARISH LIBRARY is located in Ruston, has up to 20,000 vols. in addition to periodicals, and serves the environs with two bookmobiles.

LINCOLN PARISH COURTHOUSE is a modern, red-brick structure on Louisiana Ave. built for efficiency and replacing the original building with dome and cupola that was more monumental then useful.

LINCOLN GENERAL HOSPITAL was opened in April, 1962. It has all the modern installations and 72 beds, and cost $1,500,000.

D'ARBONNE LAKE, the largest body of water in this part of Louisiana, is the principal recreation area for Lincoln and Union Parishes. It is 16 miles long, covers 13,000 acres and 130,000 acre-ft. of water, and has most of this acreage in Union. It is reached from Ruston by La 33, which passes through the village of Cedarton. The lake is fed by Comey Bayou, an outlet of Comey Lake, and has its own outlet in Bayou D'Arbonne. La 33 crosses the lake to FARMERVILLE, junction with La 2, east-west.

St. Martinville

Highways: St. Martinville is on La 31, north-south, formerly called La 25; on La 96, which connects with La 90 at Broussard, 7 *m.* west; La 347, north-south. La 31 connects with La 86 into Iberia.

Bus Line: Continental Trailways.

Railroad: Southern Pacific for freight.

ST. MARTINVILLE (23 alt., 7,153 pop. 1970; 6,468, 1960, inc. 10.6%) is the seat of St. Martin Parish and located on the Bayou Teche in the area of Acadian pioneer settlement. Acadian families came here soon after 1765, about 10 years after they had been removed from their Canadian homes by the British. The parish gained historic importance after Henry Wadsworth Longfellow's poem, *Evangeline,* swept the country, and became a valuable tourist objective with the coming of good roads and motor car touring. St. Martinville, which had only 4,614 people in 1950, passed the 7,000 mark by 1970. It is a region of primeval oaks "bearded with moss," where the Bayou Teche adds to the picturesqueness.

Sugar cane is the best crop in the parish; next come rice and cotton. Resources are salt, timber and oil. Out of the 1969 total of 29,063 people in the parish, two-thirds were in rural areas and more than one-half were non-white.

The first settler of the district seems to have been Gabriel Fuselier de la Claire, who in 1760 purchased from Rinemo, chief of a neighboring Attakapa village, a tract of land to the west of the present town. By 1764 the Marquis de Vaugine, formerly a captain in the French army, had established an indigo plantation to the south. An inventory of the De Vaugine plantation made in 1773 reveals that though living in the wilderness and surrounded by Indians, reputedly cannibalistic, these pioneers enjoyed a surprising degree of luxury. The "mansion house," like most of the first French homes, was simple, being merely a raised cottage divided into three large rooms and surrounded by galleries, with an outside court, or garden, enclosed by oak staves. But its furnishings included silver, crystal, faïence (a variety of majolica ware), and furniture carved of walnut and mulberry.

After the Spanish occupancy of 1769 the tiny settlement was made a military post and named Poste des Attakapas. The resident commandant acted as executive officer and judge for the Attakapas District and the Opelousas District until 1787.

The Attakapas District was named for its earliest known inhabitants, the Attakapas, a powerful tribe which bore the unsavory reputation of eating their prisoners of war. According to Indian tradition, in the hills three miles west of St. Martinville, a great battle was waged, shortly before the coming of the white man, in which the allied Choctaw, Alibamon, and Opelousa overcame and practically annihilated the hated Attakapas.

Between 1765 and 1800 there were steady migrations to the Attakapas District—Acadians from Nova Scotia, Canary Islanders, émigrés from France during the French Revolution, and Creole families from New Orleans. Many of these established farms and plantations in the neighborhood of the Poste des Attakapas, where they raised indigo as the staple crop and experimented with flax and hemp. Those who settled farther to the north and west took up cattle raising.

A list of the instructions to the commandant in 1797, concerning the admission of colonists, is among the archives in the courthouse. It was signed by Governor Manuel Gayoso de Lemos, and specified that a bachelor colonist must prove he was successful in the tillage of land for four years before he could secure title to homesteaded grants. If recommended by some "honorable planter," whose daughter would be given in marriage to the newcomer, the land could be secured sooner. Catholics were preferred as settlers, but others, "of great personality," were occasionally accepted. No Protestant preachers were to receive grants. To all approved colonists, 200 acres were allowed, with an additional 50 for each child born; to some, 20 additional acres were allowed for each slave owned. All grants provided that at least 10 acres had to be cultivated within a year.

During the French Revolution, many refugees who had fled to Louisiana found the village congenial and took up residence there. Regarding themselves as temporary exiles from Paris, they sought for some time to maintain their former mode of life. Their customs and scale of living caused the village to be called Le Petit Paris. Eventually, salvaged jewels and other belongings were sold and the Royalists, except those boasting titles, who married into the wealthier families, were forced to turn to trade and farming for a livelihood.

Suzanna Bossier, who in 1795 traveled through the wilds of Louisiana to St. Martinville with her father and her sister, Françoise, recorded in a letter that she found "a pretty little village . . . full of barons, marquises, counts, and countesses." A diary, kept by Françoise and quoted by George W. Cable in his *Strange True Stories of Louisiana* (1889), tells of balls where the minuet was danced and the ladies wore one-time court gowns covered with jewels; of country picnics on a lavish scale; and of gala nights at the village theater when the *Barber of Seville* was presented.

Contributing to the town's prosperity and wealth was a lucrative smuggling trade carried on with the British by way of Butte à la Rose on Atchafalaya River, and Petit Manchac on Vermilion River.

Not all the settlers around the Poste des Attakapas were Royalists;

some were ardent supporters of the new French Republic. In 1803, when Louisiana was transferred from Spain to France, discord arose between some of the loyal French and disgruntled Spanish sympathizers and French Royalists. The French Colonial Prefect, Pierre Laussat, who had arrived in New Orleans to take possession for France described the situation in a communication to Napoleon Bonaparte:

The Attakapas are peopled with French families who could not refrain from expressing their joy at our return. A native of Bordeaux, named St. Julien, who is an honest planter and much esteemed, had the impudence to head some of his letters with the word 'Citizen.' Thereupon a great conspiracy was suspected and the Spanish Governor ordered this individual to be made a prisoner and conducted here (New Orleans). In the meantime, whilst he was airing himself on his gallery at night, two shots were fired at him, one of which killed his wife. He defended himself, and his assailants, breaking six of his ribs, left him for dead. . . . The Commandant of that Poste, M. de Blanc, a military officer full of honor . . . was in New Orleans when that occurrence took place; but, as he was well known for his devotion to the French, he was deprived of his command and ordered to remain in New Orleans until further notice. In his place was put a M. Duralde, a tool of the Secretary of the Government, who makes a great parade of his exclusive and blind zeal for Spain, and who, to prove his sincerity, is the declared persecutor of all those who in his district have any sympathy for the French. . . . People shoot at each other and civil war has begun. . . . The planters, who still preserve their attachment to us, inquire of me secretly whether they must give it up.

In the fall of 1803, with the final transfer of Louisiana to the United States and the appointment of William C. C. Claiborne as first American governor, the region around St. Martinville became the County of the Attakapas. But the feud continued, and one of the first acts of the new governor was an effort to stop it.

In a letter to Secretary James Madison, May 29, 1804, Claiborne tells how the change of government had affected even religious affairs. Priests appointed by rival superiors appeared at the doors of the church in St. Martinville, each attended by a group of partisans.

The bewildering rapidity with which the country was transferred from Spain to France and then to the United States caused a great deal of confusion. Neither the laws of the United States nor its language were understood here. Robin, a French writer who lived in St. Martinville for a number of years at the beginning of the nineteenth-century, left an account of the meeting of the first grand jury in St. Martinville in his *Voyage à la Louisiane* (1807).

Criminal court had convened and the grand jury, of which Robin was the head, met behind closed doors. According to him a "stranger" presented himself and read, hastily, in "unintelligible French," an "English paper" for their instruction. The members of the jury listened attentively, but all they could make out "of the prattle" was that certain penalties were apparently prescribed "against rape, against the crimes of sodomy and bestiality, against those who illicitly cut or pull off or bite the ears, cut or mutilate the tongue, put out an eye, split nose or lip, cut or pull them out, mutilate some member, or tear the face."

Stunned by this "code for cannibals which made my hair stand on end," Robin and his colleagues reported to the judge that they found themselves "under imperious obligation of abstaining from pronouncing presently on these delinquencies." For six months afterward justice in the new County of the Attakapas was on holiday. The court refused to meet "until the new government should realize its criminals were not actually wild Indians" and had "outlined sensible principles for its guidance." Finally, the feud subsided under the efforts of Governor Claiborne and Lieutenant Hopkins.

Madame Devince Bienvenue (known as Grandmère Devince) was the daughter of Admiral de Grondel of the navy of Louis XVI. With the outbreak of the French Revolution the Admiral and his family fled to Santo Domingo and then to Louisiana. The daughter married Terville Devince Bienvenue of St. Martinville, and bore him seven sons and a daughter.

After having sent her seven sons—Terville, Théodule, Térence, Timoléon, Timecourt, Casimir, and Devince—to the defense of New Orleans in the British invasion of 1814–15, Madame Devince wrote Governor Claiborne that she regretted she did not have more sons to defend her State from the British. She also went by boat to New Orleans, where she served as a nurse. Her age at that time can only be conjectured; the next to youngest of her sons had been born January 5, 1784, and was, therefore, 31 years old when the Battle of New Orleans was fought.

After the British had been vanquished there was a victory parade in which "Grandmère" Devince was carried in a chair on the shoulders of two soldiers, and General Andrew Jackson praised her publicly for her courage and patriotism.

Shortly after Louisiana became a state in 1812, the village was incorporated under the name of St. Martinville in honor of the fourth-century French bishop, Martin of Tours. With the advent of the steamboat the town attained an important position despite its relative remoteness. The steamboat made travel in much of Louisiana not only easy but pleasant, and the village became also a fashionable summer resort. Members of the New Orleans French Opera Company summered here and, during their stay, the village had its own operas.

Beginning about 1855 a severe epidemic of yellow fever was followed by a great fire that destroyed the business district; a hurricane laid waste both houses and crops; finally came the war. Possibly the greatest damage was by the passing of the steamboat era. When the railroad first came through southwest Louisiana St. Martinville was overlooked, and some years elapsed before even a branch was established.

Much French is still spoken here, and the people are deeply attached to old ways and customs. Oldest and strongest of all these attachments is the Catholic Church. On Sunday morning Mass is announced a full hour ahead of time by the ringing of a light bell, a half-hour later a heavier one warns the townspeople once more, and, just before Mass begins, the largest bell and the two smaller ones join in an insistent but pleasant clamor, urging all to worship. Each of the bells was donated, "christened" (blessed) with much ceremony, and carried in a procession in which its "godfather" and "godmother" (the donors) played prominent parts. The Feast of Corpus Christi, celebrated here the first Sunday after Corpus Christi, is not only a religious holiday but a civic occasion.

St. Martinville cherishes a long journalistic tradition, and today two weekly newspapers, the *Teche News* and the *Democrat* are published there. In 1864, when the Union armies occupied the State, the *Courier du Teche* was printed on wallpaper, half in French, half in English. In 1927 a great flood inundated the streets with 5 ft. of water. The press of the *Weekly Messenger* was elevated above the flood and printed its editions as usual. The *Teche News* traces its history through earlier journals to 1886.

POINTS OF INTEREST

ST. MARTIN PARISH COURTHOUSE, 400 S. Main St., was built in 1853 by slave labor. It is a narrow, white cement-covered brick building in the tradition of the Greek Revival. Four fluted Ionic columns rise from the ground to the pediment of the portico and are paralleled by pilasters on the building proper. A new addition of left and right wings is in keeping with the architecture of the old building.

Old documents in French and Spanish are preserved in the courthouse and are accessible to the public. The earliest authenticated one, dated 1760, is in regard to the sale of a slave; one of the most interesting is the will of Chevalier de la Houssaye, dated 1776, together with elaborate instructions to his children for their guidance through life.

CONVENT OF MERCY SCHOOL (OLD CASTILLO HOTEL), 214 Port St., occupies probably the oldest building in what was formerly the Attakapas District; some trace it to days when it served as an Indian trading post. Only the brick framework of the original building is left. Toward the close of the eighteenth-century it housed the "White Pelican," an inn kept by a man named Morphy. According to Françoise Bossier's diary it was "a house of the strangest aspect possible. There seemed first to have been built a *rez-de-chaussée* (single-story) house of ordinary size, to which had been hastily added here a room, there a cabinet, a balcony, until the 'White Pelican' was like a house of cards . . . likely to tumble before the first breath of wind. . . . In the house all was comfortable and shining with cleanness."

An innkeeper by the name of Castillo, who succeeded Morphy, enlarged the place and added improvements; during the height of St. Martinville's fashionable period, steamboats landed passengers regularly at its door. Though continuing for years as the only hostel in the village, the inn in time grew shabby. Bought by the Convent of Mercy, it now serves as the school building of that institution. Since its restoration columns and porches have been removed; today it is a rectangular brick building painted pink, with a dormered roof and a plain façade broken only by windows and a doorway.

EVANGELINE OAK, at E. Port St. and Bayou Teche, marks the landing place of the Acadians (*see Tour 1c*) upon their arrival at the Poste des Attakapas, and tradition claims it also as the meeting place of Emmeline Labiche and Louis Arceneaux—the Evangeline and Gabriel of Longfellow's poem *Evangeline*. Cement benches have been placed beneath the tree, and there is a pleasant view out over the bayou, mantled with water hyacinths and lined with moss-draped oaks.

The CHURCH OF ST. MARTIN OF TOURS (Roman Catholic), 100 S. Main St., was built in 1832. The congregation was established in 1765 and a part of its first chapel is said to be in the present building. It is a simple structure of cement-covered brick, gray with a white trim. A square steeple rises over the front, and there is a small, octagonal cupola in the rear above the apse. Two wings make the church cruciform. The left one houses the Grotte de Lourdes, built by "Tite" Martinez, an octoroon, whose only guide in reproducing the famous French grotto was a picture. Above the altar is a century-old painting of *St. Martin and the Beggar,* by Jean François Mouchet, for which an inhabitant of St. Martinville posed as the beggar.

Facing the entrance gate of the church is the JAN MONUMENT, a brown stone figure of Father A. M. Jan, who served the parish from 1851 to 1887. To the right is the PRESBYTERY, containing church records dating as far back as 1756, and immediately in front, a small statue of St. Martin of Tours.

A remnant of the old Poste des Attakapas cemetery has been preserved at the rear of the church. Still to be seen on some of the grave markers are names and dates—among them, "Jne. Aspasie Bienvenue, Espouse de Fre. Olivier Deveron, Décédée le 27 Nov. 1811, âgée de 26 ans, Femme respectable et tendre mère (respectable woman and tender mother)." In the center is the EVANGELINE MONUMENT, posed by Dolores Del Rio, the actress, who played the role of Evangeline in the motion picture of that name some years ago, and who donated the statue to mark the grave the Emmeline Labiche, according to local tradition the original Evangeline.

French priests from Pointe Coupée and Natchitoches visited this section as early as 1755. Ten years later Father Jean François, a Capuchin, was stationed at the Poste des Attakapas as resident priest and built a chapel. One of the more noted of the earlier priests was Father Barrière, a refugee from the French Revolution, who became pastor in 1795.

The OLD CATHOLIC CEMETERY, Bridge and Cemetery Sts., succeeded the old Poste des Attakapas cemetery as burial plot for the town, in what was then the District of Pinaudville, one of the three divisions of the early village. There is a crucifix in the center and a number of the tombs are more than a century old. The "Tombe de la famille Alphonse Bienvenu" is interesting in that it has a bas-relief of a lady in the full regalia of the 1890's. An anecdote concerning another tomb has long been current. A widower of St. Martinville prayed before the grave of his wife daily, rain or shine, and eventually had a statue of himself in a praying position, clad in a raincoat, placed before the grave with an inscription to the effect that he would never remarry. Later, he did remarry, and some mischievous person broke off the head of the statue, which was later removed.

The UNITED STATES POSTOFFICE occupies the former home of Eugene Duchamp de Chastagnier, which was built in 1876 of red cypress. It is an attractive blend of Spanish and French architecture, and when the Federal Government took over the building it preserved the exterior and adapted only the interior for the postoffice. A painting of Evangeline sitting under an oak tree painted by Minetta Good, hangs in the postmaster's office.

The EVANGELINE MUSEUM was founded in 1925 by Andre A. Olivier in connection with his shop of antiques and memorabilia. As a former secretary of the Longfellow Evangeline Memorial Park Commission and principal historian of Acadian life in St. Martin Parish, he has been associated with many civic activities and has been called the poet laureate of the Acadians. The Museum is at the foot of the Teche Bridge.

St. MARTIN PARISH LIBRARY has its hq. in St. Martinville. In 1968 it reported 40,397 volumes of all categories and circulation of 130,069. It expended $63,932.

LONGFELLOW-EVANGELINE MEMORIAL PARK is located 1 m. north of St. Martinville on La 31 in St. Martin Parish. It is a park of 157 acres, partly wooded and with water courses, supervised by the State Parks & Recreation Commission. As a memorial to the Acadian settlement interest centers on the ACADIAN HOUSE MUSEUM, a small 3-story cottage built in 1765 and traditionally the home of Louis Arceneaux, the prototype of Gabriel, the lover in Longfellow's poem *Evangeline*. The house was built of handhewn cypress timbers fastened with wooden pegs. The walls are of moss mixed adobe and brick, with shutters on the windows, which had no glass when built. About 100 yards in front is the GABRIEL OAK. The house has been furnished with authentic Acadian objects. The old Cuisine, or outdoor kitchen, has been reconstructed and equipped with utensils and there is also a restored storehouse. The story of the Acadians is told here by lecturers. *Entrance fee is 50¢; children under 12 and school groups are free.*

The ACADIAN CRAFT SHOP has displays of woven articles, basketry and palmetto work, some of it purchasable, and is a craft project developed by the Extension Service of Louisiana State University. The PARK LODGE, a restaurant with country dishes, is open daily except Mondays 11–2, and 5–10. The RECREATION BUILDING is used for recreation programs and can be hired by private groups for dances and social use. *Reserve with Recreation Supervisor at Park.* The GROUP CAMP BUILDING accommodates 55 campers and 4 counselors and furnishes cooking and dining utensils but campers must bring bedding and towels. *Fee is 45¢*

per person per night for youths and $1 each for adults, with a minimum of $15. Tent and Trailer camping may be arranged for 2-week periods at $1 per night; electricity 25¢; trailers and air conditioners $1 extra per night. For these and Group Camps consult State Parks & Recreation Commission, P. O. Drawer 1111, Old State Capitol Bldg. Baton Rouge.

LOREAUVILLE HERITAGE MUSEUM VILLAGE, on La 86 7 *m.* south of St. Martinville, is a demonstration or rural history by means of shops and houses. It begins with relics of the Attakapas Indians Trading Post, showing artifacts found in local burial mounds and articles used in trading with the Indians. Objects used by French and Spanish pioneers follow, and then the exhibit moves to the period of the Acadian immigration and the development of a typical Louisiana country town. Genealogical records of families may be consulted here. *Open daily, dawn to dusk; adults, $1, children 50¢, special rates to bus groups.*

On La 345 out of Loreauville, the highway to Lake Dauterive, is the BELMONT PLANTATION HOUSE, a faithful reproduction of a mansion of the Spanish colonial period that was destroyed by fire. It is near the site of St. Maur, mentioned in Longfellow's *Evangeline.*

Shreveport

Air Services: Braniff International Airways, Delta Airlines, Trans-Texas Airways, Royale Airlines, from Greater Shreveport Municipal Airport, Interstate 20 & Hollywood Ave. Private planes and instruction from Downtown Airport, east of N. Market St., US 71. Fleetway Airline operates an air taxi service between Shreveport and Texas cities from GSMA.

Bus Line: Continental Trailways.

Railroads: Kansas City Southern-Louisiana & Arkansas Ry., Texas & Pacific Ry., Illinois Central Southern Pacific R. R., St. Louis & Southwestern Ry. Freight only.

Highways: La 1 enters state from Atlanta, runs down length of state to Grand Isle in the Gulf. US 80 main east-west, joined by US 79 near Minden, parallels I 20 completed between Monroe-Minden, eventually from Vicksburg west. Also US 71 north-south, US 171 south; La 3 from Arkansas; La 173, 511, 523, 526, 538.

Information and Accommodations: Shreveport *Journal,* evening; Shreveport *Times,* morning & Sunday; Shreveport *Sun.* Shreveport Chamber of Commerce and its Shreveport-Bossier Convention & Tourist Bureau, 529 Crockett St. (*Phone 423–6117*). Five major hotels, 30 motels; 13 hospitals, 2,617 beds; 230 churches, 32 denominations, 3 nondenominational (1969); 12 radio stations, 3 television stations.

Recreation: The city operates 36 parks and playgrounds, 2 public golf courses, 15 baseball and 2 football fields, all lighted; 30 practice baseball fields, 3 gymnasiums, 8 swimming pools, 31 tennis courts, a planetarium and two zoos. Also programs by YMCA, YWCA, Boy Scouts, Girl Scouts, etc. The new Salvation Army Boys Clubhouse at Ingleside Park accommodates 225 boys. The Andrew Querbes Park, 3500 Beverly, has 160 acres, an 18-hole public golf course, and a Tennis Center with 10 lighted courts and free instruction for students during the summer. Six private golf clubs have 18-hole courses. There are 5 public bowling alleys with 86 lanes in the Metropolitan Area. Fishing is a major sport, duck hunting a close second; well-stocked lakes can be reached in a 15 to 100-mile drive.

Spectator Sports: The Shreveport Braves, part of the eastern division of the Texas League, play ball from June through September in the Spar stadium 1700 Dove, with teams from Albuquerque, Amirillo, Arkansas, Dallas-Fort Worth, El Paso, Memphis and San Antonio. The Shreveport Oilers, a semi-pro team organized in 1968, plays in the stadium at the Louisiana State Fair Grounds. The Centenary Gentlemen of Centenary College play basketball with Gulf States Conference teams. Basketball contests are played in the Hirsch Memorial Youth Center; football in the Louisiana State Fair Grounds Stadium. The Louisiana State High School Basketball tournament and Sports Award Dinner are held in early spring. Weekly yacht races are held on Cross Lake. International Golf, Palmetto Country Club, July 4. Hilltop Motorcycle Racing Bowl, US 80. Shreveport Skeet Club, Wallace Lake Road, July.

Special Events: Holiday in Dixie, a spring festival of beauty pageant, cotillion, parades. Men's Camellia Club Show, Feb. Caddo Parish Science Show, Fairgrounds, Mar. Women's Department Club, flower show, garden party, April. Ark-La-Tex band festival, April. Louisiana Hayride, monthly program of music, spring and summer, Municipal Auditorium. Louisiana State Exhibit Museum, Fair Grounds, July. Pioneer Historical Museum Exhibits, Baptist Christian College. Art Shows, Norton Art Gallery. Band concerts, Centenary, summer. Shreveport Coin Club annual show, Convention Hall, July. Louisiana State Fair, late October. Planetarium Shows, Fair Grounds. Shreveport Symphony, 2 concerts a month, October-March. Annual programs by Civic Opera Society (2), Civic Chorus & Oratorio Society (2), Choral Ensemble (2). Shreveport Ballet, Centenary College. Shreveport Little Theater, Marjorie Lyons Playhouse, Port Players, Gas Light Players, Catholic Drama League. Shrine Circus, State Fair Grounds.

SHREVEPORT (170–280 alt., 182,064 pop. 1970; 164,372, 1960, inc. 10.8%) seat of Caddo Parish, is the second largest city in Louisiana, and the commercial center of the northwestern part of the State. It is located on the Red River, which divides it from Bossier City, which has many of the industries of the area. Its trade was built on cotton and the by-products, but its 20th century prosperity is directly related to the vast oil and gas production in Caddo and Bossier Parishes, which once exceeded that of the fields along the Gulf. Shreveport also profits by its position on the major east-west and north-south highways of western Louisiana; it is only 74 *m.* from Texarkana and its network of Texan roads. It is 185 *m.* from Lake Charles, 233 from Houston, Texas, 237 from Baton Rouge, and 316 from New Orleans. Shreveport calls its trading area Ark-La-Tex, to signify its close connections with three states.

Although a Confederate city during the Civil War it was less influenced by French settlement than was southeastern Louisiana. It attracted considerable immigration from the northern states and northern European countries, and this brought with it a predominantly Protestant influence, which lingers today even despite the later influx of Italians, Greeks, and Mexicans. There has been a substantial increase of Negroes since World War II, and in 1967 the Louisiana State Board of Health estimated that Shreveport had a total white population of 115,888 and 65,746 Negroes (*Louisiana Almanac*). In 1969 Shreveport annexed the suburbs of Southern Hills and Summer Grove, and in 1970 added several others so that the area of the city became 72,901 sq. m., or 46,656,424 acres.

When the first white explorers, Sieur de Bienville and Louis Juchereau de St. Denis, came to northwest Louisiana in 1700 they found a region of pine hills inhabited by tribes of Caddo Indians, related linguistically to the Pawnee and the Arikara of the western prairies. In the Red River Valley the Caddo built villages of dome-shaped mud and straw houses, and early explorers described them as friendly people.

During the next century few white men other than trappers, hunters, and fur traders visited the Caddo village upon whose lands Shreveport was to be built. The nearest white settlement was Natchitoches, 65 miles down Red River. About 1803 a Tennessean named Larkin Edwards settled on Coates Bluff, at the eastern end of present-day Olive Street. He acted as interpreter for the Indians in their dealings with traders. It was his land, awarded him by the Indians in 1835 in acknowledgment of his long service in their behalf, that formed the nucleus of Shreveport.

With the great western migration from the older Southern states in the early 1830's, settlers began to drift into the Caddo country and build log cabins. Prominent among them were Jacob Erwin, who became Larkin Edwards' son-in-law, and James Erwin, son-in-law of Henry Clay, who brought his family and 100 slaves from Kentucky to establish a settlement known as Erwin's Bluff, a short distance below Edwards' cabin site. About the same time Dr. William S. Bennett of New Hampshire, and James Huntington Cane arrived. Forming a partnership, these two established a trading post on the west bank of the river later known as Bennett and Cane's Bluff. Shreveport's second commercial establishment was the Catfish Hotel, used by fur traders, rivermen, and cattlemen.

By this time settlements had sprung up on the east side of the river, one north of the present town of Ruston as early as 1809, two others near Minden in 1811 and 1818. In 1828 the Parish of Claiborne, from which came Bossier, Bienville, Webster, Jackson, and a part of Lincoln Parish, was created by the State Legislature.

Traversing this territory was the Military Road, on which supplies for the U. S. Army were hauled between Alexandria and Natchitoches, and as far north as Fort Towson, in present-day Oklahoma. Because of the long haul and the labor necessary to keep the road open the War Department petitioned Congress that Red River be cleared of the Great Raft, an almost solid jam of driftwood obstructing the river for 160 miles above the present site of Campti. This formidable barrier had been in process of formation for centuries. In 1832 the U. S. Government assigned the task of opening Red River for navigation to Henry Miller Shreve (1785–1851), an American trader and steamboat builder. Born in New Jersey, Shreve was reared in western Pennsylvania, where, as a boatman, he became interested in steam navigation on the Ohio and Mississippi. He gave valuable assistance to General Jackson in 1814–15 and participated in the Battle of New Orleans. In 1815 he made the first steamboat trip from New Orleans to Louisville, violating the exclusive right to navigate the Mississippi by steam craft claimed by Robert Fulton and Edward Livingston, a monopoly that was later overruled by virtue of the improvements made by Shreve on Fulton's model. From 1826 to 1841 he served as superintendent of improvements on western rivers, after which he retired to a plantation in Missouri.

Shreve began his task of opening the Red River at Campti in 1833, employing two battering-ram-type vessels of his own invention. Within a year he had cleared the river for a distance of 80 miles, as far as Bennett and Cane's Bluff. Though he was to spend 5 more years in clearing the stream as far as Fort Towson, 720 miles from its mouth, positive results came swiftly to the little frontier settlement at Bennett and Cane's Bluff. Forty years were to pass and a great deal of money was to be spent before the Great Raft was entirely eliminated with the aid of nitroglycerine.

On July 1, 1835, at the Indian Agency House on Peach Orchard Bluff, nine miles south of Bennett and Cane's Bluff, the Caddo signed a treaty by which they transferred their territory in northwest Louisiana to the United States for $80,000. The chief of the Caddo and 24 of his braves signed for the Indians; Indian Commissioner Jehiel Brooks, for the Government. A "floating," or unidentified, section of land was reserved by the Indians for their friend and former interpreter, Larkin Edwards. The Caddo themselves agreed to "leave the United States forever, never to return." During the six-day celebration of the centennial of this event, held in Shreveport in 1935, the signing of the treaty was re-enacted on the original site, with descendants of the original signatories, both white and Indian, participating. Descendants of the Indian signatories came from Oklahoma for the occasion. The ceremonies ended with a "corn dance" by the Caddo, just as the event had ended in 1835.

Larkin Edwards selected 640 acres of land centering about Bennett and Cane's Bluff. In February, 1837, annulling a previous sale to Angus McNeil, Edwards sold his tract for $5,000 to Henry Shreve, William Bennett, James Cane, Angus McNeil, Bushrod Jenkins, Thomas Sprague, Thomas Williamson, and James Pickett, members of the Shreve Town Company, an organization formed the year before for the founding of Shreve Town. Streets were laid out and lots were rapidly bought up by Texas-bound emigrants, who passed this way in increasing numbers after Texas won its independence in 1836. The town was incorporated as Shreveport in 1839.

But the Caddo had not all left Louisiana according to agreement. Some drifted into Texas, where they became involved in difficulties with Texas pioneers. On November 21, 1838, the adjutant general of the Republic of Texas advised the Caddo Indian agent at Shreveport that the Caddo had spent the last installment of their $80,000 on arms, and were using these against the settlers in northern Texas. When trouble with the Caddo continued General Rusk led Texas troops into the parish. As a result a treaty was entered into at Shreveport, November 28, 1838. The Caddo surrendered their guns to the Texans and agreed to remain in Louisiana, to be maintained at the expense of Texas until Indian troubles were settled.

Shreveport passed swiftly from the lusty days of frontiersmen and pioneers to the picturesque and prosperous period of the steamboat and King Cotton. Flush times came to Shreveport and the whole northwest area with the agricultural development of the rich alluvial land along the river. Great plantations resembling feudal estates were established with slave labor; money was plentiful and life was gracious and gay. Every boat that docked on the levee was loaded to the Plimsoll mark with bales of cotton; and every wagon that rolled its toilsome way from the hills of Bienville, Claiborne, and Webster Parishes brought rich toll.

Shreveport gave itself over to cotton. The very streets and sidewalks were piled and cluttered with bales. Men in shirt sleeves or shabby linen dusters, wisps of cotton clinging to their beards, weighed, sampled, bought, and sold cotton—making and losing fortunes.

No battle of the War between the States was fought in or around Shreveport, but with almost the whole of southern Louisiana in the hands of Federal troops, the town became the Confederate capital of Louisiana in 1863. Sessions of the State Legislature were held in the old courthouse in 1863, 1864, and 1865. On March 7, 1863, Shreveport also became the headquarters of General Edmund Kirby-Smith, in command of the Trans-Mississippi Department, comprising the military districts of Louisiana, Texas, Arkansas, and the Indian territory. The city was the last spot to fly the flag of the Confederate States of America.

At one time there had been threat of an attack on Shreveport by Federal gunboats seeking to ascend the river as a part of Banks' Red River Campaign. In defense of the city three forts and an embankment extending in a crescent four miles along the river were built. Since few cannon were available, trees hewn to simulate formidable artillery pieces were dragged into position all along the ramparts. When General John B. McGruder saw these while on a tour of inspection, he exclaimed, "Your forts are only a humbug." Remnants of one of these forts in the northeastern section of Shreveport are now known as Fort Humbug. Fortunately for Shreveport, Banks and his invading Federal Army were turned back at Mansfield and Pleasant Hill.

Shreveport recovered rapidly from the effects of the war and embarked upon an era of prosperity and growth. The construction of railroads was resumed, and in 1873 Shreveport was connected by rail with Dallas. River traffic regained its pre-war proportions, but succumbed before the end of the century to the competition of the railroads. Streets were cleared of cotton bales and paved. Population forged ahead—from 8,009 in 1880; 16,913 in 1900; 43,874 in 1920; to 160,535 in 1966.

Showboats and barnstorming stock companies had begun to visit Shreveport about 1850. Judging from contemporary accounts the frontier town preferred Shakespearean productions to all others. A Banjo Minstrel Boat was a great favorite and its visits were eagerly awaited. There seems also to have been some local talent, as every season witnessed amateur stage productions in Brewer's Hall and the Opera House, both of which were built shortly after 1850. Crisp's Gaiety Theater, built in 1871, and the Grand Opera House, built in 1886, were also gay places. On the stage of Crisp's Gaiety, Adah Isaacs Menken launched her meteoric career in 1857 as Pauline in *The Lady of Lyons*. John McCullough, Denman Thompson, and Minnie Maddern Fiske appeared before Shreveport audiences. Tally's Opera House, a second-story hall on Milam Street also did an excellent business.

With the discovery of oil in 1906 in Caddo Lake near a point since named Oil City, Shreveport began to boom in earnest as oil men, promoters, and representatives of major oil companies flocked to exploit the fields which were opening up on all sides. In 1930 the great East Texas Field, and in 1935 the Rodessa Field, revived the slightly lagging oil industry, providing employment to thousands. But the promise of Rodessa as a boom town was not fulfilled.

Since then the fields northwest of Shreveport have produced great quantities of petroleum, natural gas, and natural gas liquids, and new wells are still being brought in. In 1963 Caddo Parish ranked first in number of wells drilled—825 and it had 500 new wells in 1962. In 1968 Caddo drilled 109 successful oil wells out of 393 in the whole State, and 6 gas wells. Production was valued at $26,324,000 in 1968. The adjoining Bossier Parish was not far behind with a valuation of $24,005,000, and this helped contribute to the prosperity of the Shreveport-Bossier City area. But the returns had dropped far behind those of the parishes along the Gulf.

Cotton has been another contributor to the welfare of the area. For years, when cotton was the top agricultural crop in Louisiana, Caddo Parish led production. When the *Louisiana State Guide* was first published in 1941, it reported that the parish led the State with 50,000 to 80,000 bales and that the annual yield within a radius of 100 miles was in excess of 850,000 bales. Since then cotton has dropped to fourth place and in some years of the 1960 decade the whole State production was only around 45,000 bales. Cottonseed oil and other byproducts are still important in this area, but they are no longer in first place.

For many years Shreveport commercial interests agitated for construction of a 9-ft. navigable channel for barge traffic on the Red River. The Chief of the Corps of Engineers, USA, in May, 1967, recommended approval of the Secretary of the Army of the barge project. Initial work covers 31 miles of the waterway, which is to extend for 294 miles and cost $523,000,000 (1967 estimate). The 9-ft. channel will be 200 ft. wide and need 9 locks and dams, one at the southern outskirts of Shreveport.

A new bridge over the Red River at 70th St. was begun in 1968 and completed in 1970. It cost $3,248,520. The Long-Allen Bridge at the foot of Texas St., crosses the Red River from Shreveport to Bossier City. It was completed in 1934 and named for Senator Huey P. Long and Governor Oscar K. Allen.

The decade of 1960–1970 saw a tremendous spurt in construction of industrial plants, office and apartment buildings, hotels and shopping centers. The biggest gain in employment came when the Western Electric Co. located its new Shreveport Works on a 278-acre tract on US 171 where Baird Road intersects Mansfield Road south of the city. By 1969 this plant employed 3,089, with an annual payroll of $22,000,000 and purchasing expenditures estimated at more than $17,000,000. Another boost came when the General Electric Co. bought 100 acres of the former Caddo Parish Penal Farm site for a plant for manufacture of underground distribution transformers that would require 800 employees by the mid-1970's. Expansion also continued at the Shreveport plant of

Baifield Industries of Dallas for the manufacture of shell casings and other forms of munitions for the Federal Government. The third largest employer in Shreveport was AMF Beaird, Inc., with 1,327 on its payroll. The Mid-Continent Steel Casting Corp. was employing 822. The Ford Motor Co. built a new battery and container manufacturing plant and by 1970 was employing 650.

Shreveport materially expanded its ability to accommodate large conventions by opening its new CONVENTION CENTER in 1965. This modern structure on Red River Parkway at Crockett St. was built adjacent to the CIVIC THEATER, a fine modern hall for the performing arts opened in February, 1965. Walker & Walker were the architects. The main convention hall can accommodate 1,000 guests at banquets and 1,200 at lectures, and a smaller hall can hold 450 for banquet and 550 for lectures. The two can be operated as one, while meeting rooms can accommodate from 15 to 125 persons each. The original cost of the convention center was $528,000.

In 1970 Shreveport built an annex to the Convention Hall linked to it by a covered walk across Crockett St. It added 7,500 sq. ft. of floor space and cost $239,000.

It is on the CIVIC THEATER that the city has lavished its best artistic talents, for construction and equipment raised the cost to approx. $1,100,000. The 1,765-seat house faces the Parkway and adjoins the Convention Center. The plain brick structure is accentuated by a façade of nine scalloped vaults rising above travertine marble columns over a 23-ft. wide terrazzo promenade. In front of the building is a circular area with a statue of Capt. Henry Miller Shreve, and a fountain that can throw a 40-ft. spray. Murals and marble plaques in the lobby commemorate Red River packets of other days as well as Shreve's famous operation of clearing the river of snags. There is also a model of a notable steamboat, the packet *Valley Stream* and an elaborate wood screen carved in what has been called steamboat gothic, so that the steamboat era is well commemorated in this civic undertaking. The Civic Theater supplants the Municipal Auditorium for symphonic music and opera and leaves that to wrestling bouts, rallies, religious revival meetings, and other spectacular events.

With the completion of the Convention Center Shreveport also obtained new hotels. To such well-established hostelries as the Captain Shreve, the Downtowner, the Holiday Inn North on Market St. were added motor hotels on Greenwood Road. A new Ramada Inn was opened in April, 1967, with 100 luxury suites. The Sheraton hotel chain arranged to occupy 12 floors of Sheraton Towers, a 32-story structure with 20 stories of offices, 250 hotel rooms, a roof-top restaurant, a 1,600-car garage, and other facilities, estimated to cost $15,000,000.

Residential construction went all the way from single apartment buildings costing $1,000,000 and up, to subdivisions that made provision for school, church, shopping center, park and swimming pool sites. Cross Lake was a desirable location and Villa del Lago, a 222-unit project, was one of those favoring its banks. Similar building of luxury apartment houses went on in the Shreve Island area. The most ambitious planners, basing their investments on projections of continuing expansion, funded subdivisions such as Town South Estates, which at its peak would have 623 houses, 700 apartment units, and 3,000 residents. The master plan for Huntington Park, 1,300 acres west of the city, visualized houses, apartments, a country club, schools, churches, and shopping centers that would cost an estimated $100,000,000 by the time it was completed in the 1970 decade.

Characterized as unique on any landscape is the FOUNTAIN, a 12-story building of circular design on Fairfield Ave. containing 221 apartments reserved for senior citizens. The elevators are located in the central core. The building comprises a restaurant, library, chapel, lounge, infirmary, woodworking shop, thermal baths, and barber shop, so that elderly residents need not venture outside its walls for any accommodation.

Shreveport has had a lively cultural life for many years, stimulated in part by the colleges. An institution of wide popularity is the Community Concert Assn., which brings to Shreveport famous operatic stars and instrumentalists, and major symphonic orchestras on a subscription basis. Highly influential in musical life is the Shreveport Symphony Society, which supports the Shreveport Symphony Orchestra, which gives two concerts a month, October to March; the Symphony Chorale, a ballet company, and two youth orchestras. The Shreveport Civil Opera Society produces two major operas a year with the participation of stars of the Metropolitan Opera Co.; during a recent season it presented *Turandot* and *Lucia di Lammermoor*. The Centenary College Choir has given programs on national and overseas tours, and annually gives its Rhapsody in View at the Convention Center, an Easter sunrise service, and Songs by Summer Starlight at Hodges Gardens. The Civic Chorus and Operatic Society gives a program during the Christmas season and in the spring. The Choral Ensemble, a woman's organization, gives two concerts a year.

Dramatics are fostered by a number of organizations. The Shreveport Little Theatre, in existence for nearly 50 years, gives six productions annually. The Barn Dinner Theatre, which performs in the round, gives 12 plays a year with a revolving New York cast. The Gas Light Players perform June through September at the State Fair Grounds, and their division, the Shreveport Savoyards, play at other times. The Jongleurs of the Drama Department of Centenary College give six performances a season in the Marjorie Lyons Playhouse. The Port Players stage six performances a year from the musical and dramatic repertory, including such works as *The Sound of Music, Harvey, Oliver,* and *Medea.*

Shreveport has a large, expanding religious population. A survey of March, 1969, found 230 churches in the city and Bossier, representing 33 denominations. It estimated that 91 percent of the community had religious affiliations; that 47 percent was Baptist, 14 Methodist, 13 Roman Catholic, 4 Presbyterian, and 3 Episcopal.

The first formal service was conducted on March 24, 1839, by

Leonidas K. Polk, the missionary bishop of the Protestant Episcopal Church who became a Confederate officer and died in battle. Six years later the Episcopalians established a congregation, followed by the Methodists, Baptists, and Presbyterians, who have had large followings ever since. The Roman Catholics founded Holy Trinity Church in 1855 (the congregation worships at 315 Marshall St.) and a Hebrew group was organized in 1859. All the major denominations are represented, and in recent years Shreveport has welcomed the Baha'i Center, Four Square Gospel, Jehovah's Witnesses, and a number of independent and nondenominational churches.

There are a number of religion-affiliated schools, including two four-year colleges, Baptist Christian College, and Centenary College; 14 kindergartens—Baptist, Episcopal, Catholic and Methodist; 8 elementary school—Baptist, Episcopal, Catholic and Seventh day Adventist; 1 Seventh Day Adventist junior high and 2 Roman Catholic high schools.

New facilities for worship and for religious education are continually being provided in the Shreveport-Bossier area. Announcements of construction and costs testify to the viability of religious life. In recent years the Queensborough Baptist sanctuary and administrative wing on Missouri Ave. cost $750,000; the First Presbyterian added a children's education wing and other facilities at $676,000; Highland Baptist built a new chapel at $500,000; Southside Baptist dedicated a new sanctuary seating 1,100 at $500,000; St. Paul's Methodist Church built classrooms costing $100,000; other extensive improvements were made by Laurel Heights Baptist, Liberty Missionary Baptist, Shreveport Seventh Day Adventist near the Municipal Airport; Mount Zion Baptist, Dunlap Presbyterian, and Nativity Lutheran, while Life Tabernacle planned a large complex at 70th St. and Meriwether Road. The Church of Christ of Latter Day Saints started a new building, and Creswell Street Church of Christ began a complex including a sanctuary seating 1,000 and an educational building. Sunset Acres Baptist Church completed a sanctuary for 1,275 which also had a choir loft for 63 and a bridal suite. The new educational wing and expanded auditorium of Sherwood Park Baptist Church was given a modern design by the architect, Roland Norman.

Numerous private secular institutions have been formed since desegregation changed the school situation. The most impressive is Shreveport Academy, opened in September, 1970, with $1,000,000 invested in buildings. It has a 47-acre tract on Flournoy-Lucas Rd., and prepared to enroll 1,200 in grades 1–12. It started with two libraries, one for elementary pupils, the other for high school students. Another complex for all grades is West Shreveport Academy, to enroll 1,200. It is a non-profit school owned by parents. Friendship Academy is a new nonsectarian school for grades 1–9. Caddo Academy has grades 1–6 and expects to expand to 12.

POINTS OF INTEREST

BAPTIST CHRISTIAN COLLEGE, 3031 Hollywood Ave., was founded in 1961 under the leadership of its first and present (1970) president, Dr. Jimmy G. Tharpe as a coeducational, four-year, liberal arts college under the sponsorship of Missionary Baptist Tabernacle, an independent Baptist church of the American Baptist Assn. The enrollment for 1969–70 totaled 611. The degree of bachelor of arts was awarded to 41 graduates on May 29, 1970. The B.A. degree includes majors in the arts and sciences, education, business administration, Bible, and physical education. A Th.B. degree is also offered, based on a program of five years study, in Bible and Christian education.

Five buildings are on the campus: College Hall, a two-story air-conditioned building, which contains classrooms and the offices of the executive vice-president, registrar, business manager, and dean of students; the Educational Building, which houses the Library and Science Laboratory and several classrooms; the Main Building contains the Auditorium-Chapel, president's office, and the school cafeteria. There are also a girl's dormitory and a boy's dormitory. The Library has nearly 20,000 volumes. The campus at present is small, but additional properties have been purchased and new buildings are planned, including a gymnasium, library, and additional dormitory facilities.

Baptist Christian College has established an Instructional Center of audio-visual aids and materials to facilitate the enrichment of teaching.

One of the chief attractions at the college is the Historical Museum, which was opened October 26, 1969. It contains the notable gun collection of Dr. A. Loyd Collins, including guns used in all periods of American history—matchlocks, wheellocks, flintlocks, percussion, and cartridge guns. It also contains a large number of old history books, school textbooks, pioneer household articles and official documents of Presidents of the United States. The college has a well-rounded physical education program, including basketball, baseball, and track, and plans for football.

LOUISIANA STATE UNIVERSITY opened its Shreveport branch in September, 1967, with 794 students registered and a faculty of 36. It began with a two-year curriculum but expansion to a four-year, degree-granting college is in the plans. The first-year's budget reached $912,980, with $840,000 appropriated by the State and the rest coming from student fees. The U.S. Department of Health, Education & Welfare donated the Nike-Hercules missile site at Stonewall to LSU for conversion to research purposes, and the Federal Housing Authority turned over the 296-unit Linwood Apartment Project for faculty and student housing. A Federal matching grant of $404,989 has been awarded LSU to help build a new liberal arts building costing $1,700,-000. Funds also have been received to be used toward a Center for Engineering & Business Administration.

The SHREVEPORT SCHOOL OF MEDICINE, associated with Louisiana State University, opened in September, 1969, with 32 students chosen out of 500 applicants. It is using the VETERANS ADMINISTRATION HOSPITAL, a $10,500,000 undertaking. The School of Medicine is to have headquarters in a 12-story structure expected to cost $20,000,000, and described as "the most costly State building ever put up in Louisiana."

A valuable addition to medical facilities is the SCHOOL FOR MENTALLY RETARDED CHILDREN established in 1964 by the Roman Catholic Church on Ellerbe Road. The land was donated anonymously by three Shreveport citizens and half the construction cost of $700,000 was allocated by the U. S. Public Health Service. Although staffed by Catholics the institution is open to all faiths.

The SHREVEPORT MENTAL HEALTH TREATMENT CENTER was able to start construction with $250,000 appropriated by the State in 1963 and a Hill-Burton grant of $250,000 from the U.S. Dept. of Health, Education & Welfare.

The SCHOOL OF NURSING of NORTHWESTERN STATE UNIVERSITY, 1427 King's Highway, was formally opened in April, 1967, in the new educational complex behind Schumpert Hospital. The institution cost $775,000, of which $264,941 was a Federal grant. The front wing of the complex houses educational facilities, administrative offices, and major mechanical equipment. The rear wing has four floors and a basement fallout shelter, the upper three floors being used for dormitories. Glass walls open on gardens and paved terraces. The School's first staff comprised a director, 14 nursing instructors, and a librarian. Students enroll at Northwestern in Natchitoches and remain there the first two years, then have their last two years at Shreveport.

SOUTHERN UNIVERSITY of Baton Rouge was authorized by the State Legislature in 1964 to establish a branch at Shreveport. It is located on a campus of 63 acres at Cooper and Blanchard Roads and offers a two-year course, especially for Negroes. In its first school year it enrolled 360. William R. Baker & Associates are architects for its new Science Bldg. which is being financed by $716,120 of State funds and $600,000 of Federal funds.

SHREVEPORT-BOSSIER VOCATIONAL TECHNICAL CENTER, 2010 Market St., was organized in 1965 to offer day and night students courses in drafting, computer technics, welding, cabinet making, electronics, automobile repairing and nursing. Audio-visual facilities are used. The original building cost $750,000; in 1970 a second building was constructed at a cost of $450,000. The Center gives instruction to about 3,000 students annually.

CENTENARY COLLEGE, 2911 Centenary Blvd., is a coeducational institution on a rolling wooded campus that places emphasis on excellence in Christian higher education and prefers small classes, preferably with a ratio of 12 pupils to one professor. It traces its origin to two separate foundations. The College of Louisiana was founded in Jackson, La., in 1825, and the Centenary College in Brandon, Miss., in 1839, under Methodist auspices. The Jackson college was bought by individuals in 1845 and donated to the Methodist Conference of Louisi-

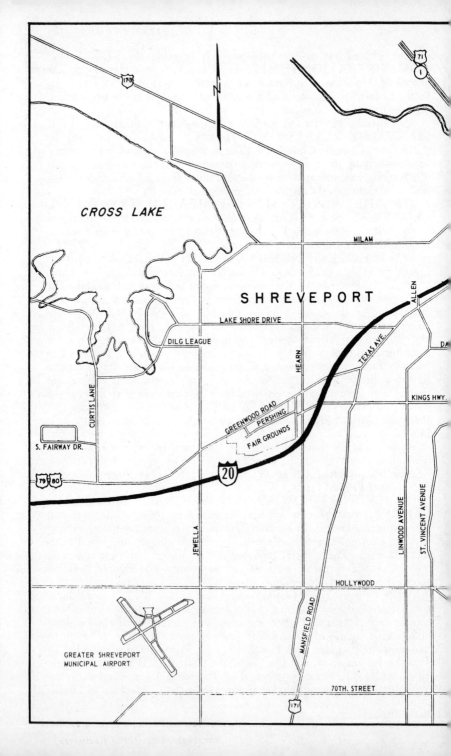

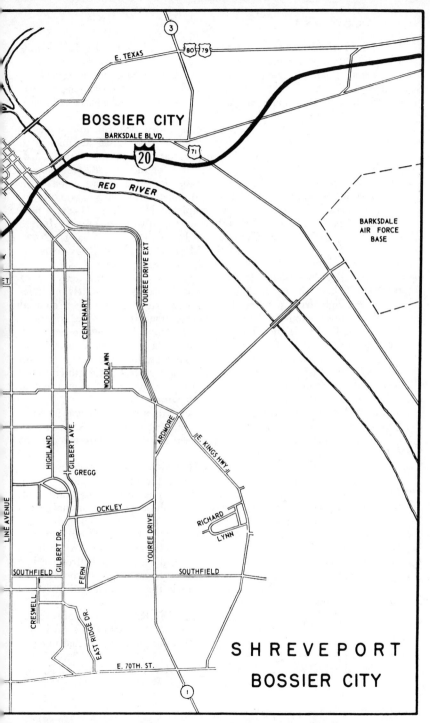

SHREVEPORT
BOSSIER CITY

Shreveport Chamber of Commerce

ana and Mississippi. The Conference then moved Centenary from Brandon to Jackson and combined the two colleges as Centenary College of Louisiana. Jefferson Davis and Judah P. Benjamin were among its students. In October, 1861, it was forced to suspend operations because all the students had gone to war. In 1907 the Methodist Conference moved the college to Shreveport.

Centenary in the 1970 spring term enrolled 806 fulltime students, 485 of them men, and some special students that raised attendance to 1,140. There was a faculty of 93. Tuition costs $1,074; room and board, $810 for men, $820 for women, with total for men $1,784, for women $1,894 a year. Although the college wishes to remain small, it has been campaigning to improve its plant, and hopes to raise $20,000,000 by 1975 for new facilities. In 1970 it completed HAMILTON HALL, a new administrative building, and the PHYSICAL EDUCATION AND ATHLETIC CENTER, a geodesic dome. The MICKLE HALL OF SCIENCE has 10 DORIC columns rising three stories and the MARJORIE LYONS PLAYHOUSE is a collection of cubes and oblongs suitable to its functions.

The college maintains close relations with the cultural activities of the area. The Centenary College Choir broadcasts regularly on television. An eight-week program of band concerts in Hargrove Memorial Amphitheater is supported by the college, the city and the American Federation of Musicians. The Marjorie Lyons Playhouse serves both city and college, and the Readers Theater gives readings in churches and schools. Film classics are shown in the Playhouse by the Shreveport Film Society. Centenary has teams competing in intercollegiate athletic contests and the Gents meet other basketball teams in the new Physical Education and Athletic Center during the winter.

Total cost of Hamilton Hall and a new athletic complex was $1,951,-300. Centenary has a long-range master plan that will cost $20,000,000, of which certain funds already have been raised by interested citizens for current construction.

The SHREVE MEMORIAL LIBRARY has its headquarters in its main building at 400 Edwards St., also the base for Caddo Parish Library. It was endowed by Andrew Carnegie. When this *Guide* was published in 1941 the library had 36,000 volumes and an annual circulation of 170,000. In 1970 it had expanded to 217,851 volumes and a circulation of more than 1,000,000, with eight neighborhood branches, two bookmobiles and the Caddo Parish collection. Films, recordings, pamphlets and periodicals enhanced its usefulness. Expenditures reached nearly $450,000. The city and parish library systems were consolidated January 1, 1970. The Broadmoor Branch Library, enlarged twice its former size, now has 13,000 vols.

The SOCIAL SECURITY ADMINISTRATION in Shreveport serves seven parishes in northwest Louisiana. It occupies its own one-story building at Youree Dr. and East Washington St., erected in 1967 at a cost of $100,000.

The BARNWELL MEMORIAL CULTURE CENTER, 501

River Parkway, was built in 1970 by the City with nearly half the cost donated by the Barnwell Family.

The MUNICIPAL AUDITORIUM, 745 Grand Ave., serves the community efficiently as the site for athletic contests and spectacles. It was erected in 1929 at a cost of $500,000, and has been kept abreast of current demands, such as getting completely air-conditioned in 1956. It seats 3,500 and has three balconies. The Louisiana Hayride and the Holiday in Dixie events are held here annually.

The LOUISIANA STATE FAIRGROUNDS have played a major part in attracting exhibits and crowds to Shreveport for more than half a century. Located southwest of Downtown, they are reached direct by Texas Ave. and Greenwood Road, the latter also the route of US 79 and US 80, with the new Int. 20 coming on the south. The principal event for years has been the LOUISIANA STATE FAIR, held annually for ten days in October, which combines fun and frolic with a large showing of agricultural and livestock products. The year-round usefulness of the Fairgrounds has been increased greatly since the HIRSCH MEMORIAL COLISEUM was opened in 1954. This huge oval arena honors W. H. Hirsch, secretary-manager of the State Fair Assn. The arena measures 120 by 240 ft., is 94 ft. high, and is covered by an immense copper roof. It houses rodeos, basket ball contests, horse shows, ice shows, tennis matches, political rallies and spectacles. It seats 9,000 and when the arena is added can seat 11,500; of the stages that can be set up the largest is 40 by 70 ft.

The PLANETARIUM is located in the State Fairgrounds Park, 2900 Edgar, 7½ acres of park and swimming pool, with an enclosed recreation center, tennis courts and picnic-playground areas. The Spitz Planetarium seats 100. Open Monday through Friday, 8:30–4:30.

The SHREVEPORT OBSERVATORY, built 1964 on the Frierson Plantation, was presented to the Board of Education by the Shreveport Astronomical Society. The circular, domed building has a 16½ in. telescope and reflectors.

The LOUISIANA STATE EXHIBIT MUSEUM, 3015 Greenwood Road (on Highways 79 and 80) is a circular building ("doughnut-shaped") housing articles, dioramas, artifacts, and examples of agricultural and industrial products of the State, maintained for public education by the Louisiana Department of Agriculture & Immigration. Its marble retunda, with exhibits on both sides of the corridor, is an eighth of a mile in circumference. There are dioramas showing an oil refinery, a sulphur mine, a salt dome (Louisiana mines 2,000,000 tons of salt annually); farm installations, waterfowl, an Indiana village, and many other forms of life and geography. Murals by Dr. H. B. Wright show the establishment of the first trading post at Natchitoches in 1714, and the cession by the Caddo Indian tribes of their lands to the United States in 1835. Among the rarities on display is the Owen Collection of Early American glassware and china, and a porcelain figurine collection of American birds made by Dorothy Doughty. Adjoining the circular building are two wings, one containing an art gallery, where paintings are changed eight times a year, historical murals, and displays of agricultural and industrial products. The other wing has an auditorium seating 400, which is frequently used by organizations. *The Museum is open weekdays 8:30–5:00, and on Saturday and Sunday afternoons. It is closed on Christmas Day.*

The R. W. NORTON ART GALLERY, located in a 40-acre park at 4700 Creswell Ave., was opened in 1961 by the R. W. Norton Art Foundation to commemorate Norton and preserve his magnificent collection of paintings and sculpture of the American West, classical art, and books. Norton had been city auditor, assistant district attorney for Caddo Parish, and developer of the Rodessa oil field, who died while attending the Democratic National Convention in Chicago in 1940. The 12 galleries contain sculptures and paintings by Frederic Remington, paintings by Charles M. Russell, Albert Bierstadt, and Hudson River, Dutch and French artists; tapestries made in 1540, Piranesi etchings, sculpture by Rodin, and other objects of similar high quality. *Tuesday through Saturday, 1–5, Sunday, 2–5, closed Monday. Free.*

GREATER SHREVEPORT MUNICIPAL AIRPORT, south of Interstate 20 and Hollywood Ave., begins the 1970–80 decade with an entirely new terminal plant. The City's Airport Authority authorized construction of a new terminal complex by Southern Builders for $4,919,-000, which with fees, relocations, new concourses and other necessities comes to $7,670,350. Of this amount the Federal Aid to Airports Program allocated a preliminary $538,238. A new fire and rescue building was designed by Walker & Walker.

DOWNTOWN AIRPORT, located on a curve of the Red River, has received a new one-story Administration Building designed by William S. Evans. Budgets for the two airports approved by the City Council for 1970 contain $691,110 in estimated revenues and $445,805 in estimated expenditures. There were 292,370 airplane boardings at the two airports in 1969.

Expansion of the CADDO PARISH COURTHOUSE, built in 1926, was voted in 1969 when the authorities allocated $1,900,000 for this purpose. They instructed the architects to work with tree surgeons to save as many of the adjacent treees as possible. The building rises in three recessed tiers to a height of 125 ft. The identical facades facing Texas and Milam Sts. have large arched entrances and Ionic colonnades of eight columns between the fourth and sixth floors.

CROSS LAKE, within the city limits, is Shreveport's principal water supply and a major recreation area as well. Water skiing is a favorite sport from May 15 to September 30. The Shreveport Yacht Club is located on the lake and has frequent competitive events and an annual regatta. It has about 100 sailboats and 90 powerboats on its roster. The lake covers 8,960 acres and holds 70,580 acre-ft. of water. Two plants treat the water for public use. A pumping station on the Twelve-mile Bayou can lift water into Cross Lake for storage.

FORD PARK, on Cross Lake, provides for the entertainment of

children with a Zoo and a Fairyland. The Zoo has bears, lions, white-tail deer, monkeys and other animals. The Fairyland, built of papier-mache, is filled with Mother Goose characters and similar inventions. Other unusual objects are a fire engine, a military tank, and a locomotive used in construction of the Panama Canal. The Zoo is open March through November, 10:00–6:45. The Cross Lake Patrol operates a Fish Hatchery near Ford Park, producing about 1,000,000 black bass, white perch, catfish, and sunfish. Deer and alligators are also on exhibition at the Hatchery.

CADDO LAKE, 18 miles north of Shreveport, is a popular hunting and fishing area and provides water for industrial purposes. It covers 32,700 acres, of which 12,000 are in Texas. Louisiana has a reciprocal fishing agreement with Texas, which permits a fisherman to cross the line between the states without penalty if he carries a license from only one. A resident of one state may buy a fishing license in the other state without being charged a fee. This affects both Caddo Lake and Lake Toledo, the latter in the huge Toledo Bend Reservoir on the Texan border, which covers 181,600 acres, of which about 100,000 acres are allotted to Louisiana.

LAND'S END, a house begun in the 1830 decade 20 miles south of Shreveport, was originally the center of Land's End Plantation of 10,000 acres. It was built by Henry Marshall, a senator in the Louisiana Legislature and representative in the Confederate Congress, who died in 1864. Seven generations of the Marshall family lived here until it was sold to Col. Henry F. Means, the present occupant. The house has period furniture, books and documents of historic interest, and is open to visitors by appointment.

Spring Ridge, southwest of Shreveport on La 525 is the site of a new Caddo Correctional Institute jail authorized in 1969 to cost $1,241,000.

Winnfield

Highways: US 167 is the main north-south highway that connects Winnfield with Ruston, 49 *m*. It is at a junction with US 84 from Natchez and La 34.

Railroads: Rock Island, Louisiana & Arkansas, Illinois Central.

Information and Accommodations: Winn Parish Enterprise, weekly. Winnfield has 2 hospitals, 2 clinics, 2 nursing homes; 1 hotel, 3 motels; 28 churches, all denominations.

WINNFIELD (118 alt., 7,142 pop. 1970; 7022, 1960), seat of Winn Parish, lies in the red clay hills of north-central Louisiana, a region of longleaf pine forests, dense canebrakes, and fertile creek bottoms. The town is built about the courthouse square, from which stretch wide paved streets lined with stately trees and comfortable homes.

The Winnfield area remained unsettled and almost unvisited by whites until about 1840, when land along the State's various rivers began to become scarce. Winn Parish was carved from a portion of Natchitoches Parish in 1852. Both parish and town were named in honor of Walter O. Winn, prominent Alexandria, Louisiana, lawyer. Winnfield was incorporated in 1855.

After the parish records were destroyed in a series of courthouse fires, Winnfield became a hotbed of lawsuits and a mecca for lawyers. Many of the State's most prominent attorneys have been products of Winnfield. The best known of these was Huey P. Long. As the late Senator Long's birthplace, Winnfield is today a shrine for many thousands of his former followers.

Winnfield is a busy distributing center for a parish that gets its chief income from lumbering, but also produces some livestock, raises cotton, mines salt, and has some oil and gas. Yet 92 percent of its 971 sq. m. is covered with long-leaf pine, and the buzz of the sawmills is heard in many places. Besides six sawmills of major size there are plants making plywood, veneers, glue, creosote products and ties. The parish gets 80 percent of its income from some form of timber. When the State Forest Festival is held here in the fall many adopt lumberman's outfits.

Besides differing from many other Louisiana parishes by its dependence on timber, Winn has one other characteristic: It is predominantly Protestant. The parish also has a Farm Bureau Organization, a Cattleman's organization and a Swine Breeders Assn. The Winn Parish Demonstration Council has 13 clubs. There are 13 4-H clubs. There is an Antique City at the Winn Parish Fairgrounds in Winnfield.

The two most famous sons of Winnfield are the Long brothers, Huey P. Long and Earl K. Long, both of whom became governors of the State and Senators. The site of Huey's birthplace is the rear lawn at 1107 Maple St., where a log cabin stood. He is buried at the Capitol at Baton Rouge, but Earl is buried in Winnfield.

Huey Long was a ready speaker, using numerous jokes and stories, with which he pointed a moral or ridiculed his opponents. He often served as the butt of his jests. Visiting the insane asylum at Jackson, Louisiana, he introduced himself to an inmate as the Governor of the State. In a fit of laughter the unbalanced one confided, "When I first came here I thought I was the President of the United States."

Generous and loyal to his friends, ruthless with his enemies, the Kingfish, as Long was known throughout the nation, gained tremendous power, and became a virtual dictator. At times he relied upon the militia to enforce his policies. Even that last stronghold of the opposition, the Old Regular organization in New Orleans, was finally forced, by verbal and legislative attack, into submission.

In the U. S. Senate Huey Long aroused the admiration, and often the animosity, of most of his colleagues through his aggressive tactics, caustic wit, utter disregard for convention, command of parliamentary procedure, and notorious filibustering to defeat or force a compromise on bills he opposed. He advocated radical measures to redistribute means of production and, as leader of the Share the Wealth movement, gained nation-wide publicity. To popularize his program he wrote *Every Man A King*. *My First Days in the White House* outlined his presidential aspirations and policies. He championed the World War I veterans and the workingman. His personality inspired either wholehearted enmity or support. It was generally understood that it was his intention either to become a presidential candidate in 1936 or wield great influence in the election. Death by assassination in the capitol at Baton Rouge in September, 1935, cut short his career.

Although during Long's governorship Louisiana spent more than ever before, State finances were kept in good condition by many new corporation, severance, and occupational taxes. To his administration Louisiana owes its free school books, fine highway and bridge systems, including the bridge across the Mississippi at New Orleans, expansion of eleemosynary and educational institutions, and many of its public improvements, including the new State Capitol in front of which Long lies buried.

POINTS OF INTEREST

The COURTHOUSE of red brick with Doric columns that served Winnfield for forty years was replaced in 1962 by a modern longitudinal structure.

WINN PARISH LIBRARY has its headquarter in Winnfield and its four branch libraries in Atlanta, Calvin, Dodson, and Sikes, Louisiana. It also operates one bookmobile. The Winnfield Library, 204 West

Main St., occupies a building of brick veneer in contemporary style, completed in 1954, and the branch libraries, which are located on or adjacent to school campuses, occupy similar buildings. With about 37,000 volumes at its disposal the Library System achieved a circulation of 231,645 in 1969, adjudged the largest in the State in relation to the population served. In addition to other activities the library sponsors a Children's Summer Reading Program, for grades 1 through 8, and awards certificates to each child who reads 12 books on his level.

The EARL KEMP LONG MEMORIAL PARK was deeded to the State in 1961. Long was three times governor and had been elected to Congress when he died Sept. 5, 1960, before taking his seat. He was a nephew of Senator Russell Long and brother of Rep. George Long. His 8-ft. statue in the park was unveiled July 4, 1963. There are shelters and fountains in the park.

The O. K. ALLEN HOUSE (*private*), NE. corner Lafayette and Pineville Sts., a modern two-story white frame house, was the home of O. K. Allen, Governor of Louisiana, 1932–36.

The JONES HOUSE (*open*), 510 Jones St., incorporates in its right wing a one-room log house set on large pine blocks which was the first courthouse of Winn Parish and originally stood where the present courthouse now stands. The cabin, now more than a century old, was moved to its present location in the 1860's, when it became the home of Robert Cassidy Jones and his bride. Jones was Clerk of Court in the parish for 28 years.

POINTS OF INTEREST IN ENVIRONS

Logging Camp, 10.2 *m.* (*see Tour 5a*). Winnfield Rock Quarry, 4.6 *m.;* Carey Salt Mine, 5.1 *m.;* Dickerson Ranch, 5.7 *m.;* Saline Lake (Northwest Fish and Game Preserve) 8.7 *m.* (*see Tour 5b*). Cedar Springs, 3.4 *m.;* Catahoula Division of the Kisatchie National Forest, 5.6 *m.* (*see Tour 15a*).

Gum Springs, 8 *m.* west on US 84, 11 tent and trailer; fireplaces, swimming, hunting. Pets on leash. Open all year, 14-day limit, fee. Kisatchie National Forest.

PART III

Tours

Grace B Dunn

Tour 1

(Gulfport, Mississippi)—New Orleans—Houma—New Iberia—Lafayette—Crowley—Lake Charles—(Beaumont, Texas) ; US 90. Mississippi
Line to Texas Line, 322.4 *m.*

Int. 10 runs parallel from Lafayette to Texas. Railroads paralleling route:
L. & N. between Mississippi Line and New Orleans; S. P. between New Orleans
and Texas Line.
All types of accommodations at short intervals.

Section a. *MISSISSIPPI LINE to NEW ORLEANS; 41 m.,*
US 90

Between the Mississippi Line and New Orleans US 90 crosses a vast
marshland. Distant margins of pines and oaks and an oddly-patterned
maze of waters combine in a broad vista.

Midway across the bridge spanning Pearl River, 37.1 miles west of
Gulfport, Mississippi, US 90 crosses the Mississippi line. The ancient
name of this stream was Tallahatchie (Ind., river of pearls). When the
French came to this section in 1699, they were told by the Indians of
a peculiar clamlike shell containing pearls to be found in the river. The
Frenchmen visualized a rich pearl trade with Paris but soon found that
their "pearls" were worthless. In spring strange music issues from the
water near the mouth of the river. According to legend, it is produced
by the ghosts of an orchestra that drowned there. In reality, it is the
"song" of spawning gaspergou (fresh-water drum).

Between Pearl River and West Pearl River the highway crosses the southern end of Honey Island Swamp. While most of this section of the island is treeless salt marsh, to the north, accessible only by boat, lies a swampy jungle (*see Tour 3A*).

In DEER ISLAND, 3.6 *m.*, a tiny village on West Pearl River, is a shrimp-canning plant.

At 8.3 *m.*, about 200 yards east of the Rigolets Bridge, is the junction with US 190. Here is a Tourist Information Office.

The RIGOLETS BRIDGE, 8.7 *m.*, crosses one of two passes connecting Lakes Borgne and Pontchartrain. The fishing here is excellent. Incoming tides bring redfish, tarpon, and sometimes small sharks, making swimming dangerous.There are strong currents at the change of tide. The Rigolets (pronounced Rig-o-lees) was discovered by Iberville in 1699. While the capital of Louisiana was at Biloxi, traders used the pass as a short cut to the Mississippi, by way of Bayou Manchac. As part of the Intracoastal Waterway (*see Tour 11D*), the Rigolets is still an important passageway for light draft boats. The name is derived from *rigole* (Fr., little canal). The Rigolets serves as the northeastern boundary of the city of New Orleans, the limits of which are the same as those of Orleans Parish, although the city proper is nearly 30 miles away.

FORT PIKE STATE MONUMENT, 9.5 *m.* is connected with Fort McComb State Monument by a narrow parkway bordering US 90. A new exhibit of ordnance and military uniforms was opened in the fall, 1970. Notable are dress and battle orders dating from the War of 1812 to the Civil War. There is also a collection of newspapers of the 1860 period.

The first fort constructed at this point was called Petites Coquilles (Fr., little shells), also the original name of the island upon which it was built. The first fortifications were erected in 1793 under Governor Carondelet, but the present structure dates from 1818, having been built by the Americans. The Confederates took possession in 1861 and the Federals reoccupied it in 1862—all without bloodshed. Old gun placements atop massive brick ramparts overlooking the Rigolets Pass, dungeonlike passages, and a semicircular moat lend an Old World feudal atmosphere.

St. Catherine's Island, which the highway traverses for nine miles westward, is noted for its fishing and duck-hunting. To the east is Lake St. Catherine, opening into Lake Borgne (really a part of Mississippi Sound); and on the west is Lake Pontchartrain, 45 miles long and 25 miles wide. It was named in honor of the Comte de Pontchartrain, French Minister of Marine under Louis XIV. The name Borgne (Fr., one-eyed) is possibly due to the fact that the lake has but one outlet. Lake Pontchartrain's waters are just salty enough to prevent its classification as a fresh-water lake; were the lake so classed it would rank close to the Great Lakes as one of the largest in the country. Along the road are many camps built on stilts. Boats and bait can be obtained.

The highway crosses CHEF MENTEUR (Fr., lying chief), 18.5

m., the second of the deep tideguts, or passes, connecting Lakes Pont-chartrain and Borgne. This pass derived its name, according to legend, from a Choctaw chief who was so confirmed a liar that his tribe banished him.

FORT McCOMB STATE MONUMENT 18.7 *m.*, is about 150 yards from the west end of the Chef Menteur bridge. It was first called Fort Chef Menteur, then Fort Woods, and finally Fort McComb. General Andrew Jackson placed a battery at this point in 1815, garrisoning it with free Negroes, and the War Department constructed the brick fort (1820–28) at a cost of about $360,000. The inner portion is a labyrinth of passageways. In the outer walls are placements for cannon and small, square openings for rifles.

The fort was garrisoned by both Confederates and Federals but was abandoned when the barracks buildings were destroyed by fire.

BAYOU SAUVAGE, 19.7 *m.*, formerly extended from Chef Menteur almost into New Orleans proper. A four-lane concrete highway now follows the old trail along the ridge of this bayou, which is now little more than a ditch. Stretching westward are cypress swamps and marshes. To the left are lands upon which extensive sugar plantations once flourished, but at present little of the area is under cultivation. General sinking of the land and consequent salt impregnation is blamed.

At 22.3 *m.* is the junction with US 11 (*see Tour 3A*).

The site of the OLD LAFON SUGAR MILL (L) is at 27.1 *m.* A brick chimney surrounded by dense underbrush is about all that remains to be seen of the vast Lafon Plantation.

The Inner Harbor Navigation Canal (Industrial Canal), 34.4 *m.*, is a deep-water channel connecting Lake Pontchartrain with the Mississippi River in New Orleans. Its construction was begun during World War I with the idea of creating another outlet from New Orleans to the Gulf but the connection was not completed. Instead the Mississippi River-Gulf Outlet was built for use of oceangoing ships. It shortened the distance into New Orleans by 40 miles at a cost of $90,000,000.

NEW ORLEANS, 41 *m. See article on New Orleans.*

Section b.   NEW ORLEANS to NEW IBERIA ; 173 m. US 90

West of NEW ORLEANS, 0 *m.*, US 90 crosses the Mississippi on the Huey P. Long Bridge and traverses a country of somber swamps, oak-wooded lowlands, serpentine bayous, straggling settlements, and occasional modern sugar factories. At Houma the route reaches its southernmost point. West of Morgan City US 90 enters the Teche country.

PROTECTION LEVEE, 4.7 *m.*, the western boundary of New Orleans, is one of a series of interior levees surrounding the city proper that were built to protect it from Mississippi River overflows and backwater from Lake Pontchartrain. Since construction of the Bonnet Carré Spillway (*see Tour 10B*), the Protection Levee is no longer deemed necessary, and the highway now cuts through it into Jefferson Parish.

On the west side of the levee is the junction with a blacktop road.

Left on this road to SOUTHPORT, 0.8 *m.*, which became known as the location of two large casinos Old Southport and Original Southport. Southport was formerly the southern limit of the ancient Village des Chapitolas (Tchoupitoula Village). In this section were the great plantations of the three Chauvin brothers, Canadians who came to New Orleans at its founding. One of these, Nicolas Chauvin de la Frenière (ca. 1720-1769), in resentment against the transfer of the territory from France to Spain, led an uprising against the Spanish in 1768 and was put to death as punishment.

Industrial plants are seen on both sides of the highway; at 5.8 *m.* are the NEW ORLEANS RIDING CLUB, and a GOLF PRACTICE FAIRWAY. Saddle horses can be rented at near-by stables.

CAMP PARAPET POWDER MAGAZINE is seen about 150 yards from the road at 6.5 *m.* The magazine is a remnant of a minor Civil War fortification begun by the Confederates as one of the defenses for New Orleans. From this point a line of earthworks extending to the river was begun, but the Union forces took it over and completed it after the capture of New Orleans in 1862. It was then developed into an extensive fortified camp, called Camp Parapet. The parapet, or breastworks, extended in a zigzag line back across where the railroad and highway now pass, a total distance of nearly two miles. The powder magazine was formerly entirely covered with earth.

ST. AGNES CHURCH, 6.7 *m.*, Roman Catholic, formerly housed Tranchina's Night Club, which closed during the depression.

The plant of the AMERICAN FROG CANNING COMPANY is at 7 *m.* Great white cement frogs blink red eyes at night on each side of the door. The lands of the company extend from the highway to the river levee, and are dotted with willow-bordered and lily-decked ponds wherein giant bullfrogs may breed amid idyllic surroundings.

At 7.5 *m.* is the junction with Central Avenue.

Left on this shell road to MAGNOLIA SCHOOL, 0.5 *m.*, formerly called Whitehall. Built by François Pascalise de Labarre in the 1850's, it is a raised cottage fronted by a wide, columned gallery and set in a grove of magnolias, cedars, and live oaks. During the War between the States Federal troops encamped on the plantation. The Labarres sold the estate and it was later converted into a gambling house. The Jesuits later took it over, using it as a retreat. The bar, now used as a sideboard, was converted into an altar. After 1931 Whitehall served as a boarding school for physically and mentally handicapped children.

US 90 turns left at 8.2 *m.*, at the junction with La 48 (*see Tour 10B*), to cross the HUEY P. LONG BRIDGE. This mighty steel and concrete structure was completed in 1935 at a cost of $13,000,000. The bridge proper, which extends from levee to levee, consists of a steel cantilever accompanied by a series of truss spans and is supported by six open dredged caissons and three pile piers. The deepest caisson rests

170 feet below sea level. The approaches on both sides are supported by steel viaduct towers and plate girders. The bridge is a combination railroad and highway structure; its total length, including railroad approaches, is 4.4 miles. The double railroad tracks are flanked by 18-foot concrete roadways, each with a 2-foot sidewalk. The height of the central pier is equal to that of a 36-story building, measuring 409 feet from the bottom of its foundation to the top of its superstructure. This bridge gives New Orleans a continuous highway to the west, via the Old Spanish Trail (US 90).

At the west end of the bridge, 10.2 *m.*, is the junction with La 18 (*see Tour 11a*), which follows the course of the river. Old houses, wells, and the remains of sugar houses are visible at intervals.

At 10.3 *m.* is the junction with a shell road extending back under the bridge approach to the river. The river at this point covers the site of FORT BANKS, a minor defense unit erected by the Federals in 1862, as a companion fort to Camp Parapet.

AVONDALE, 12.8 *m.* (4 alt.), occupies the site of the former plantation of Senator George Augustus Waggaman (1790–1843). Storage tanks and offices of the Southern Export Oil Co. and Southern Pacific Railroad yards are here.

Scattered settlements sprawl along the road. To the right the road is paralleled by the Mississippi levee. Cattle wander across the highway; motorists are warned to be careful.

WAGGAMAN, 13.8 *m.* (10 alt.), extends along part of the old Avondale Plantation.

A house, in which the *briqueté entre poteaux* type of construction is visible, is (L) at 16.6 *m.* Ruins of a sugar mill stand in the rear.

US 90 crosses the boundary line, 19.3 *m.*, between Jefferson and St. Charles Parishes. The first settlements in the latter parish were established in 1719, when a group of Germans from Alsace-Lorraine settled along the banks of the Mississippi River under the leadership of D'Arensbourg. In 1766 their numbers were greatly augmented by the arrival of 216 Acadians from Nova Scotia. The two groups soon intermingled, but the Gallic influence in religion, culture, and architecture dominated, and the Germans eventually were completely absorbed, even their names becoming Gallicized (*see Tour 10B*).

AMA, 20.9 *m.* (7 alt.), is a small village whose entire adult population is engaged in the cultivation of sugar cane.

ELLINGTON MANOR (*private*), 25.1 *m.*, a large white plantation home, was designed by the younger Gallier, noted New Orleans architect. The house has a high basement of plastered brick. The upper floor is of wood; six square wooden columns support a hipped roof, which is bordered by an elaborate cornice. Two curving stairways on the exterior mount to the gallery. The sole vestige of the gardens is a large camphor tree. Ellington Manor is on a 7,500-acre plantation formerly planted in sugar cane, but now a citrus grove. Thousands of the young orange trees are visible from the highway. Their planting was an experimental undertaking which may later greatly influence the horticultural and economic future of the State; the seedlings are of the Goudeau Sweet variety, a species suited to this region.

LULING, 25.4 m. (10 alt., 3,255 pop. 1970; 2,122, 1960), was named for a German family prominent in the community. The presence of a hotel, a bank, and several small industrial enterprises give the town a modern air which contrasts strongly with that of other settlements near by. Luling is on La 18, 3 m. from the present route of US 190.

BOUTTE, 28.2 m. (7 alt.), a small farming community, is built on reclaimed swampland.

PARADIS (Fr., paradise), 31.4 m. (6 alt.), is so-called because the surrounding country abounding in game of several kinds was thought a "sportsman's paradise."

At 32 m. is the junction with graveled La 306.

Left here 6.4 m., through a fertile truck-farming section, to (R) a drainage pumping plant, locally called SUNSET PUMP, which has been responsible for the reclamation of 108,000 acres of marshland lying between Luling and Des Allemands. At this point the road turns L. along the bank of Bayou Gauche (Fr., left), which runs through a popular fishing, crabbing, and duck-hunting area.

The oak-covered shell hillocks visible along the highway here are INDIAN MOUNDS from which broken bits of pottery and bone fragments have been excavated.

A large pool, 36.3 m., is framed by drooping branches of willows. In the spring its banks are crowded with white and colored crayfishers of both sexes and all ages. Their equipment consists of large-meshed, baglike nets baited with bits of raw meat.

DES ALLEMANDS, 36.5 m. (4 alt., 2,318 pop. 1970), whose post office name is Allemands (Fr., Germans), is on the banks of a bayou which bears the same name, and which is the source of supply for the town's one industry—the packing of sea food.

In the seafood processing plants crabs are thrown alive into huge rectangular cauldrons of boiling water. After a few minutes they are taken into a cleaning room, where girls and women deftly pick the meat from the shells, and pack it into cans which are in turn packed into iced boxes for shipment. The speed and precision of the workers in every process is remarkable. The fish-packing department is operated with similar efficiency; high catfish are skinned and dressed by hand in two or three movements.

In Des Allemands boats and supplies are available for fishing and hunting trips on Bayou Des Allemands and Lake Salvador. The SALVA-DOR WILDLIFE MANAGEMENT AREA on the northwest shore of Lake Salvador in St. Charles Parish comprises 28,469 acres and was opened in October, 1968, by the Louisiana Wild Life & Fisheries Commission. This is a fresh-water marsh area with ponds and large stands of cypress timber. A large oil field has been developed in the center of the area and its canals can be utilized for sport fishing and hunting. There are three means of access: through Bayou Segnette from Westwego into

Lake Cataouatche; through the Seller Canal to Bayou Verret into Lake Cataouatche, and through Bayou Des Allemands.

US 90 crosses Bayou Des Allemands to enter a low, flat country of bayous and cypress swamps. At every point water disputes possession with land. From spring to early autumn water hyacinths form a lavender blanket in the canals, the bayous, and around the margins of lakes. Gray Spanish moss, swinging from live oak and cypress trees, provides a somber-toned frame for the lively greens and lavenders. The descendants of the Acadians still form the predominant racial element.

Between Des Allemands and Houma, US 90 forms an approximate dividing line between an agricultural section lying to the north, where sugar cane is the chief product, and that to the south, where fishing, trapping, and oil field development are the main industries.

A sugar refinery is located at 46.3 m. (*See Tour 10B for sugar-refining process.*)

RACELAND, 46.9 m. (6 alt., 4,880 pop. 1970; 3,666, 1960), is a packing and shipping center on Bayou Lafourche, which has been called "the longest street in America" because an almost continuous community stretches for about 85 miles along its banks, from Donaldsonville to Golden Meadow, near the Gulf. The section south of Raceland's one business street lies along the west bank of the bayou, connected by a bridge with a small residential district, hidden behind the eastern bank of the levee.

Before reaching Bayou Lafourche US 90 meets La 308 (n-s). After crossing the Bayou it joins La 1 briefly to Raceland.

Between Raceland and Houma US 90 crosses several small bayous, their banks often overgrown with varicolored species of native iris.

SAVOIE'S BAYOU BLEU STORE, 55.2 m., handles the basketwork of a small group of Houma (or Ouma) Indians that live nearby. These Indians are of purer racial strain than the Houma who live farther south. Their baskets are made of natural-colored strips of cypress saplings.

HOUMA (Ind., red), 59.4 m. (14 alt., 30,922 pop. 1970), was named for a tribe of Houma Indians which originally inhabited the area. Before 1803, Joseph Hache, a Nova Scotia Acadian, took possession of a tract of land on Bayou Terrebonne which later formed the nucleus of the present town. In 1825 the country was still so wild that the police jury offered $5 a head for every "tiger" (possibly ocelot or jaguar) killed. Houma was made the seat of Terrebonne (Fr., good land) Parish in 1832. *See Houma.*

At Houma are junctions with La 24, La 56 and La 57.

Left from Houma La 57 parallels the Houma Navigation Canal southward. On the bayou live most of the Houma Indians. The Houma (*see First Americans*), a tribe of the Muskhogean family, had the crayfish for their emblem. Iberville considered this tribe the bravest of the Louisiana Indians. This section was their last stronghold. They have mixed with whites, Negroes, and other Indians to the extent that they are now denied reservation rights. They live in small houses, palmetto huts, or crude houseboats. The men fish and trap for a living, as did their ancestors; when they can, the women and children work in shrimp-packing plants. The BOUDREAUX SHRIMP AND OYSTER FACTORY, 15.3 *m.*, gives employment to many of these people.

At DULAC, 17.1 *m.*, boats can be rented for fishing in Lake Boudreaux, 2 miles east.

CLANTON CHAPEL, 18 *m.*, is a Methodist mission established in 1936; religious services are conducted in French and English. To the left of the church is the mission Indian school. In the Methodist mission school basketry and other handicrafts are included in the curriculum.

South of Clanton Chapel two roads lead through a maze of swamp and open-water country.

At 60.9 *m.* is the junction with Bayou du Large Road (La 247).

Left on this road 0.6 *m.* to the INTRACOASTAL WATERWAY.

South of CROZIER, 4.2 *m.*, La 315 parallels Bayou du Large (R). A few miles farther south the bayou bank is an almost continuous truck-farm strip.

THERIOT is a hamlet at 9.5 *m.*

The highway crosses FALGOUT CANAL, 13.6 *m.*, where boats can be rented for fishing in Lake DeCade, 3.4 miles west of Theriot by canal, Lake Theriot, 6.7 miles northwest of the canal, and Lake Mechant, approximately 10 miles down Bayou du Large.

At 19 *m.* is ST. ANDREW'S MISSION (Episcopal), where Christmas is celebrated during Lent. December 25 is the height of the trapping season, which each year finds the inhabitants of this section scattered over the vast marshes in lonely houseboats and cabins, hard at work trapping muskrat, mink, and other fur-bearing animals, and preparing the pelts for market. The trappers and their families (most of them of English-Scotch descent, though others have intermarried with the French) do not return to their bayou-settlement homes until the season is over, usually the middle of February. There follows perhaps a week of pelt selling and readjustment before their "Christmas" is observed. At community gatherings hymns are sung and prayers said, and gifts are distributed among the children. Instead of a Christmas tree, the belated celebrants content themselves with live oak boughs or saplings, covered with Spanish moss, a native holly called yaupon, and winterberries, supplemented with popcorn strings and the tinsel of manufactured decorations. In some communities school is recessed during the two-and-one-half month trapping season, and continues through most of the summer. Many families, however, strike for the coast in summer to trawl for shrimp; so that for the most part schooling receives secondary consideration, and schools are not very well attended at any time of the year.

West of Houma US 90 follows the course of Bayou Black.

GIBSON, 81.9 *m.* (11 alt.), is on the edge of the Atchafalaya Swamp. In near-by woods are deer, squirrels, rabbits, and an occasional bear. Near the center of Gibson, Bayou Chene and Bayou Black meet, forming a tiny island connected with the "mainland" by rustic bridges over a narrow canal. The towered CHAPEL on the island was built by a priest with a liking for the architecture of Holland.

AMELIA, 88 *m.* (2,292 pop. 1970), is the first village in St. Mary Parish after Assumption. Settled 1800, it was occupied by the Federals during the Civil War. About 3 *m.* west of the parish line is RAMOS, a raised cottage on Bayou Ramos, owned 1856 by H. J. Sanders and used as a hospital during the war. In 1868 it was acquired by Augustin Seger, railroad president.

BAYOU BŒUF, 88.9 *m.*, is a wide tributary of the Atchafalaya; at

90.8 *m.* it approaches the highway to parallel it for about 6 miles. Near Morgan City water hyacinths grow in profusion. Charles Tenney Jackson laid the scene of his short story, *The Man Who Cursed the Lilies* (O. Henry Collection for 1921), at Pointe au Fer, on the Gulf Coast below Morgan City.

MORGAN CITY, 96.5 *m.* (6 alt., 16,586 pop. 1970; 13,540, 1960, inc. 22.5%), is an Intracoastal Waterway port on Berwick Bay, a widening of the Atchafalaya River (Ind., long river), which is here a half-mile wide and very deep. Almost surrounding Morgan City is a network of bayous, rivers, and lakes, interspersed with fields of sugar cane and forests of cypress, tupelo, gum, and water oak. Here are excellent opportunities for game fishing and duck hunting. Morgan City and Berwick across the Bay, are the center of a large offshore and inland oil activity. About a dozen major oil companies operate from this area. Much business depends on needs of the oil industry. Also important is the expanding shrimp industry. By the discovery of new varieties and methods of taking them the shrimp industry has prospered and the waters produce more than 13,000,000 pounds of shrimp annually.

Pioneers of offshore oil drilling are commemorated by an Eternal Flame on a simulated oil derrick. A full-sized trawler, Spirit of Morgan City, celebrates the jumbo shrimp industry.

Morgan City came into being about 1850 as the western terminus of the New Orleans, Opelousas & Great Western Railroad. Here westbound passengers and freight were transferred to steamboats, to continue to Galveston and other Texas ports. The town was incorporated in 1860 as Brashear City, named for the Brashear family, upon whose plantation it was laid out. It was later renamed in honor of Charles Morgan, president of the railroad.

Because of its strategic location, Morgan City played an important part in the War between the States. The Confederates built earthwork forts—Fort Starr to the south, Buchanan to the north and Brashear across the bay—alternately held by Confederates and Federals. Gunboats were a frequent sight in the bay and fierce fighting occurred on several occasions. The forts have long since been leveled by time, and their sites are occupied by modern buildings.

In 1870 a small colony of Russian Jewish refugees was established at Morgan City. Records of 1891 speak of the town's population as being composed "mostly of foreigners and Negroes"—"foreigners" connoting almost any people other than French.

With the route of the Intracoastal Waterway passing through its southern limits, Morgan City is important as an inland port and commercial fishing center. Oysters are abundant in the lower Atchafalaya; the shells go to a local crushing plant to be used later as poultry feed and fertilizer, and in the manufacture of lime. Quantities of buffalo and catfish are packed and shipped inland to appear on restaurant tables as "trout." Morgan City is also headquarters for a flourishing fur trade whose sources of supply are the marshes to the south and southeast, where muskrat, otter, mink, and opossum are trapped in large numbers.

The town has also several small woodworking plants and furniture factories.

Boats can be rented at Morgan City at various rates for excursions to the south:

Southwest from Morgan City, by way of the Atchafalaya River and Atchafalaya Bay, to BELLE ISLE, 25 m. (75 alt.), a salt dome. The wild, primitive scenery of the island and that of Wax Bayou provided background for a motion-picture version of *Tarzan of the Apes.*

Southeast from Morgan City, in the Gulf of Mexico, to SHIP SHOAL LIGHT, approximately 55 m., where speckled trout, redfish, sheepshead, pompano, Spanish mackerel, butterfish, lemon fish, and many other salt-water varieties are plentiful. Around LAST ISLAND (or ISLE DERNIÈRE) (*see Tour 1C*), approximately 12 miles northeast of Ship Shoal Light, the fishing is equally good; Wine Island Pass, at the eastern tip of the island, is celebrated for its tarpon.

At Morgan City US 90 crosses Berwick Bay on the LONG-ALLEN BRIDGE, a 608-foot all-steel span with one of its piers sealed at a depth of 176½ feet below low water.

BERWICK, 97.3 m. (6 alt., 4,165 pop. 1970), across the bay from Morgan City, is the home port of a fishing fleet. Berwick has a boat-building plant and shrimp and oyster factories. It is a center of offshore oil exploration.

West of Berwick US 90 follows Bayou Teche, possibly a corruption of Indian name for snake. According to the Chitimacha, a snake of fabulous proportions once inhabited the region, and was slain by the tribe's warriors, its death writhings cutting out the present bed of the bayou. The bayou is the setting of Longfellow's *Evangeline.* The Gulf lies only a short distance to the south, and the Atchafalaya Basin, with its intricate system of lakes, bayous, and swamps, even closer on the north. The highway is bordered by canefields, live oaks, plantation homes, and cabins. La 182 loops from Berwick to Patterson and from Patterson to Calumet, another village on US 90.

As part of the Attakapas Settlement (*see St. Martinville*) this section was thinly populated prior to the Spanish occupancy of Louisiana (1769), just before and after which occurred migrations of French, Spanish, Acadians, and English. Along lower Bayou Teche Acadians predominate.

For 50 miles, Bayou Teche winds to the right of the highway, sometimes clearly in view, sometimes out of sight, or distinguishable only by its fringe of trees. Towns and villages are directly on the bayou, as are most of the plantation homes.

Navigable for more than 100 miles, Bayou Teche in early days formed the chief means of transportation through this section. On its surface pirogues, skiffs, and flatboats plied constantly, the flatboats usually drawn by ropes tied to horses, or by slaves who trudged along the towpath. Later regular steamboat service was maintained along all the stream's navigable reaches.

The three- to five-mile width of arable land on each side of the bayou constitutes one of the most fertile sections of Louisiana's Sugar

Bowl. Before the War between the States this was the abode of wealthy planters. Each plantation mansion was surrounded by extensive canefields and had its own sugar mill.

Before reaching Patterson turn right on La 182 to Idlewild, built 1850–54 of handhewn cypress by George Haydel. I. D. Seyburn bought it about 1875 and his grandson, E. H. Seyburn restored it 1964.

PATTERSON, 104.8 m. (9 alt., 4,409 pop. 1970; 2,963, 1960; inc. 50%), first called Pattersonville, was named for its first settler, Captain Patterson, who acquired plantations here toward the close of the eighteenth century. For many years Patterson was an important lumber center, the home of the large Williams Cypress Mill, but since the closing of the mill the town has decreased in size. It consists principally of a main street, which stretches for more than a mile along Bayou Teche.

WEDELL-WILLIAM AIRPORT, 109 m., was established in 1929 by by Harry P. Williams and James R. (Jimmy) Wedell, to handle mail and passenger planes and to design and manufacture airplanes. Mrs. Williams was before her marriage the motion-picture star, Marguerite Clark, and her home in Patterson was the scene of many brillant social functions. Shortly after Wedell, flying a Wedell-Williams machine, had broken the world's speed record for landplanes (1933), he crashed to his death while engaged in routine work. There followed in rapid succession a series of tragic accidents in which all four of the other company pilots were killed; in 1936 Mr. Williams himself met the same fate. Mrs. Williams gave the airport to the State as a memorial to her husband. Near the airport is the site of the Civil War battle of Bisland in 1863 between forces of Gen. Nathaniel P. Banks and Lt. Gen. Richard Taylor.

CALUMET, 5.6 m. west of Patterson, was built in 1870 by Daniel Thompson of Chicago and bought for a hunting lodge by Harry Williams in the 1930s. It was restored by Clarence Baughman in 1950. It has a gallery 86 ft. long across the front.

For about seven months of the year the fields to the left of the highway are green with cane in various stages of growth; in late summer the stalks reach their full height of from six to 12 feet. The light green mass of the canefields is composed of long, spearlike leaves which curl backward from central stalks. During the harvesting season (October and November), groups of Negro men and women move along the rows and with deft and rhythmic strokes of their broad cane knives cut the stalks close to the ground, strip their leaves, chop off their tops and lay them in orderly fashion in the furrows. In the late afternoon trucks and old-fashioned carts, piled high with cane and boisterous Negroes, move along the roads.

An old Negro village marks the SITE OF FAIRFAX, 113.1 m., which stood for more than 100 years before it was demolished. This was the birthplace of the late Elizabeth Bisland Wetmore (1861–1929), the novelist, and during the War between the States it was the home of her father, Thomas Bisland, a surgeon in the Confederate Army. The Bisland family fled to Natchez at the outbreak of the war. In the early months of 1863 several skirmishes were waged at their house. Mrs. Wetmore pictured the return of her family to its battle-scarred home in *A Candle of Understanding* (1902).

SHADYSIDE (*open*), 113.8 *m.*, is a three-story wooden structure with a red brick basement. There are 16 Ionic columns across the first-floor gallery and some interesting interior woodwork, including an elaborately handcarved stairway. The hipped roof, decorated with dormers, gables, and turrets, is typical of the 1890's.

CENTERVILLE, 117.4 *m.* (12 alt.) was a sugar shipping point during the years of steamboating. Now it has carbon black, gas and oil refining plants. Among its ante bellum houses are an 1855 structure called KENNEDY HOTEL 1870–1901, now owned by Mrs. Grace Barras Horton; VETTER HOUSE, owned by C. J. Peltier; FRANCES, built by the DeMarets in 1820, restored by Mrs. Edward Sutter, a DeMaret descendent. About 8 *m.* from Centerville is the SHAKESPEAR ALLEN HOUSE (c. 1853), owned by Mrs. Mae T. Burguieres. The ALICE C PLANTATION, 1 *m.* away, accounts for a house built by Jotham Bedell in the 1850's, now the plantation office, and SUSIE, built by Royal Harris, 1852.

Left from Centerville on graveled La 317, which at 1.7 *m.* reaches the bank of Bayou Salé (Fr., salty), which is follows southwestward toward the Gulf through a section known at the Bayou Salé Lands, one of the three arable ridges of St. Mary Parish. Willow trees, Cherokee roses, honeysuckle, and tall grasses grow along the curving road, with canefields lying on each side.

The Intercoastal Waterway, 7.1 *m.*, is crossed by a free cable ferry (*24-hour call service*).

At 13.8 *m.* is the junction with a narrow shell road; R. here 0.5 *m.* to NINI FISHING CAMP, where skiffs can be hired for speckled- and silver-trout fishing in East Côte Blanche Bay. La 317 ends at Salt Point.

In GARDEN CITY, 119.7 *m.* (10 alt.), is the MAY BROTHERS HARDWOOD AND RED CYPRESS MILL.

DIXIE (*private*), 120.9 *m.*, constructed inside and out of cypress, was built in 1850 by R. A. Wilkins. It is a two-story frame house painted white with green shutters, with a hipped roof and four square columns supporting a pedimented portico. Gen. Geo. E. Pickett, C.S.A. was married here. Murphy J. Foster (1849–1921), who as governor of the State fought the Louisiana Lottery and afterward served as U. S. Senator, bought the place in 1886, and it is now in the possession of his descendants.

ARLINGTON, or Old Baker Place (*private*), 122.1 *m.*, was built in the 1850's by Euphrazie Carlin, a wealthy mulatto. Since 1965 it has been owned by Carl Bauer. The pedimented portico has four fluted, wooden Corinthian columns. Wrought-iron balustrades decorate upper and lower balconies.

FRANKLIN, 122.5 *m.* (13 alt., 9,325 pop. 1970), was founded in 1800 by Guinea Lewis, a former Pennsylvanian who named the settlement in honor of Benjamin Franklin. The majority of first settlers were from the Atlantic seaboard, chiefly of English descent. There were also some French and Spanish families, among them Louis le Pelletier de la Houssaye, a descendant of Claude de la Houssaye, Prime Minister of France under Louis XV. Madame Sidonie de la Houssaye—the former's wife—gained fame as a writer on Louisiana subjects.

When Louisiana became a State (1812) Franklin was made the seat of the newly created St. Mary Parish. By 1830 the town had attained some importance as a trading and shipping point.

Probably because of the large number of settlers from the North, the majority of the residents of Franklin and of St. Mary Parish as a whole opposed secession from the Union and capitulated to Federal forces almost at the outset of the War between the States. Although the town thus escaped the ravages of conflict, Federal gunboats constantly patrolled the Teche, and from 1862 until the cessation of hostilities, all sugar cane raised in the parish was commandeered by the Federals.

The Battle of Irish Bend took place in 1863 on the Bayou Teche. Opposite the site stands OAKBLUFF, built by Edmond Rose.

Franklin's major disturbance connected with the war occurred during Reconstruction, after Colonel H. H. Pope, a former Federal officer, was elected sheriff, largely by newly enfranchised Negroes. Resentment by the armed opposition culminated in the murder of Colonel Pope and the wounding of others. Indiana, Colonel Pope's native State, offered a reward of $25,000 for the conviction of the killers, without result.

Notable houses in Franklin are the PORTER ALLEN HOUSE, 301 Main St., built in 1850 by the first mayor of Franklin, and SHADOW-LAWN, 906 Main St., built by Simeon Smith, who died in 1853. Both houses are preserved by descendants.

The FRANKLIN COURTHOUSE, Willow and Main Sts., is a brick structure topped by a clock tower with Corinthian columned porticoes on the front and both sides. It was erected in 1907, the third courthouse to occupy the site. On the front lawn to the left is the DONELSON CAFFERY STATUE, a life-sized representation of the former U. S. Senator. Senator Caffery (1835–1906) was the best type of Southern statesman, independent in his views and honest in public service to the extent that, himself a sugar planter, he could oppose the sugar bounty which would have enriched him. Senator Caffery's grandfather, the first Donelson Caffery, who was a relative of Mrs. Andrew Jackson, migrated from Kentucky in 1811 and became a planter in this section. He was once caught in a storm while on a fishing trip in Vermilion Bay and rescued by Jean Lafitte, the pirate, who sent him home with provisions and a barrel of rum. Opposite the Caffery Monument is the CONFEDERATE MEMORIAL. The H. S. PALFREY HOUSE (*private*), 200 Main St., was built in 1851 by Governor Joshua Baker and is now owned by David H. Stiel, Jr. It is a two-story frame house with four tall fluted columns supporting a pedimented portico. The GATES HOUSE, 205 Main St., long owned by the Matthew Bell family, was built by Alfred Gates in the 1850's and acquired in 1950 by Mrs. R. E. Brumby, a descendant.

Eight slender Corinthian columns uphold the hipped roof, with chimneys flanking a wide belvedere.

At 123.2 *m.* is the junction with the Irish Bend Road (La 87).

Right on this road, so named because of the wealthy Irish-Americans who established plantations along the great horseshoe bend of Bayou Teche in the nineteenth century.

The GREVEMBERG HOUSE, 0.3 *m.,* was built by Gabriel Grevemberg in 1853. It is a white two-story frame building, with four slender Corinthian columns and an upper balcony edged with a balustrade of delicate wooden spindles. A diamond-shaped window with green shutters is set in the center of the gabled front. It was bought in 1849 by the Town of Franklin.

The SITE OF HAIFLEIGH (or Sterling) PLANTATION HOUSE is at 0.4 *m.,* far back from the road and reached by a narrow lane. The home was built in 1804 by William Haifleigh, a wealthy planter whose failure to be reelected sheriff of St. Mary Parish in 1868 brought on carpetbag riots in Franklin. In 1883 the mansion passed into the possession of Senator Donelson Caffery. It burned in 1938.

OAKLAWN MANOR, 5.7 *m.* is open for a fee and a folder is available. The first Oaklawn was built in 1837–40 by Alexander Porter (1785–1844), noted Louisiana lawmaker and jurist. Henry Clay, a close friend, was often among Porter's guests. Following the War between the States the mansion passed into the hands of Colonel Robert E. Rivers, last owner of the famous St. Louis Hotel in New Orleans.

Following Rivers' tenure the mansion fell into disrepair and was finally acquired by the late Captain Clyde Barbour. While Barbour was engaged in restoring the building in 1926, it was all but destroyed by fire. The mansion was almost immediately rebuilt, however, from old photographs and descriptions.

The new Oaklawn is of brick and stone. Rising in an unbroken line across the front elevation are six large Doric columns. Wrought iron decorates both the long inner balcony of the second floor and a smaller one fronting the gabled attic windows.

Captain Barbour was a collector of antiques, and the marble-floored halls and rooms of the mansion contain many interesting items. In the Henry Clay Room is the bed in which Clay slept and in the adjoining room is a bathtub cut from a single block of marble, which he used. Some of the chandeliers and the marble flooring in the central hall came from the old St. Louis Hotel in New Orleans. In 1964 George Thomson, the present owner, refurbished it.

A driveway extending a mile and a half through a magnificent oak grove is lighted at night by electricity. Among the outbuildings remaining from early days are a small brick dairy house equipped with marble slabs and basins, and the old plantation commissary.

BALDWIN, 127.5 *m.* (15 alt., 1,117 pop. 1970; 1,548, 1960), is the sportsmen's point of departure for trips into the Côte Blanche and Vermilion Bay country. Here is the junction with La 83 (*see Tour 1E*).

Left from Baldwin on La 83, graveled, into a fertile section of St. Mary Parish called Bayou Cypremort Lands extending on both sides of Bayou Cypremort (Fr. dead cypress), so named because of cypresses killed by salt water. Near Baldwin is DARBY, built in 1813 and named for Francois St. Marc Darby, 1856 owner. On La 83, 4 m. s. of Baldwin is VACHERIE, built 1815, restored 1930 by Virgil Browne.

At LOUISA, 16 *m.,* just short of the Intracoastal Waterway La 83 turns right into Iberia Parish. Here La 319 continues south to a bathing and fishing area on the Gulf.

WEEKS ISLAND, 22.8 *m.* (150 alt.), one of Louisiana's "Five Islands," or coastal salt domes, is the site of the State's largest salt mine. The island is about two miles in diameter, nearly round, and surrounded by marsh and prairie, though separated from Vermilion Bay on the west by only 100 yards or so of sea marsh. It was formerly known as Grande Côte (Fr., large hill or crest), but later renamed for the Weeks family, of New Iberia, which owned the island and had large sugar plantations there before the War between the States. The island's surface is a series of low hills and shallow valleys, some still covered with heavy growth of timber, others under cultivation and dotted with fresh-water lakes.

WEEKS ISLAND SALT MINE, 23.2 m., is located on the western edge of the island. The shaft is more than 685 feet deep, with great depths of salt, nearly 100 per cent pure, lying below. (*For description of another salt mine, similar to this one, see Tour 2B*).

Boats and guides can be obtained at Weeks Island for hunting and fishing. There is excellent salt-water fishing in Vermilion Bay and fresh-water fishing in many of the surrounding bayous. In the late fall and early winter there is good waterfowl hunting in the marshes, and bear and deer hunting in the swamps to the east.

CHARENTON, 4 m. north of Baldwin on LA 87, and the M. P. Ry., settled as Indian Bend, is near the reservation of the Chitimacha Indians.

Across the bayou, visible from the highway at 131.9 m., is the JEAN-ERETTE OIL FIELD, which at night is spectacular because of high-flaring beacons of burning exhaust gases.

ALBANIA, 135.5 m., is a plantation bequeathed to the city of New Orleans by Isaac Delgado about 1910 for the maintenance of the Delgado Trades School and the Delgado Museums. The plantation embraces 1,100 acres planted with sugar cane and has its private refinery. The plantation house, set in a grove of oaks, was built in 1842 by Charles Grevemberg, who came to Louisiana as a French Royalist refugee, and sold in 1957 to James H. Bridges. The house is a large white frame building with six square wooden columns across the front and three dormer windows along its gabled roof. The unsupported spiral staircase in the central hallway has often been copied by architects.

JEANERETTE, 136.8 m. (21 alt., 6,322 pop. 1970; 5,568, 1960), is a typical Louisiana-French town. The business area has been progressively altered in recent years. A new CITY HALL, three times larger than its predecessor, was built and the old city hall became a police station and jail. Banking facilities have been greatly extended; a new bank, SUGARLAND STATE BANK, built its office on the site of the Dumas Moresi house. The First National Bank remodelled its headquarters and opened a new branch; the Peoples National Bank of New Iberia, and the Iberia Savings & Loan Assn., also opened new buildings. The FIRST BAPTIST CHURCH erected a new structure and the city built a new fire station.

The prevalence of black in the costumes of the older women is due both to the French opinion that the color is "chic" and to old mourning customs, still rigidly observed. Black is donned for departed grand-parents, aunts, and uncles, as well as for closer relatives; some women are rarely "out of mourning." These mourning customs are districtwide, and are not confined to Jeanerette.

English is generally spoken, but it is often an English with a definite

French accent and many colloquialisms. Common practices are the repetition of words, the reflex use of pronouns, and the addition of "yes" or "no" to a statement to give extra emphasis. "Plenty, plenty people goin' be there, yes. I'm goin' early, me!" Such colloquialisms may be heard in any town or community in this section.

Jeanerette is chiefly a market town; its principal products are sugar, oil, pecans, and pepper.

The MORESI HOUSE, 608 E. Main St., built 1870, is a two-storied house with Ionic columns and elaborate cast-iron balcony railings imported from France.

At 138.1 *m.* is the junction with the Old Jeanerette Road.

Right on this road 0.1 *m.,* crossing Bayou Teche, to BAYSIDE (*private*), surrounded by a fine grove of oaks. It is a two-story building of whitewashed brick, with six large plastered-brick, Doric columns and decorative wooden balustrades. Bayside was built in 1850 by Francis D. Richardson, classmate and friend of Edgar Allan Poe. Richardson served in the Louisiana legislature prior to the War between the States. He provided Northern soldiers with what they called "one of their best laughs" when he piled his pontoon bridge high with hay, set it afire and let it drift down the bayou in the hope that it would ignite the advancing Federal gunboats. But the Yankees merely fended the burning bridge away from their vessels with long poles, until the bridge itself had been consumed by the flames. Bayside has had many owners since that time; for years it belonged to the Sanders family, and it is still generally referred to as "the old Sanders place."

At the COMMERCIAL PECAN ORCHARD, just beyond Bayside, large quantities of paper shell pecans, one of Louisiana's chief orchard crops are raised.

About one-half mile from Bayside on this road is the FUSELIER HOUSE (private), built 1800, which was moved to its present location on Alice Plantation on a barge down the Bayou Teche.

Between Jeanerette and New Iberia the arable land along the west side of the bayou is known as Prairie au Large (Fr., wide prairie).

NEW IBERIA, 147.8 *m.* (19 alt., 30,147 pop. 1970), *see New Iberia.*

New Iberia is at the junction with La 13 and La 86.

Section c.   NEW IBERIA to TEXAS LINE; 133.6 m., US 90

West of NEW IBERIA, 0 *m.*, the route emerges from the Sugar Bowl and cuts across the southern portion of the Rice Belt. At Lafayette wide stretches of prairie lands begin, through which US 90 continues to the Texas Line. The only breaks are at points where the highway crosses the wooded basin of a bayou or larger stream, or runs through the edge of sparse pine woods. Rice fields blanket the prairie belt in light green during the growing season, in dun or tawny tints at other times of the year.

Visible in the distance at 4.2 *m.* is SPANISH LAKE, a circular body of water about five miles in diameter that has no outlet. The shore near the road is a popular spot for picnics. Snipe, ducks, and other wildfowl are hunted here.

The highway crosses the boundary of Lafayette Parish at 11 *m.* and traverses a section called Côte Gelée (Fr., frozen hills) because of the scarcity of timber needed for fuel in the days of the earlier settlers. Undulating prairies, sometimes slightly hilly, extend along both sides of the highway to within a few miles of the city of Lafayette.

Lafayette Parish, formed in 1823, originally included Vermilion Parish and was named for the Marquis de Lafayette, whose proposed visit to the United States was then stirring enthusiasm among Louisiana-French people. The first known white man to settle in the section was Andrew Martin (about 1770), an Acadian exile. There followed an extensive immigration of Martin's compatriots, and the pioneer population was almost wholly made up of them.

The Acadians transported almost intact to Louisiana the pastoral life they had led in Nova Scotia. For a time cattle raising was the chief occupation, the small patches of corn, cane, cotton, and sweet potatoes serving merely for household needs. The entire section soon became a vast expanse of crisp green turf, with herds of cattle grazing everywhere and low-roofed cabins of the settlers scattered about on the higher portions of the prairie.

The Acadian was gentle, honest, and industrious, but as a rule ambitious only for the opportunity to live his own quiet life with complete religious freedom. Expertness in riding his small ponies, dexterity in casting the lariat, and skill in playing the fiddle were his proudest achievements; his pleasures were the dance, the shooting matches, cock fights, pony races, and gossip—over a glass of wine at the roadside store, or at home drinking black coffee with a chance guest. These pioneers were not wanting in courage, and there was among them an occasional bold, adventurous spirit such as Léon Latiolais. Latiolais was a hero at the Battle of New Orleans. Entrusted with an important message from General Jackson to an officer stationed in a remote and almost inaccessible swamp, he successfully carried through his mission.

The Acadian women were excellent homemakers, ever busy at the loom. They wove the rugs, bedspreads, curtains, and linen which furnished their small but pleasant homes, and most of the household clothing was fashioned from their *cotonnade,* known both for the beauty of its weave and its durability. Even today spinning and weaving (*see Tour 2*) are continued in certain Acadian homes.

In the rural sections French or broken English is spoken, and the natives remain loyal to their traditions—the keynote of which is hospitality. The stranger is sure to be offered *café noir* (black coffee). In the true Acadian home the coffeepot never goes dry or becomes cold by day. Because of the flair of the Acadian for hospitality, many of his superstitions are connected with "company coming" signs. When a rooster crows before the home, the housewife anxiously watches the direction in which his head points, for from that direction a guest will come; a cat will also give this pertinent information by the line of its wagging tail.

In many of the gardens medicinal herbs and plants are raised, for the comparative isolation of these people from physicians has made them excel at brewing *tisanes,* or teas, to treat almost any known ill. Considered especially efficacious are the leaves, bark, and roots of the "mamou" plant (the coral tree) and the elderberry. The name of one old remedy is eloquently expressive: *onguent-des-pauvres* (ointment of the poor), composed of a mixture of laundry soap, mutton tallow, sugar, wood ashes, and turpentine. "To stop bleeding," according to an old remedy, "sprinkle sugar on the wound and then place a large spider web over the cut" (*see Folkways*).

The Acadians as a whole are deeply religious. Mass is regularly attended, though it may mean a journey of several miles on foot, and in every home there are statues of saints and palm or magnolia leaves which were blessed by the parish priest on Palm Sunday.

The Côte Gelée hills are now given over to agriculture. The farms are usually small; cane and corn are the principal products. Typical Acadian cottages are seen frequently along the highway—small wooden homes, often unpainted, and characterized by the prudent conservation of space necessary for small landowners with big families. Doors swing outward rather than inward; each cottage has a flight of garret stairs rising diagonally within the entrance porch to a space under the roof which serves as a *garçonnière* (sleeping quarters for the boys of the family); chimneys are built on the outside. The windows of these houses are occasionally without glass panes, being protected instead by batten shutters.

The BILLEAUD SUGAR HOUSE, established in 1889, is at 12.3 *m.*

BROUSSARD, 13.8 *m.* (40 alt., 1,707 pop. 1970), was named for the earliest settlers. Prominent among them was Joseph Broussard, ancestor of the present large Broussard clan of southwest Louisiana, who was commissioned Captain of the Militia and Commandant of the Acadians in the Atucapas District by the French Government in 1765. He was known far and wide as Beausoleil (Fr., sunshine) because of his smiling countenance.

PIN HOOK BRIDGE, 18.9 *m.,* crossing the Vermilion (Fr., red) River, is by the site of a small settlement important in the early days of the parish. During the French and Spanish dominations of Louisiana this was the farthest point to which English smugglers could penetrate on the Vermilion River in periods of low water to dispose of their wares. Here they tied up their boats and traded with the Indians and the scattered pioneers. The settlement, then called Petit Manchac, became the governing seat of Lafayette Parish in 1825 but shortly afterward relinquished this honor to Lafayette. Little Manchac was the name given to a number of places in south Louisiana where smuggled goods could be bought because Manchac itself was the beginning of Spanish territory. Afterward the name of the village was changed to Pin Hook. According to tradition an old restaurateur of the locality, famous for his fried chicken, sometimes found it necessary to "appropriate" his neighbors' chickens. This he accomplished by means of a long string to which was attached a bent and a piece of corn, with which the birds were lured from the yards adjoining his own. The name Pin Hook was first applied to the ingenious chef but eventually was given to the settlement also. At Pin Hook, in the spring of 1863, General Dick Taylor, retreating from Federal forces under General Banks, fought one of his most desperate rear guard battles.

At 19.2 *m.* is the junction with a graveled road.

Left here to (L) the HENRI BENDEL ESTATE (*private*), 0.2 *m.* Near the entrance gate is a small brightly colored stucco lodge. The extensive grounds, sloping down to the Vermilion River in the rear, are planted with a variety of native trees. Here in midwinter is a fine display of camellias in bloom, and in March more than 3,000 azalea shrubs mass their varied hues along the driveways and walks. Henri Bendel attained international fame in New York as a fashion designer.

LES JARDINS DE MOUTON (*adm. fee*), 19.8 *m.,* were designed by Congressman Robert L. Mouton. An azalea-banked esplanade, near the head of which is a life-size statue of a ram (*mouton,* sheep), leads from the highway to the Chateau de Capri, the residence. Behind the house are the rose gardens. There are also sunken gardens, an outdoor theatre, cypress gardens, and a parterre with a formal planting of azaleas, camellias, and boxwood. Among the statuary on the grounds are representations of Evangeline, Huey P. Long, and the Four Seasons, and a reproduction of the Manneken-Pis of Brussels. In the rear of the gardens is a mile-long Way of the Cross, each landscaped Station a memorial to a friend or relative of Mouton.

At 20.1 *m.* US 90 forks; L. here on a bypass, shorter than the main route and avoiding the center of Lafayette, to a junction with the main route at 21.5 *m.*

US 90 continues straight to the junction with a graveled road at 20.2 *m.*

Right here 0.6 *m.* to the junction with a dirt road; R. here and R. again at 0.1 *m.* to the MYRTLE PLANTATION HOUSE (*open*), 0.2 *m.* The two-story wooden house built by Dr. Matthew Creighton, who came here in 1811, has been added to by each generation. The present hall, with its hand-hewn stairway at the rear, was originally the front porch of the old house closed in with shutters and transoms made tight by a system of pulleys (which kept out the "night air," the carrier of malaria germs). On the canvas walls and ceilings of the present dining-room are landscaped scenes painted approximately 45 years ago by Charles de Buisseuil, a French artist who had worked on the old French Opera House in New Orleans. The Amaryllis garden, near the old family cemetery, is noteworthy.

On the main side road at 1.3 *m.* is the LAFAYETTE MUNICIPAL AIRPORT.

LAFAYETTE, 21.2 *m.* (38 alt., 68,908 pop.) is at junctions with La 94, La 182, US 167, and the new Interstate 10.

Right from Lafayette, on the Pont de Mouton (Fr., Mouton's Bridge) Road, graveled, to the DAN DEBAILLON PLACE (*permission to visit obtained by telephoning*) 3.9 *m.,* notable for its variety of native trees, plants, and flowers. On this 15-acre tract azaleas, camellias, irises, spirea, and various types of roses bloom among wild dogwood, redbud, and magnolia trees.

At Lafayette US 90 makes a right-angle turn and proceeds westward, with Beau Bassin on the north; to the south the land slopes gradually off into level, grassy stretches. Scattered over the prairie are clear, circular ponds of various sizes. The Acadians likened the prairies to the wide expanse of the ocean and used many nautical terms in speaking of them. A journey across the open spaces was *aller au large,* or *mettre la voile* (to set sail); and their homeland groves they called *iles*—an island being considered by them a piece of wooded ground in a prairie.

SCOTT, 26.3 *m.* (36 alt., 1,334 pop. 1970; 902, 1960), dates back to 1880, when V. Careyette, a native of France, first settled here. A story told of Scott illustrates the primitiveness of the country as late as 1881, when the first trains came through. An old settler averse to having the strange iron "beast" running wild across the prairie, conceived a plan for ridding the country of the nuisance. He covered himself with a white sheet and, as the train came snorting around the bend, jumped out from a hiding place in the tall grass. Finding after a few trials that this had no effect, he disgustedly packed his belongings and moved farther into the wilderness.

West of Scott on US 90 are occasional pecan orchards, Cherokee rose hedges (which once served as fences), China tree groves, and occasional oaks. Most numerous are the China groves, which were planted by the early settlers because they grew rapidly, provided shade in the summer, and made good firewood (when dry the wood burns as rapidly as pine). In addition the flowers were used as a moth deterrent, the China "balls" provided pop-gun ammunition for small boys, and the dried seeds were dyed and strung as beads by the girls. Often instead of cutting down the whole tree each would be thinned out—the cut limbs serving for fuel and the trunks left for future usefulness.

RAYNE, 36.8 *m.* (39 alt., 9,510 pop. 1970; 8,634, 1960), is on a plateau that divides the sugar cane country from the rice belt. Rayne has had an important place in the development of the rice industry; a new type of rice, "blue rose," was perfected on an experimental plot near by. Large irrigation interests have headquarters here. Because of the locality's abundant water supply farmers are enabled to plant without waiting for rain. Besides rice, the section produces cotton, corn, fruit, vegetables, poultry, and eggs.

A Frog Derby, in which frogs are prodded to compete, is staged annually by the Lions Club of Rayne at Crowley, during the popular Rice Festival there.

Rayne is the center of the Louisiana frog industry. The Louisiana Frog Co., 303 W. Branche St., is a major shipper of edible frogs. Many are also sent to biological supply houses, aquariums, and colleges for experimental work. Frogs to be shipped for exhibit or study are caught with nets, usually at night by trappers who use flashlights to blind the quarry. The frog season begins early in spring and lasts until hibernation.

Rayne has developed a Community Center in recent years and built a new Police Station costing $100,000.

Rayne is a typical Louisiana-French town. The northern or eastern rice buyer's first step, on coming to this section, is to acquire a knowledge of French. Here, as in other towns in this district most of the Negroes speak French, and some cannot speak or understand English.

CROWLEY, 44.7 *m.* (22 alt., 16,104, 1970; 15,617 1960), seat of Acadia Parish, calls itself the Rice Capital of Louisiana. There are 11 rice mills in Crowley and 25 within a 20-mile radius.

Rice lands are plowed in fall, harrowed in spring, and then planted by means of a low flying plane, a crop duster, which plants more than 600,000 acres of rice in Southwestern Louisiana, where the average yield is 4,000 lbs. per acre. When the green plants have reached a height of three or four inches the fields are flooded with water from two to six inches deep. Then the plant is kept half submerged for about three months until the rice has headed. Canals and drainage ditches cut the fields into plots so as to make proper irrigation possible. Powerful pumps supply water for the canals which are from eight to ten feet deep, 40 to 60 feet wide, and as much as 30 miles long.

Before harvesting irrigation is halted and the fields are allowed to dry off for about two weeks. Mechanical binders harvest the rice, stalk and all; then, after two weeks of drying, threshing machines separate the grain from the stalk. Rice is usually marketed by the "pocket"—a 100-pound bag.

At the mill the rough rice is dumped into a hopper and carried through a series of machines which clip it, grade it, and remove foreign matter. The cleaned rough rice, each grain surrounded by layers of bran in a tough hull, is passed between shelling stones. These consist of revolving discs covered with emery and cement. Centrifugal motion causes the grains to stand upright between the stones, which are just close enough together to crack the end of the hulls and free the grains without crushing them. The rice is then taken to the "paddy machine," where the hulled grains are separated from the unhulled ones.

This rice is known as brown rice, a little of which is put on the market. In the next step it is sent to the hullers, which remove the outer bran coats and germs; then the rice goes to the pearling cones, which further clean the grain. The rice is then passed on to a brush, which removes most of the inner coat, or polish. The residue from these last processes is sold as animal feed. The grain in this stage is called uncoated rice, and some is disposed of in this form. Most of it, however, passes on to the "trumbola," where it is given a coating of tallow and glucose which gives the grain a glossy finish.

The INTERNATIONAL RICE FESTIVAL in October is a most successful commercial promotion effort. It grew out of the National Festival begun in 1937, and since 1950 occupies two days and draws from 80,000 to 100,000 visitors. Sponsored by the Crowley Chamber of Commerce and supported by the State Legislature with funds for buildings, it now includes the International Frog Derby, the Livestock and Rice Exhibit, and the election of the Rice Queen. Today the City and Festival Assn. own a Festival Auditorium, a Youth Center, a Livestock Exhibition Bldg., and a Municipal Swimming Pool. The whole object is to publicize rice as a desirable food.

Records in the Acadia Parish Courthouse show that the land on which Crowley stands once belonged to the Attakapa, the chief of which tribe sold it to the early white settlers. In 1886 the 174-acre tract which comprises the present business district was sold for $80—less than 45¢ an acre. Acadians, the first settlers, had planted their small farms along the banks of streams, leaving virtually untouched the vast surrounding expanse of fertile prairie land.

The town, first named Houstch, grew rapidly after the Southern Pacific extended its line westward from Lafayette in the late 1880's. When incorporated, the name of the town was changed to Crowley in honor of Pat Crowley, a section foreman. Crowley is served by two railroads and has inland waterway communication with Gulf ports by way of Bayou Plaquemine Brule, the Mermentau River, and the Intracoastal Waterway.

Crowley is at a junction with north-south La 13, which connects 2 m. north with Interstate 10, a cross-state route to Beaumont, Texas. The city uses Lafayette Airport, 19 m. east, for regular Trans Texas flights and its LeGros Airport, 6 m. west, has runways of 4,300 ft. Southwest Louisiana Vocation-Technical School, estab. 1938, gives training in technical and business occupations, including nursing, motor car repairs, industrial electronics. The Acadia Parish Adult Education program enrolls up to 1,000 regularly.

The ACADIA PARISH LIBRARY has its headquarters and Crowley Branch on the first floor of the Acadia Parish Courthouse. It has 10 branches and one bookmoble and a collection of more than 75,000 vols. In 1969 the circulation for the parish was 233,185, the bookmobile accounting for 52,465. Over 11,000 reference questions were answered during the year.

The AMERICAN LEGION HOSPITAL is a 72-bed facility, and there are nursing homes, a mental clinic and other health agencies.

A RICE EXPERIMENT STATION (visitors admitted), 45.8 m., is conducted jointly by the Louisiana State University and the U. S. Department of Agriculture.

ESTHERWOOD, 50.7 m. (17 alt., 661 pop.), is a shipping point for rice and general farm products.

MIDLAND, 52.9 m. (22 alt.), has an irrigation plant on near-by Bayou Plaquemine Brule, warehouses, rice mills, and a small syrup factory. Fishing here is excellent.

MERMENTAU, 58.2 m. (15 alt., 756 pop.), is in the midst of the rice belt, and has the Mermentau River, which provides most of the water used for irrigation.

JENNINGS, 63.3 m. (25 alt., 11,783 1970 pop.; 11,887, 1960), first settled in 1884, was named for Jennings McComb, the engineer in charge of building the Southern Pacific Railway lines in southwestern Louisiana. Jennings is the site of the first discovery of petroleum in Louisiana (1901). The field has been in continuous production since.

Many of the early settlers came to this section from Iowa, Missouri, Indiana, and Kentucky, at the instigation of S. L. Cary, land agent for the railroad. The rest of the population is made up of people of French and German extraction and Negroes. The Germans settled in the section west of the town. The French residents have retained many of their old customs; Mardi Gras is observed annually.

Jennings has rice mills, and machine shops. The growing of Creole Easter lilies for commercial purposes constitutes one of the minor industries. The town's direct communication with the Gulf (50 miles distant) makes it a gateway to fishing grounds abounding in speckled trout, redfish, and tarpon. The countryside is the winter habitat of quail, doves, ducks, geese and snipe.

The JENNINGS PUBLIC LIBRARY in 1967 had 19,000 vols. and a circulation of around 50,000. Its Morse Collection of coral, shells, and minerals, and objects from the Near East, is notable. In 1968 the JEFFERSON DAVIS PARISH LIBRARY was established and supported by part of a sales tax.

The ZIGLER MUSEUM, 411 Clara St. occupies the former home of Fred B. Zigler, to which two wings have been added. The east wing houses dioramas by P. Ambrose Daigre, famous wildlife artist and president of the American Wildlife Studios of Baton Rouge. The main building has paintings and the west wing contains exhibitions. There is an auditorium for public use.

Jennings is at the junction with La 26 and 2 m. from Int. 10.

ROANOKE, 69.3 m. (24 alt.), was called Esterly until two brothers by the name of Booze moved here from Roanoke, Virginia, and changed its name to that of their native town. Roanoke is the birthplace of R. J. Thompson, inventor of a midget radio tube.

WELSH, 73.8 m. (25 alt., 3,203 pop. 1970; 3,332, 1960) is often the scene of Cajun (Acadian) dances, called *fais-dodos* (*see Music and Folkways*), performed to the accompaniment of the accordion, the French harp, the fiddle, and the triangle. The town was settled by Miles Welsh, who journeyed here with his family in an ox-drawn wagon. A small public library is supported by the town.

In the distance at 77 m. are seen derricks of the WELSH OIL FIELD, one of the oldest in Louisiana. Oil was discovered here in 1902.

At 79.9 m. is the junction with La 101.

Right here to LACASSINE, 0.3 m. (21 alt.). A legend says that the place was so named because a local Indian chief was fond of a drink called "cassine" which he made from berries of the yaupon.

The highway crosses the boundary of Calcasieu (Ind., crying eagle) Parish at 84.2 m. Calcasieu was formed from a portion of St. Landry Parish in 1840 and has a mixed population of Creoles, Acadians, Anglo-

Saxons, Negroes, and a few Indians. Its earliest settlers came prior to 1824, taking advantage of the Arroyo Hondo claims (*see Tour 17A*).

IOWA, 85.3 *m.* (20 alt., 1,944 pop. 1970; 1,857, 1960), in the heart of a fertile rice area, is the trade center of one of the newly developed oil fields of southwest Louisiana. This is an important location of the Shell Petroleum Company of Louisiana.

Iowa is at the junction with US 165 and 2 *m.* from Int. 10.

At 90.8 *m.* is the old LEBLEU PLANTATION HOUSE (*open*), 100 yards back from the highway, and fronted by a picket fence. The building is two stories high, with upper and lower front galleries supported by six square cypress columns. It includes in its walls materials of what is thought to have been the first dwelling built by white men in this section.

The LeBleu family has been engaged in the cattle business and has used the same brand for several generations. The original was 211. When J. C. LeBleu began using the brand he changed the second numeral to an arrow. Many years before his death in 1914 LeBleu planted the outline of his brand in narcissi in the front yard of his home.

Lafitte and his band are said to have used the barn, which was destroyed in 1918, as a meeting place. The owner of the house in 1939, "Grandma Joe" LeBleu, then 98 years old, remembered the time when she shot a "panther" that had crawled under the house, and when she fed two strangers who turned out to be Jesse James and his brother.

The Swift & Company Packing Plant, 92.2 *m.* is the center of activities in a stock-raising section from which thousands of cattle are shipped annually. The old Mexican Cattle Trail led through this district, and the pioneers opened up large ranches.

The EASTDALE MUNI GOLF COURSE, 94.6 *m.* (9 holes), is open to the public.

At 95.4 *m.* is the junction with US 171 (*see Tour 19c*).

Both sides of the highway near Lake Charles are lined with oil well supply houses. Old oil fields are constantly being extended in southwest Louisiana and new fields are being developed. Trucks loaded with pipe or oil machinery add to the heavy traffic.

LAKE CHARLES, 97.4 *m.* (13 alt., 77,998 pop.) (*see Lake Charles*).

Left from Lake Charles on South Street (La 211), paved with concrete, blacktop, and shell.

At 7.6 *m.* is the junction with a shell road. Right here 0.4 *m.* to (L) the LAKE CHARLES COUNTRY CLUB, which lies along Prien Lake, a widening of the Calcasieu River. Close-growing oaks, gums, pines, and other trees border the grounds, and the shore line is a picturesque pattern of open vistas and woodland recesses. A BOY SCOUT CAMP, 0.8 *m.*, is on the shore of the lake.

A State-operated ferry (*free; 24-hour call service*), 14.5 *m.*, crosses the Intracoastal Waterway (*see Tour 11D*).

On La 384 is GRAND LAKE (9 alt.), 18.4 *m.*, a fishing and bathing resort. The population in winter dwindles to a few caretakers and casual residents. When the river is low and the tides high, the waters of Calcasieu Lake become salty enough to bring an abundance of croakers, redfish, speckled sea trout, and other Gulf fish. Visible across the lake are the derricks of the Hackberry Oil Fields (*see Tour 1F*).

West of Lake Charles US 90 crosses the Calcasieu River, 100.2 *m.,* just below the south end of the lake which gives the town its name. From the bridge can sometimes be seen booms of logs floating downstream to sawmills farther south, or rafts of logs being towed upstream. At night lanterns are placed at intervals on the strings of logs to prevent collisions. Cypress and tupelo gum are the woods most usually cut, although forests in this section still furnish some pine. Getting logs out of the swamps gives rise to many difficulties. Lumberjacks, wearing hip boots, sometimes stand in water while sawing; sometimes they stand in boats or pirogues.

West of the river, the route runs for a short distance through a grove of willows.

At 101.1 *m.* is the junction with a graveled road.

Right here to the town of WESTLAKE, 0.6 *m.* (15 alt., 4,082 pop.), an industrial suburb of Lake Charles.

The MATHIESON ALKALI WORKS, 102 *m.,* manufactures soda ash, caustic soda, hypochlorite, liquid chlorine, dry ice, synthetic ammonia, and bicarbonate of soda.

Between here and Vinton the highway traverses a level countryside heavily wooded with pine.

SULPHUR, 108.7 *m.* (16 alt., 13,551 pop. 1970; 11,429, 1960), named for the near-by sulphur dome is at the junction with La 27 (*see Tour 1F*).

Right from Sulphur 1.1 *m.* on an asphalt-paved road through a dense pine forest to the site of a SULPHUR DOME that produced nearly 10,000,000 tons of sulphur during a period of about 20 years. The dome was discovered in 1865, at a depth of about 500 feet, by engineers prospecting for oil. Austrian, French, and American companies made several attempts to mine the deposits, but were unable to sink a permanent shaft because of overlying quicksands. In 1893 the Union Sulphur Company acquired the land and obtained the services of Herman Frasch, noted chemical engineer, to work out a method of obtaining the sulphur. The Union Sulphur Co., employing the Frasch process (*see Science*), began commercial production here in 1905. While the deposit is present to an undetermined depth, operation of the mine ceased to be profitable about 1924 and was abandoned in 1926. About 1924, petroleum, which had been originally sought at the dome, was actually found there.

At 116.2 *m.* on US 90 is the junction with a graveled road.

Right on this road to EDGERLY, 0.4 *m.* (22 alt.), an oil-field town lying near an important salt dome.

The BIG WOODS CHURCH (L), 3 *m.,* set in a large cemetery in a pine forest, is an unpainted, severely plain frame building.

VINTON, 121.7 *m.* (18 alt., 3,454 pop. 1970; 2,987, 1960), founded about 1888 by settlers from Iowa and other Midwestern States, was named for Vinton, Iowa. The discovery of oil in commercial quantities here in 1911 has been largely responsible for the growth of the town.

In the days of the sale of game (now prohibited) Vinton was a market for hunters, who shipped out great quantities of geese, ducks, snipe, plover, and other water birds. Vinton is near enough to the State Line to enjoy trade with towns of both Louisiana and Texas.

Visible in the distance at 122.7 *m.* are the derricks of the VINTON OIL FIELD.

At 125.7 *m.* is the junction with a graveled road.

Right here 2.5 *m.* to the junction with a shell road; L. on this road to NIB-LETT'S BLUFF, 5.2 *m.*, bordering a channel of Sabine River known as Old River. The Old Spanish Trail crossed the Sabine River by ferry about five miles south, in the neighborhood of what is now Orange, Texas. Before the War between the States and the coming of the Texas and New Orleans Railroad, Niblett's Bluff was a river port of consequence. During the war high breastworks were thrown up here by the Confederates. While the fort was never a scene of conflict, an epidemic broke out among the defenders in May 1863. Thirty men died and were buried within the confines of the fortifications.

The low open bluffs afford a good view of the river and surrounding swamp growths. The old road that leads to Niblett's Bluff is part of a route that was opened between this point and Alexandria during the War between the States when supply lines to Mississippi and Red River points were blockaded. The remains of the CONFEDERATE BREASTWORKS are to be seen about 1,000 feet from the river and south of the church.

At TOOMEY, 4 *m.* west of Vinton, US 90 joins Int. 10 to proceed across the Sabine River to Texas. The first town across the river is Orange, Texas, 2 *m.* south of the highway and at a junction with Texas north-south Hwy. 87. This is a station on the Southern Pacific Ry., which crosses the Sabine River on a bridge north of the highway bridge. Beaumont, Texas, is 20 *m.* west of the Louisiana border.

Early Spanish explorers called the river the "Rio Sabinas" because of the juniper trees found growing on its banks; but the French, who retained the name in a Gallicized form, attributed its origin to an incident similar to that recorded in Roman history as the "Rape of the Sabines." According to this legend, a party of Frenchmen stopped at an Indian village on the river and entertained the friendly natives aboard their boats. During the festivities, the Frenchmen, becoming intoxicated, put the Indian men ashore and made off with the women.

The Sabine River originally was the western boundary of the Neutral Ground, a strip of land set up between French and Spanish territories. After France ceded Louisiana to Spain in 1763, the river lost its status as a boundary but resumed it in 1801 when France regained the territory. After the purchase of Louisiana by the United States in 1803, the neutral strip again served as a boundary. When Mexico declared its independence from Spain in 1821, it claimed Texas, and so, nominally, at least, the Sabine became the boundary between Mexican territory and Louisiana, which in the meantime had become a State. The revolt of the Texans in 1836 made the Sabine the line dividing the Republic of Texas from the State of Louisiana. The boundary was surveyed in 1840, but although markers were set up, the line was never officially ratified by Texas or Louisiana. Both States claim sovereignty over fishing grounds and potential oil lands at the mouth of the Sabine. Louisiana claims the line runs perpendicular to the coast line out into the Gulf; Texas claims the boundary projects from the midstream line of the Sabine, which enters the Gulf at an oblique angle in a southeasterly direction. The Texas claim is based on the Treaty of Guadalupe, between Texas and Mexico, which gave Texas title to submerged land three leagues (10.3 miles) into the water. A survey of the 1840 line was made by the WPA. In 1970 a suit over this boundary was pending in the United States Supreme Court.

ᗧ•ᗧ

Tour 1A

New Orleans—Buras—Triumph—Venice—Pilottown—Pas à
Loutre Wildfowl Area—Port Eads.

This tour supplements the tours of inspection down the sides of the Mississippi River described in Tour 8 (the east bank) and in Tour 11b (the west bank), and proceeds beyond Pointe a la Hache and Venice to the farthermost passes of the Mississippi. It is primarily useful for hunters who have licenses to hunt wildfowl during the season prescribed by the Louisiana Wild Life & Fisheries Commission, which is responsible for the management of the wildlife areas and provides shelters and facilities at a number of camps. Until recent decades access to this territory was solely by boats but today there is an airstrip in the Pas à Loutre Area and at times transportation can be arranged from Venice. The use of this area by the oil industry has greatly facilitated transportation.

Motor cars from New Orleans cross the Greater New Orleans Bridge to Gretna and proceed on La 23 down the west side of the Mississippi to Venice.

BURAS, 66 m. (7 alt.) a settlement of trappers and fishermen is an important supply depot for fishermen. Here are numerous opportunities for boat rentals. The surroundings are swampy and have habitats of wildfowl and small equatic animals. This is also true of TRIUMPH, farther down.

VENICE, 80 m. (2 alt.) probably has more boats available for hunters and fishermen than any of the villages of the delta. Petroleum helicoptors have a station here. South of Venice there are no levees, the river maintaining a constant Gulf level. The narrow strips of fertile land bordering the Mississippi near its mouth are virtual islands lying between the river and the salt marshes that separate them from the nearby Gulf inlets. The settlements along the river are completely isolated and rely on river boats for their supplies and the shipment of their produce. When tropical storms threaten everyone seeks refuge in lighthouses, the only substantial, storm-proof buildings in the section.

Venice was on the main route of Hurricane Camille in August, 1969, and suffered much damage. Just below Venice is THE JUMP, socalled because here the river jumped its banks to form a new outlet; this water is now carried through Grand Pass.

The Delta area, and the adjacent parishes that extend far into the Gulf are part of Louisiana's crude oil production country, where the derricks rise both onshore and offshore. Offshore installations are numerous at Main Pass, Ship Shoal, West Desoto, Grand Isle, and along the coast.

CUBITS GAP, 87 m., is the opening for several outlets on the east side of the river. Main Pass, Octave's Pass, and Raphael's Pass extend to the Gulf through a region neither land nor water but a spongy blanket of silt, plant debris, and aquatic vegetation. The river in this region has both built up and washed away the surrounding deposits of silt, sometimes blocking its own course and cutting a new channel. In recent years, since the building of jetties to confine the stream in deep, definite channels, no new outlets have been created.

At Cubits Gap there is a central lighthouse with foghorns and other danger signals for this section. The keeper's house is the only other building at the place.

Tied to pilings in this section are what appear to be rafts, but which are actually willow mattresses used for reinforcement of caving banks in some of the passes and for contraction of the channels. The mattresses, which are made of bundles of willows woven together, are fastened by one edge to the bank and loaded at the other end with broken rock (riprap), which sinks them against the shelving bank. Sometimes the bottom of the channel is covered with mattresses to prevent scouring.

PILOTTOWN, 88 m. (1 alt.), a conglomeration of rough one-story buildings on the east bank of the river, is the headquarters of the Crescent River Ports Pilots Assn. It has a U. S. Customs Agent and a pilot station occupied jointly by river and bar pilots. The pilots and their families who once resided here and enlivened the place have since moved either to New Orleans or points near the city. Some trappers, hunters, and fishermen still make Pilottown their permanent home, but pilots remain here only for their assignments.

Bar pilots meet ships at sea and guide them through the passes to Pilottown, from which point river pilots take them into New Orleans. On outgoing trips the reverse order is followed. There is a monopoly on piloting held by certain families. For generations jobs have been handed down from father to son.

The principal flood of the Mississippi moves eastward into the Gulf through Main Pass, and Pas à Loutre (Fr. Otter pass), the rest moves through South Pass and Southwest Pass. Near the extreme end of Southwest Pass is BURRWOOD, headquarters of U. S. Engineers who supervise the jetties and maintain the dredged channel. There are a lighthouse, bar pilots station, weather bureau, and auxiliary housing, painted white.

East of the river, beginning opposite Venice, is the huge DELTA MIGRATORY WILDFOWL REFUGE. This extends down to Pas à Loutre, where the PAS À LOUTRE WATERFOWL MANAGE-MENT AREA begins. This covers all the rest of the delta lands.

The latter area is carefully supervised by the Louisiana Wild Life & Fisheries Commission in order to maintain a public hunting program that would not deplete the supply of birds. Typical is the report for the season of 1968–1969, which discloses that those taking part of the public camp hunting program took 2,472 ducks, 11 geese, and 329 coots in the allotted 30 days. Those not using the public camps but an area open to seasonal permit took 2,644 ducks, 467 geese and 100 coots. The report says: "Hurricane Camille dealt Pas à Loutre a devastating blow when she hit in mid-August, 1969. Eight of the nine public hunting camps and the entire headquarters complex were destroyed. As a result of the damages the camp hunting program was discontinued and approximately 60,000 acres of Pas à Loutre lying east of South Pass were opened hunting without special permit."

On South Pass, the original ship channel to the sea and the one still most often used, are the GARDEN ISLAND BAY OIL FIELDS, 100 m., on one of the mud lumps in the lower part of Garden (originally Gordon) Island Bay. Mud lumps are masses of river clay and silt that average about an acre in area and rise from three to ten feet above water. Some of these islands, which support no vegetation except weeds, are breeding places of the brown pelican. One lump sometimes has several hundred nesting pelicans.

PORT EADS, 102 m. (6 alt.), named for Captain James Buchanan Eads (1820–1887), builder of the first jetties of the Mississippi River, is at the end of South Pass on its east side. It is a small haven beside one of the artificial banks of rock and concrete that extend South Pass in a deep, straight channel into the Gulf. A lighthouse, pilots' station, and U. S. Engineers' quarters are its principal buildings.

Prior to 1879, shallow water and constantly shifting sandbars at the mouth of the Mississippi impeded navigation and hindered the full development of New Orleans as a port. Many methods of deepening the passes had been tried, but without success. In 1879, after five years of difficult work, Captain Eads completed the jetty system (see Science). Since the construction of the jetties, the Federal Government has deepened and widened South Pass, enabling vessels drawing 30 feet to pass through in safety.

At Port Eads there is a bar pilots' station. Bar pilots steer ships through the passes to and from the Gulf. Day or night, and in every kind of weather, pilots, using speedboats and launches, meet or leave ships in the Gulf. They must be able to swing from their boats to the dangling end of a ship's ladder as they come alongside or to reverse the operation when leaving the vessel.

Thousands of gulls hover above the water or perch on the pilings, jetties, and sandbars. Pelicans, sailing heavily or plunging unexpectedly for fish, are constantly in sight. Flocks of ducks and geese in winter and herons in summer travel back and forth among the mud flats and marshes. High in the air in late summer is the great man-o'-war, or frigate bird, and sometimes a graceful tropic-bird, or "bos'n." Out where the muddy water of the river mingles with the green of the Gulf porpoises roll and leap.

❰❁

Tour 1B

Raceland—Golden Meadow—Grand Isle; 62.8 *m.,* La 1.

Graveled and concrete-paved roadbed.
Hotels at Golden Meadow and Grand Isle.

This route, the only automobile approach to Grand Isle, parallels the west bank of Bayou Lafourche (*see Tour 11b*), a former outlet of the Mississippi River but now an almost currentless stream cut off from the river by the dam at Donaldsonville. To the left across the bayou, between Raceland and Golden Meadow, occasional sugar refineries, cane fields, and plantation homes are visible; on the right, bordering the road, is a continuous row of unpretentious houses, with small adjoining fields and gardens. The southern part of the route, from Golden Meadow to Grand Isle, traverses bleak marshes, open stretches of water, and "floating prairies" (water covered with a mat of aquatic and semi-aquatic plants). Desolate and devoid of dwellings, this section is in marked contrast with the populous upper reaches of Bayou Lafourche.

La 1 branches south from US 90 (*see Tour 1b*) at RACELAND, 0 *m.* (6 alt., 4,880 pop.) (*see Tour 1b*). The levee was built originally to protect the surrounding country from high stages of water flowing into the bayou from the Mississippi River. It has now become useless and no effort is made to maintain it. In many places the levee has worn down; long gaps are frequent.

LOCKPORT, 7.6 *m.* (7 alt., 1,995 pop. 1970; 2,221, 1960), a small shrimping town with its own canning factory, occupies both sides of Bayou Lafourche at a point where the Intracoastal Waterway (*see Tour 11D*) branches west from the bayou, connecting with Lake Long and Field Lake, popular places for fishing and duck hunting.

The Cajuns of the Lockport vicinity have several curious customs. A married woman is often referred to by her husband's first name. Thus the wives of men whose Christian names are Jacques, Philip, and Edmond are called 'Miss Jacques,' 'Miss Philip,' and 'Miss Edmond.' Trucks are sent out along the road by the owners of dance halls to transport people to the weekly dances—separate trucks for men and women in order that the occupants may be packed more closely. Before the days of automobiles, groups went to dances on barges and in boats.

Figs, plums, pears, peaches, and vegetables are widely grown and, although many families own their own pressure canners, a traveling one is sent by the parish to householders who apply for it. Some of the small sugar cane farmers crop on shares, but almost all of them have gardens, cows, and chickens.

The highway at 14.8 m. passes the derricks of the Harang Oil Field, discovered by seismograph in 1933.

LA ROSE, 19.2 m. (5 alt.), on the east side of the bayou and reached by bridge, has a small residential area on the west side. Left from La Rose to DELTA FARMS, 3 m., a small farming project developed on reclaimed land.

South of La Rose the levee banks gradually grow lower and the bayou widens out. The arable land along the bayou extends only a short distance back and the homes are close together. The natives use the levee for vegetable plots, fruit trees, and small patches of cane. Highly elevated clotheslines display family wash to passing boats.

Because of the limited farm land, cattle are pastured on the ridges and mounds that rise a few feet above the swamps bordering the bayou. Pirogues, instead of horses, are employed by the herdsmen in rounding up their hardy livestock, and trained cow hounds are used to find cattle that have bogged in muck. Dairy animals, pastured on *coteaux* (little hills) nearer the levee, go back and forth to their grazing islets through fenced-in lanes called *manches*.

CUT-OFF, 22.6 m. (4 alt.), is another shrimping village bisected by the bayou.

South of Cut-Off houses become fewer and houseboats moored among water hyacinths begin to make their appearance. Small cemeteries are seen at intervals. On the bayou, fishing luggers and trim motor launches pass frequently. Although the old-fashioned fishing luggers with their varicolored sails have been superseded by motorboats, the love of color is still seen in the blues, reds, and greens of the canvas coverings, flags, posts, and barrels of the luggers. Names display a surge of patriotism—*America, United States, Baltimore, Minnesota, Oklahoma*—with an occasional *Santa Maria, Lucretia, Christmas, Rose-C, Three Brothers, Sea Dream,* and *The Kind Father.* Passengers aboard *Polly,* a pleasure boat known to the bayou folk as *Le Bateau de Candy,* for a period of years preceding 1937, used to toss peppermint sticks to the children as the boat passed along the bayou.

With the rapid development of the oil and fish industries, much of the provincialism formerly existing along lower Bayou Lafourche is disappearing. A French patois is still quite commonly spoken, but many of the natives have adopted their own brand of English, evidenced by road signs such as, "Stop an eat, we fix you up," "Car wash and grease," and "Pants press while you hide."

GOLDEN MEADOW, 34.4 m. (2 alt., 2,681 pop. 1970; 3,097, 1960), chiefly on the west side of the bayou, is a thriving community with shrimp factories and packing sheds. A fleet of 300 fishing luggers, bringing in shrimp, oysters, speckled trout, redfish, sheepshead, and pompano, makes its headquarters here. The town is also a receiving station for fish shipments from other sections, chiefly Barataria.

Of comparatively recent origin, Golden Meadow might be described as a "boom" fishing center. Its business and residential sections have not had time to grow up to its commercial importance; they retain the picturesqueness of the old fishing village. Wooden stores and houses, interspersed with shrimp-drying platforms and packing sheds, are built on piles out over the water and other buildings crowd the highway on the inland side. Numerous houseboats bob up and down in slips or are pulled up high and dry on the bayou bank. Skiffs are moored to every available post.

Boats (fishing luggers) can be rented here, rates depending on distance. Favorite fishing grounds near by are Timbalier (Fr., kettledrummer; said to be derived from the nickname of a soldier who at the massacre at Fort Rosalie—1729—beat so vigorously on a kettledrum that a whole band of Indians ceased attacking to marvel at the strange instrument) Bay, Bay Canard Gris (Fr., gray duck), Chinese Bayou, and Bayou Landry, where white and speckled trout, Spanish mackerel, redfish, sheepshead, black mullet, and croakers are plentiful. In Timbalier Bay are tarpon, pompano, and blackfish; in Lac de L'isle (Fr., lake of the island), are black bass. There is duck hunting at all these spots, in season.

South of Golden Meadow, farms come to an end. Bayou Lafourche is wide and clear, its low banks bordered with green bushes and palmetto. Occasional shacks and outbuildings are thatched with palmetto. Level, grassy marshes, the haunt of fur-bearing animals and migratory birds, stretch away to the horizon. Although from the road these marshes appear as dry as a western prairie, they are interspersed with wet stretches and "floating prairies."

La 1 crosses Bayou Lafourche at 45.7 m. to LEEVILLE, which consists of little besides an oil field with a few scattered stores and shacks. The oil men who work here usually have living quarters farther up the bayou and travel back and forth by boat or automobile. The LEEVILLE OIL FIELD, opened in 1931, is one of the largest in the Gulf area, producing 3,863,000 bbl. in 1965.

Boats can be rented at Leeville for fishing in near-by Lake Pelican and Timbalier Bay.

Between Leeville and Grand Isle La 1 passes through marshland in which, for miles at a stretch, there are no signs of human habitation. Grassy growths, broken only by stretches of open water, and with an underlying ooze of indeterminate depth, fill the landscape as far as the eye can see, creating an atmosphere of bleakness and desolation peculiar to the unreclaimed areas of the coast. Waterfowl wing past or swim in near-by lagoons, while an occasional rabbit or opossum shares the right-of-way with the motorist. Perched on the telephone wires that line the highway brilliant blue kingfishers scream at intruders. In the warmer months white and blue herons reluctantly abandon fishing in the reed-brakes beside the road and flap awkwardly to more secluded feeding grounds.

On both sides of the approach to the three-quarter-mile-long bridge that connects it with Grand Isle is CHÊNIÈRE (Fr., oak ridge) CAMINADA, 62.1 *m.,* a low oak-covered ridge named for Francisco Caminada, a New Orleans merchant who lived during the Spanish regime. Prior to the hurricane of 1893 there was a thriving settlement here, but damage by the storm was so great that the town has never been rebuilt.

The hurricane itself did little damage to the settlement, and the inhabitants, who had gone to the mainland and Grand Isle for safety, returned to their homes when the wind fell. At nightfall, as they celebrated their deliverance with a dance, the wind suddenly veered and drove the waters of the Gulf in mountainous waves upon them. In 15 minutes the water was four feet deep. The torrent carried every-thing in its path; boats were snatched from the grasp of men struggling desperately to save their families; children were torn from their mothers' arms; and houses, swept from their foundations, floated like egg shells upon the boiling waters. For months afterwards the bodies of the victims were washed ashore. The few survivors were taken to Westwego, where the majority settled.

The bell of Our Lady of Grand Isle Church formerly belonged to the church at Chênière Caminada. It is said to have been cast in Cincinnati in the last century from 700 pounds of silver, including the crested family plate of Father Espinosa, the pastor, heirlooms of the Baratarians, and pirate loot. After the hurricane the bell was stored at Westwego. In 1905, a westbank church obtained permission to use it. En route to its destination, the bell was taken from the ox team during the night, and for thirteen years its location was a mystery. In 1918, the Baratarians, who did not want their bell to ring for any other group of people, unearthed it from Westwego cemetery and sent it to the Grand Isle church.

At the eastern end of the bridge is GRAND ISLE, 62.8 *m.* (3 alt., 2,236 pop. 1970; 2,074, 1960), one of a group of islands lying along the north shore of the Gulf of Mexico. Grand Isle is seven miles long and one and one-half miles wide. The seven-mile beach is one of the few places in Louisiana where real surf bathing can be enjoyed. From the shell road paralleling the beach a series of lanes reach back to the land-ward side of the island, which is covered with a luxuriant growth of trees and shrubs. Groves of oaks lean toward the mainland, the individual trees distorted into grotesque shapes by the lashing of the wind. Tall palms tower above the stunted oaks, and there is a dense undergrowth of palmetto, Spanish dagger, and other semitropical plants. The lanes themselves are cool green tunnels branched over with oleander, elder, and chinaberry, at the ends of which are the homes of the inhabitants. Wharves for the fishing fleet are at the eastern extremity of the island. Since the development of offshore exploration and drilling for crude petroleum Grand Island has become an important center for production. One offshore field produced 15,592,000 bbl. (42 gal.) and another 13,758,000 bbl. in 1968.

The population of the island is a mixture, of French, Portuguese, Spanish, and Filipino descent; the language, a French-Spanish patois. Many of the inhabitants, who are descendants of Lafitte's band, live in frame houses erected by their adventurous forefathers more than a century ago. They send the produce of their trucking, fishing, and trapping to New Orleans, via the same route that the pirates used in taking their smuggled goods to market.

For several years during the second decade of the nineteenth century Grand Isle served as the headquarters for Jean and Pierre Lafitte and their swashbuckling pirates. Jean Lafitte (c.1780–c.1826) may have first visited Louisiana as Captain Lafitte of the French privateer *La Sœur Chérie,* which came to New Orleans for repairs and provisions in 1804. By 1809 he and Pierre were proprietors of a blacksmith shop in New Orleans, operated by slave labor, and used as a depot for the disposal of smuggled goods. In 1811 Jean organized a band of smugglers and pirates with headquarters on the secluded islands of Barataria Bay, off the Louisiana coast. Operating about half a dozen ships sailing under the flag of the infant Republic of Cartagena, the band prospered under Lafitte's shrewd leadership. In open violation of United States revenue laws, their spoils were sold in New Orleans to merchants and planters. The U. S. Government, prior to the War of 1812, sent several ineffective punitive expeditions against the outlaws.

Three British officers visited Lafitte's stronghold in 1814, offering him immunity for past offenses, rewards in lands, and a captaincy in exchange for the Baratarians' support of the English in an attack on New Orleans. Lafitte feigned acceptance, but after gathering as much information of the British plans as possible, he promptly turned it over to Louisiana officials, and proffered his assistance to the American cause. The offer was refused, and an American gunboat was dispatched to destroy the outlaws' establishment.

From their hiding place, the pirates again offered their allegiance to the United States, and this time it was accepted. In the Battle of New Orleans the Baratarians acquitted themselves bravely and in 1815 President Madison fully pardoned them for their past crimes.

Lafitte's reformation was short-lived, however, for soon afterwards he was carrying on a more flourishing piratical trade, under the Venezuelan flag, from a new base on Galveston Island. Of Lafitte's later years little of authentic record can be found. Presumably he passed this period in piracy along the Yucatan coast, dying there of fever in

1826. According to one legend, he was buried in the little cemetery at Lafitte, Louisiana (*see Tour 11E*).

A large variety of fish swarms in the waters surrounding the island, and fishing is the chief industry and major sport. Redfish, flounder, sea trout, mackerel, jewfish, shark, swordfish, pompano, and tarpon are plentiful. A three-day Tarpon Rodeo, held during the last days of August, calls out more than 3,000 fishermen and 10,000 spectators.

Grand Isle is the first resting place for birds returning from the tropics across the central Gulf of Mexico, and many migratory bird airways converge on the island. Here the birds pause after their long flight, feeding and drinking the fresh water of island pools for a few days before resuming their northward journey. At the crest of the migration the island is literally alive with them, and ornithologists have a rare opportunity to see and study a wide variety of species. There is a fall migration when the birds return to the south, but it is not so concentrated as in the spring.

At all times of the year Louisiana's emblematic bird, the pelican, can be seen in great numbers. Herons and other aquatic fowl make their homes on the island, feeding from the waters and marshes.

The ELINOR BEHRE FIELD LABORATORY, established at Grand Isle by the Louisiana State University, is a permanent marine laboratory offering field courses in biology during the summer months.

FORT LIVINGSTON, on the southern point of Grande Terre Island, directly opposite Grand Isle, about 1 *m.* across Barataria Pass, is reached by boat from Grand Isle. Only ruins of high brick walls and a few rusted cannon remain. When Lafitte withdrew from Grand Isle in 1814, a detachment of United States soldiers occupied this spot.

Records of the War Department show that the reservation was sold by Étienne deGruy and wife to the State in 1834. The State deeded the reservation to the Federal Government in 1834. It is believed that construction started in 1835, but work progressed so slowly that the fort was not completed until 1861.

The Confederates took possession at the outbreak of the War between the States but evacuated April 27, 1862. On October 26, 1863, the 16th Regiment Main Infantry of the Federals was stationed there. After the war the fort was no longer garrisoned, and following the hurricane of 1893, which partially destroyed it, it was definitely abandoned.

BARATARIA LIGHTHOUSE, built in 1897, stands beside the fort. The lighthouse keeper and his family are the only inhabitants of the island, and their home is the only building now standing. Prior to 1893 several families lived on Grande Terre, but since the hurricane it has been left to waterfowl, sand-crabs, and the spirits ow the pirates who once roamed its coast and marshes. One lone sugar house chimney towers over the wastes at the eastern end, attesting that they were once fields of sugar cane.

Tour 1C

Houma—Bourg—Montegut—Sea Breeze—Isle Dernière, 50 *m.* Bayou
Terrebonne, by boat.

Trip to the Lapeyrouse Store can be made by automobile, La 56; there boats,
previously arranged for, can be rented for trip to Isle Dernière.
Boats rented at Houma for Isle Dernière trip include meals and bunks for party
of six or less; trip usually lasts 2 or 3 days.

Bayou Terrebonne (Fr., good earth), the principal route between
Houma and the coastal waters for boats engaged in commercial fishing,
traverses flat, fertile lands which gradually merge near the Gulf into
tidal marshes. From Presque Isle to the end of La 56, houses, stores,
and filling stations line the bayou. Boats are constantly going up the
stream with crabs, shrimp, fish, or oysters, and returning with supplies
needed by fishermen at their camps and working bases; in the winter
similar use is made of the bayou by trappers and fur buyers. The route
through Terrebonne Bay crosses shallow water dotted with small, marshy
islands.

Southeastward from HOUMA, 0 *m.* (14 alt., 30,992 pop.) (*see
Tour 1b*), Bayou Terrebonne, its low banks frequently hidden by
bushes, is bordered by fertile land only partially cultivated.

The Intracoastal Waterway (*see Tour 11D*) crosses Bayou Terrebonne at 0.5 *m.*

At 4 *m.* is the junction of Bayou Terrebonne and Bayou Petit Caillou
(*see Tour 1D*).

PRESQUE ISLE, 5.3 *m.* (*see Tour 1D*), is a small settlement
on the west bank of Bayou Terrebonne.

BOURG, 8.2 *m.* (10 alt.), a point of interchange for boat and
highway travel between lower Bayou Lafourche and the bayou district
south of Houma, occupies both sides of a canal connecting Bayou Terrebonne with the Intracoastal Waterway. The natives speak a French
patois and retain many of their original customs. Some of the residents,
like those of other towns and bayou settlements in the region, work in
the coastal oil fields. Boats can be obtained for fishing in near-by lakes
and bayous. Bourg can be reached by highway off La 56. One mile beyond Bourg La 55 goes to Montegut and some distance south.

MONTEGUT, 14.9 *m.* (8 alt.), is similar in most respects to
Bourg.

As the land below Montegut is almost at Gulf level, the waters of
Bayou Terrebonne are practically even with the surrounding wet or

muddy savannas. The view opens on progressively wider stretches of marsh or submerged prairie.

At the LAPEYROUSE STORE, 20.8 *m.*, boats are obtained by advance reservations for a trip to Last Island (Isle Dernière). Fishing parties are accommodated for a fee.

The TEXAS OIL COMPANY BASE, 21 *m.*, directs drilling operations in the oil fields south of this point.

Bayou Terrebonne flows from here to Terrebonne Bay through a region of tidal marsh in which muskrats, water birds, and other forms of aquatic life abound. Trees become rarer, appearing chiefly as dim blots on the horizon, and the air acquires a salty tang.

SEA BREEZE, 33 *m.*, at the mouth of the bayou, consists of little more than a small shrimp-drying platform and sheds in which oysters are shucked and packed in iced containers.

The western side of Terrebonne Bay, sometimes called Cat Island Lake, is very shallow, the greatest depth being about eight feet. The shore is cluttered with small, marshy islands and it is necessary to navigate carefully to avoid going aground in the shoal water.

ISLE DERNIÈRE (Fr., last island), 50 *m.*, is the most westerly of the remnants of a barrier beach that once formed a 50-mile coast line extending from the eastern boundary of Terrebonne Parish. The sea, in breaking through the former shore line, divided it into five principal islands—East Timbalier, Timbalier, Caillou, Wine, and Isle Dernière—fronting shallow bays that were cut into the land.

Isle Dernière is the most exposed of this chain and has the barest and most extensive beach. There is a shingle of small broken shells at many points on the seaward side. A fine surf breaks on the beach, which is approximately 20 miles long. The greatest width of the island is about two miles; much of it is less than half a mile wide.

There are a few camps on Isle Dernière, but no one lives there permanently. It is a continuous waste of dreary looking sand and coarse sprawling herbs, grasses, and low shrubs. One of its most characteristic summer growths is a stout bindweed, or morning-glory vine, which trails everywhere over the drift and low bushes, almost within touch of the surf. Shore birds of all kinds, including plovers and the rare curlew, feed along the beach or make long, swinging flights in flock formation from point to point. Gulls, terns, herons, and pelicans are frequent visitors or regular inhabitants. Interesting examples of marine life, such as rays, turtles, jellyfish, horseshoe crabs, and a variety of shells are found on the beach.

In ante-bellum days Isle Dernière was a fashionable resort visited by many prominent families of south Louisiana. The Trade Wind Hotel accommodated many guests and a number of cottages were built along the seashore.

On August 10, 1856, at the height of the season, a hurricane swept over the island, razing all the buildings. The low, narrow spit of sand was submerged for a time, and wind and water took a heavy toll of lives among the fashionable vacationers. More than 200 perished. The catastrophe forms the theme of Lafcadio Hearn's *Chita* (1889).

The Reverend R. S. McAllister of Thibodaux, one of the survivors of the hurricane, graphically described the storm in an article written for the *Southwestern Presbyterian,* April 9, 1891:

> About 3 o'clock in the afternoon the wind reached its climax. For many days it had been, with imperceptible accretions, gathering power; and now it seemed all the aerial currents in creation had been turned upon us, one would not think that the blast could have been stronger. Fiery lightning almost constantly illumined the heavens and deafening thunders, peal upon peal, shook our circumscribed islet to its center. . . .
> By this time the air was so filled with the flying compound of sand and rain that we could not face it, nor could we clearly see anything many yards distant. . . . The wind, coming from several directions, had driven the waters over our diminutive tract. The Gulf upon one side and the bay upon the other, were advancing upon us. Higher and higher the two seas were rising. . . .

Their house having been shattered by the wind, the Reverend McAllister and his party made their way to an old whirligig nearby. Here the desperate group clung throughout the night.

Though the water receded and they were able to find shelter on dry land, rescue ships were unable to reach them for days because of the high seas. Suffering from exposure and hunger, they were reminded constantly of the horror they had survived by the corpses and debris strewn about the island.

> The jewelled and lily hand of a woman was seen protruding from the sand, and pointing toward heaven; farther, peered out from the ground, as if looking up to us, the regular features of a beautiful girl who had, no doubt but a few hours before, blushed at the praise of her own loveliness, and again, the dead bodies of husband and wife, so relatively placed as to show that constant until death did them part. . . . And, more affecting still, there was the form of a sweet babe even yet embraced by the stiff and bloodless arms of a mother. . . .
> There were about one hundred houses on the island; not one was left, nay, not a sill nor sleeper, not any part of their foundations to indicate that buildings had once been there.

Tour 1D

Houma—Chauvin—Cocodrie; 30.7 *m.,* La 56, La 24.

Groping southward from Houma like the fingers of a misshapen hand, five bayous reach through fertile canefields and vegetable gardens to a remote wilderness of tidal marshes, the sole inhabitants and frequenters of which are Acadian or Cajun trappers and fishermen and their usually large families, with, occasionally, a family of Ouma Indian descent.

La 56 swings southeast from US 90 (*see Tour 1b*) at HOUMA, 0 *m.* (14 alt., 6,531 pop.) (*see Tour 1b*), along the west bank of Bayou Terrebonne (*see Tour 1C*).

PRESQUE ISLE (Fr., peninsula), 5.3 *m.*, is at a junction of La 56 and La 24; straight ahead on unmarked La 24, which runs along the west bank of Bayou Petit Caillou (Fr., little pebble). For several miles there are small vegetable farms and occasional fields of sugar cane.

ST. JOSEPH'S CHURCH, 14.7 *m.*, is a white frame building with a bell tower and short steeple, where the Blessing of the Shrimp Fleet, a ceremony brought from France a century and a half ago, takes place annually. Although observed for many years in Louisiana, it was for some time forgotten, but revived about 1922. The event takes place in early August, and launches the shrimping season. The celebration is a gala occasion, with the Archbishop of New Orleans officiating. More than 200 freshly painted and polished fishing boats are lined up along the bayou, their crews aboard in holiday attire, to receive the blessing.

The fleets' shrimping and fishing grounds include Lake Barré, Lake Pelto, and the open Gulf itself. Working in groups of a dozen or so, luggers, or trawlers, drag conical nets through the water, with faster ice boats standing by to rush the daily catch to canning factories or to the New Orleans market. Some shrimpers—usually those working independently without boats powerful enough to trawl—use old-fashioned seines in shallow water.

CHAUVIN, 16.6 *m.*, serves a community that stretches about 15 miles along the bayou. At this point boats or luggers can be rented with special rates for groups, and the rest of the trip made by water, if desired.

The INDIAN RIDGE CANNERY at 20.1 *m.*, is one of the pioneers in the Louisiana shrimp-canning industry (*see Tour 1b*).

Shrimp-drying platforms (*see Tour 11D*), with their cluster of bayou-side dwellings, appear at frequent intervals along the road.

South of BOUDREAUX CANAL, 20.3 *m.*, the bayou is bordered with low bushes, palmetto, and sedge. In the summer a wild mallow with delicate pink blossoms grows abundantly along the road.

The lives of the bayou people change little from year to year. Most of them speak a French patois, and many do not understand English. Housekeeping is a simple affair, particularly among the less affluent. The men of the neighborhood lend each other a friendly hand, or *coup de main,* in the building of crude huts, often thatched with palmetto, and the women aid each other in making homemade mattresses of Spanish moss. With hut and bed provided, about all else required by these people, who spend much of their lives out-of-doors, are a stove and a few cooking vessels. While few luxuries are known, no one goes hungry, with shrimp and fish abundantly at hand. A large portion of each family's income goes into boats—skiffs pridefully moored to the housefront, or, the goal of every shrimper, a lugger of his own. Storms, wrecking flimsy homes and boats, as well as taking life, are the most dreaded of catastrophes. To ward off this evil, and lesser ones as well, blessed candles and palm leaves are burned frequently before the Virgin's statue guarding each home. As a further precaution, many wear medals around their necks. This section of Louisiana is depicted in Thad St. Martin's *Madame Toussaint's Wedding Day* (1936).

The marshes throughout this region are the home of the muskrat, the trapping of which is an important Louisiana industry (*see Commerce, Industry, and Labor*). During the trapping season the trappers set unbaited traps near muskrat houses in runs, or paths, extending through half-submerged reeds. The traps are set below the surface of the water, so that the muskrat is drowned. On account of the climate the Louisiana trapper must cover his trap line regularly, usually once a day, for he cannot depend, like the northern trapper, on his catch freezing. After the muskrat is caught the trapper skins the carcass and places the hide, fur inside, on a stretching board or wire frame. It is then run through an ordinary clotheswringer to squeeze off clinging fat, and placed in the sun to dry for three or four days. The hide is then removed and packed in a burlap sack to be sent to a fur broker; frequently local fur buyers visit the trappers' camps and buy the pelts on the spot.

ROBINSON'S CANAL, 24.4 *m.*, is a popular fishing resort (*camps, boats*). Bayou and canal fishing are immediately at hand, with lake fishing one-half mile and Gulf fishing five miles away.

South of Robinson's Canal habitations thin out; open prairies serve as grazing land, and the majority of the houses are built on stilts.

The road crosses Rabbit Bayou at 28.9 *m.* At the fishing camp boats, bait, and camps are available at reasonable rates.

COCODRIE, 30.7 *m.*, is a fishing camp (*night lodgings, boats, guides*). It is near the Houma Navigation Canal, which goes into Terrebonne Bay. Visitors shout across the bayou for a skiff from the opposite side. (*Boats obtainable here in advance for trip to Isle Dernière; see Tour 1C.*)

Tour 1E

Baldwin—Charenton—Chitimacha Indian Reservation—Grand Lake; 4.1 *m.*, La 87.

Accommodations at Grand Lake during summer.

This route runs northward from Baldwin through fields of sugar cane and small vegetable farms to the Chitimacha Indian Reservation and a popular bathing and fishing resort on Grand Lake.

La 87 branches north from US 90 (*see Tour 1b*) at BALDWIN, 0 *m.* (15 alt., 2,117 pop. 1970), paralleling a curve of Bayou Teche.

CHARENTON, 3.7 *m.* (16 alt.), is a sugar cane and cotton plantation settlement in a bend of Bayou Teche. The CHURCH OF THE IMMACULATE CONCEPTION (Roman Catholic), a steepled, white frame building nearly a century old, is attended not only by white and Negro parishoners, but by Indians, who sit in pews reserved for them at the rear.

On the northern edge of the village is the CHITIMACHA INDIAN RESERVATION, established by the Federal Government in 1935, after more than 20 years of negotiation. About 60 Chitimacha (*see First Americans*) live on the 265-acre tract, the only Indian reservation in Louisiana. There are perhaps 100 other Chitimacha scattered over Louisiana and Texas whose names are retained on the tribal register. Possession of at least one-quarter Indian blood is required for reservation privileges. The Indians receive regular government payments and have been allotted small farms on which they raise corn, cane, and sweet potatoes. The homes are small, unpainted, and simply furnished, but some of the families own automobiles, trucks, and radios. A school is maintained on the grounds. In addition to the usual elementary subjects the children are taught farm management, and various handicrafts, such as Chitimacha basketry.

Among the Chitimacha marriage with Negroes is forbidden, offenders being ostracized and their names permanently removed from the tribal register. On the other hand, the tribe does not object to intermarriage with Caucasians. A white woman who married the son of the "medicine woman" and adopted the customs of the tribe, was taught the lore of medicinal herbs, so that she could succeed her mother-in-law as medicine woman, according to long-established custom. Interfamily marriages are approved, for it is believed that through them the Chitimacha strain can best be perpetuated.

Most of the reservationists speak English fairly well, though the older Indians are still more at ease in French. Few retain any considerable knowledge of their own tongue. Their dress is similar to that of other Americans within their economic class. Much tribal lore has been preserved, and the women are skilled basket makers.

A variety of cane called "piya" (*Arundinaria gigantea*) is used in making the baskets. It is split in lengthwise strips, the whole length being used for larger baskets but merely the length of a joint for smaller ones. The strips are left for eight days in the sun and dew, to render them pliable and produce a certain coloring. Natural colors predominate, and such dyes as are used are obtained by methods in use among the Chitimacha for centuries. Black, for instance, is obtained from the black walnut; red, by a process of soaking the cane in lime water, after which it is boiled with a root called *powàác* (deers' ears) and red willow bark. Some of the baskets are woven double and will hold water. Typical designs are "little trout," "worm tracks," "alligator entrails," "big blackbirds' eyes," "muscadine rind," and "rattlesnake."

There is a fine collection of Chitimacha basketry in the Louisiana

State Museum in New Orleans. Probably the most interesting specimen of Chitimacha work is a large mat more than a century old, now in the Museum of the American Indian in New York City. Before it was allowed to go to the museum, Mrs. Christine Paul, widow of a chief, made a duplicate on a smaller scale. In this mat a regular basket weave was employed, featuring the *mokc-nakc* (little trout) design. Baskets can be purchased on the reservation.

Many of the Chitimacha myths and legends have been preserved. Their creation myth attributes the origin of the earth of crayfish sent to the bottom of the primordial sea by the Great Spirit, *Thoume Kene Kimpe Cacounche,* to transport ground to the surface. To inhabit the land provided by the crayfish, the Great Spirit created men, whom he called "Chitimachas." Blessed with all good things, these god-children soon became effeminate and suffered all manner of misfortunes. Their salvation lay in tobacco, which they chewed and found soothing, and in women, who eased their toil. Fire and the bow and arrow were additional benefits bestowed on them.

Within the boundaries of their small world there were four sacred trees, located respectively at the mouth of the Mississippi, somewhere east on the coast, at the entrance of Vermilion Bay, and at Grand Lake. The cypress at Grand Lake was well known to both Indians and whites. Thunderstorms and long periods of rainy weather occurred whenever anyone splashed water on it. At several places in the Chitimacha territory there were fathomless "blue holes," into which, at certain times of the year, objects disappeared with a rushing sound. One of these holes is said to be in the vicinity of Plaquemine.

Imaginary and real animals also figure in their myths. According to one legend a monster having no nose once came out of the water and began a mad rampage, tearing up wigwams and killing Indians. A little yellow bird supposedly had the power to converse with the Indians and foretell the weather. Bears were believed to be related to human beings, and the eagle was regarded as a sacred bird.

As punishment for killing and eating a sacred white deer, a group of Chitimacha were once propelled by some invisible force out into Grand Lake, disappearing beneath the waters, never to be seen again. Some years later a canoe bearing two Indian youths capsized in the lake, and the occupants, just as they reached the point of exhaustion, suddenly felt something solid beneath them and found that they were resting safely on submerged wigwams. Righting their canoe, they marked the place with stakes and hastened home to tell of their miraculous escape. The Indians rushed to the shore and beheld two bright lights above the stakes. Ever afterward it was believed that the submerged wigwams belonged to the lost Indians. Even today there are Indians who claim to have seen dancing lights on Grand Lake.

Right from Charenton across Bayou Teche on Indian Bend, a graveled road, to CHARENTON BEACH, 4.1 *m.,* a popular bathing resort on GRAND LAKE, once called Chitimacha Lake. On the beach are a restaurant and dancing pavilion, and tourist cabins.

Twelve miles long and eight miles wide, Grand Lake is the largest lake in the Atchafalaya Basin. At intervals along its shell-lined shore are cone-shaped shell mounds, each with a large oak growing from the crest. These kitchen middens, the refuse heaps of ancient Chitimacha feasts, were built up through the years as the aborigines discarded sea food shells and bones.

((◈

Tour 1F

Sulphur—Hackberry—Cameron—Grand Chênière; 73 *m.*, La 27, La 82. Junction with Interstate 10.

Small hotels at Cameron, Creole, and Grand Chênière.

La 27, for a few miles south of Sulphur, passes through well-ordered farm lands, which merge beyond Hackberry into wide expanses of marshy meadow and open range, over which a great number of cattle and wild Creole ponies graze. Occasional *chênières* (oak-covered ridges) relieve the monotonous flatness. Paralleling the coast, numerous ridges stand out as islands in the surrounding marshland. The route here traverses excellent hunting grounds.

La 27 branches south from US 90 at SULPHUR, 0 *m.* (16 alt., 13,551 pop. 1970; 11,429, 1960, inc. 18%). Two miles south of Sulphur it has a junction with Interstate 10.

Small clusters of live oaks mark the sites of present or former homes. Many of these trees are said to have been planted in compliance with regulations under which settlers took up their claims.

La 27 crosses Bayou Choupique (Ind., mudfish) 10.5 *m.*, named for the choupique (*see Natural Resources, Flora and Fauna*). Although generally considered inedible, the choupique is eaten by some of the natives. When cooked in the same manner as other fish, its meat becomes flaky and tastes something like wet cotton. In preparing the fish it is usually soaked overnight in vinegar and olive oil to give it more substance; when smoked, it is said to be not inferior to other smoked fish.

At PORT ELLENDER, 13 *m.*, a State-operated ferry (*free; 24-hr. 20-min. service*) crosses the Intracoastal Waterway (*see Tour 11D*).

HACKBERRY, 18.2 *m.* (5 alt.), is the trade center for the near-by EAST and WEST HACKBERRY OIL FIELDS.

School funds in Cameron Parish are derived from the severance tax on oil, which is sufficient for school purposes under the regular tax program.

La 27 runs parallel with Calcasieu Lake, a saline lake 90 sq. m. in area.

South of Hackberry, La 27 traverses an unbounded expanse of marshy flats, or prairies, varied only by shrubby thickets and *chênières* visible in the distance. Almost 250,000 acres of Cameron marshes, flats, and Gulf beaches have been set aside by the State and Federal Governments as preserves for the protection of ducks, geese, and other game. Here is the SABINE REFUGE, extending west to Sabine Lake.

Canals dug in the construction of the fill for the roadbed line the highway. Tide water brings crabs into the canals, and in the warmer months many crabbers are seen along the road. Some come for sport, some for food, and others to catch crabs for market. Crabbing is a popular diversion among Louisiana folk and all-day crabbing parties are enjoyed by whole families.

At 38.2 *m.* La 27 reaches the Gulf of Mexico and makes a sharp turn to the east at HOLLY BEACH. The shore line is mostly marshy and muddy, with shell and gray sand beaches at some points. Sea pinks, evening primroses, and other wild flowers dot the sands in summer. In the marshy meadows bordering the road to the left are herds of cattle standing knee deep in the boggy prairie, munching the succulent grasses. Stock in this section remain fat the year round because of the excellent pasture and mild winters. Trucks are used to transport the cattle to market. Much of the wealth of Cameron Parish comes from the sale of beef cattle each spring. Creole ponies, small wild horses common in southwest Louisiana, are sometimes seen among the cattle.

La 27 joins east-west La 82. Westward 12 *m.* from Holly Beach it reaches Johnson's Bayou, a fishing point on Hamilton Lake, outlet for Old North Bayou. Then 15 *m.* west it crosses a toll bridge over Sabine Pass to Texas. Eastward La 82 and La 27 merge.

La 27 crosses Calcasieu Pass at 47.1 *m.* on a State-operated ferry (*free; round trip every half-hour between 5 a.m. and 8 p.m., every hour between 8 p.m. and 5 a.m.*) to CAMERON, 47.4 *m.* (6 alt., 100 pop.), seat of Cameron Parish. In the late spring, early summer, and fall, shrimp trawlers, of which there are about 50 operating out of Cameron, come up Calcasieu Pass with loads for the canning factories. In winter trappers leave the town to plod through the marshes or paddle along the bayous in their pirogues. A variety of birds are present in unusual numbers in the salt meadows and bushy marshes that surround Cameron, and ducks, geese, herons, curlews, snipe, and large plovers are often in sight of the village.

At Cameron La 27 becomes identified as La 82.

The settlements along the coast of Cameron Parish are situated on *chênières,* oak-covered ridges lying like oases slightly above the level of the surrounding marshes and coastal waters. From the clusters of low houses, small live oaks, and patches of cultivated ground, the view is unbroken across the waste that stretches dimly to the Gulf shores on the south and to the prairies on the north.

Rough comfort and a simple life are characteristic of the *chênière* communities. Most of the inhabitants in these isolated towns make their living by trapping, hunting, cattle raising, fishing, and raising vegetables, poultry, and a few fruits, principally figs and oranges, for local consumption.

Although settlement of this section began about 1840, changes have been a few and contacts with the rest of the world continue to be difficult. Until the building of the road from Sulphur to Cameron in 1932, the settlements could be reached only by boat, down either the Mermentau or Calcasieu Rivers. There is no railroad in Cameron Parish, and only a few miles of pavement. Only a few doctors administer to the ills of a people whom one physician has described as being "distressingly healthy." Few criminal cases come before the district court. The peacefulness and neighborliness of the parish is proverbial. The old jail at Cameron was often empty and it is even said that one sheriff used it to store his corn. The principal social diversion is the *fais-dodo* on Saturday nights.

CREOLE, 62 *m.* (5 alt.), is one of the oldest settlements in the parish. The residents are engaged in trapping and small farming.

At Creole is the junction of La 82 and La 27 ; continue on La 82.

OAK GROVE, 64.1 *m.,* is a small settlement.

Right from Oak Grove on the Creole Canal (*boats and guides available at Oak Grove or Creole*) and across the mouth of Mermentau River to HACK-BERRY BEACH, 4 *m.,* a favorite resort of wild geese.

La 82 crosses Mermentau River, 72.1 *m.,* on a State-operated ferry (*free; 24-hour call service*) to GRAND CHÊNIÈRE, 73 *m.* (10 alt.). The situation of this settlement is a striking one. The ridge stands out clearly beside Mermentau River, which flows between marshy flats on the north and this higher tract on the south. Small, simple homes stand among the live oaks, yaupons, and orange trees. Toward the Gulf stretches a level expanse of marshland.

Grand Chênière is a popular point for hunting parties. Accommodations are principally in the homes of the residents. Geese, ducks, rails, and snipe are abundant, and rabbits (large water hares) are so numerous and tame that they offer little temptation to sportsmanlike hunters. Before the sale of game was prohibited, market hunters came here in large numbers every winter and shipped out thousands of wildfowl.

About 10 miles east of Grand Chênière is the ROCKEFELLER WILDLIFE REFUGE. The Refuge is administered by the Louisiana Wild Life & Fisheries Commission. This immense area consists of several lakes, many acres of marshland, apparatus for maintaining water levels, and levees, canals and roads. Some areas are licensed for oil-well drilling and in order to float drilling equipment to the sites canals are dug 60 to 80 ft. wide and 8 ft. deep. When feasible roads are built. Marshes are kept to a controlled water level and areas are planted with grasses and vegetation to nourish wildfowl. Sports fishing is permitted March to October and a visitor's permit is provided free. This is a wintering area for ducks and geese and the last remaining stronghold of the alligator. The demand for alligator products has brought a decline in alligators, which are safe from hunters only in refuges. The killing of alligators has been prohibited in Louisiana since 1963. The Rockefeller Refuge maintains patrols that work the year around to guard the huge numbers of ducks and geese, as well as alligators and other wildlife.

At 106 *m.* La 82 reaches PECAN ISLAND (town) a few miles south of White Lake, a freshwater lake covering 83 sq. m. in Vermilion Parish. La 82 turns north, crosses the Intercoastal Waterway and becomes La 35, with junction with La 14 at KAPLAN.

Tour 2

New Iberia—Abbeville—Kaplan—Gueydan—Lake Arthur—Jennings; 69.2 *m.,* La 14, La 13.

Concrete-paved road.
S. P. R.R. parallels route between New Iberia and Gueydan.
Accommodations at New Iberia, Lake Arthur, and Jennings.

This route extends through south Louisiana, from the heart of the Teche country to the ancient plains of the Attakapa. Although for its entire length it lies less than 20 feet above sea level, it presents panoramas of sugar cane plantations, small fruit and vegetable farms, oil fields, bayous, lakes and marshes, cattle ranges, and—in spring or summer—half-submerged, jade green acres of growing rice.

La 14, branching west from US 90 at NEW IBERIA, 0 *m.* (19 alt.), follows the Lafitte Cut-Off, a trail used by the pirate-smuggler in bringing in contraband from vessels anchored in Vermilion Bay and White Lake.

This country was settled between 1760 and 1790 by Acadian refugees. The language of those living in more remote districts is a French-English patois all but impossible for the stranger to understand. Along the road walks an occasional barefoot Cajun, clothed in faded blue overalls and wearing a frayed palmetto hat, who nonchalantly sings:

J'ai travaillé pour les Rousseaux,	I have worked for the Rousseaus,
J'ai travaillé pour les haricots,	I have worked for the beans,
Pas d'chaussons, pas d'souliers,	Without socks, without shoes,
Pas d'argent pour m'en acheter,	Without money to buy any,
Trop catin pour m'en gagner,	Too lazy to earn any,
Le vrai moyen pour aller nu pieds.	The sure way to go barefoot.

Homes in this section are usually small frame dwellings with batten shutters instead of glass panes, outside chimneys of mud and moss adobe, and stairways rising diagonally across the porch to the *grenier,* or attic bedroom, under the low roof. In and near towns, houses are more pretentious, with red roofs—a mark of affluence. Cleanliness is an outstanding characteristic of the Acadian housewife. Though the furnishings may be modest or even poor, her home fairly shines; linens are clean, and daily scouring of floors bleaches them almost white.

In south Louisiana people often refer to Walter Coquille—self-styled Mayor of Bayou Pom-Pom (a purely imaginary municipality)—who entertained with his combination of Cajun dialect and native wit. Whenever a major political campaign looms in Louisiana "Mayor" Coquille would announce his candidacy for re-election, and New Orleans and country newspapers would publish columns in which he discussed political as well as other issues and told anecdotes, with Cajun life as the background. Typical of the anecdotes is the one about two Cajuns fishing for crabs in a pirogue:

Wat fo' you scratchin' under your shirt, ma fren, you go *une puce* (a flea)? *Non, non!* I got *un pau* (a louse)! You tink I'm a dog, me?

At 2.3 *m.* is the junction with La 329 (*see Tour 2A*).

At 9.5 *m.* is the junction with La 65 (*see Tour 2B*).

DELCAMBRE, 11.9 *m.* (12 alt., 1,975 pop. 1970) and ERATH, 14.6 *m.* (13 alt., 2,024 pop. 1970) are typical Acadian country towns. Delcambre has the unique situation of being located in two parishes, Iberia and Vermilion. One advantage is that its public library, a branch of the Vermilion Parish Library, gets support from both Iberia and Vermilion Parishes. Erath has a branch of the Vermilion Parish Library at Abbeville.

Many Acadian housewives spin their own yarn and weave fabrics for use in the home. It is generally of white or yellow cotton (nankeen), but may be of wool or a cotton-wool mixture. Though some of the fabrics are dyed in bright colors, the more typical are those ranging through shades of cream to dark brown in which white has been effectively blended. Cajun homespun is noted for its beauty and durability. The latter quality probably inspired the following song, sung by Acadian girls at their looms:

Dans les bons vieux temps,	In the good old times,
Nous dit souvent ma grand'mère,	My grandmother has often told us,
Dans les bons vieux temps,	In the good old times,
Les Jupone duraient cent ans.	Petticoats lasted a hundred years.

ABBEVILLE, 20.9 _m._ (20 alt., 10,996 pop. 1970), _see Abbeville._ Abbeville is at the junction with La 82 and US 167.

West of Abbeville are large rice fields. This region is particularly suited to rice culture (_see Tour 1c_), the level fields permitting an even depth in the water with which the young rice plants are flooded.

Some buggies and wagons have survived the automobile and motor truck in this section, and may still be met along the road. An occasional herd of cattle passes, driven by Cajun cowboys riding small ponies and using long bull whips. Many of the cow ponies are Louisiana wild horses that have been captured and broken. These small and hardy ponies, with their flashing eyes, long manes and tails, and fuzzy vari-colored coats are known by a variety of names: Creole pony (most common), Cajun pony, Creole tackey, prairie pony, and coco pony (they feed on the wild coco grass). Thousands of these wild horses have roamed the more remote sections of southwest Louisiana for the past 200 years. Being of little value, they have been left largely alone, and the hardiness of the breed and plenty of wild grass have enabled them to sustain themselves through generation after generation. In the old days wild ponies brought $2 a head, and even now, after having been caught and broken, they bring only about $10 as farm horses or $25 for those fit for the saddle.

KENNY'S COULÉE (Fr., rivulet), 22.6 _m.,_ is a narrow and tranquil branch bayou, in places surprisingly deep. Water oaks and willows arch above it, and a luxuriant growth of native iris, trumpet vines, and water hyacinths line its banks.

The ABBEVILLE COUNTRY CLUB is at 22.7 _m._

In KAPLAN, 30.6 _m._ (14 alt., 5,540 pop. 1970), is the HOLY ROSARY CHURCH (Roman Catholic), a white frame building with a square tower; the outside grotto is made of concrete rubble. In the center of town is the Kaplan Rice Mill. Kaplan and Gueydan have branches of the Vermilion Parish Library of Abbeville. Kaplan is said to be the only place in Louisiana that observes the French Bastille Day, July 14.

At 32.1 _m._ is the junction with La 13.

GUEYDAN, 45.5 _m._ (9 alt., 1,984 pop. 1970), was founded about the end of the last century, and named for Pierre Gueydan, a stock raiser who owned a 32,000-acre tract called Gueydan's Pasture. At Gueydan is the Republic Rice Mill and junction with La 91.

LAKE ARTHUR, 58.5 _m._ (8 alt., 3,581 pop. 1970), is on the northern edge of the lake of the same name, in reality a widening of Mermentau River. Lake Arthur, settled largely by people of French descent from the older sections of Louisiana, was of some importance as early as 1890, when its first newspaper, the Lake Arthur _Herald,_ was published. A long municipal pier extends into the lake, and a park stretches along the lake shore. Large moss-draped live oaks lend beauty to the town.

Lake Arthur is a popular starting point for hunting and fishing in Cameron Parish, to the south, where several camps offer accommodations at reasonable rates. Boats, guides, and equipment are obtainable along the lake front. Neighboring waters abound with fish, especially cat, which grow to enormous size.

Southwest from Lake Arthur by a 5-hour boat trip (*private boats for hunting and fishing parties chartered*) to GRAND CHÊNIÈRE (*see Tour 1F*), 40 *m.* This is a popular trip during the hunting season and an interesting one at any time. The regular boat goes down the Mermentau River, through Grand Lake. Cypress-lined shores, marshy flats, and shifting water views characterize the scenery, which has often a weird and compelling beauty.

North of Lake Arthur La 26 passes through large rice fields, where many sheep and cattle are seen in the rice stubble during the fall and winter. Stacks of rice straw are left in the fields and cattle may be seen reaching far up on them, munching the straw; sometimes an animal is half buried in the straw, eating its way into the stack.

As the highway continues north, the country becomes slightly higher and poultry farms and oil derricks are occasionally seen.

JENNINGS, 69.2 *m.* (25 alt., 11,783 pop.) (*see Tour 1c*), is at the junction with US 90 and 2 *m.* from Interstate 10.

❦❦❦❦❦❦❦❦❦❦❦❦❦❦❦❦❦❦❦❦❦❦❦❦❦❦❦❦❦

Tour 2A

Junction with La 14—Avery Island; 5.1 *m.,* La 329.

Admission fee to Avery Island and Jungle Gardens; special rates for large parties.

The Avery Island route runs through patches of rice and sugar cane and across water-splotched pastures and unreclaimed prairie lands. The high contours of the "island" are visible from the beginning of the route. This is the largest and most striking of the "Five Islands" that rise above the marshes and savannas of this region. Like the others, it overlies a coastal salt dome.

La 329 branches south from La 14, 0 *m.,* at a point 2.3 miles southwest of New Iberia, and at 3.9 *m.* turns L.

A tollgate at 5.1 *m.* marks the entrance to AVERY ISLAND (152 alt.). Nearly round in shape and with an approximate diameter of two miles, Avery Island is completely surrounded by sea marsh and swampy thickets. At the center is a cluster of small hills, comprising 1,884 acres of high land that slopes off gradually into the surrounding fringe of marsh. There are areas of virgin woodland on the island where bear and deer are still found; alligators, raccoons, muskrats, and opossums abound in the marshes and wooded areas. Every type of coastal vegetation is to be seen: floating aquatic plants in the small lagoons; mallows, cattails, bulrushes, buttonbush, willow, and wax myrtle in the marshes and half-wooded sloughs; and live oak, cypress, swamp maple, and various other trees where the soil is suitable.

For many years the island was known as Petite Anse (Fr., little cove) because of the bayou that skirts its western edge. Early writers gave it various other names, among which were Thomas Island, Marsh's Island, and Salt Island.

Salt is found some 15 to 20 feet below the island's surface and continues to an explored depth of more than a mile. Its excavation has brought to light rare animal and human relics, from which the prehistoric life of the island can be partially reconstructed. The earth here is stratified, with six to eight layers of earth crust, each representing a different period of history. At a depth of eight to ten feet the remains of extinct species, such as the mastodon, sloth, and early horse, have been found. In strata several feet deeper bits of woven matting, basketwork, pottery, etc., indicate that man existed on the island prior to these mammals. The existence of the salt springs and perhaps of the rock salt was evidently known to the aborigines, for basketry and piles of ashes were discovered in the immediate vicinity of the salt. The earliest of the material excavated was sent to the Smithsonian Institution about 1868. Both that institution and Tulane University now have collections from Avery Island.

According to John Hays, who settled on the island in 1791, there were no Indians living on it at that time, nor could any be induced to go near it because of some legendary catastrophe. John Hays rediscovered the salt springs.

Toward the close of the eighteenth century John C. Marsh, a settler from New Jersey, acquired Avery Island as a grant from the Spanish Government and established large sugar cane plantations on it. While Marsh produced salt from the springs for the use of the American army in the War of 1812, he evidently attached little importance to their development.

In 1862 rock salt was discovered at the bottom of a salt well by J. M. Avery and the island immediately assumed great importance. Two companies of infantry and a section of artillery stood guard while quantities of salt were quarried for the Confederate Army. In 1862, when the Federals sent a gunboat up the Petite Anse to bombard the mine, the vessel became entangled in the marsh some distance away and was powerless to make the attack. The salt works, however, were completely destroyed during General Nathaniel Banks' invasion of the Teche country in 1863.

Through the years the island has continued in the possession of John Marsh's descendants, being owned by various members of the Avery and McIlhenny families.

Edward Avery McIlhenny became well known for his work in connection with the establishment of Louisiana's wildlife refuges. Mc-

Ilhenny was also a writer of plantation and wildlife stories, perhaps the best known of his books being *Bird City*.

PROSPECT HILL, rising 196 feet above sea level, is the highest on the island. From the summit one can see a green expanse spreading away on every side, made up of hills and valleys, ravines, ponds, woodlands, open fields, and pastures. The developed area is mostly toward the northeast, with the larger homes occupying the high ground; workmen's cottages, hothouses, shops, and schools cluster on each side of the main road running from the entrance gate back to the salt mine on the southern edge of the island. To the east and southeast is an extensive cypress swamp, and in the distant south, Vermilion Bay. In the pasture lands lying between the bay and the higher portions of the island, herds of blooded cattle graze, including the Brahma, sacred cow of India, distinguished by the hump on its back.

JUNGLE GARDENS consist of more than 200 landscaped acres around the home of the late Edward Avery McIlhenny, on Mayward Hill, and extending down broad slopes into near-by lowlands. While there are miles of gravel roads through the gardens, they may be best viewed by walking along the winding footpaths. Native oak, redbud or Judas tree, magnolia, and dogwood grow side by side with plants brought by the island's owner from the four corners of the earth. Toward the front of Jungle Gardens, covering about 14 acres, is an oak grove. Beyond the grove lie the formal gardens.

There is a wide variety of palms, ferns, and evergreens, but perhaps the most interesting is the bamboo, which ranges from lacy, fernlike varieties to large Chinese timber cane. On one slope of Mayward Hill is a dense growth of giant bamboo, 60 feet in height. Flowers bloom everywhere at all times of the year. Bright-winged birds flit from tree to tree, Louisiana herons sun themselves on the edges of pools, and egrets spread their white wings above. Camellias, 10,000 of them, white or delicately tinted, are at their best about the middle of January. In early March, all shades and varieties of azaleas flame beneath the canopies of branching oaks. Wistaria is planted in arches, with colors shading from white through soft tones of pink and lavender to purple. In the iris beds bloom all types of the Louisiana variety and imported specimens from foreign countries. Lilies and roses bloom next and are in turn followed in the fall months by acres of chrysanthemums.

Sunken gardens and shadow pools have been constructed at numerous points. The Temple Garden is a mirror lagoon which centers around a Chinese Temple containing a statue of Buddha. Chinese lotus grows on the surface of the lagoon. In the Sunken Fern Garden, there are more than 80 varieties of fern. Beyond the Fern Garden is the Cactus Pit.

A podocarpus tree, a nearly extinct genus from whose fossilized wood has come most of the world's present supply of coal, also grows in Jungle Gardens. Near by are soap trees from India, papyrus from the Nile, papayas from the tropics, the lichee nut and finger banana from China, and the manihot, or rubber plant, from Brazil. Growing in the hothouses are exotic orchids and japonicas, dwarf wistaria from

Japan, and large red daisies from the Mountain of the Moon in equatorial Africa. Many experiments with narcotic plants have been conducted in Jungle Gardens for the U. S. Department of Agriculture.

BIRD CITY, around Willow Pond in the southeast corner of Jungle Gardens, is best viewed from the amphitheatre on the hill immediately above.

The nucleus of Bird City was McIlhenny's egret colony established in 1893. Avery Island had been the last haunt of the egret, or snowy heron, which was steadily being exterminated by plume hunters. Returning after an absence of some time, McIlhenny found them extinct even there. Going into the swamps with two young Negroes, he and his party waded in water for days, finally finding seven young birds, with which he returned and began his experiments. By 1914 the egrets had increased to more than 20,000 and today there are more than 125,000, the largest egret colony in the United States. Around the edges of Willow Pond, made of bamboo and perched on stilts, are "apartments" where the birds nest. Other birds have joined the colony —the small blue heron, summer tanager, blue jay, mocking bird, wren, thrush, and many varieties of wild duck and geese.

While some egrets remain at Avery Island throughout the year, they are most numerous in spring and early summer. Many young birds travel north during June, July, and August. In the mid-fall they reappear, but with the coming of decidedly cold weather most of them leave for the tropics, not to be seen again until the following spring.

These birds are particularly beautiful at sundown, as they seek their nests. One moment the sky is white with their wings, the next they have dropped like plummets to the low bushes and reeds around the pond.

The McILHENNY TABASCO FACTORY (*visitors admitted*) is immediately to the left of Willow Pond on the opposite side of the road. Here is packed the hot pepper sauce known as Tabasco, an exclusive product of the McIlhenny Company. The sauce was so named because the original pepper seeds were brought from Tabasco, Mexico, by a United States soldier returning from the Mexican War and presented to a member of the McIlhenny family, who experimented with the pepper on Avery Island and eventually evolved a sauce which was very well liked by his family and friends. Tabasco sauce was put on the market in 1868. In 1968 the factory observed its centennial. It operates from 7 to 5 Monday to Friday and Saturday mornings. The sauce is aged in 50-gallon oaken barrels for more than 3 years. Guides are available.

Seven hundred acres on Avery Island are sown in Tabasco pepper, and in late years the factory has met a growing demand by obtaining additional large quantities from the pepper fields of Cypress Island, in St. Martin Parish.

AVERY ISLAND SALT MINE (*visitors admitted only during periods of light operation*) is at the end of the main road. It is operated by the International Salt Company, under lease from the McIlhenny and

Avery families. After the destruction of the salt works in 1863 by Federal Forces, the mine lay idle until 1867, when mining operations began anew. In 1899 it was found expedient to tunnel at a depth of 518 feet, and since then that level has been maintained, the same shaft remaining in use. Annual production from the mine is about 100,000 tons. It has been ascertained by test borings that salt extends for 2,200 feet below the surface. In general features of operation and appearance, the mine is similar to other Louisiana salt mines.

The BLUE POND, occupying a sinkhole of the old mine that supplied the Confederate army with salt, is a deep circular pond of intense blue water (due to the salt bottom), surrounded on three sides by sloping banks and on the fourth by a steep bluff. Gum, oak, and myrtle cluster thickly along the banks.

Oil has been found on the island and the Humble Oil & Refining Co. has made public announcement that its operations do not harm the bird sanctuaries nor mar the vistas.

❧❧❧❧❧❧❧❧❧❧❧❧❧❧❧❧❧❧❧❧❧❧❧❧❧❧❧

Tour 2B

Junction with La 14—Jefferson Island 1.8 *m.*, La 675.

La 675, branching northwest from La 14 (*see Tour 2*), 0 *m.*, at a point 9.5 miles west of New Iberia, crosses the most westerly and northerly of Louisiana's Five Islands, which are really not islands in the conventional sense. Geologists call them salt domes and their origin has caused much speculation (*see Geology and Paleontology*).

JEFFERSON ISLAND, 1.8 *m.*, rises on the south from a level prairie, and is bordered on the north by Lake Peigneur. The 1,200-acre island has been known successively as Côte Carlin and Miller's Island, for early owners, Orange Island because of a magnificent grove of orange trees, and finally Jefferson Island, in honor of the noted actor, Joseph Jefferson, who owned it for many years.

Joseph Jefferson (1829–1905) bought the island in the early 1870's and built a comfortable residence which he named "Bob Acres" in honor of his favorite role. Between stage appearances Jefferson lived the life of a country gentleman, entertaining many notable figures. He was fond of painting and a number of his landscapes of the island are still extant. As ardent a sportsman as the original Rip Van Winkle (the character role that made him famous), he found ample play for this avocation in surrounding marshes. He also bred fine cattle and cultivated orchards. After his death the island continued in the ownership of his heirs until 1917, when it was sold to Lawrence Jones and J. L. Bayless, who organized the Jefferson Island Salt Company.

According to legend Jefferson Island was one of Lafitte's hiding places for treasure. In 1923 a Negro employee called Daynite unearthed a quantity of Spanish and Mexican gold and silver coins while digging a culvert.

BOB ACRES (*private*), the home built by Jefferson on the highest point of the island, now serves as a residence for the manager of the salt mine. The house is surrounded by large oaks and green shrubbery. It is a white frame one-and-one-half-story building, with an air of spaciousness and comfort contributed by wide porches and side wings. The hipped roof rises to a square belvedere, flanked on all four sides by dormer windows. A balustrade of wooden filigree work connects the square columns of the front porch. To the rear, separate from the main house, is a long low wing which formerly housed the kitchen and servants' quarters.

In *The Autobiography of Joseph Jefferson* (1904) he tells the following story about his life on the island:

As I have been living here for the past eighteen winters there is naturally some curiosity among the peasantry, both white and black, as to the precise nature of my vocation. The town near us has had no theater or hall of any kind until lately, so that the only public amusements with which they are familiar have been confined to the circus.

The country people know me very well, and it is a mystery to them what I can possibly do in a 'show,' as they call it. I had been out duck shooting and was being paddled slowly along the bayou in a canoe by my 'man Friday,' a colored boy about eighteen years of age. As a rider of buck-jumping ponies he was a wonder either with or without a saddle, and the perfect ease with which he handled a canoe made him invaluable as a guide; he would dip the paddle deep into the stream and with a firm and steady hand move the boat with great speed, and yet with such skill and so silently that he made no splash or ripple in the water. I have often sat with my back to him in the quiet of a sunset evening and listened if I could catch the slightest sound; but no, though we glided along the water like an arrow, John's paddle was quiet as a mouse.

On the excursion referred to the silence was broken by John's voice. 'Mr. Joe, will you be mad if I ax you somefen?' 'No, John, what is it?' There was a pause, then calling up all his courage he broke forth with a question which I have no doubt he had meditated upon and could contain no longer. 'What does you do in a show?' I told him that it would be rather difficult for me to explain to him what my peculiar line of business was. 'Well,' said John, 'does you swallow knives?' I told him that I had no talent whatever in that way. 'Well, your son told me that you swallowed knives, and forks, and fire, and de Lord knows what all, and I believe he was just foolin' me.' I agreed with him, saying that he was quite capable of it. 'Well, dere's one thing certain,' said John; 'you don't act in the circus.' I asked him how he could be sure of that. Here he burst into an immoderate fit of laughter, almost tipping the canoe over in his violent mirth, 'Oh, no—oh, no, sah; you can't fool me on dat. I've seen you get on your horse; you ain't no circus actor.'

During Jefferson's ownership the entire hilltop was an expanse of smooth green lawn, with avenues of magnolias and oaks leading down to the lake front. There is little left of the grove or of the once extensive fruit orchards. Canals break the once gracefully curved shore line, and scattered about are piles of debris from the mines, fallen logs, and underbrush.

JEFFERSON ISLAND SALT MINE (open on application), is one of the largest salt producers in the United States. Rock salt was first discovered here by Jefferson in 1895, while drilling for water. Shortly afterwards a contract was entered into with A. F. Lucas, discoverer of the Spindle-top oil field (Texas), but work was abandoned because of water seepage.

In 1919 Jones and Bayless began prospecting for salt on their newly acquired property, and in 1921 completed the sinking of a shaft 100 feet in circumference, then said to be the largest round mine shaft in the world. Since 1921 production has averaged 200,000 tons a year. The present working level is 800 feet below the surface, the greatest depth of any salt mine in Louisiana. It is estimated that there is enough salt at this level to last for a quarter-century at the present rate of production, and there is known to be at least 2,000 feet of salt beneath. A sloping shaft from the present 800-foot level has been sunk at an angle of 30° to a 980-foot level. Eventually, when salt on the first level is exhausted, work will progress to the second level.

An elevator, or "skip," takes sightseers down the mine to a world composed entirely of salt. Rock salt walls rise to a height of 80 feet and salt pillars support the roof of the "rooms" formed by previous excavation. Salt, ground to a fine white powder that resembles snow, lies spread underfoot or piled in small drifts; and there are mounds of newly dynamited blocks. The underground chambers stretch far back into the semidarkness, and under long lines of electric lights men and machinery are busily working in the dry atmosphere whose temperature remains between 75 and 80 degrees the year round.

The salt is first undercut by electrically driven machines and holes are drilled for charges of dynamite. It is then blasted down, loaded into cars by the muckers, and hauled by electric locomotives to the shaft. At the foot of the shaft a giant roll crusher grinds the salt, which falls to five-ton skips 100 feet below. Hoisted to the surface, the salt passes through a series of magnetically vibrated screens which grade according to size. The larger grades are loaded directly into bags for shipment, but the finer grades are reground, rescreened, and kiln-dried. Since the rock salt is 99.94 percent sodium chloride, there is no need of further refining and machines weigh the table salt grades and pack them into cartons. In the grainer plant waste salt in the form of dust is converted by grainer and vacuum processes into flake salt, used in the manufacture of cheese, butter, crackers, pretzels, and self-rising flour.

LAKE PEIGNEUR was formerly considered one of the beauty spots of the Attakapa region, but in the last quarter-century it has become partly filled with sediment, and commercial uses have marred its appearance. On one side the island rises in a 30-foot bluff above the lake and large oaks hang out over the water.

From Jefferson Island the return route is on LA 675 to La 14, then west to DELCAMBRE, site of an annual shrimp festival.

(C+ (C+ (C+ (C+ (C+ (C+ (C+ (C+ (C+ (C+ (C+ (C+ (C+ (C+ (C+ (C+ (C+ (C+ (C+ (C+ (C+ (C+ (C+ (C+ (C+ (C+

Tour 2C

Abbeville—Intracoastal City—Pecan Island; 40 *m.*, La 82 and old Intracoastal Waterway.

Boats available at Intracoastal City; reasonable rates.
Obtain permission from superintendents to visit wildlife sanctuaries; at Abbeville, for Louisiana State Wildlife Sanctuary; at Erath, for Russell Sage Game Refuge; at Youngsville, for Paul J. Rainey Wildlife Sanctuary.
Camp and restaurant at Intracoastal City.

This route runs south from Abbeville to the wildlife reservations and *chênière* settlements along the central and western coast of Louisiana. The tour is made by automobile from Abbeville to Intracoastal City, where three side tours can be made by boat through canals or on Gulf waters.

La 82 branches south from La 14 (*see Tour 2*) at ABBEVILLE, 0 *m.* (*see Abbeville*), and runs through slightly rolling land lightly wooded with a varied growth.

La 82 turns R. at 1.7 *m.* to PERRY, 2.4 *m.* (14 alt.), a settlement on Vermilion River. Formerly called Perry's Bridge, the village was named for Bob Perry, prominent planter of the section and Vermilion Parish's first representative. In 1844 Perry's Bridge became the seat of Vermilion Parish. For the next eight years a bitter controversy took place between Perry's Bridge and Abbeville over the designation of the parish seat. The honor went from one to the other at yearly elections, and outsiders were never sure about the residence of government in Vermilion Parish. Finally, in 1852, the State legislature definitely established Abbeville as the parish seat.

INTRACOASTAL CITY, 15.9 *m.* (3 alt.), on La 333, off La 82, is a settlement at the intersection of Vermilion River and the Intracoastal Waterway (*see Tour 11D*). *Fishing boats accommodating more than three persons are rented at day rates; boats for hunting at Pecan Island rented for overnight trip to party of six.*

1. South from Intracoastal City by boat (*round trip in summer made on Mon., Wed., and Sat.*) to CHÊNIÈRE AU TIGRE (Fr., oak grove of the tiger), 16 *m.*, a sand and shell ridge rising above the seamarsh and covered with small, wind-twisted live oaks and a thicker growth of buckbrush and wax myrtle. The *chênière* derives its name from the fact that a large cougar, or panther, was once killed here. Excellent fishing and a fine sandy beach make it

a popular summer resort. The duck hunting here ranks with the best in the State.

A short distance east of Chênière au Tigre is the PAUL J. RAINEY WILD-LIFE SANCTUARY (*for admission see above*), a 26,000-acre tract formerly maintained by Paul J. Rainey, international sportsman, for his own pleasure and that of his guests. In June 1924, following her brother's death, Mrs. Grace Rainey Rogers presented the tract, together with an invested fund for its maintenance, to the Audubon Society as a memorial to her brother. Like the other preserves in the region, it consists of marsh, bayous, low prairie, and sandy shore. Alligators, deer, mink, muskrat, and numerous species of waterfowl abound.

2. Southeast from Intracoastal City by boat, 3 *m.*, to the mouth of Vermilion River, where it is said Colonel James Bowie of Alamo and bowie-knife fame carried on an illicit slave trade with Lafitte. Bowie is said to have bought pirated slaves from Lafitte at Galveston (then Mexican territory) for $1 a pound, loaded them on schooners, and smuggled them into Louisiana.

Around RED FISH POINT, at about 10 *m.*, is excellent salt-water fishing. The point itself forms part of the LOUISIANA STATE WILDLIFE SANC-TUARY (*for admission see above*). This 13,000-acre tract on the west side of Vermilion Bay, part of a large section purchased for sanctuary purposes by Charles Willis Ward of Michigan and Edward Avery McIlhenny of Avery Island, was presented to the State in November 1911. In winter the sanctuary is usually crowded with wild ducks and geese and smaller birds.

On MARSH ISLAND, about 23 *m.*, is the RUSSELL SAGE GAME REFUGE (*for admission see above*). The island, 79,300 acres in area, was purchased in 1911 by Mrs. Russell Sage through the efforts of Mr. McIlhenny and was presented to the State as a permanent refuge. It is an ideal retreat for water birds, both its coast and interior being a network of grassy bayous and lagoons.

West from Intracoastal City on the mail boat (*leaves at noon on Tues., Thurs., and Sat.; returns on Wed., Fri., and Mon.*) by way of the old Intracoastal Waterway.

Approximately a mile north of the waterway, at about 27 *m.*, is SCHOONER ISLAND, which, according to tradition, was formed by the sinking of a boat by the Lafitte pirates to cut off approach to their lair on White Lake.

Entering WHITE LAKE, 32 *m.*, and crossing its east end for about seven miles, the route follows the Pecan Island Canal.

PECAN ISLAND, 40 *m.* (5 alt.), a *chênière* 18 miles long and ranging in width from a quarter of a mile to two miles, is today almost as completely isolated as when discovered over a century ago by Jake Cole, a Texas cattleman who had come to the region with several companions in search of new grazing lands. From tall trees on neighboring *chênières* they saw the distant treetops of Pecan Island. His companions refused to penetrate any further into the bog. Cole, wagering that he could reach the tree-covered oasis, set out alone. He returned the next day with his pockets full of pecans—to prove that he had actually reached the island—with the startling information that it was strewn from end to end with bleached human bones. In spite of the bone piles, the uninhabited place was exceedingly pleasant and had fine pasture land. Cole settled there with his herds and was later joined by other pioneers.

For many years the neighboring mainland knew nothing about the island and its inhabitants, though mysterious stories were circulated.

Each narrator had a different explanation for the bones found by Cole. One theory was that the island had been a retreat of the Attakapa, who brought their prisoners here, cooked them with clams, feasted at ease, and tossed the bones aside. Others held that the Lafitte pirates had habitually murdered their prisoners on the island. Another version involving Lafitte stated that he once brought several bodies of smallpox victims to the island for burial and that the entire Indian population was wiped out by the disease.

A survey by the Smithsonian Institution in 1928 of the 22 large Indian mounds that dot the island led to the conclusion that the *chênières,* had been inhabited by unknown tribes antedating the Attakapa and Chitimacha Indians of southern Louisiana. Two distinct types of culture were represented by the material excavated. Little pottery was found, but that unearthed led Henry C. Collins, archeologist for the survey, to comment that "in symmetry of form and beauty of finish, the vessels of these Pecan Islanders were surpassed by no other Indians north of Mexico, save perhaps the ancient Pueblo and Cliff Dwellers of the Southwest." The bone piles were long ago cleared away by the early settlers.

From time to time search has been made for Lafitte pirate treasure. In 1925 excited prospectors, not content with mere digging, employed dynamite, but found nothing.

Like the other *chênières* along the coast, Pecan Island is an old Gulf beach composed of crushed shells and sand, covered in places with a thin crust of rich, black loam. Its surface is undulating, with low hillocks breaking the flat expanse. Oaks everywhere rear their huge forms, gnarled and bent from their struggles with the Gulf wind.

From all sides sound the voices of terns, gulls, and other water birds, while bull alligators call from the surrounding marshes. Wooded stretches are dense with growth of oak, pecan, cypress, prickly-ash, locust, persimmon, and red-berried "firethorn." Reaching up for the limbs of the trees are numerous vines—the trumpet vine, jasmine, smilax, and most spectacular, the wild mustang grape. One of these grape vines, known to be at least 80 years old, has a stem measuring 35 inches in diameter. In the more open spaces palmetto grows in thick formation. The use of palmetto in roofing and in the weaving of wide-brimmed sun hats gives the place a tropical touch.

In its variety of wild flowers Pecan Island is one of the richest spots in the State. Growing in profusion are the water hyacinth, wild morning-glory, iris, lotus, prairie lily, swamp lily, and the yucca, or Spanish dagger; with a little searching one may find the less common violet, hibiscus, little passion flower, love-vine (dodder), evening primrose, Indian fire, cardinal flower, spiderwort, and Indian turnip.

The population shows a mixture of nationalities. The Broussards, Veazeys and Héberts represent Acadian stock; the Nunez and Bourques, Spanish; and the Fosters, Campbells, Vaughans, Winches, and Choates, Anglo-Saxon. Contrary to the usual custom in south Louisiana, where religion often separates the races, these people intermarry. Without outside aid they have developed their little settlement, providing what they consume, and virtually governing themselves.

The ROCKEFELLER WILDLIFE REFUGE begins one mile west of Pecan Island. It is operated by Louisiana Wild Life & Fisheries Commission. It extends 26.5 miles along the Gulf and about 6 miles north, to the Grand Chenier ridge. Headquarters are at Grand Chenier in Cameron Parish on La 82. The area was bought by E. A. McIlhenny of Avery Island in 1912, and sold to the Rockefeller Foundation, which in 1920 donated it to the State of Louisiana with specific requirements for operation and protection. It is now one of the largest and most valued refuges in the United States.

The ducks present in midwinter have been estimated by aerial observation as more than 400,000. There are large numbers of geese, coots, and wading birds. Nutria, muskrat, raccoon, otter and alligator are on hand the year around. The protection of wildlife against depredators, especially alligator hunters, calls for patrols. The high price paid for hides attracts poachers and night watches are kept in the season when alligators are active.

The Commission maintains biologists to study fish and wildlife. There has been intensive development of marsh impoundments, weirs, and devices to stabilize water levels to encourage growth of food plants. A levee system of 150 miles is maintained against erosion and storm damage. The hurricane of 1957 damaged or destroyed all buildings and facilities, and the office and residence were rebuilt on pilings.

Rockefeller Refuge can be reached from Abbeville on La 82, and from Kaplan, via La 35 connecting with La 82. From the west, La 27 goes south from Lake Charles and joins La 82 at Creole. It is open March 1 through September 30 for sightseeing and sports fishing. Permits may be obtained by writing to the Refuge Office at Grand Chenier. Travel is mostly by boat and there are no guided tours. Captive animals may be seen the year around without permits at Headquarters.

Tour 3

Junction with US 90—Slidell—Hammond—Baton Rouge—Opelousas —Kinder—De Ridder—(Jasper, Tex.) ; 288 *m.*, US 190.

Section a.   JUNCTION WITH US 90 to BATON ROUGE;
105.6 m., US 190

This section of the route swings westward around the northern shore of Lake Pontchartrain, through the rolling pine forests and crisp, pine-laden air of the Ozone Belt, to the blufflands bordering the Mississippi River at Baton Rouge.

US 190 branches west from US 90 (*see Tour 1a*), 0 *m.,* at the east end of the Rigolets Bridge, a point 8.3 miles west of the Mississippi Line. A Tourist Information Office is located here.

Coastal marshes, which in summer provide excellent fishing and in winter fine duck hunting, border the road for the first few miles. Runways lead from the highway to cabins and camps built out in the marsh on pilings. Guides and boats can be hired at reasonable rates.

At 2 *m.* is the junction with a graveled road.

Left 0.8 *m.* on this road to an old ferry landing; R. here about 200 yards to a small shell BEACH on the shore of Lake Pontchartrain, frequently used for swimming parties. In the oaks which hide the beach from the main road orange-flowered trumpet vines grow in profusion, and between the trees and the beach the knifelike leaves of the "Spanish dagger" jut menacingly.

SLIDELL, 9.2 *m.* (11 alt., 16,101 pop.) (*see Tour 3A*), is at the junction with US 11 and Interstate 59.

At 12.1 *m.* on US 190 is the junction with a dirt road.

Left here 0.6 *m.* to CAMP SALMEN (*visitors allowed on Saturday afternoons and Sundays only*), a Boy Scout Camp. Cabins, a swimming pool, boats, etc., accommodate boys who encamp at the place during July and August.

At THOMPSON'S STORE (L), 13.3 *m.,* on US 190, is the junction with an unmarked, graveled road.

Left here 2.4 *m.* to BONFOUCA (5 alt., 75 pop.), the center of an old French colony recorded on Spanish surveys as early as 1807. The town is near the confluence of Bayous Bonfouca (Ind., river or bayou residents), and Liberty, which unite and flow into Lake Pontchartrain. Near the lake both streams are marsh-bound, but farther upstream, particularly along the banks of Bayou Liberty, are the summer homes of many of New Orleans families. Bayou Liberty is navigable for boats and yachts as far north as Camp Salmen.

At 18.5 *m.* on US 190 is the junction with La 434.

Left here to OAKLAWN, 0.9 *m.* (10 alt.), a small summer resort on Bayou Lacombe. Yachts from the Southern Yacht Club often tie up at the small dock. The waters of the bayou are a peculiar clear brown—a characteristic of the streams of St. Tammany Parish.

LACOMBE (Fr., valley), 20 *m.* (10 alt.), is on the bayou of the same name, once the main route from this district to Lake Pontchartrain and New Orleans.

1. Left from Lacombe one block, at the point where US 190 turns R., and R. on a graveled road 0.7 *m.* to a large sawdust pile (L); L. here to a cemetery, 1.3 *m.,* containing four graves and the ROUQUETTE MONUMENT, a russet granite memorial topped by a stone cross. The base bears the inscription:

L'Abbé Rouquette of Louisiana
Chata-Ima
1813–1887
Poet—Orator—Missionary
Here Was Begun His First Work Among the Choctaw Indians.

Abbé Adrien Rouquette was born in New Orleans on February 26, 1813, of a prominent Creole family. He was early interested in the Indians but was sent to Paris to study law, which he soon deserted in favor of writing. Reputed to have been in love with a Choctaw princess who died, he eventually entered the Catholic priesthood, and in 1859 left New Orleans to devote his remaining years to missionary work among the Indians. He built his first chapel near Lacombe at Butchawa (Ind., squeezing) and later, near the same spot, established another mission, "The Nook," which he considered his home. He died in 1887 in Hotel Dieu in New Orleans, surrounded by a circle of silent Choctaw warriors who as silently followed his funeral procession to the St. Louis Cemetery. The sites of three other missions founded by Rouquette are at Ravineaux-Cannes, between Lacombe and Mandeville; Kildare at Chinchuba; and Chuka-Chaha (Ind., the night cabin), a short distance east of Mandeville. The Abbé was greatly loved by the Indians who called him Chata-Ima (like a Choctaw). Today only a few pure-blooded Choctaw live in this section.

2. Right from Lacombe, 0.6 *m.,* to the HUEY P. LONG FISH HATCHERY (*open*). Large lights swinging over the ponds serve to attract insects, which fall into the water and constitute the main food supply for more than 200,000 fish. Near the hatchery is an enclosure where quail breed in small cages among the pines.

Northwest of Lacombe US 190 travels through a wide stretch of one of the few remaining tracts of virgin pine in the State. Nearing Mandeville the route crosses Bayou Castine (Ind., flea), so named because of the number of these pests found by the Choctaw along the banks of the stream.

FONTAINBLEAU STATE PARK is entered at 25.6 *m.* This 1,000-acre tract extends to Lake Pontchartrain between Cane Bayou and Bayou Castine and has a lake frontage of approximately two miles. The area is forested with virgin and second-growth pine, live oak, magnolia, and hardwoods. A white sand beach crowded with cypress, cedar, live oak, yaupon, and palmetto extends along the lake shore. Among the recreational facilities are a large bathhouse, cottages, foot and bridle trails, and a marina. Two group camps are available to organizations; consult the State Parks & Recreation Commission, P.O. Box 1111, Baton Rouge. Outside the park proper, in an adjoining 5,000-acre area owned by the State Conservation Department, a game preserve is maintained. The combined area comprises land which from 1829 to 1852 was operated by Bernard Xavier de Marigny de Mandeville as Fontainbleau Plantation. The plantation bell, its mellow tone said to have been produced by Marigny's addition of 1,000 Spanish dollars to the molten metal of which it was cast, has been removed to the Louisiana State Museum in the Cabildo, New Orleans. Handsomely ornamented with scroll and figure work, it formerly could be heard, under favorable conditions, across Lake Pontchartrain in New Orleans. According to tradition, the bell, showing almost human loyalty to the old South, crashed to the ground the morning Lincoln signed the Emancipation Proclamation.

MANDEVILLE, 28.3 *m.* (10 alt., 2,282 pop. 1970; 1,740, 1960; inc. 31%), a popular summer resort, lies between the highway and Lake Pontchartrain. Any street crossing the highway may be followed approximately one mile (L) to the beach. Mandeville was founded about 1830 by Bernard Xavier de Marigny de Mandeville (1785–1868), who laid out a townsite on his extensive holdings and, in order to make New Orleans more accessible, established ferry service across the lake, the fare not to exceed $1. This service, under succeeding ownerships, continued up to 1936.

Marigny, a native of New Orleans, inherited a large fortune in his teens, attended school in Europe, and returned to Louisiana to engage in business, political, and social adventures. He purchased plantations, organized a bank, dealt in slaves, and financed a canal. He was a member of the Territorial and State legislatures, twice an unsuccessful candidate for governor, and a member of the Committee of Defense at the time of the Battle of New Orleans. He lavishly entertained and knew Louis Phillipe both as the exiled Duc d'Orléans visiting his father in New Orleans and later as the King of France at the French Court. Many of Marigny's business ventures failed, in part owing to huge gambling losses, and he died almost penniless.

Marigny gained a legendary reputation for his dueling. It is said he once challenged a blacksmith 6½ ft. tall, who countered with the provision that the weapons should be sledge hammers, the duel to be held in Lake Pontchartrain in six feet of water. Marigny saw the humor of the reply, bowed to the blacksmith, and ordered drinks for all present.

CHINCHUBA, 30.6 *m.,* formerly an institution for the deaf maintained by the Sisters of Notre Dame, was named for a corruption of Hachunchuba (Ind., alligator), the name first given to the bayou which runs near the institution. L'Abbé Rouquette's chapel, Kildare, which was on the bayou, has been moved to the school grounds for safekeeping. The small, square long cabin has been covered with boards to protect it from the weather.

North of Chinchuba the highway crosses three streams within four miles—Bayou Tête l'Ours (Fr., head of the bear) ; Ponchatalawa (Ind., singing hair) ; and Abita River, which the Choctaw believe was named for an old Indian.

A gate made of wagon wheels marks the entrance to the LECHE ESTATE (*private*), 32.1 *m.,* country home of ex-Governor Richard W. Leche. The house is a modern, brown-stained, shingle-trimmed lodge occupying the site of an old brick foundry in the midst of rolling pine lands.

The entrance to DASHALLO (*private*), a country estate, is at 32.7 *m.*

At 36.3 *m.* is the junction with Riverside Drive, shell-surfaced.

Left on this road, which follows the Bogue Falaya (Ind., long river) south to its confluence with Abita River, to (L) VILLA DE LA VERGNE (*private*), 0.7 *m.,* the summer home of a New Orleans family, set in a woodland tract. Along the creeks and river grow dogwood, wild honeysuckle, bright sparkleberries, and laurel. In the spring the woods are bright with heavily scented yellow jasmine and wild violets. The house is a long, low building of stuccoed brick, painted white, with a bell tower at one end and a red roof with a central dormer.

WALDHEIM, 1.2 m. (*open to public during azalea season*). The gardens have been extensively planted in a natural setting, a wooded peninsula between the Bogue Falaya and Abita Rivers.

At CLAIBORNE, 36.8 m., a suburb of Covington and the site of the first courthouse of St. Tammany Parish, is the junction with paved La 21.

Right on La 36, called the Military Road, because it was part of a trail followed by Andrew Jackson on his march from Mobile to New Orleans in 1814, to the junction with asphalt-paved La 59, 0.1 m.; R. here to ABITA SPRINGS, 3.1 m. (25 alt., 471 pop.), on Abita River. Once a well-known health resort, its popularity has waned in the last few years. The springs flow at the rate of 40,000 gallons a day.

COVINGTON, 37.2 m. (39 alt., 7,170 pop. 1970; 6,754, 1960; inc. 6%), on the west bank of Bogue Falaya and in the center of the Ozone Belt, has been the seat of St. Tammany Parish since 1828. Possessed of quiet, shady streets and a mild and bracing climate, it is a hunting and recreation resort.

The area had settlers as early as 1769. These were largely of English stock. The town was first called Wharton for an early settler. In 1813 it was incorporated and "dedicated to Thomas Jefferson by his fellow citizen, John W. Collins." In 1816 the name was changed to Covington, to honor Gen. Leonard A. Covington of Natchez, who served in the War of 1812.

COVINGTON COMMUNITY CENTER provides for tennis, baseball, and other sports, and seats 1,500. Five state parks are available including BOGUE FALAYA WAYSIDE PARK, 13 acres with beach. There are two swimming pools, five golf courses, three country clubs, and little theater and art groups. It is served by State highways 21, 25, 36, 437, and the route of the new Interstate 10 is 2 m. south of the city.

The DELTA REGIONAL PRIMATE RESEARCH CENTER for biological and medical studies of primate animals is located on a 500-acre tract near Covington. It was established in 1962 through a National Institutes of Health grant, and is operated by Tulane University. The Center's principal research programs are devoted to infectious diseases, environmental health, developmental biology, birth diseases, genetics, and behavioral problems. Buildings include the main laboratory, detached and isolation laboratories, the administration building, a large primate facility, field observation house and compound, radiation blockhouse and laboratory, service and shops building, and a power plant.

Left from Covington on asphalt-paved La 21, 6.7 m., to MADISONVILLE (10 alt., 873 pop.). In 1817 the *Western Gazetteer, or Emigrant's Directory,* stated: "Madisonville is handsomely situated on the right side of the Chefuncte (Tchefuncte) River, 2 miles above its entrance into Lake Pontchartrain. The place has not attained much importance in point of wealth or population, but it is unquestionably destined to become a great commercial city. It is favorably located for the coasting West Indian trades, having about two days' sail in going out, and about 2 weeks in coming in, the advantage of New Orleans. It is more convenient for the necessary supplies and materials for repairing vessels, and such are the local advantages of this place that the government has fixed on the site a navy yard near the mouth of the Chefuncte (Tchefuncte), where the keel of a light frigate was laid down in 1812, intended for the defense of the lakes. It is believed to be a more healthful location, and less infested with mosquitoes, than New Orleans." This information was substaintially correct.

FAIRVIEW RIVERSIDE STATE PARK is located about 2½ *m.* west of Madisonville. It has a two-story house and 96 acres on the Tchefuncte River. It was given to the State in 1960 by Frank G. Otis.

Right from Covington on unmarked road 439 to the ghost town of RAM-SAY, 3.8 *m.* A single unoccupied house, a deserted store, and the skeleton of a mill are all that remain of what was once a lumbering community alive to the thunder of falling timber and the whirl of the buzz-saw.
Right from Ramsay 1 *m.* on a graveled road across Bogue Falaya to ST. JOSEPH'S SEMINARY. The institution is operated by the Benedictine Monks and has an enrollment of about 100 students in the academic department.

LAKE RAMSAY, 3 *m.* north of Covington, is a recreational area along the Tchefuncte River, 550 acres big, and including a man-made lake of 250 acres, fed by an artesian well 3,400 ft. deep. There are 250 wooded campsites, privately operated.

West of Covington US 190 traverses sparsely settled, cut-over pine lands and small, open bogs and wooded swamps. Near Hammond are the large strawberry farms (*see Tour 9*) whose yield forms the chief source of revenue for Tangipahoa Parish.

HAMMOND, 60 *m.* (42 alt., 12,487 pop. 1970; 10,563, 1960; inc. 18.2%), is at the junction with US 51 (*see Tour 9*). Important Federal highway construction is making Hammond a center of traffic. Interstate 55 comes south from Jackson, Miss. parallel with US 51 and making a junction with US 190 at BAPTIST, 2 *m.* west. A new Interstate 12 from Baton Rouge meets Int. 55 3 *m.* south of Baptist.

At 61.3 *m.* US 51 (*see Tour 9*) branches R.

US 190 crosses Natalbany (Ind., lone bear) River into Livingston Parish, 66.4 *m.* The old spelling, Talbany, still survives with the local pronunciation "Tallbenny."

Livingston Parish was created in 1832 and named for the Livingston brothers, Robert, who urged the Louisiana Purchase from France, and Edward, the brilliant attorney who made the State his home.

ALBANY, 67.3 *m.* (41 alt., 700 pop. 1970), is a crossroads settlement.

Left from Albany on La 43 to ARPADON, 2.1 *m.*, a Hungarian colony named in honor of Arped, legendary Magyar chieftain who united the ancient nation that is now Hungary. This settlement is a striking example of a foreign group who have retained their clannishness and kept aloof, almost untouched by outside influences. In about 1896 a half-dozen lumberjacks bought the cut-over land and began to farm it. From this nucleus grew the present community, now numbering some 1,500 persons. These farmers had the foresight to diversify their crops, not depending upon strawberries alone, with the result that when the depression was felt in the berry industry, only one person in this community sought government relief. A communal life is emphasized by various community house activities, a building for this purpose having been constructed in 1931 through the efforts of their Presbyterian minister. Church work is undenominational, and classes are held in the old Magyar language. Lectures, motion pictures, and stage shows are frequently given. Young farmers rarely leave the settlement, living as their fathers, tilling the soil, and finding recreation in community gatherings.

HOLDEN, 72.5 *m.* (35 alt.), named for J. M. Holden, an early settler, was incorporated in 1910, shortly after the McCarroll Lumber Company erected a sawmill here. For a time Holden was a prosperous lumber center.

US 190 crosses Tickfaw (Ind., pine rest) River, 73 *m.*

DOYLE, 76.6 *m.* (45 alt.), was established as a sawmill town in 1907 and named the following year when the Baton Rouge, Hammond & Eastern Railroad built a station here.

LIVINGSTON, 77.4 *m.* (44 alt., 1,398 pop. 1970), was founded in 1918 as a logging camp for the Lyon Lumber Company.

WALKER, 84.2 *m.* (45 alt., 1,363 pop. 1970), was also a former lumber center. The first trail to this settlement was blazed from Amite River in 1861 by Michael Milton, who heard rumors of war and decided to leave civilization behind him. The village was first called Milton Oldfield, the name being changed to Walker in 1870, in honor of a congressman from this district.

DENHAM SPRINGS, 89.8 *m.* (50 alt., 6,752 pop. 1970; 5,991, 1960), occupies land cleared in 1804 by Alexander Hogue, a Scot from Georgia. In 1827 William Denham moved here and discovered mineral springs on his property. The village quickly became a health resort and a fine hotel was erected. During the War between the States the hotel quartered Federal troops who set fire to the building when they vacated.

BENTON FERRY BRIDGE, 92.3 *m.,* is a modern concrete structure which replaced the old ferry across Amite River. A short distance above the bridge Comite River flows into the Amite. Benton Ferry is a favorite rendezvous for picnickers, swimmers, and fishermen, many Baton Rouge-ans having camps along the two rivers.

East Baton Rouge, one of the oldest parochial divisions of the State, was established in 1811 as one of the four original Florida Parishes, and is the only one which has retained its first boundary lines. This region is made up chiefly of wooded uplands, bluffs, alluvial soils, and low plateaus which are in use for cattle raising and truck farming. Cotton, sugar, hay, oats, rice, and potatoes are the principal crops.

The pine flats end abruptly at Amite River and US 190 follows an old Indian trail west through an open, rolling country of hardwood forests.

MILLERVILLE (L), 94.9 *m.,* consists of a small group of buildings and pens used as winter quarters for travelling shows and carnivals. With its band wagons, trucks, and carnival atmosphere, the settlement is in marked contrast to other communities along the route.

HARELSON, 97.7 *m.* (50 alt.), was a chartered village with a population of 100 in 1930. It was disfranchised in 1934; the natives attribute this to a drastic cut in population due to the removal of two families, one with 14 children, the other with 13.

At 100.2 *m.* is the southern junction with US 61–65 (*see Tour 10b*), which unites with US 190 between this point and Baton Rouge (*see Tour 10b*).

BATON ROUGE, 105.6 *m.* (51 alt., 165,963 pop.)

Baton Rouge is at junctions with US 61 and La 1, 19, 30, 37, and on the route of Int. 10 and Int. 12.

Section b.   BATON ROUGE to OPELOUSAS; 61.7 m., US 190

This section of US 190 continues westward through a sparsely settled region of few farms, with great stretches of swampland spreading between the Mississippi and Atchafalaya Rivers. The greater part of these lands has been inundated many times by flood from the two rivers during high-water periods, and the section is now the scene of a new flood control system.

North of BATON ROUGE, 0 *m.,* US 190 coincides with US 61.

At 4.5 *m.* is the northern junction with US 61 (*see Tour 10a*); L. on US 190 across the Mississippi River on a bridge completed in 1940. Under the western approach is a junction with La 1.

West Baton Rouge Parish, through which US 190 runs, was inhabited by Bayogoula (bayou people) Indians when first explored by Iberville and Bienville (1699–1700). The explorers found a low, flat country of swamps, giant canebrakes, and numerous bayous—a desolate wilderness flooded each year by the Mississippi. Within a half-century there were some scattered French colonists in the region, and in 1765 there was an influx of refugee Acadians from Nova Scotia. Their first settlements were along the river. The parish was created in 1807, and was named West Baton Rouge in 1810, in order to distinguish it from the newly formed eastern parish across the river.

This area experienced a slow but steady growth until the War between the States, after which the country was hardly habitable, so harshly had it been ravaged, and so revolutionary was the change brought about by the abolition of slave labor. During late years some of the old prosperity has been regained. The area of West Baton Rouge is 134,000 acres, of which about 11,000 are planted in sugar cane. A considerable acreage is devoted to cotton and rice. Extensive stands of cypress and of oak, ash, gum, and other hardwoods are found in the swamps.

In this parish the old custom of the public dowry purse has what is probably its only survival in America. In Louisiana the custom of brides furnishing dowries to their husbands originated under Bienville, more than 200 years ago, with the arrival of the *filles à la cassette*—maidens brought from France to marry Louisiana colonists. More than a century ago Julien Poydras (*see Tour 17c*), a wealthy merchant and philanthropist, bequeathed $30,000 to West Baton Rouge and an equal amount to Pointe Coupée, the interest from the fund to be distributed among brides. In Ponte Coupée the legacy has been diverted to educational purposes, but in West Baton Rouge it continues in its original use. Poydras himself was a bachelor. It is said that when he came to Louisiana he owned little more than the pack on his back and, as the girl he loved was too poor to furnish a dowry, it was impossible for them to marry.

Any bride of Louisiana-Colonial ancestry who has been a resident of the parish for five years may share in a division of the fund, her part being determined by the number of eligible applicants. In one year when there was only a single applicant, she received the entire amount, $2,400. Her husband had been married four times previously, each of his brides sharing in the fund. It is not uncommon for a prospective bride to postpone her wedding for a year if the list of applicants is large.

KAHNS, 11.4 *m.* (23 alt.), is a sugar town supported by a sugar mill. It was in sight of Kahns, in the bend of Free Nigger Point, that the Confederate ram *Arkansas,* disabled and helpless, was blown up by her crew to prevent capture by the Federal gunboat *Essex.* The burning ram was seen by the family and guests at Westover Plantation, among whom was Miss Sarah Morgan, who wrote a graphic account of the event in her *Confederate Girl's Diary.*

At 12.2 *m.* is the ALLENDALE MILL, formerly the property of Brigadier General Henry Watkins Allen. The Allen house was burned during the war.

On clear days, at about 18.2 *m.,* the capitol at Baton Rouge is visible to the east.

ERWINVILLE, 19.6 *m.,* is a small agricultural trading settlement.

At 21.6 *m.* is the junction with La 1.

LIVONIA, 28.8 *m.* (25 alt., 611 pop.), named for a province in Russia, is a sugar settlement.

Livonia is at the junction with La 78.

Right from Livonia on graveled La 78, along Bayou Grosse Tête (Fr., big head), to several large INDIAN MOUNDS, 0.5 *m.*

West of Livonia US 190 has a junction with La 77 (north-south).

LOTTIE, 33.8 *m.* (20 alt.), is another small sugar cane settlement, surrounded by wide, fertile fields. The town came by its name in a rather unusual manner. The residents, being unable to agree upon a name, submitted a letter containing five names to the postmaster-general; he drew "Lottie." At Lottie La 81 turns north, joins La 77 at FORDOCHE.

US 190 passes through a gap in the guide levee of the Morganza Floodway (*see Tour 18A*) at 34.8 *m.*

At 40.1 *m.* is the junction with a graveled road to SHERBURNE, 3 *m.,* on Alabama Bayou, one of the best fresh-water fishing spots in the State.

US 190 crosses Atchafalaya River, 40.5 *m.,* over a steel and concrete bridge completed in 1934, and enters St. Landry Parish. Geologists believe that the Mississippi River once flowed through this channel.

At the western end of the bridge, 40.8 *m.*, is the junction with La 105 (*see Tour 18A*), running parallel with the levee.

Left on this road; guide post, 3 to 4 feet in height, mark the road and indicate the depth of high water (*see Tour 18A*).

KROTZ SPRINGS, 0.7 *m.* (30 alt., 1,435 pop. 1970), depends on fishing; gaspergou (fresh-water drum), buffalo, and catfish are marketed in considerable quantities. One sawmill and a shingle mill operate in the vicinity. There is a fine flow of artesian water, one large well supplying the entire community. The natives are largely of Acadian descent, and their old language is spoken in a majority of the homes.

West of the bridge US 190, topping a fill, or low embankment, leads across the low, wooded lands that lie in the West Atchafalaya Floodway (*see Tour 18A*).

At 44.1 *m.* US 71 branches northwest (*see Tour 18c*).

US 190 passes through a gap in the guide levee of the West Atchafalaya Floodway (*see Tour 18A*) at 47.4 *m.*, and at 48.1 *m.* crosses Bayou Courtableau (Fr., short view).

The PORT BARRÉ OIL FIELD is seen at 51 *m.*

At 53.4 *m.* is the junction with La 741, Right on this road to PORT BARRÉ, 1 *m.* (25 alt., 2,133 pop. 1970), a water terminus on Bayou Courtableau and a shipping point for a large plantation district in the upper Teche country. The town came into some prominence with the discovery of oil nearby in 1926.

OPELOUSAS, 61.7 *m.* (71 alt., 20,120 pop. 1970), is at the junction with US 167, La 31 and La 182.

Section c. OPELOUSAS *to* TEXAS LINE; *120.7 m., US 190*

West of Opelousas, 0 *m.*, US 190 continues through long stretches of rolling prairie land. The landscape shows clusters of oaks and there are many small farms.

EUNICE, 20.8 *m.* (50 alt., 11,390 pop. 1970; 11,326, 1960), the trade center of a cotton and rice district, lies in a narrow extension of St. Landry Parish between Evangeline and Acadia Parishes, at a junction with north-south La 13 and La 29. The southern border of the town is on the Acadia boundary line. Eunice was founded in 1894 by C. C. Duson and named for his wife. Crops in St. Landry Parish are led by soybeans, valued at $7,500,000 annually; cotton, sweet potatoes, rice and corn. Annual production of natural gas reaches more than 86,000,000 cu. ft., and there is big timber and pulpwood production. Eunice has a rice mill and rice driers, and profits also from employment in oil field construction and oil well drilling in the surrounding area. It is served by the Rock Island, Southern Pacific, and Missouri Pacific railroads and Continental Trailways.

The city has a 120-acre park with full recreation facilities, two municipal and one club swimming pools. It has an airport with a 3,000 ft. runway and connects with airport services at Lafayette.

The Eunice Public Library in 1967 joined the Opelousas Library in a bi-city system, unique in Louisiana (*see Opelousas*). Its library is located at 216 S. Second St. The cit, has built a new $2,000,000 hospital, a $1,300,000 high school, and a National Guard Armory. In the fall, 1967, LOUISIANA STATE UNIVERSITY AT EUNICE opened with 343 students and a faculty of 21, offering 55 courses in a new two-year college. The library and science buildings were completely equipped and a five-year budget called for the expenditure of $3,475,000 for administration-classroom, health & physical education, and cafeteria-student center buildings.

US 190 crosses the boundary of Evangeline Parish at 25.4 *m.* Named for the heroine of Longfellow's poem, the section is populated almost entirely by Acadians (*see Tour 1c*).

At 30.8 *m.* is the junction with a paved road.

Left on this road 5 *m.* to the TEPETATE (Ind., prairie) OIL FIELD, opened in 1936. The CONTINENTAL OIL VAPOR RECOVERY PLANT (*open on application*) manufactures gasoline from natural gas by means of a heat and pressure process. The plant is one of the many recovery units which have recently come into use in refineries and in oil and gas fields. Gas formerly going to waste is now processed by these units.

BASILE, 31.4 *m.* (47 alt., 1,779 pop. 1970; 1,932, 1960), was founded in 1905, taking its name from the first settler, Basile Fontenot.

Bayou Nez Piqué (Fr., tattooed nose, so called by the early settlers because the Indians in the vicinity practised the art of tattooing), 33.8 *m.,* is one of the larger streams of the prairie region of southwest Louisiana. The majority of the farms are small and devoted to truck crops including radishes, strawberries, watermelons, and potatoes. Stock raising is one of the industries of the section. Several lumber companies operate in Allen Parish and much of the cut-over land is being reforested.

ELTON (50 alt., 1,598 pop. 1970; 1,595, 1960), is at 37.5 *m.*

Right from Elton on a dirt road 3.2 *m.* to the KOASATI (Coushatta) VILLAGE, inhabited by the largest Indian tribe in Louisiana, numbering approximately 40 families and 160 persons in 1936. The tribe came from Alabama and crossed the Mississippi in 1799. By the middle of the nineteenth century they had made several settlements in Louisiana and Texas. They have retained many of their old customs and still speak the Koasati language in their homes. They attend a Congregational church (L), and their children attend a grade school conducted in the community. Many of the older children attend high school in Elton. Very few of these Indians have been successful at independent farming, but they make excellent laborers on rice farms or in the lumber industry. They have shown themselves particularly adapted to various types of woodwork. Some of the women make and sell baskets of wild cane, "pine straw" (needles), and "latanier," or palmetto.

KINDER, 46.9 *m.* (51 alt., 2,307 pop. 1970) (*see Tour 13c*), is at the junction with US 165, which runs parallel with the Missouri Pacific Railway.

West of Kinder US 190 crosses Calcasieu River, 50.3 *m.,* popular for large-mouthed bass fishing.

BELL, 61.3 *m.,* is an abandoned sawmill town.

Left from Bell on a graveled road to a large HOT SALT-WATER WELL, 1.5 *m.,* on an abandoned oil location. The water is said to have curative qualities for skin abrasions.

At BAGLEY, 71.3 *m.,* is the junction with US 171; R. on US 171, which unites with US 190 between here and De Ridder (*see Tour 19c*).

DE RIDDER, 96.6 *m.* (194 alt., 8,030 pop. 1970) (*see Tour 19c*), is at the northern junction with US 171.

West of De Ridder US 190 runs through broad stretches of desolate cut-over pine lands. Much of the denuded land is under reforestation contracts, with the Louisiana Department of Conservation superintending several large projects.

MERRYVILLE, 116.4 *m.* (85 alt., 1,286 pop. 1970; 1,232, 1960), is one of the best examples in the State of a ghost town—a vestige of a community established by lumber interests in this pine district, but deserted when the supply of timber was used up. Merryville had a population of 2,636 in 1930, but since the abandonment of many sawmills in 1933 the number has dropped.

West of Merryville US 190 leads through a partly wooded country; the road is bordered with close growths of willow, sweet gum, loblolly pine, and other fast-growing trees.

At 120.7 *m.* US 190 crosses Sabine River (*see Tour 1c*), the Texas boundary, 32 miles east of Jasper, Texas (*see Texas Guide*).

❮❖

Tour 3A

(Hattiesburg, Miss.)—Slidell—Junction with US 90; 28.5 *m.,* US 11.

Int. 59 runs parallel.
Concrete- and asphalt-paved roadbed.
Southern R.R. parallels route between Pearl River and Robert S. Maestri Bridge.
Accommodations in Slidell.

This route, emerging from Honey Island Swamp, runs south through the piney woods of the Ozone Belt to the marshland south of Lake Pontchartrain. Two miles before the State Line US 11 joins Interstate 59 for about 9 *m.*

US 11 crosses the MISSISSIPPI LINE, 0 *m.*, 78.7 miles southwest of Hattiesburg, Mississippi, midway across the bridge spanning Pearl River.

West of Pearl River the highway traverses HONEY ISLAND SWAMP, a dank jungle crisscrossed by the numerous streams of the Pearl River delta. Virgin stands of cypress, tupelo gum, and water oak choke the low-lying areas; the more elevated regions are overgrown with beech, magnolia, red gum, and oak. Here wild turkeys and deer are numerous, fish abound, and the frog population is tremendous. As the haunt of wild life the swamp is an unsurpassed laboratory for biologists and an excellent hunting and fishing ground. During the nineteenth century the island served as a hide-out for pirates. The most notorious was Pierre Rameau, who engaged in highway robbery and slave running. J. Maurice Thompson's novel, *The King of Honey Island,* is based on Rameau's life.

South of PEARL RIVER, 4.7 *m.* (31 alt., 1,361 pop. 1970; 960, 1960), a settlement on West Pearl River, US 11 runs through the pine woods of St. Tammany Parish. Numerous Indians inhabited the region at the time the parish was established in 1811; for this reason it was named St. Tammany in honor of the Delaware Indian chief of the seventeenth and eighteenth centuries, whose "wisdom in council and friendliness toward the whites," caused him to be facetiously canonized. His name was adopted in 1789 by the Tammany Society, a fraternal and benevolent organization in New York, which became a powerful Democratic political organization. Today, the parish is one of the foremost resort areas near New Orleans.

St. Tammany has valuable natural resources, particularly pine timber, white sand from river bottoms, and a combination of soils suited to the growing of vegetables, fruit, pecan, and tung trees. A great variety of plant and animal life abounds.

A new Interstate highway (Int. 12) under construction runs east-west about 4 *m.* south of Pearl River.

At 11.5 *m.* is the northern junction with US 190 (*see Tour 3a*).

SLIDELL, 12.1 *m.* (11 alt., 16,101 pop. 1970; 6,356, 1960; inc. 153%), was named for John Slidell (1793–1871), statesman and politician. Slidell was born in New York of Scottish-English parentage and came to Louisiana in 1819, where he entered the legal profession and married a Creole. In November 1845 he was appointed Minister to Mexico to adjust the strained relations then existing between that country and the United States. Mexico's refusal to treat with him increased the tension that culminated a few months later in the Mexican War. During the 1850's Slidell was the political boss of Louisiana. He wielded much influence in National affairs, and was the power behind the throne during the first three years of Buchanan's administration. He withdrew from the Senate when Louisiana seceded from the Union and accepted the post of Confederate Commissioner to France. Sailing from Havana on the British steamer *Trent,* he was arrested at sea by Captain Charles Wilkes of the U. S. sloop *San Jacinto,* and imprisoned in Boston. A strong protest by Great Britain caused the U.S. State Dept. to release Slidell and his associate, Mason. He died in exile in England after the War between the States, having received no reply from President Andrew Johnson to a request for permission to return to the United States.

Early settlers reached this section about ten years after the War between the States, but progress was slow until the advent of the railroad in 1883. The town is now the industrial center of St. Tammany Parish. Brick and tile manufacturing is the chief industry; in addition there are sawmills, creosoting plants, and shipyards.

The country adjacent to Slidell offers excellent facilities for water sports, hunting, and fishing; winding roads, rich in scenic beauty, lead to numerous picnicking and camping grounds.

Left from Slidell on the asphalt-paved Salt Bayou Road (La 1075) to (R) a small CEMETERY, 4 *m.*, interesting for its use of shells, tile, and varied, odd-shaped picket markings of graves, some of which, especially those of children, are outlined in the shape of caskets. Several have headpieces of tin-framed undertaker's notices; one a large sea shell and another a small poinsettia bush at the foot. The concrete frame of a large tomb is filled with a sandy soil in which a rosebush blooms above an outline of conch shells in the form of a bleeding heart.

At 5 *m.* is the junction with an unimproved shell road; L. here 3.5 *m.* to INDIAN VILLAGE, now merely a landing on West Pearl River, which here runs through a dense cypress swamp. About a hundred yards from the river is a broad, low Indian mound where weapons, implements, and broken bits of pottery are still found. The clay work has attracted attention from geologists for, although it is black, there is no evidence of carbonization by fire or other agents. Geology students from Louisiana State University include this mound in their field work. West Pearl River and Yellow River, which is several miles to the north and accessible only by boat, afford opportunities for fishing in Honey Island Swamp. Guides and boats are available.

Slidell connects with Int. 59 via La 493, which joins US 90 at the Lake.

US 11 crosses the eastern end of LAKE PONTCHARTRAIN, 17.5 *m.,* on the five-mile Robert S. Maestri Bridge. Bordering the highway at both ends of the bridge are camps offering facilities for hunting and fishing. Int. 10 crosses the lake independently.

At 28.5 *m.* is the junction with US 90 (*see Tour 1a*).

Tour 4

(Poplarville, Miss.)—Bogalusa—Franklinton—Amite—Clinton—Jackson—St. Francisville; 115 *m.,* La 10.

This route extends westward from the Mississippi Line through one of the States richest lumber-producing sections and the fertile northern portion of Louisiana's Strawberry Belt. Wild, picturesque spots are numerous in the Tunica Hills section in the vicinity of St. Francisville.

Midway across the bridge spanning Pearl River, 17 miles west of Poplarville, Miss., La 10, a continuation of Miss 26, crosses the MISSISSIPPI LINE, 0 *m.*

BOGALUSA (Ind., black creek), 2.4 *m.* (105 alt., 18,412 pop. 1970; 21,423, 1960, loss 14%), is an industrial town, manufacturing paper, tung oil, and lumber. It is in the heart of a heavily wooded yellow pine belt. With its carefully planned program of forest conservation and reforestation, Bogalusa has preserved one of its principal assets— lumber, and developed new wood products for its market. The Federal Government maintains an experiment station in forestry.

The Great Southern Lumber Mill, around which the city grew, was, until it closed in 1938, one of the largest in the world. During its 32-year existence the company spent more than $100,000,000 in cutting untold billions of feet of lumber.

Bogalusa is on the main line of the Gulf, Mobile & Ohio Railroad and is the northern terminus of the Pearl River Navigation Canal, connecting with the Gulf. The Crown Zellerbach Corporation employs 3,000 for its paper operations and 38 other manufactures include dairy products and food processing. The State-supported Sullivan Vocational-Technical Institute enrolls 500 adults for special training. The Community Medical Center was completed in 1962, one of three hospitals. There are 46 churches of 13 denominations. Cultural activities include a little theater, the Mill Town Players. The Pearl and Bogue Chitto Rivers provide opportunities for fishing, and wild turkey hunting is popular.

The tung tree is a native of China. The first seeds were sent to this country by the U. S. Consul at Hankow in 1902, and plantings were made in a number of Southern States. Today the industry has prospects of becoming a profitable enterprise.

In the spring the groves of low, bushy trees, with heart-shaped leaves, are covered with pink and white blossoms. In the fall, the fruit falls to the ground and splits into partitions which resemble somewhat the Brazil nut. As no domestic animal will eat the fruit or foliage, stock can be turned into the groves after the trees have grown tall enough to be safe from trampling.

Tung oil, pressed from the fruit, is used in the manufacture of paint, varnish, waterproofing, and linoleums; the meal left after removing the oil makes excellent fertilizer.

At 12.9 *m.* is the junction with a dirt road. Right on this road and L. on the first road to a LOUISIANA STATE UNIVERSITY FORESTRY CAMP, 0.3 *m.,* a group of log buildings set in the heart of a pine forest.

FRANKLINTON, 22.6 *m.* (155 alt., 3,562 pop. 1970; 3,141, 1960, inc. 13%), in the gently rolling pine hills near Bogue Chitto River, is the seat of Washington Parish. Until 1900, Franklinton, which dates from 1819, was little more than a village, accessible only by treacherous dirt roads cut through virgin forest and barren agricultural lands. The town is now the distribution point for a large district of pine, farm, and dairy country.

At 25.1 *m.* is the junction with paved La 16.

Left on La 16 to the junction with an unimproved road, 4.4 *m.; L.* here to FRICKE'S or THOMAS' CAVE (*small admission fee*), 5.8 *m.* The cave, which is in reality a gorge ranging from a few feet to 150 feet in depth, is the result of erosion caused originally by a spring. Between the valleys of the gorge rise miniature mountain peaks—clay formations of various colors with brick red predominating. Glossy green pines grow from the crags and crevices. Benches and tables are available for picnickers.

At Franklinton La 16 has a junction with La 10. La 10 then moves west to a junction with US 51 (north-south) at ARCOLA. It combines with US 51 to FLUKER, then turns west, crossing the new Interstate 55, under construction. La 16 takes a route formerly ascribed to La 10, and joins US 51 at AMITE, (130 alt., 3,563 pop. 1970).

GREENSBURG, 64 *m.* (223 alt., 652 pop. 1970), the seat of St. Helena Parish, was established in 1832 when Montpelier, 11 miles south, then the parish seat, was no longer considered a favorable location. The COURTHOUSE, in the center of town (L), is a white concrete two-story building in the modern manner.

At 74.1 *m.* is the junction with graveled La 38.

Right on La 38 to CHIPOLA, 2.6 *m.* In this section are numerous tributaries of Amite River, where the few remaining BEAVER COLONIES of the State can be seen. The beaver is rigidly protected by State laws and the colonies have increased so rapidly in recent years that the Conservation Department plans to break them up and restock other areas. Though the region is not accessible by automobile, a foot trail runs along the river banks. (*Inquire at post office for guides.*)

FLUKER'S CAVE (*directions obtainable at Chipola P.O.*), 5 *m.*, is a gorge on Dead River, an old channel of the Amite. This trip is almost impossible by car even in dry weather and should not be attempted in wet.

CLINTON, 86.2 *m.* (186 alt., 1,884 pop. 1970; 1,568, 1960), is the seat of East Feliciana Parish. Once the trading point of rich cotton plantations, Clinton is today a restful little town with shady streets and many fine old buildings of the Greek Revival period.

The COURTHOUSE, in Courthouse Square, restored in 1936, remains as imposing as when it was erected in 1841. It is a square white two-story plastered brick building with a hipped roof supported on all sides by tall Doric columns, and topped by an octagonal and domed bell tower. There are small ironwork balconies above the main entrance in the front and rear.

LAWYERS' ROW faces Courthouse Square and comprises a group of five small columned buildings constructed over a century ago. They were first occupied by 12 Clinton barristers who maintained such a splendid reputation that lawyers came from all parts of the State to hold confer-

ences in the Row. Today one of them is occupied by the AUDUBON RE-
GIONAL LIBRARY, which was established in 1963 by three parishes—
East Feliciana, West Feliciana, and St. Helena. Their building is owned
by the East Feliciana Memorial Library Assn., which formerly maintained a library and now rents its quarters for $1 a year. There are more
than 31,000 volumes and four branches, including St. Francisville and
Jackson.

The DISTRICT ATTORNEY'S OFFICE, on Bank St., two doors from
St. Helena St., is a two-room, wooden building surmounted by a pediment.

The WILLIAM BENNETT HOUSE (*open*), on Baton Rouge St., in the
southern part of town, was built about 1825. It is a story and a half with
gabled ends and covered with smooth plaster stucco. Wooden additions
have been added, but the original outline of the house is clearly marked.
The six columns and the entablature of the façade are of the Tuscan
order. The hooded rear windows and the sliding fan windows are unusual.

Baton Rouge Street forms part of the Plank Road, which dates back
to 1852, when a corporation was formed for the purpose of constructing
an all-weather plank road from Baton Rouge to Clinton and on to
Liberty, Mississippi.

The STONE HOUSE (*open*), on Baton Rouge St., south of the Bennett home, is a one-and-one-half-story plastered brick house with six
fluted Doric columns across the front. Built in 1806 by Judge Lafayette
Saunders, the house has been altered by the addition of an upper gallery
with iron grillwork.

On Bank Street, in the center of town, is the MARSTON HOUSE
(*open*), built in 1837 by Henry Marston for the Union State Bank of
New Orleans. The building served as a combined bank and bankers'
residence. It is a large, two-story structure of stucco-covered brick, with
six tall Ionic columns across the front and a small grilled balcony projecting over the large entrance.

SILLIMAN COLLEGE, on Bank St., south of the Marston home, is set
in a 10-acre grove of beech and magnolia trees and consists of three two-
story, white painted brick buildings. Each building is fronted with large
white Doric columns and all have a second-story gallery running across
the collective front. The central structure was begun in 1852 but was not
completed until after the War between the States. Two halls were
erected at a later date.

The college was incorporated in 1852 and named for William
Silliman, a member of the original board of trustees. Fifteen years later
Silliman donated the college to the Presbytery of Louisiana and it was
operated by this body until 1931. It is now a private school.

Right from Clinton on paved La 67 to the junction with a red clay road,
2.9 *m.;* L. on this road 7.6 *m.* to SWING-ALONG (*open*). The plantation was
originally called Beech Grove and was established by David Pipes, a young
cotton planter who fought in the Battle of New Orleans. The main house is a
one-story white brick cottage with green shutters, and with wings on both sides.

At 6.5 *m.* on La 67 is the junction with a graveled road; R. here 1 *m.* to the WOODWARD PLANTATION HOUSE (*private*), a two-story brick building with a portico surmounted by a porch opening on the second floor. Pilasters of dark brick rise from the foundation to the gabled roof. William Woodward built the house with slave labor in 1852–55.

PRETTY CREEK, 86.8 *m.*, on the western outskirts of Clinton, is a clear, cold stream, with a swimming hole, sandy bottom fishing hole, and a beaver dam.

At 93.1 *m.* is the junction with La 19.

Right here to WILSON, 5.7 *m.* (253 alt., 606 pop. 1970), an agricultural settlement. On this drive the country changes from pine and scrub oak thickets to rolling open pasture land abundantly watered by springs and provided with natural salt licks.

At NORWOOD, 9.3 *m.* (300 alt.) is the junction with graveled La 421; R. on this unmarked road at 14.4 *m.* is the RICHLAND PLANTATION HOUSE (*open*), built in 1820 and recently restored. It is of white painted brick with four Doric columns in the front portico.

To the R. is a one-story wing. Richland is more in the style of the manor house than most plantation dwellings of the same period.

COLONY NO. 1 of the East Louisiana State Hospital (*see below*) is at 98.4 *m.*

JACKSON, 98.8 *m.* (100 alt., 4,697 pop. 1970; 1,824, 1960, inc. 157%), in the days of the earliest settlers was called Bear Corners. Later John Horton laid out the village and called it Buncombe after his home county in North Carolina. This name was retained until after the Battle of New Orleans, when General Jackson encamped with his victorious troops on the banks of near-by Thompson's Creek, and Buncombe was promptly discarded for Jackson. In 1816 a courthouse was built and Jackson became the seat of Feliciana Parish; later, when the parish was divided, it was named the seat of East Feliciana.

The Jackson Assembly, Inc., preserves historic houses and makes restorations. The Public Library occupies the Johnny Jones store of 1850. The McKowen store of 1836, half brick, half frame, is built into a hillside. The Post Office occupies a floor of the St. Alban's Masonic Lodge Bldg., bought in 1868. The Presbyterian Church dates from 1852, the Methodist from 1854.

What is left of OLD CENTENARY COLLEGE stands four blocks north of the highway (R). This consists of the left wing and is now used as an apartment house. It is a two-story red brick building with 15 plastered brick Doric columns across the front. Six columns and several broken ones still standing to the right were part of the other wing. The rest was carted away and used in the construction of YE OLD CENTENARY INN, in the center of town; the remaining central building was demolished. The original college was called the College of Louisiana when it was established in 1825 as a State-subsidized institution. Later, in 1845, the Methodist Conference came into possession of the school and the name was changed to Centenary. Centenary numbered among its students

Jefferson Davis and Judah P. Benjamin. In 1908 the college moved to Shreveport, where it is now flourishing.

The EAST LOUISIANA STATE HOSPITAL in the eastern part of town, is a State-operated institution for mental diseases founded in 1847. It is on a 4,681-acre tract of land and has 150 buildings of varied architecture. In 1965 there were 3,329 patients. The Center Bldg., 1853, has six ionic columns three stories tall, and a cupola with a clock run by weights that descend to the basement. There are a museum of antiques and a gift shop.

Right from Jackson on unmarked graveled La 952 to the junction with an unmarked plantation road, 7.8 m.; R. on this road 1 m. to (R) THE SHADES. This house was built about 1808 on a land grant made to Alexander Scott, who came from South Carolina. Tall boxwood borders the brick walk leading to the entrance, ivy climbs over the thick white porch columns, and the flowering shrubs of an old-fashioned garden grow to the edge of the wide gallery. The two-story house is constructed of red brick. The kitchen, a wing of the main house, is flush with the ground, with cemented porches enclosed by narrow columns; iron pots hang on cranes at the immense open fireplace. There is a collection of bells made by Miss Eva Scott, late occupant, whose cousin, George Berger, now lives here. *Open by appointment.*

At 8.6 m. on La 952 is (R) HICKORY HILL (*private*); erected about 1810 by David McCants of South Carolina. The house is a tall, narrow building of red brick. On the front, four tall white plastered brick colunms rise to a fan-lighted pediment. The columns are of the Doric order, the outer ones square and the two center ones round. Both upper and lower galleries are enclosed at each end by a brick wall. During the War between the States the 15-year-old son of the family, who was home on furlough, was asleep when the house was suddenly surrounded by Union solders. A watchdog gave the alarm, but escape being out of the question, the young soldier was reminded by his sister of their childhood hideout, a platform under the attic steps, plastered underneath like the stairway walls. Young McCants was not discovered in the search, and the disappointed Federals left after appropriating some small household articles.

ASPHODEL, on La 68 4 m. south of Jackson, was built by Benjamin Kendrick in 1820 and named for the daffodil. It is a Greek Revival house with six Doric columns and two dormers on a gabled roof. It is owned by Robt. A. Couhig, who in 1968 bought the 1850 Levy House in Jackson, moved it near this house and opened it as Asphodel Inn.

La 10 crosses Thompson's Creek and enters West Feliciana Parish at 99.6 m. ELM PARK, 106.9 m. (180 alt.), is at the junction with La 421.

Right on La 421 to LOCUST GROVE, 1.5 m., built in the early nineteenth century. The big house was looted and partially destroyed during the War between the States and now only the foundation is left. The center of interest on the grounds is the shaded little cemetery which contains the grave of Sarah Knox Taylor, beautiful first wife of Jefferson Davis. Tradition has it that Sarah Knox Taylor failed to obtain permission of her father, Zachary Taylor, then President of the United States, to marry Jefferson Davis because he was a soldier, but in spite of this objection the couple eloped. During their honeymoon both contracted malaria, and, while Davis recovered from the attack, his bride of a few weeks died. The State Parks Commission has cleared away the tangle of brush which formerly concealed the cemetery and built a fence around it. Sarah Knox Taylor's grave is in the corner of the cemetery; in the center is that of General Eleazer Weelock Ripley, hero of the Battle of Lundy's Lane (1814).

At 2.2 *m.*, through two gates, is BELMONT (*open*), which was constructed toward the end of the eighteenth century on a Spanish land grant. This plantation was first called Blackwater but the name was changed shortly after the War between the States in order to commemorate the Battle of Belmont in southeastern Missouri in which several members of the family took part. It is a frame house with three gables and six square wooden columns across the front.

At 110.3 *m.* on La 10 is a junction with a plantation road. Right to ROSEDOWN PLANTATION AND GARDENS, a lavish restoration of house and grounds opened to the public in 1964 by Mr. and Mrs. Milton Underwood of Houston, Texas, who bought the place in 1956 and consulted aged documents to bring it back to its ancient splendor. Rosedown was built in 1835 by Daniel Turnbull, a cotton planter. In that year his wife Martha bought the first azaleas for the gardens in which these shrubs now flourish luxuriously. Members of the Turnbull family lived in the big white-columnned house for 120 years. The interior is filled with rare treasures in furnishings collected by the Turnbulls, including a rosewood bedroom suite intended for Henry Clay when he became President, a lost cause. Catherine Fondren Underwood in 1966 was the recipient of awards by the Southern Heritage Foundation and the Garden Clubs of America for her superb restoration. The Plantation may be reached from both La 10 and US 61 out of St. Francisville. *Visiting hours: March through August, 9–5; September thru February, 10–4; fees, gardens $2; house and gardens $3, rates for groups. Hq: Rosedown, Drawer M., St. Francisville, La., 70775.*

At 110 *m.* a short road, La 965, turns south to connect with US 61. It leads to AUDUBON MEMORIAL STATE PARK and the Oakley House, associated with John James Audubon, who lived here four months in the 1820's (*see Tour 10*).

ST. FRANCISVILLE, 115 *m.* (75 alt., 1,661 pop.), called the town "two miles long and two yards wide," is built on the crest of a ridge that slopes on both sides to wooded gullies. Bayou Sara, formerly twin town of St. Francisville, at the foot of the hill, was disfranchised in 1926. It was founded in 1790 by John H. Mills and Christopher Stewart, who established a trading post on the river which grew into one of the most flourishing ports between Natchez and New Orleans. With the advent of the railroad, trade diminished and the town gradually declined, so that now all that remains of Bayou Sara are a few wooden shacks and a tall, uninscribed monument, and these have been absorbed by St. Francisville. According to legend this monument, which lies beside the river road (L), was ordered for a grave in St. Francisville, but, after arriving by boat, it was found to be too heavy to transport up the hill, so the remains were brought down to it. Another lengend holds that it was ordered during a yellow fever epidemic by some pessimistic person who found later that his fear of an early death had been exaggerated.

Before the settlement of Bayou Sara there had apparently been little attempt to colonize the surrounding territory of what is now West Feliciana Parish. The concession of the Company of the Indies, "in the Tunicas," embracing all lands bordering on the Mississippi River in this region, was under the direction of M. de Sainte Reine, but there is no evidence of any serious move to colonize this section. There was a Fort St. Reine which existed for a brief period in the early eighteenth century, but it was abandoned in 1736. In 1765 a British surveyor, Lieutenant Rose, was sent to chart the course of the Mississippi. On his map he designates the site of Bayou Sara as "fort Ste. Reine, abandoned." About this period settlers began to acquire land grants in the more habitable portions of the region, and, when the Spaniards wrested the province from the British in 1779, the district of Feliciana had already achieved a reputation for beauty and fertility.

St. Francisville probably had its beginning about the same time that Bayou Sara was established. A part of the ground on which the former was built was granted by the King of Spain to Capuchin friars, who, about 1785, built a monastery, which was shortly afterward destroyed by fire. The land became a burial place for Catholics of the vicinity.

It is probable that the village of St. Francisville retained the name of the destroyed monastery, bestowed by the Capuchins in honor of St. Francis of Assisi.

St. Francisville's GRACE CHURCH, in the center of town, was organized in 1826. The present building, early English Gothic in style, was erected in 1858. It is a brick structure with a bell tower at the rear left and stands in a grove of moss-draped live oaks enclosed by an elaborate cast-iron fence. The churchyard cemetery contains interesting headstones, monuments, and an occasional tomb. The building was badly damaged during the War between the States by fire from Union gunboats. It is said that the young lieutenant who directed the bombardment was a staunch Episcopalian and that he was horrified when he learned that he had shelled his own church.

Probably the oldest building in St. Francisville is AUDUBON HALL, one block left of the highway in the center of town, built in 1819 for a public market, and now housing the public library and the rooms of the local Little Theater. It is a long, narrow frame structure, with simple details. In the front is a porch with slender white columns.

The St. Francisville Ferry crosses the Mississippi River to a point 5.6 miles east of New Roads (*see Tour 17c*).

Tour 5

(Natchez, Miss.)—Vidalia—Ferriday—Jonesville—Tullos—Winnfield —Natchitoches—Mansfield—(Tenaha, Tex.) ; US 84. Mississippi Line to Texas Line, 194.2 *m.*

Concrete- and asphalt-paved roadbed chiefly multilane, undivided.
Railroads roughly paralleling route: I. C., La. Midland. T. & P., between Natchitoches and Armistead.
Hotels, motels, and tourist camps in larger cities.

Section a. MISSISSIPPI LINE to WINNFIELD; 87.4 m., US 84

This section of the route, leading west from the Mississippi River, crosses fertile bottom lands laced with dark bayous, numerous lakes, and dank cypress swamps. In the vicinity of Jonesville is an unusually large expanse of swampland, which in high-water seasons is subject to inundation. Farther west the route passes the northern end of Catahoula Lake and enters the north Louisiana uplands. In ante bellum times many planters whose lands lay in Louisiana had their homes across the river in the highlands of Natchez—safe from overflow.

US 65 and US 84 cross the Mississippi line, 0 *m.*, 0.8 *m.* west of Natchez, Miss., on a ferry to Vidalia, La. The two highways are joined to Ferriday, where US 65 heads north along the Mississippi River into Arkansas, while US 84 begins its long cross-state route to Texas.

During the crossing of the Mississippi River the shifting remnant of the VIDALIA SANDBAR can be seen (R), on the Louisiana shore. In the early nineteenth century this was a popular dueling ground. Duels were fought here between Major Ferdinand Claiborne and Captain Benjamin Farar; between Abijah Hunt and Governor George Poindexter of Mississippi, in which the former was killed; between Winfield Scott, then an army captain, and a Dr. Upshaw, which arose at the former's criticism of his superior officer, General James Wilkinson. Climaxing these was the duel on September 19, 1827, between Dr. Thomas Maddox and Samuel L. Wells, in which James Bowie (*see Tour 18c*) first used his bowie knife. Neither of the principals was injured, but the seconds and several of the spectators took advantage of the meeting to settle old scores. The New Orleans *Argus* of October 1, 1827, gives the following account of the free-for-all fight that followed the rather orderly duel:

. . . [Gen. Samuel Cuney] then turned to Col. Crane . . . and observed to him that there was a difference between them, and that they had better return to the ground and settle it . . . Crane, without replying to General Cuney, or saying one word, fired a pistol at him, which he carried in his hand; but without effect . . . Crane drew from his belt another pistol, fired it at and wounded Gen. Cuney in the thigh, he expired in about fifteen minutes. . . .

Mr. Bowie, upon seeing Gen. Cuney fall, drew his pistol; Crane, after shooting Gen. Cuney, drew a third pistol; Bowie and himself exchanged shots simultaneously, but without effect: Crane fled. By this time Major Wright and the two Blanchards, from Red River, came running down from the wood with drawn pistols, when Wright stopped, took aim at Bowie, fired and missed him; he then advanced three or four paces, drew another pistol presented at Bowie, who observed to him that he was unarmed, but that if he was a man to shoot. Major M'Whorter who was near Bowie, placed an arm [pistol] in his hand—they both fired; Wright one or two seconds first, and both with effect. Mr. Bowie was shot through the breast, Wright was struck in his side, but the ball did not enter. Wright then fled, Bowie drew a knife and pursued him, and when within about ten feet of him, he received simultaneous fire from the two Blanchards, one of the balls took effect in his thigh and cut him down; observing which, Wright wheeled, when he and Alfred Blanchard drew their sword canes, rushed on and commenced stabbing Bowie, who was prostrate. Bowie scuffled for some seconds, until he gained his seat: he then reached up, caught Wright by the coat, drew him down on to him, and at one stab dispatched him; Mr. M. Wells, who had been attending on Gen. Cuney after he had fallen, observing Bowie's situation, ran to his relief, fired at Blanchard, but fortunately only wounded Blanchard in the arm. The combat here ended . . .

VIDALIA, 0.4 *m.* (63 alt., 5,538 pop. 1970; 4,313, 1960), seat of Concordia Parish, was the first settlement founded by Europeans on the western bank of the Mississippi between Pointe Coupée and the mouth of Arkansas River. About the year 1786, in an effort to counteract the British influence at Natchez, Spanish Governor Antonio de Ulloa established a post opposite that point. It was abandoned, to remain but a crossing place on the Natchez-Natchitoches overland route until Don Jose Vidal established a settlement there in 1801. Called Concord Post, the village grew slowly. When Concordia Parish was formed, the name was changed to Vidalia, in honor of Don José Vidal, who gave land for public buildings. The parish has some petroleum and natural gas, raises livestock, and has 360,309 acres in woodland. Today Vidalia is the Louisiana terminal for thousands of motorists who annually cross the Mississippi on the Natchez Bridge, route of US 65 and US 84.

Early in 1863 the Federal ship *Queen of the West* landed a force at Vidalia, in an effort to take into custody General Zebulon York. York escaped, but the town was captured and occupied by Federal troops until the close of the War between the States.

Following the opening of Gile's Bend Cutoff above Vidalia in 1933, the Mississippi shifted its course westward and threatened to undermine the levee in front of the town. To provide a wider channel for the river, a new and more secure levee was constructed in 1939 six blocks bethind the old levee. The courthouse, clerk's office, and jail on the water front were demolished, but many of the homes and business establishments in the abandoned area were moved on rollers to new sites.

West of Vidalia US 65–84 follows a great bend in the Mississippi River through fertile bottomlands planted in cotton, corn, and forage, or covered with heavy growths of hardwood.

FERRIDAY, 10.2 *m.* (60 alt., 5,239 pop. 1970; 4,563, 1960, inc. 14%), was named for John C. Ferriday, owner of the plantation on which the town was built 1903. That year an important contribution to the town's future prosperity was made by the erection of the Texas & Pacific and Iron Mountain & St. Louis Railroad shops. The town has also several cotton gins, warehouses, and a large lumber yard.

At Ferriday US 65 branches north (*see Tour 12*); L. on US 84, which roughly follows Nolan's Trace, a former cattle trail to Texas blazed in the latter part of the eighteenth century by Philip Nolan. A pioneer horsetrader, Nolan made numerous trips between Natchez and Texas, going by way of the Rapids on Red River (Alexandria) and through what are now Rapides and Vernon Parishes. His adventurous career came to a sad end near the Brazos River in 1801, where a party of Spaniards shot him and sent his ears to Chihuahua as proof of his death and of the end of his contraband trade with the Americans of Natchez. It was Nolan whom Edward Everett Hale is supposed to have portrayed as "the man without a country."

Between 12.2 *m.* and 14.6 *m.* US 84 parallels TURTLE LAKE. White egrets and blue herons are frequently seen standing in the shallow water among the cypress and willow trees.

FROGMORE, 17.7 *m.* (56 alt.), is said to have been so named by a railroad surveying party which discovered many frogs. It is a terminal of La 566. Two miles west of Frogmore La 129 starts south, passing, 7 *m.* LAKE COCODRIE (Horseshoe Lake) excellent for fishing and camping, and connecting a group of Concordia Parish villages: Monterey, 13 *m.,* Eva, 18 *m.,* New Era, 24 *m.,* and Acme, 31 *m.,* ending at the RED RIVER AREA, at the Red River.

WILDSVILLE, 24.8 *m.* (50 alt.), half hidden by trees, lies in the valley of Black River.

West of Wildsville US 84 crosses Black River by means of a bridge built in 1935 to replace a ferry which had operated at or near this point continuously since 1786.

West of La 15 and east of La 129 The Red River Wildlife Management Area of 12,600 acres in Concordia Parish is administered by the Louisiana Wild Life & Fisheries Commission in order to provide opportunities for hunting and fishing without impairment to the stocks of wildlife. This tract, opened in 1966, was augmented by 4,009 acres in May, 1968. The additional acreage has approx. 3,000 acres of forest land suitable for wild turkey and deer, and 1,000 acres of cleared pasture managed for quail, doves and rabbits.

JONESVILLE, 26.4 *m.* (54 alt., 2,761 pop. 1970), the largest town of Catahoula Parish, is thought to occupy the site of the Indian village referred to as Anilco by Hernando De Soto, who may have stopped here about 1541. Anilco lay in the angle formed by the confluence of Black and Little Rivers, where the Indians had built several large mounds on an area of 200 to 400 acres, enclosed by an earthen embankment 10 feet high and 10 feet wide. The largest of the mounds was surmounted by a truncated cone of earth 80 feet high, the second highest such mound discovered in North America. (A mound at Cahokia, Illinois, is higher.) This great mound is believed to have been the residence of the *cacique* (Sp., chief), and probably served as a temple of sun-worship. Winslow M. Walker, who conducted research in the district for the Smithsonian Institution, cites almost incontrovertible evidence that the mounds formed an Indian city or cities.

Following De Soto's presumptive visit, the mounds seem to have been deserted except for nomadic tribes that occasionally used the area as a camping site. Some historians name the mound area as the site of the last stand of the Natchez Indians (*see Tour 6*) against Governor Perier in 1730. In 1786 Don Juan Heberard established his home on the great mound and began operating a ferry across Black River. During the War between the States the cone on the great mound was cut down by the Confederates to make a nest for riflemen. From time to time the mounds have been razed, until only a small one, topped by a cemetery, and another on the river front, remain.

Jonesville, formerly called Troyville, was laid out as a town in 1871 by Mrs. F. C. Jones, whose husband had been killed in a feud. The town's chief industries are commercial fishing and lumbering.

At 26.9 *m.* is the junction with graveled La 124.

Right on this road to HARRISONBURG, 10.3 *m.* (69 alt. 626 pop.), is at a junction with La 8, which connects north with Sicily Island, La 15, (north-south) and La 84 south at Whitehall. For several decades before and after the War between the States Harrisonburg enjoyed an important steamboat trade.

The bluffs, reached by a driveway leading north a half mile from the courthouse, are the most striking feature of the local scene and afford a fine view of the Ouachita River, Harrisonburg, and the neighboring swamplands. One of the pine-covered slopes that top the bluff at this point is the SITE OF FORT BEAUREGARD, which was built by the Confederates in 1863 to prevent the ascent of Federal gunboats on Ouachita River. It was one of four forts stretching for two miles below town and more than a mile above.

On May 10, 1863, four Federal gunboats came up the river and anchored within sight of the fort. The Federals demanded unconditional surrender of the fort and surroundings, with the alternative that the fort would be shelled within an hour, giving time for the removal of women and chlidren from the locality. The Confederates replied that the women and children had already been moved and that the fort would be defended. An hour or so afterwards three of the gunboats began firing on the fort, but 150 shots failed to cause any damage aside from breaking some of the parapets. One house in Harrisonburg was destroyed and an officer in the fort was mortally wounded.

On September 4, 1863, Lieutenant Colonel Logan, commander of the fort, having only about 40 men fit for duty, determined to evacuate. Working at night, the garrison destroyed the casements, supplies, and larger guns and withdrew with the horses, mules, wagons, and three-inch guns. The Federals entered the fort after discovering the evacuation and continued the destruction, leaving little that had not been destroyed by the Confederates.

West of Jonesville US 84 parallels Little River through the hill lands and occasional pine forests of Catahoula Parish. At 36 *m.* is ARCHIE; 1 *m.* west is the junction with La 28 to Pineville and Alexandria.

JENA, 50.6 *m.* (156 alt., 2,389 pop. 1970), the seat of La Salle Parish, was incorporated in 1908. The surrounding area, a great pine forest, was called the Choctaw District during Colonial days, and Jena's earlier history is closely connected with that of the Choctaw, Natchez, and Avoyel Indians. The town's first white settlers were immigrants from South Carolina and Georgia.

Among the historic figures of this section was Richmond Nolly, an early nineteenth-century Methodist minister. It is said that wherever a company of soldiers camped, there Nolly would preach on Christianity and patriotism. He lost his life while attempting to cross Hemphill Creek in 1814.

Left from Jena on graveled La 127 which winds and dips through pine hills and creek bottoms, to NEBO, 7.2 *m.*

Left from Nebo 0.6 *m.* on graveled La 460, to HEMPHILL CREEK, a popular picnic spot. The creek has a firm bottom and a white sand beach.

At 7.9 *m.* on La 127 is the junction with a dirt road; L. here 2.5 *m.* to CATAHOULA LAKE, one of the largest fresh-water lakes in central Louisiana. It provides excellent fishing during the spring, or high-water, season. During the hot summer months, the lake and surrounding swamps are almost dry, the latter being termed "slashes" by the natives. In the swamplands grow haws, which can be made into a tasty jelly. During the winter the lake affords the best duck hunting to be found in this section.

At TROUT, 53.5 *m.* (188 alt.), are the FROST LUMBER MILL (R) and (L) the BUCHANAN LUMBER MILL (*both open on application*). It is estimated that the mills at the present rate of cutting can continue in operation for 30 years before exhausting available stands of hardwood timber.

Left from Trout on La 8, blacktop, to the PENICK INDIAN SCHOOL, 4.5 *m.*, a Government day school conducted for Indian children of the section. In addition to academic training, which extends through the seventh grade, the students receive practical instruction in crafts, economics, and homemaking.

The Indian children had practically no educational advantages until private individuals became interested and secured assistance from the Federal Government. The children of this group, descendants of the Choctaw Indians, have striking features—large, black, lustrous eyes and jet-black hair, which, according to an old settler, has "nary a curl and is dark as a corn-crow's wings."

WHITE SULPHUR SPRINGS, 9.5 *m.* was at one time popular among vacationists, who came to enjoy the "salubrious pine woods." There is no longer a resident population, but the WHATLEY HOUSE, a resort hotel, offers accommodations to 300 or 500 visitors yearly. In the early days visitors came to the springs for the mineral water, but now they come chiefly for fishing in Catahoula Lake (east), Little River (south), and various creeks.

According to a legend, Kohita, daughter of an Indian chief of the Terrebonne country, became ill and was advised by the medicine man to seek a country of pure water. Fearing for her life, the chief and his daughter, accompanied by their tribe, journeyed to these springs. On reaching the spot Kohita is said to have exclaimed, "Catahoula! Catahoula!" which in her language meant "clear water! running water!"

South of White Sulphur Springs the highway winds through beautiful pine hills and verdant creek bottoms. Timothy Flint, traveling through the region in 1835, marveled at the beauty of the forest: "I have extensively surveyed the forests of the north, of the lakes and the west," he reported in his *Journal*.

"I have seen the pine woods of New England, and many others, but this grand and impressive forest is unique and alone in my remembrance. I have seen nothing equal or to compare with it. Millions of straight and magnificent stems, from seventy to a hundred feet clear shaft, terminate in umbrella tops, whose deep and sombre verdure contrasts strikingly with the azure of the sky. Not a shrub, not a bush, nothing but grass and flowers is seen beneath this roof of verdure gently waving in the upper air. The openness of the woods is such as to allow the rider on horseback, or even in a carriage, to select his own road. Indeed the appearance is of trees planted out for a park; and deer, of which we saw more than one herd, may be descried bounding away over the undulating slopes for more than a league. The ceaseless rustle of the breeze along the wide extent of this roof, swinging like the oscillations of a pendulum, breezing and swishing on the ear, is best imagined by the shifting hues of a field of wheat in flower, when played upon by the vernal winds."

La 8 crosses Little River, 12 *m.,* which affords good opportunities for fishing and boating. Along this river are several Indian mounds built by the early tribes once inhabiting the section.

At 16.2 *m.* the highway enters the CATAHOULA DIVISION OF THE KISATCHIE NATIONAL FOREST (*see Tour 15a*).

FISHVILLE, 18 *m.* (70 alt.), has been a popular fishing and summer resort for more than a century (*bait and tackle available at reasonable rates for bank fishing*). Timothy Flint (*see Alexandria-Pineville*) lived here during the summer months and wrote many descriptions of the country in prose and verse.

Left from Fishville on a graveled road, turning L. at 0.5 *m*. and again at 1.4 *m*., to BIG CREEK CAMP AND PICNIC GROUNDS, 2.6 *m*., a recreational area developed by the U. S. Forest Service (*tables, shelters, fireplaces, bathhouses*). The chief attraction is fishing, the streams in the vicinity having an abundance of largemouthed and smallmouthed bass, sunfish, or "perch," and catfish. Various species of trees are identified by markers.

CAMP GRANT-WALKER (*not open to public*), at 18.9 *m*. on La 8, is a 40-acre tract of land (R) along Big Creek. It was deeded to the 4-H Clubs of this section by Rufus Walker of Pollock.

POLLOCK, 20.9 *m*. (120 alt.) (*see Tour 13b*), is at the junction with US 165 (*see Tour 13b*).

Back on US 84:

In TULLOS, 66.1 *m*. (106 alt., 600 pop.) *see Tour 13b,* is the junction with US 165 (*see Tour 13b*).

At 77.2 *m*. is a logging camp of the Tremont Lumber Co. The lumberjacks and their families live in bunkhouses so constructed that they can be loaded onto flatcars and moved to other locations as the timber is depleted.

WINNFIELD, 87.4 *m*. (118 alt., 7,142 pop.) *see Winnfield.* Winnfield is at the junction with US 167 (*see Tour 15a*).

Section b. WINNFIELD to TEXAS LINE; 106.8 m., US 84,
La 6, La 1

West of WINNFIELD, 0 *m*., the route winds through a section of the Kisatchie National Forest, passes to the south of Saline and Black Lakes, and crosses the fertile Red River Valley to Natchitoches. Paralleling Red River to Gahagan, the route swings west through wooded uplands to the Texas Line.

US 84 crosses the eastern boundary of the CATAHOULA DIVISION of the KISATCHIE NATIONAL FOREST (*see Tour 15a*) at 3.1 *m*.

At 4.3 *m*. on US 84 is the junction with a graveled road.

Right on this road to the WINNFIELD ROCK QUARRY (*open on application*), 0.3 *m*., the only quarry in Louisiana. It is an enormous crater-like cavity whose walls are blazing patches of red and yellow clays. The quarry was worked before the War between the States, its limestone being burned to produce free lime. Most of the present output is used in road building.

At 4.8 *m*. on US 84 is the junction with a graveled road.

Right here to the CAREY SALT MINE (*open 9–11 a.m. on Mondays*), 0.3 *m*., with an almost unlimited supply of pure rock salt (*see Tour 2B*) extending in a solid mass to a depth of 2,600 feet, over an area of approximately one square mile. The daily output is approximately 25 carloads.

The GUM SPRINGS OBSERVATION TOWER at 8.7 *m.,* affords a fine view of the surrounding timberland.

West of the tower, signs at road intersections designate various private or commerical camps on SALINE LAKE, a short distance right, a part of the Northwest Fish and Game Preserve, which, including Black, Clear, and Saline Lakes, comprises an area of 35 square miles.

US 84 crosses Saline Bayou, 20.7 *m.,* the western boundary of the CATAHOULA DIVISION of the KISATCHIE NATIONAL FOREST.

CLARENCE, 25.4 *m.* (115 alt.) is at the junction with US 71 (*see Tour 18b*) and La 6; straight ahead on La 6.

At 28.8 *m.* La 6 crosses Red River by bridge, the piers of which were built of stone battlements taken from Fort Selden (*see below*).

GRAND ÉCORE (Fr., big bluff), 28.9 *m.,* received its name from an imposing 100-foot cliff overlooking Red River. In 1829 Dr. Samuel Russell built a home on the bluff, and after Red River changed its course in 1832 a trading post was established to take over the steamboat trade that formerly went to Natchitoches. By 1850 Grand Écore had become the shipping point for all east Texas and seemed destined to become the chief port on Red River. But in 1853 yellow fever swept the town, leaving hardly a family intact. Ten years later, Federal troops sacked and burned the town as they retreated from the battles of Mansfield and Pleasant Hill.

Several poems and ballads have been inspired by Grand Écore's War between the States history, some humorous, others in a tragic vein.

At 29 *m.* is the junction with a dirt road.

Right on this road 0.1 *m.* to a fork; R. here 0.2 *m.* to another fork, leading to high poinnts on GRAND ÉCORE BLUFF, from which there is an excellent view of Red River and the surrounding country. The breastworks built by the Confederates and Federals in 1864 can still be seen.

At 0.2 *m.,* on the main side road, is a fork; L. here 0.2 *m.* to the RUSSELL CEMETERY (R), a plot enclosed by an iron fence and containing strange and ancient-looking tombs. Here is buried Colonel Louis De Russey, veteran of the Mexican War and the War between the States and builder of Fort De Russey (*see Tour 17c*).

At 2.5 *m.* on the main side road, across a creek west of the Blue Hole, several hundred yards up a precipitous bluff, is (L) the SITE OF FORT SELDEN. Only the outlines of the ramparts, a few scattered stones, and chimney mounds are still visible. The fort was established in November 1820 by companies of the 7th U. S. Infantry under Lieutenant Colonel Zachary Taylor (*see Baton Rouge*), and was named in honor of Joseph Selden, who served as lieutenant in a Virginia regiment and as captain and major in the regular army in the War of 1812. The post served as the headquarters of the Western Department of the U. S. Army, which was stationed there to protect the western boundary of Louisiana. In 1822 the department moved to Fort Jesup (*see Tour 17A*) nearer the Sabine.

A short distance west of the Grand Écore Bridge are remains of old Confederate trenches, which extend from the highway into the woods for more than two miles.

From BADIN HILL (L), 32 *m.,* formerly a high bluff on Red River but now considerably leveled, legend has it that an Indian princess, unable to marry the man she loved, jumped to her death. The legend is

Fishing and Farming

FATHER BROUSSARD BLESSES SHRIMP FLEET NEAR LAFITTE

Times-Picayune Photo

SHRIMP TRAWLERS DECORATED FOR ANNUAL BLESSING,
GRAND CAILLOU BAY

OILING WINCH ON SHRIMP TRAWLER FOR NEW SEASON

Times-Picayune Photo

JUMBO SHRIMP, A LOUISIANA DELICACY

Times-Picayune Photo

CUTTING SUGAR CANE BY MACHINERY

TYPICAL SUGAR MILL, CENTRAL LOUISIANA

E. S. Delaune Photo, Times-Picayune

DELIVERING SUGAR CANE STALKS TO BIN AT MILL

CONVEYOR BELT CARRIES CANE TO CRUSHER IN MILL

New Orleans States-Item Photo

TRADITIONAL WAY OF PICKING COTTON

COTTON BALED FOR SHIPMENT

Farm Security Administration

HARVESTING RICE

STRAWBERRY PICKING IN TANGIPAHOA PARISH

Farm Security Administration

DUCK HUNTING IN THE BAYOU, WITH DECOYS

TARPON FISHING IN THE GULF

of such frequent occurrence in Louisiana that Lyle Saxon has suggested that she jumped for a living.

NATCHITOCHES, 32.8 *m.* (120 alt., 15,974 pop.) *see Natchitoches.*

Natchitoches is at junctions with La 1 (*see Tour 17b*) and La 6 (*see Tour 17A*).

Northwest of Natchitoches the route follows La 1 (*see Tour 17b*), which unites with US 84 between Armistead and Gahagan.

At GRAND BAYOU, 62.2 *m.* (134 alt.), the route turns L. on US 84. US 84 runs for approximately four miles through the Dolette Hills, named for Pedro Dolet (or Dolette), a Creole, who in 1795 founded a settlement on near-by Bayou Adayes. The hills extend to the southeast, covering an area of ten square miles, and are thought to have appreciable deposits of coal and iron.

At 76.7 *m.* is the junction with a dirt road.

Right on this road to CARMEL, 2 *m.*, first settled by French and Spanish Creoles among whom was Pierre Boitt Lafitte, descendant of Pierre Lafitte, the Baratarian pirate. In 1886 a group of German Catholics came to the community from Waco, Texas, and established the Carmel Monastery from which the town's name is derived. Under the direction of Father Peters, a convent and a rock chapel (*see below*) were also erected. The monastery, with the exception of the chapel, was destroyed by fire in 1895.

At 3.1 *m.* is the junction with a dirt road; R. here 0.2 *m.* to (L) the IMMACULATE CONCEPTION CHURCH (Roman Catholic), a plain white frame building. In the cemetery are buried many Laffittes, Lafittes, and Laffitts, and a few Germans. Directly to the rear of the church a path leads a half mile through a wood, across a field and a creek, to the aforementioned ROCK CHAPEL. It is a small Gothic structure of native rock with a clay-plastered interior. The walls have unfortunately been disfigured with the initials of visitors. The cornerstone at the rear is inscribed: "Anno Salutis 1891."

NABORTON, 78.3 *m.,* is a farming village that was settled about 1900, around the plantation of John Nabors.

MANSFIELD, 86.7 *m.* (332 alt., 6,432 pop. 1970) is at the junction with US 171 (*see Tour 19b*).

LOGANSPORT, 106.8 *m.* (207 alt., 1,330 pop. 1970), on the Sabine River, is an agricultural town whose principal industry is the ginning and marketing of cotton grown in the surrounding territory.

Founded in the 1830's, Logansport was originally known as Waterloo and later as Logan's Ferry, after a ferryboat operated here by the Logan brothers. The town was for many years a frontier trading post, owing to its situation on a river navigable to steamboats; but much of its business was taken over by Shreveport after the Red River was cleared of the Great Raft. The completion of the Shreveport and Houston Railroad in 1885 for a time revived Logansport's prosperity. Lumber interests also helped the town to hold its own, but in 1910 a log jam formed in Sabine River, closing Logansport to navigation.

At Logansport US 84 crosses Sabine River (*see Tour 1c*), the boundary between Louisiana and Texas, 15 miles east of Tenaha, Texas (*see Texas Guide*).

❧❧❧❧❧❧❧❧❧❧❧❧❧❧❧❧❧❧❧❧❧❧❧❧❧❧❧❧❧❧❧❧❧❧❧❧❧

Tour 6

Junction with La 1—Ferriday—Clayton—Winnsboro—Monroe; 78.7 *m.*, La 15.

M. P. R.R. roughly parallels route between Junction with US 65 and Archibald.
Hotels and restaurants at Winnsboro and Monroe; limited accommodations elsewhere.

La 15 branches north from La 1 one mile west of Lettsworth in Pointe Coupée Parish and follows the river north in Concordia Parish to a point near Ferriday, where it joins US 65 until Clayton, where it branches northwest.

La 15 traverses for the most part an alluvial region of cotton plantations, hardwood forests, swamps, and natural gas fields. Much of the farming is done on the tenant, or sharecropper, basis, and there are therefore few pretentious homes in the rural areas. The most conspicuous structures are the cotton gins, lumber mills, gas recovery plants, and warehouses for cotton and other farm products.

CLAYTON, 4.8 *m.* (46 alt., 1,103 pop. 1970) is a cluster of houses centering around a cotton gin, on the east bank of Tensas River, the boundary between Concordia and Catahoula (Ind., clear water) Parishes. The village is in a semi-swampland once subject to overflow but now protected by a levee system.

Northwest of Clayton the highway crosses Tensas River into Catahoula Parish, a region of great longleaf yellow pine forests, rolling hills, occasional bluffs, and broken creek bottoms. There are many fine mineral springs, mostly sulphur, in the western portion.

French attempts to colonize the Catahoula District were retarded by trouble with the Natchez, and since the section was overrun with the latter, the French finally left the Indians largely to themselves. Under Spanish rule, Catahoula received no particular attention, the Spaniards being more concerned with the Natchez District. It was not until 1800 that settlers began to come in numbers to the section. By then the Indians were so decreased in numbers and power that resistance was negligible.

Several groups of Indian mounds have been found in this vicinity, and excavation has given grounds to the belief that Indian tribes of great but unknown antiquity inhabited the section long before Columbus discovered America. Of the people who built the mounds, little is known, although it is believed that the last to live here before the advent of the white man was a tribe of sun worshipers, possibly akin to the Natchez and Taënsa. The latter, with the Ouachita and Catahoula (*see First Americans*), roamed through this region and probably made use of the handiwork of previous races.

La 15 crosses TENSAS RIVER, 4.9 *m.*, a stream named for a tribe of Indians inhabiting the region when Iberville, in 1699, made his first journey up the Mississippi.

North of LEE BAYOU, 8 *m.* (55 alt.), La 15, built above the low ground on either side, traverses a section wooded with tupelo, water oak, cypress, and other swampland trees.

SICILY ISLAND, 16.9 *m.* (70 alt., 630 pop. 1970) is said to have been given its name by an early explorer who saw a likeness in the country to his native Sicily. The village is situated on one of the highest points of land in this section, and in times of high water from near-by streams and bayous this area becomes an island. In the 1870's the village was the scene of an attempt to establish an agricultural community of Russian Jews. Charitably minded Israelites of New Orleans and New York contributed about $8,000 to bring to Louisiana 60 persecuted and starving Jewish families (173 persons in all), from Kiev and Elizabethograd, Russia. Governor John McEnery made them generous concessions of State lands to be tax-free for two years. Only eleven of the colonists were farmers, however, and they soon began to desert the settlement to take up peddling and factory work. An overflow of the Mississippi drove the remaining ones away a few years later.

Left from Sicily Island on La 8 to the junction with a graveled road 0.4 *m.;* L. on this road, on the shore of Lake Louis, 2.1 *m.*, are several INDIAN MOUNDS, in which many artifacts have been found.

At 20.6 *m.* is the junction with a dirt road.

Right here 1 *m.* to the junction with a dirt road; L. on this road along the bluff overlooking Ditto Lake, between two small creeks, is an area supposed to be the site of the last stand of the NATCHEZ INDIANS, 1.8 *m.* The discovery of axes, cannon balls, millstones, and iron tools, the last named much disfigured by rust, all evidently of French origin, led François Xavier Martin to say: "It appears to have been among the first inhabited by the French in Louisiana, who probably abandoned it at the epoch of the massacre by the Natchez Indians." According to an article in the *Louisiana Historical Quarterly* (July 1936), this place "has been proven to a mathematical certainty" to be the site of the last stand of the Natchez against Governor Étienne Périer.

Between Sicily Island and Winnsboro the route runs through a broad and fertile region of cotton plantations. There follow a number of farm villages. PECH, 21 *m.;* WISNER, 25 *m.;* GILBERT, 30 *m.;* CHASE, 34 *m.* At the height of the cotton picking season the road is lined with a continuous procession of cotton wagons being drawn by mules to the nearest gin. Many of these wagons, which belong to Negro farmers or sharecroppers, are built on the frames of old automobiles. The vehicles of the more prosperous are equipped with tires—often discarded automobile casings—but usually the wagon wheels roll on bare rims.

At 39.9 *m.* is the junction with La 130.

Right on this road 7.1 *m.* to the junction with a dirt road, opposite a school-house; L. here and L. through a gate, 8.2 *m.*, to (R) the BRANNIN MOUND, 9 *m.*, one of the few rectangular Indian mounds in Louisiana. It is 240 feet long, 130 feet wide, and about 22 feet in height. It is relatively flat on top and probably served for signaling or sacrificial purposes.

WINNSBORO, 40.5 *m.* (65 alt., 5,349 pop. 1970; 4,437, 1960, inc. 20%), the seat and largest town of Franklin Parish, has a number of cotton gins and sawmills and is the trading center of the surrounding section.

Early settlers of what is now Franklin Parish were principally of Scottish, Irish, and English descent, coming to Louisiana from the North. More interested in hunting and trapping than in agriculture, they were not attracted to the present site of Winnsboro but rather to the district's bayou and river country, where turkey, deer, and other game was plentiful. At the time of the Louisiana Purchase, 1803, Fort Miro (now Monroe), originally a Spanish military post, was the only white community in the region large enough to merit the name of settle-ment. After 1812, however, the influx of pioneers increased, and in 1843 the parish was established and named for Benjamin Franklin. That same year Winnsboro was founded on the plantation site of J. W. Willis.

North of BASKIN, 47.2 *m.* (74 alt., 177 pop. 1970), the road passes through broad cotton fields.

La 15 passes over a bridge, 49.7 *m.*, spanning Big Creek, the Frank-lin Parish boundary at this point, and enters Richland Parish. In 1929 Richland ginned more cotton than any other parish in the State—42,000 bales. There is a huge gas field in the western part of the parish that supplies natural gas by means of pipe lines to three of the South's largest cites, New Orleans, Memphis, and Birmingham, as well as to many smaller communities. There are also valuable timber tracts.

At ARCHIBALD, 53.9 *m.* (70 alt.), a cotton gin settlement, La 15 swings west.

Opposite the Alto High School, about 300 yards (R) from the highway, is the water-filled CRATER OF A GAS WELL, 58.8 *m.*, which caught fire in 1916 and burned, out of control, until 1931. The crater, 300 feet wide and 60 feet deep, was a raging inferno consuming untold billions of cubic feet of gas. At night its glow could be seen in the sky for a distance of 50 miles, providing a spectacular landmark. The crater became a swimming hole.

ALTO (Sp., high), 59.1 *m.* (74 alt.), began as one of the early gas-field towns of this area.

The UNITED GAS PIPE LINE COMPANY PUMPING STATION, 60.7 *m.* (L), pumps natural gas from near-by fields to distant points.

The highway crosses Bœuf (Fr., ox) River at 61 *m.* and enters a swamp region long noted as fishing and hunting grounds. There is a tradition that the river was given its name because some cattle belong-ing to Mexicans were drowned here. Another account attributes the name to the great numbers of buffaloes, or bison, that once roamed this part of Louisiana. According to an article in *De Bow's Review* (1847) "the last buffalo seen in the neighborhood of Fort Miro was killed in 1803."

La 15 crosses Bayou Lafourche (not to be confused with the southern Louisiana bayou of the same name), 67.9 *m.*, and enters Ouachita Parish.

It is thought that Hernando De Soto and his party may have been the first white men to set foot in what is now Ouachita Parish. Historians agree that De Soto discovered the Mississippi, which he explored as far north as White River, crossing to the west bank and penetrating as far as middle or western Arkansas. Descending toward the junction of the Ouachita and Tensas Rivers while avoiding the swampy ground on the immediate west bank of the Mississippi, it is quite possible that he kept to the high ground near the Ouachita. It is known that the Ouachita was explored by the early voyageurs.

In 1769, when Don Alexander O'Reilly took possession of Louisiana for Spain, a census was made and the population of the Ouachita territory was found to be 110. In 1785 Don Juan Filhiol and his companions established the Ouachita Post, on what is now the site of Monroe. Later on, great land grants were made along the Ouachita, among them the huge one to the Baron de Bastrop. Soon cotton had become an important commodity, and its planters embarked upon an era of prosperity.

In 1890 Ouachita Parish had a population of 17,895. Forests of the northern portion were furnishing turpentine and lumber, and the bottomlands were producing rich crops of cotton. In 1916 gas was discovered, and paper mills, power plants, gasoline absorption units, and carbon black plants sprang up. Industries came because natural gas fuel was cheaper in Ouachita Parish than anywhere else in America. By 1930 the population had grown to 54,337; the census of 1970 counted 115,387. The parish today is dominantly agricultural in character, but industries are multiplying in the cities; the cutting of pulpwood and saw logs is an important industry in the more hilly portions, west of the Ouachita.

MONROE, 78.7 *m.* (77 alt., 56,374 pop.) *see Monroe.*

Monroe is at junctions with US 80, US 165, and Int. 20.

Tour 7

(Vicksburg, Miss.)—Tallulah—Monroe—West Monroe—Ruston—
Minden—Shreveport—(Marshall, Tex.); US 80. Int. 20 parallel most
of the distance.
Mississippi Line to Texas Line, 200.6 *m.*

Concrete- and asphalt-paved roadbed.
Railroads paralleling route: I. C., between Delta and Shreveport.
Hotels and tourist camps at larger towns; limited accommodations elsewhere.

Section a.   MISSISSIPPI LINE to RUSTON; 108.3 m., US 80

West of the Mississippi River this section of the route across north
Louisiana traverses the fertile, cotton-planted Mississippi Basin, passes
just south of the oil and gas fields in the vicinity of Monroe, and winds
through an agricultural upland country to Ruston.

US 80 crosses the MISSISSIPPI LINE, 0 *m.,* in the center of a
great steel bridge three miles west of Vicksburg, Miss. The bridge provides a panorama of the Mississippi River and its vast levee system. To
the north is DE SOTO ISLAND, created in 1876 when the river broke
through De Soto Point, cutting approximately four miles from its former
course.

When Grant laid seige to Vicksburg in 1863, De Soto Point presented an obstacle to the Federal forces, since their gunboats, stationed
north of the city, could not negotiate the point and run through the
narrow waters past the city without subjecting themselves to murderous
fire from the Confederate shore batteries. As an expedient Grant attempted to run a canal across the point but was unsuccessful. A few
years later the river accomplished by itself, in less than a day, what
Grant's engineers had attempted. Within a few hours the new channel
assumed navigable depth, and a ferryboat, the tugboat *Bigley,* and the
John B. Maude, a passenger vessel, steamed through it the same day.
The crumbling of the former peninsula is still in progress, as illustrated
by a comparison of the cutoff's width, more than 6,000 feet, with its
width at the time of the river's shift— 650 feet.

De Soto Island is often referred to as an oasis, because as a part of
Louisiana it is "wet," while Mississippi is officially "dry." For years the
only building on the island was a saloon.

DELTA, 1.5 *m.* (90 alt.), was the scene of Grant's abortive attempt
to change the course of the river during the siege of Vicksburg. Part of
GRANT'S CANAL (L), 1.8 *m.,* still remains. Through WPA funds the
site was made into a park in 1936.

Mme. C. J. Walker (née Winnie Breedlove), the wealthiest Negro woman in America at the time of her death in 1919, was born on a plantation near Delta in 1867. Her fortune, which was estimated at more than $1,000,000, was derived from the sale of a lotion she invented to remove the kink from Negro hair. Though she lived in affluence at Irvington on the Hudson, much of her wealth was devoted to the betterment of her race.

At 2 *m.*, its back facing the road, is the OLD TOWNE HOUSE (*private*), a one-story brick structure now covered with weatherboarding and painted cream with a green gabled roof. It was built to house the parish archives after the removal of the parish seat from Richmond to Delta in 1868. The change of the government seat had been necessitated when Richmond, two miles south of present-day Tallulah, was partially burned by Federal soldiers. Proud of its position as the governing center, Delta offered stubborn resistance when in 1883 it was decided to move the seat to Tallulah. Residents of the latter community, however, spirited away the records and seals at night (*a coup d'état* several times perpetrated by Louisiana residents of those days) and the executive building in Delta was vacated.

West of Delta US 80 winds through the fertile farm lands of Madison Parish, which produces almost one-third of the Louisiana oat crop.

MOUND, 7.3 *m.* (87 alt.), so called because of the number of Indian mounds in the vicinity, is a small community set in the midst of spacious farms and plantations.

THOMASTOWN, 10.5 *m.* (85 alt.), in 1938 became the headquarters of the LADELTA CO-OPERATIVE ASSOCIATION, a resettlement project established by the Farm Security Administration on five tracts of land in Madison and East Carroll Parishes.

At 16.7 *m.* is the junction with La 3030, graveled.

Left on this unmarked road to (R) the CRESCENT PLANTATION HOUSE (*open*), 2.7 *m.*, on the west bank of Walnut Bayou in a grove of tall cedar and magnolia trees. The original house was constructed about 1832; the present front section was added in 1855. It is a frame house with a gabled roof and eight square columns supporting a wide gallery. The great front doorway, flanked by French windows which extend almost to the top of the 14-foot ceiling, gives entrance to a spacious hall. A spiral stairway with a mahogany railing ascends from the rear of the hall to the second floor. The original brass knobs and locks of the door are still in use, as are the transoms of stained glass, imported from Europe. The plastered walls and the ceiling ornaments are also well preserved. It is said the dwelling narrowly escaped destruction at the hands of Grant's army as it marched on Vicksburg, when a Federal reconnoitering troop drew up before the house, and the young commander gave the order to sack and burn. As his men dismounted and prepared to obey, the front door opened and the master of the house appeared, explaining that his wife lay within, gravely ill and likely to die if unduly excited. The officer courteously heard him through, bowed, and replied, "Sir, we do not murder women; I bid you good day."

TALLULAH, 18.7 *m.* (87 alt., 9,446 pop. 1970), seat of Madison Parish, originally a lumber center, in recent years has become more prosperous from beef cattle, oil and natural gas in the parish, as well as soybeans, cotton, wheat and other farm products. It is 20 *m.* west of Vicksburg, Miss., and 5 *m.* west of the "tamed" Mississippi, on the Brushy Bayou. Its highways are US 80, US 65, and I-20; it is served by the Illinois Central and Missouri Pacific Railroads, and Continental Trailways and Arrow Coach lines. Tallulah has two airfields and connects with scheduled service at Vicksburg Airport.

The climate of Madison Parish is humid and subtropical, with a rainfall of 55.1 in. The area is popular for hunting and fishing.

An influx of settlers into the Tallulah district took place between 1830 and 1860, as people from the older Southern States were attracted by the fertile alluvial lands.

Tallulah owes its existence, according to tradition, to the whimsey of a railroad engineer who, enchanted by a widow whose plantation lay to the north of Richmond, the parish seat in the late 1850's, obligingly routed the Vicksburg, Shreveport & Mississippi Railroad through her lands. The widow's affections shifted elsewhere soon after, and the engineer gave the railroad station the name Tallulah, in honor of a sweetheart in Georgia. In 1870 a north-south line, the Iron-Mountain Railroad, was built, and as a junction of two railroads Tallulah was launched upon its career.

MADISON PARISH COURTHOUSE, in the center of town, has outgrown its original dimensions. When erected in 1887 with upper and lower galleries columns and railings, it looked like a planter's mansion, but in recent years it has been remodelled and enlarged to accommodate growing business. The iron fence that surrounded the square has been removed and part of the large Courthouse lawn has become a parking lot. The Parish Jail stands opposite the Courthouse and was built beside the old jail.

The MADISON PARISH LIBRARY is housed in the former jail, which was converted to its present use in 1945. There is one branch library at Warsaw. The book collection totaled 21,657 in 1970. The Library is a member of the Trail Blazer Pilot Library System, serving 13 parishes in Northeast Louisiana.

Tallulah is at the junction with US 65.

The area traversed for some miles west of Tallulah is replete with winding bayous and lakes of varying sizes, and is known for its fishing. In the vicinity of WILLOW LAKE (R), 21.8 *m.,* and EAGLE LAKE (R), 23.2 *m.,* are a number of camps offering accommodations, boats, and bait. The two lakes are well stocked with bream, catfish, fresh-water drum, largemouthed black bass, and crappie. Bullfrogs are numerous in this section and grow to large size; their sale as a food commodity is of commercial importance. In this region are also found wild turkey, quail, dove, deer, and occasionally bears; panthers (cougars) still prowl the more remote wilderness.

QUEBEC, 26.7 *m.* (82 alt.), on Tensas River, was once a busy steamboat landing.

TENDAL, 30.5 *m.* (88 alt.), has a sawmill providing employment for those of its residents not engaged in farming.

WAVERLY, 33.1 *m.* (83 alt.), has a cotton gin and a store. Along the highway here are numerous palmettoes whose fronds are woven into hats, baskets, and many other articles.

In HANEY'S SALOON, 37.1 *m.,* on the east bank of Bayou Maçon, is a pair of pigskin saddle holsters for cap and ball pistols which the owner, who believes they belonged to Jesse James, found in a Delhi house (*see below*), a refuge for the outlaw.

Bayou Maçon, the dividing line between Madison and Richland Parishes, was named, according to legend, for Samuel Mason, leader of the Kentucky Cave-in-Rock bandits, who was slain near Vidalia in 1803 (*see Tour 12*). Frank and Jesse James and the Younger Brothers, latter nineteenth-century outlaws, also made the vicinity their sanctuary. The stream is stocked with game fish (*boats and bait available*).

DELHI, 38.1 *m.* (96 alt., 2,887 pop. 1970), was settled before the War between the States, and is said to have been given its name by its founder, John Bishop, after he had read Thomas Moore's poem, *Lallah Rookh.* Delhi is a thriving town, with a number of cotton gins and sawmills. On La 16, three blocks north of US 80 just beyond the high school in a grove of oaks and cedars, is a house (*open*) which once served as a refuge for JESSE JAMES. The one-and-one-half-story frame house was built shortly after the War between the States by Captain Jaret, a brother-in-law of James.

At 42.1 *m.* is the junction with a graveled road.

Right on this road to the junction with a dirt road, 0.9 *m.;* L. here to the CARPENTER HOUSE (*open*), 1.4 *m.,* a one-story frame structure set on brick pillars with six square wooden columns and a shingled, gabled roof. During the 1850's the house was a popular inn on the Vicksburg-Monroe stagecoach line. The owner has a bedspread under which Jesse James slept and a slab of a tree which James shot off while practice-shooting on the porch. There is also a bed in which General Alexander Chambers of the Union Army slept.

HOLLY RIDGE, 45.8 *m.* (88 alt.), is a sawmill village lying between forks of Big Creek, in an area of dense canebrakes.

RAYVILLE, 53.6 *m.* (76 alt., 3,962 pop. 1970), the seat of Richland Parish, was named for John Ray, a citizen of Monroe who had large land holdings in this section. Rayville began its development shortly after the War between the States, when it became the junction of the Vicksburg, Shreveport & Pacific (now Illinois Central) and the New Orleans & Northwestern (now Missouri Pacific) Railroads. In 1890 and 1891 much of the town was destroyed by fire, but it was rebuilt.

The RICHLAND PARISH FAIR GROUNDS, 54.4 *m.,* has a municipal swimming pool (*free*).

BŒUF RIVER, 56 *m.,* affords fine fishing (*boats, bait, and tackle obtainable at Girard at moderate rates*); the more densely wooded sections along its winding course are the habitat of deer, bear, wild turkey, and doves.

GIRARD, 56.5 *m.* (84 alt.), the oldest settlement in Richland Parish, was founded in 1821 and named for Stephen Girard, a noted figure of the Revolutionary War period who had large property holdings in the section.

CREW LAKE, 61 *m.* (70 alt.), on the shore of a small body of water shaded by water oaks, willows, and cypress, is a fishing resort (*boats, bait, and tackle available at moderate rates*).

At 69.1 *m.* is a ridge which was virtually the only dry ground between Vicksburg, Mississippi, and Monroe during the flood of 1927, when it was possible to travel between Monroe and the Mississippi by boat.

On both sides of the road at 71.8 *m.* are buildings of the LOUISIANA BAPTIST CHILDREN'S HOME (*visitors admitted*), maintained by the Louisiana Baptist Convention for the care and education of orphans.

Standing in a grove of magnolias at 72.1 *m.* is (R) INGLESIDE (*open*). The present structure was built around a much older house. It has three stories, the first of plastered brick, the others of wood. The lower columns, 24 in number, are of iron painted white and of the Ionic order; the upper are wooden and Doric. The home is reputedly haunted; it is said that in the still of night chains clank in the attic, the plantation bell tolls, chairs rock gently, and strange melodies arise from the old piano.

At 72.2 *m.* is the junction with a blacktop road.

Left on this road 0.8 *m.* to SELMAN FIELD, an airport serving the Delta Air Lines.

The SHERROUSE HOUSE (*open*), 72.6 *m.,* is a modern two-story brick and stucco structure occupying the site of the LIMERICK PLANTATION. The original building, no longer existent, was constructed about 1809, and it also boasted a supernatural tenant. This ghost was a whimsical being who nightly removed the stair-spindles, noisily placing them on the steps. In the cemetery are buried Ephraim Knowles Wilson, first Federal Judge of Louisiana; Oliver Morgan and Benjamin Tenelle, early jurists, and others who played leading parts in the development of the city of Monroe and Ouachita Parish.

The campus of the Northeast Louisiana State College begins at 73 *m.* *See Monroe.*

At 73.5 *m.* is the junction with US 165.

Left at this junction on Powell Avenue, graveled, to (L) the MARY GOSS HOME FOR AGED NEGROES (*open*), 0.3 *m.*, established in 1932 in compliance with the will of Mary Goss, a resident of Monroe who died in 1918, leaving her estate for charitable purposes. Before her marriage Mary Goss had been a cook in a private family; afterwards she ran a small restaurant where hot catfish was a specialty. She also lent money to Negro laborers in the neighborhood at a high rate of interest, and as she grew prosperous she felt she should do something to help the race. The following is an excerpt from her will: "If the collard people build a Home for the Old Cripled, Blind and Helpless Collard Folks tha are to have two thousand dollars for Buying grounds and Building for the same out of the Cash in the Banks tha are to Have as much as twenty dollars out of every Hundred of the Rent colected of the above Property mentioned to suport said Collard Home." The institution cares for from 76 to 100 needy people 60 years of age or over.

MONROE, 76.2 *m.* (77 alt., 56,374 pop.), *see Monroe.*

Monroe is at junctions with La 15 (*see Tour 6*) and US 165 (*see Tour 13*).

US 80 crosses Ouachita River at Monroe by bridge.

WEST MONROE, (77 alt., 14,868 pop. 1970), an industrial city is located on the Ouachita River opposite Monroe in Ouachita Parish. It was originally called Cottonport. It has a mayor and five aldermen and has recently built a new $5,000,000 hospital. A center for carbon black it has a new plant of the Sid Richardson Carbon Co. capable of producing 70,000,000 pounds per year, using refinery residues from the Humble Oil & Refining Co. plant in Baton Rouge. Other important organizations are Olinkraft, Inc., large paper bag and cartons processing plant; employing 2,500; Bancroft Paper Co., Union Cotton Oil Mill. This is also a timber center and distributor for vegetables, peaches and dairy products. West Monroe has a country club and recreation program, and the annual Northeast Louisiana fair and rodeo is held here, usually in October.

Left from West Monroe at the old traffic bridge on Coleman Avenue to the OLINKRAFT PAPER MILL (*open on application*), 2.1 *m.,* one of the largest sulphate pulp, board, and paper mills in the world. Ouachita Parish has vast forests of pinewood, cheap natural gas for fuel, and excellent rail and water transportation facilities, all of which are important factors in the success of the industry.

Wood is supplied to the mill from its own forests, and from individual landowners. It is cut in lengths of 4½ feet and from 6 to 12 inches in diameter upon arrival at the mill. After the bark has been removed, the point of water saturation, suitable for the grade of paper to be made. In which it is reduced to a pulp under high steam pressure. The pulp is washed, cleaned, and placed in machines called "Jordans," which reduce it to a certain point of water saturation, suitable for a grade of paper to be made. In order that the paper may have a smooth finish, small amounts of rosin size and alum or aluminum sulphate are added. The mixture is run into an endless moving wire screen, traveling from 200 to 1,000 feet a minute, depending on the grade of paper desired. The water drains through the wire, leaving the pulp in a sheet. This sheet is then led off the wire and run between presses and onto drying cylinders. When it is about 95 per cent dry, the sheet is ironed between huge steel rollers to give the paper a smooth finish. After undergoing very rigid physical and chemical tests, the paper is wound into rolls of the proper size, or cut into sheets.

Olinkraft, Inc., maintains a complete reforestation department, planting thousands of pines every year. On the grounds is a swimming pool for the employees and their families. A spacious gymnasium has been constructed for all community activities. In addition, the company sponsors a boys' harmonica band, baseball and basketball teams, clubs for boys and girls, and a weekly newspaper devoted to mill news.

Right from West Monroe on Trenton Street to the junction with a graveled road, 1.7 *m.;* R. on this road and R. again at a junction, 3.9 *m.,* to the G. B. COOLEY HOME FOR THE RETARDED, 5.5 *m.* It was founded in 1936 as a tuberculosis sanitarium through the efforts of the Ouachita Parish Tuberculosis

Association and Captain G. B. Cooley, its chief individual sponsor; various other organizations and individuals contributed to its construction fund.

The two main buildings are in a grove at the top of a 100-foot elevation overlooking Bayou D'Arbonne. The natural beauty of the setting has been enhanced by landscaping done by the WPA. A dam across a ravine forms a lake 900 feet long, which is stocked with fresh-water fish. Other features are a reading room at one end of the dam, a rustic log hut, bandstand, vegetable garden, and a fruit orchard.

West of West Monroe US 80 enters the hill country. The predominant forest trees are pine, oak, and gum. Although cotton is the staple farm product, an effort has been made toward diversifying crop production; many farms have canefields, a grinding mill, and facilities for making syrup; sweet potatoes, tomatoes, and watermelons are also grown.

In a grove of cedars at 86.1 *m.* is (L) the house locally known as the OLD CAMP PLACE (*open*), one of the oldest houses in the region and popularly supposed to be haunted. It was built about 1855 and was once an inn on the Monroe-Shreveport stagecoach line on the Old Wire Road. As such it was the first stop out of Monroe and horses were changed here. Remodeling decreased the original two stories to one story, but nearly all materials used were from the old house—plates, joists, and sills, hewn by hand from solid pine logs. It is said that refugees of the War between the States buried gold nearby and that a murder was committed in the house.

MOUNT ZION CEMETERY, 89.3 *m.,* is one of the oldest burial grounds west of the Ouachita and all that remains of Forksville, once a prosperous community dominated by the Faulk and McClendon families. Some of the headstones bear quaint inscriptions of former years, one reading "She never turned a stranger from her door"; another "The McClendons—a people sturdy as the oak, stalwart as the pine, gentle as the brook, and enduring as the hills."

The LOUISIANA DEPARTMENT OF AGRICULTURE EXPERIMENT STATION, 91 *m.,* was established here in 1888 by the State Board of Agriculture. Affiliated with the Agricultural College of Louisiana State University, this station has been the scene of many experiments concerning dairy improvement, forage crops, and soil erosion.

CALHOUN, 91.4 *m.* (165 alt.), and CHOUDRANT, 101 *m.* (154 alt.), are small cotton-ginning towns.

RUSTON, 108.3 *m.* (311 alt., 17,365 pop.) *see Ruston.*

Ruston is at the junction with US 167 (*see Tour 15a*).

Section b.   RUSTON to TEXAS LINE; 92.3 m., US 80; Int. 20 parallels the route.

West of RUSTON, 0 *m.,* US 80 passes through hilly country broken only by the Red River Valley around Shreveport.

GRAMBLING, 5 *m.,* is the seat of Grambling College.

SIMSBORO, 10.2 *m.* (323 alt.), was formerly one of the largest lumber towns in Lincoln Parish.

ARCADIA, 18.2 *m.* (368 alt., 2,970 pop. 1970), the seat and largest town of Bienville Parish, is the trade center of an area in which the leading activities are cotton growing, lumbering, cottonseed-oil manufacturing, and the ginning and compressing of cotton. The Arcadia Salt Dome, 1 mile south of town, is known to have a tremendous potential salt production. Arcadia is at the junction with La 9 (*see Tour 16*).

AMBROSE MOUNTAIN, about one-and-one-half miles distant (R) from the highway, between Arcadia and Gibsland, is one of the highest points in the State, having an elevation of more than 400 feet. Clyde Barrow, once Public Enemy Number One, and his cigar-smoking consort, Bonnie Parker, established a hide-out in this section in 1934, and were tracked down and killed here by Texas rangers and a sheriff's posse.

GIBSLAND, 26.8 *m.* (245 alt., 1,380 pop. 1970), at the junction of the Illinois Central and the Louisiana & Northwestern Railroads, is the shipping center of Bienville Parish. Gibsland came into existence in 1884, when its site, the plantation of Dr. Gibbs, was chosen as the railroad junction in preference to the already established town of Mount Lebanon (*see below*), 2.8 miles to the south. The town is encircled by a prosperous vegetable-growing and general farming section.

COLEMAN COLLEGE (Baptist) for Negroes, in the southern outskirts of town, was founded in 1888 by Oliver L. Coleman, a Mississippi Negro. Parish training schools at Arcadia and Minden have, to a large extent, superseded this once important Negro college. College and commercial courses are still offered, however, and a theological school is maintained. The college also operates a broom and mattress factory. Recently the north building was deeded to the parish school board for a Negro high school. On the ten-acre campus is the Praying Tree, an old hickory arched in an attitude of prayer beside a spring. During the great drought of 1896, when the fields lay barren, wells dried up, and stock perished, Oliver L. Coleman prayed for rain beneath the tree. In answer to his prayer clouds formed and rain fell upon the parched earth. Sometime later, after the drought had ended, a spring bubbled up at the foot of the tree.

Left from Gibsland on blacktop La 154, unmarked, to MOUNT LEBANON, 2.8 *m.*, the first permanent settlement in Bienville Parish. In 1836 South Carolinians, attracted by great stands of timber and fertile soil, founded the town. Many of the pioneers were of the Baptist denomination, and in 1837 they built the Reheboth Baptist Church. In 1853 Mount Lebanon University was founded, receiving endowment from Baptists of Louisiana and other States. Student life must have been somewhat rowdy, for in addition to prohibiting gambling and drinking, the catalogue for the 1860–61 session decreed that "no student shall wear about his person, or have in his possession, while attending in any department of University, any pistol, dirk, bowie-knife, or dangerous weapons of any kind, under pain of expulsion." The college closed during the War between the States and never reopened.

During the War between the States Mount Lebanon was one of the three communities in the State to issue its own postage stamps. The Mount Lebanon stamp, from the hand press of the local printing shop, is today a rare and valuable philatelic specimen. It is red-brown on white paper. The wood block was carved as the stamp would ordinarily have appeared. As a consequence the stamp itself is inverted, the only instance of such an ocurrence known to philately.

The WEBSTER PARISH TRAINING SCHOOL (R), 42.2 *m.*, founded in 1922, consists of five buildings on a 30-acre campus. It offers excellent academic and occupational training facilities for Negroes of Webster Parish.

MINDEN, 43 *m.* (181 alt., 13,996 pop.) *see Minden.*

West of BAYOU DORCHEAT, 46.3 *m.*, a good fishing spot (*boats, tackle, bait*), the highway traverses a rolling wooded section which becomes more level and of lesser altitude as the Red River bottomlands are entered.

FILLMORE, 57.4 *m.*, was a thriving pre-Civil War community, but is now little more than a crossroads settlement.

At 58.1 *m.* is the junction with a graveled road.

Left on this road 0.5 *m.* to GIDDENS' CASTLE HILL, occupied by a modern frame cottage with a swimming pool. Two other buildings (*open*) house the personal collection of the late T. K. Giddens. The collection includes furniture, plaintings, and bric-a-brac. Mr. Giddens, who made a fortune in oil, was the author of a volume of memoirs. The castle for which the hill is named burned in 1936.

RED CHUTE BAYOU, 63.8 *m.*, is a good stream for fishing. The vicinity is the locale of many of Roark Bradford's Negro stories.

West of the bayou US 80 crosses the broad Red River Valley, paralleling a short distance to the south, the route of the OLD SHED ROAD. Before the construction of this unusual highway in 1874, cotton wagons were hauled with the greatest difficulty through the axle-deep mud of the valley. A corduroy road proving no better, the logs disappearing or slithering out of place in the mud, an expensive but positive method was resorted to, to keep the highway dry: a shed, nine miles in length, with eaves overhanging drainage ditches, was erected over an embanked roadway. For years thereafter, until the railroads supplanted it, the covered road was kept dry and in such good condition that it is said the mules that regularly traveled it, on sighting the shed from the hills, would bray in anticipation of easy going. Only the embankment of the old road is now visible.

At 69.8 *m.* is the junction with La 3 (*see Tour 17a*).

BOSSIER CITY, 70.9 *m.* (180 alt., 41,595 pop. 1970) is located on the east bank of the Red River opposite Shreveport, with which it is connected by bridges. It is the industrial center of Bossier Parish and the entertainment center of the Bossier-Shreveport area. Adjoining it on the south is the BARKSDALE AIR FORCE BASE. Besides US 79–80, I–20 serves both it and Shreveport. *See article, Bossier City.*

US 79–80 crosses the Long-Allen Bridge over Red River into Caddo Parish and Shreveport.

SHREVEPORT, 71.9 *m.* (225 alt., 182,064 pop.) *see Shreveport.*

Shreveport is at junctions with La 1, La 3, US 71, US 171, I–20.

At 77 *m.* on US 79–80 is the junction with a blacktop road. Right on this road 0.5 *m.* to the SHREVEPORT COUNTRY CLUB.

The SHREVEPORT POLO GROUNDS is at 78.1 *m.* and at 78.7 *m.* is the SHREVEPORT SKEET CLUB.

THE PINES TUBERCULAR SANITORIUM (*visiting hours 8–10 a.m., 3:30–8 p.m.*), 81.1 *m.*, is a private institution.

At 83.1 *m.* is the junction with a blacktop road.

Left on this road to the CADDO PARISH PENAL FARM (*open Sundays only, 9 a.m.–2 p.m.*), 0.5 *m.* The main building, an air-conditioned structure, was built of bricks salvaged when the old parish jail was razed. The institution has a capacity of 200 and is partly self-supporting.

ROSE HILL LAKE (L), 86.6 *m.,* has bathing and picnicking.
GREENWOOD, 87.4 *m.* (217 alt.), a lumber and agricultural town, was a trading post on the old wagon trail between Shreveport and Texas in the early nineteenth century. In 1855 it rivaled Shreveport in importance and an election was held to decide which should be the parish seat; Shreveport won by a single vote. To the present day a block in the center of Greenwood (R) is ownerless, having been set aside in 1855 for the parish courthouse.

Branching left from Greenwood US 79 connects with Texas 31 at DeBerry, 15 *m.*, and US 59 at Carthage, 30 *m.*

US 80 crosses the Texas Line, 92.3 *m.,* 21 miles east of Marshall, Texas, north of Int. 20. This was once the international boundary line between the United States and the Republic of Texas (*see Tour 1c*). Circular mounds, 5 feet high, were placed at regular intervals by surveyors to mark the division between the two nations.

❦❦❦❦❦❦❦❦❦❦❦❦❦❦❦❦❦❦❦❦❦❦❦❦❦❦❦❦❦

Tour 8

New Orleans—Arabi—Chalmette—Battlefield of Jan. 8, 1815—Chalmette National Historical Park—Violet—Poydras—St. Bernard, La 39.

This route extends southeastward from New Orleans down the left bank of the Mississippi River through the St. Bernard and Plaquemines Delta, one of the earliest settled sections of Louisiana. The inhabitants are descendants of early French, Spanish, and Canary Island settlers; the last named were and are still sometimes called Isleños (Sp., islanders) (*see Tour 8A*).

The countryside adjacent to the river and the numerous small bayous is fertile, supporting extensive vegetable farms, sugar cane plantations, and fruit orchards. The marsh areas contiguous to Lake Borgne are unfit for cultivation, but teem with muskrats.

La 39 swings eastward from NEW ORLEANS, 0 *m.*, on N. Claiborne Ave., turning R. on Elysian Fields Ave. and L. on St. Claude Ave.

JACKSON BARRACKS (R), 5 *m.*, extending from the highway to the river, between Delery St. and the St. Bernard Parish Line, were constructed during the administration of Andrew Jackson as a garrisoned military post for the defense of New Orleans and as a depot for interchanging troops garrisoning the river forts during the months when yellow fever was prevalent. The post was designed much in the manner of an Indian fort, with a high surrounding wall and four towers provided with rifle slots and embrasures for small cannon.

Federal troops were quartered at the barracks until about 1920, at which time the place was leased to the State of Louisiana for the housing of National Guard units. Troops have embarked from the barracks to participate in every major conflict engaged in by the United States. When Louisiana seceded in 1861 the post was taken over by the Confederate authorities but was later captured and garrisoned by Federal troops. Today Jackson Barracks maintains 14 units of National Guardsmen (about 700 men), provides warehouses for Federal and State property, and houses about 40 family of guardsmen.

The reservation consists of approximately 84 acres. Buildings ranging from large brick structures with 18- and 22-inch walls more than a century old, to small temporary sheet-iron buildings, are capable of garrisoning about 1,500 soldiers. The barracks have been remodeled and several new buildings were constructed under the WPA.

ARABI, 5.2 *m.* (6 alt.), came into being as a scattered suburb of New Orleans, in the latter half of the nineteenth century. In the 1890's, after a fire had destroyed the parish courthouse and several neighboring buildings, the town was given the name Arabi, reputedly because the incendiary activities of an Arabian sheik was at that time in the news.

Right from Arabi on Angela Ave. 0.6 *m.* to the site of the MERAUX HOUSE, 224 Angela Ave. which was badly gutted by fire in 1939. The house was erected in 1808 by David Urquhart, grandfather of Cora Urquhart Brown-Potter, the actress, and great-grandfather of Mrs. James "Fifi" Stillman. It was purchased in 1833 by Alexander de Lesseps, a wealthy sugar planter and cousin of the famous Comte Ferdinand de Lesseps who built the Suez Canal. Shortly after the War between the States the home was sold with the plantation of "Mon Secour and Mon Plaisir" to James Maumus who, upon his death, willed these estates to his daughter, Mrs. Meraux. The place was originally called the Château des Fleurs (Fr., castle of flowers), because of its gardens, which are yet crowded with native and exotic plants.

Left from Angela Ave. on N. Peters St. which follows the river.

The AMERICAN SUGAR REFINERY is said to be the second largest sugar refinery in the world. Completed in 1909, the plant occupies a 70-acre tract, a part of which was the old Roy estate and the site of La Maison des Jalousies (Fr., house of shutters). La Maison des Jalousies, so called because of the shuttered galleries surrounding it, was used as a temporary hospital for General Jackson's wounded soldiers during and after the Battle of New Orleans. The main building of the refinery is 13 stories high, and has 1,300,000 square feet of floor space; there are 1,500 employees. Six miles of railroad tracks within the yards facilitate shipping. (*For sugar industry see Tour 10B.*)

The THREE OAKS PLANTATION HOUSE (*adm. by permission of American Sugar Refinery*), 1.4 m. (L), is so-called because of the three trees growing directly in front. According to legend, General John Lewis of the Confederate Army, as a 10-year-old boy, planted two acorns to commemorate the birth in 1810 of twin brothers. By chance a third acorn was lying nearby, and from these have grown the three beautiful trees. The present ante-bellum structure stands on the site of an earlier dwelling used as a hospital in 1815, after the Battle of New Orleans. It is a cement-covered brick structure entirely surrounded by broad galleries supported by brick columns of the Doric type, which extend from the ground floor to the roof. When Admiral Farragut's fleet passed up the river to capture New Orleans in 1862, it was fired upon by a Confederate battery at Chalmette a short distance below the Three Oaks Plantation and, in the return fire, a shot from one of Farragut's gunboats destroyed one of the columns. Canon balls found lodged in nearby trees have also been traced to this engagement.

CHALMETTE SLIP, 1.6 *m.,* is a deep-water shipping terminal. There are huge dock warehouses and special equipment for the unloading of copra (dried coconut meat) from the Philippine Islands. Construction of the slip necessitated the destruction of several fine old mansions, among them the old MACARTY HOUSE, which was of special interest because of the fact that General Andrew Jackson used it as temporary headquarters during the Battle of New Orleans. Vincent Nolte, an active participant, gives a stirring account of the battle in his *Fifty Years in Both Hemispheres.* He tells of cannon balls still embedded in the Macarty house in 1838, the owners "in their enthusiasm" having "caused them to be gilt, in the year 1822." Nolte's book was one of the sources of Hervey Allen's *Anthony Adverse.* Louis Barthelemy, Chevalier de Macarty, original owner of the mansion, was said to have been a tyrannical and cruel slavemaster. On one occasion while his neighbor, Chalmette, was at breakfast, a slave sent by Macarty brought a note and a cornucopia in which Chalmette found the ear of a slave. The note read: "My friend, this is the way to treat a renegade slave." Macarty's wife was later murdered by her slaves and his daughter, Delphine (Madame Lalaurie), became known for her cruelty. *See New Orleans: the Haunted House in the Vieux Carré.*

The NEW ORLEANS RIFLE RANGE, 6.5 *m.,* for organized units of the National Rifle Association, is used primarily for training police and the National Guard.

At this point the highway bisects the CHALMETTE BATTLE-FIELD, scene of the Battle of New Orleans, January 8, 1815, the last engagement of the War of 1812, fought 16 days after peace was declared at Ghent on December 24, 1814.

The engagements of December 23, 1814, and January 8, 1815, were fought on a strip of land approximately a half-mile wide, extending three miles along the river below Chalmette Monument (*see below*).

On December 23, 1814, the vanguard of the invading British forces succeeded in advancing unseen via Bayou Bienvenue as far as the Villeré Plantation (*see below*), where Major Villeré and the detachment of Louisiana militia under his command were captured. While the British set up camp and brought up troops from their fleet at anchor in Lake

Borgne, General Andrew Jackson, having been notified of the strength and position of the invaders, mobilized his men and made plans for an immediate attack. The war-schooner *Carolina* was to anchor off the levee close to the enemy encampment and give the signal for a general attack by directing a broadside at the British. General Coffee and his Tennesseans, who are said to have marched 120 miles in two days, were to move to the cypress swamps and fall upon the British flank and rear, while Jackson and his regulars, Plauché's city volunteers, who had run all the way to New Orleans from Fort St. John (at the mouth of Bayou St. John on Lake Pontchartrain), Daquin's colored battalion, McRea's marines, and 18 Choctaw Indians were to strike along the river.

The *Carolina* moved up to the levee at 7:30 p.m. and opened fire on the unsuspecting British as they were cooking supper and preparing their bivouacs. Confusion reigned as the redcoats put out their fires and ran for shelter behind a secondary levee. Simultaneously, Jackson and Coffee advanced to the attack. In the hand-to-hand combat in the dark in which bayonets, tomahawks, hunting knives, and fists were used to advantage, the Tennesseans made murderous inroads on the British right flank, although Jackson's charge was met with stubborn resistance. After two hours of fighting, a heavy fog terminated the battle, neither side having gained any decisive advantage.

The American forces retreated 2 miles toward New Orleans during the night and established a breastwork on an abandoned canal between Chalmette and Rodriguez plantations. During the following week, while the intervening area was flooded by a break in the levee to impede an advance by the enemy, eight batteries were erected and preparations made for the British attack. Jackson now had about 5,000 men, including Jean and Pierre Lafitte's Barataria pirates. This motley crew was expected to withstand the assault of between 8,000 and 9,000 veterans of Wellington's Peninsular Campaign under the leadership of General Sir Edward Pakenham, the Duke of Wellington's brother-in-law.

The British brought up more troops and artillery. On January 1, in an effort to open breaches in the American fortifications, 24 English guns began a steady fire upon the entire extent of Jackson's line. The Americans, with 12 or 13 guns, replied with enthusiasm. Round after round rattled down the breastworks, from the river to the swamp, as the defenders of the city manned their batteries in the manner that had won for the Americans the reputation of being the best artillerymen of the day. So steady were their rounds of fire and so deadly their aim that within an hour the fire of the enemy was broken. By 3 p.m. the British ceased firing and abandoned their guns, conceding victory to Jackson's men, among whom none handled their guns better than Dominique You and Beluche, battle-scarred members of Lafitte's "hellish banditti" with whom Jackson had been loath to associate a few weeks before.

Pakenham now elected to wait for reinforcements. Jackson benefited little by the delay for, although 2,000 Kentuckians arrived, few could be put into service because of a shortage of guns and equipment.

Meanwhile rumors circulated to the effect that New Orleans was to be burned to the ground in the event of defeat.

The morning of January 8, 1815, broke with the roar of cannon and the orderly advance of the British main army. Preceded by showers of Congreve rockets, the British, carrying scaling ladders, advanced with precision and arrogant slowness. The main attack was directed to the American left, near the cypress swamp where Generals Carroll, Adair, and Coffee were stationed with their "dirty shirts," as the British called the riflemen from Kentucky and Tennessee. Grape and canister were poured into the ranks of the oncoming redcoats, while the backwoodsmen, unabashed by either the elegance or the reputation of the veterans who had harassed Napoleon Bonaparte, cut great swarths in the enemy line. Standing knee deep in mud and water, these bedraggled, tobacco-chewing mountaineers handled their "shootin' irons" with great precision and devastating efficiency. British reserves came up to keep the line intact, but the advance was checked short of the breastwork, the British retreating from the hail of fire that crackled across the plain. Pakenham, in an attempt to rally his men, was shot from his horse and carried to the rear, mortally wounded. A second rally was effected but was completely routed. By 8:30 a.m. the enemy, entirely defeated, retreated, leaving the field covered with dead and wounded. The Americans reported that only 13 of Jackson's men were killed, 30 wounded, 19 missing, as compared to British casualties of 700 killed, 1,400 wounded, and 500 missing.

CHALMETTE NATIONAL HISTORICAL PARK

Just beyond the Chalmette Slip the tall obelisk of the Chalmette Monument marks the beginning of Chalmette National Historical Park, comprising a vital section of the territory covered by the BATTLE OF NEW ORLEANS, fought here on January 8, 1815, in which Andrew Jackson and a mixed assortment of American troops decisively defeated British regulars under General Sir Edward Michael Pakenham and saved New Orleans. This, the last engagement of the War of 1812, was fought 16 days after peace was declared (but not yet ratified) at Ghent on December 24, 1814. The Park extends from the St. Bernard Highway to the River and southeast to the Fazendeville Road; there is a small segment beyond where the Chalmette National Military Cemetery begins.

Chalmette takes its name from Ignace de Lino de Chalmette, owner of the plantation on which the battle was fought. He was 60 years old at the time and with his son François fought in the ranks, while their home was burned down.

While the Park now protects an important section of the battlefield, the fighting from December 23, 1815, to January 8, 1815, took place on a strip of land about half a mile wide extending three miles along the River beyond the Chalmette Monument. Between the River and cypress swamps were located plantations of sugar cane. Years passed before much interest was shown in the site, but in 1840 the 25th anniversary brought Andrew Jackson to New Orleans for a celebration. He laid the cornerstone of a monument that was to be raised to him in the Place d'Armes, now Jackson Square, and he visited the battlefield. On January 13, 1840, a few days after his visit, the cornerstone for a monument was laid on the site of the battle.

The Jackson Monument Association tried to raise money for the monument, with little success. In 1855 the State of Louisiana bought a tract of land that included the rampart that the Americans had built along the line of the Rodriguez Canal and began to erect the monument. Work progressed slowly. In 1894 the area was placed in custody of the United States Daughters of 1776 and 1812, who cared for it until 1929. In 1907 the land was given to the United States Government by the State and the monument was completed. The U. S. Dept. of the Interior took custody in 1933. In 1939 the Chalmette National Historical Park was created and the National Park Service took over this and the Military Cemetary. In 1949 the Réné Beauregard house was added and reconstructed for the Visitor Center.

The Monument is built of brick covered with marble and has an iron spiral staircase with a brick center support leading to an observatory. It is 100 ft. 2½ in. tall; its width is 48 ft. sq. at bottom of base, 14 ft. 4 in. sq. at base of shaft. An explanatory plaque was placed by the Chalmette Chapter, United Daughters of 1812 on October 19, 1947. When the shaft was damaged by lightning the third time in May, 1937, lightning protection, with rod, was installed.

A self-guiding tour of the Park is outlined in Historical Handbook No. 29 of the National Park Service, entitled Chalmette National Historical Park, by J. Fred Roush for which address the Supt. of Documents, Government Printing Office, Washington, D.C. 20402. The following summary of sites inside the Park is partly based on it.

The VISITORS CENTER occupies the former Réné Beauregard House, which was restored in 1957. This plantation house, designed by James Gallier, Sr., had been built in 1840. It is a cement-covered brick structure of two stories with an attic and dormers. Extending along front and rear are wide galleries supported by eight doric brick columns rising to the roof. The house was known locally as *Bueno Retiro* and was occupied from 1880 to 1904 by Judge Réné Beauregard, son of General P. T. G. Beauregard, CSA. In addition to restoring the facade the National Park Service completely remodeled the interior. The house contains pictures and memorabilia of the battle. Here is a large ground map that explains the action by means of flashing bulbs and a taped lecture.

The RODRIGUEZ CANAL is a low depression in the ground that marks a former millrace, already unused when the Americans threw up a rampart of mud and timber behind it. It is on the boundary between the Chalmette and McCarty plantations. The rampart, extending along the canal to the River became the formidable barrier by means of which the Americans were able to repell the British attacks. It has been partially restored.

A marker at the River end of the ramparts indicates the location of the first three batteries, which stood on the 800 feet of land long since eroded by the River. Battery 1, had 2 12-pounders and a 6-in. howitzer; Battery 2 a 24-pounder served by sailors from the lost *Carolina;* Battery 3 had two 24-pounders served the Baratarians under Dominique You and Renato Beluche.

The rest of the batteries are properly marked along the American line. No. 4 had a 38-pounder served by sailors from the *Carolina.* Between Batteries 3 and 4 stood the Battalion of Louisiana Free Men of Color. The next (5) is known as the Victory marker, describing the importance of the victory. Then comes the Chalmette Monument.

Next on the map No. 7 locates a reconstruction of the mud rampart and Battery 5. No. 8 is Battery 6, commanded by Gen. Garrigues Flaujeac and supported by musket fire by a company of U. S. Marines and Kentucky volunteers. No. 9 is Battery 7, served by U. S. Army artillerymen and Tennessee militia commanded by Major Gen. William Carroll. The supreme effort of the British was stopped here and before Batteries 6 and 8. No. 10 designates "the mysterious gun," supported by Kentucky troops commanded by a corporal, name unknown.

No. 11 marks the left end of the American line in the swamp, held by Tennessee volunteers commanded by Brig. Gen. John Coffee. This is the last of the identified positions. The visitor then walks a short distance east on the St. Bernard Highway past Fazendeville Road to the next section administered by the Government.

This is the CHALMETTE NATIONAL MILITARY CEMETERY, which was established as a National Cemetery in 1864 and holds the remains of 15,000 veterans, 6,700 of them unidentified. It was closed for burials in 1945. In 1874 members of the Grand Army of the Republic (GAR) erected a monument in the center of the cemetery. In 1956 it was moved to the River Terminal Circle (No. 13 on the map). It bears the inscription *Dum Tacent Clamant*—While Silent, They Cry Out.

A bronze tablet, 7.4 *m.,* marks the site of the BIENVENUE PLANTATION. The Bienvenue family owned the largest concession of land in this vicinity in the late 18th and early 19th centuries; Bayou Bienvenue derived its name from the family. The old plantation home was destroyed during the Battle of New Orleans.

The ST. BERNARD PARISH COURTHOUSE, 7.7 *m.,* is a three-story concrete and steel structure with Indiana limestone facing, and granite and stone steps.

At 8 *m.* are the ruins of VERSAILLES, a plantation home built in 1805 by Pierre Denis De La Ronde, who planned to establish here a city to be called Versailles. On the shore of Lake Borgne he planned a sister city to be called Paris. Connecting the two was to be the Chemin de Paris (Fr., Paris Road). The battle and other events changed De La Ronde's plans. During the Battle of New Orleans the Versailles mansion was used as a field hospital by the British. The Paris Road became a major highway, used by La 47.

De La Ronde's nine daughters were called the nine muses and his son was known as Apollo. The family was at the town house on Chartres Street, New Orleans, when the British raided Versailles. After De La Ronde's death Versailles was sold. The house was destroyed by fire in 1876.

Extending from the roadside ruins to the river about a half-mile away is a magnificent avenue of moss-festooned live oaks popularly known as PAKENHAM OAKS, through the erroneous supposition that General Pakenham died beneath them. Part of the battle of December 23 was fought under these trees, and it was from this position that Jackson retreated upstream. The trees are sometimes ascribed to De La Ronde, but the National Park Service dates them from around 1820, after the battle.

At the riverside end of the oaks is the oil refinery of the CHALMETTE PETROLEUM CORPORATION.

At 8.1 m. is the junction with La 47, originally a part of De La Ronde's Chemin de Paris, but now called the Paris Road.

Left on this road to BAYOU BIENVENUE 3.3 m., up whose banks Pakenham marched his invading redcoats and upon which he floated his cannon. The English fleet had been anchored off the Chandeleur Islands, Lake Borgne being too shallow to accommodate the frigates. After the fleet had anchored, Pakenham sent 45 open boats manned by 1,200 men on a reconnoitering expedition. Commanding the entrance to Lake Borgne were five American gunboats manned by 182 men. The American force was defeated in a hard-fought engagement and the British were able to transport troops up Bayou Bienvenue unmolested.

At 8.8 m. on La 39 is the junction with a dirt road.

Left here 0.5 m. to the century-and-a-quarter-old LACOSTE HOUSE, in a cluster of trees, surrounded by vegetable gardens. The building was used by the British as headquarters for a battalion of infantry under the command of Major Hinds. It is a raised cottage, the lower front brick with brick archways entirely surrounding the house.

About 100 yards from the road at 9 m. is a marker designating the point from which the schooner *Carolina* poured a broadside into the British camp on December 23, 1814, giving the signal for a general attack. Although the *Carolina* floated in 50 or more feet of water, the river has shifted so that the present bank is 600 yards south of the point, making it necessary to look away from the river to the location of the *Carolina*'s former position. The British camp at the time of attack was about 300 yards north of the marker.

At 9.5 m. is the junction with a dirt road.

Left on this road 0.4 m. to the site of CONSEIL, the plantation of Jacques Philippe de Villeré, first native-born governor of the State (1816–20). It is said that Villeré's six sons and two daughters—the sons, like their father, wealthy sugar planters—were accustomed to come daily to the "mother-house," and in the beautiful garden seek their parents' counsel; hence the name Conseil. A large oil storage tank now occupies the site of the plantation home. Under a giant pecan tree, no longer standing, the viscera of General Pakenham are said to have been buried. According to legend, from then on until it was cut down or died a natural death the pecans of the tree were streaked with red. The remainder of Pakenham's body is said to have been shipped to England preserved in a barrel of rum; home-bound veterans of the campaign are supposed to have inadvertently drunk the liquor. The difficulty of preserving bodies for burial in distant lands in those days gave rise to the custom of burying the viscera of slain officers at the field of battle, and returning the rest of the body to native soil.

Major Gabriel Villeré, son of the governor, was the first prisoner taken by the British, a party of whom had approached the plantation via the Villeré Canal (no longer extant). Surprised in the home, Major Villeré was captured but escaped through a window and fled through the woods. Outdistancing his pursuers, he at length reached New Orleans and warned Jackson of the enemy's approach. On the evening following the defeat of the English, General Jackson presented Pakenham's costly sidearms to Major Villeré.

On the mile-square DOCVILLE FARM, 11.9 *m.,* grow thousands of pear, plum, peach, orange, and pecan trees. On both sides the highway here is lined with banana, oleander, and crape myrtle trees. Many varieties of honeysuckle and other vines trail from the roadside fences.

VIOLET, 13.2 *m.* (5 alt.), is at the Mississippi River end of the Lake Borgne Canal, a 7-mile channel which, when built (1901), saved light-draft vessels 60 miles between New Orleans and the Gulf. Completion of the Inner Harbor Navigation Canal at New Orleans (1923) resulted in the virtual abandonment of the earlier waterway; it is today used principally by fish, oyster, and shrimp luggers.

Boats can be rented at Violet for fishing and hunting trips on Lake Borgne, 7 miles east. In the winter ducks and geese are plentiful, while fishing is excellent the year round.

At the Lake Borgne end of the Lake Borgne Canal are the ruins of a minor fortification constructed by the War Department about 1842. It consists mainly of an octagonal brick tower, and is known variously as FORT MARTELLO, TOWER DUPREZ (or DUPRÉ), and TOWER PHILIPPON. The place was abandoned after the War between the States.

About 50 yards from the highway at 13.6 *m.* are six dilapidated brick buildings that were erected as slave quarters on the old Philippon Plantation.

POYDRAS, 15.4 *m.* (8 alt.), was named in honor of Julien Poydras (*see Tour 17c*), who established a plantation at this point in the late eighteenth century. In April, 1922, Poydras was the scene of a disastrous levee break which inundated 70,000 acres of highly productive truck farms.

Poydras is at the junction with La 46 (*see Tour 8A*).

CAERNARVON, 16.6 *m.* (7 alt.), was, in the spring of 1927, the scene of a dramatic and successful attempt to save the city of New Orleans from overflow of the swollen Mississippi River. U. S. Army Engineers and other flood-control authorities were almost unanimous in the opinion that the situation called for drastic action, and Caernarvon was decided upon as the logical place for the creation of an artificial crevasse. When the actual dynamiting began, engineers found that it was almost as difficult to destroy a stong levee as to build one. The first charge of 1,500 pounds of dynamite caused a break of only 150 feet in the levee. Repeated charges, extending over a period of several days and totalling several tons, finally widened the crevasse to 2,600 feet, through which water flowed into Breton Sound, lowering the river level at New Orleans and averting inundation of the city. Property owners of the flooded area received monetary compensation for their losses, though most of them still highly resent the choice of their lands for the sacrifice.

At 17.1 *m.* is BRAITHWAITE PARK (*free*), a 32-acre WPA-built recreation area containing picnic grounds, a bathing beach, tennis courts, a baseball diamond, and a dance pavilion.

BRAITHWAITE, 18.9 *m.* (7 alt.), was until a few years ago a thriving industrial town (1930 pop. 1,398), centering around a pulp paper mill.

Right from Braithwaite 0.2 *m.* on a shell road to ORANGE GROVE. The mansion was built in 1850 by Thomas Morgan, railroad and steamship magnate, and is of an architectural type unusual among Louisiana plantation houses. The massive red brick structure has a high pitched gabled roof and Tudor windows, and was formerly entirely surrounded by a gallery. The lower floors were originally of multicolored tile laid in intricate designs, and the mantels were of hand-carved marble. In 1867 Orange Grove was bought by Louis Fesnacht, a native of Switzerland. Fesnacht was, during the War between the States, the inventor of a balloon which he made mostly from old silk dresses and which was flown from one of the taller buildings of New Orleans. Later the plantation was bought by an English syndicate from which it received the name Braithwaite.

ENGLISH TURN, 20.4 *m.* (7 alt.), whose early name was Détour des Anglais, marks the spot where Bienville, founder of New Orleans, in 1699 succeeded through a ruse in turning back an English expedition. Bienville, who headed a very small party, told the English that the Mississippi River lay farther to the west, and that the French had established a strong fort and several settlements to the north. Discouraged, the English turned about, leaving the French in undisputed possession of the lower Mississippi Valley.

The STELLA PLANTATION HOUSE (*open*), 24.8 *m.*, is more than a century old. It is a simple brick and cypress raised cottage, with a hand-hewn shingled roof overhanging the front gallery, and supported by six square columns. The house has been restored.

Towering beyond the levee is an old smokestack, 32.7 *m.*, a remnant of the once famous BELAIR PLANTATION, owned by John Dymond who was responsible for many improvements in the technique of growing sugar cane and in the refining of sugar.

At about 35.1 *m.* the road passes through what was, during the first half of the nineteenth century, the COIRON PLANTATION. John Joseph Coiron introduced ribbon cane into Louisiana. From his plantation the planting of ribbon cane spread over the entire State, and gave new impetus to the sugar industry.

At 38.6 *m.* is the junction with a graveled road.

Left here 0.3 *m.* to Gravolet's Canal, where boats can be obtained at a moderate rental to visit the site of FORT IBERVILLE, 0.8 *m.*, Louisiana's first fortification, indicated also on early maps as Old French Settlement and sometimes merely as Old Fort. When Sieur d'Iberville learned of the meeting between his brother, Sieur de Bienville, and the English expedition at Détour des Anglais, he decided to establish French claims to the Mississippi River without delay. Accordingly, in January 1700, he sent Bienville to select a place near the mouth of the river for a settlement, and himself followed a few weeks later with soldiers, a few colonists, and supplies. In his *Journal* Iberville tells the story of the fort.

"At midnight I met my brother Bienville and six men who were eighteen leagues up the river at a place, the nearest to the sea that was not swampy, which a Bayogula whom he had brought from the village showed him as he came up the river. Here he found six or seven leagues of country which he assured us was never covered with water. On the bank was the edge of a wood, fifty paces deep, of oaks, ash, elms, plaines, poplars. The back country consists of prairies fifteen leagues deep, with occasional clumps of wood.

"I have set to work to cut down these trees and square them in order that we may build a square house, twenty-eight feet on each face, with two stories and with machicoulis, with four cannon (four pound) and two eighteen pound cannon, with a moat twelve feet across. I left my brother de Bienville, in command with fifteen men."

The subsequent history of the establishment is somewhat vague, but it is thought that a regular garrison was maintained until 1711. After the founding of New Orleans the fort was abandoned. In time knowledge of the exact site was lost, and it was not rediscovered until 1930. The ridge upon which the old fort was built is plainly visible, and the lines of the moat may easily be traced. Measurements based on early figures clearly establish the location. An old 4-pound cannonball dug from a near-by canal supplies further evidence.

At 5 *m.*, accessible only by boat through Gravolet's Canal, is OAK RIVER, a picturesque and popular fishing and crabbing spot.

ST. THOMAS' CHURCH (Roman Catholic), a modern structure 48.2 *m.*, built in Spanish Mission style, replaces the original church erected in 1820. Beside the road by a lone oak, overhung with moss, tombs stand on top of an Indian mound.

POINTE À LA HACHE (Fr., point of the axe), 49 *m.* (5 alt.). For a period of 30 years (1857–87) this was the home of the botanist-priest, Father A. B. Langlois, who collected more than 5,000 rare plants and new species of Louisiana flora in an herbarium now removed to Georgetown University, Washington, D.C. In 1892 Langlois issued a catalogue of 1,200 varieties of fungi of the region.

Point à la Hache is peopled by trappers and fishermen. Two explanations are given for the origin of the name. According to one, the spot was a refueling station in early steamboat days. Seamen and sailors were compelled to shop wood here for their ships and, disliking the task, frequently deserted. The second explanation is that the river once cut the bank at this point into the shape of a huge axe.

At Pointe à la Hache a ferry crosses the Mississippi to West Pointe à la Hache (*see Tour 11b*).

BOHEMIA, 53 *m.* (5 alt.) is the farthest south settlement on the east bank.

❖❖❖❖❖❖❖❖❖❖❖❖❖❖❖❖❖❖❖❖❖❖❖❖❖❖❖❖❖❖❖

Tour 8A

Poydras—St. Bernard—Yscloskey—Shell Beach; 15.8 *m.,* La. 46.

This route runs through the country known, since the first settlement by Europeans, as Terre aux Bœufs (Fr., land of oxen), because its first inhabitants brought with them horned cattle—perhaps the first seen in Louisiana. Here, for a century, the ox held its own against the horse because its thick hide was almost impervious to mosquitoes.

Following closely upon the founding of New Orleans (1718) the French Government granted concessions in this district to Toutant Beauregard, Adolphus Ducros, DeClouet, Delaronde, Villeré, Bernard de Marigny, DeFazende, Antonio Philippon, and others, but plantations and settlements were very slow in becoming established. Many of the above named received additional grants from Spain and in 1778 the Spanish Government granted Marigny de Mandeville a large concession of land through which much of this route lies. A number of families of Canary Islanders, more than 1,500 of whom had been sent to Louisiana in 1778 and 1779 to serve as recruits, were settled in Terre aux Bœufs by Governor Galvez. Supplies for 4 years were given them from the King's stores, and they were furnished implements with which to till the soil.

Though the Isleños (Sp., islanders), as they came to be called, had in their native land been an agricultural people, the physiographic characteristics of their new environment within a short time changed them into fishermen and trappers. They built themselves impermanent log and palm cottages raised on stilts above the bayous that served as their streets and roads. Their descendants retain many Spanish customs, and Spanish is far more often heard among them than English. In recent years many Italians have settled in St. Bernard Parish. Very few of the French descendants remain.

La 46, branches east from La 39 (*see Tour 8*) in POYDRAS, 0 *m.,* paralleling (R) Bayou Terre aux Bœufs, not navigable at this point.

ST. BERNARD, 1.6 *m.* (5 alt. about 500 pop.), was named in honor of Don Bernardo de Galvez (1746–1786). Son of a prominent officeholding family, Galvez was born in Málaga, Spain, and, before becoming acting-governor of Louisiana in 1777, fought under Don Alexander O'Reilly in Mexico and Algiers. Between 1777 and 1779, young Galvez, through the American trader, Oliver Pollock, supplied the American colonies with arms and provisions for the Revolutionary War and seized English ships attempting to stop the traffic. After the outbreak of war between Spain and Great Britain, Galvez, then Governor of Louisiana, immediately took the offensive. Recruiting a nondescript army, he easily took over the English settlements in West Florida (*see History*). Assistance came from Havana for the conquest of the forts at Pensacola. The commander of the reinforcements refused at first to attack but Galvez shamed him into action by running the gauntlet of the forts in his own small vessel, the *Galveztown*. Pensacola surrendered after a siege of several days and Galvez was acclaimed one of the military geniuses of his age. His exploits won him the title of viscount, the rank of major general in the Spanish Army, and appointment as Viceroy of Mexico. He died in a yellow fever epidemic in Tacubaya, Mexico.

The old COURTHOUSE, a three-story brick building with six Corinthian columns in the portico, was supplanted in 1939 by a new courthouse (*see Tour 8*).

At 1.8 *m.* is the TURNER HOUSE, built in 1853, a one-story cement-covered brick structure with a hipped roof and a belvedere; eight slender wooden columns rise from the front gallery. The pantry contains a secret door behind which, during the War between the States, a group of Confederate soldiers hid for several days to escape capture. Miss Mary Turner, former occupant, recalled Farragut's triumphal upriver journey, of which she had an excellent view from the observatory. Her governess, a Northern sympathizer, clapped her hands with joy at the sight and was promptly dismissed. To the rear is the private cemetery, used by the Turner family for nearly a century.

The vine-covered smokestack, 2.8 *m.,* is the remains of a sugar house at Creedmore Plantation.

The ST. BERNARD CATHOLIC CHURCH, 4.6 *m.,* occupies the site of the one built with funds donated by Governor Galvez in 1778. The original church was burned to the ground about 1917. The present stucco-finished structure is in the Spanish Mission style and has a bell tower on the left.

Opposite the church and fronting on the bayou is the ST. BERNARD CEMETERY in which were buried many of the earliest settlers. The tomb of General P. G. T. Beauregard's wife is here, bearing the inscription, "M. A. Laure Villeré, March 21, 1850." Many of the graves are adorned with glass-fronted, flower-covered stone boxes containing statues of the Virgin Mary and of the saints.

KENILWORTH (*open*), 4.8 *m.,* was originally built in 1759 as a blockhouse, or fort. Shortly after 1800 the second story was added. The wide galleries which surround the house are supported by massive brick columns, the roof by cypress colonnettes. Double doors open on the galleries and are held together by iron bolts. At the top of each of the two outside stairways which lead to the second floor are wooden doors with wrought-iron hinges. The dormers are a modern addition to the shingled hipped roof. The house is set in a grove of oak, giant pecan, fig, and other trees. Flagstone walks lead to the gateway and the old-fashioned garden. The Kenilworth Plantation covers an area a mile-and-a-half long by a quarter-mile wide, and is devoted principally to the raising of sugar cane.

Kenilworth has belonged to the Bienvenue and the Estopinal families, and at one time was owned by a Confederate soldier with the resounding name of Leonidas Montgomery Thermopylae McClung. It is said that during the Bienvenue tenure General Beauregard was presented in the home with a golden dress sword, commemorating his brilliant Mexican campaign.

There are ghosts at Kenilworth, including a headless man and a lady in white whose footprints are to be seen on the stairway the morning after the full moon.

CONTRERAS, 6.1 *m.* (5 alt.), was the birthplace of Pierre Gustave Toutant Beauregard (1818–93). Some years ago the home was demolished by vandals, who used its lumber for firewood.

P. G. T. Beauregard when 11 years old entered a military school, and later attended West Point. During the Mexican War he distinguished himself as an officer, particularly at Vera Cruz, and afterward was given charge of the construction and repair of various Louisiana forts and other defenses.

With the outbreak of the War between the States, Beauregard resigned his commission in the U. S. Army and joined the Confederate forces with the rank of brigadier general. It was at his command that the first shot of the War between the States was fired at Fort Sumter. He assumed command at Shiloh, following the death of General Albert Sydney Johnston, and led his forces to victory.

After the war he was offered command of the Roumanian Army, and later command of the Army of the Khedive of Egypt. He declined both offers and spent the remainder of his life in civil pursuits. His body lies in the tomb of the Army of Tennessee, at Metairie Cemetery, New Orleans.

Beauregard was considered one of the greatest engineers and military strategists of his time. Many of his papers and treatises were highly regarded both in America and Europe. He was the author of two books, *Maxims of the Art of War* and *Report of the Defense of Charleston.* A recent biography of Beauregard, *The Great Creole,* was written by Hamilton Basso.

At 8.8 *m.* is the junction with graveled La 300.

Right on this unmarked road to REGGIO, 0.8 *m.* (4 alt.), a village named for Chevalier François Marie de Reggio, a descendant of the princely house of Este in Italy, who was sent to Louisiana by Louis XV in 1751 and placed in command of the Arkansas Post. General Bouregard was one of his descendants.

At 2.1 *m.* La 300 passes through what was once the SOLIS PLANTATION. The original owner, Solis, was a refugee from Santo Domingo who brought with him a small wooden sugar mill with which he made unsuccessful attempts to granulate sugar. In 1791 his holdings were bought out by Antonio Mendez; and in that year, having secured the services of a sugar maker from Cuba named Morin, Mendez made sugar for the first time in Louisiana. In the following year Étienne de Boré procured cane from Mendez, hired Morin, and in 1795 produced sugar for the first time on a commercial scale.

DE LA CROIX ISLAND, 6 *m.* (4 alt.), is the supply center of one of the richest fur-producing areas in the United States, and popular fishing and duck-hunting grounds in Louisiana. The village was named in honor of the Countess Livaudais de Suan de la Croix, who built its first church and school, and was first settled by Isleños. The settlement has been devastated by hurricanes on numerous occasions; and today when there is news of an approaching storm, pictures and statues of the Virgin Mary, which are found in every home, are brought outdoors to protect the homes from disaster. Floods, mosquitoes, yellow fever, and other difficulties have combined to make the lot of the Isleños anything but an easy one. Perhaps these hardships have served to bind them closely together, for the present inhabitants, direct descendants of the pioneer Isleños, are a clannish group; nearly all are related either by blood or marriage. From November to February, when the muskrat run is on, traps and drying racks for pelts are everywhere in evidence. Along Bayou Terre aux Bœufs numerous fishing boats and pirogues are to be seen in all seasons. The bayou's banks are usually covered with drying nets, seines, and other fishing equipment. Crabbing and shrimping are other local industries.

YSCLOSKEY (*boats and guides*), 13.4 *m.* (4 alt., 500 pop.), is a trapping, hunting, and fishing center.

Yscloskey was originally Proctorville, named for Colonel Thomas Proctor, a native of Ireland who came to America in 1777. After serving as captain under General Washington Proctor in 1789 came to Louisiana with the rank of colonel, and received a grant of land from the Spanish Government. The reason for changing the name to Yscloskey is obscure. The graves of Proctor and his son, Capt. Stephen Proctor, who served in the Battle of New Orleans, were found at the base of an Indian Mound and removed to the National Cemetery at Chalmette.

St. Bernard Parish and Plaquemines Parish are the great deltaic areas of the Mississippi River, where the marshes are feeding grounds for waterfowl and small fur-bearing animals. St. Bernard has large tracts for oyster beds and shrimp, and huge areas supervised by the Louisiana Wild Life & Fisheries Commission. The Mississippi River-Gulf Outlet passes between Yschoskey and Lake Borgne on its route through St. Bernard Parish to Breton Sound. East of it is the large peninsula that forms the east shore of Lake Borgne and breaks up into dozens of islands, forming Morgan Harbor, Drum Bay and Bay Boudreau.

Many oyster-growing areas lie north of the Mississippi River-Gulf Outlet. Seed oysters are removed by dredging from the seed grounds east of the River, then transported to private leases upriver, where the seed oysters are planted and fattened for marketing. Normally this procedure starts Sept. 1 and is completed by May. There are 450,000 acres in these State-managed grounds and many have been damaged in recent years by salt water intrusion, silt and marsh grass damage. About 80 percent of the oyster production of Louisiana between the Mississippi and Atchafalaya rivers is dependable on seed oysters obtained from this area.

On August 17–18, 1969, Hurricane Camille passed over this part of St. Bernard Parish on the way to Pass Christian, Miss. The Louisiana Wild Life & Fisheries Commission estimated 30 to 40 percent of the oyster grounds was damaged. Boats and houses of fishermen were destroyed. The area had not yet fully recovered from Hurricane Betsy of 1965. Camille completely destroyed the Commission's Grand Pass Camp and Port of Entry, as well as Shell Camp on Lake Borgne.

❖❖❖❖❖❖❖❖❖❖❖❖❖❖❖❖❖❖❖❖❖❖❖❖❖❖❖❖❖❖❖❖❖❖❖

Tour 9

(McComb, Miss.)—Kentwood—Amite—Hammond (Southern Louisiana University)—Laplace; 70.1 *m.* US 51, Interstate 55.

Concrete- and asphalt-paved roadbed. Interstate 55 runs 1 *m.* west of US 51.
Illinois Central Ry. parallels route.
Complete accommodations at short intervals.

Descending from the gently rolling, pine-wooded hills of northern Tangipahoa Parish, this route crosses one of the most important strawberry regions in the United States. Traversing the swampy section that adjoins Lakes Maurepas and Pontchartrain, the route ends in the cleared sugar cane lands along the Mississippi River. This history of the communities through which the highway passes is closely linked with that of the Illinois Central Railroad, which introduced the culture of strawberries and colonized many of the settlements that line its tracks.

US 51 crosses the MISSISSIPPI LINE, 0 *m.,* 17.8 miles south of McComb, Mississippi.

KENTWOOD, 4.8 *m.* (200 alt., 2,736 pop. 1970; 2,607, 1960), was named for Amos Kent, the first settler, who came here with his family in 1854, and built a sawmill, tar kiln, and brickyard, all of which prospered. After the War between the States the spot became popular with New Orleans excursionists. Picnics and barbecues were held, and the vacationists indulged in various sports, including trapshooting. Unlike the modern trapshooters who bang away at clay pigeons, these early excursionists substituted live bats which they brought with them in boxes. In 1887 a northern promoter brought a trainload of homeseekers from the Eastern state; they settled here, and in 1893 the town was incorporated. An INFORMATION OFFICE of the Dept. of Highways is located between Int. 55 and US 51 at a junction with State 38.

The Kentwood section was once the home of Charles Étienne Gayarré (1805–1895), Louisiana historian, who lived at Roncal, on the banks of Terry's Creek, about two miles north of the present town. The house is no longer in existence. Gayarré was the author of the *Essai Historique sur la Louisiane* (History of Louisiana), published in 1846, and other works. In rapid succession he was elected to the State legislature, appointed assistant attorney general, judge of the New Orleans City Court, and was sent to the U. S. Senate. He was forced to resign almost immediately, however, because of a physical breakdown. Gayarré built Roncal shortly before the war as a summer home and depository for his possessions. At the outbreak of the war he invested his large fortune in Confederate bonds and retired to his country home. The later years of his life were marked by a bitter controversy with George W. Cable, who had aroused much local resentment by his Creole characterizations.

The KENTWOOD LUMBER MILL is at 5.6 m.

At 9.2 m. is the junction with a graveled road.

Left on this road across the railroad tracks and L. again on a narrow, road to CAMP MOORE CONFEDERATE CEMETERY AND MUSEUM, 0.8 m. A tall monument has been erected to the memory of 400 unknown Confederate soldiers who died here at a training camp during an epidemic of measles. The cemetery was neglected until 1903, when the Daughters of the Confederacy organized a Camp Moore Chapter. They acquired the land and built a log clubhouse. On May 30, 1965, they dedicated the MUSEUM in a new one-story cottage of the Louisiana farm type. *Open daily, including Sunday p.m., closed Saturday.*

TANGIPAHOA, 9.4 m. (179 alt., 469 pop. 1970), one of the oldest settlements in the parish, is unusual in that its first settlers were women. In 1806 Mrs. Rhoda Holly Singleton Mixon, locally called "Granny Mixon," and her little daughter came form South Carolina with a retinue of slaves. Mrs. Mixon purchased a large acreage, which her grandchildren subdivided and sold in 1869.

A story is told of a local planter's wife who took her personal slaves to Tangipahoa to see the first train go through on the railroad completed in 1845 from New Orleans to Jackson, Mississippi. After an interminable wait for the great event, the train finally roared into town, and, amid much whistle tooting and clatter, halted. Many of the Negroes were terrified and ran for the woods, but one ancient Negress, whose legs were no longer dependable, sought shelter beside her mistress. After eyeing the train from a safe distance and giving the situation some deep thought, she exclaimed, "Lawdy, Ah reckon he jes' did get yere; he so tired, he puffin'."

The country around Tangipahoa is chiefly devoted to truck farming and dairying.

FLUKER, 12.6 m. (151 alt.), named for Fluker Kent, member of a family that still has large holdings in the vicinity, is at the junction with La 10 (*see Tour 4*).

At 13 m. is the mill of the KENT PILINGS & LUMBER CO.

ARCOLA, 15.6 m. (137 alt.), was once called Prospect Hill because the first hills north of New Orleans are found at this point. The present name is said to have been adopted in honor of a local belle.

ROSELAND, 16.8 m. (131 alt., 1,273 pop. 1970), was founded in 1888 by a Chicago firm that owned a great part of the surrounding timber land. The influence of northern architecture and farming methods are still noticeable.

AMITE, 19.5 m. (130 alt., 3,593 pop. 1970; 3,316, 1960), is one of the older settlements of Tangipahoa Parish. Like so many other towns in this section, Amite began with the building of the railroad when families living on plantations in remote sections were attracted toward the line of tracks.

An early city ordinance prohibited pigs, chickens, and camels from running loose on the street. This ordinance, directed at a citizen who had purchased several camels from a defunct circus for use as work animals, probably included pigs and chickens in order to alleviate the embarrassment of the camel owner. Dairying, truck farming, and lumbering are the main sources of revenue here; strawberry growing is starting in this section.

Amite is at the junction (L) with La 16 (*see Tour 4*).

INDEPENDENCE, 26 *m.* (88 alt., 1,770 pop. 1970), is often called Little Italy because of its large Italian population. In the early part of this century two Italian families were imported as truck gardeners and berry growers. The venture was so successful that more Italians came to this section, until by 1914, it was necessary to install an Italian consul in the town. Independence is surrounded by strawberry farms, and from this point south to Ponchatoula the highway cuts through the center of the Louisiana strawberry belt. There is a junction here with La 40, which proceeds east of Folsom in St. Tammany Parish, 13 *m.* north of Covington.

The FLORIDA PARISHES CHARITY HOSPITAL, 27 *m.,* a porticoed brick building, formerly the Whittington House, serves the several surrounding parishes. The hospital opened in 1939.

TICKFAW (Ind., pine rest), 30.1 *m.* (64 alt., 570 pop. 1970), is chiefly populated by Italians. This is the home of the Cloud family, the originators of the Klondyke strawberry, one of the finest shipping berries on the market.

NATALBANY (Ind., lone bear), 32 *m.* (45 alt.), was the lumber center of this section until the closing of the Natalbany Lumber Mill in 1940.

At 35.2 *m.* is the junction with US 190 (*see Tour 3a*), which unites with US 51 between here and Hammond.

HAMMOND, 36.5 *m.* (42 alt., 12,487, 1970; 10,563, 1960; inc. 16%), the Strawberry Capital of America, has shady, cool streets lined with well-kept homes in groves of pine and oak. With the development of Southeastern Louisiana University it has become an important educational center.

Hammond was named for its first settler, Peter Hammond, a native of Sweden, who came to Louisiana in the early part of the 19th century. One of his old trails, first known as Hammond's Crossing, is now Thomas Street, the main street of the town.

During the War between the States a sawmill was erected here to cut timber for building a shoe factory to supply the Confederate Army, but the project was ended by the invasion of Federal troops. After the war settlement of the region progressed slowly until 1885, when the Illinois Central Railroad inaugurated a colonization program to encourage immigrants from the Northern States. Many families migrated from the North and the present population of Hammond contains a large percentage of Northerners.

During the strawberry picking season, approximately from March 15 to May 10, every available person is needed to harvest the highly perishable crop. Pickers are hired from every possible source; professional crop followers from all parts of the country are recruited and the members of whole families join in gathering the berries. The school sessions are from July to March, in order that the children may do their share. It is a big and intensive business, a $5,000,000 industry crowded into about six weeks; during this time 90 per cent of the nation's strawberry consumption is furnished by this section.

During the picking season the strawberry fields are filled with workers throughout the daylight hours. Each grower has his "row bosses" to keep tab on the pickers, who gather the berries in eight-quart racks, receiving about 25¢ a rack. At the packing shed the berries are deftly repacked in pint and quart containers, which in turn are fitted into crates and loaded into refrigerator cars.

At the end of each day the buyers gather near the center of town, where the growers' associations auction off the day's pick. The farmers keep a watchful eye on the fluctuating prices. Bids are raised silently— a nod of the head or raising of a finger punctuating the lively "lingo" of the auctioneer. Sales move swiftly; 25 to 30 carloads are disposed of in an hour's time. During the progress of the auction the loaded cars are already on their way north, being diverted to their destination by telegraphic orders.

Over-ripe berries and those softened by rain are not wasted, but are stemmed, frozen into barrels, and shipped to ice cream manufacturers, or squeezed in wine presses to extract the juice for jelly or wine.

SOUTHEASTERN LOUISIANA UNIVERSITY, which began as a small junior college in 1925, and became a four-year degree-granting college in 1938, was made a university by the act of the State legislature on June 16, 1970. Beginning with 50 students it enrolled 5,225 in the 1969 spring semester and had a faculty of 313. The remarkable growth of its physical plant in the 1960 decade gives it great opportunities for serving the cultural interests of southeastern Louisiana. The university occupies a campus of 375 acres, covered with pines and live oaks, in the northwestern section of Hammond extending to US 51.

The principal divisions of the curriculum are those of Business, with accounting and administration; Education, preparing teachers for elementary and secondary schools; Humanities, which besides the usual courses in the arts, music, languages, and psychology, has one on military science; Science and Technology, and Divisions of Nursing and of Graduate Studies. There are two semesters a year and general expenses—fees, rooms and meals—are estimated for Louisiana residents at $471 to $486 a semester; for out-of-state students, $721 to $736 a semester.

LUCIUS MCGEHEE HALL was erected as an administrative building in 1934. The SCIENCE BLDG. of 1939 received an ANNEX in 1950, and a new building was added in 1965. With the help of funds granted by Federal and State governments and a State college bond issue the college was able to erect many fine buildings. TINSLEY HALL, classrooms, was completed in 1956. The AGRICULTURAL BLDG., including a creamery, was built in 1961. The LINUS A. SIMS MEMORIAL LIBRARY, completed in 1963 at a cost of $800,000, has more than 100,000 vols. and can seat 800 students. There are two other libraries, one of them a Regional Film Library. Other new buildings are: WAR MEMORIAL STUDENT UNION, 1960; HOME MANAGEMENT, 1961; INDUSTRIAL TECHNOLOGY, 1965; BIOLOGY, 1967; CHEMISTRY AND PHYSICS, 1968; HEALTH AND PHYSICAL EDUCATION, 1969; HUMANITIES, 1970. The COLLEGE CAFETERIA, seating 1,800, received an addition that seats 3,000 more. Residence halls accommodate 1,500 men and 1,100 women, and there are apartments for married students. The State provided funds for the Tangipahoa Parish Dairy Festival Assn. to build a COLISEUM on the campus, for joint use with the university. It seats 3,600. The Computer Center, established 1965, uses an IBM 1620 digital computer.

Hammond is at the junction with US 190 and 3 *m.* from Int. 55.

At 37.3 *m.* is the junction with the Old Covington Highway (La 7).

Left on this road, crossing railroad tracks, to a fork, 0.1 *m.;* R. (straight ahead) here to the junction with a graveled road, at a sign marked "Pleasant Ridge," 1.9 *m.;* R. here to a fork, 2.5 *m.;* L. at the fork about 100 feet to Pine Lawn (R), home of LOUISIANA VETIVER FARMS. Vetiver is an ornamental East Indian grass that grows to a height of 5 or 6 feet, and has a sharp, cutting leaf and a dark, lavender bloom similar to a corn tassel. The plant is useful in landscape gardening and the roots contain a delicate perfume which is in demand by perfumers. Vetiver was imported from India years ago by Louisiana planters and has long been used by Southern women for sachets. An oddity of the plant is that the aroma is limited to the roots, the bloom and the leaves being odorless. The plant gathers the oil in its roots until the bloom has reached full perfection. The harvesting begins in November and continues through February, being done entirely by hand. Usually four men act as harvesters; one man digs about a foot around the plant with a spade, one pries it from the ground, while two others drag it out, dirt and all. The dirt is then shaken off. It is said that four men can take out and pile 500 or more plants in 8 hours. The vetiver is then conveyed to pressure washers, where it is cleaned under a pressure of 300 pounds; then sent to the combers, who rake the roots with hand cultivators to remove grass roots and other foreign matter. The roots are then cut from the clump and transferred to the tub washers, who finish the cleaning process by hand washing in running water. Next, the roots are placed on wire mesh trays and put in the sun to dry.

PONCHATOULA, 42 *m.* (25 alt., 4,545 pop. 1970; 4,727, 1960. Loss 3.9%), derives its name from the Choctaw *pashi* (hair) and *itals* (to fall)—"falling hair," the name the Indians applied to the Spanish moss growing on trees. Up to 1880 the chief occupations were burning tar, raising stock, and furnishing wood for the railroad engine, which took 8 hours for the 48-mile run from Ponchatoula to New Orleans. The water for the engine was pumped by hand at Owl Bayou, south of the town.

From 1880 to 1890, as the timber was gradually cleared, truck gardening increased and strawberries began to be grown commercially. Today, Ponchatoula is one of the leading shipping points in the State for berries and vegetables of all kinds.

Left from Ponchatoula on La 22, graveled, to PONCHATOULA BEACH (*hotel, camps, cottages, and picnic sites*), 6.4 *m.*, a resort on the banks of Tangipahoa River. Swimming, boating, and fresh-water fishing are the principal recreational activities.

South of Ponchatoula Int. 55 joins US 51. At 44 *m.* the woods abruptly give way to a wide marshlike prairie rimmed by cypress swamps. A drainage canal, edged with water maples and willows, parallels the highway.

NORTH PASS, 50.9 *m.*, flows from Lake Maurepas into Pass Manchac, and forms the northern boundary of Jones Island, a dense cypress swamp.

At both ends of the bridge spanning PASS MANCHAC, 52.7 *m.*, which connects Lakes Maurepas (R) and Pontchartrain (L), is MANCHAC (Ind., rear entrance) (10 alt.), a popular fishing and hunting center. Boats, guides, and accommodations are available at reasonable rates. Fish, crabs, and shrimp can be purchased here.

South of Manchac the highway traverses an 18-mile stretch of swamp. The variety and richness of this woodland, reflected often in bright patches of shallow water, produce a spectacular scenic effect. The prevailing gray, brown, and dark green of the swamp growth is a strong background in early spring for the clear and glowing color of ash and maple seed-leaves. Occasional canals reaching back into the swamp from the highway make interesting and beautiful vistas, often enhanced in spring and summer by sheets of the lavender bloom of water hyacinths.

At 66.8 *m.* is the junction with a graveled road.

Left on this road to FRENIER BEACH, 1.2 *m.*, a recreational resort on Lake Pontchartrain. The LOG CABIN INN, 1.5 *m.*, has limited hotel facilities. There is fine hunting (deer, rabbit, duck, and squirrel) in the vicinity. In the summer boats can be rented for fishing. Cypress groves extend to the water's edge, and there is a profusion of a giant form of native palmetto.

LAPLACE, 70.1 *m.* (15 alt., 5,953 pop. 1970; 3,541, 1960), is at junctions with US 61 and La 44. The route of Int. 10 to Baton Rouge was planned to run between Frenier and Laplace.

Tour 10

(Natchez, Miss.)—St. Francisville—Baton Rouge—New Orleans; 128.9 *m.,* US 61.

Concrete- and asphalt-paved roadbed.
Railroads paralleling route: I. C. between Mississippi Line and St. Francisville; L. & A., between St. Francisville and New Orleans; M. P. and I. C., between Baton Rouge and New Orleans.
Accommodations at St. Francisville, Baton Rouge, and New Orleans.

Section a.   MISSISSIPPI LINE to BATON ROUGE; 48.7 m., US 61

US 61 follows the route of El Camino Real (Sp., royal road) through beautiful rolling hill country to Baton Rouge. Plantation homes are to be seen at frequent intervals.

At one of the highest points (399 alt.) in Louisiana US 61 crosses the MISSISSIPPI LINE, 0 *m.,* 43.7 miles south of Natchez, Mississippi, entering the Feliciana country, settled in the late eighteenth century, and generally conceded to be one of the richest districts in the South. There are two explanations for the name Feliciana: one that it was adopted in honor of the Creole wife of Don Bernardo de Galvez, Spanish Governor of Louisiana (1777–85); another that the early settlers were so enraptured by the luxuriance of the region that they called it Feliciana (Sp., happy land).

In *Atala* (1801), Chateaubriand gave the following romanticized description of the countryside:

Suspended along the course of the waters, grouped upon the rocks and upon the mountains, and dispersed in the valleys, trees of every form, of every color, and of every perfume, throng and grow together, stretching up into the air to heights that weary the eye to follow. Wild vines, bigonias, coloquintidas, intertwine each other at the feet of these trees, escalade their trunks, and creep along to the extremity of their branches, stretching from the maple to the tulip-tree, from the tulip-tree to the holly-hock, and thus forming thousands of grottoes, arches, and porticoes. Often, in their wanderings from tree to tree, these creepers cross the arm of a river, over which they throw a bridge of flowers. Out of the midst of these masses, the magnolia, raising its motionless cone, surmounted by large white buds, commands all the forest, where it has no other rival than the palm-tree, which gently waves, close by, its fans of verdure.

A multitude of animals, placed in these retreats by the hand of the Creator, spread about life and enchantment. From the extremities of the avenues may be seen bears; intoxicated with the grape, staggering upon the branches of the elm-trees; caribou bathe in the lake; black squirrels play among the thick foliage; mocking-birds, and Virginian pigeons not bigger than sparrows, fly down upon the turf reddened with strawberries; green parrots with yellow heads, purple woodpeckers, cardinals red as fire, clamber up to the very tops of the cypress trees; humming-birds sparkle upon the jasmine of the Floridas; and bird-catching serpents hiss while suspended to the domes of the woods, where they swing like vines.

The Feliciana country differs from most of southern Louisiana in that its early settlers were largely of Anglo-Saxon, rather than Latin, origin. The predominance of this stock in the parish is reflected in its culture, its architecture, and the stubborn tenacity with which its landowners have clung to their homes in the face of tremendous odds. Many of the houses are owned by descendants of the pioneers who built them.

Between 1763 and 1770 veterans of the French and Indian War were given land grants in West Florida and settled here. After the American Revolution began hundreds of English patriots migrated to this Spanish section.

At 1.4 m. is the junction with a private road.

Left on this road 0.6 m. to WOODLAWN FARM (*private*). The original house was destroyed by fire, and with it the great hydrangeas for which the garden was noted. More than 100 camellias grow about the present dwelling. There are several barns, interesting because of their steep shingled roofs which descend to within a few feet of the ground.

At 3.4 m. is ST. JOHN'S CHURCH (Episcopal), a small frame chapel erected in 1873. The cemetery on the L. is enclosed by a cast-iron fence.

LAUREL HILL, 3.5 m. (296 alt.), takes its name from LAUREL HILL (*private*), home of the Argue family. The house was constructed between 1820 and 1830 on a Spanish grant of 216 acres. It is built of logs hewn on the place, covered with clapboards and painted a soft brick-dust red. There are six square wooden columns on the lower gallery and a smaller, partly enclosed gallery above. Outside chimneys stand at both ends of the gabled room. A brick walk leads to the entrance through a garden planted in Southern shrubs and flowers, but somehow suggesting a corner of old England.

WOODHILL FARM (*private*), 7.9 m., formerly part of Wakefield Plantation, figured in an unusual property division (*see below*). Dr. Ruffin G. Stirling, who obtained this section of the four-way partition of the estate, built the Woodhill house in 1878 from materials taken from the upper portion of the Wakefield house. To the rear, in a beautiful wood, is the DOCTOR'S SPRING, where John James Audubon and Dr. John B. Hereford spent many hours studying birds.

About 90 yards south of Woodhill Farm is the junction with graveled La 421.

Left on this unmarked road to the junction with a graveled road, 7 m.; L. here to the McCAUSLAND CEMETERY, 11.4 m., a neglected family graveyard encircled by a crumbling brick and cast-iron fence, and containing a pink marble shaft topped by an eagle protecting its nest. The monument was erected by the Federal Government in honor of General Robert McCausland (1771–1851). General McCausland lived for many years on his West Feliciana plantation.

In this section, many a visitor to country homes off the "big road" is forced to seek a night's lodging elsewhere when he finds "the creek is up." Or, perhaps, the guest may safely navigate the sandy ford, only to find himself marooned within a few hours by a raging torrent, which, in due time, will subside to a level at which the creek may be crossed by wagon and mules.

WAKEFIELD PLANTATION (*private*), 8.7 *m.*, was established by Lewis Stirling in 1833, the name being inspired by Goldsmith's *The Vicar of Wakefield*. The house was a two-and-a-half-story columned structure of imposing proportions. Lewis Stirling died in 1858 and his widow, Sara Turnbull, in 1875. Four heirs were left equal shares in the estate, with an astounding provision that the house was to be divided into three parts. Mrs. John Lobdell retained the portion that occupies the original site, and an unmarried brother made his home with her. The upper portion of the house was removed and remodeled into residences —one has since burned, but the other, at Woodhill Farm still stands. Wakefield is now a pleasant cottage with a porch across the front and six cement-covered brick columns supporting a shingled roof with a central dormer. The furniture is English, most of it having been ordered from London at the time the home was built.

Audubon, a biography of the noted naturalist and artist, by Constance Rourke, was dedicated to Miss Helene Allain, a co-owner of Wakefield.

At 9.2 *m.* is the junction with a dirt road.

Right on this road (*bad in wet weather*) to a fork, 1.2 *m.*

1. Left here 1.5 *m.* to the ISLAND PLANTATION. The old plantation house has been destroyed by fire. Island Plantation has recently been put back in cultivation. The plantation takes its name from an island that used to exist in Bayou Sara.

2. Right at the fork 3.1 *m.* to (L) a Negro church, behind which is a NEGRO CEMETERY consisting of a few wooden markers. Across the road on a hill is a WHITE CEMETERY. The proximity of the two cemeteries has caused anxiety among the Negroes, who believe that the white and black ghosts mingle. To offset the activities of the spirits, they sprinkle salt on the open fires in their cabins.

The clover-grown site of OAK GROVE, 9.6 *m.*, established in 1828 by Dr. John Hereford of Virginia, is approached by a private driveway which runs under an arch of osage orange trees. The old house burned in 1930. Two octagonal *pigeonniers* and two outhouses, including a brick schoolhouse, remain.

At 10 *m.* is the junction with a dirt road.

Left on this road 0.4 *m.* to ROSALE, once known as Egypt Plantation and also as China Lodge, established by Alexander Stirling, father of Lewis Stirling, under a Spanish grant in the late eighteenth century. The place was bought by David Barrow for his son-in-law Robert Hilliard Barrow. The original house burned in 1885. Half of the present structure was once the old schoolhouse. There is an interesting octagonal latticed wellhouse in the front yard.

At 10.6 *m.*, on US 61 is the junction with a private clay road. Right here to CEDARS PLANTATION HOUSE (*private*), 0.9 *m.*, set in a grove of cedars and oaks. It is a frame structure with six square columns across the front gallery. Azaleas, japonicas, and roses grow in the enclosed yard, in front of which is a forest of beeches, thick with dogwood, redbud, and holly.

At 11.4 *m.* is the junction with an unmarked road. Right on this road 0.7 *m.* to the site of THE COTTAGE which burned. It was owned by the descendants of Judge Thomas Butler, who bought the plantation in 1811. The Spanish document by which the land was granted, signed by the Baron de Carondelet, is dated 1795. The Cottage was a long, two-story ell-shaped frame building with four entrances opening on the front gallery. Twelve narrow octagonal posts supported the gabled roof which had four dormers, front and rear. On both sides of the ample hall on each floor were two large rooms connected by paneled double doors. There are slave quarters and a family cemetery to the rear. The Cottage stood on an oak-fringed bluff. Among the shrubs, most of which are more than 100 years old, is a huge white azalea. Alexander's Creek once ran at the foot of the bluff, but its course was diverted when the front yard began to cave in. Magnificent stands of virgin forests make up a considerable part of the plantation. General Jackson and his staff stopped here on their way north from the Battle of New Orleans and The Cottage was so crowded that the host was forced to sleep in the pantry. The Cottage was the home of Miss Louise Butler, Louisiana historian.

CATALPA (*private*), 11.7 *m.*, stands back several hundred yards from the highway in a grove of beeches and oaks. It is a white cottage with green shutters, built in the nineties on the site of the former house. The old carriage house and schoolhouse still stand.

An impressive gateway, 12.5 *m.*, marks the entrance to the site of AFTON VILLA, a Victorian-Gothic house that burned down in 1963. It is said that during the War between the States, passing Federal troops thought the entrance was the gateway to a cemetery and did not enter. The owner planted hundreds of azaleas throughout the grounds and added countless rose bushes and shrubs to the terraced gardens, which were originally laid out by a French landscape artist. These are open to visitors. Afton was a 40-room mansion believed to have been modeled after a villa near Tours, France. It was erected by David Barrow in 1849 for his second wife and built around a four-room cottage which his father constructed when he came to West Feliciana in 1820. The house was of stucco-covered cypress, painted buff with a dark red trim, and ornamented inside and out with intricately carved woodwork. The front stairway was lighted by stained-glass windows. The woodwork in the sun parlor had been painted to represent a variety of marbles; marble mantels, Dresden china doorknobs, and plaster friezes added to the ornateness of the interior, while on the exterior there were towers with miniature cannon, Moorish galleries, and cathedral windows. A moat was contemplated but rejected because of mosquitoes. The house was so named because Mr. Barrow's daughter, Mary, by his first wife, was famed in the neighborhood for her singing of "Flow Gently Sweet Afton." The family cemetery containing the tomb of David Barrow can be seen in the garden.

At 13.1 *m.* is the junction with a dirt road.

Left here 1.1 *m.*, across Alexander's Creek, to CLOVER HILL (*open*). The present house was built in the 1870's on land granted in 1798 by the Spanish Government to "Don Bernardo McDermott." Tales are told of merry gatherings at Clover Hill in the days before the War between the States. One of them concerns a barrel of whisky which always stood on the gallery of the house that preceded the present structure and was often the center of riotous entertainment. On one occasion a tardy guest arrived on the scene just in time to prevent the interment of an earlier arrival, who had lapsed into unconsciousness and had been duly declared dead by sorrowing but muddled companions. A grave had been dug by frightened slaves who realized the situation but could do nothing about it. The Clover Hill house stands near the edge of a steep bluff. The plantation has been in the hands of its present owners, the Lawrason family, since about 1883. There is an old cemetery near by.

WAVERLY (*private*), 13.2 *m.*, is a two-story white frame building with Georgian-English details. It was built in 1821 by Dr. Henry Baines, an Englishman, who married the daughter of Patrick McDermott. The latter was a miller, brought to Feliciana by Carondelet, who hoped to make a fortune by raising wheat. There are six square columns on each floor. The entrances above and below are columned and fanlighted. The wooden mantels and the molded wainscoting are admirable, and the clothes closets and built-in cupboards are unusual in Louisiana houses of the period. According to legend, "Flying Charlie McDermott" experimented with flying machines in the thirties, and on one occasion tried to launch his craft from an oak tree on the grounds. Audubon taught dancing here in the twenties.

The heirs of Dr. and Mrs. Baines held Waverly until 1921, when it was acquired by George M. Lester. Both house and garden have been carefully restored.

BAINS, 13.3 *m.* (100 alt.), is at the junction with La 66 (*see Tour 10A*).

At 14.2 *m.* is the junction with a private road.

Right on this road 0.2 *m.* to GREENWOOD is a splendid oak park. The plantation was included in a Spanish grant made in 1778 to Dr. Samuel Flower, and was owned until recently by his descendants, Mr. and Mrs. Edward Butler. The house is an irregular frame structure and the third erected on the place. The only survival of the earlier buildings is an interesting old Spanish outkitchen.

The trees of the big grove, the LEJEUNE OAKS, were planted by Madame Lejeune, who brought the acorns from the West Indies. The Lejeunes were refugees from the Santo Domingo Revolution.

US 61 crosses the tracks of the Yazoo & Mississippi Valley Railroad (Woodville Branch), 14.9 *m.*, one of the oldest railroads in the United States. This line was incorporated in 1831, and completed from Bayou Sara to Woodville about 1841. The original gauge and right-of-way are still in use, and a provision in the charter forbidding operation of trains on Sundays is enforced today.

At 15 *m.* is the junction with a private road.

Left on this road, parallel to the tracks, through an avenue of live oaks, to THE OAKS, 0.2 *m.*, a rambling post-bellum frame house with a hipped roof broken by dormers and turrets. The fence enclosing the park is covered with climbing roses, and the flower gardens are exquisite in the spring.

Diagonally across the highway from the Oaks Road is a dirt road running to the L. of a lumber yard and paralleling the tracks.

Right on this road 1.5 *m.,* to the model LIVESTOCK FARM, formerly owned by the late Governor John M. Parker.

THE MYRTLES, 15.2 *m.,* dating from 1830–50, is a long, one-and-one-half-story house with wide verandas and ornate iron grillwork. The house is set in a grove of live oaks. *Open daily 9–5 for a small fee.*

Several ghost stories are centered around The Myrtles. One concerns a little French lady in a green bonnet. She is reputed to make nocturnal visits to the guest room, lifting the mosquito bar and peering at the occupant of the bed. Another story tells of the ghost of an infant, who returns to its death chamber and cries throughout the night, or until a lighted lamp is brought into the room.

At 16.6 *m.* is the junction with La 35 (*see Tour 4*).

At 16.9 *m.* is ST. FRANCISVILLE (115 alt., 1,603 pop. 1970), (*see Tour 4*).

At 19.1 is the junction with La 965. This road leads to AUDUBON MEMORIAL STATE PARK, owned by the State and administered by the State Parks & Recreation Commission. It is being developed as a memorial to John James Audubon, who lived and worked in OAKLEY, the plantation house, in 1821. The house and land were bought from Miss Lucy Matthews, a descendant of the original owners, in 1947. *Open 9 a.m. to 4:45 p.m. weekdays, 1 to 4:45 p.m. Sundays. $1 and tax, chaperoned children free.*

Oakley has been restored to the time Audubon lived there, in the Federal Period. The Colonial Dames of America and the Daughters of the American Revolution have provided the furnishings. The detached kitchen was rebuilt. A barn is filled with historic objects. Picnic shelters are available but tent and trailer camping is not permitted.

The plantation was established under a grant dated 1770, but its owner, Ruffin Gray, died before he had an opportunity to occupy his new home. His widow moved to Oakley with her infant daughter, and in 1803 married James Pirrie. The latter built the present house between 1808–10. Oakley is a two-story frame house with a raised brick basement. There are wooden columns and balustrades on the lower gallery and permanent blinds on the upper. A curved stairway joins the two galleries. Oakley descended from Mrs. Eliza Pirrie to her grandchildren. Mrs. Pirrie engaged Audubon to teach art to her daughter Eliza at $60 a mo. plus board and room, half of his time left free for his own work. During four months Audubon painted 32 of his birds. His 13-year-old pupil, John Mason, accompanied him. Audubon was so captivated by West Feliciana that he sent to Cincinnati for his family, who joined him in New Orleans. In January 1823 Mrs. Audubon came to the parish and established a private school at Beech Woods, a plantation owned by the Percy family. She remained in West Feliciana for 7 years, during part of which Audubon also taught there.

Not far from Oakley on a dirt road is LOCUST GROVE CEMETERY, owned by the State. Here are buried Gen. Eleazor W. Ripley, who fought at Lundy's Lane (War of 1812), and Sarah Knox Taylor, daughter of Zachary Taylor and first wife of Jefferson Davis.

FAIRVIEW (*private*), 22.4 *m.,* stands on a hilltop commanding a sweeping view of the valley of Thompson's Creek. The home was erected in 1845 by Jesse Davis of Maryland. Built of bright red brick, the house is two-and-one-half stories high, with broad galleries supported by six square pillars of cypress and with white wooden railings. During the War between the States, Fairview served for a time as General Grant's headquarters, and was also used as a temporary hospital. Four hundred bales of cotton were taken from the plantation to be used in building the breastworks at Port Hudson. A restaurant has been opened here.

THOMPSON'S CREEK, 23.5 *m.*, was named for a ferryman, who, during the British occupation of West Florida, operated a ferry across the Mississippi from a landing at the mouth of the creek to the settlement of Pointe Coupée. During the Spanish regime the stream was called Rio de la Feliciana, and it is indeed more a river than a creek. Beds of quicksand make it treacherous, and after a heavy rain it becomes a torrent.

At 27.2 *m.* is the junction with La 74, graveled.

Left on this road 3.6 *m.* to the junction with a private dirt road; L. here to ASPHODEL (*open*), 3.8 *m.*, built about 1833 by Benjamin Kendrick. The house is constructed of brick covered with smooth plaster and consists of a raised central structure, flanked by two identical wings. There is a wide gallery across the front of the main building, and six Doric columns support the gabled roof, which is broken by two pedimented dormer windows. Each wing is a miniature of the central building and has a small porch with a two-columned portico. There is a plantation bell in the yard. The *asphodel* is the flower of the dead in Greek mythology.

At 27.8 *m.* is the junction with an unmarked, unimproved road which was built on the abandoned roadbed of the old Clinton & Port Hudson Railroad.

Right here 1 *m.* to LINWOOD (*private*). The house was built by General Albert G. Carter in 1838–40, and remained in possession of the Carter family until 1910. After the defeat of the Confederates the plantation was overrun by Union soldiers who burned the outhouses, sacked the big house, and partially destroyed the sugarhouse. The house is a white frame building with four heavy, plaster-covered brick columns of the Doric order across the front, and galleries upstairs and down.

US 61 enters the plateau area of East Baton Rouge Parish at 29.5 *m.* This section has been variously known as White Plains, Buhler's Plains, and the Plains of St. John. In the days of the West Florida Rebellion (*see History*) delegates from the surrounding districts met in this neighborhood and marched on the Spanish fort at Baton Rouge.

PLAINS, 30.7 *m.*, is a hamlet centered about the PLAINS PRESBYTERIAN CHURCH, a white frame building with green shutters. The land for the church property was bequeathed by the widow of John Buhler in 1829.

Right from Plains on unmarked, graveled La 272 to a large PECAN ORCHARD, 2.6 *m.*
At 5 *m.* is the junction with a graveled road; R. here 0.5 *m.* to PORT HUD-

SON (98 alt.), named in honor of James Hudson, an early nineteenth-century landowner. Port Hudson began as a trading post on the Mississippi River, at the mouth of Thompson's Creek and developed into an important shipping center. Successive encroachments of the river made it necessary to move the town to its present location. Floods and the boll weevil have put an end to the once thriving little port. Those who leave their automobiles to reconnoiter afoot may be rewarded by the discovery of old shells and battered bullets, and the remains of gun emplacements and earthen breastworks. Here the river has built a mile-wide batture, but at the landward edge stand the same high bluffs that fascinated early travellers, who gave them such names as "Painted Bluffs," "White Cliffs," and "Milk Cliffs." The siege of Confederate-held Port Hudson began in May 1863, and ended with capitulation in July, when its starving defenders stacked their arms and lowered their flag. The line of Confederate defense stretched in a crescent from the river at Sandy Creek to the river above Mount Pleasant, facing a Union line of investment 7 miles long. The best preserved of the earth-works are those thrown up by Union General Banks, and upon these a monu-ment has been erected to the Confederate dead, near the junction of La 272 and the above mentioned side road.

At 6 *m.* on La 272 is PORT HICKEY (80 alt., 20 pop.), its site now marked by a Negro cabin and a silo. The town was the fourth and last of the old river landings that once flourished in this vicinity—Thompson's Creek (app. 1765–1832), Old Port Hudson (1832–62), Alto (1863–80), and lastly Port Hickey (1880–1905). Each in turn was left stranded by the river. At the height of its prosperity Port Hickey shipped as many as 50,000 bales of cotton a year, the bales sliding down a long wooden chute from the top of the cliff to the river landing below.

At 6.6 *m.,* where La 272 turns R., is the junction with a graveled road; L. here 0.5 *m.* to a U. S. NATIONAL CEMETERY, burial place of 3,804 Union sol-diers; 3,262 of the graves are marked "unknown." The Confederate dead are buried at Port Hudson and here and there along the breastworks.

At 7.6 *m.* on La 272 is the junction with a graveled road; R. here to MOUNT PLEASANT LANDING, 0.7 *m.,* on Mount Pleasant Plantation, which was established in 1769. Between 1851 and 1858 the plantation was the property of Judah P. Benjamin, Confederate Secretary of War and State. The Mount Pleasant bluffs command magnificent views. The names of early owners of the plantation are perpetuated in Roth's Landing, Proffit's Island, and Faulkner's Lake. Faulkner's Lake, probably formed by an overflow, is enclosed by a deep forest at the south-ern edge of the bluffs. It is a refuge for a wide variety of wildlife, including hundreds of white heron, and in winter, flocks of wild ducks.

In the distance to the south of Mount Pleasant can be seen the apex of trian-gular Proffit's Island. Opposite the Island a Union sloop of war, the *Mississippi,* exploded after having been disabled and set afire by Confederate artillery at Port Hudson. When the modern battleship *Mississippi* steamed up the river in 1919 to receive her silver service at Vicksburg, she paused off Proffit's Island to fire a salute to her sunken predecessor.

At 13 *m.* on La 272 is the junction with US 61–65.

South of Plains, US 61 for a short distance follows one of the oldest roads in the district, named on a map of 1730 as Le Chemin de Proflet des Prairies (Fr., the road of Proflet of the prairies).

At 33.5 *m.* is the junction with La 272 (*see above*).

At 36.1 *m.* is a low, marshy spot once a BUFFALO WALLOW.

Stretching along the Mississippi River west of ALSEN, 39.6 *m.,* south to Scott's Bluff, is the great DEVIL'S SWAMP, named in the old Spanish records as La Cipreria de Diablo (the devil's cypress swamp). An account of the origin of this name occurs in a manuscript by Caleb Carpenter, written in 1776, and quoted by Sir Charles Lyell, president of the Geological Society of London, in *A Second Visit to the United States*. Caleb Carpenter, relative of a Louisiana friend of Lyell's declared:

A German emigrant having settled near the bank of the Mississippi, in 1776, felled, with great labour, some lofty cypresses; but, happening one day to make a false turn in his canoe, entered, by mistake, a neighboring bayou. Every feature was so exactly like the scene where he had been toiling for weeks, that he could not question the identity of the spot. He saw all the same bends, both in the larger and smaller channels. He made out distinctly the same trees, among others the very individual cypresses which he had cut down. There they stood, erect and entire, without retaining one mark of his axe. He concluded that some evil spirit had, in a single night, undone all the labour of many weeks; and seized with superstitious terror, he fled from the enchanted wood, never to return.

At 40 *m.* is the junction with a graveled road.

Right here to the OLD CHEATHAM PLACE (*open*), 0.6 *m.*, built by Oliver Cromwell Vanlandingham in 1818. The place has been modernized but axe marks are plainly visible on the great handhewn foundation timbers. The house is surrounded by live oaks which have been given the names of Confederate generals. The tree named after General Henry Watkins Allen, Confederate Governor of Louisiana, once saved the life of the owner of the house. During the War between the States Edwin Douglas Cheatham was encamped at Clinton and on one of his visits home was pursued by Yankees. Taking refuge in the tree, he remained undiscovered. After the battle of Port Hudson a detachment from General Banks' army camped here.

SCOTLANDVILLE, 43.2 *m.* (68 alt., 22,557 pop.), unincorporated and largely populated by Negroes, has the SOUTHERN UNIVERSITY AND AGRICULTURAL AND MECHANICAL COLLEGE, maintained by the State. Founded in New Orleans in 1880, it opened in 1881 with 12 students. In 1888 the Agricultural and Mechanical Department was established. In 1892 it became a Land Grant College. In 1914 it was closed by act of the Legislature, to be reestablished on a new site. This turned out to be Scotlandville. In 1922 the University was reorganized under control of the State Board of Education.

Southern University occupies a campus of 512 acres with a modern physical plant that is in process of considerable expansion. More than 30 of its buildings have been erected since 1950. A new housing complex costing $5,000,000 was opened in September, 1969, and 8 new buildings were under way in 1970. In 1969–70 it enrolled 9,114 students and had a faculty of 544. It has a branch in New Orleans and one in Shreveport. The University has an annual budget of $10,000,000 and in addition gets $2,000,000 in grants.

Southern has "active concern with minimizing the effects of educational and economic deprivation on its clientele and facilitating optimal development of each individual's potentials." There are colleges of Agriculture, Arts—with a Division of Music; Business, Education, Vocational Education, Engineering, Home Economics, and Sciences. The Graduate School was opened in 1957 and the Law School in 1947. Unless specially exempted, all students are required to take the basic course in military science under the ROTC.

A student majoring in English, history, political science or sociology may elect courses in the Black Studies Program, which "seeks to provide a comprehensive analysis with and to establish a historical perspective for the study of the black experience vis-a-vis the on-going social evolution in American society." The program aims to "explore and explode myths, ideologies, attitudes, and values associated with race relations and their impact on the future of the black people."

BATON ROUGE, 48.7 m. (see Baton Rouge). Baton Rouge is at junctions with US 190 (see Tour 3) and La 67 (see Tour 10B).

*Section b.   BATON ROUGE to NEW ORLEANS; 80.2 m.,
US 61*

South of BATON ROUGE, 0 m., US 61, united with US 190 (see Tour 3a) for 4.4 miles, leaves the blufflands, and enters the swamps that hem in New Orleans. (*Tour 10B, a longer but more interesting route, can be taken*).

At 2.6 m., where the highway sweeps right, is the junction with a blacktop road.

Left (straight ahead) here to (L) the DOWNTOWN AIRPORT, 1.2 m., equipped with a buff brick administration building, and used largely by private planes.

Opposite the airport is GOODWOOD (*open*), built in 1856 by Dr. S. G. Laycock. The land was originally granted in 1776 by George III to Thomas Hutchings, a "reduced paymaster," as he is described in the British patent on file in the parish courthouse at Baton Rouge.

Goodwood is a white, cement-covered brick structure with a hipped roof. Broad iron-railed galleries, supported by four Doric columns, extend across the front. Running water, unusual in plantation houses, was piped to all rooms, and a large zinc tub and stationary washstands were installed. Hand-painted washstands, marble mantels, and gilt window cornices remain.

At 2.8 m. is the junction with the Clay Gut Road (La 818). The road takes its name from Clay Gut Bayou, a narrow tributary of the Amite River, which flows through high clay banks.

At 4.4 m. is the southern junction with US 190 (see Tour 3a).

The BATON ROUGE COUNTRY CLUB (*members and guests only*), is at 5.4 m.

HOPE VILLA, 14.6 m. (20 alt., 100 pop.), is on the south bank of Bayou Manchac (Ind., rear entrance). During Colonial days Bayou Manchac was part of an important trade route between the Mississippi and the Gulf (see Tour 10B). At this point the bayou is navigable for small boats.

OAK GROVE, 16.2 m. (25 alt., 1,980 pop. 1970), was known as BIG SWAMP until 1908 because of an immense swampy area extending westward from the village. At Oak Grove the hill end and level lands stretch southeastward to New Orleans.

Oak Grove is at the junction with La 42 (*see Tour 10C*).

GONZALES, 22.5 *m.* (4,512 pop. 1970) is a distributing point for the heavy truck production of the East Ascension area. After the Houma Indians, Acadian refugees lived here. It was named after a settler in 1887. Petro-chemical industries are multiplying in the environs. The town profits by use of the Burnside Bulk Marine Terminal on the Mississippi. The East Ascension Central High School was completed in 1966. Gonzales is at a junction with La 44.

SORRENTO, 27.9 *m.* (17 alt., 1,182 pop.), was at one time an important lumber town, but most of the timber has been cut away. Sorrento experienced a modest boom in 1928–29 with the discovery of oil in the near-by McElroy field, which later proved unproductive.

Between Sorrento and Kenner the highway has been built through heavily wooded swamps. The concrete roadway was constructed at tremendous expense. Huge bucket dredges built an embankment 15 to 20 feet high and about 50 yards wide, thus creating deep roadside ditches whose waters soon became covered with water hyacinths. This sub-grade was then allowed to settle for several years before the final layer of concrete was poured, the result being what might be termed a floating highway.

At about 45 *m.* US 61 bisects the northeastern rim of Louisiana's Sugar Bowl. Southward to Laplace stretch the thousands of acres comprising the GODCHAUX SUGARS PLANTATION, perhaps the largest in Louisiana (*see Tour 10B*).

At 48.3 *m.* is the junction with a dirt road.

Right on this road 1.2 *m.* to the REFINERY OF THE GODCHAUX SUGARS INC. (*open on application*) (*see Tour 10B*).

LAPLACE, 53.5 *m.* (15 alt., 5,953 pop. 1970; 3,541, 1960; inc. 68%), is at junctions with La 44 which unites with US 61 into New Orleans. North from Laplace 3 *m.* on US 51 to FRENIER on Lake Pontchartrain. US 51 crosses the route of Int. 10, New Orleans to Baton Rouge, which, when completed, will parallel US 61.

At 56.9 *m.* is the junction with a road running parallel to the Bonnet Carré Spillway Guide Levee.

The BONNET CARRÉ SPILLWAY BRIDGE, 57.3 *m.,* is built over an area that has been set aside as a floodway for the Mississippi River.

At 59.2 *m.* is the junction with a road leading to Norco (*see Tour 10B*).

KENNER, 69.8 *m.* (10 alt., 29,858 pop. 1970), the business district of which lies to the right of the highway, is at the junction with La 48 (*see Tour 10B*).

NEW ORLEANS, 80.2 *m.* (4 alt., 593,471 pop. 1970), see *New Orleans*.

Tour 10A

Junction with US 61—Tunica—State Penitentiary (Angola) ; 20.1 *m.,* La 66.

The Pinkneyville Road (La 66) leads northwestward in an S-shaped curve through rolling open country to the Tunica Hills; frequent side roads extend to ante bellum mansions.

La 66 branches northwest from US 61 (*see Tour 10a*) at BAINS, 0 *m.* (100 alt.) (*see Tour 10a*), 3.4 miles north of St. Francisville.

BIG BAYOU SARA, 1.6 *m.,* crossed by a modern bridge, was formerly forded at great risk by large droves of cattle and caravans of covered wagons. The stream is normally a clear and rippling creek, but after a heavy rain is becomes a raging torrent 15 to 20 feet deep.

At 4.7 *m.* is the junction with an unmarked, graveled road.

1. Right on this narrow road 4.1 *m.* to the WEYANOKE NEIGHBORHOOD, centering about Weyanoke Plantation, established as Percy Forest about 1802 by Captain Robert Percy. The WEYANOKE PLANTATION HOUSE (*open*), a half mile left on a narrow graveled road, is a two-story frame house with a plastered front and a gabled roof. Originally a one-story log house, it is said to be the Beech Woods house in which Lucy Bakewell Audubon, wife of John James Audubon (*see Art*), conducted a neighborhood school in the early 1820's. It was at Beech Woods that Audubon found the subject for *The Wild Turkey.* The upper portion of the house was added in 1856 by Major John Towles, who had the log house rolled to its present site when he purchased the Percy estate in 1838. The story is told that the plantation mammy placed a silver spoon in the mouth of day-old Daniel Turnbull Towles, first child born in the remodeled house, and boosted him through the skylight on the new roof, to ensure that "He'd allus have high notions."

2. Left on this road by ford (*passable only at low water*) across Little Bayou Sara to (L) the HIGHLAND PLANTATION HOUSE (*private*), 0.6 *m.,* established by Olivia Ruffin Barrow in 1798. It is a raised two-story frame structure built on a bluff.

ROSEBANK PLANTATION HOUSE (*private*), 7.5 *m.,* set far back from the road on a hill, was established about 1790 by an Irishman, called by the Spanish Don Juan O'Connor, who served as *alcalde* (magistrate) of the district during the latter years of the Spanish domination of West Florida. The plantation house has undergone extensive alterations. Constructed of cypress over a high brick basement, it has long galleries across the front supported by round brick Doric columns. Iron posts connected by iron railings support the gabled roof.

At 8 *m.* is the junction with graveled La 855.

Left on this unmarked road to the junction with a graveled road, 0.9 *m.;* L. here 1.2 *m.* to the junction with a private road; L. here 0.2 *m.* to the ELLERSLIE

PLANTATION HOUSE (*open*), built in 1835 by Judge W. C. Wade. It is a square white plastered brick structure surrounded on all sides by wide upper and lower galleries; Doric columns rise from the lower-floor gallery to the hipped roof. Audubon once stayed here as a tutor for the Percy children. Ellerslie now offers accommodations for hunting parties on the private 10,000-acre tract. Quail shooting is particularly good; squirrels, rabbits, and fishing are also available.

At 3.1 *m.* on the main side road is the junction with a graveled road; R. here 0.5 *m.* to GREENWOOD, which became famous for the beauty of its symmetrical proportions and its location. The house burned down August 1, 1960. There are reports it may be rebuilt.

The acres on which the house stood were originally granted by the Spanish Government to Oliver Pollock (1737–1823), a merchant, who, with the assistance of Governor Galvez of Louisiana, financed the colonies to the amount of $300,000 during the American Revolution. An Irishman himself, Pollock met General Alexander O'Reilly, an Irishman ennobled by the Spanish king, in Havana, and, on the arrival of both in Louisiana, offered O'Reilly a cargo of flour from a ship then in port—on the general's own terms. For this generous act (the payment was $15 a barrel when the commodity was so scarce the price had risen to $30) O'Reilly gave Pollock free trading privileges in the colony, and commended him to the succeeding governors, Unzaga and Galvez. Pollock so reduced his own finances by his loans to the American colonies that he was eventually thrown into prison, and released only after Galvez went his surety for more than $130,000. The merchant left one Thomas Patterson for hostage while he recouped his fortune to pay his debts, a matter of 3 years' time. Eventually the United States repaid his entire original loans.

In the meantime he sold the plantation to the Barrow family. The plantation house was built about 1830 by William Ruffin Barrow. It was 100 feet square, built of plaster over laths, and surrounded by 24 white Doric columns of plastered brick which extended from the railed gallery to the heavily corniced flat roof. There were no upper-story galleries. The paneled cypress doors had silver doorknobs and hinges—typical of the lavish expenditures of the period.

At 8.6 *m.* is (L) the LIVE OAK PLANTATION HOUSE (*private*), built between 1808 and 1816. The two-story brick house is flush with the ground. Four squat stucco-covered brick pillars support the second-floor gallery.

ST. MARY'S CHURCH (Episcopal), 11.1 *m.*, built in 1857, is a tiny red brick chapel of modified Gothic architecture, shaded by overhanging trees at the edge of a forest.

The RETREAT PLANTATION HOUSE (*open*), 11.6 *m.*, was built in the early 1850's by Captain Clive Mulford, who named it Soldier's Retreat. Built over a high brick basement, it stands in a grove of oaks on a bluff facing Little Bayou Sara. Four round stuccoed-brick columns support the dormered roof. The kitchen stands apart from the house.

At about 13 *m.* La 66 enters the Tunica Hills, once known as the Indian Mountains. The highway follows a ridge and is bordered by deep wooded gullies. This sparsely settled section was once the haunt of the Houma, who, according to tradition, were driven out about 1706 by the more warlike Tunica. The Tunica were numerous and a source of much trouble to the early settlers. They fell victim, however, not to the white man's bullets, but to his liquor.

TUNICA, 18.7 *m.* (60 alt.), is a cluster of houses centering about a general store, at the foot of a ridge.

At 20.1 *m.* is the LOUISIANA STATE PENITENTIARY (*adm. by special permit from the superintendent of State Penitentiary, Baton Rouge*), one of the few penal institutions that are self-supporting. The penitentiary was moved to its present location from Baton Rouge in 1890. The land was formerly that of Angola Plantation and the penitentiary is still popularly known by this name. There are now more than 12,000 acres under cultivation. The institution's sugar mill, the Pelican State Factory, has an intake capacity of 1,200 tons of cane daily.

The penitentiary lands are on a broad treeless peninsula surrounded by levees except where the Tunica Hills rise abruptly. In the extreme northern portion of the tract are East Lake and Alston's Bayou, the latter named for an eighteenth-century planter, William Alston. Farther south is long and narrow Lake Angola, or "Lake of the Cross," where in 1699 Sieur d'Iberville erected a wooden cross. Pénicaut, one of d'Iberville's lieutenants, describes the scene in his *Relation:* "We sang there a Vexilla Regis on our knees, which seemed to astonish these Savages very much. We made them understand that this cross was an object greatly esteemed in our religion, and that they must take care that no harm befell it." Near by, on the bluffs above the river, was the Houma village, where in the spring of 1700 Father Du Ru, the Jesuit missionary with d'Iberville, made a model of a church which he instructed the savages to build in his absence. This chapel, the first Catholic church in the lower Mississippi Valley, was 50 feet long, and in the center of the square before it stood a great wooden cross 35 or 40 feet high, which Father Du Ru had planted.

❧❧❧❧❧❧❧❧❧❧❧❧❧❧❧❧❧❧❧❧❧❧❧❧❧❧❧❧❧❧❧❧

Tour 10B

Baton Rouge—Carville—Geismar—Burnside—Union—Convent—Lutcher—Gramercy—Reserve—Laplace—New Orleans; 120.7 *m.* La 30, La 75, La 44, connections with US 61.

Graveled roadbed between Baton Rouge and Burnside; concrete- and asphalt-paved between Burnside and New Orleans.
Railroads paralleling route: I. C., at short intervals throughout the route; L. & A., between Gramercy and New Orleans.
Limited accommodations at Convent, Lutcher, Laplace, Norco, and Kenner.

This is an alternate route (*see Tour 10b*) between Baton Rouge and New Orleans. For the greater part of its distance the highway follows the east bank of the Mississippi. Along the road are fine ante bellum mansions, former seats of great sugar cane plantations.

The route branches southward from BATON ROUGE, 0 *m.*, on St. Louis Street and its continuation, Nicholson Drive.

At 2.4 *m.* are (L) the STADIUM and handsome new buildings of LOUISIANA STATE UNIVERSITY AND AGRICULTURAL AND MECHANICAL COLLEGE (*see Baton Rouge*), on a 2-mile tract fronting on the Mississippi.

The route turns R. across the railroad tracks at 2.5 *m.* and L. along the levee at 3.1 *m.*

THE COTTAGE, 7.7 *m.,* was visited by hundreds of tourists who valued the architecture and historical associations of the place before it burned in the early 1960's. Only a couple of columns and broken walls survive to mark its site for well over a century. It was built in 1824 by Colonel Abner Duncan and presented to his daughter, Frances Sophia, and Frederick Daniel Conrad on the occasion of their wedding. It was a Greek Revival mansion set in a grove of live oaks. Twelve Doric columns enclosed a brick-paved gallery and supported a second-story gallery and a dormered roof. It had a paneled doorway flanked by fluted columns and sidelights and topped by a fanlight. Lafayette, Henry Clay, Zachary Taylor, and Judah P. Benjamin were among the guests at The Cottage.

During the War between the States an attempt to shell the house from the river was made by Federal Commodore Levin Powell, a cousin of the master of the house, Frederick Conrad. Shortly afterward Federal soldiers drove the family from the house, to occupy it for the duration of the war. It was used as a hospital and cedars still stand behind the house where the Yankees planted them to mark the graves of their dead.

At midnight of June 20, 1870, during the famous race of the *Robert E. Lee* and the *Natchez,* the steamboat *Princess,* loaded with sightseers, caught fire in the river a short distance upstream. From each bank skiffs put out to rescue passengers and crew, and on the lawn in front of The Cottage sheets were spread, upon which were poured barrels of flour. As the burned and scalded victims were brought ashore they were placed on the sheets and rolled in the flour.

The crumbling brick walls of an old sugarhouse, 13.1 *m.,* destroyed in 1930 to make way for a new levee, mark the site of CHATSWORTH, a 40-room mansion built just before the Civil War by Fergus Duplantier.

At 13.4 *m.* is the junction with La 75; R. (straight ahead) on La 75.

LONGWOOD (*private*), 13.6 *m.,* was built (L) during the Spanish occupation. The back part was added in 1835. It is a cypress building with a hipped roof supported by slender wooden columns and with iron railings on both galleries.

BAYOU MANCHAC, 15.3 *m.,* formerly connected the Mississippi River with Lake Maurepas. It was called Ascantia by the Indians, Iberville by the early French, and finally named Manchac (Ind., rear entrance) during the Spanish Domination. Sieur d'Iberville explored this country in 1699. In writing of his explorations a few years later he referred to the bayou, saying, "They have named it after my name." Fort

Bute, named for the third Earl of Bute, Prime Minister of England at the time West Florida came under British control (1763), stood at the mouth of the bayou. In 1779 it was captured by Don Bernardo de Galvez (*see Tour 8A*).

La 75 turns L. away from the river at a fork, 16.2 *m.*

At 18 *m.,* at a fork, La 75, regaining the river, turns L.

The MONTICELLO FARMS of the Louisiana State Penitentiary, 21.2 *m.,* consist of 2,500 acres of sugar cane and rice cultivated by convicts.

The CHURCH OF ST. GABRIEL in ST. GABRIEL, 21.9 *m.* (22 alt.), stands on a land grant made in 1773 in favor of "the Parish Church of Manchac." The sidewalk leading from the church to the rectory is paved with unclaimed tombstones taken from the old cemetery when construction of a levee necessitated its abandonment. Some of the slabs, bearing inscriptions in French and Spanish, date from the eighteenth century. The steps of the rectory were also built from the marble of forgotten tombs.

EVERGREEN PLANTATION (*open*), 22.2 *m.,* was established shortly after 1796 by Oliver Blanchard. The house was built about 25 years before the War between the States. It is a wooden building with a plaster-covered second-floor front. The gabled roof is supported by fluted columns of the Doric order. The hallway has a tight spiral stairway.

La 75 turns L. away from the river at a fork, 23.5 *m.*

CARVILLE, 25.5 *m.* (20 alt.).

Right from Carville on a graveled river road to the U. S. PUBLIC HEALTH SERVICE STATION No. 66 (*adm. by permission of guard at entrance*), 2.2 *m.,* better known as the NATIONAL LEPROSARIUM, the only leper colony in the United States. The site of the 400-acre colony was once part of the Indian Camp Plantation, so called because it occupied the ground of an old Houma Indian village. The plantation house, built in 1857, is now used to house administrative offices. It is an imposing structure of stuccoed brick, painted white, with a columned front. The patients, most of whom are Hawaiians, Filipinos, and Chinese, are housed in modern buildings. At present there are many recreational facilities for patients; a motion picture theater, a golf course, tennis courts, soda fountain, etc.; bicycle and automobile transportation may be used within the village. Classes are held for illiterates and weaving and leather crafts are taught as occupational therapy.

Leprosy is not hereditary and only contagious through close contact over an extended period. Small children are the exception, as they may contract it in a day. For this reason no child under ten years is allowed within the colony. Once contracted, the disease may develop within one to 75 years.

Since Biblical times, the chaulmoogra oil treatment has been the most successful. It was introduced into the United States in 1899, by Dr. Isadore Dyer, of Tulane University. Little progress has been made for thousands of years, due to ineffectual efforts to infect animals for purposes of experimentation. About 30 years ago it was disclosed that certain rodents found in Syria are susceptible to leprosy. Specimens of the rodents are now kept at the Leprosarium for experimentation and study.

It is generally believed that leprosy was brought to Louisiana by Negro slaves imported from the West Indies, and by "the flotsam of humanity" brought by John Law in his famous Mississippi Bubble project to colonize Louisiana. At any rate, in 1766, Ulloa, first Spanish governor, established the colony's first *lazaretto* at Balize, 80 miles below New Orleans, on the Mississippi. Not very successful, it was destroyed by a hurricane some years later. Then for 20 years, lepers roamed throughout the colony, unhindered. In 1785 a hospital for white and Negro was founded by Don Andres Almonester on land which became known as La Terre des Lepereaux (Leper's Land). Restrictions were lax, however, and after the War between the States, leprosy again became a serious menace. Although lepers were treated at Charity Hospital over a period of many years, attendance was not compulsory. In 1878 a pest house was established near New Orleans, but nothing definite was accomplished until 1894, when the Legislature passed a bill creating a Board of Control to provide a home and care for lepers.

So great was the dread of the disease that the City Council refused sanction of the chosen city site, and, when a 5-year lease was finally secured on the Indian Camp Plantation, patients were conveyed there at night on old coal barges, as railroad and river steamers refused to transport them. Four sisters of the Order of St. Vincent de Paul were put in charge, and with the introduction of chaulmoogra oil treatments in 1899, the Leprosarium gained nationwide recognition. In 1921 the Federal Government took it over.

The buildings of the Leprosarium are in full view of the Mississippi River, and it has long been the custom for passing steamboats to give three long whistle blasts as a salute to the inmates, who wave and cheer in response.

GEISMAR, 30.2 *m.* (20 alt.), was originally called New River, the name of an old stream that once flowed into the Mississippi. It is in the area where petro-chemical industries have expanded in recent years. Among those at Geismar are the Borden Chemical Co., methanol plant, handling 160,000,000 gallons a year, a chlorocarbon plant of Vulcan Materials Co., and a large plant for ethylene-propylene polymers of Uniroyal Chemical Co.

At Geismar is the junction of La 75 and La 73.

MOUNT HOUMAS PLANTATION, 30.4 *m.,* was the scene of a minor engagement during the War between the States. The name was inspired by the presence of several Indian mounds.

At 31.9 *m.* is the junction with an unimproved road.

Left on this road to LINWOOD (*open*), 0.5 *m.,* built on land acquired by Philip Minor in 1816. The plantation remained in the same family for three-quarters of a century. The house, which is of cement-covered brick, was abandoned after 1900 and at present the ground floor is a cow stable. Six tall Doric columns rise two stories to support a fanlighted pediment. There is a wide central hallway on each floor, the entrances to which were originally fanlighted. A one-story wing repeats in miniature the outline of the main house on one side and a long two-story wing juts out on the other. Originally the walls of the great hall and other rooms were painted with surprisingly realistic jungle scenes. Eliza Ripley, in *Social Life in Old New Orleans,* wrote of her impressions: "A great tiger jumped out of dense thickets toward savages who were fleeing in terror. Tall trees reached to the ceiling, with gaudily striped boa constrictors wound around their trunks; hissing snakes peered out of the jungle, birds of gay plumage, paroquets, parrots, peacocks everywhere, some way up, almost out of sight in the greenery; monkeys swung from limb to limb; orang-outangs and lots of almost naked dark-skinned natives wandered about. To cap the climax right close to the steps one had to mount to the floor above was a lair of ferocious lions."

BELLE HÉLÈNE, 32.7 *m.,* was originally established as the Ashland Plantation. Previous to 1838 its lands were a part of Linwood, which was owned jointly by Theophilus Minor and William Kenner. After Kenner's death, his son, Duncan built the present residence in 1841 and named it after Henry Clay's Ashland. It was designed by James Gallier.

It is a long two-story house set on brick foundations; 28 square white columns completely surround it. Duncan F. Kenner (1813–1887) was active in State politics, serving as a member in the constitutional conventions of 1845 and 1852. He served as a delegate to the secession convention held in Montgomery, Alabama, in 1861, and was appointed Confederate minister plenipotentiary to Europe by Jefferson Davis in 1865. Because of his service in behalf of the Confederacy, his property was confiscated by Federal authorities. In 1882, however, President Arthur appointed him a member of the U. S. Tariff Commission. At the age of 71 he was chairman of the Cotton Centennial Exposition in New Orleans. Ashland was recovered soon after the war and remained in the family until the latter part of the nineteenth century. It suffered much deterioration but has since been restored. *Open, small fee.*

The DARROW OIL FIELD (L), 35 *m.*, taps pools collected about a salt dome.

In DARROW (20 alt., 200 pop.), 38.7 *m.*, a ferry crosses the Mississippi to Donaldsonville (*see Tours 11a and 11B*).

The HERMITAGE PLANTATION HOUSE (*open*), 40.4 *m.*, is a square brick structure entirely surrounded by round white Doric columns of stuccoed brick, which enclose broad galleries upstairs and down and support a heavy wooden cornice topped by a hipped roof broken on the front by two dormers. The interior is *briqueté entre poteaux.* The present residence is evidently a remodeled edition of the original one, which was built in 1812 by Marius Pons Bringier for his son Michel Doradou Bringier. The Bringier men fought under Jackson at the Battle of New Orleans and the house was named after Jackson's Tennessee home.

About 1920 one of the large oak trees in the yard was blown down by a wind storm; embedded in the trunk was found an elaborately carved chest. It is said that during the War between the States a slave hollowed out a hiding place for the chest, which was to be filled with family jewels and silver at the first cry of "Yankees is comin'!"

The BOCAGE PLANTATION (*private*), 41.4 *m.*, was built in 1801 by Marius Pons Bringier as a wedding present for his daughter Françoise on her marriage to Christophe Colomb. The house was extensively remodeled in the 1840's. It is now a square structure, the lower floor brick, the upper wood. A wide entablature circles the house and completely hides the sloping roof. Eight square columns stretch across the front, the two central ones being smaller than the others.

Colomb was a native of Paris, and came to Louisiana upon the outbreak of the French Revolution, to escape the guillotine. He traced his ancestry to Christopher Columbus. Washington Irving, in his *Travels in America,* touches upon the Colomb family.

The HOUMAS HOUSE (*private*), 43.4 *m.*, popularly known as BURNSIDE, was built in 1840 by John Smith Preston of South Carolina. The house is of plastered brick, two-and-one-half stories high, with 14 Doric columns rising two stories on three sides. The hipped and dormered roof is topped by a belvedere. There are wooden railings on the second story gallery and also above the heavy cornice and around the belvedere. A wing in the rear has a carriage drive through it. The house is flanked on each side by hexagonal *garçonnières* with domed roofs. Encroachments of the river have taken a part of the magnificent live oak avenue. In 1857 the plantation was purchased by John Burnside, the Sugar Prince; upon his death in 1861, the property was left to Oliver Beirne. It was restored in 1940 by Dr. George B. Crozat and is owned by his heirs. The estate included more than 18,200 acres. The house has been used as a movie set. *Open daily 10–4, $2.50 per person.*

BURNSIDE, 43.9 *m.* (20 alt.), is a scattered community with a railroad station and a post office. This village witnessed perhaps the last stand of the mule-drawn streetcar in Louisiana. Before a ferry was available at Darrow for the crossing to Donaldsonville, railroad passengers alighted at Burnside, which was served by a tug ferry for the 5-mile trip across and up the Mississippi. A narrow-gauge track extended from the railroad station to the ferry landing, a distance of about 500 yards. On this track was an old-time mule car which had been discarded by one of the larger towns and to which an old Negro hitched a mule at train time. The driver, mule, and car presented equally ancient and dilapidated appearances; the old Negro smoking a corncob pipe while gossiping politely with the town's idlers, the animal standing asleep with ears stuck through a wide straw hat, and the quaint car, with broken window panes, warped beams, and old-fashioned straw seats. Although it would have been an easy walk to the ferry for a traveler with suitcases, few were willing to forego the opportunity to pay a small fare and be rolled slowly toward the river. For many years after the driver abandoned his line, the old car stood on its track next to the Burnside station.

Set deep in a grove of vine-covered trees (L), at 45.8 *m.,* is the TEZCUCO PLANTATION HOUSE, a raised cottage with six small square columns enclosing a wide front gallery and supporting a dormered roof. The porch railings of the front and side galleries are of elaborate wrought iron. Wistaria vines climb over the front, and two *garçonnières* flank the main building. The group was built between 1855 and 1861 by Benjamin F. Trudeau. It is frequently called the Bringier House after the family who has owned it for many years. It has been furnished with period antiques by the present owners, Dr. and Mrs. Robert Potts (*Open, slight fee*).

The section traversed for the next 40 miles of this route was originally settled by German immigrants, first among whom were John Law's Alsatians. They settled on the west bank of the Mississippi, near the site of the present village of Lucy, between 1719 and 1722. After 1728 the Germans extended their holdings and influence to the east bank, as well as up and down the river for several miles. This gave rise to the term Côte des Allemands (Fr., German coast), which was applied to the land along both banks of the river in St. Charles and St. John the Baptist Parishes. With expansion, that portion lying in St. James Parish on both banks of the river became known as the Haute (upper) Côtes des Allemands.

The French made a practice of engaging Swiss mercenaries to serve as provincial guards. Many of these, as their terms of military service expired, took advantage of liberal government offers of land and money, and settled permanently in Louisiana, largely among the Germans.

Immigrants from Lorraine (1754) and Acadians from Nova Scotia (1766) greatly extended the German coasts, and they became by far the most prosperous rural sections in Louisiana, as much by reason of the character of the settlers as of the very fertile soil. In time the French and Spanish, attracted by such prosperity, outnumbered the Germans and Swiss—the latter stock having been by this time absorbed into the Germans. Later the Germans themselves were absorbed, culturally and linguistically, into the French. Even German names became Gallicized: *Himmel* became *Ymelle; Kleinpeter, Cloinpêtre;* and *Zweig,* too difficult for the Latin tongue, was translated literally into *Labranche.*

At 45 *m.* SUNSHINE BRIDGE crosses the Mississippi to junction with La. 18. North 7 *m.* to Donaldsonville and junction with southbound La 308 on east bank of Bayou Lafourche, and 1 *m.,* with La 1, on west bank. La 44 now continues east and south.

UNION, 47.8 *m.* (18 alt.), is a river settlement marked by towering pecan trees. From the top of the levee, Negroes can be seen rowing lazily out into the current and towing in floating trees, bridge timbers, and other debris, to be cut into firewood and sold. Many of the folk living near the river use the driftwood to make Christmas bonfires, a most effective substitute for the conventional Christmas tree. Huge stacks of wood are piled about tall center poles erected on the levee and are kindled with *roseaux* (tall reeds) which crackle like firecrackers.

A group of dwellings at 48.6 *m.* exemplifies one of the earliest types of Louisiana Colonial construction—moss and mud adobe laid in between hand-hewn reinforcing timbers. The use of discarded sugar mill boilers as rain-water cisterns can be noted in this neighborhood; sprawling on short stilts, they often dwarf the modest cottages next to them.

Every half mile or so are groups of plantation buildings, some old, some middle-aged, some comparatively new. Originally roofed with hand-made shingles, many are now covered with corrugated iron.

CENTRAL, 49.3 *m.* (17 alt.), has shanties as gray as the moss that hangs from the trees; tin and corrugated iron roofs melt into dazzlingly bright skies, and long lines of clothes flap in the breeze. To the right is the unending levee, covered with scraggly grass.

At 50.7 *m.* is the junction with a shell road.

Left on this road to the HELVETIA CO-OPERATIVE SUGAR MILL (*visitors admitted*), 0.7 *m.,* constructed by neighboring planters, with Federal assistance.

At 51.5 *m.,* fronting flush on the roadway, is the COLOMB HOUSE (*open*), designed and built by Dr. Christophe Colomb, Jr., about 1835. It is a square one-story wooden building with four double sets of Doric columns across the front gallery. The hipped roof rises to a large square cupola. The house is unusual for this section in that it never served as a plantation home; its builder remained faithful to his profession as dentist, scorning opportunities to dabble in sugar. He did, however, experiment with bagasse, the pulpy, straw-like substance remaining after the juice is ground from sugar cane. He succeeded in producing a hard, clinkerlike material. An example is to be seen in the pillars of the outhouse which stands to the left of the main house. Modern chemistry has developed many uses for bagasse, chief among which is Celotex, a wallboard (*see Tour 11a*).

Here and there, in roadside pastures, can be seen bowl-shaped iron sugar kettles new serving as watering troughs.

ROMEVILLE, 51.9 *m.* (18 alt.), is a levee-side cluster of small houses and stores. Fronting on the river is the PLEASANT HILL BAPTIST CHURCH. Scattered at intervals of miles along the road are small Negro churches, chiefly Baptist and Methodist. Usually there is an ancient plantation bell hanging in a scaffold apart from the church. At wider intervals are larger Roman Catholic churches, usually painted white, with gleaming steeples.

A low swampy depression marks the NITA CREVASSE, 52.3 *m.,* caused in 1890 by a defective rice flume.

UNCLE SAM PLANTATION, 54.2 *m.,* demolished in 1940 to make way for the levee, was erected in 1841 by Judge Dominique D. A. Tureard and rebuilt in 1849, after it had been destroyed by fire, by Samuel Fagot. Until its demolition it was one of the few complete old plantation groups remaining in the State. The buildings were arranged about a central house, whose massive and classic simplicity was the keynote of all. It was a square two-story structure of plastered brick with a hipped and dormered roof supported on all sides by giant Doric columns, 28 in number. The lower gallery was paved and flush with the ground; a wide second-story gallery with a wooden railing encircled the house. On each side of the big house, one-storied *garçonnières* repeated the design. The house was flanked in the rear by two buildings which looked like miniature Greek temples; one was formerly the kitchen; the other, the office. These in turn were flanked by hexagonal *pigeonniers* with pointed roofs.

There are several explanations regarding the naming of the plantation: one is that, upon the death of the original owner, a young heir—returning from a sojourn in Europe—appeared on the scene with elegant whiskers and was nicknamed "Uncle Sam"; another is that it drew its name from the letters U. S. stamped on the sacks used in exporting sugar. The most logical is that it was called "Uncle Sam's place" by the nieces and nephews of Samuel Fagot.

ST. MICHAEL'S CONVENT, 55.6 *m.,* was the second house of the Society of the Sacred Heart to be established in Louisiana. It is a white brick three-and-a-half-story American-Gothic building with pointed dormers and a battlemented cornice. The long central building is flanked on each side by buttressed and blattlemented wings and has a wide second-floor gallery supported by narrow columns.

The convent was founded by a group of French nuns in 1825. The present building was began in 1839 but was not ready for occupancy until January, 1848. It drew the daughters of wealthy sugar planters from homes between Baton Rouge and New Orleans and maintained its positions as a first class girls' school for more than a century. It was discontinued as such following a severe storm in 1926 and was used afterward to house refugee Mexican nuns and their pupils. Abandoned as a school in 1932, the building was taken over by the National Youth Administration.

CONVENT, 55.7 *m.* (18 alt.), was named after the school. It is the seat of St. James Parish, which has some oil industries. Texaco has a refinery here with a capacity of 144,000 bbl. a day.

At Convent is the CHURCH OF SAINT MICHAEL (Roman Catholic), whose entrance is flanked by statues of Joan of Arc and St. Michael. There is a grotto constructed of bagasse by Dr. Christophe Colomb, Jr., with a shrine made of shells. The hand-carved altar was brought from the Paris Exposition of 1867. To the rear of the church is an old cemetery containing many interesting tombs, including that of Valcour Aime (*see Tour 11a*).

MANRESA HOUSE, 55.7 *m.,* a Jesuit retreat, occupies the former Jefferson College.

The buildings, with their noble proportions and dazzling whiteness in bold relief against abundant foliage, were built in the spirit of the Greek Revival. The main three-story plastered-brick structure has 22 massive Doric columns across its pedimented front which support a wide gallery. This is flanked by two modern buildings which follow the same architectural outline. Elaborate cast-iron gates mark the entrance. On each side is a square one-room structure with a columned front. To the left of the campus proper is the rectory, a pink brick structure with fluted Doric columns supporting a hipped and dormered roof.

Jefferson College was established in 1831 to take the place of the College of Orleans at New Orleans. The State contributed to its support, and as a semipublic institution it was nonsectarian. In 1842 it was partially destroyed by fire, and in 1845 the State withdrew financial support. The college struggled along until 1855, when bankruptcy closed its doors. The property was purchased at auction in 1859 by Valcour Aime, and presented to the Marist Fathers, who reopened the institution. In memory of one of his daughters, Aime built the Gothic chapel adjacent to the main building. To the right of the chapel is a tiered burial vault containing six "ovens" and topped by a cross. The college again ceased to function in 1927 and the buildings remained closed until 1931, when the property was taken over the Jesuit Order, renamed Manresa House, and transformed into a retreat.

The ZENON TRUDEAU HOUSE (*private*), 57.7 *m.,* built during the early nineteenth century, is a plastered-brick building encircled by a wide gallery. Square wooden columns rise two stories to support a heavy cornice which almost hides the low hipped roof. Octagonal *garçonnières* with pointed roofs connect with the gallery on each side of the house at the rear. Today the house is practically in ruins.

WELHAM PLANTATION HOUSE (*private*), 60 *m.,* which dates from 1835, stands close to the road. It is a brick house with six square brick columns supporting the gallery, and wooden ones bearing the roof, which is surmounted by a balustrade. The old sugar mill is now in ruins.

At 60.5 *m.* is the junction with a graveled road.

Left on this road (*impassable in wet weather*) to the junction with a dirt road, 0.6 *m.;* R. here to an INDIAN MOUND, 1.3 *m.* The mound covers an area of about a half-block and is about 50 feet high. The fact that it is composed of red clay indicates that the soil used in its construction was brought from a distance, as the land of this vicinity is of the "buckshot mud" variety. The mound is covered with moss-laden trees, and there are many excavations made by treasure hunters. At a depth of 42 feet, skeletons and palmetto leaves have been found. The elevation is locally called "the mountain." Tradition has it that the mound is filled with gold buried by Indians and by white planters during the War between the States. Natives profess to having seen "barrels of gold running down the mountain" and a "warning light like a round white ball" that rises from the ground and goes back into the mound. It is said that aynone who "has blood on his hands" (has killed someone) will never find treasure. Indian treasures (this section is reputed to be rich in them) are haunted because when treasure was buried, an Indian—preferably an enemy—was killed and buried with the gold.

Between this point and Lutcher is a narrow strip of land used almost exclusively for the cultivation of perique tobacco. It is said that all attempts to cultivate the variety elsewhere have met with failure. The tobacco is black and strong, and it is considered a proof of hardiness among the natives to smoke or chew it "straight." Approximately 1,000 acres devoted to this culture produce an annual crop of 250,000 pounds. The major portion is shipped to England, Canada, and Norway; some, however, is used domestically. Perique tobacco is the only crop grown in Louisiana under strict U. S. Internal Revenue Department supervision; before the crop can be harvested every producer is required to post a bond equal to the amount which the Government expects to collect in taxes. Perique requires three years for curing and is one of the most expensive tobaccos grown.

Perique was first grown in Louisiana by the Indians. In 1776 a group of Acadians exiled from Halifax, Nova Scotia, arrived in St. James Parish. Among them was one named Pierre Chanet, or "Perique" as he was nicknamed, who became interested in the tobacco and was the first to introduce it commercially. The descendants of Pierre Chanet and of the other Acadians have continued to be the exclusive producers and processors. Perique is used principally for blending and mixing with other and milder varieties.

At 61.5 *m.* is (L) a double row of a score or more laborers' huts. Suspended between two leaning posts, near the road, is a plantation bell whose reveille awakens the countryside for a day of labor in the fields, and whose toll, at the end of the long day's work, calls the laborers home to a supper of corn pone and pot liquor. This is the old HESTER PLANTATION; the "big house" burned about fifty years ago, but its grove of oak trees is still standing.

Along this section of the route are groves of oaks and other trees that were once the settings for plantation mansions. Some groves provide excellent picnic sites. The tree trunks are sometimes whitewashed to a height of six or eight feet above the ground—either in the belief that the whitewashing discourages ants and other insects or that it adds a neat and trim touch to the careless and haphazard beauty of the trees themselves.

Along this stretch the river has for many years cut in farther and farther to the east, eating away the land from under the proudest of the "big houses." The road itself has been moved back several times.

A group of 28 frame buildings (L), 63.1 m., all painted a dull shade of red, belong to the ST. ELMO PLANTATION.

LUTCHER, 66.1 m. (15 alt., 3,911 pop. 1970; 3,274, 1960), whose business district is reached by a side road, is a typical southern Louisiana town. Here is an old lumber mill which was responsible for the town's early growth. The population decreased with the decline in sawmill activities, and vegetable and tobacco farming took the lead in the upkeep of the remaining inhabitants. The Lutcher area produces quantities of shallots (green onions) for shipment all over the country.

At the factory of the LOUISIANA PERIQUE TOBACCO COMPANY perique tobacco is processed.

At Lutcher a ferry crosses the Mississippi River to a point 2.7 miles east of Vacherie (see Tour 11a).

GRAMERCY, 67.3 m. (15 alt., 2,567 pop. 1970; 2,094, 1960), is the home (R) of the COLONIAL SUGAR REFINERY. The KAISER ALUMINUM & CHEMICAL CORP. produces alumina here. A 3-mile road connects with US 61, north.

MOUNT AIRY (private), 68.7 m. is a raised cottage with an elaborate cast-iron outside stairway and cast-iron gallery and belvedere railings. Across the front are eight square wooden columns and three wide doors, all alike; above each door is a decorative fanlight. To the rear are several old outbuildings—pigeonniers, garçonnières, carriage houses, servants' quarters, etc. Their Trackless Way (1932), by Adèle LeBourgeois Chapin, paints an interesting picture of this and other near-by plantations.

GARYVILLE, 71.9 m. (13 alt., 2,474 pop. 1970), is a lumber town, the center of which lies to the L. along the railroad. Garyville connects with US 61, as also does Reserve.

At 73 m. is (L) SAN FRANCISCO (open), a plantation house built in 1850, whose mixture of architectural styles has produced an extraordinary example of Steamboat Gothic. The house is of plastered brick with a gallery across the front and half-way around each side supported by square brick columns. A double outside stairway with wooden railings ascends to the gallery, which has a cast-iron railing and fluted wooden Corinthian columns. These support a cornice ornamented with innumerable small windows, wooden "gingerbread," and another railing. This in turn is surmounted by a hipped roof with mullioned dormer windows. The whole is topped by a belvedere with more windows and a wooden balustrade to which lightning rods have been added. The house was completely restored in 1954. It has French and English antique furnishings, massive mirrors, china and bric-a-brac collections. Its ceilings were decorated in 1852 by Dominique Canova, whose work is in St. Louis Basilica. The house is the setting for *Steamboat Gothic* by Frances Parkinson Keyes (*open, slight fee*).

RESERVE, 75.5 *m.* (13 alt., 6,381 pop. 1970; 5,267, 1960), is the trading center and shipping point for a very productive sugar cane region. Its name is said to derive from a remark made by an itinerant merchant, presumably a Godchaux, who in an early visit took a liking to the region. "Reserve this place for me," said he. "I'll be back when I can buy it." Years later he returned to buy the land.

Noteworthy is St. Peter's Church (Roman Catholic). The building, erected about 1886, is of brick, and its gleaming white coat almost dazzles the passing motorist. To the right is a tower, with a red-capped belfry surmounted by gargoyles and containing a large chime clock. The fine rose window is a memorial to a Jewish sugar planter and philanthropist, Edward Godchaux. Religious prejudice is sometimes most apparent in small communities, and this memorial is a pleasant reminder of the friendships often formed between members of different creeds.

In Reserve is the Refinery of Godchaux Sugars, Inc. (*open on application*), one of the largest producers and refiners of sugar cane in the United States. The refinery's output is not confined to local production but includes large amounts of raw sugar imported from Cuba, the Philippines, and Porto Rico. The daily capacity of granulated sugar is 500,000 pounds. Elma Godchaux's *Stubborn Roots* (1936) is a realistic novel which uses the sugar industry of this section as a background.

A cane crop is planted by burying stalks end to end in shallow furrows during the late fall and early winter. The new growth comes from the eyes of the old stalks. The sugar cane plant produces true seeds, but these seeds are never used for commercial planting. The growing season is from April to October.

Cane cutting usually starts late in October. In some localities the harvest is preceded by the Blessing of the Cane Crop, a Roman Catholic ceremony in which the field hands and their mules, wagons, and implements are blessed to ensure a good yield. Once cutting begins, it continues at a rapid rate, in order that the crop may be out of the fields before the coming of heavy frosts. At this time the plantations are swarming with workers and every sugarhouse is going at full speed in an annual race with the weather. If there is a hard freeze before all the cane is harvested and it is impossible to complete the harvesting or windrowing within a few days, the crop remaining in the fields will be ruined; on the other hand, if the weather remains too warm, the stalk continues to grow and the sugar content is very low. On the larger plantations cane is hauled from field to refinery over a narrow-gauge railroad, with five-ton cars strung out behind a puffing "dinky." At the refinery the cane is transferred to conveyers which carry it into the building. The larger cars are unloaded by means of a derrick and "grab," but smaller ones are switched onto sidings and drawn by mules to the carriers, to be unloaded with pitchforks and rakes.

From a balcony overlooking the ponderous machinery—almost every sugar house or refinery has an observation balcony—the crushing of the juice from the stalks can be observed. High up against the wall the carrier dumps its load down a shining chute into the teeth of knives which chop the stalks into sections. The sections are then caught under the weight of rollers out of which juice runs through troughs to the clarifying system. The pulpy residue, called "bagasse," slips down another chute to a carrier which feeds it to roaring furnaces, or to a place where it is baled and stored for sale to the manufacturer of Celotex (*see Tour 11a*). On all sides are whirring wheels, sliding pistons, and whining gears, with the almost sickeningly sweet smell of crushed cane and boiling juice permeating the building.

The visitor will probably be shown to a great mixing tank, to see and taste a "strike." With a hiss of escaping steam, a curling ribbon of *masse cuite* (molasses crystals) rolls down from the vacuum pans into a vat where rotary blades stir the thick syrup, which is now ready for crystallization; through the bottom of the tank the syrup is drawn in regulated amounts into whirling centrifugals—to emerge as granulated sugar, ready to be bagged and shipped.

During the grinding season the refineries work day and night and are popular as the scene of sugarhouse parties. On such occasions the sugarhouse is especially interesting, being brilliantly lighted, bustling with activity, and filled with the odor of boiling cane syrup. The parties are sometimes elaborate, with dancing and refreshments, including a plentiful supply of eggnog; or they may consist merely of a gay crowd that moves about the plant watching the various processes and eating sugar cane. The uninitiate is warned against swallowing the cane fibre. A century ago, in the time of the open sugar kettles, it was the custom at parties to string shelled pecan halves and dip them into the boiling sugar, making a confection called *chapelets de pacanes*. Today the high point of the party usually is a chain electric shock, a prank in which the boys and girls join hands and the persons on the ends of the chain at a given signal grasp some part of the electrical equipment of the plant.

At midnight, at the end of the grinding season, the sugarhouse whistle blows and a bonfire, which can be seen for miles, is made of the cane tops. The owner of the plantation, the white mill workers, and their families and friends gather to have a gay time. The Negroes are given a beef to kill and *vin de canne* (wine of the cane), and have a celebration in their own quarters.

The modern factory is a far cry from the old-fashioned sugarhouse. Use of the centrifugal system has put an end to the colorful but inefficient open-kettle method of syrup and sugar making, whereby the *vin de canne* passed through a series of kettles called *le grand, le prop, le flambeau,* and *le sirop*. The liquid was dipped from kettle to kettle by means of big buckets swung on long poles set in rowlocks, finally reaching the smallest and hottest kettle, *la batterie,* from which emerged the syrup and a sugary substance known as *la cuite;* the latter was boiled longer than the syrup and diluted with lemon and vinegar. From the *batterie* the syrup was wheeled in little cars to the "purgery," or cooling room, poured into tanks, and stirred by hand with wooden paddles until it crystallized.

The open-kettle method of syrup making has not been completely abandoned. Occasionally, in the more isolated sections of Louisiana, can be seen an old mule, hitched to a long pole, plodding around and around a small crusher. The cane is brought from the fields in small, dilapidated wagons and fed to the crusher by hand. The juice is boiled in open kettles and a delicious syrup, or molasses, results. These antiquated mills do not manufacture sugar.

Molasses, generally speaking, is a by-product of the manufacture of granulated sugar. It is divided into three classes, known to the trade as "first," "second," and "third" molasses. These grades are determined by the proportion of saccharine matter withdrawn from the *masse cuite* and by the density to which the molasses is boiled. With succeeding "strikes" of sugar that are removed, the sweetness and quality of the molasses is lowered. First and second molasses is refined into table syrups or sold to blenders and processors. The third grade, called "blackstrap," is used in making stock feed, fertilizer, and industrial alcohol.

The VOISIN PLANTATION HOUSE, 76.6 *m.*, was built about 1785. Encroachment of the river has caused the building to be moved far back from its original site. It is of the early Louisiana plantation type—a raised cottage with spliced, mortised, and interlocked timbers between which is a filler of mud and moss, covered over with whitewashed plaster. Whenever this type of construction is encountered in Louisiana it may safely be attributed to the Colonial era. The lack of a central hallway is another indication of age. The square brick pillars which support the gallery came later. Cypress colonnettes support the dormered roof. The house is now in ruins.

The GODCHAUX BELLE POINTE DAIRY 77.9 *m.*, is one of the best equipped dairies in the State.

The rambling raised cottage, 79.8 *m.*, is probably more than a century old. Before the War between the States it was known as the ESPÉRANCE PLANTATION, later as the NEW ERA.

At 80.9 *m.* is the ST. JEANNE D'ARC CHURCH (Roman Catholic), interesting in that a statue of Joan of Arc stands atop the central tower, the cross occupying a much less conspicuous place below.

In this locality the river has been eating away its west bank rather than east. As a consequence, many of the property owners along a stretch of about two miles have been enriched by as much as 50 or 75 acres. The Mississippi frequently washes away one man's land only to bestow it upon his neighbor on the opposite bank.

LAPLACE, 81.1 *m.* (15 alt., 5,953 pop. 1970; 3,541, 1960), is a truck-farming center as well as the center of a prosperous sugar section. Laplace is at junction with US 51 (*see Tour 9*). Int. 10 was planned to pass between Laplace and Frenier.

Atop the Bonnet Carré Spillway Guide Levee, 86.3 *m.*, is an excellent view of the concrete dike of the BONNET CARRÉ SPILLWAY. At low-

Along the Waterways

SHELL OIL DRILLING RIG OFF THE GULF COAST

CATAMARAN DESIGN OIL DRILLING RIG

New Orleans Times-Picayune

INSPECTING MOTOR
ON VESSEL THAT
BORES INTO SEA FLOOR

Humble Oil & Refining Co.

AMMONIA PLANT OF OLIN MATHIESON CORP. AT LAKE CHARLES

PLANT OF THE KAISER ALUMINUM & CHEMICAL CORP. AT GRAMERCY

Humble Oil & Refining Co.
NIGHT SCENE AT HUMBLE REFINERY, NORTH BATON ROUGE

PORT ALLEN ACCESS ROUTES FROM LOUISIANA ONE
TO INTERSTATE TEN HIGHWAY AND BRIDGE

Baton Rouge Chamber of Commerce

International Relations Committee of International House

HARVEY CANAL AND LOCKS, MISSISSIPPI RIVER TO GULF

TWIN HIGHWAY BRIDGES
ACROSS LAKE PONTCHARTRAI

*Chamber of Commerce
of the New Orleans Area*

LAUNCHING VESSEL OF
THE U. S. NAVY AT
AVONDALE
SHIPYARDS
ON THE MISSISSIPPI

Louisiana Wild Life & Fisheries Commission

OIL MEN USE HAY TO MOP UP OIL SLICK IN CREEKS

PENDLETON BRIDGE ACROSS TOLEDO BEND RESERVOIR,
LOUISIANA TO TEXAS

Louisiana Dept. of Highways

EGRETS AT AVERY ISLAND

Edward Avery McIlhenny

water stage the road over the levee and across the entrance to the spill-way, between the river and the dike, can be taken, if condition of road permits. This is an emergency floodway which is put to use when the Mississippi River rises to a stage dangerous to the city of New Orleans.

The spillway, with a capacity of 250,000 cubic feet of water a second, was completed in December, 1935, at a cost exceeding $13,000,000. Its location was decided upon because this particular point is a natural basin for floodwaters, as proved by the numerous crevasses that have occurred here. In 1850 the floodwaters here were 7,000 feet wide, the crevasse remaining open for six months. In 1874 another serious break occurred at Bonnet Carré, the waters draining into Lake Pontchartrain for many months.

The idea of flood control by this method is not new. Raymond Thomassy, in *Practical Geology of Louisiana,* published in 1860, in-cluded the proposal of a spillway among other plans for checking the flood menace. There was considerable controversy as to the efficacy of the plan, some experts expressing doubt even after the construction work had been completed. These fears, however, were put to rest early in 1937. Having created havoc in some of the large midwestern cities, floodwaters surged southward and river gauges all along the line above New Orleans recorded dangerous rises. In January some of the floodgates were opened, a few weirs each day, until a great, muddy stream over a mile in width flowed toward the lake. Although the gauges upstream continued to show a steady rise, the level at New Orleans remained almost stationary and it did not become necessary to call on the spillway for its full flowage capacity, many of the weirs remaining closed through-out the high-water period.

The concrete dike replaces the old levee for a distance of 7,698 feet, and is equipped with 350 bays, or weirs, which are opened or closed by an electric crane mounted on a narrow-gauge track. The flow of diverted water is confined to the spillway limits by earthen guide levees which extend to Lake Pontchartrain, approximately seven miles to the north. The area enclosed by the spillway has been set aside as a game preserve and is reverting to a wild state, and ponds of water remaining after the water receded have become good fishing spots. More than 6,000 goats have been turned loose in the spillway between US 51-61-65 and Lake Pontchartrain to eat the grass and weeds that would otherwise retard the flow of water.

NORCO, 92.9 *m.* (9 alt., 4,773 pop. 1970), is the site of a large oil refinery of the SHELL PETROLEUM COMPANY, which has furnished recreational facilities for its employees. These include a golf course, tennis courts, a baseball field, and a swimming pool. Facing the highway is an array of modern company buildings.

Right from Norco on the river road 0.9 *m.* to the Bonnet Carré Spillway.
Facing the levee about 100 yards east of the Spillway is TREPAGNIER, site of an eighteenth-century cottage, that figured in a tragic episode. In 1811 there was an insurrection of the slaves in the parish, many of them wild Africans smuggled into the country by pirates after the importation of slaves had been

proscribed. At the news of the insurrection most of the planters fled with their families; but one of them, whose name was Trepagnier, having sent his wife and children to safety, sat with a gun on the gallery of this house and held off a group of more than 500 slaves who passed by the house and debated whether to attack. As they proceeded down the road they were met by a body of militia and 66 of them were killed in the first onslaught; many others were wounded and escaped to the woods where for days later their bodies were found. Those captured alive were brought to New Orleans for trial, their heads cut off and placed on high poles.

ORMOND, 96.5 *m.*, was built in the eighteenth century by the Butler family. The main building is a two-story structure, the lower floor of brick, the upper of wood. The house was built in the late 18th century by Pierre Tregpanier, who disappeared a few years after its completion, and was then bought by Richard Butler of the Irish house of Ormond and the "Fighting Butlers" of the American Revolution. Butler added two wings. The house was rescued from decay by Mr. and Mrs. Alfred W. Brown and fully restored and furnished.

At 97.3 *m.* is the site of the LITTLE RED CHURCH, in front and to the left of a modern stucco church built in 1921 to take care of a growing parish. As early as 1725 the Capuchin Fathers administered in this district to the needs of the German settlers from whom the territory acquired the name German Coast. In 1740 a rude log cabin church was constructed and replaced in 1806 by a red frame building, the church of St. Charles Borromeo. The Little Red Church remained standing until 1930, by which time it had become badly riddled by termites and it was decided to take it down. Church records dating back to 1754 were destroyed in 1877 when the priest's house was burned by a demented Negro. Little Red Church was a landmark for all the packets and steamers making their way down the river to New Orleans. The first glimpse of the church was a signal for paying off the roustabouts who worked on the boats and who immediately engaged in gambling which sometimes left them without a penny by the time their vessel had reached the city. In the adjoining cemetery Nicholas Noel Destréhan, the philanthropist Stephen Henderson, Sr., and many other prominent early settlers are buried. A legend is still current that the red hair of one corpse continued to grow after death and eventually made its way through the cracks of the tomb. A hundred-year-old statue of St. Charles, a gift of the Trepagnier family, has been removed from the rear of the old church and placed above the altar in the new.

DESTRÉHAN, 97.9 *m.* (12 alt.), is an oil refinery town that includes a plantation home of the same name. It was built in the beginning of the nineteenth century by Jean Noel Destréhan, a wealthy Creole merchant and planter, who served in the Territorial Legislature and helped draft the first State constitution. Porches on three sides are supported by heavy Doric columns that extend the height of the building. The line of the steeply sloping roof is broken by three small dormer windows.

At the height of his career Jean Lafitte, the pirate, was a frequent visitor to this home, and it is believed locally that a part of his wealth is buried here. His disconsolate shadow is said to haunt the house, appearing on stormy nights. At such times it comes from nowhere, points its finger at the hearth on the ground floor, then disappears.

At Destréhan a ferry crosses the Mississippi River to Luling (*see Tours 1b and 11a*).

The old PECAN GROVE PLANTATION HOUSE (*open*), 99.8 *m.,* now abandoned, is a monument to the slow, sure death that the Mississippi brings. It is a two-story structure, the lower floor of plastered-brick, the upper of wood. The entire lower floor has been razed in recent years by credulous treasure-seekers digging under its marble tiles.

Near the house formerly stood a tree which was reputed to possess supernatural powers. It was said that any animal which came under its spreading limbs would drop dead. The legend goes that on one occasion visitors from New Orleans rode to Pecan Grove and tied their horses in the shade of this tree. After inviting them into the house, their host inquired about the horses. Learning where they had been left he hurried out to move them. But, the evil powers had done their work and both were prone in death.

SAINT ROSE, 100.7 *m.* (15 alt., 2,106 pop. 1970; 1,099, 1960; inc. 91%), was, prior to the construction of the Cities Service Export Oil Company Depot, peopled mainly by Italian immigrants who engaged in truck farming and dairying. Now the majority of the inhabitants are employed by the oil company, which owns most of the homes.

KENNER, 106.3 *m.* (10 alt., 29,858 pop. 1970; 17,037, 1960; inc. 75%), was named for Minor Kenner, on whose plantation the town grew; its earliest name was Cannes Brulées (Fr., burnt canes). Kenner is the shipping center for a vegetable-growing community, and there are several small manufacturing plants. It is on the route of new Int. 10.

Since many of the inhabitants are Italian immigrants, the major events of the year are typical Italian celebrations that commemorate the memory of Saints Joseph and Rosalie. St. Joseph's Day, the 19th of March, is the one day in 40 on which rigid Lenten restrictions are removed. On this occasion every effort is expended to glorify the patron saint. Altars, decorated with fruits, vegetables, and special pastries, are erected in many homes. The day is spent in good-natured revelry and feasting, with everyone visiting the altars and receiving at each the customary offering of pastry and wine.

St. Rosalie's Day is September 4, but the celebration usually takes place the following Sunday. On that day more than 300 Italians who belong to the Order of St. Rosalie march barefooted through the streets rejoicing with music and banners. The day usually ends with an immense fireworks display which reaches its climax when a gigantic figure of the patron saint bursts into dazzling light, lingers a moment, and then is slowly consumed in flames.

In the northern outskirts of Kenner is the junction with US 61 (*see Tour 10b*).

At 110.2 *m.* is the junction with a graveled road.

Right on this road 0.6 *m.* to the COLONIAL COUNTRY CLUB. The clubhouse was originally the Soniat home, built in 1820. It is a large two-story brick house with a high, sloping roof broken by dormers. The building was considerably remodeled in 1924.

The club stands on what was once the 1,000-acre Tchoupitoulas Plantation and, in the early eighteenth century, the site of an Indian Village. The district derived its name from a small bayou called the "Chapitolas," or "Tchoupitoulas" by the French. The etymology of the name remains obscure because no one knows to what dialect it belongs. If of Choctaw origin it means "those who live at the river."

There is an interesting story connected with the early years of the Soniats at Tchoupitoulas. They bought smuggled goods from Lafitte, as many other planters did. One day, while Lafitte was there displaying his wares, Governor Claiborne and his wife arrived unexpectedly. The Claibornes were frequent visitors at the plantation, as Mrs. Claiborne was a sister of Mrs. Soniat; but Lafitte believed that he was about to be captured and fled.

HARAHAN, 111 *m.* (8 alt., 13,037 pop. 1970; 9,275, 1960), was named for W. J. Harahan, at one time president of the Illinois Central Railroad. The town grew around the yards and shops of the railroad, which have since been removed. The majority of the population is now engaged in farming and dairying. An annual "block" dance is held here in July; the concrete highway serves as the dance floor.

At 112.1 *m.* is the junction with a private road.

Right on this road 0.4 *m.* to ELMWOOD, believed to date back to 1719. It burned in February 1940, but has been restored and now houses a restaurant. Thirty-two magnificent oaks form a triple square around the house. Tradition links the name of Lafrénière with the early history of the plantation, and it is also asserted that W. C. C. Claiborne, the first American Governor of Louisiana, spent some years here.

The HUEY P. LONG BRIDGE, 112.5 *m.,* is at the junction with US 90, which unites with La 48 between the bridge and New Orleans.

NEW ORLEANS, 120.7 *m.* (4 alt., 593,471 pop. 1970) (*see New Orleans*).

Tour 10C

Oak Grove—Port Vincent—French Settlement—Sorrento; 27 *m.,* La 42, La 22.

This belt route, through a little-traveled but historically interesting section of southeastern Louisiana, affords many picnicking, camping, and fishing spots.

La 87 branches east from US 61 (*see Tour 10b*) in OAK GROVE, 0 *m.*

At PRAIRIEVILLE, 3.2 *m.,* the road forks; turn L.

At 5.7 *m.* is the site of GALVEZ TOWN, a fortified settlement that enjoyed a brief existence (1775–89) during the Spanish domination. Today scarcely a trace of it remains, and the site is a picnic ground (small fee). There is a good beach and the grounds fee includes use of a bathhouse. Hunting and fishing are good in the vicinity. An inaccurate sign, "Galvez—Original Spanish Capital of Louisiana," marks the entrance.

Galvez Town was settled during the administration of Governor Bernardo de Galvez by about 250 Isleños (Sp., islanders) (*see Tour 8A*) brought from the Canary Islands. The site chosen was the confluence of Amite River and Bayou Manchac, on the boundary between Spanish Louisiana and English West Florida. Navigation to New Orleans was afforded by the bayou itself, Amite River, and Lakes Maurepas and Pontchartrain. The first commandant was Don Francisco Collell, who conscientiously endeavored to guide the poverty-stricken and ill-equipped Isleños through their pioneer struggles, beset, as they were, by periodic famine, flood, and epidemics of malaria. In 1779, with reinforcement of the garrison incident to the opening of hostilities between Spain and England, the population of Galvez Town reached its peak, 400. That same year the Spanish garrison captured a flotilla of seven British ships loaded with foodstuffs, upon which the hungry colonists promptly feasted. Within a short time troops under Governor Galvez captured all of West Florida—a victory that spelled ruin for Galvez Town; for with the passing of British rule in West Florida went the major reason for its existence. Deprived of government support, the settlement began to disintegrate, and within a few years it was deserted. According to tradition a shipload of gold lies at the bottom of Amite River opposite the old site of Galvez Town, a part of the vast treasure that once belonged to the pirate-smuggler, Jean Lafitte.

At 7.2 *m.* is the junction with an unimproved road. Left 0.2 *m.* on this road to CLAYBANK, a bathing spot on Amite River.

East of this junction La 42 parallels the winding Amite River. The huge hoop-nets of fishermen dry in the sun beside occasional cottages.

PORT VINCENT, 8.3 *m.* (10 alt. 387 pop. 1970), is a village on the east bank, named for Vincent Scivicque, reputedly the first man to sail a schooner from Lake Maurepas up Amite River. Prior to the construction of a bridge at the point, Scivicque and successive generations of his descendants operated a ferry here; and in early days the village was called Scivicque's Ferry. By 1810 there was a thriving settlement of fishermen and farmers at the point. ST. AGNES CHURCH (Roman Catholic) was built in 1836. Port Vincent is still primarily a fishing village, although there are a number of cotton and vegetable farms in the vicinity. The catfish caught hereabouts are reputed the finest in the country. Boats can be rented at different points along the river bank. The swimming is good, though there are no bathhouses.

An interesting custom at one time common to this section involved the construction of small slatted houses over tombs in the cemeteries, presumably for protection from the weather. In the cemetery adjoining the church there are two such structures.

East of Port Vincent the route follows graveled La 42.

COLLYELL BAY, 10.5 *m.,* set in a deep cypress swamp, is in reality a lakelike bayou. The name is a corruption of that of the commandant of Galvez Town, Collell. The "bay" is crossed by means of an old-fashioned drawbridge. Boats for fishing are available. Within a few hundred yards the route leaves the swamps and enters pinelands.

At 11.6 *m.* The road turns south.

FRENCH SETTLEMENT, 14 *m.* (15 alt.), was founded about 1810 by second-generation Acadians (*see Tour 1c*), whose descendants are today almost the sole inhabitants of the village. In relative isolation, the residents of French Settlement have retained their native French, and English is spoken only with a very strong accent. No vegetables are sold in the village, as each family raises its own or borrows from a neighbor. Strawberries grown in the vicinity are excellent, although they are produced here only on a small scale.

South of French Settlement the route winds along Amite River.

AMITE RIVER, 15.9 *m.,* is crossed by a bargelike, State-operated ferryboat (*free; operates day and night on call*), which is pulled back and forth by means of a cable. At this point Bayou Pierre, sluggish and choked with water hyacinths, flows into Amite River, from 35 to 50 feet deep here and an excellent fishing spot. Camps and boats can be rented.

Southward from the ferry the road follows Bayou Pierre for about a mile through a dense swamp, emerging upon slightly higher open prairie.

At 18.4 *m.* is the junction with La 22, R. on La 22.

Left is HEAD OF ISLAND, 1.3 *m.* (5 alt., 250 pop.), a village of scattered fishermen's dwellings. Here the fishing, hunting, and swimming are good. There are no bathhouses but a bathing pen has been fenced off for children in the river. Camps and boats can be rented. Several establishments serve fish dinners.

The highway makes a sweeping curve at 22.2 *m.* and at 23.4 *m.* crosses New River, which it thereafter parallels.

SORRENTO, 27 *m.* (17 alt., 1,182 pop. 1970) is at the junction with US 61.

❧❧❧❧❧❧❧❧❧❧❧❧❧❧❧❧❧❧❧❧❧❧❧❧❧❧❧❧❧❧❧❧

Tour 11

Junction with US 190—Port Allen—Donaldsonville—Luling—Gretna
—Port Sulphur—Buras—The Jump; 203.2 *m.*, La 1, La 405, La 18,
La 23.

Concrete- and asphalt-paved roadbed, with short graveled sections.
Railroads paralleling route: T. & P., between Port Allen and Gretna; S. P., between Luling and Huey P. Long Bridge.
Hotels and restaurants at Plaquemine, Donaldsonville, and Gretna; limited accommodations elsewhere.

Section a. JUNCTION WITH US 190 to GRETNA; 130.3 m.,
La 1, La 405, La 18

This section of the route follows the tortuous windings of the
Mississippi River from its uppermost deep-water port (Baton Rouge)
to New Orleans. To the left is the levee and to the right are first
great fields of sugar cane, then truck farms. Here and there are long
lanes of live oaks leading to old plantation mansions; at times the oak
lanes lead only to weed-grown plots where magnificent homes once
stood—homes that were sacked and burned during the War between
the States. In the background to the right, for much of the distance,
are dense and swampy forests of cypress, tupelo, ash, and maple.

La 1 joins US 190 at Erwinville and turns south from US 190 (*see*
Tour 3b), 0 *m.*, under the western approach to the Mississippi River
bridge, 4.5 miles north of Baton Rouge.

MONTE VISTA (*private*), 0.8 *m.*, stands just below the levee. Six
Square plastered columns support the wide front gallery, above and
below which green-shuttered French windows open along the full length
of each story. Square wooden columns support the hipped roof. To the
left of the house is a rock garden. The rocks, a delicate jade in color,
are composed of clinker-like residue of burned bagasse (crushed sugar
cane); an old sugar kettle forms the pond. To the right is a more formal
garden. Monte Vista was built in the 1850's by Louis Favrot, and restored in 1916 by Horace Wilkinson, Jr. It contains many family heirlooms, one of which is a massive gold watch given by George Washington
to his great nephew, Charles Carter.

POPLAR GROVE (*private*), 1.3 *m.*, is partly hidden by trees (L)
between the road and levee. Viewed from a distance the building resembles a pagoda. This is due to the fact that the structure was not
intended for a plantation home, but was a feature of the New Orleans
Cotton Centennial Exposition of 1884, when it was called the Bankers'

Pavilion. Horace Wilkinson, Sr. had the building torn down and shipped by steamboat to its present site.

The HILL PLACE (*private*), 3.2 *m.*, was formerly called the HOMESTEAD PLANTATION. The house, built in 1916, is a large white structure with brick columns across the front. The former Homestead house was moved when the present building was erected, the upper story becoming the roof of a church, the lower floor, with added roof, a separate residence. The original sugarhouse of the old plantation stands to the rear.

PORT ALLEN, 4.2 *m.* (21 alt., 5,728 pop. 1970; 5,026, 1960), on the Mississippi, opposite Baton Rouge, is the seat and industrial center of West Baton Rouge Parish. The town was laid out in 1854, two miles west of St. Michel, the original parish seat founded by Michel Mahier, which was submerged by the river.

Port Allen was named for Brigadier General Henry Watkins Allen (1820–66) of the Confederate Army, who served as Confederate Governor of the State in 1864–65. At the time the Baton Rouge, Grosse Tête & Opelousas Railroad had its southern terminus here, carrying farm commodities to river packets.

Away from the river the parish raises cotton and sugar cane. Two-thirds of its people are in rural areas and whites and blacks are about evenly divided.

Port Allen is profiting by the concentration of petrochemical plants at Baton Rouge and down the Mississippi. Humble Oil & Refining has built at plant at Port Allen. A Cargill grain elevator has located there. To the south, in former fields of sugar cane, are plants of Copolymer Rubber & Chemical, Dow Chemical, B. F. Goodrich Chemical, and Sid Richardson Carbon.

The PORT ALLEN LOCK is at the terminus of the barge canal that connects with the Intrastate Waterway and thus provides a clear route free from the twistings of the Mississippi.

The route continues south of Port Allen on La 1. For a short distance the country is devoted to cattle raising. But at 7.9 *m.* is the beginning of the sugar cane lands that form part of the great Sugar Bowl (*see Tour 10B*) of south-central Louisiana.

CINCLAIRE PLANTATION (L), 8.7 *m.*, is said to be one of the best equipped sugar plantations in Louisiana.

BRUSLY, 9.4 *m.* (25 alt., 1,282 pop. 1970) probably takes its name from the past participle of the French *bruler* (to burn). The name was inspired by the burning of brush to make a clearing for a settlement. In its original form as well as colloquial corruptions the term was applied in southern Louisiana to many settlements started in this way. The main part of town lies along the river.

At 16.6 *m.* is the junction with La 77 (*see Tour 11A*).

PLAQUEMINE, 17.1 *m.* (28 alt., 7,739 pop. 1970), incorporated in 1838, took its name from the bayou which flows out of the Mississippi River through the Plaquemine Locks. Early explorers found the banks of this stream lined with persimmon trees and dined with the Indians on bread made from their fruit, which was called *pikamine* or *pliakmine,* from the Illinois Indian *piakmin* (persimmon). Bayou Plaquemine was once an outlet to the Mississippi but became unnavigable. As it is the logical waterway from the Mississippi through Grand River to the lower reaches of the Atchafalaya, the U. S. Government authorized the digging of a 10-foot channel from Plaquemine to Morgan City, and in 1909 the vast steel PLAQUEMINE LOCKS (L) were completed. There are five sets of gates designed to withstand the pressure of a 33-foot water level; the lift is 55 feet.

The Plaquemine area suffered severe damage from Hurricane Camille, August 17–18, 1969. Oil installations were broken down. The Plaquemine Public Library lost its bookmobile and 32,000 volumes by flooding.

The seat of Iberville Parish was moved from Point Pleasant to Plaquemine in 1842, and the courthouse was erected 7 years later. It is on Main St., opposite the locks, and is now known as the CITY HALL. It is a white stuccoed-brick building; the portico has four Doric columns and a wooden pediment.

ST. JOHN THE EVANGELIST CHURCH (Roman Catholic), on Main St. across from the City Hall, is a buff-colored brick building with a red tile roof, erected in 1927. Eight Ionic concrete columns support a white marble entablature.

Another of the older buildings is the MIDDLETON HOME (*private*), corner Eden and Plaquemine Sts., which came into the possession of the Middleton family in 1845 and was built some years earlier. It is of brick, painted white, with eight square brick pillars supporting the gallery and wooden ones, the roof. Three gnarled cedars stand at the entrance, and at the side is a large rose garden.

In the past sugar and lumber have been the chief support of the town, and recent oil developments in the vicinity have added impetus to its growth. Plaquemine Southwest, 1,224 pop. 1970, is an unincorporated area.

The Plaquemine ferry crosses the Mississippi to Plaquemine Point 6 a.m. to 6 p.m.

Right from Plaquemine an unmarked, graveled road leads through a sawmill district to fishing grounds on Bayou Plaquemine and Grand River. For several miles the road parallels Bayou Plaquemine (R) whose banks are lined with a continuous string of small lumber rafts.

The SCHWING MOSS GIN (*visitors admitted*) is (L) at 1.9 *m.*

INDIAN VILLAGE (also called Village Point), 7.2 *m.* (10 alt., 100 pop.), at the confluence of Bayous Plaquemine and Grosse Tête, is the site of a settlement of the Chitimacha, many of whom lived in this area until the middle of the nineteenth century (*see Tour 1E*). At Indian Village the highway makes a sharp turn L. and continues for several miles atop the levee, offering a clear view of the wide and sluggish bayou and surrounding swamps.

JACK MILLER'S STORE (L), 10.2 *m.*, is a semipublic camp at the junction of Bayou Plaquemine with the Upper and Lower Grand Rivers. There is good hunting and fishing in the vicinity (*boats and guides available at moderate rates*).

BAYOU SORREL PARK (*boats for rent at moderate fees*), 15.7 *m.*, marks (L) the end of the highway, but a shell road on the levee follows Grand River southward to its junction with Bayou Pigeon. Until the construction of the levee system of the West Atchafalaya Emergency Floodway (*see Tour 18A*), this area was accessible only by boat.

At 20.3 *m.* a small bayou (L) ends at the roadside. This stream, which formerly flowed from Lake Long into Grand River, is called Bayou Choctaw, or locally, Bayou Go-To-Hell. It is said that a party of surveyors guided by a Choctaw Indian reached the bayou near the close of a strenuous day which had proved irritating to the nerves and temper of the old Indian. The group, plying the weary native with questions, finally asked the name of the bayou; the answer was "Go to hell."

At BAYOU PIGEON (*boats at reasonable rental*), 24.4 *m.*, the bayou of the same name enters Grand River on the R. The settlement consists entirely of houseboats and levee-side dwellings. There is good hunting and fishing in the vicinity.

The scattered settlements in the swampland south of Bayou Pigeon depend for their religious services upon a chapel boat, *Our Lady Star of the Sea* (Roman Catholic), which visits each community on fixed days once a month. During the brief stay the pastor administers to the spiritual needs of the parishioners, listens to their worldly problems, and recites the news of the outside world. About 85 persons can be accommodated in the floating church, a plain white houseboat towed by a motorboat, *St. Francis Xavier*. A study and small kitchen behind the altar serve as living quarters for the pastor.

South of Plaquemine La 405, which turns right at 17.7 *m.* and left several hundred feet beyond, winds with the river through extensive sugar plantations.

The ST. LOUIS PLANTATION (*private*), 19.3 *m.*, originally the Home Plantation, was established by Captain Joseph Erwin, who came to Louisiana from Tennessee in 1807. The original house, swept away by the Mississippi River in the 1850's, was replaced by the present dwelling. It is a large white frame building with green shutters. The wide front gallery is supported by six fluted Ionic columns; Corinthian columns support the hipped roof, which is topped by a belvedere. The galleries are further ornamented with elaborate ironwork. The house is set in a lovely garden enclosed by a hedge. Erwin made and lost several fortunes, but the great crevasse and flood of 1828 completely broke him; he died the following year. His widow eventually salvaged the place, and it became the property of a great-grandson, Edward J. Gay. The sugarhouse has a daily capacity of 1,000 tons.

SOULOUQUE, 23.7 *m.*, is a settlement named for a mulatto ex-slave who became a State senator in Reconstruction days.

POINT PLEASANT, 25.5 *m.*, was the first seat of Iberville Parish. The village cemetery contains the tomb of Paul O. Hebert, Governor of Louisiana from 1853 to 1856.

The CHAPEL OF THE MADONNA, 27.2 *m.*, was established about 1890 by a pious Italian woman who thereby fulfilled a pledge to the saints at the recovery of her daughter from a severe illness. The original shrine was just large enough to shelter an altar and the officiating priest, while the worshipers stood without. In 1928, when the levee was moved, the chapel was replaced by the present equally small, square frame structure. Services are held once a year, on St. Joseph's Day.

DUNBOYNE PLANTATION (*private*), 27.9 *m.*, was established (R) during the first half of the nineteenth century by Colonel Edward George Washington Butler, who married Frances Parke Lewis, a grandniece of George Washington. The original house still stands, but has undergone several alterations. It is now a one-story frame structure with dormered roof supported by six square wooden columns.

BAYOU GOULA (Ind., bayou or river people), 29.9 *m.* (19 alt.), is on both La 1 and La 405. The Bayogoula, a Muskhogean tribe, were living in this area when the first Frenchmen came down the river, but within 50 years the survivors had left to unite with the Houma, farther south. The site of their original village was a "league (app. 3 m.) and a half from the Mississippi," near the present village, which has been moved back four times from the encroaching river. The original concession in this district was granted to Paris Duvernay in 1718, and the first step toward colonization was made the following year by Leon Dubuisson and 60 other men. Bayou Goula, at one time a prominent steamboat landing, has long been the center of a thriving sugar area. It is said that the first levees on the Mississippi River were built here.

In the vicinity of Bayou Goula, it is said, the *loup-garous* (werewolves) of Louisiana hold an annual ball. Wild dances are performed on the banks of the bayou by *loup-garous* from all parts of the State. Only a brave person, armed with a bag of salt or some live frogs, dare watch them (*see Folkways*). But even then it is dangerous, especially at the change of the moon.

The NOTTAWAY PLANTATION HOUSE (*private*), 31.5 *m.*, was built by John Hampden Randolph of Virginia, who made a considerable fortune in sugar, and in 1857 employed Henry Howard, New Orleans architect, to design the residence for him. It was named for a county in Virginia.

The huge cement-covered brick house, set in a grove of live oaks, is surmounted by a heavy cornice and rises two stories over a raised stuccoed basement. Tall square wooden columns, painted white, support the iron-railed galleries. There is a semicircular gallery on the right side and a wing on the left. Recessed and iron-barred windows add a note of solidity. The rooms are spacious and well planned; many are decorated with intricate plaster mouldings, bronze and crystal chandeliers, and marble mantels. In the north wing is a glittering ballroom decorated in white from enameled floor to plastered ceiling.

WHITE CASTLE, 33.1 *m.* (25 alt., 2,205 pop. 1970), was named for the plantation house built in the early nineteenth century for Thomas Vaughn, and used for a time as the home of his son-in-law, Governor Paul O. Hebert. The house, gabled, columned, and with encircling galleries, stood at the end of a quarter-mile driveway, bordered with weeping willows. The original site is now in the Mississippi River, the house having been moved four times, losing sections with each move until it was divided into two cottages which are now in the western part of the town.

White Castle recently completed a new City Hall and a Fire Station. It built a Water Tower, bought a gas system, and devoted funds to other civic improvements, including 42 low-rent housing units. The oil field behind White Castle continues in production and is principally owned by Shell. Industries have been multiplying across the Mississippi River and within 12 miles north and south of White Castle.

La 1 passes the fields, 33.9 *m.*, of the associated plantations that supply the CORA TEXAS REFINERY. Many of the first experiments in the manufacture of sugar occurred on Cora Plantation, which was established in 1817 by the Urquhart family. The other sugar houses in the White Castle area are Cedar Grove and Catherine.

BELLE GROVE, an ornate plantation house designed by James Gallier, Sr., and erected in 1857, and until 1914 the center of a lively social life, then fell into ruin. On Nov. 6, 1952, it burned down. Its site has been subdivided for dwellings.

CHATHAM PLANTATION, 38.9 *m.*, was established as a sugar plantation by Henry Johnson, Governor of Louisiana from 1824 to 1828, and Colonel Key, Johnson's father-in-law. The residence was destroyed by fire, but several of the beautiful live oaks which surrounded the house are still standing. The owners of Chatham entertained many famous guests, including Henry Clay, during whose visit champagne "flowed deep enough to float a battleship."

From Chatham La 1 continues southward through Lover's Lane, a stretch of road arched overhead by live oak limbs and edged with a thick growth of Cherokee roses.

HOHEN SOLMS, 39.9 *m.* (25 alt.), a small agricultural village, was formerly the center of a group of sugar cane plantations established about the middle of the nineteenth century by John Reuss, a German.

La 1 turns R. at 47 *m.* At 47.8 *m.,* is the EVAN HALL PLANTATION, purchased in 1778 by Evan Jones from the heirs of Désiré LeBlanc, who had received the land through a Spanish grant.

The route turns L. on La 405.

SMOKE BEND, 49.6 *m.* (20 alt.), according to tradition, was named by early travelers who, when they rounded a bend in the river, saw clouds of smoke rising from Indian campfires.

From Smoke Bend southward to Donaldsonville, the highway, lined with the cottages and cabins of small farmers and plantation laborers, takes on something of the appearance of a city street.

PORT BARROW, 50.8 *m.* (20 alt.), the main part of which lies along the river, was for some time after Federal occupation of New Orleans and southeastern Louisiana "a hotbed of guerillas," as General Butler put it. Small bands of Confederates harassed the Federals, swooping down suddenly upon small detachments. Most despised and hated by them was the horde of carpetbaggers that had followed upon the heels of the Union Army. About 2 months after Farragut's triumphal upstream journey, in which Port Barrow and Donaldsonville had suffered a serious bombardment, General B. F. Butler dispatched a large force to "properly subdue the guerillas"—sacking, burning, and shooting as it went.

The troops paused at Port Barrow to construct a log and earthwork fort, and on February 9, 1863, the American flag was unfurled over the new stronghold. Four months later, a small band of Confederates, chiefly Texans, staged a dramatic attack upon the fort, which was garrisoned by two or three hundred Union soldiers. In a desperate hand-to-hand struggle in which, when other weapons failed, the combatants resorted to hurling bricks, the Confederates took the fort. A few hours later Union gunboats opened fire and the Confederates quit the defenses, carrying away their dead and wounded. The Federals were very much chagrined the next morning to find only the bodies of their own soldiers in the ruins.

At White Castle La 1 proceeds due southeast, while La 405 follows the crescent made by the River. Before reaching Donaldsonville La 1 turns south, following the west bank of the Bayou Lafourche all the way to Grand Isle. At Donaldsonville is a junction with La 18, which runs along the south bank of the Mississippi.

DONALDSONVILLE, 51.9 m. (33 alt., 7,367 pop. 1970; 6,082, 1960); seat of Ascension Parish, prospers both from sugar cane and petrochemical industries. The parish produces petroleum, natural gas, and salt. The site first attracted settlers around 1750 when traders came to bargain with the Indians for furs near where the Bayou La Fourche once emptied into the Mississippi. Several miles south, where the bayou divided into two arms, was an Indian village called La Fourche (Fr. fork) des Chitimachas. In the 1760–70 decade some of the Acadians who had been exiled from Canada reached New Orleans and were granted land along the Mississippi River by the Spanish administration. In 1772 Father Angelus de Revillagodos, a Capuchin, came to look after the spiritual needs of the settlers and in 1781 helped build the first church, on the site where the present Church of the Ascension stands.

The settlement first was called Ascension. In 1806 a New Orleans Englishman, William Donaldson, bought a tract of land from the Acadians for a town site and offered part of it to the State for a capitol. He died in 1813 before any action was taken, but the State Legislature did meet there in 1830 and 1831, when the town had only 494 people. In 1822 the town had been incorporated under the name of Donaldsonville. The Catholic Order of Sisters of Charity built its convent in 1830. During the Civil War Confederate sympathizers sniped at Federal transports using the Mississippi until Admiral Farragut sent gunboats to shell the town.

A shipping center for agricultural products of the Bayou country, Donaldsonville attracted industries, most of which located across the river in East Ascension. It is served by La 1 to Baton Rouge (32 m.) and La 18 to New Orleans (60 m.); also by La 22 and La 945. The SUN-SHINE BRIDGE crosses the river to East Ascension. When the Bayou La Fourche became stagnant the community pumped 200,000 gallons of water a minute into it and revived it.

Several farmhouses built well over 100 years ago survive in the area. The BEL HOUSE downtown is notable for second-story iron grillwork, similar to that extant in New Orleans. There is a tradition that the first

Caesarian operation in the South was performed by a local doctor. The Italian community cherishes the belief that the intervention by St. Amico saved the life of a youth. The father built a chapel about 10 ft. square to honor the saint. It has been enlarged and the saint is venerated at the shrine of St. Amico on the Sunday following Easter.

The Ascension Parish Library was established in 1961. It has approx. 26,000 books and operates a bookmobile.

The Texas & Pacific Ry. serves Donaldsonville. The South Louisiana State Fair is held here annually.

The route now follows La 18.

ABENT, 54.7 m., is inhabited largely by Italian immigrant truck farmers.

The section along the Mississippi River from about 58.4 m. to the lower part of the adjoining parish of St. John the Baptist is what was always called in the early days the Côte des Allemands (see Tour 10B).

An unpretentious old plantation house, 58.9 m., embodies one of the earliest types of Louisiana construction—briqueté entre poteaux. In a great many instances unpainted weather-boarding conceals the original plastered walls. Corrugated iron often covers the old hand-hewn shingles.

A RICE FARM, 61.3 m., is today rather unusual for this section, though less than 50 years ago small rice farms were numerous along here, water for irrigation being siphoned from the river.

At intervals of a mile or two groups of old plantation bells surmounting crude scaffolds suggest the prosperous days of this plantation section before the War between the States.

The ST. JAMES CATHOLIC CHURCH, 68 m., was constructed partly from materials remaining when the original edifice was demolished. The old church was constructed soon after 1770 on land given by Don Jacques Cantrelle, Spanish commandant of St. James Parish. The original altar, statues, pews, and many other furnishings have been retained. Within, marking the Stations of the Cross, are several fine copies of classic ecclesiastical paintings. Across the road, adjacent to the site of the original church, is the old cemetery, wherein are buried members of prominent Louisiana families, notably the Romans and the Aimes.

OAK ALLEY, 74.7 m., is a magnificent plantation house of Greek Revival architecture, girdled by 28 Doric columns, each 8 feet in circumference. The house, 70 feet square, is built of brick covered with plaster painted a delicate pink. Double galleries surround it; that on the upper floor is ornamented with a painted cypress railing of unusual beauty. Fine doors at the first-floor entrance are duplicated in the second story. The columns are draped by a variety of vines, which provide a succession of multicolored blooms throughout the year. There is a dormered hipped roof surmounted by a belvedere. A double line of oaks, like the columns, 28 in number, form an avenue about 200 yards long from the highway to the residence. The largest oak is 22 ft. 9 in. in diameter.

This home—built in 1836 for I. T. Roman, brother of André Roman, Governor of Louisiana (1831–35; 1839–43)—was originally named Bon Séjour (Fr., good stay). Steamboat captains found that name difficult to remember, but the avenue of oaks furnished a distinctive substitute. Now restored to its original grandeur and furnished lavishly, it is occupied by Mr. and Mrs. Andrew Stewart. It is said that on this plantation, in 1846, a slave gardener by the name of Antoine performed the first successful pecan grafting. The garden may be visited, but not the house.

The St. Joseph Plantation House, 74.9 *m.,* of *briqueté entre poteaux* construction, was built by a Dr. Merrick, and bought by Valcour Aime as a wedding present for one of his four daughters. The steep hipped roof has three dormer windows in the front. Ten square wooden columns rise from larger brick ones which uphold the gallery.

Felicity, 75.3 *m.,* built by Aime as a wedding present for another daughter, has six large square wooden pillars and a single dormer in the low-slanting roof. Both St. Joseph's and Felicity have wide central halls with high-ceilinged rooms opening from them and Felicity boasts red Italian marble mantels.

At 76.1 *m.* is the site of the Valcour Aime Plantation, called The Little Versailles during the 30-year height of its glory centering about 1845. Here Valcour Aime (1798–1867), the "Louis XIV of Louisiana," lived the life of a feudal lord and was reputed to be the richest man in the South. He is said to have owned a table service of solid gold, which was dumped in the river to prevent Federal confiscation during the War between the States. His lavish receptions and other entertainments are remembered in St. James Parish to this day. On one occasion he won a bet of $10,000 from an epicure by serving a perfect dinner, all of which—fish, game, fruits, nuts, coffee, cigars and wines—was supplied from the immediate plantation. Aime operated a steamboat between his plantation and New Orleans for his own convenience and that of his guests, and named it *Gabriel Aime* in honor of his only son.

Although Valcour Aime's beautiful wife, Josephine Roman, bore him four daughters and a son, it was the death of this only son in 1854 of yellow fever that shadowed his declining years and turned him into a hermitlike patriarch, both loved and feared.

Experiments in sugar culture, which were recorded in full in a large diary kept by the planter, were stopped abruptly as soon as Gabriel died. A final entry, sealed with wax, when opened disclosed his last notation: "Let he who wishes continue, my time is finished—he died on September 18. I kissed him at 5 o'clock, also on the following day."

The mansion, built in 1799, was a two-story building with eight massive columns supporting the wide front galleries. Varicolored marble squares formed the floors of the first story. The floor of the gallery was made of black and white marble diamonds. The mantelpieces over the enormous fireplaces were also of marble, as were the three wide stairways that connected the floors. Secret stairways were built in the thick walls. The paved Spanish-type open court, formed by extensions of the sides of the house, was protected by deep balconies and gay awnings. The house burned to the ground in the second decade of the present century.

The chief charm of the estate was the garden, planned and watched over by a landscape gardener imported from Paris, who had 30 slaves at his command. Trees for the garden were brought from Europe, Asia, and Central America. Exotic vines came from the Orient. There were conservatories for the most sensitive foreign plants and flowers, and for growing bananas, pineapples, mangoes, and coffee. One wooded area containing a log cabin sheltered rabbits, deer, and kangaroos. A miniature river spanned by footbridges ran through the garden. Beside a small artificial lake was an elaborate small fort, where cannon boomed welcomes to distinguished guests. Children of the community staged an annual sham battle here, using oranges as ammunition. The lake and lagoons were stocked with fish; and swans, pelicans, and herons enlivened the waters. Peacocks proudly strutted through the garden, and almost every species of songbird native to the State was brought here to sing. In the midst of the garden stood an artificial "mountain" surmounted by a Chinese pagoda, and with a grotto hollowed in its base. The garden is in ruins; its rare flowers have all vanished or grown wild under a tangle of vines and weeds. The fort, in disrepair, and the dry channel of the "river," crossed by broken bridges, can still be seen. The site of the garden is marked by a tall, junglelike grove of trees. It may be explored with safety.

The ARMANT PLANTATION (R), 77.2 m., which has decreased in acreage from 12,000 to 5,000 acres, is operated by a syndicate which also controls several other large plantations in this vicinity.

VACHERIE, 77.5 m. (16 alt.), is a crossroads settlement.

Right from Vacherie on graveled La 20. For the first few miles the extensive sugar cane fields of Oak Alley Plantation are traversed.

At 9 m. is the junction with graveled La 307, the Kraemer Road (10 miles ahead on La 20 is Thibodaux. L. on unmarked La 307.

KRAEMER, 12.3 m. (5 alt.), an isolated agricultural community on narrow Bayou Chegby (also called "Chagbee" and "Chackbay") Ridge, is a typical Acadian backwater settlement with small, unpainted homes surrounded by patches of corn, cane, and cotton. The natives supplement their slender farming income with fishing, trapping, and moss picking. Farmers at work in the fields stare curiously at the rare advent of a passing automobile. In the spring the swamps on each side of the ridge are clothed in soft, fresh green foliage, and wild flowers are abundant. There are said to be more varieties of native iris in this section than in any other part of the State.

BAYOU BŒUF (Fr., ox), 19.2 m., is a small village near the mouth of Bayou Bœuf. An Indian mound here has yielded bones, bits of pottery, and arrowheads. Boats can be rented at Bayou Bœuf for fishing and hunting on Lake des Allemands (Fr., German lake), 1 mile N., and Lake Bœuf, 8 miles S. Both lakes are accessible from the village only by boat on beautiful Bayou Bœuf.

At 80.1 m. is a ferry crossing the Mississippi to Lutcher (see Tour 10B).

An example of moss-mud-cypress construction (R), 82.9 m., is especially interesting because fallen plaster has exposed structural details.

The WHITNEY PLANTATION HOUSE (private), 83.5 m. (R), is of like construction, though more elaborate; it is a raised cottage with wide galleries at the front and rear supported by square wooden pillars. The hipped roof has two dormers on the front. The hinges, bolts, bars, and other hardware are hand-made and bear scroll designs. The shuttered rear gallery and the ceiling and doors of the parlor are painted in the manner of Dresden China. The parlor ceiling has four monograms— "M.H."—painted in gratitude by an artist who, commissioned to do some work in a Catholic church near by, became ill and was nursed back to health by Mrs. Haydel, at that time mistress of the home.

The EVERGREEN PLANTATION HOUSE (*private*), 84.6 *m.*, a two-story brick structure (R), was built about 1840 by Ralph Brou in the Greek Revival style. Tall, massive stucco and brick columns of the Doric order rise from the ground to the roof and support wide galleries. The hipped roof is broken by dormer windows and surmounted by a balustrade. A single, gracefully curving exterior stairway mounts the portico to the second-floor gallery. There are large magnolia trees, and to the rear is a complete group of outbuildings, including *garçonnières, pigeonniers,* servants' quarters, barns, and carriage houses. Even the privies are built of brick and are Greek Revival in design. In the rear is an avenue of live oaks, 39 to a side, 40 ft. apart. The home is the property of Mrs. Matilda Grey.

The abandoned two-story WEGO PLANTATION HOUSE, 85.7 *m.*, fronted by eight pillars and a wide veranda, is thought to be nearly a century and a half old and is of *briqueté entre poteaux* construction. It has been moved back three times to avert destruction by the Mississippi.

Extending a half mile back from the river at 88.4 *m.* is a grove of gigantic pecan trees.

EDGARD, 89.8 *m.* (9 alt.), is the seat of St. John the Baptist Parish. Facing the highway is a two-story red brick building with iron doors. It was an old store owned by E. J. Caire and once served as a landmark for steamboats, the place being known as Caire's Landing. The building has been moved back from the river and a cornerstone commemorates the event. ST. JOHN'S CHURCH (Roman Catholic), likewise facing the highway, is a large brown brick structure with twin bell towers. To the right is an old cemetery.

LUCY, 93.3 *m.* (10 alt.), was founded in 1720 as Carlstein, one of three thriving German Coast villages settled by Alsatians.

The GLENDALE PLANTATION HOUSE, 95 *m.*, said to be more than 150 years old, is a two-story, cement-covered brick house (R) with eight square wooden pillars. The roof is hipped and dormered. The timbers of the house were hand-hewn and fastened together with pegs; the hardware was forged on the place, and the elaborate mantels were hand-carved. There is a *pigeonnier* flanking the house on each side.

KILLONA, 96.7 *m.* (11 alt.), is a quiet village whose inhabitants are engaged in the cultivation of sugar cane.

At TAFT, 99 *m.* (9 alt.), is a tower of the electric "high line," whose high tension wires cross the Mississippi River to the Bonnet Carré Spillway.

The LOCKE BREAUX LIVE OAK (R), 99.2 *m.*, has a girth of 35 feet, a spread of 166 feet, and a height of about 75 feet, and by virtue of its size is "President" of the Live Oak Society (*see Lafayette*). A private road, open to the public, makes it possible to circle the tree and continue without inconvenience. The tree stands on property now owned by the Southern Dairy Co., but formerly owned by the late Samuel Locke Breaux of New Orleans, whose interest in the tree first brought it into prominence.

The KELLER HOUSE, 103.1 *m.,* in which the Spanish and French architectural influences are clearly discernible, stands back from the highway in an ancient grove of pecan trees. The house, now called Home Place, was built in 1801. It is of brick, still covered with the original inch-thick white plaster. Round brick pillars support the gallery which completely surrounds the house; the dormered hipped roof is supported by slender round wooden columns. The woodwork throughout is hand-carved, the mantelpieces being exceptionally interesting. The dining-room on the ground floor is paved with black and white marble squares; the adjoining pantries and wine closets are iron-barred.

In the rear stands a large wooden building, which served as a hospital during the War between the States. At that time, the plantation was owned by the Fortier family, and it is still frequently referred to by their name, though the Keller family has occupied it for many years.

HAHNVILLE, 103.6 *m.* (6 alt.), seat of St. Charles Parish, presents an array of simple houses standing in large tree-shaded yards. The archives of the St. Charles Parish Courthouse contain records dating back to the first quarter of the eighteenth century.

LULING, 107.2 *m.* (10 alt., 3,255 pop. 1970), now has a 3-mile connection with US 90 at Boutte. US 90 runs parallel with La 18 to the Huey P. Long Bridge.

At Luling a ferry crosses the Mississippi to Destréhan (*see Tour 10B*).

At 122.4 *m.,* at the western approach to the HUEY P. LONG BRIDGE (*see Tour 1b*), is the eastern junction with US 90 (*see Tour 1b*); straight ahead on La 18, which for the next mile passes through a wooded section.

SEVEN OAKS (*private*), 123.6 *m.,* is an 18-room, plaster-covered brick house standing (L) under the shelter of the oaks from which its name is derived. It was built by the widow of Michael Zeringue in 1830 and was subsequently owned by other prominent families of the parish. The house is square and entirely surrounded by wide upper and lower galleries supported by white Doric columns, eight in the front and rear and seven on each side. A wooden belvedere crowns the top of the house.

La 18 crosses the Company Canal, 124.1 *m.,* on a steel bascule bridge. On the left are the lock gates that connect the canal with the Mississippi River. The canal, which is used principally to bring fish, shrimp, and oysters to market, runs southward to Lakes Salvador and Catouatche, where there are fine hunting and fishing grounds not accessible by road.

WESTWEGO, 124.5 *m.* (5 alt., 11,402, pop. 1970; 9,815, 1960, inc. 16%), so named because it was the point of departure for westbound travelers during the gold rush west. It was first settled by the Fredericks family. Until 1893 the community was a small village, but in that year the survivors of a hurricane that had desolated Chênière Caminada settled here (*see Tour 1B*). This influx marked the beginning of the town's growth. Industry centers about a shrimp-packing plant and several large alcohol manufacturing units.

The CELOTEX CORPORATION, 125.8 *m.*, a subsidiary of the Jim Walter Corporation of Tampa, Fla., manufactures building materials from "bagasse," stalks of the sugar cane after the juice has been extracted. For many decades this refuse was the subject of extensive study by sugar engineers, who sought some other use for it than as fuel in the sugar factory. In 1920 its value as a basic material for wall board was proved, and the establishment of the celotex plant resulted.

Bagasse is secured from the sugar mills of the State during the sugar-making season. It is packed in bales and piled in the fields under a tin roof until needed by the factory at Marrero. The actual manufacture begins with the cooking of the fibrous stalks in rotary cookers. The cooked fiber is discharged into a blowpit from which it is pumped to the shredders, which beat the fibrous stock through perforated steel plates. In the washers, soluble material is removed from the fibers, which are pumped to the proportioning meters. These devices control the respective amounts of wood filler, bagasse fiber, sizing, and alum in the product.

A refining engine beats out the stock so that the fibers are of the desired length and body. After it has been refined, the stock drops into the machine storage chest. It is pumped from here as required to the board machine, where water is added and the mixture felted. After going through the drier the board is finished, except for cutting to size or such operations as leveling, grooving, drilling, etc.

At 127.6 *m.* is the junction of La 45 and La 18, La 18 joins Int. 610. L. here on La 45.

MARRERO, 128 *m.* (5 alt., 29,015 pop. 1970), is named for the family of L. H. Marrero, a prominent politician of Jefferson Parish in the latter part of the nineteenth century. It original name was Amesville, derived from the Ames Plantation, a large sugar property that has since been divided into small truck farms. It was the site of a destructive crevasse in 1891. Marrero is on the west bank of the Mississippi opposite New Orleans and profits by its expansion.

HARVEY, 128.9 *m.* (5 alt., 6,347 pop. 1970), is an unincorporated community in Jefferson Parish. It was named for Captain Joseph Hale Harvey, a Virginian who in 1845 married Louise, the oldest daughter of Nicholas Noel Destréhan, owner of extensive properties, including the Destréhan Canal. An annual event here is the fair and parade held by Italian members of the community on the first Sunday of September in honor of St. Rosalie, their patron saint.

The HARVEY LOCKS link the Mississippi River and the Intracoastal Waterway (*see Tour 11D*). That portion of the waterway between the river and Bayou Barataria was known formerly as the Harvey Canal.

In 1924 the Harvey family received $425,000 from the U. S. Government for the canal and its appurtenances, which included a small lock gate. Work on the Harvey Locks was started in May, 1929, and completed in 1933 at a cost of $2,000,000. The steel and concrete lock chamber is 425 feet long and 75 feet wide. In fall and winter the canal water level is higher than the river, while in spring the river rises 18 feet or more above the canal level, necessitating high, heavy gates at each end of the lock. Construction of the locks has been an important undertaking in the commercial history of New Orleans, opening a vast new territory which now pours its quota into the city's port.

The history of the canal began in 1835, when Destréhan opened a drainage canal, which he later widened to accommodate small boats. It was constructed almost entirely by slaves, who used spades as their only tools. It lost its original name, Destréhan Canal, after its management passed into the hands of J. H. Harvey. In 1853 it was greatly deepened and widened, and in 1880 private construction of locks was started but never completed. A lock gate, used only when the canal and river were at approximately the same level, was finally completed in 1909.

HARVEY'S CASTLE, which until 1924 stood on the site now occupied by the locks, was built in 1844 by Captain Harvey as a gift for his bride. Constructed by free Negroes who lived in Free Town, now part of Gretna, it was completed in 90 days on a wager; yet when demolished it was almost as solid as when first built.

The three-story castle towered so completely over near-by structures that it came to be a landmark for river pilots, who took their bearings from the two octagon-shaped ornamental turrets on each side. Planned by Harvey and his contractor without other assistance, this house was externally much like the old State capitol in Baton Rouge, built three years later.

Above each turret was an observatory affording an unobstructed view of the Mississippi River and the surrounding country. On each floor were ten rooms, with spacious halls and 18-foot ceilings. Wide galleries ran entirely around the house on the first and second floors. From the center of the great hall, which extended to the rear of the building, rose a grand twin staircase with a beautiful walnut balustrade. The double stairway united at a landing midway between the first and second floors. Marble mantels, elaborate friezes, velvet hangings, and imported pictures made the interior indeed castlelike. There were extensive gardens with parterres, winding walks, and conservatories.

The Harvey family occupied the house until 1870. From 1874 to 1884, when the town of Harvey was the parish seat, the house served as the Jefferson Parish Courthouse. An unsuccessful effort was made to exploit the place as a pleasure resort under the name of Columbia Gardens in 1900. A chartered steamboat made regular trips from the foot of Canal Street, New Orleans, to the Castle, where dancing, sports, and sightseeing were offered as entertainment. In spite of these attractions, the venture failed after its second season, and the old home degenerated into a tenement house.

A ferry crosses the Mississippi at Harvey to Louisiana Ave., New Orleans.

Arrangements can be made at Harvey for a boat trip to the Barataria country.

East of Harvey La 23 traverses a section occupied by manufacturing plants, the most important of which are cottonseed oil refineries. The residents are principally industrial workers.

GRETNA, 130.3 m. (8 alt., 24,875 pop. 1970).

A ferry plies between Gretna and Jackson Ave., New Orleans.

Section b. GRETNA to THE JUMP; 72.9 m., La 23

Continuing to parallel the Mississippi, this section of the route runs through orange groves to a point near the mouth of the river.

South of GRETNA, 0 m., La 23 for a few miles traverses a section of former swampland that has been drained and is now used for truck farming and dairying.

BELLECHASSE, 6.3 m., a large white structure, was once the home of Judah P. Benjamin (1811–84), Secretary of State and of War for the Confederacy. Benjamin was born in the West Indies, and at the age of 14 entered Yale University. After three years of study he left without a degree and entered a commercial house in New Orleans. He soon gave up this position and began to study law in a notary's office. In 1833 he was admitted to the Louisiana Bar. Thereafter, his success was rapid. In collaboration with Thomas Slidell he published in 1834 a *Digest of the Reported Decisions of the Late Territory of Orleans and of the Supreme Court,* the earliest digest of Louisiana law. He served as U. S. Senator from 1853 to 1861.

When the Confederate States were formed, Benjamin was appointed attorney general, and later was transferred to the War Department. This proved an unfortunate appointment as he was blamed by public opinion for the loss of several battles. President Davis saved him from impeachment by appointing him Secretary of State, which position he held until the close of the war. Benjamin fled from Richmond to the West Indies, and later went to England, where his legal talents were immediately recognized. There he published his *Treatise on the Sale of Personal Property,* and in 1872 was made Queen's Counsel. He retired from practice in 1883 and died in Paris a year later. Benjamin purchased the house and plantation in 1844 from William C. Milne and, in 1846, remodeled the house.

The house is a square, three-story building. The plan of all three floors is identical. Upper and lower galleries surround the house and are supported by square box pillars of cypress. The main hallways are 16 feet wide with correspondingly high ceilings. A winding mahogany staircase ascends to the third floor from the lower hall. The interior woodwork was originally of white enamel, and all locks and doorknobs were silver plated. All of the furnishings, as well as the paintings and bronzes, were confiscated by Federal troops during the War between the

States. An old silver and bronze plantation bell with Benjamin's name inscribed on it and bearing the date October, 1858, was found in the garden. The house was falling into ruins when the Judah P. Benjamin Association bought it and arranged for its maintenance.

BELLE CHASSE, 6.4 *m.* (4 alt.), has two explanations for the origin of its name. Written as two words, it is French for "fine hunting," a fully justified title; but as one word it becomes the surname of J. D. deGoutin Bellechasse, once the owner of much property in the vicinity of New Orleans. Bellechasse commanded the troops at the transfer of Louisiana from Spain to France, and from France to the United States in 1803. At this time, Laussat, the French prefect, made Colonel Bellechasse a gift of 45 pounds of gun powder from the French stores to be used for his favorite sport—hunting. Bellechasse also helped to frame the constitution which admitted Louisiana to the Union (1812).

HEBERT CENTER is a 347-acre tract near Belle Chasse across the Mississippi River from New Orleans occupied by the TULANE RIVERSIDE RESEARCH LABORATORIES. It was awarded by the U. S. Government to Tulane University in 1963 for research and training programs in various fields, including aerospace engineering, nuclear physics, environmental sciences, water pollution, forest genetics, aquatic vegetation and fisheries sciences. The studies are a part of graduate education and are directed by the Schools of Engineering and Medicine, and the departments of chemistry, zoology, physics, psychology, geology, and botany.

Here was long the base of Seatrain, a car-ferry operated by the Missouri-Pacific and Texas & Pacific Railroads between New Orleans and New York. The loaded freight cars were lifted bodily by the crane and placed on the tracks of the ship.

ALVIN CALLEDER FIELD, opposite the Seatrain depot, is the U. S. Naval Air Station and the third airport in the New Orleans area. It has modern facilities and has lately constructed a Navy Exchange, a power check facility, and a fleet weather radar system.

The origin of the name of JESUIT BEND, 14 *m.* is undetermined, but there is a belief among the older natives that here the Jesuit Fathers first settled on coming to Louisiana. An occasional picturesque group of magnolias or moss-laden oak trees can be seen en route, once the settings of plantation homes. The tiny, willowy stalks in the fields are shallots (green onions), the growing of which is a flourishing Louisiana industry.

MYRTLE GROVE, 23.6 *m.,* was the center of a great sugar cane plantation owned by the Wilkinson family for 125 years. After the death of Theodore S. Wilkinson in 1921, the sugar mill, which had a grinding capacity of 10,000,000 pounds of sugar cane yearly, closed. Besides pursuing his career as a planter, T. S. Wilkinson was active in politics and was elected to Congress in 1866, serving two terms.

At 26 *m.* is the junction with a dirt road. Right on this road, through a beautiful virgin forest of towering interlocked oaks and cypress trees to LAKE HERMITAGE, 5.1 *m.,* where there is excellent salt-water fishing and crabbing.

The locality also affords deer, rabbit, waterfowl, and squirrel hunting. Hunting is permitted on payment of toll; the State hunting license is necessary. There is a private camp with limited board and lodging facilities. Near the small cemetery, the graves of which are marked with hand-made wooden crosses, is a picnic spot.

The small bay, 26.4 *m.,* resulted from the JUNIOR CREVASSE, an unusual break in the levee that occurred on the site of Junior Plantation in the spring of 1927. The crevasse began when an outbound 5,000-ton tanker, caught in the current, was driven head-on into the levee, its entire prow penetrating the embankment. When attempts were made to hold the bow in the crevasse to arrest the flow of water, the current caught the ship's stern, swung it around and by leverage effected an even greater break in the levee. The water rapidly widened the gap to 100 feet, and the surrounding region, most of which is sparsely inhabited marshland, was soon inundated. Although the truck farms suffered most as a result of the crevasse, when the water receded the deposit of silt remaining made the soil much richer than formerly.

Between Junior and Venice, interspersed by orange groves, are small farms devoted to the cultivation of the Creole lily.

The Creole lily (*Lilium longiflorum*) is generally called the Easter lily; its local name merely exemplifies the tendency of this section to apply the term Creole to both people and things. The flower of this special stock, which is well suited to home gardens, is said to be more vigorous, prolific, and resistant to disease than other varieties. Each stalk bears from 3 to 18 white blossoms, which reputedly last 4 or 5 days longer than those of the Japanese stock. More emphasis is placed on the production of the bulbs for shipping than on the sale of the flowers.

In the spring the blooms are nipped, allowing the bulb to retain the full nourishment of the plant juices. In midsummer the plants are dug up and the bulbs placed in a hamper protected from the sun by palmetto leaves. To prevent decay they are stored in cool, well-ventilated places, usually beneath houses. Protected against heat and fungus growth, the lily roots are shipped by express to northern cities, where they are kept in cold storage—32 to 40 degrees—through the winter. In early spring florists set them out to bloom for Easter and Mother's Day.

The row of old, two-story brick houses (L), 32.1 *m.,* the slave quarters of the former JOHNSON PLANTATION, now called WOODLAND, were built more than 150 years ago.

The house in the grove of trees to the right of the quarters is a comfortable structure with center halls and rooms on each side. Five dormers, front and rear, break the gabled roof. Though quite old, it is not the original plantation home. Bradish Johnson, original owner of Woodland, was born on Magnolia Plantation, a short distance south.

At WEST POINTE À LA HACHE, 34.2 *m.,* is a ferry (*small fee*). For ferry service blow horn or signal the operator by striking the large iron triangle.

MAGNOLIA, 35.6 *m.* is also called LAWRENCE, the official name of the post office. The former name is derived from Magnolia

Plantation, once a thriving sugar cane farm in this vicinity; the latter was the name of one of the plantation's owners. The double naming of small towns and villages is not uncommon.

Beginning here the highway runs between long groves of citrus trees—oranges, Satsumas, grapefruit, and kumquats.

About 50 yards from the highway in a grove of orange trees, is the MAGNOLIA PLANTATION HOUSE. The plantation was established about 1780 by two sea captains, Bradish and Johnson, who passing up and down the river were impressed with the altitude of the area and believed the land was adapted to the growth of sugar cane. Accordingly, they established a plantation and later erected an open kettle sugarhouse for the manufacture of sugar and molasses.

Jean Lafitte, who with his band of brigands carried on slave smuggling in the locality, is said to have been a friend of Bradish and Johnson and a guest at Magnolia. It is said domestic differences arose between the wives of the two captains and brought the prosperous partnership to an end. Johnson sold out to Bradish and purchased Woodland Plantation, a few miles north. It is interesting to note that Bradish Johnson, the son of Captain Johnson, was named for his father's partner.

The present Magnolia home was built about 1795. The house is two stories high with a large finished attic and contains ten 22-by-28-foot rooms. The walls of the house are plaster-covered brick of great thickness (2½ feet on the lower and 2 feet on the upper floor). Eight slender rectangular wooden pillars support the gabled roof.

The house might be called hand-made: the bricks are of native clay; the lumber is hand-hewn; and the interior woodwork, including the huge cypress mantels of the larger rooms, is hand-carved. All labor on the building, even the fine wood-carving, was executed by slaves.

The stack of the old sugar mill still stands. In the yard, to the rear, is the plantation bell.

In the early nineteenth century Magnolia was purchased by another sugar planter, Effingham Lawrence, who installed a vacuum process unit for the granulation of sugar. In 1873 Henry Clay Warmoth, Governor of Louisiana (1868–72), purchased a half interest in the plantation. He made a thorough study of sugar production both here and abroad, and under his ownership the plantation reached the height of its productivity.

The ex-governor was famed for his lavish entertaining and hospitality. The Grand Isle Railroad, a 60-mile line running from Buras to New Orleans, was built by Warmoth, reputedly because his wife disliked steamboats and found the horse-and-buggy trip to New Orleans too tiresome.

An amusing anecdote is told of a desk, a fine Hepplewhite of rosewood inlaid with mahogany, originally a gift to the Lawrence family from Judah Touro, philanthropist. When it passed into her hands, Mrs. Warmoth believed that it contained a secret drawer or compartment. A search revealed such a compartment containing a packet of letters and an old-fashioned jewel case. Her Negro servants were intensely interested in the jewel case, which to them suggested treasure, and crowded in as Mrs. Warmoth endeavored to open it. Suddenly she located the concealed catch and from the case there sprang a set of gold false teeth—straight into the group of Negroes, who forgot treasure in a mad scramble from the "haunted" desk. The letters had been written by Touro himself.

HAPPY JACK, 39.3 *m.,* prior to the War between the States was the center of Ronquillo Settlement, a large plantation. Shortly afterwards the land was sold in smaller lots, and a country store was opened, bearing the name Happy Jack, which thenceforth became the name of the village.

PORT SULPHUR, 43.4 *m.* (5 alt., 3,022 pop. 1970; 2,868, 1960), unincorporated, was established in 1933, and has grown into an industrial settlement. Homes of the officials and employees of the sulphur company are built around a court, each house of a different design. A plot of ground 20 by 120 feet is allotted to each employee and seed plants are furnished.

Right from Port Sulphur by boat to LAKE GRANDE ÉCAILLE (Fr., large scale), 10 *m.,* where the sulphur deposits are located.

Adjustment to local conditions was a remarkable feature of the development of the sulphur plant at Grande Écaille. The entire district, including the site of the sulphur deposits, is an open, tidal marsh. Movement of workers and materials across the boggy surfaces depended entirely, at first, on the creation of artificial waterways. To obtain the fresh water necessary for the sulphur-producing process, a pipe-line was laid from the Mississippi to the plant, and a 50,000,000-gallon earthen reservoir was constructed in order to settle and clarify the muddy river water. In the earlier operations, derricks for drilling sulphur wells were set on pilings, but since the completion of a fill over the operating area, which raised the land to an elevation of from 4 to 8 feet, derricks have been erected on mats.

The Frasch process (*see Science*) is the method employed at Grande Écaille for the removal of sulphur from the dome.

The industrial site and plant of the Freeport Sulphur Co. make up one of the largest nearly self-sustaining projects in the United States. This is accounted for by the isolation of the site and the limited transportation facilities. Among the special features of the plant that enable it to meet any requirement or emergency are a precision toolroom and a carbide shop for making ecetylene for welding.

South of Port Sulphur are vast areas of *cirier* (wax myrtle) bushes dotted with occasional trees. The production of myrtle wax from these bushes was one of the earliest of Louisiana industries. The product was used principally in the manufacture of candles. In the summer the area is sometimes visited by poachers coming to trap alligators, whose hide has become valuable for use in women's bags, men's belts and shoes. This is now illegal, for catching of alligators is prohibited at this time (1970) by conservation authorities. The alligator hunter does not shoot the reptiles on sight, but finds their haunts and lures them with meat-baited lines. When an alligator jumps from the water to seize the meat, a wire hoop is passed around its jaws, tightened, and drawn in. More daring hunters sometimes catch them with bare hands.

In and around EMPIRE, 53.1 *m.* are fine hunting and fishing grounds. The DOULLUT CANAL is named for the late Captain Doullet, its builder, operator of several packets. Early in 1936 the Doullet Canal and locks and the canal at Ostrica were purchased by the State and are now toll-free—a boon to oyster fishermen.

BURAS, 57.6 *m.* (7 alt., 500 pop.), is the orange-producing center of the State and ranks almost as high as a fishing and hunting center. Its population figure, 4,113 (1970) includes that of TRIUMPH. Here people of French, Spanish, Slavonian, Dalmatian, Chinese, Filipino, and Negro descent make Buras an interesting minature cosmopolitan melting pot. In the main, representatives of these varied extractions work side by side with little interracial antipathy. The inhabitants, with their varied costumes, picturesque trawl and other nets, fishing vessels, and oyster luggers, present an unusual opportunity to study the mingling and blending of Old World customs, viewpoints, and occupations in a New World setting.

In the northern outskirts of Buras is a settlement peopled by mulattoes, who refuse to intermarry with or live among the darker Negroes. As a result these mulattoes have established a rather exclusive residential section of their own. They refuse to share the same sections of churches with darker blacks and will send their children only to teachers with very light complexions. Among the women there is a high standard of beauty; it is said that many pass as whites. Besides the Negro blood, French, Spanish, Anglo-Saxon, and Indian are represented.

During the late eighteenth century there were several tiny settlements in the area; but it was not known by any definite name until, in 1840, seven brothers of the Buras family moved here from France. Since that time the scattered village has been called Buras. Today nearly every other inhabitant is named Buras—virtually all the whites are related either by blood or marriage.

The growth and development of the citrus industry in this region has been remarkable. An orange tree usually begins bearing after the fifth year, and an 8-year-old orchard usually pays very well. Annual profits of $1,500 an acre are not uncommon. In addition to the Louisiana naval orange, the region is noted for its Louisiana-Sweet, tangerine, Satsuma, mandarin, kumquat, and grapefruit. Until recently New Orleans consumed the bulk of the crop, but much of it is now shipped to northern and eastern markets.

At the several modern plants the fruit is first washed, dried, and polished. Then, on the grading belt, it is assorted on the basis of size, skin, color, and freedom from blemishes. Finally, the oranges are wrapped and packed under the label of the Buras Orange Growers Inc., a co-operative association to which most of the producers belong.

The orange groves extend for about 35 miles south of West Pointe à la Hache. Most groves have a depth of less than half a mile. In early spring blossoming trees perfume the air for miles around with their fragrance, and from late October to December the trees are laden with golden fruit.

The orange groves occupy only the narrow frontlands of the river.

Most of them are in large holdings that include the wooded swamp and marshlands in the rear. Some of the owners lease the trapping rights on these otherwise unproductive areas, specifying in their contracts with the trappers that they save the carcasses of muskrats and other animals for use as fertilizer in the orange groves.

The country in and about Buras abounds in voodooism. Many inhabitants, both black and white, consult the "remedy man" in preference to a qualified physician. The "remedy men" are simple folk, usually of mixed blood, who work in the fields until called upon to perform a service, which they do willingly, though rejecting any payment—not even a "thank you," as that would break the charm. Each has his favorite cures and charms: Uncle Narcisse's backache remedy is a string with seven knots tied, with elaborate ceremony, around the waist; for a teething child Uncle Emile would probably prescribe a necklace made of the vertebrae of a rattlesnake which had been buried and over which incantations had been said. Uncle Peron once directed a client whose house was haunted to get a frizzly chicken, walk backwards to the river, and throw the fowl over his left shoulder.

On the eve of St. John's Day the voodooists perform ancient rituals in absolute secrecy, allowing no outsider to attend. St. John's Day itself is a gala village holiday for all. Virtually every family gets aboard its own or a neighbor's boat and sails for the Beach, located on an island about 10 miles from Buras.

There are several oyster camps on the various little bays and bayous in the Buras area composed of dilapidated, unpainted shacks built on stilts high above the water. Life here is primitive. The possession in which each family head takes most pride is a small but seaworthy boat. The inhabitants are chiefly Slavonians and Dalmatians, many of whom have retained their Old World customs; for instance, the drinking of hard liquor or wine at breakfast. They are considered among the most honest and hard working folk in Plaquemines Parish.

Left from Buras, by passenger ferry, across the river to OSTRICA (4 alt.), a sparsely settled village peopled by oystermen, fishermen, and trappers. Here is a large semipublic fishing camp.

The cultivation of the oyster entails an amazing amount of hard manual labor, involving many steps. Wild oysters, of course, are obtained from the thousands of oyster reefs that lie off the Louisiana coasts. But these do not command the best market price, and the gathering of them requires much work in very small boats on more or less unprotected Gulf waters, so the oystermen have developed a "farming" technique.

First, the oysterman obtains empty oyster shells and transports them to carefully selected breeding grounds; these must have water of a certain degree of saltiness so that the bivalve may "spat" (spawn), "set" (attach themselves to some object—usually a larger oyster shell), and grow to maximum size. Here the shells are scattered carefully, so as to prevent overcrowding. Then, after 2 years, the new crop is gathered up, the very small oysters re-bedded on the same grounds, and the larger oysters carried to a bedding ground nearer the sea, where they may fatten and acquire the delicate flavor for which the Louisiana oyster is noted. After a period ranging from a week to 2 months the larger oysters are tonged up again, to be taken to clean grounds, usually located close to the oysterman's camp. There they are bedded closely together, so as to permit rapid loading for shipment. Several hours before the freight lugger arrives they are tonged up again, measured carefully in a standard metal basket, and dumped into the familiar 1½-bushel oyster sack.

TRIUMPH, 60.1 *m.*, is a slightly smaller edition of Buras. The village industry is the manufacturing of orange wine. During prohibition it was the mecca of wine lovers, and the site of many small illicit wineries.

Centering around a large dance hall, 62.1 *m.*, is a little settlement called FORT JACKSON, so named because of near-by Fort Jackson. The rules of conduct at the local amusement palace are reminiscent of frontier days: when a burly fisherman or oysterman dares to cast more than a passing glance at a native beauty escorted by another, a battle usually follows—with all-too-eager bystanders taking part. The brawl over, the principals shake hands and the victor claims the next dance with the lady in question.

At 62.4 *m.* is the junction with the levee road; L. on the levee road. Except during the spring and early summer, the Mississippi River here is almost blue, in contrast to its muddy waters a few miles upstream. On its brackish waters can be seen nearly every type of vessel afloat, from the pirogue to the passenger liner on its way to or from New Orleans.

At 63.6 *m.* the road runs between the old portion of FORT JACKSON, upon which construction was begun in 1815, and the later unit (L), built by the Confederates about 1861. The original, and much the larger unit, is a bastioned, star-shaped embattlement with massive brick casements, heavy bombproofs, and a surrounding moat. Since its final abandonment in 1920, a levee has been built through the fort, and some of it was destroyed. The last built unit, commanding the river, is composed largely of concrete cannon placements.

Fort Jackson and Fort St. Philip—almost directly across the river (*see below*)—figured in one of the most important engagements of the War between the States. The best military opinion of the time considered it impossible for wooden ships to oppose shore defenses of any strength. On this account, and because New Orleans was stripped of troops desperately needed elsewhere, the safety of the city was entrusted to the two forts.

On the morning of April 18, 1862, Admiral David Farragut brought a Federal fleet of 24 wooden gunboats and 19 mortar schooners within striking distance of the forts, camouflaging the masts of his vessels with willow boughs, so that the former would not betray the flotilla's position. All that day and night and for 4 successive days and nights an unceasing hail of bombs was thrown into the two besieged forts.

Meanwhile the Confederates returned the fire doggedly; but their powder was vastly inferior and their fire effected little damage. Finally, on the fifth day, Farragut ran past the forts with 17 war vessels in three divisions. As each ship passed, it poured broadside after broadside into the forts, which replied continuously. Confederate gunboats and rams entered upon the scene, some descending upon the enemy and others starting up the river. With ships moving in all directions, it was almost impossible to distinguish friend from foe. Farragut's flagship, the *Hartford,* burst into flames and it seemed that the ship was doomed; at this point Farragut is said to have cried out, "My God! Is it all to end like this?" But the discipline of the veteran sailors saved them, and the fire was soon under control. The bloodless capture of New Orleans and the mastery of the Mississippi were the ultimate results.

A legend concerning the "blood orange" originated at Fort Jackson. It is said that many years ago a young officer stationed there went across the river to call on a young lady. He overstayed his leave. The commandant reprimanded the young officer, stating that he had "to obey orders and quit running with river sluts." The young man resented this, and a heated argument followed that resulted in his courtmartial and execution by a firing squad. It happened that on the ground where the dying officer fell lay some orange seeds; within a few years a tree grow on the spot and its fruit was found to be "streaked with blood."

Fort Jackson is now a National Historical Monument. There are pits and tables, rest rooms, boating and fishing.

FORT ST. PHILIP, across the river from Fort Jackson, accessible only by boat (*make arrangements with local boat owners*), was erected in 1795, during the administration of Governor Carondelet. When Farrague made his attack in 1862, the fort was garrisoned by 700 men. During the action Federal gunboats made breaches in the walls and broke the levee so that the garrison had a difficult time keeping the water out. Fort St. Philip, with Fort Jackson, surrendered to the Federals on April 28, ten days after the attack began. It was not regularly garrisoned after 1871. During World War I it was repaired and a watchman kept there until 1923. Shortly after its abandonment the property was sold at public auction. Later, government agents learned that the historic ruins were serving as a hiding place for smuggled liquors, and the property was confiscated. Fort St. Philip is also overgrown with weeds, grass, and trees, and does not invite exploration.

BOOTHVILLE, 66.7 *m.* is a picturesque settlement of fishermen, oystermen, and trappers. It served as the locale for a novel by E. P. O'Donnel, *Green Margins.*

Left from Boothville by boat, 66.8 *m.;* to OLGA, a small settlement on an island-like section of marsh across the river from Boothville. It is inhabited by Slavonian fishermen and their families. The most desirable time to visit the place is late Tuesday or Saturday afternoon, when the riverboats are in port buying and loading oysters. These hard-working, unshaven fishermen, pulling in with luggers and skiffs loaded with oysters, present an interesting sight. The oysters are purchased from the boats, measured in wire baskets, and sacked at the wharf. The sacks are then carried one by one on the backs of Negroes to the merchants' boats.

VENICE, 72.3 *m.* at the end of the highway, is a village inhabited by trappers and fishermen. There is a small hotel here, open only during the hunting season.

At the southern extremity of the town is THE JUMP, 72.9 *m.,* an outlet to the Gulf, so named because the river broke (jumped) through at this point. The low thickets and marshes near here abound with game; geese, ducks, and rabbits are plentiful.

Tour 11*A*

Junction with La 1 at Plaquemine—Grosse Tête—Rosedale—Maringouin—Livonia; 36.6 *m.,* La 77.

T. & P. R.R. parallels route between Grosse Tête and Livonia.
Accommodations at Plaquemine only.

This route follows four bayous through one of the most fertile
regions in Louisiana. Log rafts form an almost continuous chain along
the bayou banks and small motorboats laboriously tug strings of them
to the mills.

La 77 branches west from La 1, 0 *m.,* 0.6 mile north of Plaquemine.
The route now runs northwest.

HUNTER'S LODGE (*open*), 2.2 *m.,* was built (R) about 1855 on the
site of an earlier home which had been the residence of an enthusiastic
huntsman, James Roberts. The present two-story dwelling is set flush
with the ground, with wide galleries. The lower story is plastered brick,
the upper, wood over brick.

South and west of Hunter's Lodge La 77 follows Bayou Jacob and
Bayou Plaquemine to the junction of the latter with Bayou Grosse Tête.
Crossing Bayou Grosse Tête, the route cuts northward through a densely
wooded area. These swamplands have been heavily milled and little
cypress remains, but there is a thick growth of oak, tupelo gum, and
water maple, with occasional palmetto thickets and cane brakes. On the
ridge along the bayou grow giant live oaks and magnolias; willow over-
hang the water.

The CHOCTAW CLUBHOUSE, 9.3 *m.,* is a public fishing and hunting
camp (*motorboats, skiffs, and canoes*) on the east bank of Bayou Grosse
Tête at the mouth of Bayou Choctaw. Boat trips can be made up Bayou
Choctaw to the wells of the Standard Oil Company and the salt domes
of the Solvay Process Company, which are located near the banks of the
bayou a few miles upstream.

BAY FARM, 21.8 *m.,* is the first of a long line of plantations along the
Grosse Tête ridge. This area was reclaimed from the wilderness during
the middle of the nineteenth century when Congress donated to the State
of Louisiana all swamp lowlands subject to overflow. The land was sold
to private individuals who immediately built levees to protect their

property. The soil was exceptionally rich and the planters prospered until the ravages of the War between the States, when private levees were neglected, main levees broken, and floodwaters permitted to cover the lowlands. Bay Farm was built about 1835. The plantation at first included about 2,600 acres, and the house, though built along the lines of the early Louisiana type, contained fine interior woodwork shipped from New England. Today, part of the old house stands, remodeled into a garage, at the rear of the new home. The founder of Bay Farm was Eliphalet Slack, whose descendants have always been active in fathering the development of the Grosse Tête area. It was owing chiefly to their influence that the Baton Rouge and Grosse Tête Railroad was completed in 1857, from Port Allen to a point near Krotz Springs.

GROSSE TÊTE (Fr., big head), 22.2 m. (18 alt., 710 pop. 1970), was settled in the early 1830's. It was said to have been so called by French explorers who found a large skull of undetermined species.

La 77 turns R. at 22.3 m. and L. at 22.6 m.

HOTARD (*open*), 23.2 m., was originally a two-story house built about 1815, long before the region was opened. After a storm demolished the top story, it was converted into a single-story structure and wooden additions were later made. The old part of the house is of brick painted white.

TRINITY PLANTATION HOUSE (*private*), 24.6 m., built by Dr. George Campbell of New Orleans in 1839, stands on an Indian mound at the end of a splendid avenue of live oaks. The one-and-one-half-story plaster-covered brick structure was restored by Thomas G. Markley. The interior woodwork is of hand-hewn cypress, and each room has a cast-iron mantel. On the grounds are the ruins of a sugarhouse and a slave hospital.

In ROSEDALE, 24.9 m. (15 alt., 621 pop. 1970), across the bayou, is the CHURCH OF THE NATIVITY, a Protestant Episcopal chapel erected in 1859 on the Bay Farm Plantation and moved to Rosedale by wagon when the Slack family left their home. The land on which the tiny building was re-erected was sold to the church by Dr. Campbell for $1. The building is of frame construction, brown with green shutters, with a high, steeply pitched, shingle roof. The altar, still in use, is of wood, painted and grained to resemble marble.

At Rosedale is the junction of La 77 and La 76; straight ahead on La 77.

LIVE OAKS PLANTATION, 25.2 m., was established in 1828 by Charles Dickinson of Tennessee, who was not more than 3 months old when his father, General (Dead-shot) Dickinson, was killed in a duel with Andrew Jackson. At the age of 26 young Dickinson married and brought his bride to the home of his maternal grandfather and guardian, Captain Joseph Erwin, on the Home (St. Louis) Plantation in Iberville Parish.

The old captain was fond of horse racing and cock fighting, at which he not only lost his own fortune but a good part of his grandson's as well. As compensation he deeded to his ward a plantation in the Grosse

Tête area, which, at the time, was covered with floodwaters. Undaunted, the optimistic young Dickinson climbed a tall tree, spied a solitary island, and on this island built a log cabin and, later, the present house on the same site. The residence is a white, green-shuttered frame building of two-and-one-half stories with galleries across the front supported by six square wooden pillars. The house is in a grove of superb live oaks, one of which is 27 feet in circumference. Within the grove is a slave church, built of red brick and set off with faded green blinds.

SHADY GROVE, 27.1 m., one of the numerous plantations owned by Captain Joseph Erwin, was bought from him by his son in 1828. The residence was not erected until 30 years later, when Erwin decided to make the Grosse Tête section his home. Shady Grove is a two-story brick house. The front portico has fluted wooden Ionic columns on the lower story, and Corinthian ones above. The plan called for unusually large rooms, for which Mr. Erwin gave the explanation that "he did not want to step on a child when he got out of bed." The building is now used as a school.

MOUND PLANTATION, 27.9 m., was originally composed of a number of small tracts which were consolidated by Austin Woolfolk in 1840. He built his home on a large Indian mound, one of three which were on the place at the time. During building activities a number of Indian relics were uncovered, among which was an earthenware pot containing the skeletons of two babies. The house is a rambling, single-story frame cottage, with an ell on one side. In the rear is a brick slave laundry. Many stories are told of Mr. and Mrs. Woolfolk, who were extremely popular with their neighbors and kind and thoughtful masters to their slaves. On one occasion Mrs. Woolfolk superintended the baptism of 52 Negroes, and her daughter, Lou, stood as sponsor; but a few days later her interest in their spiritual welfare was somewhat dimmed when she overheard her cook exclaim: "Law, it don't make no difference how bad us is; Miss Lou's 'sponsible for our sins."

At 30.9 m. is a bridge crossing Bayou Grosse Tête.

Right here to TANGLEWILD (*private*), 0.1 m., directly opposite the bridge. The house, a one-story, white frame building, is owned by the heirs of Barthelomew Barrow. Barrow settled in this region shortly before the War between the States and built his home in a grove of giant live oaks.

Left from the bridge on unmarked, graveled road to SUNNYSIDE (*private*), 2.1 m., a residence of the raised cottage type, with a cypress upper story over a plastered-brick basement. The plantation was first owned by Captain Jesse Hart, and since his death, about 1855, the place has changed hands several times. In the yard is a section of the old levee, built to protect the house from overflow.

MARINGOUIN, 31.2 m. (24 alt., 1,365 pop. 1970), is on the bayou of the same name, which parallels Bayou Grosse Tête for 5 miles from this point north. *Maringouin,* a word of South American or possibly Canadian origin, is vulgar French for "mosquito," and in the vicinity the standard French *moustique* is used to designate a small black gnat.

La 77 crosses Bayou Maringouin, 31.4 m., and turns R.

BELMONT PLANTATION, 32.2 *m.,* was once the property of Wiley Barrow. The old house, built in 1850 was a one-story, columned building, with galleries on all four sides, and was of considerable interest architecturally. Thirteen round brick columns and a grove of live oaks are all that remain.

EL DORADO, 34.2 *m.,* is interesting mainly for the old brick slave quarters, two-story buildings standing directly behind the white, dormered cottage that, in the middle of the nineteenth century, belonged to the members of the Barrow family.

WOODLEY PLANTATION, 35.4 *m.,* was opened by Isaac Johnson, Governor of Louisiana (1846–50), who moved to Pointe Coupée Parish from the Troy Plantation in West Feliciana Parish. Johnson and his two sons died of yellow fever in 1853. The residence on Woodley is a one-and-one-half-story frame building.

At 35.6 *m.,* opposite the ruins of a sugar factory, is the junction with a graveled side road. Right on this road 0.5 *m.* to VALVERDA, a two-story structure of bright red brick. Six tall square wooden columns, painted white, support the front galleries.

LIVONIA, 36.6 *m.* (25 alt., 611 pop. 1970), is at the junction with US 190 (*see Tour 3b*).

Tour 11B

Donaldsonville—Paincourtville—Napoleonville—Labadieville—Thibodaux—Raceland; 48.5 *m.* La 1.

Concrete-paved roadbed.
Accommodations at short intervals.

Paralleling Bayou Lafourche south from Donaldsonville, this route runs through a fertile sugar cane district. On the right, forming virtually one long rural street, are old, substantially built cottages. Bayou Lafourche was once a distributary of the Mississippi River and an important artery of commerce. A dam at Donaldsonville, however, cut off the supply of water from the Mississippi and the bayou is now merely a stagnant waterway. In its upper reaches much of the bayou's surface is covered with water hyacinths. At frequent intervals it is crossed by floating bridges, or wooden barges attached to their moorings on each side by iron chains, which the natives call "ferries." Freed from their grim duty of warding off floods, the levees are broken and irregular in places, mere loose mounds of dirt covered with long grass, shrubs, and weeds. Elsewhere they furnish thrifty natives with ground for vegetable patches or occasional fruit trees—banana, fig, peach, and orange. Here and there are small dance pavilions, built out over the bayou, where community dances are given weekly.

La 1 turns away from the river at DONALDSONVILLE, 0 *m*. La 1 runs west of the Bayou Lafourche, crossing it at Leeville. La 308 runs east of the Bayou, parallel with La 1.

On the northern edge of BELLE ROSE, 5.6 *m*. (20 alt.), is the junction with a "ferry" road leading across Bayou Lafourche.

Left on this road across Bayou Lafourche and L. on unmarked, graveled road to BELLE ALLIANCE (*private*), 0.7 *m*., a plantation home set back from the road in a dense growth of oaks and shrubbery, with the remains of a formal garden in front. The house has a high brick basement and living quarters on the second floor. Square columns extend from the brick pavement in front to the deep, molded entablature of the roof. The front porch at the second-story level is bordered by a decorative wooden balustrade. The small side porches have flat roofs supported by iron posts richly ornamented with cast-iron grillwork.

In the interior a large central hallway, plastered in soft pink, runs the length of the house, with plaster medallions over the chandeliers and a large ceiling fresco toward the back.

Belle Alliance was built in 1846 by Charles Kock as a country manor; his family spent much of their time in New Orleans and Paris, where they maintained hotel apartments.

At 0.9 *m*. is the junction with a graveled road; R. here 0.9 *m*. to the ruins of the Belle Alliance sugarhouse, once one of the most important west of the Mississippi, but now marked by crumbling brick piles and a large chimney stack. A populous Negro village, occupying former slave quarters, still clusters about it.

PAINCOURTVILLE, 10.2 *m*. (16 alt.), is near a junction with La 70, which runs west and south, west of Lake Verret, to Morgan City. One of the oldest villages of Assumption Parish, it was originally settled by Spanish families; many of their descendants still live in the section. According to tradition the village received its name from an early traveler, who in passing through was unable to obtain a single loaf of bread and therefore facetiously called the place "short-of-bread-town." One block from the highway is the ST. ELIZABETH CATHOLIC CHURCH, a large brick building with square towers rising on each side. The murals and stained-glass windows are noteworthy.

NAPOLEONVILLE, 15.8 *m*. (14 alt., 1,008 pop. 1970), seat of Assumption Parish, was named by a French settler who had fought under Napoleon. It is the site of a large salt dome. Caverns in the dome are utilized by the Mobil Oil Corp. for storage of natural gas liquids in connection with its Riverside fractioning plant. Two caverns of 300,000 bbl. capacity each are used.

In the northern part of the town is CHRIST EPISCOPAL CHURCH, built by Frank Wills of New York and consecrated by Bishop Leonidas Polk in 1853. It is a small red brick structure with a steeply pointed roof. The interior contains an interesting altar and small, old-fashioned pews.

During the War between the States, Federal troops stabled their horses in the church and used the stained-glass window above the altar as a shooting target. The glass was afterwards sent to New York and repaired so expertly that the damage could not be detected. During the storm of 1909 it was again badly shattered and again repaired.

A paved walk at the right of the church leads under an arch supporting the belfry to a cemetery, where tombs bear dates extending over a century. The family names are almost exclusively Anglo-Saxon.

The NAPOLEONVILLE COURTHOUSE on Levee St., is a buff-colored brick building with square clock tower at the center. The courthouse dates from 1896. A World War I memorial stands to the front. As early as 1807 Napoleonville was called Courthouse and it is thought that the first courthouse of the parish was situated on what is now Madewood Plantation.

ST. ANN'S CATHOLIC CHURCH, three blocks R. from the center of town, is a red brick structure erected 1909.

Right from Napoleonville on graveled La 401 to WILDWOOD PLANTATION or FRANK BERGERON HOUSE, 3 *m.*, built by James Beasley about 1836. It is a story-and-a-half wooden cottage with a porch extending the width of the house. The home is charmingly furnished in plantation style.

At 9.9 *m.* is the lower end of LAKE VERRET, a large lake in the Atchafalaya Basin. Clear and deep, it is surrounded by large trees, young willows, wild cane, and piles of snowy shells. Narrow canals and bayous branch off here and there and run back into the land, among them the Cancienne Canal, which supplies water to Bayou Lafourche. Evidence of Indian occupancy, presumably by a Chitimacha tribe, is seen in the mounds about 1 mile L. Fishing supplies can be obtained and boats rented. Black and striped bass, white perch, and catfish are caught in the lake and surrounding bayous. In the isolated swampland north and west of Lake Verret a chapel boat, *Our Lady Star of the Sea* (Roman Catholic), makes a monthly round of the bayou.

Left from Napoleonville across Bayou Lafourche by bridge; r. on La 308 to MADEWOOD, 2.1 *m.*, built 1840–1848 by Col. Thomas Pugh, one of three Pugh brothers who acquired 18 plantations. The house was bought in 1964 by Mr. and Mrs. Harold K. Marshall of New Orleans, and completely refurbished. Rare antiques and fine portraits fill the house. It is open daily, 10–5, to individuals and groups by arrangement through Napoleonville telephone (369) 7151. Madewood is a large, white two-story house of brick covered with stucco, set on a low terrace. Six handsomely fluted Ionic columns rise from the terrace to the wide entablature and gabled roof above. Surrounding the inner balcony at second-story level there is a balustrade of light wooden spindles in crossed design. On each side of the main house are connecting wings, which duplicate in miniature its chief architectural features. The interior of the house is notable. Fluted columns are grouped around the doorways leading from the large central hall, and a carved walnut staircase rises at the back. All the woodwork was made on the plantation itself, hence the name.

At 3.5 *m.* is the site of WOODLAWN, built in 1835 by Dr. W. W. Pugh. It had become diliapidated before it burned down a decade ago. It too had six formal two-story columns across the front. By the middle of the century Pugh plantations occupied much of the land on each side of the bayou. So prominent had the name of Pugh become that there was an old conundrum in the parish, "Why is Bayou Lafourche like the aisle of a church?"; the answer being, "Be cause there are Pughs on both sides of it." In the family cemetery, in a clump of live oaks in the rear, many Pughs are buried. One tomb is inscribed: "Our little Loula perished during the storm at Last Island—August 10th, 1856."

LABADIEVILLE, 24.9 *m.* (14 alt.), is thought to have been the site of the chief village of the Washi Indians, one of the four Louisiana tribes mentioned by Bienville as coming to make an alliance with him in 1699. Later it was settled by French colonists and named for Jean Louis Labadie, a pioneer resident. In October 1862, when the Federals under General Weitzel advanced down Bayou Lafourche, Labadieville was the scene of a brief pitched battle. The Confederate colonel, Armand, bravely but ineffectually resisted the 4,000 Union troops with his small force of 500 men.

The area near Labadieville was the first colonized section of the old Lafourche Settlement. French and Spanish pioneers settling here shortly after the middle of the eighteenth century were soon augmented by Acadians and a sprinkling of Germans from the near-by German Coast (*see Tour 10B*). Beginning about 1807, there was a considerable influx of Americans from the North Atlantic seaboard.

ST. PHILOMENE CHURCH (Roman Catholic) raises its tall spire in the center of town (R). It is a white cement-covered brick building erected in 1888. The cemetery in the rear is almost exclusively French. Near the center is a monument and a large tomb which contains many victims of the yellow fever epidemic of 1878.

The OLD WHITE PLANTATION HOUSE (*open weekdays, 9–5, Sunday, 1–5; closed Monday; fee*), 27.8 *m.*, birthplace of Edward Douglas White (1845–1921), Chief Justice of the United States from 1910 to 1921, is a story-and-a-half raised wooden cottage, with a brick basement. Originally taken over by the Knights of Columbus, the house is now controlled by the Chief Justice White Memorial Association, Inc. The plantation, consisting of 1,600 acres, was purchased in 1936 by the Federal Government and broken up into small farms.

The White family was among the first Americans to settle in Lafourche Parish. Judge White's father, also named Edward Douglas, served as governor of the State and as U. S. Senator. The young White attended Georgetown University at Washington, D. C., but returned to New Orleans and entered Jesuits' College at the outbreak of the War between the States. He served in the Confederate Army and was admitted to the bar in 1868. Ten years later he was made associate justice of the State Supreme Court, serving for 13 years before entering national politics as senator from Louisiana. In 1894 Cleveland appointed him Associate Justice of the United States and, in 1910, under Taft, he became Chief Justice. White was a conservative of rather gruff exterior and, although known throughout the nation, made few personal friends; only those who were able to penetrate his shell of reserve were fully ware of his kindly heart.

At 30.9 *m.* is a bridge (L) crossing Bayou Lafourche.

Left across this bridge and R. on graveled road to a green frame building with a red gabled roof (L), 0.5 *m.*, set in a live oak grove on the site of the BRAGG PLANTATION HOUSE. General Braxton Bragg (1817–76), a sugar planter in Lafourche Parish in 1856, was born in Warrenton, North Carolina, and fought in the Seminole and Mexican Wars before his marriage to Eliza Brooks Ellis of Louisiana in 1849. After resigning from the army and settling on the plantation in 1856, he served as commissioner of public works and designed much of the drainage and levee system of the State. He was an officer of the State Militia when the War Between the States started, fought in many battles, and relieved Beauregard in command of the Army of Tennessee. After the war he worked in Alabama and Texas as a civil engineer, and died suddenly in Galveston in his 59th year.

The site of the LEIGHTON PLANTATION HOUSE, 31.7 *m.*, is marked by the remains of a grove of live oaks and a large sugarhouse at the back. Here from 1842 to 1854 lived Leonidas Polk (1806–64), first Episcopal Bishop of Louisiana. Polk was born in Raleigh, North Carolina, and educated at West Point and Virginia Theological Seminary. After missionary work and European travels, he settled in the State in 1841 as Bishop of Louisiana. Through his efforts many Episcopal churches were established throughout the State (*see Religion*). He lost Leighton and most of his worldly goods in 1854, and moved to New Orleans to serve as rector of Trinity Church. At the beginning of the War between the States he accepted a commission as major general and became famous as the "fighting bishop" of the Confederacy. He was killed in an engagement at Pine Mountain, near Marietta, Georgia.

The ruins of RIDGEFIELD, 33.3 *m.*, stand in a grove of live oaks. The house, which burned in January, 1940, was once owned by Francis T. Nicholls (1834–1912), first Democratic governor of Louisiana after Reconstruction and later chief justice of the State.

THIBODAUX, 33.6 *m.* (10 alt., 14,925 pop. 1970; 13,403, 1960, inc. 11%), was the first trading post established between New Orleans and the country along the Teche Bayou. It was called Thibodauxville, in 1820 in honor of Henry Schuyler Thibodaux (1769–1827), planter and acting governor, who donated land for the courthouse, jail, and market.

In 1807 it became the parish seat, and in 1832 one of the deposit offices of the Union Bank of Louisiana. It was incorporated in 1838. It is now a distributing point for food products and profits from the sugar industry and oil refining. Irish potatoes rank high in truck products of the area. Thibodaux is on La 1, which runs down the west bank of Bayou Lafourche while La 308 follows the east bank. La 20 comes across the Bayou from the north.

The town has two schools established prior to the War between the States: MOUNT CARMEL CONVENT, 103 St. Charles Ave., and ST. JOSEPH'S COLLEGE, in the southern part of town, founded in 1855 and 1857 respectively.

ST. JOSEPH'S CHURCH (Roman Catholic) on Canal Ave., a stone-trimmed, pressed brick Renaissance structure, dedicated in 1923, is the third to serve the congregation. From 1803 until 1819, when a small frame church was erected, Mass was celebrated in private homes. Constructed of brick in 1847, the second edifice was noted for its beautiful interior. The hand-carved pulpit, executed by Joseph Koerle, a German wood carver, who settled in Thibodaux in 1860, was regarded as one of the finest examples of wood carving in the United States. The Very Reverend Canon C. M. Menard, pastor of St. Joseph's for more than 50 years, refused permission to exhibit the pulpit at the Centennial Exhibition, held in Philadelphia in 1876, on the grounds that any damage incurred would be irreparable. The church with all its art treasures was consumed by fire on the evening of May 25, 1916. The belfry alone escaped the flames. The bell, weighing 1,220 pounds, donated by the Widow E. D. White, was blessed on December 15, 1850. Recast, it still summons the faithful to services.

ST. JOHN'S CHURCH (Episcopal), Jackson Ave. and West 7th St., is a slate-covered brick structure dating from 1844. A prominent sugar planter, Judge George S. Guion, donated the land for the church and cemetery. St. John's is known as The Church of the Fighting Bishop because the parish was founded by Leonidas Polk, Bishop of Louisiana.

From 205 ST. PHILLIP STREET a rural free delivery route was started on November 1, 1896, exactly one month after the first route in the United States was established in West Virginia.

Left from Thibodaux, across Bayou Lafourche by bridge, and R. on graveled La 308 to (L) the old home of JUDGE TAYLOR BEATTIE, 0.1 m., a rambling one-story yellow wooden cottage, with carved white posts supporting an irregular roof. The place is now the home of the Thibodaux Knights of Columbus.

The RIENZI PLANTATION HOUSE (private), 0.7 m., according to legend, was built in 1796, at the request of Queen Maria Louisa of Spain, presumably as a refuge in the event of Spanish defeat in the Napoleonic wars. Some time later an Italian settler named Giovanni is supposed to have acquired the plantation, which he named in honor of Cola di Rienzi, the fourteenth-century Italian patriot. For many years the place was owned by Judge Richard H. Allen.

FRANCIS T. NICHOLLS STATE COLLEGE occupies an attractive campus of 175 acres facing the Bayou Lefourche. It opened Sept. 21, 1948, as a junior college of Louisiana State University, and became a four-year degree-granting institution under the State Board of Education by act of legislature in 1956. In 1953 it had 200 students; in 1968 it enrolled 3,836, and had a faculty of 146. The college was named for Francis T. Nicholls (1834–1912), a native of Donaldsville who was a Confederate general, governor of Louisiana, and chief justice of the State Supreme Court.

The physical plant of Nicholls is one of the most modern in Louisiana, 90 percent of the buildings having been erected since 1962, the newest of which include the LIBRARY, which houses more than 80,000 volumes, the six- to eight-story dormitories for men and women, the STUDENT UNION BLDG. and the SCIENCE-CLASSROOM BLDG.

Nicholls cooperates closely with the surrounding parishes. The Special Education Center offers cultural and remedial services in visits to the area. A high school diploma admits a student; there is no entrance examination. The college awards numerous scholarships, exemptions from fees, and loans, and part-time employment off campus is available. The Thomas Aquinas Center serves Catholic students, and nearby is a Baptist Student Union. There is a comprehensive athletic schedule and the lively student activities include an elaborate Christmas Ball, nomination of a Sweetheart of the Year, piroque races on the bayou. The yearbook is *La Piroque,* the campus newspaper is *Nicholls Worth,* and the literary publication is *Mosaic.*

ACADIA (*private*), 35.4 *m.,* a rambling yellow one-story wooden cottage, with ornate gables and dormers, is set in a grove of live oaks. This is the former home of Senator Andrew Price, built by relatives of Francis Scott Key.

At LAFOURCHE CROSSING, 38.1 *m.,* where the Southern Pacific Railroad crosses Bayou Lafourche, Confederates, led by Colonel Pyron on June 20, 1863, attacked a stockade guarding the bridge, and were repulsed with 53 killed and 150 wounded.

ST. MARY'S CHURCH (Roman Catholic), 47.3 *m.,* is (R) a brick Gothic structure built in 1888 on the site of a wooden church dating from 1850. In the cemetery is the tomb of Freddie John Falgout, 1st class seaman, who died in 1937 on the U.S.S. *Augusta* by gunfire during the Chinese-Japanese War.

RACELAND, 48.5 *m.* (6 alt., 4,880 pop. 1970), is at a junction with US 90.

❧❧❧❧❧❧❧❧❧❧❧❧❧❧❧❧❧❧❧❧❧❧❧❧❧❧❧❧❧❧❧

Tour 11C

Thibodaux—Houma; 18.7 *m.,* La 20, La 24; 17 *m.*

Concrete-paved between Thibodaux and Houma.
Accommodations at Thibodaux and Houma.

This route follows Bayou Terrebonne and Little Bayou Black through an interesting plantation country to Houma. It serves as an alternate route from Thibodaux to US 90.

La 24 branches south from La 1 in Thibodaux, 0 *m.*

DUCROS (*private*), 3 *m.,* was built just prior to the War between the States and is said to have been modeled on the Hermitage, Andrew Jackson's old home at Nashville. Set in a well-kept garden and surrounded by old oaks, it is a white two-story wooden house with eight tall square columns supporting wide galleries. The low hipped roof is bordered by a heavy cornice. A wing, with roofs sloping toward the main roof, was added on each side of the house at a later date, and the gallery extended across. Entrance doorways on both first and second floors have side lights and deep transoms, and are flanked by long, green-shuttered windows, six on each floor.

The plantation occupies a site originally granted by the Spanish Government to M. Ducros. It was sold in 1846 to Colonel Van P. Winder, who continued to add to his property until it comprised 3,300 acres, and was the first large sugar cane plantation in Terrebonne Parish. Shortly after his death Colonel Winder's widow built the present home. During the War between the States both Federals and Confederates occupied the house and encamped on the grounds. At the close of the war a picnic was held in the extensive grove surrounding the house to welcome the returning soldiers. It is said that immediately before the festivities began, Mrs. Winder was informed of the death of her youngest son, Captain Felix Winder, but courageously refused to let her grief mar the occasion. In 1872 the plantation passed to the brothers, R. S. and R. C. Woods, who had married sisters, the Misses Fannie and Maggie Pugh. The two couples lived in the mansion for 32 years and reared large families.

SCHRIEVER, 3.5 m. (17 alt.), is the headquarters of the TERRE-BONNE FARMS, INC., a 5,603-acre resettlement project established in 1938 by the Farm Security Administration. The project consists of 80 farmsteads, each having a modern five-room house, a barn, and a poultry shed. Four to five acres of each unit are farmed individually, the remainder co-operatively, with cane as the principal cash crop.

At 5.4 m. is the junction with La 20, connecting with US 90 at Gibson and going west to Morgan City.

MAGNOLIA (open), 6.7 m., is a two story building standing (R) among the flowering trees from which it takes its name. Built in 1858 by Thomas Ellis, it was used during the War between the States as a hospital by the Federals, and it is said that the soldiers used the owner's grand piano as a food trough for horses. William Alexander Shaffer bought the place in 1874 and completed the structure as it is today. The first floor front is of plastered brick, the rest of frame construction. The interior is especially noteworthy for its rosewood staircase. The kitchen is in a separate building; another outbuilding, constructed of double brick walls between which charcoal has been tightly packed, houses the cistern and was designed to keep the water cool at all times.

BELLE GROVE PLANTATION (open), 10.3 m., occupies land which was cleared by Jac Verret, under a Spanish grant. The house was begun about 1850 by Marcellus Daunis, and abandoned when nearly completed because of the tragic death of his wife in a fire. In 1881 James M. McBride bought Belle Grove from the Daunis heirs and completed it. The house, which is approached through twin rows of palms, is a two-story wooden structure with galleries on three sides supported by fluted columns of the Doric order. The hipped roof is topped by a large belvedere. The interior was executed by New York artists and woodworkers from the Pullman shops in Illinois; handsome chandeliers were designed by Stanford White, the noted New York architect, and the furniture for the 16 rooms was made to order. Hanging canvases decorated the walls of the dining room. In the two drawing rooms there are frescoes of the four seasons; cherubs play musical instruments on the ceilings. By means of folding doors the three rooms can be thrown open into one large ball-room.

At 11.9 *m.* is the junction of La 311 and La 24; straight ahead on La 24.

CRESCENT FARMS (*open*), 14.4 *m.,* was established in 1827 by William Alexander Shaffer, a pioneer from South Carolina. The plantation house has a raised brick basement, and an upper story of sturdy cypress. Six square wooden columns support the roof, which has three dormers. The house presents today a fresh white exterior, relieved by the green of shutters and latticework.

At 18 *m.* is a narrow-gauge railroad and vehicle bridge.

Right here, on the other side of the bridge, is SOUTHDOWN PLANTATION (*open*), comprised of land purchased in 1828 by Stephen Minor, who had been secretary to the Spanish Governor, Gayoso de Lemos, and who later became Governor of Natchez. For the first 2 years the entire acreage was planted in indigo; but when this did not prove profitable, cane was substituted and has been the main crop ever since. The house, originally a rambling one-story building with walls a foot thick, was built by Stephen's son, William J., in 1858 and named for the English breed of sheep raised by the family. The second story was added in 1893. The house is of brick, painted white. At each end of the front gallery are rounded turrets which reach upward beyond the roof. A colonnaded walk leads to a two-story brick building which housed the kitchen, dairy, laundry, and servants' quarters. William J. Minor, who lived here only during the cane grinding season, was noted for his lavish entertaining.

At 18.6 *m.,* across Little Bayou Black, spanned here by a pontoon foot-bridge the U. S. Government in 1925 established a sugar cane experimental station to fight a blight.

At 18.7 *m.,* in the southern outskirts of HOUMA, is the junction with US 90 (*see Tour 1b*).

(◆

Tour 11D

Canal Street Docks—Lafitte Village—Manila Village—Grand Isle, 55 *m.* Lafitte Country by boat.

This tour was formerly made by a steamboat that no longer runs. It is outlined for private boat trips and can also be reached by combining motor car and boat.

The tour traverses the Lafitte Country, so called because of its association with the Lafitte brothers, Jean and Pierre (*see Tour 1B*), whose piratical and smuggling operations were carried on in this section during the early nineteenth century. The many winding bayous, bays, inlets, and treacherous marshes of the region screened the activities of the Lafitte band, making apprehension well-nigh impossible; at the same time the waterways served as channels through which pirated and smuggled goods were brought to New Orleans and sold. Descendants of these pirates and smugglers form a large part of the population of Grand Isle and neighboring villages; most of them live simply and quietly as fishermen and trappers.

As part of the Intracoastal Waterway, the Harvey Canal and Bayou Barataria are traveled by craft of many kinds, carrying a variety of cargoes—oil barges drawn by tugboats, large motorboats loaded with produce or general freight, and small but fast luggers plying between New Orleans and the oyster beds and fishing and shrimping grounds of the Gulf Coast. The Intracoastal Waterway is the official name for the connecting series of water routes along the Atlantic and Gulf coasts of the United States between Boston and the mouth of Rio Grande River that have been dredged and improved to provide an almost completely protected passage for boats for more than 3,000 miles.

The Louisiana section was first used in August 1934, when a barge tow transported 1,400 tons of steel from New Orleans to Houston, Texas. The standard dimensions are a 9-foot depth and 100-foot bottom width. Channel markers have been posted along almost the entire waterway; where necessary the signs bear the names of connecting waterways. Mileage signs have been erected at 5-mile intervals.

In addition to its not inconsiderable commercial value, the Intracoastal Waterway might prove of immense worth in the event of war, in that foodstuffs and other commodities could be transported by water without fear of naval interference on the high seas.

For the first mile or so the Harvey Canal goes through partly reclaimed and cultivated swamplands; but soon the scene on each side of the dark and smooth waters is a green wall of cypress, willow, and other rich foliage. The canal curves R. into the winding course of Barataria, 5 *m.,* flanked with magnificent specimens of cypress, water oak, and other large trees. Moss drying on lines in front of pickers' huts can be seen at intervals.

At 7 *m.* is an artificial drainage lake, with a shell road running beside it, at right angles to the bayou.

CROWN POINT, 11.3 *m.* (5 alt.), is at a point where the bayou has two wide arms; the left arm serves as a channel, while the right, the old bed of the bayou, is used as a harbor. Fishing and moss gathering are the main activities of the village; several moss-drying establishments are on the bayou bank. Crown Point is a popular picnic site and rendezvous for fishing parties. Many yachts and other pleasure craft are moored here, in easy access to the deep-sea fishing available farther south.

At 13.1 *m.,* spanning the bayou, is the WAGNER BRIDGE, which turns laterally to permit the passage of boats. (*For points of interest between Wagner Bridge and Lafitte Village see Tour 11E*).

South of Lafitte Village, Bayou Barataria loses its identity in a fork, 22 *m.;* Bayou Rigolettes branches R. while Bayou Dupont, which the route follows, swings L.

At a fork, 24 *m.,* the route turns R. into the Duprée Cutoff Canal. The Cutoff effects a saving of about 10 miles over the old route to Grand Isle through Bayou Rigolettes, Little Lake, and Bayou St. Denis.

There are few houses along the bayou south of Lafitte Village. Salt-grass flats with oaks and cypresses in the background constitute the scenery. These unsubstantial and treacherous flats, or marshes, are called "trembling prairies" after the old French term *prairie tremblante.* In winter a few houseboats and isolated temporary huts occupied by trappers can be seen.

The LAFITTE OIL FIELD, 27 *m.,* discovered by seismograph in 1933, is believed to be situated on a deep-seated salt dome. Jets of burning exhaust gases illuminate the countryside for miles around by night, and can be seen for two miles or more by day.

The Duprée Cutoff runs through the oil field, providing a means of transportation via Bayou Barataria and the Intracoastal Waterway. Additional canals are essential because the ground will not support the weight of a man. Storage tanks and field buildings are set up on the edges of the canals, and walkways leading to various parts of the field are built on piling. Men employed in the field are domiciled in a permanent camp built on piling. Supervisors are conveyed to and from the field in an amphibian airplane.

For oil explorations in marshlands the Gulf Refining Company has developed the "marsh buggy," a combination of automobile, tractor, and boat, used to transport men and equipment on land or water. Huge pneumatic tires keep the buggy afloat. There are several variations of this vehicle in one, large steel tanks, containing enough air to allow water as well as land transportation, replace the tires.

The route turns R. into Cutlass Bayou at 31.8 *m.* and R. at 35.3 *m.* into Bayou St. Denis. At the latter junction is a wind-swept shell reef thought to be of Indian origin.

MANILA VILLAGE, 41 *m.,* was settled by Filipinos, who named the settlement after their island capital. The dozen or so red-roofed, green-painted buildings that make up the village are built upon stilts at the edge of the bayou, constituting what is called the "platform." The sustaining industry is the catching and sun-drying of shrimp.

The freshly caught shrimp are first boiled in huge rectangular pots, then dumped on open platforms to dry in the sun. Each day's catch, lying in a separate spot, has a different color: the freshly boiled group is a deep pink; that one day old, slightly lighter; two days old, still lighter; and the oldest group, bleached and colorless, is ready for the cleaning machine. The platforms are built in a series of slopes with valleys between to drain away the water in rainy weather. The shrimp are stirred at frequent intervals with long wooden rakes until completely dried; at night and during rains they are protected by tarpaulins. When dried sufficiently the shrimp are thrown into revolving hoppers which drop shells, heads, tails, and broken bits onto the floor. This residue, called "shrimp-bran," is sold as fertilizer and hog feed. The finished product is packed in barrels averaging 225 pounds in weight and sent to New Orleans for distribution; a large proportion is exported to China.

The population of Manila Village fluctuates considerably, averaging 250 at the height of the season—usually between early August and November—but dropping to a mere handful in winter, when the shrimpers, becoming trappers, leave for the muskrat trapping grounds. The town is known throughout the district as Manila Village, but a sign on the post office bears the name Cabinash. Most of the inhabitants are Filipinos, but there is a sprinkling of Mexicans, Spaniards, and Chinese.

South of Manila Village the route enters Barataria Bay, a 12-by-6-mile inlet of the Gulf of Mexico. The bay, a town, a bayou, a lighthouse, and a pass, all bear the name Barataria because of their association with the smugglers and pirates who made this locale their headquarters. Barataria is an old Romance word meaning deception.

Barataria Bay, lying between the Mississippi River and Bayou Lafourche, is the heart of the Louisiana shrimp country, embracing seven villages. Built on piling above the marshes of the bay's shores, these villages, or platforms, are owned by several companies which employ the entire adult population.

LÉON ROJAS, 42.6 m., is another shrimping platform. The population here is also of mixed races and nationalities

BAYOU CHOLAS, 43.4 m., is a platform village with floors standing six feet above the water. Not a leaf or flower breaks the view. Here, as at other platforms, cats wander at will among the baskets of live shrimp and on the platform of drying shrimp.

At times as many as three of the platform villages can be seen from the boat, separated by sheets of shining water in which porpoises (dolphins) weighing a quarter-ton disport themselves.

BAYOU DEFOND, 44.9 m., is a platform owned by Quong Sun Co., Inc., a firm composed of Cantonese. This is the oldest of the platform villages and has been here for a century.

At 46.8 m. is BASSA BASSA, for many years a prosperous platform owned and operated intermittently by Chinese.

BAYOU BRULEAU, 54.3 m., is the platform nearest Grand Isle and has daily mail service.

BAYOU RIGAUD, 55 m., named for Jacques Rigaud, the first resident of Grand Isle, who had settled there many years before the advent of the Baratarians, serves as the harbor for GRAND ISLE. At Bayou Rigaud taxicabs are available to carry passengers to the hotels.

((+

Tour 11E

Marrero (opposite New Orleans)—Lafitte Village; 21.6 *m.*, La 45.

Restaurants at lower end of tour.
Marrero is reached from New Orleans by cab across the Bridge. Some of these
places can be viewed from the decks of the steamer *Mark Twain,* which makes
daily trips over part of the route from the Canal St. Docks.

This route extends southward from MARRERO, 0 *m.,* following
La 45, into the heart of the Lafitte Country (*see Tour 11D*).
Here are located five distinct institutions related to the Associated
Charities of New Orleans, Inc. This was originally HOPE HAVEN
FARMS. The first to come into sight is the Monsignor Wynhoven
apartments, an eleven-story building of 200 apartments for the elderly,
staffed by the School Sisters of Notre Dame and opened in September,
1970. On the left of Barataria Blvd. is MADONNA MANOR and
CHINCHUBA. Madonna Manor was established in 1932 by the Cath-
olic Archdiocese of New Orleans and is staffed by the School Sisters of
Notre Dame. It is a home for dependent boys aged 5 to 13. In addition
to the Residence Bldg. there are the St. John Chapel and a school bldg.
The present capacity is 80 boys.
Chinchuba Institute for the Deaf, founded in 1890 and relocated in
Marrero in 1940, is also owned by the Archdiocese of New Orleans and
staffed by the School Sisters of Notre Dame. The two connecting buildings that house the program are located to the rear of the St. John Bosco
Chapel. There are 35 boarders and 90 day students enrolled in the school.
Hope Haven, located on the right of Barataria Boulevard, is a resi-
dence for adolescent boys who require care and supervision away from
their own homes. Founded in 1925 by Monsignor Peter Wynhoven, the
Home is operated by the Archdiocese of New Orleans. Present capacity
is 60 boys. The boys attend schools in the community. The former vocational training program was terminated several years ago.
The Archbishop Shaw High School for boys is located to the rear of
Hope Haven, fronting on Tenth Street. Opened in 1962 and staffed by
the Salesian Fathers and Brothers, the school is owned by the Archdiocese of New Orleans. Present enrollment is 650 boys.
South of Hope Haven La 45 is lined on the right and left by small
vegetable farms and occasional cane patches. At about 7 *m.* the road
enters a forest of live and water oak, tupelo gum, ash, swamp maple,
willow, and cypress trees. In the spring, roadside thickets yield wild
blackberries in abundance.
At 11.2 *m.* is the junction with a shell road.

Left (straight ahead) on this road to CROWN POINT, 0.3 *m.*, a popular picnic spot on Bayou Barataria (*see Tour 11D*). Boats for fishing can be rented.

La 45 turns L. across the WAGNER BRIDGE, 12.8 *m.*, and at a fork, 13.1 *m.*, turns R. to follow the east bank of Bayou Barataria.

West of La 45 in St. Charles Parish are two large lakes Lake Cataouatche and Lake Salvador, important to sportsmen for hunting and fishing. The Louisiana Wild Life & Fisheries Commission in 1968 acquired the Salvador Wildlife Management Area, a tract of 28,469 acres 12 miles southwest of New Orleans, which borders the west bank of Lake Cataouatche and the south bank of Lake Salvador. All forms of wildlife are controlled so that the needs of hunting will be satisfied without impairment to the stocks of waterfowl, furbearing animals, deer, alligators, rabbits and other fauna. Habitats are protected. Supplementing patrols by boats are light single-engine aircraft based at Westwego Airport. Access is by boats through three routes: (1) Bayou Segnette from Westwego via Lake Cataouatche; (2) Sellers Canal to Bayou Verret into this lake; (3) Bayou Des Allemands. There are special game regulations. Sport fishing is open all year.

LAFITTE, 15.1 *m.* (5 alt.), is named for Jean Lafitte, whose pirate village was originally 6 miles to the south. Daily mail delivery is not made on the mainland of Jefferson Parish below this point.

At 15.2 *m.*, (R), is a lane. Right on this lane, 0.1 *m.*, and R. on foot about 100 yards through a thicket of hackberry and chinaball trees to the BERTHOUD CEMETERY. Situated on an Indian shell mound, it is part of the plantation formerly owned by the Berthoud brothers, original settlers of this region. The brothers are buried at the peak of the mound, a rusted iron fence enclosing their graves. Many of the graves are marked by glass-fronted, home-made boxes containing wreaths of paper or beads, flowers, and small figures of the Virgin Mary. After dark on the evening of All Saints' Day it is customary for the people of the locality to place lighted candles on the graves; and amid the flickering lights, the shadows cast by oaks and cypresses, and the gentle lapping of the waves along the shore, the ancient ceremony of the blessing of the graves is performed by the parish priest.

The Berthoud brothers, it is said, had a mahogany longboat which they used for frequent trips to New Orleans. The boat was manned by 12 slave oarsmen, with one of the brothers acting as coxswain. Whenever a Berthoud saw a Negro shirking, he nipped off a bit of the slave's ear with a shot from a pistol carried for that purpose.

At 15.4 *m.* is a picnic spot operated by a store. On the opposite side of the bayou, at the confluence of Bayou Barataria and Bayou Villars, is ISLE BONNE (Fr., good island), an oak-covered spot dotted with Indian mounds. Bayou Barataria is the route of the Intracoastal Waterway to the point where Bayou Villars begins, the latter being the route for about a mile. A dredged canal running southwest out of Bayou Villars then becomes the route of the waterway.

Bayou Barataria is the scene of the major sports event of this region, an annual pirogue race, which usually talkes place in May. At that time hundreds of bayou folk line the course, which stretches from

Lafitte Post Office to Lafitte Village. Pirogues are dugouts cut from cypress logs, averaging 13 feet in length and 22 inches in width; they are made by their owners, who shape them entirely with the foot-adz. The handling of a piroque is most difficult for the uninitiated. So great is the skill of the bayou folk, however, that in 1937 the winning time for the 4.7-mile course was 35 minutes, 9 seconds. Community tradesmen award prizes which include cash, ham, gasoline, oil, candy, whisky, wine, gin, beer, and marine supplies.

At 16.1 *m.* is the junction with a graveled road.

Right on this road, crossing Bayou Barataria on a State-operated cable ferry (*free; 24-hour call service*), to BARATARIA, 0.2 *m.* (5 alt., 600 pop.), the home port of a fleet of shrimping vessels. A sign on the store beside the post office announces that the owners buy raw furs, moss, and alligator skins.

BAYOU DES OIES (Fr., Bayou of the Geese), 19.5 *m.,* is crossed by a high-arched wooden bridge. Bayou des Oies was in the past a favorite resting place for wild geese on the yearly migration between their northern and southern homes.

At the southern end of the bridge is (R) the LAFITTE CEMETERY, where three famous men are said to be buried. According to a fantastic local tradition the body of Jean Lafitte (*see Tour 1B*) lies here, between those of John Paul Jones and Napoleon Bonaparte. Jean Lafitte is supposed to have dispatched a fast sloop to the Island of St. Helena, where Napoleon was smuggled aboard by night and a "double" left in his place. Napoleon died on the way to America and was interred in the tiny cemetery of the Baratarians, while the rest of the world remained unaware of his fate. The legend says John Paul Jones joined the Lafittes in their smuggling operations, and died fighting their enemies. The pirates laid him to rest beside Napoleon leaving room between the two for Lafitte. No inscriptions indicate who is actually buried in the graves. The owner of the cemetery, Madame Toinette Perrin, more than 30 years ago thus described the graves to an inquirer:

Q. Is this the place where Lafitte is buried?
A. Me, I no know for true, but I tell it you like my mamma and my gran'-mère they tell it me. Yes, zat's Lafitte buried dere.
Do you know of anyone else buried here?
Some great man, I no rememb' the name, but my mamma she tell me he come from over the sea.
Was it Napoleon?
Mais, oui! Zat's ze name. I old and I don' rememb' like when I was young. But ev' year some girl from far away she come here on All Saints' Day and put candles on his grave.
What is her name?
I don' rememb', but she say he's kin to her far away, and she give me plenty money to take care zat grave.
Where does she live?
Me, I don' rememb'—but she live in a big place far off, and she come here ev' year.

LAFITTE VILLAGE, 21.6 *m.*, is the site of the original pirate settlement and rendezvous of Lafitte and his band. It is today the home port of many commercial fishing and shrimping boats; there are several private fishing and hunting clubs. La 45 terminates here on the bayou bank.

This locality offers fine fresh-water fishing; crabbing is also a popular local pastime. Usually the crabber stretches lines across the bayou, having first baited them at close intervals with fish skins or meat. He then rows across the channel in his piroque, pulls up the lines, shakes the crabs which have been attracted to the bait into a small dip net and tosses them into the boat. Recrossing the channel, he does likewise on the other line. It is a matter of record that 800 pounds of crabs have been caught in this way by one person between dawn and dusk.

A particularly fine delicacy, the soft-shell crab, is obtained here. Soft-shells are crabs that have just shed their old hard-shells. Branches of oak or wax myrtle are hung in the water near the shore, and the crabs crawl into the twigs and cling to them for the protection offered by the leaves. Once they have crawled on the branches, they are easily lifted from the water. Another way of obtaining them is by keeping hard-shell crabs in boxes or cages until they shed their old armor.

Tour 12

(Eudora, Ark.)—Lake Providence—Tallulah—St. Joseph—Ferriday; 121 *m.*, US 65.

Concrete-paved roadbed.
M. P. R.R. parallels route.
Hotels and restaurants in larger towns; limited accommodations elsewhere.

Swinging southward from the level cotton lands of southeastern Arkansas, US 65 runs along the west floor of the Mississippi Valley. Numerous oxbow lakes paralleling the highway indicate the former course of the river, which even today winds through the region in a succession of giant curves.

US 65 crosses the ARKANSAS LINE, 0 *m.*, 11.9 miles south of Eudora, Arkansas.

MILLIKEN, 3 *m.* (105 alt.), was named for an early settler supposed to have been a member of the pirate band of Captain Bunch.

ASHTABULA, 3.7 *m.*, one of the larger plantations of this area, figured prominently in the unhappy Reconstruction Era. Located in a

section which, since ante bellum days, has been predominantly populated by Negroes, Ashtabula felt the full effect of the Negro's sudden
elevation to authority. Carroll Parish (now divided into East Carroll
and West Carroll Parishes) was governed by Negro sheriffs, constables,
and other local officials; George Benham, a Republican carpetbagger,
was the parish boss. In the Ashtabula plantation home lived Simon
Witkowski, a Polish Jew who was in sympathy with the Negroes, and
Cain Sartain, a Negro politician prominent in the State legislature.

Democrats in the section were few, and when Benham became a
candidate for State senator, they were forced to resort to an interesting
expedient to prevent his election. Realizing that their weakness lay in
the overwhelming voting power of the district's Negroes, the minority
party retaliated by nominating for the office Jackwith Clay, a Negro
Democrat.

A Negro's candidacy, regardless of his party affiliation, seemed to
please the majority of the colored populace, and that fact, coupled
with zealous electioneering by the Democrats, indicated Jackwith Clay's
election. However, an eleventh-hour obstacle threw the Democrats into
panic. This difficulty was the stipulation that, notwithstanding the
favorable trend of opinion, the Democrat Clay could be elected only
by his party's payment of $500. Frantic efforts to raise this sum were
finally rewarded when an appeal to Simon Witkowski resulted in his
sending the money in gold, from Ashtabula. Jackwith Clay was duly
voted into the senate, where he cast the deciding vote which seated the
Democratic gubernatorial nominee, Francis T. Nicholls, and did much
to restore white supremacy in State government.

At 4.2 *m.* is the junction with a graveled road.

Left on this road 0.8 *m.* to the junction with the graveled River Road; R.
here to the GOSSYPIA PLANTATION HOUSE (*private*), 0.9 *m.*, named for the scientific term for the cotton plant, *Gossypium*. The plantation is devoted principally
to the production of cotton and pecans. About 200 feet from the highway (R),
surrounded by a picket fence, is the plantation home erected in 1856 by either
Don Goza, a wealthy Spanish gentleman, or his son-in-law, Charles Goff. The
two-story structure is a combination of Gothic, Spanish, and Moorish styles, its
principal Moorish feature being the square tower that rises from the front of
the hipped roof. A popular local explanation of the name Gossypia is the combination of Goza with Mississippi.

In 1863 Union soldiers took possession of Gossypia and the Goff family
escaped to San Antonio. On the approach of the Union forces, it is said that
Confederate soldiers, who had taken refuge in the house, hurled themselves from
the second story rather than be taken prisoners, and are buried in the family
graveyard near by. On the walls of the second story may be found amusing
drawings representing soldiers marching, men smoking pipes, etc., executed by
the Federals who were encamped here.

South of Gossypia Plantation the River Road parallels the levee (L) around
BUNCH'S BEND, named for Captain Bunch, an early nineteenth-century pirate of
unknown antecedents, who kept a flotilla of small but well-manned boats, one
of which is said to have been armed with a cannon.

ERIN (*open*), 7.6 *m.*, around which the road has been built, is a one-and-one-
half-story frame house set on brick pillars. It is the old home of the Barbers,
and the story goes that Major Barber kept a relay of horses, one always sad-

dled before his home, ready to gallop to Lake Providence, ten miles away, to get the latest market quotations on cotton from the wonderful new telegraph instrument which made its appearance in that town about 1885.

The VAN FOSSEN PLANTATION HOUSE (*open*), 8.4 *m.*, is a one-story frame cottage set on huge cypress blocks. Among the original furnishings was a rosewood suite which, according to legend, was made for the Napoleon House in New Orleans when Mayor Girod offered his home as a refuge for the deposed Emperor (*see New Orleans*).

At 10.4 *m.* US 65 reaches the northern extremity of LAKE PROVIDENCE and skirts its shore to the farther end. Oak, gum, and pecan trees towering skyward on the land, and gaunt, gnarled cypresses dotting the lake and its shores combine to lend this area an almost fantastic beauty.

The lake, which was formed centuries ago by a cutoff of the river, derived its name in an interesting manner. Boatmen who successfully negotiated Devil's Elbow (so called because of its treacherous currents) and escaped Captain Bunch's pirates in the bend below were safe once they reached Stack Island, opposite Stack Island Lake (Lake Providence). That accomplishment, however, was so rare as to be considered by rivermen "an act of providence." The phrase became so popular that the lake was rechristened Lake Providence.

Approximately one-half mile wide and five and one-half miles long, Lake Providence is popular for swimming, fishing, and sailing.

At 10.9 *m.* is the junction with asphalt-paved La 2.

Right on this road to (R) BUCK MEADOW (*open*), 1 *m.*, a two-story house—the front frame and the rear brick. It is but part of the original house which was a succession of rooms, one after the other, extending over a great length and including barn, carriage house, etc., under one roof. Tradition has it that the house was built in this manner so that an invalid daughter might take exercise without leaving her own rooftree. James C. Ford, the first owner of the house, won the land from his brother in a poker game. The plantation was so named because it was overgrown with buck vines.

OAK GROVE, 10 *m.* (119 alt., 1,980 pop. 1970), is the seat of West Carroll Parish. It is a prosperous community containing several large cotton gins and a lumber plant, and is the center of a trade in seed oats.

Previous to 1906, when a branch of the Missouri Pacific Railroad was run through the town, Oak Grove had been a negligible settlement called Pin Hook. It is said that during the War between the States some Federal soldiers rode up to one of the small stores and demanded to know if there was anything for sale. The storekeeper answered casually, "Oh yes, pins and hooks, pins and hooks."

During the period immediately following the War between the States the town was frequently visited by the notorious James brothers. The story was told by one of the older residents of the town of a visit made by Frank James to the home of her father. Late one evening, a handsome, curly-haired man with a lame foot, came down the bayou (Bayou Maçon) in a skiff and, approaching the house, asked if he might spend the night. The unexpected visitor made himself very agreeable, helped the children with their lessons, and regaled the family with gruesome tales and escapades of the James boys.

Whenever court is held in Oak Grove an old plantation bell is rung. This bell is mounted on a high scaffold at the rear of the courthouse. It was moved from Floyd, the original parish seat, and was once used to guide lost people back to safety from the swamp east of Bayou Maçon, as well as for a signal for social gatherings.

LAKE PROVIDENCE, 15.9 *m.* (103 alt., 6,183 pop. 1970; 5,781, 1960), is a quaint old town whose atmosphere seems to support the claim that it is the oldest Louisiana town north of Natchitoches. This belief, largely local, is based on the supposition that a log hut erected near the townsite was used as a stopping place by trappers during the original French occupancy.

During the earliest days of this section's colonization a large band of pirates and outlaws inhabited a region to the north below New Madrid (in what is now Missouri). Included in their number were members of the old Cave-in-Rock gang of Kentucky and the cutthroat, Samuel Mason, for whom Bayou Maçon is reputedly named. Driven from the New Madrid country, many of these brigands joined Captain Bunch at Bunch's Bend, established a lair on Stack Island, and made the locality a place of terror.

But after 1812, the beginning of a golden era for river ports, Lake Providence rapidly lost its notoriety and entered upon a period of commercial prosperity. By 1852 the town was a thriving port, the principal shipping point of its section, and the center of population in East Carroll Parish.

In 1863, when the Confederate batteries at Vicksburg were preventing the Federals from joining forces above and below the city, Grant, while digging a canal opposite Vicksburg (*see Tour 7a*), made an effort to extend a circuitous waterway from Lake Providence to the confluence of the Mississippi and Red Rivers, by way of Bayous Baxter and Maçon and the Tensas, Black, and Red Rivers. A canal was cut between the Mississippi and Lake Providence, a distance of one mile, but the project was abandoned as impracticable. GRANT'S CANAL lies in the northern part of the town.

The AMACKER HOUSE (*open*), 601 First St., is a one-story frame house with square wooden pillars supporting a hipped roof with ornate eaves. It was used as General James Macpherson's headquarters during the War between the States.

The EAST CARROLL PARISH COURTHOUSE, in the center of town, is a modern three-story white concrete building.

Left from Lake Providence across Grant's Canal to the junction with a graveled road, 0.6 *m.;* L. here to the ARLINGTON PLANTATION HOUSE (*private*), 0.9 *m.,* that can be seen (R) through the foliage of the oak, magnolia, and cedar trees which line its driveway. The house was built about 1841 for Mrs. T. R. Patten; in 1852 it came into the possession of General Edward Sparrow, senior senator from Louisiana in the Congress of the Confederacy. During the war Arlington was used as headquarters by several Union officers, including Generals Macpherson, McMillan, and McArthur. Tradition asserts that General Grant also used the house when he paid a brief visit to Lake Providence. The original house was one story in height and built of cypress. General Sparrow raised the house and built an under story of brick. Today wide verandas extend across the front and around the east end of the house on both stories.

At 23.3 *m.* on US 65 is the junction with a dirt road.

Left here to HOMESTEAD (*open*), 3 *m.*, built (L) in 1841 by William Benjamin. It is a one-story frame building; the wide gallery has fluted Doric columns supporting a gabled roof. At either end of the house is a large sunken brick cistern covered by a latticed summerhouse.

CONCORD (*open*), 3.6 *m.*, a two-story house set on brick pillars with square wooden pillars across the gallery, was once occupied by Richard Graham Benjamin, who was a conscientious objector to secession, and son of the William Benjamin who built Homestead. His principles brought him into disfavor and he was murdered by guerrillas.

TRANSYLVANIA, 24.7 *m.* (95 alt.), was once a busy lumber center.

STAMBOUL (*open*), 25.5 *m.*, is a one-story frame building set in a grove of pecans, oaks, magnolias, and cedars. Stamboul is noted for its splendid hand-hewn cypress timbers, all of which are mortised and pegged.

TRANSYLVANIA FARM, INC., 27.6 *m.*, 9,852-acre resettlement project established by the Farm Security Administration in 1938, consists of 147 individual farmsteads. Each farm has a modern 5-room house, a barn, and a poultry shed. In the community center are a school, a community house, a gin, a retail store, and other co-operative facilities.

ALSATIA, 29.2 *m.* (90 alt.), was also formerly a lumber town.

ROOSEVELT, 32.1 *m.* (85 alt.), owes its existence to Theodore Roosevelt's penchant for bear hunting. In October, 1907, Roosevelt and several noted Louisiana hunters stopped at a hunting lodge which had been set up on Tensas Bayou near the present village. A bearded hunter, Ben Lilley, came out of the swamps to help search for bears and, according to one account, chased a bear into a hollow tree trunk, where he held the animal by lying on his back and thrusting his feet against the bear's posterior. The rest of the party soon came up and Roosevelt got his bear. During the hunt other more dignified kills were made by the President, who does not record Lilley's feat in his account of the expedition (*In the Louisiana Canebrakes*). This expedition is said to have inspired the manufacture of the subsequently popular toy, the "teddy bear." Good roads and increasing automobile traffic have spoiled the once excellent bear and deer hunting.

SONDHEIMER, 33.6 *m.* (85 alt.), has a large lumber mill.

TALLULAH, 44.6 *m.* (84 alt., 9,643 pop. 1970), is at the junction with US 80 (*see Tour 7a*).

The TALLULAH LABORATORY (*visiting hours 8–5*), 46.5 *m.*, a group of neat gray buildings (R), is conducted by the U. S. Department of Agriculture (Bureau of Entomology and Plant Quarantine, Division of Cotton Insect Investigations). Here experts study the life histories and habits of cotton insects and means of controlling destructive species, especially the boll weevil.

The laboratory was established in 1909. Madison Parish was selected for the study of cotton insects because of its high rainfall average, moderate temperature, and areas of heavy timber draped with Spanish moss

—a combination of conditions typical of the many thousands of acres of cotton land infested at the time the station was founded. Experiments in the use of calcium arsenate for dusting cotton fields began in 1916, and it was here, from 1922 to 1930, that mechanisms for airplane dusting were perfected.

Besides the control work against the boll weevil, the station has also turned its attention to the tarnished plant bug, the cotton plant bug, the cotton flea hopper, the cotton louse, cutworms, the cotton leaf worm, thrips, flea beetles, leaf beetles, and other insects in either larval or adult stages.

At 48.8 *m.* is the junction with a dirt road.

Right on this road 0.5 *m.* to the junction with a dirt road; L. here, and L. again at 1.4 *m.*, to the SINGER WILDLIFE PRESERVE (*hunting and fishing prohibited*), 2 *m.*, through which the road partly runs. The preserve is a tract of old hardwood timber held in reserve by a large manufacturing company and placed under control of the State as a forest and wildlife refuge. The preserve is known as one of the last refuges of the ivory-billed woodpecker and is the home of a few cougars, or "panthers," some black bears, and a large number of deer. Wild turkeys are present in varying numbers, according to season and weather conditions.

The TALLULAH COUNTRY CLUB is at 48.9 *m.*

BAYOU VIDAL, 59.7 *m.,* is the northern boundary of Tensas Parish, a region said to have been visited by De Soto's expedition (1541–42). It was then peopled by the Tensa, who, according to La Salle, dwelt in eight villages.

At SOMERSET, 64.3 *m.* (83 alt.), a dirt road extends (L) 3.5 miles to a point on the river where boats can be obtained at reasonable rates to cross to Davis Island (Miss.), one-time home of Jefferson Davis.

NEWELLTON, 70 *m.* (1,403 pop. 1970, 1,453, 1960), is near the head of LAKE ST. JOSEPH. Edward Drumgould Newell settled here in 1832 and founded the town. This is inscribed on a marble arch at the Newell cemetery on La 575. There is a jct. with La 4.

Off US 65 near Newellton are the LOUISIANA DUTCH GARDENS, famous for luxuriant tulip blooms in spring, and other flowers. *Open 8–8, free.*

At 74.6 *m.* is the junction with a graveled road.

Left here to WINTER QUARTERS (*open*), 3.5 *m.*, so called because it was here that General Grant, at the time of his Vicksburg campaign, went into winter quarters. It is said to be the oldest house in the parish, but the date of its construction is not known. It is a one-and-one-half-story frame house on high brick pillars. It has antique furnishings and Civil War memorabilia.

South of 80.2 *m.* LAKE BRUIN is visible from the highway for several miles. During the summer innumerable blue herons and an occasional white egret present a beautiful picture. Small boats are available at moderate rates in LAKE BRUIN STATE PARK.

At 82.4 *m.* is an Agricultural Experiment Station conducted by the Northeast Center of Louisiana State University.

At 83.7 *m.* is the junction with unmarked, graveled La 345.

Straight ahead on La 686 to a fork, 0.6 *m.;* R. here to LAKEWOOD (*private*), 1.6 *m.,* built (R) in 1854 by Captain A. C. Watson, who commanded Watson's Battery during the Civil War. When Watson left his home in 1861 to join Lee, he drew his entire fortune of $80,000 from the banks and used $60,000 for the equipment of his regiment. The remaining $20,000 was buried on the grounds. Most of this was recovered when the captain returned from the war; but one jar containing $5,000 was missing and only brought to light in 1928 when a descendant discovered it in a garden plot near the house.

Beyond Lakewood the road continues for 10.4 miles in a scenic loop tour around the inside shore of LAKE BRUIN. Fishing opportunities are good (black bass, crappie, barfish, sunfish, catfish).

ST. JOSEPH, 85 *m.* (78 alt., 1,864 pop. 1970) is the seat of Tensas Parish and its largest town. Tensas is a fertile cotton growing area and takes its name from the Tensas Indians, who were seen by LaSalle in 1682. The principal towns besides St. Joseph are Newellton and Waterproof. Because of the change in cotton picking the preponderance of non-whites has diminished somewhat.

The main street of St. Joseph was originally part of a toll plank road. Stores along the street have been restored to their early appearance, with porches extending over the walks. The St. Joseph-Port Gibson Ferry docks 2 *m.* north on La 604 (toll). Highway markers on La 605 and 608 indicate the route taken by Union troops under Major General U. S. Grant during the siege of Vicksburg in 1863.

TENSAS PARISH COURTHOUSE is a delicately proportioned Greek Revival structure, built 1906. On the Square stands the home of Tensas Lodge, F. & A. M., built 1875, restored 1964.

CHRIST EPISCOPAL CHURCH, on the Courthouse Square, was built in 1872 in an adaptation of late Gothic. It is open daily. Its RECTORY occupies the BONDURANT House, a historic one-story structure originally the second story of Pleasant View, a plantation house built in 1852 and moved back from the engulfing river in the 1880's. The house was being shelled by a Union gunboat when Mrs. Bondurant, in order to keep her cotton from the Yankees, soaked 100 bales at Dinsmore's landing and set them afire. When the house was moved cannon balls were found lodged in the timbers. *Open last 2 weeks in March and first 2 weeks in April (fee).*

The DAVIDSON HOME is a notable town house built around an original log cabin by Joseph Moore, pioneer planter, for his daughter, Mrs. Carrie Moore Davidson, and owned by her daughter. Many original furnishings are extant (*fee*).

The TENSAS PARISH PUBLIC LIBRARY and the PLANTATION MUSEUM are located in a magnificent town house built about 1858, partially restored in 1964. The ground floor houses the Tensas Parish Library, open 8–5 Monday through Friday, 8–12 Saturday. The main floor contains the Plantation Museum, with many historical items related to the old plantation life, open weekdays except Monday, closed Labor Day to Mar. 1 (*fee*).

At St. Joseph the Mississippi River has a width of 3,300 ft., but depth varies between 9 ft. and 54 ft.

St. Joseph is still primarily dependent upon agriculture but its attractiveness is increasing as a tourist and recreation center, particularly with the development of Lake Bruin. A port elevator is in operation on the Mississippi River and a Modular home manufacturing plant has located here.

South of Cross Keys US 65 curves around the head of LAKE ST. PETER, once a large open body of water but now filled with cypress and water oak.

At 97.2 *m.* is the junction with a graveled road. This formerly led to Wavertree, a fine plantation house preserved for its antique interest, now no longer standing. At 100.1 *m.* is the junction with a dirt road.

Left on this road 0.6 *m.* to BURNS (*open*), a one-and-one-half-story frame building built in 1853 by Zenith Preston. The large rooms are plastered and frescoed. Handsome marble mantels adorn the lower floor and there are silver trimmings on the doors. In 1878, when a race riot fermented among the Negroes, the firing of the big gin house on the Burns Plantation was to have been the signal to kill all the whites and sack the house. The manager of the plantation got word of the uprising and, having been erroneously informed that the residence was to be fired, hastened his family to the gin for temporary safety. This move nearly cost them their lives. As they fled from the burning gin they encountered a cotton stack ready for pillage and loot. Fortunately, Robert Snyder, late Speaker of the House and Lieutenant Governor of the State, and the Honorable C. C. Cordill arrived with a force of 400 men from the adjoining parishes. They dispersed the mob and hanged the leaders. At the same time a ferryboat from Natchez, Mississippi, steamed up the river loaded with light infantry.

GOLDMAN, 100.6 *m.* (68 alt.), is the center of a rich cotton-growing section whose productivity is said to be unexcelled in Louisiana.

At 101.8 *m.* is the junction with a graveled road.

Left here along the levee to SOUDAN (*open*), 0.1 *m.*, a two-story frame house set (L) in a grove of cedars.

WATERPROOF, 103 *m.* (67 alt., 1,438 pop. 1970), has been moved four times because of floods and caving banks of the Mississippi River. The original site is now in the state of Mississippi. During the third flood a correspondent is said to have notified his paper that the whole region, save one waterproof knoll, was under water; the town was later rebuilt on that knoll and called Water Proof, now generally spelled Waterproof.

During the Civil War several minor skirmishes between Confederates and Federals occurred here and during Reconstruction the town and parish suffered from Negro and carpetbag rule.

The FIRST METHODIST CHURCH, oldest church in Waterproof, was built in 1871 on the banks of the Mississippi River. In 1881 caving banks threatened the structure and it was moved to its present location. The congregation was formed in 1849 and was host to the Louisiana Methodist Conference as early as 1857.

MYRTLE GROVE, located just outside of Waterproof, is believed to date from around 1812. It has been kept in fine condition and is attractively furnished with period pieces.

At 104.4 m. is the junction with the old Texas Road (La 67). Over this thousands of pioneers in covered Conestoga wagons, drove to Texas during the first half of the 19th century.

Between 109.1 m. and 113.1 m. US 65 skirts the western shore of LAKE ST. JOHN, a beautiful expanse of water noted for its fishing (*boats available at moderate rates*), and cuts southwest to parallel LAKE CONCORDIA, 115.1 m., another oxbow lake, which is hidden from the road by a levee. It was in the vicinity of Lake Concordia that the notorious highwayman, Samuel Mason, was slain by two equally infamous criminals in 1803. Mason and his gang had committed so many heinous crimes along the Natchez Trace that a reward of $2,000 was offered for Mason's capture. While hiding out in the swamps about Lake Concordia the gang was joined by John Setton, a former member, and James Mays, another highwayman. One night as Mason sat at a campfire with the two he was treacherously beheaded. At Natchez, Mason's head was presented to officials and the reward claimed; but during a delay in obtaining the money Setton was identified as Little Harpe, one who, in Kentucky and Tennessee, had earned as unsavory a reputation as the man he had decapitated. He and his accomplice, Mays, were summarily tried, convicted, and executed. Their heads were placed on poles to adorn the Natchez Trace.

At 117.6 m. is the junction with La 15, which proceeds south along the Mississippi River until it unites with La 1 near Lettsworth in Pointe Coupee Parish.

South of the junction US 65 is shaded at nearly all hours of the day by the great pecan trees of PECANIA, a 2,000-acre plantation devoted almost exclusively to pecan growing. More than 6,000 bearing trees stretch away from the road in long, straight rows.

When Louisiana was first settled pecans were found growing wild in several parts of the territory and were eaten by the Indians. Today the nut is one of the State's important agricultural products.

During the early days of pecan cultivation the planting was of seedlings grown from wild nuts. Today the seedlings are grafted and budded from choice varieties when two years old and raised in nurseries to be planted two years later, when they are from four to seven feet in height. The trees bear in their third year, but do not yield a profitable crop until their tenth or twelfth year, when they produce up to 1,000 pounds, according to their size. Pecan trees thrive best in a light, sandy loam and are usually planted from 60 to 100 feet apart in order to give them room for growth, sunshine, and cultivation. Cover crops are often planted between the trees (*see Agriculture*).

FERRIDAY, 121 m. (60 alt., 5,236 pop. 1970) at the southern end of Lake Concordia, is at the junction with US 84 (*see Tour 5a*).

€‹❖‹€‹❖

Tour 13

(McGehee, Ark.)—Bastrop—Monroe—Columbia—Tullos—Alexandria—Oberlin—Kinder—Iowa; 234.9 *m.*, US 165.

Concrete- and asphalt-paved roadbed for most of the distance.
Railroads paralleling route: M. P. between Arkansas Line and Mer Rouge;
A. & L. M. between Bastrop and Monroe; M. P. between Monroe and Iowa.
Accommodations in larger towns at hotels and tourist camps.

Section a.   ARKANSAS LINE to MONROE; 52.1 m., US 165

This section of the route runs from the Arkansas Line in a southwestwardly direction through the cotton and timber region of northern Louisiana. Between Bastrop and Monroe the route traverses natural gas fields which support numerous carbon black plants.

US 165 crosses the ARKANSAS LINE, 0 *m.*, 48.3 miles south of McGehee, Arkansas.

JONES, 3.1 *m.* (107 alt.), is a small village with a cotton gin. The LOG HOUSE (*private*), opposite the depot, is of unusual size for its type of construction. It was built in 1936 of cypress logs cut in near-by brakes. The gabled roof is covered with crude shingles hewn with adz and drawknife from cypress blocks.

The highway crosses Bayou Bonne Idée (Fr., good idea) at 6.1 *m.*

South of BONITA (Sp., pretty), 6.7 *m.* (106 alt., 533 pop. 1970), US 165 runs through forests of oak, gum, and hickory. Water-filled ditches and swamplands border the road.

GALION, 13.1 *m.* (95 alt.), is the approximate geographical center of the Morehouse Delta, a section more favorable to the growth of cotton than is the hill district to the south and west.

MER ROUGE (Fr., red sea), 19.4 *m.* (95 alt., 819 pop. 1970), the oldest town in Morehouse Parish, was settled early in the nineteenth century. According to legend French explorers saw between the bluffs lying to the north and west a sea of red sedge, and called is *Prairie Mer Rouge.* Here La 2 from the east joins US 165, which turns west.

The present townsite was included in a 1,000,000-acre tract granted by Charles IV of Spain to Baron de Bastrop in 1797. The Baron was unsuccessful in colonizing even a small portion of his vast territory and about 1805 turned his rights to much of it over to Aaron Burr, who planned an extensive colonization project (*see History*).

In 1807 Josiah Davenport, a retired Rhode Island sea captain, bought a tract in Prairie Mer Rouge from Abraham Morehouse, to whom Bastrop had transferred a part of his grant. Davenport erected the first home near what is now the village of Mer Rouge, and was followed by Morehouse, for whom the parish is named, who settled about a mile to the east.

Bordering the highway at 24.3 *m.* is a 100-acre PEACH ORCHARD, one of the agricultural ventures of this parish. The orchard was planted in 1931, under the auspices of the Bastrop Chamber of Commerce, in order to demonstrate the adaptability of this section to the growth of peach trees.

BASTROP, 26.7 *m.* (135 alt., 14,713 pop. 1970; 15,193, 1960), is almost alone among northeast Louisiana towns in that its prosperity is based not upon cotton but upon industry: paper making from wood pulp, manufacturing carbon black from natural gas, brick making, and lumbering. The presence of low-priced natural gas fuel has been largely responsible for the town's industrial development.

Following the discovery of gas in the vicinity in 1916, the town experienced a boom, and old frame structures gave way almost completely to modern brick business buildings and stuccoed bungalows. Local retail stores reflect the specialization of an urban center. A potent and inescapable reminder of Bastrop's industrial character is the pungent odor exuded by the paper mills.

The city owes its existence to bitter rivalry for the Morehouse Parish seat, after the Bastrop grant was divided into parishes in 1844. The contending towns agreed to give the seat to a new place. In 1846 a town site was laid out on 192 acres. Bayou Bartholomew enabled steamboats to carry cotton to market.

Because few inhabitants were slave owners, secession, in 1861, was generally opposed. Despite this, Bastrop sent men to the Confederate Army; out of 135, only 35 returned. Confederate and Federal troops were quartered in Bastrop, but the town escaped actual fighting.

The MOREHOUSE PARISH LIBRARY SYSTEM consists of six branches and two bookmobiles. Two of the branches are in Bastrop, where the Headquarters branch serves the central unit, in which acquisition, reference work and library programs originate. The Bastrop-Headquarters Branch was established in 1940 and moved into its present building in 1953. Its architecture is in a contemporary style.

Other branches are located in Mer Rouge, Bonita, Collinston, and Oak Ridge. Collinston is reached from Mer Rouge on La 138 and Oak Ridge from Mer Rouge on La 133. The Morehouse Parish Library maintains a general collection of books and materials for its area, including recordings, reproductions of fine paintings, and a microfilm collection of census records and Parish newspapers. It is acquiring the early files of Parish newspapers of Northeast Louisiana for microfilming, collects historical material, and maintains a genealogical section. Most of these materials are located at the Bastrop-Headquarters Branch, which in 1969 had a circulation of 65,949 books and materials. In 1969 two bookmobiles had a combined circulation of 36,839 books. The Morehouse Parish Library participates in the first regional library system in Louisiana, the

Trail Blazer Pilot Library System of Northeast Louisiana, which comprises 13 parish public library systems and three academic libraries.

Right from Bastrop on concrete-paved La 139 to the junction with a graveled road 10 *m.;* R. here to CHEMIN-A-HAUT (Fr., high road) STATE PARK, 10.5 *m.,* a 500-acre pine-forested tract situated at the confluence of Bayou Bartholomew and Bayou Chemin-à-Haut. The bayous afford good opportunities for fishing. Place for 50 tent and trailer. Facilities, bath house, rental boats. 14-day limit. Fee $1.25. Southeast on La 593 is the BUSSEY-BRAKE RESERVOIR, built by the International Paper Co. Fishing is available.

South of Bastrop US 165 descends by a gentle slope to fertile bottomlands where cotton and corn are the principal crops.

POINT PLEASANT, 28.8 *m.,* was an old steamboat landing on Bayou Bartholomew during the early steamboat era. All the cotton grown in the vicinity was for many years shipped from this point, and it was a popular rendezvous whenever the firing of a cannon announced the arrival of a boat. Planters and woodsmen with guns and hunting knives hanging on their saddles were frequent visitors. Dances were occasionally held on the boats, and fights were numerous, waged with fists, pistols, and knives. Point Pleasant had quite a reputation in the old days.

PERRYVILLE, 34.9 *m.* (55 alt), is in the center of a natural gas field. Two stations at Perryville pump natural gas from near-by fields to distant markets. There is a SOUTHERN CARBON CO. PLANT (*open on application*), one of several in this section. The plants are housed in low corrugated iron sheds within which burn gas jets, the flames coming in contact with the surfaces of steel plates, or discs. The carbon deposited on the discs is scraped into receptacles by rotating knives or similar devices. The plants can be easily identified by the dense black smoke pouring from their chimneys.

At 37.9 *m.* is the junction with paved La 11.

Right on this road is STERLINGTON, 2.3 *m.* (80 alt., 1,118 pop. 1970), formerly a farming village, but since the discovery of gas an operating base for the industry. Several companies send gas through a mammoth system of pipe lines to cities as far distant as St. Louis, Memphis, and New Orleans; other plants use gas in the manufacture of carbon black.
One of the few remaining old homes in this section is STERLINGTON. Shaded by immense magnolia and pecan trees, the house sits back from the blacktop road that crowns the protection levee at Sterlington. It is a one-story frame structure of modified Georgian design. A spacious gallery extends across the front, supported by six fluted Doric columns of solid cypress.
On the property of the Arkansas-Louisiana Gas Company, 1.3 miles south of town, once a part of Glendora Plantation, one of the most interesting Indian burial grounds in the Ouachita Valley was found by Clarence B. Moore in 1908 and 1909. Human remains, glass beads, brass ornaments, and 322 pieces of pottery were found, many of them beautiful in design.
A short distance (R) above the bridge is the STERLINGTON LOCK AND DAM (not visible at high-water stage), built by the U. S. Government to maintain a navigable depth in the Ouachita River. The locality is popular as a fishing ground, bass and catfish being especially plentiful.

Right from Sterlington, on "The Lane," a graveled road, to (L) the ISLAND CEMETERY, 2.3 *m.*, on the banks of the Bayou Bartholomew. Crumbling brick walls and heavy wrought-iron fences surround burial plots almost hidden by rank blackberry vines, weeds, and sumac. Tombstones date from 1804.

PHILLIPS, 41.9 *m.*, is the home of a SOUTHERN CARBON CO. PLANT (*open on application*).

At 45.1 *m.* is the junction with a graveled road.

Left on this road 0.6 *m.* to the JAMES A. NOE FISH HATCHERY, established by the Louisiana Department of Conservation. The hatchery is composed of a series of large ponds set in a 40-acre park. The species bred include bream, warmouth bass (goggle-eye), rock bass, black bass, and crappie. Water for the pond is pumped from near-by Black Bayou at the rate of 2,500 gallons a minute. Electric lights hanging over the ponds during summer nights attract hordes of insects, which, falling into the water, augment the food supply. Peacocks and peahens wander about the grounds, while white swans and ducks are numerous on the ponds. Frequently the caretaker provides a show at the bass pond by "calling" the fish (beating with a hammer upon a plow point) to feed them bread crumbs.

At 45.2 *m.* on US 165 is the junction with a dirt road.

Right on this road to MOON LAKE, 2.1 *m.*, and HORSESHOE LAKE, 2.7 *m.* (*cottages, boats, and bait*), popular camping and fishing resorts.

At 49.4 *m.*, in the outskirts of Monroe, is the junction with US 80 (*see Tour 7a*), which unites with US 165 into Monroe.

MONROE, 52.1 *m.* (77 alt., 56,374 pop. 1970.) *See Monroe.*
Monroe is at junctions with US 80, Int. 20 and La 15.

Section b. MONROE to ALEXANDRIA; 96 m., US 165

South of MONROE, 0 *m.*, for a considerable distance US 165 parallels the Ouachita River, passes small oil-boom towns, partially deserted reminders of a more prosperous era, and swings through a rolling wooded hill country thinned out by lumber companies and now being reforested.

The LOUISIANA TRAINING INSTITUTE (*visitors admitted*), 3.9 *m.*, is maintained by the Louisiana Department of Corrections. There are a number of main buildings, including a home for the superintendent, a dairy, outbuildings, barns, a machine shop, ample space for the growing of foodstuffs, and an athletic field, on grounds covering 697 acres. A modern gymnasium has been built. The institution can accommodate 200 boys.

The Ouachita River sweeps away to the right at 5.1 *m.* in a great curve called Buckhorn Bend—named by settlers who found a fine set of horns nailed to a tree in the bend.

BAYOU MOUCHOIR DE L'OURSE (Fr., handkerchief of a she-bear), 6.6 *m.*, leads east (L) from the highway to Petticoat and

Lafourche Bayous. Mouchoir de l'Ourse is probably an error in nomenclature, for which there are two different explanations: according to one, the name should be Machoire de l'Ourse (Fr., jawbone of a she-bear), because such a jawbone was found near the stream; more romantically, the second story relates that a gallant French explorer found a lady's handkerchief embroidered with the name "Louise" floating on the stream, and named the bayou Mouchoir de Louise. Evidence which seems to strengthen the latter account, intimating that the lady might have been bathing, is the fact that the adjoining stream is named Petticoat Bayou.

South of Bayou Mouchoir de l'Ourse the highway leads through bottomlands wooded with ash, black gum, cypress, tupelo, and various species of oak.

At 11.4 *m.* is the junction with a graveled road.

Right on this road 0.6 *m.* to the junction with the river road; L. here to the FILHIOL HOUSE (*open*), 1.3 *m.*, built (L) in 1855 by John B. Filhiol, wealthy planter and grandson of Jean Batiste Filhiol (*see Monroe*), commandant of the Ouachita Post at Fort Miro (now Monroe). It is a one-story frame house with square cypress pillars on the front porch and a fanlight in the pediment and above the front doorway. The house was originally much smaller than at present. When the additions were made Filhiol imported a French cabinet-maker to lend the interior an authentic French touch. Lumber used in the house's construction was cut from the adjacent woods, and all the ironwork such as hinges and locks were wrought in the plantation blacksmith shop. The woodwork of the front room is carefully joined with pegs, no nails having been used. This room is not ceiled, but its large rafters have been carefully smoothed and painted. The dining-room, designed to simulate the dining salon of an old river packet, is decorated with fresco and scroll-work, with windows of vari-colored glass.

Filhiol was a generous host, and is said to have ordered large bills of goods delivered at the near-by Ouachita River landing solely to allow him the opportunity of entertaining the captains. John B. Filhiol, the great-grandson of the Fort Miro commandant, is the present owner of the Filhiol home. In his possession is a *culverin,* an old firearm, which, mounted on a wooden block and bound with iron hoops, formed a part of the armament of Fort Miro in the eighteenth century.

At 23.5 *m.* is the junction with a graveled road.

Right on this road 0.7 *m.* to (L) the U. S. LOCK AND DAM No. 3 (not visible at high-water stage), built on the Ouachita River to maintain a navigable depth. The river, broad and usually placid at this point, provides excellent fishing at favorable water stages.

South of RIVERTON, 25.7 *m.* (68 alt.), a former steamboat landing, US 165 traverses a region of small lakes. Through this section gray squirrels are abundant and can frequently be seen in the trees near the highway.

South of 27.9 *m.* the road parallels an elbow of DAVIS LAKE (sometimes called Horseshoe Lake). At various places, usually indicated by signs, boats and bait are available.

US 165 crosses the OUACHITA RIVER, 30.3 *m.,* on a steel and concrete bridge constructed in 1935.

COLUMBIA, 30.5 *m.* (116 alt., 1,000 pop. 1970), is the oldest town and seat of Caldwell Parish. The site was cleared in 1827 by Daniel Humphries, a settler from the East; the first building, a store, was erected a few years later by a man named Stokes. The fertility of the soil attracted other pioneers, and presently a colony sprang up around the store. Since it was the only settlement on the Ouachita River between Monroe and the Black River towns, a number of steamboat owners and captains found it a convenient place to live. There was a good harbor, and the village became a busy port for packets from New Orleans, St. Louis, and more distant points. Farmers from the surrounding area brought cotton to Columbia to be shipped by water, frequently blocking the streets with wagons and oxcarts.

During the War between the States Federal gunboats came up the Ouachita to shell and sack Columbia, and in February 1864 it was the scene of a skirmish between Federal and Confederate forces. The town recovered after the war and regained most of its commercial prestige, only to lose it when the railroads brought about a sharp slump in river traffic. Ironically, it was a Columbia resident, R. B. Blanks, who sponsored the railroad that doomed the town's commerce. Blanks, after selling a million acres of timberland in the area at 25¢ an acre, moved to Monroe, and with Jay Gould assisted in effecting the entry of the Missouri Pacific into Louisiana.

The BLANKS HOUSE (*garden open to the public*), on the second street from the foot of the bridge, is a two-and-one-half-story frame structure almost hidden from view by a profusion of flowers, trees, and shrubbery. Immense sweet olive trees, camellias, Japanese magnolias, and hundreds of flowering shrubs, roses, lilies, and jonquils make the garden a lovely spot in spring.

South of Columbia US 165 enters rolling pine hills, the great timberland that has made the State prominent in the lumber industry. Houses, set in the surrounding pine woods, are neat and well painted. Along the highway in summer dewberries are plentiful. Opossum hunting is a popular local sport. Turkey buzzards, wheeling slowly through the skies with scarcely a perceptible movement of their wings, are a common sight. Larger towns in the area are characterized by sawmills rather than cotton gins. The Negro population is comparatively small.

GRAYSON, 35.1 *m.* (162 alt., 516 pop. 1970), is a lumber town.

A small wooded ROADSIDE PARK (*picknickers admitted*), 36.7 *m.,* was established by the Louisiana Central Lumber Company of Clarks for the popularization of forest conservation.

CLARKS, 37.5 *m.* (889 pop. 1970). It is the home of a LOUISIANA CENTRAL LUMBER COMPANY MILL (*open on application*).

OLLA, 49.2 *m.* (154 alt., 1,387 pop. 1970), was named for Olla Mills, the daughter of one of the founders. Each year the North-Central Louisiana Fair and the Louisiana Baptist Encampment are held here, the former in the fall, the latter in the summer.

National Park and Festivals

Dept. of the Interior, National Park Service

MEMORIAL MONUMENT AT CHALMETTE NATIONAL HISTORICAL PARK

RENE BEAUREGARD HOUSE, CHALMETTE BATTLEFIELD, NOW
VISITORS CENTER

GALLERY OF THE RESTORED BEAUREGARD HOUSE, CHALMETTE

RESTORED WOODEN PALISADE, CHALMETTE BATTLEFIELD

RESTORED COTTON-BALE BREASTWORK, CHALMETTE BATTLEFIELD

ENTRANCE GATE, MILITARY
CEMETERY, CHALMETTE
Dept. of the Interior,
National Park Service

U. S. MILITARY CEMETERY, CHALMETTE
Dept. of the Interior, National Park Service

HUGE MUZZLE-LOADER, RELIC OF THE WAR OF 1812

OLD CANNON AT CHALMETTE BREASTWORKS

KUBLAI KHAN FLOAT, MARDI GRAS PARADE, NEW ORLEANS

CROWDS WELCOME ANNUAL MARDI GRAS PARADE, NEW ORLEANS

FESTIVE ACADIAN COSTUMES ALONG THE TECHE

COSTUMED RIDERS OBSERVE ACADIAN MARDI GRAS

FAMOUS OLYMPIA MARCHING BRASS BAND, NEW ORLEANS

According to legend a battle once took place here between Indians and Spaniards. Defeated, the Indians fled, leaving behind a squaw and her daughter. While the Spaniards pursued the Indians, the squaw slit the throat of a sleeping guard and escaped with her daughter. Upon the return of the soldiers, the two were recaptured, killed, and buried beneath a dogwood tree.

Dogwood trees are numerous in this section. Their snowy white flowers cover the woods in the spring; but because the timber brings high prices, the trees are fast disappearing. Dogwood timber is made almost entirely into "shuttle blocks," to be recut into shuttles for textile mills.

URANIA, 53.5 *m.* (91 alt.), is the center of the URANIA FOREST, and the home of the URANIA LUMBER MILL (*open on application*), nationally known for its pioneer reforestation and conservation activities. Headed by the late Henry Hardtner, the company was organized in 1898, beginning business with 240 acres of timberland and a portable sawmill. At present the company has more than 100,000 acres of land, a modern double-band sawmill, a planing mill, drying kilns, and other properties including dwellings for employees, an ice plant, an electric light plant, and water works.

During the worst years of the depression, although operations were suspended for many months at a time, the company cared for its employees without government assistance, and there was no suffering as in other mill towns whose markets were curtailed or destroyed.

The reforestation work of the company began in the 1920's when a contract was entered into with the State to grow timber on 26,000 acres of cut-over land, the State agreeing to place the assessment for taxation purposes at $1 an acre for 40 years. This tract and others have been operated on a sustained yield basis, with at least as much timber grown each year as was cut out. The Urania Forest is protected against fire by wardens and rangers paid jointly by the State, the U. S. Forest Service, and the lumber company. Part of the company holdings has been set aside as a game and bird refuge.

For years forestry students from Yale University have completed their training here, spending several weeks each spring at a comfortable camp that has been provided for them.

Most of the lumber mills in the State have two centers of activity: a "front," or forest camp, where trees are felled and trimmed, and the mill site, where the logs are converted into lumber. The usual method of handling the logs is by means of a permanent railroad track and spurs, or temporary sections of track extending into the forest and movable to fresh tracts as the timber is cut out. At right angles to the spurs skidding roads are provided over which teams drag the logs to the track. A steam skidder on the track pulls the logs to the main line where they are lifted to flatcars. Trees growing in swamp areas in varying depths of water are taken out by means of an overhead skidder, an apparatus of ropes and cables which drags the logs to firmer ground. When the logs reach the mill they are usually dumped into a mill pond and float until needed; they are then guided to a log-slip, where an endless chain or cable carries them to the saw carriage. The larger mills have a number of band saws in gangs which cut an entire log into lumber in one forward movement. Every part of the timber is utilized by the mill. The sawdust, removed from under the saw by suction, is processed into paper and wood alcohol; the bark-covered slabs and trim from the edges are worked into laths, shingles and other similar products.

Just off the highway (R) on the premises of the Urania Lumber Company, is the tall stump of a giant cypress tree which has been fashioned into a dugout-shelter by employees of the company. The tree itself, at least 400 years old, was 118 feet tall and contained 6,000 feet of lumber. The 9-foot base of the stump, tapering now to a 6-foot, cedar-roofed top, has been hollowed out, equipped with a window and a door, made of a section cut and hinged to the trunk, and contains a gas heater, a chair, and a shelf for a lamp, books, and magazines.

Between Urania and Tullos the highway traverses the URANIA OIL FIELD. Along the road are numerous "pumpers" and "gushers," and the creeks and barren flats are covered with oil slick. Gaseous odors arise from stagnant puddles of dirty, grease-like water; occasional grotesque trees rear bare and broken branches—and in the background stands a verdant forest, presenting a refreshing contrast to the man-wrought landscape.

TULLOS, 57.4 m. (106 alt., 600 pop. 1970), is supported chiefly by oil wells in the town and vicinity. Numerous derricks, adjoining business and residential properties, can be seen near the highway. Truck farming is also of importance; thousands of dollars worth of tomatoes and other vegetables are shipped annually.

At Tullos is the junction with US 84 (see Tour 5a).

South of Tullos US 165 is lined on both sides by oil wells.

In dense swamps at 60 m. US 165 crosses LITTLE RIVER below the confluence of Castor (Fr., beaver) Bayou and Dugdemona River. Oil from the Tullos field has destroyed most of the fish in these streams, but wild game—deer, raccoon, opossum, squirrel, and wild turkey—abounds in the woods.

ROCHELLE, 60.6 m. (81 alt.), named for Henry Rochelle, who erected a lumber mill on the site in 1895, is a company town supported by the TREMONT LUMBER MILL (open on application). Every building in town belongs to the company and, with the exception of school teachers and postal employees, no one but the employees of the mill live here or are allowed to rent houses.

Rochelle has no crime problem, since any resident proving undesirable is promptly moved off the property of the company, which automatically means the town of Rochelle. No saloons or gambling halls are allowed.

GEORGETOWN, 62.5 m. (96 alt., 306 pop. 1970), formerly a farming community, now largely depends on the oil industry. Here is the junction with the Old Harrisonburg Road (La 108), which, as an Indian trail, witnessed the last flight of the Indians as they were pushed farther westward by the advance of the whites. Later, large herds of lowing Texas longhorns were driven over it to Natchez and Vicksburg slaughterhouses to be transshipped to northern and eastern markets; at the same time, moving westward, caravans of pioneer families searched for a new home on an ever-changing frontier. During the War between the States it was used as a military road alternately by Confederates and Federals.

SELMA, 64.5 *m.* (75 alt.), was once a sawmill town. HULL'S LAKE, about 2 miles southeast of Selma, according to tradition, is bottomless, a contention supported by those who have searched for the loot supposedly dropped in the middle of the lake by bank robbers pursued by a posse.

The route crosses the northern boundary of the CATAHOULA DIVISION of the KISATCHIE NATIONAL FOREST (*build fires in designated fireplaces only; keep grounds clean*) (*see Tour 15a*) at 68.3 *m.* The Federal Government has within the past few years erected a number of lookout towers in the surrounding forests, and has built many miles of firebreaks.

At 68.4 *m.* is the junction with a graveled road.

Left on this road 1.5 *m.* to LINCECUM (75 alt.), once an important sawmill town, but now little more than a railroad siding. Like many other places in Louisiana, Lincecum cherishes its legend of hidden treasure. According to local tradition at some time in the distant past an eastward-bound party of men carrying a fabulous amount of gold was attacked by Indians in this vicinity; and, though the attackers were repulsed, it was decided to bury a part of the gold, to be returned for later. Shortly afterward the men fell to fighting among themselves and all were either killed on the spot or died later from wounds. The treasure awaits a finder.

POLLOCK, 80.7 *m.* (120 alt., 341 pop. 1970), began as a trading post named Oction, about 1840. A lumber mill was later built by Captain J. W. Pollock, for whom the town was named. Most of the settlers came from Mississippi when the racial strife of the Reconstruction Period was at its height. This gave rise to the exclusion of all Negroes from the town and vicinity.

Pollock is at the junction with La 8 (*see Tours 5a and 15a*).

At 85.1 *m.,* at a church, is the junction with a dirt road.

Left on this road to a fork, 2 *m.;* L. here and R. at another fork, 3.1 *m.,* to (L) the CLEAR CREEK OBSERVATION TOWER (*visitors admitted*), 3.6 *m.*

US 165 crosses the southern boundary of the CATAHOULA DIVISION of the KISATCHIE NATIONAL FOREST at 86.1 *m.*

The LOUISIANA STATE INDUSTRIAL SCHOOL FOR GIRLS, 88.5 *m.,* was opened in 1928 and operates a 40-acre dairy and truck farm.

At 91.5 *m.* is the junction (L) with a blacktop road. Left on this road to CAMP BEAUREGARD (*open*), 0.3 *m.,* a 6,000-acre National Guard reservation. There are modern kitchen, mess halls, bathhouses, a swimming pool, garages, office buildings, rifle, machine gun, and artillery ranges, and recreational halls. During much of the year only a skeleton organization is maintained at the camp, but in July and August National Guard units from all over Louisiana meet here for military training. The reservation has been used as Civilian Conservation Corps district headquarters.

The RAPIDES GOLF AND COUNTRY CLUB is at 93.4 *m.*

GREENWOOD CEMETERY, 93.6 *m.,* serving the Alexandria-Pineville region, is a 40-acre, well-landscaped, tree-shaded tract.

At 93.8 *m.* is the junction with US 71 (city route) (*see Tour 18b*), which unites with US 165 into Alexandria.

The DAIGRE HOUSE (*open*), 94.1 *m.,* a long, low frame structure with a high gabled roof overhanging a wide front gallery, was built by Colonel Robert P. Hunter. Originally almost square in shape, it was remodeled in 1840. Many ante bellum furnishings have been retained, including a bed of cherry wood from the house of Captain J. J. Jeffries, Lieutenant Governor of Louisiana (1888–92).

PINEVILLE, 95.2 *m.* (95 alt., 8,951 pop. 1970) *see Alexandria-Pineville.*

Pineville is at the junction with US 71 (*see Tour 18b*).

ALEXANDRIA, 96 *m.* (79 alt., 41,553 pop. 1970) *see Alexandria-Pineville.*

Alexandria is at junctions with US 71 (*see Tours 15 and 18*), La 1 and La 28.

Section c. ALEXANDRIA to IOWA; 86.8 m., US 165

South of ALEXANDRIA, 0 *m.,* the route crosses the Red River basin, traverses the eastern edge of the West Louisiana uplands, and ends in the western corner of the Rice Belt.

The MASONIC HOME FOR INDIGENT CHILDREN (*open*), 4.3 *m.,* established in 1925, is a modern three-story tan brick building accommodating 100 children. A dairy and farm are operated on the 70-acre tract.

Fifty yards south of the Masonic Home is the junction with a graveled road.

Right on this road to the AARON PRESCOTT PLANTATION HOUSE (*open*), 0.7 *m.,* an early nineteenth-century one-and-one-half-story frame house with seven square wooden pillars on the front gallery supporting an overhanging roof. Old furnishings include four-poster beds, gun cabinets, silver, and quilts. In the front hall is a portrait of Mrs. Aaron Prescott painted by Theodore Moise, New Orleans artist.

Between 5.7 *m.* and 8.8 *m.* the highway traverses heavily wooded Bayou Bœuf Swamp.

US 165 crosses the northern boundary of the EVANGELINE UNIT of the KISATCHIE NATIONAL FOREST at 10.1 *m.* Picturesque vistas emerge here and there in the change from river valley to uplands, or where an occasional backwater lake comes into view.

WOODWORTH, 12.7 *m.* (86 alt.), once a lumber town, now markets gravel from near-by beds.

1. Right from Woodworth on graveled road to the WOODWORTH OBSERVATION TOWER (*open*), 4.7 *m.*
2. Left from Woodworth to the junction with a graveled road, 1 *m.;* L. here to CAMP OVERTON, 1.9 *m.,* headquarters of STATE FOREST, an 8,000-acre tract set aside for reforestation and the growing of seedlings for planting in other lumber reclamation areas. The forest covers rolling country cut by creek bottoms. Indian Creek, twisting and winding through the woods, alternately loses itself in heavy shade or reflects the sun in open glades. Among the native Louisiana trees here are cypress, three varieties of pine, white ash, sycamore, and black walnut. Although native trees are the chief concern, a constant search is maintained for foreign species that might profitably be grown in the State. About 6,000,000 seedlings are raised annually.

The Civilian Conservation Corps in the 1930's constructed roads, bridges, firebreaks, an observation tower, and camping sites. Well-marked roads in the forest lead to three fine recreation areas. Here tables, benches, and fireplaces, made of native rock set in a beautiful woodland, afford excellent picknicking facilities.

The ADMINISTRATION BUILDING, constructed by CCC men, is composed of native pine logs, peeled and varnished. The large fireplace in the main clubroom is built of stone and mud. Adjacent to the lodge are barracks for the camp workers and an observation tower.

US 165 crosses the southern boundary of the EVANGELINE UNIT of the KISATCHIE NATIONAL FOREST at 13.1 *m.*

At 15.5 *m.* is the junction with a graveled road.

The BEECHWOOD FISH HATCHERY (*open*), 1.3 *m.,* in a 221-acre tract, contains eight ponds set in groves of trees, the shores planted with shrubs and flowers. Black and warmouth bass, bream, and perch are propagated and furnished to depleted streams and lakes. The forest and hatchery are wildlife sanctuaries; wild turkeys and quail are fairly common and bear and deer are occasionally seen.

FOREST HILL, 20.2 *m.* (170 alt.), is on the site of an early Choctaw village. The Indians were friendly with the white settlers, whom they supplied with woven split-cane baskets dyed in bright colors, and leather cured and worked to extraordinary softness. About the middle of the nineteenth century the Indians abandoned the site, and the whites began to form a village, later named Bismark. When the railroad was built through in 1890, Forest Hill was substituted for Bismark.

Left from Forest Hill at the railroad station and R. at 0.1 *m.* to the junction with a graveled road, 1.1 *m.;* R. here and L. at a fork, 6.9 *m.,* to BENNETT BAY LANDING (*accommodations, boats*), 7.8 *m.,* on the shore of LAKE COCODRIE. There is excellent fishing in the vicinity during the late spring, summer, and fall, and duck, squirrel, quail, and wild turkey can be hunted in the winter. According to a legend the bottom of this lake was at one time an Indian village. While the Choctaw braves were away in battle the ground subsided and a lake covered the spot, drowning the women, children, and old men, and to this day no Indian has been known to fish in the lake's waters. Surrounded by pine forests, the lake is a shadowy expanse dotted with cypress and gum trees.

BLUE LAKE (*boats and guides available*), northeast of Bennett Bay Landing, is another fishing and hunting resort.

From Forest Hill La 112 runs northeast to LECOMPTE, 9 *m.*, on US 71.

SHADY NOOK (L), 23.8 *m.*, is a recreational spot on the banks of Spring Creek, a beautiful stream whose clear waters provide excellent fishing. Boy and Girl Scouts hold summer camps in the vicinity.

GLENMORA, 25.8 *m.* (138 alt., 1,651 pop. 1970), was supported for many years by the lumber industry, but farming is now the principal source of revenue. Irish potatoes, strawberries, beans, tomatoes, and other crops are grown. Recently the growing of tung oil trees has been introduced.

In the cut-over lands and swamps about Glenmora wild horses have ranged for approximately a century. A number of decades ago a stockman bred some of the wild mares with Percheron and Shetland stallions and obtained a greatly improved breed. Capable of withstanding a great deal of hardship, they make useful farm animals and cow ponies. So much time and energy are expended in catching and breaking the horses, however, that only a small number have been tamed. Occasionally a really beautiful animal is found, undoubtedly a throwback to the Percheron strain, but most of them are scrubs of various colors, including the arresting pinto, or "paint" pony.

OAKDALE, 37.8 *m.* (113 alt., 7,301 pop. 1970; 6,618, 1960), largest town in Allen Parish, was first called Bay, then Dunnville, in honor of William T. Dunn, who donated a half interest in 80 acres of land when the town was laid out in 1886. In 1890, when the Kansas City, Watkins & Gulf Ry. (now the Missouri Pacific) was built through the town, the name of Oakdale was substituted. The railroad tapped rich lumber resources, and the town has since been devoted half to the lumber industry and half to agriculture. Many carloads of radishes, cucumbers, strawberries, citrous fruits, and other products are produced yearly. Cut-over timber lands are now being increasingly used for grazing sheep. Oakdale is at the junction with La 10.

One of the first of its kind to be established in the United States (1927) is the DIMENSION MILL (*visitors admitted*), in the western part of town. A dimension mill is one that "sizes" lumber to meet the specifications of manufacturers. Until the idea of the dimension mill was conceived nearly all manufacturers were forced to buy lumber in standard sizes and themselves cut it into the different shapes and sizes needed. The local mill manufactures semifinished woodwork for automobiles and trucks, furniture, and many other articles.

OBERLIN, 52.4 *m.* (73 alt., 1,857 pop. 1970; 1,754, 1960), the seat of Allen Parish, is on the northeastern rim of the Rice Belt; to the north, west, and south are forests of pine, oak, sweet gum, and hickory. Three large lumber mills operate in Allen Parish.

South of Oberlin the highway bisects an extensive Satsuma orange section, a type of orange especially adapted to this locality, although not produced on a large scale. In the fall of the year the glossy deep green of the leaves in contrast with the globes of yellow fruit that weigh down the branches is an impressive sight.

KINDER, 63.1 *m.* (51 alt., 2,307 pop. 1970; 2,607, 1960), formerly a lumber center, is now supported by rice, cotton, and cattle raising. The lower levels of the longleaf pine region merge here with the lightly wooded and prairielike country to the east and southeast. On the banks of the near-by Calcasieu River are many beautifully wooded picnic sites, as well as bass fishing grounds.

Kinder is at the junction with US 190 (*see Tour 3c*).

FENTON, 73.6 *m.* (35 alt.), in Jefferson Davis Parish, is a farming community on the western rim of the rice and prairie belt. In and about Fenton the culture of Easter lilies (*see Tour 11b*) assumes the proportion of a minor industry.

South of Fenton US 165 traverses a rich rice-producing section (*see Tour 1c*).

The UNITED GAS PIPE LINE COMPANY PUMPING STATION (*open*), 76.7 *m.,* pumps natural gas from Louisiana and Texas fields to distant markets.

WOODLAWN, 79.3 *m.,* is a small farming community on the edge of the former pine timber belt. Rice and stock raising now support the village.

The IOWA OIL FIELD, 83.5 *m.,* discovered in 1929, is one of the largest potential fields in south Louisiana.

Interstate 10 now runs east-west across Jefferson Davis Parish parallel with the Southern Pacific Ry. and 1 to 2 *m.* north of US 90.

IOWA, 86.8 *m.* (20 alt., 100 pop.), is at the junction with US 90.

LAKE CHARLES, 77,918 pop. 1970, is 10 *m.* west of Iowa on US 90, and 12 *m.* west on Interstate 1 from its junction with US 165.

꘏꘏꘏꘏꘏꘏꘏꘏꘏꘏꘏꘏꘏꘏꘏꘏꘏꘏꘏꘏꘏꘏꘏꘏꘏

Tour 14

Turkey Creek—Eunice—Crowley—Junction with Interstate 10 and US 90; 64.6 *m.,* La 13.

Concrete- and asphalt-paved between Turkey Creek and Crowley.
Missouri Pacific parallels route between Turkey Creek and Crowley.
Restaurant and hotel accommodations at Eunice, Crowley, and Kaplan.

When US 71 and US 167 jointly proceed from Alexandria south, they split at Meeker, where US 167 runs south for 13 *m.,* then turns southeast at Turkey Creek. At Turkey Creek La 13 starts south.

This route extends through the Rice Bowl, whose level prairies produce more than 40 percent of the country's rice.

At about 3.8 *m.* the pine-forested, gently rolling uplands of central Louisiana give way to level and seemingly limitless prairie, checkered with occasional patches of cotton and corn. Along the highway between here and Eunice are numerous examples of Acadian cottages with outside garret staircases and with chimneys constructed of mud and moss packed in between a wooden framework.

PINE PRAIRIE, 6.5 *m.* (65 alt. 515 pop.), starts the Acadian rice country, in whose villages and towns Acadians, or Cajuns, with their distinctive customs and French-English patois, predominate. Pine Prairie, typical of their villages, is peopled with large families who gossip sociably on the porches of simple cottages.

The rice fields south of Pine Prairie are the most orderly and prosperous features of the prairies. Irrigation canals, meandering roads, and occasional thickets relieve the monotony of the level landscape.

REDDELL, 14.1 *m.* (60 alt.), is an Acadian village where cotton, not rice, is the staple crop. Small farms are the rule here, and cotton is planted, "chopped" (hoed), and picked by the farmer and his family, in contrast to mechanization.

The Acadian farmer is thrifty and industrious, and usually manages to live within his income even though his cotton or rice growing is restricted to a few acres. He operates on a strictly cash basis, and has an abhorrence of debt. Automobiles are not considered essential, and buggies are used for family outings, neighborly visits, and trips to the nearest store or Roman Catholic church. The fact that surfaced roads, except for La 13, are very scarce in this section may also account for the number of horse-and-buggy rigs. A cluster of buggies around a farmhouse usually means a wake, or perhaps butchering day.

MAMOU, 17.2 *m.* (60 alt., 3,275 pop. 1970), in the eary nineteenth century was the center of a cattle-raising district known as Prairie Mamou. Cattle raising later gave way to rice culture, and very little virgin prairie, with its luxuriant native grasses, remains. Mamou is the local name for the coral tree (*Erythrina herbacea*). A tea made from this shrub is given to pneumonia patients; the coral-red seeds are strung into necklaces by little girls. As a corruption of *mammouth* (Fr., mammoth), the name may derive from the discovery of mammoth remains in lower Louisiana. There is a junction here with La 104, east-west.

EUNICE, 27.6 *m.* (50 alt., 11,390 pop. 1970), is at the junction with US 190 (*see Tour 3c*).

In the vicinity of MOWATA, 35 *m.* (40 alt.), more intensive cultivation of land is evident, and homes are more modern in appearance, most of them lighted by electricity rather than kerosene lamps. The modernity of the region is further exemplified in the St. LAWRENCE CATHOLIC CHURCH in Mowata, a building of tan and buff-checkered stone.

The ELLIS TABERNACLE, 40.9 *m.,* a tin-roofed frame structure, is used each summer for "camp," or evangelistic meetings, by alternating religious groups. The gatherings are still very much like the old-fashioned revivals, except that the elaborate dinners are missing.

At 45 *m*. there is a junction with Interstate 10.

CROWLEY, 47.9 *m*. (22 alt., 16,104 pop. 1970), is at the junction with US 90 (*see Tour 1c*).

South of Crowley more pretentious farm houses and larger farms line the highway. Nearly every farm has a few beef and dairy cattle, and a small herd of sheep. Rice is the cash crop, but some cotton, sugar cane, and corn are grown.

The average rice farm in this section consists of about 100 acres. Water for irrigation is pumped from Vermilion River or from deep wells. Although it is about as expensive to pump water from privately owned wells as to buy water from a canal or water company, most farmers have their own wells to rely upon when the canal water becomes salty, which occurs when streams connected with irrigation systems are at low stage and water backs up from the Gulf. One-fifth of the rice crop is the usual fee of the water companies.

In this section the bane of the rice farmer is indigo, Louisiana's major crop in Colonial days. Although it is no longer planted commercially, the plant grows wild in some sections of the State. About a month after irrigation of the rice has begun, farmers begin pulling up the indigo and several native weeds of the same order; if left alone they choke out the rice. Indigo seeds mix with the rice grains and cannot be eliminated in threshing.

LELEUX, 58.2 *m*. (16 alt., 30 pop.), is little more than a post office, general store, and combination saloon and dance hall, where *fais-dodos* (*see Music and Folkways*), or Cajun "breakdown" dances, are held each Wednesday evening.

La 13 crosses Bayou Queue de Tortu (Fr., turtle tail), 57.5 *m.,* along whose banks grow irises, spider lilies, and water hyacinths.

At 64.6 *m*. is the junction with La 14 (*see Tour 2*), 2.5 miles west of Kaplan.

Tour 15

(El Dorado, Ark.)—Junction City—Lillie—Ruston—Winnfield—
Alexandria—Ville Platte—Opelousas—New Iberia; 255.8 *m.,* US 167,
US 71, La 26, La 218, La 23, La 22, La 5, US 190, La 25, La 401.

Section a.   *ARKANSAS LINE TO ALEXANDRIA; 131.6 m.,*
US 167, US 71

US 167 crosses the Arkansas Line, 17.3 miles south of El Dorado,
Arkansas, and continues due south to Alexandria through an upland
region of rolling hills mantled with pine forests. The farms, whose
chief money crop is cotton, rarely exceed 125 acres in area, and the
wooded sections are often unbroken for miles on each side of the road.
Most of the forest growth is secondary; lumbering has claimed the
virgin stands.

JUNCTION CITY, 0 *m.* (164 alt., 733 pop. 1970), lies adjacent
to Junction City, Arkansas, the State Line unevenly dividing the towns
near the southern edge of a common business district. A concrete post
on the main street (US 167) marks the boundary. About two-thirds
of the combined population of the two towns lives on the Arkansas side,
and all the churches are in that State. Each town elects its own officials.
Lumbering is the chief industry.

Here La 9 leaves US 167 and proceeds southwest to SUMMER-
FIELD, 11 *m.,* junction with La 2. It passes through the Game & Fish
Preserve of upper Claiborne Parish.

South of Junction City US 167 runs through the farming and
timber country of Union Parish. It is fine country for fruit growing;
watermelons grow to an enormous size, often weighing from 75 to 90
pounds. Sugar cane is also produced but usually in quantities sufficient
only for local domestic needs. Syrup making is one of the most interesting activities of the hill farms. This section is noted for the quality of
its hickory-smoked pork sausage and home-cured ham and bacon, recipes
for which were brought by the settlers who emigrated from Tennessee,
Kentucky, Alabama, and Georgia in the early nineteenth century.

The pioneers of this part of Louisiana were hunters and trappers
who lived in crude hand-hewn log cabins. During the winter the men
wore buckskin clothing and coonskin caps, and in summer their sons'
dress consisted largely of a single homespun shirtlike garment with one
button at the neck, which gave rise, no doubt, to the term "shirt tail
schools." The descendants of wealthy slave owners of Alabama, Georgia, and the Carolinas settled on the most fertile lands along the bayous

and rivers. Thus the early population was of two distinct types—the pioneer hunters, trappers, and small farmers, and the wealthier class.

At LILLIE, 7.2 *m.* (120 alt.), the road parallels Little Cornie Bayou. Cornie is a corruption of *corneille* (Fr., crow). West of Lillie is Cornie Lake.

US 167 crosses a branch of Little Cornie Bayou, 10.3 *m.*, uniting here with the main stream to form Big Cornie Bayou, which occasionally overflows its banks during high-water periods. At 8 *m.* there is a junction with La 15 to SPEARSVILLE.

BERNICE, 14.9 *m.* (226 alt., 1,704 pop. 1970), has a junction with La 2, which crosses the State from Mississippi to Texas.

The highway crosses Middle Fork Bayou at 19.1 *m.* and at 19.4 *m.* enters Lincoln Parish. Intensity of religious feeling is characteristic of this region, churches of Protestant denominations, especially Baptist, being numerous and well attended.

DUBACH, 23.6 *m.* (135 alt., 1,096 pop. 1970), has cotton gins, a sawmill, and a lumber yard.

US 167 crosses Bayou D'Arbonne, 25 *m.*, in all probability named for Gaspard Derbanne, a companion of St. Denis, who in 1700 traversed this section. It feeds D'Arbonne Lake.

Between 26 *m.* and 35.3 *m.* the highway traverses an Erosion Control Area, where conservation practices (strip-cropping, contour farming, reforestation, terracing, winter cover crops, sodded waterways, woodland management, gully control, and wildlife conservation) have been conducted by the Soil Conservation Service of the U. S. Department of Agriculture with the co-operation of State agencies.

VIENNA, 31.9 *m.*, is the oldest Louisiana town west of the Ouachita River and north of Natchitoches. The CEMETERY in the northern part of town (L) has interesting inscriptions on some of its monuments. One of these, on a horizontal slab in the left center of the cemetery, reads: "James H. Mays, born in Lincoln County, Georgia, November 17, 1821. Died in Ruston, Louisiana, August 9, 1911. Born spiritually, October 18, 1839, under no eyes save the Lord's and my horse's. Joined the Methodist Church on September 4, 1839, and feel that I have been an unworthy member since, but hope to join the redemmed above in the first resurrection. (Dictated by deceased.)"

Vienna, locally called "Vie-anna," is said to have been named by Georgia settlers, for a Georgia town, similarly mispronounced. Daniel Colvin and his son, Jeptha, the first settlers, came to the region in 1809. Virtually all who followed were from the Carolinas, Georgia, and Alabama. The trail blazed by the Colvins became a main road east and west, known later as the Old Wire Road, because telegraph lines were strung along it.

Following the war, Reconstruction politics divided the Vienna area into two hostile camps. Allen Greene, a leading citizen, turned Republican and become anathema to the community. In 1873 Greene wrested the State senatorship from E. M. Graham of the opposing party, and later, with the aid of Republican carpetbaggers, scalawags, and Negro voters, further overrode the wishes of the majority of whites in setting up a new parish named for Abraham Lincoln.

With the construction of the Vicksburg, Shreveport & Texas Railroad in 1883, the town of Ruston was established 4 miles south of Vienna, and grew so rapidly that the latter town—lacking rail connections—was completely eclipsed.

Left from Vienna on the Old Wire Road to the HUEY HOUSE (*open*), 0.4 *m.*, built (R) before the War between the States by John Huey. This two-story frame house, set upon pillars of native rock, was used for many years as an inn on the Monroe-Shreveport stagecoach line.

Set in a clump of cedars is a CEMETERY (R), 33.5 *m.,* in which many of the old settlers of the region are buried.

At 35 *m.* is the junction with a graveled road.

Right here to the CHAUTAUQUA SPRINGS (L), 0.8 *m.,* formerly a thriving resort area and still a popular picnic spot.

RUSTON, 36.3 *m.* (311 alt., 17,365 pop. 1970), *see Ruston.*

Ruston is at the junction with US 80 and Int. 20.

South of Ruston US 167 traverses an area of larger farms devoted to cotton and corn.

The LOUISIANA METHODIST ORPHANAGE (*open*), 37.2 *m.,* was founded in 1908 by the Louisiana Methodist Conference. It is supported wholly by voluntary contributions made in Louisiana Methodist churches on Easter Sunday and on Harvest Sunday. Educational facilities through the elementary grades are provided at the orphanage, upon completion of which inmates attend the model high school of the Louisiana Polytechnic Institute; many continue through college.

The RUSTON GOLF CLUB is at 37.9 *m.*

ANSLEY, 46.7 *m.* (191 alt.), is a sawmill town.

HODGE, 57.1 *m.* (191 alt., 818 pop. 1970), now an industrial town built around a paper company plant was originally a sawmill town. With the exhaustion of timber fit for sawmill usage, Hodge, in 1927, faced the same disintegration which had overtaken Quitman, Ansley, and scores of other mill communities. Construction of the first unit of the new plant in that year saved the community. Houses were built for employees and the village became a fair-sized town almost over night. A canning factory was constructed to enable growers to dispose of surplus produce and a herd of cattle was imported from Ohio to avert a threatened milk shortage. In recent years its population has declined.

JONESBORO, 59.3 *m.* (212 alt., 5,072 pop. 1970; 3,848, 1960), seat of Jackson Parish, is built on a high knoll. It dates from the War between the States when lumbering became an important industry. By 1908, when the parish seat was removed from Vernon, now a ghost town, Jonesboro was growing rapidly. It became the home of many of the native employees of the mill at Hodge. The two towns, which are connected by sidewalk, built a union high school midway between them.

The new COURTHOUSE occupies an elevation at the west end of the business district, the site of a fine building which was destroyed in 1936 by a gas explosion.

Jackson Parish was created by the legislature in 1845. Since there were few slave owners, the Confederate cause was none too popular with its citizens. There were, however, many men who enlisted in the Confederate Army and served throughout the war.

DODSON, 71.3 *m.* (212 alt., 457 pop. 1970), originally Pyburn, was founded about 1900 and flourished for a few years as a sawmill town, with a population of more than 2,500. By 1910, however, most of the timber in this section had been cut, and the town diminished in size.

Between Dodson and Tannehill the highway passes over a series of pine hills cut by fertile creek bottoms.

The WINONA OBSERVATION TOWER (*open*), 75.1 *m.*, is one of several similar towers in the region maintained by the State.

TANNEHILL, 77.3 *m.* (123 alt.), named for a pioneer family, was also once a thriving sawmill center.

WINNFIELD, 82.9 *m.* (118 alt., 7,142 pop. 1970), *see Winnfield.* Winnfield is at the junction with US 84 (*see Tour 5*).

At 86.2 *m.* is the junction with a graveled road. Left on this road 0.1 *m.* to CEDAR SPRINGS, a recreation center with a saltwater swimming pool and picknicking facilities.

US 167 crosses the northern boundary of the CATAHOULA DIVISION, 88.5 *m.*, largest unit (app. 800 sq. miles) of the four forest areas comprising the KISATCHIE NATIONAL FOREST. The forest embraces about 1,400 sq. miles. Its four divisions (Catahoula, Kisatchie, Vernon, and Evangeline) lie in central Louisiana and are admininstered from central headquarters at Alexandria.

Much time and effort is being devoted to replanting thousands of acres of denuded land. Many thousands of acres have been planted, largely with slash and longleaf pine—1,000 trees to the acre. The timber is generally divided into two classes: pine in the higher elevations, and various species of hardwood in the lowlands. The flora combines practically all plant life found in semitropical regions. The program will be on a sustained yield basis—"as much timber to be cut as will be grown each year." Miles of firebreaks have been constructed and a continuous lookout is maintained by tower watchers, who work in 8-hour shifts. When a fire is spotted, quick alarms effect immediate runs by rangers or workers in the section. Tower watchers live in comfortable cabins at the foot of the towers.

The U. S. Forest Service is also carrying on an extensive recreational program within the units. Camp and picnic grounds are being constructed, dams built to form lakes for swimming, fishing, and boating, and lots cleared for the erection of summer homes. The largest of these projects—Lake Valentine, near Alexandria, and Big Creek, near Fishville—have been completed. Others are contemplated at Gum Springs and Saline Lake, near Winnfield. All recreational facilities are provided free of charge. Lookout towers are open to the public. Fishing opportunities are good. State laws governing hunting and fishing apply to the forest areas.

US 167, leading through rolling woodlands, interspersed at intervals with truck farms, traverses 30 miles of the southern part of the Catahoula Division of the Kisatchie National Forest. Roads leading from the highway can be followed into the interior of the forest reservation.

At 91 *m.* is the junction with a graveled road. Right on this road to the IATT OBSERVATION TOWER (*open*), 1.3 *m.*

At 93.5 *m.* is the junction with graveled La 500. Left here 0.2 *m.* to PACKTON (161 alt.), a fox-hunting center. The sport has been popular in Louisiana since John M. Parker was governor of the State (1920–24). Increasing interest has given commercial importance to the raising and training of foxhounds. The bushy-tailed grey fox is hunted in Louisiana. A sport for more adventurous hunters is provided in the region by wolf hunting (*see Tour 5b*).

At 108.8 *m.* is the junction with La 123.

Right on this road to the junction with a graveled road, 3 *m.*; L. here to the COLFAX OBSERVATION TOWER (*open*), 3.6 *m.*

DRY PRONG, 109.3 *m.,* is one of a number of villages where singing conventions, or community sings, and revival meetings are held in brushwood arbors during the pleasant summer months.

BENTLEY, 113.9 *m.* (199 alt.), a small farming community, is on a barren, rolling plane dotted with scrub pine. The town, formerly an important lumber center, was named for Joseph Bentley, owner of several sawmills.

Left from Bentley on graveled La 8 to (L) the CATAHOULA OBSERVATION TOWER (*open*), 1.5 *m.,* at the junction with a graveled road; R. here 1.2 *m.* to the STUART NURSERY (*open*), named for the late Major Robert Y. Stuart, former chief of the U. S. Forest Service. On this 76-acre tract about 25,000,000 seedlings are grown every year, to supply young trees for the forests of Louisiana, Mississippi, and Texas.

The highway crosses the southern boundary of the CATAHOULA DIVISION of the KISATCHIE NATIONAL FOREST at 118.7 *m.*

At 120.9 *m.* is the junction of US 167 and US 71; R on US 71 (*see Tour 18b*).

ALEXANDRIA, 131.6 *m.* (79 alt., 41,557 pop. 1970), *see Alexandria-Pineville.*

Alexandria is at junctions with US 71, US 165, US 167, La 1 and La 28.

Section b. *ALEXANDRIA TO NEW IBERIA; 124.2 m.,*
US 71, US 167, US 90

This section of the route crosses the Red River Valley, skirts the west Louisiana uplands, enters the northern tip of the Rice Belt, and descends along the valley of Bayou Teche into the Sugar Bowl and Evangeline country.

Southward from ALEXANDRIA, 0 *m.*, US 71 and US 167 are joined for 20 miles as far as MEEKER. US 71 now proceeds southeast. US 167 continues south as follows:

BAYOU COCODRIE, 22.3 *m.*, forms the northern boundary of Evangeline Parish. At this point the level and highly cultivated Red River bottomlands give way to rolling forests composed originally of longleaf pine but now consisting principally of loblolly pine, oak, and sweet gum.

At 27.1 *m.* is the junction (R) with a dirt road.

Right on this road to the junction with a dirt road, 1.3 *m.*; R. here and L. at a fork, 2.8 *m.*, to JOHNSON'S LANDING, 3.2 *m.*, on the edge of Cocodrie Swamp, where directions can be obtained for visiting the ANT TOWNS in the immediate vicinity. The large reddish brown ants (*Atta texana*) live in underground colonies on sandy hilltops. The surface evidence of the colonies is a sandy patch pockmarked with mounds about 18 inches in diameter. In the vicinity of Johnson's Landing the colonies are small, averaging 15 feet in diameter, but elsewhere, in unmolested areas, nests cover as much as an acre.

There are three castes in this species—winged males and females, soldiers, and large and small workers. The last named, with the protection of the soldiers, forage for vegetation, which they snip into small bits and carry to their subterranean chambers, where it is used as bedding in fungus gardens supplying food for the colony. The ants are inactive during cold and very hot weather, but at a favorable temperature they defoliate pine and oak trees and certain types of crops. Farmers in the neighborhood have been battling the ants all their lives; they have controlled them to some extent but have never exterminated them completely. The battle is waged with dynamite and kerosene, and by digging ditches to lead water into the underground chambers to drown the eggs. In the Kisatchie National Forest the U. S. Forest Service has had some success in exterminating the ants with carbon disulphide and London purple.

Little more than a railroad siding and an old water well, 28 *m.*, is left of the once prosperous sawmill town of MERIDIAN.

TURKEY CREEK, 31.7 *m.* (72 alt.), is near the southern edge of a pine hill region that is succeeded by level, low-growing forests made up principally of hardwoods.

In Turkey Creek US 167 turns southeast, while La 13 continues south to Eunice and Abbeville. On US 167:

BAYOU CHICOT (Fr., stump), 37.5 *m.*, was named for the stream of the same name. It is thought that a Choctaw village once stood on the bank of the bayou at this point. To the right of the red brick school and the Methodist Church is the BAYOU CHICOT CALVARY BAPTIST CHURCH, the first Baptist church established west of the Mississippi. The plain frame building is still in use. The church was organized in 1812 through the efforts of the Reverend Joseph Willis, a mulatto, one of the first Protestant ministers to preach in southwestern Louisiana. Willis was reared and educated in South Carolina. He first preached in Vermilion (Lafayette) in 1804, was threatened with violence and left the State, returning in 1812.

Five miles east from Bayou Chicot to CHICOT STATE PARK, one of the largest in the South, with 6,000 acres and a lake, equipped for camping, boating, fishing, with rest rooms and shelters. Near the top of the park on La 106 is the small town of ST. LANDRY.

Bayou Chicot is at the junction with La 106, which continues east to a junction with La 29.

VILLE PLATTE (Fr., flat town), 48.4 m. (74 alt., 9,692 pop. 1970), was settled by people of French extraction shortly after the beginning of the nineteenth century; the French language is still used more commonly than English. Until recent years court was held in French. The first mayor of Ville Platte was Marcellin Garand, who had been an officer in Napoleon's army.

Ville Platte is the marketing center for the surrounding countryside. A canning factory operates day and night during the spring and fall, and there are five cotton gins. Here one finds good food and drink, and on *fais-dodo* nights the town is a gay one.

The DEBAILLON HOUSE (*open*), 53.5 m., about 200 yards off the highway, is a two-story building whose age is apparent in the exposed *briqueté entre poteaux* construction.

At 58.1 m. is the junction with a dirt road. Left on this road to the POIRET HOUSE (*open*), 0.5 m., thought to be approximately 150 years old. The plantation was established by Valentine Poiret, who came originally from France. The house has a lower floor of red brick with eight round brick columns supporting the gallery. The upper floor has a plaster-covered front and weatherboarded sides. The upper columns are of wood, and are octagonal in shape. The house is set in a grove of live oaks interspersed with magnolias.

At 61.4 m. is the junction with a dirt road. Left here to the PHILLIPS HOUSE (*open*), 0.6 m., set in a grove of oak and pecan trees. The house is of *briqueté entre poteaux* construction. At the foot of a pecan tree (R), a few yards in front of the house, is an iron contrivance which at one time served as a steam generator or coil on one of New Orleans' earliest street-cars. It was brought here years ago and fitted to a homemade locomotive, designed to pull log trains. Running to the house on the right is an old road which at one time bore wagon trains to the steamboat landing on near-by Bayou Courtableau.

At 63.2 m. is the junction of La 22 and La 5 (*see Tour 15A*); R. on La 5.

The HALFWAY HOUSE (*open*), 64 m., a dilapidated old building (R), is so called because it is halfway between Opelousas and Washington. This landmark, erected by Clément Hollier, is probably more than a century old. The lower story—flush with the ground—is of plastered brick with six square plastered-brick pillars supporting the gallery. The upper floor is of wood with square wooden pillars supporting a hipped and dormered roof.

OPELOUSAS, 67.1 m. (71 alt., 20,121 pop. 1970), see *Opelousas*.

Opelousas is at junctions with US 190 (*see Tour 3*) and La 10 (*see Tour 15B*).

The route leaves Opelousas to the east on US 190 and at 69.8 m. turns R. on La 31.

LEONVILLE, 77 *m.* (27 alt., 512 pop. 1970), largest of several mulatto settlements in eastern St. Landry Parish, was established by free mulattoes before the War between the States (*see Tour 17b*). Leonville is the center of a truck-growing community and rivals Sunset (*see Tour 15B*) in the quantity of sweet potatoes shipped annually; sugar cane and cotton are also grown. Moss is gathered from the near-by swamps and cured here before it is hauled to moss gins.

South of Leonville La 31 parallels the east bank of Bayou Teche (*see Tour 1b*), crossing to the west bank at 81.3 *m.* In this thickly settled region many homes, typically Acadian, have outside garret steps.

In ARNAUDVILLE, 85 *m.* (25 alt., 1,673 pop. 1970; 1,184, 1960), the route, recrossing Bayou Teche, turns R. on La 686 and follows the east bank of the bayou through St. Martin Parish, formed by the territorial legislature in 1807 from a part of the old colonial District of the Attakapas (*see St. Martinville*). As it exists today, St. Martin is unusual in that it is divided, by an arm of Iberia Parish, into two separate sections.

HURON (*open*), 89.7 *m.*, a well-preserved plantation home, was built prior to 1850 by Charles Lastrapes, a member of one of the old Creole families of the Attakapas country. The raised basement, now serving as the lower floor, is of dull red brick, and the second story of cypress timber, painted white.

CECELIA, 91.8 *m.* (25 alt.), is the center of a fertile section where snap beans, cabbages, sweet potatoes, and pecans form the chief crops. The village boasts the largest rural high school in the state. Just outside the southern limits is an old-fashioned open kettle syrup mill (*visitors admitted*).

At 92 *m.* is the junction of La 686 and La 31; R. on La 31. The area between Cecelia and Breaux Bridge is called GRANDE POINTE, from the great curve of the bayou. It was settled by Acadian pioneers and retains many of its earlier characteristics. In 1876 a traveler (who used the term Creole indiscriminately for all French-speaking people) described Grande Pointe as follows: "They keep up the old Creole custom of having neighborhood balls every Saturday night. The balls are generally made up of the sons and daughters of small Creole farmers who work all day and dance at night. There are not less than sixty fiddlers in this settlement. They are a merry people."

A country dance is generally known today among the Acadians as a *fais-dodo* (literally, go to sleep); possibly because the dancers stay up all night and sometimes fall asleep while still dancing; possibly because the mothers sing *fais-dodo* (lullabies) to put the younger children to sleep so that they themselves can leave the *parc aux petits* for the dance floor (*see Music and Folkways*).

Along the road are occasional fences covered with Spanish moss which has turned quite black in the process of sun-drying. Moss gathering forms one of the small but steady industries of this section. There is always a local demand for moss mattresses, and when cotton is high, manufacturers substitute moss for cotton in upholstering furniture and automobiles. A skilled picker can gather from 1,000 to 3,000 pounds a day; barefooted, he scales the trees with the agility of a monkey, and dislodges the moss with a long pole. It is estimated that the moss industry produces between $2,500,000 and $3,000,000 annually for pickers and gin operators.

Found throughout southern Louisiana, the moss has from earliest Colonial days been used for pillows and mattresses and woven into braids, for bridles, saddles, blankets, and horse collars.

Uncured Spanish moss (*Tillandsia usneoides*) is a gray and stringy growth of indefinite length, with a fine black fiber in the center surrounded by a vegetable coat. The moss is picked from tree, stacked in piles, and soaked in water or dampened periodically until the outer coating rots. The piles must be occasionally stirred to prevent spontaneous combustion. The moss is then spread out on fences and on clothes-lines to dry. When cured, the moss is black and resembles horsehair. It takes several pounds of green moss to produce one pound of the cured product. It is then ginned in much the same manner as cotton: the threads are separated; leaves, branches, and other foreign matter are extracted; and the residue packed in small bales and sold to manufacturers.

The height of the moss-picking season is from early November to April, when most of the trees on which Spanish moss grows are at least partially bare. Small dugouts called pirogues are used in the swamp areas to gather the moss and bring it to higher ground.

From the swamp regions of south Louisiana come two legends concerning the origin of Spanish moss, which the Spaniards called "Frenchmen's wig," and the French, "Spaniard's beard." One is that of an Indian mother and two children trapped by rising waters during a storm which was accompanied by sudden cold. Taking refuge in a large tree, the mother implored the moon to shine on them, lest they die. In the morning the sky had cleared and the trees were clothed in moss, giving warmth to the marooned group. "See, mother," cried the small son, "the moon heard us; see, she tore up the storm clouds and threw them down upon us, for there are none left in the sky!"

The second story is that of an Indian princess and the son of a chieftain, who were killed during their marriage ceremony by a hostile tribe. The young couple was buried beneath a gigantic oak tree. In accordance with custom, the bride's long black hair was cut and hung on a limb of the oak. A storm lashed the country that night but in the morning the hair was undisturbed. As years went on it began to grow grey, and spread from tree to tree.

La 31 crosses Bayou Teche into BREAUX BRIDGE, 99.8 *m.* (25 alt., 4,942 pop. 1970), incorporated in 1871 and named for Agricole Breaux, builder of the first toll-free bridge in the section. Breaux Bridge was an important shipping center during the steamboat era.

Somewhere within the corporation limits of Breaux Bridge nine slaves were once forced to dig a trench which served as their own grave. Early in the nineteenth century the slaves killed their master, Narcisse

Thibodeaux, and made off with his hoard of gold. Captured by a posse, the Negroes were set to digging; at a signal, a volley of shots toppled them into the ditch. One bag of gold remains to be found.

Right from Breaux Bridge on paved La 94 to PARADISE GROVE, 0.8 *m.*, containing 83 splendid old live oaks. Near the roadside, measuring 20 feet in circumference, is Archangel, a member of the Live Oak Society (*see Lafayette*).

At the ANSE LA BUTTE OIL FIELD (Fr., little bay near the hill), 3.8 *m.*, the first producing wells were found in 1902.

5.5 miles straight ahead is LAFAYETTE (*see Lafayette and Tour 1c*).

South of Breaux Bridge La 31 follows winding Bayou Teche.

The RUTH PLANTATION, 102.5 *m.*, is one of the largest sugar cane plantations in St. Martin Parish. South of Ruth Plantation, extending for several miles along the bayou on each side, is a large Negro settlement. The cabins stand on the bayou banks, shaded by large oaks and surrounded by picket fences which extend down to the water.

La 31 crosses to the east side of Bayou Teche at 104 *m.* and at 108.7 *m.* recrosses to the west side. At 110.4 *m.* is a pleasant shaded section, with masses of shrubbery growing close to the road. Wild flowers are abundant in the spring, the native iris, particularly, appearing in many hues along the highway.

At 113.2 *m.* is the junction with a graveled road. Left on this road across Bayou Teche to the ST. JOHN PLANTATION HOUSE (*private*), 0.9 *m.* The mansion was built about 1828 by Alexandre Étienne de Clouet, a descendant of the Chevalier Alexandre de Clouet, one of the early commandants at the Poste des Attakapas.

The white frame house has four tall fluted wooden columns of the Corinthian order along the front, and is topped by a hipped roof supporting a belvedere. Some of the effectiveness of the exterior has been destroyed by modern screening, which extends over the entire front. A traveler who had included the whole of the Teche country in his itinerary wrote: "General de Clouet keeps up, more than any gentleman we have visited, the best original style of Creole living; a bountiful table, an abundance of everything, excellent servants, a cordial and easy welcome to strangers, and a delicate attention to all their wants and comforts . . . His parlors, sitting room, and halls are ornamented with portraits of his paternal and maternal ancestors for several generations, and other valuable paintings." The traveler marveled at the high ceilings, and large doors and windows of the home, particularly noting a dining room and table capacious enough "to seat the patrons of a large hotel." The oil painttings referred to formed an exhibit at the New Orleans Cotton Centennial in 1885.

Leading through the grove in front of the house is an inner avenue of pines flanked by an avenue of oaks. At the extreme left of the grounds is a grove of orange trees, as yet small, but bearing fruit.

Financial troubles overtook General de Clouet after the War between the States, and the home in 1887 passed to the Levert family.

A short distance beyond St. John Plantation is a large wooded tract which served Alexandre de Clouet as a deer park.

At 114.3 *m.* is the junction with a graveled road.

Right on this road to L'ÎLE DES CYPRÈS (Fr., cypress island), 2.1 *m.*, so named because it lies between two large cypress swamps. In this section the land is divided into small farms, 20 to 40 acres, on which are planted sweet potatoes, sugar cane, corn, and peppers. The farms are owned outright, and it is said that no mortgage or indebtedness exists against any of them. The Tabasco pepper, a variety developed in Louisiana, is distinguished by its round, bushy top, yellow leaves, and short red pods. Much of the Tabasco pepper used by the McIlhenny Company on Avery Island (*see Tour 2A*) is grown on Cypress Island.

The LONGFELLOW-EVANGELINE MEMORIAL PARK (L), 114.8 *m.*, was established as a State park in 1934 (the first in Louisiana) in commemoration of Henry Wadsworth Longfellow and the heroine of his poem *Evangeline*.

According to a legend which persists in this section, Emmeline Labiche, of St. Martinville, was the original of Longfellow's *Evangeline;* and her story, as told by the natives, is almost identical, up to a certain point, with that of the heroine of the poem. In the Acadian exodus from Nova Scotia, she became separated from her lover, Louis Arceneaux, the Gabriel of the poem, and wandered over America seeking him, finally landing at the Poste des Attakapas. She found him there, but faithless to her and betrothed to another. Under the shock she lost her reason and, dying shortly afterward, was buried in the Poste des Attakapas cemetery, where her grave can still be seen (*see St. Martinville*).

The theme of Evangeline was suggested to Longfellow by Nathaniel Hawthorne, who had once considered writing a novel dealing with the wanderings of the Acadians. While writing the poem, Longfellow is known to have maintained a correspondence with Edward Simon, a young lawyer of St. Martinville who had been a student of his at Harvard, and to have received from Simon much help on local color and customs. So it is entirely possible that he knew the story of Emmeline Labiche. Although Longfellow never visited Louisiana, his descriptions of the Teche country and the ancient village of St. Martinville are remarkably accurate. They were doubtless partially inspired by a diorama of Louisiana exhibited in Boston and seen by Longfellow while he was writing the poem.

The park centers about an old Acadian cottage which stood near the home of Louis Arceneaux. The building is used as a museum to house early records and relics of the Acadians. The Acadians Craft House displays products of Acadian work.

The park lies within a 157-acre wooded tract. The State says it is open all year for a stay of 2 weeks, with space for 20 tents, 20 trailers; also tables, fireplaces, hot showers, snackbar, swimming, boating, fishing. Pets on leash. Fees: tents $1.03; trailers $1.29.

ST. MARTINVILLE, 115.5 *m.* (23 alt., 7,153 pop. 1970), *see St. Martinville.*

Left from St. Martinville on La 96 to PINE and OAK ALLEY, 2.4 *m.*, an avenue of pines and oaks which extends for nearly a mile. The alley, planted in 1829 by slave labor, originally extended to Bayou Teche and was 3 miles long.

At the end of the grove is a large sugar cane plantation owned prior to the War between the States by Charles J. Durand, who has contributed one of the section's most fantastic legends. In 1850, when the marriage of his daughter, Leontine, drew near, it is said that Monsieur Durand imported from China a quantity of giant spiders, which spun enormous webs between the trees in the grove; then he sprinkled the webs with gold and silver dust to form a glittering arch for his daughter's wedding procession. The Durand mansion is no longer standing, but old outhouses remain; these include a huge white brick barn, of a type more often encountered in New England than in the South, and an extensive slave village.

At LAKE CATAHOULA (Ind., sacred lake), 11 *m.*, in ancient times, the Attakapa held sacrificial ceremonies, dipping amulets and arrows in the water to render them effective and plunging their bodies beneath its surface to purify them. As a climax of the annual ceremony, the most beautiful maiden of the tribe was sacrificed to the Spirit of the Lake. Today the natives insist that it is haunted by the sacrificed Indian maidens and that on still days and moonlight nights their cries can be heard coming over the water. It is said, also, that the lake is subject to strange risings and fallings, often backing up precipitately, with bubbles covering its surface. Some believe that the lake, which is approximately 90 feet deep, was once part of the Mississippi River and that it is still connected to that stream by a subterranean passage. Recent showings of gas and oil in the vicinity may account for some of these phenomena. The lake, with large oaks overhanging its banks, is a restful spot, much frequented by picknickers and fishermen. Bass, perch, and other fish, as well as giant crabs, are caught here. Boats can be rented.

Vast stretches of the Atchafalaya swamp lie east of Catahoula Lake, where only the native fisherman, trapper, and lumberman are at home. The swamplands are rich in fur-bearing animals, especially mink, coon, and opossum, the annual catch in St. Martin Parish often equalling the value of the sugar or cotton crop. The lumber industry, while of decreased importance, still employs many natives. The Acadian lumberjack working in the swamp must possess unusual skill, for it is often necessary that he stand in a pirogue and pull a saw or swing an axe without upsetting his unsteady support. After the trees are cut, they are assembled into rafts and floated on the network of waterways to the mills. Neville Henshaw pictured the isolated lumber camps of the Atchafalaya in his adventure stories, *Aline of the Grand Woods* (1909) and *Painted Woods* (1924).

Lake Catahoula is connected by Crocodile Bayou with LAKE ROND, approximately 7 miles south, and LAKE DAUTERIVE, immediately below Lake Rond. These lakes are popular with fishermen, although the catch nowadays is largely commercial, consisting of buffalo, cat, and gaspergou. That even the native swamper and fisherman sometimes grow confused in the labyrinth of waterways here is evidenced by the names of two streams located near Lake Rond. BAYOU L'EMBARRAS, which flows into Lake Rond from the north, derived its name from the fact that certain swampers never seemed to learn which way to travel when they reached this annoying little stream. HA HA BAY, in the vicinity, caused equal trouble.

The OLD LABBÉ HOUSE (*private*), 117.2 *m.,* stands (L) fresh and white among sheltering oaks. Formerly a raised wooden cottage, it has been set level with the ground, and the unusually large dormer windows are obviously of recent addition. The most interesting feature of the interior is a curved stairway of stained cypress.

At 118.1 *m.* is the junction with a country lane.

Right here 1.5 *m.* to the LADY OF THE LAKE PLANTATION HOUSE (*open*), on a comparatively high strip of land, with Spanish Lake a short distance away on the front and Bayou Tortue at the back. It is said to have been built around 1800, but its combination of crudeness and nicety of detail suggests an even earlier year. The house is of the early type, consisting of a high brick basement and single story. A hipped roof broken by dormers and chimneys extends out over a wide porch which entirely surrounds the building. Tapering colonnettes rise above the small brick foundation piers, and a balustrade of slender wooden spindles encircles the house. Access to the upper floor is by two outside staircases. The walls of the building are of adobe made of a mixture of clay and Spanish moss, finished with cypress on the exterior and plastered within. The large fireplaces, one in each of the six rooms, have wide cypress mantels, carved with restraint, and are lined with cast-iron firebacks of handsome design. One of the mantels has served the present tenants for recording events; written thereon is the following:

> The high water came here the 24 of May, 1927.
> The storm knock here 16 August, 1934.
> The snow fell here 22 January, 1935.

At 121.5 *m.* on La 86 is the junction with a graveled road.

Left on this road to (L) BELMONT (*adm. 25¢*), 0.6 *m.*, said to have been built as a country residence by one of the Spanish governors and for the past 100 years the home of the Wyche family.

During the War between the States Major John Wyche entertained prominent Confederate leaders here, including General Dick Taylor, General Pratt and his staff, and Lieutenant Fauntleroy. Later, the Federal troops under Banks took possession of the home. Prior to this the Wyche family fled to Texas, carrying with them such valuables as they could get together, and a faithful overseer managed to cart off still other furnishings. But there can still be seen the old square piano, later found on the front lawn, where, minus its keyboard, it had served as a feeding trough for the Federals' horses.

Belmont is set at the back of a deep lawn, with large live oaks and masses of shrubbery forming a beautiful setting. It is a long, low one-and-one-half-story building with a lower floor of adobe weatherboarded over and painted white with a green trim. The gabled roof is set with two well proportioned dormer windows and is supported by eight square cypress pillars.

The home is tastefully furnished with period furniture in rosewood, mahogany, and walnut, and some rare crystal and china. Two large attic rooms are fitted up in Colonial style. The walls of the lower floor are hung with family portraits; noteworthy are several by the American artist, Thomas W. Wood, and one by Greuze.

Outhouses include an old plantation schoolhouse, where the Wyche children and those of neighboring plantations were taught, a *garçonnière,* and the remains of a sugar mill originally run by water from Spanish Lake, one of the two sugar mills in the State operated by water power.

At 123.1 *m.* on La 86 is the junction with a graveled road.

Right on this road to (L) the OLD DARBY PLACE (*open*), 0.7 *m.* A tangle of vines almost obscures the old entrance that is flanked by two faded green posts which once supported classic urns. The house is a raised cottage, brick below and wood above, and has now fallen into a state of complete dilapidation. The house dates back to about 1820.

According to legend, the Darby family descended from an English officer who commanded a vessel in the war of 1812. The first house built on the land was a log cabin and stood until the first François St. Mar Darby built the present structure for his son's bride, the lovely Félicité de St. Amand, a French beauty. The Darby family prospered and were among the socially élite of New Orleans, where they maintained a town house and a box at the French Opera. Each week end found the country home gay with guests and during the War between the States whole troops of soldiers from New Orleans were entertained. When the Union soldiers came it is said they rode through the house, breaking chandeliers and smashing furniture.

François and the beautiful Félicité died leaving three children—two boys, François and Octave, and one girl. The children were a trio of hot-tempered, eccentric people who were not used to misfortune and they became bitter and resentful. It is said that for years the brothers did not speak to each other although they lived in the same house. François let Octave know when his cattle had strayed into his allotted field by singing about it at the top of his voice. Octave, who sold milk, delivered it before dawn dressed in an old frock coat, a relic of better days.

The sister, it is said, promised all her share of the property to one of the brothers, leaving the other to his own jealous rages. As a last taunt a sealed will was left by the sister. After she died the "favored" brother immediately went to his lawyer to have the will probated and to his dismay found that the will was only a blank sheet of paper. François, who died in 1937, lived alone in the house for many years, cooking his meals in an open grate, and sleeping in an antique four-poster on a pile of hay. Heavily bearded, gimlet-eyed, and suspicious, he would have no truck with the outside world, and had the reputation of pursuing with an axe visitors whose personalities displeased him.

NEW IBERIA, 124.2 m. (19 alt., 30,147 pop. 1970), *see New Iberia.*

New Iberia is at junctions with US 90, La 14 and La 86.

ᗕᗕᗕᗕᗕᗕᗕᗕᗕᗕᗕᗕᗕᗕᗕᗕᗕᗕᗕᗕᗕᗕᗕᗕᗕ

Tour 15A

Opelousas—Washington; 2.3 m., La 103.

This route leads to several old plantation houses in the Bayou Courtableau region. La 182 proceeds north from US 190 at Opelousas. At 3.9 m. is the site of the LASTRAPES HOUSE, burned down in 1968. Both the manner of its construction—mud, moss, and sticks plastered between supporting timbers—and the inscription "Lastrapes—Octobre, 1801" scratched on two large bricks set in the rear wall of a brick annex, evidently added many years after the house was built, attested to the age of the place.

The great live oak cluster standing in the front yard, seemingly one gigantic tree, is in reality several individual oaks intermingled as one. It is 47 feet in girth. According to legend, at the beginning of the War between the States, a young man of the house came home one evening with seven oak seedlings. He earthed them in, intending to set them out the next day. That night he was called to war, never to return, and the seedlings grew where he left them.

WASHINGTON, 2.3 *m.* (42 alt., 1,473 pop. 1970), a quaint old town that has managed to maintain much of the dignity and charm of its antebellum days, was settled about 1800 and incorporated in 1835. Prior to the War between the States it was an important shipping point on Bayou Courtableau. Produce from the surrounding region was brought here for shipment down the bayou and through other waterways to various points on the Mississippi River and the Gulf Coast. Today the bayou is navigable only by pirogues, and the warehouses that once served Washington's thriving commerce stand in ruins along the bayou front.

The town is scattered over a group of small hills. Along Bayou Courtableau old oak and pecan trees screen many charming old homes, comfortable but unpretentious reminders of a more prosperous period.

On a moderate slope, on the western outskirts of the town, is the CEDAR HILL CEMETERY. Leading through the center of the cemetery is an avenue of moss-hung cedars. The effect produced by these closely planted trees is one of tranquillity; footfalls are muted by the soft ground and thick carpet of dead cedar sprays. Rays of sunshine filtering through the arched trees suggest the cool quiet of a cathedral. The graves are of all types, ranging from old vine-covered and sunken vaults enclosed by rusty iron fences to modern tombs.

At 2.3 *m.* is the junction with a dirt road; R. here 0.5 *m.* to (R) the WARTELLE HOUSE (*private*), approached through one of the longest and most beautiful avenues of water oaks in Louisiana. Near the center of the avenue is a slight swell that accentuates the height of the trees. In the distance to the left is the wooded Bayou Courtableau. The house is a one-story rambling, white frame structure with a dormered hipped roof. It was built in 1829 by Pierre Gabriel Wartelle, a captain in Napoleon's army, who came to Louisiana after Napoleon's exile to Elba. One of the heirlooms in the house, which is now the residence of a granddaughter of Captain Wartelle, is a medal sent to the officer by Napoleon III in recognition of his services under the Emperor. In the rear of the house is the old plantation bell.

The SPLANE HOUSE, 0.7 *m.*, also called OLIVIER, dates from the late eighteenth century. The first floor of faded red brick is set flush with the ground and has a wide entrance which leads to a hallway of imported brown flagstone. The central stairway is topped by a skylight. The second story, which is also of brick, has been weatherboarded. At a later date a central gable was constructed to provide a schoolroom for the children of the house. This projects over a narrow portico supported by round brick columns. The house is surrounded by a wooden scrollwork fence with an elaborately designed gateway. To the right of the house is an Indian mound, to the left, a large pond.

Right from Washington on paved road to the PAYNE HOUSE (*private*), 3.6 *m.*, a well-preserved, raised cottage built in 1849. The main story is of frame construction and surmounts a raised brick basement. The roof projects over a gallery running the width of the façade and is supported by six large round stuccoed-brick columns, which by their disproportionate size create an impression of massiveness for the house as a whole. A striking feature of the basement is the driveway which runs through it from the front to the rear of the house. Stairways rise on either side of the driveway entrance to a landing extending out from the gallery proper. The gallery railings are of cast iron.

MAGNOLIA RIDGE PLANTATION is located 6 *m.* north of Opelousas via La 103 on the Bayou Courtableau in Washington, La.

This fine house was built in 1830 under direction of Judge John Moore. It is a two-story house with six large columns and gallery. Both Confederate and Union troops used it as headquarters and later it was neglected. More recently it has been fully restored. The interior has original plank floors of heart pine and furnishings of the Louis XIV period. It was long known as the Old Prescott House.

ARLINGTON HOUSE, is another notable building in Washington. It was built in 1829 by Major Amos Webb. Built of brick, it has two stories and dormers, and pillars that reach only to the enclosed balcony. It is open daily, 10–5.

DES HOTELS is the name given to a big two and one-half story brick house owned by C. Kenneth Deshotels, a lawyer. It was built in the early 19th century by Jean Marie Lalanne and was a popular rendezvous in steamboat days. It retains its original French doors and window shutters. It stands at the junction of Bayous Cocodrie and Bœuf, which form Bayou Courtableau.

WOODLAND, also called Macland, east of La 10, is known as the Thistlethwaite place, since it is the home of the manager of the Thistlethwaite plantation. It has six massive plastered brick columns and a double gallery. A carriage drive runs through the lower floor to a double staircase.

Tour 15B

Opelousas—Sunset—Carencro—Lafayette; 25.7 *m.,* La 182. US 167 runs parallel with it to the east.

Concrete-paved roadbed.
Southern Pacific parallels route.
Accommodations at Opelousas and Lafayette.

La 182 runs south from OPELOUSAS, 0 *m.* (*see Opelousas*), through a level countryside checkered with well-ordered farms and wooded tracts. Neat and well-built homes bespeak the prosperity of the region.

The CEDAR LANE GOLF CLUB is at 2.6 *m.* In a cage at the rear of the clubhouse are beautifully plumed pheasants.

At 8.4 *m.* is the junction with a dirt road.

Right on this road to the CHRÉTIEN POINT PLANTATION HOUSE (*open*), 2.2 *m.,* a blood-red brick building with six white Doric columns rising across the front to the hipped roof. Three large doors, curved at the top in well-rounded arches, with windows between, open on the first and second floor galleries. The depth of the immense doorways reveals the thickness of the walls. The land was granted to Pierre Declouet by the Spanish in 1776.

Jules Baguerry, professional photographer, who once lived here, sent Hollywood a picture of the staircase at Chrétien. It was reproduced in *Gone With the Wind*.

SUNSET, 10.1 *m.* (45 alt., 1,675 pop. 1970), is the shipping point for a sweet potato growing section, the principal crop being Porto Rican yams.

At 10.3 *m.* is the junction (L) with La 93.

Left on this road to GRAND COTEAU, 1.3 *m.* (72 alt., 1,301 pop. 1970), a rambling village lying along the oak-bordered roadway. Although the English equivalent of Grand Coteau is "large hillock," the town is in nearly level country, broken chiefly by groves of trees. A slight rise, exaggerated by the general flatness of the land, probably suggested the name. Ancient trees, old-fashioned houses, and an air of quiet dignity mark the scene.

Grand Coteau owes its existence to the establishment of the Sacred Heart Academy in 1821 and the St. Charles College for boys in 1838. The two institutions trace their origin to the first definite cultural movement in the Teche valley. Grand Coteau was formerly a center of Catholic parochial and missionary activities. What is now the JESUIT SEMINARY, in the center of the town (L), had a notable existence as the St. Charles College for boys until 1922. Many prominent citizens of Louisiana received religious and classical education there. It is now one of the better known Catholic seminaries of the South. The main building, erected in 1909, is a three-story brick structure and serves as a residence and instruction hall for students and the Jesuit priests in charge. In the rear of the college are a Lourdes grotto, two parish churches for white and Negro congregations, a rectory, a parish hall, a parochial school, and the recently founded House of Closed Retreats for the clergy and laity of the diocese of Lafayette.

Left from Grand Coteau on an unmarked, blacktop road to (L) the COLLEGE AND ACADEMY OF THE SACRED HEART, 1.2 *m.,* founded in 1821 through the generosity of Mrs. Charles Smith to educate the daughters of Southern planters. She donated 100 acres to be used for a school and assumed the expense of bringing nuns from St. Louis. During ante bellum days pupils were registered from all over the South. The original schoolhouse, which was destroyed by fire in 1913, stood on the present convent grounds. The main convent, erected in 1831, is a three-story buff brick structure with fluted iron Corinthian columns supporting wide galleries, extending across the 300-foot frontage. Dormer windows surmount the roof at regularly spaced intervals, and numerous long windows are fitted with green batten shutters. Among the shrubbery that borders the wide lawns the luxuriant, century-old camellias are noteworthy. In 1914 the academy was empowered by the State to grant collegiate degrees. The convent archives contain many important records pertaining to the history of this section.

In 1866 a miracle was reported here and a feast day set aside for its observance. Mary Wilson, a young postulant in the convent, lay desperately ill, hope for her life given up. The Last Sacrament was administered and she was left alone. Shortly afterwards in a vision she saw the form of Blessed John Berchmans, a revered Jesuit priest. He assured her that he had come by God's will to cure her and that she would shortly be received into the Society as a novice. Returning to the infirmary, the Mother Superior was amazed to find the young girl entirely well, and able to resume her normal duties the next day. Before an ecclesiastical tribunal, held to pass upon facts to further the canonization of John Berchmans, Mary Wilson certified under a solemn oath to the miraculous cure.

CARENCRO, 18.1 *m.* (45 alt., 2,302 pop. 1970), derived its name from the Indian belief that a monster animal once died here, and that the air was thick with carrion crows. According to George W. Cable's *Bonaventure,* which has this section as its setting, the settlement was called La Chapelle in the early days when the mission chapel and the visiting *curé* formed the focal center of the community's life. In 1874 Pierre Cormier donated ground for a church to replace the chapel on the condition that the name "Carencro," which he deemed offensive, be changed to "St. Pierre." The villagers agreed, but in a short time they drifted back to the use of the more familiar appellation. The church has had a troubled history; the first two buildings were destroyed by fire, and the third by a tornado; the present building, the fourth, in the center of town, was erected in 1900.

South of Carencro is an area called BEAU BASSIN, named by the Acadians in memory of their beloved Nova Scotian homeland. Beau Bassin is characterized by gentle swells and long, winding ravines. Here, as in the section to the south, agriculture has superseded cattle raising, with cotton as the chief crop.

LAFAYETTE, 25.7 *m.* (38 alt., 68,908 pop. 1970) *see Lafayette.*

Lafayette is at junctions with US 90 (*see Tour 1c*) La 94 and Interstate 10.

Tour 16

(Magnolia, Ark.)—Haynesville—Homer—Arcadia—Campti; 91.5 *m.,* US 79, La 9.

Wild woodland scenery, at first dominated by bluffs, and later by rounded, pine clad hills, is the recurrent feature of this route. The hills, with their heavy deposits of iron salts, are noticeably red. Lumbering has removed much of the older pines and a great deal of the hardwood, but the region is still heavily forested. Farms have cotton, corn, and potatoes as their principal crops. Between the Arkansas Line and Homer the highway crosses oil and gas fields. North of Campti lakes and cypress brakes are found.

US 79 crosses the ARKANSAS LINE, 0 *m.,* 18.4 miles south of Magnolia, Arkansas.

At 2 *m.* are the derricks and storage tanks of the HAYNESVILLE OIL FIELD. Oil was discovered here about 1920 and the first commercial producer was brought in during March 1921.

HAYNESVILLE, 4.2 *m.* (364 alt., 3,055 pop. 1970), formerly located two and one-half miles south of its present site at a place known as Taylor's Store, was moved following the construction of the Louisiana and Northwest Railroad. Discovery of the Haynesville Oil Field considerably increased both the population and prosperity of the town.

The HOMER-HAYNESVILLE COUNTRY CLUB is at 13.7 *m.*

HOMER, 17.7 *m.* (258 alt., 4,483 pop. 1970), in a region of high, wooded hills and rugged ridges, is the seat of Claiborne Parish, the southern gateway to the Homer and Haynesville oil fields, and the center of the north Louisiana shortleaf pine and hardwood district.

The CLAIBORNE PARISH COURTHOUSE, standing in a landscaped square in the center of town, was built in 1848 in Greek Revival style. It is a square, two-story structure of brick painted white. An overhanging hipped roof, surmounted by a bell tower, is supported on all sides by plastered-brick columns of the Doric order. Homer is hq of the CLAIBORNE PARISH LIBRARY SYSTEM, which had 35,260 volumes and a circulation of 156,463 in 1968.

The HOMER OIL AND GAS FIELD lies just west of town. The first oil well here was drilled in 1919. The North Homer gas field has since added to Claiborne Parish prosperity. Deposits of siderite and limonite were found here by the Louisiana Geological Survey.

At 20.5 *m.* is the junction with La 9.

Here US 79 proceeds to MINDEN, where it combines with US 80 to Bossier City and Shreveport. La 9 turns southeast. A more direct route south is La 7. *See Section a.* Route of La 9 follows:

ATHENS, 28.8 *m.* (387 pop. 1970), is an agricultural town, the business section of which lies to the right of the highway.

Right from Athens on a graveled road 2.3 *m.* to the site of OLD ATHENS, on top of the highest hill (415 alt.) in Louisiana. A church, two cemeteries, and several frame buildings are all that is left of the old town. Settled during the 1830's, its name was the result of interest in the contemporary excavations of ancient Greek cities. This interest was reflected in the architecture of the day and in place names. Neighboring towns whose names were thus inspired are Homer, Arcadia, and Sparta.

In 1846 Athens was made the parish seat, but in 1849, after a disastrous fire destroyed the school and the parish offices, burning the records of the latter, the parish seat was removed to Homer.

MOUNT MORIAH METHODIST CHURCH (R), 34.9 *m.,* a white frame structure surrounded by oak and pine trees, was built in 1868 and was formerly the most influential Methodist church in this section.

WEST TOWN, 37.7 *m.,* a thickly settled Negro village, was almost completely demolished by a cyclone in May, 1933. The BIENVILLE PARISH TRAINING SCHOOL FOR NEGROES, a low red brick structure surrounded by white frame buildings, was erected by the Rosenwald Foundation in 1923 and provides grade and high school education.

ARCADIA, 39.1 *m.* (368 alt., 2,970 pop. 1970) (*see Tour 7b*), is at the junction with US 80 which is paralled by Interstate 20.

South of Arcadia La 9 winds through barren red clay hills and steep tree-covered slopes.

BRYCELAND, 47.7 *m.,* in a moderately prosperous farming district, is named for the Bryce family, whose plantation home once stood on the present townsite. Settled about 1890 and at one time incorporated, Bryceland is one of a number of older communities in this locality whose populations have drifted away.

Right from Bryceland on a graveled road 0.6 *m.* to the junction with a graveled road; L. here and L. again at 2.4 *m.,* on a narrow dirt road through beautiful woodlands to the SHILOH CHURCH, 5.1 *m.,* an unpainted frame building which stands on the SITE OF FREETOWN. Shortly after the War between the States a group of manumitted Negroes in the region were given government homesteads on this portion of Bryce Plantation. Independent for the first time in their lives, they began farming and started a few minor industries such as making baskets from oak splints, raising gourds for dippers and containers, and the manufacture of pottery from local clay. The white people of the area encouraged the colonists by buying both their farm produce and their handicraft, but when government aid was withdrawn, the colony disintegrated. It is said that after the Negroes had lived apart from white people for some time they began dropping conventional English and employing a dialect.

BIENVILLE, 54.3 *m.* (180 alt., 381 pop.), is a farming center.

Right from Bienville on graveled La 508 to the SITE OF SPARTA, 6.2 *m.,* seat of Bienville Parish from 1849 to 1893. The State legislature, in creating Bienville Parish in 1848, stipulated that the seat of the new parish should be located in the center of the area. The proposed site was found to be on an 80-acre tract of public land and one of the first acts of the newly organized parish was the filing of a writ of entry for the tract with the United States Land Office. This is believed to be the only instance on record of a parish (or county) obtaining a patent of land from the United States.

The choice of location, however, was most unfortunate. Set in a bed of sand so deep as to make walking difficult, and of a quality that has earned it an individual classification by geologists as "Sparta sand," the town was doomed from the start. When, in 1890, the Louisiana and Northwest Railroad extended its line to the present town of Bienville, 6 miles east, Sparta began a rapid decline. Many of its business houses moved to the new town at once, and the citizens soon followed. In 1893 the parish seat was moved to Arcadia and in 1894, the last business place in Sparta, a saloon, was closed.

Today nothing remains of the old town, and prickly pears grow in the deep, white sand.

LUCKY, 61.7 *m.,* is a crossroads settlement.

Left from Lucky on asphalt-paved La 4 to the SITE OF THE RAYBURN SALT WORKS, 5.3 *m.,* the scene of extensive mining operations during the War between the States. The surface of the Rayburn Dome is a flat, slightly swampy area of 40 or 50 acres surrounded by gently rising hills.

All the wells in the Rayburn area were operated in the same way. First they were sunk to the depth required to reach the salt water—usually 10 to 20 feet—and cased with poles to prevent caving. A crude hand pump was then set up to carry the salt water to 1,000-gallon evaporating kettles set above furnaces.

During the War between the States blockade of Gulf ports, people from many parts of Louisiana, and from Arkansas and Mississippi, came to make salt at the Rayburn and surrounding wells. Frequently the wives and daughters of Confederate soldiers brought their slaves to assist them in obtaining the precious commodity. At one time as many as 100 wells were in operation.

The route turns L. at 67.3 *m.*, at the junction with La 155, which unites with La 9 between this point and Saline.

SALINE, 70.2 *m.* (155 alt.), on Saline Bayou, settled in 1839, lies in a salt dome area. The center of a truck-growing region, it ships carload lots of tomatoes, watermelons, and Irish potatoes to Southern and more distant markets.

Between 71.4 *m.* and 78 *m.* La 9 cuts across the northwest corner of the CATAHOULA DIVISION of the KISATCHIE NATIONAL FOREST (*see Tour 15a*).

At 75 *m.* is READHIMER, junction with La 126.

Right on this road to (R) the HICKORY HILL OBSERVATION TOWER (*open*), 2.6 *m.*

CHESTNUT, 78.3 *m.* (261 alt.), is the trade center for the surrounding truck farms.

At 84.6 *m.* is the junction of La 9 and La 479; R. (straight ahead) on La 479.

Left on La 479 to the CATAHOULA DIVISION of the KISATCHIE NATIONAL FOREST (*See Tour 15a*), 7.4 *m.*

Right from GOLDONNA, 10.1 *m.* (141 alt., 250 pop.), on a narrow sandy road, to (R) the OLD DRAKE SALT WORKS, 1.4 *m.*, similar to the Rayburn Salt Works mentioned above. Near by is CAMP MARY MIMS, a 4-H Club Camp, named in honor of Dr. Mary Mims, extension sociologist at Louisiana State University. The camp has 18 cottages, a community kitchen, a small auditorium, and a swimming hole.

Here La 56 intersects La 479, and runs sw 20 *m.* to Creston, and La 9.

CRESTON, 85.7 *m.*, is a small fishing village on the shore of BLACK LAKE (*camps, boats, picnicking facilities*). Black bass, sunfish, and other fish abound in the lake.

On the southern shore of Black Lake live many "Redbones" (Louisiana name for a person of white, Indian, and Negro parentage) who, like the mulattoes of Isle Brevelle (*see Tour 17b*), live to themselves apart from whites and Negroes. Local traditions vary as to the origin of these people. According to one, they are descendants of early French explorers who intermarried with the Indians; another relates that in the sixteenth century a party of Portuguese sailors, shipwrecked in the Gulf of Mexico, made their way through the wilderness of central Louisiana and settled among friendly Indians. Presumably, these halfbreeds later intermarried with Negroes. Whatever their ancestry, the Redbones are tall and slender, have a reddish complexion, dark eyes, high cheek bones, and straight, black hair. The strange semitransparent appearance of their skin is responsible for their odd sobriquet. Strangers frequently trade and in some instances form friendships with them, but as a whole the group maintains a stoical reserve which cannot be completely broken.

South of Creston La 9 crosses Black Lake Bridge, affording a view of the lake and the surrounding country. Black Lake, and two other near-by lakes, Clear and Saline, are part of the O. K. ALLEN FISH AND GAME PRESERVE, named for the former governor of the State. This preserve comprises an area of 35 square miles and was completed in 1932 with the building of a dam across Saline Bayou.

CAMPTI, 91.5 m. (125 alt., 1,100 pop.), is at the junction with US 17–84 (see Tour 18b).

Section a. ALTERNATIVE ROUTE SOUTH FROM ARKAN-SAS TO NATCHITOCHES, LA 7

One of the highways that crosses the Arkansas border from Magnolia, Ark., and runs parallel with US 71 and US 79 is La 7, which extends from Springhill to Coushatta. At SPRINGHILL (8,000 pop. est.) it has a junction with east-west La 157. This is a center for pulp and paper, oil, resins and farm products. West of Springhill and COTTON VALLEY, is the 7,000-acre LAKE ERLING, formed by the Percy Cobb Dam. The Bayou Bodcau Wildlife Area is located here. In its progress south La 7 passes Caney Lakes, has a junction with US 79 five miles west of Minden, and after crossing Int. 20 proceeds south via SIBLEY and RINGGOLD until it meets the combined US 71 and 84 at COUSHATTA and all proceed south to Campti, Clarence, and via junction with La 6 to Natchitoches.

ᛏᛡ

Tour 17

(Lewisville, Ark.)—Plain Dealing—Shreveport—Armistead—Natchitoches—Alexandria—Marksville—New Roads—Junction with US 190; 280.1 m., La 3, US 79–80, La 1, La 5, La 299, La 30, La 49, La 93.

Railroads paralleling route: St. L. SW, between Arkansas and Shreveport; T. & P. between Shreveport and Alexandria; L. & A. between Alexandria and Torras; T. & P. between Torras and New Roads.
Accommodations in larger towns only.

Section a. ARKANSAS LINE to SHREVEPORT; 37.1 m., La 3, US 79–80

La 3, a continuation of Ark 29, crosses the Arkansas Line, 27.8 miles south of Lewisville, Arkansas, and runs due south to Shreveport through cut-over timberland and a farming region where the decline in cotton production has seen a corresponding increase in truck farming and cattle raising. Oil and gas developments have helped the industrial activities of this section.

ARKANA, 0 *m.* (244 alt.), a farming village on the Arkansas-Louisiana boundary, whose name is an abbreviation of the two States, lies almost entirely in Arkansas.

BOLINGER, 5.2 *m.* (313 alt.), a sawmill and farming village, was named for a family long identified with the lumber industry in north Louisiana.

PLAIN DEALING, 8.2 *m.* (266 alt., 2,116 pop. 1970; 1,357, 1960; inc. 55%), another sawmill and farming town, was founded in 1887 on land settled by the Gilmer family, wealthy planters from Virginia.

BENTON, 23 *m.* (210 alt., 1,493 pop. 1970), the seat of Bossier Parish, was founded just prior to the War between the States. In 1888, after a controversy with the town of Bellevue, Benton was chosen as the parish seat. Backed by a legal technicality, however, the citizens of Bellevue refused to give up the parish records; two years later they were spirited away by Benton citizens.

The Bossier Parish Library has its headquarters in Benton. It has a collection of 40,000 vols. and offers a group of reading and reference services, with recordings and periodicals. It has the cooperation of Louisiana State Library. It has branches in Bossier City, at 718 Benton Rd.; Plain Dealing, and Haughton.

WILLOW CHUTE COMMUNITY, 25.4 *m.,* and the surrounding plantation area are the scene of many of the Negro stories written by Roark Bradford.

At 35.1 *m.* is the junction of La 3 and US 79–80 (*see Tour 7b*); R. on US 79–80.

SHREVEPORT, 37.1 *m.* (225 alt., 182,064 pop. 1970), *see Shreveport*.

Shreveport is at junctions with US 79–80 (*see Tour 7b*), US 171 (*see Tour 19b*), US 71 (*see Tours 18 and 19a*) and Interstate 20.

Section b.   SHREVEPORT to ALEXANDRIA; 127.6 m., La 1

This section of the route parallels the west bank of Red River to Alexandria through a region rich in historical associations.

Southeast of SHREVEPORT, 0 *m.,* La 1 runs between Red River and Bayou Pierre for a distance of 34 miles. Early in the nineteenth century, before Captain Henry Shreve removed the Great Raft from Red River (*see Shreveport*), Bayou Pierre served as a detour for river traffic. The strip of land between the river and the bayou became known as Hart's Island, and La 1 is still referred to locally as the Hart's Island Road. The island was built up by the river and bayou. When northwestern Louisiana was settled, this land was among the first to be put into cultivation, and today plantations of from three to 15 square miles in area line the highway. At intervals hills of the ridge dividing the valleys of the Red and Sabine Rivers are visible, while at times the levee of Red River is in sight.

LUCAS, 9.7 *m.* (159 alt.), was settled by Italians who are engaged in dairying and truck-gardening for the Shreveport market.

Right from Lucas at the railroad station on a blacktop road to a path 1.9 *m.*, at the western end of the bridge crossing Bayou Pierre; L. on this path 300 yards up the bluff overlooking the bayou to an old cedar, which is said to stand near the site of the CADDO INDIAN AGENCY HOUSE (*see Shreveport*).

ROBSON, 13.4 *m.* (155 alt.), is a plantation village.

GAYLE, 15.1 *m.* (152 alt.), was named for the Gayle family, one-time owners of the land on which the village stands.

CASPIANA, 20.8 *m.* (148 alt., 250 pop.), is the center of a large pecan-growing area.

HARMON, 39.4 *m.* (153 alt.), is a shipping point for cotton and the site of an oil field.

GAHAGAN, 41.7 *m.* (134 alt.), is at the junction with US 84 (*see Tour 5b*), which unites with La 1 between here and Armistead.

ARMISTEAD, 44.5 *m.* (131 alt.), occupies a portion of what was once the 1,400-acre farm of T. R. Armistead.

At Armistead US 84 branches east, crossing Red River by bridge to Coushatta at the junction with US 71 (*see Tour 18b*).

In the vicinity of HANNA, 48.2 *m.* (161 alt.), are cotton gins and general stores. In 1932 the entire Hanna area was flooded by Red River.

POWHATAN, 58.8 *m.* (121 alt., 277 pop. 1970), is sustained chiefly by cotton and corn crops.

At 69.6 *m.,* opposite a cemetery, is a junction with a dirt road.

Left on this road to a fork, 0.2 *m.;* R. here to the SITE OF CAMP SALUBRITY, 1.8 *m.,* on a high ridge covered with oak and pine. To the west is an excellent view of Kisatchie Wold (*see Tour 17B*), a series of rugged hills. In 1844 General Zachary Taylor's "Army of Observation" was stationed 24 miles west of Natchitoches, in expectation of hostilities with Mexico. Many troops were assembled there, and the meager resources and supplies of the rough frontier camp were greatly overtaxed. For that reason, as well as to save transportation, the 4th Infantry, a part of Taylor's forces, was ordered to a new location north of Natchitoches. This location, which proved to be both beautiful and healthful, was called Camp Salubrity. U. S. Grant, who was at that time a brevet-lieutenant in General Taylor's infantry, later referred to his stay here as one of the most agreeable periods of his life.

NATCHITOCHES, 71.1 *m.* (120 alt., 15,974 pop. 1970) *see Natchitoches.* The city is at junctions with La 6 and La 1 (*see Tours 5b and 17A*).

At 71.9 *m.* is the junction with La 494, which runs parallel to La 1.

Straight ahead on La 494, which winds with CANE RIVER LAKE, a former course of Red River. The lake has been made a game and fish preserve (*closed season February 1—May 1; obtain permit, good for 7 days, at courthouse in Natchitoches*), and is stocked regularly with fish from the Federal Fish Hatchery.

Camps where boats, bait, and guides are available, are found at frequent intervals.

At 6.5 *m.* La 494 crosses Cane River Lake and parallels its south shore.

The ACHILLE PRUDHOMME HOUSE (*private*), 7.2 *m.,* behind an avenue of live oaks (R), is a century-old raised cottage, home of C. E. Cloutier.

The SOMPAYRAC PLANTATION HOUSE (*private*), 7.6 *m.,* was built (R) in the 1850's by Mrs. Emile Sompayrac. It is a one-story house of frame over mud and moss construction and is set on brick pillars. In the dining room can still be seen a punka, or old-fashioned ceiling fan, once pulled by a slave during family meals.

The NARCISSE PRUDHOMME HOUSE (*open*), 9.7 *m.,* built about 1840, is a wide one-and-one-half-story frame building with four French doors opening on the front gallery. The old underground cistern for drinking water can be seen at the front.

The BERMUDA (PRUDHOMME) PLANTATION HOUSE (*adm.*), 10.7 *m.,* is a large white frame structure set on whitewashed brick pillars in a cluster of trees and shrubs. The plantation was settled in 1718 by Emanuel Prudhomme, who planted the first cotton in Louisiana. The house was built by Phanor Prudhomme in 1821, and has since been inhabited by eight generations of his descendants. In the basement is a collection of farm, surgical, and workingman's implements dating from the War between the States.

The route crosses Cane River Lake at 10.8 *m.* and turns R. on unmarked La 119 through a section known as LA CÔTE JOYEUSE (Fr., happy coast).

MELROSE (*private*), 16.2 *m.,* is hidden (L) behind the foliage of its 3 acres of gardens. The original house, erected in 1833, is of the simple Louisiana raised cottage type, the first floor of brick and the second of wood. Modern additions to the building are two hexagonal structures, one at each side of the main building, and a rear wing. To the rear of the big house is a hutlike structure unique in Louisiana, which looks as if it belonged in Africa rather than North America. It is of whitewashed brick, square in shape, with a hipped, shingled roof that blocks the second floor from view and overhangs at the sides to such an extent as to provide shelter for wagons and teams. To the left of it is a cabin built of cypress timbers chinked with mud and moss, which was formerly a slave hospital. The house has an outstanding library of Louisiana and other Southern material, including a collection of scrapbooks compiled over many years. Many writers, research workers, and artists have worked at Melrose.

Right from Melrose on a graveled road across Cane River to ISLE BREVELLE, 0.5 *m.,* an area lying between Bayou Brevelle and Cane River. The colony of some 2,000 mulattoes who inhabit Isle Brevelle had its origin in the eighteenth century as a sanctuary for the offspring of white planters and their mulatto or Negro mistresses. In those days the children of such alliances and the mistress themselves were often manumitted and endowed with sufficient means to make them independent. They were known as "free mulattoes," or "free people of color," and many of them owned plantations and Negro slaves. As early as 1836 they lived lives of luxury; and for more than a century they have had their own church and school.

The members of the families have intermarried extensively, with the result that family names, most of them French, are repeated over and over. Today, the majority have small cotton farms. Some of their houses are of old architecture, and in the interiors hang family portraits, painted between 1830 and 1840.

Almost all of the mulattoes of Isle Brevelle are Roman Catholic, and on Sunday St. Augustine's Church, on the island, is crowded with worshipers. Some years ago the community was untouched by railroad or highway, and the roads were little more than trails along the river banks. Isle Brevelle provides the setting for *Children of Strangers,* by Lyle Saxon, a novel based on the lives of Cane River mulattoes.

MAGNOLIA PLANTATION HOUSE (*open*), 21 *m.,* on La 423, is (L) a one-and-one-half-story brick house built a few years after the close of the War between the States by Mathew Hertzog on the foundation of a former house burned during the war. The stocks in which slaves were punished can still be seen under the front gallery. Among the relics preserved is a silver tray won by the famous race horse, "Flying Dutchman," in New Orleans in 1850. The horse is buried under a large sycamore tree which stands to the left. To the right are brick slave cabins.

At 22.3 *m.* is Derry (*see below*).

At 72.9 *m.* on La 1 is (L) a U. S. FISH HATCHERY (*open; free guide service*), the only Federal fish hatchery in Louisiana. Situated along Cane River Lake, the hatchery is approximately 100 acres in area and contains 35 one- and two-acre ponds which are used for the propagation of various fresh-water game fish. Lakes and streams of Louisiana and portions of Texas, Arkansas, and Oklahoma are stocked from this station.

NATCHEZ, 77.9 *m.* (105 alt.), was the scene of the "bringing in," in 1823, of Louisiana's first gas well. While drilling for water (a novelty in that day) with hand-forged drills designed by a visiting French engineer, gas was encountered at 400 feet. Unaware of the value of gas, the plantation owner, Pierre Emanuel Prudhomme, abandoned the well.

MONTROSE, 85.9 *m.* (102 alt., 300 pop.), is a sawmill village in whose vicinity many objects of importance to botanical and paleontological research have been found. The articles include worked prints, discards, and fragments of silicated wood, some of which are believed to date from the Cenozoic Age. Petrified wood specimens have been found which are credited to the Pleistocene Age. The largest of these specimens, which has been identified as a section of palm trunk, is 30 inches high, 5 feet in circumference, and weighs 297 pounds. A few fragments show artificial chipping, attributed to aboriginal peoples. Some of the specimens discovered are on exhibit at the Williamson Museum (*see Natchitoches*).

DERRY, 89 *m.* (109 alt.), at the junction with La 119, is the center of the 6,000-acre DERRY PLANTATION. The house (*private*) is a large, ornate 50-year-old frame structure ornamented with gables, turrets, and balconies typical of the time.

South of Derry the route continues on La 1.

At 90.8 *m.* on La 1, at the western end of the bridge crossing Cane River Lake, is the junction with a dirt road.

Right on this road to a fork, 0.1 *m.;* R. here to SANG POUR SANG (Fr., blood for blood) HILL, 2.6 *m.,* a high, rocky, tree-studded hill overlooking a lake of the same name, now dry. On the shores of this lake, in 1732, a band of Natchez, fleeing from an unsuccessful attack on Natchitoches, was annihilated by the French and their Indian allies. The climb to the top is long, but the view is worth the exertion. Spread out on one side is Cane River valley, with its lush fields and winding river; on the other is a heavily wooded spot with a view of distant hills. This is an excellent picnic spot except for the lack of water.

CLOUTIERVILLE, 91 *m.* (100 alt.), occupying part of the old Alexander Cloutier Plantation, was incorporated in 1822. In the western part of town is the BAYOU FOLK MUSEUM, once the home of Kate Chopin, author of *Bayou Folk* and *Nights in Acadia*. It is a raised dwelling set in a pleasant garden.

At 98.8 *m.* is the junction with an unimproved road.

Right on this road to CHOPIN, 1 *m.* (107 alt.), the site of the OLD CHOPIN PLANTATION which Lammy Chopin bought from Robert McAlpin. It is believed by some that McAlpin, who came from New England, was the original Simon Legree of Harriet Beecher Stowe's *Uncle Tom's Cabin*. Mrs. Stowe used a plantation on Red River as the scene of her book, but it is not known that she was ever in this section of the State. One of the plantation's old slave cabins was exhibited at the Chicago World's Fair in 1893 as the original home of Uncle Tom. The place is now known as LITTLE EVA PLANTATION.

ZIMMERMAN, 110.5 *m.* (93 alt.), near the bank of Red River, is a sawmill town operated by the J. A. Bentley Company. While lumbering is the chief industry, fishing adds considerably to the community's income. Until 1935 the town was subject to inundation, and high-water marks are still visible on houses near the highway. In that year the lumber company constructed a levee around Zimmerman.

At 112.3 *m.* is the junction with paved La 121. (La 1, straight ahead, is a paved and shorter route to Alexandria but lacks the points of interest to be found on La 121).

Right here on La 121 to the BLANCHARD HOUSE (*open*), 1.4 *m.,* a low rambling frame structure (R), once the home of the late Newton C. Blanchard, former U. S. Senator (1894–97) and Governor of Louisiana (1904–08). South of here Bayou Jean de Jean, which parallels (R) the highway, has numerous cedar trees on its banks.

HOT WELLS, 5.4 *m.,* is prospering with the development of the Hot Wells Health Resort. During oil-drilling operations here about 1922 an artesian well with water of a temperature of more than 116 degrees and of some medicinal value was brought in. South of Hot Wells the highway follows (R) Bayou Rapides. There are several syrup mills in the neighborhood operated by horse power.

At 6.9 *m.* is the junction with a private road; R. here to (L) CASTILLE (*open*), 0.8 *m.,* which faces Bayou Rapides. It is a raised cottage with a gabled roof built sometime prior to 1840.

The EDEN PLANTATION HOUSE (*open*), at 7.3 *m.* on La 278, was built (L) by Benjamin Kitchen Hunter, before the War between the States. It is a one-and-one-half-story frame house.

At 9.8 *m.* La 121 joins La 28.

Right on La 28 1.7 *m.,* to the EVANGELINE DIVISION of the KISATCHIE NATIONAL FOREST. At 4.5 *m.* is the junction with a graveled road; L. here 0.9 *m.* to the junction with a graveled road; R. here and R. again at 2.9 *m.* to the VALENTINE LAKE RECREATION AREA, 3.2 *m.,* which has been developed by the U. S. Forest Service around a 70-acre lake, formed by the construction of a 600-foot dam. Facilities include docks, boat slips, a bathhouse and pavilion, camp and picnic sites, bathing beaches, cabins, and an athletic field.

At 15 *m.* on the main side route is TYRONE (*private*), an ante bellum home (L) which has been considerably remodeled. It once was the property of General Sprague of New Orleans and later of General Mason Graham. General William T. Sherman was a frequent guest here before the war. On the upstairs door of the old carriage house, to the rear, sword marks made by the Federals attempting to gain entrance are still visible.

CEDAR GROVE (*open*), 15.4 *m.,* is a one-and-one-half-story frame house, notable for the thickness of its tongue-and-groove planking. Letters and papers found in an old chimney dismantled in 1914 were at that time 156 years old. In the interior is a painting attributed to Jacques David. It shows a camouflaged Napoleon standing against a large tree which, in the illusion, appears as two trees, and looking at a tomb above which is his star of destiny. It was brought to America by Jean David.

The KENT PLANTATION HOUSE (*private*), 20.5 *m.*, is a raised cottage of plaster-covered mud and moss construction. According to local tradition it was built towards the close of the eighteenth century by Pierre Baillo. Rectangular frame wings were added in the 1820's. In the house are elaborate fireplaces and fine woodwork.

East of BOYCE, 113.3 *m.* (95 alt., 1,240 pop. 1970). La 1 traverses a swampy area of tupelo gum, willow, and heavy underbrush.

At 126.3 *m.* is the junction with US 71 (*see Tour 18b*), which unites with La 1 into Alexandria.

ALEXANDRIA, 127.6 *m.* (79 alt., 41,557 pop. 1970) *see Alexandria-Pineville.*

Alexandria is at junctions with US 165 (*see Tour 13*), US 71, US 167, La 28 and La 107, (*see Tours 15 and 18*).

Section c. ALEXANDRIA to JUNCTION WITH US 190;
115.4 m., La 1, La 452, La 114, La 417, La 93

This section of the route, leaving Alexandria on Third Street, continues along the west bank of Red River to Echo, where the highway swings away southeastwardly to skirt the Mississippi River in the northern peak of the Sugar Bowl.

Southeast of ALEXANDRIA, 0 *m.* La 1, closely following Red River, traverses a section peopled by descendants of the Acadian exiles.

The ALEXANDRIA AIRPORT is at 4.3 *m.*

ECHO, 19.1 *m.* (60 alt.), was settled in the early nineteenth century by second and third generation Acadians from the bayou region to the south (*see Tour 1c*). The name is accounted for by a story to the effect that during the days of river commerce the blasts from steamboat whistles on near-by Red River reverberated through the countryside for several minutes. French is spoken in the Echo neighborhood, particularly among the older people, and holiday festivals follow the customs of pioneer days. Hog butcherings and "beef clubs" are events in the community life (*see Folkways*).

MARKSVILLE, 31.5 *m.* (87 alt., 4,519 pop. 1970), was settled in the latter part of the eighteenth century by Acadians. It is the seat of Avoyelles Parish, named for the Avoyel Indians. During the War between the States this neighborhood saw much fighting.

In Marksville is the junction of La 452 and La 1; R. on La 452.

Left from Marksville on a concrete-paved road to a fork, 1 *m.*; R. here on a graveled road to the old breastworks of FORT DE RUSSEY (L), 3.5 *m.* During the war this fort was alternately held by the Confederate and Union forces and saw action on several occasions. The site is now a picnic spot.

At 31.7 *m.* on La 452 is the junction with a graveled road. Left on this road to the junction with a dirt road, 0.2 *m.*; R. here to MARKSVILLE PREHISTORIC INDIAN PARK, a State monument. The park is enclosed by a low earthen embankment that touches the bluff overlooking Old River at points a half mile apart. Within this area, occupying the site of a prehistoric village, are six Indian mounds. Research under the direction of the Smithsonian Institution has unearthed many relics which are now in the National Museum at Washington.

Archaeologists have assigned the Marksville People to the earliest period of Louisiana prehistory.

At 32.7 *m.* is the junction with a field road. Left here 0.4 *m.* to a TUNICA INDIAN SETTLEMENT inhabited by six families of Indians who hold their lands on the basis of grants made to their ancestors during the Spanish domination. This group, a handful of people in all, is still an organized tribe with a duly elected chief. All civil matters, as well as punishment of any member, are handled within the tribe, which retains some of the old customs. A few speak a Tunica dialect. Although they live on the 170 acres, these Indians claim that the original grand was for 1,247 acres. The property is not a reservation and the Indians are not under the supervision of the Federal Government.

Every year on a Saturday, at the beginning of the corn harvest (usually in July), an ancient festival is celebrated. A ceremony similar to Christian baptism is held in Old River, after which the Indians parade to the settlement to hold a feast in which corn is the chief item and of which no one has partaken until then.

La 1 continues southeast from Marksville through small farms peopled by Acadians. On the front porches of many of the homes hang cedar water buckets and gourd drinking cups. The Angelus is tolled at six in the evenings and on Saturday evening serves as a signal for the setting of clocks, a precaution against being late for early Sunday mass.

MANSURA, 36.7 *m.* (78 alt., 1,699 pop. 1970), is in a sugar cane and cotton-growing region.

La 1 crosses BAYOU DES GLAISES (La.-Fr., bayou of the saltlicks), 40 *m.,* which derived its name from the numerous saltlicks in the region. Immediately across the bayou is the junction with La 114.

La 114 crosses the guide levee of the WEST ATCHAFALAYA FLOODWAY (*see Tour 18A*), 42.7 *m.,* a levee-bordered corridor adjacent to the Atchafalaya River, used, when the emergency arises, to carry off highstage water from the Red or Mississippi Rivers. The levee (L) paralleling the highway in this section is a "fuse-plug" levee, which would be topped by waters reaching a stage dangerous to the higher levees confining the stream along the rest of its course.

HAMBURG, 46.2 *m.* (46 alt.), lies on the bank of Bayou des Glaises.

The majority of its settlers were immigrants from Hamburg, Germany, who were attracted to the locality by the fertility of the soil near the bayou. Dutch clover is the chief crop grown.

SIMMESPORT, 54.5 *m.* (42 alt., 2,027 pop. 1970), is a commercial fishing center on the west bank of Atchafalaya (Ind., long river) River, near the confluence of the Red and Old Rivers. Simmesport, like Melville to the south (*see Tour 18A*), is surrounded by a levee to protect it from flood waters of the Red and Mississippi Rivers. The network of small streams interlacing the section attracts many fishermen. Deer, bear, and squirrel are hunted in the dense forests and swamps.

LEGONIER, 55.5 *m.* (45 alt.), on Atchafalaya River, opposite Simmesport, is the point where General Banks and his Federal Army made a hurried crossing of the river in the spring of 1864, ending the retreat after the Red River Valley campaign.

After crossing the Atchafalaya La 1 moves on to LETTSWORTH.

Right from Legonier on unmarked, graveled La 417 to McCREA, 8.5 *m.* (40 alt.). At this point a break in the Atchafalaya, known as the McCrea Crevasse, occurred during the great flood of 1927. For a time Army engineers were seriously concerned with the possibility that the Mississippi was changing its course to the Atchafalaya Basin.

WHITE HALL (*open*), at 56.6 *m.* on La 49, was owned during the War between the States by General B. B. Simms. Many stories are told of General Simms' persuasive powers in conversation. On one occasion when two determined men came to collect a long over-due mortgage, they were so well entertained by the general that no opportunity developed in which to talk business and they went away emptyhanded. On another occasion it is said that he was seen by his wife kissing another woman. When she flew into a rage, he denied everything and said calmly, "Well, my dear, are you going to believe me or your own eyes?" "You, of course, darling," his wife replied. The Union general, Banks, used the house as his headquarters for a time. White Hall was originally more than twice as large as it is now. When it was moved back from the river in 1913 the greater part had to be left behind.

Atop the levee, at THREE RIVERS, 60.3 *m.,* is an excellent view. Here the Atchafalaya branches from Red River and Old River, or the "Mud Hole," which connects the two streams with the Mississippi, six miles southeast. Except when the Mississippi reaches flood stage and its waters back into Old River, Red River flows into both the Atchafalaya and Old River, the former normally carrying the larger volume of Red River water.

The point where the old mouth of Red River joined the Mississippi is said to be the burial place of DE SOTO. Here the great explorer fell ill and, anticipating death, appointed as his successor one of his followers, Luis de Moscoso de Alvarado. Moscoso caused the leader's body to be buried at night with great secrecy, for De Soto had led the Indians to believe that the whites were immortal. However, the Indians were aware of the commander's illness, and Moscoso, fearing they would learn the truth, had the remains disinterred and reburied in the great stream De Soto discovered. So runs the legend.

TORRAS, 64.6 *m.* (45 alt.), prior to 1831, was on the Mississippi River. It was a fast-growing port for the steamboat traffic of the Red, Atchafalaya, Black, and Ouachita Rivers until Shreve's Cutoff in 1831 shifted the course of the Mississippi to the east and cut short its development.

PHILLIPSTON (or FILSTON), 66.4 *m.,* is near the point where Captain Henry Shreve engineered a change in the Mississippi's course which became know as Shreve's Cutoff. This change shortened the course of the river by 15 miles and formed Turnbull's Island. Across the river from this point are Angola and the farms of the Louisiana State Penitentiary (*see Tour 10A*).

RED RIVER LANDING (L), 67.4 *m.,* its original site long ago eaten away by the river, was once a busy river port and a rendezvous for Mississippi River gamblers.

The RACCOURCI CUTOFF (L), 69.7 *m.,* a 19-mile short cut in the Mississippi, was made in 1848. The old river bed was named Raccourci (Fr., shortened) Old River, and the island formed, Raccourci Island. It is now uninhabited and is a popular hunting ground.

According to local belief, the ghost of an old steamboat haunts the Cutoff. On the night the river changed its course a boat entered the old channel in fog and rain. Hitting a sand bar, it backed off only to hit another. Enraged by these untimely obstructions, the pilot began to curse the boat, the crew, and the treacherous river. At the top of his voice he shouted that he'd be damned if he cared whether the boat got out or stayed in the bend until doomsday. His wish was granted. Trapped forever in the Cutoff, the old paddle wheeler can be heard on foggy nights chugging back and forth, the signal bell jangling and the pilot cursing.

ST. STEPHEN'S EPISCOPAL CHURCH (R), 71.5 *m.,* is a small, modified Gothic structure of red brick, with aborted buttresses and slender arched windows. The stained windows came from England. The church, finished in 1859, was consecrated by Bishop Leonidas Polk.

At 72.9 *m.* is the junction with unmarked, graveled La 972.

Right on this road along Bayou Latenache (L), which derives its name from a corruption of *latanier* (Fr., fan-palmetto), to the house (R) which legend refers to as the ZACHARY TAYLOR HOUSE (*open*), 2.9 *m.* Parish records show no ownership of land in Pointe Coupée by Zachary Taylor; the place was probably owned by his brother, "Colonel" William Taylor. It is a one-and-one-half-story frame house set on a high brick basement. Before the War between the States Mrs. Betty Taylor Bliss, daughter of the President, was a frequent visitor. Legend also connects the President's name with the large plantation bell. It is said that he returned from the Mexican campaign with many Mexican silver dollars and had the bell cast, using some of the silver to improve its tone.

A large section of land south of this junction once formed the LATENACHE PLANTATION. During the great flood of 1779 most of the inhabitants left the region. In 1810, when much of the land in this vicinity was granted to the Marquis de Lafayette in payment for his services in the Revolutionary War, many of the former homesteaders returned to contest Lafayette's claim. The American Government recognized the claims of certain settlers and gave them specie equal to their lost lands; others were dispossessed. Latenache Plantation was purchased from the heirs of General Lafayette by James Hopkins before the War between the States and was later acquired by James Innis, Irish immigrant. The descendants of Innis possess two of the Lafayette grants signed by President James Madison and give to James Innis on his purchase of the plantation.

LAKESIDE PLANTATION HOUSE (*private*), 76.3 *m.,* built (R) in the early 1860's for Charles Stewart, a planter, is reached through an avenue of live oaks. It is a raised cottage, brick below and frame above. Sixteen tall red brick pillars enclose the high whitewashed basement and support the gallery, which has a wide central iron stairway and delicate cast-iron railings. The low hipped roof, broken by three dormer windows, is supported by the iron pillars of the gallery.

The site of CREOLE LANDING, a busy cotton-shipping point during early steamboat days, is at 77.9 *m*. According to legend Federal and Confederate prison boats landed here to exchange prisoners, a feast and dance being held jointly. At the conclusion of the truce the vessels hoisted flags and a state of war was resumed.

The one-story frame cottage (*private*) with four gables (R), 79.3 *m.*, is the Birthplace of JOHN ARCHER LEJEUNE, commander of the 2nd Division of the U. S. Army in World War I. This Louisiana-born soldier also served in the Spanish-American War and the Occupation of Vera Cruz in 1914. After the World War Major General LeJeune was in command of the U. S. Marine Corps and later was appointed Superintendent of the Virginia Military Institute.

The OLD HICKORY PLANTATION HOUSE (*private*), 79.5 *m.*, built more than a century ago and considerably remodeled, is a raised cottage once occupied by Captain Ovide LeJeune, father of the Major General. During Reconstruction the plantation was owned by Dr. Archer at the time of a Negro uprising. The blacks planned to set fire to the house and kill the family as they fled, but the plot was revealed by a faithful Negro, who persuaded them to spare the house and its occupants. They ambushed Dr. Archer, however, and made an unsuccessful attempt to shoot him. This led to a lynching of the Negroes by the Bulldozers, a group of whites.

Between 79.6 *m*. and 86.2 *m*. the highway crosses the MORGANZA FLOODWAY, a companion outlet area to the West Atchafalaya Floodway (*see Tour 18A*).

The LACOUR HOUSE (*open*), 79.9 *m.*, whose fallen plaster reveals *briqueté entre poteaux* construction, was long occupied by Mrs. Mary Lacour, who, nearing her ninetieth birthday, recalled the visits of Federal troops to the homes in this section during the War between the States. The soldiers carried buckets of tar and a brush and, if food was scarce or the fortunes of war against them, they were likely to apply tar to the side of a house and set it afire.

MULATTO BEND, 80.1 *m.*, is an old settlement of mulattoes of French descent, many of whom now speak a French patois.

Near a cedar standing by the roadside at 80.2 *m*. is a ground cistern with a queer dome-like superstructure. Here once stood the house of "Mondu" Decuir, a clock mender and bricklayer who came to Pointe Coupée in the early 1800's. His eye was caught by a rich mulatto woman, but marriage between white and colored was prohibited by law. According to the legend, Decuir opened a vein in his arm, placed a drop of her blood in his vein, and swore that he had Negro blood in him. The marriage took place and on the records they are shown as Negroes. The small body of water across the levee is still known as "Bay of Mondu."

MORGANZA, 87.1 *m*. (35 alt., 836 pop. 1970), was named for Colonel Charles Morgan, owner of vast lands in the early nineteenth century. Colonel Morgan was a member of the first legislature convened in the newly formed State of Louisiana. In a letter to his nephew the Colonel describes a phenomenon which took place in the early morning hours of November 13, 1833. He wrote: "There came on a complete shower of stars. They fell for two hours from the clouds, as thick and fast as a July shower of rain, and continued until the sun destroyed their light . . . the earth was so illuminated at intervals that a pin could be seen at any moderate distance . . . the thermometer sank from 45 degrees to 35 degrees in an hour, the night was very fine, clear . . . the stars had a falling angle of 35 degrees from northeast to northwest." The plantation Negroes were badly frightened, and many superstitious rumors circulated among them. Later slaves reckoned their age by "the year the stars fell."

Following the Red River Valley retreat of General Banks, Federal cavalry under the command of General Emory went into camp at Morganza. This marked the closing days of the unsuccessful invasion of northwestern Louisiana.

At Morganza La 10 joins La 1 for 11 miles as far as New Roads, then crosses the River east on a free ferry.

In LABARRE, 90.8 m. (32 alt.), is a hamlet on the River Road.

STONEWALL PLANTATION HOUSE (*open*), 93.7 m., is a yellow one-and-one-half-story frame house set on a whitewashed brick basement. Two red brick *pigeonniers* flank the house in the front. An 1859 map shows this place belonging to Stephen Van Winkle (actually *Van Wickle*), and, according to legend, as Admiral Porter was passing with his gunboats he inquired as to the identity of the owner. He was told that the name was Van Winkle. "Well, wake up old Rip," said the Admiral, and a cannon ball was fired through the planter's house.

The new ST. FRANCIS CHURCH (Roman Catholic), 94.8 m., a white frame structure (R) was built in the 1890's. A mission was established at the Post of Pointe Coupée, and baptisms were recorded as early as 1728, but it was not until 1738 that Father Anselm de Langres erected the oratory at Pointe Coupée. The old church was moved three times to escape the encroachment of the water, and it was demolished in 1891 when another move would have been necessary. A model built from scraps of the old church has been preserved by Mr. James Stoneker. The altar, pews, confessional, candlesticks, and bell (bearing the date 1719) are in the new church, as are two old paintings—the *Holy Family* and a *Madonna*.

The LABATUT HOUSE (*private*), 95 m., is said not to have been remodeled since its construction by a Spaniard, Evariste Bara, more than 150 years ago. It is a raised cottage, brick below and frame above. The dining room still contains a punka. To the rear is a courtyard with an old marble sundial.

ST. MAURICE OAK, 95.1 m., was once one of the largest live oaks in the State. Several of the limbs were sawed off to make room for road and levee construction. The trunk reached 11 feet in diameter.

At the SITE OF ST. MAURICE LANDING, 95.6 m., during low water, part of the iron prow of the *J. M. White* sticks up through the sand of the batture. The steamboat was destroyed by fire in January, 1886, with a loss of more than 80 cabin passengers.

At 98.1 *m.* is the junction with a graveled road.

Left on this road 2.7 *m.* to the ST. FRANCISVILLE FERRY LANDING opposite St. Francisville (*see Tours 4 and 10a*).

The strip of river bank here was once the site of the POST OF POINTE COUPÉE, the oldest settlement on the lower Mississippi. In the early eighteenth century Canadian trappers came to this section from the Illinois country. Some of them took Indian wives and a colony was formed. In 1719 the concession at Pointe Coupée was granted to M. de Meuse. After the establishment of a military and trading post plantations were cultivated along the river bank. Before the middle of the century many of the settlers had become wealthy. The Pointe Coupée seen by the early travelers as "a village 21 miles in length" still exists today, in that there is an almost continuous line of houses along the river front; however, nothing is left of the old village, as the levee has been moved back many times.

At 100.5 *m.* is the junction of La 1 and La 10; continue on La 1.

NEW ROADS, 101 *m.* (35 alt., 3,945 pop. 1970), is on the northern shore of False River, an oxbow lake. This horseshoe-shaped body of water was once the channel of the Mississippi, and was isolated by a cutoff early in the eighteenth century. The sharp neck of land outlined by this diversion of the river was named Pointe Coupée (Fr., cut point). New Roads was first called St. Mary's. In 1847–48 the Bayou Sara Ferry Road, referred to as Chemin Neuf (Fr., new road), was constructed.

Fine homes line the bank of False River. A public pavilion and bathhouse provide bathing and dancing, and the water is usually dotted with boats of all descriptions. False River abounds with fish (*boats and bait available at moderate rates*).

In the southern part of town in front of the high school is the POYDRAS MONUMENT, a marble block topped by an urn, erected by Pointe Coupée and West Baton Rouge Parishes and the Poydras Asylum of New Orleans. Beneath it are the remains of Julien Poydras de Lallande (1746–1824), peddler, poet, planter, and philanthropist. Poydras, born in Nantes, Brittany, came to New Orleans about 1768, began his career with a hawker's box on his back in the south Louisiana parishes bordering on the Mississippi River, and soon accumulated enough capital to purchase a plantation in Pointe Coupée Parish. He is said to have entertained Louis Philippe and the Duke of Orléans in 1798. He became a close friend of Governor Claiborne and held a number of offices. Poydras died unmarried, and the bulk of his tremendous wealth was willed by him to educational and charitable institutions. Part of his fortune was set up as a dowry fund for impoverished maidens of Pointe Coupée and West Baton Rouge Parishes. Dowries are still given out in the latter parish (*see Tour 3b*). His will also provided that all his slaves should be freed 25 years after his death. This was in spite of the fact that those on Alma Plantation (*see below*) had taken an active part in the Black Rebellion. His executors, however, refused to carry out his wish in this matter and were upheld by the courts.

South of New Roads, along the west bank of False River, the high-way runs through a section called PLAIN COCHON (Fr., pig plain) from the great number of pigs that were raised there.

RANDALL OAK, 104 *m.,* stands on the site of Poydras College, where James P. Randall wrote "Maryland, My Maryland," on the night of April 26, 1861. A plaque has been erected to commemorate the event. Randall was professor of English Literature and the Classics at Poydras College. The college was established through a trust fund left by Julien Poydras, and was destroyed by fire in 1881.

South of Randall Oak, La 1 enters a plantation area rich in history and tradition. A few years prior to the Louisiana Purchase the area surrounding BAYOU CORNE À CHEVREUIL (Fr., bayou buck-horn), 105.8 *m.,* was settled by one M. Lafitte, who was inordinately fond of deer hunting. He built a rambling house and adorned the posts of the entrance gates with a pair of antlers—so that both the place and the bayou near it came to be called Corne à Chevreuil. The house was torn down soon after the War between the States.

The OLD OLIVA PLANTATION HOUSE (*open*), 105.9 *m.,* is a low hipped-roof house of adobe construction set on the bank of False River.

The NEW OLIVA PLANTATION HOUSE (*private*), 106 *m.,* was built by Disney Lacoste in the middle of the nineteenth century. Set back behind a Cherokee rose hedge, it is a one-and-one-half-story frame house. Square vine-clad plaster-brick pillars support a gallery which extends around three sides and is reached by two outside stairways. The name of the plantation is probably a corruption of Olivet, one of the earliest owners, who bought the place from a Spanish official and obtained com-plete title in 1791.

In May, 1939 Alan Wuertele, the owner, using a process developed by Ernest Kleiber of Switzerland, converted some of his sugar into synthetic rubber and pointed the way to a new industrial outlet for Louisiana's surplus sugar. By this process, sugar is oxidized with nitric acid, mixed with turpentine, and polymerized with hydrochloric acid. A rubber yield of from 78 to 83 per cent is attained. Wuertele is also the inventor of a sugar cane harvester.

PARLANGE (*open*), 107 *m.,* was built in 1750 on a land grant to the Marquis Vincent de Ternant, and is one of the oldest and most charming houses in Louisiana. Madame Ternant's second husband was Charles Parlange, a French naval officer, and the plantation has de-scended in direct line to the present owners. A dark green, cedar-lined driveway, flanked by octagonal brick *pigeonniers* painted white, leads from the highway through a grove of live oaks and pecans to the house. It is a white, green-shuttered one-and-one-half story raised cot-tage of cypress and mud and moss construction set over a brick base-ment. The house is encircled by galleries and topped by a steeply pitched, hipped and dormered roof. The ground-floor columns are of brick, and those of the second floor are of wood, slender and tapering. Wide steps lead up to the main-floor gallery, where French doors open from the living rooms. These doors have outer blinds and are surmounted by ornamental fan transoms, exquisite in detail. The furnishings of Parlange include many rare pieces of furniture, sliver, glassware, and porcelain. The slave-made implements with which the house was built have been preserved, and among them are curiously shaped brick moulds and iron tools of various kinds.

An entertaining document is the inventory of the estate of Vincent Ternant II, dated June 1842. It is in itself a comprehensive study of the structure of the plantation of the period. Among the personal effects listed was the inevitable "spit box" which, with shovel and tongs, was valued at $6; another item was "50 pairs of pantaloons of divers kinds" estimated at $50. The livestock was listed individually and by name: "Rossignol et Major" were a yoke of oxen, "Papillon," "Trompet," "Sanspareil," and "Poil Fin" were mules. The slaves were valued according to their ages and trades; Jack Blacksmith at 40 was priced at $1,000; but Thrill at 52 would bring only $200 and Uncle Tom at 80 was almost a total loss—$10. Gros Jean and Petit Jean (or Jean LeJeune) were father and son; such titles were always applied when there were two of the same name in a family. The cash assets amounted to $300,000, which was banked in metal chests. During the War between the States these chests were buried and one has never been found. Parlange served as headquarters for both General Banks, U.S.A., and General Dick Taylor, C.S.A., during the hotly contested Red River Campaign.

The AUSTERLITZ PLANTATION HOUSE (*private*), 108.2 *m.* (R), was named in honor of the battle of Austerlitz which Napoleon fought against the Austrians and Russians in December, 1805. It is a one-story frame structure set on a plaster-covered brick basement. A gallery encircles the house. There are square wooden pillars below and slender columns above. Both upper and lower entrances are fanlighted. The land on which it stands was purchased in 1783 from two Indian chiefs by Joseph Decuir, who owned vast tracts of land in Pointe Coupée Parish. The house itself dates from 1832.

PLEASANT VIEW (*open*), 109 *m.,* owned since 1867 by the Hewes family, is a high raised cottage with six square brick pillars on the lower and six slender wooden columns on the upper floor. An outside stairway rises on the front of the upper gallery.

NORTH BEND (*open*), 109.5 *m.,* is a long galleried raised cottage.

RIVER LAKE PLANTATION (*open*), 110.5 *m.,* was a grant to Isaac Gaillard but was later acquired by the Denis family, who lived there for many years. It has been remodeled by P. C. Major. Two square *pigeonniers* stand on each side of the front driveway.

At 111.1 *m.* is the junction with a graveled road.

Left on this road to the ALMA PLANTATION, 2.3 *m.* It is the property of Alma Plantation, Ltd., composed of members of the Pitcher family, whose sugar activities in Pointe Coupée Parish extend back over three-quarters of a century. Alma Plantation was once the property of Julien Poydras (*see above*). It was the center of the slave conspiracy which in April 1795 culminated in the "Black Rebellion," an uprising inspired by the success of the Santo Domingo Revolution and designed for the massacre of every white in the district—with the exception of the adult females. The failure of this plot was induced by a quarrel among the leaders over the hour at which the carnage should begin, and a disgruntled Negro warned the Spanish commandant. The ringleaders were immediately arrested, but at this the slaves rallied to save their chiefs and in the rioting that followed 25 were killed. The remaining rebels were summarily rounded up, tried and sentenced. "Sycamore Cut" on Alma Plantation is a spot which until recent years was shunned by Negroes, for it marks the grave of a white overseer who was killed by the slaves. The present, modern house (*private*) on Alma Plantation contains two of the rooms of the original house built by Poydras in 1789.

At 115.4 *m.* is the junction with US 190 (*see Tour 3b*), 2 miles west of Erwinville. La 1 remains with US 190 until Scotlandville, then turns south and follows the west bank of the Mississippi.

Tour 17A

Natchitoches—Hagewood—Robeline—Many—Pendleton Bridge, Toledo Bend Reservoir—(San Augustine, Tex.) ; 48.6 *m.,* La 6.

This route runs southwest from Natchitoches to the Texas Line over the old San Antonio Trace, or El Camino Real (Sp., royal road), one of America's historic highways. In the early eighteenth century it served as a Spanish highroad joining Mexico City, by way of San Antonio, and Los Adais. From the latter point it ran a few miles farther east to Natchitoches, the French outpost on the Red River. The trail was used by Louis Juchereau de St. Denis on his expedition to the Rio Grande and Mexico. After 1803 Moses Austin and thousands of other colonists entered Texas by way of the Trace. David Crockett and the Americans who aided the Texans in their fight for independence hurried into Texas over the same road.

La 6, leaving NATCHITOCHES, 0 *m.,* on Jefferson St., winds west through rolling hills and creek bottoms.

The highway crosses the old ARROYO HONDO (Sp., deep rivulet), 7.8 *m.,* a creek that was at one time the eastern boundary of the neutral strip of land that separated French and Spanish, and later the Spanish and American, territories. Here is SIBLEY LAKE, 2,700 acres, supplying water to Natchitoches.

HAGEWOOD, 9.1 *m.,* a small agricultural center, was settled about the time of the War between the States. A pioneer named Shaebrook, attracted to this section because of its numerous cold springs, started a tanning industry here. Other settlers followed and a community called Coldwater was soon formed. Later a Mr. Hagewood opened a post office and the village adopted his name.

Hagewood is at the junction with La 117. PROVENCAL is 5 *m.* south on 117, which passes through Kisatchie.

At 14.5 *m.* is the junction (R) with La 485 and LOS ADAIS HISTORIC PARK.

Right on this road 0.5 *m.* to the hilltop SITE OF THE PRESIDIO DE NUESTRA SEÑORA DEL PILAR DE LOS ADAIS (Sp., Our Lady of the Pillar), marked by a bronze tablet and flag pole (L) erected by the Daughters of the American Colonists in 1933. A fort was established here by the Marques de Aguayo in 1721 to protect Spanish sovereignty against French encroachment. Thirty soldiers were always on guard and cannon sent from Mexico were used for armament. The Presidio was the capital of the Province of Texas until 1773. Despite the official friction between the Spaniards of Los Adais and the French of Natchitoches, relations between the two colonies were friendly. It is said that when Governor Bustillo came to Texas in 1732 the French went to Los Adais to pay their compliments. In the same year, the Natchez attacked Natchitoches and St. Denis received aid from Bustillo, in return for which he sent the Spaniard a present of some captive women. Intermarriage between the settlers of the two posts further helped strengthen the friendship. In 1744 St. Denis died and Governor Bonea and Commandante Vallejo of Los Adais attended his funeral.

After the cession of Louisiana to Spain, Los Adais, no longer a frontier post, was overshadowed by Natchitoches. In February 1806, Captain Edward D. Turner advanced on Los Adais with 60 men and forced the Spaniards to evacuate the post and retire beyond the Sabine River, the boundary at the time. Today Los Adais is a historical park.

Atop the hill opposite the Presidio stood the Mission of San Miguel de los Adais, of which nothing now remains to mark the site. Established in 1717, three years after the French founded Natchitoches, for the conversion of the Adais Indians, it was the only Spanish mission founded in Louisiana. Some 2 years after its erection the mission was captured by French troops from Natchitoches. In 1721 the mission was recaptured and the Presidio built to protect it.

ROBELINE, 15.4 *m.* (149 alt., 274 pop. 1970), is on the main line of the Texas & Pacific Railroad in the center of a productive agricultural district. The first settlers came to this section over the San Antonio Trace in the days when the Capuchin Fathers were busy visiting the Indians in the vicinity. It is said that the town received its name from one of these early settlers. No appreciable growth was noted at Robeline until the New Orleans and Pacific Railroad built through the town in 1881. Corn and cotton are the staple crops in this area and the community is noted for its participation in State and parish fairs.

FORT JESUP, 24 *m.,* a small agricultural community, was once an important American frontier post. Founded as Cantonment Jesup by Zachary Taylor in 1822, it was the focal point of the American expansionist movement in the Southwest and the "Cradle of the Mexican War."

Two large stone pillars one block from the highway in the eastern part of town mark the entrance to the old fort, now a Sabine Parish historical park. All that remains of the original fort, which was named for Thomas Sidney Jesup, quartermaster general and later a prominent participant in the Seminole War, is one of the log buildings, recently restored, and several stone pillars near by. Stone for the foundations of the 30 or 40 buildings was quarried from neighboring hills, and lime for masonry was produced from the same source. In all, the reservation covered 25 square miles.

The United States had good reason to erect this fortification. The western boundary of Louisiana had never been definitely established, and the United States, in acquiring Louisiana, inherited a boundary dispute with Spain (*see History*).

In 1819, by the Treaty of Washington, Spain abandoned all claims to land east of the Sabine. Following the formal transfer, July 17, 1821, the United States moved in to establish order in the neutral corridor, which, during the long diplomatic wrangle, had been the refuge of outlaws, murderers, and adventurers, most of whom preyed on the swelling tide of Texas-bound emigrants. The following year Fort Jesup was established as the central stronghold on the new frontier. The site selected for the fort was on the crest of a high ridge on the watershed between the Red and Sabine rivers, strategically situated on the San Antonio Trace, a day's march from the Sabine.

During the 1830's the fort was a center of social activities. Belles and beaux danced to the music of the regimental bands or attended horse races, gander pullings, and other contests and festivals in the surrounding country.

During the revolution in Texas, troops were sent from Fort Jesup into Texas on the pretext of enforcing the neutrality laws, but the commander of the American forces, who favored annexation, gave material aid to the Texans. In response to a popular disapproval of this move President Jackson ordered the troops back to American soil. That annexation would be the signal for war with Mexico was generally recognized, and Fort Jesup was amply garrisoned to meet any emergency.

In 1844 Brigadier General Zachary Taylor, "Old Rough and Ready," was placed in command of Fort Jesup. Here he received advance notice from the Secretary of War that Texas would probably vote for annexation on July 4, 1845, and to prepare for emergencies. General Taylor was prepared, and when the word came, troops were sent from Fort Jesup, by way of New Orleans, on an expedition that resulted in the storming of Chapultepec.

The winning of the Mexican War and the moving of the border to the Rio Grande marked the end of the fort's importance. In 1846 it was abandoned as a military post and left with only a caretaker and a few guards; later it was completely abandoned.

MANY, 30.2 *m*. (242 alt., 3,112 pop. 1970), (*see Tour 19b*), is at the junction with US 171, which has been joined by La 175.

At 44 *m*. is the junction with unmarked La 476.

Left on this dirt road to BEULAH BAPTIST CHURCH, 0.2 *m*., a plain frame building marking the approximate SITE OF OLD CAMP SABINE and the OLD BLOCKHOUSE. Camp Sabine was the site of General Wilkinson's camp in 1806 when he was conducting an expedition against the Spaniards commanded by General Herrera. It was here that Wilkinson was supposed to have met Aaron Burr's emissary, Swartwout, and planned with him the details of the "Southwestern Empire." For some time conflict impended between the Spanish and American troops over the boundary of the two territories. Wilkinson and Herrera finally drew up the Neutral Ground Treaty, in which the Spaniards agreed to retire to the west of the Sabine. In 1836 General Edmund P. Gaines sent troops to construct a blockhouse and a number of warehouses here in order to strengthen the position of Fort Jesup. After Camp Sabine was abandoned, following the Mexican War, the blockhouse was converted into a church and became a noted Baptist meeting house. Some time later it was torn down and the present church was erected near the site. About 100 yards south of the church is the spring once used by soldiers stationed at Camp Sabine.

At 3.7 *m.* is the junction with a dirt road; R. here 1.5 *m.* to the junction with a dirt road; R. here to the SABINETOWN BREASTWORKS, 3.6 *m.*, on the east bank of the Sabine River, at Hooker's Bend, directly across from Sabinetown, Texas. These breastworks, now thickly overgrown, are approximately three-quarters of a mile in length and are the most extensive and best preserved in Louisiana. A line of trench 5 to 6 feet deep and topped by earthworks thrown up to an equal height, zigzags across the land in the bend in the river from river bank to river bank. The entrances of two roads, now abandoned, and protected by a "curtain," so that no break in the line is visible from the outside. The breastworks date, at least, from the War between the States, as recorded by General Edmund Kirby-Smith; but tradition has it that they were built to protect the crossing of trading caravans in Spanish times on the old San Antonio Trace.

The waters of the Sabine River contribute to the TOLEDO BEND RESERVOIR, 197,660 acres, on the boundary of Louisiana and Texas, of which about 100,000 acres are the jurisdiction of Louisiana. In place of the former Sabine River Bridge La 6 now crosses the Reservoir on the PENDLETON BRIDGE, opened 1967. The bridge is about 5 miles long and was designed and engineered by the Louisiana Department of Highways. It is made up of 180 concrete spans and four steel spans. It is classified as a drilled-foundation, concrete structure and contains more than 1,300,000 cubic yards of concrete and more than 700,000 pounds of steel. The roadway is 28 ft. wide and the road limit is 20 tons. La 6 crosses into Texas, where the route leads to Milam and San Augustine.

Tour 17B

Hagewood—Kisatchie—Junction with US 171; 41.8 *m.*, La. 117.

This route runs south from Hagewood through wooded upland country. For 22 miles the highway winds through the Kisatchie Division of the Kisatchie National Forest. Beyond the forest are bleak cut-over timber lands inhabited by timber workers, small stock farmers, and squatters.

La 117, branching south from La 6 (*see Tour 17A*) at HAGE-

WOOD, 0 *m.* (*see Tour 17A*), meanders through sparsely settled timberland. The simple rough board cottages, built of lumber sawed at one of the local mills, are roofed with heart-pine boards split from native timber. Most of the homes have wells dug by hand and the old custom of "witching for water" is still followed. Before a well is dug the local prognosticator surveys the farm with a willow twig or a peach tree limb to indicate, by the bending of the willow, the exact spot at which a vein or spring of water can be found.

PROVENCAL, 4.6 *m.* (170 alt., 830 pop. 1970), depends on corn, cotton, sugar cane, and potatoes for its main source of income. On dark, damp nights, it is said that a peculiar light resembling a ball of fire can be seen up the railroad tracks above the section house. Some of the more superstitious inhabitants believe that it is caused by the spirit of a Negro who was hanged and shot to pieces at the spot years ago; others explain it as a phosphorescent glow of some kind.

At 6.6 *m.* La 117 crosses the boundary of the KISATCHIE DIVISION of the KISATCHIE NATIONAL FOREST (*see Tour 15a*). In this forest region are stately pines and sandy hills, with occasional outcroppings of sandstone and limestone. Many cold, clear streams flow through rock-walled gorges and over sandstone ledges, forming little rapids and miniature waterfalls. Game is plentiful in the woods; quail, doves, woodcock, some wild turkeys, squirrels, rabbits, deer, and foxes are to be found. Wild honeysuckle, dogwood, wild azaleas, and the climbing yellow jasmine can be seen from February to April; in autumn the red and yellow foliage of oaks, gums, hickories, and maples outline the ridges of the heavily wooded hills. Picnic spots abound.

BELLWOOD, 13.8 *m.,* is the remnant of what was once a lumber town, before the district was taken over by the government.

The KISATCHIE OBSERVATION TOWER (*open*), 19.3 *m.,* is on one of the highest hills in the Kisatchie Forest.

KISATCHIE, 22.3 *m.* (338 alt.), has a consolidated school that serves a large rural community. The village and the Kisatchie Forest were both named for Kisatchie Creek, which flows east of the town. In John Sibley's report from Natchitoches in 1807 this name appeared as *Cossachie,* which in Choctaw means "reed river."

Left from Kisatchie on unmarked, graveled road to the junction with a dirt road, 1.8 *m.;* L. here to the KISATCHIE FALLS, 3.4 *m.* The falls, in reality nothing more than rapids, tumble over limestone and sandstone ledges, their size varying according to the season and the amount of local rainfall. Picnic tables have been erected in a grove of magnolia trees on the banks of the stream. The beauty and quiet of this secluded spot attract visitors from long distances.

At 25.9 *m.* La 117 crosses the southern boundary of the KISATCHIE DIVISION of the KISATCHIE NATIONAL FOREST.

South of KURTHWOOD, 27.7 *m.,* a sawmill town, La 117 traverses cut-over land. Logging trucks are frequently met on the highway; occasionally an ox team used for skidding or handling logs can be seen. The small houses set at intervals in clearings are generally tenanted by squatters, who are awaiting the day when the second growth of timber will be ready for cutting. In the meantime they get along as best they can, eking out a living from the land and occasionally doing a few days' work for the lumber companies. Most of the land throughout the area is owned by the large lumber companies, to whom squatters pay a token fee. Some of these people have lived so many years under this arrangement that they customarily regard the property they live on as their own. They improve their places by clearing, burning stumps, and by cultivating additional land; the more enterprising erect new farm buildings. Peculiar difficulties have arisen when these tenants have applied for government assistance for farm improvement.

Although timber work is the chief source of livelihood, many of the inhabitants supplement their incomes by raising goats and other livestock that graze on the free range amid the pines. This country is ideal for cattle, but incomes from livestock are uncertain because of the presence of the modern cattle rustler, who works by night, with the help of improved highways and modern transportation. Cattle thieves drive their large trucks into the grazing area, find a secluded by-road, load the stock and leave for a distant market. About all the owner can find is the spot where the truck left the highway and some of the tracks of his cattle. At times he finds that his cattle have been slaughtered on the spot, which makes apprehension even more difficult, since there is no tell-tale evidence of brands or other marks. In some sections irate livestock owners have organized in an effort to eliminate this hazard to their business. Sometimes a local resident is suspected of rustling, and lively feuds result.

Along the highway in this section are occasional brush arbors, where revival meetings and sometimes regular weekly church meetings are held. The congregations are usually Holiness, Apostolic, or Church of God adherents, although Methodist and Baptist groups also hold services under these arbors.

At 41.8 *m.* is the junction with US 171 (*see Tour 19b*), 0.8 mile north of Leesville.

Tour 18

(Texarkana, Ark.)—Ida—Shreveport—Coushatta—Colfax—Alexandria—Bunkie—Junction with US 190; 235.4 *m.,* US 71.

Section a. *ARKANSAS LINE to SHREVEPORT;* 38.8 *m.,* US 71

US 71 follows Red River, some distance to the east, to Shreveport. For the first ten miles the highway runs through some of the most striking upland country in Louisiana—steep red clay hills forested with pine and oak and marked by sharp outlines and strong contrasts in the colors of soil and vegetation. South of this rugged upland is the fertile, nearly level Red River bottomland, intensively cultivated in cotton. Indications of a once important lumber industry appear here and there. The oil derricks seen at intervals top the eastern edge of the Caddo Old Field (*see Tour 19a*).

US 71 crosses the ARKANSAS LINE, 0 *m.,* 32.8 miles south of Texarkana, Arkansas.

IDA, 1.1 *m.* (225 alt., 370 pop. 1970), named for the wife of an early settler, has in the past few years undergone an interesting transition. It was formerly a drowsy agricultural community, but discovery of oil in 1935 at the near-by Rodessa Oil Field gave it a temporary prosperity. In recent years it has lost people.

MIRA, 5 *m.* (200 alt.), has a junction with La 769, which connects with La 1. Black Bayou Lake lies between US 71 and La 1 southwest of Mira. Black Bayou Game and Fish Preserve is east of US 71.

HOSSTON, 9.7 *m.* (195 alt., 428 pop. 1970), marks the entrance into the Red River bottomlands. The red color of the soil is due to its iron and salt content. The principal products, in addition to cotton, are corn, potatoes, beans, peas, tomatoes, strawberries, cabbage, and beets. La 2 comes from Plain Dealing, has junction with US 71 at Hosston, runs west to terminate at VIVIAN on La 1.

South of GILLIAM, 14.4 *m.* (197 alt., 211 pop. 1970), the view on both sides of the highway remains the same for mile after mile— broad and fertile fields of cotton stretching away to the horizon. At intervals are the small houses of tenant-farmers, and, less frequently, a plantation center. La 170 connects Gilliam with Vivian.

Cotton is planted in Louisiana in March. The flower buds, called "squares," begin to develop about six weeks after planting, and the first open blooms appear about May 20. In another sixty days, under average conditions, the first bolls mature.

The picking season usually begins about the middle of August and lasts until late November or early December. Until the coming of the Rusk mechanical cotton picker, most of the cotton was picked by Negroes, each picker dragging behind him a long white bag made of Pacific duck. The cotton fields at this season were a gay sight. The bright bandannas of the Negroes, protecting them against the weather and keeping perspiration from their eyes, spotted the whitened fields with vivid spots of color; often the bandannas were topped by straw hats, painted and ornamented. Snatches of laughter and song carried clearly on the still, warm air. But when the machine came their jobs were gone. This was one cause for the movement of Negro tenant farmers to the industries up North.

Cotton gins remove the lint from cotton seed on the same principle as that of the original gin built by Eli Whitney in 1792. The teeth of rapidly revolving circular saws tear the lint from the seeds and pull it through grid openings smaller than the seeds. Revolving brushes on the other side of the grid remove the lint, while the seeds roll off into a special receptacle. The lint is then carried mechanically to the press box, where after compression by a heavy steam-operated weight, the bales, weighing approximately 500 pounds, are ready to be covered and bound. In the cotton country there is an expression that "cotton thirds itself," meaning that three pounds of picked cotton becomes one after the seed is removed at the gin.

Although many bales are sold as soon as ginned, much of the cotton is bought through local dealers and shipped to warehouses or cotton compresses, where it may be sold and resold in speculation. Louisiana cotton planters have an advantage in their proximity to New Orleans, one of the world's greatest cotton-trading centers. The New Orleans Cotton Exchange, one of the four most important cotton exchanges in the world, has a long-established reputation for reliable statistics and a traditional position in the forecasting of cotton crops.

Through the greater part of BELCHER, 19.9 *m.* (187 alt.), a farm village, the highway is bordered by huge oak, pecan, and elm trees, whose spreading branches form an arch overhead.

DIXIE, 23.9 *m.* (186 alt.), is a small collection of buildings grouped about a cotton gin.

At 35.5 *m.* is the junction with La 1 (*see Tour 19a*).

At 38 *m.* is the junction with an asphalt-paved road. Left on this road 1.1 *m.* to the SHREVEPORT MUNICIPAL AIRPORT.

SHREVEPORT, 38.8 *m.* (225 alt., 182,064 pop. 1970), *see Shreveport.*

Shreveport is at junctions with US 71, US 80, US 171, and La 1, 3, and 20.

Section b.　SHREVEPORT *to* ALEXANDRIA; *128.7 m.,*
US 71

South of SHREVEPORT, 0 *m.,* for some 25 miles US 71 parallels the east bank of Red River through rich but only partly developed farm land. Near the highway lie some truck and mixed farming lands and a wilderness of willow, cottonwood, and cypress trees on low, often wet, expanses. South of Colfax there is a constant change between upland and alluvial types of country.

BOSSIER CITY, 1 *m.* (180 alt., 41,595 pop. 1970), is at junctions with US 71 and US 79–80. *See Bossier City.*

BARKSDALE AIR FORCE BASE, 4.2 *m. See Bossier City.*

TAYLORTOWN, 13.7 *m.* (156 alt.), is a plantation village on Red River, lying between Moon and Red Chute Lakes. The former is within sight of the highway, while the latter lies three miles to the left. Both afford excellent fishing. Information and supplies can be obtained at the village store.

Left from Taylortown on La 527 to LAKE BISTINEAU STATE PARK.

ELM GROVE, 17.4 *m.* (155 alt.), was formerly an important oil town, but is today little more than a village.

Left from Elm Grove on graveled La 157 to the junction with La 154, 3.5 *m.;* R. here to LAKE BISTINEAU (*boats, bait, camp sites*), 8.5 *m.* Fishing is excellent in Lake Bistineau, particularly at its upper end. Bayou Dorcheat, which empties into the lake there, also affords fine fishing. The scenery is typical of the northwest Louisiana plantation country—wooded and gently rolling. East of the lake is the GAME AND FISH PRESERVE.

ATKINS, 20.9 *m.,* (151 alt.), is a plantation village named for the Atkins family of Shreveport, prominent in the development of northwest Louisiana.

LOGGY BAYOU, 28.6 *m.,* was an important watercourse in steamboating days. Boats entered it from Red River and passed through Lake Bistineau and up Bayou Dorcheat during high water.

At 46.1 *m.* is the junction with US 84.

Right here to COUSHATTA, 1.1 *m.* (137 alt., 1,492 pop. 1970), the seat of, and largest town in, Red River Parish, named for an Indian tribe that once inhabited this section. The first business house, a log store, was built by Paul Lisso in 1865, and the town was incorporated 7 years later. The RED RIVER PARISH COURTHOUSE, a three-story tan brick structure erected in 1929, is one of the handsomest courthouses in this section of the State. The building has a pedimented portico with Corinthian columns and is topped by an octagonal dome.

The "Coushatta Riots" occurred here in 1874, when a unit of the White League, supported by men of Red River and adjoining parishes, quelled an uprising of Negroes. The Negroes, led by unscrupulous carpetbaggers, had threatened to exterminate all native white people in the community. A landmark connected with the riot is the OLD BRICK STORE, a one-story structure with a gabled roof, near the bank of the river. The riots started at the time the store, then the first brick building in Coushatta, was being dedicated. In *Wild Work* (1880), Mary E. Bryan used these riots as the basis of a romantic novel.

West of Coushatta US 84 crosses Red River to Armistead (*see Tours 5b and 17b*).

At 60.2 *m.* on US 71 is the junction (R) with a dirt road. Right on this road 0.6 *m.* to LUVENIA SPRINGS, noted for the purity of its waters.

CAMPTI, 62.5 *m.* (125 alt., 1,078 pop. 1970), the business district of which lies to the right of the highway, is in a section of northwestern Natchitoches Parish noted for its fine fishing (*see Tour 16*). The entire town is surrounded by a fence to keep the cows in the town and out of the cotton fields. According to tradition a tribe of Indians lived in this vicinity on a large hill near the banks of Red River. Campte, their chief, became a favorite with the white settlers, who named the settlement in his honor. After the chief died his followers gradually drifted away, while the white settlement grew. It was here in 1833 that Captain Henry Miller Shreve began clearing the Great Raft from Red River (*see Shreveport*).

In Campti is the junction with La 480, to CLEAR LAKE, and La 155, which runs between Clear Lake and BLACK LAKE, good fishing area.

Southeast of Campti US 71 follows the general course of Red River through a large cypress swamp, and on into a pine hill and farming section.

CLARENCE, 69.6 *m.* (115 alt.), was called Tiger Island during and shortly after the War between the States, because of a lone tiger said to have been killed on a near-by plantation. The tiger was probably a jaguar, a species that once ranged from tropical America to western Louisiana.

Clarence is at junctions with US 84 and La 6 (*see Tour 5b*). La 6 goes west and south 8 *m.* to NATCHITOCHES, junction with La 1.

Between 75.3 *m.* and 80.3 *m.* US 71 cuts across a corner of the CATAHOULA DIVISION of the KISATCHIE NATIONAL FOREST (*see Tour 15a*).

At 82.4 *m.* is the junction with a dirt road.

Left on this road to the EBENEZER CAMP GROUNDS, 1.7 *m.*, where Union Holiness camp meetings were held every summer until the early 1920's. About 100 camps once stood here, but all that is left are several springs which have a high sulphur and magnesium content.

MONTGOMERY, 83.8 *m.* (153 alt., 923 pop. 1970), originally located two miles east of the present townsite and known as Creola Bluff, was laid out in 1850 by General Thomas F. Woodward. In 1860 the name was changed to Montgomery through the influence of a minister's wife whose birthplace was Montgomery, Alabama. Because of its location on Red River, the town soon became a thriving port. With the building of railroads it gradually diminished in importance, and now depends chiefly on agriculture. It is known for its fine watermelons.

In the southern part of town overlooking Red River is the FRENCH AND INDIAN GRAVEYARD. On a knoll on the western edge of the cemetery are three Indian graves marked by simple iron crosses. Many Confederate and Union soldiers are buried here. The latter were drowned in the sinking of a Federal transport in 1864.

Paleontologists have found many fossils in the outcropping of old sea beds in the vicinity. Crumbling of the river bank in 1895 exposed the skeleton of a pterodactyl, which, with other remains, can be seen at the Williamson exhibit, Natchitoches (*see Natchitoches*).

The TEAL PLANTATION, 98.9 *m.*, was originally a part of the Meredith Calhoun estate, which had a river frontage of seven miles. Calhoun, it is said, owned 1,600 slaves, who farmed from 6,000 to 8,000 bales of cotton each year.

COLFAX, 100 *m.* (96 alt., 1,892 pop. 1970) is the seat of Grant Parish, which was named for President Grant in 1869 by a carpetbagger legislature at the same time that the town was named for Schuyler Colfax, Grant's vice president. The parish is the site of one of the largest of four divisions of the Kitsatchie National Forest, a vast reforestation project for restocking the pine lands. The Robert Stuart Young Nursery is a Government installation near POLLOCK, east of Colfax on La 8. US 71, now runs a few miles east of Colfax, and has a junction with La 8.

Here, on Easter Sunday, April 4, 1873, occurred the bloodiest riot of the Reconstruction Period. Negroes forcibly ejected white municipal and parish officers, and the townspeople fled from their homes. After several days, with the aid of citizens from adjoining parishes, the ejected sheriff succeeded in driving out the Negroes, but only after a bloody siege. Three white men and about 120 Negroes were killed.

In the vicinity are many large pecan orchards. Red River has cut into the older portion of the town, eating away some 150 acres, including the sites of more than 30 residences.

Between 108.4 *m.* and 111 *m.* US 71 crosses the southwest corner of the CATAHOULA DIVISION of the KISATCHIE NATIONAL FOREST.

At 114.6 *m.* is the junction with a graveled road.

Left on this road to the junction with a graveled road, 0.8 *m.;* R. here to MAGNOLIA PARK (*cottages; free picknicking facilities*), 1.2 *m.,* a summer resort on Hudson Creek, which has been dammed to form a swimming pool.

At 118 *m.* is the junction with US 167 (*see Tour 15a*).

TIOGA, 121.6 *m.* (165 alt.), founded as a lumber town, was formerly named Seiss and Levin. The name is derived from the Iroquois "teyogen," meaning "a thing between two others"—believed to be Red River and Little River, or Catahoula Lake. Unlike many former sawmill centers, which are now all but deserted, Tioga has developed into an important trade center, due in part to its proximity to the U. S. Veterans' Facilities. The town is served by three railroads, the Missouri Pacific, Louisiana & Arkansas, and Chicago, Rock Island & Pacific.

The U. S. VETERANS' ADMINISTRATION FACILITIES are at 123.5 *m.* The buildings occupy the former campus of the old Louisiana Seminary of Learning. The seminary building was used as a hospital during the War between the States. In 1869 it was destroyed by fire, and the campus was made Camp Stafford, for use by the State militia. During World War I a base hospital for the care of soldiers of near-by Camp Beauregard was built on the site. The present institution was opened in 1930. Veterans of all wars of the United States are admitted for treatment. An interesting phase of the institution's work is the vocational rehabilitation of veterans. Various handicrafts, such as wood and leatherworking and weaving, are taught. In the rear is an orchard and garden whose cultivation provides exercise for the more able-bodied patients.

The institution has the atmosphere of a large resort hotel rather than that of a hospital. Bedrooms have radios and other homelike furnishings, and there is always an ample supply of newspapers, magazines, and books from the institution's library. Entertainments of various kinds —motion pictures, musicals, and dramatics—are given frequently. Recreational facilities for employees include tennis courts and a golf course.

At 124.1 m. US 71 forks (the left fork, or city route, enters Alexandria by way of Pineville and the traffic bridge); R. on US 71 across bridge.

At 125.9 m., at the north approach to the Red River bridge, is the junction with a graveled road.

Right on this road to the SITES OF FORTS BUHLOW (R), 0.1 m., and RANDOLPH (L), 0.5 m. The forts were erected in 1864 by Brigadier General Allen Thomas, commander of the Confederate forces at Alexandria, as a defense against an expected third invasion of the Red River Valley. Fifteen hundred Confederate soldiers and several thousand slaves, who had been voluntarily loaned or commandeered from plantations, worked day and night to speed construction. The fortifications were armed with nine cannon and garrisoned by several hundred men. The forts saw no action and after the war were demolished for their lumber and brick. Only the earthworks, overgrown with trees, remain.

ALEXANDRIA, 128.7 m. (79 alt., 41,557 pop. 1970) see *Alexandria-Pineville*. Alexandria is at junctions with US 165, US 71–167 and La 1.

Section c.   *ALEXANDRIA to JUNCTION WITH US 190; 67.9 m., US 71*

This section of the route swings south from Red River into the Sugar Bowl and the level, wooded bottoms of the Atchafalaya basin. The countryside presents varying views of truck farms, cotton and sugar cane fields, heavy forests, and fallow land bright with wild flowers in spring and summer. The immediate vicinity of Alexandria is populated in part by farmers of Belgian descent, whose ancestors first came to Rapides Parish in 1837. As the Sugar Bowl is entered cotton acreage decreases and sugar cane comes into prominence. Sheds housing syrup vats are to be seen along the highway, and in the syrup-making season, late fall, a colorful picture is presented by the steaming kettles, especially at night when the bright flames from pine-knot fires illuminate the area.

Southward from ALEXANDRIA, 0 *m.,* US 71 cuts across the fertile Red River Valley. At 4 *m.* is the junction with a road.

Right on this road to the HARRIS PLANTATION HOUSE (*open*), 0.2 *m.,* erected by William Harris in 1869. The house, which is set back from Bayou Robert in a grove of massive live oaks, is a one-story frame structure with seven wooden columns across the broad front porch.

Harris once became involved in a dispute with a New Orleans politician who blocked construction on a proposed road between his plantation and Alexandria. Defying opposition, Harris cut timber from his own land and built the road of planks. Recently, in an old desk, one of his descendants discovered a secret drawer containing several old pistols of unusual design, believed to have been bought at the time of the dispute.

INGLEWOOD (HARD TIMES) PLANTATION HOUSE (*open*), 5.7 *m.,* also built by Harris, is a two-story frame building set back (L) about 200 yards from the road at the end of an avenue of oaks. The hipped roof is broken by three dormers at the front and rear. Wide galleries with square wooden pillars extend across the front and halfway around the sides of the house.

On the plantation, at 6.2 *m.,* is another and older "big house," interesting in its architecture. It is a white one-and-one-half story frame building completely surrounded by a gallery with slender square wooden pillars. Adjoining the galleries on both sides on the rear are identical one-story wings with galleries on three sides. The roof of the main building is gabled, those of the wings, hipped.

Inglewood Plantation, 3,009 acres in area, is one of the most modern in the State. The workers' cabins all have running water and other conveniences. A church and school on the plantation serve their families.

MOORELAND COMMUNITY, 6.8 *m.* (75 alt.), was originally the plantation of Governor Thomas Overton Moore (1805–76). In 1860 Moore, a champion of States' rights, became governor, and in January 1861 called a special session of the general assembly, which voted for Secession. Reorganizing the State militia, he led Louisiana into the Confederacy. At the expiration of his term in 1864, Moore moved to Texas, later going to Cuba.

At 9.4 *m.* is the junction with a graveled road.

Left here to the CHAMBERS PLANTATION HOUSE (*open*), 0.2 *m.,* a long one-story white frame house (R) with a gabled roof and nine square pillars across the front gallery. There is an interesting iron gate before the house.

A few yards south of the Chambers Plantation Road is the junction with a graveled road.

Right on this road 1.9 *m.* to the junction with a graveled road; R. here to STATE FOREST, 1 *m.,* and CAMP OVERTON, 1.6 *m.* (*see Tour 13c*).

At 3.1 *m.* the main side route turns R. at a fork and crosses BAYOU LAMOURIE, 3.2 *m.,* a stream with an interesting linguistic history. Successive old maps dating from 1802 give its name as L'amoureux (the lover), Le Mourir (of death), L'Amour (love), and Lamourie, terms which seem to bear out the local tradition that the name of the bayou was derived from the fact that a young lover, plagued with unrequited love, drowned himself in its waters. It is also said that the bayou was named for an Indian chief. In the opinion of William A. Read, professor of English at the Louisiana State University, the bayou derives its name from the numerous mulberry trees which grew in this vicinity, La-mourie being a corruption of *le mûrier* (Fr., mulberry tree).

At 3.9 *m.* is the junction with a graveled road; R. here 0.7 *m.* to ASHTON (*open*), a plantation house erected in 1865 to replace an earlier mansion built on land acquired from the Indians in 1802 and first cultivated by Charles Mull-hollan. The plantation was purchased in 1854 by William Polk, who developed it profitably until the War between the States, when the old home was destroyed. Some of the pre-war buildings survive, among them the smokehouse, wood-house, and dairy, all of aged, red brick. These square-shaped outhouses, stand-ing to the rear of the house, are joined by arcades, with each unit surmounted by a spire.

The plantation house is a one-story white frame structure with square wooden pillars across the wide front gallery. Large live oaks are scattered about the grounds, and two of them named Polk (R) and Livingston (L) have been admitted as junior members of the Live Oak Society (*see Lafayette*).

Ashton contains furniture and other heirlooms of the Polk family, among which is a Duncan Phyfe table at which General Lafayette was dined by the Polks. Among other relics is the plantation bell, manufactured in 1850, which is still in use to regulate the working hours of the plantation hands.

The space between the main house and the outbuildings is a mass of flowers. A boxwood hedge planted before the War between the States borders the gar-den and forms an archway over the garden gate. Bulbs imported from Holland have been blooming in this garden for more than 50 years.

At 5.8 *m.* on La 613, marked (L) by a bungalow and a tall cottonwood tree, is the SITE OF THE SUGAR BEND PLANTATION HOUSE, home of the wealthy ante-bellum William C. C. Martin family. The Sugar Bend Plantation had a "lawn" of 8 acres that had been blessed; for 50 years not a furrow was turned, a twig broken, nor a weed pulled on the sacred plot.

The old PEGRAM PLACE (*open*), 7.5 *m.* (L), a frame structure with a hipped, shingled roof, is in a grove of live oaks. The gallery, with its square wooden pillars, extends across the front and along half the sides.

At 9.4 *m.* is the junction of La 613 and unmarked, graveled La 24.

Right on La 24 to the Stokes Nursery, 3.3 *m.* Across the road, and to the east, extend the GROUNDS OF DENTLEY, once the summer home of Colonel Thomas Jefferson Wells. Nothing remains of the buildings and the area is now a forest. Dentley was once a mecca for sportsmen; bear and deer hunts often started from here. Horse racing was popular on the Dentley track, remains of which can, with some difficulty, still be detected. Lecompte, the famous race horse, was trained here.

Left on La 24, the main side route, is CHETWOOD (*private*), 9.5 *m.* (L), built about 60 years ago by E. V. Weems, a son-in-law of James Madison Wells, former governor of Louisiana. It is a three-story frame structure surrounded by a gallery with slender wooden columns, and topped by a mansard roof broken by dormers and turrets.

In Lecompte, 10.5 *m.*, is the junction with La 112.

LECOMPTE, 15.7 *m.* (79 alt., 1,518 pop. 1970), is one of the earliest settlements in central Louisiana, although it was not incorporated until 1900. The first settlers came here from North Carolina shortly after 1800; others followed, and soon large cotton and sugar cane plan-tations were laid out. During the quarter-century preceding the War between the States this was one of the most prosperous areas of the State; today few of the large plantations are intact. Cotton, however, is still the chief interest.

In the early days slaves poled clumsy bargeloads of sugar up Bayou Bœuf, a stream winding lazily through the town. The sugar was then carried by the Ralph Smith-Smith Railroad, built in 1837, one of the earliest railroads in the South. It consisted of a string of small cars drawn by horses over wooden rails and connected Lecompte and Bayou Bœuf with Alexandria and Red River.

There are two stories concerning the origin of the name Bayou Bœuf (Fr., ox, beef, or buffalo) : according to one, the bayou was so named because a bargeload of cattle sank here at one time; according to the other, because of the great herds of buffalo that once roamed in the vicinity. Near here, in 1869, were discovered the skeletal remains of a huge mastodon with teeth four and one-half inches long and tusks six inches in diameter.

James Bowie (c. 1790–1836), Alamo hero, famed for his bowie knife, lived in the vicinity of Lecompte in the early nineteenth century and speculated in land with money made in an ingenious slave-smuggling trade with the pirate, Jean Lafitte (see Tour 2C). Bowie came to Louisiana from Kentucky with his parents about 1802 and first struck out for himself on land along Bayou Bœuf. The famous weapon, a sheathknife with a guard and a single-edged, nine-inch blade, is said to have been designed by a brother, Resin P. Bowie, and fashioned according to his instructions by a Louisiana plantation blacksmith named Snowden. The place of origin of the knife, however, has never been definitely established; both Mississippi and Arkansas contest with Louisiana for the honor. It was first used and made famous by James Bowie in the Vidalia sand-bar duel of 1827 (see Tour 5a), after which Bowie migrated to Texas, then a part of Mexico. He became a citizen of Mexico, married the daughter of the Vice-Governor of San Antonio, and lived quietly until the war with Mexico began. Up and down Texas he became known for the flourish of his bowie knife and was an important figure in clearing that area of the Mexican Army. He died in the fall of the Alamo, in 1836, his knife in his hand.

MEEKER, 18.1 m. (73 alt.), has a large sugar refinery which grinds cane from the entire section. Here US 71 turns southeast and US 167 proceeds south.

Right from Meeker, at the railroad station, on a graveled road, to the WADE JONES HOUSE (open), 0.6 m., a large two-story red brick building (R) with a hipped roof and with four wooden Doric columns on the pedimented portico. There is a porte cochère at the left and a small one-story wing on the right. A circular drive through an avenue of trees leads to the fanlighted entrance.

At 20.3 m. is the junction with a graveled road.

Left on this road, along Bayou Bœuf, to (L) NEW HOPE (open), 3 m., a plantation house built about 1816 by a member of the Tanner family. This well-preserved two-story structure, although remodeled, retains the original frame house and foundation of heavy cypress timbers. Wide porches run the full length of the upper and lower floors and slender wooden columns support the hipped roof. The furniture includes an old piano and many other interesting pieces.

Facing Bayou Bœuf, the house is set in a grove of pecan trees and an extensive flower garden in which the camellias are outstanding. There is a conservatory on the grounds (R).

At 20.4 *m.,* at the south end of a railroad trestle running parallel to the highway, is the junction (R) with a graveled road.

Right on this road 0.6 *m.* to LLOYD'S HALL (*open*), an old plantation house lately restored. The two-and-one-half-story structure is of red brick, and was constructed with slave labor. The front, veneered with lime-plaster squares, has wide upper and lower galleries supported by tall square wooden pillars and enclosed by cast-iron railings. The interior is decorated with plaster medallions in a floral motif. The rooms are approximately 18 feet in height and have moldings and woodwork of superior quality and design. Set back from the main house is the original red brick kitchen with its immense open fireplace. The old plantation bell can be seen at the rear corner of the house. The late Mrs. Docia Moore, once the mistress of Lloyd's Hall, told the story of Sally Boston, an old slave, who took a wounded Yankee into her cabin to nurse him. The soldier died and Sally, afraid to tell anyone, kept his body with her. It was not discovered until her own death many years later.

At 21.8 *m.* on US 71 is the junction with a graveled road.

Left here to WYTCHWOOD (*private*), 0.2 *m.* (R), a plantation home built of hand-hewn cypress timbers held together with wooden pines. The house has been repaired, remodeled, and added to at various times. An underground cistern built in 1824 is still in use. Between the house and the highway is a long avenue of moss-draped live oaks, and on the grounds to the left of the house stands a stately sycamore called the "ghost tree" by local Negroes, because of its white bark. One of two rows of pecan trees flanking the avenue of live oaks was cut down for firewood by Federal troops during the War between the States. The home is owned by the Munson family, whose ancestors purchased the land from the Indians.

CHENEYVILLE, 24 *m.* (63 alt., 1,082 pop. 1970), was named in honor of William Cheney, leader of a group of settlers that came here in 1811 from South Carolina. Cheneyville is a quiet, peaceful town, surrounded by cotton and truck farms.

Connected with the early history of Cheneyville is the story of a slave who bought a slave. A Negro slave named William Cooper, determined to free himself, worked overtime for years for his master and at odd jobs for other planters in order to earn enough money to achieve his ambition. Before this was accomplished he bought a Negro girl for $1,500. He married the girl and continued to save his meager earnings, but the process was slow. At length, with his wife's consent, he sold her to a near-by planter with the privilege of redeeming her at a later date, and proceeded to free himself with the money received from the sale. Being a cooper, William soon established a thriving business and repurchased his wife. He prospered, and at the close of the War between the States had acquired a store and several pieces of property in Cheneyville.

Left from Cheneyville across Bayou Bœuf to the junction with a graveled road, 0.5 *m.;* R. here to the CRESCENT PLANTATION HOUSE (*open*), 0.8 *m.,* a two-story white frame house with square wooden pillars on the upper and lower galleries. The house is set back from the road in a group of live oaks and pecans. Descendants of Captain George Benoist Marshall, who built the house in 1856, still own the plantation. The original wallpaper in the old home still covers the walls.

WALNUT GROVE (*private*), 2.1 *m.*, an ante-bellum two-story house (R) built of bricks molded by slaves on the plantation, has been remodeled. The trees from which the place derives its name have died; but fine, hand-sanded black walnut woodwork made by slave labor can still be seen in the interior. An unusual feature of the house was the tiny railroad that ran from the kitchen, which was separated from the main house, to the dining room. There is an old formal garden with brick walks.

The CHENEYVILLE OIL FIELD, 26.9 *m.*, was discovered by seismograph in 1933.

BUNKIE, 32.1 *m.* (69 alt., 5,395 pop. 1970), an agricultural center originally called Irion, was founded in 1882 by Colonel A. M. Haas, when Colonel E. B. Wheelock contracted with Green and Brogan to extend the New Orleans and Pacific Railway, later the Texas & Pacific Railway, through this section of the State. The town was named for a mechanical toy. When Colonel Haas' youngest daughter, Maccie, was just learning to talk, a friend gave her a mechanical monkey that could climb a string. In her childish pronunciation she called it Bunkie. This became her nickname and in turn the name of the town.

The alluvial lands surrounding the town yield heavy crops of cotton, sugar cane, and corn. The LOUISIANA HOOP MILL, on the southern edge of town, is a constant market for hardwood timber from the swamps. The hoops hanging on racks at this mill appear to be lengthy cylinders suspended in mid-air. Bunkie is a market also for potatoes and other farm produce, fruit, cattle, and quarter horses. A cooperative soy bean elevator was erected by 800 farmers. The Texas & Pacific Ry. serves Bunkie. Industries are based on wood products, seeds, and oil and gas fields in Avoyelles Parish.

Left from Bunkie on paved La 115 to the junction with unmarked, graveled La 25, 2.3 *m.*; to the EWELL PLANTATION HOUSE (*open*), 3.3 *m.* Originally called Clarendon, the house was erected about the middle of the nineteenth century for Martha Anne Koen by her father as a wedding present. The original house now constitutes the right half of the present structure. It is a raised cottage, brick below and frame above, with a gabled, shingled roof. An open central hallway connects it with the left half of the house, which was added at a later date.

The PEARCE PLANTATION HOUSE (*private*), 3.9 *m.* two rooms of which are more than a century old, is still occupied by descendants of the original owners. It is a white frame building, with slender square wooden pillars supporting a gabled roof, and has been extensively remodeled. There is an adjoining kitchen in the rear.

The WRIGHT PLANTATION HOUSE (*open*), 4.3 *m.*, surrounded by mammoth oak trees, is a two-story structure with a red brick foundation. The porch, with wooden Doric columns, encloses three sides. The house was built in 1835 by S. M. Perkins, and alterations in the Victorian manner were made at a later date. According to family tradition, Sam Houston was entertained here.

Right from Bunkie on La 115, to OAK HALL (*open*), 4.6 *m.*, the plantation home of Dr. W. D. Haas, a descendant of Chief Justice John Marshall. It is a modern frame structure with 14 Doric wooden columns enclosing a gallery which

extends along the front and half the sides. Set in a grove of live oaks and surrounded by extensive flower gardens, it is reached by a winding driveway
which crosses Bayou Bœuf. The bayou itself has been beautified throughout the
grounds.

MORROW, 42.3 *m.* (45 alt.), is a small agricultural center supported principally by cotton, sugar cane, and a cotton gin. In common
with other communities of this section, Morrow has suffered heavily
from overflows, due chiefly to backwater from Bayou Rouge. During the
high water of 1927 Morrow was inundated to a depth of three feet and
more, making it necessary to resort to boats.

LE MOYEN, 46.3 *m.* (37 alt.), is the center of a community of
scattered farms. The TURNER HARDWOOD LUMBER MILL employs about
300 men, most of whom are drawn from near-by farms.

LEBEAU, 51.6 *m.* (32 alt.), now a small village, was formerly the
location of a large settlement of free mulattoes, established before the
War between the States. LEBEAU CEMETERY, in the southern part of
town, has many graves decorated with artificial flowers and marked with
home-made crosses of wood nailed or wired together; other more pretentious graves are of brick, painted white. An interesting feature of this
plot is the fact that it is a mixed graveyard, used by both white and
colored, but not in separate and distinct sections—an unusual procedure
in the South. Many of the tombs bear the same family names as those
of mulatto groups at Natchitoches and Opelousas.

In Lebeau is the junction with La 10 (*see Tour 18A*), an alternate
route to the junction with US 190.

Southeast of Lebeau US 71 runs through a low, heavily wooded
section, crosisng the west levee of the WEST ATCHAFALAYA FLOODWAY
(*see Tour 18A*) at 61.3 *m.* The concrete highway, elevated about six
feet above the surrounding country, stretches for miles through dense
growths of elm, ash, gum, water oak, and other hardwoods. Here and
there are scattered cypress, and in underbrush palmetto.

At 67.9 *m.* is the junction with US 190 (*see Tour 3b*), 4 miles west
of Krotz Springs.

❧❧❧❧❧❧❧❧❧❧❧❧❧❧❧❧❧❧❧❧❧❧❧❧❧❧❧❧❧

Tour 18A

Lebeau—Palmetto—Melville—Junction with US 190; 26.7 *m.*, La 10.

This route, an alternate route (*see Tour 18c*) from Lebeau to the
junction with US 190, cuts across the West Atchafalaya Floodway,
through a low wooded section, and follows the west bank of Atchafalaya

652   LOUISIANA

River. The condition of the road is best expressed by a Cajun gentleman, who, when asked about it, replied, "He ees gra-vel road, you know, rough, plenty 'ole, but you can skip 'ole, eh?"

La 10 swings east from US 71 at LEBEAU, 0 *m.* (*see Tour 18c*).

PALMETTO, 4.3 *m.* (40 alt., 312 pop. 1970), is so named because of the profuse growth of palmettoes in the vicinity. Palmetto leaves, once used by the Indians in the construction of their huts, still serve as a thatching for trappers' cabins.

La 10 passes through the guide levee of the WEST ATCHAFALAYA FLOODWAY at 5.4 *m.* This and the Morganza Floodway were planned as part of the flood control works of the lower Mississippi Valley.

Excess floods entering the Atchafalaya River from Red River and from the Mississippi through the 7-mile Old River, 80 miles above Baton Rouge, would tax the levees beyond their capacity. There was great danger that a big flood would sweep from the Mississippi into the Atchafalaya and ruin every town and industry in the basin below. In 1954 the U. S. Corps of Engineers began an elaborate project to cut Old River off by a big dam and install controls that would move the waters without danger. Old River was cut off from the Mississippi by a dam 1,500 ft. wide at base, 100 ft. tall, and constructed of 2,160,000 cu. yds. of earth fill. A navigation lock was installed and a highway bridge built to cross the lock. This cost $67,000,000 and was completed in 1963.

At 13.3 *m.* La 10 crosses over the levee that surrounds Melville and turns left at 14.5 *m.* through a railroad underpass.

MELVILLE, 14.7 *m.* (30 alt., 2,076 pop. 1970), in 1927 stood directly in the path of an almost unprecedented flood in the Atchafalaya basin and the town was under from 15 to 25 feet of water. After the floodwaters had receded the town was completely covered with sand and silt to a depth of from 3 to 15 feet.

In Melville the tracks of the Texas & Pacific are elevated more than 30 feet. Should floods cut Melville off from road travel, the railroad would provide a means of communication.

At Melville a ferry crosses Atchafalaya River to Red Cross, 11 miles west of Morganza (*see Tour 17c*).

The route turns R. at 14.9 *m.* and R. at 15 *m.* At 15.2 *m.* is the junction of La 105 and La 10; left on La 105.

South of Melville La 105 crosses over the levee protecting Melville, 15.2 *m.,* and parallels the levee on the west bank of the winding Atchafalaya River. At intervals of 50 to 75 yards, and on both sides of the road, are upright posts, three to five feet in height, marking the road. These are necessary in order that the road may be followed during times when it is covered with water.

BAYOU PETITE PRAIRIE, 18.8 *m.,* affords opportunities for fishing and boats may be hired.

At 26.7 *m.* is the junction with US 190 (*see Tour 3b*), 0.4 miles north of Krotz Springs.

❧❧❧❧❧❧❧❧❧❧❧❧❧❧❧❧❧❧❧❧❧❧❧❧❧❧❧❧❧

Tour 19

(Atlanta, Tex.)—Rodessa—Shreveport—Mansfield—Many—Leesville
—De Ridder—Junction with US 190; 225.6 *m.,* La 1, US 71, US 171.

Section a. *TEXAS-ARKANSAS LINE to SHREVEPORT;*
44.3 m., La 1, US 71

From its entrance into Louisiana at the Texas-Arkansas corner of
the State, 11 miles southeast of Atlanta, Texas, this part of the route
runs south to Shreveport. Lying in an upland region of shortleaf pine,
the section was formerly dependent upon the lumbering industry and,
to a lesser degree, upon agriculture. The Caddo oil strike in 1906, and
subsequent greater discoveries in later years, however, have established it
as primarily oil country. For many miles southward toward Shreveport tall derricks on both sides of the highway mark the fields. A concrete
post, 0 *m.,* marks the junction of three States—Louisiana, Arkansas, and
Texas.

McCOY, 2.2 *m.* (225 alt.), was originally a lumber town. Since the
discovery of oil at near-by Rodessa, however, McCoy has been virtually
absorbed by that town. Both sides of the highway between the two towns
are lined with residences and tourist camps.

RODESSA, 4.4 *m.* (230 alt.), whose population in 1930 was but
100, changed almost overnight from a quiet village to the hectic center of
a major oil strike. The bringing in of the first gusher, in the summer of
1935, was preceded by fast-spreading rumors of the impending strike—
rumors that held Rodessa in breathless expectancy and excited the entire
State. With the bringing in of the first well, Rodessa increased in population, and in 1930 it had approx. 8,000. The census of 1970 gave it 273.

BLACK BAYOU, 5.5 *m.,* broadens 4 miles southeast of the highway to form a lagoon that affords good fishing.

MYRTIS, 7.9 *m.* (211 alt.), once a farming village, has been as-
similated by Rodessa.

South of Myrtis La 1 traverses a district whose cotton fields—to the
deep regret of their owners—are still producing excellent crops of cotton
instead of thousands of barrels of oil.

VIVIAN, 11.7 *m.* (253 alt., 4,046 pop. 1970) is the location of
offices and supply depots of several oil companies. Vivian also does a
business in lumber, cotton, and other farm products.

At 16 *m.* is the junction with unmarked, blacktop La 2.

Right on this road to JEEMS (or JAMES) BAYOU (*fishing prohibited between February 1 and May 1*), 1.6 *m.*, an excellent fishing spot for yellow bass (locally called striped bass), warmouth bass (locally called goggle-eye), and crappie, or "white perch."

From TREES CITY, 3.9 *m.*, a number of roads lead to fishing spots on Jeems Bayou, 1.5 miles SE. In Trees City is a pumping plant which sends the bulk of the production of wells in Caddo Lake through pipe lines to refineries at Shreveport and other points.

At 4.6 *m.* is the junction with a dirt road; L. here, paralleling the Texas Line, to BONHAM LANDING (*fishing prohibited between February 1 and May 1; boats and bait*), 7 *m.*, a fishing spot on Caddo Lake, a body of water cluttered near shore with cypress trees and oil derricks.

SHORELINE, 16.6 *m.* (193 alt.), is the home of the SHORELINE OIL CO. REFINERY.

OIL CITY, 20.7 *m.* (204 alt., 907 pop. 1970), the key town of the Caddo oil strike (1906), is almost the exact center of the now greatly depleted field.

South of Oil City La 1 passes through a pine-wooded district. At 24.4 *m.* the highway crosses a bridge over Caddo Lake. To the left oil derricks rise from the surface of the water.

MOORINGSPORT, 24.9 *m.* (211 alt., 850 pop. 1970), was once a stop on what is believed to have been the only inland water mail route in the country. From Mooringsport its route extended through Caddo Lake to Jefferson, Texas, a distance of about 25 miles. Although of some importance as an agricultural center and shipping point, Mooringsport is essentially an oil town.

Mooringsport was the birthplace of the singer Huddie Ledbetter (b. 1885), better known as Lead Belly, who, twice convicted and imprisoned for murder and attempted murder, sang his way out of trouble and jail to become "de king of de twelve-string guitar players of de worl'."

John A. Lomax, American ballad collector, heard Lead Belly sing in a Louisiana prison, and recorded his petition for pardon. The record was sent to the late Gov. O. K. Allen:

> In nineteen hundred and thirty two
> Honorable Governor O. K. Allen I'm appealin' to you.
> I left my wife wringin' her hands an' cryin'
> Sayin', "Governor O. K. Allen, save this man of mine."
> And Honorable Mr. Hymes looked over the pen,
> Told Governor Allen, "You've got too many men."
> Governor O. K. Allen began to turn about
> "Got to make some 'rangements to turn some of them out."
> And Honorable Mr. Hymes says to Honorable Warden Long
> "Done make some 'rangements to let the man go home."
> I know my wife gonna jump and shout
> When the train rolls up and I come steppin' out.
> Governor O. K. Allen, 'member you the rest of my life
> You studied up a plan to send so many men to their wives. Etc.

Lead Belly was reprieved in August, 1934, and was hired as a chauffeur by Lomax and his son, whom he drove around the country searching for ballads. On the trip the Lomaxes gathered material on Lead Belly's life and recorded the songs he sang. This material was worked into a volume entitled *Negro Folk Songs of Northwest Louisiana as Sung by Lead Belly* (Macmillan, 1936).

At 25.2 *m.* is the junction with a graveled road.

Left on this road to the junction with a dirt road 2.2 *m.;* L. here to a fork, 2.7 *m.*
1. Left at this fork to CAMP CADDO (*open*), 0.3 *m.*, a Boy Scout Camp on the shore of Caddo Lake. At the entrance is a home-made totem pole.
2. Right at this fork to a FEDERAL DAM 0.5 *m.*, at the eastern end of Caddo Lake. Fishing opportunities are good (*closed season between February 1 and May 1; boats and bait*).

At 41 *m.* is the junction with US 71 (*see Tour 18a*); R. on US 71 (*see Tour 18a*).

SHREVEPORT, 44.3 *m.* (225 alt., 182,064 pop. 1970) *see Shreveport*.

Shreveport is at junctions with US 79–80, US 71, US171, La 1, La 3, and Interstate 20.

Section b. SHREVEPORT to LEESVILLE; 114.1 m., US 171

South of SHREVEPORT, 0 *m.*, US 171 crosses a rolling, wooded district in which pines are the predominant forest growth. Former unrestricted cutting of timber has destroyed much natural beauty, but reforestation is in progress, and occasional virgin tracts permit visualization of the country's former beauty. Below Many the country becomes slightly more fertile, and the small cotton and corn patches of the uplands give way to larger farms.

DEAD MAN'S CURVE (R), 7.6 *m.*, is so-called because of the number of fatal accidents that have occurred here.

KEITHVILLE, 14 *m.* (205 alt.), formerly a plantation center, was named for the Keith family.

STONEWALL, 17.6 *m.* (227 alt.), founded in Reconstruction days, is named for General Thomas J. "Stonewall" Jackson.

Left from Stonewall on a dirt road to the junction with a dirt road, 3.7 *m.;* L. here and L. again at a fork, 4.1 *m.*, to ALLENDALE (*private*), 4.4 *m.* John Marshall came from South Carolina in the fifties and purchased the plantation on which a house was then standing. Two rooms, divided by an open central hall, still remain of the original 4-room house, which was constructed of square hand-hewn oak logs chinked with mud and moss. Pegs were used instead of nails.

At 21.5 *m.* on US 171 is the junction with a dirt road.

Left on this road to the junction with a dirt road, 2 *m.;* L. here 0.4 *m.* to BUENA VISTA (*private*), erected in 1861 by Boykin Witherspoon, also of South

Carolina. It is a two-and-one-half-story wooden house with octagonal wooden columns across the front. The gallery floor is detached from the columns, which have plaster-covered bases. The interior has all of the original furniture, and an interesting square staircase.

At 5.8 *m.* on the main side route is the junction with a dirt road; L. here 0.5 *m.* to LANDS END (*private*), erected in 1857 by Colonel Henry Marshall, brother of the owner of Allendale. It is a two-and-one-half-story frame house with a gabled roof. Fluted cypress columns of the Ionic order, with iron capitals, frame the gallery. The house once had two wings with a tennis court between them. The left wing contained an Episcopal chapel in which services were held before a church was erected in the community. Much of the original furniture still remains.

KICKAPOO, 24 *m.,* is a crossroads settlement.

Left from Kickapoo on graveled La 5 to GLOSTER, 1.2 *m.* (257 alt., 250 pop.), formerly a busy farming town.

ROSENEATH (*private*), 4.6 *m.,* the plantation home (R) of the Means family, was built in 1846–49. It is a two-story white frame house with square wooden pillars on the upper and lower gallery, and a galleried ell in the rear; the shingled gabled roof has an outside chimney at each end. The house contains much of the original furniture.

Right from Kickapoo on graveled La 5 to KEATCHIE (Ind., panther), 4 *m.* (338 alt., 500 pop.), named for a small tribe of Caddo Indians.

Right from Keatchie on a dirt road 1 *m.* to a path leading 75 yards, through a grove popular with picknickers, to a spring of reputedly health-giving mineral water.

Between 28.1 *m.* and 35.6 *m.* US 171 traverses an Erosion Control Area where conservation methods have been conducted by the Soil Conservation Service of the U. S. Department of Agriculture with the cooperation of State agencies.

GRAND CANE, 31.9 *m.* (306 alt.), was founded in 1848, receiving its name from a large canebrake through which its first settlers painfully chopped their way. The country surrounding Grand Cane is a fertile plateau lying between the Sabine and Red Rivers.

MANSFIELD, 39.1 *m.* (332 alt., 6,432 pop. 1970), the parish seat, is the largest town and shipping center of De Soto Parish. Founded and developed by planters of ante bellum days, Mansfield retains many traces of the old South. Its streets are broad and shaded by large trees, and its houses include a number of spacious and dignified mansions. Mansfield has been prominent at various times in the State's history; it is best known for the engagement during the War between the States (*see below*) that took place near by, the plans for which were drawn up by Generals Taylor and Mouton under a large water oak in the 900 block at the east end of Polk Street.

In the eastern part of town on Monroe Street, between Polk and Louisiana Sts., is the OLD MANSFIELD FEMALE COLLEGE, founded in 1852 and closed in 1929. The institution was a pioneer in the education of women. Its buildings were used during the War between the States as a Confederate barracks and hospital.

Located in a rolling upland country, Mansfield owes its earlier growth principally to lumbering and farming. Since 1913 the discovery of several near-by oil fields has added impetus to its growth.

Mansfield is at the junction with US 84 (*see Tour 5b*).

Left from Mansfield on Polk Street and paved La 1 to the MANSFIELD BATTLE PARK (L), 3.6 m. Here, on April 8, 1864, General Nathaniel Banks, with an army of about 25,000 Federals, was defeated by 12,000 Confederates under Generals Edmund Kirby-Smith and Dirk Taylor. The defeat resulted in the collapse of the Federals' Red River campaign, the object of which had been to gain control of the river ports, including Shreveport. Federal troops retreated to Pleasant Hill, 20 miles south. There, on the following day, the Confederates again engaged them, but neither side could claim victory. The Union forces, however, continued their retreat towards Baton Rouge. General Taylor wished to follow, but was restrained by General Kirby-Smith, who feared that without Taylor's assistance he would be unable to defend Shreveport. From the date of the Pleasant Hill battle until the surrender of the Trans-Mississippi Department, May 26, 1865, no further battles or skirmishes took place on Louisiana soil. Monuments have been erected in the park to General Dick Taylor, Lieutenant Colonel C. G. Polignac, Colonel James H. Beard, and Captain Seth Robert Field.

BENSON, 51.6 m. (259 alt.), is the southern part of De Soto Parish, was probably named for William Benson, an early planter.

CONVERSE, 57.5 m. (214 alt.), is a small agricultural town named for Colonel James Converse. Oil wells are a large factor in sustaining the town.

NOBLE, 64.8 m. (276 alt.), whose business district lies to the right of the highway, was settled in 1830 by Anglicans.

ZWOLLE, 69.6 m. (201 alt., 2,169 pop. 1970), has enjoyed increasing prosperity since the discovery of oil in the vicinity in 1928. Founded in 1896, the town was a large sawmill center. It was named for the Zwolle family. It is at a junction with La 120.

MANY, 80.1 m. (242 alt., 3,112 pop. 1970), named for Colonel Many, once in command of Fort Jesup, was established as the seat of Sabine Parish in 1843 in a region settled by a group of Belgians in 1837. It now serves as a supply station for a lumber and oil-producing district. The Spanish influence, which dates from the time when Los Adais (*see Tour 17A*) was the Spanish capital of the Province of Texas, is still evident in buildings such as ST. JOHN THE BAPTIST CATHOLIC CHURCH, in the southern part of town, a buff stucco structure with a bell tower. Today the sight of sombreros, high-heeled boots, and saddle horses gives Many a western air.

Many is at the junction with La 6 (*see Tour 17A*), the old San Antonio Trace.

FLORIEN, 89.3 m. (253 alt.), established in the late nineteenth century, was named for Florien Giauque, an Ohio lawyer who acquired thousands of acres of land here.

South of Florien on US 171 are Gandy, 92 m., and Hornbeck, 98 m., which has a junction with La 473 leading to the Toledo Bend Reservoir. At ANACOCO, 104 m., La 111 runs west past Lake Vernon and the ANACOCO GAME & FISH PRESERVE, then turns south to BURR

FERRY, a junction with La 8. When La 111 turns south La 393 leaves it and proceeds west to the TOLEDO BEND DAM, which has bottled up the Sabine River and its tributaries and created the fifth largest man-made lake in the United States.

The dam was built jointly by the Sabine River Authority of the State of Louisiana and the Sabine River Authority of Texas. It is a rolled earth fill about 11,250 ft. long, 112 ft. high, protected from erosion by soil-cement. The spillway is 838 ft. long, controlled by 11 gates, and can discharge 290,000 cu. ft. of water per second. There is a dependable yield of 1,430,000 gallons a day for hydroelectric power generation and water supply, which is shared equally by Louisiana and Texas. An indoor type of hydroelectric power plant is located in the south abutment of the dam. The power plant can generate 207,000,000 kilowatt hours annually. The reservoir normally covers 185,000 acres and is backed up 65 miles to Logansport. It has a shoreline of 1,200 miles and offers uncounted opportunities for fishing, and other outdoor recreation. The project was financed by bonds and its principal income comes from the sale of hydroelectric power.

HODGES GARDENS, a landscaped area of 4,700 acres between Florien and Leesville on US 171, were opened 1956 by A. J. Hodges, a conservationist, and are now administered by the Hodges Foundation, a nonprofit operation (Box 921, Many, La.). Thousands of azaleas, camellias, dogwoods, iris, redbuds, waterlilies, vines, mums make this an area of floral enchantment. There are elk, deer and wildfowl. Musical programs are given at Easter, May, June and Christmas. *Open daily 8 to dusk. Adults, $2, children free when with parents, school groups $1 per member.*

LEESVILLE, 114.1 *m.* (275 alt., 8,928 pop. 1970; 4,689, 1960; inc. 90%), named for General Robert E. Lee and founded in 1871, is the seat of Vernon Parish. Horse racing was once one of the chief avocations of this section. The parish itself was named for Vernon, a champion of local tracks. Lumber long has been the chief industry of Leesville, and stockraising has become important. Many of the country folk around Leesville wear boots and wide-brimmed hats reminiscent of the cattle country of the Southwest.

A cotton-picking machine invented by John and Mack Rust, Mississippians, was first demonstrated near Leesville; its development began in Vernon Parish. It mechanized the harvesting of cotton in the South.

The VERNON PARISH LIBRARY was initiated with the demonstration plan of the Louisiana State Library in 1956, and approved for taxing purposes by the community in 1957. In March, 1959, the new building, erected on Courthouse St., with Miller-Smith & Associates of Baton Rouge architects, was dedicated. It serves as headquarters for the parish library system and houses the Leesville Branch. There are also the Paul Laurence Dunbar Branch in Nona St., Leesville, and the bookmobile that visits rural areas. The Library had more than 42,000 volumes by 1970. It is closely associated with organizations and churches and provides reading guides, films, a reference service and many other benefits.

Left from Leesville on La 467, 3.3 *m.* to the VERNON DIVISION of the KISATCHIE NATIONAL FOREST. Several side roads afford opportunities for woodland drives through the forest.

At 9.8 *m.* on La 468 is the CENTRAL OBSERVATION TOWER (*open*).

Section c. **LEESVILLE *to* JUNCTION WITH US 90;**
67.2 *m.*, US 171

Left from Leesville on La 467 to the FORT POLK MILITARY RESERVATION, which occupies a part of the Vernon Division of the Kisatchie National Forest. FORT POLK can also be reached from Pickering by going left from US 171 to La 10. When World War II was heating up the U. S. Government chose 250 *sq. m.* in Vernon Parish as a site for training army recruits. Five months after acquiring the site the United States was at war, and thousands of trainees were sent to this area, which was named Camp Polk. It was also used for troops sent later to Korea. In 1962 the camp was made a permanent post as Fort Polk. Government expenditures here have had a favorable effect on the economy of the region, including Alexandria-Pineville, 47 *m.* to the northwest, which has a direct road to the area via La 28. Typical personnel and expeditures for 1966 were summarized by the Public Information Office of Fort Polk as follows: Trainees, 22,135; permanent military personnel, 14,797, of which 7,404 were dependents; civilian employees, 3,284. Military payroll $45,858,967; civilian payroll, $16,592,242. With purchases for supplies, equipment, etc., the total for 1966 reached $98,-186,988.

NEWLLANO, 2.1 *m.* (1,800 pop. 1970), was the home of the Llano Co-operative Colony, which, during its 20-year existence, attracted the interest of students of sociology and economics all over the country. For more than a decade the colony made excellent strides, then went into the hands of a receiver.

The Christian Commonwealth Colony, 5.2 *m.* was begun in 1931. Land was furnished to newcomers on a co-operative basis for a period of five years, after which time tenancy could be continued on a life lease for a nominal sum. One of the requirements was that members interest themselves in social and religious activities; a two-story log house with dormered red gabled roof was provided especially for the use of lay Christian workers, preachers, teachers, and missionaries.

PECKERING, 7.7 *m.* (242 alt.), and ROSEPINE, 15.8 *m.* (221 alt., 214 pop.), were at one time prosperous sawmill towns. The area is particularly suited to cattle, hog, and sheep raising, the mild climate allowing a long grazing period. Co-operation among the U. S. Forest Service, the landowners, and the Louisiana Department of Conservation has made possible extensive reforestation.

One problem of the pioneers of this section was the solemnizing of marriages, since magistrates and ministers were seldom available to perform ceremonies. This situation was often overcome by an interesting expedient: the prospective groom, having first consulted the parents of the girl he wished to marry, selected a home site and built a log cabin. Neighbors and friends were then invited to a supper and dance. When this celebration was over and the guests had withdrawn, the couple considered themselves duly married and remain in their new home as man and wife. Years later the State legislature, realizing this custom was still prevalent, passed an act making the children of such marriages legal heirs.

DE RIDDER, 21.1 *m.* (194 alt., 8,030 pop. 1970; 7,188, 1960), the seat of Beauregard Parish. The surrounding country is fertile, producing an abundance of corn, soybeans, sorghum, oats, rye, and other stock feeds also sweet potatoes. Citrus fruits, especially Satsuma oranges, thrive here.

One of the industries has been the extraction of turpentine and resin from the pine roots and stumps. The town is an important base in reforestation and fire prevention work.

The Beauregard Parish Library, with 43,234 vols. in 1969, circulated 122,444. It serves both De Ridder and Merryville. The bookmobile routes are given daily over KDLA party line.

De Ridder is at the junction with US 190 which unites with US 171 for 25.3 miles.

LONGVILLE, 39.9 *m.* (136 alt.), is a typical example of the ghost towns left by the lumber industry. In southwestern Louisiana there were many other towns of which no trace can now be found save some bits of rusty machinery. All the buildings were erected of wood, and after the mills ceased to operate the buildings were torn down, sold, and hauled away. In some instances, due to the development of agriculture and other activities, lumbering towns continued to exist after the timber was cut out.

The town of Longville was founded by the Long-Bell Lumber Company in 1906, and a few years later had a population of 2,000, a bank, and a post office. Today there are only some 25 families.

Between 42.1 *m.* and 43.6 *m.* US 171 passes through the Long-Bell Lumber Company's reforestation tract, which has been planted as an experiment. The long- and shortleaf pine trees in the central plot, which are surrounded by younger trees, are now about ten years old and growing rapidly. Fire breaks are plowed at regular intervals and other efforts made toward fire prevention. The 3,500-acre tract presents a refreshing contrast to the cutover land.

At 46.4 *m.* is the southern junction with US 190 (*see Tour 3c*).

Right at this junction on concrete-paved La 7 to the SITE OF KERNAN, 1.8 *m.*, in the early twentieth century a bustling lumber town. About the only trace left is the old schoolhouse (R), a white frame structure now the KERNAN BAPTIST CHURCH. Whenever a fifth Sunday occurs in any one month "Fifth Sunday Meetings" are held here, after an old-time custom of the Baptist denomination, observed especially in rural communities. On these occasions there is an all-day program, with "dinner on the grounds." These gatherings are considered important social as well as religious functions, for between hours set aside for worship relatives get together for interchange of gossip.

Interesting to note in this section is the fact that some housewives do not allow grass to grow in the front yards of their homes because they believe it untidy—every blade hardy enough to spring from the hard-packed earth is yanked out by the roots, and if there is any considerable growth, the ground is given a close and thorough shave with a hoe. The grassless yards become hard-packed, and are kept free of leaves and trash by means of "brush-brooms" made of supple switches of the dogwood tree, chosen because of its toughness. Frequently roses, jasmine, and other flowers ornament the front yards. The flower beds are often lined with matching brick, shells, or bottles; pathways are often similarly bordered.

The country graveyards of this region are usually highly decorated. On the graves are bits of broken crockery, colored bottles, shells, vases, and real and artificial flowers; it is not unusual to see a grave completely covered with large oyster shells.

DEQUINCY, 13 m. (72 alt., 3,448 pop. 1970), second largest city in Calcasieu Parish, is an important unit in the industrial life of the longleaf pine region of southwestern Louisiana. The principal industry is the extraction of turpentine and other products from the pine trunks, stumps, and roots of the cutover forest lands.

The soil of the surrounding country is adapted to the growing of truck and garden crops, fruits, and poultry. The open range of cutover forest lands furnishes pasturage for thousands of sheep and cattle. Large tracts of land have been planted with tung trees, and DeQuincy is taking part in the fast growing tung oil industry (see Tour 4).

The NEWPORT INDUSTRIES, INC. PLANT in the eastern outskirts of town, a turpentine, pine oil, and resin extraction and processing plant covering 26 acres, is said to be one of the largest of its kind; it was built at a cost of more than $2,000,000. The town has modern railroad repair shops; practically any sort of locomotive or car repair can be made here.

It is in this region that the story of the "Lost Mine of Wyndham Creek" persists, though its whereabouts are said to have been discovered by only one white person, a woman who came upon it in wandering while lost but afterwards could not retrace her steps. Indian tribes found here by the early pioneers wore ornaments of gold. They were unmolested at first but, with the arrival of thieves and desperadoes, began to be attacked and despoiled of the metal. The bandits tried to wrest the secret of the rumored hidden mine from the braves, who maintained a stolid silence. Search for the lost mine, however, has never ceased. At the end of the last century, it is said, three men who swore they would never rest until they found it, were discovered one morning brutally murdered.

GILLIS, 56.7 m., is a former logging town which had about 500 residents during the peak of its lumbering activity.

In MOSS BLUFF, 61.9 m. (18 alt.), is the MOSS BLUFF PARK (free picnicking facilities), a small triangular park enclosed by a pole fence. Across from the park a curio shop contains guns, antlers, books. At Moss Bluff boats and bait can be obtained at reasonable rates for fishing in near-by Calcasieu River.

The bridge at 62.1 m. provides a picturesque view of the Calcasieu River, upon which tugboats drawing huge rafts of timber or barges filled with oil ply their way slowly against a background of moss-hung trees. Hyacinths growing along banks add much beauty.

At 67.2 m. is the junction with US 90 (see Tour 1c), 2 miles east of Lake Charles.

PART IV

Appendices

Glossary of Terms
Used in Louisiana

ALLÉE. Fr. *allée*, an alley. A double row of trees leading from the road or river to a plantation house.

ARMOIRE. Lat. *armarium*, from *arma*, arms. A cabinet closing with one or two doors, and shelves. A wardrobe.

ARPENT. Lat. *arapennis*, or *arepennis*. A former land measure, of 100 perches, each 22 feet square.

BAGASSE. Sp. *bagazo*. The residue of sugar cane after the juice has been pressed out.

BAIRE. Fr. *barre*, crossbar. A mosquito net or bar, formerly hung about beds.

BAMBOULA. Fr. *bamboula*, a primitive African drum. A dance executed to the accompaniment of a bamboula drum.

BANQUETTE. Fr. *banquette*, a low bench. A sidewalk, so called because the early wooden sidewalks were elevated above the muddy streets.

BATTURE. Fr. *battre*, to beat. Alluvial land built up beyond the levee by the silting action of a river and exposed during low-water stages.

BATTURE-DWELLER. One who lives on a batture in a shanty built on stilts.

BAYOU. Choctaw *bayuk*, river or creek. A sluggish stream or natural canal, having its rise in the overflow of a river, or draining of a marsh.

BELLEVUE. Fr. *belle vue*, pleasant view. A belvedere.

BELVEDERE. Ital., Fr. *bello, bel*, beautiful, and *vedere*, to see. A railed platform on the rooftop of a plantation house, originally serving as a vantage point for viewing steamboats or men in the fields; sometimes enclosed as a cupola.

BIG HOUSE. Residence of a plantation.

BOUILLABAISSE. Prov. *bouiabaisso*, boiled down. Stew made of several kinds of fish, usually redfish and red snapper with crabs, shrimp, oysters, and crayfish, all highly seasoned with tomatoes and shallots in the sauce.

BOUSILLAGE. Fr. *bousilage*, mudwall. An early type of house construction in which walls were built of clay and Spanish moss laid between supporting cypress studs.

BRIQUETÉ ENTRE POTEAUX. Fr. bricked between posts. A type of construction similar to *bousillage*, except that bricks were used as fillers.

BUSTER. Popular name for the blue crab (*Callinectes sapidus*) when it is small and in the shedding stage, at which time the old shell is pried off and the crab prepared as a "soft-shell."

CAFÉ NOIR. Fr. black coffee. A dark roast, mixed with chicory, and prepared by the drip method.

CAFÉ AU LAIT. Coffee prepared with hot milk.

CAFÉ BRÛLOT. Fr. *brûlant,* burning, hot. A festive concoction of çoffee, spices, citrus peel, and burning brandy.

CAGOU. Fr. *cagot,* leprous, beggarly, indigent. Disgusted, disillusioned.

CAJUN. corruption of Acadian. Popular name for a descendant of Acadian settlers. Loosely, any country person speaking the Acadian dialect.

CAMEL-BACK HOUSE. An elongated dwelling having one story in the front and two in the rear.

CALAS. A sweetened rice cake, served with the morning *café an lait,* and formerly sold in the French Quarter of New Orleans.

CALINDA. A dance of African origin done by the slaves in Louisiana.

CARENCRO. Cajun corruption of carion crow. The black vulture, *Coragyps urubu urubu.*

CARNIVAL. Ital. *carne levare,* putting away of the flesh. The festive season preceding Lent, beginning on Twelfth Night (January 6) and ending with Mardi Gras (Shrove Tuesday).

CHAMBRE À BRIN. Fr. *brin,* linen cloth, or screen wire. A screened enclosure on a corner of a gallery.

CHARIVARI. Picard *caribari;* Med. Lat. *carivarium.* A serenade of "rough music," with kettles, pans, trays, and the like, given in derision of incongruous or unpopular marriages.

CHÊNIÈRE. Fr. *chêne,* an oak. An oak-covered ridge elevated slightly above the coastal marshes.

COULÉE. Fr. *coulée,* path. A small stream, generally dry in summer.

COMPÈRE. Fr. prefix *com,* with, and *père,* father. A term of affection or friendship.

CONGO. A very black Negro. Formerly it meant a Negro actually from the Congo.

COURTBOUILLON. Fr. *court-bouillon,* thick sauce in which fish is cooked. Redfish stew cooked with highly-seasoned gravy.

CRAYFISH BISQUE. Fr. *bisque,* thick soup. Soup made with crayfish, the heads being stuffed and served in the soup.

CREOLE. Sp. *criollo,* native to the locality. A white descendant of the French or Spanish settlers of Louisiana. As an adjective it is applied to various local items, such as Creole lilies, Creole ponies, and Creole mustard.

CUITE. Fr. *cuire,* to cook. Thick syrup, drawn just before it turns to sugar. "Sugarhouse candy."

CYPRIÈRE. Fr. *cyprès,* cypress. Cypress forest or swamp.

DAUBE. Fr. *daube,* braised meat. Pot roast.

DOG-TROT HOUSE. A small country house with a wide passageway open at both ends, running through its center; common in northern Louisiana.

ESTOMAC MULÂTRE. Fr. mulatto stomach. A kind of gingerbread.

FAIS-DODO. Fr. *dormir,* to sleep. A country dance, popular in southern Louisiana, from the *fais dodo,* "go to sleep," of children's speech.

FILÉ. Fr. *filer,* to twist. Powder prepared from sassafras leaves, an important ingredient of gumbo.

FLORIDA PARISHES. Parishes north of Lake Pontchartrain and east of the Mississippi, formerly part of West Florida.

FREE-MULATTO. A mulatto born free; that is, a person of color who was never a slave.

F.W.C. or F.M.C. These initials found in the old documents stand for Free Woman of Color and Free Man of Color.

GALLERY. Fr. *galerie;* Lat. *galeria,* gallery. A porch or balcony.

GARCONNIÈRE. Fr. *garcon,* a boy, a bachelor. Bachelors quarters, usually separate from the main house.

GARDE-DE-FRISE. Probably from Fr. *garde,* guard, and *cheval-de-frise,* spiked guard rail. The spikes projecting from rails separating two adjoining balconies.

GASPERGOU. Local corruption of *Casseburgan,* the fresh-water drum, *Aplodinotus grunniens.* It is so called because it feeds on large bivalves of the genus *turbo* (Fr. *burgau*), which it breaks (Fr. *casser*) with its teeth.

GOMBO. Variant of *gumbo.*

GRENIER. Fr. *grenier,* garret or attic. Attic bedroom of an Acadian cottage.

GRIFFE. Fr. *griffe,* origin uncertain. The child of a Mulatto and a Negro; a person having three-fourths Negro blood.

GRILLADES. Fr. *grillade,* griling or broiling. Veal rounds cooked in a well-seasoned *roux.*

GRIS-GRIS. African origin. A voodoo charm to ward off or inflict evil.

GRITS. Fr. *gruau,* grits or gruel. Hominy; served with eggs, liver, sausage, or *grillades.*

GROSBEC. Fr. *gros,* big, *bec,* beak. The night heron, *Nyctanassa violacea.*

GUMBO. Negro-French *gumbo,* from Angolan *kinkombo.* 1. Thick soup prepared with okra or filé and crabs, shrimp, oysters, chicken, ham or veal. 2. Negro-French patois.

GUMBO-YA-YA. A gathering of women at which there is much chatter.

GUMBO ZHÈBES. Negro-French *Zhèbe,* from Fr. *herbe,* herb. Herb gumbo made with greens and salt meat or ham.

HOT STUFF. Restaurant slang for various pepper sauces made in Louisiana from cayenne or tabasco pepper.

ILET. Fr. *îlet,* little island. A city square or block, so called because water stood for long periods in the ditches which drained the streets of early New Orleans, creating "little islands" of the squares.

ISLEÑO. A descendant of the Canary Islanders who came to Louisiana in the 1770's.

JALOUSIE. Fr. *jalousie,* Venetian blind. A two-battened outdoor window blind.

JAMBALAYA. Rice cooked with shrimp, sausage, chicken, or other ingredient.

KENO. A gambling game known elsewhere as lotto or bingo.

LAGNIAPPE. Sp. *la,* the, *ñapa,* from Kechuan *yapa,* "a present to a customer." A trifling present given to customers by merchants; anything thrown in for good measure.

LATANIER. Fr. derivative of Carib *aláttani,* the name of a small fan-leafed palm. The fan-palm or palmetto.

LEVEE. Fr. *lever*, raise. An embankment built along the bank of a river to prevent floods.

MAKE MÉNAGE. Local translation of Fr. *faire le ménage*. To clean house.

MARDI GRAS. Fr. lit., Fat Tuesday. Shrove Tuesday, the last day of Carnival.

MARINGOUIN. S. American *Tupi* and *Guarani*. A mosquito.

MARRAINE. Fr. *marraine*, from pop. Lat. *matrana*, from *mater*, mother. Godmother.

MINOU. Fr. *minet*, kitten. Cat.

MULATTO. Sp. *mulato*, young mule; hence, one of mixed race. The offspring of a Negro and a Caucasian.

NAINAINE. Creole diminutive of marraine, godmother.

NÉGRILLON. Fr. Diminutive of *nègre*, Negro. Negro child, pickaninny.

OCTOROON. Lat. *octo*, eight, after *quadroon*, in which the suffix is -*oon*. A person of one-eighth Negro blood; offspring of a quadroon and a white person.

PAIN PERDU. Fr. lost bread. Stale bread dipped in egg and fried.

PAPE. Fr. *pape*, pope. The painted bunting, *Passerina ciris*.

PAPILLOTES. Fr. *papillote*, curl paper. 1. Curl papers. 2. Buttered or oiled paper in which fish, especially pompano, is broiled, to retain the flavor.

PARISH. An administrative division known elsewhere as a county.

PARRAIN. Fr. *parrain*, from low Lat. *patrinus*, from *pater*, father. Godfather.

PERIQUE. Local term. Strong- flavored tobacco grown only in Louisiana.

PERRON. Fr. *perron*, from *pierre*, stone. A porch. In New Orleans, a small landing before a door.

PICAYUNE. Prov. *picaioun*. Formerly the Spanish half-real, worth about 6¼¢.

PIGEONNIER. Fr. *pigeon*, pigeon. Pigeon-house, dovecote.

PIROGUE. Sp. *piragua*, borrowed from the Carib. A dugout used in Louisiana bayous; loosely, any canoe-like boat.

POLICE JURY. The governing body of a parish.

POOR BOY. A foot-long sandwich made with French bread.

PORTE-COCHÈRE. Fr. *porte*, gate, *coche*, coach. A gateway through which vehicles enter a courtyard.

POT LIQUOR. The water in which greens and a piece of salt meat or ham have been boiled.

PRALINE. From Maréchal du Plessis praslin, whose cook is said to have invented it. A confection made of pecans browned in sugar.

QUADROON. Sp. *cuarteron*, quadroon. A person of one-fourth Negro blood; offspring of a Mulatto and a white person.

QUARTEE. Local term. Half of a 5¢ piece.

RAISED COTTAGE. An early type of plantation house set upon brick piers as a precaution against floods.

REDBONE. A person of Indian and Negro parentage.

ROUX. Fr. *roux*, brown sauce. Flour browned in butter or lard; the basis of many Creole dishes.

SHOTGUN HOUSE. A long, narrow house in which the rooms are one behind the other; so called because a shot fired in the front door would pass through all the other doors, and out at the rear.

SIROP DE BATTERIE. Cane syrup made by the open-kettle process.

SNOWBALL. A confection made with crushed ice flavored with colored syrups.

SOFT-SHELL. A crab that has shed its old shell. Soft-shell crabs are fried in deep fat and eaten shell and all.

SOIRÉE. Fr. *soir*, from Lat. *serum*, late afternoon. An evening party.

SPASM BAND. A soap-box orchestra and accompanying tap dancers, usually young Negroes, who perform on street corners in the French Quarter of New Orleans.

SUGARHOUSE. Local term. A sugar refinery.

TIGNON. Fr. *tignon*, or *chignon*, nape of the neck, from Lat. *catena*, chain. A kind of turban made with a bright-colored handkerchief.

TISANE. Lat. *ptisana*, an infusion of maple. Tea made of orange leaves or herbs, used as a specific in certain illnesses.

VIEUX CARRÉ. Fr. old square. The original walled city of New Orleans; the French Quarter, bounded by Canal Street, North Rampart Street, Esplanade Avenue, and the Mississippi River.

VOODOO. Dahomey *vôdu*, a deity. An African cult brought to Louisiana by Negro slaves; one who practices Voodoo sorcery.

WANGA. Of African origin. A spell.

ZOMBI. Congo *zambi*, a deity, Spirit.

Chronology

1519   Alvarez de Pineda explores the Gulf Coast and reports the discovery of a great river, presumably the Mississippi.

1528   Álvar Núñez Cabeza de Vaca, leader of the survivors of the Narvaez expedition, skirts the Louisiana coast, starting an 8-year trek back to civilization.

1541–42   Hernando de Soto explores the northern part of the State.

1542   May 21. De Soto is buried in the Mississippi River near the mouth of Red River.

1543   July. Luis de Moscoso and the survivors of De Soto's expedition descend the Mississippi to the Gulf of Mexico, the first Europeans to descend to the mouth of the river.

1553   Marcos de Mena, shipwrecked off the Gulf Coast, survives an Indian attack and travels through Louisiana to Mexico.

1682   April 9. Robert Cavelier, Sieur de la Salle, descending the Mississippi from the Great Lakes, erects a cross and a column at the mouth of the river, claiming the territory in the name of Louis XIV, for whom it is named Louisiana.

1685   La Salle, intending to establish a settlement at the mouth of the Mississippi, is unable to find the river and lands at Matagorda Bay, Texas.

1699   March 2. Pierre le Moyne, Sieur d'Iberville, rediscovers the mouth of the Mississippi and explores as far north as Red River.
        September. By a clever ruse Iberville's brother, Jean Baptiste le Moyne, Sieur de Bienville, turns back an English colonizing expedition at English Turn.

1700   Fort Iberville, Louisiana's first fortification, is established near Pointe à la Hache.
        Spring. Father Paul Du Ru, a Jesuit chaplain, establishes the first Catholic church in Louisiana, at the village of the Houma in West Feliciana Parish.

1712   Trading rights in Louisiana are granted to Antoine Crozat, wealthy French merchant.

1714   Louis Juchereau de St. Denis founds Fort St. Jean Baptiste (Natchitoches), first permanent settlement in Louisiana, at the southern end of the Great Raft in Red River.

1717   Crozat relinquishes his trade concession to the Company of the West, a trading company controlled by John Law. Settlers and slaves are sent to Louisiana.

Spain restricts French expansion toward Texas by establishing the Mission of San Miguel de los Adais, 14 miles southwest of Natchitoches.

1718 New Orleans, named in honor of the Regent of France, Philippe, Duc d'Orléans, is founded.

1719 Law's Company of the West is reorganized as the Company of the Indies.

1721 To protect Spanish sovereignty in the Sabine Valley Spain establishes a presidio at Los Adais, which, until 1773, serves as the capital of the Province of Texas.

1723 New Orleans becomes the capital of Louisiana, superseding Biloxi.

1724 March. The *Code Noir,* a set of laws drawn up for the regulation of Negroes in Santo Domingo, is promulgated in Louisiana. The Catholic religion is made the state faith and Jews are prohibited.

1727 August 7. Ursuline nuns arrive in New Orleans to set up a school and care for the sick.

1728 December. A shipload of *filles à la cassette* (casket girls) arrive in New Orleans to provide wives for the colonists. While being courted they are chaperoned by the Ursulines.

1729 December. New Orleans is hastily fortified following the massacre of the French by the Natchez Indians at Fort Rosalie (Natchez).

1730 French soldiers under Governor Périer, with the assistance of the Choctaw, even the score with the Natchez near Sicily Island.

1731 Louisiana becomes a crown colony under Louis XV as the Company of the Indies relinquishes its charter.

1732 The troublesome Natchez besiege Natchitoches for 22 days but are driven off by St. Denis and his garrison and annihilated at Sang Pour Sang Hill, near Cloutierville.

1735 November 16. Jean Louis, a sailor, dies, leaving his savings for the establishment of Charity Hospital in New Orleans.

1741 An epic poem is written by Dumont de Montigny, impressionable colonist.

1753 First theatrical production, *Le Père indian,* written by LeBlanc Villeneufve, is presented by amateurs at the governor's mansion in New Orleans.

1762 November 3. Louis XV makes a gift of the "Island of New Orleans" and all Louisiana lying west of the Mississippi to his cousin, Charles III of Spain.

1763 February 10. Treaty of Paris, terminating the Seven Years' War, officially confirms the transfer of Louisiana to Spain. The Florida Parishes are ceded to England, Baton Rouge becoming New Richmond.
July 9. Jesuits expelled from Louisiana and their property confiscated.

1764 Informed of the transfer to Spain, the French colonists ineffectually petition Louis XV, through the agent Bienville, to rescind the cession. Printing press set up in New Orleans.

1766   March 5. Antonio de Ulloa, Spanish commissioner sent to take over Louisiana, is coldly received at New Orleans.

1768   October 27–29. New Orleans becomes the first colonial capital to revolt against European rule as a mob of insurgents takes over the city and Ulloa sails for Cuba. For 10 months Louisiana enjoys freedom from foreign rule.

1769   August 17. Count Alexander O'Reilly, with 24 ships and 2,000 men, arrives at New Orleans to reinstate Spanish authority. The leaders of the October rebellion are executed and changes made in government, laws, and commercial regulations.

1776   Oliver Pollock, agent of the Continental Congress at New Orleans, is permitted by Governor Bernardo de Galvez to send supplies to George Rogers Clark and other American patriots fighting against the British in the western country.

Fames Willing, "Captain in the service of the united Independent States of America," using New Orleans as a base, pillages the Loyalists in West Florida.

1779   September 21. War having been declared between Spain and Great Britain, Galvez wrests Baton Rouge from the British. By 1781 all West Florida is taken over.

1788   March 21. New Orleans is almost completely destroyed by fire.

1790   April. Père Antoine, ordered to leave Louisiana, threatens to establish the Inquisition, of which he had been appointed Commissary in 1787, but is deported by Governor Miro.

1791   Louis Tabary and a company of players, refugees from Santo Domingo, present the first professional theatrical productions in New Orleans.

1793   April 25. Pope Pius VI establishes the Diocese of Louisiana, the second diocese to be established in the United States.

Caterpillar plague destroys indigo crop and for 3 weeks wreaks such havoc that indigo cultivation, temporarily abandoned, never regains its importance.

1794   December 8. Fire destroys 212 buildings in New Orleans.

December 23. The Church of St. Louis at New Orleans, rebuilt after the fire of 1788, is dedicated as a cathedral.

Louisiana's first newspaper, *Le Moniteur de la Louisiane,* is published in New Orleans by Louis Duclot, refugee printer from Santo Domingo.

1795   April. Twenty-five slaves are killed in the Black Rebellion, a slave insurrection in Pointe Coupée Parish inspired by the Santo Domingo revolution.

October 27. A treaty between the United States and Spain sets the northern boundary of West Florida, ultimately the state line east of the Mississippi, at 31° and grants Americans free navigation of the Mississippi.

The Cabildo is erected in New Orleans to house the Spanish colonial administrators.

Étienne de Boré granulates sugar on a commercial scale on his plantation (now Audubon Park) near New Orleans.

1799   Bailey E. Chaney, a Baptist minister, is arrested near Baton Rouge for conducting Protestant services among English settlers.

1801   October 1. Louisiana ceded to France by the Treaty of San Ildefonso.

1802   October 16. Free navigation of the Mississippi suspended but soon restored because of agitation among Americans.

1803   March. Announcement of the transfer of Louisiana from Spain to France is made by Pierre Laussat, colonial prefect, on his arrival in New Orleans.
April 30. Louisiana is purchased from France by the United States for $15,000,000.
November 30. Laussat formally takes over Louisiana for the French Republic.
December 20. William C. C. Claiborne and General James Wilkinson take over Louisiana for the United States.

1804   March 26. Louisiana is divided into the Territory of Orleans (south of 33°) and the District of Louisiana (north of 33°). W. C. C. Claiborne is appointed governor of the Territory of Orleans.

1805   February 17. New Orleans is incorporated.
April 19. New Orleans Library Society is incorporated.
June 16. Fifty-three Protestants, choosing an Episcopal clergyman to conduct services, establish the first Protestant church in New Orleans. October. Neutral Ground Treaty signed by General Wilkinson and General Simon de Herrera establishes the Arroya Hondo as neutral territory pending negotiations between the United States and Spain. December. New Orleans is fortified by General Wilkinson against Aaron Burr's expedition, which Mississippi authorities break up near Natchez.

1808   Pointe Coupée Parish establishes first public schools.

1810   Population, 76,556.
September 23. West Floridians, in rebellion against Spain, take over Baton Rouge and establish the West Florida Republic.
A typographical union, one of the first unions in the country, is organized in New Orleans.

1811   An insurrection of slaves in St. Charles Parish is suppressed by the militia with much bloodshed.
Louisiana's first institution of higher learning, the College of Orleans, opens in New Orleans.

1812   January 10. The *New Orleans,* first steamboat to navigate the Mississippi, arrives at New Orleans from Pittsburg. Golden era of the steamboat begins.
January 22. Constitution is adopted for admission to the Union.
April 30. Louisiana admitted to the Union.
October 12. The Half Moon Bluff Church, the first Baptist church in the State, is organized in Washington Parish.

Bayou Chicot Calvary Church, first Baptist church established west of the Mississippi, is organized by Joseph Willis, a Mulatto minister.

1815 January 8. General Andrew Jackson, with the aid of pirates and patriots, wins the Battle of New Orleans 15 days after peace was signed between the United States and Great Britain.

1819 February 22. The United States and Spain sign the Treaty of Washington, establishing Sabine River as the western boundary of Lousiana.

1820 Population, 153,407.

1821 July 17. The Arroyo Hondo, the neutral territory along Sabine River, is finally transferred to the United States and is incorporated in Louisiana.

Sacred Heart Academy, a Catholic girls' school, is founded at Grand Coteau.

Jean Jacques Audubon sets up a studio in New Orleans.

1823 Louisiana's first gas well is brought in near Natchitoches. Thought of no value, it is abandoned.

May 8. James H. Caldwell opens the American Theater in New Orleans, introducing illuminating gas.

December 9. James Brown of New Orleans is appointed minister to France by President Monroe.

1824 Julien Poydras bequeaths $30,000 each to Pointe Coupée and West Baton Rouge Parishes for a dowry fund.

1825 April 10. Lafayette visits New Orleans.

College of Louisiana (forerunner of Centenary College of Shreveport) is founded at Jackson.

1827 September 19. The Maddox-Wells duel on a sandbar near Vidalia ends in a bloody free-for-all in which James Bowie uses his famous knife.

1829 May 8. Louis Moreau Gottschalk, distinguished pianist and composer, born in New Orleans.

1830 Population, 215,739.

January 4. Seat of government moved to Donaldsonville. Bored by small-town life, the legislators, in the first act of the following session (1831), return the capital to New Orleans.

1831 April 23. The Pontchartrain Railroad, the first railroad west of the Alleghenies, begins passenger and freight service between New Orleans and Milneburg.

1832–33 Yellow fever and cholera kill 10,000 in New Orleans.

1833 April 11. Captain Henry Miller Shreve begins clearing Red River of the Great Raft.

November 13. Unusually heavy shower of meteorites. For years Negroes reckon events from "the year the stars fell."

1835 The Medical College of Louisiana (forerunner of Tulane University) is founded in New Orleans by a group of physicians.

July 1. Caddo Indians sign a treaty with the United States, relinquishing their territory in northwest Louisiana for $80,000.

1836   March 8. New Orleans, racked by dissension between Creoles and Americans, is divided into three municipalities.
       The Nachitoches *Red River Herald* scoops the press of the world with the first news of the fall of the Alamo.

1837   Shreveport is founded.
       Two printers, Kendall and Lumsden, start a 4-page newspaper, the *Picayune,* priced at one picayune (6¼¢).
       Fourteen banks in New Orleans suspend the payment of specie. Each municipality issues its own money.
       Ralph Smith-Smith begins construction of the Red River Railroad, the first west of the Mississippi, at Alexandria.
       June 22. Paul Charles Morphy, one of the world's greatest chess players, born in New Orleans.

1838   Shrove Tuesday. First Mardi Gras parade held in New Orleans.
       September 28. Henry Hobson Richardson, eminent American architect, born in St. James Parish.

1840   Population, 352,411.
       New Orleans (102,193 pop.), is the fourth largest city in the United States.

1844   National Art Gallery of Paintings established in New Orleans.

1845   May 14. Constitution is democratized; electoral franchise broadened and governor elected by direct popular vote; free public schools established and State superintendent of education appointed.
       July. General Zachary Taylor leaves New Orleans with 1,500 men for the Mexican campaign.
       November 10. John Slidell of New Orleans appointed minister to Mexico by President Polk to adjust differences.

1846   Norbert Rillieux's invention of the multiple apparatus revolutionizes the sugar industry.
       The New Orleans *Picayune,* using pony express, scoops the world on the Mexican War.

1847   East Louisiana State Hospital for Mental Diseases founded at Jackson.

1848   November 7. Major General Zachary Taylor of Baton Rouge is elected President.

1849   Baton Rouge becomes capital of Louisiana.
       Southern Yacht Club, second oldest in the United States, is organized in New Orleans.
       The Pontalba Buildings are erected in New Orleans by the Baroness Pontalba.

1850   Population, 517,762.
       McDonogh bequest provides $750,000 for the establishment of schools in New Orleans.

1851   Jenny Lind, under the management of P. T. Barnum, sings before overflow crowds on an extended engagement in New Orleans.

1852   February. The Southwestern Railroad Convention, meeting at New Orleans, selects that city rather than Mobile as the southern terminus of a proposed (eventually the Illinois Central) north-south railroad.

July 31. Additional democratic changes are written into the constitution.

Louisiana Institute for the Education of the Deaf and Dumb and Blind founded at Baton Rouge.

1853 April 7. Pierre Soulé of New Orleans is appointed minister to Spain by President Pierce.

The New Orleans Academy of Sciences, a scientific society, is founded.

In the worst yellow fever plague in the history of the State many small towns are wiped out, 11,000 persons dying in New Orleans alone.

1854 April 1. Lexington defeats Lecomte in the Great Post State Stake at the Metairie Course in New Orleans.

1856 August 10. Last Island is devastated by hurricane. More than 200 vacationers are killed.

1858 June 3–7. Know-Nothing riots in New Orleans. Mayor Waterman is impeached.

1859 September. Four thousand vigilantes break up a powerful gang of cattle thieves in a skirmish near Lafayette.

December 1. French Opera House in New Orleans opens with *Guillaume Tell*.

1860 Population, 708,002.

January 2. Louisiana State Seminary of Learning (forerunner of the Louisiana State University) opens at Alexandria with William Tecumseh Sherman president.

November 19. Adelina Patti makes her operatic debut at the French Opera House in New Orleans.

1861 January 26. Louisiana secedes from the Union, becoming an independent republic.

March 21. Louisiana joins the Confederacy.

April 12. Major General P. G. T. Beauregard of St. Bernard Parish starts the War between the States by ordering the bombardment of Fort Sumter.

April 26. "Maryland, My Maryland" is composed by James P. Randall, a homesick professor at Poydras College, near New Roads.

November 8. John Slidell, Confederate commissioner to France, is taken from the British mail steamer *Trent,* and released after British protest.

1862 March 17. Judah P. Benjamin of New Orleans is appointed Confederate Secretary of State by Jefferson Davis.

April 25. New Orleans captured by David G. Farragut and the Federal fleet.

May 1. General Benjamin F. Butler begins his dictatorial rule in New Orleans, the Federal capital of the State. The Confederate capital is removed to Opelousas and, after one session, to Shreveport.

1863 May-July. Port Hudson besieged by Federals and starved into surrender.

1864 April 8. General Banks and his Federal forces are defeated by the Confederates near Mansfield and again at Pleasant Hill, the following day.

May 13. Alexandria is fired by Federal troops and almost completely destroyed.

July 23. A Republican convention revises the constitution, abolishing slavery.

1865 January. Duncan F. Kenner of Ascension Parish is appointed Confederate minister plenipotentiary to Europe by Jefferson Davis to treat for recognition of the Confederacy on the basis of emancipation.

May 26. The last Confederate army in the field, the Trans-Mississippi, commanded by General Edmund Kirby-Smith, surrenders, Louisiana coming under complete Federal control, with the seat of government at New Orleans.

1866 July 30. Race riot at the Mechanics' Institute in New Orleans.

1867 Knights of the White Camellia form at Franklin to combat Negroes, carpetbaggers, and scalawags.

1868 March 11. Constitution is revised, granting Negroes full social and civil rights.

June 25. Louisiana is readmitted to the Union.

August 11. Louisiana Lottery established.

1870 Population, 726,915.

June 30. The *Robert E. Lee* and the *Natchez* begin their historic race at New Orleans.

1872 Shrove Tuesday. Rex, King of Carnival, parades for first time, with the Grand Duke Alexis of Russia a spectator.

1873 Easter Sunday. Three white men and about 120 Negroes are killed in a race riot at Colfax.

Through train service is established between New Orleans and Chicago.

1874 Disastrous flood; 31 parishes inundated.

August 29-30. A Negro uprising at Coushatta is quelled by the White League.

September 14. The White League defeats the Metropolitan Police in New Orleans in a bloody insurrection and gains brief control of the city government.

1876 New Orleans Lawn Tennis Club, one of the oldest in the United States, is founded.

1877 Federal troops are withdrawn and home rule is restored to Louisiana under Governor Francis T. Nicholls.

1878 Yellow fever carries off 3,800 in New Orleans.

1879 July 23. Constitution is amended to neutralize the Negro vote.

Captain James B. Eads completes the jetty system at the mouth of the Mississippi River.

1880 Population, 939,946.

1882 Baton Rouge again becomes capital of Louisiana.

Disastrous flood; 16 parishes suffer $12,000,000 property damage.

1883   Through train service, New Orleans–California begun.

1884   Louisiana State Normal College founded at Natchitoches.

1884–86   Cotton Centennial Exposition held in New Orleans.

1890   Population, 1,118,587.

Louisiana State Penitentiary established at Angola.

Louisiana becomes one of the first States to legalize prize fighting.

1891   March 15. New Orleans mob lynches 11 alleged slayers of Chief of Police Hennessey.

1892   September 7. James J. Corbett knocks out John L. Sullivan in 21 rounds in New Orleans.

1893   April 6. Andy Bowen and Jack Burke battle 7 hours and 19 minutes to a 110-round draw, longest prize fight.

October 1. Chênière Caminada devasted by hurricane.

1894   Leprosarium is established at Carville.

Louisiana Industrial Institute & College (forerunner of Louisiana Polytechnic Institute) founded at Ruston.

1895   Louisiana Lottery outlawed, moves to Honduras.

1896   November 1. Free rural delivery route, second in the United States, is established at Thibodaux.

1900   Population, 1,381,625.

1901   August. Oil discovered in Louisiana near Jennings.

Southwestern Louisiana Institute founded at Lafayette.

1902   Central Louisiana State Hospital for Mental Diseases established near Pineville.

1904   Loyola Academy, now university, founded, New Orleans.

1905   Commercial production of sulphur by Frasch process near Sulphur.

Last yellow fever epidemic.

1906   Louisiana College founded at Pineville.

Oil discovered in Caddo Lake. Shreveport booms.

1909   Plaquemine Locks are completed, facilitating navigation from the Mississippi through Grand River to Atchafalaya River.

Ralph DePalma sets an automobile speed record at New Orleans, averaging 60 m.p.h. for 50 miles.

1910   Population, 1,656,388.

December 12. Edward Douglas White of Lafourche Parish is appointed Chief Justice of the United States by President Taft.

December 24. At an international aviation tournament in New Orleans a record for the mile is set at 57 seconds.

1912   April 10. George Mestach, carrying mail from New Orleans to Baton Rouge, makes the second U.S. air mail trip.

1914   March 9. Southern University, leaves New Orleans for Scotlandville.

Picayune and *Times-Democrat* merge to form the *Times-Picayune*.

1916   Monroe gas field is discovered. Monroe booms.

The State Federation of Labor is organized.

1919   Homer oil field discovered.

December 4. French Opera House, New Orleans, burned.

1920   Population, 1,798,509.
1921   Haynesville oil field is brought in.
1923   Inner Harbor Navigation Canal opened.
1925   Louisiana State University moves to new campus in Baton Rouge.
       Southeastern Louisiana College established at Hammond.
1926   Lake Charles becomes a deep-water port.
1927   The Mississippi floods large area.
1928   Act passed providing free textbooks for public schools.
1929   May 16. An attempt to impeach Governor Huey P. Long is defeated
       by a round robin of 15 senators.
1930   Population, 2,101,593.
       U. S. Veterans' Administration Facilities are opened near Pineville.
1932   May 16. New Capitol at Baton Rouge is dedicated.
1933   Harvey Locks are completed.
1935   January 1. Tulane defeats Temple (20–14) in first Sugar Bowl foot-
       ball game. Rodessa oil field discovered. September 8. Huey P. Long
       assassinated in the Capitol at Baton Rouge. Dillard University of
       New Orleans opens. Huey P. Long Bridge dedicated, Dec. 16.
1937   Bonnet Carré Spillway used successfully to divert flood.
       The *Delgado Flash,* an airplane built by the students of Delgado
       Trades School of New Orleans, breaks the world's speed record for
       planes of its class.
1939   New Charity Hospital opens in New Orleans.
1940   New bridge at Baton Rouge dedicated.
1953   Sesquicentennial of Louisiana Purchase, New Orleans.
1957   Hurricane Audrey June 27, kills 357, injures 3,280, destroys 1,300
       houses.
1958   Federal District Court ordered New Orleans streetcars and buses
       desegregated May 21.
1960   Special session of Legislature passed 28 desegregation bills. Earl Long
       died Sept. 5, 10 days after nomination to Congress.
1962   Archbishop of Orleans ordered Roman Catholic schools to desegre-
       gate. Dr. John A. Hunter named pres. LSU.
1963   Federal Circuit Court orders high school to admit 27 blacks. Tulane
       admits 5 blacks.
1964   John J. McKeithen elected 48th governor. Louisiana gave Goldwater,
       R., 509,225; Johnson, D., 387,068. Two barges tear hole in Pontchar-
       train Causeway, bus falls into water, 6 dead, June 16.
1965   Hurricane Hilda kills 18 in Larose, 12 elsewhere, Oct. 3. Hurricane
       Betsy kills 61; sinks chlorine barge of 600 tons, Sept. 9. Natural gas
       pipeline explodes near Natchitoches, 17 dead.
1966   Harold Robert Perry first Negro to become Auxiliary Bishop of
       Orleans Parish Jan. 6. Centenary admits 4 Negroes, Jan. 31. National
       Football League gives franchise to New Orleans Saints.
1967   National Guard called out to curb school violence in Bogalusa. Ne-
       groes and K. K. K. stage rival rallies at Capitol.
1968   Gov. McKeithen reelected. Wallace polls 539,045; Humphrey

317,929; Nixon 259,715. Oil rig explosion near Buras, 11 dead. *African Star* collided with 2 oil barges below New Orleans, 21 dead. Fire in Belle Island salt mine.

1969 Hurricane Camille causes vast destruction on Gulf Coast. Plaquemine Library lost 32,000 books and bookmobile.

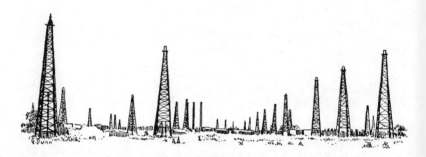

Books About Louisiana

All This is Louisiana. Photos by Elemore Morgan, text by Frances Parkinson Keyes, 1950.
Battle of New Orleans, The, by Charles L. Dufour and Leonard V. Huber, eds., 1965.
Beauregard, the Great Creole, by Hamilton Basso, 1933.
Big River to Cross, by Ben Lucien Burman, 1940.
Black Reconstruction, by W. E. B. DuBois, 1935.
Blow My Blues Away, by George Mitchell, 1971.
Cajuns on the Bayou, by Carolyn Ramsey.
Chalmette National Historical Park, by J. Fred Roush and National Park Service, 1961.
Creole Families of New Orleans, by Grace E. King, 1921.
Deep Delta Country, by Harnett T. Kane, 1944.
Delta Queen, the Story of a Steamboat, by Virginia Elfert, 1960.
Dinner at Antoine's, by Frances Parkinson Keyes, 1948.
Dynasty, the Longs of Louisiana, by Thomas Martin, 1960.
Earl of Louisiana, The, by A. J. Liebling, 1961.
Every Man a King, by C. Vann Woodward, 1964.
Fabulous New Orleans, by Lyle Saxon, 1928.
Father Mississippi, by Lyle Saxon, 1927.
Felicianas of Louisiana, The, by Marion G. Reeves, 1967.
First South, The, by John Richard Alden, 1961.
Four Civil War Stories, by Charles East *et al.*, 1961.
French Quarter, The, by Herbert Asbury.
Frenchmen, Desire, Good Children, by John Chase.
Ghosts Along the River, by Clarence John Laughlin.
Golden Age of New Orleans, The, by John S. Kendall.
Gone Are the Days, by Harnett T. Kane.
Government of Louisiana, The, by William C. Harvard, 1958.
Higher Education in Louisiana, by Commission on Higher Education, Baton Rouge, 1956.
History of Reconstruction in Louisiana, by John Rose Ficklen, 1914.
Huey Long, a Biography, by T. Harry Williams, 1969.
Jazzmen, by Frederic Ramsey, Jr., and Charles Edward Smith, eds., 1939.
Lafitte the Pirate, by Lyle Saxon, 1930.
Life of Judah P. Benjamin, The, by Louisiana State Museum, 1937.
Life on the Mississippi, by Mark Twain. Leonard Kriegel ed., 1961.

Louisiana Hayride: The American Rehearsal for Dictatorship, 1928–40, by Harnett T. Kane, 1941.

Louisiana Plantation Homes, Colonial and Ante-bellum, by W. Barrell Overdyke, 1965.

Louisiana Manpower Training Program, by State Commerce & Industry Dept. 1968.

Louisiana Oil & Gas Facts, Mid-Continent Oil & Gas Assn., 1970.

Louisiana Purchase, American's Best Buy, by John D. Chase, 1960.

Louisiana Under Ten Flags, by Louisiana State Museum, 1937.

Louisiana Voodoo, by Andre Cajun.

Master of the Mississippi. Henry Shreve and the Conquest of Mississippi, by Florence Dorsey, 1941.

Negro in Louisiana, The, by Charles B. Rousseve, 1937.

Negro Folklore, Book of, by Arna W. Bontemps, 1948.

Negro Slavery in Louisiana, by Joe Gray Taylor, 1963.

Negro, Story of the, by Arna W. Bontempts, 1948.

New Orleans City Guide, by Federal Writers Program, WPA, 1938.

New Orleans Story, The, by John Churchill Chase, 1967.

New Orleans, by Stuart M. Lynn.

New Orleans, by Oliver Evans, 1959.

New Orleans and its Environs, the Domestic Architecture, 1727–1870, by Italo W. Ricciut, intro. by Talbot F. Hamlin.

Old Louisiana, by Lyle Saxon, 1929.

Old Plantation Homes & Family Trees, by Herman B. Seabold, 1941.

One Hundred Years of Negro Freedom, by Arna W. Bontempts, 1961.

Plantation Parade, by Harnett T. Kane, 1945.

Political Tendencies in Louisiana, 1812–1852, by Perry H. Howard, revised ed., 1971.

Prehistoric Indian Settlements of the Changing Mississippi River Delta, by William J. McIntire, 1958.

Presidential Politics in Louisiana, 1952, by L. Vaughan Howard and David R. Deever.

Romance and Realism in Southern Politics, by T. Harry Williams, 1961.

Senior Citizens Look Ahead. Louisiana Commission on the Aging, 1958.

Stars in Their Eyes; Dreamers and Builders in Louisiana, by Clayton Rand.

Stories of New Orleans, by Andre Cajun.

Story of King Cotton, The, by Harris Dickson, 1937.

Story of the Riverfront at New Orleans, by Raymond J. Martinez.

Study in the State Government of Louisiana, by Melvin Evans, 1931.

Swing That Music, by Louis Armstrong, 1956.

Tales of the Mississippi, by Ray Samuel, L. V. Huber and W. G. Ogden.

Treasury of Plantation Homes, by Wesley Cooper.

White Pillars, the Architecture of the South, by J. Fraser Smith.

Historical Places

Famous Houses and Sites of Houses, Battlefields, Plantations
Numerals in circles on State maps

Index to State Map Sections

LEGEND FOR STATE MAP

U.S. HIGHWAYS _ _ _ _ _ _ _ _ _ _ _ _ _ ⬣90

STATE HIGHWAYS _ _ _ _ _ _ _ _ _ 168

CONNECTING ROADS _ _ _ _ _ _ _ _

POINTS OF INTEREST _ _ _ _ _ _ _ _ _ _ 27

FORTS _

AIRPORTS _ _ _ _ _ _ _ _ _ _ _ _ _ _ _ _ _ _

STATE PARKS _ _ _ _ _ _ _ _ _ _ _ _ _ _ _ 🌲

CAPITAL _ _ _ _ _ _ _ _ _ _ _ _ _ _ _ _ _ _ ⊛

PARISH SEATS _ _ _ _ _ _ _ _ _ _ _ _ _ _ _ ◉

NATIONAL FORESTS _ _ _ _ _ _ _ _

WILDLIFE REFUGES _ _ _ _ _ _ _ _

FLOODWAYS _ _ _ _ _ _ _ _ _ _ _

MAP SHOWING SECTIONAL DIVISION OF STATE MAP

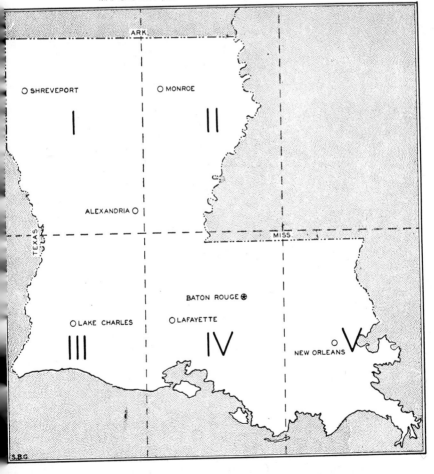

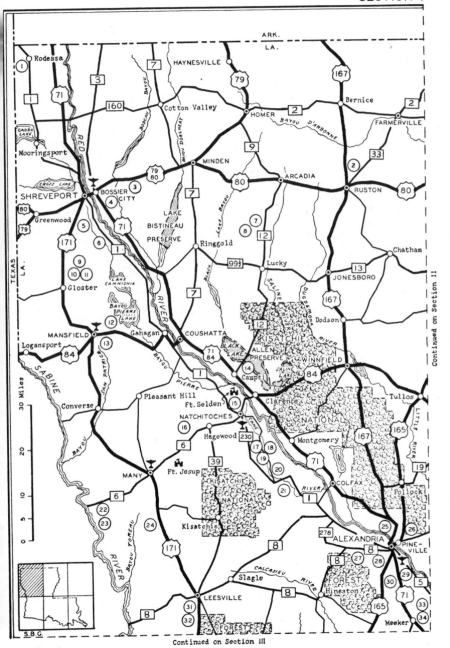

Continued on Section II

Continued on Section III

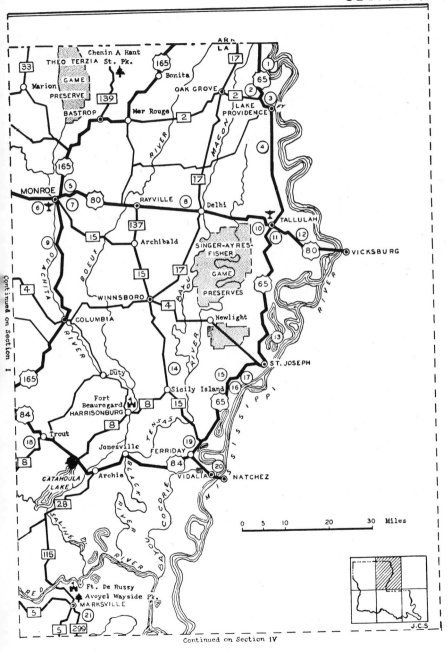

Continued on Section I

Continued on Section IV

J.C.S.

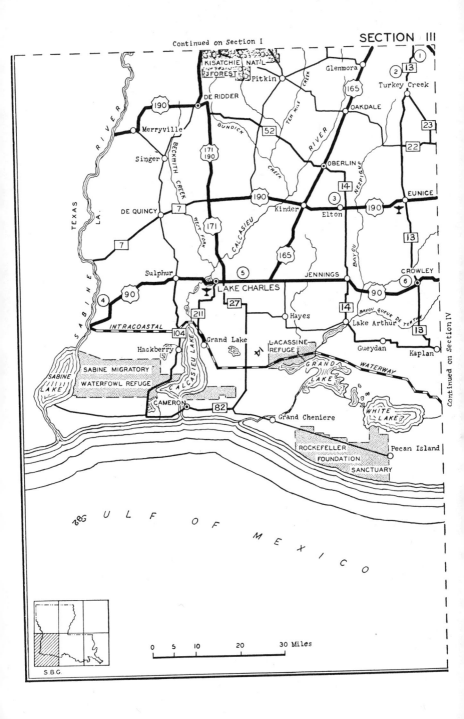

Continued on Section II

Continued on Section III

Continued on Section V

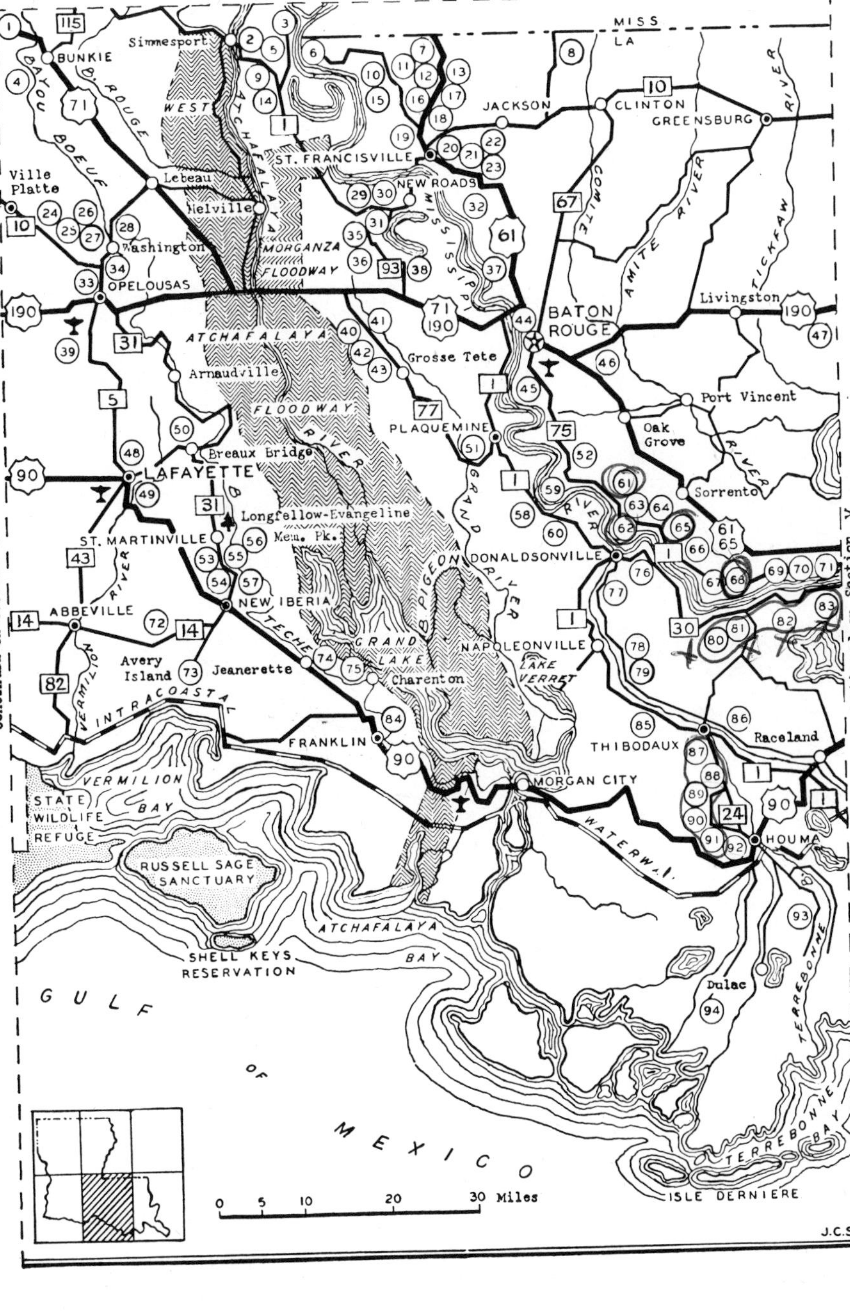

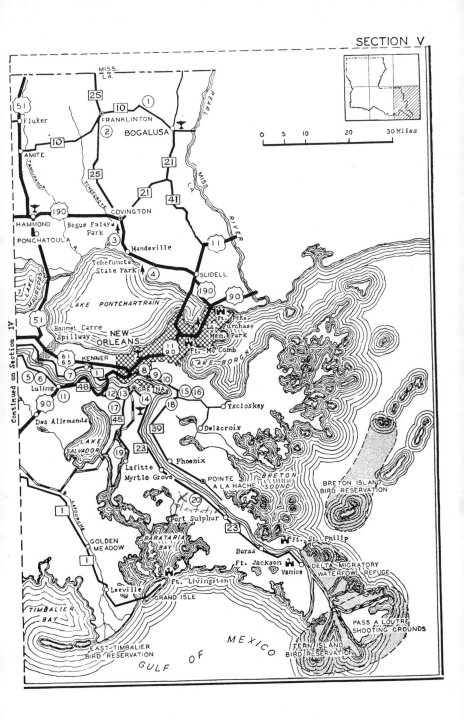

SECTION V

Index